MEXICAN LAW

Mexican Law

STEPHEN ZAMORA
University of Houston Law Center

JOSÉ RAMÓN COSSÍO
Justice of the Mexican Supreme Court

LEONEL PEREZNIETO
Universidad Nacional Autónoma de México (UNAM)

JOSÉ ROLDÁN-XOPA
Instituto Tecnológico Autónomo de México (ITAM)

DAVID LOPEZ
Member of the Texas Bar

OXFORD
UNIVERSITY PRESS

This book has been printed digitally and produced in a standard specification in order to ensure its continuing availability

OXFORD
UNIVERSITY PRESS

Great Clarendon Street, Oxford OX2 6DP

Oxford University Press is a department of the University of Oxford.
It furthers the University's objective of excellence in research, scholarship,
and education by publishing worldwide in

Oxford New York

Auckland Cape Town Dar es Salaam Hong Kong Karachi
Kuala Lumpur Madrid Melbourne Mexico City Nairobi
New Delhi Shanghai Taipei Toronto
With offices in
Argentina Austria Brazil Chile Czech Republic France Greece
Guatemala Hungary Italy Japan South Korea Poland Portugal
Singapore Switzerland Thailand Turkey Ukraine Vietnam

Oxford is a registered trade mark of Oxford University Press
in the UK and in certain other countries

Published in the United States
by Oxford University Press Inc., New York

Reprinted 2008

ISBN 978-0-19-826777-5

Preface

Publishing a book with the title *Mexican Law*, promising by implication that we will summarize an entire legal system in one volume, is an invitation to disappointment. We cannot hope to portray in a single book the richness of a legal system that has evolved over centuries, grafting European, Latin American and North American ideas onto a society with pre-Hispanic cultural patterns, established centuries before the Spanish conquest, that still reverberate in today's legal institutions. The Mexican legal system is an ornate, syncretic fabric of historical, anthropological, political and intellectual strands, a fabric that defies easy description or simplified analysis. The Mexican legal system—the laws, legal institutions, sociological and cultural norms that make up the Mexican legal *culture*—is not a seamless tapestry, nor is it a transparent one. These characteristics make the study of Mexican law a challenging enterprise, especially for a lawyer trained in the Anglo-Saxon tradition of common law; but like any intellectual challenge, dedicated study will yield rich rewards.

We offer this book as a general introduction, a point of departure rather than a definitive statement. In setting forth the outlines of Mexican law, we have attempted to provide the basic historical context from which the laws and legal institutions developed, as well as the political and economic forces that help explain why the legal system operates (or, in some instances, fails to operate) in the way that it does. A true understanding of any aspect of the Mexican legal system should begin with a reading of Mexican history, since historical events have forged every aspect of Mexican law.[1]

Since the 1980s, Mexico has experienced a political and legal evolution from an authoritarian regime to a truly democratic one. The changes have occurred at many levels, political and economic as well as legal. The roles played by legal institutions in Mexico have been altered, and they are continuing to change as this book goes to print. As one example, the Mexican Supreme Court now plays a much more prominent role in the development of Mexican law than it has ever played in the past, and this role continues to change. Another notable change has involved the trend towards increased availability of information about the Mexican government, and about the rules of law themselves. The use of computers and the availability of Internet databases have served as powerful tools in the service of transparency; one revelation of this book for the authors has been the recognition that rules of law and the processes used to apply them

[1] Many excellent English-language histories of Mexico may be found in print. *See*, for example, Meyer, M. C. and Beezley, W., eds., THE OXFORD HISTORY OF MEXICO (Oxford: Oxford University Press, 2000); Miller, R. R., MEXICO: A HISTORY (Norman, Okla: University of Oklahoma Press, 1985, reprinted 1989).

have become so readily available to the public at a moderate cost. We have attempted to make use of this by providing citations to the databases in the footnotes wherever relevant.

Our most difficult task has been to present an introduction to Mexican legal *culture*, which is virtually impossible to explain in a general treatise. A sophisticated understanding of Mexican law requires more than a technical explanation of the written laws and codes alone. Lawyers and non-lawyers often ask how Mexican law differs from US law, hoping that there might be some legal Rosetta Stone that will unlock the mysteries of Mexican law. The answer to understanding Mexican law is not simply a matter of translation of technical norms, like the conversion of a 110-volt appliance to 220-volt current. The laws and legal institutions of Mexico are interwoven with the general culture of a society that is complex, multi-faceted and not quickly understood by the non-Mexican. Guillermo Margadant, the Mexican legal historian, opined that if one transplanted the entire US legal system to Mexico, the system would still operate altogether differently south of the Rio Bravo than it does in the United States, because the history, culture, and social values of Mexicans differ from those of their neighbours in the USA.

This book is written with a certain reader in mind: a lawyer from a common law country, and in particular one from the United States. The text is necessarily general, due to the breadth of our subject; we hope that the reader will profit from an understanding of basic principles, and we have tried to include in the footnotes citations to authorities that can be consulted in expanding one's understanding. We cannot hope to elucidate details to educate those who are already experts in the areas of Mexican law that we discuss; we have attempted to portray the legal system and the rules accurately, and if in doing so we have been guilty of any misinterpretations, we hope that the readers of this book will do us the favour of providing us with their comments and criticisms.

In our personal experiences, there is a good deal of misunderstanding about Mexican law, but many of these misunderstandings are based on common stereotypes held in the United States and elsewhere. When beginning to explore another country's legal system, one is not unscathed by cultural prejudices gleaned from popular media or other sources. One such stereotype—held by people both within and outside the country—views Mexico as a lawless country where the rule of law bends to accommodate rampant corruption and political compromise. Such exaggerations ignore the many ways in which Mexican law and legal institutions function well and with admirable efficiency. True, the discrepancy between the written law and its application is well known in Mexico, and has historical roots that stretch back to colonial times. Over generations, the fatalistic acceptance of this discrepancy by the Mexican people has been a disservice to the population and an obstacle to economic and social development. Nevertheless, what may be taken as corruption or lawlessness by a visitor may simply be a misunderstanding of the Mexican legal system and of the values to which it adheres.

It has been an advantage to approach this enterprise in a co-operative, bi-national effort. Three of us are Mexican citizens, two of us are citizens of the United States. We have each provided initial drafts of several chapters, and all of us have read and commented on the drafts of others, resulting in extensive revisions of the entire text. The writing of this book has been an education for each of us, and we hope that the debates and discussions that have taken place between us in writing this book will have enriched the final product as much as they have enriched us.

The baroque entrance to the Palacio de Iturbide, which graces the cover of this book, is a fitting metaphor for this introduction to Mexican law. Like an Anglican entering a baroque cathedral, the common law lawyer who enters the world of Mexican law must become accustomed to the onslaught of rich details that surround her. Like the artwork of a dimly lit chapel, the details of Mexican law may be hidden in shadows; the observer of Mexican law, like the student of colonial art, must become accustomed to the surroundings and must spend time deciphering the meanings. For those who expend the effort, that time will be richly rewarded.

Stephen Zamora
José Ramón Cossío
Leonel Pereznieto
José Roldán-Xopa
David Lopez
May 2004

Acknowledgements

A project of this scope would not have been possible without the generous support of many individuals and institutions. At the outset, we wish to express our gratitude for the academic support of: the Instituto Tecnológico Autónomo de México (ITAM) and its Chancellor, Dr. Arturo Fernández; the University of Houston Law Center and its Dean, Nancy Rapoport; St. Mary's University School of Law and its Dean, Bill Piatt; and the Instituto de Investigaciones Jurídicas of the Universidad Nacional Autónoma de México (UNAM), and its Director, Dr. Diego Valadés, and former Director, Dr José Luis Soberanes.

Many experts volunteered to read drafts of the chapters and make substantive comments that were invaluable to us, including Cecilia Azar, Álvaro Búnster, Luz del Carmen Carrillo, Josefina Cortés, Roberto del Cueto, Ana Gaitán, Beatriz González, Daniel Guerrero, James Herget, Giselle Hidalgo, Alicia Junco, Sergio López Ayllón, Antonio de Lisi, Manuel Lizardi, Trina Lozoya, Juan Carlos Marín, Cristina Massa Sánchez, Alejandro Mayagoitia, Raúl Mejía Garza, Luis Moreno, Ewell E. Murphy, Jr, Agustín Portal, Alejandro Pucheu, Luis Santos Jiménez, Miguel Sarre, Kiyoshi Tsuru, Agustín Velázquez, Lorenza Reyes Retana, and Joaquín Rodríguez Zarza. We are also grateful to Mónica Castillejos, Mariana Cabrera, Laura Edmiston, Antonio Espinosa, Trina Lozoya, Lorely Ramírez, Dennia Trejo, and Belén Zamora for their excellent research assistance, and to Alicia Arce, Laura Lozada, and Beverly Ward for valuable secretarial support. We are also grateful to Fiona Barry, Gwen Booth and John Louth of Oxford University Press for their support of our endeavour.

We are particularly indebted to the institutions and individuals who provided significant financial assistance to support translations of a number of the chapters in this book: Mike and Teresa Baker, Joe Ryan and Yolanda Villareal Ryan, Dr. Leonel Pereznieto, Haynes and Boone, LLP, Ricardo G. Cedillo of the firm Davis, Cedillo & Mendoza, Inc., the University of Houston Law Foundation, and ITAM.

Finally, we wish to thank, and give special recognition to, three persons whose professional support was crucial to this enterprise:

Anna Rayne, of Canterbury, England, edited the typescript, improved the text, and corrected technical errors;

David Sperling, a talented legal translator who resides in Washington, D.C., translated many of the Chapters that appear in the book in a literate and technically superior style that facilitated editing and rewriting, and helped us transcend, as well as we could, the barrier that exists between Mexican legal doctrines and English-language equivalents; and most importantly,

Maria del Carmen del Rio Yermi of the Mexico City Bar, whose considerable skills as a lawyer, researcher, and editor were invaluable to us. Her perseverance and professionalism kept our ambitious project on course, and we are very grateful to her.

Contents

Table of Abbreviations: Laws, Treaties, and Legal Terms

Abbreviation acronym	English translation	Spanish
AJUSTABONOS	Federal Government Adjustable Bonds	Bonos Ajustables del Gobierno Federal
BONDES	Development Bonds	Bonos de Desarrollo
BORES-DF	Federal District Urban Renewal Bonds	Bonos de Renovación Urbana del Distrito Federal
CC	Commercial Code	Código de Comercio
CCDF	Civil Code for the Federal District	Código Civil para el Distrito Federal
CETES	Treasury Certificates	Certificados de la Tesorería
CFPC	Federal Code of Civil Procedure	Código Federal de Procedimeintos Civiles
CFPP	Federal Code of Criminal Procedure	Codigo Federal de Procedimientos Penales
CIDIP	Inter-American Specialized Conferences on Private International Law	Conferencias Privadas de Leyes Internacionales
CISG	U.N. Convention on Contracts for the International Sale of Goods	Convención sobre los Contratos de Compraventa Internacional de Mercaderías
COFIPE	Federal Code of Electoral Institutions and Procedures	Código Federal de Instituciones y Procedimientos Electorales
CPCDF	Code of Civil Procedure for the Federal District	Código de Procedimientos Civiles para el Distrito Federal
CPDF	Criminal Code of the Federal District	Código Penal para el Distrito Federal
CPF	Federal Criminal Code	Código Penal Federal

CUD	Primary Coordination Agreement	Convenio Unico de Coordinación
DOF	Official Daily of the Federation	Diario Oficial de la Federación
FCC or CCF	Federal Civil Code	Código Civil Federal
FIL	Foreign Investment Law	Ley de Inversión Extrajera
GATT	General Agreement on Tariffs and Trade	Acuerdo General sobre Aranceles Aduaneros y Comercio
GDP	Gross Domestic Product	Producto Interno Bruto
IVA	Value Added Tax	Impuesto al Valor Agregado
LA	Agrarian Law	Ley Agraria
LAN	National Water Law	Ley de Aguas Nacionales
LBM	Law of the Bank of Mexico	Ley del Banco de México
LCM	Law of Mercantile Competition	Ley de Concursos Mercantiles
LEI	Foreign Investment Law	Ley de Inversión Extranjera
LFCE	Federal Law of Economic Competition	Ley Federal de Competencia Económica
LFD	Federal Law of Rights	Ley Federal de Derechos
LFDA	Federal Copyright Law	Ley Federal de Derecho del Autor
LFEP	Federal Law of Parastatal Entities	Ley Federal de las Entidades Paraestatales
LFOPPE	Federal Law of Political Organizations and Electoral Processes	Ley Federal de Organizaciones Políticas y Procesos Electorales
LFPA	Federal Law of Administrative Procedure	Ley Federal de Procedimiento Administrativo
LFPC	Federal Consumer Protection Law	Ley Federal de Protección al Consumidor
LFRASP	Federal Law of Administrative Responsibilities of Public Servants	Ley Federal de Responsabilidades Administrativas de Servidores Públicos
LFRSP	Federal Law of Liability of Public Servants	Ley Federal de Responsabilidades de los Servidores Públicos

LFSC	Federal Civil Service Law	Ley Federal de Servicio Civil
LFT	Federal Labour Law	Ley Federal del Trabajo
LFTAIGP	Federal Law of Transparency and Access to Public Information	Ley Federal de Transparencia y Acceso a la Información Pública Gubernamental
LFTSE	Federal Law of State Employees	Ley Federal de los Trabajadores al Servicio del Estado
LGAH	General Law of Human Settlements	Ley General de Asentamientos Humanos
LGDFS	General Law of Sustainable Forest Development	Ley General de Desarrollo Forestal Sustentable
LGEEPA	General Law of Ecological Balance and Environmental Protection	Ley General del Equilibrio Ecológico y la Protección al Ambiente
LGOAC	General Law of Credit Organizations and Activities	Ley General de Organizaciones y Actividades de Crédito
LGSM	General Law of Mercantile Societies	Ley General de Sociedades Mercantiles
LGTAIP	General Law of Transparency and Access to Public Information	Ley General de Transparencia y Acceso a la Informacion Pública
LGTOC	General Law of Titles and Credit Operations	Ley General de Títulos y Operaciones de Crédito
LGVS	General Law of Wildlife	Ley General de la Vida Silvestre
LIC	Law of Credit Institutions	Ley de Instituciones de Crédito
LMV	Law of the Securities Market	Ley del Mercado de Valores
LOAPF	Organic Law of the Federal Public Administration	Ley Orgánica de la Administración Pública Federal
LOBM	Organic Law of the Bank of Mexico	Ley Orgánica del Banco de México
LOFTAJ	Federal Organic Law of the Administrative and Justice Tribunal	Ley Orgánica Federal del Tribunal Administrativo y de Justicia

LOIPAB	Organic Law of the Institute for the Protection of Savings	Ley Orgánica del Instituto de Protección al Ahorro Bancario
LONF	Organic Law of National Finance	Ley Orgánica de Nacional Financiera
LOPJF	Organic Law of the Federal Judiciary	Ley Orgánica del Poder Judicial de la Federación
LOTA	Organic Law of Agrarian Tribunals	Ley Orgánica de los Tribunales Agrarios
LOTSJDF	Organic Law of the Superior Tribunal of the Federal District	Ley Orgánica del Tribunal Superior de Justicia del Distrito Federal
LP	Law of Planning	Ley de Planeación
LPAB	Law for the Protection of Savings	Ley de Protección al Ahorro Bancario
LPDUSF	Law for the Protection and Defense of Users of Financial Services	Ley de Protección y Defensa a los Usuarios de Servicios Financieros
LPI	Intellectual Property Law	Ley de la Propiedad Industrial
LRAF	Law to Regulate Financial Groups	Ley para Regular las Agrupaciones Financieras
LRSF	Reglamentary Law of Rail Service	Ley Reglamentaria del Servicio Ferroviario
LSAR	Law of the Retirement Savings System	Ley del Sistema del Ahorro para el Retiro
MIR	Regulatory Impact Statement	Manifestación de Impacto Regulatorio
NAALC	North American Agreement on Labour Cooperation	Tratado de América del Norte de Cooperación Laboral
NAFTA	North American Free Trade Agreement	Tratado de Libre Comercio para América del Norte
NGOs	Non-governmental Organizations	Organizaciones No Gubernamentales
NOMs	Mexican Official Norms	Normas Oficiales Mexicanas
PAGAFES	Federal Treasury Promissory Notes	Pagarés de la Tesorería de la Federación
PECE	Pact for Economic Stability and Growth	Pacto para la Estabilidad y el Crecimiento Económico

PPSA	Personal Property Insurance Acts	Actas sobre la Seguridad de la Propiedad Personal
PROCEDE	Certification Program for Ejidal Rights and Titling of Urban Lots	Programa de Certificación de Derechos Ejidales y Titulación de Predios Urbanos
PROGRESA	Program for the Support of Health, Nutrition and Education	Programa de Apoyo a la Salud, Alimentación y Educación
PRONASOL	National Solidarity Program	Programa Nacional de Solidaridad
RFTS	Federal Registry of Procedures and Services	Registro Federal de Trámites y Servicios
RLFDA	Regulations of the Federal Copyright Law	Reglamento de la Ley Federal de Derechos de Autor
RLFEP	Regulations of the Federal Law of Parastatal Entities	Reglamento de la Ley Federal de las Entidades Paraestatales
RLPI	Regulations of the Intellectual Property Law	Reglamento de la Ley de la Propiedad Industrial
S. de R.L.	Limited Liability Company	Sociedad de Responsabilidad Limitada
S.A.	Corporation	Sociedad Anónima
SAR	Retirement Savings System	Sistema de Ahorro para el Retiro
SIEFORES	Investment Societies Specialized in Retirement Funds	Sociedades de Inversión Especializadas en Fondos para el Retiro
SOFOL	Limited Object Financial Societies	Sociedades Financieras de Objeto Limitado
TESOBONOS	Federal Treasury Bonds	Bonos de la Tesorería de la Federación
TRIPS	Trade-Related Intellectual Property Rights	Derechos de Propiedad Industrial Relacionadas al Comercio Exterior
UCC	Uniform Commercial Code	Código Uniforme de Comercio
UCP	Uniform Customs and Practices for Credit Documents	Costumbres y Prácticas Uniformes para Documentos de Crédito
UDI	Units of Investment	Unidades de Inversión

Table of Institutions and Organizations

Abbreviation acronym	English translation	Spanish
AAA	American Arbitration Association	Asociación de Arbitraje Americano
ANDI	National Association of Interpreters	Asociación Nacional de Intérpretes
ANUIES	National Association of Universities and Institutions of Higher Education	Asociación Nacional de Universidades e Instituciones de Educación Superior
ASCAP	American Society of Composers, Authors and Publishers	Sociedad Americana de Compositores, Autores y Publicistas
BANAMEX	National Bank of Mexico	Banco Nacional de México
BANCOMEXT	National Bank of Foreign Trade	Banco Nacional de Comercio Exterior
BANOBRAS	National Bank of Public Works and Services	Banco Nacional de Obras y Servicios Públicos
BANRURAL	National Bank of Rural Credit	Banco Nacional de Crédito Rural
BANXICO	Bank of Mexico	Banco de México
BMV	Mexican Securities Exchange	Bolsa Mexicana de Valores
CAB	Federal Conciliation and Arbitration Board	Juntas de Conciliación y Arbitraje
CAMEX	Arbitration Center of Mexico	Centro de Arbitraje de México
CANACO	National Chamber of Commerce	Cámara Nacional de Comercio
CAT	Federal Conciliation and Arbitration Tribunal	Tribunal Federal de Conciliación y Arbitraje
CEC	Commission for Environmental Cooperation	Comisión de Cooperación Ambiental
CFC	Federal Competition Commission	Comisión Federal de Competencia
CFE	Federal Electricity Company	Compañía Federal de Electricidad

CID	Interdepartmental Commission on Dissolution	Comisión Intersecretarial de Desincorporación
CIDAC	Center for Development Research (Civil Association)	Centro de Investigaciones para el Desarrollo, Asociación Civil
CNA	National Water Commission	Comisión Nacional del Agua
CNBV	National Bank Securities Commission	Comisión Nacional Bancaria de Valores
CNC	National Peasant Commission	Comisión Nacional Campesina
CNDH	National Human Rights Commission	Comisión Nacional de Derechos Humanos
CNOP	National Committee of Popular Organizations	Comité Nacional de Organizaciones Populares
CNSF	National Insurance and Surety Commission	Comision Nacional de Seguros y Fianzas
COFEMER	Federal Regulatory Improvement Commission	Comisión Federal de Mejora Regulatoria
CONACULTA	National Council for Culture and the Arts	Consejo Nacional para la Cultura y las Artes
CONACYT	National Council of Science and Technology	Consejo Nacional de Ciencia y Tecnología
CONAFOR	National Forestry Commission	Comisión Nacional Forestal
CONALITEG	National Free Textbook Commission	Comisión Nacional de Libros de Textos Gratutitos
CONAP	National Commission of Protected Natural Areas	Comisión Nacional de Areas Naturales Protegidas
CONASUPO	National Food Staples Corporation	Compania Nacional de Subsistencias Populares
CONDUSEF	National Commission for the Protection and Defense of Users of Financial Services	Comisión Nacional para la Protección y Defensa de los Usuarios de Servicios Financieros
CONSAR	National Commission for the Retirement Savings System	Comisión Nacional del Sistema de Ahorro para el Retiro
CROM	Mexican Labour Regional Confederation	Confederación Regional Obrera Mexicana
CTM	Confederation of Mexican Workers	Confederación de Trabajadores de México
DDF	Department of the Federal District	Departamento del Distrito Federal

EFTA	European Free Trade Association	Asociación Europea de Libre Comercio
FDIC	Federal Deposit Insurance Corporation	Corporación Federal de Seguros de Depósitos
FDN	National Democratic Front	Frente Democrático Nacional
FOBAPROA	Banking Fund for the Protection of Savings	Fondo Bancario de Protección al Ahorro
FONART	National Foundation for Folk Art	Fondo Nacional de Artesanías
FONATUR	National Tourism Foundation	Fondo Nacional para el Turismo
FONCA	National Foundation for Culture and the Arts	Fondo Nacional para la Cultura y las Artes
FONAPO	National Foundation for Popular Housing	Fondo Nacional para las Viviendas Populares
FOVI	Fund for the Operation and Financing of Housing	Fondo de Operacion y Financiamiento Bancario a la Vivienda
ICC	International Chamber of Commerce	Cámara Internacional de Comercio
ICSID	International Center for the Settlement of Investment Disputes	Centro Internacional para la Resolución de Controversias en Materia de Inversión
IFAI	Federal Institute for Access to Public Information	Instituto Federal de Acceso a la Información Pública
IFE	Federal Electoral Institute	Instituto Federal Electoral
IFECOM	Federal Institute of Specialists of Mercantile Competition	Instituto Federal de Especialistas de Concursos Mercantiles
IIJ	Legal Research Institute	Instituto de Investigaciones Jurídicas
IMF	International Monetary Fund	Fondo Monetario Internacional
IMPI	Mexican Intellectual Property Institute	Instituto Mexicano de la Propiedad Intelectual
IMSS	Mexican Social Security Institute	Instituto Mexicano del Seguro Social
INAH	National Institute of Anthropology and History	Instituto Nacional de Antropología e Historia
INBA	National Fine Arts Institute	Instituto Nacional de Bellas Artes

INDA	National Copyright Institute	Instituto Nacional de Derechos del Autor
INDETEC	Institute for the Technical Development of Public Finances	Instituto para el Desarrollo Técnico de las Haciendas
INDEVAL	Securities Deposit Institute	Instituto para el Depósito de Valores
INEGI	National Institute of Statistics, Geography and Information	Instituto Nacional de Estadística e Informática
INFONAVIT	Institute of the National Foundation for the Housing of Workers	Instituto del Fondo Nacional para la Vivienda de los Trabajadores
INSOL	International Insolvency Association	Asociación Internacional de Insolvencia
IPAB	Institute for the Protection of Bank Savings	Instituto de Protección al Ahorro Bancario
ISSSTE	Institute of Social Security and Services for State Employees	Instituto de Seguridad y Servicios Sociales de los Trabajadores del Estado
ITAM	Autonomous Technological Institute of Mexico	Instituto Tecnológico Autonomo de México
MP	Public Ministry	Ministerio Público
NAFINSA	National Finance	Nacional Financiera
OECD	Organization for Economic Cooperation and Development	Organización de Cooperación Económica y de Desarrollo
OMC	World Trade Organization	Organización Mundial de Comercio
PAN	National Action Party	Partido de Acción Nacional
PARM	Authentic Party of the Mexican Revolution	Partido Auténtico de la Revolución Mexicana
PCT	Patent Cooperation Treaty	Tratado de Cooperación de Patentes
PEMEX	Petroleum Mexico	Petróleos Mexicanos
PGR	Attorney General of the Republic	Procurador General de la República or Procuraduría General de la República
PNR	National Revolutionary Party	Partido Nacional Revolucionario
PPS	Popular Socialist Party	Partido Popular Socialista
PRD	Revolutionary Democratic Party	Partido de la Revolución Democrática
PRI	Institutional Revolutionary Party	Partido Revolucionario Institucional

PRM	Mexican Revolutionary Party	Partido de la Revolución Mexicana
PROFECO	Federal Consumer Protection Agency	Procuraduría Federal del Consumidor
PROFEPA	Federal Attorney General for Environmental Protection	Procuraduría Federal para la Protección Ambiental
SACM	Society of Music Authors and Composers	Sociedad de Autores y Compositores de Música
SAOF	Society of Authors of Photographic Works	Sociedad de Autores de Obras Fotográficas
SCJN	Supreme Court of Justice of Mexico	Suprema Corte de Justicia de la Nación
SCT	Secretary of Communications and Transportation	Secretaría de Comunicaciones y Transportes
SDN	Secretary of National Defense	Secretaría de la Defensa Nacional
SE	Secretary of Energy	Secretaría de Energía
SECODAM	Secretary of Government Accounting and Administrative Development	Secretaría de Contraloría y Desarrollo Administrativo
SECOFI	Secretary of Commerce and Industrial Promotion	Secretaría de Comercio y Promoción Industrial
SECONOMIA	Secretary of the Economy	Secretaría de Economía
SECTUR	Secretary of Tourism	Secretaría de Turismo
SEDESOL	Secretary of Social Development	Secretaría de Desarrollo Social
SAGARPA	Secretary of Agriculture, Livestock, Rural Development, Fishing and Nutrition	Secretaría de Agricultura, Ganadería, Desarrollo Rural, Pesca y Alimentación
SEMARNAT	Secretary of the Environment and Natural Resources	Secretaría de Medio Ambiente y Recursos Naturales
SEP	Secretary of Public Education	Secretaría de Educación Pública
SFP	Secretary of Public Administration	Secretaría de la Función Pública
SG	Secretary of Internal Affairs	Secretaría de Gobernación
SHCP	Secretary of the Treasury and Public Credit	Secretaría de Hacienda y Crédito Público
SJF	Social Justice Fund	Fondo Social de Justicia
SM	Secretary of the Navy	Secretaría de Marina
SMC	Mexican Society of Animators and Cartoonists	Sociedad Mexicana de Caricaturas

SNTE	National Union of Education Workers	Sindicato Nacional de Trabajadores de la Educación
SOGEM	General Society of Mexican Writers	Sociedad General de Escritores de México
SOMART	Mexican Society of Plastic Arts	Sociedad Mexicana de Artes Plásticas
SOMEN	Mexican Society of Music Writers	Sociedad Mexicana de Escritores de Música
SRA	Secretary of Agrarian Reform	Secretaría de la Reforma Agraria
SRE	Secretary of Foreign Relations	Secretaría de Relaciones Exteriores
SSA	Secretary of Public Health and Assistance	Secretaría de Salubridad y Asistencia
SSP	Secretary of Public Security	Secretaría de Seguridad Pública
STPS	Secretary of Labour and Social Welfare	Secretaría de Trabajo y Previsión Social
TRIFE	Federal Electoral Tribunal	Tribunal Federal Electoral
UDG	University of Guadalajara	Universidad de Guadalajara
UNAM	National Autonomous University of Mexico	Universidad Nacional Autonóma de Mexico
UNCITRAL	United Nations Commission on International Trade Law	

About the Authors

José Ramón Cossío is a Justice of the Mexican Supreme Court. From 1994 to 2003, he was Dean of the Law School at the Instituto Tecnológico Autónomo de México (ITAM) in Mexico City, and he has been a Professor of Constitutional Law and Legal Theory at ITAM since 1989. Dr Cossío Díaz has published fourteen books, as well as numerous articles on Mexican constitutional law and legal theory. In 1989, he was appointed by the Mexican Supreme Court as a member of the commission to undertake a major revision of the *amparo* laws; he has also served as an adviser on legislation to the Mexican Senate, and to numerous federal government agencies. He is a member of the Mexican National System of Researchers and of the Mexican National Academy of Sciences, from which he received the National Research Award in 1998 in social sciences. Dr Cossío holds a Doctorate of Laws from the Universidad Complutense de Madrid, and a law degree from Universidad de Colima.

David Lopez is a Partner with the law firm of Davis, Cedillo & Mendoza, Inc. From 1993 to 2001, he was Professor of Law at St Mary's University School of Law in San Antonio, Texas. During that time, Professor Lopez taught courses dealing with Mexican law, was a visiting professor at the Universidad Autónoma de Guadalajara as part of Baylor Law School's Summer Program in Mexico from 1996 to 2000, and was a frequent speaker in both the United States and Mexico on subjects relating to the Mexican legal system. Since returning to private practice in 2001, Mr Lopez's work has focused on complex international litigation and arbitration involving Mexican clients and issues of US and Mexican law.

Leonel Pereznieto is Professor of Private International Law and Comparative Law at the National Autonomous University of Mexico (UNAM), and is Of Counsel to the Mexico City law firm of Von Wobeser y Sierra, S.C. From 1993 to 1996, he served as a Commissioner of the Mexican Federal Antitrust Commission. One of Mexico's leading authorities on conflict of laws (private international law), Dr Pereznieto is an active member and former President of the Mexican Academy of Private International Law. He also serves as a member of the consulting commission on private international law of the Mexican Secretariat of Foreign Relations. He has extensive experience as an international arbitrator with the American Arbitration Association, the International Chamber of Commerce and the London Court of International Arbitrators, and is a member of the Chartered Institute of Arbitrators. Dr Pereznieto holds a law degree from UNAM, a Master's Degree from the Escuela Nacional de Administración Pública of Spain, a Master's Degree from the Institut

International d'Administration Publique of France, and a Doctorate in Law from the University of Paris.

José Roldán-Xopa is Professor of Law and Director of the Master's Programme in Administrative and Regulatory Law of the Instituto Tecnológico Autónomo de México (ITAM). He is the author of numerous books and articles on administrative law, constitutional law, the law of indigenous peoples, and economic law. He has extensive experience in Mexican administrative law, having served in administrative positions in the Government of the Federal District of Mexico City, and as an adviser on legislation to the Mexican Senate and to the federal Secretariat of the Economy. Dr Roldán holds a law degree from the Benemérita Universidad Autónoma de Puebla, a Master of Laws Degree from the Universidad Autónoma Metropolitana, and a Doctorate in Law from the Universidad Nacional Autónoma de México (UNAM).

Stephen Zamora is Professor of Law and former Dean of the University of the Houston Law Center, and is Of Counsel to the law firm Haynes and Boone, L.L.P. From 1979 to 1994, he served as Director of the University of Houston's Mexican Legal Studies Program. He has been a Senior Fulbright Professor at the Universidad Nacional Autónoma de México (UNAM), and a visiting research fellow of UNAM's Instituto de Investigaciones Jurídicas. Professor Zamora has published widely on subjects of Mexican law, US–Mexican relations, international trade law, international banking law, and international economic law, and is a member of the American Law Institute, the American Society of International Law, and the American Society of Comparative Law. Professor Zamora holds a B.A. in Political Science from Stanford University, and a J.D. from the University of California at Berkeley (Boalt Hall).

1

The History of Mexican Law

To study Mexican law without regard to Mexico's rich history would not only be boring; it would also give one a very limited understanding of the way in which the legal system functions. In the United States, a future-oriented society, legal history is an optional subject bypassed by most law students. In Mexico, first-year law students take two semesters of Roman law, and many legal subjects are taught from an historical perspective. Consequently, we begin our discussion of Mexican law with an overview of Mexican history, emphasizing the ways in which historical events have influenced the development of law.[1]

1. Pre-Hispanic Legal Cultures

To an even greater extent than its Canadian and US neighbours, Mexico inherited a rich legacy of indigenous cultures that were thriving at the beginning of the sixteenth century, when European civilizations were introduced into the 'New World'.[2] Most visitors to Mexico are aware that Spanish *conquistadores*, led by Hernán Cortes, arrived in Mexico in the early sixteenth century and quickly conquered a large indigenous empire ruled by the Aztecs. In western history books, the Spanish conquest tends to overshadow the importance and complexity of indigenous Mesoamerican cultures. The Aztec civilization was just one of the many highly evolved groups—Mayan, Zapotec, and others—that inhabited Mexico at the time of the Spanish arrival. The indigenous cultures that preceded Spanish rule were large and highly evolved, and they established patterns of communal behaviour, including a sophisticated network of rules and their enforcement, that influenced the development of law in Mexico.[3] To gain a thorough understanding of Mexican law, it is therefore useful to begin with a cursory examination of the indigenous cultures that preceded Spanish rule.

[1] For resources related to the study of Mexican history, *see* the web site of the Latin American Network Information Center of the Lozano Long Institute for Latin American Studies at the University of Texas, at www.lanic.utexas.edu/la/mexico/#history.

[2] In Canada and the United States, indigenous tribes were largely conquered and marginalized, in contrast with the colonization, conversion, and imperfect assimilation that occurred in Mexico. The European concept of 'New World' was, of course, a depreciation of the centuries-old civilizations that the Spaniards encountered.

[3] Many historians recognize the influence of pre-Hispanic norms on the indigenous population of colonial Nueva España. Thus, historian Susan Kellogg has described how the Nahua legal culture carried forward, and became subsumed in, the colonial legal system of New Spain. Kellogg, S., *Law and the Transformation of Aztec Culture, 1500–1700* (Norman: University of Oklahoma Press, 1995).

In examining the pre-Hispanic origins of Mexican law, we might begin by dispelling the notion that there is a single legal culture in Mexico. Mexico has always been a diverse country, with distinct social classes, and numerous ethnic and linguistic groups that lie outside the mainstream of the modern legal system. Over 7 per cent of all Mexicans still speak indigenous languages as their first language: Náhuatl, Zapotec, Otomí, etc.[4] Within two hours' drive from Mexico City, villages exist in which Spanish is rarely spoken, and in which cultural patterns, though profoundly influenced by modern communications, do not differ greatly from the patterns followed centuries earlier. It is not hard to imagine that the lives of many Mexicans, in particular those outside the mainstream economy, are influenced as much by customary norms of pre-Hispanic origin as they are by formal rules of law adopted by state and national governments.[5] And since the Zapatista uprising that began in the southern state of Chiapas in 1994, the Mexican government has had to acknowledge this fact by a major constitutional amendment that gives room for greater recognition of pre-Hispanic rules that govern behaviour.[6]

1.1. Pre-Hispanic Mexico[7]

Aztec culture was in full bloom when the Spanish arrived, and the drama that resulted from the confrontation of European and Mesoamerican civilizations is compelling.[8] Belying its importance in Mexican history, however, the period of Aztec ascendancy was actually quite brief, lasting from the early 1300s until the Spanish conquest of 1521.[9] Aztec rule was itself the result of conquest of

[4] Source: XII Censo General de Población y Vivienda 2000, Estados Unidos Mexicanos (www.inegi.gob.mx/difusion/español/fpobla.html). Speakers of indigenous languages reside disproportionately in several southern states: Yucatán (37 per cent of the population speaks indigenous languages); Oaxaca (37 per cent); Chiapas (24 per cent); Quintana Roo (23 per cent); Hidalgo (17 per cent).

[5] Margadant, G., *Introducción a la Historia del Derecho Mexicano* (Mexico: Editorial Esfiage, 8th ed., 1988), at 27: 'It is undeniable that the absence of democratic spirit in the [pre-Hispanic] phase, the exercise of unilateral power, without a countercurrent of ideas based on "inalienable rights of man", still explains many aspects of non-urban indigenous life, and is a key to understanding the serious difficulty of translating modern, progressive, democratic laws into tangible realities' (authors' translation). *See also* Mendieta y Nuñez, Lucio, *El Derecho Precolonial* (Mexico: Porrúa, 6th ed., 1992) at 25–27, regarding the importance of pre-Hispanic antecedents in understanding Mexican law.

[6] *See* Chapter 7 below at text accompanying notes 25–29.

[7] *See generally* Cruz Barney, O., *Historia del Derecho Mexicano* (Mexico: Oxford U.P., 1999) at 1–31; González, M., 'Historia del Derecho Mexicano', in Vol. XII, *Enciclopedia Jurídica Mexicana* (Mexico: UNAM/Ed. Porrúa, 2002) at 307, 311–320.

[8] The chronicle of Captain Bernal Díaz, who accompanied Cortes, attests to the economic, artistic, and political development achieved under the theocratic rule of the Aztec monarchs. Bernal Díaz del Castillo, *The Discovery and Conquest of Mexico* (New York: Da Capo Press, D. Garcia, ed., trans. A. Maudsley, 1996).

[9] The symbol used on the Mexican flag and on official seals comes from the mythical founding of Tenochtitlán. According to Aztec belief, a priest/follower of the god Huitzilopochtli (Hummingbird-on-the-left) instructed the Aztecs, while still wandering in central Mexico, to settle in the place where they would find an eagle perched on a cactus and devouring a snake.

competing indigenous cultures. The Aztecs as conquerors were great assimilators, and the sophistication of Aztec culture can be directly attributed to their interest in appropriating the traditions, arts, sciences, myths, and gods of earlier cultures. In this way, the Aztecs reflected their Spanish conquerors: themselves the product of Romanist, Byzantine, Moorish, and Visigothic cultural and political influences.

This penchant for assimilation of cultures is key to understanding the syncretism that characterizes the culture of the Spanish colonies in the New World. This syncretism was especially pronounced in those areas, such as New Spain, where large and well developed indigenous cultures preceded Spanish rule. It appears in Mexican language, where words of Náhuatl (the Aztec language) coexist with Spanish,[10] as well as in certain legal forms that we will examine, such as the *ejido*. The tendency to borrow and 'Mexicanize' non-indigenous concepts continues to the present day, as an examination of everything from art movements to constitutional law will attest.

1.1.1. Pre-Aztec Cultures

The Aztec culture was itself a culmination of thousands of years of mesoamerican indigenous cultures. The earliest identifiable civilizations date from 2500 B.C. Each culture was centred in a particular area of what is now Mexico, the most prominent groups being the Olmecs (1200 to 400 B.C.) in the Veracruz-Tabasco coast; the Mayas (whose golden age extends from A.D. 300 to 900, but whose culture predated the birth of Christ and extended beyond the Spanish conquest) in southern Mexico, the Yucatán, and the Central American republics; the Huastecs (A.D. 1200 to 1521) in central and northern Mexico; the Toltecs (A.D. 950 to 1150) in central Mexico; the Zapotecs (A.D. 200 to 900) in the southern region of Oaxaca; and the Mixtecs (A.D. 900 to 1500) in southern Puebla and northern Oaxaca.[11]

The Mayan civilization was the most extensive in reach. A confederation of city states (Tikal, Palenque, Copán, Chichen Itzá, Uxmal, among others), the Mayan culture extended from south-eastern Mexico to El Salvador. Mayan arts and sciences were highly developed (Mayan use of the number zero predated by centuries its use in Europe) and the Mayan legal and political systems were similarly sophisticated. The grandeur of Mayan civilization is evident in the

Aztec tradition holds that this apparition occured on an uninhabited island in the marshes of Lake Texcoco, in what is now the Valley of Mexico, in A.D. 1325, although the date may have been earlier.

[10] Numerous terms derived from Náhuatl are evidence of the syncretism of Mexican Spanish: *aguacate* (avocado), *guajolote* (turkey), etc.

[11] Another culture, referred to by the Aztecs as Teotihuacán ('Place of the Gods'), flourished in the Valley of Mexico between A.D. 200 and 900. Dominated by monumental pyramids, Teotihuacán was an impressive ceremonial city of 100,000 people, and its pantheon of gods, including Quetzalcóatl (the Feathered Serpent), was appropriated later by the Aztecs. The mysterious downfall of Teotihuacán occurred in the eighth century, and the site was later taken over by the Toltecs. Teotihuacán remains a popular destination for tourists to Mexico City.

impressive architecture of Mayan sites from Copán (in Guatemala) to Chichén Itzá (in northern Yucatán).

Mayan society was stratified, with each city state being ruled by a monarch (*halach uinic*) who was supported by a class of priests and nobles. Craftsmen, farmers, and slaves made up the bulk of the population. Mayan codices, or pictographs, that have survived the Spanish conquest portray rules of family law (monogamy was the rule, although divorce was common), laws of property and succession, and harsh criminal laws. A class of judges, or *batab*, handed down criminal judgments (from which there was no appeal), the punishment in each case depending on the social class of the defendant.[12]

The Mayan economy, dependent on agriculture (beans, squash, maize, cacao, cotton), developed an extensive trading network with other cultures in the north and south. Landholdings were chiefly communal, with individual families receiving minuscule, 400-square-foot plots for their personal use.[13]

The impressive Mayan cities in the south, which flourished after A.D. 300, experienced a vertiginous decline in the ninth century. A combination of soil depletion and disease may have placed strains on the working classes; some scholars attribute the decline to peasant insurrections brought on by the oppressive burden of supporting the growing populations of nobles and priests. After the southern Mayan cities declined, a Mayan renaissance occurred in the Yucatán Peninsula, beginning in the tenth century. In the eleventh century, Toltec tribes from central Mexico invaded the northern Mayan cities, resulting in a merging of Mayan and Toltec beliefs and arts. The Maya-Toltec civilization flourished for several centuries, but was already in decline when the Spanish arrived in the Yucatán.

1.1.2. The Aztec Empire

As already noted, the Aztecs were the inheritors of earlier cultures and traditions, in particular those of the Chichimecan and Toltecan civilizations. The Aztec Empire itself (1325 to 1521) was based on an alliance of warring tribes, in particular the *mexicas*, in the valley of Mexico.[14] By defeating local tribes, the Aztecs formed an empire of thirty-eight provinces, each recognizing Aztec supremacy. The Aztecs required periodic levies of sacrificial victims (necessary to the Aztecs' bloody religious beliefs) and exacted the surrender of lands and the payment of tribute in the form of goods and services. On the other hand, the defeated tribes were able to retain their local governments, language, and religions. Nevertheless, the resentment created by Aztec rule facilitated the Spaniards' formation of alliances with indigenous groups to confront the Aztecs.

[12] Margadant, *supra* note 5 at 14–16.

[13] *Id.* at 15; Mendieta y Nuñez, *supra* note 5 at 119–124.

[14] The Aztec Empire has been characterized as a 'triple alliance' of the kingdoms of México, Texcoco, and Tacuba, which were distinct cities of the Valley of Mexico. Each region was ruled separately by a monarch, as described below. Mendieta y Nuñez, *supra* note 5 at 35 *et seq.*

The capital of the Mexican kingdom was Tenochtitlán, a city built on a strategic but otherwise unpromising site in the marshy Lake of Texcoco. From a city of village huts, by the time of the Spanish invasion Tenochtitlán had grown to a capital of 360,000 people, one of the three largest cities of the world at that time. Tenochtitlán was supported by agricultural production in the Valley of Mexico, and by the time of the conquest it had become an impressive trading and commercial centre.

A sophisticated legal system administered by specialized tribunals supported this complex empire. By 1502, the Aztecs ruled an empire of ten million subjects organized under a complex mixture of law mixed with religious belief. Most of the law was customary and closely aligned with religion, but over time Aztec rulers (*tlatoani*) had also decreed a considerable body of laws. These laws were not codified, although at the time of the conquest, the philosopher-king Netzahualcóyotl was beginning a project of codification of laws.[15] What have come down to us as the Aztec codices are best seen as descriptive accounts or histories of Aztec life, including what we would describe as rules of law, rather than codifications of laws.[16]

As with Mayan culture, Aztec society was highly stratified, with little social mobility between classes. At the top were the hereditary nobility (*pipiltin*), the warrier elite (*teteuctin*, who were knights of noble birth), and the priests. The latter, who numbered 5,000 in Tenochtitlán by the sixteenth century, played an important role, as teachers and scholars, in the development of law. Commoners were formed into clans, or *calpullis*: groups of families organized by intermarriage. The *calpullis* held title to land, which was parcelled out to members of the *calpulli*. Each *calpulli* was governed by a council of senior men, who regulated local affairs and managed the economy. Peasants and slaves (prisoners of war, etc.) made up a significant portion of the population, and were tied to land but held little or no status or rights.

The *calpullis* were themselves organized into four major groupings, or *campans*, which elected a military leader or *tenoch*. At the founding of Tenochtitlán, the power of the *tenoch* was purely military, but over time a hereditary monarchy was established, with a king who was recognized as a descendant of the vanquished Toltec culture that had been revered by the Aztecs. Over time, this ruler, or *tlatoani*, came to be seen as a descendant of the god-king Quetzalcóatl, and he thus assumed both political and religious supremacy. Originally, the position of ruler was passed down by heredity, but gradually it became the practice that, rather than allow the *tlatoani* to choose his successor, a group of noble electors (*tlatocan*) would choose among different possible candidates which one would rule. Political rule thus emanated from the king, or *tlatoani*, the council

15 Margadant, *supra* note 5 at 17.

16 According to Margadant, *ibid.*, pre-Hispanic codices were destroyed in the religious zeal of the Spanish conquest. The primary sources of Aztec laws, such as the *Códice Mendocino*, were commissioned after the Spanish conquest.

of nobles (*tlatocan*), and the representatives of the *calpulli*. The power of the *tlatoani* was not limitless. He was influenced by 'pressure groups' of nobles and priests. In the theocratic Aztec regime, priests served as both political and religious advisers.

Much of the land was either held by the *tlatoani*, or held as public land to support the nobility, warrior, and priest classes. As already noted, the *calpulli* also owned property communally, with rights to use specific lots being handed down through particular families. The *calpulli* worked lands communally, for the payment of tribute to and support of the noble, warrior, and priest classes. It is these lands that served as the foundation of the communal *ejido* properties that formed an important institution in the Spanish conquest, and reappeared in modern Mexican property laws.[17]

Commerce and trade were highly developed, and were conducted by a merchant class that paid taxes to the king. Markets (*tianguis*, a name still employed in Mexico for communal markets) were well organized, with price controls and with commercial courts to settle disputes. Cocoa beans, copper pieces, feathers, and gold dust served as mediums of exchange.

The family was an important unit in Aztec culture, and laws regulated marriage, birth, death, and succession. Marriage was obligatory for men and women, and poligamy was practised within the nobility, where the man could demonstrate the economic ability to support more than one family.

Aztec commerce included a highly regulated market in slavery. Slaves (*tlacotin*) consisted of prisoners of war, children sold into slavery by their fathers, and voluntary sale of oneself into slavery (for payment of debts). Approximately 5 per cent of the population were slaves.[18] Farm labourers (*mayeques*) comprised about one-third of the population, had no title to land, and had no possibility for improving their status in society.

The Aztecs had a formal judicial system, with courts located in both Tenochtitlán and the neighbouring city of Texcoco. At the lower level, members of the *calpulli* elected magistrates to decide local matters. More important matters were handled by a court system administered by a supreme magistrate, who operated under the authority of the king.[19] In Texcoco, which served as the seat of appeal in non-military matters, the king's judicial authority was divided between three chambers of twelve judges who were appointed by the king. Notwithstanding this formal system for enforcing laws and deciding disputes, according to Professor Susan Kellogg the courts 'represented only a small part of

[17] Mendieta y Nuñez, *supra* note 5 at 111–114. On the modern-day *ejido* system, *see* Chapter 13 below at text accompanying notes 74 to 93.

[18] Miller, Robert Ryal, MEXICO: A HISTORY (Norman: University of Oklahoma Press, 1985) at 54.

Slavery as practised by pre-Hispanic groups was fairly benign by comparison with the institution practised in other parts of the world. Professor Borah refers to it as 'a mild affair which entitled the owner of the slave to service for life, but left the slave very substantial rights'. Borah, Woodrow, JUSTICE BY INSURANCE (Berkeley: University of California Press, 1983) at 39.

[19] Mendieta y Nuñez, *supra* note 5 at 44–46.

the broader mechanisms of social control, which relied heavily on supernatural sanctions and on families, neighborhoods and wards, work sites, and craft groups to teach and enforce rules and resolve disputes. [. . .] Merchants and presumably craft groups also exercised judicial authority over their members. [. . .] In those instances when these mechanisms failed to resolve a conflict, a case might be brought before the royal courts.'[20]

Specialized courts existed for commercial matters, religious matters, family law, and criminal matters. Aztec criminal law, as befits a military state, was harsh and bloody. The death penalty was common, and was administered with great cruelty. Tribute to the crown was administered by public officials, called *calpixqui*, who were subject to the death penalty if guilty of dishonesty. The Spanish were eventually able to exploit the resentment of conquered tribes who had been forced to pay tribute to the Aztec crown. On the other hand, these same groups, already accustomed to forced labour and the payment of tribute to a conquering tribe, were therefore made susceptible to the institution of the Spanish *encomienda*.[21]

1.1.3. *The Legacy of Pre-Hispanic Law*

Just as the Aztecs did not attempt to displace the local law of groups conquered by them, the Spanish crown authorized the continued use of pre-Hispanic rules that were compatible with those of the crown. From the sixteenth to the eighteenth centuries, the evangelization of indigenous groups by religious orders (Augustinians, Franciscans, Dominicans) was intended to displace many indigenous beliefs and customary behaviour. However, the success of the Catholic Church in converting Mexico lay not in supplanting local norms, but in accommodating them with Catholic beliefs. The same may be said of the imposition of legal norms. Indeed, certain pre-Hispanic norms have become a part of the formal legal system in Mexico. The *ejido*, a direct legacy of pre-Hispanic law that establishes rules for the communal development of agricultural lands, has survived through colonial times to the present, where it is still enshrined, albeit with recent, major modifications, as an important element of Mexican agrarian law.[22]

[20] Kellogg, *supra* note 3 at xxvii.

[21] Margadant, *supra* note 5 at 21. After the conquest, the Spanish crown allocated territories to specific *conquistadores* for exploitation and development, with permission to exact products and forced labour from the local population under the system known as *encomienda*. *See* text accompanying notes 55–61 *infra*. The *encomienda* system produced notoriously abusive treatment of indigenous groups, and certainly contributed to the disease and decline of indigenous populations after the Spanish conquest. Certain Europeans, such as Fray Bartolomé de las Casas, argued eloquently for an end to the abuses of the *encomienda*, and the institution of forced labour through *encomienda* began to be curtailed in the latter half of the 16th century, and was finally abolished by the Crown in the early 18th century. Garcia Gallo, Alfonso, 'Genesis y desarrollo del derecho indiano', in ESTUDIOS DE HISTORIA DEL DERECHO INDIANO (Madrid: Instituto Nacional de Estudios Jurídicos, 1972) at 144.

[22] *See* Chapter 13 below, text accompanying notes 74 to 93.

2. The Law of the Spanish Colonies[23]

The Spanish conquest of the Aztec Empire and other territories in the New World resulted in the eventual establishment of a highly developed colonial bureaucracy with two predominant and interrelated goals: satisfying the expansionist ambitions and demands for resources of the Spanish crown, and spreading the Catholic faith to new souls.[24] In both instances, it was clear that New Spain 'was kept subservient to the mother country'.[25]

The imposition of Spanish law in New Spain[26] was bolstered not only by the military power of conquest and occupation, but also by the religious authority of the Catholic Church. By papal Bull dated 4 May 1493, Pope Alexander VI fixed the line of demarcation of conquered territories between the kings of Spain and Portugal, thereby avoiding future conflict and bestowing upon these monarchs added justification of their jurisdiction.[27]

The *conquista* was not a simple subjugation or occupation of conquered peoples, but rather the transplantation of a political structure, a religion, and a system of laws that came directly from Spain.[28] The imposition of Spanish law was strongest in the area of public law, and in the centres of political and economic power such as Mexico City, Puebla, and others. The further one travelled from the centres of Mexico City, the more one encountered the vestiges of indigenous custom, especially in matters of purely local concern. Of course, even in the countryside, evangelization by the Catholic Church gradually influenced local matters (family law, etc.) as well.

At the outset, Spanish colonial law consisted of a transplantation of Spanish law to the New World. Gradually, the crown added numerous laws and regulations adopted specifically for the colonies. Even these, however, were laid on a foundation of Spanish law.

2.1. Spanish Law at the Time of the Conquest[29]

At the time of the conquest of Mexico, Spanish law was a confusing mixture of Roman law, Germanic law, canon law, royal decrees, and administrative

[23] *See generally* Cruz Barney, *supra* note 7 and González, *supra* note 7 at 323–352.

[24] At the outset of the conquest, Catholic theologians debated whether the indigenous peoples in the Americas possessed souls capable of salvation. Eventually, the question was resolved in the affirmative, leading to the aggressive evangelization of indigenous groups by successive waves of Augustinian, Dominican, and Franciscan ecclesiastics.

[25] Miller, *supra* note 18, at 124.

[26] The Spanish colonies were divided into two major Viceroyalties or *virreinatos*: Nueva España (New Spain), with its capital in Mexico City and governing much of Central and North America; and Nueva Granada, based in Lima, Peru, and governing much of South America. These vast territories were further subdivided into *audiencias*.

[27] Serra Rojas, Andrés, *Trayectoria del Estado Federal Mexicano* (Mexico: Porrúa, 1991) at 43. A later Bull decreed by Pope Alexander VI granted to the Crown property rights (*diezmos eclesiásticos*) in exchange for evangelization of the native peoples.

[28] Serra Rojas, *supra* note 27 at 44–45.

[29] *See* Cruz Barney, *supra* note 7 at 32–111.

practices.[30] The Iberian Peninsula, itself subject to continuous invasion and conquest until the fifteenth century, experienced the successive overlay of legal principles, one on top of another.[31]

The Iberian Peninsula had been part of the Roman Empire from 218 to 19 B.C., and as result a form of 'vulgar' Roman law was practised in the region, alongside local customary law. In the fifth century, the Roman Empire gave way to Germanic (Visigothic) invasions, and the adoption of a codification of Roman/Visigothic law in the *Lex Romana Visigothorum* in A.D. 506.[32] Visigothic rule, centred in Toledo, also produced a Visigothic code of laws (eventually known as the Fuero Juzgo) in 654, to be applied to Roman and Visigothic settlements in the region.[33]

In the interim, the extension of the Byzantine Empire into southern Spain in 554, under the rule of Emperor Justinian, brought to Spain the Justinian codification of Roman law, Justinian's Code of A.D. 564 (known as the *Corpus Iuris Civilis*). The study of Roman law, including Justinian's codification, and the subsequent rebirth of academic studies of Roman law that occurred from the twelfth to the fourteenth century, has had a profound influence on the development of private law in Spain, Mexico, and other countries that share the civil law tradition.[34] Roman law is seen as the bedrock on which Mexican law is founded, and every Mexican law student takes a basic course in Roman law during the first year of law school.[35] Under the civil law tradition as practised in Mexico, Roman law serves as an important foundation for the form of deductive reasoning employed by lawyers, academics, and judges in drawing conclusions from general principles.

During the Islamic occupation of Iberia (from the eighth to the fifteenth century), Islamic law governed political power, but Spanish subjects continued

[30] Margadant, *supra* note 5 at 28–29. The Catholic faith, having become the official religion of the Roman Empire in A.D. 380, heavily influenced the development of private law. *Id.*

[31] This multiplicity of regimes can also be attributed to the fact that political power in the Iberian Peninsula was not consolidated until 1469, with the joining in marriage of Ferdinand, King of Aragon, and Isabella, Queen of Castille.

[32] Margadant, *supra* note 5.

[33] *Id.* at 30; Bernal, Beatriz, 'Evolución Histórica del Derecho', in EL DERECHO EN MÉXICO (Mexico: UNAM, 1983) at 23.

[34] *See* Merryman, John Henry, THE CIVIL LAW TRADITION (Stanford: Stanford University Press, 1985) at 6–13.

[35] According to Beatriz Bernal, it is a mistake to think of Roman law as a single body of law. It is rather a development of legal principles throughout the ten centuries of the Roman Empire, which were eventually codified and studied at different periods of European history. The greatest codification of these principles occurred under Justinian, who commissioned not only a codification of laws, but also a *Digest* (a compilation of doctrinal writings by classical jurists) and the *Institutions* (instructional material for the teaching of law). A fourth book, composed of laws adopted after the codification, was added during the Middle Ages, and the entire collection came to be known as the *Corpus Juris Civilis* (Body of Civil Law), in contrast to the *Corpus Juris Canonici* of canon law. Bernal, *supra* note 33 at 20–22.

Beginning in the twelfth century, scholars at the University of Bologna, Italy, began to study Roman law as a source of legal science. Scholars from Spain and other regions came to Bologna, and carried Roman law back to their regions. The dissemination of Roman law throughout Europe in the 12th to the 14th century created a set of common principles known as the *ius comune*, which served as the basis of private law in most of Europe. *Id.* at 24.

to be governed in other respects by a patchwork quilt of their own laws, including the Fuero Juzgo and local, municipal *fueros* (codes).[36] The expulsion of the Moors (Granada, the final Moorish stronghold, fell in 1492) did not bring about legal unification in Spain. Instead, each region continued to apply its own *fueros*. The first of these, the *Fuero Viejo de Castilla*, was adopted in 1050. In 1255, Alfonso X (Alfonso El Sabio, or 'The Wise'), king of Castille, published the *Fuero Real*, based on earlier *fueros*, which continued to serve as supplementary laws for matters not covered in the *Fuero Real*.[37]

In 1256, Alfonso X published a new codification that was heavily influenced by principles of Roman law, sprinkled with Visigothic and canon law principles. Spanish scholars had studied in Bologna, where the glossators and post-glossators had rediscovered, and subjected to systematic study, Justinian's *Corpus Juris Civilis*. The codification produced by them, the *Siete Partidas*, served as an important type of model law both for Spain and the colonies. By virtue of the *Ordenamiento de Alcalá* of Alfonso XI, in 1348, the *Siete Partidas* were officially recognized as laws applicable to supplement other laws and regulations.

Later codifications of laws added to the confusion of overlapping laws: the *Ordenanzas Reales de Castilla* were added in 1485. In 1505, the Crown tried to prohibit the application of Roman law, in the *Leyes de Toro*; despite the prohibition, the universities continued to study Roman law and canon law, and judges continued to prefer Roman law precedents.[38]

The *Leyes de Toro* also attempted to establish a hierarchy of laws, which included most of the earlier *fueros*.[39]

Finally, in 1567, Phillip II tried to create order out of this chaos by promulgating a new codification entitled the *Nueva Recopilación*, consisting of 4,000 laws organized into twelve books. According to Guillermo Margadant, the *Nueva Recopilación* was not intended to abrogate consistent rules of earlier codifications.[40] In 1805, the *Nueva Recopilación* was replaced by the *Novísima Recopilación*, although the latter was never applied systematically in the New World.

With the exception of the *Novísima Recopilación*, this entire mass of sometimes contradictory laws applicable in the Iberian Peninsula also served as supplementary law (*derecho supletorio*) in the colonies. The ability of colonialists to understand and apply the law was weakened by the Crown's interdiction that the

[36] Soberanes, José Luis, *Una Aproximación a la Historia del Sistema Jurídico Mexicano* (Mexico: UNAM, 1992) at 37. Islamic law did influence the development of commercial and agricultural laws and practices, and left a legacy of terms still used today: *aduana* (customs), *tarifa* (tariff), *almacén* (warehouse), etc. Margadant, *supra* note 5 at 31.

[37] Margadant, *supra* note 5 at 31–32. [38] *Id.* at 34.

[39] The *Leyes de Toro* set the following hierarchy of laws:
–the *Ordenamiento de Alcalá de Henares*;
–lacking a specific provision in the *Ordenamiento*, the *fuero municipal* of the locality;
–lacking a provision in the *fuero municipal*, the *Fuero Real* of Alfonso X;
–lacking such a provision, the *Siete Partidas*:
Ots Capdequí, J.M., *El Estado Español en las Indias* (Mexico: Fondo de Cultura Económica, 1st. ed., 8th reprint, 1993) at 9–10.

[40] Margadant, *supra* note 5 at 35–36.

early universities in the New World study only Roman law and canon law. Only in 1741 did the crown decree that universities could begin to teach other laws.[41]

2.2. Colonial Law[42]

To understand the role of law in *las Indias* ('the Indies', the name given by the Crown to the New World colonies), one must appreciate the extent to which the principal law-makers, the Spanish crown and its agents, viewed the New World as the 'exclusive and personal enterprise of the [Spanish] kings'.[43] The laws of the New World were based on the laws of the Castillian crown, with all the confusion of Spanish law that is evident in the preceding pages. One element of Castillian law was clear, however: as lands were conquered, they passed automatically to the Crown, which in turn could transfer them in *encomiendas* to its agents, reserving subsoil mineral rights to the king. This pattern of control over New World resources fitted perfectly with the mercantilist notions prevalent during the period of Spanish Empire.

As early as the beginning of the sixteenth century, the Crown began to adopt laws specifically for the Indies. Over time, the political representatives of the Crown (described below) developed a body of law, termed *derecho indiano*, that was particularly adapted to the conditions of the Indies.[44] The *derecho indiano* that was developed, and eventually codified, has been characterized as casuistic, highly detailed, haphazard, adapted to local conditions, and grounded in the Catholic faith; it was also unsystematic, contradictory, and confusing.[45]

As already mentioned, the provisions of *derecho indiano* were supplemented by Spanish (Castillian) law. This was formally recognized in the first great codification of *derecho indiano*: the *Recopilación de Leyes de las Indias*, of 1680.[46] The *Recopilación de las Indias* was intended to impose order on the 200 volumes of laws and decrees that had been adopted in the century and a half of Spanish conquest.[47] These provisions were largely of a public law nature, dealing with colonial administration, finance, commerce, etc.[48]

2.2.1. Governmental Structure and Law-Making Bodies

Soon after the conquest, the Spanish crown began to create institutions to govern and administer the colonial territories. The principal law-making body for

[41] Margadant, *supra* note 5 at 35.

[42] *See generally* Cruz Barney, *supra* note 7 at 181–485; González, *supra* note 7 at 335–352.

[43] Garcia Gallo, *supra* note 21 at 124 (authors' trans.).

[44] Bernal, *supra* note 33 at 30.

[45] Dougnac Rodríguez, Antonio, MANUAL DE HISTORIA DEL DERECHO INDIANO (Mexico: UNAM, 1994) at 22; Ots Capdequí, *supra* note 39 at 12–13; Garcia Gallo, *supra* note 21 at 133–135.

[46] According to the *Novísima Recopilación*, 'in all cases, business and disputes in which it has not been decided, nor declared, what should be provided by the laws of this *Recopilación*, or by *cédulas*, provisions or ordinances given and not revoked for the Indies, as well as those decreed by our order, the laws of our Kingdom of Castille, in accordance with the Laws of Toro, shall be observed'. *Novísima Recopilación*, Ley II, tit. I. lib. II, as quoted in Ots Capdequí, *supra* note 39 at 9–10, n. 1 (authors' trans.)

[47] Garcia Gallo, *supra* note 21 at 138.

[48] Dougnac Rodríguez, *supra* note 45 at 20–21.

the colonies was the *Real Consejo de las Indias*, created in 1518 by King Carlos I (Holy Roman Emperor Carlos V) to advise the king and to legislate on matters relating to the New World colonies.[49] Located in Castille, the *Real Consejo de las Indias* had general jurisdiction over the New World colonies, and was under the direction of a presiding officer, eight *consejeros*, and various subordinate officers. The *Consejo de las Indias* was not hampered by first-hand knowledge: its members never visited the New World, but made decisions on the basis of letters, reports, and other documentation submitted by the king's agents. In addition, the king appointed periodic inspectors, called *visitadores*, to check on the administration of the colonies, the treatment of indigenous peoples, and the observance of the laws.[50]

The king's chief representative in the colonies was the viceroy (*virrey*): literally 'assistant king'. The first *virrey* in the New World was Antonio de Mendoza, who was appointed in 1535 as the chief officer of the *virreinato* of New Spain. The *virrey* was the alter ego of the king, and because of the great distance and slowness of communication, the *virrey* wielded considerable power in the New World. As chief executive and presiding officer of the *audiencia*, the *virrey* was the key source of legislative, judicial, and executive authority in New Spain.

The principal judicial body in the colonies was the *audiencia*. The first of these, the *Real Audiencia de Santo Domingo*, was established in 1511 in what is now the Dominican Republic. The *virreinato* of New Spain was eventually divided into several *audiencias*, in Mexico City, Santo Domingo, Guatemala, Guadalajara, etc. In Mexico City, the *virrey* presided over the *audiencia*, which consisted of eight to twelve members (*oidores*) appointed by the Crown. The *audiencias* heard disputes arising over the application of the laws in the colonial territories. In addition, they served legislative and executive functions on behalf of the Crown, adopting regulations to deal with matters within the jurisdiction of each *audiencia*.[51] The important feature of the arrangement is the lack of separation between the judicial, legislative, and executive functions. In essence, the executive controlled all three functions, leaving a legacy of executive control that was difficult to break even after independence, when the new Mexican Republic adopted a constitution based on the US model of separation of powers. While the powers may have been separated on paper, it took generations to make the separation effective in practice.

In matters of trade and commerce, the principal agency of the Crown was the *Casa de la Contratación de las Indias*, located in Seville. Created by *ordenanzas* of 1503 and 1510, the *Casa de la Contratación* was responsible for designing and administering a rigorous set of laws to control trade between Europe, the

[49] Garcia Gallo, *supra* note 21 at 130. Dougnac Rodríguez dates the establishment of the *Real Consejo de las Indias* as 1524. Dougnac Rodríguez, *supra* note 45 at 74.

[50] Garcia Gallo, *supra* note 21 at 131, 135–136.

[51] *See generally* Dougnac Rodríguez, *supra* note 45 at 101–137.

New World, and the Far East. All trade with the colonies was to be channelled through official ports of call: Seville, Veracruz, Cartagena, Acapulco, and Manila.

The channelling of trade with the colonies through Spain provided the Crown, and Spanish merchants, with immense opportunities for profit, as well as considerable control over the wealth (gold and silver) that was exported from the New World. After 1526, the *Casa de la Contratación* prohibited all solo voyages; instead, commerce was carried out through armed fleets (*armadas*) that sailed at specific times. These arrangements allowed the *Casa de la Contratación* to keep strict control over trade in both directions, as well as trade within the colonies.[52]

The *Casa de la Contratación* also served as a tribunal over trade matters. The archive of the *Casa de la Contratación* in Seville contains records of 300 years of Spanish imperial trade, and remains a valuable resource for historians.

2.2.2. The Indian Question

During the early sixteenth century, scholars in the Catholic Church debated whether the original inhabitants of the New World, otherwise known as 'Indians',[53] possessed souls and could thus be objects of evangelization. On the secular side, there also arose the question among legal scholars concerning the legal treatment, and juridical personality, that should be given to indigenous peoples.[54] From the beginning, the Spanish colonizers allowed indigenous groups to continue to govern their activities according to their pre-Hispanic practices, so long as these did not conflict with Spanish or canon law. This did not resolve the Indian question, however.

Not surprisingly, the Crown's agents developed theories that lent themselves to the exploitation of Indians for the profit of the crown and the *conquistadores*. Even prior to the conquest of Mexico, King Ferdinand, nicknamed '*el Católico*',

[52] *See generally* Dougnac Rodríguez, *supra* note 45 at 86–93. Spanish control over colonial trade and mining may be the high-water mark of international mercantilism. The Crown, owning all subsoil rights, granted concessions for the mining of gold and silver to entrepreneurs in the New World, in exchange for which the Crown exacted a 20% royalty (the famous *quinto real*, or royal fifth). All gold and silver was shipped back to Spain, much of it to finance Spanish wars of expansion in the Netherlands and elsewhere.

The Crown also restricted agriculture, manufacturing, and commerce in the New World. The colonies were not permitted to produce certain products, such as olive oil, that had to be imported from Europe, to the profit of Spanish traders. Even trade between the colonies was restricted. For a discussion of the trade control mechanisms applied to the Spanish colonies, *see* Zamora, S., 'Exchange control in the Spanish Empire, XVth to XVIIIth Centuries', in *Estudios Jurídicos en Homenaje al Maestro Guillermo Floris Margadant* (Mexico: UNAM, 1988) at 465–482.

[53] The imported term, or misnomer, 'Indian' has justifiably been criticized as diminishing the importance of indigenous cultures. Nevertheless, because of its common usage, we use the term 'Indian' interchangably with 'indigenous peoples'.

[54] On the development of theories covering indigenous peoples in the New World, *see* Borah, *supra* note 18 at 28–37. Eventually, the conversion of the indigenous population to Catholicism brought about greater inclusion of Indians as subject of Spanish law.

in 1512 convened a council in Burgos to consider reported abuses of indigenous peoples by Spanish settlers. The immediate result was the adoption of a theory of subjugation of Indians to the Spanish settlers (legitimized by the pontifical mandate of evangelization) and the creation of a legal vehicle, the *encomienda*, for this purpose.[55]

As subjects of Spanish law, the Indians were treated as the equivalent of minors, lacking full legal capacity and in need of 'protection'.[56] As a practical matter, of course, the Spanish colonizers were in need of labour to exploit the natural resources of New Spain. While slavery was severely circumscribed,[57] a substitute form of servitude, known as the *encomienda*, satisfied the needs of the colonizers.[58] From the very beginning, the Crown ceded extensive territories in *encomienda* to particular *conquistadores*. The *encomienda* permitted the *conquistador*, or *encomendero*, to cultivate lands and otherwise exploit the territories through the use of Indian labour. Indians inhabiting the territory of the *encomienda* were part of the package: in exchange for the obligation to 'protect' the Indians and educate them in the Catholic faith, the *encomendero* received the right to exploit their labour and exact various forms of tribute.[59]

The harsh treatment of Indians through the *encomienda*, coupled with the effects of wars of conquest and the affliction of diseases previously unknown in the New World, proved disastrous for the Indian populations. In central Mexico, in the century following the conquest, the Indian population declined from 25 million to less than a million inhabitants.[60] The abuses were exposed by protectors, such as Fray Bartolomé de las Casas and Fray Francisco de Vitoria, whose advocacy on behalf of more humane treatment, according to enlightened principles of natural law, eventually attracted the attention of the crown. Thus began a law reform movement, as early as the mid-sixteenth century, that tried to curtail the abuses of the *encomienda*. Finally, in 1718, the Crown abolished the *encomienda* altogether.[61]

The decline in the Indian population of central Mexico was reversed in the seventeenth century. In addition, interbreeding between Spaniards and Indians created a new, *mestizo* (mixed breed) population. The European and *mestizo* populations in Mexico increased from 57,000 in 1570 to 780,000 in 1793.[62] The result was a population mix that continues to this day in Mexico: a minority of European (Spanish and other) ancestry; a large *mestizo* population; and a sizeable

[55] Garcia Gallo, *supra* note 21 at 128–129. [56] Bernal, *supra* note 33 at 30.

[57] Slavery was tolerated but severely circumscribed in the colonies. Ots Capdequí, *supra* note 39 at 24–25. According to Professor Borah, the Spanish institution of slavery was much harsher than the slavery practised by pre-Hispanic cultures. Borah, *supra* note 18 at 38.

[58] On the *encomienda* generally, *see* Himmerlich y Valencia, R., *The Encomenderos of New Spain* (Austin: University of Texas Press, 1991); Simpson, L.B., *The Encomienda in New Spain* (Berkeley: University of California Press, 1950).

[59] Ots Capdequí, *supra* note 39 at 25–26. [60] Borah, *supra* note 18 at 26.

[61] *Id.* at 26–27; Garcia Gallo, *supra* note 21 at 139–141.

[62] Borah, *supra* note 18 at 26–27.

population of purely indigenous ancestry at the bottom of the socioeconomic ladder. It is not hard to imagine that the law was not applied equally to each of these groups.

2.2.3. *Colonial Courts*

As already mentioned, the principal judicial authorities in New Spain were the *audiencias*. Colonial society was highly stratified, and the colonial legal regime was not a uniform system of laws that applied equally to everyone. More than twenty special courts and judicial procedures existed for particular groups. Special tribunals and legal regimes applied to clerics, miners, merchants, universities, etc.[63] The existence of special courts, especially for clerics and the military, could mean preferential treatment depending on one's status in society.[64] As a consequence, the administration of such special rules, called *fueros*, have been controversial throughout much of Mexico's history.

Cases before the *audiencia* fell into three categories: criminal, civil, and administrative matters. Criminal matters included offences against native customs as well as against Spanish laws. As in Spain, serious crimes were punished by death and mutilation. However, as an humanitarian act, in the 1530s the *audiencia* lobbied successfully for forced labour of Indians convicted of serious offences, a practice which eventually became an important source of labour.[65] Civil cases included boundary and water disputes, both between Indians and between Indians and Spaniards; inheritance, especially inheritance of the rights of the Indian *caciques* (chiefs); and the use of forced Indian labour. Administrative cases involved complaints over the payment of taxes, and abuse of administrative discretion.[66]

Given the predominant size of the Indian population, it is not surprising that Indians were subjects of many of these court cases. What is surprising, however, is how the Indians themselves embraced litigation as a means of protecting themselves. Early on, the Crown recognized in the New World a principle that had become well established in Spain: that any person could contest administrative actions or defend property rights in the courts. As Professor Borah has noted:

> Within the Indian community, litigation before Spanish courts and petitions for administrative review and protection became the principal means of carrying on the long series of disputes unleashed by the Conquest over land, status, and virtually all other relationships. The conquerors were amazed that subjects so meek showed such ferocity and tenacity in litigation.[67]

[63] Bernal, *supra* note 33 at 31.

[64] One type of special court was not to be sought by anyone: the *Tribunal de la Santa Fe*, or Court of the Inquisition, which tried cases of heresy and was renowned for the use of torture. The headquarters of the *Casa de la Inquisición*, after independence, became the National College of Medicine, and still stands as a museum in the heart of Mexico's central historical district.

[65] Borah, *supra* note 18 at 49–50.

[66] *Id.* at 44–52.

[67] *Id.* at 40.

Of course, Spanish judges were reluctant to rule in favour of Indians against Spaniards, but that did not appear to deter Indian litigants from asserting their claims.[68]

2.2.4. *Private Law in the Colonies*

Most of the private law in the colonies was based on Spanish (Castillian) law, with the exception of special laws for special New World issues, such as marital relations between Indians and Spaniards, inheritance of *encomiendas*, laws governing Indian properties and labour, etc.[69] Spanish family law was applied flexibly to the newly converted Indians, many of whom had practised polygamy. Marital relations between Spaniards were subject to traditional Spanish law, but after continuing abandonment by Spanish colonizers of their wives in the Old World, in the *Recopilación* of 1680, the Spanish crown prohibited married men from travelling to the New World without their spouses.[70]

The legal status of women was highly circumscribed, and women played an insignificant role in public life. Single women were subject to parental authority, and married women to husbands' authority. Even the wives of colonial officials lacked the capacity to contract, and only widowhood could bring full legal capacity under civil law. Criminal penalties against women were harsher than those against men, especially in cases of adultery.[71]

In property law, the colonial administration sought to maintain the existence of communal properties. The *Recopilación* of 1680 decreed that pastures, mountains, and waters would be common property, while also providing for rights of private property.[72] Rights of expropriation were granted to religious orders to found settlements and convert the Indian population.[73] In theory, Indians could hold title to lands, but many limitations were placed on this right; for instance, lacking full legal capacity, Indians were not free to buy and sell lands even if they did hold title to them.[74] The colonial administration encouraged agricultural

[68] For a detailed discussion of Indian litigation in New Spain, *see* Kellogg, *supra* note 3.
Guillermo Margadant has published an annotated account of the proceedings of one case of Indian litigation, involving a petition for the removal of the priest from the village of Chamula, in the Valley of Mexico. *See* Margadant, G., *AUTOS SEGUIDOS POR ALGUNOS DE LOS NATURALES DEL PUEBLO DE CHAMULA EN CONTRA DE SU CURA DON JOSÉ ORDÓÑEZ Y AGUIAR PARA VARIOS EXCESOS QUE LE SUPONÍAN*, 1779 (MEXICO: UNIVERSIDAD AUTÓNOMA DE CHIAPAS/MIGUEL ANGEL PORRÚA, 1992).

[69] Ots Capdequí, *supra* note 39 at 73.

[70] *Recopilación de Leyes de las Indias*, Ley XXX, titl. XLV, lib. IX: '*Que no pase de Nueva España a Filipinas hombre casado sin su mujer, o con licencia y fianza*' ('A married man may not travel from New Spain to the Philippines without his wife or a marriage licence and guarantee').

[71] Ots Capdequí, *supra* note 39 at 95–107.
Given the limitations on women's activities, one of the few areas where an ambitious woman could find fulfilment was in the convent. One of the greatest literary figures of the Spanish colonies was Sor Juana Inés de la Cruz (1648 to 1695), a young woman born into a Spanish *criollo* family who entered the convent as a teenager. Sor Juana's writings are widely read today. *See A SOR JUANA ANTHOLOGY* (Cambridge, Mass: Harvard University Press, 1988; Alan S. Trueblood, trans.).

[72] Ots Capdequí, *supra* note 39 at 129–130.

[73] *Id.* at 134, 143–144.

[74] *Id.* at 143–144.

production by the Indians, through communal and other properties, so as to exact profits in the way of tribute (well known to the Indians since pre-Hispanic times).

2.2.5. *Eighteenth-Century Enlightenment*

Carlos II (1665–1700), the last of the Spanish Habsburgs, having failed to produce an heir to the Spanish throne, chose as his successor a member of the French Bourbon royal family, Philippe d'Anjou, who was to become Philip V of Spain. The ensuing War of the Succession, between the Austrian Habsburgs and the Spanish crown, ended in a victory for Philip V in 1713. This change in dynasty from Habsburg to Bourbon ushered in a wave of Enlightenment reforms in both the Iberian Peninsula and the New World. The eighteenth-century Bourbon Enlightenment ended the comprehensive restrictions on trade with the New World, fostering an economic revival. New administrative structures were created, reducing the domination of the *Consejo de las Indias* over the administration of the colonies.[75] The *Recopilación de Leyes de las Indias* of 1680, supplemented by new legislation, remained in effect in the Spanish colonies until the end of the nineteenth century, when Cuba, Puerto Rico, and the Phillipines were liberated after the Spanish–American War.

On the eve of Mexican independence, the movement towards constitutional limitations on monarchical authority helped bring about an end to Spanish rule over much of the colonial empire. In 1812, during the French occupation of Spain, the Spanish Cortes (legislative assembly) drafted Spain's first constitution, with *criollos* from New Spain participating as delegates in the creation of a constitutional monarchy. The Constitution of 1812 was suspended by Ferdinand VII in 1814, but reinstated in 1820. Conservatives and clerics in New Spain, alarmed by the anti-clerical provisions of the Spanish Constitution, began to favour independence from Spain, setting the stage for the establishment in 1821 of an independent Mexico, with its own set of laws and constitutions.

2.2.6. *The Legacy of Spanish Colonial Rule*[76]

The imprint of Spanish colonial rule on Mexican law and legal institutions is as prominent as the legacy owed by the US legal system to British common law. Vestiges of Spanish colonial rule are found in many contemporary characteristics of Mexican law, both private and public law, including:

(i) centralized control of government decision-making, particularly in economic matters;
(ii) governmental ownership and control of subsoil hydrocarbons and minerals;

[75] Garcia Gallo, *supra* note 21 at 142–145; Dougnac Rodríguez, *supra* note 45 at 194–195.
[76] *See generally* González, *supra* note 7 at 359 *et seq.*

(iii) special treatment for indigenous populations, and a sense of governmental responsibility in handling issues important to indigenous peoples;
(iv) lack of a solid foundation for the separation of powers between the legislative, executive, and judicial branches of government; and
(v) historically weak judicial branch of government, and limitation on the ability of judges to create legal precedent.

3. Mexican Independence and Nineteenth-Century Reforms[77]

In the early morning hours of 16 September 1810, Padre Miguel Hidalgo rang the bells in the small village church of Dolores to convene his congregation and entreat them to rise up against Spanish colonial rule. Within weeks, the uprising led by Hidalgo gathered considerable popular support in the countryside, with Indian and *mestizo* farmers attacking government forces and pillaging rich estates in North Central Mexico. Within six months, the rebels, lacking weapons and organization, were routed by the Spanish troops, and Padre Hidalgo was executed: the first martyr to Mexican independence. Jose Maria Morelos, a disciple of Hidalgo, attempted to carry on the fight for independence, but true independence did not come until 1821, when the Spanish crown, weakened by the Napoleonic Wars, could no longer maintain military and political control in the Americas.[78] Nevertheless, Mexico has long recognized Padre Hidalgo's uprising as the symbolic independence of Mexico, and Mexicans celebrate their independence each 16 September with a re-enactment by the Mexican President of the famous '*Grito de Dolores*' that Padre Hidalgo issued on that date in 1810.

Mexico's first century of independence was dominated by certain themes that influenced the political and legal development of Mexico, and were carried forward into the twentieth century. These include a constant struggle for power between conservatives, allied with the Catholic Church, who favoured consolidation of political power in the central government; and liberals, who favoured decentralization of power and the preservation of individual freedoms, reflecting the Enlightenment ideals of eighteenth-century Europe and the American Revolution.

There were also foreign interventions—military, diplomatic, and financial—that were occasionally welcomed by certain conservative groups but were resisted by a majority of Mexicans. In addition, there was the influence of strong military and political figures, *caudillos* (bosses) such as Antonio López de Santa Anna, Benito Juarez, and Porfirio Díaz, who placed a highly personal stamp on the development of Mexican public law.

[77] *See generally* Cruz Barney, *supra* note 7 at 513–619; González, *supra* note 7 at 369–438.

[78] The last Spanish viceroy, General Juan O'Donoju, arrived in Mexico in 1821, and quickly negotiated with Agustin de Iturbide, a Mexican *criollo* patriot, the Treaty of Cordoba that brought the withdrawal of Spanish troops and the recognition of an independent Mexico.

Furthermore, Mexico faced the challenge of building a viable modern economy on top of a feudal agricultural base that left a majority of Mexicans disenfranchised and impoverished. At the same time, it had an uneasy relationship with the United States, with tensions existing over territorial, economic, immigration, and political issues.

3.1. The First Constitutional Period: 1822–1855

The first of the nineteenth-century *caudillos*, Agustin de Iturbide, was a wealthy Creole military leader who had fought against the insurgents led by Padre Hidalgo. Personally ambitious, Iturbide entered into a pact, called the *Plan de Iguala*, with the last of the insurgent leaders, Vicente Guerrero. The *Plan de Iguala* succeeded in unifying Mexican independence efforts behind three broad principles: unity of ethnic and social groups; exclusive rights of the Catholic Church; and absolute independence from Spain. In August 1821, Iturbide successfully negotiated the Treaty of Cordoba with the final Spanish viceroy, the recently arrived Juan O'Donoju. This accepted most of the terms of the *Plan de Iguala*. Spanish troops were withdrawn, and in September 1821, Agustin de Iturbide entered Mexico City in triumph as the head of a governing *Junta Provisional de Gobierno*.

The junta attempted to form a constitutional congress to draft a charter for the new nation, but this effort was short-circuited in early 1822 when Iturbide's supporters succeeded in adopting the *Reglamento Político Provisional del Imperio*, establishing an imperial form of government with an elected national junta possessing certain legislative powers.[79] Iturbide was proclaimed Emperor, and while the *Reglamento* provided for a *junta instituyente* with legislative powers, Iturbide proceeded to govern like a monarch. Unfortunately, the economy of the new nation was in shambles; independence had interrupted investments in mining and agriculture, and trade with Spain had ended. Iturbide's ineffectual reign lasted only eleven months. To quell the opposition, he arrested dissident congressmen, and finally dissolved the congress in October 1822. Two months later, Iturbide's enemies, led by Antonio López de Santa Anna—the major *criollo* figure of Mexico's first half-century—succeeded in overthrowing Iturbide's Empire.

3.1.1. The Constitution of 1824

Upon the removal of Iturbide, a constitutional congress (*constituyente*) convened in 1823 to draft the first constitution for the new republic. Liberals put forth a charter that emphasized a decentralized, federal form of government, with significant power residing in the states. Not only did this reflect a rejection of the colonial model of centralized power; the adoption of a federal system with significant power for the states was also seen as the necessary condition for

[79] The *Reglamento* is reprinted in Tena Ramírez, F., *Leyes Fundamentales de México 1808–1997* (Mexico: Porrúa, 20th ed., 1998) at 125–144.

convincing numerous regions—Campeche, Tabasco, Queretaro, Zacatecas, Guadalajara, and Oacaxa—to join the new republic.

The Constitution of 1824[80] was influenced by the US Constitution, as well as by the 1812 Spanish Constitution of Cadiz. Like the United States of America, the *Estados Unidos Mexicanos* was made up of separate states (nineteen, in the case of Mexico; other states have since been added, making the current total thirty-one). The federal government of the Mexican government followed the US model, with a bicameral legislature and separation of powers between the legislative, executive, and judicial branches. The similarity ended there, however. In the United States, during the first decades of its history, the operation of this new form of government was submitted to significant tests in the courts and in the political arena. Over time, the workings of federal democracy became settled by judicial precedent and political agreement. Supreme Court decisions and amendments to the Constitution served to refine the model, without resort to *coups d'état* or violent disruptions (at least until the Civil War).

In Mexico, by contrast, the first fifty years of independence were characterized by political turmoil and the failure to build viable political institutions. Only the first elected President, the liberal Guadalupe Victoria, was able to serve his full term of office. From 1824 until the adoption of a new Constitution in 1857, thirty-seven men held the office of President. One of these men—Antonio López de Santa Anna—served as President on eleven different occasions, assuming power through a succession of *coups d'état* and questionable elections, but remaining in the President's office for a total of only nine months throughout the entire period.[81]

In reacting against the centralism of colonial Spain, the drafters of the 1824 Constitution established a form of federal republic in which the power of the central government was severely curtailed.[82] Local political bosses dominated the landscape, the federal government lacked any significant taxing power, and the individual states burdened commerce with restrictive regulations.

Within ten years, conservatives had engineered the abrogation of the 1824 Constitution, imposing instead a conservative agenda favouring centralized control. In 1836, the conservative Congress passed a new charter, known as the *Siete Leyes Constitucionales.*[83] The *Siete Leyes* provided for a unitary government and abolished the states, replacing them with *juntas departamentales* with circumscribed powers.[84]

[80] The Constitution of 1824 may be found at www.juridicas.unam.mx/infjur/leg/legmexfe.htm, under 'Documentos Constitucionales Históricos'. It is also reprinted in Tena Ramírez, *supra* note 79 at 167–195.

[81] Santa Anna was not always removed by force; he would often repair voluntarily to his *hacienda* in Veracruz, leaving his vice president in charge of operating the government.

[82] *See generally* Barragán, J., El Pensamiento Federalista Mexicano: *1824* (Mexico: Universidad Autonoma del Estado de Mexico, 1983).

[83] A copy in Spanish of the *Siete Leyes* may be found at www.juridicas.unam.mx/infjur/leg/legmexfe.htm, under 'Documentos Constitucionales Históricos'.

[84] Ortega Lomelín, F., El Nuevo Federalismo (Mexico: Porrúa, 1988) at 39–40.

Outlying regions of the new nation rebelled at this new assertion of centralized control. The most significant rebellion against central rule came from the northern territory of what is now Texas. In the 1820s, the Mexican government had encouraged colonization of sparsely settled northern territories, as a buffer against US expansion. English-speaking North Americans received large concessions of land from the Mexican government, and cultivated cotton and rice. The colonists were required to become Mexican citizens and to profess the Catholic faith; they were also allowed to import negro slaves to work their lands.

By 1830, nine thousand former US citizens had migrated to Texas; they outnumbered the Spanish-speaking population of the region by three-to-one. By the early 1830s, however, the central government had begun to curtail the autonomy of Texans to manage their own affairs, and Texans such as Sam Houston began to call for independence.[85] By 1835, a war of separation had begun. President Santa Anna gathered an army of 6,000 men to assert Mexican control; they marched to San Antonio, where a band of 150 Texans fortified themselves in an abandoned Franciscan mission known as the Alamo. Santa Anna's troops stormed the mission and killed all the insurgents; the battle cry 'Remember the Alamo' became the slogan of Texan independence. Within weeks, despite being outnumbered, the Texans had defeated Santa Anna's forces in the battle of San Jacinto, and Santa Anna was taken prisoner. With the Mexican government in disarray, the Texans declared independence, and the Republic of Texas was formed.

In 1845 tension over the United States government support of Texas' secession from Mexico eventually gave rise to armed conflict between Mexico and the United States. On 29 December 1845, President James Polk signed legislation making Texas the twenty-eighth state of the United States. Mexico refused to accede to the accession, and in January 1846, President Polk directed the US Army to invade Mexico; in 1847, a force led by General Winfield Scott fought its way to Mexico City, which it occupied for a short time. Mexico eventually surrendered, its army in disarray, and on 2 February 1848, Interim President Manuel de la Peña y Peña and a US envoy signed the infamous Treaty of Guadalupe Hidalgo with the United States. Under this treaty, Mexico gave up two-fifths of her territory: the present states of Texas, New Mexico, Arizona, California, Nevada, and part of Colorado.

The Treaty of Guadalupe Hidalgo still casts a shadow on US–Mexican relations. By many Mexicans, the loss of significant territories to an invading neighbour is still felt as symbolic one hundred and fifty years later. Mexicans are justifiably sensitive to US dominance, whether that dominance is exercised on a governmental level, through military, diplomatic, or political means, or on a private level, through the assertion of private economic power.

[85] In 1824, Texas was merged politically with Coahuila, thus diluting the Texans' political authority. In 1829, tensions increased when the government abolished slavery throughout the country. Texans also rebelled against customs regulations restricting trade with the United States. Miller, *supra* note 18 at 211–212.

Throughout this period of turmoil, the *Siete Leyes* never became an effective constitutional instrument, as control of the government continued to vacillate between conservatives and liberals. Finally, in 1847, a constitutional congress dominated by liberals adopted the *Acta de Reformas*,[86] a short document (thirty articles) that purported to restore the liberal Constitution of 1824, but with significant improvements intended to make the Constitution workable. In addition, the *Acta de Reformas* laid the groundwork for liberal reforms that were incorporated into the Constitution of 1857.[87]

Santa Anna returned to the presidency one last time in 1853, but in 1854 a group of liberals succeeded in ousting him. In the *Plan de Ayutla*,[88] they called for the convening of a new constitutional congress, and the adoption of a new charter for the Mexican republic. Thus began the period of Mexican constitutional history known as *la Reforma*, discussed in section 3.2 below.

3.1.2. Private Law During Early Independence

Mexico was unable to build a stable democratic government during this early period, but this does not mean that Mexican society functioned without legal norms. Despite constitutional crises, the Mexican Congress and the state legislatures adopted laws for the new nation. These were laid on top of the confusing mix of colonial laws and practices that had governed Mexicans for two centuries, and which continued in observance.[89] In the area of private law, the new nation followed colonial precepts that were applied according to the status of the individual in question: Spaniards and Creoles were subject to Spanish laws and customs, Indians to their own customary law (unless it offended Catholic doctrine), and *mestizos* and other classes to a mixture of the above.[90]

Finally, beginning in the 1850s, Congress began to turn its attention to the adoption of codes and laws to regulate the rights of private citizens.[91] During the first half of the century, the adherence to Spanish colonial precepts of private law was gradually abandoned, in favour of European Enlightenment doctrines that were being exported to Mexico. European influence included the impulse towards codification of private law (seen in the adoption by the French monarch of the Napoleonic Code) that began in the early nineteenth century in Europe and quickly caught the attention of legislators in Mexico.[92] Only by the end of the French intervention, 1864–1867, did Mexico achieve the political stability necessary for the adoption of a comprehensive codification of private law, with the adoption of the first Mexican Civil Code in 1871, discussed in section 3.2.2 below.

[86] A copy in Spanish of the *Acta de Reformas* may be found at www.juridicas.unam.mx/infjur/leg/legmexfe.htm, under 'Documentos Constitucionales Históricos'.

[87] *See* Fix-Zamudio, H., 'Acta Constitutiva y de Reformas, 1847, Marco Jurídico', in MÉXICO Y SUS CONSTITUCIONES (Mexico: Fondo de Cultura Económica, 1998; P. Galeana, ed.) at 198, 207–242.

[88] Tena Ramírez, *supra* note 79 at 487–498.

[89] González, M. de R., EL DERECHO CIVIL EN MÉXICO *1821–1871* (Mexico: UNAM, 1988) at 7, 25–31, 59.

[90] *Id.* at 60.

[91] Margadant, *supra* note 5 at 132–133.

[92] González, *supra* note 89 at 63–69. *See also infra* Chapter 14, text accompanying notes 2 to 6.

Nineteenth-century commercial law generally followed the pattern described above. The Spanish *Siete Partidas* and the *Ordenanzas de Bilbao*, a codification of *lex mercatoria* first adopted in Bilbao in 1429, continued to be applied by Mexican authorities in the first half-century after independence.[93]

3.2. *La Reforma* (1855–1876): The Triumph of Liberalism and the Constitution of 1857

A rejection of the conservative *caudillo* Santa Anna in 1854 was led by several *puros*, or liberal leaders, who had been exiled to the United States during the conservative ascendancy. The most famous of these was Benito Juárez, a social reformer and major architect of the liberal Constitution of 1857.

There are interesting similarities between the figures of Juárez and his US contemporary, Abraham Lincoln, both of whom are equally revered in their respective countries. Both men were of humble origin. Lincoln grew up in a log cabin in what was then the hinterland of Illinois; Juárez was a Zapotec Indian from the southern state of Oaxaca, an orphan who was educated in a Catholic seminary. They were both talented lawyers, and became effective politicians. As Presidents, they were both forced to confront civil wars that deeply divided the country.

The period of *la Reforma* began with the passage of liberal laws that were intended to curtail the power of the Catholic Church and of special interest groups. In November, 1855, the Mexican Congress, dominated by liberals after the ouster of Santa Anna, passed the *Ley Juárez*, named after Benito Juárez, then Minister of Justice. The *Ley Juárez* abolished the *fueros*, or special immunities from civil and criminal process, that were enjoyed by clerics and by the military.[94]

In June 1856, Congress adopted the *Ley Lerdo* (named for liberal Treasury Minister Miguel Lerdo de Tejada). Under this law, all religious institutions—most significantly the Catholic Church—were prohibited from owning lands beyond those strictly necessary for their operations.[95] Since colonial times, the Catholic Church had accumulated large landed estates, which it received from the Spanish crown in exchange for the efforts of Church orders (Franciscans, Dominicans, Augustinians) to convert the indigenous tribes of Mexico; from

[93] Clagett, H. and Valderrama, D., *A Revised Guide to the Law & Legal Literature of Mexico* (Washington: Library of Congress, 1973) at 127–128; Soberanes, *supra* note 36 at 147.

[94] The *Ley Juarez*, or *Ley de administracion de justicia y organica de los Tribunales de la Federación*, of 23 Nov. 1855, is discussed in Tena Ramírez, *supra* note 79 at 491. Prior to the *Ley Juárez*, as a vestige of colonial law, the clergy and the military were not subject to normal civil or criminal process, but had their own tribunals. The system led to special protections and abuses. The *Ley Juárez* limited the religious or military tribunals to matters pertaining to canon law or military affairs.

[95] The *Ley Lerdo*, or *Ley de Desamortización* of 25 June 1856, is discussed in Tena Ramírez, *supra* note 79 at 491.

testamentary donations by the faithful; and from sound administration.[96] By the end of the eighteenth century, public records showed that the Catholic Church owned half of the buildings in Mexico City, and by the mid-nineteenth century, the Church probably owned one-third of the land in Mexico.[97] Much of this land was worked as communal property by *campesinos*, peasant farmers who paid rents to support the clergy but who held considerable control over use of the land.

The *Ley Lerdo* required all corporate bodies, including the Church, to auction their agricultural lands to the highest bidder. Liberals intended not only to curtail the power of a major conservative faction, the Catholic Church; they also wished to promote a society dominated by secular institutions in which private landholders would hold property, and would invest in lands to increase productivity. Unfortunately, the liberals did not foresee that the sale of Church lands would eventually exacerbate the conditions of rural poverty in Mexico. Since many *campesinos* lacked capital or sources of credit, lands auctioned under the *Ley Lerdo* were acquired by the principal holders of wealth: the existing owners of large estates (*hacendados*) and ranchers (*rancheros*). *Campesinos*—the largest segment of the Mexican population—were forced to work as labourers under conditions dictated by absentee *hacendados* who oversaw their lands through professional administrators. Mexican rural society soon resembled the feudal European system of lord and vassal. The *campesino* population continued to grow, and to sink deeper into poverty. Occasional peasant uprisings would occur in the decades following these reforms.[98] Faced with intractable conditions of rural poverty, Mexican *campesinos* would eventually join in Emiliano Zapata's armed revolutionary campaign under the cry of '*Tierra y Libertad*' ('Land and Freedom').

A series of other laws curtailing the power of the Church and the military followed during the period 1857 to 1863; these are referred to collectively as the Laws of Reform.[99]

The liberal ascendancy resulted in the adoption of a new constitution, the Constitution of 1857,[100] based on liberal ideals of freedom of association, anticlericalism, federalism, and subordination of the executive branch to a unicameral legislature. (The liberals considered a Senate to be too conservative and centralist; however, in 1878, the Constitution was amended to include a Senate.) According to Jesús Orozco, this weakening of the presidency merely

[96] Margadant, G., *La Iglesia ante el Derecho Mexicano: Esbozo Histórico-Jurídico* (Mexico: Miguel Ángel Porrúa, 1991) at 155.

[97] Brandenburg, F., *The Making of Modern Mexico* (Englewood Cliffs, N.J.: Prentice-Hall, 1964) at 188–189.

[98] Hart, John Mason, *Revolutionary Mexico: The Coming and Process of the Mexican Revolution* (Berkeley: University of California Press, 1987) at 37–38, 357–363.

[99] The *Leyes de Reforma* are discussed and set forth in Tena Ramírez, *supra* note 79 at 638–667.

[100] A copy in Spanish of the 1857 Constitution may be found at www.juridicas.unam.mx/infjur/leg/legmexfe.htm, under 'Documentos Constitucionales Históricos'.

'forced [the President] to corrupt the Congress and to govern outside of the Constitution, with only a superficial respect for constitutional formalities'.[101]

The 1857 Constitution served as an important model for the current 1917 Constitution. Among other elements, it established a firm foundation for the *amparo* procedure that has become a major feature of Mexican judicial process.[102] *Amparo* had its origin in the early nineteenth century, when the state of Yucatan adopted a procedure to strengthen the judicial enforcement of individual rights in the state constitution of 1841.[103] In 1847, on the national level, Mariano Otero successfully promoted an *amparo* procedure, known as the *Fórmula Otero*, as part of the *Acta de Reformas* that abrogated the *Siete Leyes*. The groundwork was thus laid for including the concept of *amparo* in Articles 101 and 102 of the 1857 Constitution, and in the first federal *Ley de Amparo* of 1861.[104]

3.2.1. The French Intervention

The Mexican Catholic Church hierarchy attacked the new Constitution, with the full support of Pope Pius IX, who attempted to annul the anticlerical provisions of the charter, despite the political authority to do so.[105] With a cry of '*religión y fueros*', conservative opponents of Juárez rebelled against the Constitution, and initiated a two-year War of Reform in 1858. By 1861, liberal forces prevailed, but only temporarily. That same year, newly re-elected President Juárez decreed a moratorium on the repayment of Mexican government debts owed to creditors in England, Spain, and France, and the three governments signed a pact to recover the debts and sent military expeditions to enforce it. Spain and England quickly negotiated a settlement with Mexico, and withdrew their forces, but France had something else in mind. French Emperor Napoleon III welcomed the opportunity to re-establish its influence in the Americas. French troops invaded the country, and as they advanced to Mexico City, President Juárez set up a government in exile in Chihuahua. Napoleon III easily convinced the Habsburg Archduke Ferdinand Maximilian, younger brother of the Austro-Hungarian Emperor Franz Josef, to travel to Mexico with his young bride, Carlota, to assume the role of the French-supported Emperor of Mexico.[106]

With the support of Mexican conservatives, Maximilian was installed as Emperor of Mexico in the Spring of 1864, but he was never able to achieve full

[101] Orozco Henriquez, Jesús, 'El Sistema Presidencial en el Constituyente de Querétaro y Su Evolución Posterior', in *El Sistema Presidencial Mexicano (Algunas Reflexiones)* (Mexico: UNAM–Instituto de Investigaciones Juridicas, 1988), at 13–14 (authors' trans.).

[102] On *amparo*, *see infra* Chapter 8.

[103] Fix-Zamudio, H., *Ensayos Sobre el Derecho de Amparo* (Mexico: UNAM/IIJ, 1993) at 26. For a history of *amparo* generally, *see* Castro, J., *Garantias y Amparo* (Mexico: Porrúa, 7th ed., 1991).

[104] The first *Amparo* Law had little effect, due to the French intervention, and was eventually superseded by later *Amparo* Laws of 1869 and 1882.

[105] Margadant, *supra* note 5 at 146.

[106] The fascinating saga of Maximilian and Carlota is discussed in Krauze, E., *Mexico: Biography of Power* (New York: Harper Collins, 1997; Hank Heifetz, trans.) at 171–191.

governance over the country, and civil war marked his three-year reign. Even with the presence of French troops, Maximilian was unable to dislodge the liberals. In early 1867, Napoleon III announced the withdrawal of French troops (for financial and political reasons), and Maximilian's ill-fated Mexican Empire collapsed. Maximilian himself was taken prisoner in May, and executed in June 1867, thus ending the French intervention.

Maximilian's Empire left little imprint on the Mexican legal system *per se*: Maximilian never even succeeded in putting into effect a constitutional charter with which to govern.[107] Nevertheless, the French intervention served to reinforce Mexico's aversion to foreign influence and intervention, and in this respect it can be seen as leaving an important legacy.

3.2.2. *Private Law and Mexican Codifications*

The impulse to establish a consistent set of Mexican laws to regulate private behaviour, frustrated by the political uncertainties of the early nineteenth century,[108] finally achieved results under the leadership of Benito Juárez, with the adoption of the first civil code in Mexico, the Civil Code for the Federal District and Territory of Lower California of 1871.[109] This initial code was heavily criticized, and in 1882 President Porfirio Díaz appointed a commission to revise it. One year later, the commission submitted a new draft Civil Code, which relied in form and content on the Napoleonic Code, being subdivided into four books and 3,823 articles. This Code was promulgated in 1884, and proved much more successful than its predecessor.[110] Though limited in jurisdiction to federal territories, the federal Civil Code of 1884 (as with the 1871 Code and many other pieces of federal legislation) served as a precise model for the civil codes quickly adopted by the Mexican states in ensuing years. As noted by Clagett and Valderrama, '[i]n this fashion a more or less uniform law in this particular field has been attained'.[111] The 1884 Civil Code was replaced in 1932 by the current Civil Code for the Federal District, and by the Federal Civil Code, as discussed below.[112]

Progress towards commercial codification followed a similar pattern. In 1854, President Santa Anna commissioned Teodosio Lares to draft a commercial code, but the resulting codification was quietly abandoned in 1855 when Juárez came to power. In accordance with the liberal aversion to *fueros*, the legislature abolished the special commercial tribunals and procedures advanced in the Lares Code, and Mexico reverted to the application of commercial laws

[107] *See* Tena Ramírez, *supra* note 79 at 670.

[108] *See* text at notes 79–88, *supra*.

[109] In 1857, President Benito Juarez commissioned the eminent jurist, Justo Sierra, to draft a civil code for Mexico. Sierra followed the model of the Spanish Civil Code of 1851, itself influenced by the Code Napoleon, among others. When Juarez reassumed the presidency in 1867, the project for a federal civil code was completed and promulgated for application to federal territories. For an excellent discussion, in English, of the history of Mexican codifications of civil law, with citations to primary and secondary sources, *see* Clagett and Valderrama, *supra* note 93 at 62–100.

[110] *Id.* at 66–67.

[111] *Id.* at 62, 69.

[112] *See infra* Chapter 14, at text accompanying notes 29–34.

of Spanish origin.[113] The original Constitution of 1857 permitted the states to legislate on commercial matters, but this proved unworkable because of resulting conflicts. In 1883, Congress amended the Constitution to reserve to the federal Congress the power to legislate on commercial matters, and in 1884, Congress adopted a new Commercial Code that reinstated the commercial courts and procedures. The 1884 Code was quickly abandoned, in favour of the Commercial Code of 1889, which drew upon modern commercial codes and laws drafted in Spain and elsewhere.[114] The 1889 Code remains in effect today, despite the enormous changes that have occurred in the commercial world. In large part, the Mexican Commercial Code has been superseded or otherwise rendered irrelevant by the adoption of specialized Mexican legislation covering commercial companies, credit operations, and many other matters, as discussed below in Chapters 14, 18, and 20. Nevertheless, the Commercial Code is still authoritative in commercial matters not otherwise covered by specific legislation, and also includes procedural provisions that affect commercial litigation and arbitration.[115]

3.3. The *Porfiriato*: The Dictatorship of Porfirio Díaz (1876–1910)

After the death of Maximilian, Benito Juárez was elected to a third term as President in 1867, and to a fourth term in 1871. After Juárez's sudden death in 1872, his ally, Sebastián Lerdo de Tejada, became interim President and was elected to a four-year term soon thereafter. Lerdo solidified the liberal agenda by seeing to it that the anticlerical features of the Laws of Reform were incorporated into the Constitution. Four years later, when Lerdo announced that he would seek re-election, General Porfirio Díaz, a military hero of the campaign against the French, engineered a revolt. Díaz had earlier opposed President Juárez for attempting to establish a dictatorship, and in 1876 campaigned against Lerdo and in favour of 'effective suffrage and no reelection'. The *porfiristas* succeeded in ousting Lerdo, and Porfirio Díaz assumed power. He called a special election in 1877, and Porfirio Díaz, a popular hero, was elected President.

Porfirio Díaz initially stood for liberal ideals, and he was successful in establishing stability in the country and promoting economic growth. Ironically, however, the advocate of 'no reelection' was to become the longest ruling dictator in the history of Mexico. While he adhered to the form of a constitutional government, over the course of seven presidential terms Porfirio Díaz gradually assumed the powers of a dictator, supported by a cadre of generals who occupied the governorships of the Mexican states. He also softened the liberal opposition

113 *See* text accompanying note 94 *supra*. *See* Clagett and Valderrama, *supra* note 93 at 128.

114 *Id.* at 129–130; Soberanes, *supra* note 36 at 147.

115 *See*, e.g., Siqueiros, 'International Commercial Arbitration', in *Mexican Law: A Treatise for Legal Practitioners and International Investors*, vol. 2 (St Paul, Minn: West Group, 1998; J. Vargas, ed.) at 5–6.

to the Catholic Church, and refrained from vigorous enforcement of the Laws of Reform, earning him the support of the Church hierarchy.

Díaz and his advisers recognized that Mexico would have to attract foreign capital and foreign technology if it was going to build a modern society and economy. He was so successful in attracting foreign investment that by 1910, more than 130 of Mexico's 179 largest companies were foreign-controlled.[116] Foreign economic domination also brought favourable treatment for foreigners living in Mexico. The regime served a small elite of upper- and middle-class Mexicans, who were knowledgeable and open to foreign ideas and influences.[117] After the passage of the Laws of Reform, agricultural lands formerly owned by the Church were acquired by *hacendados*, or large landowners. The growing population of the poor—landless peasants and semi-skilled labourers—grew increasingly resentful and restless.[118]

The *porfiriato* eventually collapsed under the weight of socioeconomic inequities and political stagnation, erupting into the social and political revolution of 1910–1917. While Porfirio Díaz succeeded in modernizing parts of Mexico, the most important legacies of the *porfiriato* may not have been its accomplishments in modernizing Mexico, but the reactions that it engendered which influenced the development of law in Mexico. These reactions included antipathy towards foreign investment and foreign control of the economy; an understanding that the government should protect the disadvantaged classes, especially the landless rural population; and a deeply ingrained aversion to the re-election of government officials.

4. The Mexican Revolution and the Modern Mexican State: The Rise and Fall of the 'Perfect Dictatorship' of the PRI

In Mexico, the term *Revolución* has only one meaning: the Mexican Revolution of 1910 to 1917. The *Revolución* not only changed the political landscape; it also served as a watershed in the definition of Mexican society as a rich amalgam of European and indigenous cultures. After the *Revolución*, political leaders would instil in later generations of Mexicans the perception that as a nation, they shared a mythical common identity based on the unique characteristics of Mexicans: their *mexicanidad*, or 'Mexicanness'.[119] This sense of Mexican

[116] Hart, *supra* note 98 at 178. By the 1900s, US investors held 80% of the stock of Mexico's railroads, banks, and mining companies. *Id.* at 134, 140, 142. US investors also owned a large portion of Mexico's agricultural lands: more than 22% of Mexico's land surface at the end of the century. *Id.* at 158.

[117] Supporters of the regime included the *cientificos*, government and business leaders who subscribed to the positivist theories of French philosopher August Comte, and espoused a form of social Darwinism that justified the concentration of economic and political power in the hands of educated and wealthy elites.

[118] *See generally* Hart, *supra* note 98, at 41–51, 57–73.

[119] *See generally* Serra Rojas, A., *Mexicanidad: Proyección de la Nación Mexicana hacia el Siglo XXI* (Mexico: Porrúa, 1994).

nationalism was not fully developed or shared by most Mexicans until after the political and social upheavals of this period. Since that time, Mexican political leaders have espoused, if not practised, the social and populist ideals of the Revolution, the common identity of Mexicans,[120] and the need to follow a uniquely Mexican approach in matters, including solutions to legal problems.

The notion that Mexico underwent a complete social revolution in the second decade of the twentieth century is a myth, of course. The Mexican Revolution was fought on many fronts, by persons with many different motives. It did not terminate inequities based on social class in Mexico, and many Mexican families who were wealthy before the Revolution remained so long after the Revolution had played out. Nevertheless, the Revolution eventually brought about the adoption of a populist form of government based on middle-class values that provided greater avenues for social mobility than those that had existed prior to the Revolution.[121]

4.1. The Overthrow of Porfirio Diaz

As Porfirio Díaz neared the end of his seventh term in office, the expectation grew that he would not run for re-election in 1910. But when Díaz announced that he would seek another term, Francisco Madero, a wealthy landowner from Chihuahua, campaigned against the dictator under the banner of the No-Reelectionist Party, resulting in Madero's arrest. In July 1910, eighty-year-old Porfirio Díaz won a questionable 'landslide victory' for his eighth term as President. Madero fled to San Antonio, Texas, where he and a group of followers published a call to arms, known as the Plan of San Luis Potosí, which called for removal of Díaz and new elections.

While Madero was not a social revolutionary—his Plan did not call for land reform, or for other social reforms—his opposition to the dictator gained the support of more radical opponents. Pancho Villa in the north, Emiliano Zapata in the south, and other rural leaders led armed revolts throughout the country. The army (*federales*) was unable to control the insurrection; popular support, bred by decades of social and economic abuses, helped Villa and Zapata to recruit large bands of combatants. In May 1911, Porfirio Díaz finally signed a political agreement, the Treaty of Ciudad Juárez, in which he agreed to resign, and new elections were called. In November 1911, Madero was elected President.

[120] Not all segments of society embrace *mexicanidad* equally, of course. Mexicans include members of indigenous groups with unique cultures and languages, as well as the descendants of Europeans who fled the Second World War. However, many Mexicans take pride in a mythical national identity. The leaders of the PRI, the ruling party throughout the twentieth century, for many years portrayed itself as the voice of *mexicanidad*.

[121] Roberto Newell, G. and Luis Rubio, F., *MEXICO'S DILEMMA: THE POLITICAL ORIGINS OF ECONOMIC CRISIS* (Boulder, Colo: Westview Press, 1984) at 28. This book offers an excellent account of the political and economic effects of the Revolution.

Before leaving Mexico for exile in France, Porfirio Díaz is alleged to have stated 'Madero has unleashed a tiger, now let us see if he can control it'.[122] Unfortunately, Madero could not control the tiger. His presidency ended fifteen months after it began, when an insurrection by military leaders (supported behind the scenes by the US Ambassador to Mexico) brought about the arrest and execution of President Madero and his Vice President, Jose Pino Suárez. General Victoriano Huerta was named provisional President in February 1913, and attempted to maintain power through force, dissolving Congress and imprisoning opponents. Huerta himself was overthrown in the summer of 1914 by forces led by northern revolutionaries Alvaro Obregón and Pancho Villa. Venustiano Carranza, an educated landowner from the northern state of Coahuila, assumed the presidency.

Carranza was to remain in the presidency until 1920 (when he was assassinated), but it cannot be said that he ruled the entire country, since Villa and Zapata continued to bring about uprisings in the countryside. Zapata, with a rural base in the poorest region of the country, in particular opposed the cautious approach of Carranza. Under the banner *Tierra y Libertad* (Land and Freedom), Zapata sought to break up the large landholdings of *hacendados* and distribute land to landless *campesinos*. With Villa, Zapata, and others vying for power from the periphery, President Carranza maintained tenuous control of the government. Carranza's moderate approach was opposed by Zapata and Villa, but the former was assassinated in a surprise ambush in 1919. Carranza (assassinated in 1920), Pancho Villa (murdered in 1923), and Álvaro Obregón (murdered in 1928) met the same fate as Madero and Zapata in due course. The legacy of the Revolution would prove not to be embodied in a person, but rather in a Constitution and an ingenious political system that would govern Mexico throughout the remainder of the twentieth century.

4.2. The Constitution of 1917

In 1916, advised to institutionalize reforms and consolidate his power, President Carranza called a constitutional convention in Querétaro, a regional capital north of Mexico City. The framers (*constituyentes*) who attended the six-week convention were *maderista* middle-class liberals, with urban and professional classes well represented. Amended over 340 times since its adoption,[123] the Constitution of 1917 still governs Mexico.[124] The document drew from the Constitution of

[122] Miller, *supra* note 18 at 291.

[123] Valadés, Diego, *El Control del Poder* (Mexico: UNAM/IIJ, 1998) at 365. Dr Valadés reports that only 37 of the original 136 constitutional articles have escaped amendment.

[124] Each edition of Tena Ramírez, *supra* note 79 at 817 *et seq.*, publishes the text of the Constitution in effect as of the date of publication of the volume, with endnotes giving the original 1917 text of the Constitution, and the dates and texts of subsequent amendments. To study the amendments to Constitutional provisions, *see also* *Constitución Política De Las Estados Unidos Mexicanos, Comentada y Concordada* (Mexico: UNAM/Instituto de Investigaciones Jurídicas/Porrúa, 15th ed., M. Carbonell, ed., Cord. Miguel Carbonell, 2000).

1857: it was anticlerical, for instance, severely curtailing the powers of the Church and prohibiting Church ownership of property and its involvement in political life. In addition, however, the Constitution added a social agenda—the legacy of Zapata and others—that justified massive land reforms, controls on foreign ownership of lands, and a lengthy provision, Article 123, setting forth a broad array of workers' rights. According to Guillermo Margadant:

> This Constitution of 1917 was a multilateral declaration of war, directed at *hacendados*, bosses, the clergy and the mining companies [. . .] The potentially dangerous effects of the Constitution, however, were softened by the fact that Venustiano Carranza was able to pacify the Church and the oil companies, based on promises that, under his regime, the Constitution would not be enforced to the letter.[125]

Even after the assassination of the moderate Carranza, the social agenda—radical land reform, controls on foreign ownership, and organization of labour for political and economic purposes—was ignored by Presidents Alvaro Obregon (1920–1924) and Plutarco Elias Calles (1924–1928). The emphasis during this early period was merely on maintaining stability after a decade of turmoil.[126]

The most significant early accomplishment of the *constituyentes* was to adopt a form of government that would end the pendulum swings from legislative anarchy to dictatorial rule that had plagued Mexico in the nineteenth century. Given the country's legacy of centralized colonial rule and its history of foreign intervention and civil war, how could Mexico achieve a stable form of government that would not deteriorate into dictatorship? The principal architect of the solution to this problem was a lawyer and politician from the southern state of Chiapas named Emilio Rabasa. In 1912, Rabasa published an historical and doctrinal study of the Mexican constitution entitled *La Constitución y la Dictadura* (The Constitution and Dictatorship). In this influential book, Rabasa argued that the seeds of the Mexican tendency to migrate towards dictatorial power were sown in the Constitution of 1857. According to Rabasa, the 1857 Constitution had empowered the legislature over the executive, by adopting a unicameral legislature and limiting the President's powers. As Rabasa wrote:

> The suppression of the Senate destroyed [the equilibrium between Presidential and legislative power], not only by increasing the power of the unicameral Congress, but also by depriving the States of their equal representation in the legislative assembly. Though later establishing a Senate, the Charter still contained important defects that in practice would lead to profound conflict between branches of government, which ensured the preponderance of the legislature over the executive, thus leading to either of two extremes to deal with the omnipotence of Congress: the submission of the Executive, which establishes the dictatorship of the Congress, or a *golpe de estado [coup d'état]* that enthrones the dictatorship of the President.[127]

[125] Margadant, *supra* note 5 at 172 (authors' trans.)

[126] Newell and Rubio, *supra* note 121 at 29.

[127] Rabasa, Emilio, *La Constitución y la Dictadura* (Mexico: Cámara de Diputados, Comite de Asuntos Editoriales, 1999) at 173 (authors' trans.).

Mexican constitutional scholars note that Rabasa's ideas had a profound influence on the *constituyentes*,[128] who agreed with him that the system of government should provide for strong Presidential powers. However, where Rabasa had argued that universal, direct election of the President would make prohibitions of reelection superfluous,[129] the *constituyentes* embraced the *maderista* belief in non-reelection as a fundamental deterrent to entrenched political power. Not only did the Constitution of 1917 provide for an absolute ban on re-election of the President (Article 83), but the concept of non-reelection was also applied to federal and state senators and representatives (Articles 59 and 155-III). Indeed, throughout Mexican society, it is commonly accepted, under force of law, regulation, or customary practice, that leaders of public institutions should not be reelected, or at the least that their terms should be limited.[130]

4.3. The Consolidation of Power and the Corporatist State

By coupling the primacy of executive power with the concept of non-reelection, the Mexican Constitution of 1917 laid the foundation for the single-party form of government that has governed Mexico throughout the twentieth century. The first President to consolidate political control was Plutarco Elias Calles (1924–1928), who organized trade unions and peasant groups into effective means of populist support. Calles faced stiff opposition from the Catholic faithful, however, for he vigorously enforced the Constitution's anticlerical provisions in Articles 3, 27, and 130 (prohibiting religious education in the schools, preventing the Church from owning property, and limiting public exercise of religious services). Enraged Catholics took up arms in the *cristero* rebellion, which ended in 1929 when an uneasy truce was signed between the Church and the government. The counterbalancing of the immense power of the Mexican Catholic Church with the vigorous anticlericalism of the government would prove to be a pillar of Mexican politics throughout the twentieth century.[131]

Forced to leave office at the end of his single term, Calles controlled the country by seeing to the election of his allies as successive presidents, through whom he was able to continue cementing the foundations of a stable government

[128] *See*, e.g., Tena Ramírez, *supra* note 79 at 812.

[129] 'To prevent the taking of power in perpetuity, the concept of non-reelection of the President of the Republic has been developed [. . .] If appropriate electoral practices are adopted, such a prohibition is not only useless, but unjustified [*atentatoria*]. [. . .] One should go directly to the root of the problem, and make give effect to the people's role in Presidential succession'. Rabasa, *supra* note 127 at 164–165.

[130] Thus, for instance, the Dean of the law school at the Universidad Nacional Autónoma de México (UNAM) is allowed to serve no more than two terms of four years.

[131] Two excellent studies of the history of the Catholic Church in Mexico are Roberto Blancarte, *Historia de la Iglesia Católica en México* (Mexico: Fondo de Cultura Económica, 1992), which concentrates on the period after the *cristero* rebellion; and Guillermo Margadant, *supra* note 96. British novelist Graham Greene used the *cristero* rebellion as the background for his novel *The Power and the Glory* (New York: Penguin, 2003).

dominated by the federal power.[132] Calles can be credited with the creation of the unique political model by which the *Partido Revolucionario Institucional* (PRI) governed Mexico from 1929 to 2000. This model has been referred to as corporatism.[133] Just as a corporation engages the common interests of shareholders who buy into it, a corporatist government engages the support of competing groups by requiring them to organize within structures (federations, associations, etc.) that link them to the central government. The federal government (i.e. the President) could not only monitor the activities of every constituency, but could also use strategically the broad array of instruments available to it (government contracts, jobs, federal grants, and occasionally police power) to keep competing groups under control. By creating a strong political party, the *Partido Nacional de la Revolución* (PNR), Calles succeeded in marshalling trade unions, peasant groups, and government bureaucrats into an effective counterpoint to the centrifugal forces of local bosses, or *caudillos*, who had survived the Revolution.[134] The Church, business leaders, and large landowners were effectively neutralized, in part by the regime's ability to offer the social and economic stability that these opposing groups prized. This same formula endures, and explains the ability of the *Partido Revolucionario Institucional* (PRI), the direct successor to the PNR, to maintain political control of Mexico to the present day.

The key to the PRI's immense power from the outset was not brute force, but rather a combination of co-optation of important sectors, central control of the national economy, authoritarian tactics, and the removal of the cult of the individual under the principle of non-reelection. The last of these is key to the regime's survival. Calles himself tested this, when he attempted to direct the actions of his successor, President Lázaro Cárdenas (1934–1940). Cardenas sent Calles into exile, and throughout the rest of the twentieth century Mexican politics and government remained highly centralized and authoritarian, with the President exercising immense power over every aspect of public life and many private sector activities as well. *Presidencialismo* was the name given to this system, and no discussion of Mexican law would be complete without recognizing how it shaped the development of law.[135]

[132] During the presidency of Emilio Portes Gil (1928–1930), Congress adopted the federal Civil Code that is still, with relatively few amendments, the principal source of private law. *See* text accompanying Chapters 14 notes 29–34 *infra*. The first codification of Federal Labour Law was also adopted during this period, establishing federal domination of this important area. *See* discussion of the *Ley Federal de Trabajo* in Chapter 13, text accompanying notes 14 to 16.

[133] *See infra* Chapter 5 at text accompanying notes 1–14. *See also* Cossio Díaz, J.R., CAMBIO SOCIAL Y CAMBIO JURÍDICO (Mexico: ITAM/Miguel Ángel Porrúa, 2001) at 15–76.

[134] An evocative novel dealing with this period of Mexican history is Carlos Fuentes' THE DEATH OF ARTEMIO CRUZ (New York: Farrar, Straus & Giroux, 1991; Alfred J. MacAdam, trans.), which chronicles the life of a fictional revolutionary officer after the end of the Revolution.

[135] *See generally* Newell and Rubio, *supra* note 121 at 29 *et seq*. For many years, the essential reading on Mexican presidential power was Jorge Carpizo's EL PRESIDENCIALISMO MEXICANO (Mexico: Siglo XXI, 15th ed., 2000). First published in 1978, this book is now in its

The defining features of Mexican *presidencialismo*, and the secret to its success and longevity, were two: an assumption by the executive branch (under the control of the President) of virtually absolute power, relegating the legislative and judicial branches to lesser roles; and a temporal limitation on that power to the *sexenio*, or six-year term of office of the President, who cannot be re-elected. Power was always highly personal and coloured by the President's individual choices. While the President was bolstered by the party apparatus of the PRI, the non-ideological nature of the party itself allowed each President considerable latitude in setting policies. The limitation of presidential power to a single *sexenio* prevented the system from degenerating into dictatorship.

Swings in political and economic policies occurred from *sexenio* to *sexenio*, but they did not upset the basic power structure. This power structure was pragmatic, and was based on a refined corporatist model in which labour, the rural peasantry, industry, and government workers are organized into a broad net of confederations and congresses with which the government could negotiate (some might say manipulate). The system was controlled by a political elite, whose original members were often referred to as the 'revolutionary family', the insiders who survived the Mexican Revolution and were at the top of a complex network of alliances.

In addition to establishing the primacy of the executive branch, the Constitution of 1917 adopted a social agenda that would underscore the populist approach of the PRI-dominated government. The right to basic education (Article 3); equal rights for women, and a right to adequate housing (Article 4); land reform and control of foreign investment (Article 27); and extensive employment rights (Article 123) are spelled out in the Constitution, even if their provisions often represent aspirations rather than enforceable constitutional guarantees.[136]

Throughout the twentieth century, successive Presidents espoused the goals of the social agenda, although not necessarily taking significant steps to further these goals. By presenting itself as the party of social reform, the PRI (i.e. the government) was able to deflect more dramatic attempts at social reform by outside groups. At the same time, the federal government's paternalistic control over social welfare carried with it a strong emphasis in Mexican law on the primacy of social or public interest over individual freedoms.[137]

Lázaro Cárdenas (1934–1940) was the first post-revolutionary President to embark on a vigorous agenda of social reforms. In this respect, Cárdenas'

15th edition (2000), although much of the first edition has survived in the text. Carpizo's rather general book showed the shortcomings of the system, but was received as authoritative in government circles because it was not overly critical of the system. More recent studies of presidentialism are cited in Ugalde, Luis Carlos, 'The Transformation of Mexican Presidentialism, 1929–2000', 25 WTR FLETCHER FORUM OF WORLD AFFAIRS 115 (2001); and in Cárdenas Gracia, J., *TRANSICIÓN POLÍTICA Y REFORMA CONSTITUCIONAL EN MÉXICO* (Mexico: UNAM, 1996) at 70–91.

136 *See* Vargas, Jorge A., 'The Constitution of Mexico', in Jorge Vargas, ed., *MEXICAN LAW: A TREATISE FOR LEGAL PRACTITIONERS AND MEXICAN INVESTORS*, *supra* note 115, vol. 1 at 44.

137 Newell and Rubio, *supra* note 126 at 33–34.

presidency can be compared favourably to that of Franklin D. Roosevelt in the United States. Both leaders faced daunting economic problems brought on by worldwide depression, and both succeeded in promoting the federal government's role in providing for social welfare. During his *sexenio*, Cárdenas created a number of government agencies that would provide for social and economic welfare, including the Mexican social security system (Instituto Mexicano de Seguridad Social, or IMSS). Many of these agencies (parastatal companies included) were to participate actively in the economy, providing goods and services to the public; by the early 1980s, the large number of federal agencies and parastatal companies had a stranglehold on the economy.

The most important Mexican government-owned company was created in 1938, when President Cárdenas expropriated the properties of foreign oil companies, and soon thereafter created the government-owned enterprise Petróleos Mexicanos, or Pemex.[138] In 1937, a dispute between the oil companies and trade unions resulted in a large monetary award in favour of the workers. The oil companies refused to pay, even after the Mexican Supreme Court ordered payment. Cárdenas reacted swiftly to the companies' refusal to abide by the Court's decision, and on 18 March 1938, he announced the expropriation of the foreign oil companies. The act was applauded by the Mexican people as a declaration of economic independence (more fictional than real) and as an important demonstration that, after the Mexican Revolution, foreign interests would not continue to intervene inappropriately in Mexico.

Cárdenas also directed an ambitious campaign of land reform, forcing the subdivision and sale of large landed estates. From 1934 to 1940, the government redistributed over 18 million hectares (45 million acres) of land, more than double the amount redistributed in the previous seventeen years.[139] Much of this land was acquired in a form of communal ownership, the *ejido*, that had been common in pre-Hispanic Mexico and had become enshrined in the Constitution of 1917 (Article 27-VII).[140] While agrarian reform was politically popular, it did not liberate the rural peasantry, which became dependent on the federal government's dispensation of agricultural loans.

From 1940 to 1970, Mexico experienced a long period of political tranquility and economic growth. The corporatist system administered by the PRI became increasingly refined, and with federal domination of the major sectors of society, there was little outlet for effective opposition to government policies. The PRI's monolithic political power made application of the law an arbitrary matter. Since Congress always passed the laws and constitutional reforms he desired,

[138] On the expropriation of the oil companies, *see* Jayne, C.E., *Oil, War, and Anglo-American Relations: American and British Reactions to Mexico's Expropriation of Foreign Oil Properties, 1937–1941* (Westport, Conn: Greenwood Press, 2000); Brown, J.C., *Oil and Revolution in Mexico* (Berkeley: University of California Press, 1993); Meyer, L., *México y los Estados Unidos en el Conflicto Petrolero* (Mexico: Colegio de México, 1972).

[139] Krause, *supra* note 106 at 469.

[140] *See* text accompanying note 15 *supra*. The Mexican *ejido* is discussed in more detail in Chapter 13 at text accompanying notes 81–93, *infra*.

every President took the opportunity to place his stamp on the Constitution. As a result, the Constitution of 1917 has been amended 346 times; almost half of these amendments were adopted between 1982 and 1996.[141]

Since the enforcement of the laws lay in the hands of executive branch agencies, this left immense power in the hands of the bureaucracy. The federal government actively promoted industrialization of the Mexican economy by establishing high tariffs on the importation of consumer goods and by gradually increasing the number and power of government-owned industrial enterprises, especially in the areas of heavy industry and infrastructure (power generation and distribution, transportation, steel, etc.).[142]

4.4. The End of One-Party Hegemony

The first signs of a crack in the monolithic power of the PRI occurred in 1968, on the eve of the Olympic Games that Mexico was preparing to host (the first Olympic Games in a Latin American country). Large numbers of students organized demonstrations against the stagnant political system, intending to bring public awareness of the lack of effective democracy. On the afternoon of 2 October 1968, a peaceful student demonstration at the *Plaza de las Tres Culturas* in the Tlatelolco area of Mexico City prompted a sudden and violent response from soldiers guarding the area, some of whom opened fire on the unarmed demonstrators; hundreds of people were killed, and thousands were arrested. The word 'Tltatelolco' became synonymous with violent oppression. Anti-government demonstrations did not cease, and many people, including influential intellectuals, began to question the consensus on which the PRI's power was based.[143]

The Interior Minister who ordered the troops to quell the demonstration, Luis Echeverria Álvarez, became President of Mexico in 1970. To rebuild the consensus supporting the PRI, President Echeverria adopted leftist political rhetoric and an oppositional stance to United States interests, including foreign investment. During this period, Mexico adopted strict controls on foreign investment and transfer of technology, and the federal government asserted even more direct control of the economy.[144] The government also initiated ambitious social welfare programmes, which served to increase public spending and control of the economy. In 1976, when President Jose López Portillo

[141] Lopez Ayllón, S., *LAS TRANSFORMACIONES DEL SISTEMA JURÍDICO Y LOS SIGNIFICADOS SOCIALES DEL DERECHO EN MÉXICO: LA ENCRUCIJADA ENTRE TRADICIÓN Y MODERNIDAD* (Mexico: UNAM, 1997) at 174.

[142] For a brief overview of the import substitution policies followed by the government during this period, and their eventual collapse and abandonment, *see id.* at 90–98. For a more detailed account, in English, *see* Newell and Rubio, *supra* note 121 at 73 *et seq.*

[143] Krause, *supra* note 106 at 717–737.

[144] *See infra* Chapter 19, text accompanying notes 32 *et seq.* When Echeverría took office, in 1970, government expenditures represented 13% of the gross national product (GNP); by 1976, at the end of his *sexenio*, 40% of GNP was in government hands, and the rest was effectively controlled by government. Newell and Rubio, *supra* note 121 at 126.

(1976–1982) took office, he continued the general policies of Echeverria: increased social welfare spending; dramatic growth of the parastatal sector;[145] and the use of public debt (especially loans from foreign private banks) to fund these programmes. This was the legacy of the disturbances of 1968: '[t]he tendency to throw money at political problems rather than to solve them'[146] by opening the political system to a more democratic model.[147]

López Portillo based his programmes of social welfare spending and economic expansion (tightly controlled from the centre by the federal government) on a gamble that proved to be a bad bet: that the cost of servicing the public debt would not increase, and that continuing increases in oil prices would bring Mexico, an oil exporting nation, the prosperity it deserved. He was wrong on both counts: during the 1980s, interest rates rose dramatically, and worldwide recession drove down the price of oil. Mexico was forced to default on foreign loans; capital flight and devaluation of the peso quickly followed in the summer of 1982, and President López Portillo reacted by imposing strict exchange controls, which had not been seen since colonial times.[148] López Portillo left office as a diminished leader. His accomplishments, however, included support of electoral reforms that would eventually—without his wishing it—lead to a breakup of the PRI's monopoly of political power.

The economic crises of the 1980s began to unravel the economic and political models that had effectively maintained control of Mexico throughout much of the twentieth century: an economy relatively closed to foreign trade and foreign investment, and tightly controlled by the central government; and a closed political system that might bend, but would not break or lose its grip on the country. During the transitional presidency of Miguel de la Madrid (1982–1988), Mexico began to change direction, both in its politics and in its political economy. In 1986, Mexico embarked on a new phase in its economic history, by joining the GATT and committing itself to the dismantling of high barriers to trade.

When Miguel de la Madrid selected Harvard-trained economist Carlos Salinas de Gortari (1988–1994) to succeed him (the first economist to serve as President), the conversion from a closed and centralized economy to an open, market-driven economy was assured. Salinas was challenged in the election by a populist candidate, Cuahtémoc Cárdenas, the son of revered former President

[145] By the end of López Portillo's *sexenio*, there were over 1,100 government-owned corporations, doing everything from manufacturing steel to running hotels and cinemas.

[146] Newell and Rubio, *supra* note 121 at 265.

[147] It is an over-simplification to say that Mexico is not a democracy, just as it would be an over-simplification to say that the southern United States or the City of Chicago were not democracies during the period of single-party rule by Democrats in the mid-twentieth Century. Nevertheless, it is fair to say that Mexican-style democracy is highly managed, and has been justifiably criticized. *See*, e.g., Krauze, Enrique, *Por Una Democracia sin Adjetivos* (1986) (Mexico: Joaquśa Mortiz–Planeta, 1986); Luis Rubio, *La democracia verdadera: Información, ciudadanía y política pública* (Mexico: Cal y Arena, 1998).

[148] *See generally* Zamora, S., 'Peso-Dollar Economics and the Imposition of Foreign Exchange Controls in Mexico', 32 *Am. J. Comp. Law* at 99–154 (1985).

Lázaro Cárdenas. Many observers believe that Cárdenas had actually won the election; suspiciously, the election computers 'failed' during the voting tally, and after a period of days, when 'order' was restored, Salinas was declared the winner. The outcry, both within Mexico and in the international community, led to further reforms both of the electoral process, and of judicial challenges to elections, as discussed below in Chapter 5.

Soon after he took office, President Salinas began to accelerate the privatization of government-owned businesses (*paraestatales*),[149] which had expanded to 1,155 entities by the end of President López Portillo's administration; by the end of the Salina *sexenio*, the sale of *paraestatales* had reduced this number to 215.[150] Salinas, the Harvard economist, ushered in the era of 'economic opening' (*apertura económica)* that was calculated to convert Mexico from a centrally closed economy to an economy open to foreign trade and investment, and governed by the disciplines of free markets.[151] In addition to changes in economic policies, President Salinas engineered major constitutional changes, eviscerating land reform and permitting corporate investment in agricultural lands,[152] and culminated in Mexico's negotiation of the North American Free Trade Agreement (NAFTA) with Canada and the United States. Entering into force in 1994, NAFTA solidified Mexico's commitment to an economy based on open trade and open investment.

The entry into force of NAFTA was a major turning point in US–Mexican relations. Far from trying to guard itself against US domination, as it had throughout much of its history, the Mexican government under President Salinas chose to enter into a permanent relationship, a form of economic marriage, with the United States. The United States accounts for approximately two-thirds of all foreign investment in Mexico, and is Mexico's largest trading partner, accounting for almost 90 per cent of Mexico's exports and 61 per cent of its imports.[153] The influence of the US economy took on even more importance with the growth in importance of trade and investment in Mexico's economy after the economic opening. As a result, the Mexican economy became more dependent than ever on the economic swings of its major trading power. Conversely, for the United States, NAFTA meant that the US government would have to pay more attention to the country that was soon to become its second-largest trading power. For the first time, US, Mexican, and Canadian

[149] *Paraestatales* included not only Pemex and the commercial banks (which were 'nationalized' in 1982) but also manufacturers of basic commodities such as steel, hotel chains, food suppliers, airlines, and even cinemas. The government's direct control of a large percentage of the economy provided the Mexican President with an immense array of political appointments and contractual rights to use in buying the support of political allies.

[150] López Ayllón, *supra* note 141 at 105.

[151] For an early account of the *apertura economica*, *see* López Ayllón, *supra* note 141 at 99–106.

[152] Vargas, J., 'Mexico's Leading Revolution: An Appraisal of Its Recent Constitutional Changes, 1988–1995', 25 *Ga. J. Int'l & Comp. L.* 497, 528–540 (1996).

[153] In 2003, Mexican exports totalled 164·8 billion US dollars (146 billion were exports to the United States). Source: www.banxico.gob.mx (Indicadores Económics y Financieros), May 2004.

agencies would begin to consult on a systematic basis concerning matters of common concern. These arrangements spring from NAFTA itself,[154] as well as from the impetus that NAFTA provided to many private and public enterprises to focus their attention on expanding business links with Mexico.[155]

The last decade of the twentieth century also witnessed a political *apertura* that is still unfolding.[156] The economic changes in Mexico altered the paternalistic grip that the PRI-dominated government had held over Mexico for most of that century. The market-driven economy weakened the major source of Presidential power in Mexico: comprehensive control over the economy. The PRI's political control also became threatened, due in part to electoral reforms adopted grudgingly by the PRI in an attempt to preserve power while providing a safe outlet for opposition parties.[157] The new politics of Mexico included a new stance *vis-à-vis* the Catholic Church. Constitutional and legislative reforms in 1992[158] opened the way for 'religious associations' to own and manage and to provide for religious education in private schools—a departure from the official anti-clericalism that prevailed throughout much of the twentieth century—although the law continues to prevent religious groups from participating in the political life of the nation.[159]

By the end of the Salinas administration, the PRI had begun to lose its monolithic control over the Mexican government. Prior to 1986 the PRI had never lost any election for state governor, and the party controlled all thirty-one state legislatures. By 1994, while most state legislatures and governorships were still in the hands of the PRI, and the PRI still had a slim majority in Congress, it was apparent that lack of meaningful opposition was coming to an end, and that the elections to succeed President Salinas would be intensely competitive. Salinas selected Ernesto Zedillo Ponce de León as the PRI candidate,[160] and in the first

[154] *See* Zamora, S., 'NAFTA and the Harmonization of Domestic Legal Systems', 12 ARIZ. J. INT'L & COMP. L 401 (1995).

[155] The United States' heightened engagement with Mexico was put to the test soon after NAFTA's entry into force, when a crisis of confidence, brought on by political uncertainties (a banking crisis, the Zapatista disturbances in Chiapas, and political uncertainties) brought a dramatic drop in the exchange rate of the peso. Unlike the exchange crisis of 1982, the United States acted quickly: President Clinton, without waiting for congressional approval, approved a swap arrangement through the Federal Reserve to help bolster the peso. The US government clearly chose not to allow its new NAFTA partner to slide into economic crisis. The quick action stemmed the crisis, and within a relatively short time, the Mexican economy recovered. *See* Lustig, N., 'Los Estados Unidos al rescate de México en crisis: Repetición de la historia?', in *NUEVA AGENDA BILATERAL EN RELACIÓN MÉXICO: ESTADOS UNIDOS* (Mexico: Fondo de Cultura Económica, 1998; Verea Campos, M., *et al.*, eds.) at 443, 463–488.

[156] On the political *apertura* generally, *see* López Ayllon, *supra* note 141 at 107–130. *See also* Camp, R. A., POLITICS IN MEXICO (New York: Oxford University Press, 1999).

[157] Electoral and congressional reforms are discussed in Chapter 5 *infra*. *See generally* Rabasa, Emilio O., 'Las Reformas Constitucionales en Materia Politico-Electoral', in *OCHENTA AÑOS DE VIDA CONSTITUCIONAL EN MEXICO* (Mexico: Camara de Disputados and UNAM/IIJ, 1998; Emilio O. Rabasa, ed.) at 147–170.

[158] D.O. 28 Jan., 1992, amending Article 3 of the Constitution.

[159] Soberanes Fernandez, José Luis, 'La Nueva Legislación sobre Libertad Religiosa en Mexico (con Referencia a las Reformas de 1992)', in Rabasa, *supra* note 157 at 107–124.

[160] Zedillo was actually a last-minute, emergency candidate. Luis Donaldo Colosio, formerly Salinas' Secretary of Social Development (SEDESOL), had originally been selected as the

truly transparent election in modern times Zedillo was elected President by a narrow majority, and the PRI clung to a slim majority in Congress as well.

Like his predecessor, Zedillo was a technocrat who had never been elected to public office. Like his predecessor, he was an economist with a doctorate from a US university (Yale) who embraced the open-market policies of President Salinas. The *sexenio* of President Zedillo (1994–2000) will not be known for its economic reforms, however, but rather for legal reforms that continued the political opening and led, finally, to the defeat of the PRI as Mexico's governing party.

Two key political reforms took place during Zedillo's presidency: reforms to select the mayor of Mexico City by popular election, and reforms intended to reinforce judicial power.[161] In 1993 Congress amended the Constitution to provide that the mayor (formerly referred to as the *regente*) of the Federal District of Mexico City would no longer be appointed by the President, but would instead be elected by popular vote.[162] This move, coupled with the increased powers of the legislative assembly for the Federal District,[163] further reduced the heavy hand of *presidencialismo* by removing the President's ability to hand out federal jobs by direct appointment in the largest population centre in the country. These changes led to the PRI's loss of political power in the Federal District: the person elected in 1996 as the first mayor (*jefe de gobierno*) of Mexico City was President Salinas' presidential opponent, Cuahtémoc Cárdenas, of the leftist PRD party (*Partido de la Revolución Democrática*). In 2000 Cárdenas was succeeded as mayor by another leftist/populist PRD leader, Andrés Manuel López Obradors. In the 2003 mid-term elections, PRD candidates were elected to thirteen of the sixteen *delegado* positions, and the PRD won thirty-seven of the sixty-six seats in the Legislative Assembly. The PRI had lost control of the largest and most important electoral district in the country.

The second set of reforms involved amendments to the Constitution, in 1994 and 1997, intended to strengthen the independence and power of the federal judiciary. These reforms, discussed below in Chapter 6,[164] affected the composition

candidate of the PRI. However, on 24 March 1994, Colosio was assassinated while campaigning for the presidency in Tijuana. The assassin, Mario Aburto Martínez, was tried and convicted, and while the government contended that the assassination was an act of one individual, mystery continues to surround Colosio's murder.

161 Additional reforms during this period included a constitutional amendment to ensure the rights of the indigenous population (*see infra* Chapter 7 at text accompanying notes 24 *et seq.*); and reforms to increase the independence of the National Commission of Human Rights (*see infra* Chapter 11 at text accompanying notes 84–85); and to increase the independence of the Federal Electoral Tribunal (*see infra* Chapter 6 at text accompanying notes 37–46).

162 *See infra* Chapter 5 at text accompanying note 39.

163 *See infra* Chapter 5 at text accompanying notes 40–43.

164 *See also* Fix Fierro, H., 'Judicial Reform and the Supreme Court of Mexico: The Trajectory of Three Years', 6 US-Mex. L.J. 1, (1998); Melgar Adalid, M., 'The Supreme Courts and the Judiciary Councils', 42 *St. Louis L.J.* 1131 (1998); Vargas, J., 'The Rebirth of the Supreme Court of Mexico: An Appraisal of President Zedillo's Judicial Reform of 1995', 11 *Am. U.J. Int'l L. & Pol.* 295 (1996).

of the Supreme Court (which was reduced from twenty-one to eleven justices); created the *Consejo Federal de la Judicatura*, to provide greater independence from the executive branch over the tenure and appointment of federal judges, and over the administration of the federal judicial system;[165] and strengthened the Supreme Court's power to interpret the Constitution. Thanks to these reforms, the Mexican Supreme Court and the Courts of Appeals have exercised more power than ever in the determination of politically sensitive disputes. As often happens in Mexico, the federal reforms had repercussions in state law, as many state legislatures adopted reforms similar to the federal model.

By the time presidential elections were held in 2000, the PRI could no longer fall back on extra-legal methods of electing its candidates (vote-tampering, buying votes through jobs). The country was ready for a change. Vicente Fox, a former businessman and governor of Guanajuato, was named the candidate of the centre-right *Partido de Acción Nacional* (PAN). Vicente Fox, the former Coca Cola executive, would defeat the PRI candidate, Francisco Labastida, to become the first person from a party other than the PRI to be elected President of Mexico since the party was formed in 1929.

The legal reforms attributable to President Fox (2000-[2005]) have been modest to date. While the PRI continued to maintain a majority in the Senate after the elections of 2000,[166] no party has held a majority in the *Cámara de Diputados* during Vicente Fox's *sexenio*, and Fox has been unable to compose a coalition of legislative support; as a result, major legislative reforms have been few. The most important reforms proposed during the *sexenio* (e.g., increasing the tax base, and opening the electricity market to increased foreign investment) have been blocked by opposition from the PRI and PRD; there have been constitutional reforms since Vicente Fox became President. In the mid-*sexenio* elections of *diputados* in 2003, the PRI actually increased its number of seats at the expense of the PAN, making the prospect of major legal reform even less likely.

The *sexenio* of Vicente Fox has not lacked legal significance, however. With Vicente Fox as its leader, the PAN broke the quasi-dictatorial power of the PRI. Despite the lack of support in the legislature Vicente Fox was able to maintain political stability in the country, and should be recognized as leading Mexico into a new era of democratic government. In selecting the first non-PRI team to control the executive branch, Vicente Fox had to choose a number of persons for senior administrative posts who had had no experience in public administration; with some exceptions, most of these political appointees have been as effective as their predecessors, despite the relative inexperience of PAN leaders in governing.

[165] *See generally* Melgar Adalid, M., *El Consejo de la Judicatura Federal* (Mexico: Porrúa, 1997).

[166] In 2004 the 128 members of the Mexican Senate showed the following composition by political party: PRI, 60; PAN, 46; PRD, 16; PVEM, 5; Independent, 1.

There have also been some legislative accomplishments during this period. For the long term, the most important of these may prove to be the adoption in 2002 of the first law in Mexico to promote transparency in government by creating public access to government information. This law, the *Ley Federal de Transparencia y Acceso a la Información Pública Gubernamental*,[167] is vaguely similar to the US Freedom of Information Act,[168] and has served as a model for similar laws adopted in the state governments.[169] Transparency has not been a hallmark of government administration in Mexico, which in the past suffered from high levels of corruption and misinformation during the period of one-party rule. If the transparency law is administered effectively, it will provide long-term benefits by reinforcing the rule of law in Mexico.

Finally, the Fox administration may be credited with continuing the attempts, begun during the Salinas and Zedillo administrations, to improve public administration by trying to simplify federal regulation. As discussed below in Chapter 9, the Federal Commission for Regulatory Improvement (*Comisión Federal de Mejora Regulatoria*, or COFEMER) has systematically addressed the gargantuan task of improving the efficiency of federal regulation in Mexico.[170]

[167] D.O. 11 Jun. 2002. *See infra* Chapter 9 at text accompanying notes 93 *et seq*.

[168] 5 U.S.C. 552. For information on the US law and its administration, *see* www.usdoj.gov/foia (May 2004).

[169] *Ley de la Transparencia y Acceso a la Informacíon Pública para el Distrito Federal*, G. O. 8 May 2003.

[170] *See infra* Chapter 9 at text accompanying note 49.

2

Legal Education and the Legal Profession

PART 1: LEGAL EDUCATION

1. The Law Degree and Law Schools

A fundamental prerequisite for practising law in Mexico is a law degree (*licenciatura en derecho*) from a licensed Mexican law school.[1] This degree is roughly equivalent to a combined bachelor's and doctoral law degree in the United States. The recipient of the degree is referred to as a *licenciado*, and one respectfully addresses a Mexican lawyer as '*Licenciado*' or '*Licenciada*'. The term *licenciado* is a form of respect, even if lawyers in Mexico suffer the same jokes and criticisms as their counterparts in other countries.[2]

In 2002, 17,124 Mexicans earned the degree of *licenciado en derecho* or its equivalent. This number represents less than half the number of graduates of US law schools for the same year (38,605 graduates with J.D. degrees in the United States); these numbers correspond roughly to the relative size of the two countries' populations.[3]

In recent years, the number of institutions in Mexico offering the basic law degree has risen dramatically. Historically, Mexican legal education was centred mostly in two institutions: the law faculty of the Universidad Nacional Autónoma de México ('UNAM') and the Escuela Libre de Derecho.[4] In 1963, only about

[1] A few Mexican law schools confer the basic law degree under a name different from *licenciado en derecho*, such as *abogado* (attorney) (e.g. Instituto Tecnológico Autónomo de México, Escuela Libre de Derecho); *licenciado en derecho y ciencias sociales* (degree in law and social sciences) (e.g. Universidad Panamericana, Universidad Autónoma de Nuevo León); degree in legal sciences (*licenciado en ciencias jurídicas*) (e.g. Centro de Estudios Universitarios de Monterrey); or degree in fiscal and corporate law (*licenciado en derecho fiscal y corporativo*) (e.g. Universidad Realística de México).

[2] A Mexican curse, '*que te veas entre abogados*' (may you find yourself among lawyers), reflects the problematic relationship many Mexicans have with the legal system.

[3] Mexican figures are from Asociación Nacional de Universidades e Instituciones de Educación Superior (ANUIES), Anuario Estadístico 2002, available at www.annuies.mx, under 'servicios'. US figures are from www.abanet.org, 'Public Information Statistics'.

[4] *See* Margadant G. F., An Introduction to the History of Mexican Law (Dobbs Ferry, NY: Oceana, 1983) 352; Maxwell, R., & Goldman, M., 'Mexican Legal Education', 16 J. Legal Educ. 155, 157–58 (1963) [hereinafter Maxwell]. UNAM began legal instruction in 1553, making it the first law school to be established in the Americas. *See* Margadant, *supra*, at 125; Mendieta y Nuñez, L., Historia de la Facultad de Derecho (1956) 32. The Escuela Libre de Derecho was founded in 1912 by a group of law students from UNAM who broke away in response to interference by government and university officials in the affairs of the law

thirty law schools existed in Mexico.[5] By 1995, 180 Mexican institutions of higher education were offering the basic degree in law. Forty-six of these institutions were completely new as of 1995.[6] For 2003, according to data from the ANUIES, there are more than 500 law schools in the country.[7] Present-day law schools in Mexico range in size from giant programmes, such as the law faculties of UNAM and the University of Guadalajara to tiny programmes, such as those of the Universidad de Sahagún, Universidad Autónoma del Pacífico, and Universidad José Vasconcelos de Oaxaca, each of which had fewer than ten students in 1995. The average law school in Mexico has a total student body of 400 to 900 students.

1.1. Salient Characteristics of Mexican Law Schools

With some important exceptions, legal education is largely conducted within universities or other institutions of higher education. Law schools tend to be divisions of larger educational institutions, such as universities, institutes, or education centres. As of 1995, Mexico had only ten free-standing law programmes.[8] Together, these free-standing programmes accounted for only 2.2 per cent of Mexico's law students in 1995, and for only 1.3 per cent of Mexico's *licenciados en derecho* in 1994. Paradoxically, one of Mexico's most respected law schools is the free-standing Escuela Libre de Derecho in Mexico City.

Public law schools have dominated legal education, although this may be changing. Mexico's dominant law programmes have historically been public, i.e. created and sustained by a state government or by the federal government.[9] Only two of the twenty largest law schools in Mexico are private.[10] In recent

faculty. *See* Maxwell, *supra*, at 157; *see also* Garciadiego, Javier, 'Los Orígenes de la Escuela Libre de Derecho', 17 in REVISTA DE INVESTIGACIONES JURÍDICAS 199 (1993).The UNAM law school has long been considered the premier institution for studying law as preparation for a career in government. Other state autonomous university law schools share this distinction in their respective regions. The Escuela Libre de Derecho is highly respected for the study of 'private law', especially business law, but many private university law schools now share equal standing among lawyers.

[5] *See* Maxwell, *supra* note 4, at 158.

[6] The recent flurry of new law programmes is, in part, attributable to lenient licensing standards and the absence of meaningful accreditation at either the state or federal level. 'Mexican law schools must meet only minimal requirements before receiving permits from either state or federal authorities to offer law degree programs'. Zamora, S., 'NAFTA and the Harmonization of Domestic Legal Systems: The Side Effects of Free Trade', 12 ARIZ. J. INT'L & COMPAR. L. 401, 422 n. 40 (1995) [hereinafter 'Harmonization'].

[7] Source: www.annuies.mx/index/024html (site last visited Jan. 2004).

[8] These were the law programmes at the Centro de Estudios Universitarios; Escuela de Derecho de Atlacomulco; Escuela Libre de Derecho (Mexico City); Escuela Libre de Derecho de Puebla; Escuela Libre de Derecho de Sinaloa; Facultad Libre de Derecho; Instituto de Estudios Superiores de Yucatán; Instituto de Estudios Superiores Hidalgo; and Universidad de Sahagun.

[9] Most of Mexico's largest law schools are divisions of 'autonomous' universities, which implies a degree of independence from the government. *See* Maxwell, *supra* note 4, at 157 n. 11. For example, '[t]he National University, of course, is financially supported by the federal government, but essentially it functions under its own regulatory laws'. *Id.* at 158.

[10] These are the Universidad Tecnológica de México, and Universidad del Valle de México.

Table 2.1: The 20 largest law schools in Mexico by number of students: 2001

	Institution	*Total law students*[a]
1.	Universidad Nacional Autónoma de México	16,340
2.	Universidad Autónoma Benito Juarez de Oaxaca	7,485
3.	Universidad de Guadalajara	6,638
4.	Universidad Autónoma de Nuevo León	6,216
5.	Universidad Michoacana de San Nicolas de Hidalgo	6,052
6.	Universidad de Sonora	5,375
7.	Universidad Autónoma del Estado de México	4,525
8.	Universidad Tecnológica de México	4,345
9.	Universidad Autónoma de Sinaloa	4,091
10.	Universidad Autónoma de Guerrero	3,850
11.	Universidad Autónoma de Baja California	2,737
12.	Universidad Autónoma de Zacatecas	2,500
13.	Benemérita Universidad Autónoma de Puebla	2,354
14.	Universidad Autónoma de Tamaulipas	2,261
15.	Universidad Autónoma de San Luis Potosí	2,230
16.	Universidad del Valle de México	2,046
17.	Universidad Juarez Autónoma de Tabasco	1,982
18.	Universidad Autónoma Metropolitana	1,919
19.	Universidad Juarez del Estado de Durango	1,711
20.	Universidad Autónoma de Coahuila	1,711

[a] The number of all law students in all campuses at each institution.

years, public institutions accounted for approximately 73 per cent of all Mexican law students and about 82 per cent of all new *licenciados en derecho*. See Table 2.1.

Among public universities, UNAM has had the greatest influence on legal education in Mexico. UNAM's role is a reflection of the tradition, noted elsewhere in this book,[11] by which norms and ideas developed in Mexico City become disseminated and are accepted throughout the country. This phenomenon, less prevalent in the private business sector, is especially pronounced in public spheres, including education. By size alone (see Table 2.1), UNAM would have an inordinate influence on legal education, but UNAM's influence is due to other reasons.[12] In a country in which most law professors are full-time practitioners and part-time law teachers, UNAM has a cadre of full-time academics who have traditionally been the pre-eminent legal scholars in the country, especially in areas of public law and policy. UNAM professors have historically produced the leading legal treatises, and as recognized experts they often travel to law schools throughout the country to lecture and to teach.

[11] Regarding federalism, *see infra* Chapter 4.

[12] With seven campuses and 255,226 students, UNAM dominates higher education generally. On UNAM generally, *see* www.unam.mx.

UNAM's Facultad de Derecho, or law school, as the oldest and most prestigious law school (until recent years), has influenced the curricula of law schools throughout the country.

UNAM's Instituto de Investigaciones Jurídicas, or Institute of Legal Research, is the most important legal research centre in Mexico, and one of the most important in Latin America, and the law professors and research fellows attached to it are often invited to lecture and to teach short courses in other parts of the country. UNAM also has the largest and most influential graduate law programme in the country, with 315 lawyers enrolled in the doctoral programme in 2000. A doctoral degree has little relevance in private legal practice, but is a mark of distinction in academic circles. Only a few universities in Mexico, such as UNAM, the Universidad Autónoma de Chiapas, the Universidad Autónoma del Estado de México, the Universidad Autónoma de San Luis Potosí, the Universidad Veracruzana, the Universidad Autónoma de Tamaulipas, and the Universidad Autónoma de Puebla, among others, presently offer a doctorate in law. The largest doctoral programme is at UNAM.

There is recent evidence that the predominance of public law schools, and especially of UNAM, is waning. All forty-six of the newest law schools in Mexico are private, and a number of private law schools have displaced public law schools as the most important producers of lawyers for the private sector.[13] The decline in influence of the public law schools should not be exaggerated, but it nevertheless coincides with the relaxation of governmental authority over all aspects of society in Mexico.[14]

Licensing standards for Mexican law schools are lenient, and there is no organized system of accreditation or ongoing evaluation by external authorities.[15] No single authority in Mexico is responsible for regulating law schools and the quality of legal education. Rather, Mexican law schools are granted permits to operate by the state in which they are based or by the federal government, if based in the Federal District. Each state and the federal government retains the right to suspend or cancel a permit previously granted,[16] but there is no evidence that such action has ever been taken. Since legal education is viewed as an academic domain and not a task left to practitioners, the responsibility for ensuring the quality of legal instruction falls, ultimately, on the university administrators, university trustees, and department heads sitting over

[13] According to a survey by one of Mexico's most important newspapers, *Reforma*, the three most prestigious law schools in Mexico are the Escuela Libre de Derecho, Universidad Panamericana, and Instituto Tecnológico Autónomo de México: 'Las mejoras universidades 2003–2004', Universitarios (Suplemento Mensual), REFORMA (Mexico City), August 2003 at 24. The survey ranked UNAM sixth.

[14] *See infra* Chapter 5 on executive and legislative powers in Mexico.

[15] In the United States this role is played by the American Bar Association.

[16] In the Federal District, for example, the General Directorate of Professions of the Ministry of Education (*Dirección General de Profesiones de la Secretaria de Educación Pública*) may cancel permits to provide legal instruction in the Federal District according to the conditions established by statute. *See* Ley Reglamentaria del Artículo 50 Constitucional Relativo al Ejercicio de las Profesiones en el Distrito Federal, Art. 67.

each individual law faculty. Furthermore, since law graduates are not required to pass a bar exam,[17] there is a substantial lack of uniformity not only in the quality of legal education in Mexico, but also in the level of professional preparation of law graduates.

1.2. Law School Admissions and Curricula

In Mexico, legal education follows a twelve-year period of primary, secondary, and preparatory education in which the student earns a baccalaureate certificate (*certificado de bachillerato*). Mexican law schools uniformly require the *bachillerato* as a prerequisite for admission.[18] Many of Mexico's public universities, including UNAM, have incorporated baccalaureate-level education into their general educational programme, and students who graduate from high schools (*colegios*) that are formally incorporated into the public university are automatically admitted to the law school of that university.[19]

Students obtaining the *bachillerato* from a *colegio* outside a particular university must meet additional requirements for admission. For example, those seeking to attend either UNAM or the University of Guadalajara (Mexico's two largest law schools) must pass entrance examinations administered by each institution.[20] Further, the University of Guadalajara requires that the applicant undergo medical and psychological exams, submit to a socioeconomic evaluation and personal interview, complete an aptitude test and vocational profile, and present a letter of good conduct. The law school of the Universidad Michoacana de San Nicolas de Hidalgo, which requires only that applicants pass 'competitive selection' and a 'university induction' course in addition to possessing the *bachillerato*, is probably more representative of admissions requirements in most Mexican law schools.

Admissions to some of the private law schools are highly competitive. For example, at ITAM, 272 students apply every semester to study at the law school but only 149 are admitted. Of these, approximately forty students leave the institution or degree programme in the first semester. Another twelve or so students leave in the second semester. The rest of the students manage to complete the plan of studies or to graduate. A high percentage of ITAM students finish the law degree programme.[21]

The prevailing curriculum in Mexican law schools tracks a plan of studies created at UNAM in 1907, consisting of a five-year programme, divided into

[17] *See infra*, text accompanying notes 88–89.

[18] Certain law schools, such as those of UNAM and the Escuela Libre de Derecho, require that the student have received the *bachillerato* with a mark of eight or higher (on a 10-point scale).

[19] *See* Fix-Zamudio, H., 'Algunas Reflexiones Sobre la Enseñanza del Derecho en México y Latinoamérica', in ANTOLOGÍA DE ESTUDIOS SOBRE ENSEÑANZA DEL DERECHO 89 n. 33 (J. Witker, compilador, 1995) [hereinafter Fix-Zamudio 1995].

[20] *See id.*; UNIVERSIDAD NACIONAL AUTÓNOMA DE MÉXICO, I PLANES Y PROGRAMAS DE ESTUDIO DE LA FACULTAD DE DERECHO 57 (1993) [hereinafter Plan of Studies].

[21] 2002 Statistics from the Academic Department of Law, ITAM.

Table 2.2: Universidad Nacional Autónoma de México, Faculty of Law Plan of Studies for the Law Degree (the '1907 model' as of 1991)

First Semester	*Second Semester*
Introduction to the Study of Law	Civil Law I
Roman Law I	Roman Law II
Economic Theory	History of Economic Thought
Sociology	Criminal Law I
Third Semester	*Fourth Semester*
Civil Law II	Civil Law III
Criminal Law II	Civil Procedure
Theory of Procedure	Constitutional Law
Theory of the State	Political Science
Fifth Semester	*Sixth Semester*
Civil Law IV	Commercial Law I
Criminal Procedure	Labour Law I
Administrative Law I	Administrative Law II
Individual & Social Guarantees	*Amparo*
Seventh Semester	*Eighth Semester*
Commercial Law II	Commercial Contracts
Labour Law II	Fiscal Law
Economic Law	Social Security Law
Public International Law	Philosophy
	Private International Law
Ninth Semester	*Tenth Semester*
History of Mexican Law	Professional Ethics
Environmental Law	Social Law Clinic
Agrarian Law	Fiscal Law Clinic
Private Law Clinic	Criminal Law Clinic
Administrative Law Clinic	Elective Course
Forensic Training—*Amparo*	Elective Course

ten semesters and approximately forty courses. With the exception of several elective courses, most of the courses in the plan of studies are obligatory.[22] (See Table 2.2.)

A few Mexican law schools, such as the Escuela Libre de Derecho, have altered the semester structure or sequence of courses, but nonetheless require students to complete largely the same courses. See Table 2.3. Such standardization is attributable, in large part, to the dominant influence of UNAM as well as to the pattern of public law schools and government supervision of legal education.

[22] *See* Maxwell, *supra* note 4, at 157; Malagón, J., 'Four Centuries of the Faculty of Law in Mexico', 32 HISP. AM. HIST. REV. 442, 445 (1952).

Table 2.3: Curriculum of the Escuela Libre de Derecho (as of 2002)

First Year	*Second Year*	*Third Year*
Introduction to the Study of Law	Civil Law + seminar	Civil Law + seminar
Civil Law	Roman Law	Criminal Law + seminar
Roman Law	Political Economy	Civil Procedure + seminar
Political Economy	Theory of the State + seminar	Commercial Law + seminar
Sociology	Criminal Law + seminar	Labour Law
Introduction to Legal Research	Civil Procedure + seminar	Labour Law Procedure
		Constitutional Law + seminar
		Legal Ethics
Fourth Year	*Fifth Year*	*Elective Courses*
Civil Law	Administrative Law	Agrarian Law
Commercial Law + seminar	Private International Law	Mining Law
Constitutional Law + seminar	Fiscal Law	Securities Law
Criminal Procedure + seminar	Monetary & Banking Law	Notarial Law
Administrative Law + seminar	Mexican Legal History	Finance Law
Public International Law + seminar	Philosophy of Law	Legal English
Legal History	Thesis Seminar	

As Tables 2.2 and 2.3 reveal, traditional Mexican legal education is interdisciplinary, general, and academic, as opposed to practical professional training. About 10 per cent of the curriculum consists of courses in economics, sociology, political science, philosophy, or other non-legal fields of study. This interdisciplinary, academic approach is explained by the fact that Mexican legal education does not follow a liberal, college-level education and that law schools in Mexico are usually part of a larger department, division, school of social sciences and humanities, or of law and social sciences, of law and political sciences, or even of economic sciences. Consequently, the autonomy of law professors in making curricular revisions is limited by the appreciable interests and influence of non-lawyers and non-legal academics who control the department and university.[23]

[23] The presence of non-legal courses in the curriculum also may be attributable, in part, to the Latin American view that law is inherently interrelated to society and economics. *See* Maxwell, *supra* note 4, at 160–161.

For years, Mexican legal education has been criticized for its relative lack of practical training. As late as 1978, the typical law school curriculum involved 'no significant effort to teach lawyer skills or the use and applications of law in context'.[24] Since then, limited efforts have been made at a few schools to add clinics, seminars, or other forensic training to the 1907 model curriculum.[25] At least one institution, the Universidad Autónoma Metropolitana, constructed an ongoing 'live client' clinical programme in a poor neighbourhood, much like those one finds in United States law schools.

The most significant effort to stress practical training in Mexican legal education began in 1993, when UNAM revised its traditional curriculum to create more of a balance between theory and practice, by adding modern courses on the use of computers, foreign language, global economic integration, environmental law, international trade, and human rights.[26] (See Table 2.4.)

Elective courses include the following: bureaucracy law, military law, criminology, customs law, special crimes, maritime law, municipality law, notarial law, international economic law, intellectual property law, environmental law, electoral law, and consumer law.

To graduate under the new curriculum, a student is required to complete seventy-five courses over a period of ten semesters. To obtain the degree of *licenciado en derecho*[27] the student must in addition complete three foreign language courses and two computer courses, for a total of eighty courses. In the old curriculum, students at UNAM were only required to complete about forty courses over ten semesters to graduate.[28]

Of the eighty courses in the new UNAM curriculum, the substantial majority, fifty-nine, remain purely theoretical.[29] Four courses—the forensic training courses—are purely practical. Twelve now are a combination of theory and practice.[30] The remaining five courses (the three foreign language and two computer courses) are not classified as either theoretical or practical. Under the new curriculum, students spend from twenty-three to twenty-four hours in class per week, if one includes the foreign language and computer courses.[31]

UNAM's new law curriculum greatly increases the ability of a student to pursue specialized studies. A student can take a forensic training course in private

[24] Herget, J. and Camil, J., INTRODUCTION TO MEXICAN LAW (Buffalo, NY: W.S. Hisa, 1978) at 92.

[25] For example, UNAM first introduced mandatory clinics into its curriculum in 1977. *See* Plan of Studies, ***supra*** note 20, at 13.

[26] *Ibid.*, at 3–4. The University Council approved the new curriculum in September 1993. *See* Carvajal Contreras, M., 'Cuarto Informe de Actividades', 45 REVISTA DE LA FACULTAD DE DERECHO DE MEXICO 437, 450 (1995).

[27] And thus to be able to practise law.

[28] *See* Plan of Studies, ***supra*** note 20, at 58–69.

[29] *See ibid.* at 61–70.

[30] The twelve mixed courses are: Techniques of Legal Research, Techniques of Expression, Legal Lexicology, Mathematics Applied to the Law, Civil Procedure I, Civil Procedure II, ***Amparo*** II, Criminal Procedure, Labour Law Procedure, Fiscal Procedure, Agrarian Procedure, and Thesis Workshop.

[31] *See* Plan of Studies, ***supra*** note 20, at 61–65 and 69–70. All but five of the courses are three-hour courses.

Table 2.4: Universidad Nacional Autónoma de México, Faculty of Law Plan of Studies for the Degree of Licentiate in Law (fully effective in 2002)

First Semester	*Second Semester*
Introduction to the Study of Law	Legal Theory*
Sociology	Political Theory
Introduction to the Civil Law	Property
Introduction to Criminal Law	Criminal Theory
Roman Law I	Roman Law II
Contemporary Legal Systems*	Mexican Legal History
Economic Theory	History of Economic Thought
Techniques of Legal Research*	Techniques of Expression*
Third Semester	*Fourth Semester*
Constitutional Law I	Constitutional Law II*
Theory of the State	Theory of Procedure
Obligations	Obligations and Contracts*
Particular Crimes I	Particular Crimes II & Special Crimes
Contemporary Political Systems*	Administrative Law I
Legal Methodology*	Individual Labour Law
Legal Ethics	Introduction to Economic Law
Legal Lexicology*	Mathematics Applied to the Law*
Fifth Semester	*Sixth Semester*
Individual & Social Guarantees	*Amparo* I
Civil Procedure I	Civil Procedure II
Contracts	Family Law*
Public International Law I	Public International Law II*
Administrative Law II	Administrative Law III*
Collective Labour Law	Social Security Law
Mercantile Law	Titles of Credit
Foreign Language I	Foreign Language II
Seventh Semester	*Eighth Semester*
Amparo II*	Philosophy of Law
Criminal Procedure	Forensic Training[a]
Law of Succession	Private International Law I
Fiscal Law I	Fiscal Law II*
Administrative Law IV*	Environmental Law
Labour Law Procedure*	Agrarian Law
Credit Operations	Commercial Contracts
Foreign Language III	Introduction to Computers
Ninth Semester	*Tenth Semester*
Forensic Training	Forensic Training
Forensic Training	Elective Course
Private International Law II*	Elective Course
Fiscal Procedure*	Elective Course

(*cont.*)

Table 2.4: Continued

Ninth Semester	*Tenth Semester*
Law of International Trade*	Law of Economic Integration*
Agrarian Procedure*	Elective Course
Banking and Securities Law*	Business Management Law*
Word Processing	Thesis Workshop

* indicates a new course

[a] In the eighth, ninth, and tenth semesters, the student is required to complete four 'forensic training' courses. The six forensic training courses from which students may choose are: Private Law, *Amparo*, Labour and Social Security Law, Fiscal Law, Criminal Law, and Administrative Law.

law, *amparo*, labour and social law, fiscal law, criminal law, or administrative law. Further, a student can devote all four electives to a single field of law. For example, a student interested in criminal law can take elective courses in criminology, forensic medicine, the law of penal institutions, and criminal punishment.

1.3. The Social Service Requirement

Mexican law students must perform a prescribed amount of part-time, temporary, uncompensated work in the interest of society as a prerequisite for receiving the law degree.[32] At UNAM, students provide up to 260 hours of such work, ordinarily over a period of six months, prior to graduation. Social service programmes are created and controlled by each law school, and can entail the provision of free legal services at law school-run legal aid clinics or legal internships with a government agency. In January of each year, the law schools notify the professional licensing authorities of the names of those students who have completed the social service requirement.[33]

1.4. The Problem of *Egresados No Titulados*

In Mexico, a law student must do more than pass all required and elective courses in a school's curriculum and satisfy the social service requirement to receive the degree of *licenciado en derecho*. At UNAM, for example, the law student also must produce an original thesis or pass a written examination of general knowledge, pass an oral professional examination, establish foreign language proficiency, and demonstrate basic computer skills.[34] A person who merely completes all required courses is referred to as a 'graduate' or *egresado*.

[32] *See* Arellano García, C., MANUEL DEL ABOGADO: PRÁCTICA JURÍDICA (Mexico: Porrúa, 4th ed., 1996) at 328–329.

[33] *Id.* at 329–335.

[34] *See* Plan of Studies, *supra* note 20, at 88–89. At the University of Guadalajara, a student must complete the plan of studies, satisfy the corresponding social service requirement, produce a thesis and pass a thesis exam, and pass a professional exam in order to obtain the degree of *abogado*.

A person who meets all conditions for receipt of the *licenciatura en derecho* is referred to as *titulado* ('titled') or *licenciado*.

Many Mexican law graduates never take the final steps to secure the law degree. In 1990, 50 per cent of the *egresados* of the University of Guadalajara law school failed to complete all formalities to become *titulados*.[35] In 1995, the Dean of the faculty of law of UNAM publicly expressed concern over the large number of *egresados* from that institution who had not proceeded to the status of *titulados*.[36] In 1999 there were 24,642 *egresados* of law schools nationwide in Mexico but only 14,724 of them obtained the *licenciado en derecho* in the same year.

Several factors may explain the problem of *egresados no titulados*. First, many graduates choose to work in government jobs, politics, or private corporate positions for which a law degree is useful but not required. Second, others find in the course of their studies that law is not their proper vocation.[37] Finally, it appears that in recent years there has been a relatively limited number of professional positions available in the Mexican legal market.[38]

1.5. Law Students and Faculty

1.5.1. Mexican Law Students

In 2001, 190,338 students were attending Mexican law schools, working toward the basic law degree.[39] Fifty-two per cent were men and 48 per cent were women.[40]

Most students in Mexico are eighteen years old when they enter law school. The cost of their legal education can vary substantially, depending on the institution they attend. Like many public law schools, UNAM charges only a symbolic fee (*cuota de inscripción*) that, in 2000, amounted to less than two US dollars.[41] The cost of attending the *licenciatura* programme of the

[35] *See Titulación en la Facultad de Derecho*, 3 JURE 57, 57 (May–Aug. 1990).

[36] *See* Carvajal, *supra* note 26, at 445.

[37] A 1990 survey of students attending the Escuela Libre de Derecho revealed that most of the law students (75.3%) believed that law was their proper vocation but a significant number were unsure (20.4%) or convinced that it was not (4.2%). *See* Villalpando César, J.M., 'Para Llegar a Ser Abogado', 14 REVISTA DE INVESTIGACIONES JURÍDICAS 595, 616 (1990).

[38] *See* Lorey, David, E., THE RISE OF THE PROFESSIONS IN TWENTIETH-CENTURY MEXICO (2nd ed., Los Angeles, CA: UCLA Latin American Center, University of California, revised ed. 1994) 37–38 (discussing the general paucity of professional positions in modern Mexico).

[39] Serrano, F., LA ENSEÑANZA DEL DERECHO EN LA FACULTAD DE DERECHO DE LA *UNAM* (Mexico: UNAM, 2003) at 11.

[40] *Id.* Maria Asunción Sandoval became Mexico's first female lawyer in July 1898. *See* Mendieta y Nuñez, *supra* note 4, at 362. In 1963, only 12% of the law students at UNAM were women. *See* Maxwell, *supra* note 4, at 166 n. 51.

[41] On several occasions, the Chancellor (*rector*) at UNAM has unsuccessfully attempted to increase tuition and establish more rigorous entrance requirements. The most recent attempt to do so resulted in a year-long strike that shut down the main campus of UNAM, and resulted in a capitulation calling for a general congress to reform the University. The experience is a clear demonstration of the complexities of public higher education in Mexico, and shows that UNAM serves a political function in society as well as an educational one.

Universidad Iberoamericana, a private institution, in the autumn of 2002 was about US$3,200 per semester and of the Instituto Tecnológico Autónomo de México was about US$3,500 per semester.[42] To attend the Universidad Regiomontana, a private institution, in autumn 2000, a law student had to pay tuition fees of about US$7,200 annually.[43]

A 1990 survey of 481 students attending the Escuela Libre de Derecho suggests what might be the typical work and study patterns of Mexican law students.[44] Forty per cent of the students worked in paid employment while attending law school. The number of students who worked to earn money increased with each year of law school, and by the fifth year nearly all law students were doing so.[45] On average, students worked four hours per day, in addition to attending five to six hours of class. The amount of studying done by students diminished gradually from the first to fifth year of law school to the point that, in the fifth year, few students (only 16.2 per cent) were studying consistently. The average first-year student studied 7.6 hours per week, while the average fifth-year student studied only about half that time, 3.9 hours per week.

1.5.2. Mexican Law Faculty

The typical Mexican law school faculty consists of a small number of full-time law professors and a very large number of adjunct teachers.[46] For instance, in 1995, UNAM employed fifty-nine full-time, forty-three half-time, and 643 adjunct professors (*profesores de asignatura*) to instruct its 23,610 law students.[47]

In 2002, the Universidad Iberoamericana law school relied on only twelve full-time professors and 177 adjunct professors to teach over 900 law students. A typical adjunct professor teaches a single, three-hour course each week and devotes the rest of his or her professional time to legal practice, the judiciary, or other government work.

The prestige of law faculties is high in Mexico, but pay is meagre. Although general figures are not widely available, some information does exist about compensation at UNAM. The salary scale for full-time law professors and legal researchers at UNAM ranges from 5,000 pesos per month (about US$500) to

[42] *See* Universidad Iberoamericana (Plantel Santa Fe), at /www.uia.mx/. *See also* www.anuies.mx (both sites last visited January 2004).

[43] *See* Universidad Regiomontana, at www.ur.mx/. *See also* www.anuies.mx (both sites last visited January 2004).

[44] *See* Villalpando, *supra* note 37.

[45] Students worked in litigation firms (32.8%), in corporate firms (21.4%), in the public sector (17.3%), in notarial firms (11.9%), on their own (8.4%), in the financial sector (2.3%), in the judiciary (1.2%), or in other employment (5.2%).

[46] 'The part-time instructor is the accepted norm throughout Latin America. The view prevails that the best teachers are those actively practising law or working in the judiciary or government service at the same time.' Maxwell, *supra* note 4, at 164. The predilection to engage practising lawyers would appear to conflict with the traditional view, noted above, that the study of law is an academic, theoretical discipline. The principal reason for the use of adjunct professors appears to be economic: lack of sufficient funding in universities to support full-time law professors.

[47] *See* Carvajal, *supra* note 26, at 452–453.

10,000 pesos per month (about US$1,000).[48] Full-time professors may receive additional pay for publishing books and articles or organizing academic conferences.[49]

Law professors are hired based on their qualifications and institutional needs. Many full-time professors hold doctoral degrees in law, from either Mexican or foreign universities. Full-time professors are either contract professors (*profesores de contrato*), having no job security beyond the term of their contract, or professors with tenure (*profesores de definitividad académica*), having job and title protection (but who may still be dismissed for serious cause). To acquire tenure, a professor must develop expertise in a field of law, pass certain examinations, demonstrate good teaching skills, and defend a thesis before a panel consisting of three to five senior faculty members. In 1996, slightly more than two-thirds of UNAM's full-time professors were tenured.

Teaching methods used by Mexico's law professors vary from course to course. The traditional method of instruction, commonly known as *la enseñanza magistral* (magisterial teaching),[50] involves a lecture by the professor to a large class (sometimes hundreds of students) and no active participation on the part of the students.[51] The focus in such lectures is on a relevant code, statute, or constitutional provision and on legal readings concerning the history, purpose, and context of the provision.[52] The approach taken is often theoretical, rather than discussing practical issues and outcomes.[53] Like any other form of teaching, the magisterial approach can be well or poorly done and is not inherently defective, although legal academics in Mexico are increasingly critical of it.

Several years ago, Professor Héctor Fix-Zamudio of UNAM noted a growing tendency in Mexican law schools to use 'active learning' methods, involving the use of pedagogical devices such as questioning, dialogue, and direct conversation, working in teams or small groups, seminars, and legal clinics.[54] The new law curriculum adopted at UNAM is consistent with this trend; however, there are limits on how 'practical' Mexican legal education can become. For example, some teaching devices widely used in the United States, such as moot courts, do not transplant well into Mexican law schools because trials of the sort one finds in common law countries do not exist in the Mexican legal system. It is also

[48] In 2002, adjunct professors at UNAM were paid about US$40 per month per course.

[49] In the mid-1990s, to promote research by university professors, the federal government instituted a national system to pay stipends to Mexican academics, including law professors, who demonstrate excellence and productivity in research. This system, known as the *Sistema Nacional de Investigadores*, provides additional compensation to a limited number of full-time faculty staff.

[50] *See* Fix-Zamudio, H., METODOLOGÍA, DOCENCIA E INVESTIGACIÓN JURÍDICAS (México: Porrúa, 9th ed., 2001) 107, 124–125 (hereinafter Fix-Zamudio, 2001).

[51] *See* Maxwell, *supra* note 4, at 162.

[52] 'The common textbook resembles an American one-volume treatise rather than a collection of cases and materials.[...] The text is used as a means to understand the statutes, and it, accordingly, systematically explores the applicable legislation, giving historical and theoretical background, discussing the meaning of the provisions, and trying to reconcile any inconsistencies.' Maxwell, *supra* note 4, at 163.

[53] *See* Fix-Zamudio 2001, *supra* note 50, at 398.

[54] *See id.* at 107, 124.

important to recall that most Mexican law students work as clerks (*pasantes*) in law firms, the judiciary, the government, or legal aid clinics and, in those capacities, obtain some practical legal experience.[55]

1.6. Law School Examinations

In 1963, final examinations at UNAM ordinarily consisted of a half-hour public, oral recitation and question and answer session involving the student and professor.[56] This remained true as late as 1978.[57] The practice has now changed. Today, with the exception of the Escuela Libre de Derecho, which retains the oral examination, law school examinations at UNAM and other law schools are almost always written. During the course of a semester, students take a series of written partial examinations (*examenes parciales*) in each class. The content and form of questions on the examinations are left to the discretion of each professor.

1.7. Law Journals and Other Publications

Many of Mexico's law schools publish scholarly journals or law reviews. See Table 2.5.

The publications of the *Escuela Libre de Derecho* and UNAM were started in 1914 and 1922, respectively.[58] Unlike law reviews in the United States, scholarly legal publications in Mexico are edited by professors and legal researchers rather than by law students.[59]

1.8. Legal Research Institutes

While law professors in the United States are expected to publish scholarly articles in addition to teaching, in Mexico law is viewed as a science, and it is thought that legal research is best left to specialists working in legal research institutes.[60] Furthermore, most Mexican law professors are adjunct professors with full-time law practices, and they lack the time to conduct scholarly research for publication. For this reason, a small number of legal research centres and institutes have had an inordinate impact on the development of the law in Mexico, although this is beginning to change as private law schools achieve greater prominence.

[55] *See* Fix-Zamudio 1996, *supra* note 50, at 132.

[56] *See* Maxwell, *supra* note 4, at 167–70.

[57] *See* Herget and Camil, *supra* note 24, at 94.

[58] *See* Margadant, *supra* note 4, at 357.

[59] Maxwell, *supra* note 4, at 170.

[60] *See* Madrazo, Jorge, 'Reflexiones en Torno a la Investigación Jurídica en Mexico', 3 JURE 5, 5 (Sep.–Dec. 1990).

Table 2.5: Mexican law school publications

Institution	*Title*
Universidad Nacional Autónoma de México	*Revista de la Facultad de Derecho*
Instituto de Investigaciones Jurídicas	*Revista de Derecho Privado*
	Boletín Mexicano de Derecho Comparado
	Cuestiones Constitucionales
	Anuario Mexicano de Historia del Derecho
	Anuario Mexicano de Derecho Internacional
Escuela Libre de Derecho	*Revista Jurídica de la Escuela Libre de Derecho*
ITAM	*Revista Mexicana de Derecho Público*
Universidad Panamericana	*Ars Iuris*
Universidad Iberoamericana	*Revista Jurídica*
Universidad Anáhuac	*Revista de la Escuela de Derecho*
Universidad de Guanajuato	*Boletín Trimestral*
Universidad de Occidente	*Ciencia Jurídica*
Universidad Autónoma de Puebla	*Crítica Jurídica*
Universidad de Guadalajara	*Jure*
Universidad Autónoma de Sonora	*Lex*
Universidad Autónoma de Chihuahua	*Lecturas Jurídicas*
Universidad Autónoma del Estado de México	*Revista de la Escuela de Derecho*
Universidad Autónoma de San Luis Potosí	*Revista de la Escuela de Derecho*
Universidad Autónoma de Nuevo León	*Revista de la Facultad de Derecho y Ciencias Sociales*
Universidad Autónoma de Yucatán	*Revista de la Escuela de Derecho*
Universidad Autónoma de Querétaro	*Revista Jurídica*

Mexico's premier research centre, the Institute of Legal Research (Instituto de Investigaciones Jurídicas, or IIJ), was founded at UNAM in 1940.[61] The IIJ is located in a research park connected to the main UNAM campus, but it is independent of the law school (Facultad de Derecho), with its own director, governing board, and budget. Even though many of the IIJ's academic personnel teach courses at the Facultad de Derecho (and at other law schools in Mexico), a certain rivalry exists between the two institutions, with the IIJ being considered the leading academic research arm, and the Facultad the teaching centre.

The IIJ's law library, with 150,000 volumes, is considered to be among the best in Latin America. It is separate from the law library of the Facultad, although students have access to both. Due to the size and prestige of its

[61] F. Sánchez Román, a Spanish jurist who emigrated to Mexico, founded the Institute of Comparative Law (Instituto de Derecho Comparado) which in 1968 was renamed the Instituto de Investigaciones Jurídicas. *See* Margadant, *supra* note 4, at 353, 359.

academic staff,[62] and the quality of its publications, the IIJ has acquired an international reputation as one of the leading legal research centres in Latin America. In its sixty years of existence, the Institute has published more than 2,000 books and other monographs,[63] and it sponsors numerous national and international conferences. Three scholarly journals, the *Boletín de Derecho Comparado, Cuestiones Constitucionales*, and the *Anuario Mexicano de Historia del Derecho*, are among the leading academic journals in Mexico.

While certain IIJ publications deal with practical aspects of public or private law, much of the Institute's research and publications cover academic fields (legal history, law and philosophy, constitutional theory, etc.) and subjects of public law.[64] Because of this, and because the IIJ has been closely connected to the Mexican government,[65] the IIJ has had some influence on the development of public law in Mexico. This is both a strength and a weakness, since the IIJ has been criticized for failing to fulfil its role as an independent research centre.[66] In addition, the IIJ's relative concentration on legal history and constitutional law means that it has played an insignificant role in the development of private law, especially private business law as well as economic regulation.

With the demise of one-party rule in Mexico, and the general opening up of the economy and society,[67] prospects for legal reforms should generate a greater need for independent legal research on public and private law issues. Legal research institutes at Mexican universities other than UNAM can hope to meet some of this need. Such institutes already exist at the Universidad Veracruzana, the Universidad de Guadalajara, the Escuela Libre de Derecho, and the Universidad Autónoma de Querétaro. The Instituto Tecnológico Autónomo de México (ITAM), in response to the need for in-depth legal research into current legal issues, has created two research centres, one focusing on the administration of justice, and another on financial and monetary regulation.

1.9. Postgraduate Legal Studies

Programmes leading to a masters degree in law are generally available in Mexico. All of these are directed at Mexican lawyers who wish to specialize in particular areas of law: tax, labour law, administrative law, international trade law, etc. The basic requirements for admission are that the applicant must have

[62] According to its web site www.juridicas.unam.org.mx (last visited July 2003) the Instituto has seventy-four full-time research fellows (*investigadores*), the majority of whom hold doctoral degrees in law. Fifty-two research assistants, or *técnicos académicos*, support the Instituto's activities.

[63] Márquez Romero, R., CATÁLOGO GENERAL DE PUBLICACIONES (Mexico: UNAM-IIJ, 1999) at ix.

[64] A list of the Institute's publications can be found at the IIJ web site, *supra* note 62.

[65] Several former directors of the IIJ have held cabinet-level appointments in the Mexican government.

[66] Cossío Díaz, J.R., DOGMÁTICA CONSTITUCIONAL Y REGIMEN AUTHORITARIO (Mexico: Fontamara, 1998) 50.

[67] *See infra*, text accompanying Chapter 12 notes 1–78.

obtained the degree of *licenciado en derecho* with a grade of eight or better and must pass an entrance exam. A student can complete the masters programme over a period of four quarters (about one year). Most Mexican law schools have web sites that list graduate and undergraduate law degree programmes.[68]

UNAM, which became authorized to confer doctoral degrees in law in 1949,[69] is the most important law school in Mexico permitted to award doctorates in law.[70] A student may seek the doctoral degree in any of five fields of speciality: private law, constitutional and administrative law, social law, criminal science, or public finance.[71] To receive the doctoral degree, the student must complete twenty courses over a period of five semesters (about two years) and thereafter defend an original research thesis before a panel of five judges.[72] The doctoral programme is intended to prepare professors for university teaching, technicians for research, and specialists in diverse fields of the law.[73] Since the doctoral degree carries prestige in Mexico, especially among government lawyers, it is often sought as a means to enhance one's career in public life. By the year 2002, UNAM had awarded 628 degrees in its Doctor of Laws programme, which was inaugurated in 1950.[74]

1.10. Evaluating Mexican Legal Education

The key to understanding Mexican legal education is to appreciate the uneven quality that exists, both among law students and among law schools. The lack of both meaningful accreditation standards and ongoing monitoring of educational quality means that law schools can vary widely in the quality of their education. Since an attorney can become licensed without an objectively administered Bar exam, the consumer of legal services must assess a lawyer's competence by means other than independent certification.[75]

Both the study and the teaching of law in Mexico are predominantly part-time activities. Most law teachers are practising lawyers, and most law students are part-time law clerks. Despite this fact, there are outstanding law teachers in Mexican law schools, as well as outstanding students. While much legal education remains theoretical and removed from practice, many law students have

[68] *See* for example, Universidad Iberoamericana at www.uia.mx; Universidad Panamericana, at www.up.mx; UNAM at www.unam.mx; Universidad Autónoma Metropolitana at www.uam.mx; Instituto Tecnológico Autónomo de México at www.itam.mx; Universidad Anáhuac at www.anahuac.mx; Universidad Anáhuac del Sur at www.uas.mx; Universidad La Salle at www.ulsa.mx; Universidad de Guadalajara at www.udg.mx; Universidad Autónoma de Guadalajara at www.gdl.uag.mx; Instituto Tecnológico de Monterrey at www.sistema.itsm.mx; or Universidad Autónoma de Nuevo León at www.uanl.mx (all sites last visited July 2003).

[69] *See* Margadant, *supra* note 4, at 353.

[70] *See* Fix-Zamudio, *supra* note 50, at 151.

[71] *Id.* at 143–144.

[72] *Id.* at 153.

[73] *Id.* at 222–223.

[74] *See also* Carvajal, *supra* note 26, at 477.

[75] This may not differ entirely from the experience of other countries: passing a Bar exam does not necessarily mean that a U.S attorney is competent and keeps abreast of legal changes. More vigorous enforcement of professional responsibility does help to ensure some control, however.

the opportunity to serve as apprentices (*pasantes*) in law firms and government offices, and to learn from practising lawyers. The *pasante* system is not administered by law schools, however, and positions are not distributed evenly, since students from elite families have the connections to obtain introductions to the top law firms.

Despite weaknesses in Mexican legal education, lawyers in many fields are generally as well trained as their counterparts in other countries, including the United States. Mexican lawyers in international practice may be as sophisticated as their European or North American counterparts. Increasingly, this sophistication comes from the additional training that Mexican lawyers receive by taking a Master of Laws degree from a law school in the United States, Europe, or Canada.

The main problem of legal education in Mexico, as a part-time endeavour involving institutions with limited resources, has to do with the increasing failure of law schools, and lawyers, to have an impact on societal reforms. In the past, Mexico's government was dominated by lawyers. Mexican Presidents such as Benito Juárez, Miguel Lerdo de Tejada, José Ma. Iglesias, Miguel Alemán, Adolfo López Mateos, Manuel Avila Camacho, Gustavo Díaz Ordaz, Luis Echeverría, José López Portillo, and Miguel de la Madrid were lawyers, and lawyers dominated the political scene in Mexico throughout much of the twentieth century. As the system of authoritarian government and closed economy began to change, however,[76] the new ideas came primarily from non-lawyers, and the failings of legal education were partly responsible for this. Unlike their colleagues in economics and social science, law professors administered a system of legal education that had not changed appreciably over the past 100 years. Lacking the resources to hire full-time teaching staff, most law schools did not attempt to sponsor independent research that would develop new theories and new legal models to be tested by society. Law schools became conservative reinforcers of the status quo, and the role of legal change was taken up by economists and others. The past two Mexican presidents (Carlos Salinas de Gortari and Ernesto Zedillo) have been economists, and they surrounded themselves with advisers who were economists. The current president, Vicente Fox, is a businessman.

Unfortunately, carrying out significant reforms without sufficient input from lawyers often results in dislocations that are unforeseen by economists and social scientists.[77] The World Bank and Inter American Development Bank

[76] *See infra* Chapter 5 text accompanying notes on executive and legislative powers.

[77] Professor John Jackson has written eloquently of the contributions lawyers make in implementing economic policies:

> A word at this point might be in order as to the differences perceived by the author between a 'legal' or lawyer's approach on the one hand, and the approach of an economist or political scientist on the other. Such a word, of course, risks angering one or the other of these groups, but may nevertheless be interesting and provocative to the reader. It seems to this writer that the lawyer is often more concerned with precision, with individual problems, and with the practical limitations on realizing objectives, than his counterparts from other disciplines.

have recognized the need for legal input, after years of attempting structural adjustments in borrowing countries, with a newly founded interest in the importance of legal as well as economic development.[78] Law schools in Mexico have begun to take a harder look at legal education. Their ability to become important actors in developing legal institutions in society, however, will continue to be hampered by the lack of financial resources available to most law schools.

PART 2: THE MEXICAN LEGAL PROFESSION

2. Introduction

There are two types of legal practitioners in Mexico. Attorneys (*abogados*) make up the bulk of the profession, and fulfil the same functions as lawyers in many common law and civil law countries (litigation, commercial transactions, family practice, criminal law, etc.). Notaries Public (*notarios públicos*), who are much less numerous, combine the counselling and drafting functions of a commercial lawyer with the responsibilities of a public official charged with maintaining official records of important legal documents.[79] Each group of practitioners has its own set of admissions requirements, functions, regulatory systems, fee practices, and professional associations.[80]

3. Attorneys (*Abogados*)

Legal practice in Mexico is as varied as in most other postmodern societies. Attorneys serve as civil litigators for businesses or individuals; as corporate and

> The economist skillfully analyzes the overall or macro effects of various policies, and sees them in statistical terms. Often the political scientist does likewise. The lawyer is frequently forced to resolve individual problems, either those of particular citizens or those of a particular circumstance, often involving competing policy goals—both (or all of them) valid, but necessitating compromise. Likewise the lawyer is often a person who is asked to *implement* a policy and faces practical obstacles to such implementation. Could one say that the economist tells us what should be done, and then the lawyer worries about how to do it? In some cases, however, the lawyer is forced to (uncomfortably) play the role of the guardian of long run goals (preserving a constitution, for example) against those who strive for short term expediency.

Jackson, J.H., Legal Problems of International Economic Relations (St. Paul, Minn: West Pub. Co., 1977) at p. XVI.

[78] *See* Inter-American Development Bank, Justice and Development in Latin America and the Caribbean (Washington, DC: IDB, 1993).

[79] *See* Malavet, P., 'Counsel for the Situation: The Latin Notary, A Historical and Comparative Model', 19 Hastings Int'l & Comp. L. Rev. 389, 401 (1996) (describing the distinct 'advocacy' and 'counseling' professions in the context of the civil law).

[80] In 1992, the federal government created a third type of quasi-public official, *corredores públicos*, to relieve the backlog of commercial transactions requiring notarial services. *See infra* Chapter 18 on commercial law.

commercial lawyers; as in-house counsel to state-owned or private enterprises; as representatives of administrative or governmental agencies; as criminal prosecutors and criminal defence counsel; or as counsel for social, labour, agricultural, or neighbourhood associations.[81] Mexican attorneys also work as judicial assistants,[82] judicial appointees,[83] assistants in administrative tribunals,[84] legal researchers, government bureaucrats, or law professors.

3.1. Requirements for Admission to Practise Law

Pursuant to the Mexican Constitution, the authority to regulate the legal profession rests with each state, within its respective territory, and the federal government, within the Federal District and throughout the country in federal matters.[85] The states and federal government universally require that a person seeking to practise law obtain a licence (*cédula*) from the appropriate directorate of professions within the state or federal jurisdiction.[86] Unlike the United States and Canada, where admission to practise is limited to the state or province in which the attorney is licensed, the legal profession in Mexico is national. The Mexican Constitution mandates that professional degrees issued under the authority of any state (or the Federal District) shall be accorded full faith and credit by all other states.[87]

The General Directorate of Professions, an agency of the federal Ministry of Education, issues a licence to practise law in the Federal District and throughout the country in federal matters to anyone possessing the licentiate in law degree (*licenciado en derecho*) from an authorized institution of higher learning who registers the degree with the Directorate.[88] The issuance of the licence is purely a ministerial act and the issuing agencies have no authority to withhold a licence unless the degree presented by a person is fraudulent or otherwise invalid. Mexicans possessing a *licenciatura* are not required to sit for a Bar examination of the types administered in the United States in order to become licensed; however, in most Mexican law schools, graduates (*egresados*) cannot

[81] *See* Arellano, *supra* note 32, at 132–135.

[82] This includes attorneys working as judicial clerks (*secretarios*) and judicial notaries (*actuarios*).

[83] This includes attorneys designated to serve as trustees, mediators, executors, guardians, receivers, and arbitrators.

[84] Such tribunals include various tax courts, administrative courts, and employment boards.

[85] *See* Mexican Constitution, Arts. 4, 73, 124; Arellano, *supra* note 32, at 175.

[86] *See* Arellano, *supra* note 32, at 177. To practise in the Federal District or in federal matters anywhere in Mexico, one must obtain a licence from the General Directorate of Professions (*Dirección General de Profesiones*) in Mexico City. *See* Article 13 of the Regulatory Law of Article 5 of the Constitution Relating to the Exercise of Professions in the Federal District, published in D.O: 26 May 1945, as amended in D.O. 22 Dec 1993.

[87] *See* Mex. Const. Art. 121, section V; Arellano, *supra* note 32, at 176.

[88] *See* Mears, Rona R., 'Ethics and Diligence: A Lawyer's Perspective on Doing Business with Mexico', 22 St. Mary's L.J. 605, 644 (1991). *See also* Arts. 1, 5, 10, 11, 23 of the *Ley de Profesiones*.

obtain the law degree and become titled (*titulado*) until they pass a professional examination administered by their respective law school.[89]

3.2. Practise of Law by Foreign Citizens and by Foreign Legal Consultants

Prior to 1993, foreign citizens who wished to practise law in Mexico and who fulfilled the requirements of admission to practise were nevertheless denied licences because of their lack of Mexican citizenship. This was true even though the discriminatory practice violated the Constitution, as established by numerous decisions of the Supreme Court.[90] Foreign citizens were forced to bring an *amparo* proceeding to secure a judgment ordering their admission to practise. In 1993, the Mexican Congress amended the *Ley de Profesiones* of the Federal District in order to prohibit discrimination on the basis of citizenship.[91] Most Mexican states have similarly changed the law and practice in regards to foreign citizens who fulfil Mexican licensing requirements.

The impetus to remove obstacles to foreign citizens practising law came about in the early 1990s in the context of negotiations over the North American Free Trade Agreement (NAFTA). In NAFTA, which covers trade in services, Mexico committed itself to the elimination of citizenship requirements for practising law within two years of NAFTA's entry into force.[92] NAFTA also required each of the parties to establish a work programme to develop criteria for the qualification of foreign lawyers to practise law within each country as foreign legal consultants (attorneys not licensed to practise local law, but permitted to give legal advice so long as it is limited to foreign or international law).[93] Mexico also reserved in NAFTA certain constraints on the practice of law by US lawyers and the establishment of offices of US law firms within Mexico.[94]

[89] The professional exam consists of an oral examination before three or five professors in which the student has to defend a thesis on a specific subject, as chosen by the student and previously approved by the director of the thesis. On students who do not complete the requirement, *see* text accompanying notes 34–38 *supra*.

[90] *See* Ursúa-Cocke, Eugenio and MacPherson, William P., 'El Papel del Abogado en México', 14 REVISTA DE INVESTIGACIONES JURÍDICAS 419, 431 (1990) [hereinafter Ursúa-Cocke].

[91] *See* Arts. 15 and 17 of the *Ley de Profesiones*.

[92] *See* NAFTA Art. 1210.3, and NAFTA Annex I, page I-M-46, (Mexico) (Professional, Technical and Specialized Services). The Mexican Congress amended the law to eliminate the prohibition two years before the date stipulated in Annex I.

[93] NAFTA Annex 1210.5, section B. To this date, Mexico has not adopted legislation implementing these provisions.

[94] *See* NAFTA Annexes I, II, and VI, reservations relating to 'Professional, Technical and Specialized Services'. Since the adoption of NAFTA, negotiations concerning the liberalization of restrictions on legal services have been undertaken under the auspices of the Canadian, Mexican, and US Bar associations, as authorized by NAFTA Annex 1210.5, section B. *See* Barker, Julie, 'The North American Free Trade Agreement and the Complete Integration of the Legal Profession: Dismantling the Barriers to Providing Cross-Border Legal Services', 19 HOUS. J. INT'L L. 95 (1996); Bermann, G., Jauregui Rojas, M., Loperena Ruix, C., *et al.*, 'Mexican Lawyers going North and US Lawyers going South: Interstate Legal Practice, NAFTA and US Bar Regulations', (Moderator: Prof. Michael Gordon), 9 US-MEX. L.J. 189 (Spring 2001).

4. Characteristics of the Mexican Legal Profession

It is difficult to provide a detailed profile of the Mexican legal profession, due to the dearth of precise information.[95] According to the 1990 Census,[96] Mexico had a total of 141,539 attorneys. This compares with over 900,000 lawyers in the United States during the same time period.[97]

In 1990, 75 per cent of Mexican attorneys were male and 25 per cent were female.[98] Considering that nearly one-half of all law school students in Mexico are women, the representation of females in the legal profession should continue to grow, albeit slowly.

In 1990, 84 per cent of Mexico's licensed attorneys were actively practising law.[98] Slightly over half of these were classified as professionals, presumably meaning private practitioners. The bulk of remaining practising lawyers were working as law clerks, civil servants, educators, in business or as legal technicians. *See* Table 2.6 below.

In 1990,[100] about one-third of Mexico's lawyers earned annual salaries that were equal to three times the minimum wage (equal to about 7,500 US dollars). Forty-five per cent earned between three and ten times the minimum wage (25,000 US dollars in 1990), and only 15 per cent earned more than ten times the minimum wage.[101]

The geographic distribution of Mexican attorneys is characterized by a high degree of concentration in the Federal District and the adjoining state of Mexico, followed by concentration in a few of the country's largest states. In 1993, more than two-thirds of Mexico's attorneys resided in the Distrito Federal, and the states of Mexico, Jalisco, Veracruz, Nuevo Leon, and Puebla.[102]

Table 2.6: Employed legal professionals according to principal occupation

Professionals	61,048	51.3%
Clerks	20,335	17.1%
Civil Servants	14,550	12.2%
Educators	7,993	6.7%
Businesspeople	5,457	4.6%
Other	9,581	8.1%
Total Employed (Law)	[118,964]	[100.0%]

Source: INEGI, 55–56.

[95] *See* Clemente Valdés, S., 'Sobre los Abogados', 6 El Foro 5, 44 (1993).

[96] The figures cited on this page are from Instituto Nacional de Estadistica Geografia e Informática, Los Profesionistas En México (Mexico: INEGI, 1993) at 7. INEGI has not yet composed a similar breakdown of figures for the legal profession band on the 2000 Census.

Lawyers comprised 7.5 per cent of all Mexican professionals, ranking third behind accountants (10.6 per cent) and administrators (8.7 per cent). *See ibid.*, at 3.

[97] *See* 'The Lawyer Explosion', 81 A.B.A. J. 37, 37 (Mar. 1995).

[98] INEGI, *supra* note 96, at 7. [99] *Ibid.*, at 55.

[100] Although figures regarding the income of Mexican attorneys are scarce and unreliable.

[101] Source: INEGI, *supra* note 96 at 55. [102] Source: INEGI, *supra* note 96, at 8.

5. Regulation of the Profession

The legal profession in Mexico is not subject to a special set of ethical regulations or codes that set it apart from other professions.[103] This is in sharp contrast to the United States, in which rigorous oversight of lawyer misconduct occurs through Bar Association disciplinary proceedings, civil malpractice litigation undertaken by clients who have been injured by lawyer misconduct, and criminal process. This is not to say that lawyer misconduct in Mexico escapes sanctions; rather, Mexico depends on general civil and criminal provisions to regulate the conduct of lawyers.[104]

For example, a lawyer practising in the Federal District must comply with the provisions of the Mexican Constitution, the Federal Civil Code, the Regulatory Law of Article 5 of the Constitution Relating to the Practice of the Professions in the Federal District, the Federal Fiscal Code, other tax laws and procedures, the Federal Labour Law, the *Amparo* Law, the Federal Criminal Code, the Federal Code of Criminal Procedure, and the Federal Code of Civil Procedure.[105]

For instance, the current Federal Civil Code: (1) requires attorneys to pursue matters pending before courts conscientiously and to safeguard a client's interests in accordance with the client's instructions or as required by the nature of the case, (2) prohibits the representation of clients with competing interests in the same lawsuit, and (3) renders attorneys liable to clients for negligence, lack of skill, or bad faith, in addition to any penalty imposed on the attorney under the criminal laws.[106] If an attorney unjustifiably reveals client confidences without consent and harms the client, a variety of statutes subject the attorney to civil liability and/or criminal punishment, ranging from fines to suspension to imprisonment for a period of from one to five years.[107]

Opinions differ on the extent to which the current provisions of Mexican law are adequate to curtail lawyer misconduct. While legal sanctions exist in theory, pursuant to provisions such as those just mentioned, the reality appears otherwise: civil and criminal malpractice actions against attorneys are exceedingly rare.[108] The conflict of interest provisions of the Civil Code, cited above, are significantly weaker than those administered in US jurisdictions.

6. The Nature of Private Practice

According to the 2000 Census, 61,048 (51.3 per cent) of Mexican attorneys identified themselves as 'professionals' in private practice. Traditionally, the

[103] Voluntary codes of professional ethics have recently been adopted to instil a greater degree of professionalism by practising lawyers. *See* text accompanying notes 126–128, *infra*.

[104] *See* Ursúa-Cocke, *supra* note 90, at 425.

[105] *See* Arellano, *supra* note 32, at 175–226; Mears, *supra* note 88, at 642–644.

[106] *See Código Civil Federal*, Arts. 2588, 2589, and 2615.

[107] *See* Art. 2590 of both the Federal Civil Code and the Civil Code for the Federal District: Art. 319(II) of the Penal Code for the Federal District; and Art. 36 of the Ley de Profesiones.

[108] A survey of Mexican case-law fails to reveal a single example of the Articles cited in note 107 *supra*.

Table 2.7: Largest Mexican law firms

Firm	*No. of Attorneys*
1. Baker & McKenzie Abogados, S.C.	126
2. Basham, Ringe y Correa, S.C.	91
3. Martínez, Algaba, Estrella, de Haro y Galván-Duque, S.C.	78
4. Jáuregui, Navarrete, Nader y Rojas, S.C.	75
5. Creel, García-Cuellar y Müggenburg, S.C.	74
6. Santamarina y Steta, S.C.	71
7. Guerra González y Asociados, S.C.	59
8. Barrera, Siqueiros y Torres Landa, S.C.	50
9. Goodrich, Riquelme y Asociados, S.C.	48
10. Olivares y Cia., S.C.	48
11. Bryan, González Vargas y González Baz, S.C.	47
12. Bermúdez, Wiencke y Bermúdez, S.C.	43
13. White and Case, S.C.	40
14. Rubio Villegas y Asociados, S.C.	40
15. Ritch, Heather y Muller, S.C.	39
16. Von Wobeser y Sierra, S.C.	37
17. Franck, Galicia y Robles, S.C.	31
18. Uthoff, Gómez Vega y Uthoff, S.C.	31
19. Santos, Elizondo, Cantú, Rivera, García, González, de la Garza, S.C.	30

Source: www.martindale.com, and web sites of individual law firms, consulted January 2004.

legal market in Mexico has been composed of an overwhelming number of very small offices or partnerships of one, two, or three attorneys, and a few larger firms of over ten attorneys. As of 1978, there were only about twelve firms in Mexico City and a handful in some of Mexico's other major urban centres with ten attorneys or more, and the largest firm had fifty lawyers.[109] As of 1995, Mexico's largest law firm had seventy-four attorneys and the country's ten largest firms, ranging in size from eighteen to seventy-four lawyers, were nearly all based in Mexico City (see Table 2.7).

The small size of Mexican law firms[110] may be attributable in part to the relatively limited nature of civil litigation in Mexico. In Mexico, civil litigation is particularly unattractive because it is expensive, often very lengthy, largely controlled by the judge, and does not involve certain recovery-enhancing features such as juries and punitive damages.[111] As a result, Mexico does not share the need felt in US law firms for the large numbers of lawyers needed to handle

[109] *See* Herget and Camil, *supra* note 24, at 96.

[110] Compared with firms in the United States.

[111] *See* Simon, Henry, *When in Mexico, Use a Mexican Lawyer* (available at http://www.flash.net/òmex...perts/legal_simon_01.html); Rene Cacheaux & Dale A. Kimball, Jr., *An Overview of the Mexican Legal System* 4 (Apr. 1994) (available at http://www.flash.net/òmex...rts/legal_ kimball_01.html) [hereinafter Cacheaux]. Note that although there are no strictly punitive damages awards in Mexico, awards for 'moral damages' (*daños morales*) are

cases involving complex litigation. A second possible factor is Mexico's smaller number of large corporations with continuous legal needs of the type necessary to sustain many lawyers in large law firms.

With the entry into force of NAFTA, a number of US-based law firms have either opened offices in Mexico City, or established relationships with Mexican law firms, although this has not yet brought about the establishment of large branches of US law firms. The control of Mexican law firms is regulated by the 1993 Foreign Investment Law, although the Commission that administers that law has been generous in granting permission for 100 per cent ownership of Mexican law offices by foreign attorneys.[112] The provisions of NAFTA dealing with trade in services did not contain detailed commitments for liberalization of trade in legal services, which was left for further negotiations that were supposed to take place after NAFTA entered into force.[113] The Mexican government appointed a committee of lawyers, the *Comité Mexicano para la Práctica Internacional de Derecho* (Mexican Committee on International Law Practice), to propose draft rules for foreign legal consultants and to negotiate specific legal services commitments with its US and Canadian counterparts. However, the opposition of key members of the Committee to the large-scale influx of large US-based corporate law firms has helped stall these efforts.

6.1. Attorneys' Fees

Just as admission to the practice of law is regulated in Mexico at the state level, so too are attorneys' fees. Without exception, the states permit parties to contract freely on the amount of fees, and to allow courts or other competent authorities to intervene only in the absence of a contract.[114] In the Federal District, absent an agreement for professional compensation, 'fees shall be determined in accordance with the custom of the place, the importance of the services rendered, the matter in which services are rendered, the financial ability of the recipient of the service and the professional reputation of the individual providing the service'.[115] A Mexican attorney must be registered in a jurisdiction to be able to charge fees for work done in that jurisdiction; thus, an attorney from Veracruz with a state licence (*cédula estatal*) who works on a case in the Federal District may not charge for such services unless he also registers his law degree in the Federal District and is issued a *cédula* from the General Directorate of Professions.[116]

possible under certain circumstances as provided in the Civil Code. These awards, however, never amount to the astronomical figures often seen in US decisions. Cacheaux, *supra*, at 4.

112 *See* Art. 8, Section V, *Ley de Inversión Extranjera*, D.O. 27 Dec. 1993 (limiting foreign ownership of law firms to 49% subject to the ability of the Foreign Investment Commission to permit higher percentage ownership). This law is discussed generally in Chapter 19 below, at text accompanying notes 41–46.

113 *See* NAFTA, Annex 1210.5, Section B, and Annex II, available at www.sice.oas.org (May, 2004).

114 *See* Arellano, *supra* note 32, at 245.

115 *Código Civil*, Art. 2607.

116 *See* Arellano, *supra* note 32, at 253.

Contingency fee agreements (*pactos de cuota litis*) are not prohibited under Mexican law. However, Article 2276 of the Civil Code for the Federal District and analogous state provisions prohibit attorneys from acquiring rights in any property that is the subject of the lawsuits they are handling. Consequently, contingency agreements by Mexican attorneys take the form of agreements to be paid at the end of the lawsuit, conditional on a favourable result.[117] Further, the Code of Professional Ethics of the *Barra Mexicana* provides, with respect to contingency agreements, that the attorney's portion of any recovery should never exceed that of the client, that the attorney may charge a percentage share of any recovery only if a verdict is favourable to the client, and that, if the case is lost, the attorney should charge no fee but may recover a reasonable amount for expenses.[118]

6.2. The Role of Law Clerks

Although no formal apprenticeship is required to practise law in Mexico, as a practical matter many future attorneys spend between one and three years working for licensed attorneys as law clerks (*pasantes*). Technically, a *pasante* is a law student who has finished several semesters of coursework, but who lacks the thesis and professional examination required to obtain a law degree.[119] In view of the highly theoretical nature of legal education in Mexico, the traditional goal of clerking is for the *pasante* to obtain practical legal experience by working during law school.[120] Many states permit *pasantes* to litigate matters under an attorney's supervision. In Guanajuato, for example, a *pasante* may appear before state tribunals for a maximum of four years, so long as her law school classifies her as a *pasante* and certifies her good character.[121]

7. Attorney Professional Associations

Due in part to the constitutional guarantee of liberty of profession, membership of a professional organization of lawyers is not mandatory in Mexico but is left to the discretion of each lawyer.[122] Consequently, the number of Mexican attorneys who join Bar associations has been described as meagre.[123] In 2004, the Mexican Bar College of Attorneys (*Barra Mexicana Colegio de Abogados A.C.*), the largest and most prestigious Bar association in the country, had only 2000 members, 90 per cent of whom resided in Mexico City.[124] Most states also have voluntary Bar associations. A number of specialized Bar organizations also

[117] *See* Arellano, *supra* note 32, at 252.
[118] *See Código de Ética Profesional de la Barra Mexicana Colegio de Abogados*, Art. 36 (*infra.* note 126).
[119] *See* Arellano, *supra* note 32, at 321–322.
[120] *Id.* at 321–322.
[121] *See* Ursúa-Cocke, *supra* note 90, at 433.
[122] *See* Mex. Const. Art. 5; Arellano, *supra* note 32, at 308–309.
[123] *See* Arellano, *supra* note 32, at 308–309.
[124] Source: *Barra Mexicana Colegio de Abogados* (May, 2004).

exist, such as the National Association of Business Lawyers (*Asociación Nacional de Abogados de Empresa, A.C.*).

Despite its voluntary nature, the *Barra Mexicana* performs several significant functions. Under Mexican law, the organization has a duty to inform the General Directorate of Professions or appropriate criminal authorities of violations of law perpetrated by attorneys. In addition, it is authorized to arbitrate disputes between lawyers and clients, to represent the profession before the General Directorate of Professions, to collaborate in the development of law school curricula, to expel members who commit acts that bring dishonour on the profession, and to sanction those who fail to meet their professional obligations.[125]

In addition, the *Barra Mexicana* has fulfilled the critical task of developing and enforcing among its members a Code of Professional Ethics (*Código de Ética Professional de la Barra Mexicana Colegio de Abogados*).[126] The Code–the only such code in effect in Mexico—sets forth aspirational goals (e.g. to serve the law, aid justice, and defend the rights of clients), as well as certain essential obligations of lawyers (e.g. to work in good faith, maintain client confidences, and avoid charging fees that are excessive or which damage the dignity of the profession). Although the Code technically applies only to the group's members, its provisions are a tacit standard by which government authorities judge the conduct of all lawyers.[127] A violation of good custom may be an illegal act under certain civil or criminal statutory provisions, and therefore, at least in theory, the *Barra Mexicana*'s Code may be viewed as applicable to all Mexican lawyers, whether Bar members or not.[128]

8. Public Notaries

Public notaries constitute a special segment of the Mexican legal profession, consisting of private attorneys chosen by a state or by the federal government to provide impartial counsel to private parties and exercise certain official powers delegated to them. The Mexican notary simultaneously serves as an authenticator of legal actions, expert adviser, guarantor of title to property, tax collector, archivist, and, periodically, assistant to courts. The requirements for admission to the notarial profession are arduous and those selected are strictly regulated, both by the governmental authority from which they receive their licence and by the professional associations they are required to join.[129]

[125] *See* www.bma.org.mx (last visited January 2004).

[126] *See* www.bma.org.mx/codigo/index.html (last visited January 2004).

[127] In the Federal District, for example, the General Directorate of Professions is authorized under the law to record sanctions imposed on an attorney or any suspension of her practice and to cancel the licence of any attorney judicially declared unfit to practise. *See Ley de Profesiones*, Arts. 22, 67.

[128] Mears, *supra* note 88, at 643.

[129] On notaries and notarial law, *see* Pérez Fernández del Castillo, B., DERECHO NOTARIAL (México: Porrúa, 6th ed., 1993).

8.1. Roles of the Mexican Notary

Of the six duties notaries generally perform, those of authenticator of legal acts (*fedatario*) and expert counsellor are central. Private parties in Mexico wishing to undertake certain legal transactions, such as the conveyance of real estate, the making of wills or powers of attorney, the formation of business entities, the purchase or sale of ships or aircraft, or the payment of certain taxes, are required by law to seek the intervention of a notary.[130] In addition, parties sometimes use notaries to create official records of legal transactions (e.g. legal notifications, demands, and protests) even though the law does not require the involvement of a notary, in order to benefit from the legal presumptions that attach to notarial acts.[131]

Upon being approached by such parties, the initial task of the notary is to act as expert counsellor. *Notarios* are required to be experts in the substantive law applicable to each of the transactions they certify.[132] The notary impartially advises all persons involved in a transaction as to its proper legal form and consequences, and, as necessary, drafts the legal documents required to fulfil the transaction.[133] At this stage, the notary is the judge of the legality of the transaction and owes his ethical duty not to the parties but to the transaction.[134] The resulting product is a highly formalized document or public deed, bearing the requisite legal recitals, signatures of the parties and notary, and notarial seal.

By virtue of governmental delegation of authority for official authentication or certification (*fe pública*, literally 'public faith') of documents, the notary's act of preparation and recording of documents transforms a private transaction into an official, public act.[135] In this capacity, the notary is referred to as the *fédatario*, or certifying public official. Notarial recording endows legal transactions with the full faith and credit of the State and confers upon the instrument involved the strongest possible evidentiary value, which can be upset only by a formal judicial declaration made upon a showing of clear and convincing proof that the instrument is not genuine, does not accurately recite what the parties said, or falsely reflects that the notary complied with the formalities required for the instrument.[136]

[130] *See* Pacheco Escobedo, Albert, 'El Notario', in INSTITUTO DE INVESTIGACIONES JURÍDICAS, EL PAPEL DEL ABOGADO 139, 139 (1993); Mears, Rona R., 'Contracting in Mexico: A Legal and Practical Guide to Negotiating and Drafting', 24 ST. MARY'S L.J. 737, 751 (1993) [hereinafter Mears, *Contracting*]. In the Federal District, the sale of real estate having an appraised value of over 30,000 pesos (about US$4,000) must be established by a deed before a notary. *See Ley del Notariado para el Distrito Federal*, G.O. 28 March 2000 as amended G.O. 14 September 2000, Art. 78 [hereinafter *Ley del Notariado*].

[131] *See* 'Mexican Law for Norteamericanos', 68 L. LIBRARY J. 395, 406 (E. Weisbaum, Mod. 1975) [hereinafter *Norteamericanos*]; Malavet, *supra* note 79, at 455–456.

[132] Malavet, *supra* note 79, at 456.

[133] *See* Pérez Fernández del Castillo, *supra* note 129; Malavet, *supra* note 79, at 401–402; *Norteamericanos*, *supra* note 131, at 406.

[134] Pérez Fernández del Castillo, *supra* note 129. Malavet, *supra* note 79, at 402.

[135] *See* e.g. *Ley del Notariado*, Art. 10.

[136] Malavet, *supra* note 79, at 444; *Norteamericanos*, *supra* note 131, at 406. *See also* JOHN HENRY MERRYMAN, THE CIVIL LAW TRADITION 113–114 (Stanford: Stanford University Press, 2nd ed., 1985).

The notary's remaining duties—those of guarantor of title to property, tax collector, archivist, and judicial assistant—flow from the notary's duties as authenticator and expert counsellor.[137] In a real estate conveyance, the notary has a legal duty to investigate and verify the validity of the seller's title. In certain transactions, where fiscal laws levy a tax, the notary is required to collect the appropriate sum from the parties and remit those amounts to the government. Notaries are required by law to assist courts in reviewing instruments produced by the notaries, as necessary.

As archivist, the notary maintains a permanent record or protocol (*protocolo*) of each transaction he performs. A very intricate body of regulations surrounds *protocolos*. In the Federal District, for example, the notary's *protocolo* is formally defined as (1) the set of books in which the notary inscribes public deeds and authorizes legal acts (each book consisting of a set of sealed, progressively numbered pages) and (2) appendices and indices corresponding to the books.[138] The Council of the College of Notaries (*Consejo del Colegio de Notarios*), the notarial association of the Federal District, is responsible for dispensing the progressively numbered pages and books to its members and reporting such distributions to the government monthly.[139] The notary must keep any open books containing the *protocolo* in his office at all times, unless otherwise allowed by law, and provide sets of newly completed books to the General Archive of Notaries (*Archivo General de Notarias*) for review and certification.[140] Certified books are returned to the notary for a period of five years, after which they are sent back to the General Archive for permanent custody.[141] The General Archive of Notaries of the Federal District has been in existence and served as custodian of *protocolos* since 1525.[142]At all times, a *protocolo* remains the property of the State, entrusted to the notary only temporarily. Consequently, '[t]he State, generally through the inspector of notary offices, has absolute, unobstructed access to the *protocolo*'.[143]

While notary licences are granted to individuals, notary offices often employ a staff of several attorneys, as well as the clerks, apprentices, and secretaries necessary to process the large number of transactions that require the attention of a notary.

8.2. Requirements for Admission to Notarial Practice

For attorneys in Mexico, admission to notarial practice is regulated by the states, in their respective territories, and by the federal government, in its corresponding territory.[144] In the case of the Federal District, the Department

[137] *See* Margadant, G.F., 'The Mexican Notariate', 6 CAL. W. L. REV. 218, 227–30 (1970) [hereinafter *Mexican Notariate*].

[138] *See Ley del Notariado*, Art. 42.

[139] *See Ley del Notariado*, Art. 44.

[140] *See Ley del Notariado*, Arts. 45, 52.

[141] *See Ley del Notariado*, Art. 54.

[142] *See Mexican Notariate*, *supra* note 137, at 230.

[143] Malavet, *supra* note 79, at 447.

[144] Notarial law and registration law are both under the jurisdiction of the States of the Republic of Mexico. Although most of the States have their own laws, they are very similar, if not the same. *Norteamericanos*, *supra* note 131, at 404. In the Federal District, the

of the Federal District (*Departamento del Distrito Federal*) sets quantitative limits on the number of authorized notary offices.[145] Attaining one of these positions involves a two-step process.

First, an individual must receive the title of aspirant (*aspirante*).[146] To do this, the candidate must (1) be a Mexican citizen by birth, with full legal capacity, between twenty-five and sixty years old, and of 'good character', (2) be a graduate in law with at least three years of professional practice, (3) have been apprenticed to any notary of the Federal District during the eight months immediately before the application, (4) not have been convicted of an intentional crime, and (5) have passed the *aspirante* examination.[147] A panel consisting of three government officials and two notaries (who are appointed by the Council of the College of Notaries) serve as the 'jury' in this examination.[148] The *aspirante* exam includes a theoretical test and a practical test.[149] The theoretical part, which is held in public, involves the applicant being questioned by members of the jury. In the practical test, the applicant is required to draft one of twenty pre-designated notarial instruments. Persons receiving a mark of 70 per cent or more in the exam become *aspirantes*.[150]

When one of the limited number of notary offices becomes vacant, either by the death or retirement of the incumbent, or when a new office is created, the Department advertises the vacancy and invites applications by announcements in official publications and at least one newspaper of general circulation.[151] *Aspirantes* then arrange to complete a second examination (*examen de oposición*), also consisting of theoretical and practical tests, to attain the status of notary.[152] The *aspirante* receiving the highest score is declared the 'winner' and, within thirty working days thereafter, receives a letter of commission (*patente*) from the Department.[153] The degree of politics involved in the notarial appointment process is a point of speculation.[154]

Upon receiving a letter of commission, the new notary must obtain his *protocolo* and seal, register his seal and signature with the appropriate governmental agencies in the Federal District, deposit a bond in the amount of 10,000 times the general daily minimum wage (approximately US$40,000 in 2002), and open an office.[155] Thereafter, the notary is prohibited from undertaking any

notarial profession is administered by the government of the Federal District. *See Ley del Notariado*, Art. 1.

[145] *See Ley del Notariado*, Art. 3. As of December 2003, only 240 notarial positions were authorized for the Federal District.

[146] *See Norteamericanos*, *supra* note 131, at 405; Malavet, *supra* note 79, at 472.

[147] *See Ley del Notariado*, Art. 13.

[148] *See Ley del Notariado*, Art. 19. All members of the panel are required to be law graduates.

[149] *See Ley del Notariado*, Art. 20.

[150] *See Ley del Notariado*, Art. 23.

[151] *See Ley del Notariado*, Art. 11.

[152] *See Ley del Notariado*, Art. 21.

[153] *See Ley del Notariado*, Arts. 23, 24, 26.

[154] Clearly, at some levels politics can enter into the selection process. *See* Malavet, *supra* note 79, at 475 n. 417. In the late 1970s, Herget and Camil opined that appointment to a notarial position was 'purely political in most states'. Herget and Camil, *supra* note 24, at 97.

[155] *See Ley del Notariado*, Art. 28.

employment as a judge, private attorney in litigation, businessman, money exchange agent, or religious minister, but is permitted to accept employment as a teacher, tutor, curator, executor, judicial assistant, or arbitrator.[156]

8.3. Regulation of the Profession

Mexican notaries are subject to sweeping government regulation due to the fact that they are vested with the *fe pública*. Two of the most conspicuous features of the notarial profession are the express limits on the number of notarial offices, and geographic restrictions on their practice.[157] The limitations are designed, in part, to allow the government carefully to regulate and constantly to scrutinize notaries.[158]

In addition to these restraints, notaries are generally subject to three types of liability in the practice of their profession: (1) professional ethical liability, (2) civil liability for damages, and (3) criminal liability.[159] Professional ethical liability involves the imposition of reprimands, fines, temporary suspension, or permanent disbarment.[160] Civil liability for damages is the penalty that follows acts of malpractice, including negligent, reckless, or wilful behaviour. Criminal liability is imposed for acts of perjury, forgery, or fraud.

8.4. Notarial Fees

Notaries do not receive any salary from the government from which they obtain their authority but, instead, are entitled to recover fees and expenses from the private parties they serve.[161] Unlike attorneys' fees in Mexico, which are set by agreement between client and counsel, notary fees are set forth in a tariff (*arancel*) prescribed by law.[162] In part, this difference is due to the fact that notaries have a government-conferred monopoly on the provision of their services. Still, '[t]he limited supply of notarial services, together with the monopoly they enjoy over particular legal transactions, places them at the top of the professional and economic scale'.[163]

[156] *See Ley del Notariado*, Art. 17.

[157] Notaries of the Federal District, for example, are prohibited from performing notarial services outside of that zone. *See Ley del Notariado*, Art. 5.

[158] In the Federal District, for example, notaries are subject to annual 'general visits' by official government inspectors (upon five days' advance notice) and to 'special visits' as necessary. Infringements of the notarial law discovered during an inspection can lead to warnings, monetary sanctions, suspension of up to one year, or dismissal. *See Ley del Notariado*, Arts. 115, 116, 121, 124.

[159] Malavet, *supra* note 79, at 476.

[160] In the Federal District, a notary's letter of commission may be revoked for, *inter alia*, gross negligence in the performance of notarial duties, failure to maintain the required notarial bond, or conviction for an intentional crime. *See Ley del Notariado*, Art. 133.

[161] *See* e.g. *Ley del Notariado*, Art. 7.

[162] *See* e.g. *Arancel de Notarios para el Distrito Federal*. Notaries are prohibited by law from exceeding the delineated fees. *See Ley del Notariado*, Art. 153.

[163] Malavet, *supra* note 79, at 484.

8.5. Notarial Associations

Unlike attorneys in Mexico, notaries are required to be members of a professional association, as designated by each state or by the federal government. Notaries of the Federal District are required to join the College of Notaries of the Federal District (*Colegio de Notarios del Distrito Federal*).[164] The College had 240 members as of 2003: an astoundingly small number for a city of over 20 million inhabitants that is the economic centre of the country. The formal legal roles of notarial colleges are to draft and propose amendments to the notarial laws, and to report infringements of such laws by their members to the government.[165] In addition, the *Colegio de Notarios* handles grievances against notaries, assists the government in the selection and testing of notarial candidates, takes disciplinary actions against its members as appropriate, and publishes the Journal of the Mexican Notariate (*Revista del Notariado Mexicano*).[166]

Comparable *consejos de notarios* exist in a number of states. In addition, there are various voluntary organizations of notaries in Mexico, such as the National Association of the Mexican Notariate (*Asociación Nacional del Notariado Mexicano*) which was founded in 1955 and had over 1,200 members as of 1991, and the Mexican Academy of Notarial Law (*Academia Mexicana de Derecho Notarial*), which was founded in 1984 and whose membership includes both notaries and *aspirantes*.[167]

8.6. Evaluation and Criticism of the Notarial Process

As a general rule, Mexican notaries are highly respected for their honesty and professionalism. This is not to say, however, that the notarial system is above criticism. The delegation of governmental duties by conferring monopolies on private individuals creates two major side-effects: first, it generates significant transactional costs for trade and commerce, and second, it creates a bottleneck that may impede the timely process of important business transactions. The government could alleviate these side-effects by creating more notary offices, thus relieving the pressure on existing notaries, but it has not chosen to do so. Rather, in response to criticism from business and from intergovernmental organizations, such as the World Bank, the Mexican government created a new institution, the *corredor público*, or public commercial broker, to alleviate the backlog of business transactions held up in the notary process.

[164] *See Ley del Notariado*, Art. 151. [165] *See Ley del Notariado*, Art. 152.

[166] *See* Herget, *supra* note 24, at 98. *See also Estatutos del Colegio de Notarios del Distrito Federal; Reglamento del Consejo de Notarios del Distrito Federal.*

[167] *See* Pérez-Fernández del Castillo, B., HISTORIA DE LA ESCRIBANÍA Y DEL NOTARIADO (Mexico: UNAM, Instituto de Investigaciones Juridicas, 1983) 197–199.

9. Public Commercial Brokers (*Corredores Públicos*)

In 1992, the Mexican Congress adopted a law creating the office of public commercial brokers (*corredores públicos*), a new segment of the legal profession substantially distinct from attorneys and much like notaries, yet formally independent from both.[168] *Corredores públicos* are regulated by federal law, through the Ministry of the Economy, with the assistance of appropriate state authorities.[169] They are authorized to provide their services throughout the country, except when they act as *fédatarios*,[170] which they may only do in the state or district in which they are based.[171]

Corredores públicos perform four basic functions. They can: (1) authenticate contracts, agreements, corporate organization, or other legal transactions of a commercial nature, except those relating to real estate, (2) act as an intermediary, transmitting and exchanging proposals between businesses, (3) serve as an expert appraiser, estimating the quantity and value of property, services, rights and obligations, and (4) work as arbitrators in commercial disputes.[172] Like notaries, brokers are required by law to maintain a permanent record, called the Book of Commercial Organizations (*Libro de Sociedades Mercantiles*), of each transaction they perform.[173] The key difference between brokers and notaries is that the former act solely in the commercial field and exclusively for entities of a commercial nature,[174] while notaries may operate in non-commercial settings (sales of real estate between individuals, etc.).

Requirements for admission to the public brokerage parallel those of the notariate. An individual must qualify first as a candidate (*aspirante a corredor*) and then as a broker. To attain the status of *aspirante a corredor*, a person must (1) be a Mexican citizen, with full legal capacity, (2) have been a licensed attorney for at least two years, (3) not have been convicted of an intentional crime, and (4) have passed the examination for *aspirante a corredor*.[175] Subsequently, the individual must prove that he has practised for at least one year under a licensed broker or notary and pass a second examination (*examen definitivo*) in order to receive the title of broker.[176]

[168] *See Ley Federal de Correduría Pública*, D.O. 29 Dec. 1992, as amended 23 Jan. 1998. *See generally* www.correduriapublica.gob.mx.

[169] *See Ley Federal de Correduría Pública*, Art. 2. The federal government's power to legislate in this area is in accordance with the Mexican Constitution, which regards commercial law as matter of federal, rather than state, jurisdiction. Mexican Constitution, Article 73, Section IX.

[170] *See* text accompanying note 131, *supra*.

[171] *See Ley Federal de Correduría Pública*, Art. 5.

[172] *See Ley Federal de Correduría Pública*, Art. 6; Romero Anaya, Jaime, 'La Nueva Correduría Pública en Nuestro País', 6 El Foro 145, 146 (1993).

[173] *See Ley Federal de Correduría Pública*, Art. 16; Romero Anaya, *supra* note 172, at 147.

[174] *See* Romero Anaya, *supra* note 172, at 146.

[175] *See Ley Federal de Correduría Pública*, Arts. 8–9.

[176] *See Ley Federal de Correduría Pública*, Art. 9. Brokers' examinations are judged by a three-person jury, composed of a representative of the Ministry of Trade, a representative of the State Governor or Chief of the Department of the Federal District, and a broker designated

Mexican brokers are strictly regulated and subject to inspection by the Ministry of Economy (*Secretaría de Economía*) and, as appropriate, to written reprimands, fines, suspension, and disbarment.[177] Like notaries, brokers are required to be members of their own professional associations.[178] Unlike notaries, however, brokers are free to set their fees by agreement with their clients, although they must post a schedule of their charges for basic services.[179]

by the local college of brokers. *See Ley Federal de Correduría Pública*, Art. 10. The exams consist of a written test (involving the drafting of a commercial instrument) and an oral question-and-answer session. *See Ley Federal de Correduría Pública*, Art. 11. Unlike notarial examinations, broker examinations are not scored, but merely given a pass or fail mark. *See ibid.*

[177] *See Ley Federal de Correduría Pública*, Arts. 3, 17, 20, 21.

[178] Mexican law provides that a college of brokers (*colegio de corredores*) shall be established in each state or district having three or more brokers. The function of these associations is to support the growth of the brokerage profession, notify the government of infractions perpetrated by brokers, and assist the government in the selection and testing of new brokers. *See Ley Federal de Correduría Pública*, Art. 23. As of 2004 there were 59 brokers in the Federal District. For names and addresses of all *corredores públicos* registered in Mexico, *see* www.correduriapublica.gob.mx (last visited January 2004).

[179] *See Ley Federal de Correduría Pública*, Art. 14; Romero Anaya, *supra* note 172 at 148.

3

Sources of Law

1. Introduction

In all legal systems, judges and lawyers decide issues of legal duty and entitlement by consulting the various sources of law recognized within the legal system, including legislation, judicial decisions, custom, doctrine, and equity. Merely knowing that a society regards legislation or some other source of law as legitimate is not enough to complete the analysis, however. Judges and lawyers also must understand the relative importance accorded by the legal system to the competing sources of law and the ways in which the sources of law are thought to interrelate.

Stripped to its essential elements, the general process of making a legal determination is no different in Mexico than in the United States. Mexican judges and lawyers, like their counterparts in the United States, take a body of facts, scour the substantive legal principles found under various sources of law, and, putting the two together, assess the legal implications of those facts. For the most part, Mexican judges and lawyers rely upon the same types of law (constitutions, statutes, judicial decisions, etc.) that American judges and lawyers use.

Beyond these essential points, however, a number of significant differences do exist. First, Mexican versions of some sources of law, such as legislation and jurisprudence, differ materially from the US versions. Second, the relative importance Mexican society attaches to the various sources of law differs from the US practice; as a consequence, the hierarchies of law in Mexico and in the United States are not the same. Finally, due in part to the distinctions just mentioned, the methodologies followed by Mexican judges and lawyers to form opinions do not follow the same pattern as their counterparts in the United States. This Chapter examines each of these points.

2. Mexican Sources of Law

The names of several Mexican sources of law translate readily from Spanish to English: *constitución* translates to constitution, *legislación* to legislation, *jurisprudencia* to jurisprudence (i.e. case-law), and *doctrina* to doctrine. However, the similarity of words disguises important differences in meaning, and these differences have much to do with intangible aspects of the legal culture.[1] This section examines the Mexican definition of the following sources of law: constitutions, legislation, jurisprudence, doctrine, custom, treaties, general principles of law, regulations, equity, and administrative rulings.

2.1. Constitution (*Constitución Política*)

In both the US and Mexican legal systems, a constitution is considered to be the fundamental law of a society, an instrument that creates the underlying social and political order. Nevertheless, the Mexican approach to constitutionalism differs from that of the US in a few essential ways. First, Mexico's federal constitution (*Constitución Política de los Estados Unidos Mexicanos*) covers more subject matter in much greater detail than does the US Constitution. In contrast to the seven Articles and twenty-seven amendments that make up the US Constitution, the Mexican Constitution consists of 136 Articles (*Artículos*) and seventeen 'transitory' or technical provisions (*artículos transitorios*). In addition to organic provisions which detail the structure and institutions of the Mexican government and twenty-nine Articles providing for individual liberties (*garantías individuales*), the federal Constitution includes extensive provisions relating to political parties, sovereignty, the identities and powers of the Federal District and thirty-one Mexican states, the duties owed by citizens to Mexican society, the responsibilities of public servants, and labour and social welfare. The difference in detail becomes clear when one compares the judiciary provisions of the US and Mexican Constitutions. Article III, the Judiciary Article of the US Constitution, consists of five relatively brief paragraphs. In contrast, the judiciary provisions of the Mexican Constitution are spread over fourteen Articles which span more than twenty pages of text.

Mexico's political history and the civil law tradition—both of which give rise to a distrust of judicial law-making—account for some of the extraordinary length and detail of the Mexican Constitution. Another critical phenomenon, the uniquely political nature of the Mexican Constitution, must also be considered. Of course, the US Constitution is a political text as much as it is an organic document. The same is true in Mexico, but in a different sense. The federal Constitution is revered in Mexican society as the central place for stating in textual form the goals of the government in seeking to protect the Mexican people; in this sense, the Constitution is very much a planning document, a place for the Mexican people to signal their political priorities and to provide the means to realize objectives. The Mexican Constitution includes, therefore,

[1] In 1985, Professor John Henry Merryman published a classic text, an introduction to the mindset of a lawyer trained under the civil law system. Even though the book was aimed at an understanding of European law, it remains relevant as valuable background reading for legal systems with European antecedents. *See* John H. Merryman, *The Civil Law Tradition: An Introduction to the Legal Systems of Western Europe and Latin America* (Stanford: Stanford Univ. Press, 2nd ed., 1985).

not just the outline of a government structure, but also a social agenda (known as the 'social constitution') consisting of numerous articles in the Constitution that address social welfare, worker rights, etc. In part, this is why Mexico witnesses sweeping constitutional revision with each incoming presidential administration. Traditionally, a newly elected President has tried to demonstrate the genuineness of his commitment to address the Mexican crisis of the day—be it economic chaos, judicial corruption, electoral fraud, or whatever—by incorporating his planned reforms into the society's document-of-documents, the Constitution itself.

Legal scholars describe this difference between the US and Mexican constitutions as a *normative* versus *nominal* distinction. As a general matter, the US Constitution is 'normative' in the sense that the Constitution establishes norms that Americans expect the political and legal infrastructure to follow. As a general matter, on the other hand, the Mexican Constitution, 'has been consistently characterized by Mexican constitutional scholars as a project to be accomplished, a statement of revolutionary ideals that is nominal in that there is no intended immediate congruency between its stated aspiration and reality'.[2] This discrepancy between the stated law and the law as applied (evident at many levels, from the Constitution down) has been identified, and decried, by both Mexicans and non-Mexicans, and has given rise to efforts by public and private groups to promote the rule of law (i.e. law as a true normative principle) in Mexico.

Second, the Mexican approach to constitutional amendment differs from that of the United States. Considering that the US Constitution has been amended only twenty-seven times, American lawyers are usually surprised to learn that the Mexican Constitution had been amended hundreds of times.[3]

The breadth, detail, political role, and nominal character of the document partially explain the frequency of constitutional reform. Two other explanations are also important. First: historically, it has proven easy for Mexican leaders to amend the Constitution. Article 135 of the Mexican Constitution allows amendment upon a two-thirds vote of Congress and approval by a majority of the thirty-one state legislatures.[4] Due to the dominance of the Partido Revolucionario Institucional (P.R.I.) in both federal and state politics, and in turn the executive's dominance of the P.R.I., during most of the twentieth century Mexican Presidents were largely free to alter the Constitution at will.

[2] *See* e.g. James F. Smith, 'Confronting Differences in the United States and Mexican Legal Systems in the Era of NAFTA', 1 *US-MEX. L.J.* 85, 94 (1993).

[3] Sergio López Ayllón and Héctor Fix Fierro calculate more than 400 amendments to the Mexican Constitution since 1921, the date of the first amendment. S. López Ayllón, and H. Fix Fierro, ' "*Tan cerca, tan lejos*" *El Estado de derecho en México*' 97 *BOLETÍN MEXICANO DE DERECHO COMPARADO* (2000). The exact number of amendments depends on how one calculates each amendment, however, as explained below in Chapter 5, note 1.

[4] In contrast, under Article V of the US Constitution, ratification of a proposed constitutional amendment requires a two-thirds vote of Congress plus approval by two-thirds of the state legislatures.

With the recent departure from the one-party system, one can expect that constitutional amendments will become more difficult to achieve, and therefore less numerous. Second, the Mexican Constitution is seen as the fountainhead of all rights, duties, and procedures affecting society, and Mexican legal tradition has translated this concept into an expectation that the Constitution should be exhaustive.[5] Mexican citizens do not possess rights, and the Mexican government lacks powers, unless those rights and powers are written into the Constitution. Until recently, Mexican courts have exercised a limited ability to interpret constitutional language to support new rights or powers,[6] i.e. they have been loath to 'amend' the Constitution by interpretation. Consequently, the duty of constitutional reform falls to the Mexican Congress. In contrast, 'the United States Supreme Court has effectively "amended" the United States Constitution hundreds of times'.[7]

More recently, as a consequence of the judicial (and political) reforms described below in Chapters 5, 6, and 8, the Supreme Court has undertaken a more aggressive and creative approach to constitutional interpretation,[8] altering the balance of power that traditionally existed between the executive, legislative, and judicial branches of government.

In Mexico, as in the United States, one finds numerous state constitutions (*constituciones locales*) in addition to the federal Constitution. Generally, Mexican state constitutions deal with the same subject matter as the federal Constitution (e.g. governmental structure and institutions, individual liberties, the responsibilities of citizens and public servants) but at a state level. In a few instances, state constitutions closely track, point by point and provision by provision, the federal Constitution.[9]

As discussed below in Chapter 5, Mexico, like the United States, has a 'savings' clause that reserves to the states all powers not assigned by the federal Constitution to the federal government. Despite this similarity, state governments in Mexico have traditionally lacked both the spending power and the legislative initiative of states of the United States.[10]

2.2. Legislation (*Legislación*)

In the United States, the term legislation is generally understood to encompass only the statutory enactments of Congress and state legislatures. In contrast,

[5] *See also* Michael C. Taylor, *Why No Rule of Law in Mexico? Explaining the Weakness of Mexico's Judicial Branch*, 27 N.M. L. REV. 141, 143 (1997).

[6] Traditionally, the Supreme Court's exercise in constitutional interpretation was limited to ascertaining the 'intention of the framers' (*espíritu del constituyente*), and the Court usually adhered to the statement of motives for the constitutional reform drafted by the Office of the President.

[7] *See* Smith, *supra* note 2, at 95.

[8] J.R. Cossío Díaz, *LA TEORÍA CONSTITUCIONAL DE LA SUPREMA CORTE DE JUSTICIA* (Mexico: Fontamara, 2002) at 141.

[9] *See* Mexican Constitution, Articles 115–121, which set parameters to be followed in state constitutions.

[10] *See* Chapter 4 below at text accompanying notes 105–134.

Mexico inherited from the civil law tradition, and from its Spanish colonial heritage, a broader concept of legislation as all norms of a general, abstract, permanent, and binding character that are created by the legislative power. In practical terms, this includes statutes (*leyes* or *estatutos*) as well as codes (*códigos*) adopted by the Mexican Congress and state legislatures. Mexicans also consider certain executive branch decrees, i.e. those issued by the executive pursuant to powers expressly delegated by Congress, to fall into the category of legislation.

Mexicans draw a formal distinction between two types of statutes: regulatory laws (*leyes reglamentarias*) and ordinary laws (*leyes ordinarias*). Regulatory laws are laws that detail or amplify the content of a constitutional precept for the purpose of articulating the concepts and measures necessary to effectuate the precept.[11] One example is the Regulatory Law of Sections I and II of Article 105 of the Mexican Constitution (*Ley Reglamentaria de las Fracciones I y II del Artículo 105 de la Constitución Política de los Estados Unidos Mexicanos*) which sets forth the procedures that govern the adjudication of constitutional controversies (*controversias constitucionales*) and actions of unconstitutionality (*acciones de inconstitucionalidad*) created by Article 105. Ordinary laws are statutes that do not directly emanate from or have as their immediate purpose the elaboration of a constitutional precept. Examples include the Federal Consumer Protection Law (*Ley Federal de la Protección al Consumidor*), Federal Copyright Law (*Ley Federal de Derechos de Autor*), and Law of Investment Companies (*Ley de Sociedades de Inversion*). Organic laws (*leyes orgánicas*), which regulate the organization, attributes, and function of governmental institutions, are a species of ordinary law.[12] The distinction between regulatory and ordinary laws is important when they conflict. The Mexican Supreme Court has held that regulatory laws take precedence over ordinary laws.[13]

As discussed below in Chapter 14, codes are a key ingredient of Mexican legal culture. A code is defined as a unitary work that integrates all norms of a distinct branch of law in a systematic, comprehensive, organized, and logical manner.[14] Codes, therefore, are intended to be definitive and self-sufficient bodies of law. Although the norms stated in a code tend to be general and abstract, special care is taken to use language that is brief, clear, simple, and concise so that (ideally) the norms will be self-executing and judicial interpretation will be unnecessary.[15] Statutes differ from codes in that they deal with only a single subject or a few subjects, not an entire field of law. Compilations of US law (such as the American

[11] *See* DICCIONARIO JURÍDICO MEXICANO, vol. 3 (Mexico: UNAM-Instituto de Investigaciones Jurídicas/Ed. Porrúa, 1997) at 1978 (hereinafter 'Diccionario').

[12] Organic laws include the Organic Law of the Federal Judicial Power (*Ley Orgánica del Poder Judicial de la Federación*), the Organic Law of the Federal Fiscal Court (*Ley Orgánica del Tribunal Fiscal de la Federación*), and the Organic Law of the Attorney General of the Republic (*Ley Orgánica de la Procuraduría General de la República*).

[13] 'INSTITUCIONES DE CRÉDITO. FIANZAS QUE SE DEBEN OTORGAR EN EL AMPARO', Apéndice al Semanario Judicial de la Federación, 1917–1988, Salas y tesis comunes, at 3058.

[14] *See* Diccionario, *supra* note 11, at 488–489.

[15] *See* José Luis Soberanes Fernández, HISTORIA DEL SISTEMA JURÍDICO MEXICANO (Mexico City: UNAM 1990) 66.

Law Institute's various Restatements of the Law) differ from codes in that they do not, of themselves, carry the force of law, but rather summarize the rules that courts have adopted in different jurisdictions. In contrast, the norms in a code have legal validity because they have been adopted by a legislature, and are solidly based on democratic principles. In applying code provisions to specific cases, judges are to decide cases in accordance with the will of the legislature, by applying the criteria of 'rationalism, systematization, [and] thematic unity'.[16]

The major federal codes in Mexico today are: (1) the Commercial Code (*Código de Comercio*); (2) the Federal Civil Code (*Código Civil Federal*); (3) the Federal Code of Civil Procedure (*Código Federal de Procedimientos Civiles*); (4) the Federal Criminal Code (*Código Penal Federal*); (5) the Federal Code of Criminal Procedure (*Código Federal de Procedimientos Penales*); and (6) the Federal Tax Code (*Código Fiscal de la Federación*). The law of a typical Mexican state includes four codes: a civil code (*código civil*), a code of civil procedure (*código de procedimientos civiles*), a criminal code (*código penal*), and a code of criminal procedure (*código de procedimientos penales*). Most state codes follow the structure and language of the federal codes very closely. A few states may have an additional miscellaneous code, such as a tax code (*código fiscal*) or civil registry code (*código del registro civil*).

Codes reflect fundamental differences between the US and Mexican legal systems. The practice of codification in Mexico, which dates from the 1820s, stems from the civil law belief that 'a single, complete, coherent, and logical system of law to govern all the relationships of man to man is possible (in fact, that it already exists in at least a metaphysical sense), and that the human mind is capable of thinking it out and working it out and putting it down on paper'.[17] Thus, Mexican jurists view the development of codified systems of law that are perfect and complete as an essential element of the Mexican legal system. Self-contained codes are expected to prevent judges and others from creating rules that would contradict the spirit of the code.[18] The creation of such abstract systems of law is of secondary importance to US lawyers and judges, who take a more pragmatic approach to codes. In the United States, the emphasis is on identifying the specific rules that will govern the resolution of a legal issue, without such regard for the completeness of a code or the consistency of the result with a doctrinal model. Codifications in the United States (the Uniform Commercial Code, for example) are not viewed as self-contained and complete expressions of law.

Of course, Mexican jurists and lawyers recognize that a perfect body of law is unattainable and that the codes they fashion do not include all of the law necessary to resolve all controversies that may arise in society. Nevertheless, the

[16] Carlos de la Vega Benayas, *Judicial Method of Interpretation of Codes*, 42 LA. L. REV. 1647 (1982).

[17] Woodfin L. Butte, *Stare Decisis, Doctrine, and Jurisprudence in Mexico and Elsewhere*, in THE ROLE OF JUDICIAL DECISIONS AND DOCTRINE IN CIVIL LAW AND IN MIXED JURISDICTIONS (Baton Rouge: LSU Press, Joseph Dainow, ed. 1974) 315.

[18] Merryman, *supra* note 1, at 28–29.

devotion to codification serves several important objectives. First, codification is thought to ensure that the law and legal decisions will be based on reason, not on passion, emotion, religion, politics, or other irrational motivations. Second, codification is thought to be consistent with democratic principles in that it assigns the task of creating the law to legislators, the duly elected representatives of the people, rather than to judges, all of whom are appointed in Mexican society. Third, codification produces juridical security and certainty by reducing reliance on scattered legal norms and the arbitrary judicial application of such norms. Underlying all of these rationales for codification is a distrust of judicial power that is fundamental to the civil law.

Although legislation is formally defined in Mexico as the product of the legislative power, in the past the domination of the Mexican President in a one-party system meant that '[i]n effect, the President legislates and Congress exercises a kind of veto power'.[19] With the demise of one-party rule,[20] the executive branch has lost the ability to prescribe legislation at will, even if the Mexican Constitution still grants to the President the power to initiate legislation.[21] Even after the demise of one-party government, the executive branch can be expected to generate most legislative initiatives, since Congress lacks the personnel and other resources to assist in the drafting of complex legislation. As discussed in Chapters 1 above and 5 below, the lack of any party majority in Congress has made it very difficult for President Vicente Fox to undertake any major legislative reforms.

2.3. Jurisprudence (*Jurisprudencia*)

In the United States, there exists a general misconception that the doctrine of *stare decisis*, adherence to established precedent, plays no role or only a *de minimis* role in the Mexican legal system. While it is true that the term *stare decisis* is not used in Mexico and has none of the talismanic effects that the doctrine had in the early common law, in fact Mexican judges and administrative tribunals routinely adopt, follow, and feel themselves bound by prior judicial rulings. This practice occurs in Mexico at two levels, one formal and the other informal. In the formal sense, Mexican law expressly authorizes certain courts to issue decisions that are binding upon judges in subsequent cases, through the issuance of *jurisprudencia obligatoria* by federal courts of appeals. In such instances, the latter have no choice but to adhere to precedent. In the informal sense, Mexican judges often follow prior rulings of other courts and judges voluntarily, not because Mexican law or legal doctrine mandates that they do so but because doing so serves other purposes. These other purposes may include a desire on the part of judges to build security and certainty into Mexican law or a desire to ensure self-preservation or promotion within the judiciary. Each of these points is examined more fully below.

19 *See* Smith, *supra* note 2, at 98. 20 *See infra*. Chapter 5.
21 Mexican Constitution, Article 71, Section I.

2.3.1. *Formal Precedent in Mexico*

The first category of judicial decisions, jurisprudence, has a vastly different meaning in Mexico than it does in the United States. American lawyers understand the term to describe the abstract science of law. In Mexico, on the other hand, *jurisprudencia* stands for judicial precedent: judicial decisions that establish rules of law or of interpretation of laws that are binding on judges who subsequently decide identical or similar cases. Under the rule of *stare decisis*, courts in the United States and elsewhere in the common law world are empowered, as a matter of legal tradition, to create rules of law whenever they issue formal opinions. *Stare decisis* is a hallmark of the common law system, and is partly responsible for the power of the judiciary in the United States.

In a civil law country such as Mexico, the creation of binding judicial precedent, not being part of the legal tradition, must be established by legislation. In the nineteenth century, sensing the need to empower the courts to oversee the proper enforcement of laws by government officials, Mariano Otero, a nineteenth-century Mexican jurist and statesman from Veracruz, promoted the adoption of a procedural law, the law of *amparo*, that introduced the concept of binding precedent (*jurisprudencia obligatoria*) into Mexico. The federal Congress adopted the concept of *jurisprudencia obligatoria* in the federal *Ley de Amparo* of 1882, and it has remained a part of federal *amparo* law ever since, gaining constitutional underpinning by amendments in 1950 to Article 107 of the Constitution.[22]

The starting point in understanding judicial precedent in Mexico is the general rule that judgments of Mexican courts bind only the parties to the litigation.[23] Exceptions to this rule, though important, nevertheless represent a small minority of all the judicial opinions—and even of published opinions—rendered by Mexican courts.

Technically, two forms of *jurisprudencia obligatoria* exist in the Mexican legal system: 'single-ruling' jurisprudence (formally called *jurisprudencia por contradicción de tesis*) and 'multiple-ruling' jurisprudence (simply called *jurisprudencia*). As already discussed, single-ruling jurisprudence (the creation of binding precedent resulting from a single court judgment) is commonplace in the United States, but very rare in Mexico. Only when the highest court in a judicial hierarchy (such as the Mexican Supreme Court, or a state's highest court) decides a matter in plenary session will the rule of *jurisprudencia obligatoria* require subsequent courts to follow the single court decision. Moreover, the Supreme Court may do so only in appeals involving contradictory rulings on a point of law by inferior courts or panels. For example, the Law of *Amparo* provides that a decision of the plenary of the Supreme Court which resolves contradictory rulings by different Chambers of the Supreme Court, or by two or more Collegiate Circuit Courts, constitutes jurisprudence.[24] The same principle

[22] On the law of *Amparo, see infra,* Chapter 8.
[23] *See* e.g. Mexican Constitution, Article 105, Section I (final sentence).
[24] *See Ley de Amparo Reglamentaria de los Artículos 103 y 107 de la Constitución Política de los Estados Unidos Mexicanos*, Art. 192 (D.O. 10 Jan. 1936, as amended D.O. 10 Jan. 1994).

holds at the state level. In Jalisco, for example, any decision by the plenary state Supreme Court in an appeal involving contradictory legal rulings of two or more of its seven chambers formally binds state judges in subsequent cases.[25] Mexican law permits only a small number of other judicial and quasi-judicial bodies to establish single-ruling jurisprudence in cases of contradictory legal rulings. These include the Superior Chamber of the federal Electoral Court[26] and the plenary of the administrative courts of some states.

The second type of jurisprudence, multiple-ruling jurisprudence, is more widespread in Mexico, yet very much unlike precedent in the United States. To form multiple-ruling jurisprudence, a court must apply, interpret, or rule upon a point of law the same way in a series of cases, without interruption by any contrary ruling on that point of law. For example, a point of law sustained by the plenary of the Mexican Supreme Court in five cases by a vote of at least eight justices and without any contrary ruling constitutes *jurisprudencia obligatoria.*[27] Since the federal Supreme Court may assert jurisdiction in cases involving state law matters, under *amparo* procedures,[28] this means that rules of state law may be established most effectively by the federal Supreme Court.[29]

The multiple-ruling requirement in Mexico explains the presence of the second category of judicial decisions, *tesis aisladas*. The first, second, third, and fourth rulings on a point of law by a Mexican court do not by themselves constitute precedent but are essential steps toward the formation of precedent. In this sense, these preliminary court decisions are important and worth noting, even though they may not be formally binding. In the Mexican legal system, these pre-precedential 'isolated' rulings (*tesis aisladas*) signal that they are distinct points of decided law that have not yet become (and may never become) *jurisprudencia obligatoria. Tesis aisladas* do not carry the full weight of legal precedent, yet they are often cited by attorneys as persuasive, in the same way that decisions from a parallel jurisdiction are cited as persuasive authority in the United States.

In contrast to jurisprudence and *tesis aisladas*, judgments (*sentencias* or *ejecutorias*) are judicial decisions that have no potential to become obligatory precedent. This may be either because they are issued by courts not authorized to establish precedent or because they involve subject matter on which the law does not allow precedent to be formed. For example, as discussed below, Mexican law does not empower federal District Courts (courts of first instance) to create judicial precedent.

[25] *See Ley Orgánica del Poder Judicial del Estado de Jalisco*, Art. 239 (*Periódico Oficial* June 1997).

[26] *See Ley Orgánica del Poder Judicial de la Federación*, Art. 232-III (D.O. 27 May 1995, as amended 22 Nov. 1996) [hereinafter LOPJF].

[27] *See* LOPJF, Transitorios, Artículo Decimoquinto; Law of *Amparo*, Art. 192.

[28] *See* Chapter 8 below at text accompanying notes 6–51.

[29] This is especially true since federal Supreme Court decisions are readily available throughout the country in published and electronic form, which is not the case for state court decisions.

Under Mexican federal law, only the Supreme Court,[30] Collegiate Circuit Courts,[31] the Federal Electoral Court,[32] the Federal Fiscal Court,[33] and the Superior Agrarian Tribunal[34] may issue *jurisprudencia obligatoria* in their respective fields of jurisdiction. At the state level, ordinarily a state's highest court, its electoral court (if it possesses one), and the superior chamber of its administrative tribunal will possess some legal authority to issue jurisprudence in their respective fields of competence. In the State of Mexico, for example, the Superior Court of Justice (*Tribunal Superior de Justicia*), the Electoral Court (*Tribunal Electoral del Estado de México*), and the Administrative Court (*Tribunal de lo Contencioso Administrativo del Estado de México*) all may issue precedent according to the terms set by law.[35] In the Federal District, only the Superior Chamber of the Administrative Court of the Federal District is authorized to issue *jurisprudencia obligatoria*.[36]

Mexican legislation also intricately delineates which courts and legal authorities are bound by judicial precedent. For example, jurisprudence announced by the plenary of the Supreme Court binds the plenary and chambers of the Court itself, all lower federal courts (including the Electoral Court), all military tribunals, all state courts, all courts of the Federal District, and all federal or local administrative and labour tribunals.[37] However, as in the United States, judicial precedent established by a Collegiate Circuit Court binds all Unitary Circuit Courts, District Courts, military tribunals, state courts, courts of the Federal District, and federal and state administrative and labour tribunals *within the territorial authority of the Collegiate Circuit Court issuing the decision*.[38] Precedent established by the Electoral Court is binding only upon its Chambers, the Federal Electoral Institute, and state electoral authorities.[39] The same pattern also holds under legislation in most states.

Legislation also sets the conditions under which judicial precedents may be overruled by later courts. This may happen:

(i) by a contrary legal ruling by a vote of eight of the eleven justices of the plenary of the Supreme Court, of four of the five justices of each Chamber of

[30] *See* LOPJF, Transitorios, Artículo Decimoquinto; *Ley de Amparo*, Art. 192.

[31] *See Ley de Amparo*, Art. 193.

[32] Both the Superior and Regional Chambers of the Electoral Court may issue jurisprudence. Jurisprudence of the Regional Chambers does not officially become obligatory unless it is ratified by the Superior Chamber. *See* LOPJF, Art. 232.

[33] *See Código Fiscal de la Federación*, Arts. 259–263 (D.O. 31 Dec. 1981, as amended D.O. 23 June 1997).

[34] *See Reglamento Interior de los Tribunales Agrarios*, Art. 19 (D.O. 13 May 1992, as amended D.O. 7 July 1997).

[35] *See Ley Orgánica del Poder Judicial del Estado de México*, Arts. 139–140 (*Gaceta del Gobierno*, 8 Sep. 1995); *Reglamento Interno del Tribunal Electoral del Estado de México*, Art. 10-VI (*Gaceta del Gobierno*, 6 May 1996); *Código de Procedimientos Administrativos del Estado de México*, Arts. 289–293 (*Gaceta del Gobierno*, 7 Feb. 1997).

[36] *See Ley del Tribunal de lo Contencioso Administrativo del Distrito Federal*, Arts. 89–94 (*Gaceta Oficial del Distrito Federal*, 19 Dec. 1995).

[37] *See Ley de Amparo*, Art. 192; LOPJF, Art. 235.

[38] *See Ley de Amparo*, Art. 193.

[39] *See* LOPJF, Art. 233.

the Court, or (in the case of Circuit Court judgments) by unanimous vote of a three-member Collegiate Circuit Court;

(ii) by a single contrary ruling by five of the seven judges of the Superior Chamber of the Electoral Court; and

(iii) in state court systems, by a contrary ruling by a vote of a supermajority (e.g. three-quarters) of the judges of the state's highest court.

2.3.2. *Informal Judicial Precedent in Mexico*

Although statutorily authorized jurisprudence (in both its single-ruling and multiple-ruling versions) explains much of the adherence to precedent that occurs in contemporary Mexico, it does not account for the practice of voluntary adherence to prior judicial rulings that most commentators believe and some jurists acknowledge is widespread in the Mexican legal system. Nearly twenty-five years ago, Professor Woodfin Butte concluded that non-jurisprudential 'precedent is becoming the more important concept; the formal binding character of *jurisprudencia* is frosting on the cake'.[40] If anything, Professor Butte's characterization has become more valid with the passage of time.

Once a court authorized to create precedent interprets a point of law a certain way in three or four cases, without any intervening ruling to the contrary, Mexican judges understand that, for practical purposes, such *tesis aisladas* are likely to be followed, even if they are not obligatory. Moreover, the traditional method of judicial appointment and promotion in Mexico has served to encourage loyalty to court rulings. Historically, Supreme Court justices and the judges of the highest court of each state have been responsible for judicial promotion within their respective spheres of authority.[41] The transplantation of appointment and promotion powers to judicial councils in recent years at the federal level and in a handful of states may reduce voluntary obedience to judicial rulings; however, pressure to conform is unlikely to evaporate quickly among the Mexican judiciary.

Second, even judgments (*sentencias*) that have no possibility of becoming jurisprudence often constitute a body of informal precedent in Mexico. As a result of the Otero formula which limits the effects of rulings in *amparo* cases to the litigants (see Chapter 10 below), a federal judge (particularly a District Court judge) can face nearly identical cases or sets of facts over and over again: perhaps hundreds of times a year. For example, due to the Otero formula, a judge sitting in the Federal District may be called upon to review a claim by a taxpayer that an administrative authority has denied the taxpayer a certain exemption, despite the fact that the judge has ruled in numerous prior cases involving essentially the same facts that the agency's denial of the exemption violates the Mexican Constitution. It is a natural reaction for a judge to adhere

40 Butte, *supra* note 17, at 328.

41 Henry W. Ehrmann, COMPARATIVE LEGAL CULTURES (N.J.: Prentice-Hall, Inc. 1976) 110: 'Where concern for promotion is a fact of judicial life, one will find an understandable reluctance to stand out as a nonconformist'.

to his or her prior rulings when deciding the new claim. Considering that, as of 1996, federal district judges in Mexico were responsible for handling over 1,600 cases annually (many of which, due to the Otero formula, present virtually identical facts), obedience to prior rulings has become essential. Importantly, in these instances Mexican judges do not cite or refer by name to their earlier rulings or those of another district judge with whom they have consulted (in the way a US district judge might do in a written opinion); instead, they follow precedent without express indication that they are doing so.

The Superior Court of Justice of the Federal District (the highest appellate court in the jurisdiction that includes Mexico City) presents another interesting example of how a judgment that will never become obligatory precedent can serve as a source of law in Mexico. As a matter of law, this Court possesses no authority to establish *jurisprudencia obligatoria*; however, federal law provides for the publication in Mexico City of the Annals of Jurisprudence (*Anales de Jurisprudencia*) which records the 'most notable' decisions announced by the Court.[42] One can reasonably expect that judges of the various chambers of the Superior Court as well as the lawyers who practise before them 'voluntarily' study and rely upon the Court's prior rulings in later cases.

Finally, it is worth noting that the utility of case-law in Mexico as a guideline to interpretation of the law is limited by the extremely general and summary nature of the published opinions, as discussed in Section 3.4., below.

2.4. Legal Doctrine (*Doctrina*)

Legal doctrine in Mexico consists of the body of concepts and ideas which legal scholars formulate and present in written studies, commentaries, interpretations, or opinions.[43] Doctrine can play an important role in the formation of Mexican law by influencing the evolution of constitutional reforms, legislation (particularly codes), and jurisprudence. In addition, by explaining or interpreting the law, doctrine establishes the meaning of legal provisions or norms and, in this way, influences the application of Mexican law. Indeed, Mexican law expressly permits legal authorities to consider doctrine when making concrete legal determinations.[44] Federal law provides that the training of all federal judges and those who aspire to the federal bench shall include the study of doctrine.[45]

[42] *See Ley Orgánica del Tribunal Superior de Justicia del Distrito Federal*, Art. 160 (*Gaceta Oficial del Distrito Federal* 7 Feb. 1996, as amended 17 May 1996) [hereinafter LOTSJDF].

[43] *See* Diccionario, *supra* note 11, at 1193.

[44] *See* e.g. *Código de Procedimientos Civiles para el Distrito Federal*, Art. 395 (D.O. 1 Sep. 1932, as amended 24 May 1996); *Código de Procedimientos Penales para el Distrito Federal*, Arts. 316, 379 (D.O. 29 Aug. 1931, as amended 13 May 1996); *Código de Procedimientos Civiles para el Estado Libre y Soberano de México*, Art. 149 (9 Aug. 1937, as amended 11 Sep. 1997).

[45] *See* LOPJF, Art. 95-III; *Acuerdo General Numero 11/1996, del Pleno del Consejo de la Judicatura Federal, que Fija las Bases para el Otorgamiento de Años Sabáticos*, Art. 3(a) (D.O. 14 June 1996); *Reglamento Interno del Tribunal Electoral del Poder Judicial de la Federación*, Art. 47-III (D.O. 16 June 1997).

A similar requirement applies to all judges of the Federal District.[46] However, it is important to note that doctrine *per se* does not carry the force of law.

Ultimately, the degree of influence that doctrine has on legislators and judges depends on the authority and prestige of the author and on the support given his or her views by other prestigious scholars. Mexican legal scholars are prolific, and several institutions and authors have significant sway over the development and interpretation of Mexican law. For example, the work of the Institute of Legal Research (Instituto de Investigaciones Jurídicas) of the National Autonomous University of Mexico (Universidad Nacional Autónoma de México, or UNAM) is highly reputed and respected in Mexico. The writings of Professor Héctor Fix-Zamudio, a pre-eminent Mexican constitutional law scholar, played a key role in reforming the Law of *Amparo* and in the eventual creation of the Federal Judicial Council in 1994.[47]

The importance of legal doctrine, as explained by scholars, in interpreting Mexican law reflects the civil law tradition. From the days of the Roman law glossators, civil law courts have given considerable attention to academic commentaries in interpreting the law. In continental Europe the study of law was undertaken at universities, rather than by the instruction of practising English lawyers at the Inns of Court. Since university studies emphasized academic legal doctrine, it is not surprising that the lawyers and judges trained at the universities would resort to academic writings. This tradition continues to the present day.

2.5. Custom (*Costumbre*)

In Mexico, as in the United States, custom is defined as a body of unwritten legal norms formed through a process of general or habitual practice.[48] Whereas the legislative process is a deliberative and centralized method of creating law, the process of producing custom is spontaneous and decentralized; thus, custom is thought to violate the principles of rationalism and systematization that underlie the civil law and Mexican legal system. As a result, the use of custom as a source of law is carefully proscribed by legislation. For example, the Federal Civil Code,[49] the General Law of Securities and Credit Operations

[46] *See* LOTSJDF, Art. 180-III.

[47] *See* Mario Melgar Adalid, *El Consejo de la Judicatura Federal* (Mexico City: Porrúa 1997) 88.

[48] *See* Diccionario, *supra* note 11, at 764. Technically, the formation of custom requires two elements: one of a factual nature (i.e. objective and repetitive human acts or practices) and the other of a normative nature (i.e. attribution of normative significance to those acts or practices).

[49] The Federal Civil Code allows custom to serve as a source of law in only four instances: (1) to define the rights of beneficiaries of mountain land to cut timber and use hatcheries, *see* Federal Civil Code Arts. 997, 999; (2) to establish the implied duties of contracting parties, *see ibid.* Art. 1796; (3) to set fees for professional services in the absence of an express agreement, *see ibid.* Art. 2607; and (4) to define the terms of land sharecropping and cattle raising sharecropping contracts, *see ibid.* Arts. 2751, 2754. Moreover, Article 10 of the Federal Civil Code provides that custom may not be raised as a defence for noncompliance with the law.

(*Ley General de Títulos y Operaciones de Crédito*),[50] and the Federal Labour Law (*Ley Federal del Trabajo*)[51] provide that custom may be considered only in cases not covered by the Constitution, legislation, treaties, or regulation. One exception is Article 2 of the Commercial Code, which provides: 'In the absence of an applicable provision in this Code, the common customs of merchants shall apply'. At the state level, custom is usually available as a source of law only in those instances expressly permitted by the civil code, mercantile law, and labour law. If not expressly recognized by legislation as a source of law, custom has no binding force.

2.6. International Treaties (*Tratados Internacionales*)

Mexican law applies the definition of treaties set forth in the Vienna Convention: 'an international agreement governed by international law and concluded in written form (i) between one or more States and one or more international organizations or (ii) between international organizations, whether that agreement is embodied in a single instrument or in two or more related instruments and whatever its particular designation'.[52] The central point of controversy in the Mexican legal system with respect to treaties is their status relative to internal law.

The language of the Vienna Convention appears to accord treaties primacy over contrary domestic law. Article 27(1) of the Convention provides: 'A State Party to a treaty may not invoke the provisions of its internal law as justification for its failure to perform the Treaty'. Article 46(1) further states: 'A State may not invoke the fact that its consent to be bound by a treaty has been expressed in violation of a provision of its internal law regarding competence to conclude treaties as invalidating its consent unless that violation was manifest and concerned a rule of its internal law of fundamental importance'. Consequently, some commentators believe that under Mexican law the balance tips in favour of the primacy of treaties.[53] However, in a recent decision, the Mexican Supreme Court, in plenary session, held that, in accordance with Article 133 of the Mexican Constitution, international treaties take precedence over contradictory domestic laws, federal or state, even if the federal or state law is adopted after the treaty. According to the Court, only the Mexican Constitution is superior to international treaties within the domestic legal system.[54]

[50] *See Ley General de Títulos y Operaciones de Crédito*, Art 2-III (D.O. 27 Aug. 1932, as amended 24 May 1996).

[51] *See Ley Federal de Trabajo*, Art. 17 (D.O. 1 May 1970, as amended D.O. 21 Feb. 1988) [hereinafter LFT].

[52] *See* Vienna Convention on the Law of Treaties between States and International Organizations or between International Organizations, Art. 2 (21 March 1986), 25 I.L.M. 543.

[53] *See* Smith, *supra* note 2, at 97 (explaining that 'Mexican jurists have argued that the courts would rule that the treaty prevailed despite subsequent contradictory legislation' and that '[w]ithout question, Mexico's legal tradition and political philosophy are more deferential to international law' than is the US legal tradition); Diccionario, *supra* note 11, at 3150.

[54] P.LXXVII/99, *Amparo en revision* 1475/98. *Semanario Judicial de la Federación*, vol. X, November 1999, at 46. The Court's opinion expressly overturned an earlier *tesis aislada* of

2.7. General Principles of Law (*Principios Generales del Derecho*)

In the Mexican legal system, general principles of law constitute an extremely amorphous source of law, unavoidably ill-defined as the broadest ethical, social, or natural law principles that can be discovered through the exercise of human reason and which form the foundation of the entire legal system.[55] Examples include the rule of law, the principle of legality, the principle of equality, and the principle of security.[56]

The obligatory or normative character of these principles does not depend upon official recognition by the State but inheres in the principles themselves because they define conduct that reason proves is essential for improvement of the human condition.[57] The positive law, as a work of reason, should conform to or incorporate these general principles, expressly or implicitly. Thus, one finds in Article 14 of the Mexican Constitution the following language: 'In civil suits, final judgments shall conform to the letter or interpretation of the law, and absent this shall be based on the general principles of the law'.[58] Other bodies of Mexican law specifically designate general principles of law as a supplementary source of law for use to fill gaps in the positive law.[59] However, it does not appear that the ability of legal authorities to rely upon general principles of law as a source of law depends on express authorization in the positive law (as is the case with jurisprudence and custom).

2.8. Regulations (*Reglamentos*)[60]

In the Mexican legal system, regulations are defined as norms of a general, abstract, and impersonal nature issued by the political executive for the purpose of clarifying, complementing, or amplifying the contents of legislation.[61] Thus,

1992 that had placed federal laws and treaties on the same plane. This is the 'last in time' rule that most commentators believe to be the law of the United States. *See* E. Allan Farnsworth, AN INTRODUCTION TO THE LEGAL SYSTEM OF THE UNITED STATES (New York: Oceana Publications, 3rd ed., 1996) 62.

[55] *See* Diccionario, *supra* note 11, at 2541–2542. *See also* de la Vega Benayas, *supra* note 16, at 1657 ('These principles are either those which inspired the legal system or those which constitute superior rules of justice that are active in the whole culture of the country').

[56] *See* Soberanes, *supra* note 15, at 65.

[57] *See* 'PRINCIPIOS GENERALES DEL DERECHO. SU FUNCIÓN EN EL ORDENAMIENTO JURÍDICO', SJF, Tercer tribunal Colegiado en materia administrativa del primer circuito. Queja 93/89. Semanario Judicial de la Federación, vol. III, Segunda Parte-2, January to June 1989, at 573.

[58] Nearly identical language appears in the federal Civil Code (Article 19), the federal Commercial Code (Article 1324), and the civil codes of all Mexican states.

[59] *See* e.g. LFT, Art. 17; *Ley General del Sistema de Medios de Impugnación en Materia Electoral*, Art. 95(e) (D.O. 22 Nov. 1996); *Ley Federal de los Trabajadores al Servicio del Estado, Reglamentaria del Apartado B del Artículo 123 Constitucional*, Art. 11 (D.O. 28 Dec. 1963, as amended 31 Dec. 1984).

[60] The body of Mexican law denominated 'regulations' includes general regulations issued by agencies, as well as a variety of forms of regulation, including internal regulations (*reglamentos interiores*), decrees (*decretos-presidenciales* or *decretos-administrativos*), and official Mexican norms (*normas oficiales mexicanas* or NOMs).

[61] *See* Diccionario, *supra* note 11, at 2751.

regulations closely resemble legislation; however, an essential difference between these two sources of law is the process by which each is created. The authority of the President of Mexico to issue regulations arises from Article 89-I of the Constitution which provides that he shall have the power '[t]o promulgate and execute the laws enacted by Congress, providing for their exact observance in the administrative sphere'. State constitutions contain similar language conferring this power on their respective state governors.[62]

Because regulations derive from legislation, in theory regulations that contravene the legislation from which they originate are void as a matter of law. As a practical matter, however, historically there have been few restraints on the ability of the Mexican President to promulgate regulations that contravene legislation. A notorious example involves a foreign investment regulation issued by President Salinas in 1989.[63] Many years earlier, in 1973, the Mexican Congress passed the Law to Promote Mexican Investment and Regulate Foreign Investment which, among other things, banned foreigners from owning more than a 49 per cent interest in a Mexican company and required that the Foreign Investment Commission (*Comisión Nacional de Inversiones Extranjeras*) approve all deviations from this formula.[64] To encourage foreign investment in Mexico, President Salinas sought to eliminate the restrictions on foreign investment but faced an un-cooperative Chamber of Deputies; in 1989 he proceeded to issue a new foreign investment regulation which, despite the statute, permitted foreigners in certain circumstances to own any proportionate interest in a Mexican business, without express approval from the Commission.[65] Although the regulation was arguably unconstitutional, its legality was not challenged.

The foregoing point is counterbalanced by a relatively recent incident. In 2001, the Mexican Supreme Court declared that regulations issued by the Fox Administration affecting the distribution and sale of electricity were unconstitutional.[66] The Court ruled that, in issuing the regulations, the executive had exceeded the limitations set by the Constitution and Law of Public Service Electrical Energy (*Ley del Servicio Público de Energía Eléctrica*) on the production and sale of electricity by private parties for public use.

In the past, regulations have not always been issued in a timely manner to support new legislation. This is particularly troublesome when the regulations involve the implementation of an important law. For instance, in 1993, the Mexican Congress adopted a new Foreign Investment Law, but there were no regulations issued to cover the new law until 1998.[67] During the interim, the

[62] *See* e.g. *Constitución del Estado de México*, Art 77-IV; *Const. Jalisco*, Art. 50-VIII.

[63] *See Reglamento de la Ley para Promover la Inversión Mexicana y Regular la Inversión Extranjera* (D.O. 16 May 1989) [hereinafter Reglamento].

[64] *See Ley para Promover la Inversión Mexicana y Regular la Inversión Extranjera*, Art. 5 (D.O. 9 Mar. 1973).

[65] *See* Reglamento, *supra* note 63, Art. V.

[66] *See El Foro, Análisis crítico, No 1*, 'Reglamento de la Ley del servicio público de energía eléctrica' (Mexico: Ed. Themis, Jan. 2003).

[67] D.O. 8 Sep. 1988. On the 1993 Foreign Investment Law, *see* Chapter 19 below at text accompanying notes 42–44.

government continued to adhere to the 1989 Foreign Investment Regulations, even though they were not adapted to the new law. Under these circumstances, both government agencies and affected parties are forced to extemporize, and tend to choose practical solutions to problems of implementation.

In 2000, in the waning days of the Zedillo administration, Congress created a Federal Commission on Regulatory Improvement (COFEMER) that has had a salutary effect not only on the quality of regulatory enactments, but also on the transparency of the regulatory process. As described below in Chapter 9,[68] COFEMER has done much to improve access to information regarding regulations, both existing and proposed.[69]

2.9. Equity (*Equidad*)

Mexican law defines equity according to the Aristotelian concept, as the prudential adaptation of general legal norms to concrete cases in a manner that serves the interests of justice.[70] Equity is thought to serve as a source of law in two senses. First, it may influence judicial interpretations of legislation or other positive law. Second, it may supplement the substantive law in cases where legislation or another form of positive law is lacking. The Federal Labour Law expressly provides for such a supplementary role for equity in labour disputes.[71]

2.10. Other Sources of Law in Mexico

Several remaining sources of law—administrative rulings (*resoluciones administrativas*), administrative agreements (*acuerdos administrativos*), circulars (*circulares*), and executive agreements (*acuerdos ejecutivos*)—should be mentioned for the sake of completeness. Administrative rulings are determinations by administrative bodies which involve the application or interpretation of administrative law in response to petitions by a private party or government agency. Administrative agreements are accords between two or more executive branch organs entered into for the purpose of facilitating the execution of their duties.[72] Circulars are internal communications of governmental bodies issued by the highest authority within the body to inferiors to notify them of instructions, orders, advisory opinions, or the interpretation of legal provisions.[73] Circulars are binding upon officials of the governmental body but not on private parties that deal with the officials. Executive agreements are secondary international accords concluded by the President of Mexico based upon his foreign affairs powers that, unlike treaties, do not require senatorial confirmation to take effect.[74] Although executive agreements are becoming more common in the Mexican legal system, they remain controversial because the circumstances

[68] On COFEMER, *see* Chapter 9 below at text accompanying notes 91–96.
[69] Information on COFEMER is available at www.cofemer.gob.mx (last visited Jan. 2004).
[70] *See* Diccionario, *supra* note 11, at 1293–1294. [71] *See* LFT, Art. 17.
[72] *See* Diccionario, *supra* note 11, at 92. [73] *See ibid.* at 461. [74] *See ibid.* at 740.

under which it is constitutional to evade senatorial approval of international accords are not clear.

3. The Hierarchy of Mexican Law

Having defined the Mexican versions of the major sources of law, the purpose of this section is to explain the relative importance accorded by the Mexican legal system to these sources of law. As explained more fully below, there is a difference between Mexico's formal hierarchy of law (that is to say, the ordering taught to entry-level law students in Mexico) and Mexico's practical hierarchy of law (the relative weight in fact given the sources of law). Moreover, the Mexican legal hierarchy is not static but dynamic. This section examines why judicial precedent is the most rapidly evolving element of Mexico's legal hierarchy.

3.1. Mexico's Formal Hierarchy of Law

In the early semesters of law school, Mexican students are introduced to the country's legal hierarchy (*jerarquía del orden jurídico*) beginning with Article 133 of the federal Constitution. This states: 'This Constitution, the laws enacted by Congress, and all treaties concluded by the President and approved by the Senate, shall be the Supreme Law of the Union. The judges of every State shall be bound to the said Constitution, laws, and treaties, notwithstanding any contradictory provisions that may appear in the constitutions or laws of the States.' Further, students read introductory law school texts which typically prioritize Mexican sources of law as set out in Table 3.1.[75]

Table 3.1: Mexican Legal Hierarchy

Legal Hierarchy in Federal Matters	*Legal Hierarchy in State Matters*
Mexican Constitution	Mexican Constitution
Federal Regulatory Laws, Codes, and Treaties	Federal Laws, Codes, and Treaties
Federal Ordinary Laws	State Constitution
Federal Regulations	State Regulatory Laws and Codes
Federal Jurisprudence, Federal Administrative Rulings	State Ordinary Laws
Doctrine, Custom, General Principles of Law, Equity	State Regulations
	Municipal Laws
	State Jurisprudence, State Administrative Rulings
	Doctrine, Custom, General Principles of Law, Equity

[75] *See* e.g. Raquel Gutiérrez Aragón & Rosa María Ramos Verástegui, *Esquema Fundamental del Derecho Mexicano* (Mexico City: Porrúa 12th ed. 1997) 55–65.

As discussed above, in accordance with a recent Supreme Court opinion, the hierarchy set out above may be questioned, insofar as it places federal laws on the same level as international treaties.[76]

These models are consistent with legal ordering in the classical civil law order. Under that legal tradition, legislation is the most important and only true source of law. Legislators strive to construct codes and statutes that are comprehensive, logical, and clear so that resort to alternative sources of law is unnecessary. To the extent that other law (custom, jurisprudence, doctrine, etc.) is used in the legal system, it is used only in the narrow ways expressly permitted by legislation. Furthermore, the role of the non-legislative powers in the creation of law (i.e. jurisprudence by judges and regulation by the executive) is minor and secondary as compared to that of the legislative authority.

On the surface, Mexico's formal hierarchy of law is not very different from that of the United States. In 1996, Professor Farnsworth described the hierarchy of US legislation as follows:

(i) US Constitution;
(ii) treaties and federal statutes;
(iii) federal executive orders, rules, and regulations;
(iv) state constitutions;
(v) state statutes;
(vi) state administrative rules and regulations; and
(vii) municipal charters, ordinances, rules, and regulations.[77]

Despite their different legal roots, the two legal systems have reached the point where statutory law plays a primary role and judicial decisions (precedent or *jurisprudencia*) play an important but lesser role. Moreover, because both countries are federal in organization the law generated by central authorities is accorded supremacy over law produced by states.

3.2. Mexican Legal Hierarchy in Practice

Mexican politics, history, and legal culture have led to deviations in practice from the formal hierarchy of Mexican law set forth above. First, due to the Presidents' traditional dominance over Mexican society, legal acts emanating from the executive branch are of far greater importance in Mexico than the country's formal legal hierarchy may suggest. During much of the twentieth century, even though legislation may have been enacted by the Mexican Congress, most laws were drafted by executive branch officials, who could use the monopolistic political power of the PRI to ensure the passage of bills. Furthermore, the Mexican President's express and implicit power to create law by regulation or decree is sweeping. There have been instances in Mexican history where executive regulation has prevailed over legislation, in disregard of

[76] *See* text accompanying note 54, *supra*.
[77] *See* Farnsworth, *supra* note 54, at 61–64.

constitutional provisions.[78] The use of presidential power, or *presidencialismo*,[79] to override legal formalities has given rise to increasing calls, both internal and external, for stricter adherence to the rule of law in Mexico.[80]

Second, although some lawyers in civil law countries concede that no code or legislation can provide for all legal eventualities that might arise in practice, there are probably more gaps, conflicts, and ambiguities in the positive law (and therefore more room for judicial manoeuvring) than many lawyers will openly admit. For example, one does not find in the formal Mexican legal hierarchy any acknowledgment of the role of informal precedent (*tesis aisladas* and judgments of courts of first instance) even though these are extremely important sources of Mexican law. Indeed, informal precedent may be even more important than *jurisprudencia obligada*, due to the relatively small number of the latter as a percentage of all court opinions.

Finally, a cursory comparison of the legal hierarchies of Mexico and the United States hides the fact that federal law in Mexico overwhelms state law. Despite the liberal roots of the Constitution of 1917, since the end of the nineteenth century, governmental power in Mexico has been concentrated in the federal government, with most important matters being managed from Mexico City. Mexico's colonial and post-colonial history of centralism partially explains the sweeping scope of the federal government's sphere of real power. In addition, Mexican *amparo*, the procedural device used in the federal courts to challenge the constitutionality of acts of federal and state officials, renders all state law subject to review by federal judges. Thus, even though federal case-law is not superior to state law in Mexico's formal legal hierarchy, federal judicial precedent routinely outweighs state law.

3.3. The Increasing Importance of Judicial Precedent

Historically, Mexican judicial precedent has suffered from two major afflictions not uncommon in civil law countries: lack of access to published judicial opinions, and highly adumbrated opinions (opinions that include few facts and bland conclusions of law). While there is no effort underway in Mexico to convert to US-style judicial opinions, with their detailed and sometimes lengthy discussions of facts and law, there has been an effort in Mexico to improve the accessibility of judicial opinions to judges, lawyers, and the public at large. Without easy access to decisions, it is unlikely that courts and lawyers will rely on judicial precedent.

[78] One example of this occurred on 1 September 1982, when President José López Portillo issued a decree 'nationalizing' (i.e. expropriating) all Mexican commercial banks, without taking steps to involve Congress. Despite the questionable legal nature of the act, very few *amparo* actions have challenged this presidential action. *See infra*, Chapter 20 at note 5.

[79] For a discussion of *presidencialismo*, *see infra*, Chapter 5.

[80] *See* A La Puerta de la Ley: El Estado de Derecho en México (Mexico: CIDAC, Rubio, L., et al., eds., 1994). The full text of this book is available at www.cidac.org 'CIDAC's Books Online' (last visited Jan. 2004).

The historic inaccessibility of Mexican judicial decisions has two features: (1) the general unavailability of the physical text itself, and (2) the lack of a consistent, easy-to-use indexing system. Decisions of the Mexican Supreme Court have been published in its official reporter, the Federal Judicial Weekly (*Semanario Judicial de la Federación*)[81] since 1871. Today, all *jurisprudencia* and *tesis aisladas* of the Court, its Chambers, and all Collegiate Circuit Courts are included in the *Semanario* and in two other official publications, *Jurisprudencia por Contradicción de Tesis* and *Informes de Labores*. However, publication of a decision in the *Semanario* has historically been delayed for months or even years after the date of a Supreme Court decision, and printed copies of the *Semanario* are expensive and not readily available.

In December 1988, the Supreme Court, in an effort to improve the distribution of its reporters, created an internal administrative office devoted exclusively to the compilation, organization, and dissemination of federal judicial decisions. In 1991, the Mexican Supreme Court began to take advantage of advances in technology to disseminate judicial decisions. In that year, the Court created a compact disc (CD-ROM-IUS) containing all federal jurisprudence and *tesis aisladas* from 1917 to 1991. In its present version, IUS 6, the disc contains 190,000 *tesis aisladas* and jurisprudence from 1917 to November 1996 and sells for only about one hundred pesos (approximately US$10).[82] In 1994, the newly constituted Supreme Court swept into power by constitutional reforms intended to strengthen the judiciary[83] and immediately undertook an ambitious programme to make federal judicial decisions more accessible, stressing the use of electronic databases.[84]

[81] The *Semanario Judicial de la Federazión* is divided into a series of nine time periods or epochs (*épocas*), each containing numerous volumes, with decisions organized chronologically, not by subject matter. Beginning in the sixth epoch, each volume was subdivided into several parts (one for the decisions of the plenary of the Court, one for those of each of its chambers, and one for the decisions of the Collegiate Circuit Courts), and the pages of each part were numbered separately. There is no consistent indexing system from 1917 to the present. 'They not only change from Epoca to Epoca, but even from volume to volume within the same Epoca.' The epochs are as follows: first epoch (1871–1874), second epoch (1881–1889), third epoch (1890–1897), fourth epoch (1898–1910), fifth epoch (1918–1957), sixth epoch (1957–1968), seventh epoch (1969–1988), eighth epoch (1988–February 1995), and ninth epoch (March 1995–present). The first four epochs are called *jurisprudencia historica* and have no binding force because they pre-date the 1917 Constitution. Binding precedent under the current Constitution begins in 1918 with the fifth epoch. *See* Francisco A. Avalos, *The Mexican Legal System* (New York: Greenwood Press 1992) 21.

[82] *See* Suprema Corte de Justicia de la Nación, Publicaciones (available at http://www.scjn.gob.mx/). In 1996, the Supreme Court released a new compact disc containing jurisprudence and *tesis aisladas* relating specifically to the federal Civil Code.

[83] *See infra*, Chapter 6, text accompanying notes 9, 92–97.

[84] One can now access Supreme Court decisions on the Internet and through LEXIS. A LEXIS database, MXJTF, includes case reports of the *Tribunal Fiscal de la Federación*. The Supreme Court's website (http://www.scjn.gob.mx/ site last visited Jan. 2004) includes all *jurisprudencia* and *tesis aisladas* from 1917 to the present, both of which are updated daily. MXJUR database on LEXIS includes all decisions of the Mexican Supreme Court from 1917 to 1997 and is updated monthly.

The general availability of Supreme Court and Collegiate Circuit Court decisions is not found at other judicial levels in Mexico. Decisions by Unitary Circuit Courts and by federal District Courts (courts of first instance) are not published. State judicial bulletins periodically publish a small percentage of the opinions of the highest court of the state, but these bulletins are not widely distributed throughout the country. The passage of the Federal Transparency Law, discussed below in Chapter 9,[85] should make it possible for interested parties not only to receive copies of judicial opinions at these levels, but also to obtain other documents filed with the courts. That possibility is much less useful than systematic publication, of course.

Although researching Mexican case-law has not in any sense become easy, technological progress and the commitment displayed by the Mexican Supreme Court to improving accessibility to federal judicial decisions demonstrate a trend towards the strengthening of the judiciary.[86] Nevertheless, the difficulty of researching case-law constitutes a serious obstacle to the development of judicial precedent as a way of making interpretations of the law more consistent and application of the law more predictable.[87]

3.4. The Lack of Detailed, Well Reasoned Published Opinions

To say that *jurisprudencia* is becoming more available does not cure a separate shortcoming that makes Mexican case-law of limited use in many instances, even to experienced lawyers. The *jurisprudencia obligatoria* and *tesis aisladas* published in the *Semanario Judicial de la Federación* contain virtually no detailed description of the facts or issues presented, nor do they include a full explanation of the court's decision. They are mere summaries, usually more general than the squib notes that precede judicial opinions published in the US case reports. This is true even of important Supreme Court opinions. The failure to compose and publish full opinions is not due to laziness on the part of the courts, but rather to the overwhelming case-load faced by the federal courts,[88] making it virtually impossible to spend time composing a detailed opinion in every case. The development of *jurisprudencia* as a truly useful guide to interpretation would be helped immensely by changing that practice, permitting the courts to concentrate on publishing full opinions in a smaller number of cases.

[85] *See* Chapter 9 below at text accompanying notes 97–104.

[86] The electronic databases cited *supra* at note 84 help overcome many of the traditional indexing deficiencies. For example, the IUS 6 comes with powerful search software, which allows one to search for precedent by keyword, phrase, or chamber and epoch (*Sala-Época*). One can conduct similar searches in the databases found at the Supreme Court's website and at LEXIS' MXJUR database.

[87] In November 1996, the Supreme Court announced new guidelines intended to make case reporting clearer, simpler, and more rational. Acuerdo Numero 5/1996 del Tribunal Pleno de la Suprema Corte de Justicia de la Nación, del 18 de Noviembre 1996, Relativo a las Reglas para la Elaboración, Envio y Publicación de las Tesis que Emiten los Órganos del Poder Judicial de la Federación (D.O. 26 Nov. 1996).

[88] *See* below Chapter 6 at text accompanying notes 20–21.

4. Making Legal Determinations under Mexican Law

Once a Mexican court has established the facts of a specific legal dispute,[89] the court decides the legal issues involved by considering the various sources of Mexican law in the manner and sequence dictated by the hierarchy of law. The Mexican judge approaches the task by viewing the positive sources of law—the constitution, legislation, treaties, and regulations—as a unified, coherent, and rationally structured legal edifice. The judge's objective is 'to examine the edifice to see where in its structure his own problem will fit precisely, and if not precisely then most neatly and logically'.[90] As necessary and as permitted by legislation, the judge may resort to 'unwritten' law—jurisprudence, doctrine, custom, general principles of law, or equity—to supplement or fill gaps in the edifice.

Because the Constitution and legislation are themselves the framework of Mexican law, the judge will first scour these sources of law in search of applicable provisions. Often, the judge will find a broad but relevant provision in the Constitution and then search for a code or statute corresponding to that provision. Upon locating the relevant code or statutory provision(s), the judge, as appropriate, will seek out related regulations. If the applicable provisions and regulations are sufficiently specific and clear to conclude the legal analysis, the judge will make a straightforward decision applying the law. This probably describes the majority of legal determinations made in Mexican courts.

In those cases in which the outcome under the positive sources of law is not obvious, the Mexican judge will seek language in the positive law indicating which alternative sources of law he may consider. For example, in a case governed by the Federal Civil Code the judge would obtain guidance from Federal Civil Code Article 19 which provides: 'Civil cases shall be resolved in conformity with the letter of the law or its judicial interpretation. In the absence of law, civil cases shall be resolved in accordance with general principles of law.' In a federal labour dispute, the judge would rely upon Article 17 of the Federal Labour Law which states: 'Absent express provision in the Constitution, this law or its regulations, or in the treaties referred to by Article 6, the general principles that derive from said laws, general principles of law, general principles of social justice that derive from Article 123 of the Constitution, jurisprudence, custom, and equity may be taken into consideration'.

Unlike Mexican judges, who must look to legislation for guidance when they encounter no applicable constitutional provision, legislation, or regulation,

[89] The assumption that courts have no discretion to determine the facts of a case, that fact-finding is an automatic or objective function of judges, is as false in Mexico as it is in the United States. In many cases, the real power of Mexican courts is the ability to define the facts of a dispute because the application of legal rules is contingent on the presence or absence of various facts. The ability of courts of first instance to decide facts is somewhat constrained by the nature of civil law adjudication, which potentially permits all questions of fact to be reviewed *de novo* on appeal; however, unlike US trial judges, Mexican court of first instance judges are not constrained by the factual determinations of juries. *See generally* the discussion *infra* in Chapter 10 at text accompanying note 2.

[90] Butte, *supra* note 17, at 316.

US judges in such circumstances immediately seek relevant precedent without needing to be instructed or authorized by legislation to consider precedent.[91] If a US judge finds one decision of a higher court directly on point, the doctrine of *stare decisis* mandates that the judge apply the precedent. However, if no applicable precedent exists, the US judge is free to create an appropriate rule of law based on custom, doctrine, equity, policy, reason, or other legitimate considerations.

A Mexican judge directed by legislation, such as Article 19 of the Federal Civil Code, to consider judicial interpretation or jurisprudence as a source of law will search the decisions of the court(s) authorized by legislation to create such jurisprudence. If he finds applicable jurisprudence, he, like his US counterpart, is required to follow it, not because of the judicially created doctrine of *stare decisis* but because legislation commands him to do so. If he finds no such case-law, he turns to general principles of law as legislation requires but, off the record, does not hesitate to consider pertinent *tesis aisladas* or prior judgments of other judges. Unlike US judges, the Mexican judge who encounters a useful *tesis aislada* or judgment may follow it, not because he is legally bound to do so (unless, of course, it is that special breed of Mexican jurisprudence, *jurisprudencia por contradicción de tesis*) but because doing so serves other purposes, such as bringing certainty to the law or for his own self-preservation or promotion within the judiciary.

If a Mexican judge finds a legislative provision that governs a case but the provision is vague or contains an ambiguous term, such as 'good faith' or 'impossibility of performance', the judge will seek clarification in prior judicial decisions (jurisprudence, *tesis aisladas*, or judgments) and/or academic writings (doctrine).[92] Similarly, a Mexican judge directed by legislation such as Article 17 of the Federal Labour Law to consider custom, equity, and 'general principles of social justice' will turn to judicial decisions and/or doctrine to define what those sources of law require in a given context. Historically in Mexico, doctrine has played a larger role than judicial decisions in such situations; however, the increasing importance of case-law and the increasing reliance, noted above, on informal precedent suggests that the balance may already have shifted in favour of judicial decisions. In contemporary Mexico, doctrine is more influential in legislative chambers than it is in judicial chambers.

As this discussion reveals, the core difference between the way legal determinations are made in Mexico and in the United States is the dependence of Mexican judges on legislative instruction or direction in exercising the judicial function. This difference is consistent with the theory that under the civil law judges are

[91] 'Here lies the difference between the common law and civil law—that the foundation of the judicial function rests in the laws, whether codified or not. [...] The supremacy of the written law is consecrated in the Constitution and in the *Código Civil* itself'. de la Vega Benayas, *supra* note 16, at 1651.

[92] In interpreting legislation, the judge may also consult the statement of motives (*exposición de motivos*), usually prepared by the executive branch, which accompanies a bill being introduced in Congress.

little more than expert clerks; as noted by Professor Merryman many years ago, in practice the difference may be more formal than real.[93] Substantial room for the exercise of discretion remains in the Mexican judicial decision-making process. This is true, for example, when the judge is called upon to decide that a particular constitutional provision, legislative provision, or regulation governs a case; to interpret what the law means in the context of the facts presented; or to find the unwritten law when the legislative edifice requires supplementation. At each of these points in the decisional process, the Mexican judge, precisely like his American counterpart, seeks to do what is practical or right. This reality, together with the growing role of precedent in Mexican law, confirms what Professor Butte concluded long ago, that '[t]he differences which strongly separated civil and common law in the past are tending to become blurred and to disappear'.[94]

[93] *See* Merryman, *supra* note 1, at 47.

[94] Butte, *supra* note 17, at 315.

4

Federalism and Centrism

The Mexican Constitution of 1917, like its predecessors of 1824 and 1857, established a federal republic composed of individual states (*estados*), each possessing the power to adopt a state constitution and to enact laws that do not contradict specific provisions of the Federal Constitution. Article 115 requires the states to adopt forms of government that are 'republican, representative, popular, with the free municipality as the basis of their territorial division and political and administrative organization'. Article 43 names the thirty-one states of the federal republic (from Aguascalientes to Zacatecas) and the Federal District (*Distrito Federal*, comprising most of Mexico City) as the constituent parts of the union.[1]

Following the US model, the Mexican Constitution assigns specific powers to the federal government, and adds a 'savings clause' that reserves to the states all remaining powers that are not specifically assigned to the federal government.[2] In both constitutions, the balance of legislative and executive power between the states and the federal government, while defined in broad constitutional outline, has been open to redefinition throughout the history of each country. As a consequence, debates over the extent to which the states or the federal government would exercise power dominated the early political history of both Mexico and the United States.[3]

[1] At the time of the 1917 Constitution, the federation consisted of 28 states and the Federal District, along with two federal territories administered by the federal government: Baja California and Quintana Roo. The constitution was subsequently amended to add the states of Baja California Norte (1952), Baja California Sur (1974), and Quintana Roo (1974). The Mexican Federal Republic of 1824 consisted of 17 states. UNAM, Constitución Política de los Estados Unidos Mexicanos (Comentada) (Mexico: Porrúa, 1998) at 518–523.

[2] *Compare* Article 124 of the Mexican Constitution ('The powers not expressly granted by this Constitution to federal officials are understood to be reserved to the States') with the Tenth Amendment to the US Constitution ('The powers not delegated to the United States by the Constitution, nor prohibited by it to the States, are reserved to the States respectively, or to the people').

The addition of the term 'expressly' in the Mexican Constitution would appear to make the legal system more resistant to the encroachment of federal power into state matters than is true under the US Constitution. This has not been the case, however: during much of its history, and particularly during the twentieth century, Mexico has been characterized by a more centralized form of government than exists in the United States. Article 124 is nevertheless important, and the federal government is careful to cite specific constitutional authority to support legislation in new areas. Furthermore, as we shall *see*, one of the reasons for the large number of amendments to the Mexican Constitution has been to provide express constitutional authority for federal action.

[3] *See* Carpizo, J., 'Sistema Federal Mexicano', in 3 Gaceta Mexicana de Administración Pública Estatal y Municipal 81 (Jul–Sep 1981) ('The question of federalism was the central problem of Mexico from 1823 to 1856') [authors' translation].

At first glance, the similarity of Mexican federalism to the federal structure of the United States is obvious. Even the name given to the country, the Mexican United States (*los Estados Unidos Mexicanos*), seems to emphasize the similarity. Superficial appearances are deceiving, however. While it is true that the US Constitution served as an important model for the Mexican Constitution,[4] the manner and degree to which the federal/state balance of power has evolved differs considerably from the US model. State legislative power is an important component of the US legal system, and vigorous debates over state versus federal power are by now largely matters of historical interest. The importance of state legislative power in US public and private life is well established, even if particular ramifications of the debate wax and wane.

In Mexico, 'a country with a precarious and fictitious federal regime',[5] discussions of federalism dominate a large space in the political terrain. The need for greater decentralization has been a constant theme addressed by the federal government in Mexico even during the height of the PRI's centralist, authoritarian control. Rather than simply abandoning legislative power to the states, however, the federal government's usual approach has been to establish a plan or programme to 'co-ordinate' the decentralization, either within the federal government or between the federal government and the states. The overall result has been to maintain ultimate federal control over the states, exercised by the federal bureaucracy. Specific examples of this are discussed below.

Under Mexico's system of presidentialism (*presidencialismo*), discussed in the following Chapter, 'federal control' meant centralized control by the federal executive of government at all levels of society. As discussed in Chapter 5 below, this monolithic system of central control began to crack in the mid-1980s. Unlike previous presidents, Carlos Salinas de Gortari (1988–1994), a Harvard-educated economist, took concrete steps to reduce the central government's grip on many aspects of society. Changes in the political system—a weakening of the consensus that granted the PRI political control—forced this change. At the same time, President Salinas deserves credit for exercising a vision to effectuate real change in this regard, rather than merely paying lip service to the need for decentralization. As discussed below, his successor as president, Ernesto Zedillo (1994–2000) continued the move towards decentralization in the fields of education and public health. In 2001, by promoting reform of Article 2 of the Federal Constitution, the administration of President Vicente Fox (2000–2006) has taken important steps to assure that indigenous matters would be subject to state and local, rather than federal, power.[6]

Despite the gradual relaxation of federal power, the federal government in Mexico continues to weigh heavily in all areas of law. The continuing imbalance of federal over state power, a legacy of colonial law, is due in part to the

[4] Tena Ramírez, F., DERECHO CONSITUCIONAL MEXICANO (Mexico: Pórrua, 26th ed, 1992) at 102.

[5] *Id.* at 122.

[6] The reform was published in D.O. 14 Aug. 2001. For a discussion of the reforms to Article 2, *see* Chapter 7 below at text accompanying notes 24–29.

federal government's overwhelming share of the general fiscal power, and consequent control over public funding; in part to the availability of *amparo* as a federal remedy for all wrongs, state or federal; and in part to the centralization of the federal government and its ministries in Mexico City. These themes are discussed in more detail below. As Mexico continues to move away from an authoritarian, centralized form of government towards a more pluralistic, decentralized democracy, an important feature of this movement is likely to involve an increase in the states' abilities to govern local concerns without depending on federal resources. How this will happen, and how quickly it will take place, is open to question.

1. Historical Background

The colonial experience of New Spain provides an important background to Mexican federalism. As discussed in Chapter 1 above, until the waning days of the Spanish colonial empire, legislative and economic power were concentrated in central authorities: the *virrey* in New Spain, institutions in Spain such as the *Casa de Contratación* and the *Consejo de las Indias*, and ultimately the king himself. Beginning with the ill-fated reformist Constitution of Cádiz of 1812, however, the Spanish *cortes* introduced a decentralizing factor in colonial administration. The *cortes* abolished the position of *virrey*, and instead created provincial entities (*diputaciones provincials*) under the authority of deputies (*diputados*). Each *diputación* was to be independently administered by a group of seven *diputados*, who were to report directly to the *cortes*. From six original *diputaciones*, the number of *diputaciones* expanded until, by 1823, twenty-three *diputaciones* had been created in New Spain.[7]

The Constitution of Cádiz was eventually suspended by Ferdinand VII in 1813; nevertheless, the idea of separate provinces, governed with a certain autonomy, had been planted. When Mexico did finally achieve independence from Spain in 1822, the leaders of the independence, reacting against the oppressive centralism of the colonial regime, were ready to embrace a federal form of government based on the decentralist precedent of the *diputaciones provinciales*.[8] The adoption of federalism was a way to counteract the former centralist administrative authority of the colonial period.

While spurred by decentralist sentiment, the selection of a federal form of government at the same time served a unifying function by tying the separate territories of Mexico together in a single political union. So strong was the reaction against central authority that, in the early days of independence, a real danger existed that the separate states of the proposed union would resist any

[7] Carpizo, *supra* note 3 at 83–84.

[8] Ortega Lomelín, R., El Nuevo Federalismo (Mexico: Pórrua, 1988), at 32–33, citing Benson, N.L., La Diputación Provincial y el Federalismo Mexicano (Mexico: Colegio de México, 1955).

political union and would instead declare their independence. (The map of Mexico, with a few political turns, might have resembled the map of Central America, with numerous small, independent states with occasional political and territorial conflicts.) Indeed, in 1822 Campeche and Tabasco declared their independence, forming the Federal Republic of Yucatán; in 1823, Guadalajara and Oaxaca announced their separation from Mexico, and Querétaro and Zacatecas declared they would not be bound by acts of the constitutional congress convened in Mexico City. The constitutional congress (*constituyente*) of 1823 was able to entice the separate territories into a political union by adopting a federal model that limited the powers of the central government and left the states with a great deal of autonomy.[9]

The US and Mexican colonial experiences provide interesting contrasts. In the United States, the selection of a federal form of government was a natural way to bring together separate colonies that, from their initial establishment and throughout the colonial period, had been administered separately and held separate identities. By contrast, in Mexico federalism was a way to decentralize a strongly centralist tendency in political administration,[10] while also offering a politically acceptable form of government to local political leaders who threatened to break off into separate, independent states.

This background is necessary to an understanding of the Constitution of 1824. In reacting against the centralist model of colonial administration, the drafters of the 1824 constitution established a federal republic in which the power of the central (federal) government was severely curtailed.[11] The implementation of a strongly decentralized, federal form of government was more instinctive than scientific. In attempting to mould a federal republic, Mexico's early political leaders had little precedent to guide them. They did have the US constitutional example, but federalism was still a new invention in the United States, and there

[9] Carpizo, J., ESTUDIOS CONSTITUCIONALES, 2nd ed. (Mexico: UNAM, 1983) at 90: the federal republic 'was a necessity and actually served to unite a country that was breaking apart' [authors' translation]. *See also* González Oropeza, M., 'Introducción: El Federalismo', in J. Smith, ed., DERECHO CONSTITUCIONAL COMPARADO MÉXICO—ESTADOS UNIDOS, vol. I (Mexico: UNAM, 1990) at 219.

[10] Tena Ramírez, *supra* note 4 at 102–109.

[11] On 1 February 1823, opponents of the establishment of an empire proclaimed their rebellion against the self-declared Emperor Agustín Iturbide in a document, the *Acta de Casa Mata*, from which Mexican federalism was to take root. The Mexican Constitution was finally published on 4 October 1824. The pride of the Constitutional Congress in its achievement can be seen in the following announcement that accompanied the publication of the Constitution: 'every society should provide for itself laws that are analogous to their own customs, locality and other circumstances; . . . [should] give to its industry all available incentives, without the difficulties imposed on local industry by the colonial administration or any similar government that, located at enormous distances from the people, would lose sight of the interests of the people; . . . [should] deal with domestic matters without leaving the limits of its own state; [should], in one word, enter upon the full enjoyment of the rights of free men'. *Manifiesto* of the General Constitutional Congress of 4 October 1824, quoted in Cue Canovas, A., EL FEDERALISMO MEXICANO (Mexico: Mex Editores, 1960) at 44–45. *See also* Barragán, J., EL PENSAMIENTO FEDERALISTA MEXICANO: 1824 (Mexico: Universidad Autónoma del Estado de México, 1983); Barragán, J., PRINCIPIOS SOBRE EL FEDERALISMO MEXICANO: 1824 (Mexico: D.D.F., 1984).

was no clear understanding of the concept and its application. Only after decades of political debates, legislative action, and judicial resolutions of the US Supreme Court did federalism acquire meaning in the United States. As in the United States, Mexico had its federalist/anti-federalist contests during the first half of the nineteenth century, with Miguel Ramos Arizpe, a liberal lawyer and political theorist from Coahuila, leading the federalist forces, and Lucas Alamán, a conservative mining engineer, historian, and statesman from Guanajuato, promoting the centralist argument.

The centralists eventually prevailed, largely because the federal government in power at the time of the 1824 Constitution was so anaemic as to produce chaos. The federal government lacked any significant taxing power, while double taxation emanating from the states became a problem. States burdened local commerce with restrictive regulations, and local political bosses began to abuse the monopoly of political power. Within ten years, the vacuum at the centre of the political system resulted in a growing sentiment in favour of a more centralized form of government.[12] Coincidentally, a charismatic military leader, General Antonio López de Santa Anna, also appeared on the national scene. Santa Anna would control Mexican political life until the mid-1850s.

Santa Anna was first elected President of Mexico in 1833: the first of eleven occasions in which he would serve as president from 1833 to 1855.[13] A conservative *caudillo* and centralist, Santa Anna dissolved the Congress in 1834 and a new, conservative Congress abolished the federal system and in 1836 adopted a new constitution, known as the *Siete Leyes* (for the seven principal sections of the document). The *Siete Leyes* established a unitary form of government, abolishing the states altogether and replacing them with departmental committees (*juntasdepartamentales*) with more circumscribed legislative powers.[14] The new Constitution infuriated political leaders in the outlying territories, especially in Texas (then part of the Mexican state of *Coahuila y Texas*), where a group of English-speaking colonists took umbrage at the loss of local control over matters such as the legality of slavery, which the central forces opposed.

It is hard to characterize the period between 1836 and 1857 as either centralist or federalist. Conservative party advocates (centralists) and liberal party advocates (federalists) vied for power, but in reality the political system was too chaotic for any group to establish authority for any significant period of time.

[12] Tena Ramírez, *supra* note 4 at 111.

[13] Santa Anna loved *becoming* president, but appeared to loathe the frustrations of daily office. On ten different occasions from 1834 to 1854, Santa Anna overthrew existing presidents to claim power, each time retiring to his *hacienda* in Veracruz within a matter of weeks. On the life of Santa Anna, *see see* Yañez, A., SANTA ANNA, ESPECTRO DE UNA SOCIEDAD (Mexico: Oceano, 1982); Fuentes Mares, J., SANTA ANNA, EL HOMBRE, 4th ed., (Mexico: Grijalbo, 4th ed, 1982); Bustamante, C., APUNTES PARA LA HISTORIA DEL GOBIERNO DEL GENERAL DON ANTONIO LÓPEZ DE SANTA ANNA (Mexico: FCE, 1986); Trueba Olivares, A., SANTA ANNA, 3rd ed., (Mexico: Jus, 3rd ed, 1958).

[14] Ortega Lomelín, *supra* note 8 at 39–40; Carpizo, *supra* note 9, at 85; Carpizo, *supra* note 3 at 84.

During this period, Mexico was to lose one-third of its territory in the war of Texas independence (1836) and the United States–Mexican War of 1846 to 1848. General Santa Anna was to return from 'retirement' or exile on ten different occasions between 1836 and 1853, to take control of the presidency and establish order. He never succeeded in stabilizing the country, however, and the *Siete Leyes* never became an effective constitutional instrument.[15]

In 1856, after the final ouster of Santa Anna by liberal forces, a new *constituyente* was formed and, with liberal/federalist representation a majority, the result—the Constitution of 1857—was the creation of a federal structure with powers balanced between the federal government and the states.

In form, the 1857 Constitution is the clear model for the current Constitution of 1917 that governs Mexico. Liberal, anti-clerical, and federalist, the 1857 Constitution established a unicameral legislature[16] and a federation of states along the lines of the 1824 Constitution. Unlike the earlier constitution, however, the 1857 Constitution more clearly distributed the balance of power between the states and the federal government.

Unfortunately, the adoption of the 1857 Constitution did not signal the beginning of a stable and effective federal regime in Mexico. Internal conflicts continued: the War of Reform from 1858 to 1860 pitted conservatives against liberals, and the French Intervention (1861 to 1867) threatened to abolish democracy altogether. Only after the election of ousted President Benito Juárez to a new term in 1867 did a semblance of stability emerge. Nevertheless, for the remainder of the century, and until the overthrow of President Porfirio Diaz (1876–1910), Mexican constitutional history consisted of the gradual centralization of power under a dictator who was constitutionally suspect.[17]

By the end of the *Porfiriato*, Mexico had come almost full circle, from a centralized, authoritarian colonial regime to a centralized, authoritarian, quasi-federal regime. The Mexican Revolution would remove the dictator and restore a greater measure of democracy, but the Constitution of 1917—strictly federal in form, with significant legislative power vested in the States—would prove to be highly centralist in practice, as Mexicans gradually came to accept that the concentration of political power was necessary to overcome regional *caciquismo* and promote stability and growth.[18] To provide a measure of control over such

[15] In 1846, liberal forces took advantage of the political disarray occasioned by the US occupation to abolish the *Siete Leyes* and call for adherence to the 1824 Constitution. In the *Acta de Reformas* of 1847, a constituent assembly restored the system of states and returned to the federalist form. Carpizo, *supra* note 9 at 86.

[16] The Constitution was amended in 1874 to add a Senate.

[17] In the words of Jorge Carpizo, 'the long administration of General Porfirio Díaz turned the constitution . . . into a *traje de luces* [bullfighter's costume], a document to exhibit on public occasions, but without any real effectiveness'. Carpizo, *supra* note 3 at 86. For an interesting historical analysis of the *Porfiriato* by a leading Mexican lawyer/statesman of the period, *see* Rabasa, E., La Evolución Histórica de México (Mexico: UNAM, 1986) at 104–139.

[18] Palacios Alcocer, M., 'Las Entidades Federativas y La Constitución', in Estudios Jurídicos en Torno a La Constitución Mexicana de 1917 en su Septuagésimo Quinto Aniversario (Mexico: UNAM, 1992) at 104–139.

concentration of power, the *constituyentes* of 1917 came up with a very simple formula: the concept of no re-election. What they did not foresee, perhaps, was the effectiveness of political leaders in forging a single, broadly based political party that would blur the effective distinctions between state and federal government.

2. Federalism and the Constitution of 1917

As with the 1857 Constitution, the Constitution of 1917 established a federal system patterned after the constitutional structure of the United States. The division of federal/state power is identical in form in both Constitutions: certain clauses grant specific powers to the federal government in matters of national concern, and a general savings clause reserves all remaining power to the states. In comparing the Mexican savings clause with its US model, one sees that they are almost identical: the Mexican Constitution provides: 'Article 124. The powers not *expressly* granted by this Constitution to federal officials are understood to be reserved to the States' (emphasis added).[19]

The US Constitution provides, in Amendment X: 'The powers not delegated to the United States by the Constitution, nor prohibited by it to the States, are reserved to the States respectively, or to the people'.

In both the United States and Mexico, the constitutional structure could have led to a circumscribed federal government with the bulk of political power in the states. History has proven otherwise in both systems, however. In part because of the natural tendency for political leaders to seek national solutions to national problems, both the United States and Mexico have developed legal systems in which the federal government plays a dominant role. The principal differences between the two countries are the degree of federal monopolization of power (the federal government is even more predominant in Mexico than in the United States), and the way in which federal domination came about (in Mexico, through legislation and constitutional amendment, brought about by political monopolization of the PRI; in the United States, through legislation and constitutional interpretation). Both of these differences are explored below.

Due to Article 124, the key to examining the balance of federal/state power lies in the enumeration of specific grants of power to the federal

[19] Some experts make much of the inclusion of the term 'expressly' in the Mexican version of the savings clause. *See* Carpizo, *supra* note 9 at 94. The implication is that the power of the federal government is more circumscribed by the Mexican Constitution than by its US counterpart. In practice, there is little reason to make such a distinction, especially in light of the fact that certain express grants of power in the Mexican Constitution are extremely broad. *See*, for instance, Article 73, section X (power to legislate over 'commerce'); or Article 73, section XXIX-D (power to legislate on 'national planning for economic and social development'). In addition, Article 73, section XXX constitutes a broad 'necessary and proper' clause that allows the federal Congress to adopt any laws that are deemed necessary to carry out assigned powers.

government. The most important provisions are found in Article 73 (powers of the Federal Congress); Article 89 (powers of the president); and Articles 103 and 104 (jurisdiction of federal courts).[20] Of these, the most important by far is Article 73.

Article 73 is one of the most frequently amended articles of the constitution,[21] precisely because, as discussed below,[22] the federal government has sought to expand its legislative power and has needed the legitimizing grant of express powers required by Article 124. The numerous sections of Article 73, far from limiting the power of the Federal Congress, provide multiple grants of broad federal authority that allow Congress to act in virtually every sphere of society. Thus, among other powers, Article 73 authorizes the Congress:

—to legislate throughout the Republic on hydrocarbons, the mining industry, the motion picture industry, commerce, games of chance and lotteries, brokers and financial services, electrical and nuclear power, and to enact labor laws (section X);
—to legislate on law of the sea (section XIII), on matters of general health (section XVI), and on communication and transport (section XVII);
—to legislate on public security matters, and establish bases of coordination between federal, state and local governments in this area (section XXIII);[23]
—to establish and maintain schools throughout the republic (section XXV);
—to levy taxes on a broad array of goods and services (section XXIX-A);
—to enact laws concerning population settlements, national development planning, foreign investment and environmental protection (sections XXIX-C to XXIX-G);
—to enact laws in order to coordinate the responsibilities of federal, state and local agencies in matters of police protection (section XXIX-I);
—and to legislate on sports (section XXXIX-J).[24]

In addition, Article 122 of the Constitution authorizes the Congress to legislate for the Federal District, except on those matters expressly reserved to the Legislative Assembly (*Asamblea Legislativa*) of the Federal District.[25]

One of the most important assignments of legislative power is found in Article 73, section X, which gives the federal government the exclusive power to legislate on matters of commerce, an extremely broad field of activity that

[20] *See also* Articles 27, 74, 76, 105, 106, 122, 123, 130, and 132. Trigueros, 'El Federalismo en México: Autonomía y Coordinación de las Entidades Federadas', in DERECHO CONSTITUCIONAL COMPARADO MEXICO—ESTADOS UNIDOS, vol. I, *supra* note 9 at 247, 249.

[21] On amendments to Article 73 generally, *see* DERECHOS DEL PUEBLO MEXICANO. MEXICO A TRAVES DE SUS CONSTITUCIONES (Mexico: H. Cámara de Diputados. LV Legislatura, 1994) VIII, at 9–146.

[22] *See* text accompanying notes 31–39 *infra*.

[23] This Section was added in 1994, D.O. 31 Dec. 1994.

[24] Sections XXIX-I and XXIX-J were added to Article 73 by reforms published in D.O. 28 Jun. 1999.

[25] The power to act as the 'local legislature' for the Federal District was formerly granted to the Congress in Article 73, section VI. However, since constitutional reforms in 1993 (D.O. 25 Oct. 1993), those powers are contained in Article 122 of the Constitution, which was amended to provide for a sharing of legislative power between the federal Congress and the Legislative Assembly of the Federal District.

includes commercial transactions, negotiable instruments, the law of business organizations, securities regulation, consumer protection, economic competition, financial services, bankruptcy, maritime commerce, insurance, and intellectual property, among others.[26] The federal monopolization of commercial law occurred in 1883, when Congress amended the existing Constitution to establish exclusive authority of the federal government to legislate on matters of commercial law (*derecho mercantil*).[27]

The establishment of a single set of commercial laws under federal authority distinguishes Mexican business law from its US counterpart. While federal laws regulate the US economy, most private business transactions in the United States are governed primarily by state law; there is no federal law on incorporation, negotiable instruments, or commercial transactions in general. For the past fifty years, a nationwide movement in the Untied States towards the harmonization and codification of state commercial laws has helped to remove legal differences between states. Nevertheless, lawyers in the United States must be careful to specify in contracts and commercial instruments the law of the state to be applied, and must study that law to determine its appropriateness for the contract. In Mexico, with a single set of commercial laws for the entire country, the lawyer's work in this regard is simplified.

In addition to a broad grant of power over commerce, Article 73, section X, also establishes exclusive federal jurisdiction to prescribe and administer labour laws.[28] In the original version of Article 73, the federal Congress and the states shared the power to legislate on labour matters, and the states of Veracruz and Yucatan quickly followed suit by passing labour legislation in 1918. However, in 1929, during the presidency of Emilio Portes Gil, Congress amended Article 123 to make labour law an exclusively federal matter.[29]

When one adds the constitutional authority to legislate on planning for national economic and social development (Article 73, section XXIX-D, added in 1983) one can easily appreciate the overwhelming importance of the federal government in economic legislation. Furthermore, as we shall see below,

[26] The grant of legislative authority over commerce would appear to a US lawyer to make redundant the specific grants of legislative authority over other matters mentioned in the section, such as motion pictures, banking and credit, hydrocarbons, and mining. The reason for the apparent redundancy may lie in the perception of Mexican lawyers that *comercio* translates to general commercial law—*derecho mercantil* and the *Codigo de Comercio*—and does not necessarily include specialized economic activities such as those mentioned. The addition of the specific activities removes any uncertainty over the power to adopt federal legislation in these important industries.

[27] During the *Porfiriato*, the federal government perceived the existence of multiple state laws as burdens on the development of a modern, nationwide economy. *See generally* Chapter 18 below, text accompanying note 2. On the federal monopolization of commercial law generally, *see* Mantilla Molina, R., DERECHO MERCANTIL (Mexico: Porrúa, 26th ed., 1989); Cervantes Ahumada, R., DERECHO MERCANTIL (Mexico: Herrero, 1984).

[28] On labour law generally, *see* Chapter 13 below.

[29] De Buen, N., DERECHO DEL TRABAJO, VOL. I (Mexico: Porrua, 7th ed., 1989) at 349–357. Article 123 was amended in 1960 to add Section B, covering labour relations with government workers, and the workers of the government of the Federal District. D.O. 5 Dec. 1960.

even though the federal and state governments share taxing powers, the federal government dominates in this area as well.

In addition to assignments of federal power, the Constitution of 1917 includes important limitations on state power in Title Five ('Of the States of the Federation'), Articles 115 to 122. Article 115 establishes guidelines for the treatment of municipalities, and is discussed below. Article 116 establishes certain rules for the conduct of state government. Articles 117 and 118 prohibit the states from imposing burdens on interstate commerce by prohibiting certain types of state action—for instance, the levying of duties on interstate commerce or on the movement of persons.[30] Article 121 provides that state laws shall not have effect outside state territory, but also includes a 'full faith and credit' clause that requires states to give effect to the public acts of other states.

3. Concurrent Power to Legislate

Under the Mexican Constitution, certain matters are assigned exclusively to the federal government (e.g. commerce, Article 73, section X); some matters are assigned exclusively to the states (e.g. the adoption of laws to award professional licences, Article 5, para. 2); other matters are prohibited to the federal government (e.g. under Article 124, all matters reserved to the states); and yet other matters are prohibited to the states (e.g. restrictions on interstate commerce, Article 117).[31] In a number of important areas, however, the states and the federal government share jurisdiction to legislate. Mexican constitutional law experts make fine distinctions between the types of shared jurisdiction, distinguishing examples of coincidental jurisdiction (*facultades coincidentes*) from coexistent jurisdiction (*facultades coexistentes*).[32]

Facultades coexistentes involve instances in which the Constitution assigns separate responsibilities to each entity over the matter in question. Thus, for instance, Article 73, section XVII, assigns to the Federal Congress the power to enact laws on interstate highways (*vias generales de comunicación*), leaving to the state governments the power to legislate on local roads pursuant to the savings clause of Article 124.

Facultades coincidentes refer to instances more closely approximating what US constitutional experts would call concurrent jurisdiction.[33] In the field of

[30] Article 117, section VIII, para. 1, prohibits states from borrowing funds directly from foreign creditors.

[31] Carpizo, *supra* note 9 at 94–96.

[32] *Id.* at 94, 96; Ortega Lomelín, *supra* note 8 at 91–95.

[33] There is some debate among Mexican constitutional scholars whether the concept of concurrent jurisdiction (*facultades concurrentes*) exists in Mexican law. Jorge Carpizo understands the term to apply to instances in which the federal and state governments both have the power to legislate; in such instances, federal legislation that is adopted annuls any state laws that are also applicable. (*Cf.* the US constitutional law doctrine of preemption.) According to Dr Carpizo, concurrent jurisdiction in this sense does not exist. Federal law can never supplant state law; instead, one must conduct an exercise to determine which authority has jurisdiction to act. Carpizo, *supra* note 9 at 97–98.

social welfare, for example (e.g. health,[34] education, housing and human settlements, and environmental law) the state and federal governments share concurrent jurisdiction to legislate. If a conflict between the state and federal provisions should arise, the supremacy clause would dictate the prevalence of federal law.

To say that power is shared between the state and local governments would give a mistaken impression, however. In most areas, it is the federal government that determines the precise balance of state and federal authority in cases of concurrent jurisdiction, through the passage of enabling legislation (*leyes generales*).[35] By itself determining the balance, the Federal Congress has tended to endow the federal government with the bulk of legislative power and executive authority.

The educational system provides a good example of this. Federal, state, and local authorities share concurrent power over education (Articles 3 and 73, section XXV); however, the federal government is empowered by Article 3, section IX, to distribute powers over education between the three levels of government. Not surprisingly, the applicable federal legislation, the *Ley Federal de Educación* and the *Ley para la Coordinación de la Educación Superior*,[36] grants a virtual monopoly of the federal government over public education at the primary and secondary levels. For this reason, all public schools in Mexico (other than institutions of higher learning) are federally funded, and all public school teachers are federal employees. In education, therefore, 'concurrent jurisdiction' translates to virtual federal monopoly.[37]

Ortega Lomelín reviews the debate on whether *facultades concurrentes* exist, and fails to find a distinction between the concepts of *facultades concurrentes* and *coincidentes*. Unlike Dr Carpizo, he assumes that both terms apply to the same concept: the notion that both the federal and state governments have the power to legislate over the same matter. Neither entity can exclude the other. Ortega Lomelín, *supra* note 8 at 91–92.

[34] The health law field represents an interesting case in the allocation of federal and state power. Article 73, section XVI of the Constitution assigns to the Federal Congress the power to legislate on general health matters, leaving to the states the power to legislate on local health matters. This would appear to be an example of *facultades coexistentes*. However, over the years the federal government, through acts of legislation, has gradually increased the subject area of 'general health' and reduced the field of 'local health' matters. In 1983, by amendment to Article 4, general health became a matter of concurrent jurisdiction, with both state and federal government involvement, under the terms dictated by the federal *Ley General de Salud*. Ortega Lomelín, *supra* note 14 at 94–95. *See* the case study, 'La Descentralización de los Servicios de Salud', *id.* at 441–547.

[35] As Dr Carpizo points out, in many instances, the Constitution expressly authorizes the Federal Congress to determine the practical application of jurisdiction by federal, state, and local governments. *See* e.g. Article 3, section IX (Federal Congress to determine federal, state, and local responsibilities over education). Carpizo, *supra* note 9 at 96. Dr Carpizo refers to this as *facultad coincidente en forma restringida*, since the Federal Congress in effect controls the freedom of states to determine the extent to which they can legislate.

[36] D.O. 29 Dec. 1978.

[37] On 19 May 1992, President Carlos Salinas de Gortari announced a new programme to loosen the federal grip on public education and to decentralize education. Through this programme, the state governments became responsible for the administration of educational institutions (schools, laboratories, libraries) in each state, which were previously under the supervision of the Ministry of Education (*Secretaría de Educación Pública*) (SEP). This was

The subject of concurrent jurisdiction is of more than academic interest. As discussed below,[38] issues of federal/state power are likely to become increasingly important in Mexico as the centralized, authoritarian system recedes. States are already beginning to legislate more aggressively in fields formerly left to the federal government, such as environmental matters.[39] To the extent that state legislation differs from federal legislation in the same field, questions of pre-emption will arise. For the moment, however, the federal government will continue to determine the balance of federal and state power by exercising its authority to pass general laws in areas of concurrent jurisdiction. As long as the political system is controlled from the centre, federal authority is not likely to be challenged seriously.

4. The 'Federalization' of Mexican Law

4.1. The Political Foundations of Federal Power

As just shown, the constitutional structure of Mexico supports the weight of a vast federal government. The overwhelming power of the federal government is due to political and economic factors as well as legal ones. As we have seen, the Constitution of 1917 broadly assigns important legislative powers to the Federal Congress. In economic affairs, the federal government assumed extensive power by virtue of economic and commercial regulation as well as by direct ownership of economic and social agencies.[40] Constitutional scholars have identified other centralizing factors in Mexico as well:[41]

4.1.1. The establishment of Mexico City as a Federal Territory under the Direct Authority of the President and Congress

The *Distrito Federal* houses almost 10 per cent of the nation's population, and accounts for a large percentage of Mexico's economic activity. Until constitutional reforms on 22 August 1996, the federal government directly controlled the Federal District (D.F.); the President appointed the *regente*, or chief of the government for the D.F., and local officials had virtually no legislative authority. The President used this power of appointment not only to control the politics of the Federal District, but also as an indirect means of awarding jobs to political allies. The situation changed dramatically in 1993, when Article 122

considered a 'federalization' of education rather than decentralization, because the programme gave the states control only over the operation of educational establishments, while the federal government retains ultimate financial control, as well as control over the evaluation and regulation of education in the country (including the publication and distribution of textbooks, the preparation of educational programmes, and the distribution of materials). *See* Acuerdo Nacional para la Modernización de la Educación Básica, D.O. 19 May 1992, and PROGRAMA PARA LA MODERNIZACIÓN EDUCATIVA 1989–1994 (Mexico: SEP, 1989).

[38] *See* Section 7 below. [39] *See* text accompanying notes 78–87, *infra*.

[40] On the role of the government in the economy, *see* Chapter 12, below.

[41] Carpizo, *supra* note 3 at 133–135.

of the Constitution was amended to establish that the Federal District would, for the first time in history, elect the *regente*, who is now called the *Jefe de Gobierno del Distrito Federal*. The first election of *Jefe de Gobierno*, conducted by direct vote of the residents of the Federal District, took place in 1996, and resulted in the election of a political opponent of the PRI: Cuauhtémoc Cárdenas, a former PRI functionary and leader of the PRD Party. This represented a major fissure in the solidity of the PRI's political monopoly.

The Mexican Congress still has the power to legislate on subjects related to the Federal District, except for those subjects expressly conferred on the Legislative Assembly, which consists of sixty-six members who are also elected by the general population. The President continues to have power to propose to the Congress legislation relating to the Federal District. The 1996 constitutional amendments also reformed the public administration of the Federal District, through the establishment of centralized and decentralized agencies.

4.1.2. *Federal Jurisdiction over Labour Law*

The federal government monopolizes labour law, through the exclusive grant of authority in the Constitution to the Federal Congress to legislate on labour matters. In addition, labour unions have tended to ally themselves with political parties at the national level, and historically the unions have themselves had a centralist outlook.[42]

4.1.3. *The Use of Federal Courts, through the Federal Writ of* Amparo, *as the exclusive means to protect individual rights*

Through the widespread use of *amparo*, federal courts have exercised considerable nugatory powers over state government officials.[43]

4.1.4. *The Federal Monopolization of Numerous Social and Economic Activities*

Many important economic activities—hydrocarbons (oil and gas), public health (IMSS), electricity—are carried out directly by 'decentralized agencies' of the federal government (IMSS, PEMEX, Compañia Federal de Electricidad, etc.).

[42] On Mexican labour law generally, *see* Chapter 13 below.

[43] The writ of *amparo* is examined in more detail in Chapter 8 below. *Amparo* provides a procedure for individuals to sue in federal courts in order to contest official acts of government, either state or federal, that allegedly violate the laws or the Constitution. This has led to a centralization and federalization of judicial power, to the point of creating a bottleneck in the administration of justice, since only federal courts can declare official acts unconstitutional. Ortega Lomelín, *supra* note 14 at 187; Tena Ramírez, F., 'Del Federalismo a la Federalización: Trayectoria del Sistema Federal Mexicano', in 1 Revista Jurídica de la Sociedad de Alumnos de la Escuela Libre de Derecho 1 (1970), at 209. *See* Fix-Zamudio, H. and Cossío, J.R., El Poder Judicial en el ordenamiento mexicano (Mexico: FCE, 1996) at 138–153.

Ortega Lomelín points out that the *jurisprudencia* of the Supreme Court indicates that state courts are not entitled to pass on the constitutionality of state or federal laws under the Federal Constitution, since this is an exclusive domain of the Supreme Court. The result is to further centralize judicial power, by making the Supreme Court the exclusive arbiter of the constitutionality of state laws. He criticizes this interpretation, citing Article 133 in support of the proposition that local judges should adhere to the Constitution. Ortega Lomelín, *supra* note 8 at 194.

As discussed below in Chapter 12, the number of such agencies was dramatically reduced by the economic restructuring of the 1980s.

4.1.5. *Control of the Banking and Monetary System*

With the exclusive authority to legislate in all aspects of financial and monetary affairs (there are no state banking laws), the federal government controls the financial system. In addition, the *Banco de México*, a semi-autonomous agency of the federal government, is the country's central bank and thus controls monetary policy. Federally owned development banks, such as *Nacional Financiera* and BANOBRAS, discussed below in Chapter 20, control the allocation of credit for publicly funded projects.

4.1.6. *Other Areas of Federal Control*

One might add to this list the predominance of federal taxing power, to the detriment of state revenues, addressed in more detail below;[44] and the federal control of elections at all levels of government, as discussed in the following Chapter.

This consolidation of federal power, or 'federalization' as one of Mexico's leading constitutional scholars has called it,[45] has been made possible by the centralization of political power that took place in the 1920s and 1930s.[46] The states were incorporated into the centralized political system by political controls established within the ruling political party, thus removing any serious regional resistance to the centralization of government power. Whenever regional political leaders did begin to show some resistance to central authority, the Federal Congress (acting at the behest of the President in each case) could revert to an unusual constitutional procedure, known as removal from power (*desaparición de poderes*) and simply remove the un-cooperative state officials from office. Article 76, section V grants to the Federal Senate the exclusive power 'To declare, whenever all the constitutional powers of a state have disappeared (*desaparecido*), that the occasion has arisen for the appointment of a provisional governor, who shall call elections in accordance with the constitutional laws of the said State'.[47]

In other words, the Senate may, without the need to prove specific acts of wrongdoing, by majority vote, remove a state governor from office. Conceived originally as a way of dealing with a power vacuum that might occur in a state,[48] *desaparición de poderes* has been applied much more widely, to solve

[44] *See* text accompanying notes 106–134 *infra*.

[45] *Cf.* Tena Ramírez, *supra* note 4 at 201.

[46] *See* Chapter 1 above, Section 4.3.

[47] *See also* the *Ley Reglamentaria de la Fracción V del Artículo 76*, D.O. 29 Dec. 1978.

[48] In 1874, the Constitution of 1857, originally adopted with a unicameral legislature, was amended to add a Senate, and to endow the Senate (Article 72, Part B, section V) with the power to declare *desaparición de poderes* and to replace state governors. The impulse for the inclusion of such a provision came in 1872, when the governor of the State of Yucatán refused to vacate his office at the end of his elected term. *Desaparición de poderes* was first used in 1879, when the Senate voted to replace the governor of Colima. The provision was used 17 times from 1879 to 1914. González Oropeza, Manuel, La Intervención Federal en la Desaparición de Poderes (Mexico: UNAM, IIJ, 1983) at 45–61.

corruption in state government, to reconcile electoral problems, and—in many instances—'to serve as a corrective measure in cases where the personal and institutional relations between the state and federal governments are strained'.[49] On many occasions, the provision has been used simply to bring into line state governments that were unwilling to support the policies of the federal government.

In a detailed survey of the use of *desaparición de poderes*, Manuel González Oropeza identified sixty-three cases from 1917 to 1975 in which the Senate either employed the provision to replace a recalcitrant governor, or threatened to use the provision as a means of securing the state government's acquiescence in federal policies. Of these, only on three occasions did legitimate grounds exist for the Senate to act; in all the remaining cases, the Senate merely acted at the President's bidding to remove opposition.[50]

Constitutional scholars have identified the Senate's use of this power as a significant political problem in the federal system.[51] The provision was last used formally in 1975, in the state of Hidalgo, and since the President no longer has *de facto* control of Congress, the power to control state governors has waned. Nevertheless, *desaparición de poderes* remains a potential threat to state government officials. Thus, for instance, on three occasions in the 1990s newly elected governors, candidates of the PRI, 'voluntarily' resigned in the face of political demonstrations against their election.[52]

4.2. Federalization by Constitutional Amendment

As in the United States, the power of the federal government in Mexico increased and became more clearly defined in constitutional terms over a period of many years. In the United States, the development of a national economy in the first quarter of the twentieth century dictated a legislative response at the federal level. Even so, it was not until the New Deal of President Franklin D. Roosevelt that the federal government began to legislate aggressively. The immediate result was a constitutional crisis, as the US Supreme Court declared that the federal government had exceeded its constitutional mandate and was therefore unconstitutional.[53] Only after changes in the composition of the Supreme Court was the enlargement of federal legislative power constitutionally recognized. This recognition came about by a process of judicial interpretation,

[49] González Oropeza, Manuel, La Intervención Federal en la Desaparición de Poderes, *supra* note 48 at 88.

[50] *Id. See also* González Oropeza, M., 'Introducción: El Federalismo', in Derecho Constitucional Comparado México: Estados Unidos, vol. I, *supra* note 9 at 219, 225.

[51] Carpizo, J. and Madrazo, J., 'Derecho Constitucional', in El Derecho en México: Una Visión de Conjunto, vol. III (Mexico: UNAM–IIJ, 1991) at 1701, 1732–1733.

[52] On state and federal elections generally, *see* Chapter 5 below, section 3.2.3.

[53] *See* e.g. *Carter v. Carter Coal Co.*, 298 US 238 (1936); *Schechter Poultry Corp. v. United States*, 295 US 495 (1935). *See also* Leuchtenberg, W., The Supreme Court Reborn (New York: Oxford University Press, 1995).

rather than by constitutional amendment. In this process, the Supreme Court has served at times as a brake on the consolidation of federal power.

In Mexico, the process of federalization has occurred through repeated amendments to the Constitution. Throughout the twentieth century, the Federal Congress, at the bidding of the President, was able to enlarge its own powers by amending the Constitution whenever the Chief Executive decided that more federal power was needed. During the seventy-one years that the PRI controlled the federal legislature, and all the state legislatures, the President never experienced any real difficulty assuming more centralized powers.[54] The demise of *presidencialismo* with the election in 2000 of Vicente Fox as President has dramatically altered the ease of constitutional amendment.[55] Insofar as the federal government's domination of the states is concerned, however, the die has been cast: federal power continues to overwhelm state power, and unless this is reversed—especially as regards the states' anaemic taxing power—this is likely to remain the reality in Mexico.

Reforms to the Constitution of 1917 for the purpose of 'federalizing' governmental functions began soon after the Mexican Revolution ended. In 1921, Article 73 of the Constitution was amended to establish federal control over public education; the *Secretaría de Educación Pública* was created, and its head, José Vasconcelos, led an educational and cultural revolution in Mexico.[56] Numerous reforms followed, establishing federal control (in some cases exclusive control) over labour law, the mining industry (1929), agrarian reform (1934), the film and electricity industries (1935), labour adjudication (1942), gambling and lotteries (1947), land use and human settlements (1976 and 1983), national economic planning (1983), and environmental regulation (1987).[57] More recently, the Mexican Constitution has been amended to extend federal control over public security,[58] sports,[59] and the preservation of archeological artefacts.[60]

In all, Article 73, which largely defines the limits of federal legislative power, has been amended forty-six times since 1917;[61] section X alone has been amended ten times from 1929 to 1982.[62] When added to the 375 additional

[54] *See generally* González Oropeza, *supra* note 9 at 222.

[55] *See generally* Cossío, J.R., CAMBIO SOCIAL Y CAMBIO JURÍDICO (Mexico: ITAM/Miguel Angel Porrúa, 2001) at 213–290.

[56] On Vasconcelos, *see* Haddox J., VASCONCELOS OF MEXICO: PHILOSOPHER AND PROPHET (Austin: University of Texas Press, 1967); De Beer, G., JOSÉ VASCONCELOS AND HIS SOCIAL THOUGHT (New York: Columbia University, 1965); Crowley, F.J., THE CONSERVATIVE THOUGHT OF J. VASCONCELOS (Fl. University of Florida, 1963); A MEXICAN ULYSSES: AN AUTOBIOGRAPHY (Bloomington, Ind.: Indiana University Press, 1963; trans. and abridged by W. Rex Crawford).

[57] Carpizo, *supra* note 3 at 134–135.

[58] Amendment to Mexican Constitution, Article 73, Section XXIII, D.O. 31 Dec. 1994.

[59] Amendment to Mexican Constitution, Article 4, D.O. 28 Jun. 1999.

[60] Amendment to Mexican Constitution, Article 73, Section XXV, D.O. 21 Sep. 2000.

[61] Orozco Henríquez, 'El Sistema Presidencial en el Constituyente de Querétaro y su Evolución Posterior', in EL SISTEMA PRESIDENCIAL MEXICANO (ALGUNAS REFLEXIONES) (Mexico: UNAM-Instituto de Investigaciones Jurídicas, 1988), at 1, 59. *See also* www.diputados. gob.mx/leyinfo (last visited July 2003).

[62] Ortega Lomelín, *supra* note 8 at 102.

amendments that have been made to the Constitution, these amendments have had a powerful centralizing effect.[63]

4.3. The Importance of State Laws in Specific Areas

As the foregoing pages have emphasized, most important legislation in Mexico is federal. Nevertheless, the states do retain important legislative powers, especially in the area of private law. As a consequence, just as in the US federal system, the first question that a lawyer must ask when presented with a legal problem is which jurisdiction is responsible for the matter. Is it a federal matter, or a state matter? If it is a state law matter, which state exercises the jurisdiction to pass laws covering the activity?[64] Only after deciding which set of laws apply can the lawyer begin to solve the matter.

The states retain significant power to legislate in private law matters, and also share with the federal government (as described above) concurrent powers to legislate in public law matters. This is not to say, however, that the states have exercised these powers to create individualistic legal regimes. On the contrary, there has been a strong tendency, dating back to the last century, for the states to copy federal models in enacting their own laws. This may be natural in a country where a large percentage of the most respected legal scholars and practitioners have traditionally been found in one place, Mexico City, which is the seat of federal power. Thus, for instance, the civil codes of the Mexican states have generally been modelled after the Civil Code for the Federal District, a federal creation.[65]

Beginning in the 1970s, the federal government began to promote a more co-operative form of federalism by promoting the concept of concurrent legislative powers in certain matters. Thus, in 1983, Article 4 of the Constitution was amended to provide that the federal and state governments would concurrently share the power to legislate on matters of general public health. Article 73 was amended to add concurrent powers over human settlements (section XXIX-C, added in 1976) and over environmental protection (section XXIX-G, added in 1987). In these areas as well, however, the tendency has been for state legislators to use federal legislation as the model. For example, as discussed in the following section of this Chapter, the environmental legislation of most states is

[63] According to Ortega Lomelín, *supra* note 8 at 107, only one constitutional amendment was intended to have a decentralizing effect: the 1983 amendment adding paragraph 4 (originally para. 3) to Article 4, which authorizes the states to legislate along with the federal government on matters of general health, previously granted to the federal government only by virtue of Article 73, section XVI. For amendments to the Constitution generally, *see* www.juridicas.unam.mx/infjur/leg/constmex/hisxart.htm (last visited Jan. 2004).

[64] In matters of private law, the Civil Code of each state itself determines the persons and activities to which it shall apply, including its territorial effect. *See* Chapter 22, sections 2.2 and 2.3. *See also* Chapters 15–17 below. Article 121, section I, of the Constitution prevents the application of state laws, including the civil codes, beyond each state's borders.

[65] *See infra*, Chapter 14, Section 4.2, and Chapter 15 at text accompanying notes 3–4.

copied from the federal *Ley General del Equilibrio Ecológico y la Protección al Ambiente*.[66]

In all, the tendency to copy federal law has had a strong centralizing effect on state laws. In this way, Mexico accomplishes much more easily the harmonization of state laws that is the goal of non-profit organizations that promote the adoption of model laws in the United States.

Before examining areas in which state laws are important, a brief explanation of the form of state governments might be useful. Article 116 of the Federal Constitution requires the states to be established with a division of powers between the executive, legislative, and judicial branches. The same Article establishes that governors are to be elected for six-year terms; representatives to state legislatures are to be elected according to proportional representation (the larger the state, the greater the number of *diputados*). State legislative power is exercised by a single legislative body, the *Congreso del Estado*; a few states experimented with bicameral state legislatures, but reverted to the unicameral model. State constitutions do not usually define the legislative powers of state legislatures; because of Article 124 of the Federal Constitution, the state legislatures possess whatever legislative authority is not assigned to the federal government.[67]

To a large extent, the state legislative process reflects the federal model. State governors possess the power of legislative initiative, and most state legislation originates in the governor's office; even so, many state laws are taken from models provided by federal legislation that precedes them.

4.3.1. State Law: Civil, Criminal, and Procedural Codes

Private law subjects in Mexico—family law, contract law, civil liability (tort law), inheritance, property law—are primarily matters of state law; the same is true of criminal law.[68] Thus, each of the states has adopted its own civil code (*Código Civil*), criminal code (*Código Penal*), code of civil procedure (*Código de Procedimientos Civiles*), and code of criminal procedure (*Código de Procedimientos Penales*).[69] There is also a 'Civil Code for the Federal District' (the *Código Civil del Distrito Federal*) and a 'Criminal Code for the Federal District' (*Código Penal del Distrito Federal*),[70] which apply only in the *Distrito Federal*.

66 D.O. 28 Jan. 1988. 67 Tena Ramírez, *supra* note 4 at 136.

68 As in the United States, most criminal law in Mexico is a matter of local, i.e. state, concern; federal criminal laws exist in both countries covering areas of federal concern (e.g. crimes against federal property, on federal territory, violations of federal laws). In Mexico, the Federal Criminal Code also applies to offences within the Federal District, which holds almost 10% of Mexico's population. *See generally* Chapter 11 below.

69 For legislation of specific states, *see* www.juridicas.unam.mx (last visited Jan. 2004).

70 While the Constitution does not specifically grant the Federal Congress the power to adopt a criminal code, it does have the power, by virtue of Article 73, section XXX, to adopt criminal laws and sanctions related to federal legislation. Carpizo, *supra* note 3 at 102–104. In addition, Article 73, section VI grants the federal Congress the power to legislate in matters pertaining to the Federal District, including civil and criminal matters, which are not expressly conferred on the Legislative Assembly of the Federal District.

There has been no formal uniform law movement in Mexico for the purpose of harmonizing the civil and criminal codes of the states.[71] This may be surprising to non-Mexican lawyers, who might expect that the existence of separate codes for such important private law areas would cause conflicts and uncertainty, especially in the commercial field. Nevertheless, there are two important reasons why harmonization of state laws has not been emphasized by Mexican scholars and political leaders to the same extent as it has in the United States. First, the civil, criminal, and procedural codes in almost all of the Mexican states are modelled on the federal codes; thus, harmonization is already built into the process. Only in the most recently adopted civil codes, for instance the Civil Code for the State of Quintana Roo, are there important deviations from the federal model.[72] Second, since the federal government and federal law dominates the public law field, and society in general, if Mexicans find their legal system deficient, it is diversity rather than uniformity that is lacking.

4.3.2. *Examples of Concurrent Jurisdiction: Health and Environment*

Besides the private law and criminal law subjects just discussed, what other areas of state law are important? As already noted, federal law dominates the public law and regulatory sphere. Aside from public security (police),[73] the provision of local public works and services,[74] the maintenance of state court systems,[75] and state-sponsored educational and cultural activities,[76] there is little state legislation of major importance in the field of public law and regulation.

[71] Jorge Carpizo notes that resistance to the harmonization of state codes is due to the belief that such activity would have a centralizing effect. Nevertheless, there have been proponents of the adoption of single, nationwide civil and criminal codes. In 1967, the Instituto de Derecho Comparado (predecessor of the Instituto de Investigaciones Jurídicas) at the National University of Mexico (UNAM) published a critical study, 'Bases para un anteproyecto de Código Civil Uniforme para toda la República', that proposed the adoption of a single civil code for the country. No serious attempt was ever made to carry out such a project, however. Carpizo, *supra* note 3 at 536–540. Recently, Dr Jorge Sánchez Cordero, a Mexico City Notary Public and expert on Mexican private law, has organized a uniform law movement among notaries public throughout the country, for the purpose of harmonizing the civil obligations provisions of the state civil codes.

[72] *See* Chapter 17 below, text accompanying note 63.

[73] *See* Chapter 11 below on criminal law.

[74] Article 115, section III, lists the public services (water, sewers, cemeteries, local roads, etc.) that are the responsibilities of *municipios*, working in co-operation with state governments. States are also responsible for state highways, state parks, and promoting state tourism.

Article 116, section VI allows the federal, state, and local governments to agree on the extent to which each will carry out public works and services. Because of the federal domination of public revenues, this 'agreement' amounts in practice to federal control of public works and services. Federal domination of public works also means that the PRI can exercise considerable influence over local politicians and the electorate by granting or withholding new works and services.

[75] On state courts *see* Chapter 6 below, Section 2.6.

[76] While the states do sponsor cultural activities (museums, galleries, cultural events) the federal government dominates activities in the cultural sphere due to the preponderance of public monies available to federal cultural agencies. The *Instituto Nacional de Bellas Artes* (INBA); the *Instituto Nacional de Antropología e Historia* (INAH); the *Fondo Nacional para la Cultura y las*

During the past ten years, the federal government has focused considerable attention on the need for greater decentralization of government power. This attention is due in part to the government's reaction to internal criticism of the highly centralized system, and in part to a sincere belief that a decentralized system would work better than a highly centralized one, so long as overall central control is maintained.

In two areas, environmental protection and public health, state governments have begun to assert somewhat greater legislative responsibility.

Prior to the late 1980s, comprehensive environmental protection had been effectively ignored in Mexico, at both the state and the federal levels.[77] Vigorous protection of the environment was considered a luxury appropriate for affluent countries, but of lesser concern to a country like Mexico, with its massive problems of poverty and underemployment. Thus, even though the Federal Congress 'federalized' environmental law in 1971,[78] it failed to create an effective regulatory apparatus to implement environmental regulations. While the states, pursuant to the savings clause of Article 124, had the legislative power to adopt laws to protect the local environment, none of the states undertook to regulate environmental affairs, other than adopting local legislation to protect public health.[79]

All this changed in the late 1980s, as Mexico's environmental problems worsened and citizens' groups began to mount a campaign of public pressure both within Mexico and in the United States. In 1987, Congress responded to this pressure by amending the Constitution to grant concurrent jurisdiction among federal, state, and local governments over environmental protection.[80] In 1988,

Artes (FONCA); the *Consejo Nacional para la Cultura y las Artes* (CONACULTA); and the *Comisión Nacional para Preservar el Patrimonio Cultural* are all national in scope, and they support museums and cultural activities in every state. In the field of education, the federal government is responsible for carrying out most educational activities throughout the country other than at the university level. Each state in Mexico has its own university system, which depends largely on state funding for its existence. The federal government does fund research throughout the country, through the *Consejo Nacional de Ciencia y Tecnología* (CONACYT). On legal education in Mexico *see* Chapter 2 above.

77 For a more detailed discussion of environmental regulation, *see* Chapter 12 below.

78 In 1971, Congress amended Article 73, section XVI paragraph 4, granting Congress the specific power to legislate to prevent environmental pollution. D.O. 6 Jul. 1971. Carmona Lara, M., 'Derecho Ecológico', in vol. III, El Derecho en México, *supra* note 51 at 1645, 1669. Several months earlier, Congress had already passed the first federal environmental law, the *Ley Federal para Prevenir y Controlar la Contaminación Ambiental* (D.O. 21 Mar. 1971), using its powers to legislate on matters of general public health. The Secretaría de Salubridad was granted the principal responsibility for administering the law. In 1982 Congress enacted the *Ley Federal de Protección al Ambiente* which covered omissions issues more broadly than the previous law. This law included provisions for the preservation and protection of ecosystems and was the first to deal with environmental principles with mechanisms for socioeconomic development. *See generally* Azanza Porter, M.F., 'La Concurrencia entre la Federación, las Entidades Federativas y los Municipios en Materia Ecológica' (Mexico: Universidad Iberoamericana, 1992, unpublished *Tésis de Licenciatura*).

79 For current state legislation on health and environment, *see* www.juridicas.unam.mx.

80 D.O. 10 Aug. 1987. The 'environmental amendments' of 1987 included amendment to paragraph 3 of Article 27, and the addition of section XXIX-G to Article 73.

Congress adopted a new environmental law, the *Ley General del Equilibrio Ecológico y la Protección al Ambiente* (LGEEPA),[81] which represents the most serious attempt to date to regulate this important area.

The LGEEPA establishes the basis for federal and state concurrent jurisdiction over environmental protection.[82] In response to this invitation, twenty states have adopted environmental laws since 1988.[83] In each case, the state law has been modelled on the LGEEPA. This is not to say that the laws have been accompanied by vigorous enforcement, however. Only four states have issued regulations implementing such laws.[84] Most important, the states generally lack the revenue to establish the bureaucracies and hire the environmental scientists and technicians necessary for vigorous enforcement of environmental laws.[85] In recognition of this, perhaps, most experts interpret the LGEEPA as granting sole authority to the federal government (i.e. to the *Secretaría de Medio Ambiente y Recursos Naturales* (SEMARNAT)) the power to issue environmental standards (*normas técnicas*); the states are not empowered to issue *normas técnicas* that establish higher levels of protection than the federal standards.[86] In this respect, Mexico differs from the United States, in which the states are free to set environmental standards higher than those set by the federal government.[87]

Wherever concurrent jurisdiction exists in Mexico, the federal government, by the passage of general laws, is in the position to determine the limits of state involvement through the adoption of general laws such as the LGEEPA. In many instances, the role of state agencies is further defined through the *de facto* requirement that the states enter into *convenios de cooperación* with the federal government. Article 7 of the LGEEPA authorizes the federal and state governments to conclude such *convenios de cooperación* to co-ordinate environmental protection and enforcement of environmental laws. To date, no such *convenio* has been signed. Since the states lack the financial resources to carry out their own programmes of vigorous enforcement, environmental protection remains almost exclusively a federal matter.

Public health is the other important field in which the federal government shares concurrent power with state and municipal governments. In the nineteenth century, the power to legislate on public health was exclusively assigned

[81] D.O. 28 Jan. 1988, as amended in D.O. 7 Jan. 2000.

[82] LGEEPA Articles 4, 5, 6, and 7. Articles 5 and 6 assign regulatory powers to the federal, state, and local governments.

[83] The 20 states are: Aguascalientes, Coahuila, Colima, Durango, Guerrero, Guanajuato, Hidalgo, Estado de México, Jalisco, Morelos, Nuevo León, Oaxaca, Querétaro, Quintana Roo, San Luis Potosí, Tabasco, Sonora, Veracruz, Yucatán, and Zacatecas. Azanza Porter, *supra* note 78 at 137.

[84] *Id.* at 137.

[85] *Id.* at 148.

[86] *Id.* at 144–146, citing the final paragraph of LGEEPA Article 6. Of course, SEMARNAT could explicitly grant to the states the authority to set different (especially higher) *normas técnicas* by expressly granting that authority in the regulation issuing a *norma técnica*.

[87] In 2002, California adopted air quality legislation significantly more rigorous than the federal standards contained in the federal Clean Air Act.

to the states, which lacked, however, both the expertise to regulate activities and the resources to provide significant public health services. In 1908, at the request of President Porfirio Díaz, Congress amended the Constitution to grant the federal government the power to legislate on 'general health in the Republic' (*salubridad general de la República*), a power that was carried over into the Constitution of 1917 (Article 73, section XVI).[88]

Beginning in the 1920s, the federal government began to define its role as protector of the social welfare of all Mexican citizens, through the implementation of the *Constitución social*. An important part of this programme was the gradual federalization and centralization of public health law and health care services.[89] The first federal health code (*Código Sanitario*), adopted in 1923, defined *salubridad general* widely, giving broad powers to the federal government to set public health standards. In subsequent health codes of 1955 and 1973, the federal government increasingly monopolized health activities formerly reserved to the states, notwithstanding the conclusion of co-operation agreements between federal and state authorities. The number of personnel and financial resources available to the states declined, and what little state law existed was seldom applied.[90] The most significant element of federalization came in 1942, with the creation of the *Instituto Mexican de Seguridad Social* (IMSS).[91] In addition to providing an extensive network of public hospitals and clinics throughout Mexico, IMSS carries out educational and public health services at a national level. With more than 375,000 employees, IMSS is one of the largest government agencies in Mexico. When added to the *Secretaría de Salubridad y Asistencia* (SSA), the federal agency responsible for adopting and enforcing public health codes, federal agencies have largely monopolized the public health field.

In the early 1980s, the federal government began to reverse the trend of centralization of public health.[92] In 1981, the federal government concluded a new series of co-operation agreements with twenty states of the union, to help carry out an ambitious new programme that would bring health care to a wider segment of the population. In 1983, the Constitution was again amended to give the states concurrent jurisdiction, along with the federal government, in the provision of general health services.[93] Thereafter, on the initiative of the federal

[88] Valadés, D., CONSTITUCIÓN Y POLÍTICA (Mexico: UNAM, 1987) at 65–70. In 1861, through the implementation of the *Leyes de Reforma*, the government expropriated hospitals and similar institutions of the Catholic Church, which were turned over to the state governments and the Federal District Federal for their administration. *Id.* at 69.

[89] Ortega Lomelín, *supra* note 8 at 495.

[90] *Id.* at 447.

[91] For a more detailed discussion of IMSS, *see* Chapter 13 below, section 2.3.3. In addition to IMSS, the *Instituto de Seguridad y Servicios Sociales de los Trabajadores del Estado* (ISSSTE), created in 1959, provides health and hospital services to federal employees throughout Mexico.

[92] For a detailed discussion of the federal government's efforts to decentralize health, *see* Apéndice, 'La Descentralización de los Servicios de Salud (Crónica de un Caso)', in Ortega Lomelín, *supra* note 14 at 441–547. The author, as a former health official responsible for the decentralization programme, gives a close-up view; unfortunately, there is little criticism or objective evaluation of the process.

[93] Mexican Constitution, Article 4, para. 3.

government, a wave of pronouncements and new regulations, as well as a new *Ley General de Salud*,[94] promoted decentralization and a greater role for state governments throughout the health sector. As a result, a number of states adopted new *leyes estatales de salud* and began, with technical assistance and financial support from the federal government, to carry out public health services in co-ordination with federal agencies.[95]

These efforts have slightly reduced the federal monopoly of health activities. Nevertheless, in a system imbued from top to bottom with centralized authority patterns, it is impossible to be free of centralized control. IMSS is still the largest organization in the health sector, and it continues to be operated with a great deal of centralized, and even paternalistic, decision-making. As the following section shows, budgetary allocations to state and federal entities are determined largely by the federal government, which retains most of the tax revenues collected in the country. In short, the campaign to decentralize the government's involvement in the health sector has been carried out in such a way that the federal government does not lose overall control of this sector.

5. Municipal Law

The principal political and legal subdivisions in Mexico are:

(i) the federal government;
(ii) the states and the Federal District;[96] and
(iii) the municipalities (*municipios*).

Municipios are governed by city councils, called *ayuntamientos*, composed of elected officials (*regidores*) who are popularly elected. Both the *ayuntamientos* and the chief executive officer of the *municipio* (the *presidente municipal*) are elected in popular elections that occur, in most of the states, every three years. As with federal *diputados* and senators, these elected officials can never run for re-election for a term immediately following that in which they have served in the same position.[97]

The Constitution of 1917, unlike its predecessors, accorded specific powers and protections for *municipios* in Article 115, including the power to issue local regulations and ordinances, in accordance with general statutes (*leyes orgánicas*) that must be approved by the state legislatures. The Constitution did not, however, accord significant taxing power to *municipios*, which severely limited their ability to provide public services to their citizens, who came to expect such services, if any, from the federal government.[98] Thus, in the highly centralized

[94] D.O. 7 Feb. 1984.
[95] For current state legislation on health, *see* www.juridicas.unam.mx.
[96] The Federal District is itself divided into 16 *delegaciones*, each governed by a *delegado* who is elected by popular election of local resident voters.
[97] Mexican Constitution, Article 115, section I.
[98] *See* Tena Ramírez, *supra* note 4 at 151–153.

system of federal, state, and local government, the *municipios* suffered from being at the bottom of the political hierarchy. As early as 1922, some municipal organizations began to promote amendments to Article 115 that would give more power to the municipalities. These attempts were unsuccessful until 1983, when Article 115 underwent a significant amendment.[99] Until that date, the *municipio* in Mexico suffered from an uncertain legal status, and was subject to the whims of state and federal officials.

Much legal scholarship has been devoted to the 1983 reforms of Article 115,[100] which were intended to bolster the political, economic, and administrative position of the *municipio*, making it a more important element of a more highly decentralized governmental system.[101] The 1983 reforms: granted legal status (*personería jurídica*) to the *municipio*; confirmed the power of municipalities to issue regulations, without the approval of state governments, so long as they conform to the *leyes orgánicas* approved by the state; provided a greater guarantee of municipal control over its own treasury, and a right to receive a portion of tax revenues collected by the federal government; and granted municipalities jurisdiction over the provision of public services (see Article 115, section III), although the states may play a role in co-ordinating these functions and in setting rates for municipal services.[102]

The sum total of these reforms has been less than overwhelming. As the following section of this Chapter shows, the *municipios* have begun to receive a greater share of public tax revenues, and have therefore been able to provide more public services directly. Despite increases in the number of municipalities governed by the former opposition parties, PAN and PRD, most of the *ayuntamientos* and *presidentes municipales* remain in the hands of the PRI,[103] even though the leadership of the party in Mexico City no longer maintains the same level of centralized control over local politics that the PRI leadership once claimed. The PRI has been able to use its control over the release of tax revenues (*participaciones*) to the *municipios* so as to quiet opposition or to reward loyalty.[104]

[99] Sayeg Helu, J., FEDERALISMO Y MUNICIPALISMO MEXICANOS (Mexico: Cámara de Diputados, 1984) at 100–107.

[100] The 1983 reform was published in D.O. 3 Feb. 1983. On the 1983 reforms to Article 115, *See generally* Acosta Romero, M., LA REFORMA MUNICIPAL EN LA CONSTITUCIÓN (Mexico: Pórrua, 2d ed., 1986,); Hernández-Gaona, P., 'Derecho Municipal', in EL DERECHO EN MÉXICO, *supra* note 51, vol. III at 1509, 1534–1535, 1572–1574; *See generally* Ruiz Massieu, J., and Valadés, D., eds., NUEVO DERECHO CONSTITUCIONAL MEXICANO (Mexico: Pórrua, 1983).

[101] Article 115 was again amended in 1987 (D.O. 17 Mar. 1987), most importantly to add the first sentence to section VIII, requiring the *municipios* to adopt systems of proportional representation in order to allow greater participation by minority parties in local government. On proportional representation generally, *see* Chapter 5 below, text accompanying notes 151–168.

[102] Ortega Lomelín, *supra* note 8 at 381.

[103] As of 1999, 1,391 of the 2,426 Mexican municipalities were controlled by the PRI, representing 46% of the population. 286 municipalities were held by the PAN, 293 by the PRD, 26 by the PD (Labour Party) and 9 by the PVEM, Mexico's 'Green Party'. Federacion Nacional de Municipios de México, GEOGRAFÍA POLITICO-ELECTORAL POR MUNCIPIOS (Mexico: Dec. 1999).

[104] For instance, in 1998 the residents of Juchitán, Oaxaca, rebelled at the election of the PRI candidate as *presidente municipal*, and took possession of city hall in protest. After

6. Federalism and the Power of Taxation[105]

6.1. Background

The power to tax, basic to any realistic assessment of governmental power, has never been neatly assigned by the Mexican Constitution to each level of government. In the Constitution of 1824, the lack of authority for imposing federal taxes, as well as the imposition by the states of 'transit taxes' on the movement of goods and persons, resulted in fiscal anarchy and helped doom the first Mexican constitution.[106] Under the Constitution of 1857, the taxing authority, other than specific taxes assigned to the federal government (e.g. the power to collect customs duties), was deemed to be a concurrent power (*coincidente*) of state and federal governments, with no indication of how the power should be shared.[107]

Under the original Constitution of 1917, federal, state, and municipal taxing powers continued to be understood as undefined, concurrent powers.[108] However, beginning in 1925, the federal government has passed a succession of tax laws forcing, either explicitly or implicitly, the co-ordination of taxation by federal and state governments, and instigating a system of revenue-sharing by federal, state, and local governments.

In 1925, the *Secretaría de Hacienda y Crédito Público* (SHCP) organized the first National Tax Conference (*Convención Nacional Fiscal*) for state and federal authorities, for the purpose of defining the tax jurisdiction of each of them and to co-ordinate the collection and distribution of taxes. One result was to require the states to make a 'contribution' of a portion of their tax revenues to the federal government (from 50 per cent, the portion was eventually reduced to 20 per cent in 1930), in return for which the federal government granted 'participations' to states and municipalities in revenues collected by the federal government on mining, oil production, and income taxes.[109] This system of state participations in federally collected taxes was enshrined in the Constitution in 1942, by the addition of Article 73, section XXIX.

months of negotiation, the elected official remained in power, but the government was able to restore order by building new public works as a 'reward' for the population.

[105] *See* Díaz Cayeros, A., Desarrollo económico e inequidad regional: hacia un nuevo pacto federal en México (Mexico: Miguel Angel Porrúa, 1995).

[106] Ortega Lomelín, *supra* note 8 at 316–319.

[107] Carpizo and Madrazo, 'Derecho Consitucional', in El Derecho en México, *supra* note 51 at 1733.

[108] Carpizo, *supra* note 3 at 95, citing decisions of the Mexican Supreme Court. After some equivocation, the Supreme Court has held that Article 124 does not limit the taxing power of the federal government. Ortega Lomelín, *supra* note 8 at 103–104. *See also* González Oropeza, 'Introducción—El Federalismo', in Derecho Constitucional Comparado México—Estados Unidos, *supra* note 9, vol. I, at 219, 223. The Constitution does allocate certain specific taxing powers to the federal government alone (*see* Article 73, section XXIX), and prohibits the states from imposing certain kinds of taxes (Article 117).

[109] Ortega Lomelín, *supra* note 8 at 321–322.

By the 1950s, through the convening of subsequent national tax conferences (in 1933 and 1947) and the amendment of federal tax laws, federal and state authorities had settled into the present system of tax collection and distribution. Under this system, which has gradually been refined over the years, the states have ceded the collection of most taxes to the federal government.[110] Under the Law of Tax Co-Ordination (*Ley de Coordinación Fiscal*),[111] the federal government has sole responsibility for collecting the most important taxes: personal and corporate income taxes,[112] and value added tax (IVA).[113] Instead of imposing their own income or sales taxes, the states are granted 'participations' in the tax revenues collected by the federal government on these activities.[114] In order to receive a portion of the taxes collected by the federal government, the states are required to sign *convenios de participación* with the federal government, and to co-ordinate tax collections.[115] The federal government's practice has been to designate a fund consisting of 20 per cent of all federal tax revenues for distribution to the states. As a result of this system, the federal government retains approximately 81 per cent of the total taxes collected by the federal government in the Mexican Republic; 16 per cent of tax revenues is distributed to state governments, and 3 per cent of revenues is distributed to municipalities.[116]

The problem with this system, from the point of view of proponents of decentralization, has been that the federal government has largely determined how and to what extent tax revenues shall be collected and shared, and has appropriated the lion's share of the funds. As one commentator has described this system, 'the centralization of tax revenues at a national level has worked to the disadvantage of state treasuries; the sharing of the jurisdiction to tax has further promoted the federalization of public revenues, and the result has been federal control over the collection of the most important taxes, and federal discretion over the distribution of shares [to state and local authorities]'.[117]

[110] The *municipios* are responsible for collecting property and inheritance taxes, as well as levying charges for public services (water, sewer, etc.). According to Osornio Corres, F., ASPECTOS JURÍDICOS DE LA ADMINISTRACIÓN FINANCIERA EN MÉXICO (Mexico: UNAM, 1992) at 191–195, the property taxes collected by *municipios* are insufficient to make them financially autonomous. While the *municipios* do receive federal funds though the system of participations, described below, these funds leave the *municipios* dependent on state and federal governments.

[111] D.O. 27 Dec. 1978, as amended D.O. 13 Mar. 2002.

[112] *Ley del Impuesto sobre la Renta*, the latest version of which was published in D.O. 1 Jan. 2002.

[113] *Ley del Impuesto al Valor Agregado*, D.O. 29 Dec. 1978 as amended D.O. 31 Dec. 2000.

[114] Ortega Lomelín, *supra* note 8 at 326 *et seq*. This system was initiated in 1953, on the adoption of the *Ley de Coordinación Fiscal entre la Federación y los Estados*, D.O. 27 Dec. 1978, as amended D.O. 13 Mar. 2002.

[115] The development of this system of 'co-ordinated' taxation is discussed in Ortega Lomelín, *supra* note 8 at 327–337.

[116] *See* Merino, G., 'Federalismo fiscal: diagnóstic y propuestas' in UNA AGENDA PARA LAS FINANZAS PÚBLICAS DE MEXICO (Mexico: ITAM/Centro de Investigación en Políticas de Economia Aplicada, 2001) at 223.

[117] González Oropeza, *supra* note 50 at 9. Figures on tax distributions to municipalities are available at www.inafed.gob.mex ('participaciones mensuales para entidades federativas 1995–2003) at 223.

Table 4.1: 'Participations' Allocated to State and Local Governments (as Percentage of Total Federal Tax Collections)

1975	*1980*	*1985*	*1987*
9.3	14.8	28.3	24.0

Source: Ortega Lomelín, *supra* note 8 at 340 (using statistics from official government sources).

Table 4.2: Share of Federal 'Participations' Allocated to Distrito Federal v. States and Municipios

	1975	*1980*	*1985*	*1987*
D.F.	40.6	26.0	20.8	19.5
States and *Municipios*	59.4	74.0	79.2	80.5

Source: Ortega Lomelín, *supra* note 8 at 342 (citing official government sources).

Thus, 63 per cent of all tax revenues collected in 1900 went to the federal government; by 1966, this figure had risen to 83.4 per cent.[118] In other words, the weight of federal monopolization of public revenues has not dramatically changed in recent times.

Roberto Ortega Lomelín[119] has used government statistics to show the extent of federalization of tax revenues, while also showing a trend since the early 1980s towards turning a greater percentage of tax revenues back to the states. As shown in Table 4.1, the percentage of tax revenues allocated to the states through the system of participations in federally collected taxes has increased from 9.3 per cent in 1975 to 24 per cent in 1987. The Federal District has historically received a disproportionate share of these allocations, but in recent years (see Table 4.2) this share has declined to a level more proportionate to the Federal District's share of the national population.[120] As a result of increased federal distributions of tax revenues, state dependence on federal 'participations' also increased. Thus, federal participations only represented 22.1 per cent of total state revenues in 1975, but by 1985 this figure had increased to 49.1 per cent.[121] Municipal dependence on federal participations was even more pronounced: in 1985, federal participations to municipalities represented 57.1 per cent of total municipal revenues (up from 12.6 per cent in 1975), despite the fact that this amount represented only 5.1 per cent of all federal taxes collected.[122]

[118] Carpizo, *supra* note 3 at 101. [119] Ortega Lomelín, *supra* note 8 at 335–366.
[120] With a population of 8.6 million inhabitants, the Federal District represents about 9% of the 97.4 million inhabitants of Mexico in 2000. *See* www.inegi.gob.mx (last visited Jan. 2004).
[121] Ortega Lomelín, *supra* note 8 at 343. [122] *Id.* at 345.

One might expect the allocation of taxing power between federal, state, and local governments to constitute an accurate gauge of centralization of governmental power: the more centralist the government, the higher percentage of tax revenues allocated to the federal level. The federal government dominates the collection and distribution of taxes.[123] Nevertheless, the 'tax gauge', if taken as the sole indicator of centralization, may even underestimate the extent of central control over public spending in Mexico. In addition to tax revenues, the federal government monopolizes other sources of public income, the most important being income from public borrowing. As a result, the federal domination of public expenditure is even greater than its domination of tax revenues.

Throughout the twentieth century, the federal domination of taxes and expenditure served to enhance the ability of the PRI to use the government's economic power to punish and reward political groups throughout the country, and thus maintain political stability. Tax revenues were not distributed evenly throughout the country. Ortega Lomelín has shown that, in 1985 for example, the distribution of federal 'participations' varied greatly from state to state; Coahuila received over 90 per cent of total state revenues from the federal government, while Nuevo León received only 17.2 per cent of its revenues from federal participations.[124]

In addition to the *Sistema Nacional de Coordinación Fiscal*,[125] the federal government also makes funds available to states and municipalities for regional development programmes (including public works) through a device known as the *Convenio Único de Desarrollo* (Single Agreement on Development).[126] Begun in the 1970s (under the name *Convenio Único de Coordinación*, or CUD) as a programme to help direct economic development planning in the states, the CUD developed into an effective system for allocating federal funds to programmes and regions favoured by the federal government. Thus, in 1986, approximately 250 billion pesos (around 100 million US dollars at that time) was distributed for public works, cultural and sports activities, highways, and schools. These funds were not distributed evenly around the country, however. From 1977 to 1986, three states—Estado de México, Jalisco, and Tabasco—received 20 per cent of the funds distributed under CUDs. From 1977 to 1986, the average annual distribution of the funds *per capita* varied from a high of 3,280 pesos (Quintana Roo) to a low of 282 pesos (Veracruz).[127]

The federal government has at times attempted to decentralize the programming of CUD funds, to give more decision-making power to the states over how the funds will be used. At the same time, the rewarding or withholding of CUD funds has been used to make states adhere to federal economic programmes (such as the *Pacto de Solidaridad Económica*, an anti-inflation programme adopted in 1987).[128]

[123] As the preceding discussion shows. [124] Ortega Lomelín, *supra* note 8 at 344.

[125] Described above. [126] *See generally* Ortega Lomelín, *supra* note 8 at 282–315.

[127] *Id.* at 285–293, 294.

[128] Ortega Lomelín, *supra* note 8 at 313. On the *Pacto de Solidaridad Económica, see* Chapter 5, note 113.

6.2. The Current System of Co-ordination

Since the defeat of the PRI presidential candidate in 2000, this system of federal control has shown signs of change, but as yet they are not dramatic. The basic use of *convenios* agreed upon between the federal government and the states continues.[129] President Vicente Fox has attempted to promote a greater balance of fiscal power between the federal government and the states by shifting to the states responsibilities for public spending, while also enhancing the states' ability to fund local expenditures without depending on federal sources. Thus, in 2002, the Budget Law (*Ley de Ingresos*)[130] opened the way for the assertion of new taxing authority by the states, even though most states have as yet failed to capitalize on it, despite encouragement from the Federal Treasury Department (SHCP) to increase state tax revenues.[131]

The latest move to reduce the federal government's overwhelming domination of government spending has come from the states themselves. In July 2003, at the Tenth Annual Meeting of the National Confederation of Governors (*Confederación Nacional de Gobernadores*, or Conago),[132] Conago proposed the convening of a National Convention on Government Finance (*Convención Nacional Hacendaria*) to bring about major tax reforms to provide more opportunity for the states to be responsible for their own taxation and expenditures, and less dependent on federal government resources.[133] President Fox immediately endorsed the proposal for the Convention,[134] which was scheduled to take place in the Spring of 2004. If successful in increasing state revenues and diminishing federal control of government finances, the Convention could be a major step in decentralization of governmental authority in Mexico.

7. Federalism in Transition

Throughout the twentieth century, the PRI was able to create a broad, national coalition of political and economic forces at the command of a small group of persons, the President and his advisers. The individuals changed with each six-year regime, but the system stayed the same: corporatist, authoritarian,

[129] Information on the co-ordination of federal/state taxation can be found on the web site of the Instituto par el Desarrollo Técnico de las Haciendas Públicas (INDETEC), an organ of the National System of Fiscal Co-Ordination within SHCP. *See* www.indetec.gob.mx. (last visited Jan. 2004).

[130] D.O. 30 Dec. 2003.

[131] Consideraciones en torno a los recientes comentarios sobre el fedaralismo fiscal (Mexico: SHCP, Comunicado de Prensa 121/2002, 22 Oct. 2002).

[132] Conago serves as a forum for state governors to co-operate on common issues. The existence of this new organization, established in 1992, is itself evidence of the political opening up in Mexico. When all state governors were members of the PRI (from 1929 to 1986), there was no need for such a lobbying organization, since state/federal politics were worked out within the confines of the PRI.

[133] 'Impulsa Conago macro-reforma', *Reforma* (Mexico City), Wed. 30 Jul. 2003, at 1A.

[134] 'Respalda Fox a la Conago par air a la Convención Nacional Hacendaria', *El Financiero* (Mexico City), Thurs. 31 Jul. 2003, at 56.

ideologically flexible, centralized, and administered by an all-powerful federal government.

With the election in 2000 of PAN candidate Vicente Fox, the political system has changed dramatically. There is no clear consensus yet of the system that will replace the centralized authoritarianism, but we can venture opinions. Until 1986 no candidate other than a member of the PRI had ever won a state governorship. Today, seventeen governors are members of the PRI, ten are members of the PAN, and five are members of the PRD. State legislatures are similarly divided in political support. The breakup of the PRI's control is still too recent to have brought significant constitutional or legal changes. Over time, the demise of a single-party government should translate into a more even balance of federal and state power, with a greater assumption by state governments of authority over the welfare of their citizens. The democratization of Mexico lies not just in balancing power between parties at the federal level, but also in striking a more balanced distribution of power between municipal, state, and federal governments.

5

Executive and Legislative Powers

'La democracia es una aspiración de las generaciones futuras': Benito Juárez, as quoted on a plaque at the entrance to the *Instituto Federal Electoral.*

1. Introduction: Historical Background and Constitutional Framework

Studying Mexican law without taking into account the political system would be an exercise in unreality. Recent political changes have dramatically altered the exercise of presidential and legislative powers, and the new political reality of Mexico is still being formed. To understand Mexico's particular style of a federal republic, however, it is necessary to look into Mexico's past. Over the space of seven decades, Mexico was governed by a single political party, the *Partido Revolucionario Institucional*, or PRI, that reached into every region of the country and touched virtually every activity of social importance. In this highly centralized system, law served as a primary instrument for the preservation of political authority as well as for the maintenance of social control. Certain legal principles, such as the principle of non-reelection of the president, formed the bedrock of the legal system, and are still relatively immutable. Because of the centralized, authoritarian nature of government, the superstructure of Mexican law underwent constant transformations with a minimum of public inquiry or discussion, as the political leadership invented new ways of responding to changes in underlying political, economic, and social conditions. Even the Mexican Constitution, which is often invoked with almost religious fervour, reflects this propensity towards legal reform: the Mexican Constitution has been amended hundreds of times since its adoption in 1917.[1] In a society in which

[1] The first amendment of the Mexican Constitution of 1917 was published in the Diario Oficial on 8 July 1921. The actual number of constitutional amendments varies depending on the criteria used to calculate them. One parameter could be the number of amendment decrees, of which there have been 175 since 1917. However, many such decrees amend numerous Articles, Sections, and paragraphs of the Constitution. For example, the decree issued by President Zedillo on 31 December 1994, the most extensive constitutional amendment decree since 1917, affected 27 Articles of the Constitution. Since the election of President Fox in 2000, however, there have only been 3 amendments to the Constitution: a reduction that may be explained by the fact that Fox's party lacks a majority in Congress. The extensive number of amendments in the past were a by-product of *presidencialismo*, discussed below, and one-party rule, conditions that are not likely to return. For a more detailed approach to figures concerning constitutional amendments, the process of amendment, and the possibility of

executive and legislative powers were controlled for seventy years by a single political party dominated by the President of the Republic, both the laws themselves and the legislative process can only be understood in the context of the political background. While the PRI's domination has ended, vestiges of the system remain.

Commentators from outside the country tend to view government and politics in Mexico negatively. US commentators have a tendency to judge Mexico by how far it deviates from US political norms and practices: the greater the deviation, the greater the failure of democracy. Political scientist William Buzenberg has observed such a tendency in US news reporting on Mexican politics.[2] Mexico's political system and its form of government have always been complicated, lacking in transparency, and not easily understood by non-Mexicans.

Throughout most of the twentieth century, Mexico was governed as an authoritarian state, but it was never a totalitarian one. Political power was maintained by a complex array of instruments, the use of violence and the repression of political dissent being used relatively sparingly.[3] Indeed, for some observers, the Mexican system did not even have the feel of an authoritarian society, because competition and conflict existed at the bureaucratic level, and the general rule against re-election of public officials prevented the formation of deeply entrenched elites.[4] In 1993, Mario Vargas Llosa, the Peruvian novelist and onetime candidate for president, described the unique nature of the PRI's authoritarianism in the following terms:

> The Mexican political system is not democratic, and we should not delude ourselves about this. One should say it with all clarity if one wants to speak honestly: it is a unique system, one that does not have equivalents in the world, one that has been able to maintain a political party in power by adapting itself to the particular circumstances with a

control by the judiciary, *see* Mejía, R., *The Amendment Process in the* Mexican Constitution, (Mexico: Instituto Tecnologico Autonomo de Mexico, September, 2003). For a list of amendments in chronological order *see* www.juridicas.unam.mx/infjur/leg/constmex (last visited Jan. 2004).

[2] According to Professor Buzenberg, 'North American press coverage of Mexico's [1985] mid-term elections suffered from significant errors of exaggeration and distortion. Essentially these errors stem from lack of understanding of Mexico's political reality, and biases on the part of US reporters.' Buzenberg, W., 'The 1985 Mexican Elections And The North American Press', in *Electoral Patterns and Perspectives in Mexico* (Center for US–Mexican Studies, University of California at San Diego, Monograph series, no. 22, Arturo Alvarado Mendoza, ed., 1987) at 253. *See also* Alvarado, Arturo, *Introduction*, in *ibid.* at 1, 12: 'US reporters undoubtedly found what they were looking for, given their prejudices and predispositions, without having to try very hard'.

[3] According to Roberto Newell Garcia and Luis Rubio, Mexico lacked the qualities of a totalitarian state: maintenance of power by violence, lack of political dissent, etc. Rather, they contended that Mexico was an authoritarian state, one in which decision-making power was amassed in a ruling elite. Newell Garcia, R. and Rubio, L., *Mexico's Dilemma: The Political Origins of Economic Crisis* (Boulder, Colo: Westview Press, 1984).

[4] Philip, G., *The Presidency in Mexican Politics* (New York: St. Martin's Press, 1992) at 172.

flexibility and versatility that no other authoritarian system has been able to achieve, at least in modern history.[5]

The result is a form of democracy that would not be unfamiliar to US citizens who lived in the South during the mid-twentieth century, one in which a single, non-ideological Democratic party, by controlling all key positions of government, was able to preserve itself in power by spreading political largesse. The PRI's unlimited access to government resources (funds and jobs) allowed the political elite to purchase loyalty; when that did not work, electoral fraud was the last resort. Indeed, the PRI was even more inclusive than the Democratic Party in the South: rather than exclude certain racial or ethnic groups, the PRI attempted to fold as many social groups into its system of control as possible.

The PRI accomplished its consolidation of control by creating a corporatist, authoritarian state.[6] A number of studies have been written on how this system was constructed and how it operated.[7] In 1972, Arnaldo Córdova provided a succinct description of the Mexican-style democracy that prevailed for seventy years: 'The Mexican State built itself on a foundation of politically managed integration, by reaching out to embrace the majority of the organized sectors of society and by representing the interests of these sectors as its principal program, one that was changeable according to the circumstances and to the convergence of existing forces'.[8] In a single sentence, Córdova identified the key elements of this regime, which were as follows.

(i) *Integration* From the early days of its establishment,[9] the PRI attempted to integrate as many diverse factions as possible into its sphere of influence and control. The PRI has never had a singe ideological base. Rather, it has followed a generally populist approach. While it has concentrated its rhetoric in support of certain groups (labour unions, bureaucrats, farmers), it has generally supported other groups as well (private enterprise, large landowners), and was able to reach an accommodation with the Catholic Church. As a result of its ability to satisfy enough sectors of society, the PRI was able to avoid the formation of a large opposition movement organized around the interests of a group excluded from its concern. The PRI's dominance finally ended with the federal elections of 2000, when the PRI lost the presidency and the control of resources that went with it; the end came less from dissatisfaction with the ruling party's

[5] Quoted in Vega, Patricia, 'No hay que engañarse: El sistema político mexicano no es democrático', *La Jornada*, Tues. 4 May 1993, at 23 [author's trans.]

[6] *See* Cossio Díaz, CAMBIO SOCIAL Y CAMBIO JURÍDICO (Mexico City: ITAM/Miguel Ángel Porrúa, 2001) at 15–76.

[7] Newell Garcia and Rubio, *supra* note 3; *see also* Bizberg, Ilan and Frybes, Marcin, TRANSICIONES A LA DEMOCRACIA: LECCIONES PARA MÉXICO (Mexico: Ediciones Cal y Arena, 2000).

[8] Córdova, Arnaldo, LA FORMACIÓN DEL PODER POLÍTICO EN MÉXICO (Mexico City, Editorial Era, 1972) at 45 (author's translation; emphasis added).

[9] The PRI was first established in 1929, under the name *Partido Nacional Revolucionario* (PNR), under the leadership of Plutarco Elias Calles. *See* text accompanying notes 94–99 *infra*, and *supra* Chapter 1 at Section 4.3.

ideology, however, than from the public's desire to break with a closed system that bred corruption and inefficiency.

(ii) *Organized sectors* The early leadership of the PRI, as personified by Plutarco Elias Calles,[10] and in particular Lázaro Cárdenas, recognized the importance of constructing a stable political environment that did not depend inordinately on political bosses or *caciques*. The solution was to build political support by organizing important sectors of society into formal groups with which the government could maintain ties, both to satisfy the needs of these groups as well as to subject them to governmental control and manipulation. All major groups in Mexican society were required to organize into associations, from the mandatory trade associations to which all businesses were required to belong,[11] to labour unions, to educational and artistic groups. This corporatist model (alluded to in the *Institucional* part of the party's name) created a web of interconnections with the federal government (and the PRI) at the centre. The three principal strands of this web, referred to as the principal 'pillars' of the PRI, have traditionally been organized labour, 'popular' organizations (primarily government bureaucracy), and small farmers (*campesinos*).

(iii) *Programmes* One hallmark of the Mexican government is its penchant for programmes: in order to demonstrate its concern for the population it has adopted plans and programmes of national scope to deal with economic, social, and other issues.[12] Thus, President Salinas (1988–1994) adopted the *Programa Nacional de Solidaridad* (Pronasol), through which the government carried out social welfare programmes nationally, and the *Pacto de Estabilidad y Crecimiento*

[10] Plutarco Elias Calles was President of Mexico from 1924 to 1928, the year of Alvaro Obregón's election and subsequent assasination. Calles could not stand again immediately as President, and from 1928 until 1934, Mexico was governed by weak Presidents with Calles, the *Jefe Máximo*, exercising the real power. Calles was eventually banished from Mexico by President Lázaro Cárdenas, himself a strong President who was unwilling to suffer the countervailing powers of a former President. Since that time, no Mexican President has been challenged by a powerful predecessor. In each case, the former President has accepted, as part of the original assignment, the requirement to retire into an apolitical life, and to relinquish all vestiges of power in public life.

[11] The Law of Trade and Industry Associations (*Ley de las Cámaras de Comercio y de Industria*), D.O. 26 Aug. 1941, as amended, required virtually all business enterprises of any size in Mexico to belong to industry-wide trade associations, which facilitated the government's exercise of industrial policy. In October 1995, the Mexican Supreme Court held that the legal requirement of Article 5 of the Law of Trade and Industry Associations, which required companies with more than US$2,500 in capital stock to be members of a trade association, violated the freedom of association contained in Article 9 of the Constitution. *See CAMARAS DE COMERCIO E INDUSTRIA, AFILIACION OBLIGATORIA. EL ARTICULO 5o. DE LA LEY DE LA MATERIA VIOLA LA LIBERTAD DE ASOCIACION ESTABLECIDA POR EL ARTICULO 9o. CONSTITUCIONAL.* SJF y su gaceta, *T: P/J. 28/95, Pleno de la SCJN, Parte II*, October 1995, at 5. After the Supreme Court's declaration of unconstitutionality, Congress adopted a new Law of Trade Associations, *Ley de Cámaras Empresariales y sus Confederaciones*, D.O. 1 Jan. 1997.

[12] The love of plans and programmes is rooted in Mexican history: every major political movement or disruption has started with the announcement of a 'Plan', from the *Plan de Iguala* of the 1821 independence movement, to the *Plan de San Luis Potosí* that ushered in the Mexican Revolution. *See* Chapter 1 above.

Económico (Pact for Stability and Economic Growth) to control inflation. President Zedillo (1994–2000) adopted the *Programa de apoyo a la salud, alimentación y educación* (*Progresa*) (Programme for the support of health, nutrition, and education). With the decline in presidential power, discussed below, this aspect of government—ruling by programmes designed by the executive branch—has declined.

(iv) *Changeable* The ability to alter even fundamental policies was as important to the Mexican government and the PRI as the centralization of authority. Lacking a strong ideological base, the PRI would espouse social justice, and governmental policies would be presented as complementary to the ideals that emanated from the Mexican Revolution, which the PRI appropriated as its own victory. However, government propaganda notwithstanding, the Mexican government did not tend to follow socialist or highly redistributive policies. Some authors have even detected a conscious effort on the part of the PRI's leadership to prevent hardening of the ideological arteries by handing power alternatively to leftist or rightist presidents, to give a 'pendulum effect' that compensates for ideological swings in one direction or the other.[13] The lack of ideological focus permitted the government to capitalize on changes in societal sentiment, and to alter its policies so as to appease and forestall an entrenched opposition.

Finally, it is necessary to add a further overarching characteristic to provide an accurate view of the Mexican governmental system that prevailed throughout the twentieth century. This characteristic became referred to in Mexico as *presidencialismo*, a term that applies both to the previously unbridled (and still significant) power of the executive branch, and to the personal power of the Mexican President himself.[14] An understanding of *presidencialismo* is essential to an appreciation of the Mexican approach to separation of powers, and the subject is explored below. First, however, we must look at the constitutional model, the normative skeleton on which Mexican *presidencialismo* was constructed.

1.1. The Constitutional Framework and Separation of Powers

Title Three of the Mexican Constitution deals with the separation of powers between the legislative branch (Arts. 50–79), the executive branch (Arts. 80–93), and the judicial branch (Arts. 94–107). In this Chapter, we deal with the balance of legislative and executive powers, leaving the discussion of judicial power for Chapter 6 below.

The starting point for the study of separation of powers is Article 49, which specifies that 'The Supreme Power of the Federation is divided, for its exercise, into Legislative, Executive and Judicial branches.' This tripartite division of

[13] Philip, *supra* note 4 at 178.

[14] Some authors use the term *presidentismo* to refer to the preponderance of executive power in Mexico. *See* Patiño Camarena, F., NUEVO DERECHO ELECTORAL MEXICANO (Mexico: Ed. Constitucionalista and Instituto Federal Electoral, 6th ed., 2000) at 31, 32, 33.

governmental power into three supposedly equal branches has been a feature of Mexican law since the Constitution of 1824, which copied the principle of separation of powers that had been adopted by the US and French Constitutions, and by the 1812 Spanish Constitution of Cádiz.[15]

Despite following the tripartite form of government, during the twentieth century, the Mexican Constitution was applied so as to give clear predominance to the executive branch, for reasons that are explored below. This is true despite the prohibition contained in the second paragraph of Article 49: 'Two or more of these powers shall not be united in one single person or corporation, nor shall the legislative power be vested in one individual except in the case of extraordinary powers granted to the Executive of the Union, in accordance with the directives of Article 29'.

Article 49 was obviously intended to limit the legislative powers directly exercised by the President. Nevertheless, during the first twenty years of the Constitution, both the legislative and judicial branches granted such broad delegations of power to the executive that, in 1938, President Lázaro Cárdenas sought to reinforce the doctrine of separation of powers. The Constitution was thus amended to add the following sentence at the end of Article 49, to prevent overly broad delegations of legislative power:[16] 'In no other case shall extraordinary powers be granted to the Executive to legislate'.[17]

Despite the noble sentiments of President Cárdenas, the President retained significant 'indirect' legislative powers by virtue of the political leadership of the President in a one-party 'democratic' system. For this reason, the constitutional separation of legislative and executive powers in Mexico was, until recently, a legal fiction that did not reflect reality. While the President was careful to follow the *formal* constitutional requirements prohibiting executive incursions into the legislative arena, the political process allowed him to dictate the development of Mexican law.

After the presidential victory in 2000 of the PAN opposition candidate Vicente Fox, the President's power, as head of the PRI, to dictate legislation nationwide became a matter of historical legacy. The change has been dramatic: not only does President Fox, at the date of this publication, lack the support of a majority of Congress, it is not even clear that he can compel the support of the loosely organized PAN, his own party. The President's *de facto* power to legislate has been taken away, significantly reducing the executive branch's monopoly of

[15] De Andrea, F., 'Comentario al Articulo 49', in *Constitución Política de los Estados Unidos Mexicanos (comentada)* (Mexico: UNAM, Instituto de Investigaciones Jurídicas, 3rd ed., 1992) at 199, 201 (hereinafter Constitución Comentada).

[16] *Id.* at 199, 206. *See also* Valadés D., 'El Control Interorgánico entre los poderes legislativo y ejecutivo en México', in *El Presidencialmismo Mexicano (Algunas Reflexiones)* (Mexico: Instituto de Investigaciones Jurídicas, UNAM, 1988), at 245, 262–263.

[17] In 1951, Congress amended Article 49 to read as it does today, with the following sentence at the end of the article: 'In no case, except as directed in the second paragraph of Article 131, shall extraordinary powers be granted to the executive branch to legislate'. The second paragraph of Article 131 grants the President broad legislative powers to adopt rules regulating foreign commerce.

power. The Mexican Congress is no longer dwarfed by the presidency; and yet, since no political party has been able to construct a majority, either individually or in coalition, Congress has not been able to capture all of the power lost by the presidency. The result has been a stalemate on major legislative initiatives.

Another change in *presidencialismo* is due to consititutional reforms. On 31 December, 1994, Congress amended the Constitution to create new mechanisms of constitutional control: actions of unconstitutionality and constitutional controversies (*acciones de inconstitucionalidad* and *controversias constitucionales*)[18] that allow both chambers of the Congress, or a percentage of its members, to ask the Supreme Court to intervene and rule a presidential act unconstitutional if they consider that the President has acted beyond the scope of the powers delegated to him by the law or the Constitution. This challenge has been used rarely, but effectively,[19] and is another example of the waning of *presidencialismo*.

1.1.1. Constitutional Framework of the Legislative Branch

Following the US model, the Mexican Constitution establishes a bicameral legislature,[20] with a *Cámara de Diputados* (House of Representatives) consisting of 500 members elected from all regions of the country, including the Federal District,[21] and a *Senado* (Senate) consisting of 128 Senators: three senators from each of the thirty-one states and the Federal District, and the other thirty-two elected by the *plurinominal* system, as discussed below. From 1929 until 1997, when the PRI lost its majority in the lower house (*Cámara de Diputados*), the PRI effectively monopolized Congress through its domination of the electoral process. The PRI's former domination of Congress explains why the legislative process, explained in Section 4.3 of this Chapter, should be so similar to the US model in form, but, until recently, so different in practice from the US experience.

[18] *See infra* Chapter 8 at text accompanying notes 52–96.

[19] In 2002, the challenge was used by members of Congress against President Vicente Fox and several agencies of his administration to challenge legislation passed by Congress, and signed by Fox, that would allow greater freedom of private investment in electricity generation and distribution. *See* the Law of Public Service of Electrical Energy (Electricity Law) (*Ley del Servicio Público de Energía Eléctrica*), D.O. 3 Jun. 2002. The Supreme Court, acting pursuant to its power under Article 105, Section I of the Constitution, held that the law violated the Constitution because the President's regulation went beyond the congressional authorization contained in the Electricity Law. The decision has not been published in the *Semanario Judicial de la Federación*, the Supreme Court's official reporter, but it was published in the *Diario Oficial*: D.O. 24 May 2001.

[20] Mexican Constitution, Article 50. The 1857 Constitution abolished the Senate, as representing an elitist and conservative tendency, and Mexico had a unicameral Congress until 1874, when the Constitution was amended to restore the Senate. De Andrea, *supra note* 15 at 217, 219.

[21] Unlike the United States, in which the residents of the District of Columbia do not elect a voting member to Congress, in Mexico the Constitution provides for election by residents of the Federal District of *diputados* and senators with full voting rights. Since Mexico City's population is so large, the failure to provide voting representation in Congress would disenfranchise a much larger percentage of the national population than occurs in the United States' decision not to award voting representation in Congress to D.C. residents.

Unlike the US model, the power to propose legislation in Congress belongs not only to the *diputados* and senators of the federal Congress; the President and state legislatures also have the power of legislative initiative, by virtue of Article 71 of the Constitution. As discussed below,[22] the vast majority of all federal legislation has been drafted in the executive branch, within the presidential office or in the cabinet ministries *(secretarías)*, although this is now changing due to the political changes that have increased the power of the Congress. During the PRI's monopoly of power, legislative bills (*proyectos de leyes*) were passed with scarcely any substantive changes by the PRI-dominated Congress. Because of the overwhelming importance of federal law in the Mexican legal system,[23] the executive branch's *de facto* monopoly over the drafting of legislation gave the President an exaggerated influence over the creation of law throughout the country. When one adds to this the power of the *secretarías* to 'legislate' by the adoption, without public debate, of implementing regulations, one can easily see the reason for the centralization of legal power in Mexico. This subject is explored in more detail below, under the subject of *presidencialismo*.

As explained in section 1.1 of this Chapter, since 2000, the president's power to legislate has evaporated due to the lack of a majority by any political party in Congress; during the initial years of the administration of President Vicente Fox, the PRI and PRD held sufficient power to block most major legislative initiatives formulated in the executive branch. The waning of presidential power has also carried over into 'legislation by regulation'.

The Constitution contains numerous specific rules concerning the electoral process (Articles 51 to 60) and the legislative process (Articles 61 to 72). Articles 73 to 77 set forth the powers of Congress, including the powers assigned exclusively to the *Cámara de Diputados* (Article 74: most importantly, the review and approval of the federal budget) and the powers assigned exclusively to the Senate (Article 76). As in the United States, the Senate's exclusive powers include approval of important presidential appointments (cabinet ministers, Supreme Court justices, diplomatic personnel, etc.) and approval for the President to conclude international treaties. The Senate also served an important function in the development of Mexican *presidencialismo*: under Article 76-V, the Senate may initiate the removal of state governors by declaring that 'all the constitutional powers of a State have disappeared'. Whenever it has been used, this procedure occurred at the behest of the President, who is empowered to 'suggest' the name of a provisional governor to replace the one removed from office. As discussed elsewhere,[24] this *desaparición de poderes* was used in the past to enhance centralized control of state politics. Presidential control of state politics is probably a thing of the past, however: with the election in 2000 of an opposition presidential candidate, *panista* Vicente Fox, the

[22] *See infra*, Section 2.2.3. [23] *See* Article 73, and the discussion in Chapter 4.
[24] *See* Chapter 4, at text accompanying notes 47–49.

PRI no longer controls the presidency, and by 2002, the PRI controlled only seventeen of the thirty-one governorships and state legislatures.[25]

Finally, in recognition of the short legislative sessions of Congress,[26] Article 78 provides for a *Comisión Permanente* composed of thirty-seven members of Congress (nineteen *diputados* and eighteen senators) to make legislative decisions when Congress is not in session. Article 79 sets forth the general powers of the *Comisión Permanente* in substitution of the full Congress; while it cannot pass laws, the *Comisión Permanente* can serve important political functions, such as approving ministerial nominations by the President, calling extraordinary sessions of Congress, and approving or rejecting a presidential declaration of the suspension of constitutional guarantees under Article 29 of the Constitution.

1.1.2. Constitutional Framework of the Executive Branch

The presidency Articles 80 to 93 establish the parameters of executive governance in Mexico. The President is elected by direct, popular vote for a single term of six years, known as the *sexenio* (Articles 81, 83). Article 82 sets forth the personal requirements for the job: among other qualifications listed, the President must be at least thirty-five years old, a Mexican citizen by birth, and the child of parents who are Mexican citizens by birth.[27]

Article 83 eliminates the possibility of re-election: 'A citizen who has held the office of President of the Republic, by popular election, or in an interim nature, either provisionally or as a substitute, can in no case and for no reason again hold that office'. This principle of non-reelection, which applies to most elected officials throughout the Mexican system of government,[28] is one of the key features of the Mexican political system. In a society characterized by authoritarianism, re-election of political leaders has necessarily been an issue of major concern. The major ruptures in Mexican political history have been accompanied by outcries against presidential re-election.[29]

[25] Currently, the PAN controls eight states, the PRD five states, and a coalition of the PAN and the PRD two states.

[26] *See* note 45, *infra*, and accompanying text.

[27] Article 82 may be seen as a vestige of the Mexican fear of *intervencionismo*, after the wars and invasions of the nineteenth century. The 1857 Constitution merely required the President to be a Mexican citizen by birth. The *Constituyente* of Querétaro added the requirement that the parents must also be Mexicans by birth, the result of decades of debate over the possible influence of 'foreigners' such as José Ives Limantour, the son of French immigrants, a distinguished *diputado* and later Treasury Secretary under Porfirio Díaz. Limantour was allied to the *científicos*, who favoured the modernization of Mexico along European and US models. González Oropeza, M., 'Comentario', in CONSTITUCIÓN COMENTADA, *supra* note 15 at 340, 341.

[28] *Diputados* and senators are prohibited from being re-elected to the same position for the term immediately following the one in which they have served. *See* Article 59, discussed at text accompanying note 187 *infra*. State governors, who, like the President, serve six-year terms, can also never be re-elected to the same position. Article 116-I.

[29] For discussions of constitutional changes permitting or prohibiting presidential re-election, *see* Carpizo, J. and Madrazo, J., 'Derecho Constitucional', in *EL DERECHO EN MÉXICO: UNA VISIÓN DE CONJUNTO*, vol. III (Mexico: IIJ-UNAM, 1991) at 1701, 1762–1763; Carpizo, J., *EL PRESIDENCIALISMO MEXICANO* (Mexico: Siglo XXI, 10th ed., 1991) 56–58.

The Constitution of 1824 prohibited the president from seeking re-election immediately. Re-election was hardly a major issue, however, in the early Republic: thirty-eight men occupied the presidency of Mexico from 1824 to 1857; one of these men, Antonio López de Santa Anna, served as President on eleven different occasions between 1833 and 1855.[30] As originally adopted, the Constitution of 1857 did not include any provision limiting presidential re-election. However, in 1876, a recalcitrant military leader, General Porfirio Díaz, opposed the re-election plans of liberal President Sebastián Lerdo de Tejada, and launched a rebellion under the rubric *Plan de Tuxtepec*. A fundamental plank of Díaz's plan was the principal of non-reelection. After a period of civil skirmishes, Porfirio Díaz succeeded in installing himself as President through a *coup d'état*. In 1878, he engineered a reform of the 1857 Constitution that prohibited immediate re-election of the President. Díaz duly stepped down as President in 1880, and was succeeded by General Manuel González (1880–1884).

Porfirio Díaz's aversion to presidential re-election was short-lived. After Díaz was again elected President in 1884, he engineered successive reforms that allowed re-election for a subsequent period, and then eventually removed all constitutional impediments to re-election.[31] He gradually assumed dictatorial powers, before being overthrown by another opponent of re-election, Francisco I. Madero, who launched the Mexican Revolution in 1910 by calling for the resignation of Díaz and reinstatement of the principle of non-reelection. The Constitution of 1917, in Article 83, reasserted an absolute prohibition against re-election, only to undergo further reforms in 1927 and 1928, during the presidency of Plutarco Elías Calles (1924–1928). The second of these reforms extended the presidential term from four to six years, and only prohibited re-election for an immediately following term, but otherwise permitting presidential re-election. These reforms opened the way for President General Alvaro Obregón (1920–1924) to be re-elected in 1928. Obregón was assassinated before he could take office for his second term, and Emilio Portes Gil was the first of several 'puppet' Presidents placed in power by Plutarco Elias Calles. Finally, in 1933, the Constitution of 1917 was amended to its present form, prohibiting presidential re-election once and for all.[32] Since that time, no serious political movement has threatened to overturn this rule.

The constitutional principle of non-reelection has been the single most important factor in preventing the Mexican political system from declining into perpetual dictatorship. As the following section shows, presidential power in Mexico was relatively unbridled throughout most of the twentieth century. The inability of the President to stand for re-election was the only effective means of controlling that power, and of providing for the possibility of political change and renewal in a one-party system. Few political figures suffer such a dramatic rise and decline in power as the Mexican President. While in office,

[30] Miller, R., *MEXICO: A HISTORY* (Oklahoma: University of Oklahoma Press, 1985) 207.

[31] Barquín Alvarez, Manuel, 'Comentario', in CONSTITUCIÓN COMENTADA, *supra* note 15 at 344, 347.

[32] *Id.* at 347–348.

the President's will is tantamount to law. Once he has left office, the former President is expected to retire from political life altogether, and to keep a low profile in public. Even when the new President was chosen by his predecessor, the beginning of a new *sexenio* brought into play new actors as well as new policies.[33]

Article 89 sets forth the powers specifically assigned to the President. The President's most important constitutional powers include: the power to promulgate and execute the laws passed by Congress; the naming of cabinet ministers (*Secretarios de despacho*) and other important federal officers, including all military officers; the power to act as commander in chief (following the model of the US Constitution) and to declare war pursuant to an act of Congress; and the power to conduct foreign relations and conclude treaties, with the approval of the Senate. The Constitution does not mention, of course, the crucial political powers exercised by the President, which, during the PRI's control of government, gave the President immense *de facto* powers beyond those mentioned in Article 89.

The Secretarías de Estado and paraestatales The power of the Mexican President comes in part from the power of appointment and control over a vast federal bureaucracy. Federal employees are covered by the *Ley Federal de los Trabajadores al Servicio del Estado*[34] which implements Article 123-B of the Mexican Constitution. Under this law, government employees are classified either as employees of trust (*trabajadores de confianza*), or basic employees (*trabajadores de base*). *Trabajadores de confianza* serve in senior administrative positions, similar to political appointees in the United States; *trabajadores de base* comprise the ranks of mid- and lower-level federal employees. The President holds the power of appointment and removal of the former, who may not be members of a labour union; the latter are permitted to form unions of government employees, and may only be removed in accordance with the protections provided in the new Federal Civil Service Law.[35]

Article 90 of the Constitution deals with organization of the federal bureaucracy. Beginning in December 1917,[36] Congress passed a succession of Organic Laws (*Leyes Orgánicas*) that govern the structure of the executive branch and set forth the basic outlines of administrative law, as discussed in Chapter 9 below.[37]

The executive branch is divided into eighteen secretariats (*Secretarías*). In addition to the federal secretariats, the executive branch controls a declining

[33] The only real test of this system of forced retirement occurred in April 1936, when President Lázaro Cárdenas, annoyed by the Machiavellian interventions of Plutarco Elias Calles (the *Jefe Máximo* who had tapped Cárdenas for the presidency), deported Calles to the United States. No other former President has attempted to remain politically active or to challenge the power of the succeeding President.

[34] D.O. 27 Dec. 1963.

[35] *See* Chapter 13 below at text accompanying notes 43 to 45.

[36] *Ley de Secretarías de Estado*, D.O. 25 Dec. 1917.

[37] The current version is the *Ley Orgánica de la Administración Pública Federal* of 22 Dec. 1978, D.O. 29 Dec. 1976, as last amended in D.O. 13 Mar. 2002. The law is discussed in Chapter 9 below.

number of decentralized agencies (*paraestatales*). Secretariats and other federal agencies are discussed in more detail in Chapter 9 below.[38] During the heyday of federal government domination of the economy—the *sexenios* of Presidents Echeverría and López Portillo—*paraestatales* were as ubiquitous in Mexico as the plants of *maguey* cactus that dot the countryside. By 1982, 1,155 *paraestatales* were operating in Mexico. Government-owned companies produced steel, ran airlines, operated hotels, and owned cinemas. Many of these *paraestatales* held a monopoly over their sector of the economy. The most important example of this continues to be *Petroleos Mexicanos* (PEMEX), the state-owned oil company.

Beginning with the *sexenio* of President Miguel de la Madrid and continuing during the presidency of Carlos Salinas de Gortari, the federal government, responding to budgetary and balance of payments crises, privatized or liquidated the majority of these *paraestatales*. By 2002, after a campaign of privatizations, the number had been reduced from 1,155 to less than 300 *paraestatales*.

Finally, the government of the Federal District was also administered by the executive branch as an administrative department. Throughout much of the twentieth century, the Constitution granted to the President the power to appoint the mayor (formerly referred to as the *regente*) of the Federal District. This changed in 1993, when Article 89, Section II, and Article 122 of the Constitution were amended to provide for direct election of the *Jefe de Gobierno* (the present name for the mayor of the Federal District).[39] Furthermore, even though residents of the Federal District elected representatives to the federal Congress with full voting rights, they did not elect their own local government. This began to change in 1983, when Article 73, Section VI, of the Constitution was amended to create an Assembly of Representatives, charged with setting regulations adopted to implement laws adopted by Congress for the Federal District.[40] Further changes, creating true legislative powers, were made in 1993, when the Constitution was amended to create the Legislative Assembly for the Federal District.[41] The first *Jefe de Gobierno* elected was Cuauhtémoc Cárdenas, the leader of the opposition PRD party and the son of former President Lázaro Cárdenas: another signal that the PRI's monopoly of political power was ending. The Federal Congress still has considerable legislative power over the Federal District, such as the promulgation of the Government by-laws of the Federal District (*Estatuto de Gobierno del Distrito Federal*);[42] and the Law of Public Debt, which controls public indebtedness by the Federal District.[43] Nevertheless, under amended Article 122, *Apartado C, Base Primera* of the Constitution, the Legislative Assembly for the Federal District has the power to legislate in matters specified in the Constitution (e.g. the Penal Code for the Federal District, discussed below in

[38] The Ministries are established in Articles 26 to 44 of the *Ley Orgánica de la Administración Pública Federal*, and are discussed in more detail in Chapter 9 below.
[39] D.O. 25 Oct. 1993. [40] D.O. 3 Feb. 1983. [41] D.O. 25 Oct. 1993.
[42] D.O. 22 Aug. 1996. [43] D.O. 31 Dec. 1994.

Chapter 11; the Civil Code for the Federal District, as discussed below in Chapter 14, and environmental laws).

2. Executive Power and *Presidencialismo*

The term *presidencialismo* was coined during the twentieth century to characterize the Mexican political and governmental system, a system in which the personal authority of the President dominated all aspects of public life. Much has been written about Mexican *presidencialismo*.[44] The following discussion analyses the legal and political bases of the phenomenon, and the dramatic changes that have occurred in recent years to shift the balance of presidential and legislative power.

2.1. The Rise of *Presidencialismo*

The power of the Mexican presidency was built on a centuries-old foundation of acceptance, in varying degrees, of centralized authority. Centralized authority had been the hallmark of the colonial administration in New Spain,[45] and centripetal forces have been at work from the early days of Mexican independence.[46]

The Constitution of 1824 closely followed the model of the US Constitution, providing for an executive branch governed by a president and a vice-president, each of whom would serve for four years.[47] Despite the similarity of form, the Mexican experience under the 1824 Constitution differed radically from that in the United States. The 1824 Constitution was virtually abandoned in 1836 in favour of the *Siete Leyes*, a series of conservative laws that replaced the Constitution and increased the power of the President.[48] Nevertheless, no

[44] The classic study of *presidencialismo* was Jorge Carpizo's *El Presidencialismo Mexicano* (Mexico: Siglo XXI, 1995). *See also*, *El Presidencialismo Mexicano (Algunas Reflexiones)* (Mexico: Instituto de Investigaciones Jurídicas, UNAM, 1988); Fix-Zamudio, H., 'Las Recientes Transformaciones del Régiman Presidencial Mexicano', in IL *Congreso Iberoamericano de Derecho Constitucional* (Mexico: Instituto de Investigaciones Jurídicas, UNAM, 1992) at 215; Amparo Casar, Ma., *The Analysis of Presidentialism in Mexico* (Division de Estudios Políticos, CIDE, No. 56, 1996); Cornelius, Wayne A., *et al.*, *Mexico's Alternative Political Futures* (Center for US–Mexican studies, University of California, San Diego, 1989).

[45] *See* Chapter 1 above, at text accompanying notes 49–52.

[46] The very first political leader of independent Mexico, Agustín de Iturbide, prevailed on the first Mexican Congress to name him Emperor. Despite Iturbide's immense personal prestige as a hero of independence, ten months after assuming the 'cactus throne', liberal members of the army rebelled and overthrew him. They were led in this revolt by a young military commander from Veracruz named Antonio López de Santa Anna, who earned fame for his own dictatorial leadership on the numerous occasions in which he assumed the presidency.

[47] Orozco Henríquez, J.J., 'El Sistema Presidencial en el Constituyente de Querétaro y Su Evolución Posterior', in *El Sistema Presidencial Mexicano (Algunas Reflexiones)*, *supra* note 16 at 1, 6–7.

[48] *See* Chapter 1 above, text accompanying notes 83–84.

President—not even Santa Anna, who assumed the presidency on eleven different occasions—was able to consolidate individual power. Only Gudadalupe Victoria, the first Mexican President, was able to serve out his term of office, as thirty-seven different men held the office of President until the adoption of the 1857 Constitution. That instability prevented the early development of *presidencialismo*.

The institution of the vice-presidency has been a short-lived and negative experience in Mexican constitutional practice. The 1824 Constitution provided that the loser of the presidential election would become vice-president.[49] This ill-considered model spelled early disaster: the very first vice-president, conservative-centrist Nicolás Bravo, led an armed revolt against the first Mexican President, liberal-federalist Guadalupe Victoria. Bravo was eventually captured, imprisoned, and then exiled.[50] The 1857 Constitution eliminated once and for all the position of vice-president from the Mexican government.[51] The 1917 Constitution makes no provision for a vice-president; in case of presidential incapacitation (*falta absoluta*) Article 84 provides that the Congress shall elect an interim President, and if the incapacitation occurs during the first two years of office, the Congress shall call for a general election to choose a president to serve out the remainder of the presidential term.

As discussed in Chapter 1 above, the 1857 Constitution was heavily influenced by liberal policies. One result of this influence was the theoretical subordination of the President to the legislative branch. The 1857 Constitution provided for a unicameral legislature (the institution of the Senate was considered to be too conservative and too centralist). The President was deprived of a veto power, and could only make observations concerning legislation.[52] The urge to executive authority served to overcome the constitutional infirmities, however. According to Jesús Orozco, the weakening of the presidency merely 'obliged [the President] to corrupt the Congress and to govern outside of the Constitution, with only a superficial respect for the constitutional formalities'.[53]

Beginning with the presidency of Sebastián Lerdo de Tejada (1872–1876), a series of constitutional reforms sought to 'correct' the balance of legislative and executive power under the Constitution of 1857. In 1874, the Constitution was amended to reinstate the Senate, and to grant the President a veto power over legislation. Beginning in the 1880s, constitutional reforms provided exclusive federal authority to legislate over commerce, mining, banking, and other important economic activities, thus increasing the centralized authority of the federal government. This increase in the powers available to the central government, combined with the extensive use of emergency powers by Presidents beginning with Benito Juárez and extending to Porfirio Díaz, created optimum conditions

[49] 1824 Constitution, Article 85. *See* Rabasa, *infra* note 56, at 108–109.
[50] Miller, *supra* note 30, at 205.
[51] Orozco, *supra* note 47, at 13–14.
[52] Fix-Zamudio, *supra* note 44 at 253.
[53] Orozco, *supra* note 47 at 13–14.

for the increase of presidential power.[54] The culmination of this trend came, of course, in the presidency/dictatorship of Porfirio Díaz, who assumed office in 1876 after a *coup d'état* in protest at Lerdo's attempt to seek re-election. As we have already seen,[55] Porfirio Díaz's objections to re-election weakened the longer he remained in office, thanks to convenient constitutional reforms eliminating prohibitions against re-election, and extending the period of the presidency to six years. By 1910, when the Mexican Revolution began, *presidencialismo* had become firmly established, to the point of dictatorship.

The Mexican Revolution was fought against an individual dictator, Porfirio Díaz, and against the concept of entrenchment of power through presidential re-election. However, the Revolution was not fought to abolish a strong presidency *per se*. It may seem ironic to a non-Mexican that Emilio Rabasa, one of Mexico's most distinguished statesmen during the late nineteenth and early twentieth centuries and an opponent of dictatorship, argued in an influential book first published in 1912, *La Constitución y la Dictadura*, that the dictatorship of Porfirio Díaz was the product of a constitution that allowed the legislature to dominate the executive. This left Porfirio Díaz with only one option, to assume dictatorial powers in disregard of the constitution.[56] To prevent such a recurrence, he argued, the Mexican Constitution should provide for a strong presidency. These arguments proved persuasive to President Venustiano Carranza and to the *Constituyentes* in Querétaro. As a result, the Constitution of 1917 provided for a strong President, and weakened the legislature (for example, by providing for two annual congressional sessions, for a total of five months).[57]

While it is somewhat artificial to separate the two, the following sections set out the formal, legal bases of presidential power, and the political power of the President (which explains the overwhelming power of the Mexican President throughout most of the twentieth century).

2.2. Presidential Power Under the 1917 Constitution

2.2.1. Constitutional Bases in General

Constitutional law experts have listed the following constitutional assignations of presidential powers; for many years, these powers served to provided a solid legal basis for *presidencialismo*.[58]

[54] Orozco, *supra* note 47 at 16, 17. [55] *See* text accompanying note 25 above.

[56] Rabasa, E., *La Constitución y la Dictadura* (Mexico: Porrúa, 7th ed., 1990) at 84–85, 111.

[57] The first ordinary congressional period of sessions begins on 1 Sep. and ends on 15 Dec. The second ordinary congessional period begins on 15 Mar. and ends on 30 Apr. Mexican Constitution, Articles 65 and 66. *See* Orozco, *supra* note 47 at 19–27; Fix-Zamudio *supra* note 44 at 225–227. *See also* Carpizo, *El Presidencialismo Mexicano*, *supra* note 29 at 43–44.

[58] Osornio Corres, F.J., 'Estructura Funcional y Orgánica del Ejecutivo Federal en México', in *El Sistema Presidencial Mexicano (Algunas Reflexiones)*, *supra* note 16 at 149,

Under the current version of the much-amended Mexican Constitution, the President has the power to:

(i) introduce bills in Congress (Article 71-I);
(ii) draft the annual federal budget, to be approved by the *Cámara de Diputados* (Article 74-IV);
(iii) enter into international treaties, subject to the approval of the Senate (Article 76-I);
(iv) veto federal legislation, subject to override by a two-thirds vote of Congress (Article 72, par (c));
(v) promulgate and execute the laws passed by Congress (Article 89-I);
(vi) appoint and remove important federal officials, including cabinet ministers (Article 89-II);
(vii) appoint, with Senate approval, military officers as well as senior treasury officials (Article 89-IV and 89-V);
(viii) act as commander in chief of the armed forces and the national guard (Article 89-VI and 89-VII);
(ix) declare war, in accordance with laws approved by Congress (Article 89-VIII);
(x) call for special sessions of Congress, in agreement with the *Comisión Permanente* (Article 89-XI);
(xi) conduct the foreign affairs of the nation (Article 89-X);
(xii) provide support to the judiciary to carry out its functions (Article 89-XII);
(xiii) grant pardons to persons convicted of federal crimes (Article 89-XIV);
(xiv) present a list of three candidates for every appointment of a person to be be minister of the Supreme Court, the final selection being made by vote of the Senate (89-XVIII);
(xv) order the deportation, without a prior hearing, of any foreign citizen whose presence in Mexico is deemed 'inconvenient' (Article 33);
(xvi) carry out agrarian reform, and regulate the exploitation of natural resources (Article 27);
(xvii) enter into loan agreements on behalf of the nation (Article 73-VIII); and
(xviii) fix export and import tariffs, and establish other regulations on international trade, in accordance with powers granted by Congress (Article 131).

In addition, before the Constitution was amended in 1994,[59] the President was entitled to appoint the mayor and senior officials that governed the Federal District, the largest population centre in the country. Since the Federal District lacked its own legislative assembly (depending on the PRI-dominated Congress for legislation) the President had direct legislative and executive control over approximately 15 per cent of the country's population.

206–208; Carpizo and Madrazo, *supra* note 29 at 1701, 1755–1759, 1766–1771; Orozco, *supra* note 47 at 30–32.

[59] *See* discussion in this Chapter at text accompanying note 39.

The most obvious power assigned to the President is the administration of an immense bureaucracy in a system dominated by federal institutions.[60] In 1917, there were seven federal *secretarías* and five *departamentos*; today, there are eighteen *secretarías* and more than seventy-five *órganos decentralizados*.[61] When combined with the impressive number of government-owned *paraestatales*, these agencies give the President the power to appoint, directly or indirectly, countless government officials: a source of political largesse that Mexican presidents have used to grant favours to followers as well as to co-opt opposition leaders. According to Jesús Orozco:

> The aforementioned administrative apparatus implies a concentration of human, technical and financial resources under the executive branch, which translates into a pre-eminence over the other branches of government. All of the principal officials and employees of these dependencies and entities of the federal public administration are subject to the President of the Republic; he appoints them and removes them, gives them orders and determines the economic means at their disposal.[62]

The corollary of the power of appointment, the ability to remove officials, is also important. Indeed, the President's power to remove federal officials extended even beyond the federal executive branch, to the removal of state governors[63] and judges. The latter power, which significantly weakened the independence of the judiciary, was removed by constitutional reforms in 1982[64] and further diminished by the 1994 judicial reforms, which are discussed elsewhere.[65]

In addition to these constitutional bases, significant presidential powers emanate from ordinary legislation, some examples of which are worth highlighting here. Until the late 1980s, the President's power over the domestic economy was virtually unbridled, and represented a major instrument of Mexican *presidencialismo*. Due to economic reforms beginning in the late 1980s, which are discussed elsewhere,[66] this power is now significantly diminished, but vestiges of it still remain.

2.2.2. *The President's Economic Powers*

During the heyday of the PRI's power, Congress delegated to the President immense economic powers. Under the *Ley Federal de Entidades Paraestatales*,[67]

[60] *See* Chapter 4 above at text accompanying notes preceding note 44, and section 1.1.1. of this Chapter.

[61] *See Ley Orgánica de la Administración Pública Federal*, Article 26, D.O. 30 Nov. 2000.

[62] Orozco, *supra* note 47 at 38 (authors' trans.)

[63] *See* the discussion of *desaparición de poderes infra* in Chapter 4, and at notes text accompanying notes 47–49.

[64] In 1928, Articles 89 and 111 of the Constitution were amended to grant to the President the power to ask the *Cámara de Diputados* to remove federal judges 'for misconduct' (*por mala conducta*). D.O. 20 Aug. 1928. The power was exercised a number of times, and many judges were forced to resign rather than face the possibility of formal removal. Finally, in 1982, the provision was removed from the Constitution (D.O. 28 Dec. 1982), thus removing 'a serious obstacle in the strengthening of judicial independence'. Carpizo and Madrazo, *supra* note 29 at 1766. *See also* Orozco, *supra* note 47 at 52–54.

[65] *See infra* Chapter 6, text accompanying notes 88–104.

[66] *See* Chapter 12 below.

[67] D.O. 14 May. 1986, as amended 24 Jul. 1992 and 24 Dec. 1996.

the executive branch has direct control over decentralized agencies and government-owned businesses (*paraestatales*).[68] Beginning with President Miguel de la Madrid, and continuing in the *sexenio* of President Salinas, the federal government privatized a large number of the *paraestatales* that had been created during the Díaz Ordaz, Echeverría, and López Portillo administrations.[69] Nevertheless, even after the neo-liberal economic reforms of the Salinas and Zedillo administrations,[70] important *paraestatales* that are key elements in the economy remain government-owned, including PEMEX, which has a monopoly on petroleum exploitation and production; IMSS and ISSSTE, the social security agencies that operate public health facilities throughout the nation; CONASUPO, which distributes basic foods and other consumer goods; *Ferrocarriles Nacionales de México*, the national railroad company; the *Compañia Federal de Electricidad* (CFE) and *Luz y Fuerza*, which generate and distribute electric power; and the Mexican Postal Service.

Under the 1950 *Ley sobre Atribuciones del Ejecutivo Federal en Materia Económica*,[71] Congress delegated to the executive branch broad powers to fix prices for basic commodities and services, and even to decide which basic products should be produced. In 1976, after a dramatic devaluation of the peso, President Luis Echeverría used the law to prevent producers of goods and services from raising prices. This law was abrogated in 1992 by the *Ley Federal de Competencia Económica*,[72] but the new law included a new delegation of authority to the executive to fix prices in equally broad terms: 'The Federal Executive has the exclusive authority to determine by decree those goods and services that shall be subject to maximum prices'.[73]

For many decades, the President also possessed direct control over monetary policy, by virtue of the power of appointment and removal of officers of the Banco de México, Mexico's central bank.[74] However, in 1993, in a move to make monetary policy independent of politics, the Constitution was amended to permit the Banco de México to operate as an autonomous entity;[75] since that time, monetary policy in Mexico has been maintained with stability and without undue influence by the executive branch.

As already noted, under Article 131 of the Constitution, the Congress grants broad authority to the President to 'legislate' in matters of international trade

[68] Carpizo and Madrazo, *supra* note 29 at 1771.

[69] From 1970 to 1982, the number of *paraestatales* in Mexico grew from 471 to 1155, representing 30% of total fixed investment in the country by 1982. Sánchez González, M., 'Entorno macroeconómico frente al tratado de libre comercio', in *México y el Tratado Trilateral de Libre Comercio: Impacto Sectorial* (Mexico: Eduardo Andere and Gerogina Kessel eds., 1992) at 1, 8. By February 1990, the Mexican government had authorized the divestment of 801 of these *paraestatales*, 619 of which had already been divested. Review of Trade and Investment Liberalization Measures by Mexico and Prospects for future United States—Mexican Relations 41 (Washington, D.C.: 'US International Trade Commission', Pub. No. 2275, 1990).

[70] Discussed in Chapter 12 below, at Section 1.1.1.

[71] D.O. 30 Dec. 1950. *See* Carpizo, El Presidencialismo Mexicano, *supra* note 29 at 135–136.

[72] D.O. 24 Dec. 1992, at 9, *Artículo transitorio tercero (II)*.

[73] *Ibid.*, Article 7, para. I (author's trans.)

[74] Carpizo and Madrazo, *supra* note 29 at 1771.

[75] D.O. 20 Aug. 1993.

policy: tariffs, quotas, etc. During the many years in which the PRI controlled both the presidency and the Congress, the President's power to draft the federal budget (Article 74-IV) and to determine the federal government's level of borrowing[76] also gave the President overwhelming weight in fiscal and budgetary matters. However, with the election of *panista* candidate Vicente Fox in 2000 and the PRI's loss of a majority in Congress, the President's ability to determine the federal budget and set tax policy has been dramatically eroded. During his first two years in office, Vicente Fox, whose party lacked a majority in Congress, was unable to bring about the major tax reforms that he initially pursued, and also laboured to draft federal budgets that achieved congressional approval. The new balance of power over fiscal and budgetary matters has begun to resemble the give-and-take politics that take place between the executive and legislative branches in the United States and other countries, with a significant difference: in Mexico, the working out of a budget under these conditions is a novelty, and the practices and procedures for congressional and executive co-operation are still being tested.

2.2.3. *Legislative and Quasi-Legislative Powers of the President*

Despite preserving the formal concept of the separation of legislative and executive powers, the framers of the Constitution of 1917 were careful not to allow the legislative branch to overwhelm the executive: a danger, whether real or not, that was perceived to have encouraged nineteenth-century Mexican Presidents to assume dictatorial powers. Emilio Rabasa, Venustiano Carranza, and others believed that Mexico needed a strong President to provide leadership for the nation and for Congress. One result of this predilection for presidential power was to grant legislative and quasi-legislative powers to the President, and to create a system that permitted the executive branch to dominate the legislative process. The de facto reasons for this are explored below. At this time, we shall address certain *de jure* legislative powers of the Mexican President that contributed to the domination of Congress by the President during much of the twentieth century. (As explained above, the decline of single-party domination of Congress has eliminated such domination, at least for the time being.)

In certain instances the Mexican Constitution actually grants legislative powers to the executive branch. Under Article 73-XVI, clause 1, the *Consejo de Salubridad General*, an intersecretarial commission, is granted the power to legislate on matters of health and environment without the need for congressional approval.[77] Article 131 similarly gives the President broad powers to fix import and export duties and other trade policies, in accordance with broad delegation of power by Congress.[78] Articles 131 and 29 (emergency powers)[79] are the only

[76] Under Article 73-VIII, the Congress sets the bases on which the President may borrow money on behalf of the nation.

[77] Carpizo, *El Presidencialismo Mexicano*, *supra* note 29 at 104.

[78] *Id.* at 108–109; Orozco, *supra* note 47 at 50.

[79] Article 29 of the Constitution grants the President the power to legislate in case of emergency by virtue of general provisions and to suspend temporarily, in all the country or in

express exceptions to the principle of separation of executive and legislative powers under Article 49.

In 1938, the Constitution was amended to require congressional authorization of the President's emergency legislative power,[80] and this power has since been used just once, by President Manuel Avila Camacho, when Mexico declared war on the Axis countries during the Second World War.[81]

In addition, Article 89-I of the Constitution grants to the President the authority to 'legislate' through the adoption of regulations implementing federal legislation.[82] In important instances, the laws passed by Congress have been extremely general, thus allowing the executive branch to add considerable substance to the law through the adoption of detailed regulations.[83] Of course, the regulations adopted by executive branch agencies cannot conflict with or exceed the scope of the laws they are intended to implement.[84]

The power of the President to legislate directly, in the instances just described, is less important than the power of the President to legislate indirectly through the power of initiative. Article 71 of the Constitution states:

> The right to introduce laws or decrees belongs:
>
> I. to the President of the Republic;
>
> II. to the deputies and senators of the Congress of the Union;
>
> III. to the legislatures of the States...

Until 1997, when the PRI lost majority control in both houses of Congress, 98 per cent of the bills presented to Congress originated in the executive branch, and these were generally approved by Congress without substantial

certain places, those guarantees which could be considered as an obstacle to resolve rapidly and easily the emergency situation, and until 1938 this emergency power was used repeatedly to legislate by executive decree, with the acquiescence of the Supreme Court. Numerous important laws were adopted in this manner, including the 1929 *Ley Orgánica* of the National University (UNAM), the Ley General de Comunicaciones, the *Ley de Instituciones Financieras y de Crédito*, reforms to the *Código de Comercio*, the *Ley General de Sociedades Cooperativas*, the *Código de Procedimientos Civiles para el Distrito Federal y Territorios*, the *Ley Orgánica de Justicia Federal, the Código Agrario*, the creation of the *Comisión Federal de Electricidad*, and others. Carpizo, EL PRESIDENCIALISMO MEXICANO, *supra* note 29 at 102, citing Stephen Spencer Goodspeed, 'El papel del jefe del ejecutivo en México', in PROBLEMAS AGRÍCOLAS E INDUSTRIALES DE MÉXICO (Talleres Gráficos de la Nación, 1955) vol. VII, *passim* at 65–200. *See* also Orozco, *supra* note 47 at 49.

80 Prior to 1938, the Supreme Court had recognized that the President could exercise legislative powers pursuant to Article 29 even though Congress had not declared a state of emergency. After the reform to Article 49, it is now assumed that Congress must authorize the President to exercise emergency powers under Article 29. Carpizo and Madrazo, *supra* note 29 at 1722.

81 D.O. 12 June 1942.

82 Carpizo, EL PRESIDENCIALISMO MEXICANO, *supra* note 29 at 105–108.

83 Among the many examples, *see* the Law of Public Service of Electrical Energy (*Ley del Servicio Público de Energía Eléctrica*) and its Regulations; the General Law of Health (*Ley General de Salud*) and its Regulations; the Customs Law (*Ley Aduanera*) and its Regulations, among others.

84 Quinta Epoca, T. LXXXII, vol. VI, at. 6715 (1935); T. LXXIV, vol. V, at 3895 (1942); T. CXXII, at 28–34 (1954) and Séptima Epoca, vol. XXXIX, *tercera parte*, at 51–52; vol. LI, *tercera parte* at 81; vol. LII, *tercera parte*, at 78; vol. LIII, *tercera parte*, at 27; vol. LIV, *tercera parte*, at 31, vol. LV, *tercera parte*, at 39–40 and vol. LXI, *sexta parte*, at 53–54.

amendments, even in the case of constitutional reforms.[85] There are several reasons for the predominant role of the executive in the legislative process. First, as discussed below,[86] Congress has lacked the funding necessary to employ a significant staff that could be used to study issues and draft legislation in response to them; the executive branch, by contrast, consists of numerous bureaucracies overflowing with personnel that have the expertise to draft legislation in their specialized areas. Second, for decades, the political realities of the PRI made it difficult for significant opposition to form against the President's legislative proposals. Finally, the institutional weaknesses of Congress—for instance the non-reelection of *diputados* and senators[87] and the lack of adequate funding for congressional activities—have also contributed to the presidential domination of the legislature. As discussed in sections 3.2.2. and 4.2 below, the non-reelection of legislators means that the Mexican Congress lacks a cadre of highly professional legislators with substantive experience in different areas of legislation.[88] While citizens' groups in the United States argue for term limits and complain about the entrenchment of multi-term US congressmen and senators, one must at least concede that the legislative power exercised by such legislators serves as a counter-balance to presidential power. This counter-balance has been lacking in Mexico.

In the first post-PRI administration of President Fox, with the President's power to effect legislation dramatically reduced, Congress has able to prevent the President from passing broad legislation. At the same time, however, a Congress divided along political lines has lacked the consensus and congressional leadership to adopt an alternative agenda. Legislation that has been passed to date has been done so through negotiations carried on behind the scenes between the political leaderships of the parties.

Certain ironies occurred as a result of the operation of *presidencialismo* in the legislative process. For instance, during the past century, the veto power written into Article 72 (c) practically fell into disuse, since the President proposed almost all legislation.[89] In 2003 President Fox exercised the presidential veto for the first time in 40 years, when he vetoed the National Water Law (Ley de Aquas Nacionales).[90]

[85] Orozco, *supra* note 47 at 48–49. *Cf.* Fix-Zamudio, *supra* note 44 at 232; Carpizo and Madrazo, *supra* note 29 at 1771: '... at present it is the president of the Republic who sends to Congress the immense majority of proposed legislative bills'. *See infra* Section 4.3.

[86] *See* discussion in section 4.3 *infra.*

[87] The Constitution of 1917 permitted re-election of both *diputados* and senators, but the 1933 reforms reinserting non-reelection of the President also added the non-reelection of *diputados* and senators for the period immediately following their term in office. Mexican Constitution, Art. 59.

[88] According to Jesús Orozco, the prohibition against re-election 'has served to impede the professionalization of the legislative career and to accentuate the dependence of the legislator on the executive branch in order to obtain a position in the public administration once the legislator has concluded his period of office.' Orozco, *supra* note 47 at 50 (authors' trans.)

[89] Fix-Zamudio, *supra* note 44 at 232. Carpizo, *supra* note 29 at 89–91, footnote 24, lists the occasions on which the President of Mexico has exercised the veto power, many of which have to do with pensions and fiscal matters of lesser importance.

[90] References to the veto can be found at www.senado.job.mx/comunicacion/content/version/2003/v12diciembre.php#1. *See also* the Gaceto Parlamentaria del Senado of 2 Sept. 2003, at www.senado.gob.mx/sgsp/gaceta/?sesion=2003/09/02/1. (May, 2004).

2.3. *De facto* Bases of Mexican *Presidencialismo*

While formal legal structures may have served to support the development of presidential power, the *de facto* bases of *presidencialismo* were even more important. Political scientists have given numerous reasons for the tendency towards authoritarianism that exists in Latin America.[91] In the case of Mexico, the legacy of authoritarian government can be traced back to pre-Hispanic civilizations. True, currents of enlightenment emanating from Europe and the United States did have effects in colonial Mexico, contributing towards the independence movement and the establishment of representative democracy. The authoritarian, monarchical model was rejected, as shown in the defeat of Iturbide's imperial scheme. Nevertheless, despite periods of instability (the early Mexican Republic, the Mexican Revolution), Mexico's history gives evidence of a tendency to accept authoritarian leadership concentrated in the presidency itself. Political scientist George Philip has written of a 'Hobbesian bargain': for decades, Mexicans (who are not particularly ideological by nature) accepted a centralized power structure in exchange for the stability and economic growth that favoured influential sectors of society.[92]

Constitutional scholars in Mexico listed a number of *de facto* reasons for the personal power of the Mexican President during the PRI's monopoly of power:[93]

(i) the President was the head of the predominant political party, the PRI;
(ii) the weakness of local political bosses;
(iii) the weakness of the legislature;
(iv) the organization of farm workers (*campesinos*) and labour unions into groups supporting the PRI;
(v) the professionalization of the army, and the removal of the military from politics;
(vi) increasing centralization and federalization of tax and revenue authority, and the economic powers of the executive;
(vii) effective use of mass media to control public opinion;
(viii) the power to name important public officials, including his successor (as described below); and
(ix) the psychological element, i.e. the acceptance of a strong President by the public.

Several of these reasons are worth discussing in more detail.

[91] *See*, e.g., AUTHORITARIANISM IN LATIN AMERICA SINCE INDEPENDENCE (Westport, Conn: Greenwood Press, W. Fowler, ed., 1996).

[92] Philip, *supra* note 4 at 14–16. According to Philip, who surveyed the Mexican presidency during the period 1964–1988, there was virtually no constitutional check on presidential authority, and the Mexican President was 'an absolute monarch for six years'. *Id.* at 166 (citing Daniel Cosío Villegas, *LA SUCESIÓN PRESIDENCIAL EN MÉXICO* (Mexico: Joaquín Mortiz ed., 1975) at 19, as authority for the quotation).

[93] *See* Carpizo, EL PRESIDENCIALISMO MEXICANO *supra* note 29 at 24–25; Orozco, *supra* note 47 at 47.

2.3.1. *The Political Power of the President*

Almost from its creation (in 1929, under the name *Partido Nacional Revolucionario* (PNR)[94]) the PRI served as a 'crucial instrument of presidential control; each president has governed the party in accordance with his personal design for the national agenda'.[95] This control by one person over the party continues to mark Mexican party politics, even though the PRI has lost its electoral monopoly; as we shall see in the following section of this Chapter, this is due in part to the lack of an open, democratic system for the selection of candidates.

The political domination of the PRI was not a gradual process. From its infancy, the Party—led by Plutarco Elias Calles, the ex-President and *jefe máximo* of Mexican politics until his exile on 9 April 1936—quickly established a predominant power base from which its leaders directed the social and economic development of the nation. The PRI successfully co-opted the most powerful groups in society. While espousing revolutionary ideals, from the outset the PRI was a highly pragmatic party, immediately establishing a strong coalition of local and regional bosses (*caudillos* or *caciques*) and special interest groups.[96] From 1929, the combination of political support and electoral fraud meant that in most elections throughout the country, both state and local, the PRI candidate was virtually assured of election.[97]

Consolidation of the PRI's power was accomplished by establishing three main pillars of support: labour unions, farm workers (*campesinos*), and mid-level bureaucrats (the 'popular' organizations).[98] Plutarco Elias Calles began the process of promoting the organization of labour unions into confederations that could be counted on to support the PRI, and Lázaro Cárdenas continued this tactic with great success. Lázaro Cárdenas stepped up the pace of land reform as a way of winning the support of *campesinos*, many of whom were organized into *ejidos* and plugged into state and national

[94] The PNR was created in 1929 by Plutarco Elias Calles to impose order on the Mexican political process after the assassination of Alvaro Obregón. In 1938, the name of the party was changed to *Partido de la Revolución Mexicana* (PRM). In 1946, the Party's name was changed to the *Partido Revolucionario Institucional* (PRI). In the remainder of this Chapter, the term PRI is used to denote the party from its inception to the present.

[95] Gomez, L. and Bailey, J., (1990) 'La Transición Política y los Dilemas del PRI' 31 FORO INTERNACIONAL, 57, 64 (1990).

[96] For a discussion of the founding of the PRI, *See* Cárdenas, J., CRISIS DE LEGITIMIDAD Y DEMOCRACIA INTERNA DE LOS PARTIDOS POLÍTICOS (Mexico: Fondo de Cultura Económica, 1992) at 190, and studies cited therein. For a literary treatment of the psychology of co-optation of revolutionary ideals, *see* Fuentes, Carlos, *LA MUERTE DE ARTEMIO CRUZ* (Mexico: 1962).

[97] From 1929 to 1976, the PRI candidate for President never won less than 74% of the popular vote. Lazaro Cardenas' election was won with 98.19% of the vote. *See* Martínez Assad, C., 'Introducción', in *LA SUCESIÓN PRESIDENCIAL EN MÉXICO (COYUNTURA ELECTORAL Y CAMBIO POLÍTICO)* (Mexico: Carlos Martínez Assad, ed., Ed. Nueva Imagen, 1981) at 9, 16–17 (fold-out page).

[98] An excellent study is Roberto Newell and Rubio, *supra* note 3.

organizations.[99] The 'popular' sector was represented by the eventual formation of the *Comite Nacional de Organizaciones Populares* (CNOP), a national association of mid-level government bureaucrats.

Until the late 1980s, these three pillars, combined with the other instruments of presidential power noted above, proved sufficient to withstand the few political challenges that occasionally confronted Mexican Presidents. Of course, political leaders did not wait for the opposition to organize itself. For instance, the President has used the *desaparición de poderes*[100] to force the removal of state governors who opposed centralized policies. Similarly, professionalization of the army, begun in the late 1920s, reduced the power of *caudillos* in the military: from 1934 to 1940, under President Cárdenas, military leaders were removed from political positions in the PRI, and the Mexican military has remained largely depoliticized ever since.[101]

Two other centres of possible opposition, the Catholic Church and the entrepreneurial class, never actively supported the PRI, but nevertheless accommodated themselves to the ruling party. During the Presidency of Miguel Alemán Valdéz (1946–1952), the PRI preserved the basic rights of private ownership (despite the occasional expropriation) and bought the support of private business through the granting of government contracts and the construction of protective barriers to foreign competition. In the case of the Catholic Church, the PRI, despite the continuance of anti-clerical policies discussed in Chapter 1 above, settled into a comfortable truce in which the two most powerful institutions in Mexico avoided confrontation by being careful to operate only in their respective religious and political spheres.[102] In fact, the PRI provided important assistance to the Church, in the name of cultural patriotism, by maintaining and reconstructing sumptuous colonial churches as historical treasures: churches that the Catholic Church continues to use.

The PRI is non-ideological and composed of different interest groups; yet the internal politics of the PRI have avoided open conflict because the party has been traditionally managed in authoritarian fashion. During its long ascendancy, the leadership of the PRI—and primarily the President himself—always decided the legislative agenda, taking into account the need to satisfy different groups both within the Party and within society. Once this decision was made, the authoritarian structure of the PRI required the obedient

[99] Suárez Gaona, E., 'Legitimación Revolucionaria del Poder en México?' in *LOS PRESIDENTES 1910–1982* (Mexico: Siglo XXI, 1987) at 73.

[100] *See* Chapter 4 above, at text accompanying notes 47–49.

[101] The post-Revolutionary army included many generals with the potential to exercise military power. The Mexican army of 1927 had 159 generals for 53,000 men, i.e. or one general for every 335 men. Lázaro Cárdenas saw to the retirement of many of these generals, removing the potential for coups and political intrigues. Córdova A., *LA FORMACIÓN DEL PODER POLÍTICO EN MÉXICO* (Mexico: Ed. Era, 1972) at 51.

[102] Blancarte, R., *HISTORIA DE LA IGLESIA EN MEXICO* (Mexico: El Colegiode México/Fondo de Cultura Económica, 1992) at 415.

adherence of all party members.[103] The result was a legislative green light for the President.[104]

The President's personal authority within the PRI was also exercised in the selection of PRI candidates throughout the country, which served as an additional instrument of presidential power.[105] Lacking true party primary elections, in which large numbers of the population may vote to select a candidate, Mexican party professionals tend to hand-pick candidates for office.

The most important selection, of course, was of the presidential candidate, which for many years amounted to the appointment by the President of his successor. This method of selection of a successor, popularly referred to as the *dedazo* ('fingering'), generated a great deal of mythology, as well as serious scholarship,[106] on the process of presidential succession in Mexico. Even the terminology of presidential succession called attention to the unique pattern of this process, a process that remained mysterious because much of it occurred behind closed doors, and the principal figures refused to speak openly about it.[107] In selecting his successor, the President functioned within a closed network

[103] A well known anecdote from the presidency of José López Portillo illustrates this allegiance to the party and to the President. As discussed in Chapter 20 below, in 1982, responding to a balance of payments crisis, President José López Portillo, after consulting a handful of close advisers, chose to 'nationalize' (expropriate) all privately owned Mexican banks. On the morning of his sixth state of the union message (*Informe*), on 1 September 1982, preliminary to his public announcement of the decision, he met with his cabinet, most of whom had not been informed of the measures. The President presented the decisions to the cabinet, asking the members to sign a statement supporting these actions. Only one member of the cabinet, the president of the Mexican Export Bank, asked to speak. 'Mr. President,' he asked, 'since you want us to sign this statement, you must want to know our opinion of these measures'. The President's curt reply was negative: 'simply sign the statement'. The official and the General Director of the Bank of Mexico refused to sign, and shortly thereafter they relinquished their posts. Congress later acted to bring federal law and the Constitution into conformity with the presidential decision.

[104] During the PRI regime, all Mexican Presidents availed themselves of this *de facto* legislative power, which allowed them not only to arrange the passage of laws, but also to amend the Constitution with relative ease. The champion in this latter regard was José López Portillo, who pushed through 31 constitutional reforms on one occasion (7 October 1974), and 17 reforms on another (4 October 1977). Granados Chapa, M., VOTAR—PARA QUE?, *infra* note 131 at 30.

[105] *See generally* Carpizo, EL PRESIDENCIALISMO MEXICANO, *supra* note 29 at 191–198.

[106] Smith, P.H., LABYRINTHS OF POWER (Princeton, NJ: Princeton University Press, 1979); Castañeda, J.G., PERPETUALITY OF POWER (New York: New Press, 2000) (P.A. Smithies, trans.)

[107] During the last two years of the presidential *sexenio*, the press (encouraged by the PRI) would begin to comment on the principal government officials (ministers, or heads of agencies) who were considered to be presidenciables (that is, likely candidates for selection as the PRI candidate). These officials represented certain power groups within the leadership of the PRI, and were also referred to as *tapados* (from the verb *tapar*, to cover or place a lid on). By October of the year preceding the presidential elections (held every six years during the month of July), the list had usually been narrowed to several *tapados*. The one chosen by the President, the *verdadero* (or 'true') *tapado*, would be notified by a senior official of the PRI, usually in November, and the selection would be made public in an announcement known as the *destapamiento or destape* (unveiling). This person then became the *precandidato* (pre-candidate) who was presented at the PRI national convention held prior to the election. Once the convention had ratified the choice, as always happened, the person became the official candidate, or *candidato* of the PRI, and embarked on a national campaign to ensure election. The

of personal ties and blocs of interest groups within the PRI. The President's freedom to select the candidate was constrained somewhat by the need take into account the opinions of other members of the pyramid of power within the PRI, in order to maintain party loyalty.[108] This highly centralized system of candidate selection within the PRI broke down: a casualty of the weakening political power of the PRI, and of the electoral turmoil that accompanied it.[109] Currently, competitive, broad primary elections are still unknown in Mexico, both within the PRI and in the other political parties, but while the selection of presidential candidates to represent the PRI is not as transparent or competitive as it is in the United States, it is much less dependent on the will of a select few than previously.

2.3.2. *The President's Economic Powers*

The political powers of the Mexican President are complemented by a wide array of economic powers. This was particularly true prior to the neo-liberal economic reforms of the 1990s, discussed below in Chapter 12. Prior to that time, the Mexican government played an overwhelming role in the economy, under the general policy known as the *rectoría*, or stewardship, of the

candidato would spend months touring the country, accompanied by an entourage of PRI supporters and bureaucrats who hoped to earn important positions in the upcoming *sexenio*. The vigorous national campaign, even in times when election of the PRI candidate was assured, was a legacy of the Lázaro Cárdenas regime; Cárdenas used the campaign to learn about political conditions and to solidify political contacts throughout the country, and later candidates have done the same.

[108] 'The need to accept a compromise not only tells us something about the nature of the political process itself in Mexico, but also that the power of the President is seen as limited by other political groups'. Camp, R., 'El Sistema Mexicano y las Decisiones sobre el Personal Político', in FORO INTERNACIONAL (July–Sep. 1976) vol. 17, no. 1, at 51, 58–59. This article contains a useful general discussion of the decision-making process of presidential succession.

[109] The method of selecting presidential candidates began to change with the selection of Carlos Salinas de Gortari (President from 1988 to 1994) as the PRI's candidate. For the first time, Salinas' predecessor, President Miguel de la Madrid, publicly announced a list of 6 potential candidates (referred to as '*presidenciables*'), to test the political waters, but also to give a greater appearance of openness; after a period of public comment, de la Madrid hand-picked Salinas. For a discussion of the 1988 presidential elections, *see* Smith, Peter H., 'The 1988 Presidential Succession', in MEXICO'S ALTERNATIVE POLITICAL FUTURES (Wayne Cornelius, Judith Gentleman and Peter H. Smith, eds., Center for US—Mexican Studies, Unviersity of California at San Diego, Monograph Series No. 30, 1989) at 391.

President Salinas' selection of his successor returned to the traditional method of selecting a successor. Faced with a loss of popularity and stiff competition from a new political party (the PRD, or *Partido de la Revolución Democrática*, created by defectors from the PRI), President Salinas personally selected the PRI candidate, Luis Donaldo Colosio, who was supported by labour groups. In March 1994, four months before the election, Colosio was murdered while on campaign in Tijuana. (The murderer has never been found, and no one has been convicted of the crime.) Facing an environment of confusion and uncertainty, Presdient Salinas quickly designated Ernesto Zedillo, a former Minister of Planning and Budget, as the new PRI candidate. Since Zedillo had been Colosio's campaign co-ordinator, he had already resigned his cabinet-level post, and therefore met the constitutional requirement of not having served in government for a period of at least six months prior to the election. Zedillo was elected by a vote of 50.2% of the electorate and took office in December 1994. *See* Meyer, L., 'Prólogo', in Gómez Palacio, I., PROCESOS ELECTORALES (Mexico: Oxford University Press, 2000).

economy.[110] Under this policy, the President himself was the *rector*—the director and chief decision-maker—of all economic policies. This role was even enshrined in the Constitution, in Articles 25 and 26, and while the Presidents Salinas, Zedillo, and Fox have not exercised the full power, the constitutional underpinnings have never been removed. The President carried out these economic powers through the ministries and *paraestatales* that were at his disposal.[111] Given federal government's control of public spending,[112] the President had the power to direct the expenditure of funds throughout the country. In addition, the federal government could use its instruments of corporatist control to compel competing groups to conform to government policy.[113]

President Carlos Salinas de Gortari, an economist, began a significant restructuring of the economy in 1989, reducing the government's role and enhancing the role of private enterprise.[114] Salinas' unstated goal was to maintain political

In 2000, facing a serious challenge by candidates from the PAN and from the PRD, as well as a more transparent and honest electoral process (discussed below in section 3), President Zedillo staged a 'primary election', organized by the PRI itself, which permitted any Mexican citizen with a voting card to vote for the PRI candidate of his or her choice. Four candidates waged a public campaign, and Francisco Labastida, a former Secretary of the Interior, who was supported by President Zedillo, received the largest number of votes and was named the PRI candidate. The victory was short-lived, and Labastida, facing a swelling desire of the electorate for a change, became the first candidate of the PRI ever to lose a presidential election.

[110] *See generally* LA CONSTITUCIÓN MEXICANA: *RECTORÍA DEL ESTADO Y ECONOMÍA MIXTA* (Mexico: (UNAM)IIJ and Porrúa, 1985).

[111] *See* Orozco, *supra* note 47 at 40–45. *See also* Carpizo, EL *PRESIDENCIALISMO MEXICANO*, *supra* note 29 at 151–157.

[112] *See* Chapter 4 above, at text accompanying notes 105–134.

[113] During the height of the corporatist period, the President exercised significant *de facto* controls over the economy. For instance, in the 1980s, to combat inflation, the federal executive devised a 'Pact' to combat spiralling inflation. In 1987, President de la Madrid signed the *Pacto de Solidaridad Económica*, in which leaders of the labour, *campesino*, and business sectors agreed to hold the line against excessive wage and price increases, in exchange for the government's assurance that it would control public expenditures. (A short history of the *Pacto* can be found in 'Evolución del Pacto para la Estabilidad y el Crecimiento Económico (PECE)', EL MERCADO DE VALORES, Num. 24, 15 Dec. 1991, at 20–26.) The *Pacto* was an almost instant success, helping to reduce the annual inflation rate (measured by consumer price increases) from 159.2% in 1987 to 51.7% in 1988, and 19.7% in 1989.

The *Pacto* was not a formal agreement subject to strict enforcement through clearly measured sanctions. Neither was it entirely voluntary, however, since the government had the fiscal and regulatory powers to penalize business or labour entities that would not abide by the anti-inflationary outlines. The *Pacto* was an example of the executive's employment of its role as *rector* of the economy to secure commitments concerning the management of the economy through suasion. *See generally* Rocha Torres, Silvia Eugenia, 'Bases Constitucionales de la Concertación' (professional thesis, Universidad Iberoamericana [unpublished], 1990).

[114] Vestiges of centralized economic control remain, however. For instance, Mexican law specifically authorizes the President to fix maximum prices for a wide variety of goods and services. Under the 1950 *LEY SOBRE ATRIBUCIONES DEL EJECUTIVO FEDERAL EN MATERIA ECONÓMICA*, D.O. 30 Dec. 1950, Articles 1–3, Congress granted the President the power to set maximum wholesale and retail prices for a wide variety of basic products and consumer articles. In 1992, the current *Ley Federal de Competencia Económica*, D.O. 24 Dec. 1992 (as amended), most of which is devoted to competition law, abrogated the 1950 law but preserved the power of the President (operating through the economic secretariat) to set maximum prices for goods and services (*Ley Federal de Competencia Económica*, Article 7). Currently, the

control while loosening the government's control of the economy. From 1988 to 1994, the federal government privatized 397 *paraestatales*, as well as the eighteen commercial banks that had been expropriated by the government in 1982.[115] Unfortunately for the PRI, the relaxation of control on the economy indirectly undermined the President's political powers; the goal of maintaining an open economy and a closed polity proved unattainable.

2.3.3. *Power over the Media*

During the heyday of the PRI, the President's powers were enhanced by the government's utilization of significant *de facto* powers over the media. These powers were of three types. First, there was the ceremonial and public relations power of the presidency itself.[116] In a society in which power is highly personalized, the President can monopolize the front pages of newspapers by making speeches, announcements, dedications of programmes and buildings, etc. Second, the ministries and other executive agencies of the federal government spend considerable time and effort on public relations, selling the President's programmes as well as his point of view. In addition, the Mexican government could control the dissemination of information to the media, since at the time there was no Freedom of Information Act compelling public disclosure. As a result, investigative reporting was weak. Third, as *rector* of the centralized economy, the President exercised a certain degree of control over the 'independent' media[117] through the granting of concessions for radio and television, and the sale of newsprint by the government-owned PIPSA (*Productora e Importadora de Papel, S.A.*).[118]

The power to control the media has now been dramatically diminished. After privatizations, the government no longer owns media companies or print distributors. Additionally, in 2002, Congress adopted a public information law supported by President Fox, the Federal Law of Transparency and Access to Governmental Public Information (*Ley Federal de Transparencia y Acceso a la Información Pública Gubernamental*)[119] that provides public access to government documents; the passage of this law may prove to be the most lasting contribution of President Fox's administration, to the extent that it promotes transparency of government decision-making.

2.3.4. *The Judiciary as an Extension of Mexican* Presidencialismo

An aggressive, independent judiciary in Mexico could constitute a serious threat to the maintenance of *presidencialismo*, by holding the President and executive

principal commodities for which prices are controlled are fixed considering the monthly inflationary index published by the Bank of Mexico (*Banco de México*).

[115] *El Almanaque Mexicano* (Mexico: Ed. Grijalbo, 2000) at 178. *See generally* Salinas de Gortari, C., *Mexico, Un paso difícil a la modernidad* (Mexico: Plaza Janes Editores, 2000).

[116] *See* Carpizo, *El Presidencialismo Mexicano*, *supra* note 29 at 200–203.

[117] Before the wave of privatizations, the federal government owned newspapers, television and radio stations, and also exercised *de facto* control over television and radio stations operated by the national university, UNAM.

[118] Orozco, *supra* note 47 at 44.

[119] D.O. 11 Jun 2002. The public information law is discussed in more detail in Chapter 9 below at text accompanying notes 97–104.

agencies to the letter of the law and of Constitutional guarantees. As discussed in Chapter 6 below, until the judicial reforms of the 1990s, the Mexican judiciary lacked the independence to challenge the President on important matters. There were several reasons for this.

First, there is the limited effect of judicial decisions under Mexican law. In the United States, the rule of *stare decisis* elevates judicial opinions to obligatory rules of law that must be followed by later courts. In Mexico, which follows the civil law tradition, the general rule is that judicial decisions have no legal effect beyond the parties to the individual action.[120] Such a rule limits the power both of individual judges and of the Supreme Court. Furthermore, until the creation of the *acción de inconstitucionalidad* in 1994, the Mexican Supreme Court lacked the power to declare an executive or legislative active prospectively ineffective, a power that the US Supreme Court established for itself in 1803 in *Marbury v. Madison.*[121] Even after these reforms, constraints on the *acción de inconstitucionalidad*, especially the requirement of a majority vote of eight of the eleven ministers of the Supreme Court, have limited the effect of this power.

Second, the President's power to appoint federal judges, subject only to the formality of approval by a PRI-dominated legislature, created a judiciary sympathetic to the President's views and to the preservation of the *status quo*. Again, judicial reforms in 1994[122] replaced this power of appointment with an examination and merit system, increasing the hope, over time, of a truly independent judiciary, even if the PRI or some other party should acquire control of Congress and the presidency.

Third, as discussed in Chapter 11 below, the executive branch (that is, the Attorney General's office) has considerable discretionary power over the investigation and prosecution of criminal cases, including the power to dismiss criminal cases even after a criminal judge has found the suspect guilty.[123] Finally, as in the United States, Mexico has increasingly resorted to the establishment of federal administrative tribunals[124] to serve quasi-judicial functions in evaluating the appropriateness with which the executive branch implements the laws. These administrative tribunals—even those considered decentralized, or independent—lie within the executive branch, and have in the past shown little independence from executive authority.[125]

[120] An exception to this rule exists when the Supreme Court has adopted the same decision in five *amparo* actions in a row; in such a case, known as *jurisprudencia definida*, a rule of law is established that is to bind subsequent courts in cases involving the same set of facts. For a more detailed discussion of *jurisprudencia obligatoria*, *see* Chapter 6 below, on the judicial system.

[121] 5 US (1 Cranch) 137 (1803).

[122] *See* Chapter 6 below text accompanying notes 91–104.

[123] Orozco, *supra* note 47 at 40; *See* also Carpizo, EL PRESIDENCIALISMO MEXICANO, *supra* note 29 at 161–162.

[124] *See* Chapter 6 below, section 5.

[125] *See* Fix-Zamudio, *supra* note 44 at 301. *See* also Carpizo, EL PRESIDENCIALISMO MEXICANO, *supra* note 29 at 177; for a highly critical study, *see* La Botz, Dan, MASK OF DEMOCRACY: LABOR SUPPRESSION IN MEXICO TODAY (Boston: South End Press, 1992). (criticizing operation of *juntas de conciliación y arbitraje* in labour disputes).

2.4. Presidential Power Today: The Demise of *Presidencialismo*

The preceding pages have surveyed the foundations, both *de jure* and *de facto*, of Mexican *presidencialismo*, which was the dominant fact of Mexican political life for much of the twentieth century. The strengthening of election laws (discussed below) and the decline of centralized economic power as a result of neo-liberal reforms served to reduce the power of the Mexican presidency. Factors external to domestic politics also contributed to this. Mexico's acceptance of a North American Free Trade Agreement has encouraged an increased adherence to transparency and the application of legal rules in accordance with external criteria, leaving less room for presidential discretion. An increase in Mexico's economic integration with the United States has also brought an attendant capitulation to, if not embrace of, certain US legal models, especially in areas of business law, although Mexican leaders have been careful to find variations on the US model that fit with Mexico's unique legal culture.[126]

The demise of *presidencialismo* actually began with President Miguel de la Madrid (1982–1988), during whose presidency the corporatist state began to show signs of crumbling under the weight of endemic economic problems. President Salinas wielded considerable authoritarian power when he took office in 1988 (after a disputed election that further weakened the PRI's legitimacy as governing party, as discussed in section 3.1 below); but the mechanisms of *presidencialismo* were much weaker when Salinas left office in 1994, after six years of privatizing state-owned enterprises and opening the economy. President Zedillo (1994–2000) can be credited with having maintained political and economic stability while choosing not to reverse the decline in presidential control. Even while the PRI clung to a slim congressional majority, Zedillo chose not to exercise fully the political and legal powers that he still possessed in order to save *presidencialismo* from extinction. Zedillo's legacy will be to have presided over the burial of *presidencialismo*: something that PRI hard-liners (referred to as *dinosauros*) will never forgive.

The 2000 presidential election was fought by candidates from three major political parties: the PRI (Francisco Labastida), the PAN (Vicente Fox), and the PRD (Cuauhtémoc Cárdenas). Vicente Fox won the historic election—the first loss by the PRI in 71 years—with only 42.5 per cent of the popular vote. Facing a severely divided Congress, in which no single party holds a majority, President Fox has tried to fashion a coalition government by appointing persons from the PRI and PRD to executive positions, including cabinet posts, but he has had

[126] Examples of Mexican laws based on US models include the Federal Law of Economic Competition (*Ley Federal de Competencia Económica*), discussed in Chapter 12 below at text accompanying notes 50–78; and the Law of the Stock Exchange (*Ley del Mercado de Valores*), discussed in Chapter 20 below at text accompanying notes 57–71, among others. *See* also Zamora, S., 'NAFTA and the Harmonization of Domestic Legal Systems: The Side Effects of Free Trade', vol. 12, *Arizona Journal of International and Comparative Law* 401–428 (1995); Zamora, S., 'The Americanization of Mexican Law: Non-Trade Issues in the North American Free Trade Agreement', 24 LAW AND POLICY IN INTERNATIONAL BUSINESS (1993) at 391–459.

very limited success in this regard. At the time of writing, the lack of a majority party or coalition in Congress has converted the legislature from a rubber stamp into a brick wall of opposition for major legislative initiatives by any single group.

As an institution, the escape of Congress from domination by the presidency now allows it to set legislative goals and carry them out. It still lacks important attributes, however, to permit it to function effectively in this regard. First, Congress is divided, since no party holds a majority voting power, and no coalition of parties has yet emerged. Second, the shibboleth of non-reelection means that individual congressional leaders do not have lengthy experience or the power that goes with it. Third, Congress has not appropriated the funding necessary to hire the large staffs that Senators, *diputados*, and congressional committees would need in order to develop ambitious legislative programmes. Fourth, the very recent demise of the PRI's monopoly means that congressional leaders are still learning how to operate effectively in the new political system.

The shift in the balance of power between the executive and legislative branches was addressed by President Vicente Fox in the second state of the union message that he delivered to the Mexican Congress in September 2002.[127] Having been criticized for his failure to carry out the ambitious legislative agenda that he had promised as a candidate, President Fox laid blame on political divisions in Congress. During his first two years in office, the legislature blocked every important economic initiative of the Fox administration, including tax reforms and energy sector reforms that would give more room for foreign investment. He called on Congress to lay aside political divisions and support his legislative agenda, but there appeared little hope that this simplistic approach would be followed.[128] Rather, congressional elections in 2003 would be Fox's best hope for building political support, if PAN candidates should gain seats in Congress. Unfortunately, the PAN has no tradition of cohesion and political support behind any leader, presidential or otherwise.

3. Political Parties and the Electoral Process

The modern-day political system in Mexico can be dated from 1929, the year in which former President Plutarco Elias Calles (1924–1928) founded the *Partido Nacional Revolucionario* (PNR). The PNR was a response to the tumultuous 1920s, which were characterized by civil conflict (the *Cristero* Rebellion by conservative Catholics, the assassination of Obregón by opponents of re-election) and by the presence of competing *caudillos* in the military and in the countryside. Calles, himself a revolutionary general and *caudillo*, sought to consolidate power and bring peace to the country by creating a political party

[127] *See* www.presidencia.gob.mx (last visited July 2003).

[128] Weiner, Tim, 'His Agenda Ailing, Fox Urges the Mexican Congress to Help', *New York Times*, (Monday, 2 Sep. 2002), at A2.

that would put an end to political instability by resisting the centrifugal pull of competing forces.[129]

From the outset, the PNR was to be more than just a political party. The early leadership of the party openly espoused the goal of making the PNR coterminous with centralized government, i.e. it was intended to be the only political party of consequence.[130] Under the leadership of Calles, and later under Lázaro Cárdenas, the PNR gradually formed a solid coalition of labour, *campesinos*, and regional political bosses, and removed the army from the political arena. Over time, the PNR metamorphosed (in name and in structure) into the PRI, but at no time did the party abdicate its self-appointed role as the chief determinant of the political and electoral process in Mexico.

In this section, we look at the legal framework for political parties and elections in Mexico, with a concluding discussion of the current (and potential) roles of political parties.

3.1. The Legal Framework for Elections: 1946 to 1989

As in other areas of Mexican law, the view from outside Mexico that the PRI held totalitarian power through widespread electoral fraud and the use of violence is overly simplistic. The Mexican electoral process for much of the twentieth century lacked transparency, but allegations of fraud were probably exaggerated, and the violence that did occur (largely in the countryside) was rarely sanctioned by the central leadership of the PRI.[131] The PRI's maintenance of political control became nonetheless stifling, however. This control was the result of a sophisticated and highly complicated array of instruments. Political scientist Juan Molinar Horcasitas identified the principal characteristics of the electoral process in Mexico that assured the domination of the PRI for over seventy years:[132]

(i) a centralized electoral process, in which elections and voter registration throughout the country, at federal, state and local levels, are managed by the federal government;

[129] Rodríguez Araujo, Octavio, *La Reforma Política y los Partidos en México* (Mexico: Siglo XXI, 3rd ed., 1980) 29.

[130] Emilio Portes Gil (President of Mexico 1928–1930) has been quoted as stating at the time: 'The PNR is quite frankly a governing party. We will not delude the public, as has been done in previous times. The Revolution-turned-Government needs an instrument of agitation and defense. . . . [The PNR] will be a sincere collaborator in the administration, which will support its revolutionary agenda.' *Ibid.* at 29 [author's trans.]

[131] There have been exceptions to this statement. For instance, in 1940, PRI candidate Manuel Avila Camacho faced a serious opponent in Juan Andrew Almazán, a conservative candidate who capitalized on citizens' fears concerning 'creeping communism'. Supporters of both candidates armed themselves and gun battles occurred throughout the major cities. The result was a bloody election day, as various groups fought to take charge of the ballot boxes. *See* Granados Chapa, Miguel Angel, *Votar—Para Qué? Manual de Elecciones* (Mexico: Oceano, 1985) 87–88; José Agustín, *La Tragicomedia Mexicana* (Ed. Planeta, 1990) vol. I, at 11–15.

[132] Molinar Horcasitas, J.F., 'Elecciones, Autoritarismo y Democracia en México' (El Colegio de México, doctoral thesis, August 1989) 42.

(ii) control of the electoral process by the PRI, and a lack of effective challenges to election results by opposition parties;[133]
(iii) the fusion of the PRI with the public administration, which placed the full resources of the government at the disposition of the ruling party to buy voter support;
(iv) the absence of any single opposition party, either to the left or the right, with sufficient support to challenge the PRI;
(vi) the systematic manipulation of the electoral process by the PRI and by the electoral agencies of the federal government, for the purpose of maintaining the PRI's control, such manipulation extending even to the occasional use of electoral fraud.

The modern-day electoral regime in Mexico dates from 1946,[134] the year in which the government federalized electoral law with Congress' adoption of the Federal Electoral Law (*Ley Federal Electoral*).[135] Prior to this date, elections were conducted in a decentralized fashion, with state and municipal authorities overseeing elections in their respective jurisdictions.[136] With the 1946 electoral law, the federal government (controlled by the PRI) established a rigorous, centralized monopoly on elections, including state and local elections, throughout the country.

The 1946 law was in part a reaction to the *almazanista* threat,[137] which convinced the leadership of the PRI to impose strict controls over the formation and registration of political parties in order to avoid the sudden rise of populist opposition candidates. Under the 1946 electoral law, political parties were required to be registered before the *Secretaría de Gobernación* (today, political parties shall be registered before the Federal Electoral Institute or IFE (*Instituto Federal Electoral*)), and only candidates representing registered parties were permitted to run for election; to qualify for registration, a political party had to have at least 30,000 members nationwide, with at least 1,000 members in at least two-thirds of the states.[138]

[133] Molinar Horcasitas points to the Supreme Court's inability to judge cases involving allegations of electoral fraud. This impediment still exists, but the creation of a federal electoral tribunal has remedied the lack of oversight. *See* Chapter 6 below, at text accompanying notes 37–46.

[134] Molinar Horcasitas, taking a cue from Mexican archaeology, defines three periods in the development of the electoral process: the pre-classical period (formation of the hegemonic system, 1946–1963); the classical period (operation of the hegemonic system, from 1963–1975); and the post-classical period (1976–1985, followed by a period of crisis and decline after 1988). *Id.*, *supra* note 132, at 42. We can now add a fourth period to this, dating from the creation in 1990 of an independent Federal Electoral Institute and an independent tribunal to judge elections: the initiation of transparent democracy.

[135] D.O. 7 Jan. 1946. For a thorough discussion of Mexican electoral laws from 1946 to 1992, *see* Cárdenas, *supra* note at 96 at 160–208.

[136] Molinar Horcasitas, *supra* note 132 at 36–38. The original 1917 Constitution made no mention of political parties. A federal law of 2 July 1918, established certain requirements for the establishment of political parties, but did not set forth election rules. Cárdenas, supra note 96 at 160.

[137] *See* note 131 *supra.*

[138] Granados Chapa, *supra* note 104 at 40–41.

The 1946 law was replaced by later acts, but throughout the subsequent laws and amendments, two common features remained: the centralization and 'supervision' by the PRI-dominated federal government, and the exclusion from the electoral process of political parties that could not attain the requirements of national registration.[139]

The 1946 electoral law and subsequent legislation served to increase the PRI's control of the legislature. The most successful opposition party, the *Partido de Acción Nacional* (PAN), was able to win only twenty of the 900 races for seats in the *Cámara de Diputados* that were contested during the period 1943 to 1961.[140] Table 5.1 shows the percentage of seats won by the PRI and the PAN during this period.

Table 5.1: Percentage of seats in Cámara de Diputados won by each party

	1946	*1949*	*1952*	*1955*	*1958*	*1961*
PRI	91.16	96.60	93.79	94.41	94.41	96.6
PAN	2.72	2.72	3.11	3.73	3.73	2.8

Source: Molinar Horcasitas.[141]

In effect, because the PRI commanded a majority in all *diputado* districts nationwide, minority parties were under-represented in Congress. In 1958, *diputados* from the PAN who were elected to Congress refused to occupy their seats in protest of the electoral system.[142] The PRI's response to the growing protest was typical of the flexible approach to authoritarian power that characterized the PRI. The PRI began a long process of loosening the reins while still keeping political control, by reforming the electoral laws to promote greater representation of opposition parties, without, however, giving up the party's ultimate control of the electoral process. In 1963, the Constitution was amended[143] to provide for a new type of election of *diputados*; conforming amendments were also adopted to the 1951 Electoral Law.[144] Previously, all *diputados* had been elected from geographically outlined electoral districts, each of which elected a single *diputado* to Congress (single-member districts). Under the 1963 reform, a certain number of specially designated *diputados*, called *diputados de partido* would be allocated in the *Cámara de Diputados* for minority political parties. Each party that earned at least 2.5 per cent of the national vote in the elections for *diputado*

139 Molinar Horcasitas, *supra* note 132 at 41.

140 Granados Chapa, *supra* note 104 at 26.

141 Molinar Horcasitas, *supra* note 132 at 108.

142 *Id.* at 111.

143 The 1963 reform also placed political parties on a constitutional footing, by amending the Constitution to provide specifically for their recognition in Articles 41 and 54. D.O. 22 June 1963.

144 D.O. 4 Dec. 1951. For a discussion of the 1963 law, *see* Orozco, *supra* note 47 at 92; and De Andrea, *supra* note 29.

from single-member districts would receive 5 *diputados de partido*, with an additional *diputado de partido* for each additional 0.5 per cent of the vote earned, up to a maximum of twenty *diputados de partido*. The total number of *diputados* (300) remained the same as was established in the 1917 Constitution.

The 1963 reform was intended to increase significantly the representation of minority parties, but it failed to do so. The inability of opposition parties to achieve even 2.5 per cent of the nationwide vote led to a 1972 reform[145] reducing the percentage requirement to 1.5 per cent, and increasing the maximum number of *diputados de partido* from twenty to twenty-five. Nevertheless, aside from the PAN, the opposition parties were so weak that they failed even to achieve these minimum percentages. During this period, the PRI held over 82 per cent of all *diputado* seats, and the opposition parties together held less than 18 per cent.[146]

One reason for the weakness of opposition parties in the *diputado* elections was the drawing of electoral districts that over-represented rural areas, which had long been strongholds of PRI support,[147] as well as easy areas for electoral fraud perpetrated by rural bosses.

The PRI leaders went back to the drawing board. A new federal electoral law, the *Ley Federal Electoral of 1973*,[148] replaced the 1963 law, and again adjusted the requirements for registration of parties, for the first time requiring political parties to name delegates to the Federal Electoral Commission (*Comisión Federal Electoral)*, which was in charge of organizing elections. The latter move was obviously intended to give the impression of impartiality over elections, even though the PRI controlled the majority of votes on the *Comisión* and, thus, the electoral process.

The architect of the PRI's scheme to increase the participation of opposition parties in Congress, without threatening the ultimate PRI majority, was a brilliant politician who became José López Portillo's Secretario de Gobernación in 1976, Jesús Reyes Heroles. One year after López Portillo took office, the Constitution was again reformed to change the method of electing *diputados*.[149] Soon after, a completely new federal electoral law, the *Ley Federal de Organizaciones Políticas y Procesos Electorales*, or LFOPPE, was passed by Congress in 1977.[150] The LFOPPE adopted a mixed electoral system for the election of the federal *diputados* (a preponderant majority system, with new elements of proportional representation, or *representación proporcional*);[151] at that time, the Congress consisted of 400 *diputados* of two types: there were 300 *diputados uninominales*, who were elected by majority vote in 300 single-member districts

[145] D.O. 14 Feb. 1972.
[146] Orozco, *supra* note 47 at 94. *See also* Granados Chapa, *supra* note 104 at 29.
[147] Molinar Horcasitas, *supra* note 132 at 149.
[148] D.O. 5 Jan. The 1973 law is discussed in Cárdenas, *supra* note 96 at 163–164.
[149] Presidential Decree published D.O. 6 Dec. 1977 (reforming 17 articles of the Constitution, including Articles 51–55, relating to election of *diputados*). *See* Carpizo, J., 'La reforma política de 1977' in *ANUARIO JURÍDICO*, VI, (México, 1979) at 53.
[150] D.O. 30 Dec. 1977. [151] *See* Patiño Camarena, *supra* note 14 at 54, 55.

into which the country was divided geographically; and 100 *diputados plurinominales* (also called *diputados de represtentación proporcional*), who were elected from separate regional lists of candidates submitted by each party (known as *circunscripciones plurinominales*).[152] While each party listed candidates in the regional *plurinominal* lists, only minority parties of sufficient size were entitled to receive *plurinominal* seats. If a party won more than sixty seats in the uninominal districts,[153] it received no *plurinominal* seats. Minority parties receiving at least 1.5 per cent of the vote in all regional lists of *plurinominal* elections received a number of *plurinominal* seats that was proportional to their percentage of the *plurinominal* vote. To avoid concentration of *plurinominal* votes, and to limit the formation of coalitions that could challenge the PRI majority in Congress, the LFOPPE limited the number of *plurinominal* seats allocated to minority parties that nevertheless won a significant number of *uninominal* seats.[154]

The LFOPPE would ensure that opposition parties would hold a minimum of 25 per cent of the seats in the *Cámara de Diputados*, a level that had never been achieved since the formation of the PRI in 1929. At the same time, the PRI was virtually assured of maintaining a majority in Congress because of its *de facto* political powers. In congressional elections held under the LFOPPE (from 1979 to 1985), the total number of congressional seats never exceeded 111 of the total 400 seats (100 *plurinominal* seats plus eleven seats won in the *uninominal* elections of 1985 (nine by the PAN and two by the PARM)).[155]

Electoral reforms in 1986 and 1987 produced yet another reform of the system of electing *diputados*,[156] as the PRI continued to tinker with the electoral system in order to deflect growing criticism both within and outside of Mexico. Constitutional reforms in 1986[157] increased the *Cámara de Diputados* from

[152] The country was divided into 3 regions (*circunscripciones regionales*) for the 1979 elections for *plurinominal* seats, 4 regions in the 1982 elections, and 5 regions in the 1985 elections. For an explanation of the operation of elections under the LOPPE, *see* Orozco, *supra* note 47 at 94–95. Under the current law, there are five *plurinominal* regions.

[153] Until 1988, only the PRI fell under this rule; in the current Congress, the PRI, PAN, and PRD each have more than 60 seats. *See* text accompanying note 184, *infra*.

[154] If two or more parties with the right to *plurinominal* seats won more than 90 uninominal seats between them, then the number of *plurinominal* seats to be allocated to these parties was limited to 50% of the total (50 seats). LFOPPE, Article 3.

[155] Orozco, *supra* note 47 at 148. If the LFOPPE was supposed to correct the over-representation of the PRI in Congress, the legislation failed, and produced some curiously anti-democratic results. In the 1979 election, if one divided the number of *diputado* seats won by the total number of votes received by the party, the PRI received 1 *diputado* for every 40,508 votes cast in its favour, while the PAN only received one *diputado* for every 62,931 votes cast. Molinar Horcasitas, *supra* note 132 at 232–234. In 1988, the PRI received 1 *diputado* for every 40,098 votes cast in its favour; the PAN received 1 *diputado* for every 67,981 votes, and the PARM received one *diputado* for every 26,858 votes. *Id.* at 235.

[156] For a discussion of the 1986/87 reforms, *see* Orozco, *supra* note 47 at 95–98.

[157] D.O. 15 Dec. 1986 For more detailed information about the electoral reform of 1986, *see* Barquin, M., 'La reforma electoral de 1986–1987 en Mexico, retrospectiva y análisis', in EL CONSTITUCIONALISMO EN LAS POSTRIMERÍAS DEL SIGLO XX (Mexico: UNAM, 1988) at 324–372.

400 to 500 members, by increasing the number of *diputados plurinominales* from 100 to 200. This remains the configuration currently in force.

In early 1987, Congress abrogated the LFOPPE and adopted a new electoral law to implement the reforms: the Federal Electoral Code (*Código Federal Electoral*) of 1987.[158] One of the innovations of the 1987 *Código Federal Electoral* was the creation of a special adjudicatory body, the *Tribunal de lo Contencioso Electoral*, for handling elections disputes. As with other electoral bodies, the Tribunal lacked independence from the PRI, and was eventually replaced by an independent tribunal placed within the judicial branch, rather than under the executive branch, as discussed below.[159]

The 1986 Constitutional reforms were designed to increase the number of opposition seats in the *Cámara de Diputados* (from 400 to 500) while still ensuring that the PRI would have an absolute majority. This was accomplished by allowing all parties receiving at least 1.5 per cent of the national vote, including the PRI, to compete for the 200 *plurinominal* seats (increased from 100 *plurinominal* seats before the 1986 reform).[160] Each party received the number of *plurinominal* seats that corresponded to the percentage of votes cast for the party on the regional lists, but to avoid an exaggeration of the PRI's majority in the *Cámara*, an amendment to the Constitution placed a limit of 350 total seats in the *Cámara* that could be held by a single party.[161] To facilitate the PRI's maintenance of an absolute majority in the *Cámara*, the Constitution provided that the party obtaining the highest number of *uninominal* seats and at least 35 per cent of the *plurinominal* vote nationally would receive a sufficient number of *plurinominal* seats to achieve an absolute majority in the *Cámara*, as well as an additional two *plurinominal* seats for each percentage of the vote above 35 per cent (up to 60 per cent of the total seats in the *Cámara*). The PRI expected easily to win the most *uninominal* seats and more than 35 per cent of the *plurinominal* seats. For a period of time, this complicated electoral system, worthy of an Academy Award for political tinkering, continued to allow the PRI to maintain a majority in the *Cámara de Diputados*, while allowing minority parties to increase their representation. The PRI demonstrated that it was willing to undertake electoral reforms to enhance the fairness of the electoral process without entirely losing its grip on political control.

The first opportunity to test the 1986/87 reforms came in July 1988, when general elections were held for Congress and for the presidency.[162] The economic

[158] D.O. 12 Feb. 1987. [159] *See* text accompanying notes 189–205 *infra*.

[160] Mexican Constitution, Art. 54-II (a), D.O. 14 Feb. 1972. Currently, to compete for *plurinominal* seats, a political party must present candidates in at least 200 of the 300 *uninominal* elections, and must win at least 2% of the national vote for the regional lists of *plurinominal* circumscriptions. *See* Article 54 of the Constitution.

[161] Mexican Constitution, Art. 54-IV. This Article was amended to set a limit of 300 as the number of total seats in the *Cámara* that could be held by a single party.

[162] For a succinct discussion of the 1988 elections, *see* Smith, Peter H., 'The 1988 Presidential Succession in Historical Perspective', in Cornelius, Gentleman and Smith, *supra* note 109 at 391 *et seq*.

crises of the 1980s, coupled with a serious rift within the party,[163] brought an electoral challenge to the PRI, both from the right and from the left. PRI candidate Carlos Salinas de Gortari was declared winner of the presidential election,[164] despite the unsuccessful attempts of opposition candidates to contest the election in the *Tribunal de lo Contencioso Electoral*.[165] Even so, the narrow margin of victory (50.74 per cent, *versus* 31.06 per cent for FDN candidate Cuauhtémoc Cárdenas, and 16.81 per cent for PAN candidate Manuel Clouthier) was by far the closest ever for a PRI presidential candidate up to that date.[166]

The 1988 elections also provided the PRI with its smallest majority ever in the *Cámara de Diputados*. The PRI lost sixty-seven of the 300 *uninominal* seats, almost as many as the seventy-two seats it had lost in all *diputado* elections held from 1946 to 1985.[167] The PRI added twenty-seven seats from the *plurinominal* list, for a total of 260 seats in the *Cámara*, a legislative majority. For the first time, however, the PRI had an insufficient number to guarantee the two-thirds majority needed to adopt constitutional amendments without the support of *diputados* from opposition parties. The PAN won 101 seats in the *Cámara* (thirty-eight *uninominal* and sixty-three *plurinominal*); and the FDN coalition, the forerunner of the PRD, won 139 seats (twenty-nine *uninominal* and 110 *plurinominal*).[168] A crack in the PRI's hegemony had begun to appear.

The decline of popular support for the PRI in 1988, and the ineffectiveness of the PRI's constituent organizations to deliver a healthy majority, ushered in a new political era. During his *sexenio*, President Salinas (1988–1994) devoted most of his energies to economic, rather than political, reform. Salinas appeared to understand that electoral reforms had already gone far enough to bring down the PRI's monopoly, and instead he hoped that the economic prosperity promised by the imminent entry into force of NAFTA would translate into a new coalition of supporters of the PRI. The PRI also hoped that by allowing increased representation to minority parties, it could relieve the pressure for more major reforms while still maintaining the party's control of government. As the following sections show, this was not to be the case.

[163] During the pre-election manoeuvrings, a faction within the PRI that sought a more open political system, the *corriente democrática* (democratic current), attempted to wrest party control from PRI traditionalists. The *corriente democrática* proved unsuccessful in democratizing the PRI, and some influential PRI members—most notably Cuauhtémoc Cárdenas, the son of Lázaro Cárdenas, and Porfirio Muñoz Ledo—left the PRI to form a leftist coalition party known as the Frente Democrático Nacional (FDN), the forerunner of the current Partido Revolucionario Democrático (PRD).

[164] On the day following the balloting, Secretario de Gobernación Manuel Bartlett announced that the results could not yet be made public, since the new computer system that had been devised to count the ballots had 'gone down' ('*se cayó el sistema*'). Two weeks later, the official announcement was made showing that the PRI candidate had won. Some commentators have alleged that the election results were manipulated to ensure a PRI victory. Despite vigorous demonstrations and protests against the results, President Salinas de Gortari was sworn in as Mexican President on 1 December 1988.

[165] *See* text accompanying notes 192–193 *infra*.

[166] Molinar Horcasitas, *supra* note 132 at 345–346.

[167] *Id.* at 349.

[168] Orozco, *supra* note 47 at 148.

3.2. The Current Electoral Regime: COFIPE

The constitutional regime for federal elections in force today is virtually the same as that which was in force for the 1988 elections, described above. However, the contentious election of 1988 elicited another series of electoral reforms in 1989 and 1990. In 1989, Congress again amended the Constitution, making minor adjustments to make the electoral process appear more honest and transparent.[169] In 1990, Congress adopted the *Código Federal de Instituciones y Procedimientos Electorales* (COFIPE),[170] which replaced the 1987 *Código Federal Electoral*. The electoral process briefly described below is governed by the COFIPE, which is still in force.

In accordance with the legal tradition of Mexico, the COFIPE is intended to be a complete, self-contained code, covering virtually all aspects of federal elections, from the registration of voters and political parties, to the conduct of elections, to the process for contesting election results.

3.2.1. Organization and Oversight of Federal Elections

Both the registration of political parties and the organization of federal elections are carried out by the Federal Electoral Institute (*Instituto Federal Electoral*, or IFE), which under the COFIPE replaced the *Comisión Federal Electoral*. IFE was established as an 'autonomous' and permanent agency of the federal government.[171] IFE is controlled by a *Consejo General*,[172] which meets in ordinary sessions every three months to set general policies for elections. A permanent secretariat of IFE, governed by a *Junta General Ejecutiva*, oversees the day-to-day functioning of IFE; the chief permanent officers are a *Director General* and a *Secretario General*, who are appointed by the *Consejo General* of IFE.[173]

IFE is national in scope. In organizing federal elections on a national scale, it oversees a system of local executive committees (*juntas locales ejecutivas*) which are permanent agencies of the IFE, and local councils (*consejos locales*) that function only during the federal electoral process; both are responsible for carrying out elections in each state, under guidelines established by the central

[169] The constitutional reforms were published in D.O. 6 Apr. 1989. For a discussion of the limited effect of the 1989 reforms, *see* Cárdenas, *supra* note 96 at 173–178, and Patiño Camarena, *supra* note 14 at 55–61.

[170] D.O. 15 Aug. 1990, at 3, *as amended*, D.O. 3 Jan. 1991, at 2 (minor amendments to Articles 13, 15, 127, and 366).

[171] COFIPE, Article 70.1.

[172] The *Consejo General* of the IFE is presided over by a *consejero presidente*, who is elected by a vote of the *Cámara de Diputados*, by a two-thirds majority, from among candidates proposed by the parties represented in Congress. In addition to the *consejero presidente*, the *Consejo* includes eight additional *consejeros* elected by the *Cámara de Diputados*: COFIPE Article 74. This complicated system of governance of the IFE is intended to ensure impartiality in the electoral process. For a discussion of the selection of the membership of IFE bodies, *see* Alcocer, Jorge, 'IFE: Legalidad y conflicto', NEXOS (vol. XIV, Num. 164, Aug. 1991), at 11, and Gómez-Palacio, *supra* note 109 at 43–70.

[173] On the governance of IFE, *see generally* COFIPE, Articles 82–97.

organs of IFE.[174] In addition, IFE oversees 300 *juntas distritales permanentes*, one for each *distrito uninominal*, and Distrital councils (*consejos distritales*), which function during election periods to oversee elections in each *diputado* district.[175] Voting takes place in *casillas*, or polls, supervised by citizens appointed by the local and district councils (*consejos locales y distritales*).[176] The election results are computed by the local and district councils,[177] and under Article 60 of the Constitution, the IFE is charged with certifying the election results. Each of these electoral bodies is composed of a combination of IFE officials, representatives of registered political parties, and local citizens.

Voters in federal elections must be registered with the *Registro Federal de Electores*, which is organized and maintained by a corresponding *Dirección Ejecutiva* within IFE.[178] The list of voters qualified to vote in each election is called the *padrón electoral*.

COFIPE also regulates the allocation of radio and television time to political parties,[179] and contains provisions concerning the financing of political parties and electoral campaigns.[180] In both of these areas, the government maintains the appearance of impartiality towards political parties. For many years, despite formal controls on campaign finance, the PRI enjoyed a favourable position by virtue of its control of government agencies and spending programmes. Critics of the PRI argued that social welfare programmes such as the *Programa Nacional de Solidaridad* were used by the PRI to reward or punish communities that vote with the PRI; such programmes do not constitute 'campaign funding' *per se*, but were identified with the PRI nonetheless.[181]

[174] COFIPE, Articles 99–107. *See* Lara Sáenz, Leoncio, 'El Nuevo Sistema Electoral Mexicano' in CUADERNOS CONSTITUCIONALES MÉXICO-CENTROAMÉRICA (No. 3, Centro Estudios Constitucionales México-Centro América, 1992) at 14–15.

[175] COFIPE, Articles 108–117; Leoncio Sáenz, *supra* note 174 at 15.

[176] COFIPE, Articles 118–124. [177] Lara Sáenz, *supra* note 174 at 12.

[178] COFIPE, Articles 142–164. [179] COFIPE, Articles 42–48.

[180] Under the COFIPE as currently drafted, political parties are entitled to receive funding from the federal government (as determined by the Consejo General of IFE) sufficient to finance the minimum campaign costs for *diputados* and senators: COFIPE, Article 49. However, other than a provision for exemption from taxes (COFIPE, Articles 50–52), and the prohibition of contributions from foreign persons or political parties (COFIPE, Articles 49(c), 25.1(c), and 38.1(n)), COFIPE does not place restrictions on the receipt of private funding by political parties.

The financing of political parties is currently a subject of debate and possible legal reform. *See generally* ASPECTOS JURÍDICOS DEL FINANCIAMIENTO DE LOS PARTIDOS POLÍTICOS (Mexico: UNAM-IIJ, 1993) esp. Part Three, 'El Financiamiento en la Legislación Electoral Mexicana y Propuestas para una Nueva Regulación Jurídica de la Financiación de los Partidos Políticos en México'.

[181] While it was still in control of government, the PRI also had a *de facto* advantage in political advertising. Even today, anyone travelling in the Mexican countryside will notice the political signs and painted walls displaying the names of party candidates in a country that always seems to be holding elections. Before the late 1990s, the signs for PRI candidates were professionally painted in the most prominent places in a rural town or regional city, while the signs for opposition parties were generally smaller, less numerous, and less prominent. After the 2000 elections, with the opening of the system, this has changed, with all major parties spending more on political advertising with a chance to sway public opinion.

3.2.2. *Presidential and Congressional Elections*

Presidential elections The President is elected by a direct nationwide vote every six years. The presidential candidate must be nominated by a national political party duly registered before the Federal Electoral Institute (*Institute Federal Electoral*). The elections take place on the first Sunday of July, and the candidate who is elected President is the person who obtains the majority vote of the citizens registered in the *Padron Electoral* (Register of Voters) who voted in the election. Unlike in the United States, there is no electoral college in Mexico: the President is elected by direct majority vote. Nor is there a requirement of an absolute majority; the person who receives the highest number of votes in the election is elected President, even if the candidate receives less than 50 per cent of the vote.

Election of diputados Under Article 54 of the Constitution, the *Cámara de Diputados* consists of 500 members who are elected for a period of three years, 300 from *uninominal* districts distributed geographically throughout the country, and 200 from national *plurinominal* lists (see section 3.1 above[182]) which results in representation that is proportional to the votes received by all parties that garner more than 2 per cent of the vote. As under the 1988 electoral regime, each registered party submits a list of *plurinominal* candidates for each of five regions of the country. *Diputado* elections are held every three years, also on the first Sunday in July.

As discussed in section 3.1 of this Chapter, the election of *diputados* underwent a long period of reform managed by the PRI for the purpose of increasing minority party representation without losing political control. Unfortunately for PRI loyalists, the reforms were more successful than envisaged. In the elections of 2000, the PRI not only lost the presidency, it also lost, for the first time since 1929, a majority in the *Cámara de Diputados*.[183] Indeed, after the 2000 elections, while the PRI still held a majority of the seats in the Senate, no party held a majority of the *Cámara de Diputados*. After the most recent congressional elections, held in July 2003, the PRI holds the largest number of seats in the *Cámara de Diputados*, with 222 seats, compared to 151 seats for the PAN, 95 seats for the PRD, and 28 seats for other parties.[184] This represented a major loss not only for the PAN, but also for President Vicente Fox, whose hopes of major legislation in the final three years of his *sexenio* were dampened.

Senatorial elections During the many years of electoral reform just described (from 1917 to 1993), the configuration of the Senate and the election of Senators was left virtually untouched, and the PRI's historical majority was undiminished. Senators are elected for six-year terms, with half of the Senate seats up for election every three years (Article 56 of the Mexican Constitution). Before 1996, two senators were elected from each state and from the Federal

[182] *See supra*, text accompanying notes 143 to 162.
[183] EL ALMANAQUE MEXICANO, supra note 115 at 254. *See* also www.ife.gob.mx.
[184] On 2003, *see* www.diputados.gob.mx (site visited Jan. 2004).

District, but the number of senators increased as states were added to the Republic. Thus, in 1949, there were fifty-eight senators; in 1952 there were sixty; and in 1976 sixty-four.

In 1996, President Zedillo supported a constitutional amendment[185] to increase the size of the Senate by increasing the number of senators elected from each political subdivision. Zedillo's idea, supported by the liberal faction of the PRI and in line with the opening up of the *Cámara de Diputados*, was to increase the participation of minority parties in the Senate, while still maintaining the PRI's historical majority in that body.

Since the reforms in 1996, the Senate has consisted of 128 senators, who are elected in the following manner. Three senators are elected from each state and from the Federal District, but in an unusual form of election. The elections of federal senators are contested by each qualifying political party submitting a list of two candidates in each state to the IFE. When the election is held, voters vote not for individual senatorial candidates, but rather for the party list. The party that receives the highest number of votes in this election is entitled to two seats in the Senate, in representation of the particular state. The third senator selected will be the first candidate listed in the list of the party receiving the next highest number of votes. Finally, thirty-two additional senators are elected by national elections in which senatorial candidates are listed by party affiliation in a single national *plurinominal* ballot. The winning senatorial candidates are selected in direct proportion to the percentage of the votes received by each candidate in the election, without being connected to any particular state.

This new system of electing senators effectively eliminated the PRI's historical majority in the Senate, but at the cost of an incredibly complicated formula that many people fail to understand. After the 2000 elections, the PRI held sixty of the 128 senatorial seats in the Congress, while the PAN held forty-six seats, and the PRD fifteen seats.[186]

One final aspect of senatorial election deserves mention. In the United States, one-third of the members of the US Senate are elected every two years, each for a period of six years. Thus, the US Senate does not change dramatically from election to election. In Mexico, however, aside from a brief period of staggered elections in the late 1980s and early 1990s, the general rule has been that senators are elected in the same national elections as the president, and they serve a single, six-year term that coincides with the presidential *sexenio*. Some experts have criticized this timing, since it reduces the importance of the mid-term elections of *diputados*, held every three years, and places too much emphasis on the sexennial elections.

[185] D.O. 22 Aug. 1996.

[186] The PRI's control of municipal governments has also been reduced. In 2002, of the 2,447 municipal governments (*ayuntamientos*), the PRI controls 1,129 municipalities, while the PAN controls 417 municipalities, and the PRD 236 municipalities; others are governed by coalitions of PAN and PRD or PRI and PRD.

No re-election One major difference between Mexico and the United States, as well as other democratic countries, involves the constitutional prohibition against re-election, which continues to apply to virtually all elected officials in Mexico, at both the state and federal levels.[187] Thus, when Mexico elects *diputados* every three years, they replace the entire body of the lower house. The Senate is renewed every six years.

The principle of non-reelection grew out of presidential politics and a desire to forestall dictatorship.[188] It resulted in a brilliant (if ultimately flawed) system in which a series of Presidents from the same political party could have absolute power for seventy-one years, without inflicting on the country a rigid system dependent on the power of one person alone. Ironically, however, the extension of non-reelection to Congress has prevented the development of a highly professional corps of experienced legislators, whether from the PRI or from other political parties. Rather than limiting presidential power, non-reelection has served to weaken the effectiveness of Congress as a counterbalance to the presidency. Under the newly competitive political system in Mexico, it still remains to be seen if, and how, the Mexican Congress will become an effective source of leadership.

3.2.3. *State and Municipal Elections*

The organization of state and local elections conforms largely to the process described above for federal elections. State and local elections are held in conformity with the constitution and electoral laws of each state. Elections of state officials (governors, state *diputados*, and municipal *ayuntamientos*) are held on different dates throughout the year, always on dates other than the dates for federal elections.

State electoral laws generally parallel the federal model. Each state has its own set of electoral bodies (*consejos estatales electorales*) to organize and oversee state elections. In most states, the *Registro Federal de Electores* serves as the voter registration list for state elections as well, although some states require separate registration for state elections.

Until the late 1980s, the PRI dominated state elections as much as it did federal elections. However, the same process that weakened PRI domination at the federal level had an effect on state elections. Over time, Mexican voters became disenchanted with the PRI's performance and sought a change in leadership. At the same time, increased transparency in elections made it difficult for the PRI

[187] Mexican Constitution, Art. 83 (non-reelection of president); Article 59 (non-reelection of senators and diputados to succeeding terms); Article 116-I, par. 3 (non-reelection of state governors); Article 116-II, par. 2 (non-reelection of state *diputados* to succeeding terms). On non-reelection of the president, including historical precedent, *see* Carpizo, EL PRESIDENCIALISMO MEXICANO, *supra* note 29 at 56–58; Carpizo and Madrazo, *supra* note 29 at 1762–1763. On non-reelection in general, *see* Diego Valadés, *supra* note 16 at 252–253.

[188] *See* Chapter 1 at text accompanying notes 127–130. *See generally* Ugalde, L.C., THE MEXICAN CONGRESS: OLD PLAYER, NEW POWER (Washington, D.C.: Center for Strategic and International Studies, 2000) at 97–120.

to maintain control by illegal means. This was especially true in the states in Northern Mexico; far from Mexico City geographically, these states have resisted political and economic domination imposed from the capital, and have been based on a greater appreciation for private enterprise. The first governorship lost by the PRI occurred in Baja California in 1986, and began a trend of inroads into PRI political domination of the states. By 2002, the PRI still controlled the governorships in seventeen states in Mexico: Campeche, Coahuila, Colima, Chihuahua, Durango, Guerrero, Hidalgo, Mexico, Oaxaca, Puebla, Quintana Roo, San Luis Potosí, Sinaloa, Sonora, Tabasco, Tamaulipas, and Veracruz. The PAN controlled eight primarily northern states: Aguascalientes, Baja California Norte, Querétaro, Guanajuato, Jalisco, Morelos, Nuevo León, and Yucatán. The PRD controlled four states: Baja California Sur, Michoacán, Tlaxcala, Zacatecas, as well as the Federal District. And a coalition formed by the PAN and PRD controlled two states: Chiapas and Nayarit. In 2002, the PRI controlled 1,129 municipalities, while the PAN and the PRD controlled 416 and 236, respectively.

3.2.4. *Contesting Elections*[189]

Even under the PRI's hegemony, the public belief, both in Mexico and in the United States, was that the PRI's success in federal and state elections came only through electoral fraud perpetrated by its supporters. Even in the PRI's heyday, however, electoral fraud was neither universal nor homogeneous; it appears to have been used selectively, was often not directed by the leadership of the PRI, and was most common in rural areas at the fringes of the system of election controls.[190] Nevertheless, the public's perception of widespread electoral fraud, and the likelihood that fraud does exist, were serious obstacles to Mexico's political development, and contained the seeds of political instability. As the corporatist structure of Mexico gave way to more competitive political and economic systems, the PRI began to lose the support of monolithic groups (labour, *campesinos*, government employees), and had to resort to ever more sophisticated methods of deception to ensure power. In the process, as one commentator noted at the time, '[t]he situation has reached the point that the PRI always loses—to the opposition if the latter wins the vote, and through a discredited electoral system when it attracts majority support'.[191]

[189] For a discussion of jurisdiction over electoral matters, see the discussion of the Federal Electoral Tribunal in Chapter 6 below at text accompanying notes 37–46. The Federal Electoral Tribunal has published an extensive overview of the evolution of electoral disputes. *See* EVOLUCIÓN HISTÓRICA DE LAS INSTITUCIONES DE LA JUSTICIA ELECTORAL EN MÉXICO (Tribunal Electoral del Poder Judicial de la Federación, 2002).

[190] *See* Molinar Horcasitas, *supra* note 132 at 6. *See also* Alvarado Mendoza, Arturo, 'Introduction', in ELECTORAL PATTERNS AND PERSPECTIVES IN MEXICO (Center for US–Mexican Studies, University of California at San Diego, Monograph series No. 22, 1987; A. Alvarado Mendoza (ed.), at 1, 7: 'the government's absolute control over the electoral process allows it to manipulate vote totals so as to ensure victory for its candidates'.

[191] Molinar Horcasitas, *supra* note 132 at 31 (authors' trans.).

The narrow election of President Salinas in 1988,[192] which was widely considered to have been secured fraudulently, represented a turning point. Opposition parties contested the election of President Salinas and of congressional candidates in the Federal Electoral Tribunal, but to no avail: the Tribunal decided the allegations by confirming the victory of the PRI for the presidential elections.[193] Public criticism mounted, and it became apparent, even to the leadership of the PRI, that a trustworthy system for contesting elections and for penalizing fraud was needed to restore confidence in elections.

Initially, reforms to the process of challenging elections were more cosmetic than effective. In stark contrast with the United States, where the federal courts have gone to great lengths to enforce constitutional and legal rights surrounding elections, the courts in Mexico have never played an important role in elections, for the legal, historical, and political reasons discussed below in Chapter 6.[194] Prior to 1986, Congress was the sole judge of the authenticity of its own election: the only way for political parties or candidates to contest federal elections was in accordance with Article 60 of the Constitution, by asking the *Colegio Electoral* of either the Senate or the *Cámara de Diputados* to examine irregularities. If satisfied, the *Colegio Electoral* could refuse to seat a candidate who had won a contested election. Needless to say, the PRI-dominated Congress controlled the process. As amended in 1977,[195] Article 60 did permit appeal against decisions of the *Colegio Electoral* to the Supreme Court. However, given the historical reluctance of the Supreme Court to assert its jurisdiction in political cases,[196] it is not surprising that the Supreme Court never actually decided such a case. Indeed, since the *Colegio Electoral* was empowered to override the Court's decision, the insertion of a role for the Supreme Court was seen as potentially weakening the Court's prestige.[197]

Additional constitutional amendments in 1986[198] brought two important reforms to the method of contesting federal elections. First, they abrogated the portion of Article 60 that inserted a role for the Supreme Court in overseeing the *Colegio Electoral*. In place of the Supreme Court, Article 60 provided, for the first time, that an 'independent' electoral tribunal would review the proper conduct of elections. Consequently, the *Código Federal Electoral* of 1987 created a *Tribunal de lo Contencioso Electoral* (Court of Electoral Disputes) as an

[192] *See supra*, text accompanying note 159.

[193] For information regarding the electoral process of 1988, *see* Domínguez, J., and Poiré A., TOWARD MEXICO'S DEMOCRATIZATION: PARTIES, CAMPAIGNS, ELECTIONS AND PUBLIC OPINION (New York: Routledge, 1999) and 'Imágenes Sociales en el proceso electoral de 1988' in REVISTA DE CIENCIAS SOCIALES Y HUMANIDADES (Año 8, Número 16, June–December, Mexico, 1988).

[194] The constitutional guarantee of *amparo*, which allows private citizens to contest the act of any government official or agency, is not available to contest political elections. *See* Chapter 6 below, text accompanying note 37, and Chapter 8, n 76 and accompanying text. Thus, the system of electoral tribunals discussed below is the only legal way to contest electoral fraud in Mexico.

[195] D.O. 6 Dec. 1977.

[196] *See* Chapter 6 below.

[197] Orozco, *supra* note 47 at 98.

[198] D.O. 15 Dec. 1986.

'autonomous' agency to review electoral irregularities.[199] The autonomy of the Tribunal was a fiction, however; in addition to the PRI's control of nominations to the Tribunal,[200] decisions of the *Tribunal de lo Contencioso Electoral* was subject to congressional override, since its decisions could be overridden by a simple majority vote of the *Colegio Electoral*, and therefore vetoed, in effect, by the PRI.

The first test for the *Tribunal de lo Contencioso Electoral* came in the general elections of 1988, in which widespread instances of electoral fraud are alleged to have contributed to the narrow victory of President Carlos Salinas de Gortari and of a number of PRI congressional candidates. Despite these allegations, the Tribunal resolved the appellations and complainants' briefs against the presidential, the *diputados*, and senatorial elections, and certified the questionable election of President Salinas.[201]

Complaints over the ineffectiveness of the electoral tribunal led to further reforms in 1989, when Article 41 of the Constitution was amended. As a result of these amendments, in 1990 the COFIPE was promulgated and the Federal Electoral Tribunal (*Tribunal Federal Electoral*, TRIFE) was created as an autonomous jurisdictional entity. Nevertheless, these reforms failed to satisfy those who criticized the lack of independence of the *Tribunal Federal Electoral* and the lack of aggressive oversight of the electoral process,[202] since Congress still had the power to override a decision of the Tribunal. Furthermore, since the magistrates of the *Tribunal Federal Electoral* were selected by the *Cámara de Diputados* from among a list of candidates put forward by the President,[203] the President, who still controlled Congress, could hand-pick sympathetic magistrates. In 1993, new electoral reform of Articles 41 and 60 of the Constitution was adopted in order to establish clearly that the decisions of the Federal Electoral Tribunal are definitive and non-appealable.[204]

Finally, in 1996, President Zedillo succumbed to widespread criticism of the Federal Electoral Tribunal by supporting new constitutional reforms. Article 99 of the Constitution was amended to replace the Federal Electoral Tribunal with the institution that now oversees electoral disputes, the Electoral Court of the Federal Judicial Power (*Tribunal Electoral del Poder Judicial de la Federación*). This Electoral Court is discussed in detail below in Chapter 6, at section 2.5.1. As the name suggests, the independence of this Tribunal from the elected branches of government was achieved by placing it within the judicial branch, and making the selection of magistrates by a method similar to the selection of

[199] *Código Federal Electoral* [of 1987], D.O. 12 Feb. 1987, Article 352.

[200] The Tribunal was composed of 7 *magistrados numerarios* and 2 *magistrados supernumerarios*, all of them appointed by the political parties.

[201] As a result of the 1988 elections, the *Tribunal de lo Contencioso Electoral* was bitterly criticized, and brought calls for reforms that would strengthen the objective review of elections. *See* Patiño Camarena, *supra* note 14 at 542.

[202] *See* Cárdenas, *supra* note 96 at 180; Woldenberg, J., 'Que Sera y Que Fué de la Legislación Electoral?' NEXOS, vol. 15, no. 170 (Feb. 1992) at 37, 39.

[203] COFIPE, Article 268.1.

[204] D.O. 3 Sep. 1993.

federal judges. This latest reform appears to have finally secured the independence that an elections tribunal needs, and the Electoral Tribunal has been credited with dramatically improving the reliability of Mexican elections, as evidenced by the federal elections in 2000.[205]

The *Tribunal Electoral del Poder Judicial de la Federación* has Regional Tribunals located in five different regions of the country. These Regional Tribunals have the jurisdiction to investigate and rule upon the validity of allegations made by political parties and candidates of irregularities in elections. In most instances, such tribunals have placed a high burden of proof on those contesting state elections, and have been reluctant to overturn election results.

The operation of the Federal Electoral Tribunal has helped improve considerably the honesty and transparency of the electoral process in Mexico. In the elections of 2003, despite a number of contested elections, the public accepted the honesty of the process.

3.3. Political Parties

Describing Mexican democracy as a 'one-party system' throughout the twentieth century may be an overstatement, but it is almost accurate. While other political parties have long existed, they were rendered inconsequential by the combination of elements, discussed in this Chapter as well as in Chapter 1 above, that gave the PRI a virtual monopoly of political power. Unlike the system that prevailed in the Soviet Union, however, the Mexican system permitted the open functioning of opposition political parties for which there was, at least in theory, no impediment to a takeover of power by democratic election. The political reforms that took place during the final decades of the twentieth century were an attempt by leaders of the PRI to strengthen representative democracy without losing control of the government; they succeeded in the former, and failed in the latter.

Numerous reforms during this same period to the manner of registration and representation of political parties accompanied the electoral reforms. One constant element of Mexican politics remained, however, and continues to apply: Mexican law prohibits political parties from establishing ties with foreign persons or political entities.[206] Article 24 of the COFIPE sets forth the legal requirements for an organization to be considered as a national political party: (i) it must formulate a declaration of principles, an action programme, and by-laws for the regulation of the party's activities; and (ii) it must have 3,000 members in at least ten states, or 300 affiliates in at least 100 *uninominal* electoral districts, but in any case the number of members in the country should be no less than 0.13 per cent of the *Padrón Electoral Federal* of the previous election.

[205] *See* Chapter 6 below, text accompanying notes 45–46.
[206] COFIPE, Article 38.1 (n).

These reforms, coupled with an erosion of the PRI's power base and spreading dissatisfaction with the efficacy of PRI-style democracy by the population at large, greatly strengthened the position of opposition parties, and eventually helped usher in a system of representative democracy in which three major political parties vie for power.

After the defeat of the PRI candidate in the 2000 elections, the political terrain in Mexico consists of three major political parties, none of which has been able to secure a solid majority in Congress.

After the 2000 elections, the PRI continued to hold the largest number of seats in the Congress, with 208 seats in the current *Cámara de Diputados* and sixty-one seats in the Senate. Having lost the presidency and a majority control of Congress, the PRI is searching to find a new power base to replace the base of support it formerly enjoyed with labour unions (less powerful today), *campesino* groups, and government employees. The PRI is divided between leaders of the old guard, referred to as 'dinosaurs', who wish to re-establish the *modus operandi* of past regimes, and newer leaders who are still looking for a political base.

The PAN (*Partido de Acción Nacional*), created in 1939, began to achieve electoral success in the northern states, which were farther removed from the influence of the PRI-dominated federal government. The PAN favours neo-liberal economic policies and a strong role for the private sector. Historically, the PAN leadership was centred in the northern states, and did not have a strong central leadership. The PAN lacked true political power until the election of *Panista* Vicente Fox to the presidency in 2000. Vicente Fox has not been able to reform the PAN into a cohesive party, and the PAN, like the PRI, is still undergoing changes in its governing structures.

The PRD (*Partido de la Revolución Democrática*) began as a splinter group of the PRI, and espouses many of the policies that the PRI espoused in its heyday: strong central control of the economy; economic and political independence from foreign influence, especially from the United States; and strong regard for social welfare policies.

The political spectrum shows the PAN to the right of centre, the PRI in the centre, and the PRD to the left of centre.

A major obstacle to the enhancement of representative democracy in Mexico has existed within the political parties themselves. The PRI was always highly centralized, with decisions on all aspects of party politics (from the selection of candidates to the development of policies) being controlled from the centre (the President), and emanating outward. Until the federal pre-electoral process of 2000, there were no primary elections to select candidates;[207] instead, the *dedazo*

[207] In 1964, Carlos Madrazo, then president of the PRI, tried to institute direct primary elections for the selection of PRI officials and candidates. Opposition from traditionalists led to the ouster of Madrazo. Gómez and Bailey, *supra* note 95 at 65. In 2000, the PRI engineered a national 'primary' election to select the PRI candidate from a group of four candidates offered to the public at large. Francisco Labastida Ochoa was the winner of the primary (*pre-elección*), with a majority vote over Manuel Barlet, Roque Villanueva, and Roberto Madrazo.

(appointment of a candidate by party leaders) has operated at all levels of the party, in federal, state, and local politics. Such a system is a natural obstacle to fresh ideas and new political actors.

The major opposition parties have generally been no more democratic in their internal procedures than the PRI. Indeed, they appear to be modelled on the PRI structure, with central committees making all major decisions on candidates and policies.[208]

For this reason, to manage a real shift away from authoritarianism in Mexico, political leaders must do more than reform the electoral system. In addition, they must enhance the powers of those institutions that counterbalance the federal executive: the federal legislature and judiciary, and state governments. During the second half of the twentieth century, the Mexican Congress served merely as a rubber stamp for the President's own legislative programme, providing an easy path for the maintenance of Mexican *presidencialismo*. In the next section, we will examine weaknesses in the legislative process, and ways in which the legislature could be developed into a more important political and legal force.

4. Congress and the Legislative Process

As set forth in the Mexican Constitution, the formal exercise of legislative power in Mexico follows the model adopted from the US Constitution. Federal legislative power is held by a bicameral Congress,[209] to which the Constitution assigns specific legislative powers,[210] reserving all other legislative powers to the states.[211] The consideration and adoption of legislative bills also follows a formal pattern similar to that in the United States, with a simple majority of both houses required to pass a bill into law, which is then 'promulgated' by the President and published in the *Diario Oficial de la Federación*.[212]

As often happens, the legal-formalistic similarities between US and Mexican legislative practice gave rise to significantly different legislative practices and traditions due to political differences. First, as shown elsewhere,[213] the

[208] Cárdenas, *supra* note 96 at 200.

[209] Mexican Constitution, Art. 50. The liberal Constitution of 1857 established a unicameral legislature, with a *Cámara de Diputados* but no Senate, the latter body being considered a repository of conservatism. The Senate was reinstated in constitutional reforms of 1874. Diego Valadés, *supra* note 16 at 249. The Mexican states all have unicamerel legislatures of relatively small size. The largest state legislature, that of the Estado de México, has 45 state *diputados*, while the smallest legislature (Colima) has 9 *diputados*. Hernández Gaona, P., 'Comentario al Artículo 116', in Constitución Comentada, *supra* note 15 at 509.

[210] Mexican Constitution, Art. 73. *See supra* Chapter 4, text accompanying notes 21–24. *See also* Articles 74 (powers exercised exclusively by the *Cámara de Diputados*), and Article 76 (exclusive powers of the Senate).

[211] Mexican Constitution, Art. 124.

[212] Mexican Constitution, Art. 72. For a discussion of the formal legislative process, *see* Schroeder Cordero, F., 'Comentario al Artículo 72', in Constitución Comentada, *supra* note 15 at 288–292.

[213] *See* Chapter 4, Section 2.

'federalization' of Mexican law has increased the power of the federal Congress at the expense of state legislatures. Consequently, in general, federal law has been much more important in Mexico than has state law. Second, until the recent election of Vicente Fox in 2000, the congressional legislative process was largely a formality without political significance. The final section of this Chapter addresses the changes that have taken place in recent years that have changed the role of Congress, to place it much further towards the forefront of legislative policy.

4.1. The Political Background

During the PRI's reign (1929–2000), political factors weakened the role of the Mexican Congress. The dominance of the PRI in the election of senators and *diputados* assured a PRI majority in both houses of Congress. The lack of internal democracy within the PRI meant that elected members of Congress voted in accordance with the President's wishes, and not necessarily in the best interests of their particular consitutuents. Opposition to the 'Party line' would not only spell the end of a *diputado*'s career within the Party, it would also result in less favourable treatment for the *diputado*'s district.[214] Congressional opposition to the President was also weakened significantly by the non-reelection of members of Congress, as discussed below, which made it difficult for *diputados* and senators to build strong political bases.

The conditions that weakened Congress have substantially changed. In the elections of 2000, the PRI lost not only the presidency, but also a majority of the votes in the *Cámara de Diputados*, although they continued to hold the highest number of seats in the Senate. Since 2000, no party holds a majority either in the *Cámara* or the Senate, and therefore legislation can only be adopted by the building of a coalition of support from more than one party. In this way, the Mexican legislative process has begun to resemble that of the United States, but with several important differences. First, because of non-reelection, discussed below, individual members of Congress lack the ability to develop expertise and legislative allegiances over time. Second, since congressional power is still new, the mechanisms of professional lobbying are still being developed. Ironically, or perhaps because of the lack of any solid majority, Congress has become a more important institution. Election of the leaders of each party in each house has now become front-page news, as individual senators and *diputados* have become more important in the process.

4.2. Congress and the Principle of Non-Reelection

One reason for the weakness of federal and state legislatures continues to this day: the broad principle of non-reelection that underscores Mexican politics.

[214] Carpizo, *El Presidencialismo Mexicano*, *supra* note 29 at 115.

The qualifications of individuals for election as a federal Senator or *diputado*[215] rule out the re-election of members of Congress to the same position for a period immediately following their term of office.[216] This principle, long an element of presidential politics in Mexico, was made applicable to *diputados* and senators in the constitutional reforms of 1933.[217] Non-reelection also applies to state legislators, by virtue of Article 116-I and 116-II of the Constitution. Non-reelection of members of Congress was seen as a way of breaking up political blocs and ending the '*continuismo*' that removed elected officials from the desires of their constituents,[218] an argument that is gaining force in the United States in support of constitutional limitations on the re-election of legislators.

Ironically, the inability of members of Congress to seek re-election has seriously weakened the legislative branch. First, non-reelection means that congressional members (especially *diputados*, who serve only for three years) always lack experience. Critics of the system have pointed therefore to the lack of professionalism within the legislative branch.[219] Second, it is not possible for a *diputado* or senator to build a power base as a legislator. There are no Ted Kennedys or Russell Longs in Mexico, no multi-term legislators with long experience in legislative politics who know how to push difficult legislation through Congress, or to impede its adoption. In the past, PRI *diputados* and senators naturally catered to the President's wishes, in a desire to secure an important job in the next administration.[220] Today, with a weakened executive, *diputados* and senators who are members of the President's party (currently the PAN) are much less likely to follow the dictates of the President than in the past.

There have been sporadic movements to alter the rule against re-election of legislators,[221] but the principle appears to be firmly etched in the Constitution.

4.3. The Legislative Process

The Mexican Congress is constitutionally required to meet for five months each year, the first ordinary period of sessions beginning on 1 September and ending on 15 December, except in a presidential election year, in which case the session may be extended until 31 December; and the second ordinary period of sessions beginning on 15 March and ending on 30 April of the same year.[222] Such short legislative sessions (the United States Congress usually meets for over ten months in each year) are a measure of the historical weakness of the Mexican

[215] Mexican Constitution, Art. 55 (qualifications for *diputado*), Article 58 (qualifications for senator are the same as for *diputados*, but the minimum age for senator is 25 years old on day of election, as opposed to 21 years for *diputados*).

[216] Mexican Constitution, Art. 59.

[217] D.O. 29 Apr. 1933.

[218] González Oropeza, M., 'Comentario al Artículo 59', in CONSTITUCIÓN COMENTADA, *supra* note 15 at 250.

[219] Orozco, *supra* note 47 at 115–116.

[220] *Id.*

[221] In the 1960s, labour leader Vicente Lombardo Toledano, head of the PPS, led an unsuccessful attempt to remove the prohibition in order to allow the development of career legislators. Granados Chapa, *supra* note 104 at 21.

[222] Mexican Constitution, Arts 65 and 66.

Congress:[223] since the executive branch had overwhelming control of the legislative process, the need for debate and deliberation by Congress was limited.

When Congress is not in session, the Constitution authorizes a special commission, the *Comisión Permanente*, to act on behalf of Congress, including calling for special sessions of Congress. When a special session of Congress (which are rare) is called, a vote of three-fourths of the members present is required for a bill or resolution to be adopted.[224] The *Comisión Permanente* is also empowered to receive legislative bills (*iniciativas de leyes*) from the executive branch, the states, or individual *diputados* or senators, and to pass them to legislative committees for the preparation of a draft report, in order to be discussed during the subsequent period of sessions.[225] The greater balance of power between the executive and legislative branches in recent years has enhanced the role of Congress, as well as the roles of individual members of Congress. The limited congressional sessions may have to be reconsidered if Congress is to undertake coherent legislative programmes.

The legislative process begins with the introduction of a bill (*iniciativa de ley*)[226] in either the *Cámara de Diputados* or the Senate.[227] Senators and *diputados* are not the only ones who can initiate legislation; both the President and the state legislatures share the power to introduce bills directly in Congress.[228] As previously mentioned,[229] the vast majority of legislation emanates from the executive branch, and in the past the Congress served as a rubber stamp for PRI

[223] Prior to 1986, Congress was only endowed with a single legislative session, from 1 September to 31 December. In that year (D.O. 7 Apr. 1986), Articles 65 and 66 were amended to provide for two sessions. De Andrea, *supra* note 16 at 410.

[224] Mexican Constitution, Art. 67.

[225] The *Comisión Permanente*, which is composed of 37 members: 19 *diputados* and 18 senators elected by their respective chambers at the end of each ordinary session, represents the legislature in times when Congress is not in session. Mexican Constitution, Art. 78.

[226] Legislation is generally grouped in the following categories:

- *leyes reglamentarias de los artículos constitucionales*, or laws that provide more specific rules for the implementation of certain articles of the Constitution. *See*, for instance, *Ley Reglamentaria del Artículo 5 Constitucional relativa al ejercicio de las profesiones en el D.F*, D.O. 26 May 1995; *Ley Reglamentaria del Artículo 27 constitucional en el ramo del petróleo; Ley Reglamentaria del Servicio Ferroviario*, D.O. 12 May 1995;
- *leyes orgánicas*, or laws that set forth the structure and principal powers of federal agencies. *See*, for instance, *Ley Orgánica del Poder Judicial de la Federación*, D.O. 26 May 1995; *Ley Orgánica del Congeso General de los Estados Unidos Mexicanos*, D.O. 3 Sep. 1999 and 7 Dec. 2001; *Ley Orgánica del Banco Nacional de Comercio Exterior*, D.O. 20 Jan. 1996;
- *decretos* (decrees), based on the executive power to 'legislate' in order to modify, complete or derogate the federal legislation. For example, *Decreto que establece, reforma, adiciona y deroga diversas disposiciones de la Ley del Impuesto sobre la Renta y del impuesto sustiutivo del crédito al salario*, D.O. 31 Dec. 2002;
- *reglamentos* (regulations), adopted by executive branch agencies to implement federal legislation, such as: *Reglamento de la Ley del Servicio Público de Energía Eléctrica*, D.O. 31 May 1993.

[227] The federal budget is submitted exclusively to the *Cámara de Diputados* for legislative approval. Mexican Constitution, Arts. 74-IV and 75.

[228] Mexican Constitution, Art. 71. [229] *See supra*, text accompanying note 85.

law-making. Insofar as budgetary laws is concerned, this power of executive initiative has been express.[230] More recently, Congress has taken a more active role in exercising its oversight and approval of the budget.

An *iniciativa de ley* received from the executive branch is referred to a legislative committee, or *comisión*, which studies the bill and drafts a report (*dictamen*) that accompanies the bill when it is referred to the respective chamber. (Except for budgetary laws, either chamber, or *cámara*, can be the *cámara de origen*, or originating chamber, for legislation; the bill is then passed to the other chamber as reviewing chamber or *cámara revisora*.) Once both chambers of Congress approve, the bill is sent to the President. If the President has no comment, then the law is promulgated and published in the *Diario Oficial de la Federación*, usually within a matter of days.[231] The President may choose to veto the bill, in which case it is referred back to Congress, which may override the veto with a two-thirds majority vote.[232] As mentioned earlier,[233] the exercise of the presidential veto has been rare in Mexico, but is not unheard of. If the President fails to act on a bill that has been approved by Congress for a period of ten business days, the bill will be considered approved by the President.[234]

The Constitution provides for the formation of congressional committees, and expressly grants to the Congress the power to require government ministers and heads of agencies to appear in hearings before Congress to answer questions concerning bills (*iniciativas de ley*) or other matters concerning their agencies.[235] Theoretically, the committee structure would allow considerable legislative input into the legislative process through the hearing process. This has not been the case in the past, however. Most legislative hearings are not public. However, thanks to the transparency available through the Internet, *iniciativas de ley* are now generally published on the World Wide Web,[236] but

[230] Mexican Constitution, Art. 74-IV, para. 2. *See* Carpizo, *supra* note 29 at 144–145. Article 74-IV, para. 2, requires the presentation of the budget by 15 November which gives the *Cámara de Diputados* a brief 45 days to approve the budget by the end of the legislative session. As a result of the short time, and the lack of staff, congressional oversight of the budget is minimal. Alcázar, Josefina, 'Diputados pobres, Ejecutivo rico', *Este País* (No. 9, December 1991) at 27, 28.

The relative paucity of *iniciativas* that originate in the legislature itself can be explained in part by the lack of legislative staff necessary for studying and drafting complex legislation, as explained below. The executive agencies, on the other hand, are heavily staffed with experts in all areas of government activity.

While Congress may lack the practical ability to initiate complex legislation, it has found the political strength to block initiatives that begin in the executive branch. President Vicente Fox (2000–2006), the first President in modern memory to face an independent Congress, has seen many of his major legislative reforms blocked by Congress, and has had difficulty getting congressional approval of the federal budget.

[231] Mexican Constitution, Art. 72, para. (a). Mexican legislation is available in Spanish online at www.diputas.gob.mx and www.juridicas.unam.mx. The *Diario Oficial* is available on www.gobernacion.gob.mx, 'Sistema de informatión legislativa'. (All sites last visited Jan. 2004.)

[232] Mexican Constitution, Art. 72, para. (c).

[233] *See supra*, text accompanying note 89.

[234] Mexican Constitution, Art. 72, para. (b).

[235] Mexican Constitution, Art. 93.

[236] Legislative bills may be found at www.senado.gob.mx, 'Gaceta Parlamentaria', and at www.diputados.gob.mx, 'Servicios parlamentarios'.

printed copies of draft bills are not generally made available to the public for comment. Newspapers usually are aware when major legislative reforms are under discussion, and often publish rumours concerning their content. The public's first opportunity to study the reforms usually occurs when the reforms are published in the *Diario Oficial* after their adoption. This lack of prior public comment, which used also to be true of draft regulations adopted by executive agencies, weakens the legislative process. Under the increased transparency of administrative law, discussed below in Chapter 9,[237] regulatory acts must now be made available for public comment prior to adoption by federal agencies.

Another limitation on the independence of the legislature is the lack of funding to support an adequate staff and to ensure professional administration of congressional affairs. Consequently, not only does Congress lack experienced, professional legislators, it also lacks a sufficient number of experienced staff to assist in drafting and studying legislation.

Most parliaments in other countries have permanent professional bodies of parliamentarian advisers; in Mexico, however, legislators are assisted by *ad hoc* and part-time personal advisers (*asesores*) who are not members of their staffs and are not able to devote their full time to legislative research. Moreover, in most cases, there are only two parliamentary advisers for each Congress committee, insufficient to research, review, and analyse all the legislative projects under review by the committee. The Mexican Congress is also assisted by the legal research of the Legislative Research Institute (*Instituio de Investigaciones Legislativas*). However, unlike the Congressional Research Service in the United States, which is a true research arm of the US Congress, the Mexican Legislative Research Institute has served a limited function of organizing academic events and publishing studies related to parliamentary procedure and congressional organization. To make the Mexican Congress a more effective generator of legislation, it should adopt a budget that could support a specialized staff of permanent parliamentarian advisers who would be responsible for researching draft legislation, and conducting public hearings on important subjects under consideration by Congress.

[237] *See* Chapter 9 below, at text accompanying notes 97–104.

6

The Judicial System

1. Introduction

For a lawyer trained in the United States, the Mexican judicial system is a study in both similarities and contrasts. Two fundamental principles of governmental authority, federalism and the separation of powers, give form to the basic court structures of both nations. Thus, in Mexico, as in the United States, one finds that judicial power is distributed between independent but interrelated systems of federal and state courts. Moreover, at the federal and state levels in Mexico, as in the United States, the judiciary constitutes a distinct branch of government, formally independent of the executive and legislative branches. Beyond these core analogies, however, the US judiciary and the Mexican judiciary are more different than they are alike.

Many of the differences between the two judiciaries are attributable to differing legal traditions in the two countries. The common law's precept that law is to be formulated by judges has meant that judges in the United States enjoy considerable power and prestige. This power is based in part on a rigorous application of the common law principle of *stare decisis*, which permits court rulings to be binding on courts in subsequent cases brought within the same jurisdiction,[1] and in part on the acceptance of court rulings as binding other branches of government.[2] As developed in the United States, the common law's broad vision of what constitutes an appropriate exercise of judicial authority is the foundation for a judiciary that, in meaningful ways, acts as a counterweight to the executive and legislative powers, defending the liberties of citizens and preserving the integrity of the Constitution. In contrast, the civil law tradition de-emphasizes the role of the judge, eschews judge-made law, and instructs judges to refrain from policy decisions while applying legal norms adopted by the legislature and codified. The civil law tradition's premiss of subservience of courts to the other branches of government is responsible, in part, for a Mexican judiciary substantially less prestigious, less independent, and less powerful than that of the United States.[3]

[1] *See* Merryman, J., The Civil Law Tradition: An Introduction to the Legal Systems of Western Europe and Latin America (Palo Alto: Stanford University Press, 2nd ed., 1985) at 34.

[2] In the hallmark case of *Marbury v. Madison*, 1 Cranch 137, 2 L. Ed. 60 (1803), the US Supreme Court held that federal courts have the power to declare acts of the other branches of government (in that case, an act of Congress) unconstitutional and, therefore, null and void.

[3] As used here, judicial independence entails what Professor Fiss labels 'political insularity' of the judiciary, enabling the judiciary to act as a countervailing force within the larger

Mexico's civil law tradition does not, however, completely explain a judiciary that has not defended individual liberties and constitutional order on the scale people in the United States have come to expect of their courts. The reasons for the endemic deficiency of Mexico's judicial system lie in the country's unique and complex historical, ideological, cultural, and political traditions. Such traditions include the Spanish colonial practice of unifying executive, legislative, and judicial powers in a single organ, the *audiencia*; a history of dominance of public life by the political executive; and the powerful forces of centralism that have shaped Mexico's legal landscape.[4]

Coming from a legacy of centralized executive power, Mexicans have never been accustomed to the presence of a powerful, independent, and aggressive judiciary. Almost since its inception in the 1917 Constitution, the contemporary Mexican court system has been considered inefficient, ineffectual, or even corrupt;[5] however, matters in Mexico reached a level of unprecedented crisis in the early 1990s. As violence and organized criminal activity in the country grew, and as the police became increasingly corrupt, public insecurity rose and the lack of confidence in the ability of the courts to dispense justice became increasingly intolerable. By the 1994 presidential campaign, opposition parties, Mexican intellectuals, lawyers, judges, and some members of the ruling political party agreed that the need for fundamental judicial reform had become urgent.[6]

The impetus to strengthen the judicial power coincided with the general political opening of Mexico. During the late 1980s, a consensus developed among Mexicans that major political reforms were needed, after decades of authoritarian government.[7] Economic liberalization without political reform, the model adopted by President Carlos Salinas de Gortari, proved insufficient. Still,

governmental system. *See* Fiss, O., 'The Right Degree of Independence', in *TRANSITION TO DEMOCRACY IN LATIN AMERICA: THE ROLE OF THE JUDICIARY* (Boulder: Westview Press, Irwin Stotzky, ed., 1993), at 55, 56.

[4] *See* Chapter 1 above, on Mexico's legal history, and Chapter 5 above, on Mexico's executive branch.

[5] *See* Lanz Cárdenas, T., 'Retos de la Administración de Justicia en materia de Seguridad Pública y Procuración de Justicia' in *LA JUSTICIA MEXICANA HACIA EL SIGLO XXI* (Mexico: UNAM & Senado de la República, LVI Legislatura, 1997) at 75. For general information about the Mexican Court system *see generally* Cossío Díaz, J.R., *LA TEORIA CONSTITUCIONAL DE LA SUPREMA CORTE DE JUSTICIA* (Mexico: Fontemara, 2002); Kozolchyk, B., 'Mexico's Political Stability, Economic Growth and the Fairness of Its Legal System', 18 *CAL. W. INTL L.J.* 105, 111, 113 (1997).

[6] *See* Cossío Díaz, *supra* note 5, Chapter I; Rubio, L., et al., *A LA PUERTA DE LA LEY: EL ESTADO DE DERECHO EN MEXICO* (1994) 58 [hereinafter Rubio]; Soberanes Fernández, J.L., 'Reflexiones para una Reforma Judicial en México', 17 *REVISTA DE INVESTIGACIONES JURIDICAS* 283, 283, 288 (1993).

[7] This consensus is evident in the elections of July 1988, in which the power of the opposition grew in the Mexican Congress and the ruling *Partido Revolucionario Institucional* (PRI) lost several important municipal elections. In 1989, for the first time in sixty years, an opposition party (the *Partido Acción Naciónal*) won the governorship of a state (Baja California). *See* Margadant, G., *INTRODUCCIÓN A LA HISTORIA DEL DERECHO MEXICAN* (Mexico: Editorial Esfinge, 13th ed., 1997) at 270.

it took a major devaluation and the ensuing economic crisis of 1994 to bring the country's top political leaders to realize that revolutionary change in the economic realm alone was not enough; rather, sweeping change in political practice and the judiciary were also crucial to national progress. Political leaders began to see that a competitive, market-oriented economy demanded a court system that could efficiently and impartially resolve commercial disputes.[8]

Mexico's judicial inadequacies were seen as products of several key shortcomings, including a lack of judicial independence; a Supreme Court overwhelmed by thousands of inconsequential cases and the time-consuming duty of administering the entire federal court system; the need for a system for effectively disciplining corrupt and incompetent judges; and the proliferation of administrative courts which operated outside the formal judicial framework and at the expense of judicial authority. Thus, in late 1994, President Ernesto Zedillo proposed constitutional amendments making radical changes in Mexico's federal judiciary. Under *la Reforma Judicial* of President Ernesto Zedillo, which took effect on 1 January 1995, the Supreme Court was restructured, the bulk of its administrative and disciplinary duties were shifted to a new institution (the Federal Judicial Council, or *Consejo de la Judicatura Federal*),[9] the Court's jurisdiction was altered to allow it to focus more on constitutional issues, and a new procedural device (the 'action of unconstitutionality') was created to allow for meaningful challenges of government abuses. The 1994 reforms and Mexico's new political climate were designed to assure the Supreme Court's independence from external political pressure, and to help the bolster independent and efficient administration of the courts. Nine years after the reform, it is apparent that the reform has been partly successful, but that reforming an entire system on a national scale will take decades rather than years.

2. Structure of the Mexican Court System[10]

The structure of Mexico's federal court system is defined by the federal Constitution and by a handful of federal laws. The most important law, the Organic Law of the Federal Judicial Power (*Ley Orgánica del Poder Judicial de la Federación*, or LOPJF),[11] is the functional equivalent of Title 28 of the United States Code, which codifies the US federal Judiciary Act. Similarly, the judicial

[8] Professor Margadant attributes the social reforms of the late 1980s and 1990s to pressure from international economic forces. *See* Margadant, *supra* note 7 at 271–272. Some analysts *see* Mexican judicial reform as part of a general pattern of judicial reform in Latin America in the 1990s, brought about by forces of globalization and the new world economic order. *See* Fix-Fierro, H. and López-Ayllón, S., 'The Impact of Globalization on the Reform of the State and the Law in Latin America', 19 *Hous. J. Int'l L.* 785, 787 (1997).

[9] *See* Cossío Díaz, J.R., *Jurisdicción federal y carrera judicial en México* (Mexico: UNAM, 1996) at 82.

[10] For general information on the federal court system, *see* www.scjn.gob.mx, and www.cjf.gob.mx. Information on state courts can be found at www.juridicas.unam.mx.

[11] D.O. 22 Nov. 1996.

structure in Mexican states is defined by each state's own constitution and laws, including a state judicial code.

2.1. Structure of the Federal Court System

Articles 94 to 107 of the federal Constitution identify and define the institutions that embody Mexico's federal judiciary. For most of Mexico's history, the country's federal court system, like that of the United States, has consisted of a three-tier structure, with courts of first instance, intermediate courts of appeal, and a Supreme Court at the top.[12] The 1994 reforms, and a further set of constitutional changes in 1996, added two new institutions to the federal court structure, which depart from the US model. In its present form, Article 94 of the Constitution vests federal judicial power in a Supreme Court of Justice, a Federal Electoral Court, Collegiate and Unitary Circuit Courts, District Courts, and the Federal Judicial Council. As discussed below, the Federal Judicial Council was added in 1994 to improve the quality of judges and the administration of the courts, and the Federal Electoral Court was added in 1996, to fill the void that had long existed because of the basic assumption under Mexican law that the federal courts lacked jurisdiction to deal with disputes involving electoral matters.[13]

2.2. Supreme Court (*Suprema Corte de Justicia de la Nación*)

The Mexican Supreme Court is composed of a Chief Justice (*Presidente de la Suprema Corte*) and ten associate justices, called *ministros*, who are organized into two chambers (*salas*) of five justices each.[14] Each chamber of the Court adjudicates cases according to subject matter. As of 2001, the First Chamber (*Primera Sala*) had jurisdiction over criminal and civil matters, and the Second

[12] Tracking the US Judiciary Act of 1789, the Mexican Constitution of 1824 divided federal judicial authority among district courts, intermediate appellate courts, and a supreme court. The 1857 Constitution preserved the three-tier structure of federal courts. Until the recent reforms, the 1917 Constitution followed the same basic outline of judicial institutions. In 1951, the Collegiate Circuit Courts, discussed below, were created to relieve the case overload of the Supreme Court. *See* Fix-Zamudio, H. and Cossío Díaz, J.R., *El Poder Judicial en el ordenamiento mexicano* (Mexico: Fondo de Cultura Económica, 1996) at 156–157.

[13] *See* text accompanying note 42, *infra*.

[14] In its original form, the Constitution of 1917 provided for a Supreme Court consisting of 11 justices who met exclusively in plenary sessions. In 1928, the Constitution was amended to increase the Court to 16 justices who were organized into 3 chambers. As the workload of the Court increased, Congress again increased the size of the Court, and in 1934, 5 more justices were added and the Court was reconfigured into 4 chambers. In 1951, the size of the Court was expanded again, to total 21 full justices plus 5 supplementary justices (*ministros supernumeraris*), divided into 5 chambers. This remained the Supreme Court's configuration until the 1994 reforms. Ironically, the reforms—intended to bolster the efficiency and independence of the Court—required the dismissal of all 21 justices and all supplementary justices then sitting. The President then nominated a new set of 11 justices (one of whom was carried over from the prior Court), according to the appointment and approval procedures discussed at note 93, *infra*. On the 1994 judicial reforms, *see generally* Fix-Zamudio and Cossío Díaz, *supra* note 12.

Chamber (*Segunda Sala*) had jurisdiction over administrative and labour disputes. All other cases within the Court's jurisdiction, including special constitutional disputes and suits challenging the constitutionality of certain governmental actions, are handled by the full Court sitting in plenary session (*sesionando en pleno*). Decisions by the Court when sitting *en banc* and by each chamber are by majority vote, unless otherwise specified by law.

Unlike US Supreme Court justices, who are appointed for life, Mexican Supreme Court justices serve fifteen-year terms and are prohibited from being reappointed to the Court. Salaries of the justices, as well as those of all lower federal court judges and members of the Electoral Court and Federal Judicial Council, are constitutionally shielded from reduction during their terms of office.[15] During their terms of office, Supreme Court justices are prohibited from holding any position in the federal executive or legislative branches, state government, or of a private nature, except for unpaid positions in scientific, educational, literary, or charitable organizations. Violation of these prohibitions is punishable by loss of one's seat on the Court, together with all related benefits and privileges. Justices are also prohibited from acting as attorneys or representatives in any matter before the federal courts during the two years following their retirement from the Supreme Court. The same prohibitions applicable to Supreme Court Justices apply to circuit judges, district judges, members of the Federal Judicial Council, and judges of the Superior Chamber of the Electoral Court.

The *Presidente*, or 'Chief Justice', of the Mexican Supreme Court is elected every four years by a vote of all of the justices sitting *en banc*, and may not be re-elected to serve a consecutive term.[16] The *Presidente* is responsible for the administration of the Supreme Court and is involved in the administration of the rest of the federal judicial system generally. The *Presidente* works and votes as a judge in the plenary of the Court, but is not a member of either of its two chambers and does not participate in their deliberations.

Before the 1994 reforms, the practice of appointing politicians or personal friends of the Mexican President to the Supreme Court as a springboard to political office severely damaged the Court's independence, competence, and integrity.[17] In part to end this practice, the Constitution now provides that, for one year prior to appointment and for two years following retirement, no justice may serve as a Secretary of a federal ministry, head of an executive branch department, Attorney General of the Republic, Attorney General of the Federal District, Senator, Federal Representative, Governor of any State, or Chief of the Federal District.[18] Moreover, Article 95 of the Constitution expressly states that

[15] Mexican Constitution, Art. 94.

[16] LOPJF, Art. 12. On 1 Feb. 1999, Ministro Genaro Góngora Pimentel was elected Chief Justice. Each chamber elects a Chief Judge of the Chamber (*presidente de la sala*), who is responsible for carrying out within the Chamber tasks parallel to those which the Chief Justice performs for the full Court.

[17] *See generally* Cossío Díaz, *supra* note 5 at 131–134.

[18] Mexican Constitution, Art. 95(VI) and Art. 101, para. 3.

Supreme Court nominees should be persons who have served the administration of justice with efficiency, ability, and integrity, or who, as judges, have distinguished themselves by their honesty, competence, and professional achievements. Aside from not holding one of the foregoing political offices, a person seeking appointment to the Court must be a Mexican citizen by birth, be of good reputation and not convicted of a felony or crime involving deception, be at least thirty-five years old, have possessed a law degree from an accredited institution for at least ten years, and have resided in the country during the two years prior to appointment.

Other important defects that weakened the Supreme Court as a constitutional tribunal involved the Court's inability to resolve cases in a timely fashion, due to the overload of cases, and limitations on the Court's authority to issue binding interpretations of the Constitution. After many years of legal and constitutional reforms, the Court's influence in counterbalancing the executive and legislative branches is finally beginning to be felt. In 1951, Congress adopted legislation creating the Collegiate Circuit Courts, granting them jurisdiction over a number of *amparo* cases that were formerly under Supreme Court jurisdiction, in particular direct *amparo* actions in civil matters. In 1987, the Mexican Constitution was amended to strengthen the Supreme Court's role as interpreter of the Constitution by granting the Court the power to decide the constitutionality of any law. In 1994, the Constitution was again amended to further bolster the Supreme Court's role as an authoritative interpreter of Mexican law by granting the Court exclusive jurisdiction over the most important constitutional controversies.[19] Finally, in 1999, Article 94 of the Constitution was amended to permit the Supreme Court to improve judicial administration by delegating certain types of cases to the Collegiate Circuit Courts, through *Acuerdos* (agreements) administered by the Supreme Court through decisions made *en banc.*[20]

As a result of these reforms, the case overload has been significantly reduced. The Supreme Court delegated 1,024 cases to the Collegiate Circuit Courts in 1999, 532 cases in 2000, and 601 in 2001. Prior to 1994, the Supreme Court received approximately 6,000 new cases each year, and maintained a docket of approximately 7,800 cases. By comparison, in a typical year, the US Supreme Court disposes of about 6,500 cases.[21] Unlike its Mexican counterpart, however, the US Supreme Court disposes of most of these cases without significant review, under the rule of *certiorari* by which the US Court may choose not to accept the appeal. For this reason, the US Supreme Court issues

[19] *See* Chapter 8 below, on judicial procedures to enforce the Constitution.

[20] The *Acuerdos* allow the Supreme Court to delegate to the Collegiate Circuit Courts cases that involve issues that do not raise important constitutional questions, but rather involve the application of rules already well established by the courts. *See* Cossío Díaz, *supra* note 5, at 143. Since the 1999 reform, more than 15 *Acuerdos* have been issued.

[21] *See* Administrative Office of the United States Courts, Judicial Business of the United States Courts: 1996 Annual Report of the Director (1997), at 82.

80 to 100 published opinions in a given year. In contrast, cases filed with the Mexican Supreme Court, unless 'removed' by means of the *Acuerdos* discussed above, must be decided by the Court. Since the 1999 reforms, the Supreme Court receives approximately 3,000 cases per year, and maintains a docket of approximately 5,000 cases.

Limitations on the Supreme Court's ability to issue opinions that are binding on courts in deciding subsequent cases also prejudiced its importance in the Mexican legal system. As discussed elsewhere,[22] under the *Fórmula Otero* there is no general rule of *stare decisis* in Mexico. A judgment of the Supreme Court is only binding as *jurisprudencia obligatoria* if five consecutive judgments applying the same rule are decided by a vote of at least eight of eleven ministers in cases decided in plenary session, or four of five ministers in cases decided by *salas*.[23] Cases that do not achieve this status may be persuasive (*tesis aisladas*), but do not have to be followed by judges in deciding subsequent cases. Since the 1994 reforms, the Supreme Court's issuance of *jurisprudencia obligatioria* has increased.[24]

Finally, as a further limitation on its role as an authoritative interpreter of the law and the Constitution, the Mexican Supreme Court lacked a *Marbury v. Madison* rule: the recognition of the general principle, long established in the United States,[25] that court judgments are binding on other agencies of government beyond the judicial branch. This defining principle of judicial power was absent in Mexico until 1994,[26] when a limited *Marbury v. Madison* principle was adopted in important constitutional cases. Discussed in more detail in Chapter 8 below, the 1994 Constitutional reforms permitted the Supreme Court to hand down constitutional judgments that are binding on all branches of government, in limited types of cases, and only when the Supreme Court meets in plenary session and adopts a decision by a special majority of at least eight of eleven justices.[27]

Even after the reforms of 1994 and 1999, far too many cases end up in the Supreme Court to permit the Court to concentrate on constitutional matters of national significance. For instance, the Court is called upon to act as

[22] The distinction between Supreme Court decisions that are formally binding and decisions that only have persuasive value is discussed in Chapter 3 above, on sources of Mexican law.

[23] Judgments of the Supreme Court that resolve conflicts arising between Circuit Courts are also considered binding. Judgments of Collegiate Circuit Courts are considered binding if 5 consecutive judgments applying the same rule have been approved by the unanimous vote of each panel of Collegiate Circuit Courts. *See* Article 192 of the *Ley de Amparo Reglamentaria de los Artículos 103 y 107 de la Constitución Política Mexicana*, D.O. 10 Jan. 1936, as amended D.O. 10 Jan. 1994, D.O. 8 Feb. 1999, D.O. 9 Jun. 2000, and D.O. 17 May 2001.

[24] During the period 1 January 2001 to 30 December 2001, the plenary of the Supreme Court issued 130 judgments having precedential value (*tesis de jurisprudencia obligatioria*), and another 22 judgments having persuasive value (*tesis aisladas que no integran jurisprudencia obligatoria*). During this same period, the Court's two chambers issued 187 binding judgments and 350 persuasive judgments. *See Informe de Labores que rinde el Ministro Genaro David Góngora Pimental 2001. Suprema Corte de Justicia de la Nación.* These figures compare with 3,700 judgments in the year 2001.

[25] *See supra* note 2, and accompanying text.

[26] For criticism of the limited nature of judicial judgments, *see* Gudiño Pelayo, M., REFLEXIONES EN TORNO A LA OBLIGATIRIEADAD DE LA JURISPRUDENCIA (Mexico: SCJN, 2000) at 10.

[27] *See* Chapter 8 below, at text accompanying notes 92–96.

a court of first instance in hundreds of cases annually (930 in 1995 and 674 in 1996); in contrast, the US Supreme Court acts as a court of first instance in only eleven or twelve cases per year. The Mexican Supreme Court is called on to issue opinions in thousands of cases each year, compared with the eighty or ninety opinions of the US Supreme Court that are published each year. As a result, the Supreme Court does not have the time to fashion well reasoned opinions to support its judgments, and for the most part the only opinions, or *tesis*, available in publication are extremely general summaries of the Court's opinion, which are virtually useless in providing insight into the Court's reasoning.

In the future, if Mexican political leaders wish to increase the Supreme Court's role as a true constitutional court, they will have to adopt reforms to permit a greater volume of cases to be decided by lower federal courts and by the state courts. Reducing federal jurisdiction, especially limiting the availability of *amparo* in cases involving state law issues, would bring a dramatic improvement, but would go against the sacrosanct nature of *amparo* as a bastion of civil rights protection.

One result of the high volume of cases is a deficiency in the quality of judicial opinions issued by the Supreme Court. As discussed in Chapter 3 above, the Mexican Supreme Court does not compose lengthy judicial opinions in the style of US courts. Rather, Supreme Court judgments (*sentencias*) consist of lengthy transcripts of arguments considered by the Court. While copies of these judgments are kept on file at the Supreme Court offices in Mexico City, they are not easily available for consultation by lawyers. The Court's 'opinions' (*tesis* and *jurisprudencia obligatoria*) that are published in the official Supreme Court Reporter, the *Semanario Judicial de la Federación*, and which are available at the web page of the Supreme Court,[28] are actually highly reduced summaries, or 'squibs', of the Court's final judgment; the summaries do not repeat the facts of the case before the Court, and are often so generally drafted (by clerks of the Court) that they provide little insight into the precise way in which a rule was applied. The Supreme Court should be encouraged, either by law or by practice, to compose and publish fully reasoned *tesis*, with a description of the facts of the case and the full reasoning behind the judgment, rather than mere summaries. The Supreme Court does not have the time to compose and publish a full opinion in each case, but it could do so in the most important cases. Not only would this help promote certainty and predictability in the application of the law, it would also impose discipline on the justices to support the outcomes of cases decided by the Court.

2.3. The Federal Appellate Courts: Collegiate and Unitary Circuit Courts (*Tribunales Colegiados y Unitarios de Circuito*)

As in the federal judicial system of the United States, federal courts in Mexico are divided into geographical circuits, each of which contains both collegiate and

[28] *See* www.scjn.gob.mx (site visited Jan. 2004).

unitary circuit courts. By 2004, ten years after the 1994 judicial reforms, the number of intermediate courts in Mexico had grown to 167 collegiate circuit courts and 64 unitary circuit courts in 29 circuits nationwide.

The jurisdiction of the circuit courts is discussed in more detail below. As a general rule, the collegiate circuit courts review *amparo* cases involving final judgments of any Mexican court, while unitary courts review judgments of federal district courts in civil and criminal cases. Collegiate courts are composed of three judges (*magistrados*), while unitary courts have one judge only. As opposed to the *ad hoc* panel system used to decide cases in the US Courts of Appeals, the same three judges of a particular collegiate court in Mexico form a standing panel that hears all cases that come before the court. Circuit court judges must meet the qualifications required of Supreme Court justices and they must have practised law for at least five years. Mexican circuit judges serve an initial six-year term, at the end of which time they may be ratified and retained, or promoted to a superior post, or, by implication, dismissed.[29] Once a *magistrado* has been retained beyond the initial six-year term, he or she can only be removed for cause.

Although the 1917 Constitution provided for unitary circuit courts, collegiate circuit courts were not created until 1951. Prior to that time, nearly all unsuccessful petitions for *amparo* eventually found their way to the Supreme Court, monopolizing its business and causing a serious backlog of undecided cases. The collegiate courts were created to relieve the Supreme Court of a large part of this burden by taking on all *amparo* appeals that involved procedural errors of lower courts, leaving to the Supreme Court those appeals in which a lower court made an error of substantive law. The distinction between procedural and substantive error proved elusive and unworkable, however, and eventually the jurisdiction of the collegiate courts was expanded to include all types of *amparo* appeals, other than those involving important questions of constitutional interpretation.

Mexican federal circuit court judges outnumber their counterparts in the United States and, on average, handle far more cases. In 2001, for example, 263,000 matters were pending before Mexico's 214 collegiate and unitary circuit court judges, an average of 1,182 cases per judge.[30] In the same year, 57,464 cases were filed before the 179 judges of the US circuit courts of appeals, an average of only 315 cases per judge.[31]

2.4. Federal District Courts (*Juzgados de Distrito*)

The district courts are Mexico's federal courts of first instance. Each court (*juzgado*) is presided over by a single district judge (*juez de distrito*). Federal

[29] Mexican Constitution, Art. 97; LOPJF, Art. 106.

[30] This included 225,357 matters in the collegiate courts and 37,649 in the unitary courts. *See Informe de Labores que rinde el Ministro Genaro David Góngora Pimentel 2001 supra* note 24.

[31] *See* Administrative Office of the United States Courts, 'Press Release: Federal Courts Caseload Continues Upward Spiral' (12 Mar. 1997) (available at http://www.uscourts.gov (site visited Jan. 2004)) (hereinafter 'Federal Courts Caseload').

district judges must meet the qualifications required of Supreme Court justices, except that they need only be thirty years of age and must have practised law for at least five years. District judges serve an initial six-year term, at the end of which time they may be ratified and retained, promoted to a superior post, or, by implication, dismissed.

As of 2004, there were 278 federal district courts in Mexico, spread throughout the country, more or less in accordance with the concentration of the population. As explained more fully below, district courts possess federal subject matter jurisdiction (civil, criminal, and administrative), including the broad allocation of jurisdiction in *amparo* cases (civil and criminal), as discussed below in Chapter 8.[32]

Despite a larger caseload, federal district judges in Mexico are outnumbered by their US counterparts. In 2001, for example, 302,104 non-bankruptcy matters were filed before the 665 federal district judges in the United States, an average of 454 cases per judge.[33] In the same year in Mexico, 248,442 matters were pending before the country's 252 district judges,[34] an average of 985 cases per judge, a slight improvement over the 1990 average of 1,600 cases per district judge, but still an immense caseload.[35] It is unrealistic to expect even the most competent and energetic of judges to dispense justice when he or she must handle almost 1,000 cases annually. One result of the heavy caseload is a tendency for Mexico's federal district judges to dismiss a large number of their cases on technical grounds, rather than to resolve them on the merits.[36]

2.5. Specialized Courts and Related Institutions

2.5.1. *The Federal Electoral Court* (Tribunal Federal Electoral)

Historically, the Law of *Amparo* (*Ley de Amparo*)[37] has barred Mexican federal courts from adjudicating controversies over the constitutionality of electoral laws, or the legality of election results and activities surrounding federal elections. Originally, Mexican law required these disputes to be filed before a special administrative tribunal, the Federal Electoral Court (*Tribunal Federal Electoral*), which was established in 1990 during the Presidency of Carlos Salinas de Gortari.[38] The Federal Electoral Court was a quasi-autonomous administrative tribunal organized under the executive rather than the judicial branch. All members of this court were appointed by the President, and its decisions could be reviewed and reversed only by the electoral colleges

[32] The jurisdiction of the federal district courts is discussed in more detail in Chapters 8 and 10 below.

[33] Source: Federal Courts Caseload, *supra* note 31.

[34] *See Informe de Labores que rinde el Ministro Genaro David Góngora Pimentel 2001*, *supra* note 24 at 340.

[35] *See* Rubio, *supra* note 6, at 76.

[36] *See id.* at 78.

[37] *See* Article 73 of the *Ley de Amparo Reglamentaria de los Artículos 103 y 107 de la Constitución Política Mexicana*, D.O. 10 Jan. 1936, as amended, D.O. 10 Jan. 1994, D.O. 8 Feb. 1999, D.O. 9 Jun. 2000, and D.O. 17 May 2001.

[38] *Código Federal de Instituciones y Procedimientos Electorales*, D.O. 15 Aug. 1990, as amended D.O. 31 Oct. 1996, D.O. 22 Nov. 1996, and D.O. 23 Jan. 1998.

of the Mexican Congress, never by the federal courts. Given the inherently political nature of congressional decisions, this gave one pause before accepting the unbiased outcome of electoral disputes, and for this reason the Mexican electoral system was subject to much criticism. The performance of the Federal Electoral Tribunal in the face of serious allegations of electoral fraud in the presidential elections of 1988, which resulted in the election of Carlos Salinas de Gortari, lent credence to the criticism.[39]

President Zedillo's 1994 judicial reforms did not include any amendment subjecting federal elections or election laws to judicial review, despite the rhetoric that the reforms were intended to secure the separation of powers and assure respect for constitutional guarantees, including that of free, genuine, and regular elections.[40] Nevertheless, in 1996, on the heels of widespread criticism, President Zedillo pushed through Congress a constitutional amendment to expand the Federal Electoral Court's authority, and to make it more independent of the President by transferring it from the executive branch to the judicial branch of government. Article 99 of the Constitution now declares that the Electoral Court of the Federal Judicial Power (*Tribunal Electoral del Poder Judicial de la Federación*), formally renamed to distinguish it from the prior non-judicial body, is the supreme judicial authority in federal electoral matters, with the exception of challenges to the constitutionality of electoral laws, which fall within the exclusive jurisdiction of the Supreme Court.[41] The Federal Electoral Court is charged with guaranteeing the legality of electoral activity and election results in Mexico by adjudicating disputes concerning federal congressional elections, the presidential election, allegations that any federal electoral authority has acted illegally, allegations that certain acts abridge the political-electoral rights of Mexican voters, and any other matter provided for by law.[42]

The Federal Electoral Court, which is based in the Federal District of Mexico City, consists of a Superior Chamber (*Sala Superior*) composed of seven judges (*magistrados electorales*), and various regional chambers (*Salas Regionales*) composed of three judges each.[43] Disputes concerning a presidential election

[39] *See* Rossell, M., *La Reforma Política en México y el Tribunal Federal Electoral* (Mexico: Joaquín Porrúa, 1988) at 37; De la Peza, J.L., 'El Tribunal Electoral del Poder Judicial de la Federación y el Estado de Derecho', 4 *Actualización jurídica* 1 (1997); Pérez-Fernández del Castillo, G., 'Reforma del Estado, Reforma Política', 3 *Actualización Jurídica* 1 (1997); Mateos Santillán, J.J., 'Los fraudes electorales del siglo XIX, una lección para el siglo XXI' 10 *Revista Jurídica Jalisciense* 4 (1994).

[40] Mexican Constitution, Art. 41, D.O. 5 Feb. 1917, as amended D.O. 20 Mar. 1997.

[41] Mexican Constitution, Art. 105, II, as amended D.O. 22 Aug. 1996. *See* Cossío Díaz, J.R., 'Artículo 105', in *Constitución Política de los Estados Unidos Mexicanos, comentada y concordada* (Mexico: UNAM & Porrúa, 15th ed., 2001) at 157.

[42] The Federal Judicial Council, discussed *infra*, at notes 47–53, includes a special Commission that is responsible for the administration, supervision, and discipline of the Electoral Court and its personnel. This Commission is composed of the Chief Judge of the Federal Electoral Court, a second judge from the Superior Chamber of the Electoral Court (who is selected by lot), and 3 members of the Federal Judicial Council.

[43] LOPJF, *supra* note 9, Arts. 185, 187, 192. In 2001, the Electoral Court had 5 regional chambers in Guadalajara, Monterrey, Jalapa, Toluca, and Mexico City. Judges of the Superior Chamber serve a ten-year term (non-renewable), and must meet the qualifications required of

may be filed only in the Superior Chamber. Cases involving federal congressional elections are brought initially in the regional chambers, and can be appealed only to the Superior Chamber. Decisions of the Federal Electoral Court within its field of authority are final and not appealable; however, the Supreme Court acting *en banc* may review any decision of the Federal Electoral Court that contradicts a prior Supreme Court ruling on the constitutionality of a particular electoral activity or election result. With some exceptions, decisions by the Superior Chamber are by majority vote. Decisions by the regional chambers are also by majority vote.

Since the laws were amended in 1996, the Federal Electoral Court, along with the *Instituto Federal Electoral* (IFE),[44] has had a profound effect on Mexican electoral politics. It is generally accepted that the presidential elections of 2000, which resulted in the election of the first non-PRI candidate, for seventy-one years, were the most transparent and accurate elections in Mexican history. The Federal Electoral Tribunal has not only adjudicated matters alleging electoral fraud, it has also taken a relatively aggressive stance to ensure compliance with campaign finance laws.[45] Thus, in June 2002, the Federal Electoral Court made formal demands on Mexican banking regulators to force financial institutions to provide information to IFE about suspected violations of campaign finance laws during the 2000 federal elections, despite resistance from the Mexican Banking and Securities Commission.[46]

2.5.2. *The Federal Judicial Council* (Consejo de la Judicatura Federal)

Prior to the 1994 constitutional reforms, the Supreme Court, in addition to having to decide thousands of cases annually, was responsible for appointing and disciplining all lower federal court judges, administering the federal judiciary, creating new circuit and district courts, and setting federal subject matter and territorial jurisdiction. One of the cornerstones of the 1994 reforms was to create the Federal Judicial Council, in order to shift almost all of the Court's administrative and disciplinary burdens to this new institution.[47]

Supreme Court justices. Mexican Constitution, Art. 99. Judges of the regional chambers serve an eight-year term (which may be extended if promoted to a higher post), and must meet the qualifications required of judges of the collegiate circuit courts. All judges of the Federal Electoral Court must have knowledge of electoral matters and must not have been a registered candidate for elective office or in the management of any political party in the 6 years prior to appointment. *See* LOPJF, Arts. 212 and 213.

44 *See* Chapter 5 above, on the executive and legislative powers.

45 For an evaluation of the performance of the Federal Electoral Court, *see* Fix-Zamudio, H. and Fix-Fierro, H., *El Consejo de la Judicatura* (Mexico: UNAM, 1996) at 61–70; Fix-Zamudio, H., *Breves reflexiones sobre el Consejo de la Judicatura* (Mexico: Consejo de la Judicatura Federal, 1997) at 30.

46 'Colocan a CNBV contra la pared', *Reforma*, Tues., 25 June 2002, at 1-A.

47 For more information on the Federal Judicial Council, *see generally* Melgar, M., 'El Consejo de la Judicatura, eje de la Reforma Judicial', 6 *Revista jurídica* (1996); Melgar M., 'La reforma al poder judicial, evaluación del Consejo de la Judicatura Federal', 2 *Diálogo y debate de cultura política* 7 (1999); Melgar, M., 'Mexican Justice towards the 21st century. The Federal Council of the Judicature, formation, branches and operation', 6 *US-Mexico Law Journal* (1998); Fix-Zamudio and Fix-Fierro, *supra* note 45; Roldán, J., 'La nueva

Formally, the Federal Judicial Council is responsible for the administration, supervision, and discipline of the federal judiciary, with the exception of the Supreme Court and Electoral Court. Pursuant to Article 94 of the Constitution, this includes the power to determine the number, division into circuits, territorial jurisdiction, and, as necessary, specialization by subject matter of the circuit and district courts. The development of an effective disciplinary mechanism was especially critical, because prior to 1995 no credible method of enforcing judicial responsibility existed.[48] The possibility of impeachment by Congress provided no real incentive for proper judicial conduct, and the Supreme Court was so overburdened with cases and other administrative duties that its ability to supervise the judiciary was extremely limited.

The Council consists of seven councillors (*consejeros*), including the *Presidente* of the Supreme Court (who serves as the President of the Council), three councillors designated by the Supreme Court *en banc*, two persons designated by the Senate, and a final person designated by the President.[49] The Constitution requires councillors to serve with independence and impartiality; thus, councillors appointed by political officials are not intended to act as representatives of the authority that appointed them.

The Council functions *en banc*, in standing commissions, and in *ad hoc* commissions.[50] Decisions concerning the appointment, assignment, and removal of circuit and district court judges must be made by the Council sitting *en banc*. With some exceptions, decisions by the Council when acting *en banc* are by majority vote of the councillors present (LOPJF Article 76). All decisions of the Council are final and unappealable, except for decisions concerning the appointment, assignment, and removal of judges, which may be reviewed by the Supreme Court to assure that they comply with applicable federal law. Each commission consists of three councillors, one from among those drawn from the judiciary and the other two from among those appointed by the President and Senate (LOPJF Article 77). Decisions by the commissions are by majority vote (LOPJF Article 78).

Since the Council was installed on 2 February 1995, it has aggressively undertaken to perform its duties. Between that date and August 1997, the Council created seventeen new collegiate circuit courts, four new unitary circuit courts, and fifteen new district courts.[51] This expansion of the lower federal

organizacíondel Podes Judicial de la Federacíon', in *La Defensa de la Constitución* (Mexico: Fontamara, 1997) at 127–155.

[48] *Ibid.* at 66–68.

[49] The councillors elected by the Supreme Court are designated among the circuit court judges and the district judges by the majority of at least 8 votes. The senatorial and presidential designees must be persons who have distinguished themselves by their ability, honesty, and integrity in the exercise of judicial activities. All councillors must meet the qualifications required of Supreme Court justices. Except for the Chief Justice, councillors serve five-year terms and may not be nominated to serve a subsequent term. *See* Mexican Constitution, Art. 100.

[50] *See* LOPJF, Art. 77. The Council has standing commissions on administration, judicial careers, disciplinary matters, creation of new organs, and appointments, supervision, and administration of the Federal Electoral Court. The latter are discussed *supra*, at note 38.

[51] Source: www.cjf.gob.mx (site visited Jan. 2004).

courts by a margin of about 13 per cent in two years was remarkable, considering that creating new courts in a short period of time is difficult because appropriate funds must be allocated in the judiciary's budget and qualified persons must be found to fill the benches. By December 2001, the Council had made ninety-five circuit court reassignments, sixty-two district court reassignments, fifty-two new circuit court appointments, and ninety-three new district court appointments.

With respect to supervision of the federal judiciary, by December 2001, the Council had re-appointed twenty-six circuit judges and ninety-two district judges who had reached the end of their initial six-year terms. The Council refused to ratify five circuit judges and three district judges.[52]

With regard to its disciplinary function, the Council found that the judicial reforms of 1994 led to a large rise in the number of administrative complaints filed against federal judges and clerks; however, a majority of these complaints sought review of judicial rulings and were not proper administrative complaints. By December 2001, the Council had resolved 259 administrative complaints, only forty-five of which were found to have merit. Of these, most were not serious and warranted only warnings or admonitions. Two cases led to the dismissal of federal judicial employees. In other cases, eleven federal district judges were suspended for fifteen days, and ten matters were referred to the Attorney General for criminal prosecution. In twelve cases, complainants were fined for filing frivolous complaints.[53]

The Organic Law of the federal judiciary creates several auxiliary bodies to aid the Council in carrying out its duties, including the Federal Judicial Institute (*Instituto de la Judicatura Federal*)[54] and the Office of the Judicial Inspector (*Visitaduría Judicial*), created in 1996. The role of the Institute is to improve the knowledge, skills, and training of federal judges as well as of those who aspire to the federal bench. It sponsors educational programmes, develops means of evaluating judicial performance, and participates in the competitive examinations (*examenes por oposición*) that persons seeking judicial appointment are required to take, as discussed below. Inspectors from the Judicial Inspector's Office (all of whom are circuit or district court judges temporarily reassigned from their benches) are required to inspect each circuit and district court at least twice annually and to report any irregularities they discover to designated authorities. During 2001, the Office conducted 443 inspections, including 154 of collegiate circuit courts, 60 of unitary circuit courts, and 229 of district courts.[55]

2.5.3. *Structure of the Courts of the Federal District*

The Federal District of Mexico (*Distrito Federal*), which encompasses Mexico City, is the most important judicial district in the country. Not only does

[52] *Informe de Labores que rinde el Ministro Genaro David Góngora Pimentel, 2001, supra* note 24 at 340. [53] *Ibid.*

[54] For information, *see* www.ijf.cjf.gob.mx (site visited Jan. 2004).

[55] *Informe de Labores que rinde el Ministro Genaro David Góngora Pimentel, 2001, supra* note 24 at 340.

the region contain over 9 per cent of Mexico's population,[56] it also serves as the seat of the country's governmental and economic power. This leads to a disproportionately large volume of civil and criminal filings in this one region.

Just as federal law in the United States provides for a distinct court system in the District of Columbia to handle civil and criminal matters of a non-federal or local nature, federal law in Mexico has established a system of courts in the Federal District which adjudicate matters of a local character. Thus, within the Federal District, one finds both federal courts and local courts of the District itself, each operating within their own separate (but sometimes overlapping) jurisdictional spheres. The structure of the courts of the Federal District is set forth in the Mexican Constitution and various federal laws, including the Organic Law of the Superior Court of Justice of the Federal District (*Ley Orgánica del Tribunal Superior de Justicia del Distrito Federal*)[57] and the Governmental Statute of the Federal District (*Estatuto de Gobierno del Distrito Federal*).[58]

Article 122 of the federal Constitution distributes the political authority of the Federal District among three governmental branches: an Assembly of Representatives (*Asamblea de Representantes*), a Chief of the Government of the Federal District (*Jefe de Gobierno del Distrito Federal*), and a Superior Court of Justice (*Tribunal Superior de Justicia*). The judicial branch consists of the Superior Court (the highest court in the system), and courts of first instance (*juzgados de primera instancia*), courts of the peace (*juzgados de paz*), and a Judicial Council of the Federal District (*Consejo de la Judicatura del Distrito Federal*). There are no intermediate appellate courts between the *Tribunal Superior* and the courts of first instance. These courts apply the local law (private law, criminal law, etc.) that is applicable to the territory of the Federal District.

The Superior Court consists of a Chief Judge (*Presidente*) and sixty judges (*magistrados*) who are organized into twenty chambers of three judges each.[59] Judges of each chamber rule on cases either individually or in three-member panels.[60] The plenary of the court, which consists of all forty-nine judges,

[56] *See* INSTITUTO NACIONAL DE ESTADÍSTICA GEOGRAFÍA E INFORMÁTICA (INEGI), CONTEO DE POBLACIÓN Y VIVIENDA 2000 (available at www.inegi.gob.mx (site visited Jan. 2004)) (8.6 million out of a total of 97.4 million people in 2000).

[57] D.O. 7 Feb. 1996.

[58] *Estatuto de Gobierno del Distrito Federal*, D.O. 26 Jul. 1994.

[59] Each chamber adjudicates appeals according to subject matter. As of 2002, there are 9 civil chambers (*Salas Civiles*), 8 criminal chambers (*Salas Penales*), and 3 family law chambers (*Salas Familiares*). *See* www.tsjdf.gob.mx (site visited Jan. 2004). The Chief Judge of the Superior Court is elected every 4 years by a vote (by secret ballot) of the judges who have been on the court a minimum of 3 years, and may not be re-elected to serve a consecutive term. Each chamber of the Superior Court elects a Chief Judge of the chamber who serves a one-year term and is barred from re-election for the following year. The Chief Judge is a member of the plenary of the Superior Court but not of any chamber.

[60] Panels are mandatory in appeals from final judgments of the courts of first instance, from decrees of the lower criminal courts that affect the liberty of the defendant, and from orders of the lower family courts concerning child custody.

resolves conflicts that may arise between the chambers, makes rulings of a general legal nature, and reviews cases pending in any chamber that may merit plenary examination. Decisions by the court when sitting *en banc* or by chambers when acting as a panel are by majority vote.

Judges of the Superior Court must meet the same qualifications required of Mexican Supreme Court justices and, in addition, must have distinguished themselves in the practice of law or as a judge, preferably in the Federal District. No appointee to the court may have served as Chief of the Federal District, Secretary General of the Federal District, Attorney General of the Federal District, or as a member of the Assembly of Representatives for one year prior to appointment. Judges of the Superior Court serve an initial six-year term, at the end of which time they may be ratified by the Assembly of Representatives and retained.

Below the Superior Court lie courts of first instance divided by subject matter.[61] The Civil Courts (*juzgados civiles*) have jurisdiction over property disputes if the amount in dispute exceeds 6,000 pesos, business disputes if the amount in dispute exceeds 20,000 pesos, and matters of a civil nature not within the jurisdiction of any other court of first instance.[62] The Criminal Courts (*juzgados penales*) have jurisdiction conferred upon them by federal criminal law. Family Courts (*juzgados familiares*) adjudicate family law matters (e.g. disputes relating to the validity of marriage, divorces, the division of marital property, paternity, child custody, and guardianship), matters of succession, and issues relating to mental or physical incapacity. Landlord-Tenant Courts (*juzgados de arrendamiento inmobiliario*) have jurisdiction over disputes involving leased premises, regardless of whether the property involved is used for housing, commercial, industrial, or other purposes. The Judicial Registration Court (*juzgado de inmatriculación judicial*) presides over disputes concerning the registration of real property. Each court of first instance consists of only one judge.[63]

Below the courts of first instance lie the justices of the peace, who are distributed among the political precincts (*delegaciones*) of the Federal District.[64]

[61] As of 2001, there were 190 courts of first instance of the Federal District. This included 66 criminal courts, 62 civil courts, 40 family law courts, 21 landlord-tenant courts, and 1 judicial registration court.

[62] At 2002 exchange rates, 6,000 pesos equalled approximately US$600 and 20,000 pesos equalled approximately US$2,000. The jurisdictional floor of the Civil Courts of first instance automatically rises each year to reflect inflation.

[63] These judges must be Mexican by birth, be at least 30 years old, possess a law degree and law licence, have practised law for at least 5 years, have resided in the Federal District or metropolitan area during the 2 years prior to appointment, be of good reputation and not convicted of a felony or crime involving deception, and have excelled on the examination required of applicants to the post.

[64] The Federal District is divided into 16 geographical *delegaciones*. A *delegación* may include more than 1 justice of the peace. In 2002, there were 40 criminal and 28 justices of the peace in the Federal District.

These single-judge courts have jurisdiction over civil or criminal matters of lesser importance, or mixed jurisdiction.[65]

The final component of the court system of the Federal District is the Judicial Council of the Federal District (*Consejo de la Judicatura del Distrito Federal*), which is very similar to the Federal Judicial Council.[66]

2.6. Structure of the State Courts

The fact that Mexican states did not formally exist until 1824, after independence from Spain, is crucial to understanding the relative powerlessness and inferiority of state government and state courts in modern Mexico.[67] In the United States, the thirteen colonies pre-existed the nation formed in 1789 (some by as much as 150 years), and the limited powers delegated to the central government were extracted from powers previously held by the colonies and their citizens. Mexico's founders adopted the United States federal model, theoretically dividing power among a central government and multiple states, but they also faced the challenge of forming these political units without the precedent of any analogous colonial structure. Instead, as explained in Chapter 1 above, Mexico's founders received a legacy of history, culture, and politics shaped by highly centralized government. As a result, centralism has characterized the balance of power between the federal and state governments in modern Mexico much more than it has in the United States.

The dominance of the federal government in legal matters in Mexico carries over into the judicial branch, and has contributed to the weakness of state judicial systems generally. The states cede much budgetary authority to the federal government, and state agencies, including the judiciary, are generally underfunded.[68] Salaries paid to state judges and clerks are low,[69] and the state courts have a reputation for being inefficient, dependent on antiquated technology, and more susceptible to corruption than the federal courts. Still, the state courts are an essential part of the Mexican judiciary since the overwhelming majority

[65] Justices of the peace in civil matters may adjudicate property disputes with an amount in dispute up to 7,000 pesos and business disputes with an amount in dispute up to 50,000 pesos. Regarding criminal matters these courts have jurisdiction over offences that involve no imprisonment as well as those involving a maximum penalty of up to 2 years' imprisonment.

[66] *See generally* Fix-Zamudio, H. and Fix-Fierro, H., 'El Consejo de la Judicatura en las entidades federativas. Una evaluación de su marco normativo y diseño institucional', in 2 *Dialogo y Debate de Cultura Politica* 7 (1999).

[67] *See* Parkes, H. B., *A History of Mexico* (Boston: Houghton Mifflin Company, 1966) chapter 1.

[68] According to a recent study conducted by ITAM University in Mexico City, the percentage of the annual state budget allocated to the judiciary varies from a high of 2.38% in Veracruz, to a low of 0.56% in Michoacan. 'Calificaciones de Ejecutabilidad de Contratos Mercantiles e Hipotecarios', published by Moody's Investor Service, Global Credit Research, April 2002, at 21. Of course, as explained in Chapter 4 above, the states lack general taxing authority, and state budgets are generally small and dependent on allocations of federal revenues.

[69] In 2001, the monthly salaries of state court trial judges varied greatly by state, from a high of 35,000 pesos (approximately 3,500 US dollars) in the relatively wealthy State of Mexico, to a low of 10,982 pesos in the State of Nayarit. *Ibid.* at 22.

of lawsuits that arise in Mexico between private parties are filed in state courts.[70] For example, in 1997, 98.9 per cent of all cases initiated in the Federal District were filed in local courts, not federal courts.[71]

Judicial reform in Mexico cannot succeed if the state courts continue to be deficient. In 1987, Congress attempted to fortify the state courts by amending the federal Constitution in order to establish that state judges must meet the same qualifications as federal judges, and that the salaries of state judges shall be adequate and irreducible. However, the reforms proved largely unsuccessful, as governors continued to appoint and remove state judges, and state governments continued to underfund the state judicial branches. As a result of the 1994 reforms, the federal Constitution now requires that state judges meet most of the qualifications required of Supreme Court justices and must not have served as Governor, state Attorney General, or state legislator during the year prior to appointment.[72]

The perceived weaknesses of the state court system, and the heavy overlay of federal *amparo* jurisdiction,[73] help explain why a sizeable number of the judgments issued by state courts continue to end up in the federal courts.[74] Well functioning, modernized, and adequately funded state courts that competently and impartially resolved disputes could reduce the caseload of Mexico's federal courts enormously. A narrowing of *amparo* jurisdiction, to prevent the use of the federal courts simply to give the losing party an additional appeal from state courts, would also help, but would be a significant departure from the general belief that *amparo* should always be available to attack any wrongful official act. Because of these weaknesses, the concern of some is that the substantial attention devoted to federal judicial reform in recent years will bring about further federal judicial control at the expense of local judicial improvement.[75]

Article 116 of the federal Constitution mandates that state authority be divided into executive, legislative, and judicial branches, but otherwise leaves to each state the liberty to adopt the court system it wishes. For the most part, Mexican states have adopted the hierarchy employed in the Federal District, which includes a superior court of justice, courts of first instance, and courts of minor jurisdiction but no intermediate appellate courts.[76] One example of this typical Mexican structure and one exception are examined below. Information

[70] No analogue to diversity jurisdiction exists in the Mexican legal system. Therefore, cases that arise purely under state law and involve citizens of different states cannot be initiated in federal court in Mexico in the same way as diversity cases can be filed in federal court in the United States.

[71] *See* Rubio, *supra* note 6, at 59–61.

[72] Mexican Constitution Art. 116-III. The federal Constitution also provides that state judicial nominees should be persons who have ably and efficiently served the administration of justice or who have demonstrated their honesty, competence, and achievement in other branches of the legal profession. Art. 116-III, para. 4.

[73] The use of *amparo* to provide federal review of all state judicial decisions is discussed in Chapter 8 below, at text accompanying note 10.

[74] For example, in 1992, nearly 37% of all judgments issued by the Superior Court of Justice of the Federal District were appealed to federal courts. *See* Rubio, *supra* note 6, at 61.

[75] *Id.* at 59.

[76] This was the court structure present in 1994 in the states of Baja California, Baja California Sur, Campeche, Chiapas, Chihuahua, Colima, Durango, Guanajuato, Guerrero,

on specific states, including state constitutions and legislation, is now available on the World Wide Web.[77]

The State of Mexico (*Estado de México*), which adjoins the Federal District, is the country's most populous and economically important state.[78] In this state, judicial power is exercised by a Superior Court of Justice, courts of first instance, and small claims courts (*juzgados de cuantia menor*).[79] The Superior Court consists of nine regional chambers (*salas regionales*) spread over three geographical regions within the state. Each regional chamber consists of three judges (*magistrados*)[80] and is assigned appeals of either civil, family law, or criminal jurisdiction. The plenary court consists of all twenty-seven judges of the regional chambers plus the Chief Judge of the court, and ordinarily meets monthly to determine jurisdictional and administrative matters.

Like the regional chambers, the courts of first instance of the State of Mexico are divided by subject matter into civil courts, family law courts, and criminal courts.[81] Each court of first instance consists only of one judge.[82] The small claims courts of the State of Mexico have jurisdiction over minor civil and criminal cases.[83] Each small claims court consists of only one judge.[84]

Hidalgo, Jalisco, México, Michoacán, Morelos, Nayarit, Nuevo León, Oaxaca, Puebla, Quintana Roo, San Luis Potosí, Sinaloa, Tabasco, Tamaulipas, Tlaxcala, Veracruz, Yucatán, and Zacatecas.

[77] *See* 'Legislación de las entidades federativas' at www.juridicas.unam.mx/infjur/leg (site visited Jan. 2004).

[78] The state of Mexico had a population of more than thirteen million people in 2000 and contributes more to the country's gross national product (GNP) than any other state, generating nearly 20% of the nation's industrial production. Winsor, A., *The Complete Guide to Doing Business in Mexico* (New York: American Management Assoc., 1994) at 46.

[79] The state's court structure is set forth in its constitution (*Constitución Política del Estado Libre y Soberano de México)* and its statutes, including the Organic Law of the Judicial Power of the State of México (*Ley Orgánica del Poder Judicial del Estado de México*). *See* 'Legislación de las entidades federativas' at www.juridicas.unam.mx/infjur/leg (site visited Jan. 2004). As of 1997, there were 103 courts of first instance and 80 small claims courts in the State of Mexico.

[80] Judges of the Superior Court must be citizens of the State of Mexico, be Mexican by birth, have inhabited the state for at least 3 years, have served in the state judiciary or be of recognized professional or academic merit, have possessed a law degree for at least 10 years, and be of good reputation and never convicted of a felony or crime involving deception. No appointee to the Superior Court may have served as Governor, state Attorney General, Senator, federal representative, state legislator, or mayor for one year prior to appointment. Judges of the Superior Court serve fifteen-year terms.

[81] The civil courts of first instance have jurisdiction over civil and commercial disputes with an amount in dispute in excess of 500 times the minimum daily wage applicable in the state. The family law courts of first instance have jurisdiction over all family law matters as well as disputes concerning succession. The criminal courts of first instance adjudicate all criminal matters except those within the jurisdiction of the small claims courts.

[82] Judges of the courts of first instance are held to the same qualifications as judges of the Superior Court, except that they need be only 28 years old and have possessed a law degree and practised for only five years. They serve six-year terms, at the end of which time they may be ratified by the state Judicial Council to serve 1 additional term or, by implication, be dismissed.

[83] This includes civil and commercial disputes in which the amount in dispute does not exceed 500 times the local minimum daily wage, and criminal cases in which the sanction consists of a warning, the posting of a bond, a fine, or imprisonment and a fine as provided for by law.

[84] Judges of small claims courts must meet the same qualifications as judges of the Superior Court, except that they need be only 25 years old and possess a law degree. They serve three-year

The State of Coahuila borders Texas and is home to many of the in-bond plants (*maquiladoras*) established by US companies in recent years. Unlike most Mexican states, Coahuila possesses a court system that consists of a Superior Court of Justice, intermediate appellate courts (*Tribunales Unitarios de Distrito*), and courts of first instance.[85] The Superior Court consists of seven judges (*magistrados*)[86] and functions in plenary session or in six unitary chambers. The plenary Court determines the number, territorial jurisdiction, and subject matter jurisdiction of the lower state courts. Each chamber is assigned jurisdiction over either criminal appeals or civil and family law appeals.

In response to the federal initiative for judicial reform, several Mexican state judiciaries have adopted a judicial council based on the model of the Federal Judicial Council discussed above.[87] (Two states, Coahuila and Sinaloa, had judicial councils even before the 1994 federal reforms.) For example, the Judicial Council of the State of Coahuila (*Consejo de Judicatura del Estado*) has exclusive authority to nominate, inspect, and discipline members of the state judiciary. It is composed of seven members, including the Chief Judge of the state Superior Court, the state Attorney General, an attorney appointed by the state legislature, the most senior judge of the intermediate appellate courts, the most senior judge of the courts of first instance, and the deans of the college of notaries and bar association of the state capital.

3. Methods of Selection, Promotion, and Removal of Judges

The methods of selection, promotion, and removal of judges obviously affect the degree of independence enjoyed by judges, as well as the relative power held by the co-ordinate branches of government. A judiciary in which judges are selected, promoted, and removed at the pleasure of the political executive can never be a true defender of individual liberties (especially in cases where executive officials are accused of abridging constitutional rights), or a protector of the constitutional order. Historically, the *presidencialismo* which dominated Mexico

terms, at the end of which time they may be ratified to serve another three-year term or, by implication, be dismissed.

[85] The structure of Coahuila's court system is set forth in its constitution (*Constitución del Estado de Coahuila*) and various statutes, including the Organic Law of the Judicial Power of the State of Coahuila (*Ley Orgánica del Poder Judicial del Estado de Coahuila*). *See* 'Legislación de las entidades federativas' at www.juridicas.unam.mx/infjur/leg (site visited Jan. 2004). In addition to the courts named above, Coahuilan law provides for guardianship councils for minors (*consejos tutelares para menores*) and conciliation courts (*juzgados de conciliación*).

[86] Judges of the Superior Court must be citizens of Coahuila, Mexican by birth, be at least 35 years of age and under 65 years of age, have resided in Coahuila for at least 5 years (unless absent for reasons of public service), have a law degree and at least 5 years of practice, and be of good reputation and not convicted of a felony or crime involving deception.

[87] *See generally* Fix-Zamudio and Fix-Fierro, *supra* note 66. Twenty-six of the 31 Mexican states have state judicial councils based on the federal model.

for most of the twentieth century[88] included unbridled powers over the appointment and retention of judges.

In the United States, the American Bar Association and state and local bar associations play a major role in the selection of judges.[89] In contrast, the Mexican legal profession plays no meaningful role in the selection of Mexican judges. One reason is that membership in Mexican bar associations is purely voluntary[90] and, consequently, such groups tend to be small and relatively powerless.

A major impetus of the post-1994 judicial reforms at the federal and state levels was the desire to remove the dominance of the executive branch by creating judicial councils within the judicial branch, and assigning to them the task of making key decisions concerning the selection, promotion, and removal of judges, sometimes with and sometimes without requiring legislative approval. In addition, Mexico began to formalize judicial career systems involving competitive examinations and judicial education in an effort to improve the qualifications and competence of jurists, as well as to remove politics from appointments and promotions. Nevertheless, even after the 1994 constitutional reforms, one still can identify at each level of the Mexican court system different devices for ensuring that the political executive (and sometimes the legislature) retains considerable authority over the selection, promotion, and removal of judges.[91]

3.1. Appointment of Federal Judges

3.1.1. Supreme Court

Prior to the 1994 reforms, the Mexican President appointed Supreme Court justices with the approval of the Senate, just as is done in the United States today. Unlike the US Supreme Court, the Mexican Supreme Court, in turn, appointed judges to the lower federal courts. These methods of federal judicial selection caused two major problems. First, because the PRI dominated the Senate, and the President dominated the PRI, the Senate could do little more than endorse presidential nominations, and the President's control of the process impaired the Court's independence from the executive.[92] Second, the appointment of judges to the circuit and district courts consumed time and energy that the Supreme Court could instead have devoted to resolving disputes.

[88] *See* Chapter 5 above, at text accompanying notes 15–19, 58–93.

[89] *See* Abraham, H.J., *The Judicial Process: An Introductory Analysis of the Courts of the United States, England, and France* (Oxford: Oxford Univ. Press, 6th ed., 1993) at 25–28.

[90] *See* Chapter 2 above at text accompanying notes 122–124.

[91] Judicial independence generally is accepted as a value to be attained in Mexico; however, as Professor Fiss warns, '[a]n independent judiciary can be a threat to democracy'. Fiss, *supra* note 3, at 56. In all countries, including the United States, national preservation and political reality require that numerous elements of political control remain over judicial officers. *See id.* at 58–62 ('It is thus apparent that even the mythic independence of the United States federal judiciary is substantially constrained').

[92] For more information about the appoinment of federal judges *see* Cossío Díaz, *Las Atribuciones no Constitucionales de la Suprema Corte*, *supra* note 47 at 101–105.

Ironically, to strengthen the Supreme Court's independence, significant reform presented the dilemma of having to remove from office the members of a Supreme Court that the society viewed as subject to undue presidential influence. President Zedillo resolved the matter by including in the 1994 reforms a requirement that all twenty-one existing justices retire, effective from 1 January 1995. To fill the new Supreme Court, the President then submitted the names of eighteen persons to the Senate, from which the Senate, by a two-thirds vote taken on 26 January 1995, selected eleven justices to serve staggered terms.[93]

Future vacancies on the Supreme Court are to be filled using a substantially revised method of appointment designed to increase the Senate's role in the process and to subject nominees to greater public scrutiny.[94] Article 96 of the Constitution provides that the President shall submit a list of three nominees to the Senate for each vacancy on the Court. Within thirty days thereafter, the nominees are to appear before the Senate and that body, by a two-thirds vote of the members present, is to designate one of the nominees to fill the vacancy.[95] If the Senate fails to act within the time allowed, the President shall select one of the three nominees to fill the vacancy. In case the Senate timeously rejects all three nominees, the President shall submit a list of three new nominees for consideration by the Senate. If the Senate rejects all three nominees on the second list, the President is to designate one of the new nominees to fill the vacancy.

During their fifteen-year terms (which are not renewable), Supreme Court justices may only be removed from office in accordance with Title IV of the Mexican Constitution.[96] Title IV, which deals generally with the discipline of federal officials including all members of the federal judiciary, provides for impeachment when officials, in the exercise of their duties, commit acts or omissions that harm the public interest.[97]

[93] D.O. 31 Dec. 1994. Two justices served until 30 Nov. 2003, 2 will serve until 30 Nov. 2006, 2 will serve until 30 Nov. 2009, 2 will serve until 30 Nov. 2012, and the remaining 3 justices will serve until 30 Nov. 2015. This process of removing existing justices and appointing new justices was not without controversy, including allegations that the President fixed the selection by submitting to senators in the PRI a secret list of his 11 choices, in addition to the public list of 18 candidates. *See* Taylor, M.C., 'Why No Rule of Law in Mexico? Explaining the Weakness of Mexico's Judicial Branch', 27 *N.M. L. Rev.* 141, 159 (1997).

[94] *See* Article Eleventh, Transitory Articles of the LOPJF, D.O. 26 May 1995.

[95] The thirty-day deadline for senatorial action on Supreme Court nominees appears arbitrary and designed to inhibit extensive public scrutiny of nominees. In fact, the January 1995 Senate confirmation proceedings leading to appointment of the 11 new Supreme Court justices 'left much to be desired'. Taylor, *supra* note 90, at 160–161.

[96] Prior to the 1994 judicial reforms, impeachment of federal judges, and of Supreme Court justices in particular, was possible by vote of a simple majority of Congress; however, removal in this fashion was rare. In practice, the primary means of removal of Supreme Court justices was unilateral termination by the President who, thereafter, would proceed to appoint a replacement to the Court. For this reason, President Zedillo's decision to force retirement of the entire Supreme Court in 1994 was viewed with suspicion.

[97] Officials may not be impeached merely for expressing ideas. In addition to serving as a basis for impeachment, official misdeeds may be punishable by criminal and administrative sanctions. To pursue criminal charges against a Supreme Court justice, a judge of the Superior Chamber of the Electoral Court, or a member of the Federal Judicial Council for offences committed during the individual's term of office, the Chamber of Deputies must first declare

3.1.2. Lower Federal Courts

Pursuant to Article 97 of the federal Constitution, judges of the federal circuit and district courts are to be appointed and assigned to their seats by the Federal Judicial Council.[98] As mentioned previously, the judges of these lower federal courts serve an initial six-year term, at the end of which time they may be ratified and retained, or promoted to a superior post, or, by implication, dismissed.[99] If a federal circuit or district judge is retained or promoted, he or she may be removed from office only by impeachment, under the process described above for Supreme Court Justices, or by mandatory retirement at the age of seventy-five.

Entry into and promotion within the lower federal judiciary is regulated by means of a 'judicial career system' (*sistema de carrera judicial*), organized according to principles of excellence, professionalism, objectivity, impartiality, independence, and seniority.[100] Persons seeking appointment to a federal circuit or district court seat must participate in a competitive examination. At the discretion of the Federal Judicial Council, examinations may be open to anyone (*examen libre*, or open exam) or limited to judicial employees (*examen interno*, or internal exam). Only sitting district court judges may take the internal examination to become a circuit court judge and only Supreme Court, circuit court, and district court clerks may take the internal examination to become a district court judge. According to statistics of the Federal Judicial Council,[101] during 2000 one open (*libre*) examination took place with the participation of judges, academics, and lawyers specializing in procedural law. In addition, there were four internal examinations administered for vacancies of circuit court and

(by a majority vote of the members present) that there are grounds upon which to proceed. Only if the Chamber of Deputies so votes may the appropriate federal authorities prosecute the matter. Mexican Constitution, Art. 111.

Impeachment proceedings begin in the Chamber of Deputies where, following a trial, the accused official may be impeached by a vote of a simple majority of the representatives present. The proceedings then move to the Senate which, acting as a sentencing jury (*jurado de sentencia*), determines an appropriate sanction by a vote of two-thirds of the senators present. The penalties for impeachment include removal from office and prohibition from future public service. The decisions of the Chamber of Deputies and Senate may not be appealed.

[98] In making initial appointments to a circuit or district court, when several judicial positions are vacant, the Federal Judicial Council is to consider the results of the competitive examination; courses completed at the Federal Judicial Institute; the time working for the judicial branch or professional experience; the judge's performance of official duties; and academic degrees and advanced studies. *See* LOPJF, Art. 119.

[99] In determining whether to retain a circuit or district court judge at the end of the six-year term, the Federal Judicial Council is to consider: the judge's performance of official duties; the results of periodic evaluations; academic degrees and advanced studies; whether the judge has been sanctioned for grave misconduct; and other factors of a general nature specified by the Council at least 6 months prior to the review. LOPJF Art. 121.

[100] Law clerks and secretaries play important roles in the Mexican courts, and the federal judicial career system also applies to judicial clerks (*secretarios*) and assistants (*actuarios*) as well as to judges.

[101] The figure is cited in an *acuerdo* of the Federal Judicial Council, available at www.cjf.gob.mx/organizacioncjf/acuerdos (site visited Jan. 2004).

district court judges. Eighty-five circuit court judges and one hundred and seven district court judges were appointed during this period.

Mexican law provides that the five applicants for a judicial post with the highest grades on a preliminary written test shall be allowed to take practical written and oral examinations which are graded by a jury consisting of a member of the Federal Judicial Council, a federal judge (either of a circuit or district court depending on the seat to be filled), and a law professor appointed by the Judicial Institute. Ultimately, the jury selects a winner based on the applicant's performance on the examination, courses completed at the Judicial Institute, seniority within the judiciary, and academic degrees and advanced studies, if any. Once informed of the winner, the Judicial Council sitting *en banc* makes the appointment by majority vote. Reassignments of sitting circuit and district judges are to occur based on the judge's completion of courses in the Judicial Institute, seniority, academic degrees and advanced studies, performance on judicial evaluations, and professional discipline and development.

In 1996, the Judicial Council conducted the first competitive examinations for the appointment of circuit and district court judges in the nation's history.[102] Because the competitions were internal, only sitting district judges were tested for circuit court appointments and only federal judicial clerks for district court appointments. The competitions included four phases: a test of general legal knowledge, evaluation of each aspirant's academic merit, a practical test, and an oral and public examination. The first two phases of the competitions were strictly anonymous, which is a crucial point considering that prior appointments to the lower federal courts were criticized as being based on favouritism rather than objective merit.[103] Moreover, numerous persons within the judicial branch, including judges, members of the Judicial Institute, law professors, and members of the Council, actively participated in the process. By means of these first competitive examinations, fifty-two new circuit court judges and sixty-two new district court judges were appointed.

The early experience under the new federal system of judicial appointments has been positive. Federal judges appear to be exercising their judicial authority independently, bolstered by the weakening of executive control. The Supreme Court has shown considerable independence and authority by deciding important cases that have affected political, social, and economic developments.[104] While budgetary appropriations for the federal courts have not been as high as

[102] Information concerning competitive examinations is available at the Federal Judicial Council's website, www.cjf.gob.mx (site visited Jan. 2004).

[103] *See* Soberanes, 'Reflexiones para una Reforma Judicial en México' *supra* note 6, at 286.

[104] The most important decisions of the Supreme Court in recent years include: judgment invalidating Article 1 of the Decree of the Federal Branch by virtue of which the contributors importing or commercializing beverages sweetened with fructose not derived from sugar cane were exempted from the payment of a special tax. SJF, 9th, Pleno, Tomo XVI, P. 1049 (2002); judgment declaring unconstitutional amendments to the Regulations of the Electricity Law (D.O. 24 May 2001), by which President Fox had attempted to promote private investment in electricity generation. SJF, 9th, Pleno, Controversia 22/200 (2002); and judgment declaring unconstitutional the extradition of any person located within Mexico, in cases in which the

some members of the federal judiciary would have hoped, the compensation of federal judges has become significant enough to make this a respectable career and to attract outstanding candidates. The same cannot be said for the state courts, however; with some exceptions, budgetary allocations for state judicial systems are still inadequate. There are also some lingering problems. Furthermore, tension has arisen between the Supreme Court ministers and members of the Federal Judicial Council over the supervisory functions of the Federal Judicial Council and the imposition of administrative sanctions on the ministers of the Supreme Court, which some ministers contend are beyond the constitutional powers of the Federal Judicial Council. The lesson to be drawn from Mexico's experience is clear: the reform of an entire judicial system can only be accomplished by many years of sustained effort and by a consensus of political support for the judiciary as an institution.

3.1.3. Federal Electoral Court

Judges of the Superior Chamber and regional chambers of the Federal Electoral Court are nominated by the Supreme Court and selected by the Senate, by a two-thirds vote of the members present. The Supreme Court, sitting *en banc* and by simple majority vote, submits a list of three persons to the Senate for each vacancy on the Electoral Court.[105] As is true for all federal judicial officers, judges of the Federal Electoral Court may be removed from office only by impeachment in accordance with Title IV of the Constitution.

3.1.4. Federal Judicial Council

As explained previously, the Federal Judicial Council consists of the Chief Justice of the Supreme Court, a collegiate circuit court judge, a unitary circuit court judge, a district judge, two persons appointed by the Senate unilaterally, and a final person appointed by the President unilaterally. The two circuit court judges and the district court judge are selected by lot from among the sitting circuit and district court judges. All appointees to the Council, except those named in 1995 (who will serve staggered terms), are to serve five-year terms. During their terms of office, councillors may be removed from office only by impeachment in accordance with Title IV of the Constitution.

The rigour with which the Council (including those councillors appointed by the Senate and President) has performed its administrative, supervisory, and

accused is charged in the foreign jurisdiction with a crime punishable by life imprisonment (considered a violation of the constitutional right to rehabilition). SJF, 9th, Pleno, Tomo XIV, p. 15 (2001). These and other cases may be found at www.scjn.gob.mx (site visited Jan. 2004).

[105] *See* Aguinaco, J.V., *El Nuevo Poder Judicial de la Federacion* (Mexico: Suprema Corte de Justicia de la Nación, 1997) at 69–70. To fill the new Electoral Court, the Supreme Court, in August 1996, announced that it was accepting applications and received responses from 292 qualified applicants. Following initial screening and interviews, the Supreme Court formed a list of 3 names for each seat on the Electoral Court, which it submitted to the Senate on 23 October 1996. The Senate appointed judges to the Electoral Court from the Supreme Court's list in November 1996. D.O. 28 Nov. 1996.

disciplinary functions in its initial years has been impressive. Judicial appointments at the federal level have largely been removed from outside political influence, and appointments have been made on the basis of individual abilities of candidates. Assuming this continues, the Council will do much to fortify the federal judiciary.

3.1.5. Courts of the Federal District

Judges of the Superior Court of the Federal District are appointed by the Chief of the Federal District with the approval of the Assembly of Representatives. They serve an initial six-year term, at the end of which time they may be ratified by the Assembly of Representatives and retained or, by implication, dismissed. If ratified, judges of the Superior Court may be removed from office only by impeachment in accordance with Title IV of the federal Constitution, by mandatory retirement at the age of seventy-five, or due to physical or mental incapacity.

Entry into and promotion within the lower courts of the Federal District is regulated by means of a judicial career system that parallels the system used in the federal courts since the 1994 reforms. Persons seeking appointment to a court of first instance or justice of the peace court must participate in a competitive examination (*concurso por oposición*) consisting of written and oral portions graded by a four-person jury. The jury delivers the names of the persons with the five highest scores to the Judicial Council of the Federal District for its use in appointment and promotion. Judges of the courts of first instance and justices of the peace serve an initial six-year term and, at the discretion of the Judicial Council, may be reappointed to serve one or more additional six-year terms. At any time, the Judicial Council may determine that a judge of the Federal District should be removed from office for just cause (*causa justificada*) and seek to have the judge impeached as provided for by Title IV of the federal Constitution.

Members of the Judicial Council of the Federal District are appointed by the Assembly of Representatives to serve five-year terms and may be removed from office only by impeachment in accordance with Title IV of the federal Constitution.[106]

3.2. State Courts

The methods for selection, promotion, and removal of state judges can vary considerably from state to state. The traditional approach in Mexico has been a reflection of the pre-1994 system of federal judge appointments: the governor appoints judges to the state's highest court, after legislative approval, and the judges of the state's highest court, in turn, appoint all lower court judges. As

[106] *See* Fix Fierro, H., 'El Consejo de la Judicatura en las Entidades Federativas. Una evaluación de su marco normativo y diseño institucional', in *DIALOGO Y DEBATE DE CULTURA POLITICA* 2, 7 (Mexico, 1999).

with the former federal system, this method of selection has been criticized for granting substantial power to the state executive and jeopardizing the independence of state judges.[107]

Joining the wave of federal reforms, twenty-six Mexican states have created judicial councils patterned on the Federal Judicial Council, to improve judicial selection. For example, in the State of Mexico, entry into and promotion within the state judiciary is regulated by means of a judicial career system that parallels the system used in the lower federal courts and Federal District. Using this system, the state Judicial Council appoints all state judges with the approval of the state legislature. Coahuila has a hybrid system, with judges of the Superior Court appointed by the governor (with the approval of the state legislature) from a list of candidates created by the state judicial council. Judges of Coahuila's lower courts are then appointed in the traditional manner by the Superior Court.

As a general rule, state judges in Mexico may be removed from office only by impeachment by the state legislature or due to mandatory retirement at a constitutionally designated age or as a result of physical or mental incapacity. State court judges are also subject to impeachment under federal law, but only for grave violations of the federal Constitution or federal law, and in such instances, decisions of impeachment by the federal Congress are solely declaratory and are to be communicated to the state legislatures so that they may proceed appropriately.[108] Short of removal from office, all state judicial officers are also subject to professional sanctions, including admonishments, warnings, fines, and temporary suspension.

4. Federal Jurisdiction

The jurisdiction of the federal courts in Mexico is defined primarily by Articles 103 to 107 of the Constitution and by the Organic Law of the Federal Judiciary (LOPJF). Federal jurisdiction falls into two broad categories: *amparo* jurisdiction, and other cases involving subject matter assigned by the Constitution or by federal law to the federal courts. Unlike US law, Mexican law does not provide for federal jurisdiction based on diversity of citizenship (i.e. on the basis that plaintiff and defendant are citizens of different states of the union).

4.1. Federal Question Jurisdiction

4.1.1. Exclusive Jurisdiction of Federal Courts

Disputes within the exclusive jurisdiction of the federal courts include admiralty cases,[109] cases in which the federal government is a party,[110] cases involving

[107] For general information about states constitutional law *see* Arteaga Nava, E., *Derecho Constitucional Estatal* (Mexico: Porrúa, 1988) at 342.
[108] Mexican Constitution, Art. 109, III.
[109] Mexican Constitution, Art. 104-II.
[110] *Ibid.*, Art. 104-III.

diplomatic or consular officials,[111] federal criminal cases,[112] appeals from federal administrative courts,[113] federal–state and interstate jurisdictional conflicts,[114] and, by virtue of the 1994 judicial reforms, certain special cases called Article 105-I constitutional controversies (*controversias constitucionales*) and Article 105-II actions of unconstitutionality (*acciones de inconstitucionalidad*), both of which are discussed below in Chapter 8.

4.1.2. Concurrent Jurisdiction of the Federal Courts

Article 104-I (A) of the Constitution gives the federal courts, state courts, and courts of the Federal District concurrent jurisdiction over civil and criminal cases that involve the enforcement or application of federal laws or international treaties, provided that such cases affect only the rights of private parties. In such instances, the choice of forum is left to the plaintiff. Thus, a lawsuit between two companies that involves the application of federal commercial law can be brought in federal or state court depending on the plaintiff's preference. In addition, all cases involving negotiable instruments, or those related to the execution of a commercial contract, can be brought before either a federal or a state court, depending on the plaintiff's preference.[115]

4.1.3. Amparo *Jurisdiction*

Since Chapter 8 below contains a detailed discussion of *amparo*, this section merely sets forth the salient jurisdictional features of this important procedure. *Amparo* encompasses a set of federal judicial procedures by which any private person (individual or enterprise) may contest the action of a government agency or official, either at state or federal level, on the ground that the action is unconstitutional. Under the *Amparo* Law, the federal courts are empowered to issue what amounts to an order (*fallo de nulidad*) preventing the governmental defendant from carrying out the contested action.

As discussed below in Chapter 8,[116] the Supreme Court has interpreted the constitutional guarantee of due process broadly to include within the scope of *amparo* protection the misapplication of any law, state or federal. Court rulings

[111] *Ibid.*, Art. 104-V.

[112] This includes offences provided for by federal law or international treaty, offences committed by a federal official or employee in the exercise of his duties, all crimes which hinder the exercise of any federal power, and crimes by or against federal election officials. In addition, the federal courts have exclusive jurisdiction to hear extradition proceedings and requests for authorization to tap private communications.

[113] Article 104-I(B) of the Constitution grants the collegiate circuit courts exclusive jurisdiction to hear appeals from federal administrative courts, that is, from the Federal Fiscal Court and Administrative Court of the Federal District. *See* section 5, *infra*.

[114] *See* Mexican Constitution, Art. 106.

[115] Mexican Constitution, Art. 104, I (A). On commercial litigation, *see* Chapter 18 below. Despite having jurisdiction, in practice federal courts often look for technicalities on which to dismiss commercial cases, in essence removing them to the state courts for resolution.

[116] *See* Chapter 8 below, at text accompanying notes 13–14.

are included in the definition of 'acts of a governmental official',[117] and for this reason any court judgment (including judgments by state courts interpreting state laws) are reviewable by federal courts under *amparo*, since an erroneous application of a principle of state law is deemed to be a violation of due process.

Federal *amparo* jurisdiction derives from Articles 103 and 107 of the Mexican Constitution. Article 103 grants federal courts jurisdiction over controversies arising out of: (1) laws or government acts that violate individual rights, (2) laws or acts of federal authorities that encroach upon or restrict the sovereignty of the states or the jurisdiction of the Federal District, and (3) laws or acts of state or Federal District authorities that invade the jurisdiction of the federal government. Article 107 opens by delineating procedural limitations on *amparo* actions. Article 107, together with other federal laws, specifies the jurisdiction of the Supreme Court, circuit courts, and district courts over different types of *amparo* actions. As part of the effort in 1994 to reshape the Supreme Court into a true constitutional court, Article 107 was amended to provide the Court the authority (*la facultad de atracción*), on its own initiative or at the request of a collegiate circuit court or the Attorney General of Mexico, to take from lower federal courts any *amparo* case that merits special attention because of its overriding importance. In addition, the 1994 amendments conferred upon the Supreme Court expanded authority to enforce federal *amparo* rulings.[118]

Three features of *amparo*, although developed in more detail in Chapter 8, deserve special mention here: (1) the limited effect of *amparo* judgments beyond the parties involved in a dispute; (2) the application of *amparo* as a generally available avenue of final appeal from state court judgments; and (3) the monopolization of federal courts by *amparo* cases.

The 'Otero *formula*' *and the limited effect of* amparo *judgments* Under Article 107 of the Constitution, only a party who is directly aggrieved by a governmental act may initiate an *amparo* case. Article 107 also sets forth the *Otero* formula, by which judgments in *amparo* cases do not have effect beyond the individual(s) involved in the case before the court, unless the court concludes five consecutive judgments based on the same ruling, which creates *jurisprudencia obligatioria*.[119] The *Otero* formula is a basic feature of Mexican *amparo* law, but

[117] The Court's rationale was that the failure to apply state law correctly constituted a violation of the constitutional guarantee of due process contained in the 1857 Constitution. *See* Fix-Zamudio, H., *Ensayos Sobre el Derecho de* Amparo (Mexico: UNAM, 1993) at 28. When Congress passed legislation to prohibit the use of *amparo* against state court judgments, the Supreme Court declared the legislation unconstitutional and continued the practice. *See id.* at 29, n. 35.

[118] As amended, Article 107-XVI provides that if, after *amparo* is granted, a government official repeats the challenged act or otherwise attempts to evade a federal court's ruling and the Supreme Court believes such noncompliance to be inexcusable, the official shall immediately be removed from office and forced to appear before a district judge.

[119] Article 107-II of the Constitution, which states the *Otero* formula, provides that a judgment in an *amparo* case shall limit relief to the private individual who brought the complaint, without making any general declaration with respect to the law or act in question. On the *Otero* formula, *see* Chapter 8 below, at text accompanying notes 17–20. On *jurisprudencia obligatoria*, *see* Chapter 3 above.

it also severely limits the rule-making effect of judicial judgments. For this reason, in order to strengthen the Supreme Court's power to interpret the Constitution, several Mexican scholars have called for elimination of the *Otero* formula in favour of Supreme Court rulings of general effect when a law or official act is held to be unconstitutional.[120]

Amparo *and the interpretation of state law* The ability of federal courts, via *amparo*, to review any state court judgment has shifted the balance of judicial power in favour of the federal courts in Mexico. By permitting federal courts to second-guess every judgment of a state court through *amparo*, regardless of whether the underlying substantive law is state or federal, Mexican law weakens the power of state courts. In contrast, in the United States, doctrines such as 'the adequate and independent state ground' doctrine preserve state independence and fortify the role of state courts as the definitive voice on questions of state law.[121] The result in Mexico has been a centralization and federalization of the judicial system that parallels other areas of Mexican law.[122] This overlay of federal judicial authority could be reduced by limiting *amparo* to the most egregious violations of due process that emanate from state law actions, but such a reduction is unlikely given the reverence for *amparo* in Mexico.

Amparo *and the monopolization of federal courts* The sweeping breadth of the controversies which can be brought to the federal courts as *amparo* cases under the Mexican 'due process clause' has caused this device to overwhelm federal dockets. In 2001, for example, 219,663 *amparo* suits and only 3,379 non-*amparo* civil suits were filed in the federal district courts.[123] Most of the federal suits that are not *amparo* cases involve family law or labour law matters, while tort litigation is almost non-existent.[124] Thus, the federal judicial system in Mexico serves primarily to permit individuals to contest government action. Lawsuits between private parties are a smaller percentage of all federal cases. Moreover, traditional distrust in the ability of courts to act impartially may also account for the relative lack of private recourse to courts to settle disputes.

The vast flow of *amparo* cases has shaped the development of the federal judicial structure itself. By virtue of its breadth, *amparo* made the Mexican

[120] *See* Fix-Zamudio, H., *Introduccion al Estudio de la Defensa de la Constitucion en el Ordenamiento Mexicano* (Mexico: UNAM, 1994) at 65–66; Cárdenas Gracia, J., *Transicion Politica y Reforma Constitucional en Mexico* (Mexico: UNAM, 1994) at 167–168.

[121] Under the adequate and independent state ground doctrine, the US Supreme Court lacks authority to review a state court judgment if the judgment rests on two grounds, one of which is federal and the other non-federal in character, and the non-federal ground is independent of the federal ground and adequate to support the judgment. *See Murdock v. City of Memphis*, 87 U.S (20 Wall.) 590 (1875).

[122] *See* Chapter 4 above.

[123] *El Informe de Labores Que Rinde el Ministro Genaro Góngora Pimentel 2001* (Mexico: Poder Judicial de la Federación, 2001), Statistical Annex at 4 and 13. *See also* Noriega, A., Lecciones de Amparo (Mexico: Porrúa, 6th ed., revised by Soberanes Fernández J.L., 2000) vol. 1 at 235–300.

[124] *See* Rubio, *supra* note 6, at 59.

Supreme Court the ultimate court of appeal for all cases, state and federal. Prior to the 1950s, the Court's calendar gradually became clogged with cases of little constitutional import, preventing it from acting purely as a constitutional court. In 1951, Congress created the collegiate circuit courts in order to relieve the Supreme Court of some of this burden. Despite this change, by 1960, the Supreme Court's backlog stood at 8,000 cases, and by 1965, reached 16,000 cases.[125] Further reforms in 1967, 1968, 1983, and 1987 systematically reduced the Supreme Court's *amparo* jurisdiction and amplified the role of the collegiate circuit courts. The decision in 1994 to create the Federal Judicial Council and transfer to it most of the Supreme Court's administrative duties was inspired by the continuing need to reduce the Court's workload and transform it into a constitutional court.

4.2. Article 97 Investigative Authority

Article 97 of the Constitution, as amended in 1994, ambiguously grants the Supreme Court jurisdiction to investigate cases involving grave violations of human rights.[126] This provision authorizes the Supreme Court (on its own initiative, or in response to a request of the President, one of the houses of Congress, or of a Governor of a state) to appoint one or more of its members, or a circuit or district court judge, or one or more special commissioners, to investigate any act or acts that may constitute a grave violation of any individual right. In such cases, the Court may issue a declaration in such matters, but is otherwise powerless to remedy abuses. The provision has been seldom used to date.[127]

[125] *See* Fix-Zamudio, H., 'La Suprema Corte de Justicia como Tribunal Constitucional', in *Las Nuevas Bases Constitucionales y Legales del Sistema Judicial Mexicano: La Reforma Judicial 1986–1987* (Mexico: UNAM & Porrúa, 1987) at 379.

[126] Prior to the 1994 amendment, Article 97 conferred on the Supreme Court the power to investigate any act or acts that constituted the 'violation of any individual guarantee'. *See* e.g. *Constitución Política de los Estados Unidos Mexicanos* (Mexico: Editores Mexicanos Unidos, S.A. 1987) 83. The precise meaning of the 1994 change in the language of Article 97 to cases of 'grave violation of human rights' is unclear.

[127] In September 1995, Mexican President Ernesto Zedillo requested the Supreme Court to investigate the murder of 16 peasants on 28 June 1995 in the municipality of Aguas Blancas, in the state of Guerrero. In June 1996, the Supreme Court issued an opinion articulating the scope of its power to investigate any violation of individual guarantees in connection with the subject matter. GARANTIAS INDIVIDUALES, MARCO LEGAL DE INTERVENCION DE LA SUPREMA CORTE DE JUSTICIA DE LA NACION EN LA AVERIGUACION DE GRAVE VIOLACION DE AQUELLAS, SJF, 9ª epoca, Tesis LXXXVII/96, T. III, June, 1996. The Supreme Court found that local authorities had failed to produce satisfactory answers to allegations of human rights violations and other abuses, and consequently the Court held that it was competent to investigate the alleged human rights violations pursuant to the power conferred in the second paragraph of Article 97 of Mexican Constitution and in Article 11 of the LOPJF. Ministers Juventino V. Castro and Humberto Ramos Palacios were appointed as special commissioners for that case. The outcome of the investigation is discussed in Informe de los Ministros Juventino V. Castro y Castro y Humberto Román Palacios sobre el caso Aguas Blancas, SJF y su Gaceta, 9ª epoca, T. III, June 1996, at 470 *et seq. See also* Morineau, M., 'Aguas Blancas, estudio de un caso de aplicación del segundo párrafo del Artículo 97 de la Constitución Política de los Estados Unidos Mexicanos', in *Boletín Mexicano de Derecho Comparado* (Mexico: UNAM, 2000) 89.

Article 97 further provides that the Supreme Court is empowered to investigate on its own initiative any act or acts that may constitute electoral violations, but only in those cases which could place in doubt the legality of the entire election process of the President or Congress. If it chooses to investigate an election, the Supreme Court's power under Article 97 is limited to providing the results of its investigation 'to the competent authorities', presumably the *Tribunal Electoral.*

5. Administrative Courts

State and Federal administrative tribunals, which are under the authority of the President or state governors, decide a large number of disputes (including some of the most politically charged matters, such as labour disputes), despite the fact that they lie in the executive rather than the judicial branch. Mexico resembles the United States in this regard. For well over a century, the US Supreme Court has tried, without success, to articulate a principle to explain why congressional grants of adjudicatory authority to non-Article III tribunals do not violate the separation of powers.[128] The continuing reliance on non-judicial tribunals is significant because these tribunals have historically been prone to the influence of the co-ordinate branches of government. Ultimately, of course, the decisions of administrative tribunals are subject to potential judicial review via *amparo directo*.[129]

5.1. Federal Administrative Courts

As discussed above in Chapter 1, during Mexico's colonial period, numerous tribunals were designed to handle disputes between the colonial administration and individuals. During the nineteenth century, after Mexico won independence, attempts were made to establish administrative courts within various government agencies, with little permanent success. Instead, Mexicans, using the newly invented *amparo* procedure turned to the federal courts to contest arbitrary or illegal agency actions. This reliance on *amparo* helps explain why the Constitution of 1917 made no provision for the creation of administrative courts. By the mid-1930s, however, it became apparent that the federal courts could not handle the volume of *amparo* cases contesting administrative action.

[128] In *Murray's Lessee v. Hoboken Land and Improvement Co.*, 59 US (18 How.) 272 (1855), the Supreme Court crafted a public rights/private rights distinction that ultimately proved unsatisfactory. In *Crowell v. Benson*, 285 US 22 (1932), the Court applied a constitutional facts/jurisdictional facts formula that also failed the test of time. In *Northern Pipeline Construction Co. v. Marathon Pipe Line Co.*, 458 US 50 (1982), the Court tried to justify grants of authority to Article I courts using theories based on historical and essential attributes. More recently, in *Commodity Futures Trading Commission v. Schor*, 478 US 833 (1986), the Court enunciated a purposes test but conceded that no formalistic or unbending rules were possible in this field of constitutional law; at best the Court can weigh a variety of considerations to assess the legality of jurisdictional grants to non-Article III courts.

[129] *See* Chapter 8 below, at text accompanying note 42.

Beginning in 1964, there were several proposals to establish a single federal administrative court with general jurisdiction over all disputes arising out of the actions of federal administrative agencies, but none of these proposals has succeeded. Instead, administrative tribunals were created from time to time to deal with disputes arising within specific agencies. As a consequence, if a party wishes to contest a federal administrative action in modern Mexico, the method for doing so depends on the presence or absence of a specific administrative court with authority to review the action. If such a tribunal exists, the party's first recourse is to exhaust administrative appeals and, thereafter, if still unsatisfied, to seek review of the administrative action in federal court by means of *amparo*. If no appropriate administrative court exists, the party may immediately seek the review of an administrative action by initiating an *amparo* suit.

5.1.1. Federal Court of Fiscal and Administrative Justice (Tribunal Federal de Justicia Fiscal y Administrativa)[130]

The Federal Court of Fiscal and Administrative Justice (*Tribunal Federal de Justicia Fiscal y Administrativa*) (Federal Fiscal Court), the first administrative court established in modern Mexico, was created by Congress in 1936[131] to reduce the burden of *amparo* suits before federal courts contesting decisions of the federal taxing authorities. The Federal Fiscal Court remains the most important administrative tribunal in Mexico. The jurisdiction, organization, and operation of the Federal Fiscal Court are governed by the Organic Law of the Federal Fiscal Court[132] and the Federal Fiscal Code.[133] In essence, the Fiscal Court operates much like the federal judiciary operated prior to the 1994 constitutional reforms.

Pursuant to these statutes, the Federal Fiscal Court has jurisdiction over cases challenging final rulings of federal agencies which: (1) determine that a tax obligation exists, (2) deny a tax refund, (3) impose fines for violation of administrative regulations, (4) deny or reduce pensions or other benefits to members of the armed forces or their families, (5) involve social security benefits within the authority of the Government Employees Institute for Security and Social Services (*Instituto de Seguridad y Servicios Sociales de los Trabajadores del Estado*), (6) concern the interpretation or enforcement of public works contracts undertaken by federal agencies, (7) award damages against federal employees in their official capacities, or (8) impose administrative sanctions on federal employees. The Federal Fiscal Court may also adjudicate cases brought by federal authorities to annul administrative decisions in favour of a private party, so long as such decisions concern any of the foregoing tax, pension, social security, public works, or other matters.

130 *See generally* Pérez, L.M., 'El anhelo cumplido: El Tribunal Federal de Justicia Fiscal y Administrativa', in 1 *Ratio Iuris* 6 (2001).

131 *Ley de Justicia Fiscal*, D.O. 27 Aug. 1936.

132 *Ley Orgánica del Tribunal Federal de Justicia Fiscal y Administrativa*, D.O. 15 Dec. 1995, as amended D.O. 30 Dec. 1996.

133 *Código Fiscal de la Federación*, D.O. 31 Dec. 1981, as amended D.O. 15 Dec. 1995.

Finally, in accordance with the Organic Law of the Federal Fiscal Court and Article 94 of the Trade Law (*Ley de Comercio Exterior*), the Federal Fiscal Court also has jurisdiction to review decisions by Mexican customs or other officials of the Treasury or Economic Secretariats over international trade matters.[134] In connection with customs issues, Article 203 of the Customs Law (*Ley Aduanera*)[135] states the jurisdiction of the Federal Fiscal Court over all final resolutions of the customs authorities against private parties. Article 3 of the Customs Law defines customs authorities as those who have the administrative functions related to the importation or exportation of goods, and which are competent to exercise the powers granted on the Customs law.

The Federal Fiscal Court consists of a Superior Chamber (*Sala Superior*) and a number of regional chambers (*salas regionales*).[136] The Superior Chamber is composed of eleven judges (*magistrados*) and operates *en banc* (*en pleno*) and in two sections (*secciones*) of five judges each.[137] The plenary of the Superior Chamber designates the number and location of regional chambers, resolves jurisdictional conflicts that may arise between the regional chambers, establishes the precedent (*jurisprudencia*) of the court, and decides the most important fiscal cases brought within the system, either due to the amount in controversy or the substantive issues in the case. The sections resolve fiscal controversies arising out of international trade or treaties (such as disputes involving the avoidance of double taxation), and other matters established by law. The regional chambers, which consist of three judges each, are dispersed throughout eleven geographical regions[138] and adjudicate all disputes within the jurisdiction of the Federal Fiscal Court except for those assigned to the Superior Chamber and its Sections.[139]

All judges of the Federal Fiscal Court are appointed by the President with the approval of the Senate.[140] Judges of the Superior Chamber serve an initial six-year term, at the end of which time they may be re-appointed once to serve nine additional years. Judges of the regional chambers serve an initial six-year term, may be re-appointed to serve a second six-year term, and, if re-appointed again, may serve until they reach the mandatory retirement age of seventy. During their terms of office, judges of the Federal Fiscal Court may only be removed by impeachment in accordance with Title IV of the Mexican Constitution.

[134] *See* Article 11, XI, of the the *Ley Orgánica del Tribunal Federal de Justicia Fiscal y Administrativa, supra* note 130, and the *Ley de Comercio Exterior*, Art. 94., D.O. 27 Jul. 1993.

[135] *Ley Aduanera*, D.O. 15 Dec. 1995, as amended in D.O. 30 Dec. 1996; D.O. 31 Dec. 1996; D.O. 31 Dec. 1998; D.O. 4 Jan. 1999; D.O. 31 Dec. 2000; and 1 Jan. 2002.

[136] As of 2001, the Federal Fiscal Court had 32 regional chambers.

[137] The person elected Chief Judge (*Presidente*) of the court does not serve in either section.

[138] As of 2001, 11 of the 32 regional chambers were located in the Metropolitan region (which includes the Federal District and state of Morelos) and another 3 were situated in the Hidalgo-Mexico region (which includes the states of Hidalgo and Mexico).

[139] Cases are distributed among the regional chambers according to plaintiffs' 'tax domicile'.

[140] To be a Federal Fiscal Court judge, a person must be a Mexican citizen by birth, be at least 35 years old, be of good reputation, have been licensed to practise law for at least 10 years, and have practised tax law for at least 7 years.

The Federal Fiscal Court's principal power is the authority to reverse administrative decisions by declaring administrative rulings illegal and therefore null and void. Certain final judgments of the regional chambers may be appealed to the Superior Chamber; other judgments of the regional chambers are reviewed by collegiate circuit courts using the procedure of *amparo directo*.[141] Appeals of final judgments of the Superior Chamber are filed in a collegiate circuit court in the Federal District. Judgments of the collegiate circuit courts in cases from the Fiscal Court are generally final and not appealable; however, appeal to the Supreme Court is available in instances where the collegiate circuit court declares a law unconstitutional or bases its judgment on a direct interpretation of the Constitution. In addition, the Supreme Court may use its power of 'attraction' to assume jurisdiction over any appeal of a Fiscal Court judgment pending in the collegiate circuit courts that merits Supreme Court review.[142]

5.1.2. Federal Labour Boards (Juntas de Conciliación y Arbitraje)

A special system of adjudication outside of the federal and state courts exists for all labour disputes, including those between a government agency and private party, and those between private employers and employees. Ostensibly, a separate system of labour law tribunals was created to give special attention to the vindication of workers' rights after the Mexican Revolution. In fact, critics of Mexican labour law have questioned the effectiveness of settling labour disputes in administrative tribunals rather than in the courts, alleging that government and business interests dominate the administrative adjudication.[143] US labour advocates lobbied vigorously to make labour law enforcement a condition for ratification of the North American Free Trade Agreement.[144]

Adjudication of labour disputes is discussed in more detail below in Chapter 13. As pointed out in that Chapter, labour law is a federal matter in Mexico, and the Federal Labour Law applies to all labour relationships within the country. Labour disputes, however, are administered by boards at both the state and federal levels. Labour disputes between private employers of national or federal significance and their employees are adjudicated by the Federal Conciliation

[141] *See* Vázquez Alfaro, J.L., *EVOLUCION Y PERSPECTIVA DE LOS ÓRGANOS DE JURISDICCION ADMINISTRATIVA EN EL ORDENAMIENTO MEXICANO* (Mexico: UNAM, Instituto de Investigaciones Jurídicas, 1981) at 64 n. 338, 177, 262 *et seq.*

[142] *Ley Orgánica del Tribunal Federal de Justicia Fiscal y Administrativa, supra* note 130, Arts. 16-V and 20, and the *Código Fiscal de la Federación*, Art. 239-A, I (B), D.O. 31 Dec. 1981, as amended.

[143] *See* De Buen, C., 'Nuestras Juntas de conciliación y arbitraje', in *EL TRABAJO, EL DERECHO Y ALGO MAS* (Mexico: Porrúa, 1999) at 113–118.

[144] The North American Agreement on Labor Cooperation, a supplemental agreement to the North American Free Trade Agreement between Canada, Mexico, and the United States, commits each country to guarantee the enforcement of its own labour laws, and provides an avenue for complaints to be lodged with the NAFTA Labor Commission for persistent failures to enforce worker rights. For information on the North American Commission on Labor Cooperation, *see* www.naalc.org (site visited Jan. 2004).

and Arbitration Board (*Junta Federal de Conciliación y Arbitraje*).[145] Labour disputes between federal agencies and their employees are handled by the Federal Conciliation and Arbitration Tribunal (*Tribunal Federal de Conciliación y Arbitraje*).

The *Junta Federal de Conciliación y Arbitraje* (Federal Arbitration Board) is composed of a Chief Judge, appointed by the President, plus one representative for workers and another for management. The Federal Arbitration Board is based in the Federal District, although most of its dispute settlement activities are conducted by numerous federal special boards (*juntas especiales federales*) that are scattered throughout the country.[146] Each federal special board consists of three arbitrators representing workers, management, and the government. The government representative on each board is appointed by the Mexican Secretary of Labour, while representatives of workers (*trabajadores*) and management (*patrones*) are elected at meetings held for this purpose. Members of the boards serve six-year terms.

The Federal Conciliation and Arbitration Tribunal (CAT) functions in plenary session, in three chambers (*salas*) based in the Federal District, and, as deemed necessary, in auxiliary chambers (*salas auxiliares*) located in state capitals. The plenary Tribunal consists of all judges of the three permanent chambers plus a Chief Judge who is appointed by the President.[147] The plenary body is authorized to arbitrate collective bargaining disputes between unions of federal employees and federal agencies, to grant or cancel union registration, and to resolve internal union conflicts. Each permanent chamber is composed of three judges, one appointed by the federal government, one by the workers, and one by agreement of the first two appointees.[148] They handle disputes between individual employees and federal agencies as well as any other matters assigned to them by the plenary Tribunal. The auxiliary chambers resolve the same types of individual cases but concerning federal employees working outside of the Federal District, in the various states.

[145] Mexican Constitution Art. 123, Part A, XVIII to XX. Employers of national or federal importance include, for example, the textile, electrical, film, mineral, hydrocarbon, petrochemical, automotive, railroad, tobacco, and banking industries, firms controlled by the federal government, firms performing under a federal government contract or concession, and firms located in a federal zone. Mexican Constitution Art. 123, Part A, XXXI; Federal Labour Law (*Ley Federal de Trabajo*), Art. 527.

[146] As of 1994, there were 65 federal special boards in Mexico, 19 of which were located in the Federal District alone.

[147] The Chief Judge of the CAT and chief judge of each chamber serve six-year terms. Persons appointed by the federal government and workers may be freely removed by their respective appointing authority.

[148] The judge appointed by agreement of the government and worker appointees functions as the chief judge (*presidente*) of the chamber. All judges of the CAT must be Mexican citizens, at least 25 years of age, and not convicted of a felony or intentional crime. In addition, the chief judges and appointees of the federal government should have possessed a law degree for 5 years and have practised labour law for at least 3 years at the time of appointment. The worker appointee should have been a civil service employee in the federal government for at least 5 years at the time of appointment.

Adjudication of labour disputes in Mexico has a long tradition in Mexico, and has functioned at least well enough to have avoided major strikes in recent years. This is not to say that the system is above criticism, primarily for the role of the Mexican government in effectively controlling the boards so as to offset the potential power of workers.[149]

5.1.3. *Other Federal Administrative Tribunals*

Agrarian tribunals Under Article 27 of the Constitution and federal law, the Superior Agrarian Tribunal (*Tribunal Superior Agrario*) and Unitary Agrarian Tribunals (*tribunales unitarios agrarios*) resolve disputes arising out of federal agrarian reforms.[150] The Superior Agrarian Tribunal consists of five judges and is based in the Federal District. The lower agrarian courts each consist of a single judge and are dispersed among several territorial districts throughout the country. The agrarian judges are appointed by the Senate from a list of candidates submitted to it by the President. As discussed below in Chapter 13, Mexican agrarian reform laws have been vastly modified, but this system of tribunals still exists to deal with issues arising from past reforms.[151]

Military courts The courts of military justice prosecute members of the armed forces for violations of the Code of Military Justice (*Código de Justicia Militar*).[152] Military courts consist of the Supreme Military Court (*Supremo Tribunal Militar*), the War Councils (*Consejos de Guerra*), and military judges.

The Supreme Military Court is composed of a Chief justice and four judges who hold the rank of brigadier general (*general de brigada*). The Supreme Military Court serves as a court of first instance for the most serious military cases, and also resolves jurisdictional conflicts between the military judges who try lesser infractions. The members of the Supreme Military Court are appointed by the *Secretario de la Defensa Nacional* (National Defence Secretary) with the consent of the President.

War Councils (*Consejos de Guerra*) try cases of military misconduct involving violations of military discipline, and may be ordinary or extraordinary, depending on the severity of the offence. Military judges handle jurisdictional conflicts of the war councils and have jurisdiction over crimes with a penalty less than one year of imprisonment, suspension or discharge.[153]

The system of military justice has remained largely beyond public scrutiny until recently, although the National Commission on Human Rights, discussed below, has investigated reported human rights abuses for which the military is allegedly responsible. In 2002, the Mexican Congress adopted a new public

[149] *See* Chapter 13 below, at text following note 38.

[150] *See* Mexican Constitution Art. 27-XIX; *Ley Orgánica de los Tribunales Agrarios* (D.O. 26 Feb. 1992, as amended D.O. 9 July 1993).

[151] *See* Chapter 13 below, at notes 45–55.

[152] Mexican Constitution, Art. 13. *See also* the *Código de Justicia Militar*, D.O. 28 Aug. 1933.

[153] *See* Fix-Zamudio and Cossío Díaz, *supra* note 12, at 204–214.

information law, the *Ley Federal de Transparencia*,[154] which resulted in the public release of documents related to the disappearance of numerous Mexican dissidents during the 1960s and 1970s. This new information is likely to bring greater public scrutiny of military justice.

5.1.4. Federal Agencies with Quasi-Judicial Functions

As discussed elsewhere, a traditional hallmark of the Mexican legal system is heavy reliance on governmental control over the enforcement of public laws,[155] leaving relatively little scope for private parties to use the judicial system to assert their rights under antitrust, environmental, or other public laws. This contrasts with the United States, where lawsuits by private persons and public interest groups are common in these same fields. In Mexico, disputes over the application of important laws to protect the public are handled almost exclusively by administrative agencies. The Federal Consumer Protection agency, the Federal Environmental Agency, the Federal Competition Commission, the National Banking Commission, and the National Human Rights Commission[156] are administrative agencies that settle disputes or conflicts between individuals, or between individuals and government agencies, but they are not considered administrative tribunals under Mexican law.[157]

The role of the Federal Consumer Protection Agency (*Procuraduría Federal del Consumidor*) is to promote and protect the rights of consumers and ensure fairness in dealings between merchants and customers.[158] It is based in the Federal District and has delegations in each state. The Commission is empowered to monitor merchants' compliance with federal laws, to receive consumer complaints, and to arbitrate and mediate disputes between consumers and merchants. The rulings of the Commission have the force of law and, in appropriate cases, may include fines on merchants.

The Federal Environmental Protection Agency (*Procuraduría Federal de Protección al Ambiente*), an *órgano desconcentrado* within the Secretariat of Environment and Natural Resources, is headquartered in the Federal District but also has delegations in each state.[159] The Agency, acting through various units and the state delegations, conducts environmental inspections, receives and investigates citizen complaints concerning violations of federal environmental law, prosecutes persons or firms that violate such law, acts as a

[154] *See* Chapter 9 below, at text accompanying notes 97–104.

[155] *See* Chapter 12 for discussion of governmental *versus* private enforcement.

[156] The Human Rights Commission is an autonomous constitutional institution. Mexican Constitution Art. 102, para. B.

[157] According to José Ovalle Favela, the agrarian, fiscal and administrative, labour, and military tribunals are the only true administrative tribunals in Mexico. *See* Ovalle Favela, J., TEORÍA GENERAL DEL PROCESO (Mexico: Oxford University Press, 4th ed., 1998) at 233–239.

[158] *See Ley Federal de Protección al Consumidor*, Art. 20 (D.O. 24 Dec. 1992, as amended D.O. 24 May 1996).

[159] *See Acuerdo que Regula la Organización y Funcionamiento Interno del Instituto Nacional de Ecología y de la Procuraduría Federal de Protección al Ambiente*, Art. 31 and Transitory Art. 2 (D.O. 17 Jul. 1992).

conciliator in environmental disputes between private parties, and may impose administrative sanctions or other remedial measures for environmental infractions. The effectiveness of this method of enforcing environmental laws, which has been called into question, is discussed in more detail below in Chapter 12.

The role of the Federal Competition Commission (*Comisión Federal de Competencia*) is to maintain competition in the domestic economy by preventing and eliminating monopolies, practical monopolies, and other restrictions on market efficiency.[160] (Competition law, which is relatively new in Mexico, is discussed in more detail below in Chapter 12.) The Commission, which consists of five commissioners, has the authority to investigate the existence of monopolies and other prohibited business concentrations, resolve cases within its jurisdiction, impose administrative fines for violations of the law, suspend illegal business activities, and order the partial or total disintegration of illegal economic concentrations.

The National Banking and Securities Commission (*Comisión Nacional Bancaria y de Valores*) supervises and regulates financial institutions in Mexico, including financial holding companies, banks, credit institutions, stock houses, investment societies, credit unions, savings and loan associations, and currency exchange houses.[161] The Commission's Governing Board (*Junta de Gobierno*), which consists of ten members, is empowered to license, inspect, and suspend the operations of financial institutions; to intervene administratively in such entities; and to impose fines on firms and individuals that violate federal banking law. Complaints regarding the provision of financial services are handled by the National Commission for the Protection and Defence of Financial Service Users (*Comisión Nacional para la Protección y Defensa de los Usuarios de Servicios Financieros*, CONDUSEF).

The National Human Rights Commission (*Comisión Nacional de Derechos Humanos*, or CNDH) has jurisdiction over complaints related to human rights violations committed by federal authorities, except for judicial officers.[162] Created in 1990 as a response to complaints of alleged human rights abuses from critics within and outside Mexico, the CNDH consists of a President (*Presidente*, also referred to as the 'Ombudsman'), executive-secretary, and five inspectors-general. The President is the most important figure in the CNDH, and over the years has assumed the role of a major spokesperson on human rights issues within Mexico. The CNDH is authorized to receive complaints, conduct investigations, formulate non-binding recommendations for submission to appropriate law enforcement authorities, and mediate disputes between complainants

[160] *See Ley Federal de Competencia Económica*, Art. 2 (D.O. 24 Dec. 1992).

[161] *See Ley de la Comisión Nacional Bancaria y de Valores*, Arts. 2 and 3 (D.O. 26 Apr. 1995).

[162] *See Ley de la Comisián Nacional de Derechos Humanos*, Art. 3 (D.O. 29 June 1992). The Commission was created in 1990 by amendment to the Constitution, Art. 102, para. B. *See generally* www.cndh.org.mx (site last visited Jan. 2004).

and offending government authorities. Significantly, the CNDH is expressly prohibited from reviewing judicial decisions, labour disputes, and acts and decisions of electoral officials. It has no legal power to compel government agencies to provide information to it, and the resolutions of the Commission may call for action, but the CNDH has no legal power of enforcement.[163] As a result, the CNDH was criticized from the outset for failing to have sufficient teeth. Since the President of the CNDH was initially appointed by the President, and the office funded by the then PRI-dominated Congress, the CNDH was careful not to be overly aggressive, and for this reason it was criticized by human rights activists. The independence of the CNDH was enlarged in 1999, when Congress amended the Constitution to provide that the President of the Commission would be selected not by presidential appointment, but by a two-thirds vote of the Senate.[164] The CNDH has played an increasingly significant role in focusing the attention of the government and the public on the protection of human rights in Mexico. This does not prevent human rights groups from criticizing it for not being more aggressive, and for the lack of enforcement powers available to it.

5.2. Administrative Court of the Federal District

The many governmental entities that dispense local public services within the Federal District are housed under the Public Administration of the Federal District (*Administración Pública del Distrito Federal*).[165] Sitting alongside the Public Administration is an autonomous tribunal, the Administrative Court of the Federal District (*Tribunal de lo Contencioso Administrativo del Distrito Federal*), which has jurisdiction to decide controversies between private parties and agencies of the Public Administration.[166]

The Administrative Court is composed of a Superior Chamber (*Sala Superior*), three regular chambers (*Salas Ordinarias*), and auxiliary chambers (*salas auxiliares*). The Superior Chamber consists of five judges (*magistrados*) and each regular and auxiliary chamber consists of three judges. The Superior Chamber issues the judgments (*jurisprudencia*) of the court, hears appeals from decisions of the lower chambers, reviews rulings of the lower chambers that conflict, establishes guidelines for the distribution of cases among the chambers of the court, and determines the locations of each of the lower chambers. The lower chambers serve as courts of first instance for private parties who wish to challenge administrative acts or omissions of agencies of the Federal District, to

[163] Resolutions of the CNDH can be found on the Commission's web site, www.cndh.org.mx (site visited Jan. 2004).

[164] Mexican Constitution, Art. 102, Part B, para. 5, amended D.O. 13 Sep. 1999.

[165] *See generally Ley Orgánica de la Administración Pública del Distrito Federal*, D.O. 30 Dec. 1994, as amended D.O. 29 May 1996.

[166] Mexican Constitution Art. 122, Part C, Base Quinta; *Estatuto de Gobierno del Distrito Federal*, Art. 9, D.O. 26 July 1994, as amended D.O. 22 Nov. 1996; *Ley del Tribunal de lo Contencioso Administrativo del Distrito Federal*, Art. 2, D.O. 19 Dec. 1995.

dispute rulings by District authorities that a tax obligation exists, or to complain that an agency of the District has refused to comply with a court judgment.[167]

The Administrative Court can declare the acts or determinations of administrative agencies void on the grounds that the agency in question lacked jurisdiction to act, failed to comply with legal formalities, violated or misapplied the law, or acted in an arbitrary, excessive, capricious, or manifestly unjust manner. Such a declaration renders the administrative act invalid and relieves private parties of any duty to comply with it.[168] In addition, the court can order administrative authorities to modify, revoke, or annul an act or decision not in compliance with the law.

Judges of the Administrative Court are appointed by the Chief of the Federal District with the approval of the Assembly of Representatives. Judges serve six-year terms, at the end of which time they may be ratified by the Assembly and retained, or promoted within the court or, by implication, dismissed. If retained or promoted, judges of the Administrative Court may only be removed from office by impeachment in accordance with Title IV of the federal Constitution or due to mandatory retirement at the age of seventy-five or physical or mental incapacity.

5.3. State Administrative Courts

Beginning in the 1950s, some Mexican states, such as Hidalgo, the State of México, Nuevo León, Sinaloa, Tamaulipas, and Veracruz, created fiscal courts (tribunales fiscales) modelled on the Federal Fiscal and Administrative Court, with jurisdiction limited to state taxation matters. In 1987, Article 116 of the Mexican Constitution was amended to permit states to establish general administrative tribunals with authority to settle controversies between state administrative authorities and private parties. Since then, several states (including Baja California, Guanajuato, Guerrero, Hidalgo, Jalisco, México, Querétaro, Sonora, Veracruz, and Yucatán) have established administrative tribunals designed after the Administrative Court of the Federal District. Other states have no administrative tribunals, in essence directing citizens to the federal courts through *amparo* procedures to protest rulings by state agencies.

All Mexican states possess state labour tribunals (*juntas locales de conciliación y arbitraje*) with jurisdiction to adjudicate all matters not specially delegated to the federal government, such as labour disputes involving state employees, municipal employees, or employees in localized industries. As a general rule, state labour tribunals parallel the federal CAB in terms of organization, function, and composition.

In 1992, the federal Constitution was amended to require that each state create a human rights commission patterned after the National Human Rights

[167] In addition, the lower chambers adjudicate cases filed by agencies of the Federal District contesting rulings by the local taxing authority that favour taxpayers.

[168] *See Ley de Procedimiento Administrativo del Distrito Federal*, Art. 25 (D.O. 19 Dec. 1995).

Commission to receive and investigate complaints against state and local authorities.[169] In addition, some Mexican states have established electoral tribunals modelled on the Federal Electoral Tribunal. These state tribunals adjudicate disputes concerning electoral activity or election results at a state and local level. In Jalisco, for example, the Electoral Tribunal (*Tribunal de lo Contencioso Electoral*) may issue binding decisions that may only be modified by the Electoral College of the state legislature (*Colegio Electoral del Congreso del Estado*), not by the state Supreme Court. The judges of the Electoral Tribunal are appointed by the state legislature based on lists presented by registered political parties.

6. Conclusion

Although the judicial systems of Mexico and the United States are based on common precepts of federalism and the separation of powers, distinct political, historical, cultural, economic, and legal traditions in the countries have produced judiciaries vastly different in structure and operation. As in the United States, one finds in Mexico parallel bodies of federal and state courts with separate but sometimes overlapping authority; yet, due largely to forces of centralism, the relatively late formation of Mexican states, and the federal procedure of *amparo*, a steep imbalance of power favouring the federal judiciary exists in Mexico.

The judiciaries of the two countries also differ sharply in the way they function. The allocation of cases in the United States tips heavily toward federal and state trial courts, leaving the supreme courts to participate in only a tiny fraction of all suits. In contrast, Mexican collegiate courts (including supreme courts and intermediate appellate courts) are required to adjudicate so many suits that they probably exceed the ability and energy of even the finest jurists. The burden of processing thousands of disputes monopolizes the appellate judges' time and efforts, and means that the appellate courts as a whole, even the Mexican Supreme Court, have been more important as mechanisms for settling individual disputes than as rule-creating institutions. In contrast with the United States, where the rule of *stare decisis* gives broad effect to court judgments, in Mexico the *formula Otero* limits the rule-making power of judges, and therefore limits the effect of court judgments, even Supreme Court judgments, on the development of the law in Mexico. With the exception of an occasional Supreme Court judgment in an action of unconstitutionality,[170] or a rare *tesis de jurisprudencia obligatoria*, most Supreme Court judgments receive little attention. Nevertheless, the Supreme Court's power is certainly on the rise, and it is increasingly common for the Court to decide important matters

[169] Mexican Constitution, Art. 102-B, D.O. 28 Jan. 1992.

[170] *See* Chapter 8 below, at text accompanying notes 92–96.

of constitutional interpretation that affect the allocation of power between the states and the federal government, and other matters that have significant importance for the development of Mexico's political and legal systems.

Because of the burden of processing thousands of cases a year, the Supreme Court opinions that are published in the *Semanario Judicial de la Federación* tend to be generally worded pronouncements that give only general reasons for a ruling, rather than a detailed discussion. This generality, coupled with the lack of publication of lower court and state court opinions, makes case research in Mexico a marginally productive activity in comparison with the common law system in the United States.

7

Constitutional Guarantees of Individual Rights

1. Introduction

Most modern governments have distinguished themselves from their predecessors by establishing a set of fundamental rights to protect the individual from abuses of state power. Concern for individual rights is the product of an ongoing process that dates back to the roots of the nation state, and has given rise today to intense examination at the national, regional, and international levels. The evolution of individual rights under Mexican law began when the country gained its independence from Spain in the early part of the nineteenth century. Respect for individual rights survived a period of social upheaval as a result of the Mexican Revolution that began in 1910 and ended with the adoption of the Constitution of 1917. In the second half of the twentieth century, Mexico's co-operation with international initiatives to promote the protection of individual rights resulted in adherence to a number of human rights treaties that further promoted a respect for individual guarantees. Political changes in the late twentieth century—the dissolution of authoritarian government by a single political party—also contributed to increased adherence to protection of individual rights.

Even though the texts of the different constitutions and international treaties may purport to establish a highly progressive system for the protection of individual rights in Mexico, in the past the enforcement of these 'guaranteed' rights has been deficient. A variety of reasons may account for the inconsistency between what the Mexican Constitution says and what actually transpires in practice, but two major points stand out. First, adherence to the rule of law in Mexico has often been seen as an aspiration, rather than a reality, and judges, government officials, and private citizens were often unwilling, or unable, to be aggressive in enforcing constitutional rights.[1] This discrepancy between what the law says and how it is applied can be traced back to colonial times.[2] Second, under the influence of Roman law, the civil law tradition followed in Mexico dictated a circumscribed role for judges. Under the civil law tradition, since the meaning of laws is seen as self-evident to a trained jurist, judges are to apply laws according to the meaning that is inherent in the law. Judges are therefore reluctant to engage themselves in expansive enforcement of

[1] *See* Rubio, L., *et al.*, *A La Puerta de la Ley* (Mexico: Cal y Arena, 1994) Chapter 5.

[2] *See* Chapter 1 above, Section 2, esp. at text accompanying notes 45, 51.

constitutional guarantees, which would also be seen as an anti-democratic usurpation of power.[3]

In short, fundamental rights in Mexican law can be viewed in two different lights: first, under the bright light of the prolific influx of provisions written into the texts of Mexico's evolving Constitutions and the signing of an impressive number of international treaties in order to provide for a wide range of civil rights and liberties; and second, under the dim light of a small body of judicial and academic writings in the field. In view of such circumstances, it is not surprising that attempts by Mexican scholars to elucidate these rights consisted mainly of describing legal texts, with cursory allusions to judicial decisions, and much of the commentary by Mexican legal scholars developed as an academic debate unrelated to events transpiring in everyday life. This is gradually changing, thanks to the newly competitive political system and to the greater transparency that characterize Mexico in the twenty-first century.

2. Evolution of Constitutional Rights

The enforcement of constitutional rights can be divided into three historical phases in Mexico: the liberal phase, the social phase, and the human rights phase. As the judicial and political systems matured, each new phase built upon the prior phase by incorporating new elements into the body of Mexican law.

The protection of constitutional rights must be viewed against the background of a society plagued with immense economic disparities between classes and problematic social conditions. Hence, a peculiar name for the rights of individuals has emerged during the historical development of the Mexican Constitution: *garantías individuales*. The term 'individual guarantees' is broader than the term 'civil rights' which is used in the United States to signify constitutional guarantees. The term *garantías individuales* reflects the effort to consider such things as work, health, housing, and land as rights guaranteed to the individual by the Mexican Constitution in order for society to achieve a fairer distribution of wealth. In this Chapter, we refer to *garantías individuales* as 'constitutional protections', 'constitutional rights and liberties or freedoms' or 'civil rights and liberties', with the caveat that these English language renditions are to be understood from an entirely different perspective than their meanings imply at the present time in the context of US constitutional law.

Throughout Mexico's history, political leaders have debated the extent to which the Constitution should be used as an instrument of social justice in Mexico, by 'guaranteeing' social 'rights'. The desire for social justice was a major cause of the Mexican Revolution of 1910, and as we shall see, the resulting Constitution of 1917, still in force, incorporates a number of constitutional

[3] *See* Cossío Díaz, J.R., *La teoria constitucional de la Suprema Corte de Justicia*, II, (Mexico: Fontamara, 2002) at 48.

'guarantees' that relate to social equality and justice. Not all of these 'guarantees', such as the right of adequate housing, have been backed up by deeds, due either to a lack of resources, or to a lack of will on the part of government leaders. That failure has in some cases been due to lack of resources, lack of will on the part of government leaders, or the lack of a strong system of mandatory constitutional interpretation by the federal courts.

2.1. Independence and Reform: The Liberal Phase of *Garantías Individuales*

Before Mexico achieved its independence, two important documents were adopted by the Spanish *Cortes*: the 'Constitution of the Spanish Monarchy' of 1812 (Constitution of Cadiz) and the 'Constitutional Decree for the Freedom of Mexican America' (*Decreto Constitucional para la Libertad de la América Mexicana*) of 1814 (known as the Constitution of Apatzingán). Both purported to guarantee certain rights of the individual, making these documents important precursors to Mexican law under independence. The Constitution of Cadiz was partially and provisionally applicable in Mexico until 1821, when Mexico achieved independence. The Constitution of Cadiz formally eliminated the concept of inequality between Spaniards and those born in Nueva España, whether *criollos*, *mestizos*, or indigenous peoples, by considering that all free individuals born and living in Spanish territories were considered members of the Spanish nation. It required the government to guarantee civil liberty, equality, security, property, and other 'legitimate rights' to all members of the Spanish nation. The Constitution of Cadiz was not a comprehensive or well organized catalogue of guarantees, but rather a sporadic recognition of these rights throughout the entire text.

The second document, known as the 'Constitution of Apatzingán'—in essence, a declaration that never assumed the force of law—was drafted in a more systematic manner, drawing on different elements of the Constitutions of the United States, the French Declaration of 1789, and the Constitution of Cadiz.[4] The Constitution of Apatzingán stated in general terms (Article 24) that the main function of government was to preserve equality, security, property, and liberty in order to guarantee the happiness of its people and inhabitants and, for this purpose, a set of specific rights was set forth in a precise and orderly fashion (Articles 25–40).

The Mexican Constitution of 1824,[5] as noted in Chapter 1 above, adopted many elements of the US Constitution, including the silence of the US

[4] Torre Villa, E., 'El Decreto Constitucional de Apatzingán y sus fuentes legales', in BOLETÍN MEXICANO DE DERECHO COMPARADO, VOL. X (Mexico, No. 28–29, January to August, 1997) at 76–77 and 83–85.

[5] This is the 'Constitución Federal de los Estados Unidos Mexicanos', Tena Ramírez, F., *LEYES FUNDAMENTALES DE MEXICO* (Mexico: Porrúa, 1985) at 167–195. The 1824 Constitution is also available at www.juridicas.unam.mx, 'Legislación Federal', 'Documentos Constitucionales Históricos'. (Site visited Jan. 2004.)

Constitution on the preservation of individual rights, until the adoption of the US Bill of Rights in 1791. Mexican constitutional protections were limited to a disjointed group of rights such as prohibition of torture or of cruel and unusual punishment, or protection of the inviolability of the home. In contrast with the 1824 federal Constitution, the constitutions of the Mexican states established several different types of rights,[6] including rights related to the security of individuals and the protection of private property, prohibition of retroactive application of laws, guarantees of due process, etc.

After the Constitution of 1824 was enacted, two rival factions with opposing notions of government soon emerged: liberals, led by Manuel Crescencio Rejón, who were in favour of a republican, representative, democratic, and federal form of government with significant decentralized powers assigned to the states; and conservatives, led by Fray Servando Teresa de Mier who espoused a centralized, Catholic, and ultimately monarchical system of government. The struggles between these two factions shaped the political life of the country over the course of the nineteenth century. In 1835, the conservatives temporarily triumphed and adopted a set of political documents known as the Constitutional Foundations (*Bases Constitucionales*); in 1836, conservative leaders adopted the Seven Constitutional Laws (*Siete Leyes Constitucionales*). Both documents served as a *de facto* abrogation of the 1824 Constitution.[7]

The principal rights set forth in these two documents were: due process; the principle of *non bis in idem* (no one shall be tried twice for the same crime, known in the Anglo-American tradition as 'double jeopardy'); freedom of movement; freedom of expression; and the right to hold property. Based on the general concept of government that was strongly centralized, the *Siete Leyes* was a blueprint for a new Political Constitution of the Mexican Republic, which would be produced in 1842,[8] and which listed *garantías individuales* together for the first time.[9]

The 1842 draft Constitution was never adopted, however. In 1847, the liberals regained power, and brought about the adoption of the Constituent and Reform Act (*Acta Constitutiva y de Reformas*), reinstating the Constitution of 1824 and, along with it, a more decentralized federal system of government.[10] The 1847 *Acta*

[6] Carrillo Prieto, I., 'Las declaraciones de derechos en las primeras constituciones de las entidades federativas' in *Anuario Juridico* vols. III–IV (Mexico: UNAM, 1976–1977), at 9 *et seq.*

[7] Both texts can be found in Tena Ramírez, *supra* note 5 at 202–204 and 204–248. On the *Siete Leyes Constitucionales*, *see* Chapter 1 above, at text accompanying notes 83–84.

[8] For the text of the 1842 draft Constitution, *see* Tena Ramírez, *supra* note 5 at 307–340.

[9] A minority opinion was presented opposing the Draft of the Constitution, arguing in favour of a more systematic approach to *derechos individuales* ['individual rights'], which were divided up into 4 broad categories: personal freedom, property, security, and equality. This new way of organizing the *garantías* was to become the forerunner of the Constitutions of 1857 and 1917. A second Draft emerged after the minority opinion was put forth, and an attempt was made to try to reconcile the differences between the two versions. This new draft, the 1843 'Organic Foundations of the Mexican Republic' (*Bases Orgánicas de la República Mexicana*), incorporated the idea of the First Draft of the Constitution of 1842 by grouping the most important rights or *guarantías* together in a single article of the Constitution.

[10] Tena Ramírez, *supra* note 5 at 472–477.

Constitutiva y de Reformas did not include individual guarantees of rights itself, but left to the legislature the task of defining constitutional protections of freedom, security, property, and equality. The 1847 Act did, however, introduce the term 'rights of man' (*derechos del hombre*), and it created, at the federal level, the *amparo* proceeding, as a federal judicial procedure by which an individual could defend his or her constitutionally guaranteed liberties and protections in court.[11]

The *Acta Constitutiva* was the first step in a series of legislative reforms that resulted in the adoption of the federal Constitution of the United Mexican States in 1857.[12] The 1857 Constitution drew heavily on the arguments and draft measures that had been proposed over the course of the nineteenth century by both liberals and conservatives. It adopted the classical liberal ideals recognizing the rights of man 'as the foundation and the object of social institutions' (Article 1), and instituted the prohibition of slavery; freedom of education, work, and industry; freedom of expression of ideas; freedom of the press; freedom of petition; freedom of association; the right to bear arms; freedom of movement; equal protection under the laws; application of general principles of law in the absence of a law or custom on which to base a decision; prohibition of retroactive application of the law; guarantee of due process; protection against arbitrary acts by public officials; and protections related to certain types of punishments and property rights.[13]

Garantias individuales were incorporated into the Constitution to prevent agents of the state and federal governments from abusing authority in their dealings with private citizens. Liberals claimed that these rights were inherent to all human beings,[14] and they recognized the need for a judicial procedure, the *amparo*, to guarantee their protection. As was the case in many countries during the nineteenth century, the main purpose of constitutionally guaranteed rights was to place restraints on the conduct of the state, thereby safeguarding the freedoms of those who lived within the borders of the nation.

During the long presidency of General Porfirio Díaz, the government's role in preserving individual rights was limited, and significant abuses occurred, especially in the countryside.[15] As the dictatorship calcified, protection of individual guarantees was generally ignored. Ironically, it was during this same period that the Supreme Court developed the basic doctrines surrounding the use of *amparo* to protect constitutional rights.

[11] On the history of *amparo*, *see* Chapter 8 below.

[12] Tena Ramírez, *supra* note 5 at 606–629.

[13] These 'rights of man' were amended in 1873, 1883, 1898, 1901, and 1908.

[14] Some of the leading jurists from the second half of the 19th century strongly supported this concept of fundamental rights. Thus, Isidro Montiel y Duarte claimed in his *Estudio sobre garantías individuales*, that the basic rights that individuals possess by simple virtue of their existence, as well as the means set forth under fundamental law to ensure enjoyment of these rights, are what is properly called *garantías individuales* ['constitutional protections']. Montiel y Duarte, I., *ESTUDIO SOBRE GARANTIAS INDIVIDUALES*, 5 [facsimile edition] (Mexico: Porrúa, 1991) at 6.

[15] Hart, J.M., *THE COMING AND PROCESS OF THE MEXICAN REVOLUTION* (Berkeley: University of California Press, 1987).

2.2. The Revolution of 1910 and the Constitution of 1917: The Social Phase

The struggle led by Francisco I. Madero, which began in 1910 as an offshoot of an earlier 'liberal' democratic movement, quickly escalated into a widespread struggle waged on several different fronts headed by different leaders. One of those fronts focused on a group of social demands that had been woven into the Platform of the Mexican Liberal Party of 1906 by revolutionary leaders such as the Flores Magón brothers, Vázquez Gómez, and Pascual Orozco. In 1916, when the framers of a new Mexican Constitution met in Querétaro to adopt a new charter, they fell into two major schools of thought regarding society and the state.[16] One school, led by Felix Palavicini, viewed law as a manifestation of prevailing ideas at the time of the Revolution: that is, the traditional protection of individual rights of a general nature, such as freedom of speech, or freedom from unauthorized arrest. The other school, under the leadership of Antonio Díaz Soto y Gama, felt that the constitution should incorporate a strong social agenda, including changes that would favour the working classes and peasants, such as land reform, labour guarantees, and guarantees of social welfare.

The debates in the constitutional Congress were initially dominated by the general liberal agenda of Venustiano Carranza, but once discussion began to focus on constitutional protections, the debates became more focused on the social agenda. The core protections of the Constitution of 1857 were kept intact in the Constitution of 1917, but in addition, a group of social 'rights' was added whose purpose was not just to prevent the state from violating individual rights, but rather to remedy social inequalities. These social rights expressly provided for in the Constitution included: free elementary school education (Article 3); land grants to towns that had been dispossessed of land (Article 27); and minimum labour standards in order to improve working conditions (Article 123). These social rights can be viewed as belonging to one of two types: rights that imply a clear commitment on the part of the state to grant material benefits, such as the right to free elementary education; and rights that must be preserved by private citizens, such as worker rights that should be observed by employers and land owners.

Social rights have been immensely important over the course of the twentieth century, insofar as these rights have served a variety of purposes for the PRI regime. From its inception, the PRI proclaimed itself to be the sole heir to the revolutionary movement, and the protection of social rights was the most tangible proof of such a claim. To demonstrate its monopoly, the PRI created a network of permanent institutional relationships with the groups these rights were designed to protect: the workers and peasants.[17] In the end, incorporating social rights into the Constitution did not have the effect that delegates to the Constituent Congress expected: redistributing wealth in Mexico. Instead, the 'social constitution', coupled with the domination by the President and the

[16] Cossío, Díaz., J. R., *Constitución Tribunales y Democracia* (Mexico: Themis, 1998) at 241.

[17] *See* Chapters 1 and 5 above.

PRI of all levels of government, served to bolster the PRI's monopoly of social welfare programmes, and thus maintain control over workers and peasants.

Of course, many of the social rights written into the Constitution represented, in principle, heavy expenditures by the federal government. During the populist governments of Luis Echeverría Álvarez (1970–1976) and José López Portillo (1976–1982), the right to health care, decent housing, the right to transmit and receive information, and protection of families and juveniles were enshrined in the Constitution, and the government created and expanded federal agencies to carry out these and other social rights. After Mexico experienced severe economic hardships in the late 1970s and early 1980s, the inability of the PRI to meet social welfare demands contributed greatly to the party's loss of legitimacy.

2.3. The Era of Human Rights

To the civil liberties of the 1857 Constitution and the social rights of the 1917 Constitution, in the 1940s Mexico began to add another type of individual rights based on a series of human rights treaties to which Mexico became a party. Under Article 133 of the Constitution, the rights set forth in these treaties theoretically became part of the nation's body of law, ranking just below the Constitution in the hierarchy of the legal system. The following section sets forth the characteristics of each type of constitutional protection: civil liberties or individual rights (*garantías individuales*), social rights, and international human rights.

3. Constitutionally Guaranteed Civil Rights and Individual Liberties (*Garantías Individuales*)

Constitutional protections in the Mexican system are characterized by several basic common elements, following a method of classification widely used in the civil law tradition. In this section, we address only the most common characteristics of these protections, or *garantías individuales*. Constitutional guarantees are expressly included in Articles 1–24, 27, and 28 of the Constitution.[18] Due to their constitutional status, these protections are the supreme law of the country, and any regulation, state or federal, that contradicts any of these articles, is invalid. Similarly, any ruling or decision issued by a public official at any level of government, such as judges, legislators, administrative authorities, etc., must adhere to the requirements and prohibitions set forth in the Constitution. Any violation of constitutional rights may constitute grounds for judicial protection under the *amparo* procedures, which can be brought by private citizens against a wide variety of public officials[19] due to alleged abuses of authority.[20]

[18] SJF, 5a, T. I, at 337, 26 Sep. 1917.

[19] The Supreme Court of Justice has stated many times that the *garantías individuales* are in effect solely and exclusively with relation to public officials. On this issue, *cf.* SJF, 5a, T. XXVII, 16 Oct. 1929, p. 1063; 5a, T. XXXI, 24 Apr. 1931, p. 2429; 5a, T. XLV, 25 July. 1935, p. 1533.

[20] For a discussion of the *amparo* procedure *see* Chapter 8 below.

In interpreting constitutional protections of individual rights, the Mexican Supreme Court follows the general tradition of the Mexican judiciary in avoiding what is referred to in the United States as 'judicial activism', that is, judicial interpretations of general constitutional provisions, such as 'due process' or 'equal protection', to mandate far-reaching decisions that establish rules of law. Interpretations of similarly vague provisions in the Mexican Constitution have not led to similarly aggressive judgments. The Mexican Supreme Court has held that, because individual rights emanate from the Constitution, a constitutional guarantee must not be interpreted in an absolute sense, but rather in keeping with the other provisions of the Constitution.[21]

3.1. Equal Protection (*Garantías de igualdad*)

The right of equal protection prevents agents of the State from issuing laws or regulations or setting any precedent that singles out individuals on the basis of personal characteristics (age, sex, race, etc.) or social or political status. The main provisions include the following:

(i) protections conferred by the Constitution shall apply to all individuals within the United Mexican States, including foreign citizens found within the territory of Mexico (Article 1);
(ii) slavery shall be prohibited (Article 1);
(iii) prohibition against discrimination based on ethnic origin, nationality, gender, disability, social or health conditions, religion, opinions, preferences, civil status, or any other discrimination against human dignity or individual rights or liberties (Article 1);[22]
(iv) men and women shall receive equal treatment under the law (Article 4);
(v) no person shall be conferred titles of nobility nor shall titles be inherited, and those conferred abroad shall not be recognized (Article 12);
(vi) no individual shall be tried under laws that deprive a defendant of his or her rights nor tried in special tribunals (Article 13); and
(vii) the State may not become a party to international treaties of extradition of political prisoners or slaves or any treaty that may alter constitutional protections (Article 15).

In the United States, the enforcement of constitutional guarantees (civil rights) such as equal protection has generated a considerable gloss of constitutional interpretation, especially in light of the remnants of discrimination that exist in society. This is due in large part to the fact that the US Supreme Court has given a broad interpretation to the scope of equal protection. In the United States, a violation of equal protection may be found even if the actor is a private party; so long as there is state participation in any form ('state action') in

[21] *Cf.* SJF, 5a, T. I, 26 Sep. 1917, p. 337; 5, T. LXXIV, 28 Oct. 1942, p. 2535.
[22] Article 1 was amended D.O. 14 Aug. 2001.

recognizing or supporting the activities of a private party (e.g. licensing of a business that discriminates against a particular race), the private act may be ruled unconstitutional. In addition, the US courts have ruled that not only *de jure*, but also *de facto* discrimination may violate the constitution.

By contrast, in Mexico, the constitutional guarantee of equal protection is much more limited. While the guarantee does prohibit any *governmental* act, either *de jure* or *de facto*, that violates a constitutional guarantee, it does not generally apply to private acts. Thus, for instance, if a private urban bus company operates a public bus line that refuses to accept passengers of a particular race, a person denied access may not bring an *amparo* action directly to enforce the guarantee of equal protection, because the defendant is a private party; this is true even though the bus line may have been licensed by public authorities. The only recourse for the complainant is to bring a civil action or administrative action, based on the civil codes or on a law. If a federal or state court issues a judgment denying a remedy, the complainant may then bring an *amparo* action, and the act of the judge in deciding the case will be sufficient to satisfy the Constitution's implicit requirement of state action. This is true even after the constitutional reforms related to the expansion of the rights of indigenous persons,[23] which added an adamant non-discrimination principle to Article 1 of the Constitution. As a result of this requirement that the defendant in an *amparo* action must be a public official, equal protection claims in Mexico have not been common. Those cases that do appear in the *jurisprudencia* tend to involve tax matters.

3.2. Protection of the Rights of Indigenous Peoples

One consequence of the Zapatista rebellion in Chiapas during the mid-1990s[24] was a re-examination of the rights of indigenous peoples under the Mexican Constitution. The Zapatista rebellion raised the profile of the debate over the extent to which the Constitution should recognize that indigenous communities ought to be allowed the right to follow practices that predated the Spanish Conquest even when these practices arguably deviated from national norms.[25] Congress adopted reforms to Articles 1, 2, 4, 18, and 115 of the Constitution,[26] in an attempt to recognize the pluricultural composition of Mexico based on the existence of indigenous communities with social, economic, political, and cultural institutions of their own. Before the reforms, Article 4 stated in very general terms that the State must recognize and protect indigenous cultures and customs. In the constitutional reform of 2001, the subject of guarantees of indigenous rights was transferred to the present Article 2 of the Constitution,

[23] *See infra*, text accompanying notes 24–28.

[24] *See* Chapter 1 above, at text accompanying note 155.

[25] For a discussion of the issues leading up to the constitutional reforms, *see* Cossio Díaz, J.R., *et al.*, DERECHOS Y CULTURA INDÍGENA: LOS DILEMAS DEL DEBATE JURÍDICO (Mexico: Miguel Angel Porrúa 1998).

[26] D.O. 14 Aug. 2001.

which formerly contained only the prohibition of slavery (now contained in Article 1).[27] The amended Article 2, which is now three pages long, guarantees the right of free determination and autonomy for indigenous peoples and their communities (including rights of women). In those municipalities in which indigenous peoples make up a majority of the population, Article 2 requires that the form of local government, and the rules governing the population, shall be according to indigenous rules of governance and customs, rather than by the rules dictated by Article 115 of the Constitution. This is a surprising development, and departure from the norm of rules of governance, including constitutional rights, established on a national basis. For this reason, perhaps, Article 2 leaves the implementation of this 'conversion' to indigenous rules of governance to the local legislatures of each state. Of course, the local rules of indigenous governance must give way to the hierarchy of Mexican laws: they cannot conflict with constitutional rights, nor can they contradict higher laws (federal laws, state constitutions, or state laws).[28]

These constitutional amendments were vigorously debated before eventually being adopted by Congress.[29] The proponents of greater rights for indigenous peoples were dissatisfied with the vague and general nature of the provisions, while opponents of the effort were concerned that accepting greater autonomy for indigenous groups would undermine the general rule of law applicable to everyone. While the amendments were ratified by the requisite number of states (eighteen), ironically, those states with the largest indigenous populations—Oaxaca, Chiapas, and Guerrero—refused to ratify the amendments, because they had already adopted legislation dealing with their indigenous populations, and felt that the reforms contradicted their own regimes. Now that the constitutional reforms have been adopted, all states must abide by them.

3.3. Individual Freedoms (*Garantías de Libertad*)

Individual freedoms are designed to review the content of any legal norm (legislative or judicial) that would deprive individuals of human liberty in violation of the constitution. The following constitutional protections are usually considered to be liberty-related *garantías*:

(i) freedom to form a family of any size (Article 4);
(ii) freedom to work and to engage in commerce (Article 5);
(iii) freedom to express thoughts or ideas (Article 6);
(iv) freedom of the press (Article 7);

[27] The amendment also added a third paragraph to Article 1 of the Constitution, to prohibit discrimination based on ethnic origin or nationality, gender, age, different abilities, social or health conditions, religion, opinions, preferences, civil condition, or otherwise.

[28] *See* Cossio Díaz, J.R., 'La Reforma Constitucional en Materia Indígena', in LOS PROBLEMAS DEL DERECHO INDÍGENA EN MÉXICO (Mexico: CNDH, 2001), at 145–176.

[29] *See* Rabasa Gamboa, E., DERECHO CONSTITUCIONAL INDÍGENA (Mexico: Porrúa 2002) at 81–92, 159–167.

(v) the right to petition (Article 8);
(vi) freedom of assembly and of association (Article 9);
(vii) the right to bear and own arms (Article 10);
(viii) freedom of movement (Article 11);
(ix) freedom of communication and of correspondence (Article 16);
(x) freedom of religious belief (Article 24); and
(xi) freedom of competition in economic matters (Article 28).

Certain of these individual freedoms correspond to the civil liberties guaranteed in the Bill of Rights of the US Constitution, and are examined below.

3.4. Protection of Property Rights (*Garantías de Propiedad*)

Article 27 of the Constitution recognizes three forms of property under Mexican law: public property, private property, and social property. With regard to the first two, the first sentence of Article 27 states: 'Ownership of land and water contained within the limits of national territory originally belong to the nation, which has had and has the right to transfer dominion thereof to private citizens, constituting private property'. Part VII of the same Article recognizes the legal status of common and community lands (*tierras ejidales y comunales*) that make up 'social property'.

For many foreigners, Article 27 is one of the most significant and widely cited articles in the Constitution. It protects property rights, by including a 'takings' clause (Article 27, second sentence) that guarantees to private parties that expropriation of property can only occur to benefit the public,[30] and upon payment of compensation. Expropriations are also governed by the Expropriation Law (*Ley de Expropiación*),[31] which requires that compensation be paid in local currency (i.e. Mexican pesos)[32] as soon as the expropriated property is transferred to the State (Article 19). The amount should be calculated in accordance with the tax value of the expropriated property as determined by Mexican tax authorities (Article 10); however, if there is a significant difference

[30] In 1940, the Supreme Court ruled that expropriation means 'that dominion of real property is transferred from a private citizen to the State, so the latter may satisfy some purpose of public utility'. *Semanario Judicial de la Federación*, 5ª época, tomo LXV, p. 4450, 12 May, 1940. To demonstrate a public purpose, the state must show: (i) the existence of a public need; and (ii) that the property to be expropriated will meet the public need. The public utility purpose should also be specific, and, social welfare should be considered in expropriation cases. *See* Burgoa, I., *Las Garantías Individuales* (Mexico: Porrúa, 1995) at 470–485.

[31] D.O. 25 Nov. 1936.

[32] The investment provisions included in NAFTA Chapter 11 provide additional protections to foreign investors from Canada and the United States. Thus, NAFTA provides in Article 1110 that expropriations must be for a public purpose, non-discriminatory, in accordance with international law, and upon payment of adequate compensation, as well as other protection. For a discussion of the investment provisions of NAFTA, *see* Aguilar Alvarez, G., and Park, W., 'The New Face of Investment Arbitration: NAFTA Chapter 11', 28 Yale Int'l LJ 365 (2003). NAFTA also grants to foreign investors access to dispute resolution mechanisms to enforce these provisions (NAFTA Articles 1115–1137). The NAFTA text is available at www.sice.oas.org (site visited Jan. 2004).

between the tax value and the market value of the expropriated good, the Expropriation Law grants the owner a right to solicit from a federal District Judge a determination of the amount of compensation in accordance with the fair market value of the property.

But Article 27 goes far beyond this. It is not by accident that the Article begins with a declaration that private persons receive their property rights from the state: as a legacy of colonial rule,[33] the underlying notion of Mexican law is that private citizens' rights are derived from and secondary to the property rights originally claimed by the nation. The reason why private property is subject to these rules dates back to the new concept of private property that emerged from the Constitution of 1917. The Mexican Supreme Court issued a succinct ruling in this regard, stating that '[t]he essential reforms that have come about as a result of the Constitution [that are now] in force, do not involve an absolute and exclusive right of the individual, but rather a right that is subordinate to or conditional upon collective needs'.[34]

This premiss of political philosophy, as well as Mexico's history of foreign intervention,[35] helps explain why important limitations on individual rights of ownership are set forth in Article 27, to the occasional frustration of Mexican and foreign investors.[36] This historical background also helps explain the fourth paragraph of Article 27, which states that natural resources generally, and all subsoil mineral rights, including petroleum and all hydrocarbons, belong to the nation, rather than to the owner of real property on which the natural resources are found.[37]

Finally, in addition to guaranteeing property rights and limitations on private ownership, Article 27 has also served as the constitutional basis for systematic land reform through the breakup of large landholdings (*latifundios*).[38]

[33] *See* Chapter 1 above, at text accompanying notes 42–44 (ownership of territories by the Spanish Crown, which ceded property rights to its subjects).

[34] SJF, 5a, T. II, 31 Jan. 1918, p. 2.

[35] *See* Chapter 1 above, section 3.

[36] Under Article 27, foreigners may not acquire ownership of lands and waters or obtain mining or water rights, unless they agree to consider themselves as Mexican nationals for the purpose of the acquisition of the property. This 'Calvo Clause' provision is discussed in more detail below in Chapter 16, at text accompanying notes 49–52. Foreigners may not acquire, under any circumstances, real property located within 100 kilometres of the nation's borders or within 50 kilometres of the coast, but they may acquire the use of such properties as beneficiaries of a trust. According to Article 27, Sections II and III, religious associations, certain types of charitable institutions, and corporations may only acquire rural properties that are indispensable to their corporate purpose. Prior to constitutional reforms in 1992, religious associations could not hold title to real property of any kind; this blanket prohibition was amended by D.O. 28 Jan. 1992. Corporations could not own agricultural properties until 1992, when Congress amended Article 27, Section IV, to permit corporations to own agricultural lands if authorized by their articles of incorporation. Article 27, Section V, states that banks may not hold, either in ownership or in receivership, more property than is absolutely necessary for them to do business.

[37] On the colonial law background, *see* Chapter 1 above, at text accompanying notes 42–43.

[38] On land reform, *see* Chapter 13 below, section 4. *Latifundios* are considered to be any expanse of land privately owned by one person that exceeds the limits of a 'small property' as defined in Article 27, Section XV of the Constitution. These limits vary according to the available natural resources and productivity of the land in question, with limits varying from 100 hectares for highly productive land to 800 acres for mountainous or heavily forested land.

3.5. Due Process Protections

The Mexican Constitution includes several provisions that promote, at least on paper, adherence to the rule of law. These rights are designed to regulate the types of acts that federal, state, and local government agencies may perform, by defining which acts may be performed by which agency, and the legal procedures to be followed.[39] The general conditions and requirements to which a governmental official or agency is subject are known as guarantees of legal security (*garantías de seguridad jurídica*). They are similar to the protections that exist under the due process clauses of the United States Constitution. Some of these rights are discussed in Chapter 10 below on civil procedure and Chapter 11 below on criminal law and procedure.

Such rights include prohibition against retroactive application of laws (*irretroactividad legal*) (Article 14); the right to be heard in court (*audiencia*) (Article 14); the right to strict adherence in criminal matters to the exact codified descriptions of crimes and punishments as they appear in valid criminal codes (*legalidad en materia penal*) (Article 14); the right to civil decisions being based on the law, precedent or, in the absence of either of these sources, general principles of law (*legalidad en material civil*) (Article 14); the right to require the governmental authority to show a basis in the law and the facts in order to issue warrants (*fundamentación y motivación*) (Article 16); protection against arbitrary detention on criminal charges (Article 16); access to justice (Article 17); and the right to due process of the law in criminal matters (Articles 18 to 23).

3.6. Freedom of Education

The first part of Article 3 of the Constitution establishes that primary and secondary education shall be obligatory[40] and available to all without charge. The Constitution also establishes that the education imparted by the State shall be secular (or independent from any religious doctrine), in order to guarantee the freedom of religion provided for in Article 24. This is one of the most controversial constitutional precepts in recent Mexican history, concerning differing opinions about the role the State and the Church should play in the education of children. The controversy surrounding this issue dates back to the liberal reforms of the mid-nineteenth century,[41] and reached a turning point during the debates on the draft of the Constitution of 1917. The framers eventually agreed

[39] Schmill Ordoñez, U., EL SISTEMA DE LA CONSTITUCIÓN MEXICANA (Mexico: Manuel Porrúa, 1971) at 404–405.

[40] The obligation contained in Article 3 refers to the obligation of the State to provide free primary and secondary education for all children, including the provision of free text books, the construction and maintenance of schools, and the payment of salaries and granting of social services to teachers and administrative personnel of public schools. However, there is no general obligation for students to remain in school after a certain age. Figures on schooling vary by region: in Nuevo León, the average citizen receives 9.8 years of schooling, while in Chiapas and Oaxaca, the average citizen receives 5.8 years of school. In 1999, 10% of Mexicans were illiterate. INEGI, Censo 2000, www.inegi.gob.mx (site visited Jan. 2004).

[41] *See* Chapter 1 above, Section 3.2.

that not only would public education be secular, but also that private citizens would not be permitted to impart any form of religious education, even in private schools, a prohibition that extended equally to religious associations, including the Catholic Church. This was a surprising result for such a Catholic nation, but was considered necessary to counteract the immense power of the Catholic Church.

The tension over religious education has waxed and waned over the course of the twentieth century.[42] Soon after the adoption of the 1917 Constitution, a bitter confrontation with the Catholic Church led to the gruesome struggle between Catholics and the State known as the Cristero War.[43] Beginning in the early 1920s, Secretary of Education José Vasconcelos initiated a nationwide effort to combat literacy, building rural schools, establishing federal control, and hiring thousands of new teachers. After Vasconcelos, the federal government took virtual total control of public education at the primary and secondary levels, until constitutional amendments in 1992 reversed this.[44] Vasconcelos was the first to use public funds strategically to support cultural activities, hiring artists such as Diego Rivera to paint murals in public spaces that extolled Mexican history and populist values. Government support for cultural enterprises for public consumption has been constant throughout the twentieth century; this function has also served as one of the methods by which the PRI, so closely associated with the government, could portray a populist stance.

The highly secular and increasingly socialistic model of public education reached its apogee during the presidency of Lázaro Cárdenas, gradually settling into a truce between the state and the Catholic Church in which thinly veiled religious education was offered in private schools and overlooked by the state. Article 3 of the Constitution was amended in 1934 to provide that education in Mexico shall be 'socialistic', which was interpreted to recognize the public interest of the state in overseeing the content of eduction, more than an ideological position. In 1946, Article 3 was again amended to remove the term 'socialistic' from the education provisions.

This discrepancy between the constitutional prohibition of religious education and *de facto* practice was finally abolished in 1992. On the initiative of President Carlos Salinas de Gortari, not known as a particularly religious

[42] *Cf.* Solana, F., Cardiel Reyes, R. and Bolaños Matinez, R. (Coord), *Historia de la Educacion Publica en Mexico* (Mexico: Fondo de Cultura Económica-SEP, 1982).

[43] *See* Chapter 1 above, at text accompanying notes 131.

[44] In 1992, amendments to Article 3 made state governments responsible for the direct administration of educational institutions (schools, laboratories, libraries) that were previously under the supervision of the Secretariat of Public Education (*Secretaría de Educación Pública*, or SEP). D.O. 5 May 1993. The federal government kept control over the evaluation and regulation of education in the country, however, through the edition and distribution of textbooks, preparation of educational programmes, distribution of materials, and evaluation of education in general, among others. In addition, the financing of primary and secondary education depends primarily on federal funding, since the states lack the taxing power to fund public schools. On federal–state relations in education, *see* Chapter 4 above, at text accompanying notes 36–37, 56, and 76.

person, Article 3 was amended to remove the prohibition on private religious education.[45] For the first time since the Mexican Revolution, religious groups could now establish religious schools. The secular nature of public education remains, however: there is no debate over prayer in the schools in Mexico, where such a suggestion would be an unthinkable intrusion on the power of the state.

3.7. Freedom of Employment

The first part of Article 5 of the Constitution provides that 'no person shall be prevented from dedicating himself [or herself] to whatever profession, industry, commerce or work that suits him [or her], as long as it [such activity] is lawful'. Article 5 also allocates to the states the right to regulate the professions.

Mexican case-law is rich in Supreme Court opinions on the subject of freedom of employment. The Supreme Court has ruled that freedom of employment must adhere to the provisions of Article 123 of the Constitution (which includes numerous workers' rights);[46] that freedom of employment may not infringe the rights of other persons or be contrary to the public interest;[47] that government employees may not seek protection under freedom of employment provisions because these employees are not engaged in professional practice or involved in industry or business;[48] that legislation prohibiting any type of employment must be reasonable and the legislature must feel 'compelled [to enact such a law] due to social demands of such a pressing nature that [the legislation] cannot be delayed, or in order to thwart activities that contravene proper morals or customs';[49] and that general restraints on freedom of employment can only be enacted by law.[50]

In general terms, freedom of employment refers to the right of any individual to perform any lawful job of his preference, without any pressure or prohibition from the state or its authorities. Article 5 expressly prohibits the issuance of any law, regulation, or decree, or the exercise of any act of authority, that would restrict individuals from freely exercising this right. In addition, Article 5 of the Constitution provides that no individual should be required to perform work without fair compensation, nor without his or her previous consent; payment of compensation to a person may only be prevented when so ordered by a judicial order, under a judgment supported by law.

Article 5 is also the source of a constitutional 'freedom of commerce' provision. According to the Supreme Court, the underlying goal of Article 5 is to prevent the enactment of any constraints on commerce 'that have no other purpose than to impinge upon an individual's right to freely practice an occupation in such a way that[. . .] makes it difficult to engage in business'.[51] On the other

[45] *See* the discussion in CONSTITUCIÓN POLÍTICA DE LOS ESTADOS UNIDOS MEXICANOS—COMENTADA (Mexico: UNAM-IIJ, 1997) vol. 1 at 30–31.

[46] SJF, 5a, T. III, 21 Oct. 1918, p. 1096.

[47] SJF, 5, T. VII, 2 Jan. 1920, p. 8.

[48] SJF, 5a, T. XVII, 26 Oct. 1925, p. 1103.

[49] SJF, 5a, T. LXI, 5 Sept. 1929, p. 4025.

[50] SJF, 8a, T. VI, 8 Oct. 1990, p. 227.

[51] SJF, 5a, T. IV, 14 Feb. 1919, p. 337.

hand, the Court has also said that sanctions imposed on businesses for violations of regulations cannot be considered violations of freedom of commerce,[52] even though these regulations may require that business be conducted under certain conditions or prohibit certain forms of business activity in certain locations.[53] Added together, the Supreme Court's rulings show an unwillingness to challenge governmental action as a violation of Article 5 if it can be shown that a legitimate state regulatory interest is furthered by the prohibition or restriction.

As noted in Section 5 below, effective freedom of employment is related to the 'social rights' written into Article 123 of the Constitution. As in the case of those rights, the recognition of the 'freedom to work' that is guaranteed by the Mexican Constitution must be evaluated in the light of an economy that has long suffered from a surplus of unskilled and semi-skilled labourers. This condition has generated high levels of unemployment and underemployment, and a concomitant lack of labour productivity as the production of new jobs in the economy failed to keep up with the growth in population. As a result, there is uneven enforcement of worker protections under Mexican law. In general, the higher the profile of the employer (large companies, foreign-owned companies, etc.) the greater the likelihood for strict enforcement of worker protections. However, in the 'informal economy' of small, individually owned businesses (a large segment of the Mexican economy) there is a constant temptation by both workers and employers to ignore the worker protections and freedoms 'guaranteed' by law and the Constitution.

3.8. Freedom of Speech and Publication

The first part of Article 6 of the Constitution describes freedom of speech in the following terms: 'The expression of ideas shall not be the subject of any judicial or administrative inquiry, except in cases where it constitutes an assault on morals, a third party's rights, incites an offence, or disturbs the public order'. Article 6 is interpreted to cover oral and visual freedom of expression, by conversations, speeches, conferences, debates, or any other kind of means of expression, such as artistic expression (including music, painting, sculpture, cinema, television, and radio)[54] other than through written words.

Article 7 of the Constitution covers freedom of expression in writing, including the writing or publication of books, newspapers, magazines, booklets, or any other kind of publication.

The freedoms protected by Articles 6 and 7 are subject to certain exceptions, as in other countries. Thus, when an oral or artistic expression, or a publication, constitutes an assault on privacy, morals, or public peace, a court may impose an administrative fine of 500 pesos and imprisonment for one to eleven

[52] SJF, 5a, T. VIII, 4 May 1921, p. 885.
[53] SJF, 5a, T. IX, 26 Aug. 1921, p. 418; 5a, T. XLV, 24 Aug. 1935, p. 3455.
[54] SJF, 5a, Vol. 97–102, (*Tribunales Colegiados de Circuito*), 18 Jan. 1977, p. 144.

months, aside from any civil liability for defamation (*daño moral*) of an injured party.[55] No objective criteria have been developed, either by the courts or by law, to distinguish the exact circumstances in which these exceptions might apply, and much has depended on the discretion of judges and government officials. The Law of Publication (*Ley de Imprenta*) of 1917,[56] which still regulates Articles 6 and 7, has never been amended, despite being outdated.[57]

Despite these shortcomings, the federal courts have occasionally intervened to safeguard freedom of expression. For example, the courts have said that statements designed to proselytize in favour of a political party cannot constitute a crime *per se*, and it would therefore be a violation of freedom of speech to prohibit such political expression.[58] Since radio and television are the most powerful media for the dissemination of ideas, federal courts have held that the award of concessions of these media cannot remain under government control without judicial scrutiny.[59] The granting of rights to a new television channel or the cancellation of concessions already in use may only be done to avoid a monopoly that restricts freedom of speech or the control of such media by persons who may offend public morals or attack the private lives of individuals.[60]

During much of the twentieth century, freedom of expression was often sacrificed in favour of the political hegemony of the PRI, which had numerous extra-legal and extra-judicial techniques to control the media and silence serious opposition.[61] For instance, in the heyday of government control of enterprises, if a newspaper were critical of the PRI it would lose lucrative advertising revenue earned from hundreds of government- (i.e. PRI-) controlled enterprises. The PRI-dominated government also had a monopoly on the sale of newsprint, and a newspaper could find itself without the paper to print its upcoming edition if it was overly critical of the government. Since the government controlled allocation of television and radio concessions, it could choose to deny or cancel licences of critical opponents.

For many years, the PRI was adept at creative uses of the law to protect its power. Thus, there has long been an unwritten rule that the media was to avoid overt criticism or ridicule of the person of the President while in office; this would quickly change after a President left office, however. In 1993, when an enterprising company began selling rubber masks with a caricature likeness of then-President Carlos Salinas de Gortari, the Attorney General of Mexico

[55] *Ley de Imprenta*, Articles 10 and 11, D.O. 12 Apr. 1917. *Daños morales* for defamation are covered in Chapter 17 below, section 6.4.3. [56] D.O. 12 Apr. 1917.

[57] For more detailed information about freedom of expression *see* Villanueva Villanueva, E., DERECHO MEXICANO DE LA INFORMACIÓN (Mexico: Oxford University Press, 2000).

[58] SJF, 5a, T. XXXVIII, 10 May 1933, p. 220.

[59] *Semanario Judicial de la Federación*, 5a, T. 169–174, 6th Part (Collegiate Circuit Courts) 13 Apr. 1978, at 119.

[60] SJF, 5a, Vol. 109–114, Sexta Parte (Tribunales Colegiados de Circuito) 25 Jan. 1978, at 120.

[61] Isolated examples of successful defence of the right of political expression exist. *See*, for example, the discussion of judicial enforcement of constitutional guarantees that took place in Yucatan in 1933, in Cossío J.R., *et al.*, EL PODER JUDICIAL DE LA FEDERACIÓN Y LOS MEDIOS DE COMUNICACIÓN: SENTENCIAS *(1836–2001)* (Mexico: Porrúa, 2002).

confiscated the masks for a violation of law: appropriation of the image or personality of another without permission or compensation.

These controls on political expression have virtually disappeared, along with the PRI's monopoly of government. Today, the media and the press in Mexico are highly independent and generally free from government coercion.

3.9. Freedom of Association

The first part of Article 9 of the Constitution provides that 'the right to associate or assemble peacefully for any legitimate purpose shall not be abridged'. Freedom of association also grants citizens the right to form or to be members of political parties in accordance with Article 41 of the Constitution.

There were two distinct periods of judicial interpretation of the right of association in the twentieth century. Originally, the Supreme Court held that the right to associate was to be given a restrictive interpretation, being limited to the ability of individuals to create associations to carry out lawful purposes. The significance of the Court's interpretation lies in the fact that the Mexican political system, beginning in the late 1930s, was highly corporatist. As discussed elsewhere,[62] Mexican society was organized into industrial, professional, and trade corporations or associations that served as agents of political representation and exercised some control over persons and activities within their jurisdiction, through mandatory membership of labour, management, and communal farm organizations. Ironically, far from promoting the right to associate freely, the constitutional provision was originally held to underscore the compulsion of groups to associate with a corporatist form of government, which made it compulsory for everyone to belong to the association of one's respective trade or profession.[63] At the same time, the PRI was able to stifle independent associations, especially labour unions, which were a main pillar of the PRI's support. As a result, the Secretary of Labour would generally not register independent labour unions that were perceived as threats to the PRI; if not registered, the nascent labour union would lack personality to bring an *amparo* action.[64]

In response to increasing pressures for democratization, in 1992 the Supreme Court changed its interpretation of Article 9, holding that mandatory membership of chambers of commerce violated the right of association. The Court held that not only did Article 9 assure the right to form an organization or join one that is already in existence, but it also included the right *not* to associate.[65] In the wake of this landmark opinion, many of the entrenched corporatist mechanisms are vulnerable to challenge. Thus, in the states of Jalisco and Oaxaca,

[62] *See* Chapters 1 and 5 above. [63] Cossío Díaz, *supra* note 16 at 203.

[64] Cossío J.R., CAMBIO SOCIAL Y CAMBIO JURÍDICO, I, (Mexico: Porrúa, 2001) at 53.

[65] Even though the opinion has been reiterated on several occasions, the first time it was issued was on 30 June 1992 and, in 1995, it became mandatory legal precedent (*jurisprudencia*). On this subject, *cf.* SJF, 9a, T. II, October 1995, p. 5.

state bureaucrats have challenged a state law requiring public employees to join the 'official' state employees' union.[66]

There are important constitutional limitations on freedom of association. For instance, foreign citizens are prohibited from associating or assembling for political purposes, or for the purpose of criticizing Mexican law or Mexican authorities[67] (Mexican Constitution, Article 33, second paragraph). In anticlerical Mexico, the same prohibition exists for religious leaders (Mexican Constitution, Article 33). Article 9 of the Constitution limits the freedom of association to carry out insurrections or other illegal activities against the government.

3.10. Right of Access to the Courts

One of the most frequently invoked rights in Mexican courts is the *garantía de audiencia*, or the constitutional right to have one's day in court. According to the second paragraph of Article 14, no one shall be deprived of life, liberty, or property, possessions, or rights, except by means of a trial held in a previously established court, during which all essential procedural formalities are complied with, in accordance with laws issued before the fact. This provision, along with the first sentence of Article 16 (discussed in the next section), recognizes rights that are analogous to the guarantee of due process protection under the Fifth and Fourteenth Amendments to the US Constitution.

The wording of this constitutional protection is complex, and has therefore given rise to considerable interpretation by the Supreme Court. Although the Constitution does not provide specifically for the right to a 'prior hearing', the Supreme Court has interpreted Article 14 to mean that judicial officers must give private citizens the opportunity to be heard in their own defence before being deprived of liberty or property.[68] The Supreme Court has also interpreted Article 14 to establish a right for private citizens to mount an effective defence to state action, by 'providing them with full and proper disclosure of all information or exhibits that may be used by judicial officers to make a finding based on the law and the facts, otherwise, only a poor defense could be mounted and proper and cogent arguments and evidence could not be presented or introduced'.[69] The Supreme Court has also ruled that, during all stages of any judicial proceeding, certain rules must be observed: defendants must be formally apprised of the initiation of the proceedings, of the issues that will be the subject of discussion,

[66] *Cf.* Cossio Díaz, ***supra*** note 16 at 111.

[67] This prohibition on foreign involvement in Mexican politics is important in a country which suffered numerous interventions by the United States during the 19th and 20th centuries. It is underscored by Article 33 of the Constitution, which permits the President to deport any foreign citizen, immediately and without protections of due process of law if, in the words of the Article, the President finds the presence of the foreign citizen 'inconvenient'.

[68] SJF, 5a, T. LXXXVIII, Tercera Parte, p. 30.

[69] SJF, 5a, 103–108, Sexta parte (TCC) 20 Sep. 1977, p. 36 (authors' trans.).

and of the possible consequences of the proceedings; defendants must also be informed that they may assert their right to mount a defence and to have any claim made by any party substantiated, and defendants must be afforded an opportunity to present arguments after the evidentiary stage has concluded; a limit must be set on the length of the proceedings; and finally, the appropriate judicial officer must expressly describe how the parties are to comply with the judgment.[70] Finally, a statement that a law or regulation is in the public interest does not prevent parties from challenging the law in court.[71]

The constitutional protection provided by Article 14 is most often enforced through *amparo* proceedings, as discussed in Chapter 8 below. The protections of Article 14 apply to foreign parties as well as Mexican citizens, and set out the principle that the government may not deprive persons of life, liberty, property, or constitutional rights without providing an opportunity for judicial proceedings to contest the action and pursuant to laws published before such action takes place.

3.11. Protection Against Violations of Due Process (*Garantía de Legalidad*)

The first paragraph of Article 16 of the Constitution provides a guarantee against violations of due process performed by public officials, known as *garantía de legalidad*, and is responsible for most of the thousands of *amparo* cases that are brought before the federal courts each year to contest arbitrary or illegal government action.[72] Article 16 prohibits any act of authority that is inconsistent with any law or ruling issued by a governmental agent or agency that is not in keeping with the applicable law or regulations. The protection has been interpreted broadly by the Supreme Court, to apply not only to all laws and regulations in force in Mexico, at any level of government; it also protects persons against individual actions by public officials that constitute violations of laws or the Constitution. There is no requirement that the law allegedly violated must be of a federal nature; violations of state and local laws and regulations give rise to a federal action of *amparo* to vindicate this due process right. Article 16 even gives the federal courts a basis to serve as appellate courts that can overturn the opinions of state courts in the application of purely state law. For this reason, critics of centralized power in Mexico have decried the extensive use of *amparo* as an infringement on states' rights.[73]

[70] SJF, 5a, T. VII, January 1991, p. 153.

[71] SJF, 7a, 103–108, Primera Parte, 22 Nov. 1977, p. 75.

[72] For a detailed discussion of *amparo* proceedings, *see* Chapter 8 below. In 2000, there were 114,264 *amparo* cases before the Collegiate Circuit Courts; 1,209 *amparo* cases before the Unitary Circuit Courts; and 180,222 before the Federal District Judges; approximately 75% of these cases dealt with allegations of violations of Article 16. *See* www.scjn.gob.mx (site visited Jan. 2004).

[73] For instance, judicial reformers have complained of the use of *amparo* actions to prevent the removal of corrupt or incompetent state judges.

According to the language of Article 16, 'no one shall be disturbed in his person, family, domicile, papers or possessions, except by virtue of a written order [issued] by the competent authority, in which a basis in law and in fact is set forth for the proceeding'. Any individual or group of individuals physically present in Mexico may claim the protection of this and every other constitutionally guaranteed right, in accordance with Articles 1 and 16 of the Constitution. The language of the provision is so broad that protection applies to practically any type of property or possession.

Pursuant to Article 16, all acts of authority must be issued by the competent public office having jurisdiction over the subject matter; moreover, any act of authority must be duly supported by a legal provision expressly mentioned in writing (*fundamentación*), and the act must specify the way in which the facts, circumstances, and procedures conform to the law in question (*motivación*).[74] Finally, the act of authority should be issued in a written order signed or issued by the competent public authority. If any of these requirements is not fulfilled, the act would be considered as violating individual guarantees, and an affected party federal court may issue an order rendering the act null and void.

It is important to note that *amparo* actions may only be brought against public officials or agencies; they are not available to challenge actions against private persons or enterprises. If a private company infringes upon one's constitutional rights, then the appropriate form of judicial action will depend upon the particular circumstances of the infringement.

3.12. Voting Rights

The discussion of constitutional guarantees would not be complete without considering the status of voting rights under Mexican law. Under the legal systems of most other countries, these rights have the status of constitutional protections.[75] Under Mexican law, however, while Article 35 appears to confer a right to vote and to stand for election, for many years the Supreme Court ruled that the judicial branch may not interfere in political affairs,[76] since to do so would violate the separation of powers assured in Article 49.[77] This political philosophy led the Court to rule that 'acts that infringe on political rights are not grounds for *amparo* proceedings, because [such rights] are not constitutional protections (*garantías individuales*)'.[78] Since a petition for *amparo* is

[74] SJF, 5a, Vol. 14, Tercera Parte, p. 37, 20 Feb. 1970; Vol. 80, Tercera Parte, p. 13, 7 Aug. 1975, Appendix to SJF, 1917–1988, Segunda Parte, Salas y Tesis Comunes, tesis 902, p. 1481. For a more detailed discussion of these elements, *see* Chapter 9 below, at text accompanying note 80.

[75] *See* Biscaretti di Ruffia, P., *INTRODUCIÓN AL DERECHO CONSTITUCIONAL COMPARADO* (Mexico: Fondo de Cultura Económica, 1996) at 699.

[76] SJF, 5th, Pleno, T. III, p. 1246 (1918). *See also* Moctezuma Barragán, J., *JOSÉ MARÍA IGLESIAS Y LA JUSTICIA ELECTORAL* (Mexico: UNAM, 1994).

[77] *See* Arteaga Nava, E., *DERECHO CONSTITUCIONAL* (Mexico: Oxford University Press, 1999) at 345.

[78] *Cf.* e.g. SJF, 5a, T. VIII, 16 Feb. 1921, p. 389; SJF, 5a, T. XXIV, 9 Nov. 1928, p. 598.

the only practical means for a citizen to assert voting rights, the Supreme Court's restrictive interpretation essentially removed voting rights cases from the federal courts.

Despite the judiciary's passivity, Mexicans are not left entirely without the means to contest violations of the right to vote. Beginning in the 1980s, under growing criticism at home and abroad, the PRI-dominated federal government began to move towards electoral reforms that would provide a greater voice for opposition parties in government. In 1990, as a response to allegations of fraud in the election of President Carlos Salinas de Gortari, the Mexican Congress created the Federal Electoral Tribunal (*Tribunal Federal Electoral*) as an autonomous agency within the executive branch to settle election disputes. Opposition leaders continued alleged control of the tribunal by the executive, and in 1996, Congress amended the Constitution to incorporated the Federal Electoral Tribunal into the judicial branch. The tribunal was renamed the *Tribunal Electoral del Poder Judicial de la Federación* (Electoral Tribunal of the Federal Judicial Branch),[79] and was empowered to decide all cases involving allegations of illegality in federal elections of *diputados*, senators, and the Mexican President, as well as to review appeals from judgments resolutions of state electoral tribunals and protect the political and voting rights of individuals. The Federal Electoral Tribunal is empowered to review the legality of decisions and acts undertaken by electoral officials, but it lacks authority to decide any question related to the constitutionality of electoral laws or regulations, which is a matter for the Supreme Court determination.[80] In extreme cases, the Federal Electoral Tribunal has the power to overturn an election, and to order a new election,[81] such as have occurred in the states of Guanajuato, Yucatán, and Tabasco.

4. Social Rights

A unique feature of the Mexican Constitution is the attention devoted to the recognition of 'social rights'. A product of the Revolution of 1910, these rights represented a substantial departure from the standard subject matter that had been incorporated into Constitutions of other countries of the world up until that time. Social rights were initially conceived by the Constitution's framers as a restraint on the ability of powerful individuals to act against the interest of the socially disadvantaged. Accordingly, in order to improve the condition of peasants and workers, the federal government was empowered: to ban and punish unfair monopolization of land (*latifundios*) (Article 27); to divide up the

[79] Information on the Federal Electoral Tribunal may be found at www.trife.gob.mx.

[80] D.O. 22 Aug. 1996. For more detailed information on the electoral laws, *see* Chapter 5 above, Section 3. *See also* Patiño Camarena, F. Nuevo Derecho Electoral Mexicano (Mexico: Editorial Constitucionalista and Instituto Federal Electoral, 6th ed., 2000).

[81] *Ley Organica del Poder Judicial de la Federacíon*, D.O. 22 Nov. 1996, Art. 189.

land of private citizens among landless members of a community by creating common farmlands and settlements (*ejidos* and *comunidades*) (Article 27);[82] and to prevent the imposition of unfair working conditions (Article 123). Originally, social rights could be characterized as restraints on the conduct of certain individuals in order to protect the disadvantaged; any administrative or judicial infringement on these constitutionally guaranteed social civil rights was legitimate grounds for seeking judicial protection via *amparo* proceedings. However, with the exception of an implied obligation to provide primary (and later secondary) education to all citizens free of charge,[83] these rights did not imply a positive obligation on behalf of the state.[84]

In the early 1970s, under the leadership of President Luis Echeverría, new subject matters, also known as 'social rights', were incorporated into the Constitution for an entirely new purpose. Having become President during a time of political protest, Echeverría's response was to deflect criticism and recreate public support by adopting a wide range of new social welfare policies. In addition, he oversaw the incorporation by constitutional amendment of a second block of newly established social rights which made the state responsible for providing certain benefits or entitlements, such as the right to protection of the family (i.e. freedom to create a family of any size at any time), the right to decent housing, protection of the rights of juveniles and protection of the right to health care (Article 4); the protection of the right to information;[85] and the obligation of the State to promote integral rural development (Article 27).[86] These rights differ from earlier social rights because, as legal scholars and the judiciary have reasoned, they do not create an absolute obligation on the state or federal governments to guarantee them; rather, governments can only be expected to implement programmes that address these social rights if they possess the economic resources available to do so. Consequently, these entitlements could not be demanded through an *amparo* proceeding.[87] Rather than constituting a constitutional mandate to bring about a more fair redistribution of wealth, these hortatory provisions have proved largely rhetorical, and have been used in the past by PRI-dominated governments to present the appearance of a governmental concern for social welfare that has not often been carried out in practice.

[82] On land reform laws, *see* Chapter 13 below, Section 4.

[83] *Cf.* SJF, 5a, T. LXVII, 7 June 1940, p. 2702.

[84] The only exception to this statement is the obligation of the State to provide free elementary education, which had been established at the time of the drafting of the original text of the Constitution of 1917.

[85] Regarding the right to information, the Supreme Court ruled that a court cannot require a government agency to provide information to a private individual upon request, unless the law expressly provides for this. *Cf.* SJF, 7a, T. X, 15 Apr. 1995, p. 44. In the wake of new policies after 2000 to promote transparency, Congress adopted a new Information Law that fulfils this requirement of legislation to direct government agencies to divulge information. This law is discussed in Chapter 9 below, at text accompanying notes 97–104.

[86] During that same period, Article 28 of the Constitution was modified in order to establish the right to protection of the consumer which, in a strict sense, cannot be considered an entitlement.

[87] SJF, 8a, T. X, 4 June 1992, p. 272.

5. Human Rights

Following the emergence in the 1940s of a worldwide human rights movement, the Mexican state ratified a variety of international human rights treaties that have been incorporated into domestic law in accordance with the provisions of Article 133 of the Constitution. This Article states that treaties entered into by the President of the Republic and ratified by the Senate shall become 'the supreme law of the land throughout the Union' together with the Constitution and the laws that emanate therefrom. With regard to general compliance with constitutional precepts, human rights treaties may not violate any constitutionally guaranteed civil right (*garantía individual*) and, specifically, must conform to Article 15 which establishes that Mexico may not become a party to any international treaty that provides for the extradition of political prisoners or slaves or that abridges the scope of any of the constitutional protections (*garantías individuales*). Consequently, any other rights covered in any treaty executed by the state that do not violate the provisions of Article 15 of the Constitution shall become part of the body of law and all authorities shall adjust their conduct so as to respect these rights. Should it be found that any instrument or agent of the government or of the judiciary had breached the terms of a human rights treaty, the individual so harmed may file a double *amparo* suit, arguing both violation of the principle of legality of public acts (protection against arbitrary acts of public officials), which appears in the first paragraph of Article 16 of the Constitution, and failure to adhere to the provisions of the treaty itself.

Mexico is a party to thirty-eight international human rights treaties that are global in scope,[88] as well as nine regional human rights treaties.[89] This is not to say that the rights established in these treaties are fully recognized by the courts, however. For one thing, Mexico has filed reservations to some of the key human rights conventions because their provisions deviate from principles established in the Mexican Constitution.[90] Thus, while human rights treaties may in theory

[88] The most important human rights treaties to which Mexico is a party can be found at www.cndh.org.mx (site visited Jan. 2004). *See also* Corcuera Cabezut, S., *Derecho Constitucional y Derecho Internacional de los Derechos Humanos* (Mexico: Oxford University Press, 2000).

[89] The regional treaties include the Inter-American Convention on the Granting of Civil Rights to Women; the Inter-American Convention on the Granting of Political Rights to Women; the American Convention to Prevent and Punish the Crime of Torture; the Convention on Asylum and the Convention on Political Asylum; the Convention on the Nationality of Women; the Convention on Diplomatic Asylum; the Convention on Territorial Asylum; and the Convention to Prevent and Sanction Acts of Terrorism Taking the Form of Crimes against Persons and Related Extortion that are of International Significance. *See* www.cndh.org.mx (site visited Jan. 2004).

[90] Mexico has ratified 38 human rights treaties, and has filed reservations to 8 of these. Four of these reservations were filed with regard to the International Pact on Civil and Political Rights; 3 were filed concerning the American Convention on Human Rights; 2 were filed to both the Convention on the Status of Foreigners and the Convention on Nationality; and 1 reservation was filed with regard to each one of the following international instruments: the Convention on

carry the force of law in Mexico, in practice they are rarely, if ever, enforced by Mexican courts.

6. Constitutional Rights of Foreign Nationals

The Mexican Constitution grants foreign nationals a broad range of constitutional rights. Under Article 1, 'In the United Mexican States all persons shall enjoy the rights granted by this Constitution, which shall not be abridged nor suspended, except in cases and under circumstances that are established by the Constitution'. According to Article 33, 'Foreign nationals have the right to the constitutional protections (*garantías*) that are granted in Chapter 1, Title 1 of this Constitution'. In principle, therefore,[91] the Mexican Constitution provides protection of the basic civil rights and liberties, social rights, and human rights to all inhabitants of the country, be they nationals or foreigners.[92]

There are five exceptions to the preceding underlying precept regarding the rights of foreign nationals on Mexican soil. The first exception is found in Article 8 which grants the right of petition in political matters only to Mexican citizens. The second exception relates to the right of association for the purpose of participating in the political affairs of the country (Article 9), which cannot be exercised by foreigners. Third, freedom of movement of foreign nationals can be restricted by an administrative decision, as long as the decision is in keeping with laws on immigration, emigration, sanitation, and pernicious foreigners (Article 11). The fourth exception, stated in Article 12, is that titles of nobility, prerogatives, and inherited honours granted by any other country shall have no effect in Mexico. Finally, Article 27, section I, restricts the ability of foreigners to acquire direct dominion over land and waters that are in the prohibited zone (within 100 kilometres of any border, or within 50 kilometres of any coast),[93] and places relative restraints on acquisition of lands on Mexican soil elsewhere by requiring that foreign nationals appear before the Secretariat of Foreign Relations and agree (under oath) to be considered Mexican nationals with respect to their property and not invoke the protection of their governments.[94]

In addition, the broad constitutional protection enjoyed by foreign nationals is also qualified by the first paragraph of Article 33, which gives the Mexican

the Nationality of Women; the Convention on Territorial Asylum; the International Pact on Economic, Social and Cultural Rights; and the Convention on the Elimination of All Forms of Discrimination against Women. Source: www.cndh.org.mx (site visited Jan. 2004).

[91] SJC, 5a, T CIX, 10 Aug. 1951, p. 1330.

[92] Since the regulatory laws of Articles 4 and 5 of the Constitution established that foreign nationals could not engage in professional activities in Mexico, an interesting dilemma existed for many years. Subsequently, however, the Supreme Court has ruled on several occasions that such a provision was contrary to Article 5 of the Constitution which allows for broad freedom of work and, for this reason, the Court ruled in favour of the petitioners in many cases of requests for *amparo* brought on this issue. On this subject, *cf.* e.g. SJC, 5a, T. CXIV, 28 Nov. 1952, p. 477.

[93] *Cf.* SJC, 5a, T. CIV, 8 May 1950, p. 1348.

[94] *Cf.* SJC, 5a, T. LXXX, 14 Apr. 1944, p. 577.

President the authority 'to make any foreigner whose stay it deems undesirable to leave the country, immediately and without any need for any prior judicial hearing'. The federal courts have interpreted this power on several occasions, and have held that the President must provide legal and factual grounds for resolving to expel a foreigner in this way;[95] a foreign national may bring an *amparo* suit to claim a violation of constitutional protections that may have been committed in relation to the expulsion decree.[96] However, even though the *amparo* claim may be admissible, motions to suspend execution of the expulsion decree are not to be granted.[97] This provision has served as a deterrent to political involvement or to government criticism by the many foreign citizens to whom Mexico has given asylum over the course of the twentieth century.

7. Suspension of Individual Liberties

Under Article 29,[98] in extreme situations, the President is granted the power temporarily to nullify certain rights or all rights at a given point in time and for a length of time to be determined by these authorities. Such a declaration would have three major effects: first, federal and local authorities would no longer be required to follow the precepts of constitutional protections in performance of their duties; second, any legal provisions of inferior rank to the Constitution (laws, treaties, court judgements, etc.) could be created without observing these precepts; and third, individuals may not bring *amparo* suits to counteract violations of any suspended rights.[99]

The reasons for such a dramatic suspension of rights are circumscribed by the provisions of Article 29. A declaration of suspension of constitutional rights would be proper in the following circumstances: a military invasion of the country, a 'grave disturbance of the public peace', or any other event that 'puts society in grave danger or conflict'.

Although broad language is used to describe the circumstances in which a suspension can be declared, in principle this is justified because the purpose of this provision is to enable authorities to confront a situation that is as extraordinary as the measures being taken to combat it. In fact, the power to suspend individual guarantees under Article 29 has been exercised only once. This was in 1942 when, on the occasion of Mexico's entry into World War II, President Ávila Camacho partially suspended the rights and liberties guaranteed in Articles 4–7, 9–11, 14, 16, and 19–21 of the Constitution.[100]

[95] *Cf.* SJC, 5a, T. CX, 3 Oct. 1951 p. 112.

[96] *Cf.* SJC, 7a, Vol. 187–192, Sexta Parte, 4 July 1984, p. 74.

[97] SJF, 5a, T. XV, 2 July 1924, p. 25; Appendix to SJF, *1917–1975*, Tercera Parte, Segunda Sala, tesis 395, p. 652.

[98] *See* D.O. 13 June 1942.

[99] The second part of Article 29 also grants to the President the power to legislate in cases where constitutional rights have been suspended due to an emergency.

[100] *See* D.O. 13 June 1942.

The reluctance to suspend individual liberties is due both to the political constraints of such drastic action, and to the procedural constraints placed by Article 29 on the exercise of such a suspension. Only the President of the Republic can call for the suspension of constitutional rights, and before doing so, he must obtain prior consent of all the Secretaries of the cabinet,[101] of the administrative departments,[102] and of the Attorney General of the Republic. The measure must then be submitted to and approved by the Congress of the Union (both the Chamber of Deputies and the Senate) or, should these bodies be in recess, by their Permanent Commissions.

In addition, the suspension of constitutional rights should be duly circumscribed in terms of geographical coverage, the constitutional protections to be suspended, the effect on individuals, and the duration of the suspension. Coverage of the suspension, according to the powers granted by the Constitution, may encompass the entire country or just selected parts of domestic territory; however, the suspension may only take effect at the site of the invasion, 'grave disturbance' or events that 'put the country in grave danger or conflict'.

In principle, the Constitution permits suspension of rights if the exercise of these rights could effectively constitute an 'obstacle to confronting the situation readily and speedily'. Legal scholars have debated whether the right to life may or may not be suspended. Some experts argue that the right to life underlies all other rights and, consequently, may not be suspended; others say that the right to life is simply like any other right of the individual (Article 14) and, as such, may be suspended. There is no clear answer to this question, but it is evident that the early framers of the Mexican Constitution also grappled with this dilemma: the right to life could not be suspended under the Constitution of 1917, and yet, during the debates of the Constituent Congress of 1916–1917, this prohibition was lifted.

Article 29 establishes that under no circumstances can the suspension of rights be applied specifically to an individual and, accordingly, suspension decrees must be worded in general terms. This requirement derives specifically from another provision of Article 29, which states that suspension decrees must be made up of general resolutions, meaning provisions of a general, abstract, and impersonal nature.

Finally, on the subject of duration of suspensions, the Constitution states that the suspension of rights should last for a defined period of time. No further

[101] In accordance with Article 26 of the Organic Law of Federal Public Administration, at this time there are 18 Secretariats of State (the major government agencies equivalent to US Departments): Internal Affairs; Foreign Affairs; National Defence; Navy; Public Security; Treasury and Public Credit; Social Development; Environment and Natural Resources; Energy; Economy; Agriculture, Livestock, Rural Development, Fishing, and Nutrition; Communications and Transportation; Comptroller and Administrative Development; Public Education; Health; Labour and Welfare; Agrarian Reform; and Tourism.

[102] With the legal transformation of the Federal District [Mexico City], at this time no administrative departments exists within [the organizational structure of] the federal public administration.

elaboration is provided on this issue. However, based on the language of the Article, it is possible to extrapolate certain limitations: first, the duration of the suspension must coincide with the duration of the cause or event that gave rise to the request for suspension; and second, a specific date, known to all, must be set for termination of the suspension. If it should prove to be impossible to foresee the termination date of an event, the suspension may remain in effect until such time as the event or cause comes to an end.

8. Conclusion

Over the last two decades of the twentieth century, the protection of individual rights and liberties in Mexico was strengthened in direct proportion to the decline of the PRI's authoritarian power. Constitutional rights have long been inscribed in the Mexican Constitution, but were not always defended vigorously. Organic changes to judicial power (in the appointment of judges, discussed in Chapter 6 above, and in the jurisdiction of the Supreme Court, discussed in Chapter 8 below) have been responsible for a greater adherence to the rule of constitutional law in the protection of individual rights,[103] reinforcing freedom of association and freedom of speech.[104] There is still considerable room for improvement, especially in the ability of individuals with lower incomes to assert their rights in courts. Mexico has lagged behind the United States in the use of citizens' groups (non-governmental organizations and others) that employ the civil system (lawsuits, electoral politics, civil protest, education) to fight for individual rights. This is a legacy of Mexico's authoritarian and corporatist past, but that is likely to change. In the more open democratic environment of today, non-governmental organizations, unaligned with political parties, are becoming increasingly important to Mexico's future.

[103] *See* Cossío, J.R., *La Teoria Constitucional de la Suprema Corte de Justicia*, II, (Mexico: Fontamara, 2002) at 43.

[104] *See* Cossío *et al.*, *supra* note 61 at 109 *et seq.*

8

Judicial Procedures to Enforce the Constitution

1. Introduction

This Chapter describes the mechanisms built into the Mexican legal system to safeguard the supremacy of the Constitution over conflicting laws and governmental acts. The procedures discussed here—*juicios de amparo, controversias constitutionales*, and *acciones de inconstitutionalidad*—are both complex and unique to the Mexican legal system. In contrast with US constitutional practice, the procedures available for enforcement of the Mexican Constitution are not part of the ordinary judicial process, but are separate from all other judicial proceedings. In the United States, judicial review can be exercised during any judicial proceeding by judges, state or federal, at all levels of the judicial system.[1] Despite the influence of the US Constitution on many aspects of the Mexican Constitution, constitutional enforcement in Mexico follows the European civil law tradition, by which enforcement of constitutional principles can only take place in special proceedings that are the sole jurisdiction of courts with specific jurisdiction over constitutional matters.[2] It is by means of the three procedures discussed in this Chapter that the supremacy of the Constitution guaranteed by Article 133 is ensured.

The mechanisms for enforcing the Constitution have undergone major changes since the judicial reforms of 1994, which were discussed above in Chapter 6 and are dealt with in more detail below. Prior to that date, while Mexican lawyers extolled the virtues of the *amparo* system, there were significant deficiencies in judicial enforcement of basic rights. The recent reforms have corrected some, but not all, of these deficiencies.

Judicial enforcement of the Constitution may be divided into three major subjects. Section 2 of this Chapter deals with *amparo*, or the protection of individual constitutional rights. Section 3 deals with 'constitutional controversies', or disputes between competing governmental authorities. Section 4, on *acciones de inconstitucionalidad*, discusses the most recent of the forms of judicial

[1] Rotunda, R., and Nowak, J., *Treatise on Constitional Law* (St Paul, Minn: West Group, 1999) vol. 1 at 40–41.

[2] *See generally* Fix-Zamudio, H., 'La justicia constitucional en lbero América y la declaración general de inconstitucionalidad', in *Latinoamérica: Constitución, proceso y derechos humanos* (Mexico: Miguel Angel Porrúa, 1988) at 337 *et seq.*; Cossío Díaz, J.R., *La Teoría constitucional de la Suprema Corte de Justicia* (Mexico: Fontamara, 2002) chapter II.

reform, created in 1994 as a mechanism of challenging unconstitutional laws adopted by the Congress or by state legislatures.

Judicial enforcement of the Constitution, suspect during the PRI's authoritarianism, has now improved in Mexico, thanks to procedural reforms as well as to the increased independence of the judiciary, as discussed above in Chapter 6.[3] In recent years, the federal judiciary has played an increasingly important role in resolving governmental conflicts (between the President and state governors, between the Congress and the President, etc.)[4] representing a fundamental change in the balance of powers in Mexico.[5]

2. The *Juicio de Amparo*: Petitions for Judicial Protection against Violations of Constitutionally Guaranteed Rights of the Individual

2.1. Significance of the *Juicio de Amparo*

Before trying to understand the complicated rules and procedures that embody *amparo*, one must first grasp the importance of *amparo* to the Mexican legal system. It is no exaggeration to say that the record of adherence to the rule of law in Mexico is in direct proportion to the effectiveness of federal courts in using the *amparo* procedures, since it is by means of *amparo* that individuals are protected by the courts against governmental abuses of authority. The use of *amparo* is widespread: according to the Chief Justice of the Supreme Court, in 1997 Mexican federal courts heard a total of 343,162 *amparo* suits throughout the country.[6] The number of *amparo* suits brought each year has steadily risen,[7] as citizens have increasingly resorted to the federal courts for judicial protection of their constitutional rights. The sheer volume of *amparo* cases has not necessarily translated into strict adherence to the rule of law, however, for reasons discussed below.

The widespread use of *amparo* is due to a broad interpretation of the constitutional guarantees (*garantías individuales*) that the procedure is designed to protect. *Amparo* provides protection to such a broad range of individual rights that most acts undertaken by government agencies or officials are subject to *amparo* review. By virtue of Articles 12 and 16 of the Constitution, all acts of government officials are subject to due process (a broad concept by itself) and must conform with applicable laws, treaties, and administrative regulations.

[3] *See* Chapter 6 at section 3.

[4] Cossío Díaz, J.R., CAMBIO SOCIAL Y CAMBIO JURÍDICO (Mexico: Miguel Angel Porrúa, 2001) chapter IV.

[5] *See also* Cossío Díaz, J.R., RÉGIMEN AUTORITARIO Y DOGMÁTICA CONSTITUCIONAL (Mexico: Fontamara, 2000).

[6] Suprema Corte de Justicia de la Nación, Anexo al Informe anual de estadística 1997, Mexico, 1997.

[7] For example, in 1990, 50,028 matters of direct *amparo* and 22,748 of *amparo* reviews were heard by Circuit Court Panels. By contrast, in 1997, 98,435 direct *amparo* cases and 45,270 *amparo* reviews were heard by Circuit Courts. *Ibid.* at 31.

Thus, almost any final act of any government official at the federal, local, municipal, or Federal District levels, and within each branch of government (legislative, executive, and judicial), is susceptible to challenge under *amparo* law. For example, the failure of a public official to observe an administrative regulation may become a violation of 'constitutional guarantees' by contravening Articles 12 and/or 16, providing grounds for abrogation of the official act by an *amparo* judgment.

Amparo petitions may be filed to challenge the constitutionality of numerous types of acts: procedural errors in constitutional reforms (e.g. lack of a proper quorum in Congress for approval of a reform); laws passed by the Federal Congress or by state legislatures; administrative rules issued by the President of the Republic or governors of states; final judgments handed down by the courts of any state, the Federal District, or the Federal government; arbitrary arrests conducted by police; resolutions issued by any administrative authority; expropriations of assets, etc. *Amparo* has become so crucial to litigation that in many judicial and administrative proceedings the parties are not as interested in the outcome of the ordinary process itself as they are in using the regular trial as preparation for a subsequent *amparo* suit. For this reason, the *amparo* suit to be brought subsequently has a direct bearing upon the procedural strategy adopted in the underlying lawsuit.

Mexican legal scholars take great pride in the *amparo*, a uniquely Mexican legal institution.[8] Federal judges are generally considered to be fair and independent in deciding *amparo* cases, the courts are considered to be accessible, and there is generally a high level of compliance by public officials with the courts' final judgments. On the other hand, if we compare judicial interpretation of fundamental rights in Mexico to that of other countries of the world, there are glaring deficiencies. Critics consider the *amparo* procedures to be overly complicated and unwieldy, which translates to high costs for litigants and therefore unequal access to justice. Judges are also criticized for giving inconsistent results (bearing in mind, as discussed below, that a single *amparo* decision is only binding on the parties before the court).

At the end of the 1950s, and again in the 1970s, Mexican courts became inundated with *amparo* cases,[9] and in dealing with the backlog, they began to deem many petitions for *amparo* inadmissible based on a strict interpretation of procedural requirements. Far from a streamlined process, *amparo* gradually turned into a subtle and intricate tapestry of legal nuances. Even though the technical requirements have been relaxed by recent judicial reforms, the complexity of *amparo* procedures continues to be cited as a major obstacle for

[8] *Amparo* procedures based on the Mexican model have been adopted by a number of Latin American countries. Fix-Zamudio, H., 'El juicio de amparo en Latino América', in *LATINOAMÉRICA: CONSTITUCIÓN, PROCESO Y DERECHOS HUMANOS*, Fix-Zamudio, ed., (Mexico: Miguel Angel Porrúa, 1988) at 273 *et seq*.

[9] *See* Molina Pasquel, R., 'Algunos problemas relacionados con el rezago de la Suprema Corte', REVISTA DE LA FACULTAD DE DERECHO, Num. 3–4 (July–Dec. 1951) at 11–40.

litigants, since many attorneys lack the competence to obtain the protection their clients seek. *Amparo* cases call for the technical expertise of specialized legal counsel who tend to command high attorneys' fees, thus rendering this recourse unavailable to people of limited means. Other criticisms of *amparo* involve disagreement over the concept of government 'authorities', to whom the procedure applies; the rules governing the filing of motions; the binding effect of judgments on the parties; and the lack of clear definition of the different types of *amparo*, which are discussed below.

A final criticism relates to the way in which *amparo* serves to ensure the predominance of the federal courts over the state judiciary. Because decisions of state court judges are considered official acts subject to *amparo* review, the federal courts are empowered to review all decisions of state courts; this is known as 'judicial' *amparo*. After a final judgement has been rendered in any criminal, civil, labour, or administrative matter in any state district court, any party who feels that any of the rights or protections conferred upon individuals by Article 14 of the Constitution has been violated may petition a panel of Circuit Court judges to issue a ruling on the constitutionality of the state judge's decision. This is true even if the state court's decision was based entirely on state law, since an error in the application of state law becomes a federal constitutional matter by denying due process or equal protection. This exclusive authority of the federal courts to interpret and review the bulk of state laws has led to calls for decentralization and streamlining of the judiciary,[10] and continues to generate tension between federal and state courts.

Past efforts to reform the *amparo* system have been largely ineffectual. In the face of domestic and foreign criticism of civil rights abuses, in the early 1990s President Salinas created the *Comisión Nacional de Derechos Humanos* (National Human Rights Commission)[11] to supplement the *amparo* system in

[10] In a document called the 'Declaration of Querétaro', signed on 10 Nov. 1994, by the chief judges of the Superior Courts of Justice of all the states of the Federation and the Federal District of Mexico City, state court judges decried the subordination of state courts to the federal courts, causing inefficiency and preventing judges from disposing of cases in a speedy fashion. Among other suggestions, the judges called for federal courts to assume jurisdiction over cases involving concurrent jurisdiction (discussed in Chapter 6 above, at text accompanying note 115), which represent 50% of the cases brought before local and state authorities. (The state of Nayarit went even further: in July 1996, the highest court of that state unanimously held that state courts would refrain from hearing commercial cases until the federal courts with jurisdiction in the state of Nayarit share the caseload in commercial matters involving concurrent jurisdiction. *See* Amlonz, Agustín, 'Alcanzar la impunidad y la inconsequencia de los poderes', *Proceso*, 15 Sep. 1996, at 32.) To decentralize and speed up the *amparo* process, the judges called for the creation of local state supreme courts that would handle *amparo* review of court decisions in matters that do not deal with true constitutional issues. *See* Cossío Diaz, J.R., 'Federalismo judicial', in *Este País*, Nov. 1996, at 34–36.

[11] The Commission lacks enforcement power, and can only bring public opinion to bear on human rights abuses. The head of the National Human Rights Commission, or *Presidente*, is often referred to in the popular press as the 'Ombudsman'. The first Ombudsman was Dr Jorge Carpizo, a respected constitutional law scholar, who later served as Attorney General and Secretary of the Interior. Subsequent heads of the Commission have been similarly respected jurists with close ties to the government. Despite these political ties, the Human Rights

strengthening adherence to the rule of law by government officials.[12] More recently, in late 1999, the Supreme Court appointed a commission[13] to prepare the draft of a new *amparo* law that would simplify and improve the administration of *amparo* cases. The commission submitted a draft of a new *amparo* law to the Supreme Court in April, 2001;[14] even though the commission produced a draft, there has been little Congressional support for the initiative.

2.2. Historical Background[15]

Today's *amparo* proceeding has evolved over the past two centuries. As Mexicans began to plan for independence and constitutional government, they contemplated adopting a constitution and laws, under the influence of US and French models, that would contain provisions for defending the rights of man through judicial review and the protections provided by *habeas corpus*.[16] The use of *amparo* was established early on as the principal means of accomplishing this.

Commission has maintained a generally favourable reputation for serious investigation of human rights abuses. For a discussion of the National Human Rights Commission, *see* Chapter 6 above at text accompanying notes 162–164. *See also* www.cndh.org (site visited Jan. 2004).

[12] On 5 June 1990, President Salinas issued an Executive Decree creating the National Human Rights Commission. D.O. 6 Jul. 1990. On 29 January 1992, Congress adopted an amendment to Article 102, Section B, of the Constitution, giving the National Human Rights Commission constitutional status. D.O. 28 Jan. 1992. During congressional debates on the amendment, Victor Marín Orduna Muñoz, a *diputado* of the National Action Party (PAN), stated the following: 'many members of the Federal Judiciary hold that the National Human Rights Commission is not necessary because individual rights and human rights in Mexico are already safeguarded by the *amparo* process. True though this may be, we must also recognize that although the *amparo* proceeding has been in existence for more than 100 years in Mexico and has operated and shall continue to operate, we cannot fail to recognize that the *amparo* process has turned into an extremely formal, extremely rigid structure and that for someone to be able to file a petition for *amparo*, he or she must have access to the services of a good attorney, an expert in that field of the law and, unfortunately, gentlemen, experts in this area charge a lot of money. The recourse of the *amparo* process is not available to just anyone, due to the high cost that it entails.' *Cámara de Diputados* of the H. Congress, Derechos del Pueblo Mexicano, tomo X, 4a. Ed., p. 207.

[13] The commission consisted of 2 Supreme Court Justices (Román Palacios and Silva Meza), 2 appellate judges (Esquinca and Saloma), 2 academics (Fix-Zamudio and Cossío Díaz) and two litigators (Quijano and Zaldívar).

[14] Proyecto de la Suprema Corte de Justicia de la Nación de la Ley Reglamentario de los Artículos 103 y 107 de la Constitución Política de los Estados Unidos Mexicanos (Mexico: SCJN, 2001).

[15] The *amparo* procedure has received much attention from scholars. For a full discussion of the history and operation of *amparo*, *see* Azuela, M., '*El amparo y sus reformas*', in *El pensamiento jurídico de México en el derecho constitucional* (Mexico: Manuel Porrúa, 1961) at 68 *et seq.*; Barragán Barragán, J., '*Algunos documentos para el estudio del origen del juicio de amparo, 1812–1861*' (Mexico: UNAM, Instituto de Investigaciones Jurídicas, 1987) at 295; Ortiz Ramírez, S., *Derecho constitucional mexicano: sus antecedentes históricos, las garantías individuales y el juicio de amparo* (Mexico: Cultura, 1961) at 628.

[16] A synopsis of the most important of these legal provisions can be found in Fix-Zamudio, H., *Justicia Constitucional, Ombudsman y Derechos Humanos* (Mexico: CNDH, 1997) at 153–159.

The earliest example of *amparo* dates back to the Political Constitution of the State of Yucatán enacted on 16 May 1841. The architect of the *amparo* procedure in that Constitution was Manuel Crescencio Rejón, who drew his inspiration mainly from Alexis de Tocqueville's work, *La Démocratie en Amérique* of 1836. Under the 1841 Constitution of Yucatán, petitions for judicial protection (*amparo*) were admissible only in cases of unconstitutional acts. When claims dealt with unconstitutional laws and decrees enacted by the legislature or decisions issued by the governor, *amparo* petitions were filed before the state Supreme Court; in cases involving state officials, suits were brought before local judges; and, when claims were lodged against local judicial officials, the request was filed before their judicial superiors. In contrast with present-day *amparo*, this process in mid-nineteenth century Yucatán was not separate from ordinary judicial proceedings, and no specialized courts were created with exclusive jurisdiction in *amparo* cases. Instead, all judges were granted the power to refrain from enforcing any law or act that ran contrary to the provisions of the Yucatán Constitution.

The next important development occurred in 1847, with the adoption by the federal Congress of the Act of Reform of the Federal Constitution of 1824 (*Acta Constitutiva de Reformas*), which was drafted by Mariano Otero.[17] Article 25 of this Act stated that:

> The courts of the Federation shall afford protection to [*ampararán*] any inhabitant of the Republic in the exercise and preservation of the rights granted to him or her by this Constitution and constitutional laws, against any attack by the legislative and executive branches, whether of the Federation or of the States; said courts being limited to providing protection in the specific case that is the subject of the process, without making any general statement regarding the law or act that gave rise to the protection.[18]

The provision of Article 25 that limits the effect of an *amparo* action to the parties involved in the specific case before the court, without nullifying the law itself or affecting persons who are not parties to the suit, has become known as the *Fórmula Otero*, which continues in force to this day.

Under the *Acta de Reformas*, the new *amparo* procedure quickly achieved a measure of success. Government officials generally complied with *amparo* judgments, and the right of *amparo* became closely intertwined with the rights and liberties conferred upon individuals by the Constitution. As a result of this early success, the drafters of the Constitution of 1857 were inspired to include the *amparo* procedure in the Constitution itself, and the

[17] Despite a short life, Mariano Otero (1817 to 1850) was to have a significant impact on Mexican public law. As a young man, he was elected to the Mexican Congress, and in 1848 he became Minister of Internal and Foreign Affairs in the liberal government of President José Joaquín de Herrera. In 1847, during the discussions alluded to in the text, Otero expounded the theory that *amparo* judgments should only be binding on the parties to the case decided before the court. Since that time, this limitation has been known as the *Fórmula Otero*.

[18] The Act may be found at www.juridicas.unam.mx (site visited Jan. 2004) at 'Legislación Federal Mexicana', 'Documentos Constitucionales Históricos'. *See also* Tena Ramírez, F., LEYES FUNDAMENTALES DE MÉXICO (Mexico: Porrúa, 20th ed., 1998) at 475.

procedure has held constitutional status ever since. The *amparo* process established in the Constitution of 1857 underwent major transformations in the *Amparo* Laws of 1861, 1869, and 1882, and in the Federal Codes of Civil Procedure of 1897 and 1908. Under these procedures, *amparo* petitions could be filed before federal district court judges at the trial level (upon first hearing), and before the Supreme Court of Justice on appeal (upon review). *Amparo* thus became a broad system of protection of the rights of man enshrined in the Constitution.

The principal issue debated during this period was whether to permit *amparo* petitions to be filed against court judgments, which could be considered violations of Article 14 of the Constitution. The arguments in favour of this concept, *amparo judicial*, as it came to be known, questioned the impartiality of the local courts; the arguments against criticized the centralization of power and the potential for backlog of cases before the Supreme Court.[19] In the end, the supporters of judicial *amparo* prevailed, and ever since, the use of *amparo* to contest local court decisions has clogged the federal courts with cases. Many of the reforms to the *amparo* procedure and to the federal courts have been occasioned by the case overload that resulted from judicial *amparo*.[20]

Articles 103 and 107 of the Constitution of 1917 incorporated most elements of the *amparo* procedure, including judicial *amparo*, that had been developed previously. Since the adoption of the 1917 Constitution, four major reforms of the *amparo* process have come about.

The first important change involved the organizational structure and jurisdiction of the federal courts. Circuit court panels of judges (*Tribunales Colegiados de Circuito*) were created (1951), and the jurisdiction of the Supreme Court was reformed (1951, 1968, and 1988) to direct *amparo* cases to the federal District Courts and Courts of Appeal, allowing the Supreme Court to engage itself increasingly with *amparo* cases that raised significant constitutional issues.

Another group of changes pertained to the procedure of *amparo* actions, and resulted from Supreme Court opinions that were eventually incorporated into revisions of the *Amparo* Law.

In 1963, several provisions were adopted in order to protect the rights of the members of common farmlands or communities (*ejidatarios* or *comuneros*), guaranteed in Article 27 of the Constitution. These reforms eventually led to the incorporation of a special section (*Libro Segundo*) into the *Ley de Amparo*, which afforded protection to this specific segment of the population.

Finally, in 1988, state and local courts were denied the power to directly interpret the constitutionality of laws or to refrain from enforcing or applying laws that were contrary to the Constitution.

[19] *See* Rabasa, Emilio O., *El Artículo 14 estudio constitucional y el juicio constitucional: orígenes, teoría y extensión* (Mexico: Porrúa, 1969).

[20] *Cf.* Fix-Zamudio, Héctor and Cossío Díaz, José Ramón, *El poder judicial en el ordenamiento jurídico mexicano* (Mexico: Fondo de Cultura Económia, 1996).

2.3. Procedural requirements in *Amparo* cases

Access to judicial protection of constitutional rights may be asserted by any private party, whether a Mexican or foreign citizen, through *amparo*. This procedure may be used not only by individuals and private persons, but also by *personas morales*, that is, by corporations, associations, or other legal entities. Government officials and agencies may not bring an *amparo* action, except in cases when property rights (*intereses patrimoniales)* have been violated by another government agency or by a law.[21]

This section highlights certain procedural requirements that must be observed in proceeding with an *amparo* suit.[22]

2.3.1. The Rule of Materiality (Base Material)

The first requirement of admissibility of an *amparo* action is known as the rule of 'materiality' (*base material*), which is established by Articles 103 and 107, Section I of the Constitution. Under this rule, requests for *amparo* are only admissible when violations of constitutionally guaranteed rights are committed by government authorities. Supreme Court and Circuit Court opinions have shed light on the meaning of this requirement, by defining, for purposes of *amparo*, the terms 'authorities' and 'acts of authority' (official acts). According to the case-law, for purposes of *amparo*, the term 'authorities' encompasses all persons who hold positions of public power, whether legally or *de facto*, and who, consequently, are *materially* able to perform official acts or duties, as a result of the public office they hold.[23] The Circuit Courts of Appeals have held that 'acts of authority' (official acts) should be understood as conduct of officials or employees of government or autonomous (decentralized) agencies who, as their official duty, unilaterally impose obligations on private individuals, either by modifying existing obligations or by abridging rights of the individual.[24]

2.3.2. The Rule of Jurisdiction (Regla de Competencia)

The second requirement, called the 'rule of jurisdiction' (*regla de competencia*), is that *amparo* suits may only be heard by the federal judiciary, i.e. by the Supreme Court (sitting *en banc* or in panels), by the Circuit Courts (either unitary or collegiate), or by District Court judges.[25]

[21] *Amparo* Law, Article 9.

[22] The *Amparo* Law contains many complicated procedural requirements that are spread throughout the law. *See generally* Bazdresch, L., *El Juicio de Amparo: Curso General* (Mexico: Trillas, 3d ed., 1997) at 43–45.

[23] Appendix to the SJF, 1917–1918, Segunda Parte, Salas y Tesis Comunes, tesis jurisprudencial 300, p. 519.

[24] Informe de Labores de 1988, Tercera Parte, Tribunales Colegiados de Circuito, p. 187.

[25] As an exception, local judges may hear *amparo* cases, only in accordance with Article 37 of the Law of *Amparo*, which states that such judges may do so in order to assist the federal judiciary and that this may only be in cases involving violations of the constitutionally guaranteed individual rights (*garantías individuales*) that are set forth in Articles 16, in criminal matters, 19 and 20, Sections I, VIII and X, paragraphs one and two of the Federal Constitution.

2.3.3. *Injury to the Claimant*

The third rule refers to 'harm to the claimant', and holds that Mexican citizens or foreign nationals (including domestic or foreign corporations) that bring an *amparo* action must claim some harm to their legally protected interests, and may not simply file a challenge to findings-of-fact or to uncertain events that may take place at some future date. On this subject, the Supreme Court has held that, for the purposes of *amparo*, a person is considered to have been harmed when his or her legally protected interests, such as person, property, or assets, are directly harmed as a result of any law or official act.[26]

2.3.4. *Rule of the Action* (Base de Acción)

The fourth rule, known as the *base de acción*, or 'rule of the action', requires that *amparo* suits must be brought either by an interested party or by a legal representative thereof; that the complaint must be filed in writing and must meet certain standards of form; and that established procedures must be diligently followed by the appropriate court.

2.3.5. *Unappealable Acts of Government Officials*

The fifth rule involves two major requirements. First, claims may only be filed against a government official, not against acts performed by private individuals (Mexican Constitution, Article 103; *Amparo* Law, Article 1). Second, the act or decision that is the subject of the complaint must be unappealable; in other words, all other means of legal recourse must have previously been exhausted (Mexican Constitution, Article 107, Section III; *Amparo* Law, Article 73, Sections XIII and XIV).

2.3.6. *Nexus between Complaint and Official Act* (Base de la Sentencia)

The sixth rule requires that there must be a clear and direct link between the complaint and the official act complained of (*base de la sentencia*); the case may only be decided on the basis of evidence that the government official in question had at his or her disposal in order to decide the matter; and, the official act must specifically affect the person who filed for judicial protection (*amparo*), since under the *Fórmula Otero*,[27] judges may not give redress to the general population for laws or acts that gave rise to the *amparo* petition.

2.3.7. *Temporary Suspension of Official Acts*

The seventh requirement is known as the rule of 'suspension', and provides that execution of the official act that is being challenged may be stayed or postponed by the court, either at the court's initiative or at the request of an interested party, until the *amparo* case is resolved. The Supreme Court has held that when suspension is ordered by the court, the status quo must remain as it was

[26] Apéndice al SJF, 1917–1988, Segunda Parte, Salas y Tesis Comunes, p. 2092.
[27] *See supra*, text accompanying notes 17, 18.

at the time the suspension was decreed, and the court must not order restoration to the status quo before the (alleged) violation of the Constitution took place, because the latter remedy can only be the result of the final judgment of the *amparo* case.[28]

2.3.8. *Economy in Litigation*

Finally, another governing principle commonly mentioned by Mexican legal experts is the rule of 'procedural economy in litigation'. According to this principle, if during the course of ordinary litigation (whether civil or criminal) a party alleges that any of its constitutionally guaranteed rights has been violated, the affected party must wait until final judgment is handed down before filing an *amparo* petition, to prevent several hearings on interlocutory motions holding up normal development of the underlying trial.

2.4. Types of *Amparo*

2.4.1. *Indirect and Direct* Amparo

A major obstacle to understanding *amparo* has to do with its sheer complexity. Professor Héctor Fix-Zamudio, one of the leading constitutional law scholars in Mexico, has referred to the *amparo* as:

> a federation of procedural instruments, each serving a specific protective function, which in turn determines a series of particular aspects that cannot be understood except by separate analysis. In fact, in Mexican *amparo* law we find five distinct functions, since *amparo* can be used to protect personal liberty; to counteract unconstitutional laws; as a means of challenging judicial rulings; to file claims against acts and decisions of the administration in power; and, lastly, to protect the social rights of peasants who operate under the regime of agrarian reform.[29]

Mexican courts and legal experts identify two broad categories of *amparo*, according to the number of procedural levels (*instancias*) or courts involved in the process: 'indirect' and 'direct' *amparo*.[30]

Indirect amparo This encompasses all two-stage procedures that begin at the District Court level and move up either to the Circuit Court, or in some instances, all the way up to the Supreme Court; the procedural track that the case follows depends on the subject matter of the challenge. As explained below,[31] the subject matter of indirect *amparo* claims is as broad and diverse as the processes designed to resolve the claims. By means of indirect *amparo*, challenges can be lodged against the constitutionality of legal provisions that apply to the general population (*amparo contra leyes*), against most administrative

[28] SJF, Apéndice 1917–1985, Octava Parte, p. 490. Also *see* related thesis on page 491 of the same compilation.

[29] *See* Fix-Zamudio, *supra* note 8 at 30–31 (authors' trans.)

[30] The Supreme Court has established that a single act may not be indiscriminately subject to both a direct and an indirect *amparo* claim, since the admissibility of direct *amparo* precludes admissibility of the indirect type. Apéndice al SJF, 1917–1988. Segunda Parte, Salas y Tesis Comunes, p. 278.

[31] *See infra*, Section 2.4.2.

decisions resulting from proceedings other than a trial (*amparo administrativo* and some types of agrarian *amparo*), and against arbitrary detention (*amparo habeas corpus*). After a request for *amparo* is filed by an individual, a District Court Judge presides over and hears the first stage of an indirect *amparo* proceeding. The first stage involves serving notice on the government official allegedly at fault; setting a date for the hearing known as a 'constitutional hearing' (*audiencia constitucional*); receiving the briefs or written reports that must be filed by the government official in question; holding the hearing; and issuing the final decision (*resolución definitiva*).[32] This *resolución definitiva* may be appealed by filing a motion to review before the Supreme Court, provided that the case involves a challenge to the constitutionality of a law that applies to the general population; in all other instances, appeal must be made to the Collegiate Circuit Courts. This process of review before the Supreme Court or Collegiate Circuit Court resembles any other appeals process: one Supreme Court Associate Justice or Circuit Court Judge, as the case may be, takes his or her turn drafting a proposed judgment which, in turn, is discussed and eventually approved by the appropriate body sitting *en banc*.[33]

Direct amparo This encompasses all processes that must be heard in a single stage before panels of Circuit Court judges.[34] This type of *amparo* is the process designed for individuals to assert their right to judicial protection against a decision of any Mexican court at any level of government, local, state, or federal, in either criminal, civil, administrative, or labour matters, and is also known as 'judicial *amparo*' (*amparo judicial*). The Supreme Court has ruled that direct *amparo* cases challenging final court judgments can only be brought by individuals who were party to the underlying case; individuals who were not party to that case who wish to challenge the same judgment must seek federal protection before District Court judges by indirect *amparo*.[35]

The procedure followed in direct *amparo* cases before the Circuit Court panel begins with the filing of the request for protection (*amparo*) against a judicial official who issued what is believed to be a faulty act or ruling. Aside from the complainant (*quejoso*), the parties to the suit are the judicial official whose ruling is being questioned, acting as the defendant in the proceeding, and the opposing party in the underlying trial, who is given the name of 'harmed third party' (*tercero perjudicado*). After the submissions of the parties are received,

[32] On average, it takes 4 months in this type of case for the final decision to be handed down. On this topic, *see* Estudio de la creación y comportamiento de las cargas de trabajo de los órganos jurisdiccionales del Poder Judicial de la Federación, Suprema Corte de Justicia de la Nación, Tomo I, 1997.

[33] It usually takes the Supreme Court from 60 to 90 days to hand down a decision when sitting *en banc*, and from 40 to 60 days when sitting in smaller panels; it takes Circuit Court panels approximately from 2 to 3 months to do likewise. *Ibid.*

[34] Direct *amparo* cases are always filed with a Tribunal Colegiado de Circuito. The only exception to this is when the Supreme Court uses its power of 'attraction' under Article 107 of the Constitution (discussed in Chapter 6 above at text accompanying note 142) to hear an *amparo* action that raises important constitutional questions.

[35] Apéndice al SJF, 1917–1988, Segunda Parte, Salas y Tesis Comunes, p. 277.

one of three Collegiate Circuit Court judges on the panel hearing these cases takes his or her turn in drafting the final proposed judgment, which is discussed and voted upon by the rest of the panel.

Under direct *amparo*, the final judgment is unappealable, except when the complainant challenges the constitutionality of a law, or when the Circuit Court has taken it upon itself directly to interpret a constitutional provision. In such cases, the Supreme Court has sole jurisdiction to hear what is known as 'direct *amparo* on review' (*amparo directo en revisión*), by which the Court is to issue a ruling exclusively on the constitutional precept or issue in question (Mexican Constitution, Article 107, Section VIII).

2.4.2. Categorization by Underlying Subject Matter

In addition to categorizing *amparo* as either direct or indirect, legal scholars have analysed separate classes of *amparo* proceedings according to the *subject matter* each type is designed to protect. This analysis is preferred here, as being more analytically relevant. Nevertheless, in the following analysis of *amparo* according to subject matter, the reader must be aware that certain subjects may lend themselves either to direct or indirect *amparo*, as those terms have just been explained.

Amparo contra leyes: *petitions for judicial protection against unconstitutional laws* *Amparo contra leyes* allows the court to review, in a single stage, the constitutionality of legal provisions that apply to the general public.[36] This includes the constitutionality of constitutional reforms (only in cases involving challenges to errors of procedure in adoption of the reform, such as lack of ratification by the required number of states, and challenges based on the substance of the reform); the constitutionality of laws issued by the federal Congress, by the state legislatures or by the Federal District, or by the President of the Republic acting under Articles 29 and 31 of the Constitution (state of emergency, other special conditions); the constitutionality of international treaties entered into by the President of the Republic and approved by the Senate; and the constitutionality of regulations issued by the President of the Republic, by governors of the states, or by the mayor of the Federal District of Mexico City (Mexican Constitution, Article 107, Section VIII).

Amparo review of the constitutionality of any laws, treaties, or regulations begins when a claim is filed by the affected individual before a District Court judge against the government official or officials who issued the provision (called the 'responsible party', or *persona responsable*) who becomes the defendant in the suit. In cases involving a legal provision which, merely by being enacted, compromises the constitutional rights of the claimant, the request for

[36] According to the Supreme Court, when judicial protection is sought against the unconstitutionality of laws (*amparo contra leyes*), the complainant may challenge only the particular provision of a law that is considered to be unconstitutional, and need not challenge the whole body of the law in which the allegedly unconstitutional precept or provision is found. Informe de Labores de 1989, Primera Parte, Tribunal Pleno, p. 584.

amparo must be filed within thirty days from the time the provision goes into effect. In cases involving official acts of a government that are executed on the basis of a provision that is called into question, the request must be filed within fifteen days of the date of performance of the act.

Unlike the general rule in *amparo*,[37] which requires the complainant to exhaust all remedies before recurring to *amparo*, in an *amparo contra leyes*, the complainant may seek judicial protection against unconstitutional laws directly before a District Court Judge without exhausting administrative or other remedies. The importance of resolving the constitutionality of a law of general application justifies direct recourse to the courts in *amparo contra leyes* in these cases.

As noted above,[38] judgments by Collegiate Circuit Courts in cases of direct *amparo* are not appealable, unless they involve the constitutionality of a law or an interpretation by the Collegiate Circuit Court of a constitutional provision, in which case appeal from the Circuit Court decision may be made directly to the Supreme Court, in a procedure called 'direct *amparo* on review' (*amparo directo en revisión*). Indeed, it is possible for a Collegiate Circuit Court to refuse to decide a case that has important constitutional implications, preferring instead to send the case directly to the Supreme Court for review. Appeals to the Supreme Court in such cases are intended to promote uniformity in constitutional interpretation of laws and regulations that apply to the general public.

Even though *amparo contra leyes* deals exclusively with laws and regulations that apply to the general public, the *Fórmula Otero* requires that any *amparo judgment* rendered by the court does not apply to the population at large, but only to the individual who filed the claim. When this type of judicial protection is granted, the legal provision ceases to apply to the claimant by virtue of the court's decision; furthermore, that provision may never be applied to the complainant by any judicial officer at any later date. The result is to severely limit the effect of *amparo* judgments, an outcome that is dealt with at the end of this section.

Habeas corpus amparo *Amparo* can also be brought against acts that endanger the life of a person, infringe one's personal liberty, or violate Article 22 of the Constitution (prohibiting cruel and unusual punishment, excessive fines, and confiscation of property). This type of request for *amparo* can be brought by any individual and may be filed either in written form or orally by appearing before a judge at any time. Additionally, should the offended party be unable to appear or to file on his or her own behalf, the request may be filed by any other person in representation of the affected party. This request is submitted to a District Court judge, who may issue an injunction (*suspensión del acto*) to stay the act being challenged, or take any measure that may be required to bring the complainant before the court to ascertain his or her well-being.[39]

[37] *See supra*, Section 2.3.5. [38] *See supra*, Section 2.4.1, final paragraph.

[39] In some instances, state and municipal court judges may assist in *amparo* cases. In areas where no District Court judge sits, a person may file a *habeas corpus amparo* request before a judge of any level. In these circumstances, state and municipal judges are empowered to receive

Administrative Amparo (amparo strictu sensu) This permits an individual or legal entity to seek protection of his or her constitutionally guaranteed civil rights and liberties (*garantías individuales*) against acts of government officials when no other formal judicial or administrative process has been established for this purpose, except in cases involving acts committed by agrarian officials or acts that affect the liberty or integrity of the individual, which are the subject of *habeus corpus amparo* and agrarian *amparo*. (When a formal judicial process exists to tend to such violations of individual rights, these claims are the subject of judicial *amparo*, described above.[40]) Administrative *amparo* is designed to safeguard a large number of civil liberties, such as the freedoms of expression, assembly, association, etc., that may be committed by a broad array of federal, state, Federal District, or municipal administrative officials. Procedurally, administrative *amparo* is heard in a two-stage process identical to the one described above concerning *amparo contra leyes*.

Originally, administrative *amparo* was very broad and important, because there were very few federal or local courts with special jurisdiction to oversee the legality of official administrative acts at all levels of government. Subsequently, however, Congress and state legislatures created many administrative tribunals for this purpose, with the power to hold public officials accountable to the law and the Constitution for their official acts. Moreover, case overload in the area of administrative *amparo* has been gradually alleviated due to a shift in the procedural track that these cases follow. Before an individual may resort to filing a request for administrative *amparo*, all other remedies and means of appeal provided for by the different codes of procedure in force must have been exhausted.[41] Administrative proceedings are heard by administrative courts (*tribunales administrativos*),[42] and judgments handed down by these courts are appealable by judicial *amparo*.

Agrarian amparo: *Judicial Protection Against Violations of Agrarian Reform Law* As noted in Chapter 1 above, the Mexican Revolution and the Constitution of 1917 emphasized the plight of the disadvantaged, particularly the rural peasants and the working classes. Many felt that a procedure was needed to protect peasants whose land was under the communal farm regime (*ejidos* and *comunidades*) in order to provide ready access to defence of peasants' rights through the *amparo*. The Supreme Court ruled that, given the national importance of the agrarian problem,[43] agrarian *amparo* was needed to

the complaint, order a temporary stay of the act in question and, subsequently, pass the case file on to a District Court Judge, thus setting the ordinary procedure into motion. *Ley de Amparo*, Art. 38.

[40] *See* text following note 43, *infra*. [41] *See supra*, Section 2.3.5.

[42] The main administrative courts are the Tax Court of the Federation (*Tribunal Fiscal de la Federación*) and the Administrative Law Court of the Federal District (*Tribunal de lo Contencioso Administrativo del Distrito Federal*). Nevertheless, note that besides these courts, other courts that have local jurisdiction operate in some states such as in Baja California, Colima, Guanajuato, Guerrero, Jalisco, México, Michoacán, Morelos, Nuevo León, Querétaro, Sonora, and Yucatán. On this subject, *see* Fix-Zamudio and Cossío Díaz, *supra* note 20 at 482.

[43] SJF, 1917–1988, Primera Parte, Tribunal Pleno, pp. 386–387, Apéndice.

protect the interests of the rural peasantry by enforcing their rights under agrarian laws. In this way, the inhabitants of these settlements would not be rendered defenceless out of ignorance when government officials attempted to ride roughshod over their constitutional rights.

In 1963 and 1976, Congress amended the *amparo* laws to accomplish this purpose. The reforms were intended to keep procedural formalities to a minimum; for this reason, in agrarian *amparo*, the presiding judge must, on his or her own initiative, correct any errors found in the complaint, arguments, or motions. The judge must allow leaders or authorities of the communal farms or communities to present a simplified complaint, and must gather or collect on behalf of the complainant any evidence that may be lacking and that may be required to decide the case. Additionally, the deadlines for filing such complaints are extended to thirty days when individual *ejidatarios* or *comuneros* are filing suit; there is no deadline at all in suits on behalf of an entire community.

Amparo judicial: *protection against unconstitutional judicial decisions* The last type of *amparo*, also heard in a single stage before a panel of Circuit Court Judges, is the legal remedy sought by individuals and legal entities in opposition to allegedly unconstitutional final judgments (or other decision terminating a proceeding) that is issued by any court in the nation. Petitions for judicial protection (*amparo judicial*) may be filed if it is believed that, during the course of legal proceedings, violations were committed of any provision contained in the last three paragraphs of Article 14 of the Constitution, which provides:

> No-one may be deprived of life, liberty or of their property, possessions or rights, except by means of a legal proceeding held before a previously established court, in which essential formalities of procedure are complied with and in accordance with laws issued prior to the act.
>
> In criminal trials, it is prohibited to impose by simple analogy, and even by compelling reason, any punishment that is not decreed by a law exactly applicable to the offence in question.
>
> In civil trials, final judgment shall conform to the letter [of the law] or to the juridical interpretation of the law, and in the absence thereof, shall be based on general principles of law.

Two types of violations of constitutional rights are subject to challenge via *amparo judicial*: first, procedural errors (errors *in procedendo*), meaning a departure from established procedure during the course of the suit, such as failure to serve proper notice, admission of improperly obtained evidence, etc; and second, errors in the judgment itself (known as errors *in judicando*), which pertain directly to irregularities in the judgment itself (incorrect application of the law). In both cases, the claimant must establish that, at some point of the judicial proceeding, the judge did not strictly adhere to the law, and consequently, at least one of the constitutionally guaranteed rights set forth in the above-quoted paragraphs of Article 14 was ignored. The ultimate goal of the complainant is to have a court vacate the judgment in question, and send the case file back to the trial judge or court that was responsible for issuing it, in order for a new decision to be handed down in conformity with the *amparo* judgment.

2.5. The Effect of an *Amparo* Judgment

Amparo cases may result in one of three possible consequences: a granting of the petition for judicial protection, after the court determines that a violation of constitutional rights has occurred; a denial of the petition, after the court determines that there has been no violation of rights; or a dismissal of the case on technical or procedural grounds (lack of standing, etc.).[44]

The granting of *amparo* protection for violation of constitutional rights does not carry with it the power of the court to award damages to the complainant; the courts do not possess such power under the *Amparo* Law.[45] A complainant who has been injured by governmental action may, however, bring a civil action in tort;[46] in such a case, the *amparo* judgment may serve as important evidence in a later civil trial, but there is no formal *res judicata* effect. In addition, in 2002, Congress amended Article 113 of the Constitution to provide that the state and federal government agencies could be held strictly liable for damages caused to private parties by improper government actions.[47]

In theory, the effect of a successful *amparo* action is limited to the negation of governmental action, and does not contemplate the court ordering a government official or agency to perform a positive act. There are many occasions, however, in which an *amparo* proceeding is brought to challenge a government agency's refusal to approve a request by the complainant, and an *amparo* judgment, in requiring that the refusal be nullified, in fact requires positive action. Nevertheless, it is important to distinguish the nugatory effect of *amparo* judgments from the positive *mandamus* orders of common law courts in the United States.

Article 107, Section II of the Constitution and Article 76 of the Law of *Amparo* incorporate the *Fórmula Otero*, mentioned previously,[48] which severely limits the effect of *amparo* judgments. Under Article 76 of the *Amparo* Law, judgments rendered in *amparo* proceedings 'shall only deal with the individuals or private or public corporate entities, that file the petition for *amparo*, and may only aid and protect them [such individuals or entities], should the petition be admissible, in the specific case pertaining to the complaint, and the ruling on the law or act that gave rise to the complaint may not be applied to the general population'. Thus, even in cases where *amparo* is sought against laws that apply to the general population, the effects of the final decision only apply to the moving party, though such effects are binding on all public officials insofar as the petitioner is concerned.

[44] Fix-Zamudio, H., 'Breve Introducción al Juicio de Amparo' in *Ensayos Subre el Derecho de UNAM*, Instituto de Investigaciones (Mexico: Jurídicas, 1993) at 63–64.

[45] The *Amparo* Law fails to include any provision empowering the award of damages by the courts.

[46] *See* Chapter 17 above, Section 6.

[47] D.O. 14 Jun. 2002.

[48] *See supra*, text accompanying note 11.

With regard to the enforcement of *amparo* judgments, after a petition is granted, the government official whose act has been overruled is required to comply with the decision within twenty-four hours of being served notice to do so, when the nature of the act makes such swift compliance feasible; otherwise, steps towards compliance with the judgment must at least be initiated within this timeframe.[49] In case of non-compliance, the District Court judge or the Circuit Court panel that ruled in the *amparo* case shall directly call upon the government official to comply, and should such a call go unheeded, the judge or panel shall call upon the official's superior to do likewise. If the previous measures do not lead to compliance, or if it is shown that the responsible government official has repeated the act that was deemed unconstitutional, the case file shall be sent to the Supreme Court to proceed in accordance with the provisions of Section XVI of Article 107 of the Constitution. In such circumstances, the Supreme Court may remove the non-compliant official from office, bring the official directly before a district judge for arraignment on charges of crimes against the administration of justice, grant a reasonable amount of time to comply with the judgment, or hold a hearing on a motion for substitute compliance, unless it can be shown that if the judgment were executed, the harm thus caused to society would greatly outweigh any benefits obtained by the complainant.

Finally, the Supreme Court has held on several occasions that when a public official is accused of non-compliance with an *amparo* judgment, the petitioner must file a special appeal known as a *recurso de queja*.[50] According to the Supreme Court, in order to grant a motion to hold such a hearing, the petitioner must allege that absolutely no steps have been taken towards compliance with the *amparo* judgment, when such judgment involves affirmative performance of an act that the official had failed to carry out; or the petitioner must claim that the government official has persisted in the conduct that constitutes a violation of constitutional rights, when such a judgment calls upon the official to cease such behaviour.[51]

2.6. Criticisms of *Amparo* as an Effective Mechanism

Amparo has been an important mechanism for defending the rights of individual Mexicans against governmental abuse. The *amparo* process has many shortcomings, however. First, since *amparo* may only be used against governmental authorities, it offers no protection against the curtailment of constitutional rights by important non-governmental actors in society: political parties, news media, private associations, labour unions, businesses, etc. For instance, if a shopping centre refused to allow people of a certain race or religion to enter the premises, an *amparo* action could not be brought to seek a remedy. Second,

[49] Apéndice al SJF, 1988, vol. III, p. 1206.
[50] Apéndice al SJF, 1917–1988, Primera Parte, Tribunal Pleno, p. 382.
[51] Apéndice al SJF, 1917–1988, Primera Parte, Tribunal Pleno, p. 828.

amparo may only be directed against constitutional violations; violations of international treaties to which Mexico is a party, such as human rights treaties, may not be addressed through *amparo*, even though treaties are considered part of the supreme law of the land. Third, the procedural complexities of *amparo* make the procedure expensive, and therefore inaccessible to many persons. The courts have imposed high standards of proof of the elements of *amparo* (see above, Section 2.3), making the process precarious, slow, and technically difficult. Fourth, the *Fórmula Otero* has been criticized for unduly limiting the effect of court judgments in interpreting and enforcing the Constitution. On the other hand, the limited nature of *amparo* judgments does give the federal courts licence to deal with many individualized cases without worrying about the broader implications of the judgment. Finally, proponents of federalism in Mexico (increased states' rights) have pointed to the fact that the *amparo* system provides the federal courts the final say on matters of state law, and is an extension of centralization of power by the federal government; if one wants to research interpretations of the Civil Code of Jalisco, one consults federal case-law. A related criticism is that *amparo* is so broad that it needlessly clogs the federal courts with cases that do not really address constitutional protections, but simply represent the chance for a party who has suffered an adverse judicial judgment or other act to have one more appeal. This is often simply used as a delaying tactic in civil disputes that have little to do with constitutional guarantees.

3. *Controversias Constitucionales*: Disputes Between Competing Authorities over the Constitutionality of Laws, Official Acts, or Delineation of Borders

As noted above, the *amparo* procedure is only available to private parties and, with one minor exception,[52] the procedure cannot be used by government entities to contest unconstitutional laws or acts. For this purpose, a separate procedure, known as *controversias constitucionales*, exists to resolve disputes between competing authorities over the constitutionality of laws, official acts, or borders. It is by this process that many political disputes that arise throughout the nation between the different levels of government and among the different branches and agencies of government are settled.

The procedure known as *controversias constitucionales* was established in the Constitution of 1917, but was limited in effectiveness because of the restrictive nature of the measure (only disputes between states, or between political powers, could be brought) and because there was no implementing legislation to make it effective. In 1994, as a by-product of Mexico's move away from centralized, authoritarian control, Article 105 of the Constitution was amended[53]

[52] *See supra*, note 21 and accompanying text.

[53] D.O. 31 Dec. 1994.

to increase the effectiveness of the procedure, through three significant reforms: broadening the categories of parties that may participate in *controversias constitucionales*; giving general effect to judicial judgments concluded under the procedure; and adopting a new law, the *Ley Reglamentaria de las Fracciones I y II del Artículo 105 Constitucional*,[54] to create special procedures governing such cases. As a result, most political conflicts can now be resolved by the courts, and since 1995, 700 *controversias constitucionales* have been filed with the Supreme Court.[55]

Controversias constitucionales are intended to settle any dispute that may arise between government authorities: conflicts between federal and state authorities, between authorities from different states, and between authorities from different branches of government (legislative *versus* executive, executive *versus* judicial, etc.). To understand why it was established, we must first review two underlying principles of the Mexican Constitution: federalism and the principle of separation of powers.

Article 40 of the Constitution defines the Mexican system of government as a federal state in which laws of national application, at the federal level, coexist with a system of local laws that apply in the geographical subdivisions of the Federal District, the states, and municipalities. The principle of the separation of powers is set forth in Article 49 of the Constitution,[56] which establishes that legislative, executive, and judicial functions are to be carried out by different agencies of government under a single body of law, and such agencies may only perform duties expressly conferred upon them by the Constitution or by law.

Before extensive judicial reforms in December 1994,[57] the Supreme Court issued a number of opinions clarifying the application of this procedure, holding that the Supreme Court had original and exclusive jurisdiction over *controversias constitucionales*.[58] 'Citizen suits' are not permitted under this procedure, the Supreme Court having held that private individuals have no standing to bring actions of this type;[59] *controversias constitucionales* can only be brought at the request of a party authorized to bring such an action in accordance with the Constitution and the *Ley Reglamentaria*.[60] No state may rule on the validity of laws established in another state.[61] The Supreme Court has also held that a genuine court proceeding (*juicio*) must be held in these disputes,[62] during which the petitioner must demonstrate a legal interest at stake.[63] When cases involve conflicts between branches of government of the same state, a violation of the federal Constitution would have to be involved.[64] Regarding

[54] D.O. 11 May 1995.

[55] *See* 'Informe de Labores del 2002 que Rinde el Ministro Genaro David Góngora Pimentel' (Mexico-Suprema Corte de Justicia de la Nación, 2003).

[56] Articles 116 and 122 mandate separation of powers for the state and Federal District governments as well.

[57] *See* Chapter 6 above, at text accompanying notes 9, 17–28.

[58] S.J.F., 5a., T. II, p. 644; 5a., T. II, p. 1046; 5a., T. III, p. 729; 5a., XXXVI, p. 1067.

[59] S.J.F., 7a., vol. 66, primera parte, p. 35; 7a., vol. 175–180, primera parte, p. 35; 8a., T. III, primera parte, p. 49.

[60] S.J.F., 5a., T. XCI, p. 1798; 5a., T. XCVI, p. 2278.

[61] S.J.F., 5a., T. CXXVI, p. 495.

[62] S.J.F., 5a., T. II, p. 1046.

[63] S.J.F., 5a., T. XV, p. 595.

[64] S.J.F., 5a., T. VIII, p. 409.

the rules that govern procedure in such disputes, the Supreme Court has held that, if no regulatory law or statute (*ley reglamentaria*) is in effect for this purpose, the Federal Code of Civil Procedure shall govern the case.[65]

3.1. Historical Background

Mexico's adoption of a specialized procedure to resolve interstate and interbranch conflicts of a constitutional nature can be traced to the US Constitution.[66] According to Article III, Section 2 of the US Constitution, in matters to which the federal government is a party, any federal court can hear the case under ordinary rules of procedure, whether the case is brought by a private individual or by a state. However, in disputes between two or more states, the US Supreme Court has original jurisdiction.

Historical roots of the *controversia constitucional* can also be found in Article 137 of the Mexican Constitution of 1824, in several provisions of the Constitutional Laws of 1836, and in Article 115 of the *Bases Orgánicas de la República* of 1842. As in the case of *amparo*, Mariano Otero was instrumental in promoting the adoption of this procedure. In drafting provisions for the Act of Reforms of 1847,[67] Otero expounded on the need to allow the federal government to annul state laws that would infringe the Constitution. The Act of Reforms established a mechanism for federal control over unconstitutional state laws through complicated provisions that assigned roles to the federal and states legislatures, in addition to the Supreme Court.[68] The 1857 Constitution (in Article 98) also dealt with *controversias constitucionales*, although this precept was considered inadequate by legal scholars of the day, since it did not grant the Supreme Court exclusive jurisdiction.[69]

The framers of the 1917 Constitution viewed a strong Supreme Court as a necessary element of a federal system of government. The Supreme Court was to protect constitutional rights of persons through the *amparo* process, and should also be empowered to decide jurisdictional and other controversies arising between different governmental authorities. Consequently, Article 105 of the original Constitution of 1917 included a key term, which was added during the debates of the constituent congress, to grant sole and original jurisdiction to the Supreme Court in the second of these matters: 'It is incumbent *only* upon the Supreme Court of the Nation to hear controversies that arise between two or more States, between the branches of government of a same State regarding

[65] S.J.F., 5a., T. II, pp. 644 and 1046; 5a., T. III, p. 769.

[66] *See* Cossío Díaz, J.R., 'LAS CONTROVERSIAS ENTRE ESTADOS EN EL DERECHO ESTADOUNIDENSE', IN EL FORO, novena época, tomo X, número 1, primer semestre de 1997, at 25–53.

[67] *See supra*, note 18.

[68] *See* Articles 22 to 24 of the Act of Reforms of 1847, and Tena Ramirez, *supra* note 18 at 474–475. The Act of Reforms is also available at www.juridicas.unam.mx, 'Legislación Federal', 'Documentos constitucionales históricos'. (Site visited Jan. 2004).

[69] Ramón Rodríquez, DERECHO CONSTITUCIONAL (Mexico: Universidad Nacional Autónoma de México, 1978) at 690, 691. (Facsimile publication of the second edition, 1875.)

the constitutionality of its acts, and conflicts between the federal government and one or more States, as well as those in which the federation [federal government] is a party' (emphasis added). This provision remained unchanged from 5 May 1917 until 31 December 1994, but was infrequently used. From 1917 to 1994, fifty-five disputes were brought: fourteen disputes arose between the federal government and a state; twenty-two between branches of government within the same state; one between states; twelve between several municipalities and a state; and one between a single municipality and a state.[70]

On 5 December 1994, President Ernesto Zedillo sent to Congress a bill which included, among several other proposals, changes to Article 105 of the Constitution. The statement of motives (*exposición de motivos*) accompanying the President's draft bill contained the explanation that strengthening the Supreme Court as a constitutional tribunal: 'calls for granting the Court more power to enforce its decisions; calls for broadening the Court's jurisdictional authority to issue rulings on the constitutionality of laws that affect the general population in order to settle controversies between the three branches of government and to act as a guarantor of federalism'.[71]

3.2. Types of Disputes Subject to *Controversias Constitucionales*

There are four types of disputes that may be settled by means of *controversias constitucionales*.[72]

(i) The first type involves disputes between two different jurisdictions over the constitutionality or legality of laws that apply to the general population or official acts (e.g. when the President objects that a law adopted by a state legislature constitutes an incursion into federal executive powers). This type specifically involves disputes between different levels of government or two separate entities at the same level, such as between the federal government and a state or the Federal District; between the federal government and a municipality; between two states; between a state and the Federal district; or between the Federal district and a municipality or two municipalities of two different states (Mexican Constitution, Article 105, section I, paragraphs a, b, d, e, f, g).

(ii) The second type of dispute entails controversies that arise between different branches of government, either at the federal level or from two different jurisdictions, over the constitutionality or legality of laws that apply to the general population, or official acts. In the words of Article 105, section 1(c), this includes disputes between 'the Executive branch and the Congress of

[70] *See* CONSTITUCIÓN POLÍTICA DE LOS ESTADOS UNIDOS MEXICANOS, COMENTADA Y CONCORDADA, vol. IV (Mexico: UNAM—Instituto de Investigaciones Jurídicas, 15th ed., 2000) at 125 (hereinafter CONSTITUCIÓN COMENTADA).

[71] The constitutional reform was published in D.O. 31 Dec. 1994.

[72] Cossío Díaz, J.R., 'Similitudes y diferencias entre las controversias constitucionales y las acciones de inconstitucionalidad', in Cossio Díaz, J.R. and Pérez de Acha, L.M., eds., *LA DEFENSA DE LA CONSTITUCION* (Mexico: Fontamara, 1996) at 65–79.

the Union; the former and either chamber of the latter or, when applicable, the Permanent Commission, whether [the Congress] is acting as the legislative body of the federal government or of the Federal District of Mexico City'—or between agencies of a state and a municipality of another state (Mexican Constitution, Article 105, section I, paragraphs c and j).[73]

(iii) The third type of controversy takes place between two different branches of government within the same jurisdiction, such as between two government agencies of the same state, a state and one of its municipalities, or two agencies of the government of the Federal District, when the constitutionality of laws of general application or official acts is called into question (Mexican Constitution, Article 105, section I, paragraphs h, i, and k).[74]

(iv) Finally, *controversias constitucionales* can be used to resolve border conflicts between federal entities and/or the Federal District, as was the case recently in suits filed by the states of Quintana Roo against Campeche, and Colima against Jalisco (Mexican Constitution, Article 105, Section I, paragraph d).[75]

The Constitution provides in general terms that *controversias constitucionales* may arise between the above-mentioned branches or levels of government, but places no restrictions on the type of legal provisions that may be the subject matter of such disputes. Therefore, the laws, decrees, or regulations involved in such disputes may be directed either towards the general population, or towards a particular individual or group of individuals. Thus, this process could be used to call into question the constitutionality of reforms of the Constitution (based on errors of procedure, such as lack of proper quorum, etc); or to challenge decrees of suspension of individual rights and laws issued under extraordinary powers granted to authorities in a state of emergency under Article 29 of the Mexican Constitution. The procedure may be used to challenge federal, state, and municipal laws, international treaties, state constitutions, and administrative regulations, as well as rulings, decrees, or official acts directed towards specific individuals.

[73] Before the reform of 1994 was implemented, the Supreme Court of Justice issued inconsistent rulings in cases involving municipalities with regard to recognition of their standing to be a party in these cases, often casting doubt upon whether municipal governments could be considered a legitimate branch of government (S.J.F., 5a., T. IV, p. 729; S.J.F. 5a., T. XLV, p. 3577; S.J.F., 5a., T. XLVIII, p. 349; S.J.F., 9a., T. III, March 1996, p. 262).

[74] The Supreme Court has refused, on several different occasions, to recognize the standing of public officials who claimed to be government authorities, and the Court has held that only persons who could prove their 'legal, unquestionable, indisputable status as such' could act as public authorities (S.J.F., 5a., T. XIV, p. 458).

[75] The Supreme Court has held that claims of encroachment upon the powers of the federal government and the states are valid subject matters for *controversias constitucionales* and were not admissible in *juicios de amparo* (S.J.F., 5a., T. III, p. 769; 5a., T. XXXVI, p. 1067), and that such claims could not be filed directly before the Supreme Court through the procedure known as direct *amparo* on review (discussed at paragraph preceding Section 2.4.2, *supra*) (S.J.F., 8a., T. III, primera parte, p. 49).

Certain types of disputes cannot be submitted to the Supreme Court as *controversias constitucionales.* These include any election-related laws or acts;[76] situations that involve the decision by a governmental authority, in the proper exercise of its discretion, to carry out an official duty, such as Congress' decision not to pass a law; and decisions issued in what is known as a 'political trial', i.e. Mexico's process of impeachment of elected and politically appointed officials (Article 110 of the Constitution). The Supreme Court has also recently held that it does not have jurisdiction to settle claims brought against acts that allegedly violate state constitutions or local laws, since, according to the Court, such a duty is incumbent upon the local constitutional authority or the state legislatures.[77]

3.3. Rules of Procedure for *Controversias Constitucionales*

A *controversia constitucional* begins when a government branch or agency, as the moving party *(actor)*, files a complaint *(demanda)* with the Supreme Court of Justice, naming as defendant *(demandado)* the branch or agent that 'has issued and enacted the general legal provision or announced the act that is the subject of the controversy'.[78] The complaint may also name third parties that have been harmed, including any jurisdiction or branch or agent of government that could be adversely affected by any judgment which may be handed down in the case. Additionally, the Attorney General of the Republic is required to take part in all *controversias constitucionales* to protect 'the interest of the Constitution'.[79]

The Regulatory Law of Constitutional Controversies (*Ley Reglamentaria de las Fracciones I y II del Artículo 105 Constitucional*) establishes the following time limits for the filing of complaints:

(i) in cases involving a challenge to an official act or decision, the complaint must be filed within thirty days, counting from the day after the effective date of the decision in question, or counting from the time the general population learned of the effects of the decision, or from the time the moving party claims to have become aware of the decision;

[76] The following section, on *acciones de inconstitucionalidad*, challenges the constitutionality of election laws themselves, and the Federal Electoral Tribunal (*see* Chapter 6 above, Section 2.5.1) was created to deal with alleged violations of electoral laws.

Since *amparo* requests have been declared unavailable in electoral matters, no sound scholarly legal writings exist in Mexican jurisprudence that specifically define this area of the law. In January 1995, the Supreme Court decided a case brought by several members of the *Asamblea de Representantes del Distrito Federal* (the legislative body of Mexico City) against the Law of Citizen Participation (*Ley de Participación Ciudadana*) and, in so doing, issued a definition of the term 'electoral matters'. The Supreme Court stated that this subject encompasses matters 'that establish the rules under which selection and appointment is carried out, by means of citizens voting and within a democratic process, of the persons that are to act as the heads of the branches of government in representation of the people, at the federal, state and municipal and Federal District levels'. SJF, 9a, T. III, Pleno, Mar. 1996, p. 84.

[77] *See* SJF G, T III, March 1996, p. 320.

[78] *Ley Reglamentaria de Las Fracciones I y II del Artículo 105 Constitucional*, Article 10, Section II.

[79] *Ley Reglamentaria* Article 10, Section IV.

(ii) in cases involving challenges to laws applying to the general population, the claim must be brought within thirty days of the date the law is published or of the date the law is first applied; and
(iii) in cases of territorial disputes, complaints must be filed within seventy days, counting from the effective date of the law or from the realization of the act that gave rise to the conflict.[80]

The procedure for *controversias constitucionales* takes place in four stages. In the first stage, the Chief Justice of the Supreme Court appoints an Associate Justice who will hear the case and draft a proposed judgment upon conclusion of the hearing. Then, in the absence of blatant grounds for dismissal,[81] the defendant is required to respond within a thirty-day period, and any other parties involved in the case are notified to provide them with an opportunity to present their own arguments in the matter. In the third stage, the presiding Associate Justice sets a date for and conducts the evidentiary hearing. Finally, after the hearing is held, the presiding judicial officer prepares a draft judgment, which is submitted to a vote of the Supreme Court in plenary session. The majority vote required for decisions by the Supreme Court varies with the type of *controversia constitucional* presented. For example, a state law challenged by the federal government requires a minimum of eight votes out of a total of eleven, whereas a federal law challenged by a state requires only a simple majority to be ruled unconstitutional.[82]

When a *controversia constitucional* is pending, even before final judgment is rendered, the presiding Associate Justice may issue a decree of suspension of the acts or provisions in question, either on his own initiative or at the request of the moving party. Such a suspension can only apply to a specific individual (not to the general population) and can only be issued if national security or public safety, the national economy, and the basic institutions of law and order are not jeopardized by the suspension, and if adverse effects on society do not outweigh the benefits that would be obtained by the claimant if a suspension were to take effect.[83]

3.4. Effects of Judgments in *Controversias Constitucionales*

Due to the political and legal importance of *controversias constitucionales*, the procedures for enforcing judgments of this type are complex and subject to numerous controls.[84] In its final judgment, the Supreme Court is required

[80] Article 73, Section IV of the Constitution empowers the Congress to approve any agreements between two or more states that have resolved a border dispute by agreement.
[81] Regulatory Law of Constitutional Controversies, Article 19, sets forth certain instances when *controversias constitucionales* are inadmissible (*improcedente*), such as against Supreme Court decisions, in electoral matters, when a parallel dispute is pending, when the law in question is no longer in force, etc.
[82] *Ley Reglamentaria* Article 72.
[83] *Ley Reglamentaria* Article 14.
[84] *See* CONSTITUCIÓN COMENTADA, *supra* note 70, vol. IV at 125.

to identify the legal provision or official act that is the subject of the dispute. Should the case warrant it, the Supreme Court must provide an evaluation of the evidence introduced by the parties (*valoración de las pruebas*), state the guiding legal principles used in reaching the judgment, set forth the reasoning behind the ruling, define the scope and effects of the judgment, and specify the reasons for its holding.[85] If the claimant prevails, the Court must set a deadline for the defendant to execute the action ordered in the judgment.

When the federal government challenges state or municipal laws or regulations, when states challenge municipal regulations, or when a branch of government challenges laws affecting the entire population within its jurisdiction, at least eight Supreme Court Justices must vote in favour of the challenge for the law to be declared unconstitutional with relation to the general public.[86] When municipalities challenge state or federal laws or regulations, or states challenge federal laws or regulations and the required majority of Supreme Court Justices votes in support of the challenge, such laws or regulations cease to apply only within the territory of the state or municipality that won its case. Finally, when a dispute involves decrees or official acts directed at a specific individual or individuals, the effects of the judgment apply only to the disputing parties.

Section I of Article 105 of the Constitution and Article 45 of the Regulatory Law of Constitutional Controversies establish that the effective date of judgments in *controversias constitucionales* shall be determined by the Supreme Court and that, except in criminal matters,[87] judgments may not by applied retroactively.

The law requires notice of a final judgment to be given to all parties to the case, and such notice should be published in its entirety, together with the individual opinion of each Supreme Court Justice, in the *Semanario Judicial de la Federación*.[88] This is a departure from the normal rule of judicial opinions, of which only a very brief summary is published in the *Semanario*. When a statute is declared invalid, the judgment must be published in the *Diario Oficial de la Federación* and in the official instrument of the state or municipality where laws were made public.[89]

[85] The Supreme Court is required to correct 'any errors it may notice in citations of precepts invoked [by the parties] and shall examine all of the reasoning put forth by the parties in order to resolve the issue at hand', and to cure any errors that may appear in the complaint, the answer, arguments, or alleged damages. *Ley Reglamentaria*, Article 39.

[86] *Ley Reglamentaria*, Article 42. If a majority of 8 votes is not reached in disputes involving statutes of general application, the Supreme Court sitting *en banc* is required to dismiss the case.

[87] *See infra* Chapter 11 at text accompanying notes 24 and 59.

[88] *Ley Reglamentaria* Article 43. On *jurisprudencia* generally and the effect of Supreme Court judgments, *see* Chapter 3 above, Section 2.3. *See also* De Silva Nava, Carlos, *La Jurisprudencia. Curso de Actualización sobre el Juicio de Amparo* (Mexico: UNAM, 1996) at 102–144; Cabrera, Lucio, 'La Jurisprudencia', in *La Suprema Corte de Justicia y el Pensamiento Juridico* (Mexico: S.C.J., 1985) at 225–267.

[89] *Ley Reglamentaria* Article 44.

Finally, in accordance with the provisions of the first two paragraphs of Section XVI of Article 107 of the Constitution, the Supreme Court must oversee compliance with its judgments regarding *controversias constitucionales*, and the Court is to resolve any instances of non-compliance or repetition of any acts that were the subject of the dispute. Any government official who fails to comply with a judgment or repeats an act deemed to be unconstitutional may be removed from office and brought directly before the appropriate District Court Judge.[90] However, the official may request a hearing on a motion for substitute compliance if, 'by executing the judgment, the harm that would come to society or third parties would greatly outweigh any benefits obtained by the complainant'.[91]

In cases involving laws that apply to citizens in general, as soon as the judgment of nullification is handed down, the law is immediately considered unconstitutional and such a law ceases to have effect. In cases where a government authority continues to apply a law ruled unconstitutional, a new suit would have to be brought to elicit another ruling of unconstitutionality; however, an official who is personally responsible for applying an unconstitutional law would be subject to punishment.

3.5. Evaluation

The process known as *controversias constitucionales* has become an important mechanism for resolving political conflicts. Prior to the political and judicial reforms of the 1990s, conflicts between federal and state entities, or between different government agencies or officials, would be resolved behind closed doors, in the offices of the President. The judicial system was marginalized from these conflicts. When coupled with reforms designed to increase the independence and professionalism of the judiciary, the use of judicial processes such as *controversias constitucionales* increases the transparency in the exercise of governmental power, and contributes to the development of the rule of law in Mexico.

4. *Acciones de Inconstitucionalidad*: Challenges to the Constitutionality of Laws *A Priori*

The third procedure available to uphold the Constitution is the *acción de inconstitucionalidad*, which may be loosely translated as a 'challenge to the constitutionality of laws'. The *acción de inconstitucionalidad* has no historical roots in Mexican law; it was created as a reaction to single-party rule in Mexico

[90] *See* S.J.F., 8a, T. VIII, p. 7.
[91] Mexican Constitution, Articles 105 and 107, Section XVI.

for seventy-one years, another product of the effort to control the undue accumulation of political power by the PRI. Introduced by an amendment to Article 105 of the Constitution in December 1994,[92] the *acción de inconstitucionalidad* was based on European models imported from Italy, Spain, and Germany.

Section II of Article 105 of the Constitution provides for a process whereby certain branches of government or subgroups thereof, or the executive committees of political parties (constitutionally recognized as agents of society), may go before the Supreme Court to argue against the constitutionality of laws that apply to the general population. Put bluntly, the *acción de inconstitucionalidad* provides an opportunity for a disaffected political group—a minority political party, for example—to challenge a law adopted by the majority party, or by a coalition of parties. The process also permits other agencies, such as the Attorney General of the Republic (who is charged with preserving the Constitution, much like the US Solicitor General) or political parties (in their capacity as groups that serve the public interest) to call into question legislation approved by the parliamentary majorities so that the Court may determine whether or not such laws are constitutional.

4.1. General Rules

There are three distinguishing characteristics of *acciones de inconstitucionalidad* that separate this procedure from *juicios de amparo* and from *controversias constitucionales*.

First, in *acciones de inconstitucionalidad*, the moving party need not prove that an offence has actually been committed or that a person has been adversely affected in order for the challenge to be admissible. It is enough for the moving party to allege in abstract terms (theoretically or hypothetically) that the potential exists for violation of a constitutional provision. If the claimant succeeds in convincing the Supreme Court that such a law contradicts a constitutional provision, the law in question would cease to apply to the general population.

Second, only certain bodies (groups of legislators, political groups, and the Attorney General of the Republic) have standing to bring *acciones de inconstitucionalidad*.

Third, the *acción de inconstitucionalidad* must be filed before the law that is challenged actually comes into force.

The procedures involving *acciones de inconstitucionalidad* are similar to *controversias constitucionales*,[93] although some important differences set them apart.

[92] D.O. 31 Dec. 1994.

[93] *See* Cossío Díaz, J.R., 'Similitudes y diferencias entre las controversias constitucionales y las acciones de inconstitucionalidad', in Cossio Díaz and Pérez de Acha, *supra* note 72 at 65–79.

4.1.1. *Limited Standing and Subject Matter*

According to Article 105, Section II of the Mexican Constitution, only the following institutions or persons have standing (i.e. are legally qualified) to file a challenge to the constitutionality of legislation (*acción de inconstitucionalidad*):

(i) a total of 33 per cent of the members of either the federal *Cámara de Diputados*, of the federal Senate, of state legislatures, or of the Legislative Assembly of the Federal District;
(ii) the Attorney General of the Republic; and
(iii) the leadership of political parties registered at either the national or state levels.

The *subject matter* of *acciones de inconsitucionalidad* may vary, but in each case, these challenges may only be filed against laws that apply to the general population. In broad terms, legislative acts in Mexico can be divided into two categories: laws or decrees. Only laws enacted in accordance with established procedure of either the federal Congress, the State legislatures, or the legislature of the Federal District may be challenged via *acciones de inconstitucionalidad*; *decretos* may not be challenged by this procedure.[94]

A party qualified to bring these challenges before the Supreme Court may only do so when laws enacted by certain bodies are the subject of the challenge. For example, members of the *Cámara de Diputados* may question either federal or Federal District laws issued by the general Congress of the Union; however, they may not challenge any laws issued by either Chamber of Congress when the Senate or the *Cámara de Diputados* exercises its sole discretion in such matters as review of public accounts, approval of the budget and expenditures, or any other matter listed in Article 74 of the Constitution (Mexican Constitution, Article 105, Section II). The same rules that apply to members of the *Cámara de Diputados* also apply to members of the Senate, except that, under Article 76, Section I of the Constitution, the Senate is granted sole discretion to challenge the constitutionality of provisions of international treaties. Members of state legislative bodies or of the Legislative Assembly of the Federal District may challenge laws or legal provisions issued by their same body (Mexican Constitution, Article 105, Section II).

Article 105, Section II, paragraph (c), confers upon the Attorney General of the Republic the right to challenge federal, state, municipal, or Federal District laws, and international treaties. The Attorney General has total discretion to challenge any law that applies to the general population regardless of the issuing body, and therefore may even challenge provisions issued by either Chamber of Congress in exercising its sole discretion pursuant to Articles 29 (suspension of constitutional guarantees during state of emergency) and 131 (relating to the establishment of customs duties) of the Constitution.

[94] A law (*ley*) is a legislative act that applies to the general population, while a decree (*decreto*) is a legislative act that applies to a particular individual.

Finally, federally registered political parties (i.e. those accredited by the *Instituto Federal Electoral*) may, through their respective national executive committee, file an *acción de inconstitucionalidad* in order to challenge the constitutionality of federal or state election laws. Similarly, the executive committee of a political party registered at the state level may file challenges 'against electoral laws issued by the legislative body of the State that granted them their registration' (Mexican Constitution, Article 105, Section II, paragraph (f)). Thus, an *acción de inconstitucionalidad* is the only valid means of judicial challenge to the constitutionality of election laws in the Mexican legal system, since *juicios de amparo* and *controversias constitucionales* expressly exclude consideration of electoral disputes.

4.2. Rules of Procedure for *Acciones de Inconstitucionalidad*

The procedures to be followed in *acciones de inconstitucionalidad* are set forth in the *Ley Reglamentaria*. The complaint must be filed within thirty days of the day after the law is published in the *Diario Oficial* or, as the case may be, in the appropriate state register. Following the Italian model, the Mexican Congress adopted a rule requiring that these challenges be brought *before the law or legal provision in question comes into force.*[95] Other rules of procedure in *acciones de inconstitucionalidad* are virtually the same as those followed in *controversias constitutionales*.

4.3. Effect of Judgments

Judgments in *acciones de inconstitcionalidad* may lead to invalidation of the challenged provision, provided that a majority of at least eight of the Justices of the Supreme Court vote in favour of the challenge (*Ley Reglamentaria*, Article 72). Since the ultimate purpose of this process is to enforce strict adherence to constitutional principles in legislative acts, if a majority of eight votes is not achieved, the case is dismissed; a judgment of dismissal may be published in such cases, but it carries no legal effect.

Declarations of invalidity of laws in *acciones de inconstitucionalidad* apply to the general population and, consequently, as soon as the Supreme Court decides in favour of invalidation, the law in question immediately ceases to be in force. *Controversias constitutionales* differ markedly from *acciones de inconstitucionalidad* in the geographical scope of the effects of the decision. For example, in a *controversia constitucional*, if a state challenges a federal law that applies to the general population, or if the federal government questions a state law, annulment of the law only applies to the particular state involved in the suit; by contrast, in *acciones de inconstitucionalidad* the effects of the declaration of invalidity apply wherever the unconstitutional law was in force.

[95] *Ley Reglamentaria*, Article 60.

Therefore, in cases involving challenges to federal laws, such a declaration leads to a total repeal of the law throughout the nation.

As in the case of *controversias constitucionales*, the Mexican Constitution prohibits retroactive application of judgments of invalidity in *acciones de inconstitucionalidad*, although criminal matters constitute an exception to the general principle of non-retroactive application of laws. Similarly, the same rules regarding non-compliance with judgments issued in *controversias constitucionales* apply to judgments handed down in *acciones de inconstitucionalidad*. In contrast with the rules applying to *controversias constitucionales*, for *acciones de inconstitucionalidad* the *Ley Reglamentaria* expressly prohibits both the repetition of any act ruled invalid due to the unconstitutionality of the underlying law that gave rise to the act, and the enactment of a law previously ruled unconstitutional (*Ley Reglamentaria*, Article 71).

Since the adoption of *acciones de inconstitucionalidad* in 1995, ninety-one cases have been brought to the Supreme Court.[96] Of these, the Supreme Court has declared twenty-six laws unconstitutional.

[96] Database of the *Suprema Corte de Justicia de la Nación*.

9

Administrative Law

1. Introduction

Mexican administrative law governs: the structure, organization, functions, and operation of governmental agencies; the laws and procedures to be followed by these agencies in carrying out their functions; and the judicial interpretation of laws and regulations that govern them. In a system that values deductive reasoning, the separation of legal principles and structures into distinct, formal categories is important, since categorization helps determine the foundations from which analysis of a specific legal problem may proceed. In the case of administrative law, legal principles are determined according to the organization and structure of a legal act, rather than by the agency that undertakes them. Thus, administrative acts can be undertaken by legislative, judicial, or executive agencies; the determining factor is not the agency, but rather the procedure for issuance of the administrative act, or the nature of the act.[1]

Administrative law encompasses a large and diverse group of public agencies that are dependencies of the executive branch of government; it also encompasses judicial and legislative entities that have administrative functions, such as the Federal Judicial Council, which is discussed above in Chapter 6, and the Secretariats of the Chambers of the Mexican Congress.

This Chapter covers all subgroups of government administration at the federal, state, and municipal levels. Each level of government has its own administrative agencies, which are either subordinate to the executive branch (as a centrally controlled, decentralized, or quasi-governmental entity) or are autonomous. However, due to the complexity and breadth of this field, it is impossible to cover the entire field of Mexican administrative law in a brief introductory Chapter. To simplify matters, this Chapter concentrates on the organization and operation of the federal administration.

As noted above in Chapter 5, the executive branch of the Mexican federal government has dominated the other branches, and has held sway over state and local governments. This domination reached its apogee during the administrations of Presidents Echeverría (1970–1976) and López Portillo (1976–1982) during which the federal bureaucracy swelled with the growth of numerous quasi-governmental or parastatal agencies (*entidades paraestatales*) that carried out activities ranging from commercial air transportation to the management of cinemas. In recent years, however, the monopoly of power exercised by the federal executive branch has dramatically diminished, for political reasons

[1] *See* Fraga, G., *Derecho Administrativo* (Mexico: Porrúa, 38th ed., 1998) at 61.

that are discussed above in Chapter 5. While the federal executive still weighs heavily, the federal Congress, no longer dominated by the President, has asserted more independent control over legislation. Judicial reforms begun in 1994 have also caused the judiciary to exercise greater power in controlling administrative acts, although the widespread use of *amparo*, discussed in the preceding Chapter, has long been an avenue for judicial control of administrative acts.

2. Organizational Structure of the Federal Government

In Mexico, the executive power resides in the President of the Republic and all subordinate entities: a vast bureaucratic complex that includes a wide range of public and government-owned entities. While most federal agencies respond to presidential authority, in recent years there has been a tendency to detach certain agencies from the hierarchical relationship of subordination to the executive branch of government. Accordingly, several entities have been granted autonomy and removed from the chain of command under the executive branch or under the agencies of the central administration, and have been conferred more autonomous decision-making powers. Pursuant to the Constitution, the chief executive officers of these entities have the authority to act independently of the President. Examples of such 'independent' agencies include the Bank of Mexico,[2] the autonomous universities,[3] the human rights commissions,[4] and the Federal Electoral Institute.[5] This autonomy must be viewed against the

[2] Paragraph 6 of Article 28 of the Constitution states: 'The State shall have a central bank that shall be autonomous in the exercise of its functions and in its administration'. Article 28 was amended in 1993 to add this paragraph, in order to make monetary policy more independent of political controls. D.O. 23 Aug. 1993.

[3] The autonomy of public universities has been long established as a formal matter, even if the practice of autonomy is more complicated, as noted above in Chapter 2. Under Part VII of Article 3 of the Constitution, '[public] universities and institutions of higher learning which are granted autonomy by law, shall have the authority and responsibility of self governance, shall fulfil their purposes of education, research and dissemination of culture in accordance with the principles of this article, respecting academic freedom in teaching and research and free examination and discussion of ideas; shall determine their own curricula and programs; shall set the hiring, promotion and tenure policies of their own faculty, and shall administer their own assets'.

[4] In 1992, the Constitution was amended to empower Congress and the State Legislatures to establish entities for the protection of human rights, which shall have the power to file independent, non-binding, public recommendations, complaints, and denunciations before the respective authorities. Article 102, Section B, added D.O. 28 Jan. 1992. This provision was adopted at a time in which the Mexican government was under pressure at home and abroad to depart from one-party rule, and to abandon authoritarian tactics that did not respect individual rights.

[5] By D.O. 6 Apr. 1990, in reaction to criticism of the PRI's domination of the electoral process, the Constitution was amended to create an autonomous public entity called the Federal Electoral Institute (*Instituto Federal Electoral*), which has the status of an independent corporation and operates under its own set of rules and organizational structure. Mexican Constitution, Article 41, Part III. On the operation of the Federal Electoral Institute generally, *see* Chapter 5 above, Section 3.2.1. *See also* Cárdenas Garcia, J., *et al.*, *Estudios jurídicos en torno al Instituto Federal Electoral* (Mexico: UNAM, 2000) at 67; Carbonnel, M., 'El Instituto Federal Electoral: Una aproximación a su integración y funcionamiento', in 5 *Concordancias, Estudios Jurídicos y Sociales* 58 (No. 8, May–Aug. 2000).

pattern of authoritarian control that has long been a part of Mexican political and legal history.[6] During the period of the PRI's ascendancy, formal independence was qualified by the immense political and budgetary power of the President. Thus, while UNAM is autonomous and therefore 'independent', the University continues to be entirely dependent on budgetary allocations from the federal government, over which the executive branch still exercises much control. In recent years, political reforms, and accompanying legal and constitutional reforms, have strengthened the independence of such agencies by increasing the transparency of the legal process and reinforcing the rule of law. Nevertheless, the independence of government entities still varies, depending on the agency and its importance to government policy.

In accordance with Article 90 of the Constitution, public administration in Mexico is composed of governmental and quasi-governmental agencies as follows:

Cabinet-level ministries Known as *secretarías de estado*, each of these is headed by a Minister or *Secretario*. There are currently eighteen such *secretarías* and the *Consejería Jurídica del Presidente*, as established by the Federal Law of Public Administration.[7]

Government agencies (órganos gubernamentales) These are attached to *secretarías*, such as intersecretarial commissions, e.g. the *Comisión Intersecretarial para el Fomento de la Industria Maquiladora*, and the *Comisión Ejecutiva de Turismo*.

Administrative departments (departamentos administrativos) However, legal reforms in 1997 removed the only existing administrative department, the *Departamento del Distrito Federal* (DDF), which previously governed the Federal District, and no other administrative departments have since been created.[8]

Quasi-independent agencies (órganos desconcentrados) These are semi-autonomous institutions that lack legal personality and are placed under the overall authority of Secretariats, on which they depend for funding.

Decentralized agencies (organismos descentralizados) These have legal personality and their own source of funding through direct budgetary appropriations or other sources. Examples include the *Instituto Mexicano de Seguridad Social* (IMSS), the *Instituto Mexicano de la Propiedad Intelectual* (IMPI), *Petróleos Mexicanos* (PEMEX, the national oil company), and the *Comisión Federal de Electricidad* (CFE, the national electricity company).

[6] *See* Chapters 1 and 5 above.

[7] *See Ley Orgánica de la Administración Pública Federal* (LOAPF), Art 26 of D.O. 30 Nov. 2000.

[8] *See* D.O. 4 Dec. 1997. Prior to this date, the DDF was administered as a federal governmental agency, headed by a mayor, called the *regente*, who was appointed by the President of Mexico. As part of the political opening and increased democratization of Mexico, Article 122 of the Constitution was amended in 1996 to provide for self-governance of the Federal District, through the election of a Legislative Assembly, and to provide for election of the *regente* by popular election. Since that date, the Federal District is no longer considered administratively as a department of the central government administration, but rather as a political entity similar to a state. For a discussion of the governance of the Federal District, *see* Chapter 5 above, at text accompanying notes 39–43.

Government-owned corporations (empresas de participación estatal mayoritaria) These are established as *sociedades anónimas* or *sociedades civiles* in which the government is the majority shareholder. This type of vehicle is used for areas of priority development, such as the Mexican Export Bank (*Banco Nacional de Comercio Exterior*, or BANCOMEXT), *Nacional Financiera*, (NAFINSA), the government's principal development bank, or government-owned commercial ventures, such as petrochemical companies.[9]

Government-owned trusts (fideicomisos) These are established to carry out cultural or social welfare activities. Examples include the *Fondo Nacional para la Cutltura y las Artes* (FONCA), which promotes culture and the arts; the *Fondo Nacional de Artesanías* (FONART), which promotes the production and sale of Mexican handicrafts; and the *Fondo Nacional para el Turismo* (FONATUR), which promotes Mexican tourism.[10]

Government agencies are subject to the hierarchical principles of law discussed above in Chapter 3, and may only exercise the powers delegated to them in legislation and regulations. Administrative law is governed by the general principles set forth in Articles 80 to 93 of the Constitution. The principal federal laws include the Organic Law of the Federal Public Administration (*Ley Orgánica de la Administración Pública Federal*, or LOAPF);[11] the Mexican Administrative Procedure Act (*Ley Federal de Procedimiento Administrativo*, or LFPA);[12] the Law of Government Planning (*Ley de Planeación*);[13] the General Law of National *Property* (*Ley General de Bienes Nacionales*);[14] the Law of Acquisitions, Leasing and Services of the Public Sector (*Ley de Adquisiciones, Arrendamientos y Servicios del Sector Público*);[15] the Law of Public Works (*Ley de Obras Públicas y Servicios Relacionados con las mismas*);[16] the Law of Expropriation (*Ley de Expropiación*);[17] the Federal Law of Liability of Public Servants (*Ley Federal de Responsabilidad de los Servidores Públicos*);[18] the Federal Law of Transparency and Access to Public Information (*Ley Federal de Transparencia y Acceso a la Información Pública Gubernamental*), recently adopted to promote transparency;[19] and the Federal Law of Administrative Responsibilities of Public Servants (*Ley Federal de Responsabilidades Administrativas de los Servidores Públicos*).[20] In addition, agencies must conform to the laws and regulations applicable to the particular type of agency involved in administrative action. Thus, government-owned entities (*paraestatales*) are subject to the Federal Law of Quasi-Governmental Entities (*Ley Federal de las Entidades Paraestatales*, or LFEP).[21]

[9] The *sociedad anónima* and *sociedad civil* are discussed below in Chapter 19 at Sections 2.1 and 5, respectively.
[10] On *fideicomisos* generally, *see* Chapter 16 below, Section 2.7.1.
[11] D.O. 29 Dec. 1976, last amended D.O. 13 Mar. 2002. [12] D.O. 4 Aug. 1994.
[13] D.O. 5 Jan. 1983. [14] D.O. 8 Jan. 1982, as amended 29 Dec. 1999.
[15] D.O. 4 Jan. 2000. [16] D.O. 4 Jan. 2000. [17] D.O. 25 Nov. 1936.
[18] D.O. 31 Dec. 1982, last amended 13 Mar. 2002. [19] D.O. 11 Jun. 2002.
[20] D.O. 13 Mar. 2002.
[21] D.O. 14 May 1986, as amended, 24 Jul. 1992 and 24 Dec. 1996.

The jurisdictional authority of each agency (*competencia*) consists of two equally important elements: the powers granted to a government agency, and the limitations on the agency's operations. Acts that fall outside the jurisdictional capacity or are beyond the scope of powers of a government agency or one of its officials are considered to be illegal (*ultra vires*) and, therefore, are potentially subject to annulment or revocation. It would also be improper for an administrative act to be performed without an agency having previously been duly created in accordance with the law to perform such an act, or to act without the authority to do so or, having such authority, to exercise it improperly; any of these instances would constitute grounds for annulment or revocation of administrative acts (under the *amparo* procedures discussed above in Chapter 8), and may even give rise to liability on the part of public servants.[22]

Under the Constitution, the President is responsible for executing laws issued by Congress, and for enforcing strict observance thereof in administrative practice.[23] Article 90 of the Constitution also establishes that the federal government administration shall consist of centrally controlled agencies, independent agencies, and quasi-governmental entities (*entidades paraestatales*) created by Congress. The LOAPF sets forth the specific powers delegated by the President to the *secretarías de estado* and to the administrative departments.[24] Legislation creating quasi-governmental entities (*entidades paraestatales*) will typically establish how much control the federal executive branch may exercise over their operations.[25] The laws establishing federal agencies also shall determine the relationships between quasi-governmental entities (*entidades paraestatales*) and the federal executive, or between these entities and the *secretarías de estado* and the Administrative Departments.[26]

The Office of the Attorney General of Mexico (*Procurador General de la República*, or PGR) has a unique character among agencies of the federal government. Prior to 1994, the PGR was considered one of the cabinet-level

[22] Annulment of administrative acts and liability of public servants are covered below in this Chapter.

The *ultra vires*, and therefore revocable, nature of an agency's acts was demonstrated in an unusual case arising under the North American Free Trade Agreement (NAFTA), to which Mexico, Canada, and the United States are parties. In this case, a company complained to NAFTA authorities that Mexico's Trade Secretariat (SECOFI, the predecessor agency of the Secretariat of the Economy) had levied an antidumping duty against its product in a manner that contravened Mexican law and the applicable provisions of the NAFTA. The complainant asked that a dispute resolution panel be convened under NAFTA Chapter 19, to review SECOFI's duty assessment. In a surprising decision, the NAFTA panel ruled in favour of the complainant, without addressing the technical elements of the trade dispute; rather, the panel held that the department within SECOFI that had assessed the antidumping duty had not been created in accordance with the legal requirements of Mexican administrative law, and therefore any action taken by the department was null and void. *See* In re Mexican Anti-Dumping Investigation into Imports of Flat-Coated Steel Products From the US, MEX-94-1904-01, available at www.sice.oas.org/dispute/nafta.

[23] *See* Mexican Constitution, Art. 89, Section I.

[24] *See* LOAPF, Arts. 1, 27 to 42, where the powers granted to each Cabinet minister are set forth.

[25] Mexican Constitution, Art. 90, para. 1.

[26] Mexican Constitution, Art. 90, para. 2.

ministries under the authority of the President. The dependence of the Attorney General (*Procurador*) on presidential authority may create difficult conflicts of interest: as enforcer of the nation's laws, particularly in cases involving other executive agencies or their officials, or even the President, the *Procurador* is expected to act independently of political influence. At the same time, the PGR is the government's lawyer, defending government agencies in cases brought against them by affected parties. Just as the United States Attorney General is sometimes criticized for making political decisions in determining the prosecution of federal crimes, in Mexico the *Procurador* has often been accused of failing to prosecute laws vigorously when government officials might be implicated.[27] As part of Mexico's transformation in 1994 from authoritarian control to a society based on the rule of law, Congress amended the LOAPF to remove the PGR as one of the agencies listed in LOAPF Article 1 as being subject to central control. The reforms may have been more cosmetic than effective: they did not alter the PGR's nature or administration. The *Procurador* continues to serve at the pleasure of the President; the PGR has not been immune from allegations of corruption or ineffectiveness that in the past plagued other Mexican government agencies.

The central government administration is hierarchical, with the Office of the President located at the top of the pyramid-like structure.[28] This vertical chain of command[29] establishes a clear relationship of authority between the different levels of the government. The President possesses the inherent power of appointment and removal of officials in subordinate agencies, the power of command, the power to make decisions, the power of oversight, the power to discipline subordinates, the power of review and the power to resolve conflicts of jurisdiction.

Cabinet-level ministries occupy the second level in the hierarchy of federal administration. Article 26 of the LOAPF creates the following Secretariats of State, the principal agencies of the Mexican federal executive branch, which are equivalent to US Departments and to cabinet ministries in other countries. These government agencies have equal rank in the hierarchical structure of government, and their chief executive officers are appointed and removed by the President of the Republic.[30] Together with the Office of the Legal Counsel of the Federal Executive, the following *secretarías* make up the presidential cabinet:

- *Secretaría de Gobernación* (SG) (Secretariat of Internal Affairs);
- *Secretaría de Relaciones Exteriores* (SRE) (Secretariat of Foreign Affairs);

[27] In the United States, this conflict has been dealt with by the creation of a controversial office, the Office of the Special Prosecutor, to investigate suspected crimes by high-level officials, including the President. The law authorizing the appointment of a special prosecutor has since lapsed, and was not renewed after the controversial investigation of President William Clinton, and others accused of breaking securities laws prior to President Clinton's assumption of office.

[28] *See* Fraga, *supra* note 1, at 164.

[29] Known as the *regla de la instrucción*.

[30] LOAPF, Arts. 4 and 10 and Mexican Constititution, Art. 89, part 2.

- *Secretaría de la Defensa Nacional* (SDN) (Secretariat of National Defence);
- *Secretaría de Marina* (SM) (Secretariat of the Navy);
- *Secretaría de Seguridad Pública* (SSP) (Secretariat of Public Security);
- *Secretaría de Hacienda y Crédito Público* (SHCP) (Secretariat of the Treasury and Public Credit);
- *Secretaría de Desarrollo Social* (SEDESOL) (Secretariat of Social Development);
- *Secretaría de Medio Ambiente y Recursos Naturales* (SEMARNAT) (Secretariat of the Environment and Natural Resources);
- *Secretaría de Energía* (SE) (Secretariat of Energy);
- *Secretaría de Economía* (SECONOMÍA) (Secretariat of Economy);
- *Secretaría de Agricultura, Ganadería, Desarrollo Rural, Pesca y Alimentación* (SAGARPA) (Secretariat of Agriculture, Livestock, Rural Development, Fishing, and Nutrition);
- *Secretaría de Comunicaciones y Transportes* (SCT) (Secretariat of Communications and Transportation);
- *Secretaría de la Función Pública* (SFP) (Secretariat of Public Administration);[31]
- *Secretaría de Educación Pública* (SEP) (Secretariat of Public Education);
- *Secretaría de Salud* (SSA) (Secretariat of Health);
- *Secretaría de Trabajo y Previsión Social* (STPS) (Secretariat of Labour and Welfare);
- *Secretaría de la Reforma Agraria* (SRA) (Secretariat of Agrarian Reform);
- *Secretaría de Turismo* (SECTUR) (Secretariat of Tourism).

In accordance with the LOAPF, each *secretaría de estado* is headed by a Secretary, who is the chief executive officer, and staffed by: undersecretaries; a chief administrative officer; directors general and deputy directors (*subdirectores*); department, section, and desk chiefs and assistant chiefs; and other officials listed in the respective internal regulations (*Reglamento Interior*) of the agency or in other legal provisions.[32]

Secretarios de estado are appointed by the President, who also has the power to remove them; unlike in the United States, appointments of cabinet ministers are not subject to the approval of any body of Congress. According to Article 91 of the Constitution, the Secretary must be a Mexican national by birth and at least thirty years of age.

[31] SFP is the name now given to the government accounting agency referred to as the *Secretaría de Contraloría y Desarrollo Administrativo* (SECODAM) [Secretariat of the Comptroller and Administrative Development]. *See* D.O. 10 Apr. 2003.

[32] Listed hereafter are the dates of publication in the *Diario Oficial* of the last reform of the internal regulations of the principal executive agencies of the federal government: SHCP, 24 Dec. 2001; SECONOMÍA, 10 Aug. 2000; SFP (formerly SECODAM), 16 Jul. and 29 Nov. 2001; SEP, 26 Mar. 1994; SEDESOL, 13 Sep. 2001; SG 2 Mar. 2000 and 30 Jul. 2002; SSA, 15 Sep. 2000 and 5 Jul. 2001; SM, 19 Jul. 2000 and 5 Mar. 2001; STPS, 21 Dec. 2001; SEMARNAT, 5 Jun. 2000 and 4 Jun. 2001; SCT, 7 Dec. 2001; SRA, 10 Aug. 2001; SE, 4 Jun. 2001; SAGARPA, 10 Jul. 2001; and ST, 15 Jun. 2001. SDN is regulated by the Organic Law of the Mexican Army and Air Force. D.O. 26 Dec. 1986.

Aside from broad duties set forth in the Constitution (see Articles 92 and 93), the LOAPF also establishes general powers that each federal executive agency is entitled to exercise. Legislation enforced or implemented by *secretarías de estado* also establishes jurisdictional and other parameters for agency action.

Co-ordination of agency action takes place through either standing or *ad hoc* Intersecretarial Commissions (*Comisiones Intersecretariales*) authorized by Article 21 of the LOAPF and set up under federal executive agreements.

Some of the more important commissions are:

- the Intersecretarial Commission on Government Finance (*Comisión Intersecretarial de Gasto Financiamiento*);
- the Intersecretarial Commission on Privatization (*La Comisión Intersecretarial de Desincorporación*);
- the Intersecretarial Commission on Civil Service (*La Comisión Intersecretarial de Servicio Civil*);
- the Consultative Intersecretarial Commission on Public Works (*Comisión Intersecretarial Consultitiva de la Obra Pública*); and
- the Intersecretarial Commission to co-ordinate activities of agencies entrusted by law to conduct research on and protect archeological, historical, and artistic property that comprises the nation's cultural heritage.

In addition, President Vicente Fox has created a group of advisers to serve as co-ordinators of federal agency action, to promote and evaluate the administration's overall policy initiatives. Pursuant to Article 8 of the LOAPF, these co-ordinators are to give technical assistance and advice to government agencies in the co-ordination of their activities.[33]

2.1. Semi-Autonomous Agencies of the Federal Government (*La Desconcentración Administrativa*)

A highly centralized government, such as that which has dominated Mexico for decades, represents a significant challenge for governmental efficiency, especially at an operational level. Mexico has responded to the inefficiencies of centralized, hierarchical government by the creation of semi-autonomous federal agencies that are similar to (and to some extent modelled on) the administrative agencies of the US federal system (Federal Communications Commission, Securities Exchange Commission, etc.). This phenomenon is referred to as *desconcentración administrativa*, which might be translated as 'deconcentration', although that term has little meaning to a common law lawyer. The term denotes a type of decentralization: *desconcentración* involves the transfer of executive power from higher-level agencies to a lower-level office

[33] Co-ordinators of the federal government include the following offices: the General Co-ordinator of Social Communication; the General Co-ordinator of Public Opinion and Image; and the General Co-ordinator of Advisors in Public Policy.

within the central government administration, thus diminishing direct hierarchical control.[34]

Órganos desconcentrados lack independent legal personality; they generally lack budgetary independence, but they maintain some autonomy over decisions within their jurisdiction. Two types of *órganos desconcentrados* exist in Mexico: (1) those agencies whose chief executive officer is subordinate to the upper levels of the hierarchical structure, and (2) those agencies that are technically not accountable to superior bureaucratic authority in exercising decision-making powers.

This first type of *órgano desconcentrado* consists of agencies that are created by cabinet-level secretariats, and remain connected to the umbrella of activities within the jurisdiction of the particular secretariat.[35] Examples of this type of agency include the National Institute of Immigration (*Instituto Nacional de Migración*), which is within the jurisdiction of the Secretariat of Internal Affairs (SG); and the National Institute of Anthropology and History (*Instituto Nacional de Antropología e Historia*, known as INAH), which is under the Secretariat of Public Education.

The second type of *órgano desconcentrado* is generally created by a law or an executive order or decree which either contains an express provision creating the agency, or implicitly charters such an agency by virtue of the technical, operational, or budgetary independence granted to it. Examples of these types of agencies include the Federal Antitrust Commission (*Comisión Federal de Competencia*),[36] the Tax Administration Service (*Servicio de Administración Tributaria*),[37] the National Commission on Banking and Securities (*Comisión Nacional Bancaria y de Valores*),[38] and the National Energy Regulatory Commission (*Comisión Nacional Reguladora de Energía*).[39] These are enforcement agencies, rather than policy-making agencies; as such, they are *desconentrados* so as to be able to carry out their functions independently from other agencies. Several of these agencies are new, and reflect a level of

[34] *See* Serra Rojas, A., DERECHO ADMINISTRATIVO, VOL. I (Mexico: Porrúa, 11th ed., 1982) at 507. *See also* Acosta, M., TEORÍA GENERAL DEL DERECHO ADMINISTRATIVO (Mexico: Porrúa, 11th ed., 1993) at 422, who defines *desconcentración* as 'a form of administrative organization in which the "empowered" agency (*órgano desconcentrado*) is granted, by means of a materially legislative act (law, regulation), certain limited powers of decision and execution, that enable it [the agency] to act more swiftly, efficiently and flexibly as well as having greater autonomy in the management of its own budget, although the hierarchical link to the higher level agency does not cease to exist'.

[35] LOAPF, Art. 17 states: 'In order to [achieve] the most effective service and efficient handling of matters within their scope of duties and responsibilities, the Secretariats and Administrative Departments may create *órganos desconcentrados* that shall be hierarchically subordinate to the Secretariats and shall have the specific authority to decide the particular matters within their territorial confines that may be determined in each case in accordance with applicable legal provisions'.

[36] *See* www.cfc.gob.mx (site visited Jan. 2004).

[37] *See* www.sat.gob.mx (site visited Jan. 2004).

[38] The National Commission on Banking was created by presidential decree published in D.O. 24 Dec. 1924, and the National Commission on Securities was created by decree on 26 Apr. 1946. Both agencies were later consolidated into one. *See* D.O. 28 Apr. 1995.

[39] D.O. 31 Oct. 1995.

independence from hierarchical influence that was relatively unknown during the heyday of authoritarian government and *presidencialismo* discussed above in Chapter 5.

2.2. Quasi-Governmental Agencies (*La Administración Paraestatal*)

The largest number and greatest variety of independent agencies are quasi-governmental entities. Pursuant to Article 3 of the LOAPF, the following entities belong to the quasi-governmental branch of the government, known as the *administración paraestatal* (parastatal sector):

- de-centralized agencies (*organismos descentralizados*);
- government-owned corporations (*empresas de participación estatal*), including banking, finance, and insurance institutions; and
- government-owned trusts (*fideicomisos*).[40]

Such quasi-governmental, or parastatal, agencies are governed by the Federal Law of Quasi-governmental Entities (*Ley Federal de las Entidades Paraestatales*, known by its Spanish acronym, LFEP); by the regulations adopted pursuant to it (known also by its Spanish acronym, RLFEP);[41] and by the applicable statutes and presidential decrees that create such entities.

Thousands of such agencies have been created over the years, to carry out activities in strategic areas involving public or social services, including public health services. As noted previously in this Chapter, the apogee of the parastatal enterprise occurred during the administrations of Presidents Echeverría (1970–1976) and López Portillo (1976–1982). By 1982, 1,155 *paraestatales* had been established.[42] The scope of parastatal 'public services' became so extended that few sectors of society were unaffected by these agencies, which engaged in activities ranging from cultural affairs to commercial enterprises.

As neo-liberal economic policies took root in Mexico, during the 1990s, many of these *paraestatales* were sold to private investors, folded into other federal agencies, or dissolved. At present, there are approximately 250 decentralized agencies, government-owned corporations, and public trusts that belong to the federal government and are subject to the LFEP.[43] The most important of the remaining quasi-governmental entities are *Petróleos Mexicanos* (PEMEX), the state-owned oil company; the *Compañia Federal de Electricidad* (CFE), the state-owned power company; *Aeropuertos y Servicios Auxiliaries*, which operates airports; the *Consejo Nacional de Ciencia y Tecnología* (CONACYT), which is

[40] Government-owned trusts, established in certain sectors of public interest, are to be distinguished from the private trusts discussed in Chapter 18 below.

[41] *Reglamento de la Ley Federal de las Entidades Paraestatales*, D.O. 26 Jan. 1990, amended 7 Apr. 1995.

[42] *See* Rogozinski, J., *La privatizacion de las empresas paraestatales: Una Vision de la Modernizacion de Mexico* (Mexico: Fondo de Cultura Económica, 1993), at 45.

[43] A list of quasi-governmental agencies can be found at www.presidencia.gob.mx (site visited Jan. 2004).

similar to the United States National Science Foundation, and supports research; the *Loteria Nacional para la Asistencia Pública*, the national lottery; the *Institutio Mexicano de Serguridad Social* (IMSS), which operates public hospitals throughout the country; and its counterpart for government employees, the *Instituto de Seguridad y Servicios Sociales de los Trabajadores del Estado* (ISSSTE); the *Instituto del Fondo Nacional para la Vivienda de los Trabajadores* (INFONAVIT), which funds workers' housing; the *Banco Mexicoano de Comercio Exterior* (BANCOMEXT), Mexico's export bank; and numerous others.

Organismos descentralizados have their own legal personality *(personería juridical)* and are autonomous from any other agency in the federal system. They may be created either by Congressional statute or by presidential decree.[44] Each parastatal agency has a governing board or its equivalent, a director general, and an auditor or inspector general (*Comisario Público*). The first two agents act as governing and administrative bodies, and the third as an oversight body.

2.2.1. Organizational Structure and Governance of Decentralized Parastatal Agencies

Decentralized parastatal agencies are governed by the following bodies: a governing board; a chief executive officer; and an Inspector General (*Comisario Público*).

Governing Board The governing board of a decentralized parastatal agency has between five and fifteen members, and is presided over by the relevant *Secretario de Estado* or by a person appointed by the Secretary.[45] The governing board must include representatives of the SHCP (*Secretaría de Hacienda y Crédito Público*), representatives of the *Secretaría* that has jurisdiction over the field in which the agency operates, and representatives of the private or social sectors who are experts in the same field (Article 17 of the RLFEP). The following may not be members of the governing board: the director general of the entity;[46] spouses, relatives, or in-laws of any members of the governing board or of the director general; persons who have pending litigation with the particular entity; persons convicted of crimes against public assets; persons disqualified from engaging in commerce or from serving in public office, employment, or commission; and deputies and senators, as set forth in the provisions of Article 62 of the Constitution.

[44] *See* LFEP, Arts. 14 and 15. For an example of a statute creating a *parastatal* agency *see* the decree creating *Petróleos Mexicanos* (PEMEX), D.O. 7 Jun. 1938.

[45] In accordance with Article 16 of the RLFEP, the governing boards of quasi-governmental entities that are deemed by the federal executive to deal with priority areas must be presided over by the lead Secretary of the co-ordinating group of the sector; the governing board of all other entities shall be presided over by a public servant appointed by the lead Secretary of the co-ordinating group of the sector.

[46] The exclusion of directors general from the governing board does not apply to the *Instituto Mexicano del Seguro Social* (Mexico's national health care agency), the *Instituto de Seguridad y Servicios Sociales de los Trabajadores del Estado* (the Federal Government Employees' Health and Social Service Administration), the *Instituto del Fondo Nacional de la Vivienda de los Trabajadores* (INFONAVIT) (the federal public housing authority), nor other analogous institutions. LFEP, Art 19, part 1.

The governing board has the powers conferred on it by the law or decree that created it, including the power to issue its own organic law (*estatuto orgánico*) (LFEP Article 15). Article 58 of the LFEP also grants governing boards broad powers to carry out the agency's operations.

Director general The director general possesses broad powers, and in most cases the directors general of parastatal agencies have dominated their agencies' policies and operations.[47] While the director general is not immune from persuasion from high levels of the federal bureaucracy, he or she is often charged with managing a large bureaucracy and extensive operations. While the heads of agencies such as the IMSS or ISSSTE have in the past been political leaders, and even presidential hopefuls, increasingly these positions are being taken up by persons with technical expertise in the field in which the agency operates.

The director general is appointed by the President of the Republic or this power of appointment may be delegated by the President to the co-ordinating Secretary of the sector. The director general must be a Mexican citizen, must have previously served in a high level decision-making post which required managerial skills and expertise, and must not be disqualified from holding the position due to any of the impediments that apply to sitting on a governing board (LFEP Article 21).

Inspector/auditor general (comisario público) Oversight of decentralized parastatal agencies is conducted by a principal inspector general/auditor and a substitute, who are appointed by the Secretariat of Public Administration (SFP, formerly known as SECODAM, an agency similar to the US General Accounting Office). Under LFEP Article 60, the *comisario público* acts as an external auditor, evaluating the entity's general performance, assessing the propriety of the disbursement and investment of funds, the use of general revenues, and requesting information on these and other aspects. In addition to the *comisario público*, each agency must also employ an internal auditor, or *auditor interno*, within its organizational structure, to support efficient management and compliance with laws and regulations, under guidelines established by the SFP (formerly SECODAM) (LFEP Article 62).

These provisions are designed to prevent inefficiency and corrupt practices within parastatal entities. While such controls have had some effect, they must try to overcome a legacy of corruption in Mexican government that turned into an epidemic in the second half of the twentieth century. During the heyday of centralized control, government-owned enterprises were responsible for managing billions of dollars in activities, as buyers and sellers of goods and services, and the possibilities of personal gain were tempting. For example, both the management and the labour leadership of PEMEX were accused of corrupt practices that benefited highly placed officials; a former director general of PEMEX was even convicted of corruption in the late 1980s. The level of

[47] *See* LFEP Arts. 21 to 23 for the enumeration of and limitations on powers of directors general.

corruption has declined, in part due to the dramatic reduction in the number of government-owned enterprises. Nevertheless, in a recent report, *Transparencia Mexicana*, a private organization, concluded that government corruption costs the Mexican economy 2.5 billion US dollars per year.[48]

The government of President Vicente Fox has attempted to combat corruption through the adoption of federal legislation to promote openness in government. At Fox's urging, in 2002 Congress passed the Federal Law on Transparency and Access to Information, which is discussed in Section 6 below. The Fox administration also capitalized on the creation, at the end of the Zedillo *sexenio*,[49] of the Federal Regulatory Improvement Commission (COFEMER)[50] to help lobby within government for transparency in regulation.[51] In addition, SFP has undertaken a campaign to assure that all federal procedures are available to the public on the World Wide Web.[52]

2.2.2. *Special Rules Governing Government-Owned Enterprises* (Empresas de Participación Estatal)

Throughout much of the twentieth century the Mexican economy was highly centralized, and the government played a direct role in many sectors of the economy through the operation of government-controlled corporations.[53] Even under the neo-liberal, free-market policies of more recent government administrations, government-owned corporations continue to play significant roles in the economy. Examples of prominent government-owned enterprises include *Nacional Financiera* (NAFINSA), the government's principal development bank; the *Banco Nacional de Comercio Exterior* (BANCOMEXT), the Mexican export bank; and the *Banco Nacional de Obras y Servicios Públicos* (BANOBRAS), which finances public works.

Government-owned enterprises are generally incorporated as shareholding corporations (*sociedades anónimas*) in which the shares are wholly owned by the government or by a government agency.[54] In some instances, the government owns a majority of the shares, and a minority interest is held by enterprises that have an interest in the sector in which the government-owned enterprise

[48] *See* www.transparenciamexicana.org.mx/transparencia2.htm; Arellano-Gault, D., 'Corruption in Mexico Under the New Regime: Why Is It Still So High?', at www.aspanet.org/publications/columns/archives.

[49] *See* Chapter 12 below, at text accompanying note 14.

[50] *See* www.cofemer.gob.mx. LFPA, Title Three A (Tercero A) (Articles 69A to 69Q), 'On regulatory improvement', was adopted as part of the original LFPA, but it was not until amendment of the LFPA, after the election of Vicente Fox, that COFEMER was created with a mandate to implement an organized plan of regulatory transparency and improvement. D.O. 19 Apr. 2000, amending LFPA.

[51] *See also infra*, text accompanying notes 94–95.

[52] *See* www.funcionpublica.gob.mx. *See also* www.cofemer.gob.mx, '*prontuario jurídico*'. (Sites visited Jan. 2004.)

[53] *See* Chapter 12 below, at text accompanying notes 1–8.

[54] Examples of wholly owned state enterprises include BANCOMEXT, and e.g. *Petroquímica Cangrejera S.A. de C.V., Petroquímica Cosoleacaque S.A. de C.V.* Government-owned enterprises can also be established as limited liability companies (*sociedades de responsabilidad limitada*), co-operative enterprises (*sociedades cooperatives*), national credit enterprises (*sociedades nacionales de créditto*), civil corporations (*sociedades civiles*), or civil associations (*asociaciones civiles*). On the characteristics of such forms, *see* Chapter 19 below.

operates.[55] Enterprises with minority participation by the federal government are rare, since the government generally refuses to take an ownership interest in an enterprise it does not control.[56] Pursuant to Article 46 of LOAPF, the capital stock of a government-owned enterprise shall include a special series of certificates that can only be underwritten by the federal government.

Government-owned enterprises are governed by the following bodies: a board of directors or its equivalent; a chief executive officer (usually called the director general); and inspector/auditors (*comisarios públicos*).

Board of directors The composition of the board of directors is determined by the by-laws of the corporation, which themselves must conform to the enabling legislation authorizing creation of the government-owned corporation. The LFEP requires that the board of directors must include representatives of *secretarías de estado* or other government agencies responsible for the relevant sector, who must account for more than half of the total membership on the board. Directors are appointed by federal executive, and must be either public servants or private citizens with expertise in the area.[57] The board of directors shall exercise the powers granted by the corporation's by-laws and enabling legislation, provided that such provisions are consistent with the provisions of the LFEP and RLFEP regarding boards of directors of decentralized agencies. The members that represent the governmental shareholders must constitute more than half the Council.

Chief executive officer The requirements, method of appointment, and powers of the chief executive officer (*director general*) of a government-owned corporation are the same as those established by law for the directors general of other decentralized agencies, although the by-laws of the government-owned enterprise or the law that governs the particular class of corporation may provide otherwise.[58]

General auditor (comisario público) Government-owned corporations must have a permanent general auditor (*comisario público)* who is appointed by the SECODAM, in addition to any other auditors required to be appointed in accordance with the by-laws or other applicable laws. The powers of these inspector/auditors general are similar to those of the inspector/auditors general of decentralized agencies.[59]

2.3.2. Merger, Dissolution, and Privatization of Quasi-Governmental Entities

The LFEP establishes rules for federal government intervention in the operations of *paraestatales* entities in certain instances. Thus, whenever the possibility exists

[55] Examples include the news agency *Notimex, S.A. de C.V.*, the government information agency.

[56] *See* Martínez, R., DERECHO ADMINISTRATIVO I Y II (Mexico: Oxford University Press, 4th ed., 2000) at 155. Pursuant to Article 67 of the LFEP, when the federal government owns between 25% and 50% of the shares of an enterprise, SECODAM shall designate a public investment auditor to oversee the government's investment.

[57] LFEP, Arts. 9 and 34.

[58] LFEP, Arts. 37 and 38.

[59] LFEP, Art. 63.

of a merger or dissolution of the corporation, the government official responsible for co-ordinating the sector in which the enterprise operates[60] may intervene during the merger or dissolution in order to determine how such transactions shall take place, taking into consideration the best interests of the public, the shareholders, and the employees. Intervention of the co-ordinating group of the sector in these instances shall operate under the rules and regulations established by the SHCP for this purpose.

In 1982, a total of 1,155 quasi-governmental federal entities existed in Mexico; by 1990, only 213 of them remained in existence.[61] These statistics show how aggressively the federal government pursued a policy of dissolving or transferring (including by privatization) government-owned enterprises during the administrations of Miguel de la Madrid (1982–1988) and Carlos Salinas de Gortari (1988–1994).

The procedures surrounding the dissolution or transfer of a government-owned enterprise are complex, and the economic conditions have not always been amenable to easy dissolution or privatization. Some dissolutions or transfers have been conducted smoothly and without controversy, while others have either elicited public criticism, or have failed to attract sufficient interest to bring about a successful sale of assets, as in the case of some privatizations.[62]

Various federal agencies may take part in the process of dissolution or transfer, particularly the co-ordinating office of the sector involved, the SHCP, and the Intersecretarial Commission on Dissolution or Transfer (*Comisión Intersecretarial de Desincorporación*, or CID).[63] The CID is presided over by the Secretary of the Treasury (SHCP), and includes representatives of the Secretariats of the Economy, Labour (STPS), the Secretariat of Public Administration (SFP, formerly SECODAM), and the person in charge of the agency that co-ordinates the particular sector to which the government-owned agency belongs. Pursuant to the RLFEP, at the recommendation of the co-ordinating group of the sector, the SHCP submits a proposal for dissolution or transfer to the President for consideration; the proposal must also be endorsed by the CID (RLFEP Article 6).

The CID is responsible for overseeing the dissolution or transfer of assets. It defines overall policies and strategies, and establishes rules of procedure and oversight of the process. Such rules are complicated, because they involve the many areas of concern involved in these cases, from guidelines for the appraisal of the entity to be disposed of, to financial models, grants of concessions or permits, dissemination of information to the public and to interested parties, and many other details. In each case, the Commission appoints a special

60 *See supra*, text accompanying note 43.

61 Secretaría de Hacienda y Crédito Público, *Unidad de Desincorporación de Entidades Paraestatales* (Mexico: Secretaria de Hacienda y Crédito Público, April 1991) at 12.

62 The most important recent privatizations involved the telephone company, *Teléfonos de México*, in 1990; the sale of the steel company *Altos Hornos de México*, in 1991; and the sale of government-owned banks, described below in Chapter 20, at text accompanying notes 5–6. *See generally* Rogozinski, *supra* note 42 at 165 *et seq.*

63 The CID was created by presidential agreement and published in D.O. 7 Apr. 1995.

commissioner to carry out the dissolution or transfer, who is required to report to it.[64] Dissolution or transfer of assets may be carried out in several different ways: dissolution, liquidation, merger, or transfer of ownership, either to a private party or to another governmental entity.

Under Article 134 of the Constitution, when a government-owned entity is privatized (i.e. sold to a private investor), a procedure of public bidding (*licitación pública*) must be conducted in order to guarantee the best possible terms of sale for the state. The exception to this rule is when such a procedure is not the most suitable way to guarantee the best terms of price, quality, opportunity, or other relevant factors, in which case the pertinent law shall determine the procedures to be followed in order to guarantee the best terms for the state.

In general, privatization begins with a proposal prepared by the agency in charge of co-ordinating the sector in which the quasi-governmental entities operates. This agency's proposal is then analysed by the Intersecretarial Commission on Government Finance, which evaluates the financial viability of privatization and makes recommendations concerning the way in which the assets will be transferred. If the Treasury Department (SHCP) then authorizes privatization, the CID designates the credit institution (normally a government-owned bank) to operate as sales agent on behalf of the federal government. Details concerning the sale are then designed by the CID and published in the *Diario Oficial de la Federación*. Bids are submitted to representatives of the SHCP and the agent bank, and the receipt of bids is notarized by a public notary. The agent bank analyses the bids, and submits its analysis to the CID, which makes a recommendation for acceptance of the bids. Once the bid amounts are paid into the Treasury and the sale is complete, the CID requests the SHCP to remove the enterprise from the public registry of parastatal agencies.[65]

2.4. Public Trusts (*Fideicomisos Públicos*)

In addition to government-owned corporations, the government has employed a separate vehicle, the trust, or *fideicomiso público*, to carry out certain programmes. Mexican governments (state and federal) use the *fideicomiso público* when they wish to establish an agency that benefits social welfare but is of a non-commercial nature. *Fideicomisos públicos* are found in agriculture, housing, tourism, and education, although among others; examples include the National Fund for the Promotion of Tourism (FONATUR), the National Fund for Popular Housing (FONHAPO), and the National Fund for Folk Art (FONART).

A *fideicomiso* is a creation of commercial law[66] that has become incorporated into administrative law as a way of realizing certain activities or fulfilling

[64] Art. 6 of the Agreement that created the Intersecretarial Commission on Dissolution or Transfer, D.O. 7 Apr. 1995.

[65] *See* Rogozinski, *supra* note 42 at 49–109.

[66] According to Article 346 of the General Law of Negotiable Instruments and Credit Operations (*Ley de Títulos y Operaciones de Crédito*), D.O. 26 Aug. 1932, as amended, by virtue of a trust, the trustor earmarks certain assets for a specific legal purpose, and entrusts the realization of that purpose to a fiduciary institution (trustee).

specific duties (LOAPF Article 47). The structure of a *fideicomiso* is similar to that of other government entities, with a director general who may also serve as the trustee (*delegado fiduciario*)[67] of the *fideicomiso*. The *fideicomiso* is assisted by a technical committee composed of expert advisers, who are public employees. The technical committee is chaired by the cabinet Secretary responsible for the sector in which the public trust operates, and the committee includes officials from governmental entities related to the subject area of the trust. A minority of the committee may include non-government members who represent important public and private interests.

As quasi-governmental agencies, *fideicomisos públicos* are not to be confused with the private trust or *fideicomiso*, which is discussed elsewhere in this volume.[68]

Fideicomisos públicos trusts are created when the federal government, represented by the SHCP, enters into a trust agreement with an institution that is legally qualified to be a fiduciary or trustee.[69] Typically, when the SHCP creates the *fideicomiso público*, it transfers funds to the trustee which serve as the initial assets (*patrimonio)* of the *fideicomiso*.

The trust agreement establishing the *fideicomiso público* sets forth the rights and duties that the fiduciary or trustee may exercise in connection with the assets placed in trust; and the rights of any institutions or third parties that may be created by the terms of the trust agreement. The trust agreement also specifies the rights reserved by the trustor and, if applicable, the powers to be granted to the technical committee (LFEP Article 41). The trust agreement must also specify any additional powers that may be granted to the technical committee, including the right to approve or disapprove actions by the trustee, as a check on the latter's actions (LFEP Article 44).

The dissolution of public trusts is similar to that of private *fideicomisos*. According to the LFEP, the government has the principal right to revoke public trusts, although this does not preclude the rights of third parties to do so, except when trusts are mandatory,[70] or when the nature of the trust does not allow revocation (LFEP Article 45). After dissolution of a trust, the SHCP or the technical committee issues guidelines to carry out the dissolution. Once this phase is completed, dissolution is formalized by executing a dissolution agreement (RLFEP Article 9).

[67] In private trusts, the *delegado fiduciario* is usually a bank employee, but in the case of public trusts, the same person usually serves as director general and *delegado fiduciario*, who has a joint responsibility to the bank and to the government administration.

[68] *See* Chapter 18 below.

[69] Only certain institutions, preferably national credit institutions (banks), or occasionally the Mexican central bank (*Banco de México*), may serve as trustee (*ficudicario*). *See* Martinez, *supra* note 56 at 166.

[70] For example, under Article 97 of the Ley Agraria, the National Trust Fund for the Promotion of Common Farmlands (*Fideicomiso Fondo Nacional de Fomento Ejidal*) is authorized to receive all expropriated lands that have not been used for the purposes specified in the law, and therefore dissolution of the *Fondo* would require an act of Congress.

Recent dissolutions include the controversial dissolution of the *Fondo Bancario de Protección al Ahorro*, or FOBAPROA, which had been created by the Mexican central bank (*Banco de México*) as a bail-out mechanism for overly indebted Mexican banks.[71]

3. Administrative Acts and Their Regulation

Administrative acts refer to particular actions and decisions by governmental agencies that trigger the application of a complex set of regulations and controls. Thus, the characterization of an act as an administrative act may have important consequences.

According to Mexican legal scholars, an administrative act is 'a unilateral declaration of will, understanding, or judgment, of an administrative body, carried out in the performance of administrative duties, which has a direct, concrete legal effect'.[72] Excluded from the category of administrative acts are legislative and jurisdictional acts, and agreements entered into by governmental agencies, either with other agencies or with individuals. Legal consequences may also occur in response to administrative silence or inaction if a law specifically states that lack of agency action will result in either acceptance or denial of a matter.[73] Such 'negative action' is known as *silencio administrativo*, and is tantamount to the commission of an administrative act.

3.1. Requirements for Issuance of Valid Administrative Acts

Administrative acts are governed not only by the laws and regulations applicable to each agency, but also by the Federal Law of Administrative Procedure (*Ley Federal de Procedimiento Administrativo*) (LFPA).[74] The LFPA applies to acts, procedures, and decisions of bodies of the central and parastatal administration; it does *not* apply to fiscal or financial matters, the liability of public servants, electoral or economic matters, agrarian and labour justice, or to public prosecutors in the performance of their constitutional duties (LFPA Article 1).

Attention to formal details is taken seriously in Mexican administrative law, just as in other areas of Mexican law.[75] This may be due to an abiding sense

[71] *See* Chapter 20 below, at text accompanying note 29.

[72] Delgadillo, L. y Espinoza, L., Compendio de Derecho Administrativo (Mexico: Porrúa, 3rd ed., 2002) at 231. Miguel Acosta Romero has defined an administrative act as 'a unilateral and external manifestation of will, that expresses a decision of a competent administrative authority, in the exercise of public power. This decision creates, recognizes, modifies, transmits, declares or extinguishes rights or obligations, is generally executive and its purpose is to satisfy the public interest.' Acosta, *supra* note 34 at 718.

[73] *See* e.g. LFPA, Art. 17 (if 3 months pass without agency resolution of a matter, it will be understood that the resolution is negative).

[74] D.O. 4 Aug. 1994. The LFPA of 1994 was Mexico's first comprehensive administrative law, and was modelled on Spanish law. Major amendments to the LFPA occurred in 2000. D.O. 19 Apr. 2000. On the evolution of Mexican administrative law, *see* Cortés, J., 'Orden Jurídico Administrativo y mejora regulatoria', in Este País (no. 40, Nov. 2002) at 1.

[75] *See* Chapter 15 below, at text accompanying notes 14–15.

that in a legal culture not known for efficiency, forthrightness, or transparency, formal requirements may be an important bastion against arbitrary action.

Article 3 of the LFPA establishes the requirements that must be observed by an agency in issuing administrative acts that are considered to be legally valid and effective. Failure to comply with any of these requirements is a ground for nullifying the administrative act, as discussed in Section 9, below.

Article 3 of the LFPA also enumerates the requirements for issuing valid administrative acts. Some of the most important requirements are the following:

The act must be issued by a competent body, by a public employee; should such a body consist of several officials acting in a group, the act must meet the formal requirements set forth in the law or decree that empowers the agency to issue the act (LFPA Article 3, Section I). This requirement is sometimes referred to as the *principio de legalidad.* The agency must possess the jurisdictional capacity (*competencia*) to act: that is, the act cannot exceed the range or scope of powers established by law (subject matter and territorial jurisdiction, timeliness, and hierarchy of authority). Jurisdictional capacity can be created by the Constitution, a statute, administrative regulation, international treaty, or by acts of delegation of authority,[76] administrative pre-emption (*avocación*),[77] or administrative co-ordination.[78]

The object of the administrative act must be sufficiently specific, including the act's precise application in time and place, to be precise and foreseeable (LFPA Article 3, Section II). The object of the administrative act is understood as the substance or content of the act, that is, the creation, transfer, modification, recognition, or abandonment of rights and obligations carried out by the government.[79]

The act must be in the public interest and serve a public purpose (LFPA Article 3, Section III). This requirement serves as a restraint on the discretionary powers of administrative officials and as a guideline for their performance. There is obviously an element of subjectivity inherent in this requirement. If the administrative act is not in the public interest, this may amount to an abuse of power (*abuso de poder*), which is one of the grounds for annulment of administrative acts. For example, if the award of a public contract for the construction of a freeway is not carried out by the *Secretariía de Comunicaciones y Transportes* (SCT) according to a public bidding process, as required by law, the act would be considered not to be in the public interest, and the SCT would be guilty of an abuse of power.

[76] *See* LOAPF, Art. 16. Agreements to delegate authority must be published in the *Diario Oficial de la Federación.*

[77] *Avocación* (a form of pre-emption) applies when a superior official undertakes the powers of an inferior agent in the hierarchy. This power is usually spelled out in the Internal Regulations applicable to each *secretaría de estado*, and can usually be found on the web site of each *secretaría.*

[78] The federal government has entered into numerous co-ordination agreements with states of the Republic, by which the state or municipal authorities shall carry out acts that fall within the scope of federal powers or jurisdictional capacity. An example of this is found in Art. 14 of the Law of Fiscal Co-ordination (*Ley de Coordinación Fiscal*), D.O. 27 Dec. 1978, last amended 13 Mar. 2002, which authorizes state officials to collect taxes on behalf of the federal government.

[79] *Cf.* Acosta, *supra* note 34 at 728.

The act must be recorded in written form signed by the representative of the authority that issues it, except in cases in which the law authorizes another form of issuance (LFPA Article 3, Section IV). This requirement is established by Article 16 of the Constitution, which provides that no person may be disturbed in their person, family, domicile, papers, or possessions, except by virtue of a written order from the competent authority that states the bases in fact and law for the proceeding.

The act must be grounded in the law and supported by the facts (fundamentación y motivación) *(LFPA Article 3, Section V).* The grounding of an administrative act in fact and in law is one of most litigated subjects in the Mexican courts. An act is only valid if there is consistency between the points of law and the points of fact in the argument put forth by the authority in the case at hand. This is referred to as 'due basis in law and fact' (*debida fundamentación y motivación*). In the words of the one Mexican appellate court, '[t]o be grounded in the law means that the precise legal precept applicable to the specific case must be set forth, and grounded in the facts means that the particular circumstances, reasons and immediate causes that have been taken into consideration to issue the act must also be precisely set forth. Also, a correlation must exist between the causes cited in the act and laws that apply thereto; that is to say, that the hypothetical elements of the law must match the specific facts of the case.'[80] For example, the Mexican Supreme Court has held that an order of attachment of property (*embargo precautorio*) is not grounded in law and fact if the order is overly general and merely alleges irregularities, but does not specify the particular law and facts that merit application of the attachment. In such cases, an *amparo* action may be brought to nullify the act.[81]

The act must be issued in conformity with the provisions of the LFPA. This requirement obliges an agency to observe the procedures established by applicable laws and regulations, as well as the procedures set by the LFPA, in carrying out an administrative act. Administrative agencies often adopt particular regulations that set forth procedures specific to their administrative acts; such procedures complement, and must be in conformity with, the LFPA.

The main procedural requirements under the LFPA include the following:

(i) Administrative proceedings must be conducted in keeping with the principles of economy, swiftness, efficiency, legality (the rule of law), proper service of notice, and good faith (LFPA Article 13).
(ii) Authorities may not require that any formalities be met other than those expressly set forth in the law (LFPA Article 15).
(iii) Officials are required: to request an appearance before the agency only when such action is required by law; to request during verification visits any

[80] SJF, 8ª, T. XVI, Segundo Tribunal Colegiado del Quinto Circuito, June 1992, p. 49.

[81] SJF, 6ª, 3ª Sala, at 80. (*Acto Administrativo Carente de Motivación o Fundamentación. Amparo Total y No Para Efectos. Amparo en revisión 230/94. Flora Alimentos, S.A. de C.V. 12 de enero de 1995. Unanimidad de votos. Ponente: Gullermo Baltazar Alvear. Secretario: José Luis Solórzano.* (Administrative act lacking in *motivatión* or *fundamentacíon*).

records, documents, and information from individuals that may be needed to assist in deciding the case; to report to individuals on the status of the proceedings and provide them with a copy of the report; to admit any evidence introduced by individuals and receive their arguments or pleadings; to permit access to records and files; and to facilitate the exercise of individuals' rights and fulfilment of their obligations (LFPA Article 16).[82]

According to Article 17 of the LFPA, administrative authorities may not exceed a period of four months to settle matters that fall within their jurisdiction, unless otherwise specified in an applicable legal provision. Should an agency fail to act or respond within the required time limits, such inaction shall be taken as a denial of a request put before it (*negativa ficta*). The putative denial that is established in the LFPA operates when the statute that governs the subject matter does not expressly set forth how an authority's silence shall be understood, thus constituting a type of substitute denial. The regulatory law pertaining to the subject matter may also establish putative approval (*afirmativa ficta*). Putative denials and approvals have both become more common in recent years, as a result of the federal government's attempts at deregulation.

The LFPA contains additional provisions (Articles 19 to 69) specifying which parties have a stake in the proceedings, in which circumstances administrative officials may be precluded from hearing a case and must recuse themselves, the terms and length of proceedings, access to records and information by the parties, service of notice and filing of challenges, as well as initiation, procedures, and completion of the administrative proceeding.

The act must be issued without any error regarding the object, cause, or purpose of the act (LFPA Article 3, Section VIII). In Mexican law, error is considered to be a false assessment of reality.[83] When error affects the rights and obligations that are the object or substance of the act, this is a ground for annulment of the act. The cause or motive of the act is considered to be the prior factual and legal circumstances that give rise to the administrative act.[84]

The administrative act must be issued without fraud (dolo), *that is to say, without any criminal intention, wilful malfeasance or malicious failure to fulfil one's obligation, or violence (LFPA Article 3, Section IX).* The official who issues the act must act with free will. If the official is coerced into issuing an act,

[82] Pursuant to the recently adopted Federal Transparency and Information Law, discussed *infra*, at text accompanying notes 97–104 persons outside the government are guaranteed access to information held by government agencies. Exceptions to access exist, and experience in the operation of this new act is limited to date.

[83] The concept of error as a legal defect or impediment has received considerable attention in the field of civil law, where legal scholars have classified the different types of error: errors of fact, errors of law, errors of calculation, and errors of account (mathematical mistakes). *See* e.g. Domínguez, J., *Derecho Civil, Parte General: Personas, Cosas, Negocio Jurídico e Invalidez* (Mexico: Porrúa, 3rd ed., 1996) at 593.

[84] According to Gabino Fraga, the motive of the act is the 'antecedent [prior event] that gives rise to it [the act], is the legal or factual relationship foreseen by the law as the necessary reason for administrative action'. Gabino Fraga, *supra* note 1 at 270.

or is led into error by another party, this will be considered as fraud, and will justify annulment of the act.

4. Procedures for Nullification (*Nulidad*) and Voidability (*Anulabilidad*) of Administrative Acts

The previous section set out the ground rules for issuing valid administrative acts. This section discusses the procedures to be followed in declaring improperly issued acts invalid.

Mexican law establishes two separate forms of invalidity of administrative acts: nullification (*nulidad*) and voidability (*anulabilidad*).

4.1. Nullification (*nulidad*)

Nullification (*nulidad*) applies when omissions or irregularities exist in the requirements specified in Sections I to XI of LPFA Article 3, including those listed above (LFPA Article 6). When this occurs, a superior official in the hierarchy of the agency in which the act was issued should declare the act illegitimate and non-executable. Private parties are not obliged to comply with the act, and public employees must record their opposition to executing the act, setting forth the legal grounds and facts for their refusal to execute such an act. The effects of declarations of nullification shall be retroactive: the act is considered nullified from the moment of its issuance, and all legal effects of the act are deemed invalid. If the defect that causes nullification is cured, the act may later become valid. Nullification does not preclude the issuance of a new act, which may be valid so long as it does not contain similar defects.

If an act subject to nullification has already been carried out, and if it is impossible to undo the effects of the act, the public employee that issued or ordered the act may be liable for damages that arise therefrom.[85]

4.2. Declaring an Act Voidable (*Anulabilidad*)

Under LFPA Article 7, an act may be declared voidable (*anulabilidad*) in cases involving less serious omissions or irregularities with regard to the elements and requirements of administrative acts, which are set forth in LFPA Article 3, Sections XII to XVI. Administrative acts that are declared voidable are more easily cured than those that have been nullified. A declaration of voidability does not prevent the act from taking effect; such an act is considered valid and executable if the administrative agency cures the defect in the issuance of the act by the agency. Both private parties and public agencies must comply with a voidable act once the defect has been corrected, and the act shall have retroactive

[85] On the liability of public employees, *see* Section 7, *infra*.

effect and shall be treated as if it had always been valid. Until the defect is corrected, the administrative act is not effective, and may be challenged in court by a petition for *amparo*.

4.3. Procedures for Declarations of Nullification or Voidability

Declarations of nullification or voidability may be issued by the administrative authorities, or by an interested party (LFPA Article 14). The Mexican legal system has a wide variety of procedures available to private parties for this purpose. Regulatory laws themselves may establish procedures of administrative appeal that may be heard by the same administrative authority that issued the act or by a superior in the hierarchy.[86] Alternatively, challenges to administrative acts may be heard through procedures other than the ordinary appeals process of the agency in question, such as the following:

(i) a hearing before a specialized administrative law judge in the Federal Fiscal Court;[87]
(ii) the *amparo* procedure (discussed above in Chapter 8); or
(iii) other procedures available under international treaties, such as the use of dispute resolution panels under NAFTA.[88]

4.4. Revocation of Administrative Acts

In addition to nullification of an act on the ground of irregularities in the act's issuance, as discussed above, Article 11 of the LFPA states that an administrative act may be revoked by the agency under certain circumstances. Revocation of an administrative act may come about as a result of an administrative appeal, or at the initiative of the issuing agency.

Under LFPA Article 11, revocation of an administrative act may occur in the following circumstances.

(i) when the act has fulfilled its purpose; for instance, the authorization needed for an archaeological treasure to be temporarily exported for an exhibition expires as soon as the artefact is returned to Mexico;
(ii) when the deadline for which the act was issued expires; for example, the permission for a foreign tourist to remain in Mexico for ninety days expires as soon as the period has passed;
(iii) when completion of the act is conditional upon an event, and this condition is not met; for example, the admission of a student to a public university

[86] For example, under the Customs Law, a party who wishes to appeal an administrative act may file a request for administrative revision before the customs authority that issued the act, or it may file a nullification procedure before the Federal Fiscal Tribunal.
[87] *See* Chapter 6 above, Section 5.1.2.
[88] *See*, for example, NAFTA, Art. 1904, providing for panel review of decisions by Mexican trade officials regarding antidumping and countervailing duty decisions. Information on binational panels reviews under NAFTA may be found at www.sice.oas.org.

may be conditional on the satisfaction of certain requirements that the student fails to meet;

(iv) when the interested party drops the claim, if such party is the exclusive beneficiary of the act and such a waiver does not operate to the detriment of the public interest;

(v) when it is in the best interest of the public for the act to be revoked in accordance with the law that regulates the subject matter.

5. Regulatory Reform and Transparency

The political and economic 'opening' (*apertura*) that began during the last decade of the twentieth century[89] eliminated the worst excesses of authoritarian, one-party rule under the PRI. The *apertura* also had a salutory effect on administrative law. Reform of administrative law was dictated by Mexican political leaders' realization of the need to carry out administrative reforms that would increase bureaucratic efficiency, predictability, and transparency, to complement the conversion of the economy from a centralized, state-planned model to a free market economy. Private business and investment thrives under such conditions, which were seen as necessary to the new political economy. Economic reformers also wished to reduce the high levels of corruption that had plagued Mexican government, and to increase transparency to make it easier to prevent criminal acts undertaken by government officials and private parties.[90]

5.1. Regulatory Reform

As discussed below in Chapter 12, the administration of President Carlos Salinas de Gortari (1988–1994) began a vigorous policy of regulatory reform to transform the centrally planned economy to accommodate more efficient regulatory practices associated with a free market economy. Beginning in 1989, the Secretariat of Trade and Industry (formerly SECOFI, now the *Secretaría de Economía*) issued new regulations covering economic activity,[91] and the President announced the creation of a new Unit for Economic Deregulation to promote these new policies.[92]

Further reforms were carried out at the end of the administration of President Ernesto Zedillo. In April 2000, the LFPA was amended[93] to introduce a new section dealing with improvement of the regulatory environment. The most important innovation of the 2000 administrative reforms was the creation of the

[89] *See* Chapter 1 above, at text accompanying notes 149–170; Chapter 5 above, at text accompanying notes 126–128, 206–208; and Chapter 12 below, at text accompanying notes 1–8.

[90] *See* Arce, C. and López, S., 'La manifestación de impacto regulatorio', in *Proyectos de Reformas Legales e Interpretación de las Normas Existentes* (México: BMA-Themis, 2002) at 1535.

[91] *See* D.O. 9 Feb. 1989.

[92] *See* D.O. 3 Mar. 1989.

[93] *See* D.O. 19 Apr. 2000.

Federal Regulatory Improvement Commission (*Comisión Federal de Mejora Regulatoria*, or COFEMER) as a semi-autonomous agency within the Secretariat of Economy.[94] COFEMER is advised by a council made up of the Secretaries of the Economy, Treasury (SHCP), Public Administration (SFP), Labour, and the Legal Counsel to the President; other federal officials designated by the President (governor of the Bank of Mexico, the chairman of the Federal Competition Commission, and the Attorney General for Consumer Affairs); and representatives from the business, labour, agricultural, and academic sectors. The relative autonomy of COFEMER has given it an aggressive stance *vis-à-vis* other federal agencies, the regulatory performance of which it monitors.

COFEMER is charged with reviewing all draft regulations, and proposals to amend regulations, before they are finalized by the federal agency proposing them. COFEMER's review is intended to ensure that the proposed regulations are in accordance with the laws, and the regulations can survive a cost–benefit analysis (LFPA Article 69-E). In proposing the new regulation, the agency must submit a Manifestation of Regulatory Impact (*manifestación de impacto regulatorio*, or MIR), similar to an environmental impact statement, to assess the impact of the regulation on society. The MIR concept, developed by the governments of OECD countries, provides a framework for conducting a cost–benefit analysis of specific government regulations. In evaluating the agency's MIR, COFEMER will review: the consistency of the regulation with its regulatory objectives; the empirical information (statistical, scientific, or legal) that justifies adoption of the regulation; the effect that the regulation will have on competition and access to markets; and the effect on consumers and small and medium industries, among other things. In carrying out its mission, COFEMER is assisted by a staff of economists, lawyers, and other professionals. In addition to evaluating regulatory impact statements, COFEMER fulfils an important function in promoting transparency of regulation. An example is the Federal Registry of Government Regulations and Services (*Registro Federal de Trámites y Servicios*), which uses the Internet to make detailed information available to any person who seeks to find out about federal regulations of any activity.[95] In addition, COFEMER enforces the requirement that any federal regulation must be made available for public comment at least one month prior to adoption of the regulation. COFEMER is still in its infancy, but the early experience has been generally favourable, and has begun to influence regulatory reform in some of the states.[96]

[94] *See* LFPA, Art. 69-A to 69-G. For information on COFEMER, *see* www.cofemer.gob.mx (site visited Jan. 2004).

[95] Access to the *Registro Federal de Trámites y Servicios* (RFTS) is through the agency's web site, www.cofemer.gob.mx (site visited Jan. 2004). By law, federal regulations or agency requirements that are not registered in the RFTS cannot be enforced by federal agencies.

[96] *See* Informe Anual COFEMER 2001 (Mexico: Cofemer, 2001), and reports on the agency web site. *See also* Consejo Coordinador Empresarial, CALIDAD DEL MARCO REGULATORIO EN LAS ENTIDADES FEDERATIVAS MEXICANAS. ESTUDIO COMPARATIVO *2000* (Mar. 2001) and 'Indicadores de avance en los programas bianuales', available at www.cofemer.gob.mx (site visited Jan. 2004).

5.2. Transparency

The most recent addition to Mexico's package of regulatory reforms involves the adoption in 2002 of the Law of Transparency and Access to Governmental Public Information (*Ley Federal de Transparencia y Acceso a la Información Pública Gubernamental*, or LTAIGP).[97] The Federal Transparency Law was an integral part of President Fox's attempt to curtail government corruption, and if enforced vigorously, could prove to be one of the most significant outcomes of the Fox administration. The Law and the regulations that support it[98] are intended to guarantee access by all persons to information held by any agency of the *federal* government—whether the agency belongs to the executive, judicial, or legislative branch. The Law is subject to exceptions, and the government may withhold certain confidential information, in accordance with specific standards set forth in the Law and the Regulations.[99] The Law also covers access to information concerning private persons, and includes provisions protecting against indiscriminate dissemination of such information (LTAIPG Articles 20 to 26). According to LTAIGP Article 15, the maximum term that a public document may be withheld under these provisions is twelve years.[100]

The Transparency Law created the Federal Institute of Access to Public Information (*Instituto Federal de Acceso a la Información Pública*, or IFAI),[101] an independent federal agency with operational, budgetary, and decision-making autonomy, which was established to assure the proper administration of the Law by federal executive branch agencies (*Administración Pública Federal*).[102] The Institute is governed by five commissioners who are appointed by the President of the Republic, with the approval (*no objección*) of the Senate. The commissioners serve for a single term of seven years, and can only be removed for cause. IFAI issues general regulations to be followed by federal agencies in establishing the

[97] D.O. 11 Jun. 2002. More information on the Federal Transparency Law can be found at www.cofemer.gob.mx, '*Transparencia y acceso a la información*'. (Site visited Jan. 2004.)

[98] *Reglamento de la Ley Federal de Transparencia y Acceso a la Información Publica Gubernamental*, D.O. 11 Jun. 2003, available at www.ifai.org.mx, 'Marco Normativo'. (Site visited Jan. 2004.)

[99] According to Arts. 13 and 14 of the LTAIPG, exceptions exist: to protect public safety or national security; when release of the information would damage international relations or economic, monetary, or financial stability; when release would risk the life, safety, or health of any person; when release would prejudice law enforcement, criminal enforcement, the administration of justice, tax collection, or the control of immigration, among others. Private information (such as trade secrets or private financial records) are also excepted.

[100] LGTAIP, Art. 15. The 12-year period may be extended when circumstances justify it. Art. 26 of the Regulations provide that the 12-year period shall begin to run when the information becomes classified.

[101] IFAI is a principal source of information on the Federal Transparency Law. *See* www.ifai.org.mx (site visited Jan. 2004).

[102] Only agencies of the executive branch are subject to regulations of the IFAI. The judicial and legislative branches are responsible for adopting their own organs and rules for administering the Transparency Law, as are independent subjects of the federal power, such as the *Banco de México*, the *Comisión Nacional de Derechos Humanos*, the *Instituto Federal Electoral*, autonomous universities, etc.

rules by which they should process requests for release of information,[103] although each agency is responsible for establishing its own procedures in accordance with the guidelines of IFAI. The person soliciting information must bear the cost of its reproduction and transportation (LFTAIPG Article 27).

Denials of requests for release of information may be appealed to IFAI, either directly or by filing the appeal through the office (*unidad de enlace*) of the federal agency denying the request (LTAIPG Articles 40–48). IFAI has sole authority to consider the appeal.

As is often the case in Mexico, a number of states, and the Federal District, have adopted transparency laws in response to the passage of the Federal Transparency Law.[104] At the date of this writing, it is too soon to evaluate the Law's long-term effects. Early reports indicate that most federal agencies are complying with the law, although there have been newspaper reports of some intransigence by certain agencies.

Transparency is a revolutionary concept in Mexican public administration, which has long made decisions that were seldom open to any objective inquiry. Nevertheless, the long-term implications of the adoption of transparency laws for the improvement of public administration and control of corruption are obvious, and adoption of the Federal Transparency Law may prove to be the most striking accomplishment of the Fox *sexenio*.

6. Evaluating the Effectiveness of Administrative Challenges and Appeals

The procedures discussed in this Chapter provide significant safeguards for citizens against arbitrary or illegal governmental actions. This conclusion is at odds with the general perception, both within Mexico and abroad, that government officials in Mexico are not subject to stringent controls, and that the government itself has not adhered to the rule of law in carrying out its functions on behalf of the citizenry. As a vestige of single-party rule, the opinions held by many Mexican citizens continue to be highly critical of public agencies and those who run them.

The stereotype of the corrupt or incompetent Mexican government official is increasingly at odds with reality. The waning of the PRI's authoritarian power has been accompanied by a growth in the professionalism of a new style of civil servant: well educated and skilled in subjects that are in demand in modern governmental agencies.

[103] *See*, for example, '*Recomendaciones para la identificación de información reservada* o *confidencial por parte de las dependencias y entidades de la administración pública federal*', D.O. 1 Apr. 2003.

[104] Transparency laws of certain Mexican states, and of the Federal District, can be found at www.juridicas.unam.mx, '*legislación de entidades federativas*'. (Site visited Jan. 2004.)

The efficiency and honesty of public administration has also been aided by the gradual strengthening of the judicial system, and by the proliferation of administrative tribunals, as discussed above in Chapter 6. As the federal judiciary is strengthened, the use of *amparo* as a weapon against bureaucratic abuses has become more important than ever, as federal judges are increasingly willing to overturn agency actions that do not conform with the law.

The professionalism of Mexican governmental bureaucracies has been compromised in the past by the absence of a general law providing civil service protection (e.g. employment security and other safeguards) to federal employees. Without civil service protection, a federal employee's continued employment has often depended on his or her allegiance to superiors, tempting workers to overlook or ignore abuses. Finally, in 2003, Congress adopted the first Federal Civil Service Law (FCSL)[105] with the intention of promoting increased job security and professional standards for government employees. Under the new Law, only the top levels of officials in federal agencies (secretary, under-secretary [*subsecretario*], and *oficial mayor*, heads of agencies, or their equivalent) will be considered political appointees, and therefore subject to removal without cause (FCSL Article 7). All other federal employees, from the level of director general down, will receive civil service protection (*servidores públicos de carrera*): that is, they are guaranteed 'stability and permanence in service under the terms and conditions of the Law' (FCSL Articles 5, 10). This change is calculated to improve public administration in Mexico, by providing greater stability and professionalism of government workers, who will be less subject to removal due to changes in political leadership.

While the Federal Civil Service Law only covers federal agencies,[106] it is expected that the states and the Federal District will adopt similar laws in an attempt to improve public administration at the state level.

7. Liability of Public Servants and Government Agencies

Public employees are subject to political, administrative, criminal, and civil liability, and agencies themselves may be subject to administrative sanctions for acts or omissions that injure private parties.

[105] *Ley del Servicio Profesional de Carrera de la Administración Pública Federal*, D.O. 10 Apr. 2003, also discussed in Chapter 13 below, at text accompanying note 43.

[106] The Federal Civil Service Law applies to agencies directly dependent on the executive branch, such as *secretarías* and their subordinate organizations. Quasi-independent agencies, such as those discussed in Section 2.2. *supra* (e.g. PEMEX, IMSS, etc.), are expected to establish their own separate civil service system based on the Federal Civil Service Law, and on the *Ley del Servicio Público de Carrera de la Administración Pública del Distrito Federal*, published in the *Gaceta Oficial* of the Federal District 13 June 2000 and available at www.assembleadf.gob.mx (site visited Jan. 2004).

7.1. Liability of Public Employees

In accordance with Article 108 of the Constitution, the following officials are considered public servants for purposes of liability: popularly elected representatives of government; members of the federal judiciary, including the judiciary of the Federal District; officials and employees of government agencies; and, in general, any person who performs a government job, serves in a position or commission of any type in the federal government or the Federal District, as well as officials of the Federal Electoral Institute who are responsible for acts or omissions they commit in performance of their respective duties. The state constitutions specify the persons who are considered public employees of the state and municipalities; these include state governors and legislators, judges, and other public employees of state or municipal agencies.

This Chapter focuses on liability for violations of federal laws, by federal, state, or municipal employees. Similar rules of liability exist under state law for violations of state, rather than federal, laws.

Mexican law establishes different types of liability applicable to public officials for non-performance of obligations established by law; for commission of acts or omissions that are considered crimes; or for commission of acts or omissions that cause damage to third parties. Federal and state laws distinguish between the political, criminal, civil, and administrative liability of public servants.

7.1.1. Political Liability

The Mexican Constitution provides for a process of 'political trial' (*juicio político*), or impeachment, of government officials[107] who, in the performance of their duties, are guilty of committing acts or omissions that are detrimental to fundamental public interests or the proper performance of governmental duties.[108]

[107] According to Article 110 of the Constitution, the following officials may be removed by *juicio político*: members of Congress (senators and *diputados*); justices of the Supreme Court; counsellors of the Federal Judicial Council (and of the Judicial Council for the Federal District), cabinet ministers (*secretarios de estado*); heads of administrative departments; heads of government and legislative representatives (*diputados*) of the Federal District (Mexico City); the Attorney General of the Republic; the Attorney General of the Federal District; federal Circuit Court and District Court judges; judges of the Federal District; the president, counsellors and the executive secretary of the Federal Electoral Institute; magistrates of the Federal Electoral Tribunal; and directors general and their equivalents of decentralized agencies, majority state-owned enterprises, government-owned corporations, and public trusts (*fideicomisos*).

[108] According to Article 50 of the Federal Law of Liability of Public Servants (*Ley Federal de Responsabilidades de los Servidores Públicos*) D.O. 31 Dec. 1982, as last amended 13 Mar. 2002, the following instances are detrimental to fundamental public interests or to the proper performance of governmental duties: assaults on democratic institutions; assaults on the republican, representative, or federal form of government; serious and systematic violations of constitutionally guaranteed individual and social rights; assaults on the freedom of suffrage; illegal assumption of authority; any violation of the Constitution or federal laws when serious damage is caused to the Federation, to one or several states of the Federation, or to society, or that causes any disturbance to normal operations of institutions; any serious omissions or

Impeachment, or *juicio político*, is a federal cause of action: state governors, state and local legislators, magistrates of State and Municipal Superior Courts of Justice, and members of local judicial councils may only be subject to federal impeachment by *juicio político* for serious violations of the federal Constitution or federal statutes, or for mismanagement of federal funds and resources. In cases in which the federal Congress votes to impeach a state official for violation of federal law, the matter may be referred to the state legislature for sanctions in accordance with the state constitution and laws.

Impeachment proceedings are governed by the last three paragraphs of Article 110 of the Constitution, and by the more detailed provisions of Articles 5 to 24 of the Federal Law of Liability of Public Servants (*Ley Federal de Responsabilidades de los Servidores Públicos*, or LFRSP). Impeachment trials are conducted before both houses of Congress. The Chamber of Deputies (*Cámara de Diputados*) receives the charges and presides over the preliminary stages of the trial, acting as the investigatory and prosecutorial body. The Senate acts as the trial court and either votes to convict or acquit. Verdicts in political trials may not be challenged, not even by *amparo* proceedings.

When a public servant is convicted in a *juicio político*, the punishment may consist of removal from office of the public servant, and disqualification from ever serving again in public office, government jobs, posts, or commissions, or other positions of a public or governmental nature. As in the United States, impeachment is rarely used in Mexico. The most recent case involved the impeachment and conviction of Jorge Díaz Serrano, Senator, who was impeached in 1983 for acts committed in connection with the PEMEX operation when he was Director of PEMEX.

7.1.2. Criminal Liability

Under Section 2 of Article 109 of the Constitution, the commission of a crime by a public servant during his or her term of office shall be prosecuted and punished in accordance with the criminal laws. The Federal Penal Code establishes the following types of criminal behaviour in cases involving public servants: improper exercise of public service,[109] abuse of authority,[110] collusion of public servants,[111] improper use of power or authority,[112] extortion by a public official,[113] intimidation,[114] abuse of office,[115] influence peddling,[116] bribery,[117] embezzlement,[118] and illegal enrichment.[119] Punishment for any of these

failure to act that bring about any of the preceding effects; and systematic or serious violations of plans, programmes, and budgets of the federal government or of the government of the Federal District, or of laws that determine how federal and Federal District economic resources shall be managed.

[109] Federal Penal Code (FPC), Art. 214. [110] FPC, Art. 215. [111] FPC, Art. 216.
[112] FPC, Art. 217.
[113] FPC, Art. 218. This offence applies to a public servant who, under the guise of a tax or other legitimate payment, demands money, stocks, services, or any other thing that he or she knows to be improper. [114] FPC, Art. 219.
[115] FPC, Art. 220. [116] FPC, Art. 221. [117] FPC, Art. 222.
[118] FPC, Art. 223. [119] FPC, Art. 224.

offences may include imprisonment, fines, forfeiture of illegally acquired gains, removal from public office, and disqualification from future public office; the extent of the punishment will vary with the severity of the offence.

The President of Mexico, during his term of office, may only be prosecuted for treason or for commission of serious crimes against public order.[120] Any criminal trial of the President for such a crime shall take place before the Senate.

Criminal prosecution of public servants is carried out by the Office of the Attorney General (PGR). Before a high-ranking public servant[121] can be subjected to criminal process, Article 111 of the Constitution requires that the Chamber of Deputies of the Mexican Congress, by majority vote of the members present, declare that sufficient grounds of wrongdoing exist to prosecute the defendant, thus stripping the public servant of official immunity. The process before the Chamber of Deputies is known as 'declaration of admissibility' (*declaración de procedencia*), commonly referred to as *desafuero*. That process involves the establishment of a commission, the *comisión instructora*, composed of four *diputados*, which studies the case and presents its findings to the Chamber. If the Chamber of Deputies decides that there are insufficient grounds to justify prosecution, the proceeding is dismissed. In such a case, however, the public official may still be prosecuted after he or she leaves office if grounds for prosecution exist. If the Chamber does approve the *declaración de procedencia*, the public official is handed over to the Attorney General and is usually removed from office during the criminal process. If acquitted, the defendant may be reinstated after trial.

Once the declaration of admissibility is issued by the Chamber of Deputies, the public servant in question ceases to enjoy immunity from prosecution and is subject to the jurisdiction of the criminal courts.[122] The successful prosecution of a *desafuero* of a high-ranking public official is complicated by the divisions that currently characterize the Mexican Congress, but some notorious cases have resulted in successful use of the process.[123]

In the past, during the PRI's unchallenged political hegemony, these procedures were very rarely used, and the public became accustomed to the impunity

[120] Mexican Constitution, Art. 108. *See* Barragán, J., *EL PRESIDENTE MEXICANO Y EL SISTEMA DE RESPONSABILIDAD AL QUE ESTÁ SUJETO* (Guadalajara: Universidad de Guadalajara, 2001) at 107.

[121] Pursuant to Article 111 of the Mexican Constitution, high-ranking officials include senators and *diputados*, Supreme Court justices, judges of the Federal Electoral Tribunal, counsellors of the Federal Judicial Council, cabinet ministers (*secretarios*), heads of administrative departments, and the Attorney General, among others.

[122] Article 111 of the Constitution reserves to the federal Chamber of Deputies the power to declare, by absolute majority of the members present in session, whether there are sufficient grounds to proceed with criminal prosecution of those high-ranking government officials that are listed therein.

[123] In 2002, Carlos Romero Deschamps, a *diputado* affiliated with the PRI, was accused of the misuse of PEMEX funds to support the campaign of the PRI presidential candidate in the 2000 elections. As a *diputado*, he could not be prosecuted for the alleged crime without first being tried by the Chamber of Deputies under *declaración de procedencia*. At the date of publication, the Chamber of Deputies has not yet ruled on the matter.

of public officials. Since the demise of single-party politics, there is hope that government officials will be held to standards of the law. President Vicente Fox, like several of his predecessors, has tried to campaign against wrongdoing and corruption in government, and with the breakup of political power there is greater hope than ever that this will succeed. The PGR and SFP (formerly SECODAM) have become more diligent than ever in investigating and prosecuting government officials.[124]

7.1.3. *Civil Liability*

Prior to 2000, governmental agencies were immune from civil liability for damages to private parties caused by government misconduct. In 2000, Congress amended Article 113 of the Constitution to restrict governmental immunity, and to permit an agency of the federal government to be held liable for damages caused to private persons. No regulatory law has yet been adopted in order to implement this change, and until such a law is passed the civil liability of a federal government agency or public servant is based on the Federal Civil Code. The constitutional amendment applies to both state and federal government agencies: under the transitory article to the amendment, both state and federal governments have until 1 January 2004, to adopt implementing legislation.[125]

Because of the amendment to Article 113, when a public servant causes damage to another person in the exercise of his or her official duties, the government must indemnify the injured party. Liability shall be joint, i.e. shared between the government and the public servant, in cases of malicious failure to fulfil obligations or wilful malfeasance (*dolo*), and shall be subsidiary in all other instances. The government is only obliged to indemnify the injured party if the public servant who caused the injury does not have sufficient assets to cover the damages awarded.[126]

The government's liability for payment of damages may also be predicated on the criminal misconduct of public servants. Accordingly, Section VI of Article 32 of the Federal Penal Code states that the government is jointly liable for crimes committed by public servants with criminal intent (*dolo*) in the performance of their duties, and the government is liable as a subsidiary (as explained in the previous paragraph) when crimes are committed or when damage is caused through negligence.

[124] According to a report in 2003 by SECODAM, during the first 2 years of the administration of President Fox (2000–2002), 13,133 allegations of misconduct were filed in administrative proceedings before SECODAM (now SFP) against 9,220 public servants. Of this total, 659 resulted in warnings; 3,470 resulted in administrative warnings (*amonestaciones*); 1,297 cases resulted in dismissal from office; 2,392 resulted in suspensions; and 1,834 resulted in fines (*multas*). During the same period, criminal complaints were filed against 278 government employees, resulting in 152 convictions, and 76 public officials serving prison sentences. *See* the 'Informe de labores que presenta Francisco Barrio Terrazas' (SFP, 31 Mar. 2003), www.funcionpublica.gob.mx 'Renditión de Cuentas' (site visited Jan. 2004).

[125] D.O. 14 Jun. 2002. [126] Federal Civil Code (FCC), Art. 1927.

Civil liability of the government or public servants can be adjudicated through the following procedural means:

(i) a civil trial, in which the judge determines the criminal liability of the public servant and amount of damages to be paid;
(ii) adjudication as part of a criminal trial, in which the criminal judge may order the defendant to pay civil damages to the injured party, in addition to any sentence of imprisonment or criminal fines;[127]
(iii) an administrative proceeding designed to determine the administrative liability of a public servant. Under Article 33 of the Federal Law of Administrative Responsibilities of Public Servants (LFRASP), an injured party may report the infraction to the agency responsible for the public servant, or to SFP. If the agency acknowledges liability, it will order the appropriate disbursement necessary to compensate the injured party, thus obviating the need for the individual to resort to the courts or any other agency. If the agency refuses to pay damages or the amount does not satisfy the claimant, he or she may assert the right to collect damages before the Federal Administrative Tribunal and Fiscal Justice[128] or before a civil judge.[129] The government may claim reimbursement from the public servant for damages paid to the injured party; or
(iv) a recommendation of the National Commission of Human Rights (CNDH, after the Spanish acronym), in which the Commission may propose that the agency responsible for damages indemnify the injured party; since the CNDH has no authority to order compliance with its recommendations, the agency may accept or reject the proposal.[130] When a recommendation of the CNDH is accepted by the agency involved, the agency is only required to pay the specific amount recommended by the Commission, and shall issue the respective payment order.[131]

7.1.4. Administrative Liability

In 2002, Congress adopted a new Law of Federal Liability of Public Servants (*Ley Federal de Responsabilidades Administrativas de los Servidores Públicos*, or LFRASP)[132] as part of the campaign led by President Vicente Fox to combat corruption in government. The LFRASP does not deal with the political, criminal, or civil liability of public servants, for which the LFRSP is still the controlling law. The LFRASP regulates: the duties of public servants; behaviour that will be considered illegal; penalties; and administrative procedures. SFP (formerly SECODAM) is charged with administering this disciplinary regime.

127 FCC, Art. 32.

128 LFRASP, Art. 33 and Organic Law of Federal Administrative Tribunal and Fiscal Justice (OLFATFJ) Art. 23, Part X.

129 LFRASP, Art. 33.

130 For a discussion of the CNDH, *see* Chapter 6 below, at text accompanying notes 162–164.

131 LFRSP, Art. 77 bis, final para.

132 D.O. 13 Mar. 2002.

LFRASP Article 35 provides for the establishment of a Registry of Property of Public Servants (*Registro Patrimonial de los Servidores Públicos)* to facilitate the monitoring of financial activities by government employees. All public servants are required to file a report of their holdings with SFP, which administers the registry; SFP (formerly SECODAM) has received thousands of such reports since the law was passed.[133] The law allows the National Banking Commission (*Comisión Nacional Bancaria)* to provide banking information to the government concerning the accounts of public servants liable for damages, if requested by an appropriate government official.

Mexicans have long told tales of vast fortunes earned by corrupt government officials.[134] The creation of a public registry of property owned by public servants shows the extent to which the Mexican legal system is changing.

[133] From 1 January to 31 August 2003 SFP received 269,485 such filings, a 3.5% increase over the same period of 2002. www.funcionpublica.gob.mx/doctos/informe03 (site visited Jan. 2004).

[134] *See* e.g. González, J., *Lo Negro del Negro Durazo* (Mexico: Posada, 1985) at 14, a popular account of the wealth accumulated by the one-time police chief of Mexico City.

10

Civil Procedure

PART I: CIVIL PROCEDURE

One of the distinctions commonly made between the common law and civil law traditions involves differences in judicial procedure.[1] In this Chapter, the reader will note many elements of procedure that are shared by both legal traditions. However, there are also major differences, as explained below.

The absence of juries In Mexico, as in most civil law countries, there is no jury trial in civil or criminal cases.[2] The judge serves as both finder of facts and interpreter of the law. The judge is expected to have the experience and the judgement to form conclusions without being prejudiced by evidence that is irrelevant or of questionable probity. For this reason, the rules of evidence in Mexico are not as extensive as those in the common law, which are deemed necessary to avoid improper influence of a jury of laymen.

The role of the judge Mexican civil and criminal procedure follows the basic concept of the civil law tradition in which the judge serves as both finder of fact and interpreter of law. Lawyers for the litigants present evidence to clerks of the court. The Mexican judge may also order, on his or her own initiative, the gathering of evidence, although this is unusual (for instance, the judge may decide to visit a location that is crucial to the litigation). Unlike the common law system, where much of the litigator's role involves strategies to organize and resent evidence, in Mexico the judge and the clerks of the court are entirely responsible for organizing the evidence in such a way that the judge may evaluate it and make a decision.

The lack of a concentrated, public trial A key feature of common law (and a corollary of the jury system) is the use of the public trial, which takes place during a concentrated time period (usually days or weeks) after months or years of preparing evidence. Trial lawyers in such a system expend considerable energy defining the strategies to be used for the presentation of evidence to a jury, and the arguments that may influence the jury's decision. In Mexico, by contrast, the 'trial' (*juicio*)—in the sense of the period during which evidence is gathered and evaluated—takes place sporadically over a period of months or even years. A civil court

[1] *See generally* Merryman, J.H., THE CIVIL LAW TRADITION: AN INTRODUCTION TO THE LEGAL SYSTEMS OF WESTERN EUROPE AND LATIN AMERICA (Palo Alto: Stanford University Press, 2d ed., 1985) at 34–38, 111–132.

[2] The only use of a jury in Mexico is in criminal cases involving crimes committed by means of the press, crimes against public order, or against national security. Articles 56–67 of the *Ley Orgánica del Poder Judicial de la Federación*, D.O. 26 May 1995.

of first instance in Mexico receives evidence (much of it written) over a period of several months, according to specific phases set forth in the procedural codes. In Mexico, the principal work of the litigator (*abogado litigante*) consists of filing initial pleadings, and presenting written and oral evidence; and occasionally making written and oral arguments (*alegatos*) after presentation of evidence.

Civil litigation is primarily a written process Due to the lack of a jury and the periodic gathering of evidence over a lengthy period of time, civil litigation in Mexico is primarily a written process. The court of first instance transcribes oral testimony, compiles documents and other written evidence, and forms a voluminous file (*expediente*) that is used to establish the facts of the case. In such a system, it is considered possible for an appellate court, viewing the *expediente* for the first time on appeal, to review and overturn the lower court's determinations of facts as well as its application of the laws.

Lack of contingency fees As in most countries of the world, Mexico does not permit civil litigators to charge contingency fees. This fact, coupled with the lack of a jury system and severe limits placed on the amount of damages that may be awarded in personal injury suits, helps to explain the relative lack of tort litigation in Mexico.

1. Sources and Interpretation

The law of civil procedure in Mexico governs the process by which Mexican courts and related institutions resolve disputes arising out of matters governed by the civil codes.[3] Article 55 of the Code of Civil Procedure for the Federal District (*Código de Procedimientos Civiles para el Distrito Federal*) provides that 'this Code shall govern the filing and resolution of matters before ordinary courts, [and] legal recourse or the right to challenge may not be waived by agreement of the parties nor can the rules of procedure be altered, modified or waived'. In addition to the codes of civil procedure, the law of civil procedure includes the organic laws of the respective judiciary systems (state or federal), case-law (*jurisprudencia*), and general principles of law.[4]

The provisions of the Code of Civil Procedure for the Federal District do not provide any guidelines for the interpretation of procedural rules. This silence makes it necessary to resort to the general rule set forth in paragraph 4 of Article 14 of the Constitution, which establishes that in 'civil trials, final judgments

[3] *See generally* Ovalle Favela, José, *Teoría General del Proceso* (Mexico: Harla, 4th ed., 1996), at 58.

[4] Words to this same effect can be found in Article 19 of the Federal Civil Code and of the Civil Code for the Federal District. The Supreme Court has defined general principles of law as 'well known, indisputable, juridical truths, of a general nature, as their name so indicates, produced or selected by the science of Law, in such a way that the judge can provide a solution that the legislator himself would have pronounced had he been present, or would have established, had the case been foreseen; provided that the these "principles" are not out of harmony with nor contradict the laws whose gaps or omissions [the principles] are supposed to fill'. SJF, 5a, T. LIV, Tercera Sala, 1957, p. 2641.

shall be in accordance with the letter or the legal interpretation of the law, and in the absence thereof, shall be based on general principles of law'.[5] Additionally, Articles 18, 19, and 20 of the Federal Civil Code (hereinafter 'FCC') and identical provisions in the Civil Code for the Federal District (hereinafter 'CCDF') also contain rules that may aid the interpretation of procedural rules. For example, FCC Article 18 provides that 'silence, obscurity, or inadequacy of the law do not authorize judges or courts to fail to resolve a controversy'. FCC Article 19 follows Article 4 of the Constitution by stating that civil disputes submitted to courts of law 'shall be resolved in accordance with the letter of the law or its legal interpretation. In the absence of a law, they shall be resolved in accordance with general principles of law'. FCC Article 20 stresses the principle of equal treatment of parties in the judicial process, in accordance with the general principles of Article 13 of the Constitution.

2. Evolution of Procedural Law

As noted elsewhere in this book, Mexican independence did not lead to the invalidation of all Spanish law in Mexico. The Law of 23 May 1837, expressly provided that civil law suits would be decided in accordance with Spanish laws, provided that these provisions were not in conflict with the legal institutions adopted since independence. It was not until 9 December 1871 (soon after the adoption of the first Mexican Civil Code, of 1870) that the Mexican Congress adopted the first Mexican Code of Civil Procedure, which was based on the Spanish Code of Civil Procedure of 1855. The 1870 procedural code was replaced in 1884, after the adoption of the new Civil Code of that date. Both 1884 codes, civil and procedural, were replaced in 1932 by the codes that, with minor changes, remain in force today. The procedural code, the Code of Civil Procedure for the Federal District, known by its Spanish acronym, CPCDF,[6] has had the greatest influence on civil procedural law in Mexico.

At the federal level, Codes of Civil Procedure were adopted on 6 October 1897 and 26 December 1908, and both followed the general model of the local procedural codes for the Federal District. The present Federal Code of Civil Procedure (*Código Federal de Procedimientos Civiles*, or CFPC) was issued on 31 December 1943 and has been in effect since 27 March 1943. The CFPC is important not only because of its technical content, but also because it applies directly to civil matters which are under the jurisdiction of the federal courts, including those to which a federal agency is a party.[7] Consequently, the CFPC serves as a supplemental text

[5] Even though this constitutional precept refers expressly to the 'final judgment' [of a suit], it is clear that the rule of interpretation contained therein is applicable in general to all judicial rulings.

[6] *Código de Procedimientos Civiles para el Distrito Federal, Gazeta Oficial*, 16 Jan. 2003 (hereinafter CPCDF).

[7] On the jurisdiction of federal courts in civil matters, *see* Chapter 7 above, Section 4.

to a variety of federal statutes, such as the Law of *Amparo*, the Federal Labour Law (*Ley Federal del Trabajo*), Federal Law of Workers at the Service of the State (*Ley Federal de los Trabajadores al Servicio del Estado*), and the Fiscal Code of the Federation (*Código Fiscal de la Federación*).

As discussed above in Chapter 7, the Mexican federal system gives rise to the coexistence of two judicial systems, federal and state. Consequently, thirty-three codes of civil procedure are in effect in Mexico: one for the courts of each state, one for the courts of the Federal District, and one for the federal courts throughout the country (the Federal Code of Civil Procedure). Despite this multiplicity of procedural codes, the content and overall approach of the different codes do not differ significantly.

The most important procedural code is the 1932 Code of Civil Procedure for the Federal District (CPCDF), which is applied by the local territorial courts of the Federal District (as opposed to the Federal Courts located in the Federal District). First adopted in 1932, at the time of the entry into force of the Civil Code itself, the CPCDF was heavily influenced by Spanish law, and has served as a model for the majority of state civil procedural codes. Because it has served as a national model, and due to its importance as the procedural code for courts serving the largest population in Mexico—that of Mexico City, D.F.—we refer repeatedly to the CPCDF in this Chapter, with occasional references to the Federal Code of Civil Procedure. Excellent secondary research materials exist for both codes.[8]

A second type of procedural code is made up of the 1934 Code of Civil Procedure for the State of Guanajuato and the 1942 Federal Code of Civil Procedure (*Código Federal de Procedimientos Civiles*). The structure and content of both these codes were influenced by Italian doctrine. A final family of procedural codes consists of the codes of the States of Sonora (1949), Morelos (1955), Zacatecas (1965), and Guerrero (1993), which are modelled on the proposed 1948 Code of Civil Procedure for the Federal District, which was never adopted.

3. Classification of Civil Cases (*Juicios Civiles*)

In Mexico, civil cases are classified either as 'ordinary' (*juicios ordinarios*), when the subject of litigation involves general civil claims, or as 'special' (*juicios especiales*), when litigation deals with claims in specific areas of civil law. The CPCDF further divides ordinary cases into two categories: ordinary civil suits (*juicio civil ordinario*), which involve claims of larger monetary value and are explained in detail in this Chapter, and small claims (*juicio ordinario de mínima cuantía*).[9] Special cases deal with the following topics: special summary procedures for

[8] Gómez Lara, C., *Derecho Procesal Civil* (Mexico: McGraw-Hill, 2000).

[9] Small claims cases involve civil property disputes where the value of the claim does not exceed 182 times the minimum general daily wage in force for the Federal District. CPCDF Art. 2, *título especial*.

enforcement of monetary claims (*ejecutivo*), mortgage foreclosure (*hipotecario*), eviction (*desahucio*), arbitration, estates and inheritances (*sucesorios*), bankruptcy (*concurso*), family matters, and controversies in the leasing of real property (*arrendamiento de inmuebles*).

3.1. Ordinary Civil Suits (*Juicios Ordinarios Civiles*): The Stages of Civil Procedure

3.1.1. Pre-Filing Stage (Etapa Preliminar)

The initial stage of a civil lawsuit may begin prior to the filing of a complaint. Thus, a preliminary stage (*etapa preliminar* or *etapa previa*) may occur when the parties engage in three types of preliminary discovery or pre-filing motions (*realización de medios*).

The first type is called *preparatorios del proceso*, which occurs when a party attempts to clarify a doubt concerning the case, remove an obstacle, or cure a defect before the complaint is filed. Examples of this are: obtaining the admission or denial (*confesión*) of a potential defendant concerning facts relevant to the lawsuit; the production of property or of a document to be used as evidence; or prior examination of witnesses whose testimony will be useful to the construction of the complaint.[10] *Preparatorios del proceso* are somewhat similar to the pre-trial discovery that is notorious in US civil lawsuits, in which the judge before whom a complaint has been filed may issue orders compelling a party to make documents or testimony available to an opposing party. In the Mexican case, a judge may also order a party to submit documents or other proof to the court pursuant to a request by a litigant; such evidence is delivered to the court, and may be viewed by other litigants.

The second type of pre-filing measure consists of filing with the court motions for interim equitable relief (*medidas cautelares*). This motion is filed to ensure execution of final judgment, should the court rule in favour of the plaintiff. Examples of *medidas cautelares* include a requirement that the defendant post a bond, or a court order of temporary attachment of property. A plaintiff may also include a request for such measures as part of the complaint.

3.1.2. Opening or Introductory Stage (Etapa Expositiva)*: Statement of Claim or Response*

The first, or introductory, stage of the formal civil proceeding is known as the *etapa postulatoria* (also called *etapa expositiva* or *etapa introductoria*). The purpose of this stage is for the parties to state their cases to the court, including the facts and laws on which their claims and defences are based. This stage is carried out by the filing of the complaint (*demanda*) by the plaintiff (*demandante*, or actor) and the filing of an answer by the defendant (*demandado*). The judge must rule on the admissibility of the complaint, and must serve the

[10] SJF, 9a, Tribunales Colegiados de Circuito, T. II, Feb. 2001, p. 557.

defendant with a notice to answer (*emplazamiento*). If the defendant asserts a counterclaim (*reconvención*) the plaintiff must also be served a copy thereof in order to file an answer to the counterclaim.

The right to be heard in court: the complaint (demanda)

The constitutional right to judicial relief[11] requires the filing of a complaint (*demanda*) that fulfils several formal requirements. The formal requirements of a complaint are set forth in CPCDF Article 255 and CFPC Article 322, and include the need to state the official name of the court where the complaint is to be filed; the name of the plaintiff and a mailing address to receive notices; the name of the defendant and his or her domicile; the subject of the claim, and the factual and legal basis for the suit; and the signature of the plaintiff or plaintiff's legal representative. All documents in support of the claim must be attached to the complaint, including: documents that demonstrate the breach of rights asserted in the complaint;[12] documents that justify the claim and refer to the facts set forth therein; documents that accredit the legal representation of any person who appears on behalf of another, as legal or conventional representative; and copies of the complaint and attachments served upon the defendant.

Service of process on defendant (emplazamiento) *and defendant's right to file an answer* (contestación)

Just as the plaintiff has a right to file suit, the defendant must have the opportunity to answer the complaint, and to gather and introduce evidence to support a defence.[13] Once a court admits a complaint, as having fulfilled the formal requirements of the law, the *actuario*, an employee of the court, must notify the defendant that a complaint has been filed, providing the defendant with a copy of the complaint and accompanying documents. Such notice is called *emplazamiento* (CPCDF Article 259; CFPC Article 327). After receiving notice, the defendant is granted a period of time—nine days for ordinary civil suits—to answer the complaint (CPCDF Article 256; CFPC Article 329 and 330). If the defendant fails to file an answer (*contestación)* within the deadline for its receipt in accordance with the relevant procedural code, the judge may hold the defendant in default for failure to answer the complaint (*declarar en rebeldía* or *contumacia*) (CPCDF Article 271; CFPC Article 332). In such cases, the judge also

[11] Article 17, paragraph 2, of the Constitution states that 'All persons have the right for justice to be administered to them by courts that shall be expeditious in imparting justice within the deadlines and the terms that the law may set, issuing their decisions in a prompt, complete and impartial manner'. Both the general right of access to the courts and the specific rights to file suit and to mount a defence are based on this constitutional provision.

[12] SJF, 9a, Tribunales Colegiados de Circuito, T. II, Jan. 2001, p. 527.

[13] *See* the second paragraph of Article 14 of the Constitution, which provides that 'nobody shall be deprived of life, of liberty, of property, possession or rights, except by means of a judicial proceeding [*juicio*] conducted before previously established courts, in which the essential formalities of procedure are fulfilled'. SJF, 7a, Tercera Sala, T. X, 109–114, 4th part, at 12 (1970).

issues a ruling of admission by default, or implied admission (*confesión ficta*),[14] and the judge may then order attachment of the defendant's personal or real property, if necessary to preserve the money or property that is the subject of the suit.

The defendant may follow one of several strategies in filing an answer (*contestación*). The defendant may file an 'acquiescence to the claim' (*allanamiento a la demanda*), by which the defendant accepts the claims of the plaintiff,[15] making it unnecessary to continue the proceeding. The judge may then summon the parties to appear and issue a final judgment. Alternatively, the defendant may present an affirmative defence, denying the facts or the application of the law referred to in the complaint (*oposición de excepciones*) and alleging facts and arguments in support of the defendant's motion to dismiss the case. Possible defences (*excepciones*) include, for example, an allegation that procedural requirements have not been met (*excepciones procesales*),[16] or an objection to the court's admission of the complaint on the basis of the facts or substantive law as stated in the plaintiff's claim (*excepciones sustanciales*).[17] The defendant may also file a counterclaim against the plaintiff (*reconvención* or *contrademanda*), on matters related to the complaint; such counterclaims must meet the prerequisites of a complaint (*demanda*), but the judge may refuse to

[14] In accordance with the last paragraph of CPCDF Article 271, 'the facts of a complaint that [a defendant] fails to answer shall be presumed to be admitted'. This rule does have exceptions, inasmuch as the paragraph cited here also states that an unanswered complaint is not considered to establish the facts alleged in the complaint when the case involves matters affecting: family relations; the marital status of persons; the leasing of urban real estate for habitation, when the defendant is a tenant; or when service of process is carried out by legal notice published in a newspaper (*emplazamiento por edicto*).

[15] SJF, 7a, Tercera Sala, T. 175–180, p. 19.

[16] Procedural requirements are understood as 'the group of conditions whose presence or absence is necessary for the valid integration and development of the procedural relationship'. Examples include the jurisdictional authority of the court to hear the case (*competencia*), legal capacity of a party to the suit (*capacidad procesal*), representation and standing of the parties to the case (*representación y legitimación*), *res judicata* (*cosa juzgada*), whether an identical case is pending in another court (*litispendencia*), admissibility of the claim (*procedencia de la vía*), proper service of notice (*emplazamiento*), and expiration of the statute of limitations on the claim (*caducidad de la pretensión*). Failure to comply with procedural requirements can either be argued on a motion put forth by the defence, or may be brought up by the judge. Ovalle Favela, *supra* note 3 at 71–80.

[17] *Excepciones sustanciales* 'consist of extinguishing, modifying or impeding facts put forth by the defendant as an argument to challenge the substantive legal relationship alleged by the plaintiff as the basis of his or her claim'. Ovalle Favela, *supra* note 3 at 81. The CPCDF does not specifically list substantive defences, which are based on legal theories grounded in the civil codes. Examples of substantive defences include that a debt has been paid (*pago*), accord and satisfaction (*dación en pago*), set-off of debts (*compensación*), merger of rights (*confusión de derechos*), forgiveness of a debt (*remisión de la deuda*), novation, revocation (*revocación*), loss of property owed to another party (*pérdida de la cosa*), lapsing of the statute of limitations (*prescripción*), expiration of a statutory or prescriptive period (*término extintivo*), settlement, agreement or pledge to not demand payment (*promesa o pacto de no pedir*), waiver of right, nullification, rescission, and legal invalidity (*inexistencia*), among others. De Pina y Castillo Larrañaga, *PRINCIPIOS DE DERECHO PROCESAL CIVIL* (Mexico: Porrúa, 27th ed., 2003) at 157.

admit a counterclaim if the judge feels that it is not grounded in the law or the facts.

Pretrial conference and pretrial settlement (Audiencia previa y de conciliación)

After the filing of a complaint and an answer, the judge proceeds to set a date for the pretrial conference (*audiencia previa*), which must take place within the ten days following the answer to the complaint or the filing of the counterclaim, if appropriate. This preliminary hearing or pretrial conference is intended to serve several purposes: (1) to help the parties reach a settlement (*conciliación*) with the aid of a court-appointed mediator (*conciliador*), who must prepare and propose to the parties trial alternatives to litigation; (2) to examine and resolve issues pertaining to procedural requirements, in order to cure the proceedings of any procedural defects; (3) to help define the subject of the suit and the issues that the suit raises (which may involve application of foreign law or customary law); to allow the judge to rule on the admissibility of evidence that was offered in the opening written briefs, and to order any necessary measures to prepare or gather such evidence for introduction into the court record.[18] If the parties reach a settlement, and if the judge approves the settlement agreement, the settlement will have the same legal force as a final decision of the court (i.e. *res judicata).*

3.1.3. *Evidentiary Stage* (Etapa Probatoria)

The second stage of the civil litigation process is the evidentiary stage or *etapa probatoria*, in which the parties prepare and introduce evidence to the court. The evidence (*las pruebas*) comprises 'the collection of elements of knowledge that are provided in the process and aid in proving the facts or rights claimed by the parties, under the legal rules in force'.[19] The court's final decision in a case must be based on facts that are proven through the evidence introduced by the parties[20] or requested by the judge.[21] It is the sole responsibility of the judge to direct or conduct the evidentiary stage on his or her own without the involvement of intermediaries.[22] Only facts can be admitted into evidence, and these

[18] SJF, 8a, Tribunales Colegiados de Circuito, T III, p. 157. Jan.–June 1989.

[19] Arellano García, Carlos, Derecho Procesal Civil (Mexico: Porrúa, 5th ed., 1998) at 220.

[20] SJF, 8a, Tribunales Colegiados de Circuito, T IV, p. 428.

[21] CPCDF Article 279 permits the judge to order on his or her own initiative the gathering and introduction of any evidence the court deems useful to ascertain the truth with regard to the facts in dispute. This discretionary power of judges can be exercised at any time during the proceeding, from the evidentiary stage until pronouncement of final judgment. This discretionary power not only allows an order to gather additional evidence to add to that already offered by the parties, but also includes the power to order that new evidence be gathered and introduced by the parties, provided that the new evidence pertains to the facts in question and that the procedural rights of the parties are respected in gathering and introducing this evidence, particularly the right to participate in the presentation of the evidence and the right to object to the probative value of the evidence.

[22] The principle of the judge directly conducting the production of evidence without any intermediary is inconsistent with actual practice in Mexican civil procedure, in which the judge delegates to the clerk of the court (*secretario de acuerdos*) the responsibility of conducting most evidentiary hearings and procedures, without the judge being present.

may include evidence of usage or custom. The opinion of an expert (*perito*) is also admissible to aid the court in making factual determinations.[23]

The evidentiary stage involves several steps: an offering or proposal of evidence by the parties; admission or rejection by the judge of evidence proposed by the parties; preparation or gathering of the evidence; examination of the evidence that has been admitted; and weighing or evaluation of the evidence, which is set forth in the preamble (*considerandos*) of the judgment.

The judge will use instruments of proof (*medios de prueba*) to help ascertain the evidence in a case. Article 289 of the CPCDF, though no longer in force, contained a list of instruments of proof, including admission of the facts (*confesión*), public and private documents, expert opinions (*dictámenes periciales*), judicial recognition or inspection (*reconocimiento o inspección judicial*), testimony of witnesses, photographs, photocopies, fingerprint records, and in general any element contributed by scientific discovery, reputation, presumption, or any other means that may be convincing to the judge. In 1986, this article of the CPCDF was amended,[24] and Article 289 now simply states that 'any elements that may be convincing to the judge concerning the facts in dispute or in doubt are admissible as means of proof'.

Both the CFPC and the CPCDF contain rules governing the offering of evidence. The Mexican rules are more straightforward and less exclusionary than those in the USA. The relative permissibility of Mexican rules is not so surprising when one realizes the extent to which the Mexican judge controls the gathering and evaluation of evidence: there is no jury to be swayed by irrelevant testimony or other prejudicial evidence. This is not to say that the offering of evidence in Mexican courts is informal. As is evident elsewhere in Mexican law, there is a high degree of formality in the way in which evidence is presented. For instance, oral questioning of witnesses is highly formalized, as required under the procedural codes (CPCDF Article 360; CFPC Article 562).

Once the judge declares the evidentiary stage open, the judge only receives evidence for a period of ten days; after that, only evidence that was unknown to the parties may be admitted by the judge, up until the time that a final judgment is entered.

A major difference between the civil litigation process in Mexico and that in the United States has to do with the lack of an open trial in Mexico: that is, the lack of an oral proceeding in a courtroom open to the public during a brief time period in which all the evidence is adduced. In accordance with the civil law tradition, in Mexican 'trials' the gathering of evidence is conducted over a period of months (the periods are prescribed in the codes of civil procedure) by clerks of the court. There are few, if any 'hearings' (*audiencias*). The taking of

[23] Only facts in dispute are required to be substantiated by evidence, and therefore the following types of facts do not need to be proven: admitted facts (i.e. facts stipulated by the parties, or *hechos confesados*); facts that are matters of common knowledge, of which the court can take judicial notice (*hechos notorios*); and facts that have a legal presumption in their favour.

[24] D.O. 10 Jan. 1986.

testimony from witnesses is similar to the taking of a deposition in a US lawsuit: witness statements are transcribed by a clerk of the court in the court's offices, and usually lawyers for all parties are present and are allowed to ask questions. Witnesses may be questioned by the clerk of the court, or by the judge. The testimony becomes part of the written documents, or *expediente*, that comprise the evidence in the case.

Since the 'trial' in Mexico begins as soon as a case is filed, there is no 'pre-trial discovery', the process in US litigation in which litigants may enlist the power of the court to compel the production of evidence by the opposing party. In Mexico, 'discovery' takes place during the evidentiary stage, when the judge may order the production of evidence.

Finally, it is noteworthy that, just as in most US jurisdictions when foreign law is relevant to a lawsuit, proof of the foreign law must be presented into evidence. CPCDF Article 284*bis* establishes that a court must apply foreign law just as the judges of the foreign jurisdiction would apply it, without precluding the parties from presenting arguments to establish the validity (*existencia*) and interpretation of the foreign law invoked. The second paragraph of that provision adds that the court may make use of official reports in order to understand the language, validity, sense, and legal scope of foreign law. The court may request such reports from the Mexican Foreign Service, or it may order the taking of any evidence that may be deemed necessary to the understanding of the foreign law, or admit any evidence that the parties may introduce for this purpose.

3.1.4. Closing Stage (Etapa Conclusiva)

In the closing stage, the parties state their closing arguments, and the judge issues a final judgment, thus terminating the trial stage or first instance (*primera instancia*) of the process.

Arguments (alegatos)

In presenting their arguments, or *alegatos*, the parties try to convince the judge that the evidence presented proves the facts as alleged by the plaintiff or defendant, and that a legal basis exists for every piece of evidence that was introduced. The judge must hear the parties' claims and defences before issuing final judgment.[25] Each party's argument should include a brief account of the facts and a detailed analysis of the evidence presented; a showing of how the laws cited by the party are applicable to the facts alleged; and the precise legal basis for the judge to rule in the party's favour. The arguments may be expressed orally, at the conclusion of the period in which the court receives evidence, or in written form, in which case the code does not specify at what point in the procedure the parties must do so.

[25] Arguments are not considered part of the lawsuit itself, but serve to assist the judge in arriving at a final decision. SJF, 8a, Tribunales Colegiados de Circuito, T. VI, p. 53, 2 Feb. 1995.

Judgment (sentencia)
The judgment 'is the decision that the judge or the court pronounces to resolve the merits of the case, conflict or controversy, which signifies the end of the process'.[26] According to CPCDF Article 86, final judgments must meet several formal requirements, including a statement of the case name and number, the legal and factual bases for the ruling, as well as the signatures of the judge and the clerk of the court. Federal Code of Civil Procedure (CFPC) Article 222 also provides minimum requirements for judgments, which must contain, 'in addition to the requirements common to any judicial ruling, a succinct account of the issues raised and of the evidence provided, as well as the applicable legal considerations, based on both laws and scholarly writings, encompassing therein the reasons for ordering or not ordering payment of costs, and shall conclude by resolving very precisely the points that are subject to the consideration of the court and, when appropriate, setting the time period for judgments to be carried out'. The judgment, which resolves the conflict submitted to trial, becomes final and binding when it may no longer be challenged by any other means; it then becomes *res judicata*.

In addition to the requirements set out in the Codes, final judgments must also conform to the constitutional requirement of stating a basis in the law (*motivación*), which emanates from the provisions of Articles 14 and 16 of the Constitution and applies to all acts of authorities. This requirement means that the judge must examine and weigh each piece of evidence introduced during the proceedings and, based on this examination and evaluation, determine the facts that support the judgment.[27]

In theory, then, the duty to find a legal basis to support judgments cannot be fulfilled merely by citing articles of the applicable law, or general legal principles that the judge deems applicable; rather, the judge must also set forth the precise reasoning that supports the judgment.[28] Despite this requirement, lawyers trained in the US common law system will find Mexican judgments (not only from courts of first instance, but also appellate judgments) to lack the level of highly detailed factual and legal analysis that appears in many judicial opinions published in the United States. The common law rule of *stare decisis* forces US courts to issue such detailed judgments, since the application of law to specific facts (the 'holding') creates rules that are binding on later courts. By comparison, Mexican court judgments, at both the lower and appellate levels,

[26] Fix-Zamudio, Héctor, 'Derecho Procesal', in EL DERECHO (Mexico: UNAM, 1975), at 99.

[27] The Supreme Court has held that the 'judge has the duty to examine every piece of evidence admitted to the record, in order to determine, along with the result of the judge's analysis, whether or not the facts forming the basis of the rights being claimed or of the defenses put forth have been proven and to what extent they have they been proven'. SJF, 8a, Tribunales colegiados de Circuito, T. XII, (1993) at 410.

[28] This was the opinion handed down by the Supreme Court: 'a simple citation or quoting is not sufficient, in a decision, in order to consider the decision based in law, but rather it is necessary that pertinent arguments be set forth which help to establish the corresponding decision'. SJF, 7a, Tercera Sala, T: 145–150, p. 462.

generally only bind the immediate parties to the suit. As discussed above in Chapter 3, most judicial opinions in Mexico are not published, and even Supreme Court opinions, which are published in the *Semanario Judicial de la Federación*, are difficult to research and to interpret, by comparison with US standards.

4. Appeal (*Etapa de Impugnación*)

After the court records a judgment, the parties have a right to appeal, by initiating an appeals stage or 'second instance' (*segunda instancia*).

4.1. Methods of Appeal

Methods of appeal (*medios de impugnación*) consist of procedures that allow a re-examination, in whole or in part, of the lower court's judgment. At the outset, it is important to distinguish between appellate review in the United States and appellate review in Mexico. In the United States, appellate courts must accept the factual determinations made at the trial stage, unless the factual determination is unreasonable or unsupported by the evidence; the US appellate process, then, is predominantly limited to addressing errors in application of the law to the facts as found at trial. In Mexico, by contrast, the appellate court is permitted not only to review possible errors in law, but may also review factual determinations, and may reject or alter factual determinations made by the court of first instance if it is clear that the lower court misinterpreted the evidence, a more liberal standard for effecting review of factual findings.[29] This distinction in appellate review is a common difference between the common law and civil law traditions. In the latter, there is generally no jury and no concentrated trial in open court, and the process of establishing the facts is primarily a written one; in such a case, an appellate court is as capable as a judge of first instance of viewing the written evidence and transcripts of testimony

With few exceptions,[30] all lower court decisions are subject to challenge by appeal to an appellate court within the state or federal system. Appeals are classified as ordinary, special, or exceptional. Ordinary appeals (*medios de impugnación ordinarios*) include a motion to appeal (*recurso de apelación*), and a motion for reconsideration of an interlocutory order of a trial judge (*recurso de*

[29] Ovalle Favela, J., Derecho Procesal Civil (Mexico: Oxford University Press, 1999), at 238–261.

[30] The CPCDF excludes certain types of decisions from appeal: CPCDF Article 23 (judgments in small claims cases); CPCDF Article 426–III and IV (decisions regarding questions of jurisdiction); CPCDE Articles 99, 277, 285, and 298 (decisions relating to admissibility of evidence or examination of witnesses); and CPCDF Article 527 (rulings regarding execution of judgment). While not subject to the civil appeals process, these decisions may give rise to an *amparo* claim. As discussed in more detail above in Chapter 8, *amparo* claims are admissible against rulings the execution of which may cause irreparable damage, in accordance with Article 114–IV of the Law of *Amparo*.

revocación), a motion for reconsideration of an appellate court's decision (*recurso de reposición*). Special appeals (*medios de impugnación especiales*) include the *recurso de queja* (discussed below),[31] which can only be used to challenge the types of decision set forth in CPCDF Article 723; and the *recurso de responsabilidad* (judicial impropriety), a civil action which is filed against a judge for violating the law either negligently or through 'inexcusable ignorance' (CPCDF Article 728). An exceptional appeal (*medio de impugnación excepcional*) includes an 'extraordinary appeal' (*apelación extraordinaria*), which can be filed even after a case has been adjudicated, i.e. after a case has been declared *res judicata*. This Chapter focuses on the most common type of appeal, the ordinary appeal.

4.2. Ordinary Appeals

An ordinary appeal is the most common form for seeking review of a trial court decision. Generally speaking, both final judgements and interlocutory rulings can be appealed in the Mexican legal system. CPCDF Article 689 recognizes the right to appeal for litigants who feel they have been harmed as a result of a lower court error (*agravio*). Ordinary appeals must be filed in written form with the judge responsible for issuing the judgment, within six days of an interlocutory ruling and within nine days of a final judgment.

The motion for appeal is presented to the judge of first instance, who forwards the appeal to the appropriate appellate court, which will agree to consider the appeal if it meets the formal requirements for appeal of a judgment or ruling. In such cases, a stay of execution (*suspension de ejecución)* of the trial court judgment may or may not be granted by the appellate court. There are two possible courses of action. The first, known as *efecto devolutivo* and referred to in the code as '*en un solo efecto*',[32] is a procedure whereby the trial court's decision remains unaffected by the appeals process. This is similar to an appeal without a stay of execution in the Anglo-American system. Thus, for example, if the lower court judgment orders one party to pay a sum of money to the other by a given date, the payment must be made even though an appeal is pending. In general, appeals are granted without a stay of execution of the lower court judgment. However, when a law expressly provides for a stay of execution of judgments such as the one in question, the appellate court may order a stay under a procedure known as *efecto suspensivo*.

The process for filing a motion of appeal against a final judgment issued in an ordinary lawsuit (*juicio ordinario*) is divided into five phases: (1) receipt of the appeal by the court, consideration of admissibility of the appeal, and

[31] CPCDF Article 723 sets forth the instances in which a *recurso de queja* may be admissible: against a judge who refuses to admit a suit or fails to recognize by operation of law the legal capacity of a litigant prior to serving notice of suit; against an interlocutory ruling for execution of judgment; against a denial of leave to appeal; and in other cases prescribed by the law.

[32] CPCDF 694.

determination of the effects of the motion; (2) statement of causes for the appeal;[33] (3) review of the evidence; (4) arguments; and (5) final decision by the appellate court. During an appeal against a final judgment, the parties may not introduce new evidence, other than evidence of an event that took place after the trial began and gave rise to a motion for dismissal; introduction of evidence that was available but not introduced prior to the original judgment is not allowed (CPCDF Article 294).

As with the proceedings in the lower court, the appellate process is primarily a written one. It is common, however, for the parties to present oral closing arguments, and they are called to appear in court for pronouncement of appellate judgment. The hearing to pronounce final judgment on the appeal must take place within fifteen days of the date of issuance of the notice of such hearing, and may be extended for another eight days if the court has to examine voluminous documentation.

Appellate court decisions must fulfil the same requirements as the final judgment of a trial court. However, the appellate court judgment need not examine all aspects of the trial court judgment, but instead considers the specific points of the judgment that are challenged by the appellant. The appellate court may rule in three possible ways: (1) it may uphold the trial court final judgment, when it considers the causes for appeal (*agravios*) stated by the appellant to be groundless; (2) it may partially modify the trial court judgment if it deems that one or several of the reasons for appeal are well founded, but that these points do not affect the entire judgment; or (3) it may completely overturn the final judgment of the trial court if it considers that the cause(s) for appeal are all well founded and require the appealed judgment to be entirely set aside. In the latter two instances, the appellate court will remand the case to the trial court for proceedings consistent with the appellate court's decision. It is very rare, in Mexico, for an appellate court to reverse a lower court judgment and order judgment for the respondent. Rather, such cases are usually remanded for further consideration by the lower court, including the receipt of new evidence, in accordance with the appellate court decision.

4.3. Reconsideration of Interlocutory Orders (*Recurso de Revocación*)

Parties may also file a motion for reconsideration of a trial court's interlocutory orders in a civil case, through the process known as *recurso de revocación*. This motion is filed before the same trial court judge who issued an order, requesting the judge totally or partially to modify the original order.[34] A *recurso de revocación* cannot be used to challenge a final judgment, however, since CPCDF

[33] The Supreme Court has interpreted that '*Agravios* must be understood as the reasoning related to the circumstances that, in a court case, lead to proving a violation of the law or an inaccurate interpretation of the law'. SJF, 8a, Pleno, T. LXXX, p. 14.

[34] A similar procedure, known as *recurso de reposición*, exists to allow motions to request reconsideration of appellate court decisions.

Article 683 provides that judgments cannot be overturned on reconsideration by the same judge that issued them. Final judgments may only be challenged by *recurso de apelación*, or appeal to an appellate court.

5. Ordinary Small Claims Proceedings (*Juicio Ordinario de Mínima Cuantía*)

The final section of the CPCDF governs small claims proceedings that must be followed in civil matters before the justices of the peace of the Federal District. Civil lawsuits involving property claims whose value or monetary amount does not exceed 182 times the general minimum daily wage in effect for the Federal District, known as *juicios de mínima cuantía*, or small claims, are heard in this type of court proceeding. Justices of the peace (*jueces de paz*) have jurisdiction not only to hear small claims, but also to conduct certain commercial proceedings governed by the Code of Commerce, under concurrent jurisdiction granted to these courts pursuant to section I of Article 104 of the Constitution.[35] The civil jurisdictional authority of justice of the peace courts does not include authority to hear the following types of proceedings, regardless of the amount of money involved: family law and inheritance matters, matters involving leases of real property, and bankruptcy proceedings.

Small claims courts were created to provide access to justice for the poor. (Parties are not required to be represented by attorneys, but in most instances they are.) The procedure before small claims courts permits procedural freedom (*libertad de formas*), which allows the parties significant latitude in complying with procedural formalities. Cases are conducted orally, the stages of the procedure are compressed into a shorter period of time, and formal rituals are not required for the introduction of evidence or arguments. The predominantly oral form of small claims trials extends not only to the evidentiary hearing and closing arguments, but also to the complaint, which may be presented orally or in written form, as well as the judgment, which may be orally issued by the judge at the end of the evidentiary and argument hearing.

6. Special Civil Proceedings (*Juicios Especiales*)

6.1. Family Courts

Judges are granted greater discretionary power in conducting proceedings and gathering evidence for cases involving family relations and the marital status of

[35] This constitutional provision grants federal courts the jurisdictional authority to hear 'all controversies of a civil or criminal nature that arise concerning compliance and application of federal laws or international treaties to which the Mexican State is a party. When said controversies only affect private interests, the moving party may choose to have the case heard by either local or Federal District judges and courts.'

persons than are judges who preside over ordinary civil suits. Since the rights in dispute in these cases cannot be relinquished, parties are not free to dispose of them at their own discretion without the intervention of a court.

Prior to the 1970s, family law matters were decided by the state civil courts. Since such matters were considered of private, rather than public interest, it was generally understood that this was not an area appropriate for government intervention in the furtherance of public policy. Family matters were considered to be just another type of civil law matter.

Change began to occur in February 1971, when special family law courts were created and granted the jurisdictional authority to hear both trials and *ex parte proceedings* (*procedimientos de jurisdicción voluntaria*) pertaining to family relationships and the marital status of persons, as well as probate matters.[36] In February 1973, a new Title 16, 'Family Controversies' (*De las controversias del orden familiar*), was added to the CPCDF, in recognition that family law matters are matters of public interest (*de orden público*). Title 16 established general principles for all family-related proceedings, and included the following significant changes: (1) family court judges were given new power to issue final judgments with *res judicata* effects regarding marital status, such effects extending to third parties who may not have participated in a proceeding; (2) when the petition affects family relations or the marital status of persons, and a party fails to appear or provides an incomplete answer to the complaint, the party will be presumed to have filed a denial to the complaint, as opposed to the prior rule of admission by default (*confesión ficta*); (3) family court judges were granted the discretionary power to intervene on their own initiative in matters that affect a family, especially when minor children and child support are involved; and (4) the obligation was imposed on the courts to appoint a public defender when a party in a family law suit has no legal counsel, provided that the opposing side has an attorney. In December 1983, an additional reform provided that all judges hearing any family matter are obliged to cure or correct any deficiency or error committed by any of the parties in their legal arguments.[37]

6.2. Arbitration Proceedings (*Juicio Arbitral*)

Arbitration (*juicio arbitral*) is a proceeding designed to bring about the settlement of disputes, in which a third party, the arbitrator (*árbitro*), may not only propose solutions to the parties (as is done in out-of-court mediation (*conciliación*)), but

[36] D.O. 24 Mar. 1971.

[37] Aside from the special rules for all trials and proceedings concerning family relations, Title 16 of the CPCDF established a new type of special proceeding, whereby the following family matters can be brought before a family law court: (1) disputes over payment of alimony; (2) determination of impediments to enter into marriage; (3) disputes between spouses regarding the administration of marital property, and the education of children; (4) disputes between spouses, parents, and guardians; and (5) 'all similar family matters that call for judicial intervention' CPCDF Article 942.

may also issue a binding resolution, known as a *laudo arbitral* or 'arbitral award'. Unlike the ordinary judicial process, arbitration is based on the binding nature of an agreement entered into between the parties to submit a dispute to the decision of an arbitrator. This agreement may take the form of an arbitration commitment (*compromiso arbitral*) made after a dispute has arisen, in which the parties mutually agree to submit the dispute to arbitration; or by the use of an arbitration clause (*cláusula arbitral*) in a contract, under which the parties agree to submit future disputes arising out of the contract to arbitration. The two types of arbitration differ in timing and form. In both situations, the mutual agreement of the parties makes it possible for an arbitrator to settle the dispute; however, once the contractual clause or the agreement to submit a conflict to arbitration has been established, the parties' acceptance of the award issued by the arbitrator is binding. The CPCDF only makes express reference to commitments to submit to arbitration after a dispute arises (*compromiso arbitral*), although the rules that apply to this type of agreement can usually be applicable to an arbitration clause in a contract as well.

In deciding a dispute, the arbitrator should apply the applicable law, based on accepted rules of conflicts of law (*derecho internacional privado*),[38] including the law chosen by the parties. The CPCDF also allows the parties discretion to authorize the arbitrator to resolve the litigation without strictly adhering to the law, but rather to base the award on the principles of equity.[39]

In principle, anyone who is qualified to exercise his or her civil rights may enter into an agreement to submit disputes in business dealings to arbitration. Nevertheless, the following types of matters are expressly prohibited by law[40] from being submitted to arbitration for dispute resolution: (1) the right to receive support; (2) divorce, whether contested or uncontested, except for separation of jointly owned marital property and other issues of a purely pecuniary nature; (3) nullification of matrimony; and (4) marital status.

6.3. Summary Procedures for the Enforcement of Judgments (*Juicios Ejecutivos*)

Juicios ejecutivos are summary procedures in which a party seeks, by means of attachment and sale of a debtor's property, to collect unpaid or outstanding loans or credit that are recorded and evidenced by a certificate of title (*título*) which has legal force to serve as proof.[41] The types of special summary proceedings covered by Mexico's civil procedural legislation are civil proceedings to enforce monetary judgments, special foreclosure proceedings, and special eviction proceedings.

Civil judicial proceedings are also covered in Chapter 18 below, which discusses their importance in commercial transactions.[42]

[38] Arbitration is also covered in Chapter 22 below, at text accompanying notes 58 to 64.
[39] CPCDF Article 220.
[40] CFPC Article 615.
[41] Ovalle Favella, *supra* note 3 at 314.
[42] *See* Chapter 18 below, Section 4.

6.3.1. Civil Enforcement of Monetary Judgments (Juicio Ejecutivo Civil)

Valid documentary proof of the plaintiff's right to execute on a debtor's property (*título ejecutivo*) is the essential requirement for filing a *juicio ejecutivo civil*. The courts have defined proof of the right of execution, or *título ejecutivo*, as 'the document that constitutes legal proof of credit for purposes of execution' and have established that the debtor/creditor relationship must be individualized (i.e. a specific individual or entity must be identified as the creditor, and likewise for the debtor), the debt must be payable (the debt must be overdue and no conditions preventing collection may be in effect),[43] and the debt must be liquidated (i.e., the amount and currency of payment must be apparent from the debt instrument). Examples of *títulos ejecutivos* are an official copy of a public document issued by a judge or notary (*escritura pública*), an admission of indebtedness (*confesión de la deuda*), a stipulation (*convenio judicial*), and a final judgment rendered by a court of law. The procedure is divided into three phases: (1) attachment, (2) payment, and (3) sale and execution in satisfaction of judgment (*sentencia de remate y ejecución*).

6.3.2. Special Mortgage Foreclosure Proceedings (Juicio Ejecutivo Hipotecario)

Special mortgage foreclosure proceedings are used whenever a party seeks to create, extend, or alter a mortgage, or to pay off creditors in the order of priority guaranteed by the mortgage agreement. To use this summary procedure, the loan must be recorded in a publicly registered document, and payment must be due. When a creditor seeks payment, or preferential treatment in payment of a mortgage loan, the creditor must submit the mortgage deed or a certified copy of the document in which the mortgage loan is recorded.[44] The main stages of special mortgage foreclosure proceedings are issuance and registration of the mortgage note, opposition, and sale and execution of judgment (foreclosure).[45]

6.3.3. Eviction Proceedings (Juicios de Desahucio)

Litigation between landlords and tenants over notices to vacate the premises of leased property for failure to pay rent is heard in special eviction proceedings.

6.4. Proceedings Involving a Person's Estate or Total Assets (*Juicios Universales*)

Juicios universales involve the estate or the totality of property rights of a person, whether an individual or a corporation (*persona moral*). These proceedings

[43] SJF, 5a, Tercera Sala, T. XXXIV, p. 2113.
[44] De Pina y Castillo Larrañaga, *supra* note 17 at 562.
[45] *See* Chapter 18 below, at text accompanying note 146.

may be *mortis causa*, by reason of death, such as probate proceedings, or *inter vivos*, such as personal bankruptcy proceedings (*concurso de acreedores y de quiebra*).

Commercial bankruptcy under the *Ley de Concursos Mercantiles* of 2000 is covered below in Chapter 19.[46]

Personal bankruptcy occurs when a non-merchant debtor suspends payment on civil, liquid, and enforceable debts. There are two types of personal bankruptcy: voluntary or involuntary (*concurso voluntario* or *concurso necesario*). *Concurso voluntario* occurs when the debtor willingly releases his or her property to satisfy debts owed to creditors. In this case, the debtor simply files a written document, in lieu of making an appearance, and attaches a statement of assets and liabilities (excluding assets that are not subject to attachment and foreclosure[47]), indicating the name and domicile of the debtors and creditors, and providing an explanation of the reasons for non-payment of the debt.

Concurso necesario is held when two or more creditors file a claim in court, after a payment period has lapsed, against the debtor and have not found enough assets to cover the amount of the outstanding debts and legal expenses. In this case, the debtor must file a statement of assets and liabilities with the judge, stating the names and domiciles of his or her creditors and debtors; should the debtor fail to file this statement, a trustee (*síndico*), acting as administrator of the property, shall do so.[48] When the process is finished, all remaining creditors' claims against the debtor are extinguished by the bankruptcy.

6.4.1. *Probate of the Estates of Deceased Persons* (Juicios Sucesorios)[49]

Probate proceedings are known as *juicios sucesorios*, and their purpose is the transmission of the assets of the owner of an estate to his or her heirs and legatees. These proceedings may be *juicio sucesorio intestado*, an intestate succession proceeding, when the owner of the estate has passed away without leaving a valid will; or they may be *juicio sucesorio testamentario*, based on a valid will (a testate probate proceeding). When the owner of the estate has left a written will, transfers of the property making up the estate must conform to the stipulations of the will. The phases of *juicios sucesorios* include the recognition of rights of inheritance, the formulation of an inventory and appraisal of property in the estate, estate administration, and division and distribution of the property of the estate.

[46] *See* Chapter 19 below, text accompanying notes 77 *et seq.*

[47] Certain family possessions, such as the family home, are not subject to attachment. CCDF Art. 727; FCC Art. 727.

[48] These proceedings consist of four phases: (1) declaration of default or bankruptcy and initial securing of property; (2) acknowledgement and determination of priority rights to debt repayment (*graduación de créditos)* during which the *síndico* or trustee is appointed; (3) sale of property; and (4) distribution and payment. On this topic, *see* Alcalá-Zamora, N., *Derecho Procesal Mexicano* (Mexico: Porrúa, 1976) at 133.

[49] On the law of succession, *see* Chapter 16 below, Section 3. *See also* Ovalle Favela, *supra* note 3 at 402.

PART II: COMMERCIAL PROCEDURE (*DERECHO PROCESAL MERCANTIL*)[50]

7. Introduction

According to section X of Article 73 of the Mexican Constitution, the Mexican Federal Congress has the power to enact legislation relating to business and commerce, including procedural laws and rules. Nevertheless, even though commercial law is exclusively federal, the federal Congress chose not to create specialized commercial courts with jurisdiction over commercial disputes. Indeed, the jurisdictional authority to hear and solve commercial litigation was granted exclusively to the state and local courts under the 1884 amendment to Article 97 of the Constitution of 1857. With the enactment of the 1917 Constitution, jurisdiction over commercial disputes became concurrent between the federal and local courts.[51]

In exercising its exclusive power to legislate on commercial matters, Congress originally produced a single Commercial Code, the *Código de Comercio* of 1889, as the law applicable in this area. As discussed elsewhere in this volume,[52] over the course of the twentieth century, Congress passed numerous commercial laws, many overlapping with each other, and overlapping and replacing parts of the Commercial Code. Similarly, the procedural rules of commercial law are spread among several different bodies of law at different levels of government. The most important set of laws with regard to commercial procedural law in Mexico is the Commercial Code itself, the *Código de Comercio* of 1889 (hereinafter CC), which is still in force today. Book 5 of this Code, titled 'Commercial procedures' (*De los juicios mercantiles*), contains most rules of commercial procedure applicable today but, as we shall see, these rules must be read in context with other applicable procedural laws.

The starting point in understanding commercial procedure is the realization that commercial cases are decided by the normal civil law courts in the state and federal judicial systems, and therefore the relevant code of civil procedure governs the dispute. However, under CC Article 1049, commercial procedural law may *also* apply, when the nature of the act from which the litigation arises is commercial. A single act may appear to be of a commercial nature to one party and of a civil nature to the other party. To resolve this potential dispute, the Commercial Code (CC) provides that when the act in question is of a commercial nature in the view of *any of the parties*, litigation must be resolved by applying the rules of commercial procedure (CC Article 1050).[53] Many of these

[50] On commercial litigation, *see also* Chapter 18 below, section 4.

[51] Mexican Constitution, Art. 104, Section I. In practice, plaintiffs resort more often to local courts than to federal courts, which occasionally gives rise to conflicts between these two court systems.

[52] *See* Chapter 18 below, at text accompanying notes 4–20.

[53] The preference for commercial procedure was espoused in the Commercial Code itself, under the principle that 'commercial procedure, preferably to any other type, is the conventional [procedure]'. Commercial Code, Art. 1051.

'procedural' rules in the Code of Commerce are actually of a substantive nature, while others govern elements of proof and procedure.

The Commercial Code recognizes the discretionary power of the plaintiff in regards to filing, advocating, and establishing the subject of the suit, and enables the parties to agree on the application of commercial rules of procedure to which the court and the parties must adhere.[54] When the parties disagree on the application of commercial procedural law, the rules of Book 5 of the Commercial Code are to be applied, and these rules are to be given the status of rules supplementary to the will of the parties. Lastly, in the absence of a stipulation on a matter in dispute and of a provision in Book 5 of the Commercial Code, 'the respective local law of procedure shall apply'.

Another source of commercial procedural law is the General Law of Instruments and Operations of Credit of 1932 (*Ley General de Títulos y Operaciones de Crédito*, or LGTOC).[55] This law contains provisions on motions and defences (*excepciones*) that may be raised against actions stemming from instruments of credit; on procedures that must be followed to seek payment and repayment, replacement or restoration of bearer instruments of credit that have been lost or stolen, and on the procedure for sale of property or negotiable instruments given as collateral, amongst others (LGTOC Article 8.)[56] Finally, commercial bankruptcy proceedings under the *Ley de Concursos Mercantiles* are discussed below in Chapter 19.

8. Ordinary Commercial Proceedings (*Juicio Ordinario Mercantil*)

Unless a dispute between parties involves exceptional procedures due to the a particular commercial law, such as the *Ley del Mercado de Valores*, commercial disputes between parties must follow ordinary procedures. Ordinary commercial procedures involve the same stages as ordinary civil procedure, discussed above.[57]

[54] It is necessary to state that Art. 1052 of the Commercial Code prescribes that 'the courts shall be subject to the procedure that is agreed upon by the parties, provided that [the agreement] is formalized in a public document, certificate of a *corredor público*, or before the judge that is hearing the claim at any stage of the suit, and the essential formalities of procedure are respected'.

[55] D.O. 27 Aug. 1932.

[56] Additionally, the Federal Law of Consumer Protection of 1992 (*Ley Federal de Protección al Consumidor*), D.O. 24 Dec. 1992, contains several provisions that regulate aspects of commercial procedure. This law establishes the Federal Special Prosecutor's Office for the Consumer (*Procuraduría Federal del Consumidor*) as a decentralized agency, with the jurisdictional authority to act as mediator, arbitrator, or even as prosecutor on behalf of consumers in conflicts between consumers and service providers or producers. This law also regulates mediation and arbitration procedures that must be followed by the Office of the Special Prosecutor for Consumers. The Law of the National Banking Commission (*Ley de la Comisión Nacional Bancaria*), D.O. 28 May 1995, and the General Law of Insurance Institutions of 1935 (*Ley General de Instituciones de Seguros*), D.O. 18 July 1990, and [the Federal Law of Fiance Institutions of 1950 (*Ley Federal de Instituciones de Fianzas*) D.O. 16 Jan. 2002, also provide for the use of mediation and arbitration proceedings.

[57] *See supra*, Section 3.1.

In commercial proceedings, the plaintiff must refer in the complaint to all public and private documents that are relevant to the suit, as well as whether these documents are available or not, and must file with the court any of those documents that are in his or her possession.[58] The plaintiff must also offer proof of having requested any relevant documents he or she was unable to obtain for the proceedings.[59] The plaintiff must provide the full names of the witnesses present when the events set forth in the complaint took place, and must provide a single copy of the complaint, of which the court must serve notice on the defendant. After the complaint has been admitted, the defendant is served with notice to produce an answer within nine days. Within three days of the receipt of the answer, the plaintiff is summoned for a court appearance to rebut the defendant's answer, to offer the testimony of any witnesses who were present during the events described in the complaint, and to submit documentary evidence related to the facts of the controversy.[60] As is the case under ordinary civil procedure, the Commercial Code provides that any type of defence motions or arguments must be asserted at the same time as the answer and may not be offered subsequently, unless the motion involves events that occurred after the events cited in the complaint (*hechos supervenientes*) (CC Article 1061).

In the answer to the complaint, a counterclaim (*reconvención*) may be filed, a copy of which must be provided for the opposing side within nine days. After the defendant answers the counterclaim, the counterclaimant is summoned for hearing, in order to make his or her case known. The judgment in the underlying suit and the counterclaim are both argued and resolved at this same proceeding.

After the complaint has been answered, the judge sets the date for the evidentiary stage to begin, according to the nature of the matter under dispute. In general, the evidentiary hearing should take place within forty days following notice of the hearing (CC Article 1383). The first ten days of this period are used for the offering of evidence (*ofrecimiento de pruebas*), and the following thirty days are for filing the evidence (*desahogo de pruebas*) with the court.[61] When evidence must be gathered outside of the venue of the proceeding, terms of sixty or ninety calendar days shall be granted, at the request of the party, when the evidence is located within the Republic or outside the country, respectively (CC Article 1384).

In ruling on the admissibility of the evidence, the judge must reject any questions submitted by the plaintiff or defendant in the list of interrogatories of witnesses (*pliego de posiciones*)[62] that are not relevant to the dispute. After the

[58] CC Art. 1061. [59] SJF, 9a, Tribunales Colegiados de Circuito, T. II, p. 583 (1995).

[60] CC Arts. 1194, 1198, 1203, 1205, and 1207.

[61] A party who wishes to move for an extension of the evidentiary period must do so within the period set by the judge for the offering of evidence (*ofrecimiento de las pruebas*), and the judge has the discretion to grant or deny the extension based on the arguments of the parties. If both parties agree to an extension, it shall be granted for whatever period is agreed on, not exceeding 90 days.

[62] If the list of interrogatories (*pliego de posiciones*) or the interrogatories of witnesses with the corresponding copies are not presented either, the evidence may not be admitted.

evidentiary stage has concluded, the parties may view the evidence gathered by the court and, usually within a period of three days, they must present their closing arguments. After this period, whether or not the parties have presented their closing arguments, by operation of law the judge must serve notice of appearance of the parties at a hearing, to be held within fifteen days of such notice, to hear the final judgment of the court (CC Article 1390).

9. Appeals from Judgments in Commercial Cases

Several avenues are available to the parties to challenge judgments under commercial procedure.

9.1. Clarification of Judgment (*Aclaración de Sentencia*)

Aclaración de sentencia is only available with regard to final judgments; its purpose is for the judge to clarify contradictory, ambiguous, or obscure words used in the ruling; the judge is not permitted to change the essential points of the judgment (CC Article 1332).

9.2. Motion to Appeal (*Recurso de Apelación*)

As a result of an appeal, the higher court may either uphold, modify, amend, or reverse the decisions of the lower court that are appealed. The filing procedure for these remedies is similar to procedures in non-commercial civil matters.[63]

9.3. Motion for Reconsideration of a Trial Court Interlocutory Order (*Recurso de Revocación*)

Non-appealable court orders may be reversed by the issuing judge or by the judge who replaces the original judge in hearing the matter (CC Article 1334).

9.4. Motion for Reconsideration of an Appellate Court Decision (*Recurso de Reposición*)

This motion is made to the same appellate court that issued the decision.

10. Summary Enforcement of Judgment in Commercial Cases (*Juicio Ejecutivo Mercantil*)

Summary proceedings for the enforcement of commercial claims are available when the complaint seeking enforcement is based on a document that allows

[63] *See supra*, Section 4.2.

for summary enforcement as a consequence of non-performance. These claims may stem from different types of documents, which may be divided into two groups. The first group consists of documents of a public nature, such as final court judgments, public instruments, court-supervised admissions of indebtedness, and judicially recognized private documents and contracts. The second group is made up of documents of a private nature, such as arbitration awards and instruments of credit regulated by the General Law of Instruments and Operations of Credit (*Ley General de Títulos y Operaciones de Crédito*, or LGTOC). Commercial enforcement proceedings consist of the following three phases: (1) attachment; (2) payment or opposition; and (3) sale of property and execution of judgment (*sentencia de remate y ejecución*). These stages are similar to ordinary civil proceedings, discussed above.[64]

[64] *See supra*, text accompanying notes 26–28 and Chapter 22 below at text accompanying notes 71–83.

11

Criminal Law and Procedure

Mexican criminal law is rooted in the Constitution, which sets forth the civil rights (*garantías individuales*) that all officers and agencies of the criminal justice system must protect. In addition to establishing the basic organizational structures of the federal judiciary,[1] the Mexican Constitution also creates the federal prosecutorial body (*Ministerio Público Federal*)[2] and the Office of the Public Prosecutor of the Federal District (*Ministerio Público del Distrito Federal*)[3] The Constitution establishes the essential elements of due process (*formalidades esenciales del procedimiento*),[4] and also provides for specialized systems of criminal enforcement: military justice, which is imparted when violations of military codes are committed;[5] juvenile courts, which have sole jurisdiction to hear matters of underage offenders;[6] and political, criminal, and administrative liability of public servants.[7]

Mexicans have often been cynical about the honesty and efficiency of their own judicial system, and this cynicism has been applied to both the criminal justice and civil justice systems.[8] While the criminal justice system is not as arbitrary as the harshest critics suggest, there has been a general recognition by political leaders in Mexico of the relationship between criminal justice and the endemic corruption that has plagued Mexican public life for generations. While recognizing Mexico's sovereignty and the sensitive nature of this subject, external agencies such as the multilateral development banks and the US Agency for International Development have offered support of judicial reform efforts in Mexico. Within Mexico, most of the reform efforts to date have focused on the need to promote the professionalism and independence of federal and state judges.

An additional matter of concern (the Achilles heel of law enforcement in Mexico) has to do with a grudging acceptance of the relative impunity of police officers for violations of the law and of constitutional guarantees. While the procedure known as *amparo* is supposed to correct illegal behaviour by police

[1] *See* Chapter 6 above, Section 2.1. [2] Mexican Constitution Art. 102.

[3] Mexican Constitution, Art. 122, Section D.

[4] Mexican Constitution, Art. 14, second paragraph II.

[5] Mexican Constitution, Art. 13. [6] Mexican Constitution, Art. 18.

[7] Mexican Constitution, Articles 108 to 114. *See also* the *Ley Federal de Responsabilidades de los Servidores Públicos*, D.O. 31 Dec. 1982, as last amended 13 Mar. 2002.

[8] Criticism of criminal law enforcement in Mexico can be found in the annual reports (*informes*) of the National Human Rights Commission (*Comisión Nacional de los Derechos Humanos*). *See* www.cndh.org.mx (site visited Jan. 2004). *See also* Sarre, M., SEGURIDAD COMUNITARIA Y JUSTICIA PENAL FRENTE A LA DEMOCRACIA, LA DIVISION DE PODERES Y EL FEDERALISMO (Mexico: El Colegio de México, 2001).

and other officials,[9] many instances of abuse of police power never reach the courts. The weakness of law enforcement and prosecutorial services, discussed below, undermines a criminal justice system that is theoretically as just and efficient as that in most modern societies.

1. Criminal Law[10]

1.1. Historical Background

After gaining independence, Mexican political leaders focused their attention on political organization, and criminal laws dating back to colonial times simply remained in force. In 1835, the first criminal code to take effect in Mexico was enacted in the State of Veracruz. During the French intervention (1864–1867), the government of Emperor Maximilian at first adopted the French criminal code; an effort by Maximilian to commission a new Mexican criminal code ended with his premature death. Finally, in 1868, President Benito Juárez ordered the creation of a commission to draft a federal criminal code, which resulted in the adoption by Congress of the Federal Criminal Code of 1871, which closely resembled the Spanish Criminal Code of 1870.

The Criminal Code of 1871 remained in force until the end of the Mexican Revolution. As mentioned above, the Constitution of 1917 included a number of provisions relevant to the application of criminal law, but as a result of the revolutionary turmoil, no progress was made with regard to enactment of a new criminal code until 1925, when President Plutarco Elías Calles named a commission to draft a criminal code for the Federal District and federal territories (*Código Penal para el Distrito y Territorios Federales*), which was published on 15 December 1929. However, this draft code was heavily criticized,[11] and was never put into effect.

Soon thereafter, President Emilio Portes Gil appointed a new commission, which produced the Federal Criminal Code that is in effect today. This code, the *Código Penal para el Distrito Federal en materia de fuero común y para toda la República*

[9] On *amparo*, *see* Chapter 8 above.

[10] The principal treatises on criminal law in Mexico are: Márquez Piñero, R., *Derecho Penal y Globalización* (Mexico: Porrúa, 2001); González Salas, R., *La Teoría Del Bien Jurídico en el Derecho Penal* (Mexico: OUP, 1999); López Betancourt, *Delitos En Particular. Introdución al Derecho Penal* (Mexico: Porrúa, 1999); Díaz de León, M.A., *Código Penal Federal Con Comentarios* (Mexico: Porrúa, 1998); Benítez Treviño, V., *La Reforma Procesal Penal Y la Defensa de Los Derechos Humanos en Temas de Derecho Procesal* (Mexico: UNAM, IIJ, 1996); Silva Silva, J.A., *Derecho Procesal Penal* (Mexico: OUP, 1995); Colín Sánchez, G., *Derecho Mexicano de Procedimientos Penales.* (Mexico, Porrúa, 1993); Castellanos Tena, F., *Lineamientos Elementales de Derecho Penal* (Mexico: Editorial Mexicana, 1991); Porte Petit, C., *Apuntes de la Parte General de Derecho Penal* (Mexico: Porrúa, 1991); Pavón Vasconcelos, *Derecho Penal Mexicano* (Mexico: Porrúa, 1986).

[11] *See* e.g. Jiménez de Asúa, L., *Tratado de Derecho Penal*, I, (Buenos Aires: Losada, 2nd ed., 1964) vol. 1 at 1163–1164.

en material federal,[12] or Federal Criminal Code, was enacted on 13 August 1931 under President Ortíz Rubio and went into effect on 17 September of that year.

Due to the highly centralized nature of the Mexican federal system, most state criminal codes and criminal procedure in Mexico were modelled on the Federal Criminal Code and federal procedural laws. Consequently, this Chapter concentrates on the major provisions of the Federal Criminal Code (referred to hereafter as CPF). The reader must keep in mind, however, that each state has its own criminal code and code of criminal procedure which apply to crimes committed within the state.[13]

Prior to 2002, the Federal Criminal Code also applied to local criminal matters in the Federal District of Mexico City. However, in 1993, Congress amended Article 122 of the Constitution[14] to grant to the Legislative Assembly for the Federal District the power to legislate on local civil and criminal matters. In response, in 2002, after much discussion, the Legislative Assembly adopted the first Criminal Code for the Federal District (*Código Penal para el Distrito Federal*),[15] which follows general concepts of the Federal Criminal Code, but with important deviations.[16] In this Chapter, we occasionally refer to the Criminal Code for the Federal District, but focus primarily on the Federal Criminal Code that served as its model.

Co-operation between federal and local prosecuting authorities exists, but depends upon the optional signature of special co-operation agreements.[17] Of course, both state and federal courts and law enforcement agencies are required to respect the civil rights (*garantías individuales*) set forth in the Mexican Constitution.

1.2. Sources of Criminal Law

The Federal Criminal Code (CPF) is made up of two books. The first book deals with general aspects of criminal law, such as the definition of a criminal offence, types of criminal offenders, and degrees of punishment. The second book sets forth the specific elements of all criminal offences (*tipo penal*) and their applicable ranges of punishment.

Mexican criminal law and procedure coexist at two jurisdictional levels, federal and state. Accordingly, Article 73, section XXI of the Constitution grants to the federal Congress the power to define the acts that constitute crimes and misdemeanours against the federal government, and to attach an appropriate

[12] D.O. 2 Jan. 1931, since amended on numerous occasions.

[13] The relevant criminal codes and codes of criminal procedure of the 31 Mexican states can be found at www.juridicas.unam.mx.

[14] D.O. 25 Oct. 1993.

[15] *Gazeta Oficial* of the Federal District, 16 Jul. 2002.

[16] For example, the Criminal Code for the Federal District, unlike the Federal Criminal Code, contains rules regarding abortion (Articles 144–148), artificial insemination, and genetic engineering (Articles 149–155).

[17] Articles 12 and 19 of the *Ley Orgánica de la Procuraduría General de la República*. D.O. 16 Apr. 1996.

punishment to each offence. This constitutional provision also confers upon federal courts the ability to hear, at their discretion, matters involving acts that constitute violations of state criminal codes when such offences are committed in connection with federal offences. Pursuant to the provisions of Article 124 of the Constitution (the 'savings clause'), the appropriate state legislature has the power to establish as a violation of state criminal law any conduct that the federal Congress has not determined to be a federal crime, so long as the state law does not infringe upon constitutional guarantees.

Article 1 of the Federal Criminal Code states that the Code shall apply to criminal offences committed within the Federal District that are the jurisdiction of local courts, and to crimes committed throughout the Republic that are under the jurisdiction of the federal courts. Article 50 of the Organic Law of the Federal Judiciary[18] lists the following types of criminal offences as being within the *exclusive jurisdiction* of the federal courts: (a) offences set forth in federal laws and international treaties; (b) extraterritorial offences listed in Articles 2 to 5 of the Federal Criminal Code;[19] (c) offences committed overseas by Mexican diplomatic agents; (d) offences committed in embassies and foreign missions; (e) offences of which the federal government is a victim; (f) offences committed by a federal public servant or employee in the performance of his or her duties; (g) offences committed against a federal public servant or employee; (h) offences perpetrated in connection with or against the operation of a federal public service, regardless of whether or not said service is removed from the authority of the central government (*descentralizado*) or performed by a private concessionaire (*concesionado*); (i) offences that hamper the exercise of a power granted exclusively to the federal government; and (k) offences committed by or against federal electoral or party officials.

In order to distinguish between federal and state offences, the Federal Criminal Code lists the specific federal criminal offences over which federal judges assigned to criminal courts have jurisdiction when cases fall within the categories of offences contained in Article 50 of the Organic Law of the Federal Judiciary. State judges have jurisdiction to hear cases involving any violations that are not covered by the categories of this Article.

For example, if the offence of lewd and immoral behaviour (*ultrajes a la moral pública*) is committed by a private citizen in the State of Jalisco, then prosecution belongs to the local jurisdiction (*fuero común*) and the case is heard in the state court. On the other hand, if the circumstances of the same offence match any of the categories set forth in Article 50, such as lewd and immoral behaviour carried out on a Mexican vessel at sea or on a foreign vessel docked

[18] *Ley Orgánica del Poder Judicial de la Federación*, D.O. 12 Nov. 1996.

[19] Articles 2–5 of the Federal Criminal Code (*Código Penal Federal*) establish, for example, that Mexican criminal legislation shall apply in cases involving crimes committed outside of Mexican borders or in locations not belonging to Mexico that are intended to have effect in the Republic; crimes committed on board vessels by Mexican nationals or foreigners in Mexican consular offices, at high sea on board domestic vessels, or on board a foreign vessel anchored in a domestic port or in Mexican territorial waters.

in a Mexican harbour, or if the same offence is committed by a Federal public official, then the case falls under the jurisdiction of the federal courts.

The Federal Criminal Code includes a comprehensive list of criminal conduct, as set forth in Articles 123–429.[20] Article 6 of the Federal Criminal Code addresses any offences that are not covered elsewhere but are set forth in special laws or international treaties, establishing that 'these [laws and treaties] shall be applied taking into account the provisions of Book I of the Penal Code and, as the case may be, any relevant provisions from Book II'. The general provisions of Book I of the Federal Criminal Code also apply to all special criminal laws. Therefore, if a defendant is prosecuted for a crime contained in a special criminal law, such as the Federal Tax Code,[21] the judge must follow the general principles set forth in Book I of the Federal Criminal Code. A considerable number of special criminal laws have been enacted in Mexico, and numerous international treaties pertaining to this area of the law have been ratified by the Mexican government.[22]

1.3. Judicial Precedent in Criminal Matters (*Jurisprudencia*)

As a general rule, the legal precedent established in judicial opinions, or *jurisprudencia*, is recognized under certain conditions as a source of law applicable to all levels of the Mexican legal system.[23] Nevertheless, in keeping with the due process provisions (*principio de legalidad*) enshrined in Article 14 of the Mexican Constitution, judicial opinions cannot create or establish new crimes or criminal penalties, but serve only to clarify the courts' interpretation of a criminal law, or to invalidate a provision of criminal law by declaring it unconstitutional. In interpreting Article 14 of the Constitution, the Circuit Courts have ruled that *jurisprudencia* may apply retroactively to benefit an individual.[24]

In contrast to the US Supreme Court, the Supreme Court of Mexico has not had a major impact on the refinement or development of rules of criminal procedure through its interpretation and application of federal constitutional principles. To the contrary: in the past, the Mexican Supreme Court has followed a conservative approach, refusing to strike down procedural practices by government authorities

[20] The list includes the offences listed in the Annex to this Chapter.

[21] Articles 82–98 of the Tax Code (*Código Fiscal de la Federación*) refer to crimes such as smuggling and tax evasion.

[22] Some treaties relating to criminal law, such as the International Covenant on Civil and Political Rights of 1966 and the Inter-American Convention on Human Rights of 1969, simply reinforce the civil rights of a nation's citizens. Other international agreements, such as the Single Convention on Narcotics of 1961 and the Convention on Psychotropic Substances of 1971, set forth the obligations of the signatory nations to exert their influence in keeping with the goals of the treaty, and thus require domestic legislation establishing the elements of the crimes covered by the treaty.

[23] On *jurisprudencia* generally, *see* Chapter 3 above, Section 2.3, and Chapter 6 above, at text accompanying notes 22–24.

[24] SJF, 9a, Tribunales Colegiados de Circuito, T. III, July 2000, p. 964.

that might arguably constitute violations of constitutional rights.[25] For this reason, human rights critics have accused the Supreme Court of over-representing the state's interests in criminal matters.

1.4. Geographical Scope of Federal Criminal Law

The Federal Criminal Code (*Código Penal Federal*, or CPF) is applicable 'in the entire Republic for offenses within the jurisdiction of the federal courts' (CPF Article 1). The CPF is also considered to apply to acts that are initiated, prepared, or committed overseas, when such acts have an effect, or are intended to have an effect, on Mexican soil; offences committed in Mexican embassies or consulates overseas; and offences committed on board domestic vessels by Mexican nationals or foreigners on high seas, on board domestic or foreign vessels anchored in a domestic port, or in Mexican territorial waters (CPF Articles 2 and 5).

1.5. Overview of Criminal Offences

Criminal offences consist of: the commission of a prohibited act, the failure to perform an act that should have been performed, or the failure to perform part of some act. Criminal offences are often classified according to the gravity of the offence, as either a felony (*delito grave*) or a misdemeanour (*delito no grave*).[26]

According to criminal law theory, a criminal offence must satisfy three requirements: (a) the act in question must be legally codified as a criminal offence (*tipo penal*); (b) there must be an unlawful nature to the criminal conduct (*antijuricidad* or *ilicitud*); and (c) guilt must be attributed to the offender (*imputabilidad*).

1.5.1. El Tipo Penal: *Elements of an Offence and the Applicable Punishment*

All substantive criminal statutes are made up of two components: the description of the specific antisocial acts or failures to act that constitute the elements

[25] *See* e.g. SJF, 7a, Vol. 187–192, segunda parte, pag. 25, 13 Sep. 1984 (failure to provide legal counsel to an accused during the period of *averiguación previa* does not violate constitutional rights); SJF, 7a, Vol. 175–180, segunda parte, 5 Sep. 1983 (a confession may be considered valid even though a lawyer representing the accused may not have been present, and even though coercion may have been used).

[26] Article 194 of the Federal Code of Criminal Procedure, discussed below, lists the following criminal offences as felonies or serious crimes (*delitos graves*): serious negligent homicide; treason against the nation; espionage; terrorism; sabotage; piracy; genocide; aiding and abetting the escape from prison of convicts or defendants; tampering with lines of communication; illegal use of air transport facilities; crimes against health (drug-related offences); corruption of minors; pandering or procurement; exploitation of the body of a minor in the sex trade; forgery and alteration of currency; rape; armed robbery on roads or highways; murder; kidnapping; armed robbery; extortion; and business transactions with profits of illegal origin. Felonies also include the offences listed in Articles 83-III, 83bis, and 84 of the Law of Fire Arms and Explosives (*Ley Federal de Armas de Fuego y Explosivos*), D.O. 11 Jan. 1972, as last amended 24 Dec. 1998, which include torture and trafficking in undocumented persons.

of a criminal offence, and the description of the specific punishment and the sentencing range for that offence.[27] In Spanish-speaking nations, this description is called the *tipo penal*. Mexican criminal law requires that the *tipo penal* must exactly match the behaviour of the offender, a characteristic known as *tipicidad*. This requirement is rooted in the *principio de legalidad*, or respect for due process of law that protects citizens against the arbitrary behaviour of public officials, and is mentioned in paragraphs 2 and 3 of Article 14 of the Constitution.

The Federal Criminal Code recognizes three situations in which behaviour that normally would be classified as a criminal offence is considered to be lawful. The first situation is when an individual acts in self-defence, known in Spanish as 'legitimate defence' (*legítima defensa*). A person who rightfully defends himself or herself does not commit a crime by resisting a wrongful, imminent act of aggression in order to protect one's own or someone else's legally protected interests. There must be an actual need for this defence; the means employed must be reasonable; and the person under assault or who is being defended, prior to the act, must not have unjustifiably provoked the assault.[28]

The second situation in which otherwise criminal conduct may be acceptable is known in Mexican law as 'state of necessity' (*estado de necesidad*), which is akin to the Anglo-American concept of 'extenuating circumstances',[29] and is applicable when a legally protected interest of an individual is under real, present, or imminent danger. The danger must not have been wilfully caused by the actor; there must be no other means at the disposal of the actor to save the legally protected interest that he or she is attempting to preserve; and the actor must not have a legal duty to confront the danger. In *legítima defensa*, the actor uses force to resist an attack by another person. In *estado de necesidad*, on the other hand, the action taken by a person who has been threatened consists not of a direct attack on a person threatening him or her, but rather an act that would otherwise be a violation of a third party's rights. Examples of *estado de necesidad* would include the otherwise illegal transfer of funds to someone in violation of money-laundering legislation, under the threat of being killed for failing to do so; where a shipwreck survivor takes a lifejacket from another person in order to save his own life; or a case in which a person trespasses on private property in order to escape a violent dog.[30] In each of these instances, the law may excuse, in whole or in part, the commission of an otherwise criminal act.

The final situation in which behaviour legally recognized as criminal conduct may be excused is in performing a duty or exercising a right, as when a police

[27] SJF, 5a, Primera Sala, T. CXXXI, 1953, p. 121.

[28] SJF, 8a, Tribunales Colegiados de Circuito, T. XIV, 1994, p. 650.

[29] SJF, 7a, Primera Sala, Nos. 175–180, Segunda parte, Aug. 1983, p. 61.

[30] Carranca y Trujillo, R., *Las Causas Que Excluyen la Incriminación, Derecho Mexicano y Extranjero* (Mexico: Porrúa, 1944).

officer, in fulfilling his or her law enforcement duties, must use violent means to subdue a violator of the law.

1.5.2. The Unlawful Nature of Criminal Conduct (Antijuridicidad)

Criminal conduct comprises behaviour that is contrary to law and presupposes an existing law that prohibits such conduct.[31] No matter how unfair or harmful the conduct may be, no criminal punishment can be imposed if it does not appear in a law or code as an offence.

1.5.3. Attribution of guilt (Imputabilidad)

Furthermore, only a person who has the capacity to comprehend the unlawful nature of his or her conduct and of behaving in accordance with that understanding (*sujeto imputable*) can be held liable for a criminal offence. In cases involving mentally impaired defendants, offenders are not excused from the application of the criminal laws; however, the law provides for possible reduction of sentence or application of therapeutic security measures as alternatives to incarceration.[32]

1.6. Degree of Guilt of the Criminal Offender (*Culpabilidad*)

Culpability, or guilt, has been one of the most complex areas of Mexican criminal law, and has been characterized in many different ways. Criminal intent and state of mind (*dolo* in Spanish, *mens rea* in Latin) are important concepts in Mexican criminal law, as is criminal negligence (*culpa*), or acting out of carelessness or recklessness. The first paragraph of Article 9 of the Federal Criminal Code defines the concept of criminal intent (*dolo*) by stating that 'a person acts with criminal intent (*dolo*) when such person is aware of the elements of a crime, or foreseeing the crime as a possible result of his or her conduct, attempts or accepts the realization of the act described by the law'. Criminal intent is present when the offender knows what he or she is doing, and is aware that this action is a crime (i.e. he or she is aware of the content of the *tipo penal*), and also desires the result of the crime that he or she is committing.[33]

In Mexico a person acts with *dolo* if he or she knowingly commits the elements of the crime. As in the United States, ignorance of the law does not exonerate one from the commission of a crime if the actor is aware of the material elements, or *tipo penal*, that make up an offence.

[31] 'Based on the constitutional principle that there is no crime or punishment without a prior law, criminal law defines various types of crimes, indicates the characteristics of each criminal violation, and sets forth the nature of punishment and extent and duration of imprisonment. Crime, punishment and means of imprisonment are, therefore, essential concepts of criminal law.' Álvaro Bunster Briseño, 'Derecho penal', in DICCIONARIO JURÍDICO MEXICANO, vol. II. (Mexico: UNAM-Porrúa, 1997) at 1021.

[32] *See* CPF Article 15, Section II.

[33] On criminal intent, *see* Muñoz Conde, F., DERECHO PENAL, PARTE GENERAL (Valencia: Ediciones Tirant lo Blanch, 1996).

Normally the level of criminal intent is set forth in the criminal law, since most crimes can only be perpetrated intentionally. Different types of criminal intent exist. Direct criminal intent (*dolo directo*) is present when the offender desires and achieves the criminal result. 'Eventual criminal intent' (*dolo eventual*) occurs when the offender does not specifically intend to commit a crime but does think of the criminal act as a possible result of his conduct and chooses to accept this risk.[34]

Mexican criminal law also recognizes guilt based on criminal negligence, or *culpa*. *Culpa* is defined by CPF Article 9, second paragraph: 'A person acts with criminal negligence (*culpa*) when the result of his or her actions has been previously codified as a criminal offence, such person did not foresee such conduct even though it was foreseeable, or such person foresaw such conduct trusting that it would not come about, and it came about by virtue of a violation of the person's duty to take care, that the person should or could have observed such care in accordance with the circumstances and conditions of the person'. A determination of criminal negligence (*culpa*) has a direct bearing on punishment, and therefore judges should be careful to assess the degree of guilt with which the offence was committed.[35]

After the judge has determined whether a crime was committed wilfully (with *dolo*) or with criminal negligence (*culpa*), the judge must impose a sentence and any security measures he or she may deem fair and appropriate within the limits set forth by law, and in accordance with the degree of seriousness of the unlawful act and the degree of guilt of the perpetrator (CPF Article 52). (Sentencing is discussed in more detail below in Section 1.7.1.)

1.7. The Offender (*El delincuente*)

A criminal offender is an individual who takes part in a criminal offence and can be classified as belonging to one of two categories: either the principal or chief perpetrator of a crime (*autor*), or an accessory to a crime, known in Mexican law as 'criminal involvement' (*participación delictiva*). CPF Article 13 sets forth the following eight forms of involvement in criminal offences: agreeing to or preparing for the realization of a crime; sole perpetration of an offence (*autoría material*); joint perpetration (*coautoría*); incitement to commit a crime or procuring an innocent agent to commit the crime (*autoría mediata*); wilfully causing others to commit a crime or to mastermind a crime (*autoría intelectual*); being an accessory to a crime, or wilfully aiding and abetting in the commission of a crime (*complicidad*); prior to execution of a crime, promising to aid and abet the principal perpetrator after the crime is committed (*complicidad*); or

[34] An example of *dolo eventual* would be the case of a torturer who brutally interrogates a suspect, knowing that the death of the suspect is an (albeit unwanted) possibility. *Dolo eventual* can be compared to the concept of recklessness in US law.

[35] Mexican criminal law is based on a presumption of innocence; therefore, the burden of proving guilt rests on the prosecutor (*el Ministerio Público*). SJF, 6a, Primera Sala, T. LV, March 1959, p. 21. *See also* the discussion of burden of proof in the discussion of criminal procedure, *infra*, at text accompanying note 67.

involvement with other perpetrators, without prior agreement, when the precise result of the involvement of each party cannot be determined (*complicidad correspectiva or autoría indeterminada*).

1.8. Criminal Punishment (*La Sanción Penal*)

Since criminal liability is individual and non-transferable, punishment may only affect the person convicted and his or her property. Article 22 of the Constitution prohibits all cruel and unusual punishments,[36] including implicit prohibition of any punishment that goes beyond the person and property of the offender,[37] and explicitly bans imposition of excessive fines[38] and improper confiscation of property.[39]

As a general rule, corporations or other legally chartered entities are not subject to criminal prosecution *per se*, since the essential element or requirement of guilt cannot be attributed to such entities. Nevertheless, CPF Article 11 provides for imposition of criminal punishment upon corporations when some member or representative of a corporation or association (*persona moral*) commits a crime 'with the means that are provided for such a purpose to the member by the same entity, in such a way that the crime is committed in the name of or under the protection of the corporate representation or to the benefit thereof'.[40] The punishment in such cases may involve suspension from doing business or dissolution of the association, partnership, or corporation (government agencies are not subject to this provision) if the judge rules that such measures may be necessary in order to maintain public safety.[41]

A criminal judgment does not of itself impose civil liability on the offender to the victim. However, as in the United States, a criminal act may give rise to civil liability under the provisions of the relevant civil code.[42] In such cases, a criminal conviction may serve as definitive proof (*res judicata*) of facts in a subsequent civil action.[43]

[36] Article 22 prohibits mutilation and punishments that affect one's public honour, as well as branding, whipping, flogging or beating, torture and 'any other cruel and unusual punishment'. In addition, Mexico is a party to the International and American Conventions to Prevent Torture and Other Cruel, Inhuman and Degrading Punishment or Treatment. *See* López Bassols, H., Los Conceptos Básicos del Derecho Internacional Público Contemporáneo (Mexico: ITAM, 2000). *See also* the Federal Law for the Prevention and Punishment of Torture (*Ley Federal para Prevenir y Sancionar la Tortura*), D.O. 27 Dec. 1991.

[37] *See also* SJF, 5a, Pleno, T. VII, 1920, p. 136.

[38] *See also* SJF, 9a, Tribunales Colegiados de Circuito, T. III, Feb. 1996, p. 418.

[39] This last part of Article 22 was the product of constitutional reforms in 1996 that provided for imposition of criminal punishment without the requirement of a direct link between the conduct of the offender and the consequences of his conduct which result in the commission of a crime. Seizure of assets is not available in order to combat organized crime, but can be used if the alleged owner cannot provide positive proof of the lawful origin of the property in question.

[40] SJF, 9a, Tribunales Colegiados de Circuito, T. II, Sep. 1995, p. 594.

[41] CPF Article 11.

[42] *See* Chapter 17 below, at text accompanying notes 59–61.

[43] *See* e.g. Article 327, Section VIII of the Code of Civil Procedure for the Federal District (*Código de Procedimientos Civiles para el Distrito Federal*) (a public document filed by the

1.8.1. Sentencing Guidelines (Principios de Individualización de la Pena)

In keeping with the principle of individualization of punishment (*individualización de la pena*), judges set the sentence within a range of sentences provided in the Federal Criminal Code for the specific crime committed. CPF Article 51 instructs the judge to consider 'the external circumstances of execution and the particular circumstances of the criminal', i.e. the offence and the person who commits it. CPF Article 52 directs the judge to consider the seriousness of the offence and the degree of guilt of the offender (*los principios de gravedad and culpabilidad*) in sentencing, as well as factors such as how much damage was caused, or to what degree the victim's life was put in danger; the nature of the conduct and the means used to carry out the criminal conduct; the circumstances under which the offence was committed; the manner and degree to which the perpetrator was involved in the unlawful act; characteristics of the offender and of the victim (e.g. their age, upbringing, schooling and educational levels); the behavioural patterns of the offender prior to commission of the crime; the socioeconomic status of the offender; whether the perpetrator belongs to an indigenous ethnic group; the defendant's behaviour after committing the offence; and the state of mind or physical condition the offender may have been in when the crime was committed.

1.8.2. Types of Punishments and Security Measures

CPF Article 24 provides for the following types of punishment and security measures: imprisonment; treatment on release;[44] work release (*semilibertad*) and community service; commitment to in-patient care or treatment on release for persons declared legally insane who, therefore, are immune from criminal prosecution (*inimputables*), and for people who are habitual narcotics users; confinement to a particular location; banishment from a particular location; monetary punishment or fines; seizure of instruments, objects, and products of the crime; warning and threat of a harsher sentence should the offender repeat the offence; warning and threat of being sentenced as a repeat offender if re-arrested on the same charge, which would carry a stiffer sentence; pledge to not commit any further offences; suspension or deprivation of rights; disqualification from holding office or other positions or exercising certain professions, jobs, or duties; removal or suspension from office or from a job; special publication of the sentence in the local press; probation (monitoring of the offender by an authority); suspension from doing business or dissolution of partnerships or companies; guardianship for juveniles; and asset forfeiture (seizure of property obtained from illegal enrichment). Most Articles of the CPF establish the applicable punishment for each *tipo penal*, in accordance with the punishments listed in Article 24.

judicial power serves as irrebuttable evidence in subsequent proceedings; therefore, a judgment entered by a criminal judge constitutes definitive proof in subsequent civil cases. Federal Code of Civil Procedure, Art. 407.

[44] Treatment on release allows the convicted person to be placed under the supervision of a correctional authority, who arranges for educational and/or psychological treatment.

1.8.3. *The Death Penalty* (Pena de Muerte)

In theory, Mexico recognizes the possibility of capital punishment in certain cases: treason against the nation in wars with foreign nations; murder of a parent; premeditated murder with certain aggravating factors; arson; kidnapping; armed robbery on highways and roads; and piracy.[45] Despite this constitutional possibility, however, no federal or state legislation currently provides for imposition of the death penalty, and the death penalty is never imposed in practice.[46] Most Mexicans are opposed to capital punishment since it is considered inhumane.

1.8.4. *Imprisonment*

Imprisonment consists of deprivation of liberty a minimum of three days, and a maximum of forty years (fifty years in cases involving: intentional homicide stemming from a rape or robbery committed by the offender; intentional homicide in an inhabited residence, after breaking and entering into the home (CPF Article 315bis)); aggravated homicide (CPF Article 320); and kidnapping and murder of the victim (CPF Article 366, in fine).[47] Pursuant to the Constitution, prison terms must be served in penitentiaries, penal establishments, or any other facilities that may be designated by the agency in charge of the execution of punishments.

Federal penitentiaries are administered by the *Secretaría de Seguridad Pública*,[48] while those convicted of state crimes serve sentences in state-administered prisons. In theory, Mexican criminal law and procedure emphasize the rehabilitation of criminals, and this is one of the factors that the judge must take into account in sentencing (CPF Articles 51 and 52). The concept of rehabilitation of criminals into society, or *readaptación social*, focuses attention on job training and education of the criminal, and is mandated in Article 2 of the Law of Minimal Standards of Social Readjustment for Convicts (*Ley de Normas Mínimas sobre Readaptación Social de Sentenciados*).[49] Despite the theory, just as in the United States, there is little hard evidence in Mexico that the prison system successfully rehabilitates criminals. Jail conditions in Mexico vary widely, and while the federal government has built new penitentiaries, many state prisons and local jails are dramatically inadequate.

[45] Mexican Constitution, Article 22. The death penalty is prohibited for crimes of a political nature. Military law allows for capital punishment for serious military crimes and has been used several times over the course of Mexican history.

[46] The death penalty has not been applied in Mexico since 1957, when Francisco Ruíz was executed in the state of Sonora after having been found guilty of first degree murder, kidnapping, and rape. On the death penalty in Mexico, *see* Arriola, J.F., *La pena de muerte en México* (Mexico; Trillas, 1999).

[47] Originally, the Federal Criminal Code stipulated that the maximum amount of time that a sanction could deprive someone of liberty was 30 years. The general maximum of 40 years was established as a result of the reform enacted in 1954. D.O. 31 Dec. 1954. The maximum of 50 years, for the crimes listed above, was the product of a later reform. D.O. 30 Dec. 1988.

[48] *See* Article 2 of the *Ley Orgánica de la Administración Pública Federal*. D.O. 19 Dec. 1976.

[49] D.O. 19 May 1971.

1.9. Termination of Criminal Liability

CPF Articles 100 to 115, entitled 'Lapsing of Criminal Liability' (*Extinción de la Responsabilidad Penal*), set forth the circumstances under which the government is precluded from prosecuting an offender or from carrying out a sentence. The circumstances listed in these articles are death of the offender; amnesty; presidential pardon; pardon granted by the victim (only applicable in certain types of cases); recognition of innocence; rehabilitation; running of the statute of limitations; fulfilment of the sentence or punitive measure; or passage of a more lenient law after a sentence under old legislation.

A few of these circumstances require further explanation. For example, criminal liability is strictly of an individual nature; it cannot be transferred to others, and cannot therefore outlive the offender. However, while the death of the defendant or convict prevents further prosecution, the termination of criminal liability does not extend to compensation of victims for damages resulting from the crime, nor to seizure of property that was the product or the object of the crime.

In accordance with the provisions of Section XXII of Article 73 of the Constitution, Congress has the legal authority to grant amnesty for crimes that are under the jurisdiction of the Federal courts, although such amnesty does not relieve the criminal from the duty of reparation for damage. A criminal punishment is considered terminated when a criminal is granted a pardon. Only the President of the Republic has the power to grant a pardon (*indulto*); other officials, such as state governors, are not empowered to pardon a criminal. Presidential pardons are possible provided that 'the conduct observed by the convict reflects a high degree of social readjustment (*readaptación social*) and his or her release does not represent a danger to public tranquility and safety', which must be corroborated in a report filed by the agency responsible for execution of the punishment (CPF Articles 94 to 98). Perpetrators of the following crimes may *not* be granted a presidential pardon: treason against the nation, espionage, terrorism, sabotage, genocide, crimes against public health (drug-related offences), rape, premeditated crimes that attempt to or put an end to the life of others, and kidnapping, as well as recidivism of voluntary offences (*delito intencional*) (CPF Article 97). In practice, presidential pardons are almost never granted.

When evidence appears that supports the innocence of a person who has been convicted of a crime, a special appeal may be made to the judge who sentenced the accused; based on the judge's review, the court may issue an order overturning the conviction. Acknowledgement of innocence occurs when evidence of the following is put forward: that the convict did not commit the crime for which time is being served; that the conviction was supported by evidence that was subsequently discredited; that more than one person has been convicted for the same crime in different proceedings, and proof is offered that it was impossible for both or all of the persons to have committed the crime; that one person is convicted for committing the same criminal act in two or more different proceedings, in which case the most lenient sentence takes effect.[50]

A person may be tried and convicted of a crime so long as the statute of limitations for the crime has not expired by the time a criminal proceeding is initiated. The statute of limitations begins to run at the time the crime is committed, and varies in length according to the applicable punishment: the more serious the crime, the longer the possible punishment and statute of limitations. For example, when cases involve a term of imprisonment, the statute of limitations is equal to one half of the entire prison term, and this term can never be less than three years.[51]

2. Criminal Procedure[52]

As with substantive criminal law, federal legislation has heavily influenced state laws of criminal procedure. Space here does not allow a discussion of the criminal procedure of all the states, so this Chapter discusses federal criminal procedure, since it has served as the model for criminal procedure in most of the states.

At the outset, we wish to call attention to a misconception that many lawyers trained in the common law have about Mexican criminal procedure: the belief that the Mexican judicial system views a person accused of a crime as 'guilty until proven innocent'. This characterization of burden of proof is erroneous: as discussed in Section 2.2.1 below, the prosecutor in Mexico has the burden of establishing the guilt of the accused. Mexican criminal prosecution does differ from that in the United States in many important ways, but it does not relieve the prosecution of proving guilt.

While Mexico does not place the burden of proving innocence on the defendant, there are other aspects of Mexican criminal justice that have earned justifiable criticism. As in other areas of Mexican law, the operation of criminal justice does not always conform to the letter of the law, and the guarantees written into the Constitution are not always observed. In every country errors in criminal prosecution sometimes occur. In Mexico, however, the criticism has been especially harsh.[53] Much of the criticism focuses not on the courts

[50] SJF y su Gaceta, 9a, Primera Sala, T. III, Feb. 1997, p. 193.

[51] CPF Article 105. In cases for which the law permits a private criminal complaint (*querella*) to be filed (*see infra*, text accompanying note 69) the statute of limitations begins to run 1 year from the time the complainant becomes aware of the offence, but in no case may the statute of limitations run for more than 3 years from the date the crime was committed. CPF Article 105. The Federal Law against Organized Crime (*Ley Federal contra la Delincuencia Organizada*), D.O. 7 Nov. 1996, considerably extended both the statute of limitations and the length of punishment in cases involving organized crime, doubling both the length of time of the statute of limitations and the maximum prison terms in these cases.

[52] Most of the texts cited *supra*, in note 10, cover criminal procedure as well as criminal law.

[53] *See* e.g. Sarre, M. and Figueroa, F.A., 'Perspectives on the Right to Fair Trial in Mexico', in Weissbrodt, D., and Wolfrum, R., eds., *The Right to a Fair Trial* (Germany: Springer, 1998) at 85–114.

themselves, but rather on the law enforcement officers—prosecutors (*ministerio público*) and police—who are responsible for bringing criminals to justice. The Judicial Police (*Policia Judicial*), especially at the state level, have been particularly criticized for violating the law with impunity in the treatment of persons accused of crime, and others.

One often hears Mexicans speak disparagingly of police officers. The *mordida*, or bribe, is a common act associated with Mexican police. Mexican criminal penalties are harsh, but the combination of harsh penalties and 'flexible' enforcement gives a great deal of power to police officers to exact bribes in exchange for overlooking an infraction, large or small. Standards of professionalism by police are undermined by low salaries, which make it difficult to attract persons with adequate education and training, and provide an incentive for taking bribes.

Finally, one troublesome aspect of Mexican criminal justice has to do with criminal prosecution that is related to civil litigation. Even before private parties were allowed to lodge a criminal complaint (*querella*),[54] a merchant or business that found itself in a business dispute could attempt to secure a criminal indictment against an opponent, by asserting that the opponent had committed criminal fraud or some other criminal act. By arresting the party charged with the 'crime', the complainant could compel a settlement. Hopefully, as the criminal justice system continues to improve and become independent of the executive branch, this practice will cease.

2.1. Constitutional Protections in Criminal Procedure[55]

The Constitution guarantees that certain civil rights of the individual must be respected during the preliminary inquiry or investigation (*averiguación previa*), which is conducted by the Ministry of the Public Prosecutor (*Ministerio Público*), as well as during the criminal proceeding or trial (*proceso penal*) conducted by the judge.

2.1.1. *Banning of Special Tribunals*

As noted in Chapter 1 above, during the nineteenth century, liberals opposed the special treatment received by certain sectors of society (clerics, the military) that were insulated from normal judicial process by the existence of special tribunals (*fueros*).[56] The liberal Constitution of 1857 banned *fueros* in a provision that has been carried forward verbatim into Article 13 of the 1917 Constitution, which states that 'no one can be tried under laws that strip a person of rights

[54] *See* discussion *infra*, at text accompanying note 69.

[55] Mexican civil rights law can be traced to the Constitution of 1857, the provisions of which influenced the constitutional protections adopted in the Constitution of 1917. Over the course of the twentieth century, numerous constitutional reforms have been adopted, some intended to confer broader rights and freedoms on individuals, and some to expand the powers of the authorities to combat organized crime.

[56] *See* Chapter 1 above, at text accompanying note 94.

(*leyes privativas*) nor by special tribunals'.[57] Article 13 has been interpreted as prohibiting the creation of ad hoc or special tribunals *ex post facto* to cover specific criminal conduct.[58]

2.1.2. *Retroactive Application of Laws*

Article 14, paragraph 1, of the Constitution prohibits retroactive application of laws, stating that 'no law shall take retroactive effect to the detriment of any person'. The words 'retroactive effect to the detriment' have led the Supreme Court to endorse a corollary to the prohibition: when a law is enacted that benefits the defendant, or is more favourable to the defendant than the law under which he or she was tried, the favourable law must be applied by the court and adminstrative agencies.[59] This disposition is also provided in Article 56 of the CPF.

2.1.3. *Due Process of the Law* (Formalidades Esenciales del Procedimiento)

In all judicial proceedings, officers of the court must adhere to 'essential formalities of procedure' as guaranteed in the second paragraph of Article 14 of the Constitution. This concept is similar to the 'due process of law' principle of the US Constitution, and requires the observance of all procedures intended to ensure that defendants enjoy full exercise of their rights to be heard in court, that they can defend themselves effectively, and that they may take part in their own defence. These essential formalities of procedure entail receiving notice of the controversy or dispute; having access to the courts; the opportunity to prove any claim or defence; having the ability to present arguments as may best suit the interests of the defendant; and the right to legal assistance or defence.[60]

2.1.4. *Rule of Law* (Principio de Legalidad)

Observance of the rule of law in criminal matters can be summed up by the Latin aphorism ***nullum crime, nulla poena sine lege***: 'there is no crime or punishment without prior law'. The third paragraph of Article 14 of the Constitution, taken from the Constitution of 1857, establishes that 'in criminal trials, it is forbidden to impose, by simple analogy, and even by process of deduction (*mayoría de razón*), any punishment that is not decreed by a law exactly applicable to the offence in question'. Thus, in criminal proceedings,

[57] The constitutional prohibition does not preclude specialized tribunals with jurisdiction over tax laws, administrative matters, labour law, or electoral laws.

[58] SJF, 5a, Primera Sala, T. XXVII, p. 1140.

[59] SJF, 8a, Tribunales Colegiados de Circuito, Aug. 1994, p. 67.

[60] The criminal law does not specifically list such formalities. Case-law (*jurisprudencia*), however, has established that 'the following [elements] are necessary in order to guarantee an adequate defence before the defendant may be deprived of liberty, and generally speaking, these formalities can be translated into the following requirements: (1) notification of the initiation of the procedure and of its consequences; (2) the opportunity to offer and collect and introduce all evidence or exhibits on which to base the defence; (3) the opportunity to argue; and (4) the issuing of a decision to settle the matters being argued'. SJF, 9a, Pleno, T. II, Apr. 1996, p. 133.

a judge may not convict a person of a crime by extrapolating from a general principle, even when logic appears to support such a conviction; rather, the court may only convict on the basis of a law that lists the precise elements found in the offence in question.

2.1.5. *Double Jeopardy*

Protection against double jeopardy is established in Article 23 of the Constitution, which states that 'no one may be tried twice for the same offence, regardless of whether the person is acquitted or convicted at trial'. This principle, known in Latin as *non bis in idem* ('not twice for the same thing'), is applicable once a judge gives a final judgment in a criminal case. The court's judgment is binding on the prosecutor's office (*Ministerio Publico*), which may not reopen the preliminary inquiry (*averiguación previa*) nor retry the case.[61]

2.1.6. *Additional Constitutional Protections*

Article 16 of the Constitution sets forth the two requirements that must be fulfilled in order to initiate a criminal proceeding: first, the prosecutor must submit proof that a crime has indeed been committed (*corpus delicti*), known in Spanish as *el cuerpo del delito*: and second, there must be sufficient evidence to show that the suspect is probably guilty of the crime (*probable responsabilidad*). Article 17 of the Constitution prohibits private individuals from taking the law into their own hands to retaliate against a criminal act or to demand a right through the use of violence, and also makes it illegal for any officer or agent of the judiciary to charge money for any service related to the administration of justice. Article 18 of the Constitution sets forth how suspected criminals must be investigated and prosecuted, as well as how sentences must be imposed and served out by convicts.

Article 19 establishes that a suspect may be held in custody for a maximum term of seventy-two hours before a judicial authority must issue a pre-trial detention order. Such an order must be supported by the two elements mentioned above: proof of the commission of a crime (*el cuerpo del delito*), and evidence that the suspect probably committed the crime (*probable responsabilidad*). Article 20 establishes constitutional protections of defendants during the criminal proceeding, which include the right to be released on bail (with exceptions); protection against intimidation, solitary confinement, and torture; the right of defendants to learn the name of their accuser; the right to introduce evidence and present witnesses; and the right to be tried in a public hearing.

Article 21 of the Constitution introduces the Ministry of the Public Prosecutor (*Ministerio Público*), placing this office under the authority of the

[61] In rulings concerning the prosecution of one person for two different illegal acts of the same nature, the courts have stated that if the evidence shows that both acts were committed on different occasions (even though the same crime is involved), this does not constitute a violation of the principle of *non bis in idem*. SJF, 8a, Tribunales Colegiados de Circuito, T. XII, Oct. 1993, p. 251.

executive branch of the government and conferring upon it sole responsibility for investigating and prosecuting criminals under federal law. (Section 2.2.1 below examines the role of the prosecutor in greater detail.) Article 21 grants the courts the exclusive power to impose punishments. Finally, Article 22 makes it illegal for punishments to extend to persons other than the individual responsible for the crime.

2.2. An Overview of the Criminal Trial

Federal criminal procedure is governed by the Federal Code of Criminal Procedure (*Código Federal de Procedimientos Penales*, or CFPP),[62] as well as by other relevant laws, such as the Organic Laws of the Federal Judiciary (*Leyes Orgánicas del Poder Judicial de la Federación*).[63] Every state has its own code of criminal procedure, all of which are based on the CFPP. Criminal courts in the Federal District are subject to the Code of Criminal Procedure for the Federal District (*Código de Procedimientos Penales del Distrito Federal*).[64]

2.2.1. *The Public Prosecutor* (Ministerio Público)

The role of the prosecutor, known in Mexico as the *Ministerio Público*,[65] is assigned to the *Procuraduría General de la Républica* (Office of Attorney General of the Republic, or PGR) for crimes committed throughout the Republic that are under the jurisdiction of federal courts (federal crimes) and to the *Procurador de Justicia*, or state attorney general, for crimes prosecuted before the state courts. The Attorney General of Mexico is called the *Procurador General de la República*, and the state attorney general is the *Procurador de Justicia*.

The role of the prosecutor is arguably more crucial to the administration of criminal justice in Mexico than it is in the United States. This is due in part to the fact that, unlike the United States, Mexico does not employ a grand jury or similar independent body to make decisions about whether to indict persons for important crimes. In the past, the decision whether to begin criminal proceedings was traditionally left entirely to the prosecutor (*ministerio público*). If a public prosecutor decided not to initiate criminal action, no criminal indictment could proceed. However, in 1994, Congress amended Article 21 of the Constitution[66] to permit victims of crimes to challenge a decision by a state or federal public prosecutor not to prosecute a particular crime or a particular person. In practice, such a challenge will be carried out by the filing of an *amparo* action.

[62] D.O. 29 Aug. 1931, as amended. [63] D.O. 26 May 1995.
[64] D.O. 29 Aug. 1931, as amended.
[65] *See* Mexican Constitution, Section A, Article 102. The office of Public Prosecutor, based on the French model, first appeared in the Mexican Constitution of 1857 as a weak and undefined position, but subsequently took on greater importance in the Constitution of 1917.
[66] D.O. 31 Dec. 1994.

As in the United States, Mexican criminal procedure is accusatory in nature: the government lodges criminal charges and bears the burden of proving the guilt of a suspect when a crime has been committed. Article 21 of the Constitution[67] has been widely interpreted as granting to the *Ministerio Público* a virtual monopoly over bringing criminal actions. This monopoly consists of three functions over which the Ministry has sole jurisdiction: (1) the investigation of crimes; (2) the decision whether to prosecute an alleged criminal offender (in light of the evidence gathered during the preliminary inquiry, or *averiguación previa*); and (3) the formal act of charging or indicting an alleged criminal before a court of law.

The following sections discuss how the criminal process works *in theory*. In most countries the application of criminal justice does not always coincide with the theory, and this is particularly true in Mexico, a country that has laboured in recent years to promote adherence to the rule of law. Criticism of the Mexican criminal justice system focuses on corruption and incompetence of the principal actors in the system. The *Ministerio Público* has often been criticized for its lack of independence from the executive branch, since the *Procurador General de la República*, who heads the *Ministerio Público*, is appointed by the President. Since indictment cannot take place without action by the *Ministerio Público*, the executive branch has been criticized for the selectivity of its decisions whether to investigate and prosecute crimes. Although the honesty and professionalism of judges are improving, the judiciary is still criticized for failing to provide efficient and impartial justice, and this is especially true in the state criminal justice system.

The judicial system operates its own police force, at both the state and federal levels: the *Policia Judicial*. Unfortunately, the judicial police has earned a reputation for violence, corruption, and violation of human rights. In sum, while recent governments in Mexico have attempted to improve the criminal justice system, problems of corruption and inefficiency are so endemic that it will take decades for the full benefits of reform to be realized by society.

Finally, as also in civil procedure (discussed above in Chapter 10), the criminal procedure employed by Mexico differs markedly from that of common law countries such as the United States. Several of these differences are worth noting at the outset:

Lack of trial by jury The use of a jury is virtually unknown in Mexico; only in cases involving the crime of treason is the defendant entitled to trial by jury.[68]

Written proceedings Because there is no jury, most of the criminal process consists of the filing of written documents. Even the testimony of witnesses is usually taken by a clerk of the court and reduced to writing, although judges

[67] Article 21 of the Mexican Constitution states in part that 'investigation of crimes and prosecution of criminals is the responsibility of the Ministry of the Public Prosecutor, which shall be aided by a police force that it shall have under its immediate authority and command'.

[68] Mexican Constitution, Article 20, Section VI. The procedures to be used in convening juries in such cases are covered in CFPP Articles 308–350. These provisions are rarely (if ever) used.

may occasionally question witnesses to clarify a question of fact. The prosecutor must be present during such questioning, and the defendant has the right to remain silent, as well as the right to representation by defence counsel, either his own or a court-appointed lawyer.

Relatively open rules of evidence Because there is no jury that may be prejudiced by improper evidence, the rules of evidence that the judge must follow are very general and permissive, although the Mexican penchant for adherence to form is observed.

The role of the judge In the United States, criminal trials usually involve a jury, which makes final determinations of facts before the judge forms a criminal judgment by applying the law. The US judge serves as an impartial and inactive participant in the offering of evidence, which is left to the prosecutor and the defendant. In the criminal process in Mexico, the role of the judge is considerably different. In Mexico, since juries are not used, the judge is responsible for making final determinations of fact, in addition to applying the law. The judge's role is potentially a more active one. For instance, the judge may at his own initiative order production of evidence, and also has discretion to extend the evidence gathering phase to permit full consideration of proof.

2.2.2. *The Stages of Federal Criminal Procedure*

Overview of the criminal process As is common in the civil law tradition, most criminal proceedings in Mexico are conducted in written form, and oral hearings are not common. Unlike the adversarial criminal proceedings in a common law system, where the judge is a passive arbiter, in Mexico the criminal judge directs the collection of evidence after a defendant has been formally charged. Criminal judges may even make site visits to verify evidence (*inspección judicial*) such as a visit to a hospital to observe a victim's injuries, or to a doctor's office to witness a medical examination performed by an expert medical witness. The judge may call for oral hearings (*audiencias*) from time to time, at which the judge may examine witnesses. The taking of evidence, rather than taking place in a concentrated period of trial, may be spread out over the entire phase of the criminal process and is referred to in Mexican criminal law as the *proceso penal*, the defendant being called the *procesado*.

Criminal proceedings in Mexico are set in motion by a proceeding known as the *consignación*, when the Public Prosecutor (*Ministerio Público*) puts the offender under the disposition of the competent criminal judge, once it has conducted a preliminary investigation and gathered sufficient evidence to convince the judge to hear the criminal case and issue an arrest warrant if the defendant is still at large. This *consignación* is similar to arraignment in the US system; however, at this point in the proceeding the judge relieves the prosecutor of control over investigation of the case.

Next comes the stage of *preinstrucción*, in which probable cause is determined and the bond status of a defendant is set (similar to the preliminary hearing and detention hearing in the US system). In contrast with US criminal procedure, before a suspect can be held in preventive detention and the process continue, a hearing is held in open court during which the judge advises the defendant of his or her rights and of the charges he or she is facing, and appoints defence counsel (*declaración preparatoria*). At this hearing, the judge must take the defendant's statements regarding the facts of the case, as well as the statements of witnesses for the prosecution, who may be cross-examined by the defence.

A detailed but not verbatim transcript is made of the proceedings by the clerk of the court. The process then moves to the evidentiary (*instrucción*) stage, during which all exhibits and testimony are gathered (*practicar diligencias*), adduced (*desahogo de la prueba*), and examined by both parties and the judge in detail (*calificar el valor de la prueba*). This investigative and evidence-gathering phase may last for several months, with the judge overseeing the gathering of evidence. Evidence may be presented in written or oral form; if oral statements are taken, a transcription is prepared and placed in the files. After the *instrucción* is formally closed, the prosecution and the defence offer their respective conclusions or arguments (*conclusiones*) regarding the law and the facts. The process culminates in the rendering of the final judgment (*sentencia*) in writing (usually either a conviction or acquittal) and in the case of a conviction the judge orders the applicable punishment.

Preliminary Inquiry (Averiguación Previa) Criminal proceedings in Mexico are set into motion by notification to the *Ministerio Público* that a crime has probably been committed. The *Ministerio Público* may receive a complaint (*denuncia*) from one of three sources: (1) any individual who wishes to file a complaint with the *Ministerio Público*; (2) the victim of a crime, or his or her legal representative, through the filing of a *querella*,[69] or private criminal charge; (3) the police, who, after initiating a criminal investigation, or arresting someone caught committing a crime, may notify the prosecutor of the need to begin an *averiguación previa*.

According to Articles 16 and 19 of the Constitution, during the preliminary inquiry, before the Public Prosecutor may obtain an arrest warrant for the defendant, the prosecutor must prove to a reasonable degree of certainty (1) the existence of the *corpus delicti* (i.e. the fact that a crime has been committed), and (2) that the suspect is probably guilty of the crime (*probable responsable*).

Corpus delicti (*cuerpo del delito*) has been defined by Mexican courts as the 'group of objective or external elements that constitute the material elements set forth in the legal description of the offence specifically set forth by

[69] On *querella, see generally* Arila Bas, F., EL PROCEDIMIENTO PENAL EN MÉXICO (Mexico: Porrúa, 21st ed., 2001) at 66, 68–75; Gouzález Bustamante, J.J., PRINICIPIOS DE DERECHO PROCESAL PENAL MEXICANO (Mexico: Porrúa, 5th ed., 1971) at 127–131. Crimes such as fraud, extortion, trespass, etc., that cause damage to the victim may only be investigated by the Public Prosecutor after the filing of a *querella* by the victim. SJF, 8a, T. XII, Tribunales Colegiados de Circuito, Dec. 1993, p. 540.

criminal law'.[70] Probable guilt has been defined in case-law in these terms: 'the authority must confirm whether there exists no lawful justification in favour of the suspect and that there is sufficient information to prove the suspect's probable guilt'.[71] 'Probable guilt' can only be established if the suspect: (1) acts with criminal intent (*dolo*, discussed above) or with criminal negligence (*culpa*, also discussed above); and (2) there is no evidence that the defendant acted out of self-defence or under a state of compulsion (*estado de necesidad*), or was exercising a right or performing a duty or obligation.

Arraignment (consignación *and* preinstrucción) If the Public Prosecutor is convinced that the evidence presented to it show the existence of *cuerpo del delito* and *probable responsabilidad*, the prosecutor may formally initiate a criminal action against the suspect (*el probable responsable*), but must do so within forty-eight hours from the time the report of the crime or the private complaint is filed.[72] This is done by presenting the results of the preliminary investigation to a judge, in a hearing known as the *consignación*.[73] The purpose of the *consignación* is to decide the bond status of the defendant during trial, and to determine probable cause in order to proceed with the criminal process. Up until the time of the *consignación*, the Ministry of the Public Prosecutor operates as an independent authority and does not have to account directly to any judicial officer. By the act of *consignación*, the prosecutor's office becomes the moving party in the case, and from that point on, all of its actions fall under the scrutiny and direction of the judge who has jurisdiction over the case.[74]

Unlike an arraignment in the United States, *consignación* may take place in two ways: either in the presence of the defendant (*consignación con detenido*) or without the presence of the defendant (*consignación sin detenido*). When the hearing is held in the absence of the defendant, not only must the Public Prosecutor formally present the charges to the judge, but it must also request that an arrest warrant (*orden de aprehensión*) be issued against the defendant.

[70] SJF, 9a, T. XII, Tribunal Colegiado de Circuito, Sep. 2000, p. 735.

[71] SJF, 8a, T.I, Segunda Parte, Tribunal Colegiado de Circuito, Jun. 1988, p. 451.

[72] This deadline of 48 hours can be doubled in cases involving organized crime, in accordance with the provisions of Article 16 of the Constitution and Article 134 of the Federal Code of Criminal Procedure.

[73] This hearing has no exact equivalent in US law, and is actually a cross between a request for an arrest warrant (which in the US is usually performed by a law enforcement officer acting at the instruction of a prosecutor), an initial appearance (although in the Mexican *consignación*, the defendant may not have been apprehended yet), an arraignment hearing before a judge, and a detention hearing all rolled into one.

If the two elements are not present, the prosecutor may decide not to continue the prosecution at this time, and the case is filed away in an act known as an 'administrative dismissal' or 'stay of investigation' (*sobreseimiento administrativo*). Finally, if the Public Prosecutor's office feels that there is insufficient evidence to prosecute someone, but that it may be possible to obtain more evidence in the future, the prosecutor may file the case in a special category. In such cases, the preliminary inquiry is not permanently terminated, but rather the the prosecutor's office reserves the right to reopen the case, amounting to what is known in US criminal procedure as a 'dismissal without prejudice' (in Mexico, *sobreseimiento provisional* or *temporal*).

[74] SJF, 8a, Tribunales Colegiados de Circuito, T. I, Jan.–Jun. 1995, p. 797.

In issuing an *orden de aprehensión*, the judge authorizes the judicial police, acting at the direction of the Public Prosecutor, to take the suspect into custody. A judge may not issue such a warrant unless the Public Prosecutor makes a formal request for such action and, in so doing, fulfils the requirements called for in Article 16 of the Constitution.

The *consignación* gives rise to the first formal stage of a criminal proceeding, called the *preinstrucción*, which is similar in many ways to the preliminary hearing and detention hearing in the US system. This stage begins with the issuance by the judge of a ruling known in Mexico as *radicación* or *cabeza del proceso*, the purpose of which is to open the case and declare that the court will hear the case and, in so doing, will assume the obligation of enforcing all rights and civil liberties granted by the Constitution to both the defendant and the victim. When the defendant has been arrested and is before the court (*consignación con detenido*), the judge immediately declares the case formally open (*radica*). When the defendant has not yet been arrested (*consignación sin detenido*), the judge may delay issuance of the formal order to hear the case (*auto de radicación*) for up to three days after the Public Prosecutor's request for arraignment is received. In the latter case, the judge must decide within five days of the *auto de radicación* whether or not an arrest warrant shall be issued. Within seventy-two hours of the time when the defendant is placed at his or her disposal, the judge must issue a decision whether to continue the criminal prosecution, or to dismiss the case due to the failure to find either *cuerpo del delito* or probable guilt.[75]

During the process of *consignación*, the Public Prosecutor is required to present to the judge all the evidence that has been gathered against the accused. The accused does not have a right to present evidence or arguments during the *consignación*.[76] In cases involving crimes punishable by incarceration, a preventive detention order (*auto de formal prisión*) is issued for the purpose of holding the defendant in custody over the course of the criminal proceeding. If the crimes with which the defendant is charged are not punishable by imprisonment, the judge issues an order to stand trial on personal recognizance (*auto de sujeción a proceso*).[77]

If *cuerpo del delito* and *probable responsabilidad* have not been established, the judge may issue an order known as a 'release order for want of prosecution' (*auto de libertad por falta de elementos para procesar*); such an order is tantamount to a simple delay in prosecution until such time as further evidence is collected.

[75] The term of 72 hours set forth in the Constitution may be doubled at the request of the defendant or defence counsel. Federal Code of Criminal Procedure, Article 161.

[76] *See* García Ramírez, S., CURSO DE DERECHO PROCESAL PENAL (Mexico: Porrúa, 1977).

[77] Both of these orders must expressly list the charges for which the defendant shall stand trial pursuant to Article 19 of the Constitution, which establishes that all criminal trials 'must be for the crime or crimes stated in the formal order of imprisonment (*auto de formal prisión*) or [order] to stand trial (*de sujeción a proceso*). If, after the criminal process has begun, it should appear that a crime has been committed other than the crime for which the defendant is being tried, this crime must be the subject of a separate inquiry, which does not preclude consolidation of cases at a later date, should such be warranted.'

Alternatively, the judge may issue an 'order of absolute freedom' (*auto de libertad absoluta*) if he determines that any element of the charges has not been reasonably substantiated; in this instance, basic elements of the crime are missing, and the defendant cannot be prosecuted.

Evidentiary stage (Instrucción) The *instrucción*, or evidentiary stage, begins when the judge issues either an *auto de formal prisión* or an *auto de sujeción a proceso*. The *auto* serves as an indictment listing the exact criminal offence or offences with which the defendant is being charged (*objeto del proceso*), and concludes when the judge formally declares the end of the evidentiary stage. The purpose of this stage is for the parties to introduce relevant evidence to aid the court in ruling on the alleged criminal acts. The judge may admit any lawful evidence, including confessions, public and private documents, expert testimony, judicial and ministerial or government agency inspection reports, testimony or sworn statements of witnesses or legal presumptions, or inferences (circumstantial evidence).

Final review of evidence, closing arguments, and final judgment (Juicio) After all the evidence has been introduced and evaluated, the judge officially closes this stage and opens the stage known as the *juicio*. This stage is made up of two parts. During the first part, in closing arguments, the Public Prosecutor refines and clarifies the charges against the defendant and the defence counsel reiterates and sums up the defence. During the second part, the court evaluates the evidence introduced in the case, takes into consideration the arguments of the parties, and hands down a final judgment (*sentencia*). If the judge finds that the Public Prosecutor has failed to present sufficient evidence to establish the guilt of the defendant, then the case against the defendant will be dismissed. If the prosecutor's case inculpates the defendant, the judge will find the defendant guilty.

If the judge finds the defendant guilty, he will conclude the first phase (*primera instancia*) of the criminal process by sentencing the defendant to a punishment that conforms to the particular circumstances of the crime and the individual situation of the defendant, known as 'individualizing the sentence' (*individualizar la pena*). The judge will also determine any damages or restitution to be awarded to the victim.[78] The most common judgments are conviction (*sentencia condenatoria*);[79] or a judgment of acquittal (*sentencia absolutoria*), ordering the release of the defendant because insufficient evidence was presented to prove that the crime was committed.

[78] Under Article 29 of the Federal Code of Criminal Procedure, restitution or reparation of damage caused by the offence has been elevated to the category of a 'public punishment' (*pena pública*). Consequently, a judge may impose restitution as part of the judgment in a criminal proceeding, and when this occurs, the Public Prosecutor is charged with enforcing the restitution. The victim is therefore not required to bring a separate action grounded in tort (*responsabilidad extracontractual*) apart from the criminal proceeding.

[79] In 1997, 19,220 people were convicted and sentenced to federal prisons; during the same period, another 42,138 people received sentences of incarceration in local or state jurisdictions. México Social, 1996–1998, División de Estudios Económicos y Sociales, Banco Nacional de México, S.A., 10th ed., 1998, p. 526.

2.3. Appeals Against Criminal Convictions

2.3.1. Intermediate Appeals (Segunda Instancia)

Several different recourses are available to parties who wish to challenge criminal court decisions. They may either request the same court to reconsider its own decision, or resort to a higher court to review the decision of the lower court.[80] Federal criminal procedure establishes four types of ordinary appeals for this purpose: motion for reversal of a court's own decision (*recurso de revocación*); motion for appeal (*recurso de apelación*); motion to review a denied appeal (*recurso de denegada apelación*); and appeal based on the failure of a judge to follow proper procedure (*recurso de queja*).

The most common recourse or review proceeding in Mexican criminal law is the motion for an appeal (*recurso de apelación*), in which a higher court reviews the decision of a lower court and the record of the proceedings (*constancies procesales*) and either upholds, overturns, or modifies the decision. Such a review may occur when a party files a *recurso de apelación*, the purpose of which is to examine whether the judge below applied the law properly and observed the relevant rules governing evaluation of evidence. The appeal may also charge that the account of the facts was tainted during the earlier proceedings, or that the decision was not grounded in the law and the facts. Only judgments that have not yet achieved the force of law (i.e. decisions that have not reached the point of *res judicata* (*cosa juzgada*)) may be appealed. A court's preventive detention order (*auto de formal prisión*) becomes *res judicata* three days after it is issued by the judge, and a final judgment becomes *res judicata* five days after it is issued. Thus, a notice to appeal either decision must be filed prior to the expiration of these short periods.

The right to appeal decisions in criminal trials is granted in the Federal Code of Criminal Procedure, or in the procedural codes of the states or Federal District, only to the following parties: the Public Prosecutor; the defendant and his counsel; and the victim or his or her legal representatives (when such persons have been recognized by the trial court judge as co-accusers or third party accusers (*querellantes*)). The following types of court decisions may be appealed: acquittals of a crime; dismissals or suspensions of the proceedings (or dismissals without prejudice); rulings that uphold the constitutionality of detention; arrest warrants and preventive detention orders (*autos de formal prisión*); orders to stand trial on release (*auto de sujeción a proceso*); dismissals for want of prosecution or lack of evidence (*auto de falta de elementos para procesar*); rulings on the admissibility of evidence; granting or denying of release on bail or bond or release for disappearance or vanishing of evidence or information; denials of requests for search warrants; precautionary measures or bond, bail, or collateral intended to keep the defendant from absconding during the trial; rulings on jurisdiction and venue; and denial of a request for

[80] González Bustamante, Juan José, PRINCIPIOS DE DERECHO PROCESAL PENAL MEXICANO (Mexico: Porrúa, 3rd ed., 1959), p. 264.

an arrest warrant, which may only be appealed by the Ministry of the Public Prosecutor.[81]

2.3.2. *Additional Procedures Available to Criminal Defendants for Violations of Constitutionally Guaranteed Rights* (Garantías Individuales)

In addition to the normal appeals process, the Mexican Constitution provides two additional judicial procedures, one judicial, and one quasi-judicial, by which criminal defendants may challenge the actions of courts and criminal justice authorities: *el juicio de amparo*, and complaints of human rights abuses (*quejas*) to the National Commission of Human Rights (*Comisión Nacional de Derechos Humanos*).

Amparo Review: Petitions for Protection against Violations of Constitutionally Guaranteed Individual Rights *Amparo* proceedings are established in Articles 103 and 107 of the Constitution and are regulated by the Law of *Amparo* of 1936 (*Ley de Amparo* de 1936). By means of this process, any individual whose constitutionally guaranteed civil rights (*garantías individuales*) have been violated may seek protection by filing suit before an appropriate federal court, which may order the challenged judgment or judicial order to not be applied or enforced.

The *amparo* procedure is discussed in more detail in Chapter 8 above. For the present purposes we confine ourselves to those elements of *amparo* that apply in criminal cases. In criminal matters, a petition for *amparo* may only be filed at the request of the aggrieved or injured party. However, if this party is unable to file the petition, the request for protection under *amparo* may be filed by the duly designated legal representative of the injured party; or by a relative or other person, when cases involve: acts that put the life of the petitioner in jeopardy, attacks on personal freedom outside of a judicial proceeding, deportation, banishment or exile, or any of the acts prohibited by Article 22 of the Constitution (cruel and unusual punishment, etc.).

Article 11 of the Law of *Amparo* refers to 'responsible authorities' (*autoridades responsables*) against whom *amparo* petitions may be filed. The *Ministerio Público* is a special case, since it ceases to be an independent authority when it officially brings criminal charges in the act of *consignación* (arraignment) before the appropriate judicial officer, and becomes at that point a party to the case, and therefore no longer a 'responsible authority' subject to *amparo* judgments.[82]

Petitions for *amparo* in criminal matters must normally be filed in written form, but in certain instances, listed in Article 117 of the Law of *Amparo*, they

[81] CFPP Articles 366 and 367.

[82] Before the *consignación*, during the preliminary inquiry (*averiguación previa*), the Public Prosecutor acts with judicial authority, i.e. with certain adjudicatory powers or the right to adjudge and have the judgment carried out; consequently, during this stage of a criminal proceeding, the *Ministerio Público* is considered a 'responsible authority' subject to *amparo*, and maintains this status when it proceeds to arrest the defendant at the instructions of the judicial authority which issues the arrest warrant.

may be brought orally in an appearance before a District Court judge: for instance when cases involve acts that endanger the life of the petitioner, attacks on the personal liberty of the petitioner outside of a judicial proceeding, deportation, banishment or exile, or any of the acts prohibited in Article 22 of the Constitution.

After the petition for *amparo* has been filed, it is taken under advisement by the District Court judge, who either agrees to apply *amparo* review, or refuses to do so in cases where the petition is without merit or lacks an element essential for *amparo*. When the judge accepts the petition for *amparo*, the authority responsible for the challenged decision must file a response explaining its actions, along with the records of the proceedings (*constancias)*. Afterwards, both parties have the opportunity to submit written exhibits and offer oral testimony at a hearing, in which written closing arguments are given; the Public Prosecutor has an opportunity to be heard at this time, before the judge makes the final decision. If the request for *amparo* is denied, that decision may be reviewed before the appropriate *Tribunal Colegiado de Circuito*, or before the Mexican Supreme Court of Justice when the constitutionality of a law or regulation of general application is challenged.

If the petitioner fears that the act being challenged will be carried out before an *amparo* order is issued, he or she may request that the District Judge stay execution of the act.[83] This stay of execution may be ordered at the same time as the petition for *amparo* is filed, in which case it is of a temporary nature; after the *amparo* defendant (the alleged responsible authority) receives notice and has an opportunity to be heard, such an order may continue in effect for the remainder of the proceeding. This suspension or stay of execution of the challenged act may be issued at the initiative of the court when cases involve acts that may deprive the petitioner of his or her life, or involve deportation, banishment, or any of the acts prohibited in Article 22 of the Constitution, or any other act that, if executed, would make it impossible for the complainant to achieve redress of the violated civil right. Should such a case arise, it is mandatory for the District Court judge to issue the stay of execution in the same written decision in which he or she agrees to hear the case, and the judge is required to advise the responsible authority to comply immediately.

The National Commission of Human Rights (La Comisión Nacional de Derechos Humanos) During the 1980s, increasing public dissatisfaction with the authoritarian rule associated with single party control of government led the PRI, by the end of the decade, to create institutions that would reinforce the public's confidence in government. One such institution, created by a decree signed by President Carlos Salinas de Gortari on 5 June 1990, was the National Commission of Human Rights (*La Comisión Nacional de Derechos Humanos*), sometimes referred to in Mexico by the English term 'ombudsman'. The CNDH, as it is known by its Spanish acronym, was not endowed with enforcement

[83] *See* Articles 122–124*bis* of the Law of *Amparo*.

powers, and therefore did not represent a direct threat to the authorities in office. Nevertheless, the Commission was given broad responsibility to investigate allegations of human rights abuses throughout the country, and from the outset the CNDH defined 'human rights' broadly, to include violations of constitutional guarantees of civil rights.[84]

The initial presidents of the CNDH were appointed by the President of Mexico, who also had considerable practical control over the Commission's budget. Questions concerning the true independence of the CNDH led Congress, in 1990, to amend the Constitution in order to make the Commission less dependent on the executive branch, by establishing a constitutional basis for the CNDH and similar state commissions. Article 102, Section B, of the Constitution requires the federal Congress and the State legislatures to establish human rights agencies within their respective jurisdictions. To make the CNDH more independent of the executive branch, the Constitution provides for election of the president of the CNDH by direct vote of the Senate. The federal and state commissions are to hear complaints against administrative acts or omissions committed by any government authority or public servant (with the exception of violations of human rights committed by the Federal Judiciary, which are heard by the Supreme Court, and electoral or labour matters). Federal and state human rights commissions, in response to complaints from private citizens and citizen groups, issue non-binding recommendations and denunciations that are sent to the authorities complained against. These recommendations and denunciations, when issued, are made public, and are considered to carry some political force.

The CNDH publishes periodic studies and an annual report on its activities.[85] In the area of criminal law, it serves as a brake on the abuse of the criminal process by the *Ministerio Público*, for which it serves as a watchdog. With a staff of over 800, the CNDH is able to undertake investigations related to the criminal process throughout the country, and while it has not eliminated abuse, optimistic observers hope that it will have a long-term effect on improving the process. For the individual defendant, the value of the CNDH is limited to the ability to use information gained in an investigation as the basis of an *amparo* suit.

2.4. Special Systems of Criminal Justice (*Regímenes Especiales*)

As noted in Chapter 1, above, in Mexico's early history separate systems of justice, called *fueros*, applied to different, and sometimes favoured, sectors

[84] For a more detailed discussion of the Commission, *see* Chapter 8 above, text accompanying notes 11–12, and Chapter 6 above, text accompanying notes 162–164.

[85] The total number of complaints received by the National Commission of Human Rights was 53,319 between 1990 and 1997, 43,903 of which have been resolved pursuant to the provisions of the Constitution and the Law and Regulation of the National Commission of Human Rights. During that same period, 787 recommendations issued by that agency were complied with. México Social, 1996–1998 (Mexico: Banco Nacional de México, 10th ed., 1998) at 545–546.

of society, such as the Church and the military. The liberal reforms of the mid-nineteenth century did away with most *fueros*, and these reforms were carried forward into the Constitution of 1917. However, special criminal procedures do apply in four specific instances that depend on the character of the criminal act or the identity of the actor.

2.4.1. *Military Justice* (Fuero Militar)[86]

Military justice represents the only comprehensive exception to the interdiction in Article 13 of the Constitution against special tribunals. The Supreme Court has ruled that special characteristics of the armed forces, which include the army, the air force, and the navy, justify the existence of a special system of rules and regulations applying only to these institutions.[87] The separate system of military justice does not amount to immunity for crimes, but is rather a distinct system of adjudication and sentencing.[88] Military law may only be applied to members of the armed forces who commit crimes or misdemeanours that represent violations of military laws while on active duty. These military offences or violations of military law are codified as criminal conduct in the Code of Military Justice of 1933 (*Código de Justicia Militar*)[89] which sets forth the elements of these offences and the punishment applicable to each offence, sets up the organizational structure of the military courts, and contains provisions regarding execution of sentences.[90] Articles 203 to 453 of this Code list crimes against the internal or external security of the nation, and against the existence and security of the army, as well as offences committed in performance of military duties, offences against military duty and decorum, and crimes that may be perpetrated against the administration of military justice. The punishments set forth in the Code of Military Justice include imprisonment, suspension from employment, discharge from the military, and death: although there has been no execution.

2.4.2. *Juvenile Justice*[91]

According to federal laws and the law of the Federal District, when an individual turns eighteen years of age, he or she becomes subject to the adult criminal

[86] For a discussion of Mexican military justice, *see* Bermúdez, F.R., COMPENDIO DE DERECHO MILITAR MEXICANO (Mexico: Porrúa, 1996).

[87] SJF, 7a, Primera Sala, T. 115–120, Aug. 1978, p. 51.

[88] The death penalty is still on the books in the code of military justice in Mexico, although it has otherwise been removed from criminal codes in Mexico. On the other hand, jail terms are less lengthy in military sentences than in the civilian system. For example, for military crimes, prison terms may only last up to 20 years, whereas in the civil justice system, jail terms may last up to 50 years in cases of serious felonies.

[89] D.O. 31 Aug. 1933.

[90] According to Article 13 of the Constitution, it is a constitutionally guaranteed right of a civilian who jointly commits a crime with a member of the armed services to be tried by civilian courts.

[91] On juvenile justice generally, *see* Saenz, F.W., 'Debido proceso y principios procesales en la justicia penal garantista para la adolescencia', vol. 8 REVISTA MEXICANA DE PREVENCIÓN Y READAPTACIÓN SOCIAL (May–Aug. 2000) at 73–97; Sánchez Galindo, A., 'Criminología y justicia de menores', vol. 2 CRIMINALIA (REVISTA DE LA ACADEMIA MEXICANA DE CIENCIAS PENALES (May–Aug. 1996) at 95–118.

justice system.[92] According to these laws, offenders under eleven years of age are to be provided with social services, and are not subject to criminal conviction. However, Article 6 of the federal Law for the Treatment of Juvenile Offenders of 1991 (*Ley para el Tratamiento de Menores Infractores*)[93] establishes that individuals between eleven and eighteen years of age are subject to special federal courts for juvenile offenders. Most states have also followed the federal model in terms of juvenile justice. Juveniles are assisted by Guardianship Councils (*Consejos Tutelares*), who are responsible for the care and protection of juvenile defendants.[94] The courts have ruled that Juvenile Courts and the Guardianship Councils are not true public authorities, but rather act as substitute parents and guardians. Juvenile courts are not deemed to impose true sentences on juveniles, and the procedure followed in these cases is not of a criminal nature, as juveniles are not considered to be defendants in the strict sense of the term.[95]

2.4.3. *Organized Crime*

In accordance with the 1996 modifications to Article 16 of the Constitution,[96] organized crime was officially classified as a criminal offence which, in turn, brought about procedural changes regarding the apprehension of suspects of organized crimes. In the same year, Congress passed the federal Law against Organized Crime (*Ley Federal contra la Delincuencia Organizada*).[97] According to the first paragraph of its Article 2, organized crime is committed when 'three or more persons agree to organize, or organize themselves to carry out, on a permanent basis or repeatedly, conducts that in themselves or together with other conduct, have the purpose of or result in committing one of the following offences . . .' The offences listed in Article 2 consist of both federal and state crimes such as terrorism, crimes against health (drug-related offences), forgery or alteration of currency, conducting transactions with resources of unlawful origin, stockpiling of or trafficking in weapons, trafficking of illegal aliens, organ trafficking, armed robbery, kidnapping, trafficking in minors, and vehicle theft. With the exception of the last four offences listed above, criminals suspected of committing these crimes shall be investigated, pursued, prosecuted, and punished in accordance with the provisions of this law. For a defendant to be subject to federal criminal process for the common crimes of armed robbery, kidnapping, trafficking of minors, and vehicle theft (normally the jurisdiction of the state or local courts), not only must the offence be committed by a person engaged in organized crime, but the Federal Public Prosecutor must also exercise its power to prosecute when local crimes are connected to federal

[92] In several states, individuals are tried as adults from either 16 or 17 years of age.

[93] D.O., 24 Dec. 1991. The Law for the Treatment of Juvenile Offenders is in effect for the Federal District in the local courts of general jurisdiction and for the entire Republic in matters under federal jurisdiction.

[94] *See* Federal Law of Juvenile Justice (*Ley para el tratamiento de menores infractores para el Distrito Federal en material común y para toda la República en material federal*), D.O. 2 Aug. 1974.

[95] SJF, 8a, Pleno, 86–2, Feb. 1995, p. 18.

[96] D.O. 3 Jul. 1996.

[97] D.O. 7 Nov. 1996.

crimes (*facultad de atracción*), as authorized under Section XXI of Article 73 of the Constitution. In these instances, the Federal Public Prosecutor and the federal courts have jurisdiction to hear such cases, but under no circumstances can they request or impose a harsher punishment than those set forth by law for these crimes under state or local law.

The punishments applicable to organized crime-related offences are found in Article 4 of this law. In order for the punishment to fit the crime, the law differentiates between perpetrators of these crimes whose involvement is of an administrative, managerial, or supervisory nature, and other types of involvement, setting harsher punishments for the upper echelon of criminal organizations: a maximum of forty years in prison, 'without precluding punishments from being imposed that may be appropriate for other crimes committed'.

The attempts by Congress to strengthen the federal laws as a deterrent to organized crime have, to date, had limited effect. Mexico's battle against organized crime is not only hampered by a lack of resources; it is also burdened by the endemic corruption that has existed at many levels of government, including the criminal justice system. The destructive presence of corruption in government has been recognized by many Mexicans, and recent governments have made the eradication of corruption a major goal. Their success in accomplishing this goal has been frustrated by the simultaneous increase of organized crime activities on a global scale, and by the large sums of money available from drug trafficking that are available to bribe officials in many countries.

2.4.4. *Criminal Liability of Public Servants and Employees*

Section 2 of Article 109 of the Constitution states that 'the commission of crimes by any public servant shall be prosecuted and punished in keeping with criminal legislation'. Public servants and employees may be held liable for crimes committed during their terms of office or employment; the statute of limitations for prosecuting such crimes is generally three years, although other periods apply to certain offices listed in Article 111 of the Constitution.

To avoid prosecution intended to harass high-ranking officials, Article 111 of the Constitution requires that certain public officials may only be prosecuted if the Chamber of Deputies of the Mexican Congress, by majority of the members present, votes to impeach the public official, that is, votes that the defendant shall stand trial in the appropriate jurisdiction.[98] If the Chamber of Deputies

[98] Article 111 of the Mexican Constitution states that 'in order to prosecute Senators or Deputies of the Congress of the Union, Justices of the Supreme Court of the Nation, Judges of the High Court of the Electoral Tribunal, Counsellors of the Federal Judiciary, Secretaries of the Cabinet, Chiefs of Administrative Departments, Deputies to the Assembly of the Federal District, the Chief Executive of the Government of the Federal District, the Attorney General of the Republic and the Attorney General of the Federal District, as well as the Presiding Councillor and the Electoral Councillors of the General Council of the Federal Electoral Institute, for the commission of offences during the time of their tenure in office, the Chamber of Deputies shall declare, by absolute majority of the members present, whether or not there are sufficient grounds to prosecute the defendant'.

decides that grounds are insufficient to justify prosecution of the public official, the proceeding against the official is concluded. However, a decision by the Chamber of Deputies not to recommend prosecution does not prevent such public servants from being prosecuted at a later date after they have finished serving their term in office, or after resigning their post; in other words, the resolution of the Chamber has no permanent effect on the grounds for the charges. This feature, the possibility of submitting government officials to criminal prosecution or civil litigation after they have left office, has become increasingly important due to the political opening up of Mexico. Even former Presidents have been questioned about their activities during their presidency, or while they served in other executive positions prior to their presidency.

If the Chamber declares that sufficient grounds exist to move forward against the defendant, the official is handed over to the proper authorities. As a result of impeachment (*declaración de procedencia*) by the Chamber of Deputies, the public official is removed from office during the entire course of trial. Should the defendant be acquitted, he or she may be reinstated in office; however, if the defendant is convicted and the case involves an offence committed during performance of official duties, the convicted official may not be afforded the benefit of a pardon. The sentences in these cases are imposed in accordance with the same punishments set forth generally in the criminal laws, and when offences involve illegal enrichment on the part of the perpetrator or damages caused to government property, punishments are adjusted in keeping with the amount of profit obtained and damage caused by the unlawful conduct.

ANNEX
CRIMINAL OFFENCES LISTED IN ARTICLES 123–429 OF THE FEDERAL CRIMINAL CODE

- Treason against the nation (high treason);
- espionage;
- sedition;
- mutiny;
- rebellion;
- terrorism;
- sabotage;
- conspiracy;
- piracy;
- violation of immunity of parliamentarians and diplomats and conscious violation of the neutrality of the nation;
- violations of the duties of mankind toward prisoners of war and the wounded;
- genocide;
- aiding and abetting in the escape from prison of convicts or defendants;
- violation of the terms and conditions of a criminal sentence;
- possession, manufacture, trafficking, or stockpiling of prohibited weapons; criminal association;
- assaults on lines of communication;
- tampering with the mail;
- illegal use of air transport facilities;
- disobedience, contempt of court or of an administrative authority, and resistance;
- prevention of execution of a federal public work or service;
- breaching of official seals (e.g. when someone breaks the seals that have been placed by administrative authorities to close a certain establishment, such as a restaurant, for violating labour, health or other regulations);
- crimes against federal public officials;
- desecration of national emblems (flag, seal, anthem);
- production, possession, trafficking, proselytism (recruitment) and other narcotics-related acts; endangerment of infecting another person with an illness;
- lewd and immoral behaviour ('offences against public morals'), corruption of a minor or of a mentally or physically disabled person;
- exploitation of persons or sexual pandering or procuring;
- incitement or instigation to commit a crime and advocating such criminal behaviour or any vice;
- divulging secrets; improperly serving in public office or position;
- abuse of authority (non-performance or improper performance of normal duties), conspiracy of public servants;
- improper use of discretion and power; extortion of an individual by a public official;

- intimidation of a potential witness against a public official or an individual who is in a position to report a public official for wrongdoing;
- improper awarding of contracts, concessions, franchises, exemptions, authorization, etc;
- influence peddling;
- bribery;
- embezzlement of federal public funds;
- illegal enrichment;
- improper exercise of the law (using force to exercise a right or against a right being asserted);
- inappropriate and incompetent behaviour of legal counsel, employers, and litigants;
- forgery, counterfeiting, and destruction of currency, bearer bonds, documents of public credit, seals, keys, stamps or dies for minting of coins, trademarks, weights, measures, and documents;
- false testimony in judicial proceedings and in official reports; use of assumed or fabricated names or domiciles;
- usurping public office or posing as a professional without proper credentials;
- improper use of decorations (honours, medals) uniforms, hierarchical ranks, badges, pins, and acronyms;
- crimes against consumers and federal government property;
- sexual harassment;
- sexual abuse;
- statutory rape (sexual intercourse with juveniles);
- rape;
- incest;
- adultery;
- crimes against the institution of marriage (false attribution of parenthood or marital status, switching of infants at birth, providing false information regarding blood relationship in order to gain access to an inheritance), and bigamy;
- violations of laws on burials and exhumation;
- threats;
- trespassing or unlawful entry into a home;
- battery;
- murder;
- abortion;
- abandonment of persons;
- family violence;
- assault and other simple physical violence;
- libel;
- slander;
- illegally depriving someone of their liberty and other constitutional protections;
- abduction;

- robbery or theft;
- abuse of confidence;
- fraud;
- extortion;
- crimes of businessmen undergoing bankruptcy proceedings;
- dispossession of real property or water rights;
- destruction of property; being an accessory to a crime after the fact or harbouring a criminal;
- carrying out business transactions with resources from illegal origin;
- electoral crimes;
- environmental crimes; and
- infringements of copyrights or of intellectual property rights.

12

Regulation of the Economy and Environmental Regulation

1. Regulation of the Economy

1.1. Introduction

With a legacy of centralized, authoritarian government, it is not surprising that Mexico's economy should have been dominated by government control throughout the twentieth century. Centralized control reached its apogee under the presidencies of Luis Echeverria (1970–1976) and José López Portillo (1976–1982) when the federal government controlled the economy, either directly or indirectly. However, as in many other countries, the Mexican economic model of government intervention and import substitution crumbled under the pressure of the external debt crises of the 1980s. During the presidency of Carlos Salinas de Gortari (the first economist to serve as President of Mexico, from 1988–1994), Mexico dismantled much of the structure of the state-controlled economy. While the federal government still dominates certain areas of the economy (e.g. the production and distribution of hydrocarbons and electricity), free markets have come to prevail in most sectors of the economy, and the borders have opened to both trade and investment.[1]

The restructuring of the Mexican economy, which actually began during the presidency of Miguel de la Madrid (1982–1988),[2] relied on three main pillars: privatization of publicly owned companies, domestic deregulation, and the establishment of a new legal regime for a free market economy.

1.1.1. Privatization

The argument in favour of privatization is rooted in neoclassical economic theory, which advocates free markets and a *laissez-faire* state, and which views individuals and private agents as the most suitable means for improving social

[1] For an analysis of Mexican government intervention in and control of the economy, *see* Ortiz Mena, A., *El desarrollo estabilizador: reflexiones de una época* (Mexico: Fondo de Cultura Económica, 1998).

[2] Facing severe balance of payments pressures in 1982, Mexico was forced, at the outset of the de la Madrid administration to resort to IMF balance of payments assistance. By this time, the IMF and its sister agency, the World Bank, had begun to embrace economic deregulation as a key to long-term economic health, adding to the pressures for economic reform. On the subsequent reforms that took place during the presidency of Carlos Salinas de Gortari, *see* the account of Salinas' Finance Minister, Pedro Aspe, in Aspe Armella, P., *El camino de la transformación económica* (Mexico: Fondo de Cultura Económica, 1993).

welfare. By expanding and strictly enforcing property rights, and by allowing the free operation of market forces to promote efficiency, the government has a less adverse effect on business and, consequently, private interests have greater opportunities to generate economic growth. Eliminating government regulation also serves to relieve society of the tax burden needed to employ an inefficient and unproductive bureaucracy.

Mexico was one of many Latin American governments to embrace this neoclassical economic model during the last two decades of the twentieth century. The first Latin American government to do so, in Chile, adopted free-market economics with a vengeance.[3] Mexico followed a more cautious approach, consonant with the populist politics of the PRI and the fear that complete deregulation would throw the country into economic chaos. Political realities—for instance, opposition to privatization of the energy sector, especially in the area of oil and gas—also dictated caution in the use of free market policies.

In 1982, when Miguel de la Madrid inherited the leadership of a bankrupt government, the parastatal sector in Mexico was made up of 1,155 entities. Many of these entities, such as PEMEX, the state-owned petroleum monopoly, engaged in important activities. However, the government also owned and managed airlines, hotels, railroads, shipping companies, commercial movie theatres, and other activities in which the need for governmental ownership was highly questionable. President de la Madrid began the process of selling state-owned enterprises, partly in response to IMF and World Bank urging. Privatizations reached their crescendo under Carlos Salinas de Gortari, the Harvard-trained economist who took up the banner of *apertura económica* when he took office in 1988. In his National Development Plan of 1988–1994, President Salinas stated that 'privatization and downsizing of [public] entities, aside from providing greater opportunity for participation of the social and private sectors, helps to free up public resources in order to pay greater and better attention to strategic and priority areas. Privatization does not mean a retreating of the State, nor giving up the areas for which it is responsible; hence, a strong State does not need to be complex: the modernity of a nation is measured by the fluidity with which private and public affairs move along.'

By the end of the Salinas' administration, only 213 government-owned entities remained in existence.[4] By 2002, 203 state-owned enterprises still existed, including 80 *organismos descentralizados*, 101 state majority-owned enterprises (21 of these enterprises were in the process of de-incorporation at the time), and 22 public trusts (*fideicomisos*).[5]

Most of the privatizations were carried out during the administration of President Salinas under the direction of the *Secretaría de Hacienda y Crédito*

[3] *See* Hachette, D., and Lüders, R., *La privatización en Chile* (Panama: Centro Internacional para el Desarrollo Económico, 1992).

[4] Rogozinski, J., *La privatizacion de empresas estatales* (Mexico: Fondo de Cultura Económica, 1993) at 7.

[5] *See* the list of *entidades paraestatales* of the federal government in D.O. 2 Aug. 2002.

Público (SHCP) and the Intersectarial Commission on Public Finance.[6] The privatizations of government-owned commercial enterprises were successful in reducing the immense fiscal burden of supporting hundreds of state-owned concerns, with thousands of government employees. The sale of such enterprises also produced revenues that were used to reduce government debt, and improved the efficiency of the privatized companies, which now had to compete in the market place.[7] Nevertheless, high-profile privatizations, such as those involving the commercial banks, were criticized both on ideological grounds (by those who still favoured state control of the economy) and for the way in which the privatizations were carried out.[8]

1.1.2. Economic Deregulation

The second pillar of Mexico's economic restructuring involved economic deregulation. Since most commercial and economic law in Mexico is federal, deregulation involved a fundamental change in attitudes towards the central government's role in the economy. The height of central government regulation took place at the beginning of the administration of Miguel de la Madrid (1988–1994). In 1983, President de la Madrid sent to Congress a constitutional amendment that added two new articles, Articles 25 and 26, which raised to a constitutional principle the government's role as *rector de la economía* (guide of the economy), and required the government to adopt national economic plans.[9] These articles and the government's role are discussed in more detail below.

Under the dire economic conditions faced by President de la Madrid, a central role for the government could be understood. His predecessor, President López Portillo, had 'nationalized' the banking system, and had imposed strict exchange controls to control capital flight. A standby arrangement with the IMF, concluded in 1986,[10] had imposed numerous conditions on the government to deal with the balance of payments and external debt crises facing the nation at that time.

[6] *See* Aspe Armella, *supra* note 2 at 170. In 1995, President Zedillo regularized the oversight of privatizations through the creation of an Inter-secretarial Commission on Privatization (*Comisión Intersecretarial de Desincorporación*) made up of the Secretary of the Treasury (SHCP), the Secretary of Commerce and Industrial Promotion (SECOFI, now Seconomía), the Comptroller and Administrative Development (SECODAM), the Secretary of Labour and Welfare (STPS), with the Chairman of the Federal Commission on Competition (*Comisión Federal de Competencia*) as *ad hoc* member. D.O. 7 Apr. 1995.

[7] *See id.* at 154–187.

[8] Among other criticisms, the government was accused of selling the banks to investors who were inexperienced in banking, and of failing to provide an appropriate regulatory regime for the newly privatized banks. *See* Manrique Campos, I., 'El caso de las empresas públicas en el sector financiero mexicano', in Ramon Martinez Escamilla *et al.*, eds., *CRISIS ECONÓMICA? FIN DEL INTERVENCIONISMO ESTATAL?*, Instituto de Investigaciones Económicas (Mexico: UNAM, 1996); and Solís Rosales, R., *DEL FOBAPROA AL IPAB: TESTIMONIOS, ANÁLISIS Y PROPUESTAS* (Mexico: Universidad Autónoma Metropolitana/Plaza y Valdés, 2000) at 15–20.

[9] Commentaries on these articles are contained in *CONSTITUCIÓN POLÍTICA DE LOS ESTADOS UNIDOS MEXICANOS—COMENTADA* (Mexico: UNAM-Instituto de Investigaciones Jurídicas, 2000), vol. I, at 356–368 (hereinafter *CONSTITUCIÓN POLÍTICA COMENTADA*).

[10] *See*, Vázquez Pando, F., *LA CRISIS DE LA DEUDA Y LOS DESEQUILIBRIOS CONSTITUCIONALES* (Mexico: Escuela Libre de Derecho/Miguel Angel Porrúa, 1995) at 76.

By the time Carlos Salinas became president, Mexico was no longer subject to the conditions of the IMF standby arrangement that had been concluded in the early 1980s. Having been educated as an economist, Salinas embraced free market economics. In undertaking to restructure Mexico's economy, he viewed deregulation as a key element in preparing Mexican businesses for international competition that would confront them once the borders were open to trade and investment (the third pillar of Salinas' plan). President Salinas undertook to dismantle the interventionist economic policies of the federal government that had long characterized the political economy of Mexico. He also began to reverse the policies that had allowed inefficient producers to thrive in Mexico under government protection, culminating in the negotiation and entry into force of the North American Free Trade Agreement (NAFTA) in 1994. Salinas' policies brought increased competition, and more efficient production, but they also caused many smaller companies to go bankrupt, adding to the unemployment that has long plagued the economy. By the time Salinas left office in 1994, the economy was much more open and competitive, but poverty, under-employment, and unequal distribution of income remained.

President Ernesto Zedillo (1994–2000), also an economist, embraced the neoliberal economics of Salinas, and sought to institutionalize them, under the Programme of Industrial Policy and Economic Deregulation (Deregulation Programme).[11] To make this programme effective, Zedillo issued a Resolution (*Acuerdo*) calling for increased efficiency in business regulation,[12] with guidelines for easing restrictions on business activities and time limits for authorizations. At the end of his *sexenio*, in March 2000, President Zedillo sent to Congress a proposed reform of the Federal Law of Administrative Procedure, which was readily adopted,[13] creating the Commission on Regulatory Improvement (*Comisión de Mejora Regulatoria*, or COFEMER), a semi-autonomous agency with technical and operational autonomy within the *Secretaría de Economía*.[14]

By the time Vicente Fox was elected President in 2000, much economic restructuring had already been done. The accomplishments of the Fox administration to date have been maintaining economic stability, promoting continuing economic reform, and promoting transparency in government operations. As already noted, the Federal Commission on Regulatory Improvement (COFEMER) was established at the end of the Zedillo administration. Thus, at the outset, a priority for President Fox was to appoint a technically capable staff to manage COFEMER, and try to realize the promise of regulatory improvement. To demonstrate the importance of continued regulatory reform, President Fox issued his own Federal Programme for Regulatory Improvement,[15] and in his

[11] D.O. 24 Nov. 1995.

[12] *Acuerdo para la desregulación de la actividad empresarial*, D.O. 24 Nov. 1995.

[13] D.O. 19 Apr. 2000.

[14] On COFEMER, *see* www.cofemer.gob.mx (site visited Jan. 2004) and *see* text accompanying notes 51, and 94–95, *infra*.

[15] D.O 17 Jan. 2003.

government's National Development Plan 2001–2006, he emphasized the need for regulatory reform to improve economic efficiency.[16]

Fox's regulatory reforms have been hampered by an inexperienced leadership in certain agencies, as well as by the failure of the administration to develop a new, viable model of political leadership to replace the authoritarianism of the PRI. There have been gains, although they have been modest to date. One of the most important gains may prove to be the passage in 2002 of the Federal Transparency Law (discussed above in Chapter 9, Section 5.2.). If it fulfils the expectations of its sponsors, this law—the first 'government information law' ever adopted in Mexico—will do much to improve not only regulatory efficiency, but honesty as well.

2. Establishing a New Legal Framework for a Free Market Economy

Mexico operated under an authoritarian, government-controlled economic regime during much of the twentieth century, and the laws affecting business and trade reflected that closed model. There was no antitrust law to speak of, since monopolies were virtually assured tacit or open protection. International trade law was rudimentary, since trade in most goods (other than petroleum) was relatively insignificant. During much of the twentieth century, economic regulation was carried out by direct government action or intervention.

With Mexico committing to a free-market economy in the 1980s, it soon became apparent that the legal regime regulating business and the economy was woefully inadequate to a modern, market-oriented economy.[17] Thus, beginning in the late 1980s, Congress began to adopt a series of laws, some of them based on US or other foreign models, to regulate business activity in the new, open economy in which private investment was to play a much larger role. These laws included the first competition law, the Federal Law of Economic Competition (*Ley Federal De Competencia Económica*),[18] which drew liberally from US antitrust laws,[19] and is discussed in greater detail later in this Chapter.

After its accession to the General Agreement on Tariffs and Trade (GATT) in 1986,[20] Mexico was also forced to adopt a number of laws to promote international trade that would make the Mexican regime governing international trade more similar to that in other countries making up the GATT system.

[16] *Plan Nacional de Desarrollo* 2001–2006, Sections 4.6, 6.3.2 (*Objeto* 2, (g), p. 152), D.O. 30 May 2001, available at www.economica.gob.mx, '*Marco Normativo*', '*Diversas Disposiciones*' (site visited Jan. 2004).

[17] *See* Witker, J., *Derecho de la competencia en América: Canadá, Chile, Estados Unidos y México* (Mexico: Fondo de Cultura Económica, 2000) at 23–25 (discussing privatization of airlines and telecommunications companies without sufficient regulatory structure).

[18] D.O. 24 Dec. 1992.

[19] *See* Witker, *supra* note 17 at 93.

[20] D.O. 17 July 1986. Mexico also adopted the GATT Code on Technical Barriers to Trade (D.O. 20 Apr. 1988), and the Customs Valuation Code (D.O. 25 Apr. 1988).

These included a new Law of Foreign Commerce (*Ley de Comercio Exterior*);[21] the adoption of a Mexican Antidumping Law, in accordance with the GATT Antidumping Code;[22] and changes in other laws in order to bring Mexico into compliance with GATT codes on technical barriers to trade and customs valuation.[23] With Mexico's accession to membership in the WTO (referred to as OMC in Mexico),[24] the country has adopted the obligations that make up the Uruguay Round Agreements, and are therefore automatically incorporated into Mexican domestic law, by virtue of Article 133 of the Constitution.[25]

In addition to its membership in the WTO, Mexico has entered into a number of regional free trade arrangements as part of a strategy, which began under President Salinas and continues in subsequent regimes, to promote Mexico as an important export platform. The most important of these, the North American Free Trade Agreement (NAFTA),[26] has created a successful free trade area that includes Canada, Mexico, and the United States. Subsequently, Mexico entered into free trade agreements with Chile; Venezuela and Colombia; Uruguay; Bolivia; Costa Rica; Nicaragua; Israel; El Salvador, Guatemala and Honduras; the EFTA countries (Iceland, Liechtenstein, Norway, and Switzerland); and the European Union.[27] Mexico's adherence to these free trade agreements, especially NAFTA, have forced Mexico to amend a number of laws that govern matters, such as international trade, foreign investment, intellectual property rights, etc., that are covered by provisions of the free trade agreements.

3. The Government's Role in Guiding the Economy (*Rectoría Económica*)

Several articles of the Mexican Constitution set limits on government regulation of business and the economy. Mexican legal scholars refer to these, Articles 25, 26, 27, and 28, as the 'economic chapter of the Constitution'. Articles 25 and 26 assert the federal government's authority to establish guidelines for economic development, and to carry out 'democratic planning'. These Articles are written in broad, hortatory terms; for the most part, they serve as political underpinnings for central government regulation of the economy (by both executive and legislative branches) rather than as specific allocations of power.[28]

[21] D.O. 27 July 1993. [22] D.O. 21 Apr. 1988.

[23] Mexico adopted the GATT Code on Technical Barriers to Trade (D.O. 20 Apr. 1988), and the Customs Valuation Code (D.O. 25 Apr. 1988). [24] D.O. 4 Aug. 1994.

[25] *See* the discussion of incorporation of treaties into Mexican law, Chapter 3 above, at text accompanying notes 52–54. [26] D.O. 20 Dec. 1993.

[27] A list of the countries with which Mexico has concluded Free Trade Agreements, as well as copies of the official texts, may be found at www.economia.gob.mx, '*Negociaciones comerciales*', '*Tratados*'. (Site visited Jan. 2004.)

[28] The federal government certainly used central economic planning and control long before Articles 25 and 26 were added to the Constitution in 1983. In a way, the specific mention of central economic regulation in Articles 25 and 26, rather than relying on the legislative powers mentioned in Article 73, serve to forestall the kind of conflict that arose in the United

There is one exception to this, however: the fourth paragraph of Article 25 specifies that the public sector, through the federal government, shall have direct control over certain activities that are deemed 'strategic' by the Constitution.

3.1. Strategic Activities

Article 28, paragraph 4, provides that the following areas are strategic activities, which must be carried out exclusively by the federal government: mail, telegraph, and radiotelegraphy services; petroleum and other hydrocarbon fuel extraction; the manufacture of basic petrochemicals; radioactive minerals and nuclear power; and electrical power generation.[29] Article 28, paragraph 4, also provides that other activities may be designated as strategic, through new legislation or amendments to existing laws.

The fundamental characteristic of strategic activities is that they are the *exclusive* province of the Federal government. Either the government itself or a quasi-governmental agency (*organismos descentralizados*)[30] must carry out these activities. Examples of such agencies include PEMEX, the Federal Electricity Commission (CFE), and the *Instituto Mexicano del Seguro Social* (IMSS), among others. The designation 'strategic' implies an absolute exclusion of private individuals from carrying out these activities. Nevertheless, in line with the trend in recent years to reduce the government's immense power over the economy, in recent years the Congress has amended Article 28 to reduce the number of strategic areas reserved to the State. In 1995, paragraph 4 of Article 28 was amended to remove rail transport and satellite communications from the list of 'strategic' activities.[31] Similarly, the regulatory laws that govern strategic areas have eased restrictions on involvement of the private sector, paving the way for private investment in these sectors.[32]

States, during the administration of President Franklin D. Roosevelt, when the Supreme Court held repeatedly that the federal government lacked the authority under the Commerce Clause of the US Constitution to regulate economic activities on a national scale. The Supreme Court's interpretation of the Commerce Clause, of course, eventually became expansive.

[29] Article 28 of the Constitution should be interpreted in conjunction with Article 27 of the Constitution, which sets forth the state's control over and ownership of natural resources, especially of subsoil minerals and hydrocarbons. *See* especially paragraph six of Article 27, which states that: 'in matters involving petroleum and solid, liquid or gaseous hydrocarbons, no concessions or contracts shall be granted, nor shall any contracts or concessions that may have been granted previously, as the case may be, continue in force, and the Nation shall utilize those products, in accordance with the provisions that the respective regulatory law sets forth. It is the sole responsibility of the Nation to generate, conduct, transform, distribute and supply electric power for the purpose of public utilities. In this area, no concessions shall be awarded to private individuals and the Nation shall benefit from the assets and natural resources that may be required for this purpose.'

[30] *Cf. Ley Federal de Entidades Paraestatales* (LFEP) Article 14, Section II, D.O. 14 May 1986 (the purpose of *organismos descentralizados* shall be to carry out strategic activities).

[31] D.O. 2 Mar. 1995. For a discussion of this reform, *see* CONSTITUCIÓN POLÍTICA—COMENTADA, *supra* note 9 at vol. I, p. 397.

[32] *See*, for instance, the relaxation of government control over petrochemicals and electric power generation. With regard to petrochemicals, Article 3 of the *Ley Reglamentaria del*

3.2. Priority Activities

In addition to *strategic activities*, which are reserved exclusively to the State, the Mexican Constitution establishes a category of activities known as 'priority activities', in which government may: carry out the activity solely, join with private investors to carry out the activity; or grant a concession for a private enterprise to carry out the activity. In any case the federal government has an important regulatory role because the investment involves vital public services.

Several models exist for providing priority activities, as follows.

(i) The State may carry out the activity exclusively, without permitting private participation. Examples of this include the National Sports Lottery (*Lotería Nacional or Pronósticos Deportivos*).[33]

(ii) The State may perform the function of a producer of goods or provider of services through one of its agencies or entities, without excluding private companies from performing such an activity as well. Examples of this include the *Comisión Nacional de Subsistencias Populares*, or CONASUPO, which buys basic agricultural products and sells them to needy persons.

(iii) The State may participate in joint ventures with private individuals or companies to carry out such activities under several different types of association. An example of this is Port Authorities, or railroads in areas of low density (such as the *Ferrocarril del Istmo de Tehuantepec*, S.A. de C.V.).

(iv) A private enterprise may carry out the priority activity under a concession granted by the government. In such cases, the government may furnish goods or provide services related to the priority activity, and may grant subsidies or incentives (*externalidades*) that affect the priority activity carried out by the private enterprise. Examples of private performance of public services include railroads, banks, telephone companies, airports, toll highways, etc. When public services are carried out by private enterprises, the federal government (and, when applicable, state governments) are supposed to monitor the

Artículo 27 Constitucional en el Ramo del Petróleo, D.O. 29 Nov. 1958, reduced to 9 the number of derivatives of petroleum considered to be basic petrochemicals, and therefore reserved to the state: ethane, propane, butane, pentane, hexane, heptane, raw materials for carbon black (*negro de humo*), naphtha, and methane (from domestic hydrocarbon deposits). D.O. 13 Nov. 1996. With regard to electrical power generation, private investment was permitted when the electricity produced by such an investment is not sold directly to the public, but is sold to a government-owned public utility. Amendments to Article 3 of the Law of Public Utilities of Electrical Power (*Ley del Servicio Público de Energía Eléctrica*) provided that certain types of electric power generation shall not be considered as public utilities: generation of electric power to meet one's own needs, co-generation or small-scale production; generation carried out by independent producers for sale to the Federal Electricity Commission (CFE); electricity bound for export, derived from co-generation, independent production, or small-scale production; import of electric power by individuals or corporations for the sole purpose of meeting their own needs; and generation bound for emergencies stemming from power outages in public utilities. D.O. 22 Dec. 1993.

[33] Before a public service can be provided by the State, a constitutional provision must so stipulate or Congress must pass an enabling statute for this purpose. Mexican Constitution, Article 28, paras. 2ff.

services to ensure that the public's needs are met and that services are provided in accordance with applicable laws.[34] The Constitution specifically provides for the possibility of subsidizing such activities.[35]

3.3. Public Services

The most obvious form of governmental economic intervention, under any political economy, relates to the provision of basic services to the general public.[36] Mexico continues to provide many basic public services directly by the means of government-owned companies. While certain basic public services have been privatized (the administration of ports and airports, railroads, potable water in certain areas, etc.) others continue to be provided directly by government agencies. These include electricity transmission and distribution (CFE, and *Compañía de Luz y Fuerza del Centro)*, distribution of water in many cities, certain forms of urban transport (e.g. the subway service in Mexico City), etc.

The Mexican Constitution sets forth certain basic services that the State *must* provide: basic education (Article 3), electric power (Article 27, paragraph 6), water and sewage, public lighting, public sanitation, food markets and wholesale food supply, cemeteries, slaughterhouses, parks and public gardens, public security, and transportation (by municipalities, Article 115, Section III). Certain federal[37] and state and municipal laws[38] are also in effect that declare certain functions as public services.

Unless prohibited by law or the Constitution, a public service may be provided either directly by the government, or by the government granting a concession to a

[34] *Cf.* Serra Rojas, A., DERECHO ADMINISTRATIVO, VOL. *I* (Mexico: Porrúa, 11th ed., 1982) at 107.

[35] The last paragraph of Article 28 of the Constitution states that: 'subsidies may be granted to priority activities, when they are of a general, [and] temporary nature and don't substantially affect the finances of the Nation. The State shall oversee their implementation and evaluate the results.' Subsidies for public services have been common in the past, as the PRI government used public funds, including petroleum earnings, to buy populist support for agriculture subsidies, food support programmes, etc. Subsidies persist under the the more recent, neoliberal regime, but they are now more tightly controlled and represent a smaller portion of the federal government budget.

[36] *See* Fraga, G., DERECHO ADMINISTRATIVO (Mexico: Porrúa, 26th ed., 1987) at 22.

[37] A few examples of these services declared by federal law are the postal service, which is defined as reception, transportation, and delivery of correspondence as per Article 2 of the Law of the Postal Service (*Ley del Servicio Postal*), D.O. 20 Aug. 1986; the service of public electric utilities, as per the previously cited Law of Public Electric Utilities (*Ley del Servicio Público de Energía Eléctrica*), D.O. 22 Dec. 1975.

[38] Public services in Mexico City are regulated by the Law of Public Property and Service (*Ley del Régimen Patrimonial y del Servicio Público*), D.O. 23 Dec. 1996, which provides in Article 129 for the possibility of expropriation of property to fulfil the public service. *See also* Article 2 of the Law of Transportation of the Federal District (*Ley de Transporte del Distrito Federal*), D.O. 20 Dec. 1995, which provides authority for the government of the Federal District to carry out public transportation services, either directly or by granting concessions to private enterprises. Currently, public bus transportation in Mexico City is carried out by private enterprises, while subway transportation is carried out by a decentralized agency of the Federal District government.

private enterprise. Some services, e.g. electricity distribution, cannot be contracted out to private concerns, due to constitutional or other legal restrictions.

3.4. Special Laws Governing Concessions in the Provision of Public Services[39]

Where concessions to provide public services are allowed, the penultimate paragraph of Article 28 of the Constitution sets forth the authority for granting the concessions:

> The State, adhering to the law [and] when such action is in the public interest, shall grant concessions for the provision of public services or management, use and benefit of property owned by the Federation, except in the circumstances set forth therein. The laws shall set the terms and conditions that ensure efficiency in the provision of services and the [social] utilization of the property for the benefit of society, and shall avoid irregular practices and concentrations [unlawful conglomeration of economic power or monopolies] that go against the best interest of the public.

As stated above, the State is precluded from granting concessions for provision of public services *in strategic areas* to private individuals, and such services must be provided exclusively by the State. With regard to *priority areas*, concessions for provision of public services may be awarded if the law so permits, and private individuals will have access to any supports, such as subsidies or incentives that may be applicable. In areas of public services other than strategic or priority areas, services may be either provided by the State or awarded to private individuals in concessions.

When the law provides for the possibility of awarding a concession of a public service to a private individual and the administrative authority decides to avail itself of such an option, the concession must be carried out in such a way as to promote efficient services and avoid improper concentration and abuse of monopoly power in the exercise of the concession. Consequently, although the Constitution permits certain public services to be provided by the State under monopolistic conditions, when services are provided by private individuals or companies, irregularities, monopolies, and undue accumulation of economic power in the hands of one or a few individuals must also be avoided. When monopolies are a natural consequence of the grant of a concession (for example, when the concessionaire must invest in considerable infrastructure) the laws covering the activity generally require public bidding, and other controls to prevent the abuse of monopoly power.[40]

4. Central Economic Planning

Article 26 of the Constitution charges the federal government to promote national development by creating a system of 'democratic planning' (*planeación*

[39] For a discussion of government concessions in Mexican law, *see* Fraga, *supra* note 36 at 242 *et seq*.

[40] *See*, e.g., *Ley Reglamentaria del Servicio Ferroviario (LGSF)* Article 9, D.O. 12 May 1995.

democrática). Adopted during the early years of the de la Madrid administration, this Article expresses in very general language what is clearly a key role of any modern government: to promote and direct economic development. Indeed, central economic planning had been exercised by the government since the early days of the PNR, predecessor to the PRI, long before the adoption of Article 26 in 1983.[41]

Federal economic planning is carried out through the periodic issuance of a National Development Plan (*Plan Nacional de Desarrollo*), which serves as the basis of more detailed economic programmes adopted by the executive branch during the period of the plan. According to the Law of Planning (*Ley de Planeación*), the President of the Republic is required to adopt a National Development Plan, covering all relevant sectors of the economy, within seven months of entering office.[42] The National Development Plan covers the period of a presidential *sexenio* (six years), and usually consists of a five-year plan issued in the second year of the *sexenio*.[43]

The National Development Plan is implemented in four different ways.

4.1. Mandatory Implementation (*Ejecución Obligatoria*)

Mandatory implementation is directed at centrally controlled and quasi-governmental agencies of the federal government (PEMEX, CFE, COFEMER, IMSS, etc.) that are under direct governmental control, and are required to carry out programmes in accordance with the objectives of the Plan.

4.2. Implementation in Co-Ordination with the States (*Ejecución de Coordinación*)

Implementation in co-ordination with the states encourages states and state agencies that are not under direct control of the federal government to adhere to the Plan, and to participate in the programmes stemming from the Plan. The federal executive has many instruments that can be used to convince state governments to carry out policies in accordance with the National Development Plan. The most important of these is the federal government's overwhelming domination of tax revenues in Mexico, which it distributes to the states in accordance with federal policy objectives.[44]

[41] CONSTITUCIÓN POLÍTICA—COMENTADA, *supra* note 9, vol. I, at 363.

[42] *Ley de Planeación* (LP), Article 21, D.O. 5 Jan. 1983.

[43] *See* e.g. *Plan Nacional de Desarrolo* 2001–2006, *supra* note 16.

[44] *See*, for example, the Agreement on Administrative Collaboration in Federal Fiscal Matters, celebrated between SHCP and the State of Jalisco, D.O. 26 Jun. 2003. Under this agreement, the SHCP agreed to restore to the state 100% of IVA revenues (value added taxes), which represent a federal tax, that are collected by the state government as agent of the federal government.

4.3. Private and Social Sector[45] Implementation (*Ejecución de Concertación*)

Private and social sector implementation involves the use of federal agencies, working with private enterprises as well as social groups (labour unions, *ejidos*, co-operatives, etc.) to carry out goals of the Plan. This type of implementation of the Plan involves the use of 'pacts of economic solidarity' (*pactos de solidaridad económica*). An example is the Pact for Economic Stability and Growth (*Pacto para la Estabilidad y el Crecimiento Económico*, or PECE), signed by President Salinas in 1987 with leaders of the labour, agricultural, and business sectors, by which private enterprises, labour, and government agencies agreed to moderate prices and salary increases in order to limit Mexico's monthly inflation rate to 2 per cent by the end of 1988.[46] Such Pacts are no longer common, after the economic and political opening up that has taken place.

4.4. Rule-Related Implementation (*Ejecución de Inducción*)

Rule-related implementation consists of the design and implementation of regulations that create favourable conditions for promoting the type of economic behaviour the government deems beneficial to economic development. Thus, the federal budget (*Presupuesto de Egresos*), the programmes and budgets of quasi-governmental agencies, tax legislation proposed by the executive branch, and administrative acts of government agencies must all be consistent with the objectives and priorities of the Plan.[47] Through this type of implementation, the federal government asserts its immense power to guide and influence economic development by providing incentives or disincentives to economic agents.[48] Examples of this include the policies for pricing the use of natural resources, such as water, depending on the scarcity of the resource, the use and conservation to which it is put, etc.[49]

The model of national planning just described conforms to the corporatist, authoritarian form of government that held sway until the end of the PRI's single-party control, but it seems anachronistic in the open, free-market economy that the current political leadership of Mexico appears to embrace. National Development Plans, in accordance with the constitutional and legal precepts briefly described above, are more than a curious anachronism, however. While the weight of the federal government over the economy has been reduced, it is still considerable, and a pronouncement through the National Development

[45] The term 'social sector' in Mexico refers to trade union organizations and *ejidos* or common farmlands, which came into being as a result of agrarian reform.

[46] *See* Aspe Armella, *supra* note 2 at 29.

[47] *Ley de Planeacíon*, Art. 40.

[48] In addition to regulating business, the government may, in certain instances authorized by law, set price limits for certain goods on the market that are considered necessary for the domestic economy, and may set rules for distribution of goods to avoid unnecessary intermediation by markets. Mexican Constitution, Article 28, para. 3.

[49] *Ley Federal de Derechos* (LFD) Art. 223, D.O. 1 Jan. 2003.

Plan of the administration's future course in economic and social policies is invaluable information, assuming the Plan is an honest expression of policy. In using the Plan to advertise its economic and social policy course, the government acts in an uncharacteristically open way in a society in which transparency of government operations has not been the general rule. We might conclude that, as in many other areas of law, the model followed by Mexico is a hybrid one: a form of mexicanization of foreign legal influences (such as free-market policies) that conform to a particular Mexican stamp.

5. Regulation of Economic Competition

Mexico has long had both constitutional (Article 28) and legislative prohibitions[50] of monopolies and other practices that restrict economic competition. However, antitrust law in Mexico was virtually a dead letter until the adoption in 1992 of the comprehensive Federal Law of Economic Competition (*Ley Federal de Competencia Económica)*,[51] or LFCE, from its Spanish acronym.[52] For many years, as a relatively non-competitive society with governmental controls over many aspects of the economy, antitrust law was unnecessary. In the past, if the government wished to promote or deter particular behaviour, it could use its position as a buyer or seller of goods, regulator of prices, or political power to carry this out. In the 1990s, when the government began to privatize enterprises and promote a free-market economy, it became necessary to create a regime in which anti-competitive practices could be controlled and outlawed. Almost overnight, Mexico had to invent a system of competition law.

In language that has remained unchanged since 1917, the second paragraph of Article 28 of the Constitution prohibits monopolies and monopolistic practices, and authorizes the adoption of laws to punish such illegal acts. Article 28 goes on to state:

> the authorities shall efficiently investigate any cornering of the market or hoarding of basic consumer goods in the hands of a single individual or of a few individuals for the purpose of raising prices; any agreement, procedure or combination of producers, industrialists, merchants or service providers, who in any way do anything to prevent free competition among each other and oblige consumers to pay inordinately high prices and, in general, do anything that constitutes an improper exclusive advantage in favour of one or several specific individuals to the detriment of the public in general or any social class.

The LFCE, which serves as the current regulatory statute of Article 28, repealed previous laws that had not been actively enforced.[53] The Federal Competition Law

[50] The *Ley Orgánica del artículo 28 Constitucional en material de monopolios*, D.O. 31 Aug. 1934.

[51] D.O. 24 Dec. 1992, effective 23 Jun. 1993.

[52] Witker, *supra* note 17 at 91–92.

[53] In addition to the repeal of the Organic Law cited in note 50, *supra*, the Federal Competition Law also repealed the following: the Law on the Powers of the Federal Executive

must be read in conjunction with the Regulations of the Federal Law of Economic Competition (*Reglamento de la Ley Federal de Competencia Económica*)[54] and the Internal Regulations of the Federal Commission of Economic Competition (*Reglamento Interior de la Comisión Federal de Competencia Económica*).[55] Unlike in the United States, there are no state competition laws, and the Mexican Supreme Court has held that the federal Congress has sole authority to legislate on competition.[56]

The purpose of the LFCE is to 'protect the process of competition and free access to compete by preventing and eliminating monopolies, monopolistic practices and other restraints on efficient operation of the marketing of goods and services'. All private and public interests are subject to the LFCE, including agencies of federal, state or municipal governments, associations, professional groups, trusts, or any other form of participation in economic activity. [57]

5.1. Monopolistic Practices

The LFCE classifies monopolistic practices as either absolute or relative.

5.1.1. Absolute Monopolistic Practices

Absolute monopolistic practices are those that are sufficiently anti-competitive to constitute outright violations of the competition law; they are therefore similar to the concept of *per se* violations of US antitrust laws.[58] LFCE Article 9 defines absolute monopolistic practices as contracts, agreements, arrangements, or combinations of competing economic agents among or between each other, whose purpose or effect is any of the following: (a) to set, raise, agree upon, or manipulate the sale or purchase price of goods or services at which these items are to be offered or purchased on the markets, or to exchange information for the same purpose or with the same effect; (b) to limit the production or distribution of goods or services; or (c) to divide or distribute market shares for goods or services; (d) to agree upon or co-ordinate involvement in public bidding, auctions, contests, or other competitive proceedings. The CFC has taken

Branch in Economic Matters (*Ley sobre Atribuciones del Ejecutivo Federal en Materia Económica*) D.O. 30 Dec. 1950; the Law of Industries of Transformation (*Ley de Industrias de Transformación*), D.O. 13 May 1941, and the Law of Associations of Producers for the Distribution and Sale of their Products (*Ley de Asociaciones de Productores para la Distribución y Venta de sus Productos*) D.O. 25 Jun. 1937.

[54] D.O. 4 Mar. 1998. [55] D.O. 12 Oct. 1993.

[56] In a recent decision, the Supreme Court held that the federal Congress has exclusive jurisdiction to legislate on matters relating to economic competition. SJF at 9a, T. XVI, Sep. 2002, at 254 (Primera sala). [57] LFCE, Arts. 2 and 3.

[58] *See* Levy, S., 'Notas sobre la nueva Ley Federal de Competencia Económica', in EN TORNO A LA LEY FEDERAL DE COMPETENCIA ECONÓMICA (Mexico: UNAM-Instituto de Investigaciones Jurídicas, 1994) at 67. *Per se* violations of US antitrust law are 'agreements whose nature and necessary effect are so plainly anticompetitive that no elabrote study of the industry is needed to establish their illegality'. *National Society of Professional Engineers v. US*, 435 US 679, 692 (1978).

enforcement of the law seriously. For instance, in 1996 the CFC considered six cases involving absolute monopoly practices, establishing sanctions in five of them. Most of the cases had to do with price-fixing and manipulation of bidding.[59] In 2002, the CFC investigated twelve cases of this type, imposing sanctions in eight of them.[60]

5.1.2. Relative Monopolistic Practices

According to LFCE Article 10, relative monopolistic practices are those acts, contracts, agreements, or combinations whose purpose or effect is or may be improperly to displace other agents in a market, substantially prevent them from having access to markets, or which may establish exclusive advantages in favour of one or several persons, in the instances listed in Article 10. These practices include anti-competitive distribution agreements, the imposition of fixed prices or other conditions on distributors, tying arrangements, agreements not to distribute competing products, and other types of anti-competitive arrangements.

In order for *relative monopolistic practices* to be considered violations of the law, the alleged responsible party must have substantial power[61] over a relevant market,[62] and the practices must involve goods and services that belong to that market (LFCE Article 11). The prohibition of relative monopoly practices is similar to the 'rule of reason' applied under US antitrust law.[63]

5.2. Mergers and Acquisitions: Improper Concentration of Economic Power

The LFCE defines accumulation of economic power (*concentración*) as mergers, acquisitions of control, or any other act whereby companies, associations, stock shareholders, 'social groups' (*sector social*, that is, labour unions, *ejidos*, or other such organizations), or trusts are consolidated when the parties involved

[59] *Informe Anual de Competencia Económica* 1995–1996, Chaper III, '*Prácticas monopólicas y otras restricciones a la competencia*', available at www.cfc.gob.mx (site visited Jan. 2004).

[60] The companies receiving sanctions included Archer Daniels Midland Company; Arman Reimer Corp; F. Hoffman La Roche, Ltd; *Grupo Modelo*; and the *Cámara Nacional de la Industria Tequilera*. *See Informe de Competencia económica* 2002, '*Apéndice estadístico*', available at www.cfc.gob.mx (site visited Jan. 2004).

[61] Whether an agent has substantial power over a relevant market depends on the following factors: market share and whether or not he or she is able unilaterally to set prices or restrict supply on the market without competing agents being able to counteract said power; the existence of barriers to market entry; the existence and power of competitors; access to supply sources; recent behaviour; and other criteria that the regulatory law of this Article may establish (LFCE Art. 13).

[62] On the factors used to determine whether a market qualifies as a 'relevant market' (*mercado relevante*), *see* LFCE Art. 12 (e.g. possible substitution of other goods or services, costs of transport and distribution, and other factors that may limit access to alternative sources of supply).

[63] García Rodríguez, S., 'Reflexiones Comparativas de la Ley Federal de Competencia Económica. La regla per se y la regla de la razón', in *En torno a la Ley Federal de Competencia Económica*, *supra* note 58 at 50–53.

are competitors, suppliers, customers, or other economic agents. Unlawful or improper accumulation of economic power is defined as any of the preceding arrangements whose purpose is to diminish, harm, or prevent free competition of the same or substantially related goods and services.[64]

To determine whether such forms of economic concentration are illegal, the governmental authorities must take into account the following factors: whether the concentration confers or may confer upon the merging or acquiring party the power to fix prices unilaterally, or substantially restrict supply on the relevant market, without competitors being able to counteract said power; whether the concentration has as its purpose the improper displacement of other economic agents, or preventing such agents from having access to the relevant market; or whether the purpose is to substantially facilitate execution of any monopolistic practices listed in the Law.[65]

Concentraciones represent the largest category of cases in which the CFC has intervened. For instance, in 1996 the CFC investigated 166 cases of *concentración*, opposing 146 of such mergers and acquisitions.[66] In 2002 the CFC investigated 229 *concentraciones*, but only opposed two mergers and acquisitions, and imposed conditions on five such *concentraciones*.[67]

5.3. Enforcement of the LFCE

Historically, the enforcement of antritust law, like that of environmental law, has differed significantly from the mode of regulatory law enforcement in the United States. In the United States, in addition to administrative (governmental) enforcement of competition laws, the private sector plays an important 'quasi-regulatory' role: non-governmental parties (companies, consumer groups, etc.) are accustomed to filing law suits seeking to enjoin anti-competitive behaviour, or to recover damages caused by such behaviour. In Mexico, by contrast, the enforcement of competition laws is almost entirely dependent on governmental enforcement through an administrative body.[68] The Federal Competition Commission (*Comisión Federal de Competencia*, or CFC), an office of the Secretariat of Economy (*Seconomía)*, is the governmental authority responsible for enforcement of the LFCE. The CFC enjoys operational and technical autonomy, and has discretionary power to issue decisions on antitrust matters without being required to seek the approval of the Secretary of Economy or other officers of *Seconomía*.[69] This attribute of independence is important, since the CFC is virtually the only antitrust enforcer in Mexico, and since other government agencies are themselves subject to the antitrust laws.

[64] LFCE Art. 16. [65] LFCE Art. 17.

[66] CFC *Informe* 1995–1996, *supra* note 59. [67] CFC *Informe* 2002, *supra* note 60.

[68] While civil liability for anti-competitive acts is theoretically available, such litigation is rare in Mexico. Private parties do play a role in enforcement, as described below (*see infra* text accompanying notes 72–74).

[69] The CFC is a quasi-independent agency (*órgano desconcentrado*), and is therefore semi-autonomous from the federal executive branch. *See* Chapter 9 above, Section 2.1.

The CFC is made up of five members who are appointed by the President for ten-year terms.[70] Members meet in weekly sessions. All decisions are made on the basis of a simple majority of votes; when only four members vote, and there is a tie, the Chairman has the casting vote.[71]

The CFC has been delegated broad authority under LFCE Article 24 to perform the following functions. It can investigate the existence of private monopolies, governmental monopolies, practices, or forms of conglomeration of economic power prohibited by the LFCE; in conducting such investigations, it may request any pertinent information or documents from private individuals and other economic agents that may be required. It can establish mechanisms to combat and prevent private and governmental monopolies, unlawful practices and forms of conglomeration of economic power. It is also empowered to resolve disputes involving anti-competitive practices, impose administrative penalties for violations of the LFCE, and report to the Ministry of the Public Prosecutor any criminal conduct pertaining to free competition. The CFC can report on whether programmes and policies of the federal government administration conform to the principles of free competition, and issue opinions at the request of the federal executive branch as to whether proposed laws and regulations conform to the principles of free competition. Alternatively, it can issue, at its own discretion, non-binding opinions on whether laws, regulations, and resolutions currently in force, or previously issued decisions, executive or administrative orders, and administrative acts are conducive to free competition; prepare and implement internal procedural and organizational manuals for the Commission; and co-operate with other government agencies in the process of entering into international treaties, agreements, or covenants regarding free competition rules and policies. The CFC can also undertake any other duties that the LFCE or other laws or regulations may confer upon it.

The CFC may take action either on its own initiative, or at the request of a party involved in a case. In cases involving relative monopolistic practices and unlawful conglomeration of economic power, the interested party must file a request before the Commission to investigate the case. Once the complaint is filed, a summons stating the basis for the investigation along with a copy of the complaint is sent the alleged violator, who has thirty calendar days to respond and introduce evidence in defence of its actions; after all the evidence is gathered, a date is set within a further thirty calendar days to present oral arguments; once the case file has been completed, a final ruling is handed down within sixty calendar days.[72]

While the LFCE clearly defines a role for private parties in *initiating* antitrust proceedings, private parties must depend on the government administration (the CFC) to prosecute the case, judge the violation, and carry out any resulting penalties. This contrasts with the US experience, where an affected party can

[70] Under the transitory articles to the LFCE, the initial appointments of commissioners were made at one time for terms of two, four, six, eight, and ten years. [71] LFCE Art. 25.
[72] LFCE Art. 33.

bring a claim directly to the courts to judge the violation of antitrust laws. The enforcement mentality in Mexico, like that in many civil law countries, differs from that of the United States. In Mexico, as in other areas of regulation, the control of anti-competitive practices is regarded as something beyond mere private interests, and engages the public interest, which the government is expected to protect. This predilection for governmental, rather than private, enforcement of antitrust law is even written into Article 28 of the Constitution, which states that 'the law will severely punish, and the [governmental] authorities will effectively prosecute' every concentration of monopoly power or attempt to control a market. Thus, anti-competitive practices are addressed administratively, through fines and other sanctions. This also helps to explain why the CFC is not expected to settle disputes between private parties, nor is it empowered to order a violator of the antitrust laws to compensate a party injured by such activity. If an individual or company is injured by the anti-competitive practices of another, then the injured party may *theoretically* seek damages in the civil courts for extracontractual (tort) liability, although as yet such actions are rare.[73] Insofar as society as a whole is injured, the CFC has a separate responsibility to enforce the law, and in this regard it has generally earned a good reputation for having done its work acceptably, in an objective and professional manner. The work of the CFC has accordingly increased. In 1996 the CFC investigated 319 cases of possible antitrust violations; by 2002 1,651 cases were pending before the Commission, 1,360 of which dated from that same year.[74]

5.4. Sanctions and Enforcement Powers

Article 35 of the LFCE empowers the CFC to impose any of the following penalties:

(a) suspension, correction, or termination of the monopolistic practice or improper conglomeration of economic power;[75]
(b) total or partial break-up of an improper merger or concentration, without precluding imposition of a fine, should the case so merit;
(c) a fine[76] of up to the equivalent of 7,500 times the minimum daily wage[77] in effect for the Federal District for having borne false testimony or provided

[73] The CFC is empowered to establish the extent of damages suffered by parties, and this amount may be submitted into evidence in a subsequent civil action for damages under the extracontractual (tort) liability provisions of the civil code. On extracontractual (tort) liability, *see* Chapter 17 below, Section 6.

[74] CFC *Informe* 2002, *supra* note 60.

[75] For example, in 2002, the *Cámara de la Industria de la Masa y la Tortilla de Yucatán*, a trade association, agreed to an increase in the price of tortillas, a basic Mexican staple. The CFC investigation showed that the producers had engaged in price-fixing, and ordered the businesses envolved to set new prices based on supply and demand. *See* CFC *Informe* 2002, *supra* note 60.

[76] In cases of repeat offenders, the assessment of a fine may result in an additional fine of up to double the amount of the original fine. LFCE Art. 35, last para.

[77] The minimum daily wage is a common measure used in Mexico for assessing fines or penalties. The minimum daily wage for the Federal District is published annually in the *Diario Oficial*. In 2002 this was 43.65 pesos, equal to 4.35 US dollars. D.O. 26 Dec. 2002.

fabricated information to the Commission, in addition to any criminal liability for which the person may be held responsible;

(d) a fine of the equivalent of up to 375,000 times the minimum daily wage in force for the Federal District, for committing any absolute monopolistic practice;

(e) a fine of up to the equivalent of 275,000 times the minimum daily wage in force for the Federal District, for committing any relative monopolistic practice, and a fine of up to the equivalent of 100,000 times the minimum daily wage in force for the Federal District, in any of the instances set forth in section VII of Article 10 of the Law;

(f) a fine of up to the equivalent of 100,000 times the minimum daily wage in force for the Federal District, for not reporting the consolidation of economic power when required to do so by law;

(g) a fine of up to the equivalent of 7,500 times the minimum daily wage in force for the Federal District, for any individual who directly participates in monopolistic practices or in a prohibited concentration of economic power in representation of, on behalf of, or at the direction of a corporation.

A motion to reconsider any penalty may be filed before the Commission within thirty days following the date that the decision is handed down. The lack of a response to such a motion on the part of the Commission is to be interpreted as reaffirming or upholding the original decision (LFCE Article 39). In 2001 the CFC imposed penalties on thirty-two firms, with total fines in the amount of 11.9 million pesos (approximately 1.2 million US dollars); in 2002, nineteen firms were fined, for a total of almost 5 million pesos (approximately 500,000 US dollars).[78]

6. Environmental Regulation

6.1. Introduction

The General Law of Ecological Equilibrium and Environmental Protection (*Ley General del Equilibrio Ecológico y la Protección al Ambiente*, or LGEEPA)[79] and related regulatory enactments[80] make up the general regulatory framework pertaining to ecology and the environment. The LGEEPA has been amended on

[78] CFC *Informe* 2002, *supra* note 60 at 87. [79] D.O. 28 Jan. 1988.

[80] *See* e.g. Regulatory General Law of Ecological Equilibrium and Environmental Protection regarding Environmental Impact, D.O. 30 May 2000; Regulatory General Law of Ecological Equilibrium and Environmental Protection regarding Hazardous Wastes, D.O. 25 Nov. 1988; Regulatory General Law of Ecological Equilibrium and Environmental Protection regarding prevention and control of pollution in the atmosphere, D.O. 25 Nov. 1988; *Reglamento de la LGEPA en materia de Auditoria Ambiental*, D.O. 12 Nov. 2000; *Reglamento de Areas Naturales Protegidas*, D.O. 30 Nov. 2000. These regulations and other aplicable laws may be found at www.semarnat.gob.mx '*Normatividad y Leyes*' (site visited Jan. 2004).

a number of occasions, and underwent a major overhaul in 1996, in order to define better the appropriate jurisdictional competencies of federal, state, and municipal authorities (since environmental affairs are matters of concurrent jurisdiction). The 1996 amendments also made changes in environmental policies, and broadened the scope of public involvement in environmental protection.[81] In addition, in 1996 the Federal Criminal Code was amended to include a new chapter on environmental crimes.[82]

The LGEEPA was adopted pursuant to Article 73 of the Mexican Constitution.[83] Environmental regulation is an area of concurrent jurisdiction: federal, state, and municipal governments all have the power to regulate activities that affect health and the environment. Nevertheless, because of the vastly superior resources of the federal government, federal regulation predominates in this area.

The adoption of the LGEEPA in 1988 marked Mexico's first real attempt to regulate environmental quality. Mexico had adopted environmental laws prior to that date, but in a country with immense problems of economic development and under-employment, the regulation of polluting industries took a back seat to economic expansion. Even with the adoption of the LGEEPA, Mexico was slow to enforce its environmental laws with rigour.[84] However, the negotiation of NAFTA in the early 1990s served to focus attention on Mexico's lack of environmental protection, and the supplemental North American Agreement on Environmental Co-Operation, which became part of the NAFTA 'package', lent international emphasis to effective regulation in this area.[85] The North American Agreement on Environmental Co-Operation required Canada, Mexico, and the United States to adopt laws to protect the environment, and to provide effective means to enforce those laws; it also created a new intergovernmental agency, the

[81] *See*, Brañes, R., *Manual de derecho ambiental mexicano* (Mexico: Fondo de Cultura Económica, 2nd ed., 2000) at 112.

[82] D.O. 13 Dec. 1996, adding Federal Criminal Code Arts. 414–423. The provisions establish the following acts as crimes: causing injury to natural resources by carrying out dangerous activities without taking sufficient precaution; introducing into Mexican territory plants or animals, or their products, that carry contagious diseases that can endanger plants, animals, or the ecosystem of Mexico; introducing genetically modified organisms that may harm Mexican ecosystems, etc.

[83] Article 73, section XXIX-G grants Congress the power to 'issue laws that establish concurrency of jurisdiction of the federal government, the governments of the states and municipalities, with regard to environmental protection and preservation and restoration of ecological equilibrium'.

[84] *See* Brañes, *supra* note 81 at 107.

[85] North American Agreement on Environmental Cooperation, available at www.sice.oas.org, 'Trade Agreements', 'NAFTA'. (Site visited Jan. 2004.) *See generally*: *Greening NAFTA: The North American Commission for Environmental Co-Operation* (Stanford, Calif: Stanford University, 2003, D. Markell and J. Knox, eds.); Behre, C., 'Mexican Environmental Law: Enforcement and Public Participation Since the Signing of NAFTA'S Environmental Co-Operation Agreement', 12 J Transnat'l L & Policy 327 (2003); Granbert, J., 'Giving Meaning to New Trade-Linked "Soft Law" Agreements on Social Values' 6 UCLA J Int'l L & For. Aff. 425 (2002). For a study of the possible effects of NAFTA on the environment, *see* *Comercio y Medio Ambiente: Derecho, Comercio y Política* (Mexico: Instituto Nacional de Ecología/Centro Mexicano de Derecho Ambiental, J. R. Bracamontes, ed., 1995).

Commission on Environmental Co-Operation (CEC), to carry out the activities set out in the NAFTA supplemental agreement.[86]

The increased attention generated by the NAFTA opening also served to promote interest in creating new players on the Mexican environmental scene: the non-governmental organizations, or NGOs, that have become important watchdogs of environmental regulation in Mexico. NGOs had little place under the old Mexican corporatist model, in which the PRI monopolized and controlled the representation of the public interest; but since the dismantling of the PRI, they have become increasingly active and important in environmental, human rights, and other matters. The consciousness of the Mexican public has been awakened to environmental issues, and political parties now include environmental policies in their campaign platforms.[87]

6.2. Federal, State, and Local Jurisdiction over the Environment

The LGEEPA establishes the jurisdictional authority of federal, state, Federal District, and municipal governments with regard to environmental protection of the atmosphere (Articles 11–116), water systems (Articles 117–133), the soil (Articles 124–144), hazardous activities (Articles 145–149, and 150–153 for hazardous wastes and management of dangerous materials), nuclear energy (Articles 150–153), and other forms of pollution (Article 154). The federal government agency charged with environmental protection has changed names numerous times since the adoption of the LGEEPA, and is now called the *Secretaría del Medio Ambiente y Recursos Naturales*, or SEMARNAT.[88]

In addition to requiring formulation of a national environmental policy, the LGEEPA directs the federal government to set environmental policies for and regulate territories or properties under federal jurisdiction,[89] including the marine environment, and to promote sustainable use and development of forest resources, domestic waters, flora and fauna, and other natural resources. The federal law also regulates the management and disposal of hazardous wastes, as well as air pollution emanating from federal territories. The LGEEPA

[86] The CEC, located in Montreal, Canada, is led by the environmental ministers of the 3 NAFTA countries, and includes a secretariat dedicated to carrying out the CEC's programmes. Information on the CEC, its activities, and related programmes, is available at www.cec.org (site visited Jan. 2004).

[87] For a listing of web sites of environmental NGO's active in Mexico, *see* www.greenpeace.org.mx, '*Ligas de interés*'. One political party, the 'Green Party' (*Verde Ecologista de México*), was formed around concern for the environment; in the elections of 2003, the *Verde* Party received 4% of the popular vote nationally. *See* www.ife.org.mx. *See also* www.pvem.org.mx (all 3 sites visited Jan. 2004). *See also* Carvajal Isunza, G. and Quadri de la Torre, G., *Partidos políticos y medio ambiente, Guía para electores 2003* (Mexico: Centro de Políticas Públicas para el Desarrollo Sustentable, A. C., 2003) at 20–21.

[88] *See generally* www.semarnat.gob.mx (site visited Jan. 2004).

[89] LGEEPA Art. 28 defines the public works and activities that are considered to be of federal jurisdiction, including dams; telecommunication lines; oil, gas, and other pipelines; the petroleum and petrochemical industries; the chemical industry; and the steel, sugar, and cement industries, all of which are of exclusively federal jurisdiction.

requires the federal government to maintain a National System of Reporting on the Environment and Natural Resources (*Sistema Nacional de Información Ambiental y de Recursos Naturales*), and to issue recommendations to federal, state, or municipal authorities to bring about compliance with environmental legislation. Environmental matters that affect two or more states (or a state and the Federal District) also come within federal jurisdiction;[90] since few, if any, environmental matters are confined to a single state, this last jurisdictional basis serves as a broad delegation of federal jurisdiction.

In addition to the federal government, states and municipalities have the power to regulate the environment within their geographical jurisdictions, and the LGEEPA contains provisions that attempt to define this jurisdiction.[91] LGEEPA Article 11 instructs federal, state, and local government agencies to enter into agreements so that local authorities may assume federal responsibilities, such as the management and surveillance of natural protected areas under federal jurisdiction, or control of low-risk toxic waste disposal, since state or municipal authorities may be effective environmental law enforcers. [92] The goal of effective co-ordination and decentralization has been elusive, however. The uneven distribution of governmental resources between the federal and state governments, and among the various state governments themselves, has meant that many states lack the infrastructure and expertise required to undertake effective environmental monitoring and regulation. The presence of SEMARNAT delegations in every state and the Federal District has not been sufficient to remedy this.[93] Most environmental regulation is still carried out by the federal government, which has concluded co-operation agreements with the states. This explains in part why there is no federal case-law resolving conflicts in jurisdiction.

[90] LGEEPA Art. 5, Section XX.

[91] Under LGEEPA Art. 7, states may regulate matters within their borders that are not specifically allocated to the federal government, including air pollution and other sources of pollution from fixed and mobile sources that are not under federal jurisdiction. They may also regulate land use in conjunction with municipalities. States are responsible for the collection, transportation, treatment, and disposal of solid and industrial wastes, other than hazardous materials, which are regulated by the federal government. States may regulate water use and water pollution, and may also resolve environmental problems that arise between two or more municipalities.

LGEEPA Art. 8 defines the regulatory scope of municipalities; as with states, municipalities are generally given the authority to regulate behaviour within their geographical borders, so long as they are not matters allocated exclusively to the federal government, like regulation of hazardous materials or pollution caused by federal facilities or on federal territories.

The Federal District has virtually the same regulatory authority as a state and municipality combined.

[92] For instance, under an agreement concluded between SEMARNAT and the State of Mexico, the latter has agreed to administer and monitor the exploitation of forests within the State in accordance with federal laws. *See* www.semarnat.gob.mx (site visited Jan. 2004).

[93] *See* www.semarnat.gob.mx, 'SEMARNAT *en los estados*' (site visited Jan. 2004). A list of the state delegations of SEMARNAT and their personnel can be found at www.semarnat.gob.mx, '*Directorio*'.

6.3. Tools of Environmental Policy

The LGEEPA establishes the following means of implementing environmental policies:

(a) environmental planning;[94]
(b) adoption of national, state, and local environmental programmes;[95]
(c) adoption of economic instruments (tax, financial, or market-oriented measures);[96]
(d) environmental regulation of human settlements (*asentamientos humanos*);[97]
(e) requiring environmental impact statements;[98]
(f) issuing official Mexican environmental standards;[99]
(g) encouraging environmental self-regulation and audits;[100] and
(h) encouraging environmental research and education.[101]

6.4. Maintaining Biodiversity[102]

Mexico boasts many coastal and interior regions that are endowed with a rich array of plant and animal life, including many endangered species of animals and

[94] LGEEPA Arts. 18 and 19. The National Development Plan contains a special chapter on environmental policy for sustainable development and the obligation to formulate an Environmental Sector Programme. *See Plan Nacional de Desarrollo* 2001–2006, *supra* note 16, at section 4.5.

[95] *See* LGEEPA Art. 19bis. For federal programmes currently in effect, *see* www.semarnat.gob.mx, '*Mapa del Sitio*', '*Programas y Proyectos*'. (Site Visited Jan. 2004.) The Government of the Federal District has also adopted an Environmental Law (*Gaceta Oficial* 13 Jan. 2000), which is administered by *Secretaría de Medio Ambiente* (*see* www.sma.df.gob.mx).

[96] LGEEPA Art. 22.

[97] LGEEPA Art. 23 sets 9 guidelines that must be followed in drafting environmental regulations for human settlements, or *asentamientos humanos*. Under Mexican law, *asentamientos humanos* are similar to metropolitan areas, that is, they represent continuous population centres, notwithstanding political boundaries. *See Ley General de Asentamientos Humanos* (LGAH) Art. 2, D.O. 21 Jul. 1993.

[98] LGEEPA Art. 28 requires that an environmental impact statement must be conducted when public works or other business activities are carried out where they may cause an environmental imbalance and violate the limits and terms established by law to preserve the environment.

[99] LGEEPA Art. 36. Official Mexican Standards, or *normas oficiales mexicanas* (known by their Spanish acronym NOM) are public statutes or laws directed to the general population that are issued by SEMARNAT (Secretariat of the Environment and Natural Resources) for the purpose of setting the technical standards and permissible limits that must be observed in carrying out activities subject to environmental regulation.

[100] Producers or companies may voluntarily adopt systems of environmental self-evaluation and audit to improve environmental performance, monitor compliance with environmental laws, and promote preventive measures. LGEEPA Art. 38 to 38bis 2.

[101] LGEEPA Arts. 39–41.

[102] In addition to the LGEEPA, other federal laws protect biodiversity. The Wildlife Law (*Ley General de la Vida Silvestre*, or LGVS) (D.O. 3 Jul. 2000). The LGVS regulates activities that affect wildlife. *See* LGVS Art. 4.

Mexico is also party to a number of international treaties to promote wildlife protection. *See* e.g. the 1993 Rio Convention on Biodiversity, D.O. 7 May 1993. *See* Carmona, M., 'Derecho ecológico', in *Enciclopedia Jurídica Mexicana*, Vol. III (Mexico: UNAM-Instituto de Investigaciones Jurídicas/Ed. Porrúa, 2002).

plants. The adoption of the LEEPA was designed, in part, to provide increased protection to these valuable natural resources by authorizing the creation of protected natural areas and other measures designed to protect wildlife and plant life, by imposing bans on activities that endanger plant and animal life, by creating refuges for wildlife, including marine wildlife, etc. (LGEEPA Articles 45–87). Protected natural areas include biosphere reserves, national parks, natural monuments, natural resource protection areas, wildlife and plant life protection areas, wildlife sanctuaries, federal and state parks and reserves, and zones of ecological protection in population centres (LGEEPA Article 46). Parks and reserves established by the federal government are maintained by the National Commission of Natural Protected Areas (*Comisión Nacional de Áreas Naturales Protegidas*, or CONANP), a quasi-independent agency within SEMARNAT.[103]

State parks and reserves, and zones of ecological preservation in population centres, may be established by governments of the states or the Federal District; all other types of protected natural areas must be established by the President of the Republic (LGEEPA Article 57). Such parks and reserves impose restrictions on property owners, but also provide fiscal incentives for protection of such areas.[104]

6.5. Citizen Involvement in Environmental Protection, Regulation, and Enforcement

For many years, critics who attacked the lack of environmental law enforcement in Mexico decried the federal government's monopoly over environmental law enforcement (discussed below), and the lack of information available to citizens' groups interested in monitoring the government's performance in this regard.[105] Before the adoption of the LGEEPA in 1988, private citizens and NGOs had no standing to complain of non-compliance with environmental laws and standards, and were left without access to the information necessary to monitor environmental law enforcement.

The LGEEPA changed this, at least in theory. LGEEPA Article 158 established the basis for citizen involvement in promoting public awareness of environmental problems, and in 1996 the LGEEPA was amended to promote more citizen involvement in environmental protection,[106] through increased consultation with businesses, private citizens, and NGOs. Before this change, the role of

[103] *See* www.conanp.gob.mx (site visited Jan. 2004).

[104] According to SEMARNAT, there are 148 areas of Natural Protected Areas, comprising 17 million hectares (41 million acres) of land: www.conanp.gob.mx, '*Lo que hacemos*'. (Site visited Jan. 2004.)

[105] Tapia Landeros, A., 'Resquicio legal para una . . . tala ilegal disfrazada?', LEX DIFUSIÓN Y ANÁLISIS, SUPLEMENTO ECOLOGÍA, Año VIII, no. 97, July 2003, pp. IV–VII.

[106] Brañes, *supra* note 81, at 166. For instance, CONANP has concluded agreements and undertaken projects with citizen groups. For instance, Sempra Energy Global, through its Mexican subsidiary, funded the construction of a visitor centre in the national park of San Pedro Mártir. *See Informe* CONANP 2002, www.conanp.gob.mx (site visited Jan. 2004).

private citizens and citizen groups in Mexico was severely limited; by contrast, in the United States, private citizens and NGOs can initiate environmental lawsuits.[107] Mexican citizen groups could call environmental problems to the attention of authorities, and could try to collect information on environmental problems to educate the public and lobby the government to improve environmental protection. However, private citizens who were not directly affected by environmental violations had no standing to compel enforcement of the laws.

In 1992[108] SEDESOL, the predecessor of SEMARNAT, created the Office of the Federal Attorney General for Environmental Protection (*Procuraduría Federal de Protección al Medio Ambiente*, or PROFEPA),[109] a quasi-independent agency within SEMARNAT. After the 1996 reforms to the LGEEPA, a citizen or group of citizens (e.g. an NGO, *ejido*, or trade union) may file a complaint (*denuncia popular*) with PROFEPA, alleging acts or omissions that harm the environment, and may constitute violations of environmental laws.[110] If PROFEPA agrees to take jurisdiction over the case, it will conduct an investigation, take evidence from the alleged offender, and may also conduct studies or request academic institutions, research centres or agencies of the public, social, and private sectors to conduct studies, file reports, and issue expert opinions, as well as receive evidence from the complainant. If an investigation demonstrates acts or omissions committed by federal, state, or municipal authorities, the Federal Prosecutor's office may issue non-binding, independent recommendations that are made public. When appropriate, the parties involved may hold a settlement hearing to resolve the matter. If administrative offences or crimes come to light as a result of the investigation, PROFEPA may itself file charges before the appropriate authorities (LGEEPA Articles 191–204).

The problem with this system lies in the discretion that exists in the office of PROFEPA to prosecute citizen complaints aggressively. Absent authorization in a special law, which does not generally exist, the citizen or group that makes a *denuncia popular* has no standing to bring suit.

6.5.1. *Public Access to Information*

The effectiveness of public involvement in environmental protection depends to a large degree on the public's access to information available to the federal and state agencies. The LGEEPA delegates to SEMARNAT the task of developing

[107] Garrett, T., 'Citizen Suits' in ENVIRONMENTAL LITIGATION (J. Kole *et al.*, eds.) (Chicago: ABA Publishing, 1999) at 83–107.

[108] D.O. 4 Jun. 1992.

[109] *See* www.profepa.gob.mx (site visited Jan. 2004). *See generally* PROFEPA, *Informe Annual* 2002, available on this web site.

[110] LGEEPA Arts. 189, 190. The complaint must state the identity of the complainant, the acts, facts, or failure to act that are the subject of the complaint, the identity of the alleged offender, and evidence of the claim. The complaint may be made by telephone and, in this case, must be subsequently confirmed by the complainant. The Federal Prosecutor's office may keep the identity of complainants secret for security reasons or when such a measure is in the best interests of the complainant (LGEEPA Arts. 189 and 190). *See also* Art. 118 of the SEMARNAT Internal Regulations, D.O. 21 Jan. 2003, available at www.semarnat.gob.mx, '*Normatividad y Leyes*' (site visited Jan. 2004).

a national environmental reporting system for the purpose of registering, organizing, and disseminating up-to-date information on national environmental concerns. SEMARNAT is also required to make public all recently enacted or issued statutes, official Mexican standards (NOMs), decrees, regulations, resolutions, decisions, and other administrative acts, as well as general information pertaining to the environment that may be generated by the federal, state, or municipal governments or international documents (treaties or conventions) relating to the environment (independently of the official announcement of the above documents and information in the *Diario Oficial de la Federación*) or in other official instruments of dissemination (LGEEPA Article 159bis 2).[111]

The right of private individuals to environmental information is not absolute. Access to such information may be denied when such information is deemed by law to be classified or, because of the nature of the information, dissemination would constitute a breach of national security; when the information requested relates to issues that are the subject of a judicial proceeding, inspection, or surveillance operation that have yet to be decided or concluded; when the information has been provided by third parties who are under no legal obligation to provide it; and when information pertains to inventory or stocks and inputs and processing technology, including descriptions of industrial processes (Article 159bis 3 and bis 4). In addition, with the passage in 2002 of the Federal Transparency Law[112] all federal government agencies, including SEMARNAT and PROFEPA, must abide by the provisions of the law that guarantee public access to information.[113]

6.6. Inspection, Monitoring, and Enforcement

While state and local agencies and officials have the power to enforce laws under their jurisdiction, SEMARNAT continues to be the principal agency responsible for enforcement of environmental laws in Mexico. SEMARNAT may, at its discretion, conduct inspections and monitoring of activities regulated by law. To exercise this power, SEMARNAT must adhere to the procedures set forth in the Constitution (Article 16) and in the Federal Law of Administrative Procedure (*Ley Federal de Procedimiento Administrativo*).[114]

Individuals or companies subject to these inspections are required to provide SEMARNAT officials access to the premises that are the subject of the inspection, and to provide any type of information that may be requested, except for information dealing with industrial property. Should a company refuse to allow access to its facilities, the authorities may request assistance from law enforcement agents in order to gain access.

[111] *See* www.semarnat.gob.mx (site visited Jan. 2004).

[112] *See* the discussion of the Law in Chapter 9 above, at text accompanying notes 97–104.

[113] *See* e.g. www.semarnat.gob.mx, 'Transparencia en la Semarnat' (site visited Jan. 2004).

[114] On the Federal Law of Administrative Procedure, *see* Chapter 9 above, at text accompanying note 12, and text following note 74.

SEMARNAT can require a person or company to take the necessary measures to come into compliance with environmental laws and regulations, including respective permits, licences, authorizations, or concessions.[115] The party being inspected has the right to present evidence and arguments on its own behalf. SEMARNAT's order must state the corrective measures to be taken to cure the deficiencies or irregularities, the maximum period of time granted to the violator to comply with the order, and penalties to be imposed on the violator for failure to comply.[116]

When the risk of an environmental imbalance, serious damage to natural resources, or pollution with dangerous effects on public health or on ecosystems arises in any region, SEMARNAT has the authority to order that any of the following safety measures be taken: temporary closing down, partial or total, of the source of the pollution or of the facilities involved; precautionary securing of toxic materials, wastes, or residues, wildlife or plant specimens, products or by-products of species or the genetic material thereof, or of forest resources;[117] and any other actions that may serve to prevent deleterious effects on the environment.

SEMARNAT has the authority through PROFEPA to order and enforce penalties for violations of the LGEEPA and its subsidiary regulations, including failure to comply with an enforcement order issued by SEMARNAT pursuant to an inspection. Possible penalties include fines; temporary or permanent, partial or total closure; administrative arrest for up to thirty-six hours; seizure and suspension; or revocation of concessions, licences, permits, or authorizations (LGEEPA Article 172). Imposition of these penalties may be challenged via a motion for reconsideration or for review of judgment (*recurso de revisión*) before SEMARNAT (LGEEPA Articles 176–181).[118]

Environmental law enforcement in Mexico, while improving, continues to be hampered by a lack of resources available to SEMARNAT, PROFEPA, and other agencies of the federal and state governments charged with enforcing the laws. Since private citizen suits are difficult to bring, this lack of governmental resources (which must also be used to address endemic problems of poverty,

[115] LGEEPA Arts. 161–169.

[116] For example, Metamex Peñoles corporation, a foundry located in the industrial corridor between the States of Durango and Coahuila, was required to take corrective action to reduce high lead emissions that were adversely affecting the quality of life of the surrounding population. *La jornada*, Mexico, D.F., 14 June 1999, at 38.

[117] According to data published by PROFEPA (*Informe Anual* 2000), in 2000 PROFEPA undertook 7,020 inspections of forests; in 5,045 of these there was lack of compliance with environmental laws, resulting in 3,811 fines for a total of 49 million pesos (approximately 4.9 million US dollars).

[118] However, when concessions, licences, permits, or authorizations have been granted by authorities other than SEMARNAT, SEMARNAT must file a request to the granting authority for suspension, revocation, or annulment of administrative acts issued by other secretariats or entities under the rules of such agency. For example, if the Comisión Nacional del Agua (CNA) grants a concession to use water from a river for an industrial use, and if SEMARNAT can show that the concession violates environmental laws or regulations, it can request CNA to cancel the concession.

underemployment, etc.) weakens environmental protection. The federal and state governments might do well to enter into partnerships with business and environmental groups to address environmental protection comprehensively, altering the traditional reliance on law enforcement only by governmental agencies.

7. Natural Resources Law

7.1. Water Law

Mexico is a country of great geographical diversity, from the lush, tropical regions of the south and southeast to the semi-arid lands of the north. Water is plentiful in subtropical areas in which farming is difficult due to terrain or climate; water is scarce in some of the most important agricultural areas, where rainfall is sporadic.[119] It is not surprising, therefore, that water law should be important.

The importance of water resources is recognized in Article 27 of the Constitution, which begins with the admonition that 'Property interest in lands and waters found within the territorial limits of the Nation belong originally to the Nation, which has the right to transmit ownership in them to private parties in the form of private property'. Section 5 of Article 27 lists as property of the Nation territorial seas, lakes, rivers, etc., and contains provisions about the use and exploitation of surface and subsoil waters.[120]

[119] Approximately half of Mexican territory is tropical or subtropical, with precipitation averaging 2,400 cubic millimetres per year, while in the semi-arid climates, rainfall is only 100 cubic millimetres per year. *See* Carmona, *supra* note 102 at 588. *See generally* www.cna.806.mx, 'Estadísticas del Agua de México' (site visited Jan. 2004).

[120] Article 27, Section 5, of the Constitution states that the following are property of the Nation: '. . . waters of territorial seas to the extent and in the terms set by international law; interior marine waters; lake and estuary water that is permanently connected to the sea; interior lake water of natural formation that is linked directly to constantly flowing streams; waters of rivers and their direct or indirect tributaries from the point in their bed where the first permanent, intermittent, or torrential waters start, to their delta or point of entry into the sea, lakes, lagoons, or estuaries on domestic soil; those waters of constantly flowing or intermittent streams and their direct or indirect tributaries, when their course or bed, in its entirety or partially, serves as a border of the national territory or of two federal entities, or when it [the bed] runs from one federative entity to another or crosses the dividing line of the Republic and a neighbouring country, or when the edge of the banks serve as a boundary between federal entities or of the Republic with a neighbouring country; spring waters that emerge from beaches, maritime zones, river beds, channels or banks of lakes, lagoons, or estuaries that belong to the nation, and those [waters] that are extracted from mines; the basins, beds, or banks of lakes and interior streams to the extent that is set forth in the law. Waters of the subsoil can be freely brought to the surface through artificial works and be appropriated by the owner of the land; but, when the common good so requires or if this affects other forms of utilization, the federal executive branch may regulate the extraction [of this water] and utilization and even establish zones of prohibition for this and any other waters belonging to the nation. Any other waters not listed above shall be considered an integral part of the property of the land through which they run or in which their reservoirs are found; but should such waters be located on two or more different properties, utilization of these waters shall be considered of public benefit [*utilidad publica*] and shall be subject to the laws issued by the states.'

The principal law regulating this subject is the Law of Domestic Waters (*Ley de Aguas Nacionales*, or LAN)[121] and by its regulatory law.[122] The LAN regulates the extraction, use, and management of both surface and subterranean waters, distribution and control of these waters, as well as preservation of the quantity and quality of water required to achieve sustainable development.

7.1.1. *Regulatory Authorities*

Pursuant to the LAN, the qualified authorities in matters of water resources are as follows.

The National Water Commission (Comisión Nacional del Agua) The National Water Commission (*Comisión Nacional del Agua*, or CNA)[123] is a quasi-independent agency (*órgano desconcentrado*) of SEMARNAT and, after the federal executive, is the ultimate authority in federal water maters. Its duties and responsibilities are broad, as detailed by Article 6 of the LAN: to administer and safeguard all domestic waters and national property related thereto (beaches, riverbeds, river banks, etc.); to conduct planning and studies for, construct, operate, conserve, and maintain federal hydraulic works, either directly or through contracts and concessions with third parties; to issue concessions, assignments, or permits authorized by the LAN; to recognize property rights and create and maintain the Federal Public Registry of Water Rights (*Registro Público de Derechos del Agua*); to settle disputes and, as the case may warrant, act at the request of the users as an arbitrator in the resolution of disputes related to water; to exercise prosecutorial powers in the administration, determination, liquidation, charging, fee collection, and monitoring of contributions and any other uses the CNA may be assigned; to issue Official Mexican Standards (*Normas Oficiales Mexicanas*) in water management; to interpret the LAN for administrative purposes, and to apply punitive measures and to issue acts of authority in matters that are not the exclusive right of the President of the Republic; and to issue declarations concerning water rights on government property, which must be published in the *Diario Oficial*.

The CNA is headed by a Director General, who directs the work of the CNA and acts as its legal representative. The Director General is appointed by, and serves at the will of, the President.

Watershed Councils (Consejos de Cuenca) After obtaining approval from the Technical Committee, the CNA is responsible for forming watershed councils to liaise between the CNA and federal, state, and municipal agencies, and representatives of the users of a particular watershed, for the purpose of formulating and implementing watershed management programmes and water works. The councils, made up of representatives of CNA and of state and local authorities, also have the duty of working out agreements with users regarding temporary limitations on existing rights in order to be able to cope with emergency

[121] D.O. 1 Dec. 1992. [122] D.O. 12 Jan. 1994.
[123] *See* www.cna.gob.mx (site visited Jan. 2004).

situations, extreme scarcity, over-utilization, or reserves (Article 13). By 2002, twenty-six *consejos de cuenca* had been established throughout Mexico.[124]

7.1.2. *Right to Use or Benefit from Government-Owned Waters*

Regulation of the use of government-owned waters is divided into two categories: waters of free use and benefit; and waters that require a concession to private enterprise (*concesión*) or to a government agency or quasi-governmental agency (*asignación*).[125]

The first category involves surface water belonging by law to the nation, whose extraction, use, and benefit is freely available to any resident of the Republic, provided that manual (rather than mechanical) methods are employed to obtain the water, the water is for domestic use or watering livestock, and the water is not diverted from its course nor causes any alteration in quality or significant decrease in flow. No concession is required either for the extraction of inland marine water (e.g. an inland bay) or of Mexican territorial coastal waters utilized for these purposes. Similarly, government-owned water contained in the subsoil may be freely brought to the surface by artificial devices, except when, in the best interest of the public, the Federal Executive opts to regulate extraction and utilization by reserving exclusive rights thereto and prohibits such extraction. All such uses, of course, are subject to regulation under the environmental laws.

The second category consists of any water not included in the first category, whose extraction, use, and benefit by individuals or corporate entities may only be come about under concession granted by the federal executive branch through the Commission. A concession confers upon the concessionaire the rights: to extract, use, or benefit from government-owned water and property related thereto; to carry out any construction works or perform any labour necessary to exercise the right to extract, use, or benefit from the water, always at the expense of the concessionaire; and legally to obtain any easements over property that are indispensable for the utilization or removal of the water, such as drainage ditches or aqueducts (LAN Article 28). Concessions may be transferred (LAN Article 28); they remain in effect from five to fifty years, and may be extended for a further period of the same length of time (LAN Article 24).

Concessions are often granted for agricultural or industrial purposes, such as water to cool machinery in a factory. The concessionaire's duties include the obligation to build any facilities and perform any labour required for the extraction, use, or benefit of the water under the terms and conditions set forth in the LAN and its respective regulations; to verify proper execution of construction and labour in order to prevent any adverse effects on third parties or on hydraulic operations of the supply sources of the watershed; to operate, maintain, and preserve any facilities that are required for the stability and security of dams, spillway control, and other infrastructure; to permit inspection by the

[124] *See* www.can.gob.mx. 'Participación ciudadana' (site visited Jan. 2004).
[125] *See* LAN Arts. 17–20.

Commission of hydraulic works, and to permit the reading and verification of the proper operating order of meters and other activities that may be required to attest to compliance with the provisions of the law (LAN Article 29).

When the beneficiary is a government office or agency, or a quasi-governmental agency, a special type of concession called an *asignación* may be granted by the Commission. *Asignaciones* may be made to federal, state, or local agencies. Examples include drinking water for a municipality, or water to operate a hydroelectric plant.

7.1.3. Penalties for Violation of the LAN

The LAN sets forth the offences for which violators of the LAN may be penalized. Examples include discharging waste water, in violation of the provisions of the LAN, into government-owned collecting pools or bodies of water; allowing waste water to seep into government-owned or other property so as to pollute the subsoil or aquifer (punitive measures for this offence do not preclude imposition of other health-related or environmental protection penalties); extracting, using, or benefiting from government-owned waste water without complying with the Official Mexican Standards regarding quality and the particular conditions established for such a purpose; extracting, using or benefiting from government-owned water in excess of volumes permitted to users; occupying channels, canals, federal zones, or protected zones without a concession from the Commission; bringing subterranean water to the surface for the concessionaire's own use or for a third party in prohibited zones or reserves without the permission of the Commission; supplying government-owned water for human consumption that does not meet quality standards; disposing of or dumping, in violation of the law, garbage, dangerous or toxic substances, or sludge that are the by-products of waste water treatment processes, into rivers, river or stream beds, channels, marine waters, or other reservoirs or streams of water, or allowing materials or substances that pollute waters of the subsoil to leak out; and blatantly wasting water in violation of the law (LAN Article 119).

The penalties applicable to such offences are fines that may range from the equivalent of 50 to 10,000 days of the general minimum wage in force for the Federal District. Other penalties include closure of facilities or eviction from unlawfully occupied property (LAN Articles 20–122).

7.2. Forestry Resources

Mexico's forestry resources pale by comparison with those of the United States and Canada, yet they are substantial, and important to the Mexican economy. Forestry lands capable of exploitation in Mexico amount to 21.6 million hectares (52 million acres) of which the government has to date authorized the harvesting of 8.6 million hectares (21 million acres).[126]

[126] *See Informe* PROFEPA 2002, at 8, available at www.profepa.gob.mx (site visited Jan. 2004).

Mexico's forest resources are governed by a new Forestry Law (*Ley General de Desarrollo Forestal Sustentable*, or LGDFS)[127] which abrogated the former Forestry Law.[128] It is the principal law governing this matter; however, the LGEEPA is also applicable as a supplementary law. The LGDFS is designed to regulate and promote conservation and management of the forest resources of the nation, in order to create favourable conditions for sustainable development.

The new Forestry Law defines forest resources as natural, artificial, or induced forest vegetation, their products or residues, as well as the soil of forestland or land particularly fit for forest cultivation (LGDFS Article 7bis, Section XXV). Regulation of forests has no effect on the rules of ownership of the resources, which are determined by the ownership of the land on which the forests are located; thus, such resources may be the property of an *ejido*, a community, individuals, or corporations (LGDFS Article 5).

The new law represents a major institutional restructuring. It establishes concurrent jurisdiction among federal, state, and municipal government agencies, and guidelines for co-ordination. Under the LGDFS, the federal government is responsible for the major elements of forestry management: setting major policies, issuing regulations (such as *normas oficiales mexicanas*, or NOMs, and technical standards), providing permits for exploitation of forests on federal lands, maintaining databases and providing public information, providing permits for exploitation of forests on federal lands, etc. (LGDFS Article 12). States are permitted to adopt their own forestry laws, and to administer policies within their territories that do not conflict with federal laws. States are encouraged to enter into co-operative agreements with relevant federal agencies to maximize forestry management (LGDFS Articles 13–15).

SEMARNAT is the agency responsible for enforcing the LGDFS and its regulations (LGDFS Article 16). The LGDFS also created two new forestry bodies. The first, an agency within SEMARNAT, is the National Forestry Commission (*Comisión Nacional Forestal*, or CONAFOR),[129] designed to promote forestry conservation and management. The second body, a co-ordinating group known as the National Forestry Service (*Servicio Nacional Forestal*), was created to help co-ordinate the activities of agencies involved in forestry management and conservation at different levels of government (LGDFS Articles 8–9). The National Forestry Service is made up of representatives from SEMARNAT, SDN, SAGARPA, and the National Forestry Council (CONAFOR, an agency), the Director of PROFEPA, representatives of state governors and the Federal District, and the heads of state forestry agencies.

[127] D.O. 25 Feb. 2003. The LGDFS and supporting regulations may be found at www.semarnat.gob.mx, 'Normatividad y Leyes' (site visited Jan. 2004).

[128] *Ley Forestal*, D.O. 13 Dec. 1996; modifications published on 22 Dec. 1996 and 20 May 1997.

[129] CONAFOR is made up of representatives of the Secretariats of SDN, SHCP, SEDESO, SECONOMIA, SAGARPA, SECTUR, SEMARNAT, and SRA, as well as the director of the CNA. *See* www.conafor.gob.mx (site visited Jan. 2004).

7.2.1. *Exploitation of Forest Resources*

Based on the types of forest resources available in Mexico and the range of activities conducted on forestlands or land fit for forest cultivation, the LGDFS establishes several different ways for SEMARNAT and other forestry agencies to intervene in forest management and control, by placing limitations on exploitation.[130] SEMARNAT also has the power to grant authorization for logging on forestlands or land fit for forest cultivation, whether the land is owned by the government or by a private party. CONAFOR is responsible for the registration of forestry experts in charge of exploiting or protecting forest resources (LGDFS Articles 58–72). The law also creates a forestry management fund to promote better sustainable forestry development (LGDFS Articles 127–141).

7.2.2. *Penalties and Enforcement*

If SEMARNAT determines that forest ecosystems are in danger of imminent damage or degradation, SEMARNAT may, at its discretion, take any of the following security measures: precautionary securing of forest resources and raw materials, as well as property, vehicles, utensils, tools, equipment, and other instruments directly associated with the action or omission that gives rise to imposition of such a measure; temporary, partial or total, closure of facilities, machinery, or equipment for use, storage, or processing of forest resources and raw material, or closure of the premises or facilities where the acts that may be causing damage to the biodiversity or natural resources is taking place and the temporary, partial or total, suspension of utilization or extraction of resources, of forestation, of deforestation, or of the activity in question (LGDFS Article 161).

SEMARNAT also has the legal authority to impose penalties for violations of the law. The violations include conducting any type of business, work, or activities in violation of regulations regarding forestry; preventing authorized personnel of SEMARNAT from conducting on-site inspection visits or technical audits; utilizing forest resources, forestation, and reforestation in violation of the applicable regulations; forestation for purposes of commercial production in substitution of natural vegetation of forestlands, in violation of the applicable regulations; and a number of other violations listed in LGDFS Article 163.

SEMARNAT may impose a range of penalties for violations, including warnings; fines; temporary, partial or total, suspension of authorization for utilization of forest resources; revocation of authorization or of forest registration; seizure of raw materials, instruments, machinery, and equipment, or of the premises or facilities where such forestry activities are carried out; and temporary or definitive, partial or total, closure of facilities, machinery, and equipment of facilities where the unlawful activities are being conducted (LGDFS Article 164).

[130] *See* www.conafor.gob.mx, 'zonas forestales' (site visited Jan. 2004). For instance, the law prohibits the planning of commercial species of forests in substitution of native plants, except when biodiversity is not adversely affected or the vegetation is of little value. LGDFS Art. 85.

In fulfilling its responsibilities under the law, SEMARNAT faces serious obstacles. PROFEPA, which oversees compliance with the laws, has only 222 inspectors to oversee a total of 63.8 million hectares (154 million acres) of forests. According to SEMARNAT, there are over 100 critical areas of threatened deforestation and other concerns, the most serious of which are found in remote areas of *ingobernabilidad*, that is, where governmental authority is marginally present. These include forests in Michoacan that serve as a reserve for the Monarch butterfly, the Lacandon rainforest of southern Chiapas, the Chimalapas region in Oaxaca, the National Park of Zoquiapan in the State of Mexico, and the region surrounding the famous volcanoes, Ixtaccihuatl and Popocatépetl, in Puebla. PROFEPA has recently reported some success in increasing compliance with the law in some of these areas.[131]

[131] *Informe* PROFEPA 2000, at 8, available at www.profepa.gob.mx (site visited Jan. 2004).

13

Labour Law, Agrarian Reform, and Social Welfare

1. Introduction

After the adoption of the Constitution of 1917, the Mexican government gradually assumed the roles of the sole provider of welfare benefits to the needy,[1] and an active mediator on behalf of the poor. At the Constituent Congress of 1916–1917, supporters of an aggressive welfare state (or *estado social*) faced serious opposition, which continued after the Constitution was adopted. This tension persisted throughout the course of the twentieth century, and while the PRI-dominated government during this period espoused a paternalistic, welfare-state agenda, the reality of government action has varied from presidential administration to administration, shifting with the winds of non-ideological politics of the PRI. At the millennium, the PRI's absolute domination of Mexican politics was replaced by a multi-party system in which business-oriented (PAN), pragmatic (PRI), and populist labour (PRD) parties vie for political control, and Mexico's adoption of an open, market-oriented economy has reduced, but not eliminated, many elements of the welfare state policies adopted by PRI governments in the past.[2]

The politics of the social welfare state became known in mainland Europe and Latin America after the end of World War II, but the term carries a variety of meanings. There are important differences among those constitutions that espouse the welfare state (*estado social*), and the Mexican Constitution, which has a number of peculiarities in its particular expression of the social agenda. Labour rights are at the centre of social welfare rights, but this Chapter also explores other aspects of the welfare state, including agrarian reform, education, housing, and health.

[1] While some Catholic charities do exist, the Catholic Church, despite extensive involvement with the poor in rural and urban Mexico, has done relatively little to address problems of poverty. Of course, the Catholic Church in Mexico, having lost all of its own properties to expropriation (*see* Chapter 1 above) generally lacks the financial resources to address social concerns.

[2] On political change, *see* Chapter 5 above, Section 3.3. On the change in economic policies, *see* Chapter 12 below, at text accompanying notes 1–16.

2. Labour Law

2.1. Historical Background

During the nineteenth century, Mexico had no specialized labour legislation, and this area of the law was regulated exclusively by application of the Civil Code to labour contracts. At the Constituent Congress of 1857, Ignacio Luis Vallarta argued the dangers of empowering labour by inserting labour rights in the Constitution of 1857, and his views prevailed. In Vallarta's view, the Constitution should simply proclaim the freedom to work; detailed regulation of the subject would hamper industry and the efficient circulation of capital, and should therefore be excluded.[3] However, as industries (especially mining and agriculture) developed during the long period of the Porfiriato (1876–1910), abusive labour practices gave rise to labour conflicts. In 1906, miners from the foreign-owned Cananea Copper Company in Sonora demanded better treatment, including fair wages, and the failure to meet these resulted in a famous strike that ended in a bloody massacre. One year later, a second violent strike arose in the textile industry, this time in Rio Blanco, Veracruz, and despite the intervention of President Porfirio Díaz this strike also ended in bloodshed.

In response to these events, political parties began to call for labour legislation, and in the few years prior to the Revolution of 1910 the first labour laws in the country were enacted, but at the state rather than federal level.[4] Porfirio Diaz's government ignored the need for labour legislation, and it was not until the constitutional debates of 1916–1917 that the decisive step was taken in this direction at the national level.

The Constituent Congress of 1916–1917 underwent two distinct ideological stages. Overcoming the opposition of President Carranza, who favoured small government and decentralization, those who advocated strong federal programmes to achieve social justice and welfare, which had been goals of the Revolution, were able to incorporate progressive ideas into the final draft of the Constitution. The eventual result was the adoption of Articles 3, 4, 27, and 123, the last being a highly detailed compilation of specific workers' rights, as discussed below.

[3] On this subject, *see* De la Cueva, M., *Derecho Mexicano del Trabajo, Vol. I* (Mexico: Porrúa, 1954) at 92–95.

[4] The platform of the Mexican Liberal Party, headed by the Flores Magón brothers, published on 1 July 1906, contained 13 specific proposals to create federal labour legislation. Nevertheless, the first Mexican labour laws were enacted at the state level; these were the Law of Professional Risks of 1904 of José Vicente Villada, the governor of the State of Mexico, and a law signed in 1906 by the governor of the State of Nuevo Leon, Bernardo Reyes. On this subject, *see* Castorena, J.J., *Manual de Derecho Obrero* (Mexico: Castorena, 1973) at 45–47. After the overthrow of Porfirio Díaz in 1910, many state labour laws were enacted: in the states of Coahuila in 1912; Veracruz in 1914; Yucatan in 1915; and in Hidalgo and Zacatecas in 1916. *Id.* at 47–48.

Mexican constitutional law scholars have extolled this 'social constitution', which includes specific provisions focusing on the welfare of workers. Adopted in the same year as the Russian Revolution, when the world was beginning to focus on oppressive working conditions, the Mexican Constitution of 1917 was an extremely progressive document. In practice, however, the labour protections included in the Constitution have proven impossible to enforce consistently, for economic and political reasons. Like certain other provisions in the Mexican constitution, the 'guarantees' written into Article 123—the right to work, limitations on the workday, the right to a minimum wage—have served as targets or aspirations, rather than as enforceable rights. As we shall see, labour law itself became an important element of the control mechanisms used by the PRI to maintain political control through selective enforcement of the laws.

2.1.1. *The Federalization of Labour Law*

Labour legislation in Mexico has its roots in Article 123 of the Constitution.[5] In 1929, Congress decided to do away with overlapping federal and state labour laws by replacing municipal and state labour laws with one federal law that would pre-empt state legislation in this field.[6] Subsequent constitutional reforms of Articles 73 and 123 paved the way for enactment of the first Federal Labour Law of 1931 (*Ley Federal de Trabajo*), referred to by its Spanish acronym, LFT. After undergoing numerous changes over the years, in 1970 the original LFT was replaced by a new Federal Labour Law[7] that, with many modifications, remains in force today.

As governmental bureaucracies grew, so did the need to regulate labour relations between government agencies and their employees. Thus, in 1938, the

[5] Art. 123 is highly detailed, and there has been a tendency to refine and amend its provisions in order to accomplish social ends. From the time the Constitution of 1917 came into effect, Art. 123 has undergone 9 amendments. The most important of these are:

- (i) D.O. 6 Sep. 1929 (amending part XXIX to provide for the Law of Social Security (*Ley del Seguro Social*), in order to provide disability, life, unemployment, work-related illness, and accident benefits to workers);
- (ii) D.O. 5 Dec. 1960 (adding Part B, which extended worker rights to state and federal governmental employees); however, this reform became effective in 1965; D.O. 28 Dec. 1965;
- (iii) D.O. 21 Nov. 1962 (amending Part A to define clear standards regarding the length of the work day, child labour, minimum wages, profit sharing, and social insurance);
- (iv) D.O. 14 Feb. 1972 (amending section A to require all companies to 'provide comfortable and hygienic living accommodations to workers', obligations that would be fulfilled by means of contributions made by employers to a nationwide housing fund (INFONAVIT));
- (v) D.O. 31 Dec. 1974 (defining the length of the work day, overtime pay, occupational health and safety conditions, and placement of workers);
- (vi) D.O. 9 Jan. 1978 (introducing the requirement that employers must provide training to workers); and
- (vii) D.O. 23 Dec. 1986 (setting specific minimum wage requirements).

[6] Art. 123 of the Mexican Constitution was amended in D.O. 6 Sep. 1929.

[7] D.O. 1 Apr. 1970, as last amended 23 Jan. 1998.

federal Congress enacted the Charter of Workers at the Service of the Powers of the Union (*Estatuto de los Trabajadores al Servicio de los Poderes de la Unión*) to regulate labour–management relations between government employees and the agencies that employed them. In 1963, this law was replaced by the Federal Law of Workers at the Service of the State (*Ley Federal de los Trabajadores al Servicio del Estado*), the regulatory law of Part B of Article 123 of the Constitution,[8] which is still in force today.

2.1.2. The Development of the Corporatist Labour Model, 1917–1997

It is impossible to understand the role of labour law in Mexican society without understanding the political environment of the corporatist, single-party system in which the law developed. President Lázaro Cárdenas' creation of the Party of the Mexican Revolution (*Partido de la Revolución Mexicana*), the predecessor of the PRI,[9] in 1938 laid the groundwork for the pattern of corporatism that has marked the Mexican form of government. The term corporatism refers to a system of government in which the society is organized into industrial, social, and professional organizations that serve in theory as instruments of political representation, but which in fact may operate to control the activities of persons who come within their jurisdiction.[10] In Mexico, this system served to control the political landscape through a political/electoral machine with the strongly organized backing of the masses, particularly peasants and workers. With the exit of the military from the political arena in 1940,[11] the PRI relied on three major segments of society as the three 'pillars' of the ruling party: workers, rural peasants (*campesinos*), and the popular sector or general masses. The laws and regulations adopted throughout the twentieth century to govern the activities of these different sectors of the population reflect this corporatist system, and gave rise to an authoritarian and paternalistic system of governance that, despite shortcomings, was relatively effective. The 'labour pillar' of this support was central to the PRI's control of society, and became a means both of distributing benefits to groups and individuals and of controlling dissent.[12]

[8] *Cf.* Margadant, G., HISTORIA DEL DERECHO MEXICANO (Mexico: Esfinge, 1990) at 246–248.

[9] The PRM was preceded by the Partido Nacional Revolucionario created by Plutarco Elías Calles in 1928, which laid the early foundations of corporatism. *See* Lajous, A., LOS ORÍGENES DEL PARTIDO ÚNICO EN MÉXICO (Mexico: UNAM, 1981) at 196–203.

[10] On corporatism in Mexico, *see* Bizberg, I., ESTADO Y SINDICALISMO EN MÉXICO (Mexico: Colegio de Mexico, 1990) at 210; Bizberg, I., 'La crisis del corporativismo mexicano', in FORO INTERNACIONAL, vol. XXX, No. 4, Apr.–June, 1990; and Trejo Delarbe R., CRÓNICA DEL SINDICALISMO EN MÉXICO *(1976–1988)* (Mexico: Siglo XXI, 1990) at 74. *See* also Chapter 1 above, Section 4.3.

[11] On 10 Dec. 1940, Manuel Ávila Camacho, for the first time, excluded members of the military from the Party of the Mexican Revolution (PRM). *See* Garrido, L.J., EL PARTIDO DE LA REVOLUCIÓN INSTITUCIONALIZADA, LA FORMACIÓN DEL NUEVO ESTADO EN MÉXICO *(1928–1945)* (Mexico: SEP, 1986) at 388–395.

[12] Cossío Díaz, J.R., CAMBIO SOCIAL Y CAMBIO JURÍDICO (Mexico: ITAM/Miguel Angel Porrúa, 2002), chapter 1.

An example of this system can be seen in the government's dealings with federal government workers. The Charter of Workers at the Service of the Powers of the Union, the first labour code for government employees, (*Estatuto Jurídico de los Trabajadores al Servicio de los Poderes de la Unión*) went into effect in December 1938.[13] This law established rules for government employees in positions of trust and management (*trabajadores de confianza*), and provided for recognition of only one union within each governmental department. The individual government unions were organized into the Federation of Unions of Workers at the Service of the State (*Federación de Sindicatos de Trabajadores al Servicio del Estado*). Under this system, one had no choice but to join the only union allowed to represent workers of one's occupation, and expulsion from the union was tantamount to losing one's job.

Non-government workers, for whom labour–management relations are governed by the provisions of Section A of Article 123 of the Constitution, were subject to an arrangement of domination similar to that of government workers. The earliest example of this system can be found in the Federal Labour Law of 1931.[14] Under this law, workers' unions had the right to have an employer remove a union worker from a job if the worker quit or was expelled from the union, provided that the worker's contract contained a clause (known as an 'exclusion clause', or *cláusula de exclusión*) stipulating such an agreement. Another notorious worker control clause, known as the 'admission clause' (*cláusula de admisión*), was commonly inserted in labour agreements, and required membership of a particular union as a prerequisite to being hired. Exclusion clauses and admission clauses gave union leaders considerable control over dissident factions. As discussed below, on 17 April 2001 the Mexican Supreme Court finally ruled that such clauses are violations of the right to work contained in Article 5 of the Mexican Constitution;[15] throughout much of the twentieth century, however, admission and exclusion clauses were considered valid, and they served to solidify the power of certain 'government-approved' labour unions and labour leaders.

The LFT of 1931 established that unions could form federations and confederations, and that the Secretariat of Industry, Commerce, and Labour would be responsible for the registration and accreditation of such organizations. This was the foundation of the classic model of corporatist organization, an official link between the organization (union) and the government. Labour federations became the principal vehicles not just for organizing worker demands, but also for co-opting union leaders and controlling labour militancy. The leaders of these federations—Luis Morones, Vicente Lombardo Toledano, and Fidel Velázquez, among others—became important figures in Mexican politics, not

[13] D.O. 5 Dec. 1938.

[14] D.O. 28 Aug. 1931, which was later superseded by the Federal Labour Law of 1970.

[15] *See* the discussion *infra*, at text accompanying note 32. For a discussion of admission and exclusion clauses, *see* Cossío Díaz, J.R., CONSTITUCION, TRIBUNALES Y DEMOCRACIA: COLECCIÓN DE ENSAYOS JURÍDICOS (Mexico: Editorial Themis, 1998) at 111.

just as advocates for the workers they represented, but also as backstage supporters of the PRI's political agenda.[16]

The Federal Labour Law of 1970 kept the corporatist machinery in place, preserving the ability of labour unions to write exclusion clauses and admission clauses into labour agreements, in accordance with Articles 371 and 395 of the LFT of 1970. Organized labour was assimilated into the PRI as a major component of the party's grass roots support. Union leaders who co-operated with the PRI received benefits (job security, access to decision-makers) that loyal actors in the corporatist system would receive.

2.2. Part A of Article 123 of the Constitution: Labour Rights in the Private Sector[17]

Mexican labour law is set forth in the lengthy provisions of Article 123 of the Mexican Constitution, and in the more detailed provisions of the Federal Labour Law (LFT). Mexican labour law is administered by the Secretariat of Labour and Social Protection (*Secretaría de Trabajo y Previsión Social*), often referred to by the acronym STPS.[18]

As mentioned earlier, the original text of Article 123 of the Constitution recognized certain rights of workers in general. In 1960, when Part B of that same Article was added (dealing with relations between government agencies and their employees), the original text of the Article 123 became Part A. Part A regulates labour relations of 'workers, day workers, employees, domestic employees, craftsmen and, in general, all labour contracts', and the LFT of 1970 serves as the Regulatory Law for Part A only (LFT Article 1).

[16] The most important labour federations were the CROM and the CTM. Founded in 1918, the CROM (*Confederación Regional Obrera Mexicana*), led by Luis Morones, grew rapidly during the 1920s and claimed 2,250,000 members by the time President Calles was elected in 1924. By virtue of the CROM, the state controlled the labour movement after the Revolution, by offering social benefits in exchange for political loyalty.

The CTM (Confederacion de Trabajadores de México) was founded in 1936, and by the early 1950s it had become the largest labour federation in Mexico. Its founder was Vicente Lombardo Toledano, a lawyer and philosopher who was elected to the Mexican Congress three times, was a candidate to the Mexican Presidency in 1952, and a leader of the Popular Socialist Party (*Partido Popular Socialista*, PPS). In 1940, Fidel Velázquez became the leader of the CTM, a position he held until his death in 1997, at the age of 97. 'Don Fidel' maintained strong centralized control over the policies, including strikes, of its constituent unions. Today, the labour unions affiliated with the CTM represent 4.7 million workers. *See* www.uom.edu.mx/trabajadores/29aguilarl.htm (site visited Jan. 2004).

For more information on the CTM, *see* *Historia de CTM 1936–1990: El movimiento obrero y el estado mexicano*, vols. I and II (Mexico: UNAM-Instituto de Investigaciones Sociales, Facultad de Economía, 1990) and Lombardo Toledano V., *Escritos del movimiento obrero* (Mexico: UOM, 1975).

[17] On Mexican labour law generally, *see* De la Cueva M., *El Nuevo Derecho Mexicano del Trabajo* (Mexico: Porrúa, 7th ed., 1981); and De Buen, N., *Derecho del Trabajo I y II*, (Mexico: Porrúa, 2000). For a comparative overview of labour law in Mexico, Canada, and the United States, *see* Commission for Labor Cooperation, North American Agreement on Labor Cooperation, *Labor Relations Law in North America* (2000).

[18] *See* www.stps.gob.mx (site visited Jan. 2004).

Part A contains general employment law provisions, as well as those on collective bargaining. A lawyer from the United States will be immediately struck by the length and detail of Article 123. With thirty-one detailed sections, Part A of Article 123 includes many provisions that are subjects of labour laws in other countries, rather than constitutional principles. As we shall see, not all of the rights contained in this Article have been enforced as guarantees, due to both economic and political reasons.

2.2.1. *Substantive Rules of Labour Law*

The original Constitution of 1917 included a number of specific protections for workers in Article 123, and later amendments to the Constitution added to these rights. The rights are to be implemented, however, by the LFT.

Scope of the LFT The scope of the LFT—labour law (*derecho laboral,* or *derecho del trabajo*)—is very broad. For the US lawyer, the term 'labour law' refers to laws governing labour unions and collective bargaining. However, under the LFT 'labour law' includes both collective bargaining and what would be called 'employment law' in the United States: that is, laws regulating any employment relationship, including individual employment.[19]

In principle, the LFT applies to all employment relationships, except those involving government employees (state and federal). Thus household employees, skilled professionals, and employees of large corporations are all covered by its terms. However, as discussed in the concluding section to this Chapter, enforcement of workers' rights has been haphazard, at best, due to the economic pressures that attend a country that has suffered from endemic unemployment and underemployment. Small businesses in Mexico's 'informal' sector, which make up a sizeable portion of the economy, often ignore regulatory laws, including labour protections. On the other hand, large corporations, both Mexican and foreign-owned, are generally subject to stricter enforcement of labour laws. In addition, the importance of large companies to regional and national economies gives them a high profile that subjects them to stricter scrutiny by authorities. Even so, the protections and guarantees written into the LFT may be ignored by both workers and employers. Much depends on the industry in question, but particularly in industries that rely on unskilled or

[19] The LFT defines 'worker' (*trabajador*) as an 'individual who performs a subordinate personal job for another individual or company' (LFT Art. 8). Work (*trabajo*) is defined as 'any human, intellectual or material activity, irrespective of the degree of technical preparation required by each profession or skill' (LFT Art. 8). Employer (*patrón*) is defined as 'the individual or corporation that utilizes the services of one or several workers' (LFT Art. 10). The employment relationship is defined as 'the performance of a personal job that is subordinate to another person, in exchange for payment of wages', regardless of the act that gives rise to the relations (LFT Art. 20). SJF, 8a, T. VII, Tribunales Colegiados de Circuito, p. 424.

According to LFT Art. 21, the law assumes that there is a contract and a labour relationship between one who performs a personal job and one who receives the benefit thereof. Interpreting LFT Arts. 20 and 21, the Supreme Court has concluded that the contract does not necessarily have to be in written form. SJF, 8a, T. VIII, Tribunales Colegiados de Circuito, p. 291.

semi-skilled labour (of which there has traditionally been a surplus in Mexico) the pressure on workers to earn a subsistence wage causes many businesses, and the workers themselves, to ignore labour protections.

Employees of quasi-public agencies, such as the government-owned oil company (PEMEX) and the Federal Electricity Commission (*Comisión Federal de Electricidad*), are covered by Part A of Article 123, rather than Part B. In other words, they are treated as private, rather than government, employees for purposes of the application of the LFT.

Worker protection under the LFT In addition to covering the procedural aspects of labour law, the LFT establishes a number of substantive rules to protect workers. In accordance with Article 123, Part A, Sections I to XV, of the Mexican Constitution, LFT Article 5 sets forth numerous prohibitions, including the following: against employing minors under fourteen years of age; against forcing workers to work longer than eight hours on day shifts and seven hours on night shifts;[20] against imposing overtime on minors under sixteen years of age; against paying wages below the legal minimum wage;[21] against delaying payment of wages to workers for more than a week; against setting rates of pay for employees at restaurants, bars, or stores; against requiring employees to purchase consumer goods in specific establishments with their wages; against withholding wages as fines; against violating the principle of 'equal pay for equal work';[22] against employing minors under seventeen years of age for night shifts or work after 11 pm; and against inducing a worker to waive any rights granted to him or her by the Constitution or by statute.[23]

The Constitution and LFT also establish certain positive obligations on employers,[24] including the obligations: to grant workers a day of rest for every six days that they work; to grant pregnant workers six weeks' maternity leave both before and after giving birth; to share company profits with workers;[25] to

[20] SJF, 9a, T. II, Segunda Sala, p. 311.

[21] Minimum wages vary according to geographical areas or specific branches of industry, commerce, or to special professions. Minimum wages are set by Regional Commissions and submitted for approval to the National Commission of Minimum Wages (LFT Arts. 90–94). The level of minimum wage in Mexico is a reflection of an oversupply of labour. As of March 2003, the minimum daily wage in Mexico City was 43 Mexican pesos (equal to approximately 4 US dollars).

[22] The Mexican Circuit Court of Appeals has held that wages consist of cash payments by means of a daily quota, fees, receipt of salary, right of habitation, bonuses, commissions, benefits in kind, as well as any other benefit provided to a worker in exchange for his or her work. *Cf.* SJF, 9a, T. V, Tribunales Colegiados de Circuito, p. 285. With regard to the previous thesis, *cf.* SJF, 8a, T. V, Tribunales Colegiados de Circuito, p. 626.

[23] Mexican Constitution, Art. 123, part A, Sections I–XV, and LFT, Art. 5.

[24] Mexican Constitution, Art. 123, part A, Sections I–XV and LFT, Art. 5. LFT Art. 132 establishes additional obligations of employers towards workers.

[25] Profit sharing refers to the amount of money that workers are entitled to receive of the profits made by their employer during the fiscal year, based on a percentage of the number of days worked times the wages that a worker would make during that same fiscal year; the percentage is determined by the National Commission for the Sharing of Workers in Profits of Companies (*Comisión Nacional para la Participación de los Trabajadores en las Utilidades de las Empresas*), and is usually around 10%. On this subject, *see* Apéndice al SJF, 1995, 8a, T. V, Cuarta Sala, 1995, p. 202.

provide workers with comfortable and sanitary housing accommodation;[26] to pay workers at double wages when they are required to work more than a normal work day; to provide training to workers; to grant annual paid vacation leave of at least six work days per year to all workers that have been employed for more than a year;[27] and to compensate workers for accidents at work and work-related illnesses.[28]

As discussed at the end of the preceding section, not all of these positive obligations are fulfilled in practice, due to economic realities. Those that require significant investment, such as the provision of adequate housing, are viewed as aspirations rather than legal commitments.

The obligations on the part of workers are set forth in LFT Article 134, and basically amount to a list of types of misconduct that constitute grounds for rescission of an employment contract or termination, as discussed below.

Articles 182 to 353 of the LFT apply to special jobs or particular categories of workers, such as jobs performed by women or minors, positions of trust or management, jobs on seagoing vessels or aircraft, of railroad workers, truckers, farm workers, agents of commerce, professional athletes, actors and musicians, delivery workers, domestics, hotel employees and employees of analogous establishments, home businesses, doctors in residency, and university workers. These provisions must be read as modifications of the general rules due to the special risks or other characteristics of these particular categories of workers.

Duration of the employment agreement, termination, and rescission One major difference between US and Mexican labour law involves the length of the employment relationship. The United States has historically recognized a common law principle that employment contracts are terminable at will by either party: a rule that has been severely limited in more recent years, diminishing employers' overwhelming power over employees.[29] In Mexico, by contrast, the employment relationship may remain in effect either for specific periods of time or indefinitely; when the length of time is not specified, the relationship shall be deemed to continue indefinitely. Employment for limited periods of time must be justified either by the nature of the job to be performed, or because one

[26] Pursuant to Art. 123, Part A, Section XII of the Constitution, employers are obliged to provide workers with comfortable and sanitary living accommodation, and the same provision allows employers to fulfil this obligation by contributing to the national housing fund. In accordance with the terms of the LFT, fulfilment of such an obligation shall be made by contributing 5% of a worker's wages to the National Housing Fund (*Fondo Nacional de Vivienda*), which is administered by the National Institute of Housing for Workers (INFONAVIT) (*Instituto Nacional de la Vivienda para los Trabajadores*).

[27] The LFT sets a minimum amount of vacation time: after the first year of service, vacation time shall accrue in two-day increments each year for the first 3 years of service, reaching a maximum of 12 days at that time. After that, vacation time shall accrue in two-day increments for every 5 years of service (LFT Art. 76).

[28] Additionally, LFT Art. 6 establishes that any other laws and regulations or clauses in international treaties that directly benefit workers shall be applicable and enforceable.

[29] Farnsworth, A., *Farnsworth on Contracts* (New York: Aspen, 2nd ed., 1988) vol. I at 102–105.

worker is replacing another permanent worker on a temporary basis (LFT Articles 35–37). When one employer is replaced by another, as when a business is sold, the new employer shall be held jointly liable with the former employer regarding the rights of workers that are inherent to such a relationship (LFT Article 41).

Although requirements regarding the duration of labour relations are broad, relationships may be suspended, rescinded, or terminated under certain circumstances. According to LFT Article 42, *suspensión* is legal when a worker: catches a contagious disease; is temporarily disabled due to accident or illness (unless such condition does not constitute a job hazard); is placed in preventive detention and is subsequently acquitted of the charge(s); is arrested; is required to perform services or fulfil any duties set forth in Article 5 of the Constitution (services, such as electoral duties, that are compulsory for citizens); or is appointed to serve on any labour adjudicatory body.

Employment may be *terminated* only under strictly defined conditions: by mutual consent of the parties; because of death of the worker; for physical or mental disability or a patent inability of the worker properly to perform the job; or due to the termination of the works or the fulfilment of the term for which the worker was employed (LFT Article 53). A worker's employment can also be terminated by termination of the collective labour contract of work, if there is an economic failure by the employer to sustain employment;[30] by *force majeure*; by exhaustion of a natural resource on which the line of business depends; or by legally declared bankruptcy (LFT Article 434).

Employment may also be terminated by *rescission*. In contrast to termination, rescission is available to either the employer or the employee when either breaches the employment contract, or when one party violates a provision of the Federal Labour Law. An *employer* may rescind a labour contract for cause under the following circumstances: misrepresentation of the worker's qualifications; when a worker commits an offence of moral turpitude or act of violence, or threatens, slanders, or abuses the employer, his family, or the management of the company; when a worker damages company property; when a worker jeopardizes the security of the company or the safety of other employees; commissioning immoral acts on company grounds; divulging trade secrets or releasing confidential information about the company; when a worker is absent for more than three days within a period of thirty days; employee disobedience; failure to adopt safety measures; appearance at work while intoxicated or under the influence of drugs; an employee's criminal conviction; and for any other analogous reason that may be as serious as any of the foregoing (LFT Article 47). Employers must give written notice to the worker regarding any rescission of

[30] This justification for termination is similar to the 'layoffs' ordered by US companies, but is subject to strict scrutiny in accordance with LFT Arts. 433–439, and is also subject to collective bargaining agreements, where applicable. LFT Arts. 900–919, which set out the procedures for 'economic termination', are very complex, and for this reason they are rarely used as a justification to terminate.

the employment contract and, if the employer fails to do so, removal from the job shall be considered unjustified. A worker whose contract is terminated or rescinded without just cause is entitled to severance pay or, in some cases, reinstatement.[31]

A *worker* may rescind the labour contract or relationship: for misrepresentation of working conditions; when the employer, his family members, or management commits an offence of moral turpitude or act of violence against the worker or his family, or threatens to or perpetrates similar acts; when the employer reduces the worker's wages or the worker does not receive his or her wages on time; when the employer maliciously damages the worker's tools; when the employer places the worker in serious danger or fails to take proper safety and sanitary measures; when the employer carelessly jeopardizes the safety of the premises or of workers; and any other situations that may be analogous to the previous points (LFT Article 51). The worker is entitled to resign within thirty days following the act that is grounds for rescission, and is entitled to receive severance pay in accordance with the provisions of LFT Article 50.

2.2.2. *Private Sector Collective Bargaining*

Collective bargaining is covered in Part A of Article 123 of the Constitution, and in LFT Articles 354–385. The LFT recognizes the right of workers to form labour unions and federations, and the right of businesses to form employer unions (trade associations).[32] Workers may create a union without any prior authorization with a minimum of twenty individuals, although they are required to register before the appropriate labour authorities in order to be able to exercise certain types of powers (LFT Articles 364–370). Employer unions must be made up of at least three employers. Unions are granted considerable freedom to draft their charters and by-laws, to elect officers, and to acquire property, but they may not take part in religious matters or do business or exercise a profession for profit (LFT Article 378). Individual labour unions may form federations or confederations, which must be registered with the STPS.

Types of collective bargaining agreements The LFT recognizes two types of collective labour relations: the *contrato colectivo de trabajo* (collective bargaining agreement) and the *contrato ley* (contract law). A *contrato colectivo de*

[31] If the worker is fired without just cause, any one of the following situations may arise, depending on whether the worker chooses reinstatement or severance pay: (a) if the worker chooses severance pay and wins the case, he shall be entitled to payment of all accrued benefits, severance pay equivalent to a total of 3 months' wages, a seniority bonus of 12 days per year of service, and payment of all unpaid wages due since the date of termination until the date of total compliance with payment of the award; (b) if the worker chooses reinstatement and it is granted by the employer, the employee is entitled to all of the payments of accrued benefits and wages required in scenario (a); and (c) if the worker chooses reinstatement and it is not granted by the employer, the worker shall be entitled to severance pay of 20 days of wages for each year of service, as well as to payment of all amounts stated under point (a) (LFT Art. 48).

[32] Pursuant to LFT Art. 356, unions are associations of either employers or workers created for the study, improvement, or defence of their respective interests.

trabajo is defined in LFT Article 386 as 'an agreement entered into by and between one or several unions of workers and one or several employers, or one or several employer unions, for the purpose of establishing the terms under which work shall be performed at one or more companies or establishments'. A single labour union[33] negotiates the agreement with management on behalf of the employees. The contract must be in writing, and it must contain certain information and prescribe certain rules of employment: the name of the contracting parties and the companies involved, the length of time the contract shall remain in effect, length of the work day, days of rest and vacation time, wage rates, clauses regarding training and instruction, rules for serving on the commissions set up by law, and anything else upon which the parties may agree (LFT Article 391). The *contrato colectivo de trabajo* may not abridge a fundamental right of workers, and may not set standards below the minimums provided for in the Constitution and applicable statutes.

According to LFT Article 395, a collective bargaining agreement may stipulate that 'the employer shall exclusively admit as workers any persons who are members of the contracting union' (the 'admission clause') or that 'the employer shall remove from the job any [union] members that may quit or resign from or are expelled from the contracting union'. This ability to fire employees who leave the union is called the 'exclusion clause'. As discussed previously,[34] admission and exclusion clauses strengthened certain labour leaders and stifled dissent and competition. Finally, on 17 April 2001 the Mexican Supreme Court, in response to an *amparo* petition,[35] held that LFT Articles 395 and 413, which permit exclusion clauses in labour agreements and contract laws, violated the right to work provisions of Articles 5, 9, and 123A of the Constitution. The LFT has not been amended since that resolution.[36] Nevertheless, the decision has been a further incentive to the development of independent trade unions not affiliated with labour confederations that were allied with the PRI.[37]

Admission and exclusion clauses were not the only rules of Mexican collective bargaining law that strengthened the power of certain labour unions and federations; the *contrato ley* also added to the concentration and centralization of union power in Mexico. LFT Article 404 defines the *contrato ley* as 'the agreement entered into by and between one or several unions of workers and several employers, or one or several unions of employers, in order to establish the terms under which the job must be performed in a specific branch of industry,

[33] In cases where more than one labour union represents workers in a company, the union with the majority membership among the employees of the company, shall be considered the main party to the collective labour agreement (LFT Art. 388).

[34] *See supra*, text accompanying note 13.

[35] SJF, 9a, T. XIII, Segunda Sala, Tesis 2a, LIX/2001, May 2001, p. 443, *amparo en revision* 1124/2000.

[36] *See* Lastra Lastra, J.M., 'Inconstitucionalidad de la cláusula de exclusión', in LIBERTAD SINDICAL: CLÁUSULA DE EXCLUSIÓN (Mexico: UNAM, 2002) at 39.

[37] *See supra*, note 16.

and declared mandatory in one or several states, in one or several economic zones that encompass one or more of said entities, or in the entire territory of the nation'. In other words, the *contrato ley* is a kind of 'super collective bargaining agreement' that covers worker conditions in an entire industry, and usually encompasses many labour unions and companies. The *contrato ley* differs from the individual collective bargaining agreement because it covers an entire branch of an industry. The *contrato ley* is filed before the Labour Ministry (*Secretaría del Trabajo*) and must be entered by all employers in the sector; it should not last for more than two years. The *contrato ley* served an important corporatist function for the PRI,[38] since it facilitated the consolidation of labour into a highly structured apparatus that was controlled from the top. The *contrato ley* became prevalent in the textile, sugar, and liquor industries, as well as certain manufacturing sectors, all of which are important to the Mexican economy. The tide has changed, however. Currently, few Mexican workers are covered by agreements of *contrato ley*; employers consider them cumbersome, and labour unions are increasingly unwilling to cede individual control by entering into a *contrato ley* with a group of unions and employers.

There are special requirements for entering into a *contrato ley*. A request for enactment of a *contrato ley* may only be made to the STPS or to a state governor or a governor of the Federal District by the unions that represent at least two-thirds of the unionized workers 'of a branch of industry or several states, in one or more economic zones, that encompass one or more of said entities or in the entire territory of the nation' (LFT Article 406). After receipt of such a request for certification of a *contrato ley*, the STPS, the governors of the States, or the Mayor (*jefe de gobierno*) of the Federal District must verify that the required majority has been obtained. If the STPS, governor, or Mayor considers that the proposed *contrato ley* may be in the best interests of the industry, the relevant employer associations and labour unions must then convene general meetings of their members who will be covered by the *contrato ley*, who must vote to accept it. If the *contrato ley* is approved at these meetings, notice of the approval must be published in the *Diario Oficial de la Federación*, or in the official gazette of the corresponding state. Upon publication, the *contrato ley* becomes effective in all companies within the industry included under the agreement, regardless of any individual collective bargaining agreements that may have previously been entered into, unless the terms of the individual collective bargaining agreements are more beneficial to the worker than those of the *contrato ley*[39] (LFT Article 417).

While the *contrato ley* may be used to strengthen labour's voice in a particular industry, the abuses that occur under its widespread use are readily apparent. The *contrato ley* has contributed to the monopolization of power by the specific union or federation that controls an industry. In addition, certain worker's benefits are

[38] On Mexican corporatism, *see* Santos Azuela, H., DERECHO COLECTIVO DEL TRABAJO (Mexico: Porrúa, 2nd ed., 1997), at 310.
[39] Apéndice al SJF, 5a, T. V, Cuarta Sala, 1995, p. 77.

included in such agreements which are beyond the financial capability of small or new enterprises.

The right to strike Article 123, Section XVIII of the Mexican Constitution guarantees the right of workers to strike,[40] and Articles 440–469 of the LFT establish the rules by which workers, acting through their labour representatives, may conduct a strike. Strikes are legal when their purpose is to strike a balance between the different factors of production by reconciling the rights of labour with the rights of business; to obtain fulfilment of the provisions of a collective bargaining agreement or of a *contrato ley*, or to obtain a revision of either of these; to support the strike of another labour union or industry, i.e. to hold a sympathy strike; and to demand revision of contractual wage rates (LFT Article 450). For their part, employers may legally lay off employees provided that a state of overproduction has been reached at a plant and, in an effort to maintain prices at an affordable level, prior approval has been obtained from the Board of Conciliation and Arbitration (*Junta de Conciliación y Arbitraje*).

A strike may be called after filing a notification with the relevant *Junta de Conciliación y Arbitraje*, in accordance with the requirements provided in LFT Article 452. The employer shall be notified of the strike within twenty-four hours of the filing of the notification, and the employer has forty-eight hours to prepare its response. The President of the *Junta de Conciliación y Arbitraje* then calls the parties for a conciliation meeting designed to help them reach agreement. If the parties do not reach agreement, the *Junta* will resolve the dispute by issuing a decision, or *laudo*, which declares a strike either legal or unjustified. In the latter case, the strike must be suspended by labour leaders.[41]

Strikes have been uncommon in Mexico, due in large part to the control of the labour movement by the PRI. Since the economic and political opening up of Mexico, labour strikes have continued to be rare, because of the continued willingness of labour unions to negotiate with large companies. During the Presidency of Vicente Fox, strikes have not been a significant problem for enterprises.

2.3. Part B of Article 123 of the Constitution: Labour Rights of Government Employees

As previously mentioned, in 1960 Congress amended Article 123 of the Constitution to add Part B in order to provide for regulation of labour relations between state and federal government agencies and their employees. Sections I–VI and Section IX of Part B confer on government employees rights that are similar to the rights provided for in Part A of Article 123. These include: maximum length of the work day; mandatory weekly rest days; adherence to the principle of equal

[40] Strikes are illegal when a worker commits violent acts against persons or property, or when the nation is at war and establishments and services are under the control of the government. Mexican Constitution, Art. 123, Section A, part XVIII.

[41] LFT Arts. 451–465.

pay for equal work; protection of wage rates; vacations (although twenty days per year of service are granted to government employees); and job security.

Most federal government agencies and their employees are not subject to the LFT, but rather to the Federal Law of Workers at the Service of the State (*Ley Federal de los Trabajadores al Servicio del Estado*, hereinafter LFTSE).[42] The states and the Federal District have all adopted laws that cover employees and agencies of the states, the Federal District, and local governments. The LFTSE is very similar to the LFT, with the important exception that government employees are divided into two categories: *trabajadores de confianza*, who serve in positions of higher authority in government agencies (similar to political appointees); and *trabajadores de base*, which includes all others. Under LFTSE Article 8, *trabajadores de confianza* are excluded from the provisions of the Law, as are members of the armed forces, with the exception of the civil employees of the Secretariat of National Defence and the Secretariat of the Navy. Foreign Service officers are also excluded from the application of the LFTSE, but employees of the Secretariat of Foreign Relations who are not Foreign Service officers are covered by the LFTSE.

The Mexican Constitution addresses job security of federal government employees in Article 123, Part B, Sections VII and VIII, establishing rules for appointments to government positions, based on a system of promotional grades that takes into account the employee's knowledge, skills, and seniority. In fulfilling this obligation, the LFTSE establishes a system of promotional grades for government employees, and LFTSE Articles 47–66 deal with rules relating to job security. Unlike the United States, however, where most government employees (other than senior political appointees) are covered by civil service laws providing a measure of job security, state and federal government employees in Mexico, except for the Judicial Branch, have not in the past been protected by civil service laws. The absence of such protection has made it difficult to promote efficiency and honesty in government bureaucracies. Finally, in 2003 Congress adopted the Federal Civil Service Law, or Law of Professional Civil Service for the Federal Public Administration (*Ley del Servicio Profesional de Carrera en la Administración Pública Federal*)[43] which established mandatory rules of job security for all federal

[42] Most federal government employees are covered under the provisions of Part B of Art. 123, or under the Federal Law of Workers at the Service of the State (*Ley Federal de los Trabajadores al Servicio del Estado*), D.O. 28 Dec. 1963 as last amended on 23 Jan. 1998. However, employees of the following federal entities are NOT covered by the Provisions of Part B of Art. 123: PEMEX; UNAM; the Federal Power Commission (*Comisión Federal de Electricidad*, CFE); and the Mexican Institute of Social Security Service (*Instituto Mexicano del Seguro Social*, IMSS). Employees of these agencies are covered under Part A of Art. 123 of the Constitution and the LFT. However, employees from some state agencies, e.g. the Institute of Social Security and Services of the Workers at the Service of the State (*Instituto de Seguridad y Servicios Sociales de los Trabajadores del Estado*); the National Institute of Housing (*Instituto Nacional de la Vivienda*); National Institute of Indigenous (*Instituto Nacional Indigenista*); the Banking and Values National Commission (Comisión Nacional Bancaria y de Valores); and others, are covered by the Federal Government Workers' Law.

[43] D.O. 9 Apr. 2003.

government agencies subject to this new law.[44] Some Mexican states have adopted similar civil service laws to protect state employees.[45]

2.3.1. Unionization of Government Employees

Just as the LFT gives workers the right to unionize, all government employees, whether state or federal, have the right to be members of labour unions. As in the private sector, more than one labour union may represent employees of a given government agency.[46] Subsequent to the Supreme Court's decision holding exclusion clauses unconstitutional,[47] a government employee who is expelled from a union cannot therefore be dismissed from government employment.

In the past, government employee unions were extremely powerful, and formed a major pillar of support for the PRI. The teachers' union, or *Sindicato Nacional de Trabajadores de la Educación* (SNTE),[48] is the largest labour union in Latin America, representing 1.4 million public school teachers throughout the country. University professors belong to their own unions, such as the *Sindicato de Trabajadores de la UNAM* (labour union of UNAM employees, including professors).

Employees of government-owned corporations are deemed to be covered by Part A of Article 123, and the rules of collective bargaining described in section 2.2.2 above (private collective bargaining) apply to such unions.[49]

2.3.2. The Right of Government Workers to Strike

Government employees may avail themselves of the right to strike when a government agency commits a violation of the rights enshrined in Article 123, Part B, Section X. This right is also dealt with in LFTSE Articles 92–109. However, a major difference exists between the rights of government employees and those in the private sector. Employees of a private company may strike over specific differences, such as fulfilment of the provisions of a labour agreement or *contrato ley*, or wage increases. Before government employees can strike, however, there must be a 'general and systematic violation of rights', in accordance with

[44] Public school teachers are not covered by this law. For the list of federal laws covering teachers, *see* www.sep.gob.mx, 'Dirección General de Asuntos Jurídicos', 'La Educación y sus Normas Jurídicos' (May, 2004). All federal agencies are subject to the Federal Civil Service Law, with the exception of employees of the Office of the President, members of the armed forces, employees of the national security system, Foreign Service officers, medical and paramedical employees, and certain others (Federal Civil Service Law, Art. 8). The Federal Civil Service Law also excludes senior political appointees, as discussed in Chapter 9 above, at text accompanying note 103.

[45] For state laws, *see* www.juridicas.unam.mx, 'Entidades federativas' (site visited Jan. 2004.)

[46] *See* the *amparos* decided by the Supreme Court, SJF, 9a, T. V, pleno, Jan. 1997, p. 117. *See* generally Cossío Díaz, J.R., 'Sindicalización burocrática y activismo judicial', *Este País*, No. 66, Sep. 1996, at 28–30.

[47] *See supra*, text accompanying notes 34–37.

[48] *See* www.snte.org.mx (site visited Jan. 2004). In the first half of the twentieth century a number of teachers' unions existed, but in 1943 the Secretary of Education, Jaime Torres Bodet, in a classic example of corporatist organization, prevailed on labour leaders to form a single national union, the SNTE, to simplify government–labour negotiations in the education sector.

[49] *See supra*, note 41, regarding the special rules of application for autonomous agencies.

LFTSE Article 94. Instances of general and systematic violations have been extremely rare, and for this reason the right of government employees to strike, while available in theory, has rarely been used.

2.3.3. *Social Security Protection for Government Employees*

Part B of Article 123 also establishes the basis of the federal system of social security protection for government employees, similar to the system established for workers of the private sector. In the case of private sector employees health, insurance, and other security benefits are administrated by the Mexican Institute of Social Security Services (*Instituto Mexicano del Seguro Social, IMSS*),[50] while in the case of government employees such social security benefits are administered by the Security and Social Services Institute of the Government Workers (*Instituto de Seguridad y Servicios Sociales de Trabajadores del Estado*, ISSSTE).[51] This protection includes coverage of accidents at work, work-related illnesses, maternity leave, retirement, disability, old age, and death.

In addition to these benefits, the Mexican government provides federal workers with a broad range of services that US government employees would be surprised to receive. Thus federal government employees receive automatic health insurance and medical prescription coverage administered by a system of hospitals maintained by ISSSTE. More surprisingly, many government agencies also own and provide vacation centres and discount stores for the benefit of their employees and their families. Federal government employees also benefit from affordable housing, through a fund (FOVISSTE) established to provide financing for such housing. The furnishing of such benefits was a natural consequence of the corporatism by which the PRI dominated Mexican politics during the second half of the twentieth century.

3. Labour Law Enforcement and Adjudication of Labour Disputes and Worker Claims

Given the surplus of labour in Mexico,[52] it is not surprising that a discrepancy exists between what the Federal Labour Law mandates and what is actually enforced. Highly critical studies of Mexican labour law decry the failure to enforce the law as it is written,[53] and US and Canadian concern about lack of

[50] *See* www.imss.gob.mx (site visited Jan. 2004).
[51] *See* www.issste.gob.mx (site visited Jan. 2004).
[52] Unemployment figures issued by the Mexican government in February 2003 tend to show the unemployment rate at 2.8%. *See* www.inegi.gob.mx (site visited Jan. 2004). INEGI's figures are unrealistic, however. INEGI counts any person as 'employed' who earns even one peso per day in the 'informal economy', such as the many street vendors who abound in Mexican cities. 'Para el INEGI, ellos son empleados', *Reforma* (Mexico City), 26 July 2003, p. 1A. Vast underemployment in Mexico reduces the productivity of labour and depresses wages.
[53] LaBotz, D., *Mask of Democracy: Labor Suppression in Mexico Today* (Boston: South End Press, 1992).

enforcement of Mexican labour law resulted in the tripartite North American Agreement on Labour Co-Operation that supplemented the North American Free Trade Agreement.[54]

The *Secretaría de Trabajo y Previsión Social* (STPS) is responsible for enforcing Mexican labour law, although the agency has traditionally concentrated more on general initiatives to improve job training and labour productivity than on aggressive enforcement of the LFT. As a result, most labour law enforcement is carried out through adjudication of employment disputes or collective bargaining actions that are submitted to special labour tribunals known as *Juntas de Conciliación y Arbitraje*, which have been created pursuant to state and federal laws and are administered by the STPS.

3.1. Labour Tribunals: *Juntas de Conciliación y Arbitraje*

Labour and employment disputes in Mexico are not settled by the judicial system, but rather by a special set of arbitral boards that lie outside judicial power. This method of adjudicating labour matters was written into the Constitution of 1917, which created the boards of conciliation and arbitration that are established in Part A, Section XX of Article 123, drawing from European models. These boards, called *juntas de conciliación y arbitraje*, are made up of one representative from each of three categories: government, business management, and labour.[55] In the beginning, the submission of labour disputes to *juntas de conciliación y arbitraje* was voluntary, and the boards were simply viewed as mediators.[56] Under current law, however, submission of disputes to labour boards is obligatory.[57]

The LFT's rules apply to labour disputes that arise at the federal, state, or Federal District levels. The LFT's rules are applied by *juntas de conciliación y arbitraje* at both the state and federal levels. In 1927 President Plutarco Elías Calles established the first Federal Board of Conciliation and Arbitration (*Junta Federal de Conciliación y Arbitraje*), laying the foundation for the composition and functioning of these bodies. The LFT of 1931 provided for the creation of several adjudicative bodies to mediate labour disputes and to settle those disputes in which labour arbitration was mandatory.[58]

[54] The North American Agreement on Labor Co-Operation, as well as annual reports and other information on the NAALC, can be found at www.naalc.org. On the NAALC generally, *see* Toledano H., *et al.*, LABOR RELATIONS LAW IN NORTH AMERICA (Washington, D.C.: North American Commission on Labor Cooperation, 2000), available at www.naalc.org, 'Publications'. (Site visited Jan. 2004.)

[55] *See generally* Fix-Zamudio, H., and Cossío Díaz, J.R., EL PODER JUDICIAL EN EL ORDENAMIENTO MEXICANO (Mexico: FCE, 1996) at 256–257.

[56] In 1918 the Supreme Court decided that these boards lacked the jurisdictional capacity to hear labour disputes relating to performance or fulfilment of labour contracts, although it reversed itself in 1924 and finally granted jurisdiction to these bodies in such matters. SJF 5a, T. II, 8 Mar. 1918, p. 773.

[57] *Juntas de conciliación y arbitraje* have exclusive jurisdiction over labour disputes, either individual or collective. If a labour dispute is submitted to a judicial tribunal, it will be dismissed for lack of jurisdiction.

[58] *Cf.* Fix-Zamudio, and Cossío Díaz, *supra* note 55, at 257–262.

The current labour law, the LFT of 1970, carried forward the settlement of disputes by both federal and local boards.[59] Federal and local labour boards carry out similar functions, too numerous to list here, but they differ in jurisdiction. Pursuant to the provisions of part XXXI of section A of Article 123 of the Constitution, federal boards have jurisdiction to hear matters related to textiles; electricity; the movie industry; rubber; sugar; mining; metallurgy and steel; hydrocarbons; petrochemical products; cement; lime; automotive parts; chemicals; paper and pulp; vegetable oils and fats; packaged, canned, or bottled food products; beverage production; railroads; basic lumber; the glass industry; tobacco; and banking and credit services.[60] Since Article 124 of the Constitution states that any jurisdictional authority that is not expressly conferred upon federal bodies shall be understood as being the sole jurisdiction of the states, state boards of conciliation and arbitration may hear labour disputes pertaining to any subject not specifically assigned to federal boards under Article 123, Part A, Section XXXI. Most states have created and provided funding for state *juntas de conciliación y arbitraje*.

3.2. General Outline of Labour Dispute Procedure[61]

Whether they involve collective bargaining disputes or allegations of violation of individual employment rights, labour claims and disputes are heard in a single stage before a *junta de conciliación y arbitraje* (federal or local) having jurisdiction over the matter. Proceedings are predominantly oral; the members of the *junta*, the claimant, and the defendant are present at the hearings, which generally creates a sense of immediacy. Written motions and other procedural formalities usually observed in judicial proceedings are dispensed with in

[59] Federal and state labour arbitration boards are also discussed in Chapter 6 above, at notes 128–135.

[60] Under the Federal Labour Law, federal *juntas de conciliación y arbitraje* also have exclusive jurisdiction to hear disputes related to: enterprises that are either directly administered by the federal government or that have been detached from the government administration; enterprises that do business under a federal contract or concession, and industries that are in some way connected to such enterprises; and enterprises that perform work on federally owned property, in areas that are under federal jurisdiction in territorial waters or within the exclusive economic zones of the nation. Federal *juntas de conciliación* also have exclusive jurisdiction to apply public labour laws in matters that affect two or more states, or a state and the Federal District (an example is electricity); to hear matters regarding collective bargaining contracts that have been declared mandatory in more than one state; to hear matters pertaining to the obligations of management to provide education and training to workers, as well as to create safe and healthy conditions in the workplace.

[61] Rules of procedure for *juntas de conciliación y arbitraje* are set out in LFT Arts. 870–991, and the same rules are mandatory for both federal and state or local *juntas*. *See also* Chapter 6 above, at notes 128–135. For an authoritative discussion of labour procedure, *see* Salmorán de Tamayo, M.C., 'Jurisdicción y derecho procesal del trabajo', in EL DERECHO LATINOAMERICANO DEL TRABAJO, vol. II (Mexico: UNAM, 1974) at 114 *et seq*; Santos Azuela H., DERECHO COLECTIVO DEL TRABAJO (Mexico: Porrúa, 2nd ed., 1997); De Buen, D., DERECHO PROCESAL DE TRABAJO (Mexico: Porrúa, 3rd ed., 1994).

matters presented to the *juntas de conciliación y arbitraje*, in order to allow a full examination of workers' claims.

Individual and collective bargaining proceedings generally follow the same procedure. The proceedings are initiated by the filing of a petition before the appropriate board, which identifies the parties to the dispute. The petition is usually filed by an individual employee or by a labour union, represented by an official of the union. After the petition is filed, the board must set a specific date and time for a pre-trial settlement hearing. The defendant is served with notice of this hearing date and is warned that failure to appear shall be considered a refusal to settle as well as an acceptance of the demands of the claimant.

If the parties fail to reach a settlement at this hearing, a new stage of the proceedings begins in which the petition is filed once again, and may be broadened or amended; defence motions are heard; and the parties are permitted to respond and file counterclaims. When these preliminary motions are completed, the board summons the parties to an evidentiary hearing.[62] After this hearing has concluded, the board grants the parties forty-eight hours to present written closing arguments. Next, each party submits to the *junta* a draft arbitration award which includes a summary of the main points of each of the previous stages. If the board concurs with the proposed award, a hearing is held to discuss and vote on the resolution of the dispute. Decisions of the *juntas de conciliación y arbitraje* are final and not subject to appeal, although they may (and often do) give rise to *amparo* actions.[63]

This system of labour law 'enforcement', through arbitral tribunals, leaves much to be desired. The tripartite representation of labour, employer, and government as members of *juntas de conciliación y arbitraje* means, in practice, that the government representative governs the dispute: another example of the way in which corporatism is woven into the legal system. Critics also point out that *juntas de conciliación y arbitraje* lack the precision of judicial tribunals: their composition favours negotiated settlements, rather than a precise application of rules and enforcement of the labour laws. They further point to the relative lack of independence of the *juntas de conciliación y arbitraje*, which are administered by STPS, and do not fall under judicial power. For this reason, some experts argue for abandonment of the current system in favour of extension of the jurisdiction of federal and state courts to labour disputes, or at least the incorporation of the *juntas* into the judicial branch.[64]

[62] Generally, the following types of evidence may be introduced: confessions, documents, testimony, expert testimony, on-site inspections, and circumstantial evidence. *See* LFT Art. 776.

[63] The only way to challenge this judgment is via the *juicio de amparo*, a petition for judicial protection from violations of the constitutionally granted rights of the individual, discussed above in Chapter 8. An *amparo* petition must be directly filed before a Tribunal Colegiado de Circuito (Federal Circuit Court of Appeals) pursuant to the provisions of Art. 158 of the Law of *Amparo*.

[64] *See* Cavazos Flores, B., *40 Lecciones de Derecho laboral* (Mexico: Trillas, 1998) at 73; De Buen, N., *Derecho del Trabajo* (Mexico: Ed. Porrúa, 1992) at 125.

3.3. Disputes between Government Employees and Agencies

The Constitution of 1917 did not originally provide for regulation of labour relations between the government and its employees, although President Lázaro Cárdenas signed legislation in the 1930s that attempted to create an arbitral system for government employees.[65] Effective dispute settlement did not begin until 1960, when Part B of Article 123 was added to the Constitution;[66] in 1963 Congress adopted the regulatory law of Part B, the *Ley Federal de los Trabajadores al Servicio del Estado* (LFTSE).[67] Title Seven of the LFTSE (Articles 118–147) specifies that individual, collective, and inter-union disputes are the jurisdiction of the *Tribunal Federal de Conciliación y Arbitraje*, which resolves all disputes concerning federal government workers.[68] In 1995 Congress amended the organic law of the federal judiciary to establish that disputes between the federal judiciary and its employees are to be decided by the *Consejo de la Judicatura Federal* (discussed above in Chapter 6) and that any disputes between the Supreme Court and its employees shall be resolved by the Supreme Court.[69]

Disputes between state government agencies and their employees are submitted to state *juntas de conciliación y arbitraje*, as established by the legislation of each state.[70]

During the hegemony of the PRI, strikes by government employees were extremely rare. In addition to informal means of control, the law requires a showing of regular and systematic violation of worker rights before a strike is justified (see Section 2.3.2 above). Criticism of the *Tribunales Federales de Conciliación y Arbitraje* is similar to that voiced for the arbitral bodies that operate in the private sector.[71]

4. Land Reform and Agrarian Rights

4.1. Background

Until the mid-twentieth century, the Mexican economy was dependent on agriculture and mining, a legacy of colonial times. Given the accumulation of agricultural

[65] In 1938, President Lázaro Cárdenas signed the Charter of Workers at the Service of the Powers of the Union (*Estatuto de los Trabajadores al Servicio de los Poderes de la Unión*, D.O. 5 Dec. 1953) which for the first time established an arbitral tribunal and arbitration boards for workers.

[66] Presidential Decree of 21 Oct. 1960, published in D.O. 5 Dec. 1960.

[67] D.O. 27 Dec. 1963.

[68] Both the Mexican Supreme Court and the *Tribunal Federal de Conciliación y Arbitraje* (TFCA) have ruled that the TFCA has exclusive jurisdiction to decide labour disputes involving government employees. SJF, Apéndice 1988, Cuarta Sala, 1988, p. 3183. TFCA Laudo: Exp. No. 180/961. *Jefe del Departamento del Distrito Federal v. Sindicato Nacional de Trabajadores del Distrito Federal. See also* TFCA Laudo: Exp. No. 425/61. *Pablo Castillo Cervera v. Secretario de Gobernación.*

[69] *See* LOPJF, Art. 10, Section 9.

[70] All states, including the Federal District, have established state *Juntas de Conciliación y Arbitraje*, similar to the federal model. *See* www.stps.gob.mx/stps1/stpsvp.htm. State legislation on labour relations may be found at www.juridicas.unam.mx (both sites visited Jan. 2004).

[71] *See supra*, text accompanying note 60.

properties in the hands of relatively few families and the destitution of rural peasant farmers (*campesinos*) it is not surprising that issues of land ownership received much attention at the Constitutional Congress of 1916–1917.[72] The constitutional debates took place against a background of revolutionary ideals (the battle cry of Emiliano Zapata and his followers was '*Tierra y Libertad*') that sought radical reforms, including land expropriation on a major scale, which were resisted by some of the constitutional framers.

The final result was the adoption of a lengthy provision, Article 27 of the Constitution, that guarantees private property rights but establishes significant limitations on land ownership and exploitation. Article 27 begins with a pronouncement that all property located within the territory of Mexico belongs originally to the nation, which has the right to transmit ownership rights to private parties. This sets the tone for the lengthy third paragraph of Article 27, which provides the foundation for government control over and limitations of private ownership, including authorization for Congress and state legislatures to adopt laws establishing the maximum amount of land that one person or company could own; how expropriation would be conducted and how expropriated land was to be divided up; and the amount of compensation owed to owners whose properties were expropriated. Article 27 also established a constitutional foundation for a form of communal property, the *ejido* (discussed below) that had its origins in pre-Hispanic indigenous cultures. Finally, Article 27 established the parameters for ownership of land, forest, and water resources for rural population centres.[73] Article 27 has been amended sixteen times, and the 1992 amendment, discussed below, effectively ended the period of rural land reform in Mexico.

4.2. Land Reform: 1917–1992[74]

Even before the Constitution of 1917 was ratified, on 16 January 1915 President Venustiano Carranza issued a decree that declared null and void numerous transfers of communal lands that had taken place during the Porfiriato dictatorship. This decree was eventually incorporated into the third paragraph of Article 27,[75] and laid the foundations for subsequent laws that would implement campaigns of agrarian reform. However, despite the

[72] Rouaix, P., *Génesis de los artículos 27 a 123 de la Constitución Política de 1917* (Mexico: PRI, 1983). According to historian John Mason Hart, nineteenth-century liberal reforms forced the divestiture of Church-owned properties that had previously been leased to local farmers. These properties were confiscated and sold to the highest bidders, leading to vast accumulations of land in *haciendas* owned by rich *hacendados*, many of them absentee owners. Hart, J.M., *Revolutionary Mexico* (Berkeley: University of California Press, 1987).

[73] Section VII , as amended on 6 Dec. 1937.

[74] On Mexican land reform laws generally, *see* Calva, J.L., *La disputa por la tierra* (Mexico: Fontamara, 1993) at 27; Mendieta y Núñez, L., *El problema agrario de México* (Mexico: Porrúa, 1968) at 41.

[75] Fix-Zamudio, H., *Setenta y cinco años de evolución del Poder Judicial en México* (Mexico: INERM/FCE, 1988) at 323–324.

adamant desire of proponents, effective land reform and the breakup of large landholdings did not happen immediately. The first law adopted on the subject, the Law of Communal Lands (*Ley de Ejidos*) of 28 December 1920 was repealed by President Obregón soon after he took office in 1921. It was not until the presidency of Plutarco Elias Calles (1924–1928) that meaningful distribution of agricultural lands began to take place. During the Calles presidency, 3 million hectares (7.4 million acres) of land (triple the amount distributed under Obregón) were expropriated[76] from large landholders (both Mexican and foreign) and redistributed to individuals and to communal farms (*ejidos*). The largest land redistribution was to take place under President Lázaro Cárdenas (1934–1940), when almost 18 million hectares (44 million acres) were expropriated and redistributed[77] pursuant to the *Código Agrario de los Estados Unidos Mexicanos* of 1934.[78] Successive codes refined the land reform system, eventually resulting in the adoption in 1971 of the Agrarian Reform Law (*Ley Federal de Reforma Agraria*),[79] which remained in force until major constitutional reforms in 1992 effectively ended Mexican agrarian reform, as discussed below.

The 1971 Agrarian Reform Law established a limit of 100 hectares (247 acres) as the maximum size of agricultural property that could be owned by one person, in accordance with the limits established in Article 27 of the Constitution.[80] In addition, the Mexican government attempted to use the Agrarian Reform Law not only to bring about land reform, but also to generate conditions that would raise productivity in Mexican agriculture. The Secretariat of Agrarian Reform became responsible for the enforcement of Agrarian Reform Law, the elimination of *ejidos*, and the authentication of property ownership.

In authorizing land redistribution and controls on the creation of new large landholdings, the Agrarian Reform Law had an unintended effect of limiting private investment in agriculture. As the following section shows, the existence of the *ejido* made private investment irrelevant in many agricultural zones. Furthermore, Article 27 of the Constitution prohibited ownership of agricultural lands by corporations (*sociedades mercantiles*), as a way of preventing wealthy families from reasserting their control of the countryside by using corporate vehicles. These measures, unfortunately, were severely to limit the productivity of Mexican agriculture, which could only survive through an elaborate system of price supports and controls maintained by the PRI-dominated government.

[76] Miller, R., *Mexico: A History* (Norman, Okla: University of Oklahoma Press, 1985).
[77] *Id.* [78] D.O. 20 Mar. 1934. [79] D.O. 22 Mar. 1971.
[80] Art. 27, Section X, as amended on 12 Feb. 1947, established the minimum surface measurement of an individual unit of land that could be awarded to a peasant. According to Section XV of Art. 27, a small farm would be defined as land for agricultural use that did not exceed 100 hectares of irrigated land or high quality wetlands, or their equivalent in any other type of land used for farming or raising livestock.

4.3. Communal Farmlands: The *Ejido*

The breakup of large landholdings went hand in hand with the creation of a new form of landholding, the communal farm or *ejido*. Created pursuant to Section VII of Article 27 of the Constitution, the *ejido* had its origins in pre-Hispanic indigenous culture. Indigenous pre-Hispanic cultures preserved agricultural land in communal landholdings, called *calpuli* by the Aztecs. *Calpuli* lands were a form of permanent joint tenancy; no person had any individual interest in any piece of property. In the modern-day *ejido*, however, the *ejidatario*, or individual member of an *ejido*, receives a particular piece of land (*parcela*) to cultivate; if he does not use the land productively, it may be taken from him and given to another person.

In accordance with Article 27, lands registered as part of an *ejido* could never be alienated; they were considered to be the permanent property of a local group or community: the residents of the *ejido*. Not only could *ejido* lands not be sold, they could not be pledged in guarantee of loans, since foreclosure and sale was impossible.[81]

The *ejido*, which was governed by the federal Agrarian Reform Law, normally includes: the land necessary for agricultural purposes (cultivation, animal husbandry); land used for residential purposes; school lands; and other communal property needed to satisfy the community's needs. The *ejidos* themselves had legal personality and were granted rights over specific lands, which were registered before the National Agrarian Registry (*Registro Agrario Nacional*) by the Assembly of *ejidatarios* (members of the *ejido*). While formally having much in common, *ejidos* differed from locality to locality, according to ethnic, cultural, and economic histories. Some *ejidos* had operated as communal entities even before the Mexican Revolution, while others were newly created by law.

By 1991, 27,399 *ejidos* existed in México, with a population of 2.7 million *ejidatarios*, which controlled 16.6 million hectares (41 million acres) of agricultural land.[82] While providing a measure of stability to the countryside, however, the *ejido* system also contained inherent weaknesses. The inability to alienate property made it impossible to secure loans for farm improvements, and the *ejido* became dependent on only one source of funding, a government-owned agricultural bank called Banrural: another example of Mexican corporatism.[83]

4.4. Failure of the Land Reform System and the 1992 Constitutional Reforms

If measured by the total acreage of land redistributed from large landowners to peasant farmers, Article 27 and the agrarian reform laws represent an important accomplishment. Between 1970 and 1980 the federal government

[81] Mexican Constitution, Art. 27 prior to the 1992 reforms.
[82] INEGI, VII Censo Ejidal, 1991, available at www.pa.gob.mx (site visited Jan. 2004).
[83] On corporatism in Mexican governance, *see* Chapter 5 above, Section 4.3.

expropriated and distributed 12 million hectares (30 million acres) of agricultural land to peasant farmers, including distributions to *ejidos*.[84] Unfortunately, neither the redistribution of land nor the creation of *ejidos* satisfied the country's needs for agricultural productivity. Agricultural production by small farms is less efficient than large-scale farming. In addition, the inability of *ejidos* to pledge property, and the inability of corporations to engage in agricultural production, made it difficult to finance capital improvements to enhance productivity. A drive through the Mexican countryside, dotted with ploughs pulled by oxen and other picturesque bucolic scenes, were testament to the lack of agricultural investment and low productivity of labour in many rural areas. With some exceptions, the overall lack of private capital investment in agricultural production consigned Mexican farm workers to centuries-old farming techniques. The widespread use of oxen and donkeys may have been picturesque for tourists visiting the countryside, but they did not translate into high wages and productivity.

As with labour law, agrarian law was administered by the PRI in a paternalistic and populist fashion, and it contributed to the strengthening grip of the ruling party over the Mexican political scene. The PRI drew much of its strength among the rural peasantry from the conditions of abject poverty that pervaded peasant life, and from the lack of any competing institution that demonstrated ongoing concern for the rural poor. Even the Catholic Church, a powerful institution throughout Mexico, has refrained from taking an active role in alleviating rural poverty. The PRI, operating through governmental agrarian agencies, monopolized the field of rural welfare, and thus succeeded in creating broad grassroots support in elections, obtaining votes in exchange for preferential treatment or favours (*clientelismo*).[85] In keeping with this practice, the *Confederación Nacional Campesina* (CNC), or National Peasant Confederation, was created in 1935 as the organization responsible for unifying and bringing peasants into the party fold by acting as a social advocate for land distribution and for the improvement of rural conditions.

Agrarian reform, and in particular the redistribution of agrarian lands, represented a major achievement of the Mexican Revolution. While vast differences of wealth still exist in Mexico, the concentration of wealth in rural areas, where a vast percentage of the population lives, was alleviated by limiting the size of individually owned ranches and farms, and by the establishment of the *ejido* system of communal properties. In the 1970s the federal government established a government-owned bank, Banrural, that helped small farmers finance agriculture production and improve their lands. Seventy years of agrarian reform had a salutary social effect, by giving small farmers more control over their lives, but it did not improve the productivity of Mexico's agricultural

[84] www.ciesas.edu.mx/bibdf/ini (site visited Jan. 2004).

[85] *Cf.* Cossío Díaz, J.R., 'El orden jurídico (corporativo) mexicano y el cambio democrático II', in *Este País*, no. 79, Oct. 1997, at 51–56.

sector, which lagged far behind that of neighbouring countries Canada and the United States.

By the end of the 1980s virtually all the large landholdings in Mexico had been redistributed. As Mexico began to turn from a centrally controlled economy to one based on private enterprise and investment, the paternalistic attitude towards the countryside became increasingly out of step with the overall economic strategy promoted by Presidents Salinas de Gortari and Zedillo (who served as Secretary of Public Education under President Salinas). By 1992 these economic reformers were ready to replace the politics of land redistribution and of paternalistic, centralized support of basic agriculture.

4.4.1. 1992 Reforms[86]

Agrarian reform came to an abrupt end on 6 January 1992, when Article 27 of the Constitution was amended, repealing the provisions pertaining to land redistribution.[87] The goal of these amendments was to attract more investment to the countryside, by removing restrictions on alienation of communal lands and on the use of corporate forms of investment. Under previous laws, *ejidos* were treated as sacrosanct communal lands that could not be sold or threatened with foreclosure. With the reforms of 1992, a new Agrarian Law (*Ley Agraria*) was adopted in 1992,[88] abrogating the Federal Agrarian Reform Law. Pursuant to the new Agrarian Law, *ejidatarios* can now vote to pledge their lands as security for loans, or to form partnerships with outside interests.[89] Moreover, *ejidatarios* can transfer their individual land rights to other members of the *ejido*, although no individual can own more than 5 per cent of the total land of the *ejido* or exceed the maximum size of a small farm established by law.[90] *Ejidatarios* can vote to sell or rent their lands, and can obtain financing from credit institutions, provided that these institutions are qualified to use land belonging to *ejidos* as collateral for loans.[91]

The most important provisions of the new Agrarian Law are as follows.

(a) The government's constitutional obligation to redistribute agricultural land was terminated by the 1992 reforms of Article 27. As a result, private landowners who make capital investments in agricultural lands no longer risk being expropriated.

(b) Land rights disputes between *ejidatarios* and private landholders are now settled by Agrarian Tribunals, rather than by the Federal Secretariat of Agrarian Reform.

(c) *Ejidatarios* can obtain individual certificates of title to their land parcels if their *ejido* agrees to participate in the PROCEDE (*Programa de Certificación*

[86] For a study of the agrarian law reforms after 1992, *see* Zepeda, G., TRANSFORMACIÓN AGRARIA (Mexico: CIDAC/Miguel Angel Porrúa, 2000).

[87] D.O. 6 Jan. 1992.

[88] D.O. 26 Feb. 1992.

[89] *See Ley Agraria* (LA), Arts. 23, Section IX, 50, and 75.

[90] LA, Art. 47.

[91] LA, Art. 51.

de Derechos Ejidales y Titulación de Solares Urbanos) a governmental programme created to certify title to rural property.

(d) *Ejidatarios* who have had their boundaries certified have the right to sell, rent, or sharecrop their property, or mortgage it as collateral for loans.

(e) *Ejidatarios* are no longer required to work their parcels personally.

(f) Individual farmers are limited to 254 acres of irrigated land.

(g) No single *ejidatario* can acquire through purchases more than 5 per cent of land in any *ejido*.

(h) *Ejidatarios* can form joint ventures with outside investors.

(i) Foreign entities may invest in *ejidos*, provided that they do not own more than 49 per cent of the capital of the entity created.

While *ejidatarios* may not form themselves into a corporation, they may form any kind of partnership, whether civil or commercial, desired to ensure the development of their lands, or for the commercialization and transformation of the *ejido*'s products or services.[92]

Finally, the 1992 constitutional amendment abrogated the former prohibition of ownership in agricultural lands by corporations. Under the current law, a Mexican corporation may own an unlimited amount of agricultural land if such ownership falls within the corporate purposes as specified in the corporation's bylaws. A foreign corporation may not directly own agricultural lands in Mexico, although there is no prohibition of foreign ownership of a Mexican corporation that owns agricultural lands, so long as the land is not located in the prohibited zones along the coasts and borders of Mexico.[93]

4.5. Dispute Settlement of Agrarian Reform Actions

As land redistribution waned, most disputes have involved the protection and administration of *ejidos*. For many years such disputes were resolved by administrative bodies within the *Secretaría de Reforma Agraria*, although Mexican legal scholars argued that agrarian disputes should be resolved by the judicial system. The 1992 reform put an end to any argument on this matter: Section XIX of Article 27 states that 'Any pending matter that may arise between two or more communities or population centres (*núcleos poblacionales*) regarding the limits of plots of land on *ejidos* or *comunidades*,[94] regardless of the origin of these *ejidos* or *comunidades*, are the jurisdiction of the federal judiciary; as are any disputes relating to possession of land on *ejidos* and *comunidades*'. This reform empowered Congress to create federal courts with sole jurisdiction to handle agrarian disputes; these *tribunales agrarios* operate

[92] LA, Art. 50.

[93] On the restrictions on foreign ownership of lands along coasts and borders, *see* Chapter 16 below, Section 2.7.1.

[94] The term *comunidad* refers to a communal grouping that has indigenous origins. *Comunidades* preceded adoption of the 1917 Constitution which created the *ejido*, and are subject to the same rules as *ejidos*.

under simplified rules of procedure,[95] and final judgments are subject to *amparo* procedures.

5. Other Government Welfare Practices

5.1. The Mexican Welfare State

As discussed in Chapter 1 above, throughout the twentieth century the PRI was able to maintain political control in part by portraying itself as a patriarchal protector of the needy: the sole embodiment of the ideals of the Mexican Revolution. Neither the Catholic Church nor private philanthropy has contributed meaningfully to the protection of the vast numbers of Mexicans living below the level of poverty.[96] Instead, to the extent that poverty has been addressed institutionally at all, it has occurred through the creation of a social welfare infrastructure composed of federal agencies dominated by the federal executive branch.

Although numerous social 'rights' were written into the Constitution (e.g. the rights to health protection and adequate housing, or the rights of children to adequate food and health written into Article 4), it was impossible, absent a radical socioeconomic revolution, for the PRI to satisfy such rights as if they were entitlements, rather than goals or aspirations. If the PRI had attempted to guarantee such rights and failed, it would have lost control of government. Supporters of this system justified the government's stance by stressing the political nature of the Constitution, holding up the Constitution as a political instrument rather than a socioeconomic blueprint; in this view, social rights and constitutionally mandated social programmes could only be implemented to the extent that resources were available. Since such social rights were not fully guaranteed, the government was able to maintain flexibility in administering social welfare, and was not subject to challenge over eligibility, scope of rights, etc.

[95] *See Ley Orgánica de los Tribunales Agrarios* (LOTA), D.O. 26 Feb. 1992; internal regulations of these tribunals were published in D.O. 8 May 1992). LOTA, Art. 2 states that the agrarian tribunal system will consist of a Superior Agrarian Tribunal headquartered in Mexico City, and of trial courts presided over by a single judge which would be spread throughout the nation. These trial-level tribunals are responsible for hearing all controversies stemming from application of agrarian law, which includes matters related to *ejidos*, the organization of *ejidos*, limits, quality, and use of lands, waters, and forests belonging to *ejidos*, the creation of new *ejidos*, *comunidades*, rural partnerships, and small holdings of land, forests, and waters.

Agrarian disputes follow a simple procedure. The proceedings are set in motion by the filing of a petition, followed by the issuing of a summons to the defendant and a response to the petition. The court then holds a hearing on defence motions and takes evidence, during which the judge has broad latitude to examine the parties and witnesses. At the conclusion of the hearing, a judgment is handed down, which can be reviewed on appeal by the Superior Agrarian Tribunal. Decisions issued by the trial courts and by the Superior Agrarian Tribunal may be challenged in *juicios de amparo directo* before a Circuit Court Panel.

[96] According to the World Bank's *World Development Report 2000/2001: Attacking Poverty*, over 26.3 million Mexican citizens, or 27% of the population, live below the level of extreme poverty, which is defined as a *per capita* income of US$1.00 per day.

This is not to say that the PRI failed entirely to fulfil its role as social welfare agent. To the contrary, over the years the PRI was able to construct a network of agencies to carry out sometimes ambitious social welfare programmes that were affordable under budgetary constraints. We focus here on two of the most important: education and health care.

5.2. The Right to Education

On 11 December 1916 the constitutional framers submitted to the Assembly the draft report on Article 3 proposed by Carranza.[97] The draft envisaged mandatory and free primary education, but the principal debates focused on 'freedom of education': that is, whether religious education should be restricted or prohibited.[98] The version of Article 3 that was finally adopted included a severe restriction on religious education: 'Education shall be free, but public education shall be secular, as shall primary, secondary and higher education in private schools. No religious organization or cleric of any faith may create or manage primary schools'.

Free education at the elementary and secondary school levels is the one social right written into the Constitution that has been most widely given effect.[99] As is the case in other areas of Mexican law, this has been done through the 'federalization' of the subject matter. Unlike the United States, in which public schools are financed and administered at the state and local levels, public education in Mexico is primarily federal, administered by the *Secretaría de Educación Pública* (SEP) and funded out of the federal government budget. Since the 1992 constitutional reforms to Article 3, state and municipality governments have been responsible for the *administration* of the educational establishments located in their jurisdictions (schools, libraries, or laboratories). However, the federal government continues to serve as the principal source of funding for primary and secondary public education; federal funds are distributed to the states and Federal District for administration by local authorities, along with additional funds provided by localities. The Federal government continues to maintain control over the evaluation and regulation of education at all levels; over the distribution of free text-books for primary and secondary levels; and over curricular programmes.

[97] *Diario de los Debates*, 11 Dec. 1916, pp. 370–371.

[98] *Diario de los Debates*, 13 Dec. 1916, pp. 436–437. The debates mainly focused on whether the Catholic Church should be allowed to offer education. The discussion featured two different schools of thought regarding freedom of education: those who wanted the government to decide whether to ban parochial school education, and those who favoured leaving that choice to parents, which implies the freedom to establish any type of schools. Many framers, influenced by the calls for social justice underlying the Revolution, believed that the state had the right as well as the obligation to control basic aspects of social life, including education, which should not be left to private choice.

[99] For more detailed information in connection with the freedom of education *see* Chapter 7 above.

Of course, it is one thing to guarantee the existence of public schools for all children, and quite another to provide the quality of education that children need. Despite the constitutional guarantee of free primary and secondary education, and despite the construction of schools throughout the country, the federal government has never been willing to provide an education budget that can keep up with the population growth and still provide quality education. (As in the United States, the existence of private schools has helped alleviate the challenge of providing a quality education for all, but these schools are only available to the middle and upper classes; the urban and rural poor are left with underfunded public schools taught by underpaid teachers.) Because of high birth rates, the number of school-age children has always been a relatively large percentage of the Mexican population,[100] placing a burden on society to generate the tax base to support quality schools for the millions of youngsters who enter the school system each year. Thus, while the amount budgeted for education (based on 1996 prices) grew from $7.9 million pesos in 1963, to $46.3 million pesos in 1978[101] this increase in fact failed to keep up with increases in the school-age population and in inflation. Indeed, in terms of percentage of the federal budget, the budget for education *decreased* from 21.83 per cent of the total budget in 1963 to 8.15 per cent in 1978.[102] The amount spent on education in 1999 was 181 billion pesos (approximately 18 billion dollars), equivalent to 5.54% of the gross domestic product.

Under the 1993 General Law of Education (*Ley General de Educación*)[103] the federal government has attempted to redress inequities in public education for groups and in regions that are economically or socially disadvantaged. The main measures include: special attention to schools in remote or low-income urban areas; support for teachers who work at schools in these areas; providing special educational services for students who drop out of the regular educational system; a distance learning system of education; scholarship programmes; and providing incentives for non-profit organizations and teacher co-operatives involved in education.

5.3. The Right to Health Care

Beginning in the mid-1970s, Article 4 of the Constitution underwent a series of amendments to strengthen the social welfare provisions of the Constitution. One such amendment added paragraph 4 to Article 4, and established that all

[100] In 2000 the number of school-age children was 19,700,930, which represents 20.2% of the total population of Mexico. The birth rate has declined in recent years, thanks to government support of family planning.

[101] *Mexico Social, 1994–1995* (Mexico: División de Estudios Económicos y Sociales, Banco Nacional de México, S.A., 1996) (figures based on 1996 prices).

[102] *Ibid.*

[103] *Ley General de Educación*, Arts. 32–36, D.O. 13 July 1993, as last amended on 13 Mar. 2003.

persons are entitled to protection of their health, and that the law would define the rules, terms, and conditions for access to health care services.[104]

The right to health care has its roots in the type of rights granted to workers by Article 123 of the Constitution. In September 1929 Section XXIX of Article 123 of the Constitution was amended to provide the basis for the enactment of a social security law that could provide payments for disability, old age, involuntary termination of work, work-related illness and accident insurance, and other types of related insurance.[105] It was not until 1943, however, that the *Ley del Seguro Social* (Social Security Law)[106] was finally enacted, initially for the purpose of protecting workers, as provided under Article 123. The Social Security Law was eventually extended to protect subjects such as peasants, disadvantaged groups, bureaucrats, and others not necessarily covered by the provisions of Article 123. In 1960 Section B was added to Article 123 of the Constitution, establishing the basis for a specific health care system for workers at the service of the state (federal, state, and municipal government).

In Mexico, the government social security system has long provided health care to citizens through a social security system. Unlike in the United States, this health care is primarily carried out by hospitals maintained by government agencies and physicians who are on the public payroll. The social security system also included a rudimentary form of retirement fund, although in 1992 the federal government adopted a law creating a new, more ambitious system of retirement funds: the *Sistema de Ahorro para el Retiro*, or SAR.[107]

The National Health Care System (*Sistema Nacional de Salud*) is made up of four institutions covering four major subgroups of the population. The IMSS

[104] D.O. 3 Feb. 1983.

A further amendment to Art. 4 established the 'right' of all families to enjoy decent and suitable housing, stating that the law would determine the instruments and supports required to reach this objective. D.O. 7 Feb. 1983. The main provisions regarding the right to housing are set forth in Sections A and B of Art. 123 of the Constitution, which deals with housing for workers. Legislation has been adopted to support this right, such as the *Ley del INFONAVIT*, D.O. 24 Apr. 1972, and the *Ley sobre el Sistema Nacional de Asistencia Social*, D.O. 9 Jan. 1986. Separate federal agencies, INFONAVIT and FOVI, have been created to administer public housing programmes. Aside from the provisions of Art. 123, however, there has been no clear attempt by the Mexican government to fulfil this 'right to housing', which has been interpreted not as an entitlement, but rather as a goal dependent upon the availability of public resources. Lack of available housing in Mexico is a serious problem today, since the pace of new housing construction has not kept up with population growth in the country. This has translated into a chronic housing shortage, which has contributed to the increase of an average occupancy rate per home from 4.9 in 1929 to 5.8 in 1990. As occupancy rates show, not even a dramatic increase in new public housing construction from 1983 to 1990 has solved the problem: a total of 2,020,575 new units built (with public and private funds) during this period compared to a total of 511,044 units built in 1971–1979. *ESTADÍSTICAS HISTÓRICAS DE MÉXICO* (Mexico: INEGI, 1990). The answer to adequate housting in Mexico is likely to come from the improvement of the mortgage lending market (there is no secondary market to speak of) and the increased availability of private lending to families of moderate income, rather than with publicly financed housing.

[105] Soberanes Fernández, J.L., 'Regímenes de seguridad social en el derecho mexicano', in *LA SEGURIDAD SOCIAL Y EL ESTADO MODERNO* (Mexico: IMSS/FCE/ISSSTE, 1992) at 176–187.

[106] D.O. 21 Dec. 1995, as last amended 21 Dec. 2001.

[107] *See* Chapter 20 below, at text accompanying notes 85–89.

(*Instituto Mexicano del Seguro Social*)[108] covers workers employed by private enterprises; the ISSSTE (*Instituto de Seguridad y Servicios Sociales de Trabajadores del Estado*) covers persons who provide service in government agencies;[109] the IMSS covers workers employed by PEMEX, the state-owned oil industry; and the Secretariat of National Defence and the Secretariat of the Navy provide medical care to the members of the armed forces through the Institute of Social Security for the Mexican Armed Forces (*Instituto de Seguridad Social para las Fuerzas Armadas Mexicanas*). In each of these systems, cover is extended to the family members of the workers or their beneficiaries. The segment of the population that is entitled to receive these health care benefits is called the *población derechohabientes* (the eligible population) and this group includes, in addition to those groups listed above, pensioners and their family members. Other citizens, known as the *población abierta* (open or uncovered population) consists of persons who may have access to certain health care services through institutions like the Secretariat of Health and state or municipal institutions.[110]

The Mexican system of public health care appears admirable when compared with the United States, where an aversion to public health care exists. This is especially true given the level of poverty that exists in Mexico, and its relative lack of fiscal resources. The Mexican system, especially the IMSS and ISSSTE, are nevertheless criticized for failing to provide quality health care, and those who can afford to do so often use private hospitals and doctors, even if they are eligible to use the IMSS or ISSSTE systems.

108 On IMSS, *see* www.imss.gob.mx (site visited Jan. 2004).

109 For information on ISSSTE, *see* www.issste.gob.mx (site visited Jan. 2004).

110 In 1944, the population that used the National Health Care System was made up of 53% eligible persons and 47% 'open population'; in real terms nationwide, the number of persons who see national health care system doctors is 84% of the eligible population, 48% of the open population, and 68% of the entire population. MÉXICO SOCIAL, 1994–1995 (Mexico: División de Estudios Económicos y Sociales, Banco Nacional de México, S.A., 1996); *see also* Laurel, A.C. and Ruiz, L., *¿PODEMOS GARANTIZAR EL DERECHO A LA SALUD?* (Mexico: Universidad Autónoma Metropolitana, 1996) at 23.

14

The Civil and Commercial Codes

1. Introduction

As noted in Chapter 1 above, Spanish law continued to be used throughout Mexico even after the country gained its independence. It would take many years for leaders in the new nation to adopt legal regimes suited to local circumstances. The fledgling nation's pressing need for consolidation of political power led Mexico's early leaders to focus their attention on developing structures of *public law*: legal forms for regulating relations between the government and its citizens, and between governmental entities. The development of *private law*, the laws that govern relations between individuals, associations, and corporations, was another story altogether. The survival of Spanish legal sources was much more prevalent in private law than in public law, and owed much to the Spanish legal training of the first Mexican jurists, who were grounded in doctrines of Justinian Roman Law.[1] In areas of private law, some attempts were made to change or repeal prior laws, as a logical corollary to the politically charged agenda of the independence movement. Nevertheless, the legal order established by the Spanish to govern private affairs was not immediately displaced by Mexico's break from the mother country. It would take many decades (and the development of intellectual resources) for the new nation to graft its own legal models on those inherited from Spain. Eventually, Mexico would develop its own laws governing private affairs and commercial matters, adapting European models to fit local needs.

2. Codification in Europe

European governments underwent considerable changes following the French Revolution, due to two major forces: the need to prevent social unrest that could lead to further uprisings, and the rise to power of enlightened rulers who held a broader vision of society and culture. Legislation enacted between the early eighteenth and the late nineteenth centuries was, to a great extent, the product of that period of enlightenment.

As European governments became more responsive to their inhabitants, there emerged a growing need to simplify the content and number of laws and,

[1] Ots y Capdequí, José María, *Historia del Derecho Español en America y del Derecho Indiano* (Madrid: Ed. Aguilar, 1964) at 349.

particularly, to provide access to laws.[2] In an effort to achieve these goals, the legislative bodies of European countries of the eighteenth and early nineteenth centuries set out to classify and systematize uses, customs, ordinances, decrees, and jurisprudence, subsequently publishing the fruits of their endeavour in the form of codes.[3]

The most important of these codes governing subjects of private law was the French Civil Code of 1804. This code is often referred to as the *Code Napoleon*, after Emperor Napoleon Bonaparte, during whose reign the French Civil Code was adopted as a means of establishing a set of rules that could be understood and applied at all levels of society. The original *Code Napoleon* was divided into three books. One book dealt with the status of persons and relations between persons, including marital status and legal competency, birth, domicile and family relations, matrimony, divorce, and filial relationships. A second book covered 'property and the different modifications of ownership'; and a third book focused on 'the different forms of acquiring ownership'. This logical organization of the major principles of civil law[4] and the dissemination of civil codes in published form gave people access to the law, and coincidentally promoted academic discussion and political debate.

The codification movement was founded on the theory that codification of private law should clearly set out the most important rules governing private relations. Drafters of the civil codes, including the *Code Napoleon*, attempted to define these rules in terms that were understandable to non-lawyers, so that all parties involved may become more aware of their rights and obligations. Codification efforts involved attempts to construct an entire, self-contained body of rules that would serve to govern all aspects of private relations through a structured collection of interconnected rules.[5]

The initial codifications of private law in Europe and the Americas have gradually evolved along with socioeconomic changes, but this type of evolution

[2] This was not the first time such a task was undertaken; centuries earlier, canon law had been developed by the Church as the 'first modern Western legal system'. *See generally* Berman, J.J., *La formación de la tradición jurídica de Occidente* (Mexico: Fondo de Cultura Económica, Mexico, 1996) at 211.

[3] The wave of codification in Europe, which yielded the Commercial and Civil Codes, was the result of a conjunction of prevailing interests, including those of the *bourgeoisie* whose prosperity was linked to the development of rules to promote commerce and private property. Gonzalez, Ma. del Refugio, 'Comercio y Comerciantes en México en el Siglo XIX', in *Centenario del Código de Comercio* (Mexico: UNAM, 1991) at 225.

For a discussion of the development of civil codes in nineteenth-century Europe, *see* Valladao, H.T., *Derecho Internacional Privado* (Mexico: Ed. Trillas, 1987) (trans. Leonel Pereznieto Castro) at 174 *et seq.*

[4] 'Civil law', also referred to as 'private law', was the term commonly used in contrast with 'public law'. The conceptual distinction between the two types of law was valid until shortly after WWI, when certain fields of the law underwent a transformation as a result of state intervention in the economy. Fields such as labour law, which until that time had fallen largely under the realm of private law, became areas in which the state desired to be more involved in order to defend the rights of labour. Such was also the case of the defence of the rights of minors.

[5] On codification of the civil law generally, *see* Zweigert, J., *Comparative Law* (Oxford: Oxford University Press, 3rd ed., 1994).

moves slowly. Civil and commercial codes have gradually evolved, especially in countries with legal systems that allow judicial precedent (*jurisprudencia*) to play an important role, as has been the case in most countries of Europe and in a few Latin American countries such as Argentina, Uruguay, and Chile. In most Latin American countries, including Mexico, judicial precedents continue to play a minor role in the development of codified law.[6]

The codification movement in Europe extended to rules of civil and commercial procedure, which were codified during the nineteenth century to establish the rights of litigating parties and define the powers of judges and other authorities. Procedural codification can be useful in controlling abuse of judicial authority, but it may also act as a strait-jacket to judicial reform. The excessive formality brought about by codification has sometimes been stifling and may lead to sacrificing justice in favour of procedural conformity. There is a tendency for legal systems based on codified law to become bogged down by the weight of their own formality in attempting to confront the most pressing needs of society. Countries with highly evolved systems of codified law have found a way to remedy these shortcomings: by giving judicial precedent a major role in interpreting the rules contained in the codes, in order to remain in step with the changing times.

3. Codification of Commercial Law in Mexico

By the mid-nineteenth century Mexico had begun to emerge from the political disruptions of early independence. The development of commerce and urban life prompted the need for a modernized body of laws to govern commercial matters. Finally, by 1854 Congress had adopted the first Commercial Code in Mexico, the Lares Code (*Código Lares*), after Teodosio Lares, the cabinet minister who championed its adoption. The Lares Code adhered to the European tradition of exhaustive and comprehensive codification of laws.[7] For the first time in its history, Mexico had a set of commercial rules that reflected the particular circumstances of the economy and society. Unfortunately, the Lares Code had a short life. One year after it went into effect, the Code was annulled by the government of General Antonio López de Santa Anna. In 1855 his successor, President Ignacio Comonfort, repealed all of Santa Anna's legislation, and in 1863, during the French intervention, the Emperor Maximilian re-enacted the Lares Code, but its formal legal effectiveness was as short-lived as the Emperor's reign. Nevertheless, Juan B. Pardo, a treatise writer of the times,

[6] On the development of Mexican *jurisprudencia* on issues of civil law, *see* Pereznieto, Leonel, Derecho Internacional Privado, notas sobre el principio territorialista y el sistema de conflictos en el derecho mexicano (Mexico: UNAM, 2nd ed., 1980) at 27 *et seq*.

[7] 'This body of law—the Commercial Code of 1854—was influenced by the Spanish Code of 1829, from which it copied its organizational structure and almost every one of its provisions'. Barrera Graf, J., 'Codificación en México, antecedentes del Código de Comercio de 1889, Perspectivas', in Centenario del Código de Comercio, *supra* note 3 at 72 (authors' trans.).

reasoned that the reinstatement of the liberal government in 1856 left the Lares Code as 'the only Code in force in most of the States of the Federation'.[8]

The Lares Code was eventually replaced by the Code of Commerce of 1884. The 1884 code drew from the Lares Code, which itself had been influenced by modern commercial codes developed in France and Italy in the middle of the century. Implementation of the 1884 Code 'changed in our country the traditional [. . .] subjective structure of mercantile laws, a tradition followed both by Spanish colonial legislation as well as the first texts of an independent Mexico [. . . ; Mexico came] to adopt the objective French model of commercial acts'.[9] Earlier commercial rules placed greater emphasis on the characteristics of the businessman or trader, i.e. on the person who was registered to enter into acts of commerce. In the 1884 Code, on the other hand, the focus shifted to the act of commerce itself; a commercial act was determined by the nature of the act itself, rather than by the characteristics of the parties who entered into it. This tendency to focus on the act as opposed to the person carrying out the act continued well on into the future. Thus, under Article 4 of the Commercial Code of 1889, private parties may be subject to the Code if they undertake acts that are defined as commercial acts.

By the last decade of the nineteenth century, Mexico was in the midst of a long period of economic growth under Porfirio Diaz, the dictator who ruled Mexico until 1910. Merchants and landholders who supported the Diaz regime sought to strengthen the legal regime that would preserve property rights and the enforcement of contracts, especially since the economic growth under Diaz was not uniformly distributed throughout society. The result was the adoption by Congress of the Code of Commerce of 1889. Despite massive economic and societal changes since its adoption, this Code remains in force as the basic commercial law of Mexico: a nineteenth-century Code in a twenty-first century economy.

The principal difference between the 1884 and 1889 Commercial Codes was the greater inclusiveness of the latter; while the 1884 Code only considered individuals as merchants, the 1889 Code included companies, including foreign corporations, as merchants subject to the Code.[10] Aside from establishing rules generally to cover generic acts of commerce, the 1889 Code also provided specific rules governing particular types of commercial transactions, such as commercial sales, secured financing, and insurance. The 1889 Code was quite advanced for an expanding society on the threshold of a new century.

The 1889 Code of Commerce covered the basic areas of commerce known at the time, including commercial transportation of goods by land, maritime commerce, bankruptcy and suspension of payment, and commercial procedure. As the economy developed throughout the twentieth century, however, many specialized forms of commerce developed. Rather than attempt to carry out multiple amendments to the Code of Commerce, Congress chose to adopt from

[8] *Id.* at 73. [9] *Id.* at 69. [10] González, *supra* note 3 at 240.

time to time specialized legislation on many types of commercial activities. These laws include the General Law of Title and Credit Operations,[11] the General Law of Corporations,[12] the Law of Bankruptcy and Suspension of Payments,[13] and other specialized commercial laws that are discussed below in Chapters 18 and 20. Specialized legislation adopted subsequent to 1889 takes precedence over the Code of Commerce, and has in fact rendered the 1889 Code—which is discussed in more detail in Chapter 18—an antiquated set of substantive provisions that are only occasionally applied as supplementary rules.[14] As a result, the 1889 Code of Commerce serves primarily as a source of procedural rules governing commercial litigation, as well as a source of supplementary rules applicable to those commercial activities that are regulated by more specific laws, such as the *Ley General de Sociedades Mercantiles*, or corporations law, discussed below in Chapter 19, or the *Ley General de Títulos y Operaciones de Crédito*, discussed below in Chapter 20.

Despite the antiquated nature of the Commercial Code, there has been little support for a movement to replace it with a modern code. The most recent reforms of the Commercial Code were adopted in 1993,[15] to reinforce the rules governing commercial arbitration and to define more clearly the rules regarding jurisdiction in commercial matters.[16] The basic rules of the Commercial Code are still sound, and much of the law of specific commercial transactions has been set forth in subsequent laws covering specific types of transactions.

4. Codification of Civil Law in Mexico

4.1. Historical Background to the Civil Code of 1870

Although there is some difference of opinion,[17] it appears that the first Mexican Civil Code was adopted soon after independence in the State of Oaxaca in 1828, with subsequent civil codes being adopted by the states of Zacatecas (1829) and Veracruz (1835).[18] These early, local codifications of private law

[11] *Ley General de Títulos y Operaciones de Crédito*, D.O. 27 Aug. 1932, as amended.

[12] *Ley General de Sociedades Mercantiles*, D.O. 4 Aug. 1934, as amended.

[13] *Ley de Concursos Mercantiles*, D.O. 12 May 2000.

[14] *See* Commercial Code Art. 1: 'Commercial transactions shall be governed only by this Code and by other applicable commercial laws'. *See also* e.g. *Ley de Títulos y Operaciones de Crédito*, Art. 1 (credit operations are commercial acts).

[15] D.O. 22 Jul. 1993.

[16] For a discussion of the rules of commercial arbitration, *see* Chapter 18 below, Section 4.2.

[17] *Cf.* Vázquez Pando, *infra* note 21 at 393; Díaz Jerónimo, 'La Posesión en el Derecho y en la Jurisprudencia Mexicana', XVI Revista de la Facultad de Derecho de Mexico at 321 (No. 62, April–June 1966); and Rojas, Isidro, 'La Evolución del Derecho en México', in IV (4th Epoca) Boletín de la sociedad Mexicana de Geografía y Estadística at 298 *et seq.* (1897).

[18] *See Código Civil, libro segundo para el Gobierno del Estado libre de Oajaca, Oajaca*, México (Imprenta del Superior Gobierno, directed by Antonio Valdéz y Mayo, 1928); *Proyecto de Código Civil* introduced at the 2nd Constitutional Congress of the Free State of Zacatecas, by the Commission charged with its drafting, printed in the Oficina del Gobierno,

represented attempts to adapt Spanish legal doctrines to more modern, enlightened private law doctrines developed in Italy and elsewhere.[19] These early codes were eventually replaced, and had little influence over later codifications.

In 1857[20] the liberal government of President Benito Juarez commissioned Don Justo Sierra, a leading intellectual, to draft a federal Civil Code, which was completed in 1860. Ten years later, after the end of the French Intervention and the restoration of liberal government under the 1857 Constitution, the Sierra draft was enacted on 8 December 1870, taking effect on 1 May of the following year. This was the first civil code adopted by the Mexican federal Congress, and applied throughout the country, although various states began to adopt their own civil codes around this time. The 1871 Civil Code represented a step forward in the legitimacy of the Mexican state as a society governed by law[21] (a concept that has nevertheless proven elusive throughout its history).

The Mexican Civil Code of 1870 is thus of European origin,[22] drawn primarily from the *Code Napoleon* (French Civil Code of 1804),[23] with influences from Roman law, Spanish legislation of the colonial era, and the civil codes of Austria, Portugal, the Netherlands, and Sardinia.[24] In varying degrees, these

under the direction of Pedro Piña, Zacatecas 1829; *Proyecto de Código Civil* introduced at the 4th Constitutional Congress of the State of Veracruz, Jalapa, Veracruz, Mexico, Blanca y Aburto, 1835.

[19] Siliceo Camacho, F., *El Derecho Internacional Privado en el Derecho Civil* (Mexico: UNAM, 1936) at 8.

[20] An important precedent is worthy of mention: in the Decree of 28 Oct. 1853, Art. 6 established that 'documents from outside the Republic shall have herein [in this Republic] the authenticity that the law confers upon them, being granted by the form prescribed by the laws of the country in which they are granted and by the authorities and officials to whom they [the authorities and officials] entrust such task'. This essentially established the principle of *locus regit actum*, which says that when a legal transaction complies with the formalities required by the laws of the country where it takes place, the transaction is also valid in the country where it is to be given effect, although by the law of that country other formalities may be required. This principle is echoed in Art. 34 of the law of 27 Jan. 1857: 'Any act of [a change in] marital status, registered in a foreign country, shall be authentic if it has been recorded as provided for by the law of the nation in which it was entered into'.

[21] Vázquez Pando, F.A., 'Notas para el Estudio de la Historia de la Codificación del Derecho Civil en México de 1830 a 1834', 4 Revista Jurídica (July, 1972) (Universidad Iberoamericana) at 382 (discussing the tendency towards codification that developed in the early days of Mexican independence).

[22] On the history of the civil code, *see* Aguilar Gutiérrez, A., 'Sintesis de Derecho Civil', in *I Panorama del derecho Mexicano* (Mexico: UNAM) 12 (1965); Borja Soriano, M., *Teoría General de las Obligaciones, Vol. I* (Mexico: Porrúa, 6th ed., 1968) at 20; Macedo, P., 'El Código de 1870. Su importancia en el Derecho Mexicano', in 3 *Revista Jurídica* (July 1971) (Universidad Iberoamericana) 248.

[23] According to one nineteenth-century authority, the adoption of the Mexican Civil Code was the natural result of the virtually unanimous acceptance of the French Civil Code by European and Latin American nations, and was intended 'to unify, with regard to such an important subject, the numerous Spanish laws that continued to be in effect for a long time among us'. Verdugo, A., *Derecho Civil Mexicano, Vol. L* (Mexico: Facsímil 1885) at 10. For further background to codification of the Code of 1870, *see also* 'La Reseña Histórica de la Codificación en México', IV El Derecho (No. 17, 25 Apr. 1870) 335.

[24] According to Luis Mendez, one of the code's drafters, the 1870 Code was also influenced by Florencio García Goyena's draft Civil Code of 1851, which was published in 4 volumes in 1852, in Madrid, Spain. Mendez, L., 'La verdad histórica sobre la formación del Código Civil',

codes incorporated ideas from the European enlightenment,[25] which viewed law as rational and egalitarian (at least on paper), with individual rights of central concern.[26] Of course, Mexico in the late nineteenth century was far from an enlightened country,[27] but that did not prevent liberal idealists from adopting legislation that, at least in theory, coincided with a free society.

The 1870 Civil Code was eventually replaced in 1884, when the federal Congress adopted a new Civil Code applicable to federal matters. The 1884 Code consisted of an 'almost simple, albeit careful revision of the previous Code of 1870, without any important innovation other than that of introducing the freedom to make a will'.[28]

The 1884 Civil Code remained in force until 1932, when it was replaced by the Civil Code for the Federal District for Local Matters and for the Entire Republic in Federal Matters.[29] This Code has had the most far-reaching influence on civil law in Mexico, as it has served as the principal model for the civil codes adopted by the Mexican states.

4.2. The Civil Code of 1932 and Subsequent Variations

The rules established in the 1932 Civil Code remain largely in effect throughout Mexico, not by direct application, but rather because the rules of the Civil Code for the Federal District have been repeated almost verbatim in every civil code adopted in the country. The published commentaries on private law in Mexico are dominated by books and articles that analyse the 1932 Code, and because of the similarity of its provisions with those of state codes, this commentary is often cited as a secondary authority in discussions of the provisions of state civil codes. Unfortunately, reliance on treatises based on the 1932 Code,

a letter first published in REVISTA 'EL FORO', 26 June 1873, reprinted in VOL. I, *LA CIENCIA JURÍDICA, TALLERES DE LA LIBRERÍA RELIGIOSA* (1897) at 28 *et seq*. The Brazilian jurist Haroldo Valladao also claims that the Garcia Goyena draft also influenced the 1870 Code, as did the Austrian, Portuguese, and Chilean Codes. Valladao, H., *ESTUDOS DE DIREITO INTERANCIONAL PRIVADO* (Rio de Janeiro: ed. Livrária José Olimpo, 1942) at 14.

25 *See generally* Reyes Heroles, J., *EL LIBERALISMO MEXICANO* (Mexico: UNAM, 1957); Ramos, R., *LOS LIBROS QUE LEYO DON MIGUEL HIDALGO Y COSTILLA* (Univ. de Guanajuato, 1953); López Cámara, F., *LA GENESIS DE LA CONCIENCIA LIBERAL EN MEXICO* (Mexico: UNAM, 1969); Bravo Ugarte, J., *HISTORIA DE MEXICO*, vol. III (Mexico: ed. Jus, 3rd ed., 1962) at 14 *et seq*. *See also* Ignacio Carrillo Prieto: 'The new ideas [of the enlightenment] shook the foundations of the Spanish Empire, when the enlightened clergy decided to support in America the efforts of the Criollo intelligentsia to decide autonomously their own life style'. *Influjo del Derecho Natural en las Constituciones de la Indepencia*, Thesis, Facultad de Derecho, 1970, UNAM, at 295.

26 On the development of civil law in the Age of Enlightenment, *see generally* Glenn, H.P., *LEGAL TRADITIONS OF THE WORLD* (Mexico: Oxford University Press, 2000) at 116–135.

27 For a discussion of the late nineteenth-century seeds of Mexican revolution, including social unrest, *see* Hart, J.M., *REVOLUTIONARY MEXICO: THE COMING AND PROCESS OF THE MEXICAN REVOLUTION* (Berkeley: University of California Press, 1987).

28 Macedo, P., 'La evolución del derecho civil', in LA EVOLUCIÓN DEL DERECHO MEXICANO (Mexico: Ed. Jus, 1943) at 67.

29 The 1932 Civil Code was published in D.O. 26 May 1928, but by its own terms, it entered into force on 1 Oct. 1932 (Artículos Transitorios—Primero).

and on the current CCDF and FCC, has become increasingly problematic as state legislatures have begun to adopt civil code provisions that do not conform strictly to the centralized model of the Federal District of Mexico, as is the case with the civil liability provisions of the Civil Code of Quintana Roo, or the family law provisions of the Codes of Hidalgo and Veracruz.

In 2000 a major change in Mexican civil law ended the application of a single Civil Code to federal matters throughout the country as well as to local matters in the Federal District.[30] In 1996, Congress amended Article 122 of the Constitution to grant to the Legislative Assembly for the Federal District the power to legislate on civil and criminal matters (formerly the prerogative of the federal Congress). This amendment took effect on 1 January 1999,[31] and in May 2000 the PRD-led Assembly adopted a new version of the Civil Code (hereinafter the CCDF)[32] that is applicable to matters of local jurisdiction within the Federal District. Shortly thereafter, President Zedillo promulgated a new version of the 1932 Code[33] for matters of federal jurisdiction throughout the country (hereinafter the Federal Civil Code, or FCC). Both Codes retain over 95 per cent of the rules, contained in the 1932 Civil Code, verbatim, with the CCDF deviating from the 1932 Code primarily in matters of family law. Most state civil codes also closely follow the provisions of the 1932 Code.[34]

The 1932 code adopted the structure of the French Civil Code, although unlike its predecessors, this Code is made up of four books, dealing with persons and their legal relationships (Book One); property rights (both personal and real property) (Book Two); inheritance (Book Three); and obligations (contractual and non-contractual) (Book Four). While the 1932 Civil Code mirrored the earlier codes, it was also influenced by the revolutionary process of 1910–1928. For instance, it zealously protected the territorial jurisdiction of the nation, a logical reaction to the foreign interventions that preceded the revolution. For example, Article 12 of the 1932 Code provided that Mexican laws applied without distinction to any person physically located on Mexican soil, leaving no room for any foreign law to be applied by courts in Mexico. (Article 12 remains virtually unchanged in the CCDF, but has been amended in the FCC to open the way for application of foreign law.) The territorialism

[30] *See* Chapter 22 below, at text following note 12.

[31] *See* the discussion in CONSTITUCIÓN POLÍTICA DE LOS ESTADOS UNIDOS MEXICANOS—COMENTADA Y CONCORDADA, Vol. IV, (Mexico: UNAM-IIJ, 15th ed., 2000) at 331.

[32] The decree adopting the new *Código Civil para el Distrito Federal* was published on 25 May 2000, in the *Gaceta Oficial del Distrito Federal.*

[33] D.O. 29 May 2000.

[34] The adoption of a separate Civil Code for the Federal District, distinct from the FCC, may be attributed to political factors. Thanks to the adoption of a greater margin of self-rule for the Federal District, and to free elections of officials who had formerly been appointed by the President, the Federal District began to achieve independence from the federal government, and from the President in particular. Since this time, government of the Federal District has been dominated by a leftist/populist party, the *Partido de la Revolución Democrática* (PRD). In recent years, the PRD-led government has undertaken legal reforms that are often influenced by federal models, but include unique features. This is true of the adoption of the CCDF of 2000, which included numerous reforms in areas, including family law, that attempted to 'modernize' the traditional civil code provisions.

reflected in the post-revolutionary civil code was intended to protect the country from undue external influence, and therefore it is not surprising that, until recently, the Mexican legal system insulated itself from legal currents and doctrines in other parts of the world. To open up would be to subject the system to criticism.[35]

Chapters 15, 16, and 17 below deal in more detail with the substantive rules of the civil codes. This introduction serves merely to highlight certain basic themes.

An increased concern for social welfare that emerged from the Mexican revolution found its way into the Civil Code of 1932, especially in matters involving persons and families. For instance, separation of marital property remained in effect only if spouses expressly mutually agreed on such an arrangement; otherwise it was assumed that an arrangement of joint ownership of marital property had been chosen. The economic level of either spouse was immaterial, and unless the parties specified otherwise, all property owned by the bride and groom at the time of marriage automatically became jointly owned. Rules such as these represented important new protections for women. The parameters of divorce were broadly expanded to include voluntary divorce. Children born out of wedlock were granted the same status and rights as those born in wedlock. These last two reforms represented radical departures from the previous codes.

The changes made with regard to ownership and possession of property were also radical for the time. The Code broke with 'the subjective criteria of the classical school of thought regarding possession and embraced the objective theory of the German and Swiss Codes',[36] as well as the Italian Code. Under the new rules, property ownership and possession was understood as serving a social function. Thus, the 1932 Code protected the property rights of persons whose possession of property fulfilled the function that such property was destined to serve.[37] Thus, protection of *possessors* of property, as opposed to owners of title, was a new and radical concept. As a result of this new concept, acquisition of property through adverse possession (squatters' rights) became an important form of acquisition of real property in Mexico. The Code also recognized the principle of good faith in acquisition of real property. The first rules pertaining to intellectual property were also included in the new Code, and time periods for the enjoyment of exclusive privileges derived from patents were established.

In the field of inheritance, the right to inherit could no longer be asserted beyond the third generation (i.e. great-grandchildren had no claim against the great-grandparent's estate) and in cases where no heirs come forth, the Code established forced inheritance for the public benefit. The holographic or

[35] Pereznieto Castro, L., *DERECHO INTERNACIONAL PRIVADO, NOTAS SOBRE EL PRINCIPIO TERRITORIALISTA Y EL SISTEMA DE CONFLICTO EN EL DERECHO MEXICANO* (Mexico: UNAM, 2nd ed., 1981) at 21–50.

[36] Macedo, *supra* note 28 at 90 and 91.

[37] *See*, for examples, Arts. 830 and 831 of the Federal Civil Code.

hand-written will was added as an acceptable way of making a last will and testament, along with the traditional form of appearing before a notary public. The rights of illegitimate children to inherit were established, as were those of common law wives who were not legally married to someone else.

These liberal advances in the substantive rules did not mean, however, that the Civil Code was uniformly applied in keeping with the noble social principles that motivated some of its provisions. Failings in the judicial system, incompetent lawyers, limited recourse to legal representation by the poor, and interference by public officials considerably diminished the social welfare benefits of the more enlightened Code rules.

Finally, in the area of obligations, the 1932 Code created a distinction between civil contracts and civil obligations that are non-contractual, more clearly distinguishing these types of obligations than had previously been the case. The relatively few sources of obligations appearing in the older Codes were expanded to include six categories of obligations stemming from the following: contracts, unilateral declarations of consent, unjust enrichment, business management, unlawful acts (intentional and negligent) (i.e. torts), and employer liability for worker safety.[38]

4.3. The Lack of Amendment of the Civil Code

The forward-looking Civil Code of 1932 was a major achievement of the early twentieth century, but the common law lawyer who reads the Code today will find many of the provisions very general, and on first reading almost simplistic. The language of many of the Articles seems out of place in the age of computers and rapid technological change. In fact, the texts of the civil codes currently in force in Mexico are virtually the same as that of the 1932 Code. Despite dramatic socioeconomic and technological changes, the 1932 Civil Code (now the FCC) has been amended only twelve times in seventy years, and most of these changes have been minor. (It is true that the adoption of specialized legislation in certain areas has supplemented and updated the civil codes.[39]) The lack of amendment contrasts with the numerous (over 350) amendments of the Mexican Constitution.

In fact, the lack of frequent amendment is considered to be a positive hallmark of the Civil Code. There is an abiding belief in the immutable character of the Code's rules, perhaps a vestige of the notion that these rules represent an expression of natural law. Because many of the Code's provisions are worded generally, judges have room to apply the rules in order to deal with situations not contemplated by the Code's drafters, without violating the central doctrinal principles that are considered to give the Code its timeless authenticity. Much of Mexico's legal education is based on training lawyers to understand how to

[38] Macedo, *supra* note 28 at 92–93.

[39] *See*, for instance, the *Ley del Contrato de Seguro*, or Law of Insurance Contracts, which is discussed in Chapter 20 below at text accompanying note 75.

apply the deductive reasoning (discussed below) that is essential to application of the civil codes in Mexico. Far from being considered an antiquated set of rules, the Civil Code is seen as a sort of 'constitution' of private law; like the vaguely worded US Constitution, the Civil Code serves as a set of fundamental principles that prevent judges and legislatures from straying too far from the enlightened principles on which the legal instrument is based.

5. The 'Code Mentality' in the Interpretation of Mexican Law

Lawyers from common law countries are usually aware that the civil law tradition places a great deal of importance on codifications of law, in particular on the codification of private law in the civil codes. Accompanying this appreciation is a vague understanding that this emphasis on codes helps to explain an approach to legal problem-solving by the lawyer trained in the civil tradition that differs from the approach followed by common law lawyers. As Professor John Merryman has pointed out, common law countries have also embraced codification, and yet it is true that the civil law tradition has much greater reliance on comprehensive codes than the common law tradition.[40]

The central concept of the civil codes, which is followed to a lesser extent in other codifications in Mexico, is that a code is a complete and comprehensive statement of all laws relevant to a given subject. In an age of specialization, and in countries (such as the United States) that follow pragmatic and casuistic approaches to problem-solving, it is hard to appreciate the value placed on a comprehensive code answering all possible problems. For the Mexican lawyer, the value is obvious: the civil codes serve an almost constitutional function in defining private rights, and all other laws affecting the activities of persons and corporations are grounded in the codes. The Mexican lawyer, by comparison, may view the common law approach to problem-solving as overly rhetorical and pragmatic, and lacking in stability.

Certain qualities of legal analysis in Mexico may be associated with the fundamental position that the Civil Code holds in Mexican legal education and legal practice. These qualities include the following.

(i) *An emphasis on classification and categorization* The Civil Code is a highly structured collection of rules, reflecting the mentality of the Code's drafters (influenced by European predecessors) and their efforts to organize the rules according to an internal logic compelled by the understanding of civil law as a legal science. Thus, the 3,074 Articles of the Civil Code are arranged into four books (*libros*), which are themselves divided into numerous titles (*títulos*), with each title further subdivided into many chapters (*capítulos*). The Mexican law student is taught that each rule must be read in relation to other rules, and to

[40] Merryman, J., *The Civil Law Tradition* (Stanford: Stanford University Press, 2nd ed., 1985) at 26–33.

its position in the Code. This emphasis on structure and classification of rules is reflected in the Mexican lawyer's approach to legal analysis. When first presented with a legal problem, the initial task of the lawyer is to classify the problem, to place it into the appropriate category under the Civil Code so that analysis can proceed. Such an approach may seem overly doctrinal and formulaic to the common law lawyer; to a Mexican lawyer, the casuistic analysis of the common law lawyer may seem unstructured and poorly grounded in doctrine.

(ii) *Deductive reasoning* The Mexican lawyer trained in civil law employs *deductive reasoning* in solving legal problems that arise under the codes. As just noted, the lawyer will initially determine which articles of the Civil Code or Commercial Code apply to the matter at hand, and by studying these articles and the relationship between them, will arrive at a preliminary conclusion. The reasoning process will employ the use of logical deductions that emanate from the language of the Code's articles and from the philosophies that underlie them; case-law (*jurisprudencia*) will be consulted, as discussed below, but case-law can only be instructive if one understands the theories that underly the codes. This type of reasoning is honed in Mexican law schools, which concentrate on teaching legal theories rather than on analysis of judicial opinions or practical applications of the law to specific case scenarios. This process differs considerably from the *inductive reasoning* that dominates common law analysis. When faced with a legal problem, the common law lawyer proceeds quickly to the study and analysis of cases, using the many research tools available for finding, among the thousands of judicial decisions published each year, cases that deal with the issues under consideration. The common law lawyer draws 'the law' from these cases, even in matters governed by statute, since case-law provides a gloss of mandatory judicial interpretation.

(iii) *The relevance of case-law and scholarly writings* The Mexican lawyer may indeed use research into *jurisprudencia* (case-law) and the writings of legal scholars[41] to help interpret the Code's provisions and to inform the deductive reasoning process. Nevertheless, case-law is often of limited use in interpreting Civil Code provisions, because of the relative paucity of mandatory precedent (*jurisprudencia obligatioria*) governing civil law matters.[42] Of course, lawyers do cite judicial decisions (*tesis*) even though the decision does not give rise to mandatory precedent. However, even if relevant decisions are found among the decisions published in the *Semanario Judicial de la Federación*, they may lack sufficiently detailed discussions of facts and application of law to serve as a meaningful guide to the problem at hand. The technology now exists to post the detailed reasoning behind a court's decision, but the Supreme Court has not seen fit to provide for this. As a result, the only practicable way to learn about

[41] Lawyers and judges commonly cite as authorities non-Mexican experts on civil law, due to the similarity of civil code provisions in many countries. French, Italian, and Argentinian authorities are frequently cited.

[42] For a more complete discussion of Mexican case-law and mandatory precedent, *see* Chapter 3 above, Section 2.3.

the detailed discussions underlying a Supreme Court decision is to go to the Court's archive to secure a hard copy. For this reason, a detailed discussion of a legal concept contained in a published book or article written by a respected legal scholar or practitioner may be cited by lawyers or judges in support of a legal conclusion. In the end, the Mexican lawyer must usually fall back on his or her basic understanding of the underlying logic of the Civil Code.

15

Family Law and the Law of Persons

1. Introduction

Despite its history of church–state conflict, Mexico remains a predominantly Catholic country in which most citizens adhere to traditional Catholic views regarding the family.[1] Indeed, in Mexico the family is almost as revered an institution as the Catholic Church. Not surprisingly, this reverence for the family is reflected in the laws surrounding the status of persons and the family in Mexican law. In a society with a meagre safety net of social welfare services, the Mexican family serves as an alternative, informal social security system. Unfortunately, there is also an element of myth involved in preserving a traditional notion of the Mexican family. During the past several decades, Mexico has faced the same sociological pressures that have led to the breakdown of family structures and values in other societies: rural poverty, the uprooting and migration of people seeking employment, and an increased incidence of divorce.

The law surrounding the status of persons and families in Mexico is governed by the individual civil code applicable in each territory, i.e. in the Federal District or the particular state of the union. As discussed earlier,[2] the state civil codes in Mexico are highly uniform, having for the most part adopted verbatim the provisions of the Civil Code for the Federal District of Mexico City. This dependence on the Civil Code for the Federal District has waned, however, and in recent years there have been significant changes in the civil codes of some states that set them apart from the Mexico City model. Thus, for instance, the Civil Codes of Tamaulipas and of Hidalgo departed from the federal code by granting the same legal rights to spouses in a common law marriage as exist in a conventional marriage. Chihuahua modified its Civil Code to confer greater rights to wives. Quintana Roo, which became a state in 1974, adopted a civil code in 1980 that introduced sweeping reforms with regard to civil liability. Despite these departures, the 1932 Civil Code applicable to the Federal District

[1] In contending that Mexican family law reflects traditional Catholic values, we do not ignore the syncretism that characterizes the Catholic faith as it is practised in Mexico. The farther one recedes from large cities, the more one is exposed to popular Catholic beliefs that have been shaped by, and reflect strong vestiges of, pre-Hispanic religious practices and cultural beliefs. While these beliefs may not be officially endorsed by the Catholic hierarchy, they are nevertheless followed in local communities, and influence behavioural practices generally, including family matters.

[2] *See* Chapter 14 above, section 4.2.

and Federal Territories[3] has rarely been amended, despite major changes in Mexican society and economy, and it has served as the model for civil codes throughout the Mexican states.[4]

The 1932 Civil Code for the Federal District remained in force, with very few amendments over the years, until 25 May 2000. On that date, the Legislative Assembly for the Federal District adopted a new Civil Code to be applicable only within the territory of the Federal District.[5] This Civil Code, hereinafter referred to as the CCDF, is very similar to the 1932 Civil Code, its principal changes having to do with family law. When the CCDF was transformed into a purely local code, applicable only to matters in the Federal District, the federal Congress adopted an identical version of the 1932 Civil Code as the Federal Civil Code (FCC) applicable to federal matters and to federal territories.[6] For this reason, the FCC is applicable as a supplementary law to commercial law matters, since commercial law is exclusively federal in Mexico.[7] Since questions of family law and the law of persons are governed by local law, the civil code of the state of residence (or the Federal District) applies to such matters. However, the FCC does apply as a residual code in respect of the status of foreign citizens, in accordance with Article 73, Section XVI, of the Constitution. The FCC also applies to all matters related to the application of international treaties to which Mexico is a party.

The adoption of the 'new' CCDF was carried out by an opposition party, the PRD, which won control of the Federal District in the late 1990s, and wished to assert its independence from the PRI's legislative authority; in short, politics, rather than a desire for reasoned reform, compelled the adoption of the new CCDF.[8] Most of the changes made to the CCDF appear in the area of family law, and many of these involve changes in terminology without a dramatic change in substance. For that reason, the new CCDF is not likely to have a great effect on state civil codes.

This Chapter focuses on the Federal Civil Code (*Código Civil Federal*), or FCC, although we will occasionally refer to the rules of the CCDF when these differ from the FCC. In fact, most articles of the CCDF retain the same numbering, and the exact language, of the FCC. As the continuation of the 1932 Civil Code, the FCC is still the model code for private law in Mexico, and most legal treatises on legal doctrines contained in the civil codes are based on this Code.

[3] D.O. 26 Mar. 1928, which entered into force 1 Oct. 1932.

[4] *See* Chapter 14 above, section 4.2.

[5] *Gazeta Oficial* of the Federal District, 25 May 2000. The change in the CCDF is discussed in Chapter 14 above at text accompanying notes 30–34.

[6] D.O. 12 May 2000.

[7] *See* Chapter 18 below, section 1.1.

[8] In the past, the federal Congress, dominated by the PRI, had sole authority to adopt legislation for the Federal District. When Article 73, Section VI, and Article 122 of the Constitution were amended in 1993 (D.O. 25 Oct. 1993), to permit election of a Legislative Assembly for the Federal District, Congress created a new opportunity for opposition leaders to promote legislation specifically tailored for the Federal District. After much debate, the legislative assembly for the Federal District adopted a 'new' Civil Code that is largely based on the 1932 model.

1.1. Historical Background

The Mexican Civil Code, like its counterparts in Latin America, was largely based on the French Civil Code of 1804 (*Code Napoleón*), a set of rules that represented enlightenment ideals that contrasted with the more conservative private laws that had been applied in the Spanish colonies. Chile and Argentina adopted French-based Civil Codes in 1854 and 1875, respectively, and these codes influenced the content of similar codes adopted in other countries in Central and South America. The first Civil Code of Mexico, modelled on the French *Code Napoleon*, was adopted in 1870, replaced in 1884, and replaced again in 1932, when the current FCC entered into force. Although Mexico did not directly import the Argentinian version of the civil code, Argentinian legal authorities (especially the writings of Argentinian jurists) have long been consulted for instruction on principles of civil law, and have been cited by Mexican courts, for two reasons: both Codes are based on the French model; and there is great respect in Mexico, as in Latin America generally, for the high quality of Argentinian legal scholarship.

Like its Latin American counterparts, the Mexican Civil Code echoed a European philosophy towards persons and family which was in keeping with the liberal thinking of the day. As often happens in Mexico, however, the foreign model eventually became 'Mexicanized', and in the twentieth century Mexico continued to be influenced more by European civil law than by Latin American developments.[9] Beginning with the liberal reforms of the last half of the nineteenth century, and continuing through the Mexican Revolution, the European-based principles of family law underwent significant re-examination, as a consequence of the secularization of Mexican law and the need to meet the demands of different social strata of Mexican society. In 1856 the anti-clerical Laws of Reform secularized the institution of marriage, establishing marriage as a civil contract to be registered with the state and rendering the religious ceremony of marriage an act without legal significance. This was the first step towards eventual recognition of divorce, although this did not occur until 1915, when Congress adopted a new Law of Family Relations that recognized divorce for cause, rights of children born out of wedlock, and rights under common law marriages (*concubinato*).

2. The Law of Persons: Applicable Law[10]

Article 12 of the Federal Civil Code (FCC) sets forth the following general choice of law rules in matters governing persons and families. As noted below

[9] For a discussion of differences between the Mexican Civil Code and other Latin American nations, *see* L. Pereznieto, 'La tradition territorialiste en Droit international dans les pays d'Amerique Latine', in 1985 vol I *Recueil des Cours de L'Academie de Droit International* (Leiden: 1985) at 275 *et seq*.

[10] On Mexican choice of law rules, *see* below Chapter 22, Conflict of Laws. For a more detailed discussion of Mexican law applying to persons, *see* Pereznieto, L. and Silva, J., *Derecho Internacional Privado, Parte Especial* (Mexico: Oxford University Press, 2000), chapter 4.

in Chapter 14, the FCC has been used as a model by most state civil codes; in addition, the FCC applies to the personal and family law issues affecting foreign persons, since this is a matter of federal jurisdiction.[11]

FCC Article 12 states:

> Mexican laws apply to all persons within the Republic, as well as to acts and events that take place within Mexican territory or under its jurisdiction, and to those persons who submit themselves [or their acts] thereto, *unless [Mexican] law provides for the application of a foreign law, or the application of foreign law is otherwise provided by treaties or conventions to which Mexico is a party* (emphasis added).

The italicized words were added in 1988 reforms to the CCDF, as discussed in Chapter 22 below, Section 2.3. As a result of this change, the Federal Civil Code retains a territorial base for choice of law, while at the same time opening the possibility for recognition of the application of the laws of other jurisdictions, either because of the parties' selection of the aplicable law, or because of choice of law rules aceptable under international law or international treaties.

According to Article 13, section II of the FCC, questions of legal capacity, marital status, custody, and financial support are to be determined in accordance with the law of the person's domicile. The first part of this Chapter deals with two related concepts that are fundamental to the law of persons: capacity (*capacidad*) and the legal status of persons (*personalidad jurídica*). We then turn to specific topics such as birth, matrimony, the different forms of relationships between parents and children (known as *filiación*), divorce, and guardianships. Regulation of inheritance and property is discussed in the following Chapter.

2.1. Natural and Artificial Persons (*Personas Físicas* and *Personas Morales*)

The FCC distinguishes between natural and artificial persons (*personas físicas* and *personas morales*). *Persona física* refers to an individual or natural person, whereas *persona moral* refers to an artificial or fictional 'person', such as a group of individuals with a particular purpose (associations, partnerships, corporations, etc.).

Personas físicas are defined in the FCC on the basis of their legal capacity (*capacidad jurídica*) i.e. the ability to be regarded as the subject of a right or the object of a duty. According to FCC Article 22, a person acquires legal capacity at birth and loses legal capacity at death. However, Article 22 also states that a person acquires legal rights—referred to in Mexico as *capacidad jurídica de goce*, or enjoyment of rights—at the time of conception. Thus, an unborn child cannot enter into a contract, but may be the beneficiary of a contract or of an inheritance.

[11] Mexican Constitution, Art. 73, Section XVI.

The term *persona moral*,[12] or artificial person, encompasses a wide variety of entities that are enumerated in seven different categories under FCC Article 25:

I. The nation, the Federal District, states, and municipalities;
II. other corporations of a public nature recognized by the law;
III. corporations of a civil or business nature;
IV. trade unions, professional associations, and other entities listed in section XVI of Article 123 of the Federal Constitution;
V. co-operatives or mutual benefit corporations;
VI. associations other than those listed above that pursue political, scientific, artistic, recreational, or other lawful purposes, provided such purposes are recognized by law; and
VII. foreign corporations, pursuant to the terms of Article 2736.[13]

According to FCC Articles 26 and 27, institutions with legal personality may exercise all of the rights that are deemed necessary to fulfil the purpose of their institution, and they are bound by decisions taken by their governing bodies in accordance with the laws, charters, and rules that govern them.

Mexican law is prone to excessive formality with regard to the power of representation,[14] and requires anyone who attempts legal representation of a *persona moral* to have been granted the power of representation by the governing board or person designated by the rules of the corporation or association, under the exact terms set forth therein. If the formalities of legal representation are not strictly followed, the power of representation is considered invalid.[15] Thus, for instance, a Mexican court of law will not permit an officer of a corporation to represent the corporation in acts related to a lawsuit (e.g. answering a complaint) without proof that the person has proper power of attorney. In Mexican litigation involving corporations, lawyers commonly use the strict requirement of proof of representation as a trial tactic, requesting the judge to demand not only a document that evidences the grant of power of

[12] On *persona moral* generally, *see* Pacheco, A., *La persona en el Derecho Civil mexicano* (Mexico: ed. Panorama, 1991) at 46 *et seq.*

[13] On Mexican foreign investment law, *see* Chapter 19 below, section 4. Any association, domestic or foreign, that presents itself as a corporation will be considered a *persona moral*, even though such an entity may not have been duly incorporated by charter. On the other hand, should a company call itself a corporation but not meet the legal requirements of incorporation, Mexican law provides that all members of the partnership or company are jointly and severally liable. *See infra*, Chapter 19 at text following note 28.

[14] *See*, Pérez Fernández, B., *Representacion, poder y mandato* (Mexico: ed. Porrúa, 1996), at 100–101.

[15] *See generally* Novoa, C., 'Jurisprudencias emitidas por la Suprema Corte de Justicia sobre el otorgamiento de poderes en el extranjero, de conformidad con el Protocolo sobre uniformidad del Régimen legal de los poderes', in 1 Revista Mexicana de Derecho Internacional Privado at 137 *et seq.* (Oct. 1996); Velasco Sánchez, L., 'La formalidad de los poderes otorgados en el extranjero', in 4 Revista Mexicana de Derecho Internacional Privado at 5 *et seq.* (Apr. 1998). *See also* Pereznieto and Silva, *supra* note 10, at chapter 15.

attorney, but even proof that the person or body that granted the power was itself duly appointed and authorized to do so. Mexican attorneys representing foreign corporations must sometimes ask members of the board of directors of the foreign corporation to prove that they were properly elected and acting within their authority when they granted power of attorney to answer a complaint, before the court will accept the representation. Given the time limits in litigation, this can be particularly vexatious.

It is important to remember that under Mexican law, legal principles established in the civil codes operate as an important body of supplemental law that may apply to artificial persons in the field of commerce or business. Since Mexican commercial law is of a federal nature, should a controversy or doubt arise that is not covered by the specific provisions of the Commercial Code (*Código de Comercio*) or of the General Law of Business Corporations (*Ley General de Sociedades Mercantiles*) the law is to be determined in accordance with the provisions of the FCC.[16]

2.2. Characteristics of *Personas Físicas* and *Personas Morales*

2.2.1. Legal Capacity

Legal capacity refers to the legal system's recognition of the capability of natural or artificial persons to acquire rights and duties. (In Mexico, as in most Latin American legal systems, the term used to denote legal capacity in the case of *personas morales* is '*personalidad juridica*.') According to FCC Article 22, *personas físicas* acquire legal capacity at birth. However, FCC Article 22 also makes clear that a person may acquire legal rights as of the date of conception, such as the right of inheritance. *Personas morales*, such as corporations or civic associations, acquire legal capacity upon registration of the act of incorporation in the Public Registry, as discussed below.

Mexican law distinguishes between, on one hand, the capacity to be regarded as the subject of a right and/or the object of a duty (*capacidad de goce*), which the individual acquires from the moment of conception and, on the other hand, the capacity to exercise one's rights independently of other persons (*capacidad de ejercicio*), which is acquired when a person reaches the legal age of adulthood (in Mexico, at eighteen years) and is capable of carrying out legal manifestations of consent.[17] Persons who have reached adulthood are assumed to have legal capacity unless a court of law has declared otherwise, due to lack of mental capacity, alcoholism, drug addiction, etc.

Name of an Individual or Corporate Name (Nombre o denominación social)
Legal capacity involves the official recognition of the name of a natural or

[16] FCC Article 1; Commercial Code Article 2.

[17] *See* CCDF Article 24 'An adult has the power to dispose freely of his person and of his property, absent limits imposed by law'. *See also* Domínguez, J.A., DERECHO CIVIL, PARTE GENERAL, PERSONAS, COSAS, NEGOCIO JURÍDICO E INVALIDEZ (Mexico: ed. Porrúa, 1992), at 135 *et seq*; *Amparo en Revisión* 613/97; SJF, 9a, T. VII, Jan. 1998, p. 1092.

artificial person through registration in the civil registry (*registro civil*) that is maintained within each state and in the Federal District. In the case of individuals, birth certificates registered with the civil registry must show the first, middle, and last names of the person, as well as the father's and mother's names.[18] By putting a certificate of birth on record, a person acquires the right to defend the use of his or her legal name, should the name be unlawfully used by another person. The Mexican Supreme Court ruled that this is 'one of the rights of the legal status of human beings [*personalidad humana*], which just as other rights of this type, cannot be renounced or disposed of'.[19]

Personas morales, including corporations, must following specific procedures to acquire names that are recognized under law. As discussed below,[20] any association or company wishing to become incorporated in Mexico must first obtain permission from the Secretariat of Foreign Relations (SRE). Such permission establishes a record of the corporation's official name, which is then registered in the charter granted by the notary public or *corredor público* who records the charter.[21] Registration of the corporate name with the SRE is separate from registration of a trademark, and does not automatically provide trade mark protection. (On registration and protection of trade marks, see Chapter 21 below.)

Domicile Domicile refers to the territorial location of both natural or artificial persons. In a federal system such as Mexico's, domicile serves as the basis for determining what law is applicable to a person for purposes of defining marital status, property rights, etc.

Establishing the place of domicile According to FCC Article 29, 'the domicile of natural persons [*personas físicas*] is the place where they habitually reside and, in the absence thereof, the place of their main centre of business'. According to Article 29, habitual residence exists when a person resides in a place for more than six months. The Supreme Court of Mexico has interpreted Article 29 to contain two key components: the *fact* of habitual residence, provable by objective evidence; and the *intent* voluntarily to reside in a particular place.[22] FCC Article 30 goes on to define 'legal domicile' for individuals as 'the place

[18] As in much of Latin America, Mexicans automatically acquire both their father's and mother's last names, with the father's last name appearing first in order. Thus, as an example, if Juan Gómez Sánchez marries Ana López Moreno, and they have a daughter named Maria, she will be Maria Gómez López. If Maria marries Antonio Garcia Robledo, her name will become Maria Gómez López de Garcia. Many Mexicans use the father's last name as their principal surname.

[19] *Amparo civil directo* 9262/50; SJF, 5a, T. CIX, p. 242.

[20] *See infra*, Chapter 19.

[21] *See generally* Pereznieto, Leonel, DERECHO INTERNACIONAL PRIVADO, PARTE GENERAL (Mexico: Oxford University Press, 7th. ed., 2000) at 82 *et seq*. In accordance with the opinion issued by the Supreme Court of Mexico in *Amparo en revisión* case number 20441/30, 'all corporations acquire their individual status by means of their corporate name'. SJF, 5a, T. XLVI, p. 1011.

An individual's name or company's name has no effect on any prior right that may have been granted with regard to trade marks or trade names, which involves a separate process, as described below in Chapter 21. However, the date of registration of the corporate name can be used as legally admissible evidence of an intellectual property right in any matter regarding such rights.

[22] *Competencia civil* 86/97; *Informe* 1987, Parte II, 7a, p. 192.

where the law sets his or her residence for the exercise of his or her rights and the fulfilment of his or her obligations, even though in fact he or she may not be present there'. The Civil Code also establishes special rules of legal domicile for certain categories of individuals.[23]

Domicile is important in litigation, since it may be used as a basis for a court to assert jurisdiction over a party.[24] Domicile is also used as a basis for determining the law applicable to the status and rights of *personas físicas*. According to FCC Article 1, section II, the law of the place of domicile determines matters such as birthright, legal capacity, marriage, divorce, and inheritence.[25]

Establishing the domicile of *personas morales*, such as corporations, is much less straightforward, because of overlapping provisions in various laws.[26] According to the first paragraph of FCC Article 33, the domicile of artificial persons, such as corporations, is the place 'where their administration is established'.[27] In matters involving corporations, the provisions of the FCC concerning *personas morales* give way to the overlapping provisions of the General Law on Business Corporations (*Ley General de Sociedades Mercantiles*, or LGSM). LGSM Article 6, section VII, provides that the corporate charter (*estatutos*) must state the place of domicile, that is, either a State of the Republic or the Federal District.[28] The Supreme Court of Mexico has held that the domicile established in the corporate charter shall be presumed to be the legal

[23] FCC Article 31 (minors share the domicile of parents or guardians; military personnel have the domicile of the place they are stationed; public servants are domiciled where they perform their duties for more than six months; foreign diplomats are deemed to be domiciled where they lived in Mexico, etc.).

[24] *See* Article 24, section IV, of the Federal Code of Civil Procedure (*Código Federal de Procedimientos Civiles*), recognizing jurisdiction in civil cases involving personal liability or marital state on the basis of domicile. *See also* Article 156, section IV, of the Code of Civil Procedure for the Federal District.

[25] In the case of foreign citizens, FCC Article 12 states that persons present in Mexico shall be governed by the provisions of the Federal Civil Code, unless foreign law or the law of a treaty indicates otherwise. FCC Article 13, section II, makes clear that the place of domicile governs matters of 'civil status' (marriage, divorce, etc.) of all persons. Therefore, it is clear that a married couple domiciled in Houston will not be subject to federal law regarding divorce, etc., since the law of their place of domicile, Houston, will take precedence. (A more difficult case arises if a couple is separated, and the spouses have different domiciles.)

The Federal Civil Code applies to the status of foreigners throughout the Republic of Mexico. Strangely, the Civil Code for the Federal District, when separated from the Federal Code in 2000 (*see* Chapter 14 above at text accompanying notes 30–34) amended Articles 12 and 13 to state that the CCDF shall apply to *all* persons present within the Federal District, without any mention of the exceptions stated in FCC Articles 12 and 13.

[26] The domicile of corporations, and the laws applicable to them, is discussed generally in Chapter 19 below. For tax purposes domicile of artificial persons is considered 'the place where the main business administration is located'. Article 19, section II, Federal Fiscal Code.

[27] FCC Article 33, second paragraph, states that if the principal offices of a corporation are located outside the Federal District, but the corporation conducts business within the Federal District, the Federal District shall be considered the corporation's domicile for the purposes of the transactions performed within the Federal District. *See also* CCDF Article 33, second paragraph. CCDF Article 33 provides that 'branch offices that operate in places other than where the home office is based, shall be considered to be domiciled in those places for the fulfilment of obligations incurred by the branch offices themselves'.

[28] Frisch, P. W., SOCIEDAD ANÓNIMA MEXICANA (Mexico: Oxford University Press, 4th ed. 1999) at 159.

domicile, even if the corporation's principal place of business is in a state other than that set forth in the charter.[29] The domicile may be changed provided that the rules of the corporation are amended to reflect such modification.[30]

3. Civil Status (*Estado Civil*) of Persons

The legal status (*personalidad jurídica*) of individuals, including their capacity to enjoy rights and fulfil obligations (*capacidad de goce*), and their capacity to accomplish legal acts on their own behalf (*capacidad de ejercicio*), is closely tied to certain events and acts that stem from marital status. These events are considered key concepts in Mexican law, and include birth, marriage, divorce, different forms of filiation, and guardianships.[31]

In the area of civil status, the strong hand of the Catholic Church makes its mark on Mexican law. According to statistics gathered by the Mexican Institute of Statistics (INEGI), in the 1990 census approximately 90 per cent of the Mexicans surveyed professed the Catholic faith as their religion.[32] Despite the history of anti-clericalism that has characterized Mexico from the mid-nineteenth century,[33] as the following paragraphs show, Mexican laws governing subjects of concern to the Catholic Church (marriage, divorce, abortion, etc.) reflect traditional Catholic values.

3.1. Birth

As mentioned above, FCC Article 22 provides that legal capacity of persons is acquired at the moment a person is conceived. All persons born in the Federal District must be registered before a judge of the Civil Registry of the place where they were born within six months of their birth (FCC Article 55). Should the child be presented as having been born in wedlock, the civil registry shall record the full names, domiciles, and nationalities of the parents, the names and domiciles of the grandparents, and the names of two witnesses who must appear when the birth certificate is issued (FCC Articles 58 and 59).

The FCC establishes four different types of parental recognition that may be entered on a birth certificate. The first type involves a child born out of wedlock. In such cases, to be recognized as parent, the father must expressly

[29] 'C.H. Buckley', S. in C., 8 Aug. 1927, SJF, 5a, T. XXI, p. 355: 'The domicile of a business corporation is that which is set forth in its corporate charter, without precluding admission of evidence to the contrary, and should the charter say nothing in this regard, the domicile shall be considered to be the place where management or administration of the business of the company is located; however, even though the principal place of business is located in a certain place, the legal domicile shall be the domicile established by the corporate charter'.

[30] LGSM Articles 182 and 190.

[31] For a historical discussion of family law in Mexico, *see* Chavez A., M.F., 'La familia en la legislación mexicana', in 23 Jurídica (Universidad Iberoamericana) 381 (1994).

[32] *See* www.inegi.gob.mx/estadistica/sociodem (site visted Jan. 2004).

[33] *See* Chapter 1 above, Section 3.2.

request that his name appear on the birth certificate;[34] the mother, on the other hand, does not have the right to refuse to recognize the child (FCC Article 60). The second type of recognition applies if the child is the product of adultery; the name of the father may be entered on the certificate, but the name of the mother may not be if she is married and lives with her husband (FCC Article 62). Thirdly, if a child is born to a married women who lives with her husband, 'in no case, nor at the request of anyone, may the judge of the registry enter [on the birth certificate] as the father anyone else except the husband, unless the husband does not recognize the child as his own and a final judgment of a court of law has been issued declaring this to be so' (FCC Article 63). Finally, 'a child born as a result of incest may be recognized. Parents of a child born in this circumstance have the right to have their names entered on the birth certificate, but it shall not be stated thereon that the child is the product of incest' (FCC Article 64).

According to Mexican law and practice, the birth certificate is the most important document of identification for persons conducting matters with public agencies, and is the main document employers inspect when hiring employees.

3.1.1. Abortion

Ironically, the legality of abortion, an extremely divisive issue under the law of the United States, was until recently a settled question under Mexican law. Due to the immense influence of the Catholic Church in Mexico, abortion was generally outlawed by the state penal codes as a form of homicide.[35] In Catholic doctrine a person's soul is created at the time of conception, and abortion is therefore a mortal sin, tantamount to murder. Mexico is predominantly Catholic, and no alternative religion or atheistic movement has seriously challenged this dogma and attempted to overturn the opprobrium connected with abortion. In Mexico, if abortions take place they do so surreptitiously, to escape the condemnation of society.

The law concerning abortion in Mexico is slowly changing, and being decriminalized in limited instances. For instance, in 2002 the Legislative Assembly of the Federal District adopted a Penal Code for the Federal District[36] that, for the first time, contained a specific chapter regarding abortion (CPDF Articles 144 to 148). Article 148 of this Penal Code sanctions abortion following rape or artificial insemination without the consent of the mother if her life is in danger, or when the foetus has congenital abnormalities.

3.2. Marriage and Marital Property

Despite the importance of the religious ceremony of marriage for most Mexicans, it is the civil ceremony of marriage—a formal civil act performed by a judge of the Civil Registry in accordance with strict procedural requirements—that makes

[34] According to the appellate courts, 'it is not enough that on the certificate in question only the name of the parent [progenitor] be recorded, but rather it is necessary that the parent appear at the act of registration'. SJF, 9a, T. V, March 1997, Tesis VII. 1o. C. 10C, p. 809.

[35] *Código Penal para el Distrito Federal*, Art. 144.

[36] *Gaceta Oficial del Distrito Federal*, 16 Jul. 2002, as amended.

a marriage legally valid and binding.[37] (Later in this Chapter we discuss the recognition of common law marriages (*concubinato*) in Mexico.) Marriages that take place in a foreign country and are binding according to the laws of that country are recognized in Mexico under the conflicts of law principle that 'the form of legal acts shall be governed by the law of the place in which they are celebrated'.[38] Thus, if two Mexican citizens decide to marry while on a visit to Houston, Texas, that marriage will be recognized in Mexico if the marriage is considered valid under the laws of the state of Texas.[39]

Marital property[40] may be either jointly owned (*sociedad conyugal*) or separately owned (*separación de bienes*); either before or at the time of entering into marriage, the parties are free to agree upon either arrangement by concluding an agreement (*capitulaciones*) that sets forth the marital property regime.[41] The marital agreement on property (*capitulaciones matrimoniales*) must be filed with the judge at the time of the ceremony. Most married couples dispense with the filing of this agreement, and it is then understood that marital property is to be jointly owned.[42] In such instances, however, property owned by the bride and groom *prior to marriage* will be considered separately owned.

To enter into an enforceable agreement of joint ownership of property at marriage (*sociedad conyugal*), recognizing that property owned separately before marriage would become jointly owned upon marriage, the parties must adhere to the formal requirements established by FCC Article 189.[43] If the

[37] Regarding the formal requirements of a civil marriage, *see* FCC Articles 97–113. As a throwback to Roman law, the FCC provides for the enforceability of antenuptial gifts (*donaciones ante nupciales*) under conditions established in FCC Articles 219–231. The FCC also provides for enforceability of written promises to marry (*esponsales*), but the relevant provisions (FCC Articles 139–145) were abrogated in the 2000 revisions to the CCDF. 25 D.O. May 2000. Nowadays, written *esponsales* are uncommon, but a ceremony to announce an engagement is still common.

[38] *See* CCDF Article 13, section IV. *See also* Pereznieto and Silva, *supra* note 10, at chapter 4.

[39] FCC Article 161 states that within 3 months of their return to Mexico, Mexicans married outside the country must register their marriage in the Public Registry of the place in which they become domiciled, in which case the marriage is recognized under Mexican law retroactively, from the date of its celebration; if not registered within 3 months, legal effect will only be given to the marriage from the time of its registration. CCDF Article 161 is more emphatic, requiring the parties to register the marriage within 3 months, and making no mention of later registration.

[40] On property law generally, *see* Chapter 16 below.

[41] The Mexican Supreme Court has held that 'the marriage contract must be entered into under the arrangement of [either] joint ownership or under separation of property', and 'the arrangement of ownership of property in marriage is left to the free contracting of the spouses'. *Amparo directo* 8357/61, SJF, 6a, T. LXXXIV, Cuarta Parte, p. 82.

[42] FCC Articles 182ter and 183. For a detailed discussion of marital property regimes, *see* Baqueiro R. E. and Buenrostro B. R., DERECHO DE FAMILIA Y SUCESIONES (Mexico: Ed. Harla, 1989) at 83 *et seq.*

[43] On joint ownership, *see* FCC Article 206*bis*.

CCDF Article 189 states:

> Marriage agreements in which joint ownership of property is established must contain:
>
> I. A detailed list of real property that each spouse brings into the partnership, listing the value and any outstanding liens;

parties wish to provide for separate property (*separación de bienes)* of property acquired *after marriage*, this may be accomplished by the parties signing *capitulaciones* to this effect, and including a list of the separate property of each spouse.[44] As already noted, if the bride and groom contract marriage without entering into a contract of *capitulaciones*, the marital property acquired after marriage shall be jointly owned, but property that was separately owned by either of the parties prior to marriage shall be deemed separate property.

The prenuptial agreement establishing marital property rights may be amended or terminated by joint agreement of the parties, who may convert from joint ownership to separate ownership, or vice versa (FCC Article 186). In addition, the agreement can be terminated by one spouse, provided that termination is based on certain grounds.[45] (Property rights after the death of a spouse are discussed in the following Chapter, under the topic of inheritance.)

3.3. Annulment and Divorce

Mexican law provides for annulment of marriage in certain instances set forth in CCDF Articles 235–263, which include cases involving incest, coercion, or existence of a prior marriage that is still valid. Marriage can also be annulled for failure to follow the formal procedures dictated by the CCDF:[46]

> II. A list of specific personal property that each spouse brings into the partnership;
> III. An itemized report of all debts that each spouse has upon entering into marriage, stating whether the [marital] partnership shall be responsible for them or only for those [debts] that are incurred during marriage, whether by both spouses or by either one of them;
> IV. An express declaration as to whether the marital partnership is to include all assets of each spouse or just part of them, specifying in the second instance which assets are to become jointly owned;
> V. An explicit declaration as to whether the marital partnership is to include all assets of the spouses or just their products. In either case, the part of the assets or of their product belonging to each spouse shall be clearly determined;
> VI. A declaration as to whether the product of the work of each spouse shall belong exclusively to the one that performs it, or whether he or she shall share that product with the other spouse and in what proportion [it shall be shared];
> VII. A definitive declaration as to who shall be the administrator of the partnership, clearly setting forth the powers conferred upon him or her;
> VIII. A declaration as to whether future assets that may be acquired by the spouses during matrimony belong exclusively to the acquiring party, or whether they should be divided up among them [both spouses] and in what proportion;
> IX. The rules for liquidation of the marriage partnership.

[44] *See* CCDF Articles 207–217.

[45] *See* CCDF Article 188: termination at the request of a spouse if the administrating partner, through dishonesty or wilful negligence, seriously diminishes the joint estate; if the administering partner, without express consent of the spouse, cedes joint property to creditors; if the administering partner files for bankruptcy, or is declared bankrupt; or for other reasons considered justifiable by a competent agency having jurisdiction.

[46] CCDF Article 249. *See generally* Baqueiro and Buenrostro, *supra* note 42 at 127 *et seq.*

For a traditionally Catholic country, Mexico has adopted quite liberal rules governing divorce. This was not always so. The first Civil Codes of Mexico, adopted in 1870 and 1884, failed to include any provision for divorce. Divorce first appeared in the Law of Family Relations of 1915,[47] and the CCDF of 1932 included provisions on divorce (Articles 266–291) that remain in force with few changes to this day. The existence of a liberal regime has not translated into a high incidence of divorce, however: the National Institute of Statistics and Demographics (INEGI) calculates that the divorce rate in Mexico was 8.7 per cent in 1970, but actually declined to 6.5 per cent in 1998.[48] Mexico continues to be a society in which the importance of marriage and family in a Catholic country underlies a strong societal antipathy to divorce. Of course, these values are less evident in the large population centres of Mexico City and Monterrey, where divorce has become increasingly common.

Divorce in Mexico is governed by Articles 266–291 of the FCC, which has been adopted in most of the thirty-one Mexican States. In 2002, however, the Legislative Assembly for the Federal District made numerous changes to its rules of marriage and divorce, adopting a Civil Code for the Federal District that is separate from the Federal Civil Code.[49] These deviations were intended to modernize the civil code provisions, but did not make a fundamental change in divorce law.

Mexican law provides for two types of divorce: divorce by mutual consent, and divorce for cause. Divorce by mutual consent (*divorcio voluntario*, also called *divorcio administrativo*) is governed by FCC Article 272; such a divorce may be granted by an administrative judge, or *juez de Registro Civil*, in the place of domicile. Divorce by mutual consent may be granted if at least one year has lapsed since the marriage took place, and only when the parties have no children, and have decided mutually to submit to an administrative divorce (FCC Articles 266, 267 (section XVII), and 272–276). Divorce for cause (*divorcio necesario*) is authorized by FCC Article 267, may occur upon the petition of one spouse, and may be based on any one of the twenty different grounds for divorce established in FCC Article 267.[50] Both types of divorce require the

[47] *See supra*, text following note 6.

[48] According to statistics of INEGI, the government census bureau, the divorce rate in Mexico was (divorces per 100 marriages) 3.2 in 1971, 4.4 in 1980, 7.2 in 1990, 7.4 in 2000, and 8.6 in 2001: www.inegi.gob.mx/información estadística (site visited Jan. 2004).

[49] *See* Chapter 14 above at text accompanying notes 30–34.

[50] FCC Article 267 provides as follows:

> [The following] are grounds for divorce:
> I. Duly proven adultery committed by one of the spouses;
> II. The wife giving birth, during matrimony, to a child conceived before entering into this contract, and who is declared illegitimate by a judge;
> III. The husband proposing to prostitute his wife, not only when the husband does so directly on his own but [also] when it is proven that he has received money or any other remuneration for the express purpose of permitting someone else to have intercourse with his wife;
> IV. One spouse inciting or using violence towards the other to [get her or him] to commit a crime, even though the crime is unrelated to sexual depravity or excess;

filing of a petition for divorce (*demanda de divorcio*) before a family law judge (*juez de lo familiar*) in the jurisdiction in which the married couple resides.[51]

Divorce dissolves the marital bond, and also results in the separation of jointly owned marital property. Where the parties have entered into a prenuptial agreement, the separation of property must take place before a notary public, in accordance with the provisions of the agreement. Where no such

[50] (*cont.*)

V. The husband or the wife committing immoral acts for the purpose of corrupting their children, as well as tolerance of corruption;

VI. Contracting syphilis, tuberculosis or any other chronic or incurable disease, that may also be contagious and hereditary, and [a spouse] being affected by incurable impotence after entering into marriage;

VII. Suffering from incurable mental illness, provided that the spouse has been committed or declared mentally ill by a judge (*declaración de interdicto*);

VIII. Absence from the marital home for more than six months without good reason;

IX. Absence from the marital home due to a cause that is sufficient to file for divorce, if the separation continues for more than a year without the spouse that separated [ever] filing for divorce;

X. A legal declaration of absence, or a legal declaration of the presumption of death, in [certain] cases of exception it [a legal declaration of the presumption of death] is not needed for the declaration of absence to be admissible;

XI. Cruel treatment, threats or serious defamation of one spouse to another;

XII. Unjustified refusal of a spouse to fulfil his or her obligations as set forth in Article 164, without it being necessary to first exhaust the remedies [intended to bring about] their fulfilment, as well as non-compliance, without good cause, by either of the spouses, with a final judgment in the case of Article 168;

XIII. A slanderous accusation made by one spouse against the other, which is a crime that carries a maximum sentence of more than two years in prison;

XIV. One of the spouses committing a crime, other than political crimes, that brings shame upon the persons, for which he or she must serve a prison term greater than two years;

XV. Habitual gambling or intoxication or improper and persistent use of enervating drugs, when this [activity] threatens to ruin the family or constitutes continuous reason for marital discord;

XVI. A spouse committing an act against someone physically or against their property that would be punishable, when it [the act] involves a stranger, provided that such an act is punishable by law with a prison term greater than one year;

XVII. Mutual consent;

XVIII. Separation of spouses for more than two years, independently of the original motive of the separation that may be argued by either one of them [the spouses];

XIX. One of the spouses committing violent family conduct against the other or towards the children of both or of one of them. For the purposes of this article, family violence is understood in accordance with the terms set forth by Article 323 of this Code;

XX. Unjustified non-compliance with decisions of administrative or judicial authorities that have been issued so that the spouse obliged to do so corrects acts of family violence toward the other spouse or the children.

[51] When spouses are separated and living in different jurisdictions, the petition for divorce may be filed in the jurisdiction in which either spouse resides.

agreement exists, the separation of property is overseen by the judge, who will issue a decree declaring the separate property of each spouse, and dividing any communal property acquired during the marriage in an equitable way between the two spouses.

In the divorce decree (*sentencia de divorcio*), the judge provides for the amount of child support; decides who shall exercise parental authority (*patria potestad*); and decides who shall have custody of the children (FCC Article 283). Mexican law distinguishes between the latter two concepts. *Patria potestad* (in Latin, *patria potestas*)[52] or parental authority, derives from Roman law and implies '[t]he whole group of powers—which also entail duties—conferred upon those who exercise them (parents, grandparents, adoptive parents, as the case may be) for the protection of non-emancipated minors[53] with regard to their person and property'.[54] The judge normally awards *patria postedad* to both parents upon divorce, and only in extreme cases, usually based on lifestyle, is one parent deprived of parental authority. On the other hand, custody (called *guarda y custodia* in most Spanish-speaking countries) refers to the personal care of a minor child or incompetent adult, and it is understood that the ex-spouse who takes on this obligation is entitled to child support from the other ex-spouse.[55]

Custody is generally understood as a temporary right. Mexican judges usually award custody to the mother, especially in the case of young children, with the father being granted visitation rights or temporary custody for periods of vacation, etc. Once the divorce decree is issued, both parents may have parental authority (*patria potestad*), but only one may have custody; or one of the parents may lose parental authority as well as custody and the other may only have visitation rights.

In cases of contested divorce, 'the judge, taking into consideration the circumstances of the case, such as the spouses' capacity to work and their economic situation, shall issue a judgment sentencing the guilty party to payment of alimony [*alimentos*] to the innocent party'[56] (FCC Article 288). In cases of divorce by mutual consent, the woman shall have the right to receive alimony over a period of time equal to the length of the marriage, provided that she lacks sufficient income to support herself and does not remarry or enter into a common law marriage (FCC Article 288). The same conditions apply to the man, should he be unable to work.

[52] Regarding *patria potestad*, *see*: Baqueiro and Buenrostro, *supra* note 42 at 223 *et seq*.

[53] The term 'non-emancipated minor' refers to persons who are under the age of adulthood (18), or who have been declared by a judge to be legally incompetent due to a mental or physical incapacity.

[54] De Pina Vara, R., *Diccionario de Derecho* (Mexico: Porrúa, 1992) at 400.

[55] When custody is awarded to a third party, such as a grandparent, both ex-spouses must provide child support to the third party.

[56] The term *alimentos* refers to a sum of money deemed by the judge to be necessary for the maintenance and support of the divorced spouse.

According to FCC Article 288, if divorce gives rise to damages or losses suffered by the innocent spouse, the guilty spouse shall be held responsible for them 'as author of the unlawful act (*hecho ilícito*)', i.e. as someone liable for a civil wrong that gives rise to damages under the civil code.[57] For example, a victim of spousal violence could bring a civil action against the wrongdoer under FCC Article 1910 (CCDF Article 1910) for injuries suffered as a result of the violence.[58]

3.4. Filiation

The Supreme Court of Mexico has defined filiation as the 'origin of children with respect to the parents, which brings as a consequence different correlative and reciprocal rights and obligations, giving rise to parental authority (*patria potestad*)'.[59] Paternity and filiation are intimately connected to the reciprocal rights and obligations that exist between spouses and between parents and children, affecting individuals and their property interests.[60]

The CCDF recognizes four main types of filiation, or parent–child relationship:[61]

(i) *legitimate filiation* or *matrimonial filiation* (*filiación matrimonial*), the result of a child being born in wedlock;
(ii) *illegitimate*, or *extra-marital filiation* (*filiación extramatrimonial*) refers to cases in which a child is born out of wedlock, and the father–child relationship is recognized, either through voluntary recognition by the father, or by a court ruling;
(iii) *legitimation* (*legitimación*) refers to cases in which a couple, after marriage, recognize that they are parents of a child born prior to their marriage; and
(iv) *adoption*, in which, unlike the first three types of filiation, there is no biological connection between the parents and the minor child, and a relationship of family kinship is legally granted to the adopting parents and adopted son or daughter as if they were the biological parents.

3.4.1. Legitimate Filiation

The FCC operates under a strong assumption that the offspring of spouses are children born in wedlock. Children born within 180 days of the date of contracting marriage, and children born within the three hundred days following the dissolution of marriage, are presumed to be legitimate children.[62] The

[57] The topic of *hechos ilícitos*, similar to common law tort liability, is discussed below in Chapter 19.

[58] For a discussion of moral damages, *see* Chapter 17 below, section 6.4.3.

[59] SJF, 5a, T. XXV, p. 816. [60] *Ibid.*

[61] *See generally* Elías A.E., PERSONAS Y BIENAS EN EL DERECHO CIVIL MEXICANO (Mexico: Porŕua, 1997) at 21 *et seq.*

[62] CCDF Article 324. Dissolution must result from the death of the husband, an annulment of the marriage contract, or divorce. In the last two instances, the term of 300 is counted from the day on which the spouses actually separated pursuant to the judicial decree.

presumption of children being born in wedlock is established in almost absolute terms by the FCC: a father cannot fail to recognize children born in wedlock, with only one exception: where it was physically impossible for the husband to have had intercourse with his wife during the first 120 days of the 300 days preceding the birth (FCC Article 325). If the facts of this exception are not proven, then the father must recognize the child even if he alleges that the mother committed adultery, and despite the fact that the mother affirms that the child is not the husband's.[63]

The FCC provides for settlement of paternity disputes through compromise or arbitration with regard to financial rights stemming from matrimonial filiation (FCC Article 339).

3.4.2. *Establishing the Legitimacy of Children*

According to FCC Article 354, '[s]ubsequent marriage of the parents makes the children born before celebration [of marriage] considered to be born in wedlock'. The FCC, however, makes establishing the legitimacy of children born out of wedlock contingent not only upon the parents subsequently getting married, but also on the parents expressly recognizing the child or children before getting married or during the marriage,[64] with 'both [parents] recognizing [the child or children] in any case [either] together or separately' (FCC Article 355). Even though recognition may be given subsequent to the marriage ceremony, the children's rights are recognized to exist as of the date that the marriage is entered into (Article 357), and this right is extended to the descendants of children who pass away before the marriage is formalized (FCC Article 358).[65]

3.4.3. *Filiation of Children Born Out of Wedlock and Proof of Paternity*

The FCC recognizes three types of filiation of children born out of wedlock. The first type is maternal filiation, based on the fact of a mother's giving birth to a child, which establishes legal filiation to the mother (FCC Article 360). The second type of filiation of children born out of wedlock involves voluntary acknowledgement of the paternity of a child. The third type of filiation involves a declaration of paternity issued by a court of law.

Voluntary acknowledgement of filiation The power to acknowledge the paternity of a child is far-reaching under the FCC. For example, parents may acknowledge parenthood of an unborn child or a child who has died and left

[63] If a woman remarries before 300 days following the dissolution of a prior marriage (FCC Article 158), and has a child within that period (FCC Article 334), the law considers the husband from the dissolved marriage to be the father of the child. However, if the child is born after 180 days of the second marriage, then the legal presumption is that the child is from the second marriage, even if the birth occurred within 300 days of dissolution of the first marriage. FCC Article 334, Section II.

[64] Baqueiro and Buenrostro, *supra* note 42 at 203 *et seq.*

[65] The Mexican Supreme Court, in a case involving a request of inheritance, has held that birth certificates may not be sufficient, in and of themselves, to prove a child's filiation to his or her parents. It may also be necessary for the moving party to produce a copy of the parents' marriage certificate. *Amparo directo* 500/95; SJF, 9a, T. II, October 1995, Tesis XI. 2p. 18 C, p. 551.

descendants (FCC Article 364). Nonetheless, the effects produced by voluntary acknowledgement of parenthood only apply to the person who acknowledges paternity of the child, and are not extended to the other progenitor (FCC Article 366).[66] Voluntary acknowledgement of paternity of a child born out of wedlock must be made by means of one of the forms specifically set out in FCC Article 369.[67]

If the person who acknowledges paternity of child born out of wedlock is married, he or she may not acknowledge paternity and take a child born outside of marriage into the matrimonial domicile without prior permission from his or her spouse (FCC Article 372). If a married woman gives birth during marriage to a child fathered by someone other than her husband, the biological father is not permitted to acknowledge paternity of the child, unless the husband refuses to recognize paternity and a court order has also been issued declaring that the child is not the husband's (FCC Article 374).

Court-ordered recognition of filiation The FCC grants to an illegitimate child, or to the descendant of an illegitimate child, the opportunity to prove paternity (that the child is the offspring of the biological father) through an investigation conducted pursuant to FCC Article 382.[68] An illegitimate child or his or her descendants can also investigate and attempt to prove maternity, 'but the investigation will not be permitted when it is designed to attribute maternity

[66] *See also* CCDF Article 370: 'When the father or the mother separately recognize children, he or she may not, at the time of the act of recognition, reveal the name of the person with whom he or she had the child, nor state any circumstances whereby this person could be identified. Words [to this effect] contained in the revelation shall be expunged *sua sponte* [on the court's initiative], so they will remain absolutely illegible.' The Supreme Court applied this provision in *Valdovinos de Barrero María*, 28 October 1930; SJF, 5a, T. XXX, p. 1188.

[67] Any of the following documents is sufficient: birth certificate; a special certificate (*acta especial*) issued by a judge of the Civil Registry; a public document [official record] issued before a notary public, or an official agent (corredor público); a last will and testament; or evidence of a direct or express confession before a court of law.

[68] *See* CCDF Article 382:

> The investigation of paternity of children born out of wedlock is permitted:
>
> I. In cases of abduction, statutory rape, and rape, when the date of the crime is consistent with that of conception;
>
> II. When the child has enjoyed the status of being the son or daughter of the alleged father;
>
> III. When the child was conceived during the time in which the mother lived under the same roof as the alleged father, as a married couple;
>
> IV. When the son has written evidence (*principio de prueba*) in his favour against the alleged father.

As mentioned in the previous Chapter, in 1932 the CCDF departed from the prior versions of the Civil Code by providing for recognition of children born out of wedlock. The 1932 Code finally recognized the widespread practice in Mexican society, dating back to colonial times, of children being born outside of marriage. Although having children outside of marriage may have been condemned officially by the Catholic Church and by conservative society in general, it was nevertheless common, particularly in rural areas. To alleviate the problems arising from illegitimacy, the Civil Code of 1932 for the first time permitted illegitimate children to use the courts to establish their parentage and related rights.

[of an illegitimate child] to a married woman'.[69] This provision is an example of the reverential status granted to the Mexican mother;[70] it is plainly calculated to protect married women and reinforce traditional family values.

The FCC provides important rights to illegitimate persons whose parentage is recognized by the biological parent or parents. Upon securing a favourable court order, children born out of wedlock are entitled to bear the first and last name of the father and mother who recognize them as well as to receive child support and to inherit property from their estate (FCC Article 389). Since this provision gave the same status to children born out of wedlock as to those born in wedlock, the CCDF of 1932 was harshly criticized at the time of its adoption. Nevertheless, the Supreme Court has been liberal in recognizing the rights of illegitimate children.[71]

The CCDF also recognizes the legal effects of another widespread practice in Mexican society, *concubinato*, commonly known in the United States as common law marriage. *Concubinato* is recognized not only in the Civil Codes but also in other laws,[72] and children of common law marriages have rights that are similar to those that arise under marriage. According to CCDF Article 383, the following children are 'presumed to be the children of the common law husband (*concubinario*) and wife (*concubina*): I. Children born after 180 days from the time the common law marriage began; and II. Children born within 300 days following the day common life ceased between the common law husband and wife'. However, in order for rights under a common law marriage to be recognized, neither spouse may be a party to a valid marriage during the *concubinato*.

The 2002 Civil Code adopted for the Federal District added Chapter XI of Book Five, in which certain rules were added that could be interpreted as furnishing property rights for spouses in a common law marriage. Thus, CCDF Article 291*ter* states that 'the rights and obligations inherent in a legal marriage shall govern a common law marriage, to the extent applicable'. Similarly, CCDF Article 291*quater* states that 'common law marriage establishes alimony and inheritance rights between common law spouses'. These provisions could be interpreted as granting property rights to a common law spouse, although no case-law has yet been generated interpreting them.

[69] CCDF Article 385. Despite the prohibition quoted in the text, an investigation may proceed if the alleged maternity can be inferred from a civil or criminal judgment. CCDF Article 386.

[70] The Mexican mother is revered not only as the foundation of a strong family, but the bedrock of society. If one hears that someone '*no tiene madre*' (does not have a mother), it means that whatever the person has done is beyond the pale.

[71] In 1969, the Supreme Court ruled that although CCDF Articles 352 and 353, which preserve the property rights of children, apply expressly to children born in wedlock, nevertheless 'they provide equal protection to natural children [i.e., biological or illegitimate children], by virtue of the well known principle of analogous application, where the same legal reason exists, the same provision of the law should exist'. *Apéndice* 1917–1985, SJF, 7a, T. VI, Cuarta Parte, Tercera Sala, p. 71 (26 June 1969).

[72] *See*, for example, Article 501, section III of the Federal Labour Law, D.O. 21 Dec. 1995, which recognizes the rights of the common law wife in the case of the death or disability of her common law husband. *See also* the Social Security Law, D.O. 21 Dec. 1995, Article 130.

Finally, the reader should note that children also have certain rights with regard to recognition of filiation. For example, should the child who is the subject of an act of recognition be of adult age, he or she must expressly consent to recognition (FCC Article 375). On the other hand, should the child be a minor, consent must be given by the guardian and, should no guardian have been previously appointed, the court shall appoint one specifically for this purpose (FCC Article 375). If filiation of a minor child was recognized by a guardian, the child may 'challenge the recognition when he or she reaches legal age' (FCC Article 376).

Custody of children born out of wedlock The Civil Code has special provisions concerning the custody of children born out of wedlock. For instance, when parents who do not live together both recognize a child in the same proceeding, an agreement must be reached on which parent shall be granted custody. Should the parents fail to reach such agreement, the judge shall decide who has custody (FCC Article 380). Appellate courts have held that when children are born out of wedlock and the parents later separate, and do not agree on custody, a family court judge shall have the power to award custody according to the best interests of the child.[73]

If the parents of a child born out of wedlock recognize the child at separate times, custody shall be exercised by the first parent to recognize the child, unless the parents agree on who shall have custody and their agreement is approved by the court (FCC Article 381).

3.4.4. Adoption

The Mexican law of adoption[74] has undergone significant changes in recent years, due to Mexico's adherence to several international conventions that directly or indirectly influence the laws of adoption.[75] As a result, in 1998 the Mexican Congress adopted reforms to the Civil Code for the Federal District, adding Article 410-E, to modernize the law governing this subject matter;[76] this change has been carried over into CCDF Article 410-E.

Under the FCC, both married and unmarried adults of twenty-five years and older are qualified to adopt in Mexico, provided that the age difference between

[73] *Amparo directo* 3080/90; *Semanario Judicial de la Federación, Octava Época*, T. VI Segunda Parte-1, p. 200.

[74] Both minors and incompetent adults are treated in the chapter on adoption in the Civil Code. Nonetheless, we refer in this Chapter of the book specifically to minors, since they are the subject of most adoptions.

[75] *See* the Inter-American Convention on Conflicts of Laws regarding Adoption of Minors, in effect for Mexico as of 21 August 1987; the U.N. Convention on the Rights of Children, in effect for Mexico as of 25 January 1991; and the Hague Convention on the Protection of Minors and Cooperation regarding International Adoption, in effect in Mexico as of 24 October 1994.

See generally Siqueiros, J.L., 'La convención relativa a la protección de menores y a la cooperación en materia de adopción internacional', 23 JURÍDICA (UNIVERSIDAD IBEROAMERICANA) 313 (1994). *See also* Pereznieto and Silva, *supra* note 10, at chapter 8.

[76] D.O. 28 May 1998.

the adoptive parent and the adopted child is at least seventeen years (FCC Articles 390, 391).[77]

International adoptions (adoptions of Mexican children by foreign citizens) may take place in either of two ways: when the foreign citizen is a Mexican resident (*inmigrado*), the procedures described later in this Chapter for Mexican adoptions are followed. Otherwise, when a foreign party attempts adoption under the law of his or her home country, regulation of adoption engages rules of international law, including applicable treaty law.[78] Such treaties generally provide that the applicable law governing the adoption shall be the law of the legal place of domicile or habitual residence of the adopting party. If an adoption is conducted under the FCC and the adopting party subsequently changes countries, the law of the new domicile shall apply; it would be against the interests of the minor for Mexican law to continue to apply when the life-long relationship between the adopting parent and the adopted child is subject to a different law.

The FCC establishes two types of adoption: simple adoption (*adopción simple*) and full adoption (*adopción plena*). Simple adoption produces ties only between the adopting parent and the adopted child (FCC Article 402), and does not create rights and obligations *vis-à-vis* other members of the family, including biological children. In full adoption, the adopted child is given the same status as a biological son or daughter, and adoption creates legal ties to all members of the family of the adopting parents (FCC Article 410-A). Traditionally, simple adoption was the principal type of adoption recognized by the FCC. As a consequence of Mexico's becoming a signatory to international treaties on adoption, and following implementation of reforms to the FCC in 1998, full adoption was included as another possible type of adoption under Mexican law. These international agreements also helped make it possible to turn simple adoption into full adoption (FCC Article 404).

When an adoption case is heard in Mexico, the presiding judge must obtain the authorization or consent of the following persons and institutions, as circumstances may require (FCC Article 397).[79] When a person legally exercises parental authority (*patria potestad*) over the minor, this person must consent to the adoption. If a guardian (*tutor*)[80] has been appointed by a court, the guardian must give consent. In the absence of either a person exercising *patria potestad* or a guardian, the person who has had the minor child under his or her care for more than six months and who has treated the child as a son or

[77] In the case of adoption by a married couple, only one of the spouses must be at least 25 years of age, but both must be at least 17 years older than the adopted child. FCC Article 391.

[78] *See* treaties listed in note 75 *supra*. Article 133 of the Constitution requires courts to give effect to the provisions of these treaties. *See generally* Pereznieto Castro, Leonel, 'El Articulo 133 Constitucional, una relectura', in 25 JURÍDICA (UNIVERSIDAD IBEROAMERICANA) 265 (1995).

[79] The Supreme Court has ruled that, if proper authorization or consent is not provided, such non-compliance constitutes a violation of the Constitution: 'In order for an adoption to take place, the parents or guardians or those that have the minor in their care must be heard from, otherwise, Articles 14 and 16 of the Constitution are violated'. SJF, 5a *Época*, T. LXXIV, p. 1675 (19 Oct. 1942).

[80] The institution of guardian (*tutor*) is discussed in the next section of this Chapter.

daughter must give consent. Finally, in the absence of all of the above cases, the Office of the Public Prosecutor (*Ministerio Público*) located in the legal place of domicile of the adopted child must authorize the adoption. If the minor was taken in by a social welfare institution, the institution must also consent to the adoption. Should the minor be older than twelve years of age, the judge may also request the consent of the child (FCC Article 397).

The entenado: a form of de facto adoption The Civil Code provides for recognition of the rights of persons who have cared for a child since infancy, even if they have no blood relationship or kinship tie to the minor child, in recognition of a widespread practice in Mexican society. As a result of the extreme poverty suffered by large segments of Mexican society, many parents feel compelled to entrust their children to the care and custody of other people. This extreme measure may be taken either because the parents lack the means to support the child, or the mother wishes to conceal from conservative Mexican society the fact of having a child out of wedlock or of having given birth as a single mother. The rights of the carers in such situations (known informally as *entenado*, the name given to the minor who is under care) have become recognized by law. In recognition of the *entenado*, the FCC grants rights to a woman who has had a child under her care since infancy, to whom she has even given her name, and whom she has publicly presented as her son or daughter. This amounts to a type of *de facto* adoption. According to FCC Article 378, in such cases the child 'shall not be taken away from [the woman], unless she consents to handing him or has over or she was obliged to hand him or her over by final judgment of a court of law'. Oddly enough, FCC Article 378 expressly grants rights to women, but this does not rule out the possibility that a male carer might earn similar rights by analogy.

3.4.5. *Guardianship*

In this section we outline four types of guardianship of minors that are recognized under Mexican law: *tutela, guardia, curador*, and *patria potestad*.

Tutela, best translated as 'guardianship', is defined as the protection of a person and of a person's property when that person is incompetent or incapable of caring for himself or herself (such as a minor), and he or she is not subject to the parental authority of someone else (*patria potestad*). In contemporary Mexico, guardianship is most often undertaken, not by private persons, but rather by public agencies: public defenders, agencies of juvenile advocates, juvenile court judges, guardianship councils, or the public prosecutor's office.[81] Thus, the employment of guardianships has shifted from the private realm to become an institutional system used by the state to watch over the interests of the unprotected minors or incompetent adults.[82]

[81] *See* CCDF Article 452. And *see* Baqueiro and Buenrostro, *supra* note 42 at 237.

[82] A chapter was added to the FCC on 30 December 1997 for the regulation of abandoned children left in the care of a welfare or charitable institution, which assumes the functions of guardianship of any minor children that it takes in. FCC Articles 492–494.

Pursuant to the provisions of the FCC, the exercise of guardianship is subject to the oversight or intervention of a conservator (*curador*),[83] the family court judge and the local council of guardianships (FCC Articles 454, 536). The *curador* is a legacy of Roman and French law, and is a person designated by the judge to ensure that a guardian is properly caring for the child. In practice, however, the *curador* is a government employee who is rarely engaged in close supervision of the child.

The FCC distinguishes between three types of guardianships, as follows.

(i) A *testamentary guardianship* (*tutela testmentaria*) refers to guardianship of a minor child arising out of a will that expressly specifies that a particular person is to serve as guardian of the children of the deceased (FCC Article 470). It is possible for guardianship to be created by the testator solely for the purpose of administration of the testator's estate on behalf of the incompetent person (Article 473).

(ii) A *statutory guardianship* (*tutela legítima*) occurs when a minor is not otherwise left under any type of guardianship (e.g. no guardian was named in a will, or the will is declared invalid). This type of guardianship is created by operation of law. Under the provisions of the FCC, statutory guardianship consists of two types: 'when there is no one to exercise parental authority nor a testamentary guardian' and 'when a guardian must be appointed because of a divorce' (FCC Article 482). Statutory guardianship may only be exercised by the relatives of the incompetent person, and the FCC creates an order of preference among relatives: top priority is given 'to siblings, with preference for those [siblings] that are on both sides' [i.e. not half-brothers or half-sisters] and in the absence of siblings, any other relative 'up to and including the fourth degree of kinship' (FCC Article 483).

(iii) A *court-appointed guardianship* (*tutela dativa*). When no guardian has been named pursuant to a will, and no other person is entitled to statutory guardianship, a family court judge may designate the guardian (FCC Articles 495 and 497). Minor children of at least sixteen years of age are entitled to appoint their own guardian, subject to the approval of the person they name and the judge of the family court hearing the matter (FCC Article 497).

If the guardian (*tutor*) or the conservator (*curador*) do not carry out their duties responsibly and in accordance with the law, they may be dismissed by order of the court (FCC Article 463).

Comparing guardianship with patria potestas (parental authority) or *guarda (custody)* In general, the rights and obligations of guardians must be understood in relation to two related institutions: parental authority (*patria potestas*) and custody (*guarda*).

[83] The *curador*, or conservator, is 'the person designated to defend the rights of the incompetent, in law suits or outside of them, exclusively in cases in which their rights are in opposition to those of the guardian; to watch over the conduct of the latter, informing the judge of matters the conservator deems to be harmful to the ward'. De Pina, *supra* note 54 at 207.

Guardianship (*tutela*) is a concept of Roman law in which the care of an incompetent person is entrusted to an adult person of legal age who is not the parent of the minor or incompetent person. Parental authority (*patria potestas*) is a right that may be asserted *only by parents or grandparents* in order to care for and represent their children.[84] Derived from Roman law, *patria potestas* constitutes the most comprehensive right that can be exercised over incompetent persons, and is designed precisely to protect the interests of the children.

Guardianship arose under Roman law to deal with situations in which the minor was without parents or grandparents. In contrast to *patria potestas*, the guardian is not the parent of the incompetent person or minor, but rather is the *legal representative* and does not necessarily take care of the ward (*pupilo*).

Custody (*guarda*) implies a lesser responsibility than guardianship or parental authority. Custody, in Mexican law, simply involves the personal care of the incompetent person or minor, and always implies a temporary status under which the person exercising custody has no legal power of representation on behalf of the incompetent person (*minor*). A hypothetical example of custody is a father stripped of parental authority (*patria potestad*) by a judgment of the court, but who for some reason must temporarily take care of his child. Another example is a person not related to the incompetent person either by blood or marriage, but who has been entrusted with the care of the incompetent person or minor.

Obligations of the guardian It is the obligation of the guardian to support and raise the minor, to provide the necessary resources for the betterment of the minor, to take inventory of all property and administer the estate of the minor, and to represent him or her in any legal proceedings (FCC Article 537). Even though the guardian may put the minor under the care and custody of a person other than the guardian, the ward must always be under the supervision of the guardian and the above-mentioned obligations must be fulfilled. When the guardian is appointed, the judge and the guardian shall jointly set the amount of money that must be dedicated for the support and education of the minor (see FCC Article 538).

The financial interests of the minor, such as those relating to the sale of properties from the estate transferred to the minor, must be approved by a judge of the family court (FCC Articles 564 and 566). The guardian is precluded from conducting any business with the minor (FCC Article 569), nor can the guardian accept the assignment of any creditors' rights against the ward (FCC Article 572) or make donations in the name of the ward (FCC Article 576).

The guardian must file a detailed annual report of his administration to the judge of the family court in charge of the case (FCC Article 590). Once the guardianship has terminated, either by judicial order or because the minor has reached legal age, the guardian is obliged to return all assets from the guardianship to the judge or to the former minor (FCC Article 608).

[84] The Supreme Court has ruled that, in accordance with legislative intent, '*patria potestas*, as a general rule, must be exercised by the two parents jointly, and only as an exception may it be exercised by only one [parent]'. *Amparo directo* 2627/71; SJF, 7a Época, Tercera Sala, T. LI (Cuarta Parte), p. 59 (15 Mar. 1973).

16

Property Law and Inheritance Law

1. Introduction

Property law and the law of inheritance (*sucesiones*) are private law subjects covered by the civil codes applicable in each Mexican state or federal territory. The second and third books of the Federal Civil Code (Articles 747 to 1791) set forth the basic rules of property and inheritance. While the rules of property and inheritance are matters of local law, and are thus governed by the civil code of the state or Federal District, this Chapter refers to the Federal Civil Code (FCC) (originally enacted in 1928, and until 2000 applicable both to the Federal District and to federal matters generally, as explained above in Chapter 14) since the FCC has served as such an important model for the civil codes of the individual states, and has therefore served as a 'model law' in property law matters.

While property law is private law, private property rights are subject to an important overlay of federal and state law. For example, the Mexican Constitution forbids foreigners from owning full title to land near the borders or coastlines, and federal land reform legislation, also rooted in the Constitution, has long placed restrictions on the private ownership of large landholdings. This Chapter focuses on the private law of property ownership, as well as the most important federal laws on the subject.

1.1. Historical Background

Mexican private law traditionally divided the regulation of property into three categories: ownership, possession, and intellectual property. In 1956, however, intellectual property law (covered below in Chapter 21) ceased to be regulated by the Civil Code for the Federal District (CCDF), after the adoption of the first copyright law (*Ley de Derechos de Autor*),[1] which was enacted at the federal level and applies nationally. This Chapter therefore focuses on ownership and possession of both real and personal property.

The foundations of Mexican property law were laid under Roman law, which considered the right of property ownership inviolable and sacred.[2] Throughout

[1] *Ley Federal sobre el Derecho de Autor*, 24 Dec. 1996, as amended D.O. 19 May 1997 (amending Article 231, Section III).

[2] Macedo, Pablo, 'Derecho Civil', in *Evolución del Derecho Mexicano (1912–1942)* (Mexico: ed. Jus, 1943) at 88.

history, the ownership and control of real property has determined other rights as well; thus, in medieval times, feudal possession of property provided an entitlement for a selected few and servitude for many others. Feudal concepts of real property ownership were transferred to New Spain by the Spanish Crown, which undertook to allocate property use and ownership by grants to Spanish explorers (*conquistadores*) and others, and largely disregarded the ownership rights of the indigenous cultures they subdued.[3] Even after Mexican independence, property ownership remained effectively feudal, with large land-holdings, or *haciendas*, held by a small number of families and peasant farmers tied to the land by subsistence needs. The Mexican Revolution was fought, in part, by Emiliano Zapata and others who wished to break with this legacy, by expropriating large landholdings under the slogan 'Land and Freedom' (*Tierra y Libertad*) and distributing land to rural workers.[4]

The framers of the Constitution of 1917 were divided on the extent to which the new charter should actively do away with large landholdings. Most of the framers were bureaucrats, teachers, and political cognoscenti, rather than large landowners, but they were nevertheless wary of rampant expropriation. There was, however, a general agreement on the need to redefine the concept of real property ownership, to provide a basis for future policies that would control, if not eliminate, inequities in property ownership. This new mentality stressed, at least in theory, the community obligations of property owners.[5] Based on this new interpretation of ownership, the ultimate owner of real property became the state, which conferred property rights on individual owners but with the underlying notion that such owners had a responsibility to use the property in the service of society as a whole. This concept is known in Mexico as the 'social function' of property ownership, and is enshrined in the lengthy Article 27 of the Constitution, which states at the outset 'Ownership of the lands and waters that lie within the limits of the national territory belong originally to the Nation, which has had and continues to hold the right to transfer control of them to private persons, constituting private property'. The 'social function of property' serves as an underlying justification for governmental intrusions on private ownership to promote public welfare. Examples of such governmental intrusion include land reform laws, the regulation of the *ejido*, and adverse possession, all of which are discussed below. The government's ownership of subsoil minerals, a direct legacy of Spanish colonial rule, is also discussed below.

[3] *See* Chapter 1 above, at Section 2.2.

[4] Mason Hart, John, *REVOLUTIONARY MEXICO: THE COMING AND PROCESS OF THE MEXICAN REVOLUTION* (Berkeley: University of California Press, 1987), at 252 *et seq.*

[5] This mentality is reflected in the comments of Macedo, *supra* note 2 at 88 and 89: 'ownership is [viewed as] a social function and the individual ceases to be an end and becomes a means. A means of fulfilling, to the extent that his business may permit, the destiny of the greater society of which he is a part; a means of fulfilling, to the fullest extent, his own destiny.'

1.2. Governing Law

Pursuant to Article 121, section I of the Mexican Constitution, legal questions concerning rights to personal and real property are governed by the law of the place where the property is physically located.[6] This rule is reiterated in FCC Article 13, section III: 'The establishment, recognition, and termination of property rights (*derechos reales*) over real property, as well as contracts for rent and contracts for temporary use of such property, and [of] personal property, shall be governed by the law of their location, even if the owners are foreign nationals'. The Federal Code of Civil Procedure (Article 568) similarly establishes that the Mexican courts have exclusive jurisdiction over real property located within Mexican territory. As a consequence, any foreign judgment regarding real or personal property that is located in Mexico will not be given effect by a Mexican court, even if the foreign court has applied Mexican law in making its judgment.[7]

In matters involving intangible property, such as trade marks or contract rights (an insurance policy, or a bank's interest in a loan, for example), the applicable laws include the *Ley General de Títulos y Operaciones de Crédito*,[8] the *Ley de Propiedad Industrial*,[9] the *Ley de los Derechos de Autor*,[10] the *Ley de Instituciones de Crédito*,[11] and the *Ley General de Organizaciones y Actividades Auxiliares de Crédito*,[12] among others.

Judgments rendered by the courts of a Mexican state that enforce rights over property (either real estate or *derechos reales*[13]) located in another Mexican state are to receive full faith and credit only if the law of the state in which the real property is located provides for such enforcement (Mexican Constitution, Article 121, section III). Thus, parties to a mortgage contract celebrated in the state of Sonora covering property located in the state of Baja California may agree that the contract shall be governed by the law of Sonora, and a party may secure a judgment based on this contract in a court of the state of Sonora. The Sonora judgment will only be enforceable in Baja California, where the property is located, if the law of Baja California provides for such enforcement, i.e. if a judge in Baja California does not refuse to enforce the judgment as contrary to Baja California law. This is due to the language of the Full Faith and Credit Clause, Article 121, section III, which states that the judicial judgments of one state shall be given effect in the state in which the property is situated 'if the laws [of the latter] so provide'. This vague language creates the potential for

[6] *See also* Mexican Constitution, Articles 115, section IV(a) (state and municipal power to tax property); and Article 122, Base Primera, section V(h) (power of Legislative Assembly of Federal District to legislate on civil law matters, including property).

[7] *See* Article 568 of the Federal Code of Civil Procedure, which grants 'exclusive jurisdiction' to Mexican courts in matters involving real property located in Mexico. *See generally* Pereznieto, L., DERECHO INTERNACIONAL PRIVADO (Mexico: Oxford University Press, 7th ed., 2000) at 203 *et seq.*

[8] D.O. 27 Aug. 1932.

[9] D.O. 27 Jun. 1991.

[10] D.O. 24 Dec. 1996.

[11] D.O. 18 Jul. 1990.

[12] D.O. 14, Jan. 1983.

[13] On *derechos reales*, *see infra*, text accompanying notes 15–18.

non-enforcement of judgments by sister states, since few states, if any, have specific laws that are controlling, and the Supreme Court has not clarified the meaning of Article 121's qualification 'if the laws so provide'.

1.3. Classifications of Property: Tangible and Intangible, Personal and Real Property

According to the Federal Civil Code, any object not excluded from commerce by law can be subject to ownership[14] (FCC Article 747). The FCC divides property into two general categories: tangible property (*bienes corpóreos*) and intangible property (*bienes incorpóreos*). *Tangible property* consists of physical things, either movable goods or real estate. *Intangible property* includes creditors' rights (*derechos de crédito*), as well certain intangible rights that pertain to tangible property, known as *derechos reales*, or by the Latin term *jus in re*. Thus, a seller of goods by instalments normally retains a creditor's right (*derecho de crédito*), as well as a property right (*derecho real*) or security interest in the physical goods themselves. The *derecho de crédito* entitles the seller to collect the debt, while the *derecho real* entitles the seller to repossess the goods upon the buyer's default.

Tangible property is subdivided into personal property (*bienes muebles*), which is movable; and real property (*bienes inmuebles*), i.e. land, buildings, fixtures, streams, trees, etc. (See FCC Article 750.)

In property law matters, Mexican legal scholars and case-law make a distinction between *derechos personales* (rights emanating from a particular obligation between two or more persons, similar to the common law concept of *in personam* rights and obligations) which may be linked to property; and *derechos reales*, or rights to possession that are exercised over the property itself (whether personal property or real property, similar to rights *in rem*). This important distinction is characteristic of civil code countries, and in Mexican law it is applied in dogmatic fashion.[15]

[14] FCC Articles 748 and 749 state that objects may be excluded from commerce either by their nature or by law.

[15] *Derechos personales* are of limited scope, and require particular conduct from individuals, such as granting 'the creditor the power to demand that the debtor perform something (*prestación*) or refrain from doing something (*abstención*) relating to property'. Rojina Villegas, R., COMPENDIO DE DERECHO CIVIL (Mexico: Porrúa, 1997), vol. I, at 130 (authors' trans.). Such a creditor's right is enforceable against a debtor, but not necessarily against third parties. *Derechos reales*, by contrast, are exercised over property directly, and are enforceable against third parties. *Id.* at 45.

The Mexican Supreme Court has referred to the distinction between *derechos personales* and *derechos reales* in the following terms:

'The power that a person, called the creditor, has to demand of another person, called the debtor, is a "personal right" [*derecho personal*], which is also known by the name *obligación*. One of the forms of transfer of "personal rights" is assignment of rights or credit interests.[. . .] On the other hand, the direct and immediate juridical power that a person has over a thing for his or her total or partial economic use, to the exclusion of third parties, constitutes what are known as "real rights" [*derechos reales*] and the transfer of these rights has two sources: either

In Mexican law, a *derecho real* involving real property rights must be evidenced by a document (either a certificate of title or a contract that describes the real property) that names a particular person or entity as the owner of property right. This document must be registered before a notary public located in the place where the property is located, or in the place where the contract assigning the *derecho real* was made.[16] A property right over either real property or personal property is characterized in the same way as the property itself.[17] Thus, FCC Article 750, section XII, states that *derechos reales* over real property (*bienes inmuebles)* are themselves to be considered real property; thus, a mortgage interest in real property is itself considered a real property right. Similarly, property interests that pertain to movables or personal property (*bienes muebles*), such as security interests in goods, are themselves considered personal property. (See FCC Articles 753, 754.) Shares of stock of corporations and partnerships are also considered property interests (*derechos reales*) over personal property (*bienes muebles*) (FCC Article 755). Property interests in any property that is not considered real property, such as vessels of all types (FCC Article 756), or copyrights (FCC Article 758), are treated as property interests in personal property (*bienes muebles*) (FCC Articles 756, 758, and 759).

As we shall see, this characterization of property rights has certain practical implications. For instance, in matters involving *derechos personales* (*in personam* rights, explained above), the applicable law is the law of the place in which the *person affected*, or the debtor, is located; in the case of *derechos reales*, the applicable law is the law of the place in which *the property* is located. This distinction is not always clear, however, in cases involving the assertion of rights to personal property.[18]

2. Subjects Covered by the Property Provisions of the Civil Codes

The civil codes of the state and federal governments in Mexico are similarly structured, and follow the patterns and theories of the Napoleonic Code. The

by succession, upon death of the owner, or by an agreement to transfer dominion, such as sales contracts, barter contracts, or gifts.' SJF, 9a, Tribunales Colegiados de Circuito, T. IV, Oct. 1996, p. 585.

[16] The notary public has the power to record documents celebrated within his or her locality. Thus, a notary public in Mexico City, D.F., can record a contract involving the sale of real property located in Baja California, so long as the parties conclude the document before the notary in Mexico City. In every case, however, the document should also be registered in the Public Registry of the place where the property is located.

[17] Domínguez Martínez, J.A., LOS *ASPECTOS DE ESENCIA DEL FIDEICOMISO MEXICANO* (Mexico: Porrúa, 2nd ed., 1996) at 313–314.

[18] The distinction between *derechos personales* and *derechos reales* was discussed in an *amparo* decision in 1994. In that case, a federal appellate court held that an action against a

Second Book (*Libro Segundo*) of the Federal Civil Code deals with property (*bienes*), rights to both real property and personal property, which includes movable property (goods) as well as intangible property. *Libro Segundo* is separated into chapters that deal with: posession and use of property, real and personal; easements covering real property (*servidumbres*, such as those involving rights of way, drainage, or access to water); and usufruct (*usufructo*), which covers the right to use and enjoy property. Rules governing mortgages of real property appear in Title Fifteen of the Fourth Book (Obligations) of the Federal Civil Code (FCC Articles 2893–2943). The chapters governing usufruct and mortgage cover both real property and personal property, although provisions governing creditors' rights and copyright only apply in the case of personal property.[19]

2.1. Registration of Property

As a general rule, any legal act that affects *real property* must be registered in the public register of property of the state in which the property is located. Most states in Mexico have modernized their public registries of real property through computerization, but certain states still maintain records manually, which can generate errors and uncertainty.

Transactions involving personal property (chattels or goods, and intangible property) are often registered in either local public registries (in the case of chattels or intangible property) or in federal registries, such as patents registered by the *Instituto Mexicano de la Propiedad Industrial* (IMPI) or the copyrights registered with the *Instituto Nacional de Derechos de Autor* (INDA), which are discussed below in Chapter 21. Technically, three important types of transactions are *required* to be recorded in public registries, for the purpose of providing legal notice to third parties: (1) when the sale of the personal property is subject to a condition subsequent (*condición rescisoria*) that may nullify the sale upon the occurrence of a prescribed condition (FCC Article 2310, section II); (2) when the purchaser's possession of personal or real property is subject to a seller's reservation of a security interest (*derecho real*) in the property under the sale contract (FCC Article 2312);[20] and (3) when a loan is secured by an interest in personal property (*contrato de prenda*) in cases not involving purchase money security interests (FCC Article 2859). In these three instances, a transaction involving personal property must be recorded if it is to be effective against third parties.

gratuitous bailee of personal property is an assertion of *derechos personales* against the bailee; in contrast, a contract action against a *bailee for hire* should be considered an assertion of *derechos reales*. SJF, 8a, Tribunales Colegiados de Circuito, T. XIV, Dec. 1994, p. 356.

19 De Ibarrola, Antonio, *Cosas y sucesiones* (Mexico: Porrúa, 5th ed., 2001) at 627.

20 A seller who retains a security interest in goods in accordance with FCC Article 2312 retains title to the property, and the buyer acquires possession only. As in the United States, retention of title by the seller facilitates repossession and resale by the seller. Such arrangements are common in automobile financing.

In all other transactions, registration is not required; however, parties may nevertheless register a transaction involving personal property as a means of ensuring proof of the transaction in case of subsequent claims either by a contracting party or by third parties.

2.2. Mortgage Lending and Security Interests in Real Property: The *Hipoteca*

Mexico has a surprisingly undeveloped mortgage market for a sophisticated market economy. This is especially true in residential mortgage lending (*préstamos hipotecarios)* where a homebuyer will rarely be able to borrow more than 20 or 30 per cent of the purchase value of a home, notwithstanding an excellent credit rating. There is a very limited secondary mortgage market (i.e. bundling and resale of mortgage obligations) due to the lack of uniformity in lending practices among primary mortgage lenders, the lack of a reliable credit reporting system nationwide, and complications with judicial enforcement of mortgage interests.

There are several reasons for the relatively undeveloped mortgage market, some of which involve the Mexican market, and some its legal structure. In the former category, long-term lending has been relatively unattractive in Mexico, due to the history of volatility in inflation rates, interest rates, and exchange rates. With such uncertainties, long-term lending becomes a risky business. In addition, until recently, Mexico lacked a national system to investigate and certify the creditworthiness of borrowers.[21] Problems involving the legal structure have included the fallibility of the system of registration of title to real property, which gave rise to property disputes. Title insurance is expensive and sometimes non-existent. Finally, and perhaps most importantly, the procedures that allow lenders to foreclose on real property in case of default are cumbersome and time-consuming; coupled with the omnipresence of *amparo* challenges and the lack of confidence in the honesty and efficiency of the judicial system, mortgage lenders in Mexico have rarely resorted to foreclosure of real property, but have instead tended to reschedule troubled debts.

The Mexican government has worked with the World Bank and other agencies to study these problems, but no dramatic solutions have yet been devised. Instead, the federal government has filled the void for mortgage financing by providing government lending programmes, such as INFONAVIT.[22]

Commercial loans are generally governed by the provisions of the Commercial Code, as well as by more specific legislation adopted subsequent to the Code. The

[21] In 1996, Dun & Bradstreet and Trans Union established a credit reporting system called Buró de Crédito. For information on the system, *see* www.burodecredito.com (site visited Jan. 2004).

[22] INFONAVIT, the *Instituto del Fondo Nacional de la Vivienda para los Trabajadores* was established in 1972 for the purpose of financing low- and middle-income housing. *See generally* Villaseñor, S., 'El Infonavit, organismo fiscal autónomo', in 6 Cuadernos del Instituto de Investigaciones Jurídicas (UNAM) p. 30 (no. 18, Sep.–Dec. 1991).

rules of the Federal Civil Code, including those covering contracts (FCC Articles 2856–2892), supplement these provisions. In addition, Title Two of the *Ley de Títulos y Operaciones de Crédito* (CC Articles 259–414) sets forth rules on credit operations, payments, etc. that may also be applicable. The Commercial Code also establishes procedural requirements applicable to the enforcement of credit obligations (Book Five, Titles One to Three of the Comercial Code, Articles 1049–1414*bis*, 20).[23]

FCC Article 2893 defines a mortgage (*hipoteca*) as a real property guarantee that gives a payment preference to the creditor. The FCC provisions date from the nineteenth century, and while they establish a legal basis for the *hipoteca* that is theoretically well established, the mortgage lending laws are considered by many legal experts to be outdated.

Because of the outdated mortgage finance laws, the market for mortgage financing in Mexico is very small, in relation to both the size of the economy and the needs of the population. According to a World Bank Development Report published recently, in 2000 the ratio of outstanding mortgage loans to GDP in Mexico was 5.2 per cent, as compared to an average of 33 per cent for fifteen countries of the OECD.[24] The averages in Canada and the United States, Mexico's NAFTA partners, is even higher: 41 and 44 per cent, respectively. The World Bank report cited problems in the legal aspects of secured lending and foreclosure of loans as a major obstacle to development of a viable mortgage market.[25] The government housing entities (INFONAVIT, FOVI, and FOVISSSTE) which provide housing credits to subscribers, help fill the void, but represent a vestige of centralized government control that is increasingly out of step with the rest of the economy.

In the early 1990s, the Mexican government began to work with the World Bank to address these shortcomings. The first project involved a loan of 450 million US dollars from the World Bank and IDA to the Government of Mexico to fund a 'Housing Market Development Project'. The loan included regulatory reforms of the Housing Fund for Commercial Banks (FOVI), and technical assistance to study the improvement in the home mortgage market, including the study of legal and structural reforms to help build a secondary mortgage market.[26] The project was completed without any significant change in the methods of enforcing mortgage contracts, although the Mexican government has continued to work with the World Bank and the InterAmerican Development Bank to address these issues.

[23] On the Commercial Code provisions, *see* Chapter 18 below, Section 4.1. On the law of financial institutions generally, *see* Chapter 20 below.

[24] *See* the World Bank Sector Report, 'Mexico—Low income housing: issues and options', at www.worldbank.org, 'Development Reports', Report No. 22534-ME, 9 Sep. 2002, at 28, which includes a discussion of reforms needed in the mortgage financing market (site visited Jan. 2004).

[25] *Ibid.* at 31. According to the report, mortgage foreclosures require about 5 years for resolution: a good example of the inefficiencies exacerbated by the possible use of *amparo* as a strategic litigation tool.

[26] *See* www.worldbank.org, 'Mexico News', 'Lending Projects' (site visited Jan. 2004).

2.3. Security Interests in Personal Property (Movable Goods, or *Bienes Muebles*)

Until recently, Mexico was not a market-driven economy. Government price controls, anti-competitive practices, and closed markets characterized many sectors of the economy. In such an environment, the legal regime for both consumer and business lending remained relatively undeveloped. The laws governing registration of security interests in personal property were drawn from centuries-old rules governing real property, which have themselves failed to keep up with modern methods of property financing. With the opening of Mexican markets during the 1990s, reforms of the legal regimes governing commercial and consumer lending have been advocated by businesses, as well as by international financial institutions such as the World Bank. With the growth of the middle classes and retail consumer markets during the second half of the twentieth century, the need for streamlined commercial lending laws became apparent. In 2000 Congress amended the *Ley General de Títulos y Operaciones de Crédito*, the Commercial Code, and the *Ley de Instituciones de Crédito*, to introduce a new system of secured financing for movable goods, in order to expedite perfection and enforcement of security interests.[27] Further reforms were adopted in 2003.[28]

These reforms introduced, for the first time in Mexico, legal models developed in the United States and incorporated into Article 9 of the Uniform Commercial Code. Thus, Articles 346–380 of the LGTOC introduced the concept of the pledge without transfer of possession (*prenda sin transmisión de posesión*),[29] a form of secured financing that is widely accepted in many countries. Before this reform, if a creditor loaned money to a debtor, to be secured by an interest in the debtor's movable property, the security interest would only be valid if the creditor took possession of the property as collateral. This antiquated form of pledge was obviously useful for most modern security transactions, in which the debtor wishes to remain in possession of property (automobiles, equipment, inventory), and will only give up possession to the creditor in case of foreclosure. To overcome this, creative lawyers created forms of fictional 'bailments' (*depósito)* in which the creditor would agree to place the goods 'on deposit' with the debtor. To do away with the inefficiencies inherent in this model, and in response to pressures from financial institutions and government agencies alike, Congress amended Articles 346–380 of the LGTOC to allow the

[27] D.O. 23 May 2000. On the reforms of 2000, *see generally*, 'La ejecución de la prenda sin trasmisión de posesión', in 9 Revista Mexicana de Derecho Internacional Privado 87 Nov. 2001). *See also* the articles collected in 13 Revista Mexicana de Derecho Internacional Privado y Comparado 9 (April 2003). On commercial lending generally, *see also* Chapter 18 below, at text accompanying notes 116–125.

[28] D.O. 13 Jun. 2003.

[29] According to LGTOC Article 346, the *prenda sin transmisión de posesión* is considered a *derecho real*, or property right.

creation of an enforceable security interest in movable property that is retained by the debtor or by a third party.[30]

2.4. Transfer of Title to Personal Property and Real Property

Other than transfers of property by inheritance (*sucesión*), which are discussed below, most transfers of property ownership in Mexico are accomplished pursuant to contract, usually a purchase and sale contract (*contrato de compraventa*) (FCC Article 2248).[31] The rules of contracts are found in either of two sources: in the contract rules contained in the Book on Obligations of the relevant civil code applicable to the contract (many of which are modelled on provisions of the FCC); or contract principles contained in the Commercial Code, regarding the sale of personal property that may be characterized as a commercial transaction. Thus, for instance, if a person purchases an automobile in the state of Jalisco, the contract will be governed by the Civil Code of the state of Jalisco. However, if a *private company* buys a shipment of tequila in the state, the contract will be characterized as a commercial transaction, and the rules of the Commercial Code will govern the contract, as supplemented by the relevant rules of the Federal Civil Code (since commercial transactions are matters of federal legislative jurisdiction) and, if necessary, by supplementary rules of the Civil Code of Jalisco. All contracts for the sale of movable property concluded by *government agencies or government-owned entities*, such as PEMEX or CFE, are also governed by the Commercial Code and by the Federal Civil Code, rather than by the civil code of the locality.

When a transfer of *real property* is carried out pursuant to a contract, formal procedural requirements must be fulfilled in a notarized document issued by an accredited notary public. After the transfer of real property is properly notarized, it must be recorded in the Public Registry of the place where the real property is located.[32]

[30] The reforms also created a new form of trust, or *fideicomiso de garantia*, that could be created to place title of personal property with a fiduciary, such as a bank, in order to facilitate foreclosure. LGTOC Articles 381–414. Unfortunately, the expense of employing a *fideicomiso de garantia* makes this vehicle impractical for securing loans, except in the case of large equipment loans, etc.

[31] Property can also be transferred: by a barter contract (*permuta*) (FCC Article 2327); by gift (*donación*) (FCC Article 2384); or by adverse possession (*prescripción*) (FCC Articles 1135–1180), discussed *infra*, in Section 2.5. In addition, uncommon forms of transfer of property ownership include *occupancy* (*ocupación*), where the real property involved is not owned by the person who occupies it, whose occupancy is permitted by the owner; *accession* (*accesión*), when an accessory piece of property is acquired after having acquired ownership of the main property; *alluvion* (*aluvión*), which is the gradual buildup of property along river or stream banks as a result of the deposit of residual material that comes from another property; *avulsion* (*avulsión*) occurs when the river deposits a recognizable portion of another property; and finally *accretion*, caused when the course of a river or stream changes and affects a property.

[32] *See* Article 24, Section VII of the Federal Code of Civil Procedure, D.O. 24 Feb. 1942, as amended.

2.5. Adverse Possession (*Prescripción Positiva*)

Mexican law also provides for acquisition of property by *adverse possession*, known as *prescripción positiva*. This form of acquiring property was included in the Civil Code of 1932 (the predecessor of the Federal Civil Code). *Prescripción* is covered by FCC Articles 1135 to 1180; this section discusses only the most important details of the doctrine.

Prescripción positiva is covered in FCC Articles 1151–1157.[33] (The Federal Civil Code also includes provisions on *prescripción negativa*, which is similar to the common law doctrine of statutes of limitations that curtail judicial enforcement of rights after the lapse of certain periods of time, depending on the type of rights under consideration. See FCC Articles 1158–1164.) Under FCC Articles 1152 and 1155, a claimant who has been in *peaceful* and uninterrupted possession of real property for a minimum of five years, where such possession has been known to the public or has been recorded in the Public Registry as the claimant's property for that period of time, may seek a court order declaring the claimant the rightful owner of the property. The ruling of the judge must be certified by a notary public and must be recorded in the Public Registry of property of the place where the real property is located. Where possession has *not been peaceful* (i.e. has been contested), or has been *in bad faith*, adverse possession must occur for a continuous period of ten years or more, counted from the time when the act of takeover (bad faith possession) first occurred. These facts must also be proven before a judge. (FCC Articles 1151–1152.)

Adverse possession of movable property is also possible under Mexican law. According to FCC Article 1153, the period required for adverse possession of movable property is three years of 'peaceful and uninterrupted possession', when the party in position acts in good faith, and five years in the case of possession by bad faith.[34]

Adverse possession in Mexico often arises in the context of squatting (*invasión de tierras*) of rural lands by *campesinos* unable to house or maintain their families. *Invasión* of urban properties also results from migration of poor workers to urban centres that are not equipped to house the influx of residents. Legal action by landowners to dispossess unauthorized occupants of lands can be both lengthy and costly, but it is necessary in order to forestall adverse possession.

2.6. Expropriation of Property for Public Purposes

It is not surprising that Mexico, a country with a dramatic history, should have experience of expropriation of property. Most instances occurred in the distant past, in an effort to free the country from the inordinate influence of large

[33] Regarding adverse possession and its historical background, *see*: Elías Azar, Edgar, PERSONAS Y BIENES EN EL DERECHO CIVIL MEXICANO (Mexico: Porrúa, 1997) at 459 *et seq*.

[34] On bad faith, *see* the discussion of *dolo* in Chapter 17 below, Section 3.

landholders. Lands owned by the Catholic Church were expropriated during the liberal reforms of the second half of the nineteenth century (1856),[35] and land reform laws that followed the Mexican Revolution (1910–1917) resulted in the expropriation of agricultural lands during the first half of the twentieth century.[36] More recently, the federal government expropriated Mexican-owned private banking institutions in 1982, as a response to the financial crisis of the time, although it sold the banks back to the private sector twelve years later.[37] Foreign-owned property has rarely been expropriated, the most pronounced examples being: the expropriation of large foreign-owned agricultural estates in the first half of the twentieth century; expropriations of foreign mining concessions in 1937; and expropriations of the foreign-owned oil companies in 1938, which resulted in negotiated settlements for compensation paid to the foreign oil companies.[38] There have been virtually no expropriations of foreign-owned property, with or without compensation, since 1938.

Article 27 of the Mexican Constitution states: 'Expropriations can only be carried out for a public purpose and by [payment of] indemnification'. Any attempt at expropriation may be challenged in federal court, through *amparo*, for failure to fulfil the requirement either of public purpose or indemnification. A federal court may order the suspension of an expropriation proceeding for failure to meet these prerequisites.

In addition to constitutional protections, investors from the United States and Canada enjoy protections under the North American Free Trade Agreement (NAFTA). NAFTA Article 1102 guarantees national treatment for investors from a NAFTA party, and Article 1103 guarantees most-favoured nation treatment to such investors. NAFTA Article 1105 states that '[e]ach Party shall accord to investments of investors of another Party treatment in accordance with international law, including fair and equitable treatment and full protection and security'. NAFTA Article 1109 guarantees the right to transfer funds related to investments, and Article 1110 states that no party may expropriate property of a NAFTA investor except for a public purpose, on a non-discriminatory basis, in accordance with international law, and on payment of fair compensation. NAFTA chapter 11 creates a mechanism for NAFTA investors to enforce these rules through the establishment of ad hoc dispute resolution panels, in accordance with NAFTA Articles 1115–1138. In case of an alleged expropriation, or other violation of international law, NAFTA investors may initiate an arbitral proceeding against the offending government, either under the World Bank's International Centre for the Settlement of Investment Disputes (ICSID), or under the UNCITRAL rules for international arbitration. In the short history of the provisions, several notorious cases have been brought against the Mexican government (as well as against the United States and Canadian governments)

[35] *See* Chapter 1 above, Section 3.2. [36] *See* Chapter 13 above, Section 4.2.

[37] *See* Chapter 20 below, text accompanying note 5.

[38] On the expropriation of the oil companies, *see* Chapter 1 above, at text accompanying note 137, and commentaries cited in note 137.

based on alleged 'regulatory expropriations': that is, the adoption of regulations that the investor contends are tantamount to an expropriation, as well as to a violation of the controversial standard established in NAFTA Article 1105.[39] One such case resulted in an award of 16 million US dollars against the Mexican government, although the panel's award was partially overturned by a Canadian court.[40]

2.7. Limitations and Restrictions on Ownership of Real Property

Article 27 of the Constitution begins with the declaration that the ownership of real property resides originally with the State, which concedes private property rights to groups or individuals. This characterization of property is grounded in Mexican history. From the very outset of the Spanish conquest, real property (even the name connotes royal origins) originated in the Crown: the *conquistadors* claimed lands in the New World on behalf of the Crown, which granted concessions to individual *encomenderos* to exploit. On the other hand, the Mexican Revolution was motivated in part by a desire to rid the country of foreign ownership and the oppression of large landholdings, and made way for a patriarchal government that assumed responsibility for social welfare.

With these historical origins, it is not surprising that private ownership of real property in Mexico is subject to limitations and restrictions. Thus, Article 27, section XV, limits the size of rural landholdings and has served as the basis for land redistribution, which is discussed elsewhere.[41] Furthermore, just as the Spanish Crown owned all rights to subsoil natural resources, the Mexican Constitution of 1917 reserved all subsoil mineral and hydrocarbon rights to the state.

2.7.1. *Government Ownership of Subsoil Rights*

Article 27 of the Constitution establishes general rules concerning the ownership of waters and subsoil mineral rights, and reflects Mexico's colonial heritage, in which the Spanish Crown was deemed to possess all subsoil mineral rights.[42] Article 27 broadly sets forth the principle of ownership by the federal government ('the Nation') of virtually all useful classes of minerals and organic

[39] The uncertainty of agreed rules of customary international law, or even of international treaty law, in regards to treatment of foreign investment contradicts the apparent simplicity of the Article 1105 standard, 'treatment in accordance with international law'.

[40] *See Metalclad v. United Mexican States* 40 ILM 36 (2001), also available at www.worldbank.org/icsid/cases/awards. Aguilar Alvasez, G., and Park, W., 'The New Face of Investment Arbitration' 28 YALE J. INT'L L. J. 365, 375–377 (2003). Information on chapter 11 proceedings can be obtained at the following web sites: www.worldbank.org/icsid; www.naftaclaims.com; www.sice.oas.org; and www.naftaclaims.com. (all sites visited Jan. 2004). On NAFTA chapter 11 dispute settlement generally, *see* Pérez Correa, C. F., 'Crónica de una expropiación no anunciada: el laudo dictado en el Arbitraje Estados Unidos Mexicanos vs Metalclad Corporation', 9 REVISTA MEXICANA DE DERECHO INTERNACIONAL PRIVADO 115 (Mar. 2001).

[41] *See* Chapter 13 above, Section 4.2.

[42] *See* Chapter 1 above, text accompanying notes 42–43, 76.

materials (including petroleum, coal, and natural gas) from which minerals or other products may be extracted. Article 27 states that these ownership rights are inalienable, although the state may grant concessions for their exploitation, and does so in the case of mineral exploitation. An important exception to the granting of concessions exists, however. In regards to petroleum and gas exploitation, and the exploitation of radioactive minerals, Article 27 not only forbids the granting of concessions, but expressly requires the government to exploit these deposit natural resources.[43]

The prohibition of private concessions, whether to Mexican or foreign companies, was included in the original Constitution of 1917. However, the United States government refused to recognize the new government of Mexico if these provisions were enforced.[44] In pragmatic fashion, Mexico declined to enforce the constitutional prohibitions until 1938, when President Lázaro Cárdenas authorized the expropriation of foreign oil companies,[45] and from that date, the constitutional prohibitions on private investment in hydrocarbons have been zealously enforced. In 1938 President Cárdenas created Petroleos Mexicanos (PEMEX), the government-owned company that holds a monopoly on the exploration, production, marketing, and sale of oil and gas, and of basic petrochemicals.[46] As a result, a private landowner in Mexico has no right to exploit subsoil resources located on his property. To the contrary, the federal government has an inherent right to exploit the natural resources located on private property, either directly or by concession to a third party, under conditions that are set forth in the applicable regulatory laws.[47] If PEMEX, or some other government or private entity, causes damage to a person's property as a result of exploration and production, the person may bring a civil action for noncontractual liability under Articles 1910 to 1934 of the Federal Civil Code. Environmental laws similarly protect public lands from environmental damage, and require restoration of lands. Furthermore, when PEMEX carries out exploration and production it is required by the Petroleum Law to protect and

[43] Article 27 states: 'As regards petroleum and solid, liquid or gaseous hydrocarbons or radioactive minerals, no concessions or contracts may be granted, nor may any such concessions that have been granted [previously] remain in effect, and the Nation will carry out the exploitation of these products, under terms to be set by the relevant regulatory law. The Nation has the exclusive right to generate, conduct, transform, distribute and store electrical energy for public use. In this matter no concessions to private parties may be granted, and the Nation will exploit properties and natural resources to this end. The Nation is also in charge of the exploitation of nuclear fuels for the generation of nuclear energy and the regulation of its use for other purposes.'

[44] Pereznieto, L., DERECHO INTERNACIONAL PRIVADO, PARTE GENERAL (Mexico: Oxford University Press, 7th ed., 2000) at 82.

[45] *See* Chapter 1 above, at text accompanying note 137, and commentaries cited in note 137.

[46] On PEMEX generally, *see* Randall, L., THE POLITICAL ECONOMY OF MEXICO OIL (New York: Praeger, 1989).

[47] PEMEX is subject to the *Ley Orgánica de Petróleos Mexicanos y Organimos Subsidiarios*, D.O. 16 Jul. 1992, as amended; the *Ley General de Bienes Nacionales*, D.O. 8 Jan. 1982, as amended; as well as a broad array of laws and regulations that may be found at www.pemex.com, at 'La Empresa: Marco Normativo' (site visited Jan. 2004).

restore the landowner's property.[48] PEMEX's record in maintaining the surface environment is spotty, however, in part because of the under-funded nature of PEMEX operations.

The restriction on private sector involvement has been particularly important in Mexico's political economy, due to the dependence of the government on revenues generated by PEMEX. PEMEX is one of the largest oil companies in the world, but its record for operational efficiency has been abysmal. This is due in large part to politics. The federal government has found it easier to depend on PEMEX revenues than to raise taxes to support government spending. As a result, PEMEX is under-capitalized. At the same time, protection of the government monopoly has allowed PEMEX to survive with an over-sized workforce and the inefficiencies that result from lack of competition.

PEMEX remains the last great bastion of central economic control after the neo-liberal economic reforms of the 1990s. Even with Mexico's conversion to a relatively open market economy, no serious attempt has been made to relax PEMEX's vertical and horizontal monopoly of oil and gas exploration, production, and distribution within the country. This is due in part to the federal government's reliance on oil export revenues to balance the federal budget. To the disappointment of US and other foreign oil companies, there appears to be no major political force in Mexico willing to remove this shibboleth of federal economic and political power.

2.8. Foreign Ownership of Real Property

Foreign persons (individuals or corporations) have the right to acquire full title to real property in Mexico, although there are important qualifications of this right. First, under Article 27 of the Constitution, any foreign person who invests in real property must file in advance a written document with the Secretariat of Foreign Relations demonstrating that the investor agrees to subject himself to Mexican law (i.e. an agreement in conformity with the 'Calvo clause').[49] Second, as explained below, a foreign person may not acquire title to real property near a Mexican border or coastline. Finally, as also discussed below, corporations may only acquire lands that are used in carrying out their corporate objectives. In addition, as explained in Chapter 13 above, because of Mexico's land reform laws, limitations on the size of agricultural properties owned by individuals apply indirectly to corporations; thus, a corporation may only own agricultural land to the extent that the total area owned by the corporation does not exceed the amount of property that could be owned by all the shareholders individually.

[48] *Ley Reglamentaria del Artículo 27 Constitucional en el ramo del Petróleo*, D.O. 29 Nov. 1968, Arts. 7, 10.

[49] Foreign Investment Law (*Ley de Inversión Extranjera*), D.O. 27 Dec. 1993, Art. 10-A. Information on the registration requirements can be found at www.sre.gob.mx/juridicos (site visited Jan. 2004).

2.8.1. *Beneficial* (Quasi) *Ownership of Real Property by Foreign Individuals in Coastal and Border Areas: The* Fideicomiso

One of the important legacies of the Mexican Revolution—a desire to rid the country of foreign intervention—is firmly enshrined in the Constitution of 1917, which proscribes foreign ownership of real property within what is called the 'forbidden zone' (*zona prohibida*). The full language of Article 27, section I is:

> Only Mexicans by birth or naturalization and Mexican corporations have the right to acquire ownership of lands, waters, and related property rights or to obtain concessions for the exploitation of mines or waters. The State may concede the same rights to foreigners, so long as they agree with the Ministry of Foreign Relations to consider themselves as Mexican nationals with respect to such rights, and not to invoke the protection of their governments insofar as these rights are concerned; under penalty, for failing to comply, of forfeiting to the Nation the properties they had acquired. *In no event may foreigners acquire direct ownership of lands and waters located within one hundred kilometers of the borders or fifty kilometers of the beaches* [emphasis added].

Despite the prohibition on foreign investment in the forbidden zone, the Mexican government has long made available forms of property ownership other than full title to help attract productive investment in these prime development areas. Since 1971 foreign nationals have been expressly authorized to acquire the use and enjoyment of rights over real property located within the forbidden zone by entering into a long-term trust agreement (*contrato de fideicomiso*) with a Mexican bank.[50] This real estate *fideicomiso* has evolved over time. In the original Foreign Investment Law of 1973, the trust agreement was limited to thirty years' duration, and some uncertainty existed concerning the right to renew the trust. This uncertainty has been resolved in the current Foreign Investment Law of 1993 (*Ley de Inversión Extranjera, or* LIE),[51] which establishes that a *fideicomiso* covering property in the restricted zone may last for fifty years, and is renewable (LIE Article 13). These real estate trusts have become common vehicles for foreign owners of residential property (resort homes or retirement homes).

Foreign companies are also subject to the constitutional limitations on ownership in the forbidden zone, but they face additional restrictions as well. Foreign corporations are not permitted to establish *fideicomisos* directly, but may only invest in property in the forbidden zones through ownership in Mexican corporations which themselves must enter into the real estate trust agreement. In accordance with Article 10 of the LIE, Mexican companies whose charters prohibit ownership of shares by foreign persons or companies can acquire property in the forbidden zone, since there is no threat of foreign control. In addition,

[50] The *fideicomiso* has its origin in the trust laws of the United States, and has acquired a long tradition in Mexican law. For more information on the *fideicomiso, see* Chapter 9 above, Section 2.4., and *see generally* Batiza, R., *Principios Básicos del Fideicomiso y de la Administración Fiduciaria* (Mexico: Ed. Porrúa, 2nd ed., 1985); and Domínguez Martínez, *supra* note 17.

[51] D.O. 27 Dec. 1993.

LIE Article 10 permits Mexican companies *without* a foreigners' exclusion clause to own property in the forbidden zone if they have agreed to a Calvo clause limitation of their recourse to diplomatic protection.[52]

There are three parties to a *fideicomiso* contract involving real property. The *fideicomisario* is the beneficiary of the trust, and is usually a foreign citizen who, because of the prohibition of Article 27, cannot otherwise hold title to real estate in the forbidden zone. The builder or seller of a residential or commercial property, known as the *fideicomitente*, is the person who initially holds title, and who transfers title to the credit institution and possession of the property to the trust beneficiary. Finally, the trust is established in a credit institution, which serves as *fiduciario*, or fiduciary agent, of the transaction, and which holds title to the property, as recorded in the Public Registry of Property of the location of the real property. The *fideicomisario* pays the purchase price of the property to the *fiduciario* (credit institution); the credit institution acquires title to the property by transferring the sale price to the original owner or builder, or *fideicomitente*. The bank's exposure as *fiduciario* is limited, and for this reason the fees payable to a bank that serves as *fiduciario* are moderate, generally in the order of 1 per cent of the purchase price, with more moderate administration fees paid annually during the life of the *fideicomiso*. On the other hand, the bank may also extend a loan to enable the *fideicomisario* to acquire the property interest; in such cases, the bank's interest is secured by the fact that title to the property is held by the credit institution, albeit for the benefit of the *fideicomisario*.

Article 17 of the LIE permits foreign citizens (individuals and corporations) to establish trusts, or *fideicomisos*, for the acquisition of real property for any of the following purposes: to undertake a wide range of tourism activities, including both public activities (hotels, etc.) and private activities (residences);[53] and to undertake industrial activities (broadly defined), provided that the beneficiary of the *fideicomiso* is a foreign-owned company with direct investment in Mexico and the property is not located in a major industrial area, or is a *maquiladora* (in-bond manufacturing company).[54]

As beneficiary of the *fideicomiso*, the *fideicomisario* has virtually the same rights as an owner of real property, including the right to use and enjoy the property, and to earn income from the property, either directly or through third parties (LIE Article 12). The *fideicomisario*'s interest in the *fideicomiso* can be sold to a third party, whether Mexican or foreign, person or company; in such instances, the third party acquires the interest for the period of time remaining of the original fifty-year period of the trust.

[52] LIE Article 11. Under LIE Article 10, section I, Mexican corporations owned in whole or in part by foreign nationals that wish to acquire property rights within the restricted zone, by use of *fideicomiso*, must also file within 60 days an acceptance of the Calvo clause provision with the Secretariat of Foreign Relations, and must certify that the real property involved is intended for non-residential activities.

[53] LIE Article 19 lists the types of activities.

[54] *See* LIE Articles 5, 6, and 28.

To give an example, in the typical use of a *fideicomiso* for a tourism development, a Mexican corporation with an 'exclusion of foreigners' clause in its charter acquires real property located near a Mexican beach resort for the purpose of building a resort condominium. The Mexican corporation enters into a *contrato de fideicomiso* that will transfer title to the real property to the credit institution. With title to the real property as guarantee, the bank makes a construction loan to the Mexican developer, who becomes the *fideicomitente*. (The Mexican developer typically begins to sell the condominium apartments while they are under construction.) A foreign citizen may acquire trust beneficiary rights to the apartment through a *fideicomiso*, by signing a *contrato de fideicomiso* between the developer, the trust beneficiary, and the bank and by paying the purchase price to the credit institution. (As stated previously, the bank may also provide a loan to the purchaser, in exchange for a security interest in the real property.) The bank issues in return a *certificado de participación inmobiliaria* to the purchaser as *fideicomisario*. The certificate serves as evidence of the purchaser's interest in the property, title to which is held in trust by the bank for his benefit. After using a portion of the purchase price to repay the bank's construction loan to the developer, the bank will forward the remainder, or profit, to the developer.

A similar process is used for the construction of industrial plants owned by foreign corporations within the forbidden zone. The typical industrial project involves the construction of a *maquiladora*, or in-bond assembly plant, within 100 kilometres of the border with the United States.[55] It is important to note, however, that the foreign corporation could enter directly into a *fideicomiso* arrangement, and may do so by establishing a Mexican subsidiary, with the subsidiary serving as *fideicomisario*.[56]

3. The Law of Inheritance

The law of inheritance, like the law relating to property generally, is governed by local law, that is, by the civil codes of each state of the Republic, and of the Federal District. In most instances, matters of inheritance are governed by the civil code of the jurisdiction in which the person was domiciled at the time of death.[57] Since the Federal Civil Code (FCC) rarely applies to matters of

[55] The *maquiladora*, or in-bond assembly plant, is a product of US and Mexican customs laws that permit components to enter Mexican territory to be assembled into finished products and re-exported to the United States, with US customs duties being charged only on the value added. This allows US and foreign companies to use Mexican labourers, at a relatively small cost, to manufacture labour-intensive products. On *maquiladoras* generally, *see* Rein, R., 'Maquiladoras and Their Legal Regime', in vol. 1, *Mexican Law: A Treatise for Legal Practitioners and International Investors* (St. Paul, Minn: West Group, Jorge Vargas, ed., 1998) at 191–230.

[56] *Ley General de Títulos y Operaciones de Crédito*, D.O. 14 Sep. 1932, Art. 383.

[57] *See* Article 24, section VI, of the Federal Code of Civil Procedure; and Article 156, section V, of the Code of Civil Procedure for the Federal District.

succession,[58] this section refers primarily to the Federal Code for the Federal District (CCDF), which closely follows the provisions of the FCC. However, when the state of domicile of the deceased (e.g. Nayarit) is other than the state in which property is located (e.g. Jalisco), the courts of Nayarit will apply the Civil Code of Nayarit, but the judge may choose to follow the procedural rule of the Federal Code of Civil Procedure in administering the estate, for the simple reason that if the ruling is challenged via *amparo*, the federal court will be more likely to give effect to the Nayarit court's ruling.

Mexican inheritance law has been largely influenced by Spanish law, and indirectly by French law which drew from principles established under Roman law. Mexican law recognizes two types of inheritance: testamentary succession *(sucesión testamentaria)*; and intestate succession (*sucesión intestamentaria*), also known as legitimate succession (*sucesión legítima*).

3.1. Testamentary Succession

The CCDF defines a will (*testamento*) as an 'individual, revocable, and free act, whereby an able person disposes of his [or her] property and rights and declares or fulfils duties for after his [or her] death' (CCDF Article 1295). Mexican law does place certain limitations on the freedom of a testator (*testador*) to dispose of property by will. These limitations pertain mainly to the duty to leave means of financial support for six different types of persons (CCDF Article 1368). Thus, a testator *must* leave support (*alimentos*)[59] for the following: descendants under the age of eighteen whom the testator has a legal obligation to support at the time of his or her death;[60] descendants of any age who are unable to work; a surviving spouse[61] if the spouse is unable to work and does not have sufficient assets to support him- or herself, so long as the surviving spouse does not remarry and continues to 'live honourably' (unless the testator expressly excuses the spouse from fulfiling these conditions); surviving parents or grandparents (*ascendientes*); and for the testator's siblings and other relatives to the fourth degree, if the siblings or relatives are under eighteen years of age, or are unable to work and do not have sufficient assets to cover their needs. If a will does not provide support for any of these categories of person, such a person may ask a court to nullify the will in order to obtain support (CCDF Article 1374).

There are several other limitations on a testator's freedom to dispose of property. According to CCDF Articles 1323–1325, the following persons may not inherit property: a doctor who took care of the testator during his or her

58 *See* e.g. FCC Art. 1328 (establishing a requirement for reciprocity for foreigners to inherit property).

59 As used in this context, *alimentos* refers to food, clothing, housing, and health care. In regard to minors, *alimentos* also includes education costs. FCC Article 308.

60 On the obligation to support minors, *see* FCC Articles 303 and 306.

61 If the testator was not married, but lived with a person as if they were spouses for the 5 years prior to the death of the testator, and if that person was not married, the latter may have the same right to support as a surviving spouse. *See* FCC Article 1635.

last illness (if the will was made subsequent to such illness); a notary public or witnesses who participated in the formalization of the will; a spouse, sibling, or relative of such persons; or a notary who took part in the formalizing of the will.

The CCDF sets forth certain basic rules regarding the content of wills. A will is a valid legal act even if it does not specify the appointment of an heir, or even if the heir does not accept the inheritance or is incapable of inheriting. (CCDF Article 1378). The will is a strictly personal act; even though the language of the will may be drafted by a person other than the testator, the testator alone must sign the will (CCDF Article 1295). The testator may change or revoke the will at any time (CCDF Article 1295).

Reflecting the attention to legal formalities noted elsewhere in this book, a will is considered a formal legal act, and is only valid if the will meets the formalities and conditions set forth in the Civil Code (CCDF Articles 2344 and 2406). Furthermore, a holographic will (a will personally drafted by someone without any attention to formalities, but with the intent to dispose of property upon death) is only valid in Mexico if the instrument is deposited within the notarial archives (*Archivo General de las Notarías*) and otherwise conforms to the requirements of the Civil Code (CCDF Articles 1550–1564).

Finally, a will may be nullified if evidence is submitted showing that the intent of the testator was not freely expressed, either because of violence, error, deceit, fraud, or threats against one's spouse or family (CCDF Article 1485).

3.2. Intestate Succession (*Sucesión Intestamentaria*, or *Sucesión Legítima*)

The Civil Code for the Federal District contains provisions dealing with intestate succession: inheritance of property from persons who have not made a will, or from persons who have failed to make known their choice of heir. According to CCDF Article 1599, intestate succession takes place in the following circumstances:[62]

(i) when the deceased has not made a will, or when a will is totally or partially null and void;
(ii) when a testator has not provided in the will for the disposal of all of his or her property;
(iii) when heirs have failed to fulfil a condition imposed on them;
(iv) when the heirs die before the death of the testator, repudiate the inheritance, or are incapable of inheriting property, and no substitute heir has been named;
(v) when a will has been totally or partially revoked;
(vi) when a will has expired as may be the case in certain types of will that are subject to a certain time limit, such as a private will (*testamento privado*) (Article 1571) or a military will (*testamento militar*) (Article 1582); and
(vii) when a will has been destroyed or opened early or when it has been altered (Articles 1548 and 1563).

[62] For a broader explanation of intestate succession, *see* Arce y Cervantes, J., *De las Sucesiones* (Mexico: Porrúa, 3rd ed., 1992) at 163 *et seq*.

The CCDF sets forth the general rules regarding the priority of inheritance in cases involving intestate succession. Thus, the closest relatives exclude more distant relatives (CCDF Articles 1609, 1631, and 1632); relatives of the same degree inherit in equal parts (CCDF Article 1605); if children only survive the death of a parent, every child inherits equally (CCDF Article 1607); a surviving spouse has inheritance rights equal to that of a child (CCDF Article 1611). Of course, this provision applies only to property that is separately owned by the deceased; it does not affect the rights of a surviving spouse to community property, which are described above in Chapter 15.

Finally, in contrast with the United States, Mexico has no estate tax, either at the federal, state, or municipal level. This may help to explain the relative concentration of wealth in Mexico. Despite the lack of tax revenues to support public spending, Mexican political leaders have not chosen to endorse such a tax.

3.3. Judicial Procedures Relating to Succession

The procedures surrounding property rights on succession are similar to the common law concept of probate. Administration of a deceased's estate is carried out under the authority of an executor, or *albacea*, who may be designated in the decedent's will, or may be appointed by a judge.[63]

A petition for probate of an estate is generally filed in the state court (or court for the Federal District) having jurisdiction over the estate, i.e. the court where the deceased's domicile is located. Even in cases in which the federal and state courts have concurrent jurisdiction (for instance, when the estate includes property under the control of the federal government[64]), cases brought before the local courts often end up in federal court due to the expansive jurisdiciton available under *amparo*.[65] Probate requires that the party requesting probate provide written notice to every person who may have an inheritance claim on the estate. Probate is a highly formalistic procedure, and for this reason there are ample opportunities for parties contesting the disposition of an estate to delay the proceedings of the *juicio sucesorio*. In general, the disposition of an estate under testamentary succession is less prone to delay than disposition of intestate succession, due to the heightened possibility of conflict between possible heirs in the latter case.

[63] The *albacea* is responsible for making an inventory of the decased's property, for making decisions regarding the administration of property in the estate, and reporting thereon to the supervising judge. The *albacea* is also responsible for making any payments necessary to preserve the property, and for filing the petition for probate (*petición de juicio sucesorio*) (FCC Art. 1706 CCF).

[64] *See supra*, text following note 40.

[65] On *amparo* jurisdiction, *see* Chapter 8 above.

17

Contracts and Other Obligations

1. INTRODUCTION

The previous Chapter dealt with the law of property, known as *jus in rem*. This Chapter deals with the law of obligations, also known as *jus in personam*, or 'rights against a person'. These categorizations are symptomatic of the civil law tradition. Legal problems are classified as being subject to property laws (formally referred to as *estatutos reales*) or to the laws of obligations (*estatutos personales*) and the Mexican civil codes have separate books for these laws. In modern business dealings such a distinction may seem antiquated, especially when one considers the importance of intangible forms of property such as debts, securities, intellectual property rights, and so on. Nevertheless, the distinction remains an important part of Mexican legal analysis, even though many legal problems have issues that overlap both categories.

In the Mexican legal system, as in other systems of codified law, contract law is regarded as only one branch (albeit the most important branch) of *in personam* obligations. Obligations are viewed as stemming not only from contracts voluntarily entered into, but also from one's status (e.g. as a fiduciary agent, a corporate officer, etc.) and from negligent or intentional misconduct, including violations of criminal law. An Argentinian jurist defines the law of obligations as 'a legal relationship by virtue of which one party (the debtor) has the legal duty to perform a certain task in favour of the other party (the creditor)'.[1] Obligations are linked to a person's property (*patrimonio*), or more specifically to a person's entire estate (*universalidad de los bienes*), under a concept known as *patrimonio universalidad jurídical*, which refers to the totality of property legally held by a person.[2]

The law of obligations is central to any legal system, and in civil law countries such as Mexico the term encompasses concepts derived from Roman law that serve as the root principles for many legal areas of practical importance, including modern commercial law. The inclusion of concepts that date to Roman times lends an air of doctrinal formality to the legal analysis of obligations in Mexico, in contrast to the practical, problem-oriented approach

[1] Alterini, A., *et al.*, DERECHO DE LAS OBLIGACIONES CIVILES Y COMERCIALES (Buenos Aires: Abeledo Perrot, 1996) at 14. The original definition of obligations in Roman law, which forms the basis of Mexico's legal system, takes in the concept of credit. Book III, Title XIII of the Institutes of Justinian reads as follows: '*obligatio est iuris vinculum, quo necessitate adstrirgimur alicuins solvendae rei secundum nostrae civitatis iura*' (obligation is a legal relationship, whereby we are constrained by the need to pay something, according to the laws of our city).

[2] *Id.*

commonly employed by common law lawyers and judges in the United States and elsewhere. Some of these concepts are discussed below, in the section entitled 'Basic Elements of Obligations'.

2. Sources of the Mexican Law of Obligations

As with other subjects of private law, such as family law, property law, and the law of inheritance, obligations are governed by the Mexican civil codes, specifically by the fourth book (*Libro Cuarto*) of the applicable civil code. As private law, in the Mexican federal system the law of obligations is governed by the civil code applicable to the particular state or federal jurisdiction in which an obligation arises, with the Federal Civil Code applicable to federal matters throughout the country.[3] Thus, to give two examples, obligations arising under a contract entered into in Mexico City between two private parties will be subject to the Civil Code for the Federal District (CCDF), unless the parties have indicated in the contract that the law of another jurisdiction will control the agreement;[4] obligations stemming from a personal injury suffered in Guadalajara will be subject to the Civil Code for the state of Jalisco, unless the injury occurred on federal property.[5]

The civil codes are not the only laws that apply to many types of obligations. Many types of transactions, whether of a contractual or non-contractual nature, are also subject to specialized legislation adopted by the federal and state government to regulate particular types of private obligations. For instance, the Federal Consumer Protection Law, or LFPC (*Ley Federal de Protección al Consumidor*[6]), establishes many rules of contract law[7] and tort law[8] designed to protect consumer interests. The Commercial Code, or *Código de Comercio* (discussed below in Chapter 18) also contains rules that apply to commercial contracts. The Negotiable Instruments Law, or *Ley General de Títulos y Obligaciones de Crédito* (also discussed in Chapter 18); corporations law, or the *Ley de Sociedades Mercantiles* (discussed in Chapter 19); and numerous other specialized laws also have rules that affect private obligations. When such specialized laws apply, their provisions take precedence over the more general provisions of the civil codes; the civil codes nevertheless serve as supplementary rules applicable to such specialized activities or transactions.[9]

[3] On the application of the separate civil codes, *see* Chapter 14 above, section 4.2.

[4] Choice of law clauses are valid under CCDF Article 13, section V.

[5] *See* Mexican Constitution, Article 104, and FCC Article 13.

[6] D.O. 24 Dec. 1992.

[7] For instance, LFPC Article 82 provides remedies to a consumer, including rescission, for breach of warranties in a contract.

[8] *See* LFPC Articles 82 and 92, establishing strict liability (*responsabilidad objetiva*) for damages caused by defective products. *See* Ovalle Piedra, Julieta, 'La responsabilidad civil por productos en México, Canada y Estados Unidos', (thesis, UNAM 2001) at 148–149.

[9] The law determining supplementary rules, or *ley supletoria*, are essential to the general doctrine of the civil law tradition that a judge may rely on general principles of law if an applicable law is unclear or insufficient. *See* FCC Article 18, and Article 14 of the Mexican Constitution

The Mexican civil codes list six separate sources or types of obligations, as set out in the first six chapters of Title One (*Título Primero*) of the Fourth Book of the Civil Code (*De las obligaciones*):[10]

(i) contractual obligations (*contratos*);
(ii) unilateral manifestation of intent (*declaración unilateral de la voluntad*);[11]
(iii) unjust enrichment (*enriquecimiento ilegítimo*);[12]
(iv) business management (*gestión de negocios*);[13]
(v) unlawful acts, also known as extra-contractual obligations (torts) (*obligaciones que nacen de actos ilícitos*); and
(vi) workers' compensation (*riesgo professional*).[14]

This Chapter focuses on the first and fifth types of obligations, which correspond generally to the common law subjects of contracts and torts.

3. Basic Elements and Terminology

Before examining specific types of obligations, it is worth setting out some basic elements of obligations, and to define some of the terms that are commonly used in the analysis of obligations.

('apply the general principles of law to resolve disputes of a civil nature, where an express law is lacking'). Morineau, O., EL ESTUDIO DEL DERECHO (Mexico: Porrúa, 2nd ed., 1997), at 444.

[10] *See* Borja Soriano, M., TEORÍA GENERAL DE LAS OBLIGACIONES (Mexico: ed. Porrúa, 2000) at 389 *et seq*.; Rojina Villegas, R., DERECHO CIVIL MEXICANO, vol. 1, Obligaciones (Mexico: ed. Porrúa, 1985) at 177 *et seq*. Borja Soriano and Rojina Villegas remain the leading authorities on the Mexican law of obligations, despite the fact that neither text has been significantly revised in decades. The original Borja Soriano text was published in 1939, and the Rojina Villegas text in 1962. More recent authorities include Bejarano Sánchez, M., OBLIGACIONES CIVILES (Mexico: Oxford University Press, 5th ed., 1997); De La Peza, J.L., DE LAS OBLIGACIONES (Mexico: McGraw-Hill, 1997).

[11] Unilateral manifestation of intent is traditionally broken down into two types: public offerings (such as public bidding) (*oferta*), and last wills and testaments (*testamento*). The rules set forth in this section of the civil codes serve generally as supplementary rules for more specific laws that regulate these subjects.

[12] This chapter includes provisions that are similar to the common law doctrines of unjust enrichment or *quantum meruit*, but also applies to illegal payments or commissions. FCC Article 1882 states that, 'He who without good reason becomes richer to the detriment of another person is obliged to indemnify that person for the impoverishment in the amount that he has become richer'. In contract disputes in Mexico, parties often claim both unjust enrichment and improper payment when the service provided does not meet the terms agreed upon in the contract or when the agreed service is delivered but is not properly performed, and therefore requires some type of redress.

[13] Business management applies when a person improperly interferes (*interviene*) in the protection or preservation or administration of another person's assets or property without the appropriate legal representation (i.e. without proper power of attorney or proxy granted by the appropriate third party). This source of obligation could more precisely be called 'mismanagement of another person's business affairs', and most commonly arises when an employee exceeds his or her authority in the performance of duties entrusted to the employee.

[14] Chapter six includes three Articles (1835–1837) dealing with workers' compensation, covering the liability of employers for workers' injuries suffered in the workplace. These Articles have been superseded by labour laws and social welfare legislation.

All obligations recognized by Mexican law include three basic elements: an active subject, the creditor (*acreedor*); a passive subject, the debtor (*deudor*); and a third element, *objeto de la obligación*, which may be translated as the basis of the obligation.

3.1. The Creditor (*Acreedor*) and the Debtor (*Deudor*)

Any relationship of obligation will involve two distinct parties, the creditor (*acreedor*) and the debtor (*deudor*). Thus, in contracts, the *acreedor* may be the party to whom a performance is due, and the *deudor* the party who owes the performance. In extra-contractual obligations (torts), the *acreedor* is the injured party, and the *deudor* is the party responsible for the act or condition that caused the injury.

Under traditional civil law analysis, 'obligation' connotes reciprocity of rights as well as duties on the part of both parties, creditor and debtor. This concept is not unlike the traditional common law rule of 'mutuality of obligation', that is, both parties to a contract possess rights as well as owe obligations of performance.

3.2. The *Objeto*: Subject Matter or Basis of the Obligation (Legal Duty)

Any obligation must spring from some basis or subject matter (*objeto*) that has been established either voluntarily or involuntarily. When obligations are based on contract, the *objeto* may involve either giving something (*obligaciones de dar*, e.g. pledging something or providing collateral) (FCC Articles 2011–2026); doing something (*obligaciones de hacer*, e.g. tendering delivery of goods) (FCC Article 2027); or refraining from performing an action (*obligaciones de no hacer*, e.g. pledging not to acquire something or not to sell property offered as security) (FCC Articles 2028). *Objeto* is similar to the common law concept of legal duty.[15]

3.3. *Causa*

Causa is the term used to indicate the ultimate purpose for undertaking an obligation, and applies not only to contracts, but to obligations in general. *Causa* is related to the common law concept of intent. Thus, if a seller agrees to sell merchandise that he does not possess nor intends to acquire from a third party, the buyer may request annulment of the contract due to a failure of *causa*.[16]

[15] For a broader discussion of legal duty, *see* Alterini, *et al.*, *supra* note 1 at 57 *et seq.*

[16] *Causa* should not be confused with the concept of causation, which is discussed in Section 5.6. *infra*.

3.4. The Relationship that Gives Rise to an Obligation (*Vínculo de la Obligación*)

Vínculo de obligación refers to the relationship between the creditor and the debtor, and is established when the obligation is created. In Latin American law, a distinction is usually made between the relationship itself and the legal duty that arises from it: the *objeto*, as discussed above.

3.5. Civil Liability (*Responsabilidad Civil*)

If an obligation exists and has not been fulfilled or extinguished, for example, if a contract provision has not been performed, or if an injury to another has been caused by a negligent act, then the obligation may give rise to civil liability, *responsabilidad civil*. Civil liability may either be contractual or non-contractual (*extra contractual*).

3.6. *Dolo*

Dolo is a key concept in civil law. It is similar to the common law concept of intentional or wilful misconduct, and is associated with bad faith of the actor. *Dolo* may exist in contractual obligations when one of the parties makes a material misrepresentation to induce another to enter into the contract (FCC Article 1815). The presence of *dolo* usually results in the nullification of an act.

An example may serve to clarify how the above elements interact. In a contract of sale, the *acreedor* (seller) has an obligation to deliver goods and the right to receive payment. The *deudor* (buyer) has an obligation to pay the price and the right to receive conforming goods. The *objeto* refers to the legal duty to perform an obligation established in a contract, and gives rise to a relationship (*vínculo*) of obligation between buyer and seller, for the purpose of fulfilling a legal objective or *causa*. Failure by the seller to deliver the goods as agreed results in *responsabilidad civil*, which the buyer can redress by filing a civil action in a court of law. If the seller has acted with intent to deceive the buyer (*dolo*) he may also be guilty of a crime of fraud.

4. The Relevance of Case-Law (*Jurisprudencia*) to Contract and Tort Analysis

The drafters of the Napoleonic Code, which served as the model for the Mexican Civil Code, wished to establish a body of rules that were self-evident in application, and would leave little or no room for interpretation by the courts. Two centuries later, it is apparent that this goal was unrealistic: with technological and other changes, what may have seemed like self-evident and self-contained rules are impossible to apply to many situations in real life without interpretation or extrapolation.[17] In this regard, Mexican lawyers will rely on: their understanding of the basic philosophy of the Civil Code; the opinions of authorities in scholarly works; and, to a much lesser extent, case-law (*jurisprudencia*). The usefulness of *jurisprudencia* in interpretation of the law of obligations is weakened by the fact that most Mexican judicial opinions are not published, and the opinions that are published (those of the Supreme Court and of the Federal Courts of Appeals) are extremely general and often lack insight into the specific facts or detailed arguments that decide a case.[18]

While few sources on Mexican contract law exist in English, the reader of Spanish may consult treatises that examine the subject in detail.[19] The common law lawyer, accustomed to a casuistic, fact-based approach to legal analysis exemplified by treatises (hornbooks) published in the United States, will likely find Mexican legal treatises lacking in practical applications and short on factual analyses. Instead, Mexican treatises tend to be laden with doctrine and jurisprudential context, with references to other academic writings. This is a clear demonstration of the difference in legal reasoning between civil law and common law analysis. It is nonetheless true that Mexican authorities, courts and lawyers alike, rely heavily on the published writings of legal experts. As in other areas of private law, Mexican lawyers often consult non-Mexican authorities (Argentinian, Spanish, and French, in particular), to the extent that they discuss common principles that appear in the civil codes.[20]

5. The Law of Contracts

Most obligations today arise out of contract. The importance of contract is reflected in the Mexican civil codes; for instance, the vast majority of the 1,282 Articles in Book Four of the Federal Civil Code ('*De las obligaciones*'), comprising almost half of the entire Civil Code, are devoted to rules governing contractual obligations of one form or another.

Unlike the Uniform Commercial Code in the United States, whose provisions apply only to certain contracts (sales of goods; leases; banking transactions), the contract rules set forth in the civil codes *theoretically* apply to *all* contracts in Mexico, whether concluded between private individuals, between individuals

[17] To the US lawyer, this conclusion is most evident with regard to the relatively few Civil Code articles applicable to liability for personal injuries (i.e. Mexican 'tort law'), the rules of which, derived from the *Code Napoleón*, are extremely general. *See infra*, discussion at section 6.

[18] *See* Chapter 3 above, section 2.3.

[19] The leading treatises on the law of obligations in Mexico are: Rojina Villegas, *supra* note 10, vols. 1 and 2; Borja Soriano, *supra* note 10. Note, however, the comments in note 10 about the freshness of these treatises. *See also* Magallón Ibarra, J. M., Instituciones de Derecho Civil, 6 vols. (Mexico: Porrúa, 1987).

[20] *See*, e.g. Urbano Salerno, M., Contratos Civiles y Comerciales, (Mexico: Oxford University Press, 2002); Colmo, A., De las obligaciones en general (Buenos Aires: Librería y Casa Editora de Jesús Méndez, 1928); Rezzoinco, L.M., Los contratos en nuestro derecho civil (Buenos Aires: S/E, 1950).

and government entities, or between large corporations; whether they involve merchants or non-merchants; and whether they involve the sale of goods, sale of intangibles, promises to perform services, or other types of contractual obligations. (See Article 1859 of the Federal Civil Code.) It is important to note, however, that the civil code provisions are *displaced* by more specific provisions for types of contracts covered either by other parts of the civil code, or by specific laws adopted for such contracts. Thus, commercial contracts are first subject to the more specific rules of the Mexican Commercial Code (*Código de Comercio*), and the state and federal civil codes apply as *supplemental rules* to the extent that a matter is not dealt with in the Commercial Code.[21]

Contracts for the sale or lease of real property, and other obligations directly related to real property (*propiedad inmobiliaria*), are covered by Book Two of the Federal Civil Code (Articles 747–1180), and for such contracts the rules stated in Book Four are only supplementary rules.

It is impossible to provide a thorough grounding in Mexican contract law in a single chapter, and we have limited our discussion to the most general outlines of the civil code procedures surrounding Mexican contractual obligations. More detailed analyses can be found in Spanish-language treatises.[22]

Applicability of the U.N. Convention on contracts for the international sale of goods In 1988 Mexico ratified the United Nations Convention on Contracts for the International Sale of Goods, often referred to as CISG.[23] The Convention applies automatically to contracts for the sale of goods in which a Mexican party contracts with a party from a foreign country that is also a signatory to the CISG. The CISG was adopted to harmonize basic aspects of international contracts for the sale of goods, and has been successful in this regard, although many of the CISG rules are vague and subject to differing interpretations by national courts.[24]

The CISG applies *automatically* to a contract for the sale of goods between a Mexican contracting party and a foreign party from another contracting state, unless the parties exclude the application of the CISG in their contract.[25] There is no precedent for a Mexican court giving effect to the CISG where the parties have chosen to specify its application to a contract to which it would not otherwise apply. Since the United States has also ratified the Convention, the CISG will, unless excluded, automatically apply to a contract between a Mexican

[21] A contract is considered commercial in nature if it is carried out for the purpose of making a profit. Rodríguez y Rodríguez, Joaquín, *Derecho Mercantil* (Mexico: Porrúa, 2001) at 508.

[22] This chapter provides a brief introduction to the substantive law of contracts. For more detailed analysis, *see* Sànchez Medal, R., *De los Contratos Civiles* (Mexico: Porrùa, 1993) 16th ed.; Rojina Villegas, R. *supra* note 10, vol. IV; Lozano Noriega, F., *Cuarto Curso de Derecho Civil*, Contratos, (Mexico: Asociación Nacional del Notariado Mexicano, A.C., 1994) 6th ed.; Pérez Fernández del Castillo, *Contratos Civiles* (Mexico: Porrúa, 1995) 3rd ed.

[23] 22 February 1988.

[24] On the CISG, *see* Adame Godard, J., Contratos Internacionales en América del Norte (Mexico: UNAM/McGraw-Hill, 1999); Honnold, J., *Uniform Law for International Sales Under the 1980 United Nations Convention* (The Hague: Kluwer, 3rd ed., 1999).

[25] CISG Article 6 authorizes the parties to opt out of application of the Convention.

buyer and a US seller, or between a Mexican seller and a US buyer, without regard to where the contract was concluded. The CISG will also apply to a contract between a foreign company and a Mexican government agency for the purchase or sale of goods.

The CISG takes precedence over local rules, but even where the CISG does apply, the applicable civil code will serve as a basis of supplementary rules. In addition, as stated in its Article 1, paragraphs 2 and 3, the CISG does not contain rules concerning the capacity of the parties to contract, nor rules concerning the transfer of property, so these subjects will be governed by the civil code applicable to the transaction.

5.1. Contract Formation

The Federal Civil Code (FCC)[26] requires only two elements to create an enforceable contract in Mexico: 'consent' (*consentimiento*), and 'a basis (*objeto*) that can serve as the subject matter of the contract'. (FCC Article 1994). This is not to say, of course, that all contracts that fulfil these two elements are enforceable. For example, FCC Article 1795 lists four circumstances that invalidate such contracts: legal incapacity of one of the parties; invalid consent (*vicios del consentimiento*);[27] the unlawful nature of the subject matter (*objeto*); and 'consent has not been manifested in the form required by law'. This last element reflects the attention to formal details that underlies much of Mexican private law.[28] While the general rule is that no special form of a contract is required,[29] in concluding contracts, the parties must always be careful to consult the particular requirements of the Civil Code itself. Thus, while there is no general rule stating that a contract must be in writing, some types of contracts must be not only in writing and signed but also registered by a *Notario Público*.[30] One should also consult any specialized laws that may apply to the particular contract in question for special requirements of form or registration.[31]

[26] For reasons stated in Chapter 14 above, section 4.2., this Chapter focuses on the Federal Civil Code, which is copied virtually verbatim throughout the Republic.

[27] On *vicios del consentimiento*, *see* FCC Articles 1812–1823, discussed in Rojina Villegas, Rafael, DERECHO CIVIL MEXICANO, Introducción y Personas, vol. I (Mexico: Porrúa, 1990) 6th ed. at 371.

[28] Excessive formalism is discussed in Chapter 14 above, at text following note 6, and Chapter 19 below, section 3 (esp. 3.4. and 3.5.).

[29] *See* FCC Article 1832: 'each party is bound in the way and by the terms to which each intended to be bound, without specific formalities being required for the contract to be valid, except for certain instances that are expressly set forth by the law'.

[30] *See*, for instance, FCC Article 2317, requiring contracts for the sale of real estate to be signed before witnesses and ratified by a notary public or a judge. The second part of Book Four of the FCC, Articles 2316–2963, establish particular rules applicable to 'diverse types of contracts', and the third part of Book Four contains particular rules applicable to credit agreements. For a discussion of the *notario público*, *see* Chapter 18 below, section 2.3.

[31] For example, the *Ley General de Títulos y Operaciones de Crédito*, or LGTOC, establishes special requirements for registration of certain promissory notes or letters of credit. *See* e.g. LGTOC Article 81.

The US lawyer will notice that Mexican law does *not* require one element that is commonly required for enforceability of contracts under common law: consideration. Under the doctrine of consideration, a promise is not enforceable under contract law unless it is supported by a bargained-for exchange; that is, the promisee must suffer a detriment in exchange for the promise. The principle effect of this requirement is to make donor promises unenforceable, unless the promisee has suffered a detriment based on justifiable reliance on the promise.[32] In Mexico there is no such requirement. Thus, a contract to promise to sell property is binding, even if the promisee has not offered anything in return. (See FCC Articles 2243–2247.)

5.2. Contract Interpretation

FCC Article 19 states that 'Civil law suits should be decided in accordance with the letter of the law or its judicial interpretation. In the absence of a law, disputes will be settled in accordance with general principles of law'. Despite the reference in Article 19 to judicial interpretation, as we have mentioned elsewhere,[33] under the civil law tradition of Mexico judges are not expected to exercise a great deal of leeway in interpreting laws. Mexican judges tend to exercise conservatism in interpreting the language of contracts; judges are generally loath to depart from the 'plain meaning' of the law as it was taught to them in law school.

FCC Articles 1851–1857 set forth basic rules of interpretation for contracts, and these rules have generally been followed in the state civil codes. Thus, FCC Article 1851 states that a contract should be interpreted in accordance with the intention of the parties; FCC Article 1853 states that the court should favour an interpretation that will give validity to the contract, etc. Judges are to interpret contracts in accordance with the usages and customs of Mexico (FCC Article 1856), although international commercial contracts may be interpreted in accordance with international customs and usages.

5.3. Matters Affecting Contract Performance

Rules pertaining to the performance of contracts are contained in numerous parts of Book Four (*Obligaciones*) of the Federal Civil Code. Book Four is separated into three Parts: Part One (Obligations in General); Part Two (Of the Different

[32] *See* American Law Institute, Restatement of Contracts (Second):
Section 17: 'A contract requires a bargain in which there is a manifestation of mutual assent to the exchange and a consideration.'
Section 17(1): 'To constitute consideration, a performance or a return promise must be bargained for.'
Section 17(2): 'A performance or return promise is bargained for if it is sought by the promisor in exchange for his promise and is given by the promisee in exchange for that promise.'

[33] *See* Chapter 3 above, at text accompanying note 15.

Types of Contracts); and Part Three (Creditors' Preferences). Thus, Title Four of Part One (Articles 2062–2184) deals with the effects of obligations in general, and includes rules concerning payment, the effects of non-performance, etc.; these rules apply, if not displaced by more specific rules, to all kinds of contracts. Title Five of Part One (Articles 2185–2223) deals with termination of obligations, and Title Six (Articles 2224–2242) deals with nullification.

The Second Part of Book Four (Articles 2243–2963) is divided into sixteen *Títulos*, or Titles, each of which applies to a different type of contract.[34] Thus, to answer a question concerning the rules governing a particular contract of sale, the lawyer will consult first the language of the contract itself, which establishes the rules agreed upon by the parties. The lawyer will next consult any specialized legislation applicable to the type of contract (such as securities laws, in the case of a sale of securities). Finally, the lawyer will consult the general provisions of Part One, Book Four of the Federal Civil Code, as well as the Provisions of Title Two to Part Two ('On Sales'), FCC Articles 2248–2326. Note that the latter provisions apply to sales of intangible property as well as to sales of goods. Finally, the lawyer may have to consult specialized legislation relating to particular types of sales.

The rules set forth in the civil codes may generally be altered by agreement of the parties; thus, as is the case with Article II of the Uniform Commercial Code of the United Status, the rules stated in the civil code are 'default rules' applicable in the absence of a contrary agreement of the parties as set forth in the contract of sale. The major exception to this rule is contained in FCC Article 6, and similar provisions of the state civil codes, which render unenforceable any provisions agreed upon by the parties that would be contrary to law or public policy, or that would defeat the rights of third parties.

FCC Articles 2062–2118 contain general provisions concerning performance and non-performance of obligations. These provisions are not limited to contractual obligations, and theoretically apply to obligations in general. However, by their nature (many of the articles deal with forms of payment or other matters relevant to contract), most of the articles have little relevance to extra-contractual obligations (torts).

Many of the provisions regarding contract payments are similar to concepts in other legal systems, including the United States. However, one idiosyncrasy of payment in the fulfilment of obligations does exist under Mexican law. When

[34] The sixteen Titles of Part Two are: I. *De los Contratos Preparatorios* [Agreements to Agree]; II. *De la Compraventa* [Sales]; III. De la Permuta [Barter] IV. *De las Donaciones* [Gifts]; V. *Del Mutuo* [Mutual loans]; VI. *Del Arrendamiento* [Rental Agreements]; VII. *Del Comodato* [Gratuitous bailments]; VIII. *Del Depósito y del* Secuestro [Deposit and Attachment Contracts]; IX. *Del Mandato* [Contracts of Power of Attorney]; X. *Del Contrato de Prestación de Servicios* [Service contracts]; XI. *De los Asociaciones y de las Sociedades* [Contracts regarding Associations and Societies]; XII. *De los Contratos Aleatorios* [Aleatory Contracts]; XIII. *De la Fianza* [Bonding and Guarantee Contracts]; XIV. *De la Prenda* [Security Agreements on Movable Property]; XV. *De la Hipoteca* [Mortgage Agreements]; and XVI. *De las Transacciones* [Settlement agreements].

parties stipulate in a contract to payment being made in Mexico in foreign currency, for example in US dollars, Article 8 of the Mexican Monetary Law (*Ley Monetaria*)[35] applies. According to this provision, 'obligations of payment in foreign currency, acquired inside or outside the Republic, to be fulfilled within [the Republic], shall be paid by delivering the equivalent amount in Mexican currency at the exchange rate that is in effect at the place and time in which the payment is to be made'. Thus, if a contractual agreement is made anywhere in the world for payment in dollars, or in any other currency, and payment is due within Mexico, Mexican law gives the debtor the right to pay the obligation in Mexican pesos at the exchange rate applicable on the date the obligation is to be paid.[36]

5.4. Non-Performance of Contractual Obligations: Defence and Conditions

FCC Articles 2104–2118 contain the principal rules concerning non-performance (*incumplimiento*) of an obligation, whether contractual or non-contractual. According to one authority, '[n]on-performance means refraining from delivering the thing owed or from providing the service that [a person] is obliged to perform, as well as performance of something that the debtor was supposed to cease from doing'.[37] Breach or non-performance gives rise to remedies, as discussed below.

Delay in the performance of an obligation is governed by FCC Articles 2104 and 2080, which state:

Article 2104. He who is obliged to perform an action and ceases to perform it or does not perform it in accordance with what has been agreed upon, shall be responsible for damages and loss of loss of income (*daños y perjuicios*) under the following terms:

I. If the obligation was to be fulfilled by a certain date, liability shall start to run as of that date;

II. If the obligation was not contingent upon a time certain, the provisions in the final part of Article 2080 shall be observed.

He who breaches an obligation not to perform an action shall pay damages and loss of income based on the mere fact of the breach.

Article 2080. Should no time limit have been set for making payment in a case involving obligations to give something [*obligaciones de dar*], the creditor may not demand payment until thirty days after the issuance of a demand for payment (*interpelación*), either by court order, or extrajudicially, before a notary or before two witnesses. When obligations to perform some act or service are involved, payment must be made whenever the creditor demands it, as long as the necessary amount of time has elapsed for performance of the obligation.

[35] D.O. 27 Jul. 1931.

[36] Regarding this Law and other related legal provisions, *see* Pereznieto C., L., *DERECHO INTERNACIONAL PRIVADO, Parte General* (Mexico: Oxford University Press, 1998) at 171 *et seq.*

[37] Martinez Alfaro, J., *TEORÍA DE LAS OBLIGACIONES* (Mexico: Porrúa, 2nd ed., 1991) at 198 (authors' trans.).

In the case of time-limited or fixed-term obligations, default begins from the time the non-performance of the obligation comes about. However, if the time for performance is not certain, the Civil Code requires the creditor to send the debtor a notification of demand for payment (*interpelación*), following the procedures set forth in FCC Article 2080. The notification can be made either by a judge or, should the creditor prefer not to deal with the court system, he or she may compose a demand for payment before either a notary public or two witnesses. Once the debtor has received the written notification of the demand for payment (*la interpelación*), time begins to run.

Mexican contract doctrine provides for a defence to an action for non-performance known as *contrato no cumplido*, which is similar to the doctrine under common law contract law of failure of substantial performance (material breach). Under this doctrine, 'the dependence that exists between the respective obligations of parties to a *contrato sinalagmático* [i.e. a bilateral contract, one in which reciprocal obligations exist] makes it possible for one of the parties not to fulfil his obligation if the other party refuses to perform his'.[38] This defence comes from the Roman law principle of *non adimpleti contractus* (non-fulfilled contract). When it is asserted, the contract may be suspended; if a non-complying party refuses to fulfil its obligation, then the innocent party may proceed either to enforce or to rescind the contract, as discussed below. According to Borja Soriano, 'the *non adimpleti contractus* defense applies to all mutually binding [bilateral] contracts where there exists a double obligation, a credit and a debt [. . .] but the defence implies that execution of the obligations of the contracting parties must be simultaneous and it is not available when [the two parties'] performance is consecutive'.[39]

5.5. Defences for Non-Performance: *Force Majeure* and Failure of Conditions

Non-performance of a contract may be excused in two major instances: when the party's failure to perform was caused by events beyond the party's control (*force majeure* or *cas fortuit*); and when the fulfilment or non-fulfilment of a condition excuses performance.

5.5.1. Fuerza Mayor *and* Caso Fortuito

Western legal systems, civil and common law, traditionally provide a contracting party with an excuse for non-performance if performance was made impossible, or impracticable, due to some act or event. This doctrine is commonly referred to as *fuerza mayor* (*force majeure*, in its French origins). According to Mexican legal doctrine, *fuerza mayor* is an 'event outside the conduct of the debtor and that takes place independently thereof with such force as to be impossible to be overcome so that it discharges the debtor of responsibility for

[38] Borja Soriano, *supra* note 10 at 494. [39] *Id.*

performance of the obligation'.[40] The term *fuerza mayor* is usually understood as dealing with events such as acts of nature (fires, floods, storms, etc.) and is related to the common law term 'acts of God', but it may also arise due to acts of man, such as government prohibitions, etc.

Caso fortuito (from the French *cas fortuit*, meaning unforeseen event) is a doctrine of excuse similar to *fuerza mayor*, but does not involve any human action that prevents performance or renders it impossible. *Caso fortuito* has been defined as 'an event that the parties failed to foresee, but even if it had been foreseen, it could not have been avoided'.[41] Non-performance of a contract due to *caso fortuito* occurs when the debtor (contracting party) is capable of performing (that is, performance has not become physically impossible) but the circumstances under which a party was expected to fulfil an obligation prove to be entirely different from those that were foreseen by the parties when they entered into the agreement.

Taken together, *fuerza mayor* and *caso fortuito* are similar to the common law doctrine of impracticability, under which performance of a contract is excused if, in the words of section 2-615 of the Uniform Commercial Code, 'performance as agreed has been made impracticable by the occurrence of a contingency the nonoccurrence of which was a basic assumption on which the contract was made'.

The Federal Civil Code contains numerous provisions relating to *fuerza mayor* and *caso fortuito*. For instance, FCC Article 2017, section V, states that where property is to be transferred to the debtor, the loss of property by operation of *fuerza mayor* or *caso fortuito* will render the obligation to transfer property excused, but the risk of loss falls on the creditor, unless the parties have agreed otherwise. The Federal Civil Code also contains numerous other provisions that engage the concepts of *fuerza mayor* and *caso fortuito* (see e.g. FCC Articles 2431, 2435, 2483, etc.).

5.5.2. Conditions

FCC Articles 1938–1952 set forth rules for obligations that are subject to conditions. According to FCC Article 1938, an obligation is conditional 'when the existence or performance [of an obligation] depends upon a future or uncertain event'. As in the common law, the Civil Code provides for two basic types of conditions: condition precedent (*condición suspensiva*) and condition subsequent (*condición resolutoria*).

Under FCC Article 1939, the condition is precedent (*suspensiva*) when the existence of the obligation depends on its performance or fulfilment. The obligation does not arise until the condition exists.[42] An example of a contract subject to a *condición suspensiva* is one in which the obligor guarantees to the obligee the performance of debtor (payment of a sum of money, for example).

[40] De Pina, R. and de Pina Vara, R., *Diccionario de Derecho* (Mexico: Porrúa, 1992) at 296.
[41] *Id.* at 148.
[42] *See* Borja Soriano, *supra* note 10 at 397.

The failure of the debtor to make payment is a *condición suspensiva* of the obligation to perform under the guarantee agreement. The obligor's performance is deemed 'suspended' (*suspensiva*) while the debtor still has time to pay the debt. Contracts subject to condition precedent are highly useful in commerce. For instance, two companies may enter into a merger agreement that is subject to a *condición suspensiva* to the effect that the merger and related contracts will not become effective until the fulfilment of certain conditions, including approval of the merger by the Federal Competition Commission (CFC); the Commission has ruled that such conditional agreements are acceptable under the Federal Law of Economic Competition.[43] If the Commission does not approve the merger, the merger and related agreements are not enforceable.

FCC Article 1940 defines a condition subsequent (*condición resolutoria*) as one in which, once the condition occurs, 'the obligation is fulfilled, and matters revert to the way they were, as if that obligation had never existed'. In other words, occurrence of the condition causes an obligation to disappear. For example, the seller of equipment, such as a crane, may insert in the contract of sale a *condición resolutoria* that the contract may be rescinded upon the occurrence of a condition: the buyer's failure to make a timely payment. Upon rescission, the seller may reclaim possession of the crane. The Supreme Court has held that such a *condición resolutoria* is enforceable not only against the buyer but also against third parties.[44]

5.6. Contract Remedies

General remedies for breach of contract are covered in FCC Articles 2104–2162, which are based on rules adopted under the French *Code Napoléon*. Of course, in addition to the remedies provided in the civil codes, specialized legislation exists, such as the Federal Law of Consumer Protection (*Ley Federal de Protección al Consumidor*).[45] According to Article 2104, one who fails to perform an obligation, or performs the obligation in a manner that fails to conform to the contract, is liable for the 'damages and losses' (*daños y perjuicios*) caused by such a breach. The Civil Code makes a distinction between these two terms: according to FCC Article 2108, the term *daños* (damages) means 'the loss or reduction [in value] caused to a property interest by non-performance of an obligation'; *perjuicio*, on the other hand, is similar to lost profits, and is defined by FCC Article 2109 as 'the deprivation of any lawful earnings that would have been obtained by the fulfilment of the obligation'.

[43] Comisión Federal de Competencia, Annual Report 1993–1994, at 26. For a discussion of Mexican competition laws and the role of the Commission, *see* Chapter 13 above, section 5.

[44] Supreme Court of Justice of the Nation. Novena Epoca. Instancia: Tribunales Colegiados de Circuito. Fuente: Semanario Judicial de la Federación y su Gaceta. Tomo I, junio de 1995. Tesis: VIII, 1°1C. P. 524. N° de registro: 205,084, Aislada. Materia Civil. Amparo. Amparo en revisión 4/95. José Luis Velarde Pérez y Quirino Benjamín Narcio. 28 April 1995, Unanimous Opinion. Writing for the Court: Marco Antonio Arroyo Montero. Clerk: Julio Jesús Ponce Gamiño.

[45] D.O. 24 Dec. 1992, as amended.

The concept of *daños* dates back to Roman law, and may include physical damage to personal or real property, as well as a reduction in property value caused by a breach. Thus, if a seller delivers non-conforming materials to a factory, causing physical damage to the factory's machinery, the seller will be liable to pay *daños*, an amount in monetary damages sufficient to restore the machinery to the condition it was in before the physical damage occurred. In addition, the seller may be liable for *perjuicios*, or the loss of earnings suffered by the factory owner because of inability to operate the factory while the machinery was inoperable.

5.6.1. Causation Requirement

To recover monetary damages, the non-breaching party must prove a causal link between the breach and the injuries incurred. According to FCC Article 2110, '[d]amages and loss of income (*daños y perjuicios*) must be the immediate and direct consequence of non-performance of the obligation, whether they have actually been caused or would necessarily be caused [by the breach]'. Mexican courts take this requirement seriously, and have interpreted Article 2110 as a strict requirement to prove a direct relationship between the breach and the injuries allegedly caused by it. Thus, the Mexican Supreme Court has held that it is insufficient for a buyer to prove damages for a seller's breach by providing copies of invoices for similar goods purchased from other buyers at a higher price, without some additional proof that such goods were actually purchased in substitution for the goods not delivered.[46] The issue of causation also arises in extra-contractual obligations, which are addressed below

5.6.2. Liquidated Damages Clauses and Penalties

As with common law contracts, Mexican law gives effect to liquidated damages clauses (*claúsula penal*) that are voluntarily entered into by the parties to a contract (FCC Articles 1840, 2117). Since proof of damages is as difficult in Mexico as it is in other countries, liquidated damages clauses are useful and relatively common. According to FCC Article 1842, where a contract contains a valid liquidated damages clause, the creditor is not required to prove actual damages.

An important limitation exists on the enforcement of liquidated damages clauses. First, FCC Article 1843 states that the amount set forth in a liquidated damages clause cannot exceed the value of the underlying obligation. Furthermore, as is also the case under common law contracts, Mexican courts will not enforce a liquidated damages clause in cases in which the liquidated

[46] *Amparo* directo 7300/85. Purina, S.A. De C.V. 13 January 1988. Five vote majority. Writing for the Court: Mariano Azuela Gïtrón. Clerk: Lourdes Ferrer Mac Gregor. SUPREMA CORTE DE JUSTICIA DE LA NACION, Octava Epoca; Instancia: Tercera Sala; Fuente: Semanario Judicial de la Federación; Tomo: I Primera Parte; page 289; Genealogía: Informe 1988, Segunda Parte, Tercera Sala, tesis 79, p. 126; No de Registro: 207,549; Aislada; Materia(s): Civil.

amount set by the parties is out of proportion to the actual damage suffered. In other words, clauses which are intended to penalize the breaching party, rather than compensate the victim of the breach, are not enforceable. This conclusion is based on the language of FCC Article 2117, and from the definition of *daños* and *perjuicios* as compensatory in nature, as set forth in FCC Articles 2107–2110. Finally, the second paragraph of FCC Article 2117 states that if the obligor's performance consists of the payment of a sum certain, the liquidated damages resulting from such a failure to pay may not exceed the 'legal rate of interest', which is currently set at 9 per cent by FCC Article 2394, unless the parties agree otherwise in the contract. FCC Articles 1844 and 1845 also permit a judge to reduce the amount due under a liquidated damages clause in proportion to the amount of the underlying obligation that has been partially performed by the obligor.

5.6.3. *Specific Performance of Contracts: Attachment and Foreclosure in Satisfaction of Judgment*

CFPC Articles 400–503 contain rules relating to judicial enforcement of civil judgments (*ejecución*), attachment of property pursuant to judgment (*embargo precautorio*), and foreclosure of property (*remate*). Where the plaintiff has secured a judgment against the defendant, the judge may issue a writ of execution (*auto de ejecución*), ordering the debtor to comply with the obligation to perform, if this is possible; if the debtor does not comply, the debtor's assets may be attached to assure payment of damages (referred to as *embargo precautorio*) (CFPC Articles 401 and 402).

Other examples of specific performance exist under Mexican law. Article 525 of the Code of Civil Procedure for the Federal District[47] authorizes the court to issue an order requiring the defendant to convey real or personal property to the plaintiff or a third party, and if this is not done, the court may order a judicial official (*actuario*) to carry out the order of conveyance using public force, if necessary.

5.6.4. *Recission as an Alternative to Enforcement of a Contract*

Non-performance of an obligation may not only give rise to damages; it may also serve as a cause for rescission of a contract. The party who has suffered a breach of contract may choose *either* to enforce the contract and collect damages (*daños y perjuicios*), *or* to rescind the contract.[48] A rescission clause, known as a '*pacto comisorio expreso*', may also be written into contracts in Mexico. Under this clause, the parties agree that the contract will be rescinded if either of the parties does not fulfil their respective obligations.[49] When the *pacto comisorio expreso* is used, the parties may agree to a time limit for serving written notice of non-fulfilment to the breaching party in order to provide a last chance to fulfil obligations. Should this party (the obligor) not comply before the term expires, the other party (obligee) may declare the contract

[47] D.O. 21 July 1993. [48] FCC Art. 1949. [49] Borja Soriano, *supra* note 10.

rescinded by sending notice certified by a notary public to the place of business of the obligor (FCC Art. 1949).

The non-breaching party must be careful to gather evidence of the non-performance in order to substantiate the rescission, if necessary. Nonetheless, when a party rescinds a contract for non-fulfilment of contract and subsequently files suit for damages and lost income, the case will almost always end up in court. Rescission does not remove the obligee's entitlement to damages caused by the obligor's non-performance. In such a law suit, not only must the plaintiff prove that the defendant did not comply with the contractual agreement, but also that such non-compliance prevented performance of the plaintiff's obligations under the contract.

5.6.5. *Statute of Limitations*

The Federal Civil Code establishes a ten-year statute of limitations (*prescripción negativa*) as a general rule for the enforcement of obligations (FCC Article 1159). However, there are important exceptions to this general rule. For example, a two-year statute of limitations applies in matters listed under FCC Article 1161 (e.g. an action by a commercial vendor to recover the price of goods, see FCC Article 1161, section II), and actions for the payment of rent (FCC Article 1162).

6. *Responsabilidad Extracontractual*: Non-Contractual Obligations (Torts)

Much of Mexican contract law may seem recognizable to a common law practitioner. The same is not true of Mexican 'tort law'. The approach to non-contractual liability for intentional or negligent misconduct by persons or entities (known in Mexico as *responsabilidad extracontractual*) is dramatically different in Mexico from that in the United States. The latter country is known for imaginative theories of liability and for multi-million dollar judgments awarded in thousands of cases filed each year and argued before civil juries; legal representation of plaintiffs and defendants in US courts is lucrative, and the legal doctrines are constantly being refined. In Mexico, on the other hand, tort law is little changed from the scant, general principles that were incorporated from the French Civil Code of 1804. The same rules of liability, highly general and relatively undeveloped, have been applied for many decades; because of severe limitations on the amount of damages recoverable in personal injury actions, Mexican lawyers tend to ignore *responsabilidad extracontractual* as an area of law practice worthy of their attention. As Professor Jorge Vargas has written, 'no reputable law firm in Mexico handles personal injury cases resulting from a tortious act'.[50] The reasons, Vargas notes, are cultural as

[50] Jorge Vargas, 'Tort Law in Mexico', in vol. 2, *Mexican Law: A Treatise for Legal Practitioners and International Investors* (St. Paul, Minn: West Group, 1998) at 214.

well as legal: Mexican society has traditionally been less confrontational than US society, and Mexican tort victims are usually satisfied with compensation from corporate tortfeasors for medical expenses and other direct losses, rather than rushing to file a lawsuit.[51] (Some of this reticence, however, may have to do with a traditional lack of confidence in the judicial system.)

The Mexican aversion to aggressive application and development of tort law is further evidence of an important contrast between Mexican and US approaches to the role of law in society. The US legal system reflects a society that prizes individualism; individuals are encouraged to use self-help methods, including litigation, to preserve their rights, including their right to be free of interference and injury by others. By contrast, the Mexican legal system reflects a more paternalistic society, in which the government agencies are expected to intervene when necessary to protect those who have been injured or disadvantaged. Prosecution of individual rights, through the courts, is uncommon, and this is particularly true where personal injury is involved. Thus, if a disastrous accident (an aeroplane crash, or an explosion) occurs in Mexico, causing death and injury to many people, the matter is often settled outside of the courts, with the responsible party or the party's insurer paying moderate compensation to the victims.

As the following discussion shows, while the Mexican civil codes include rules creating tort liability, these rules are expressed in very general terms. The *jurisprudencia* (case-law) is often unhelpful in interpreting them, since the published opinions (*tesis*) of the Supreme Court and Federal Appellate Courts are themselves vague and the facts of the cases are not usually reported. If one combines the simplicity of the doctrines and limitations on damages with two other factors—the lack of civil juries, and the conservative attitudes of judges in resisting creative interpretations—it is easy to see why there is little tort law in Mexico. US courts have increasingly been called upon to apply and interpret Mexican tort law, as the expansion of tourism in Mexico has brought a rise in the number of personal injury actions filed against hotels, tour operators, automobile rental companies, and transportation companies. For the reasons just stated, these cases are usually filed in US courts if the plaintiff can find a basis of jurisdiction there (presence of corporate affiliates, advertising activities, etc.). Because of the relative lack of authoritative commentary in Mexico, either by courts or scholars, US judges are often left with a relatively unclear direction in applying the general provisions of the Mexican civil codes, leaving room for more 'creativity' than might actually occur in most Mexican courts.

6.1. Theories of Tort Liability (*Responsabilidad Extracontractual*)

Articles 1910 (liability for wrongful acts) and 1913 of the Federal Civil Code (strict liability for use of dangerous instruments) are the principal sources of

[51] *Id.*

tort liability in Mexico. Other articles cover liability in specialized situations, and are not discussed here.[52]

Corporate entities (*personas morales*) are liable for damage caused by their employees in carrying out their work (FCC Articles 1918, 1924), as are hotel owners for damage caused by their employees (FCC Article 1925). The liability of minors may be imputed to parents, guardians, or others who have authority over them (FCC Articles 1919–1921). Separate provisions also exist for the liability of employers to their employees for work-related injuries (FCC Articles 1935–1937), although in these cases both liability and compensation are also regulated by the more detailed provisions of the Federal Labour Law, as discussed above in Chapter 13.

6.1.1. Liability for 'Wrongful Acts' (FCC Article 1910)

FCC Article 1910 sets forth the most basic rule of tort liability in Mexico:

> He who, acting improperly [*ilícitamente*] or against proper customs [*buenas costumbres*], causes damage to another, is obliged to make reparation for it, unless [such person] proves that the damage came about as a consequence of the fault or inexcusable negligence of the victim.

The bulk of Mexican tort law hangs upon this spare frame. The Civil Code itself carries virtually no provisions elucidating the key terms, and as discussed above, there is very little *jurisprudencia* that provides insight into their application to specific cases. Nevertheless, the language is virtually unchanged from that which appeared in the *Code Napoleón* of 1804, and for this reason, comparative academic sources (French, Spanish, Argentinian) have helped round out a meaning. For instance, the term *ilícitamente*, translated as 'improperly' above, could be taken to mean 'unlawfully'. However, such a term connotes the violation of a law, and legal experts make it clear that a person may be held liable even though no specific law has been broken. According to Bejarano, the term *ilícito* refers to 'unlawful, culpable, and harmful conduct, which brings upon its perpetrator the obligation to repair the damage and gives rise to the civil liability of the perpetrator. Stated in other terms: an *hecho ilícito* is a culpable violation of a legal duty that causes damage to another and gives rise to civil liability.'[53]

The principles established in Article 1910 are broad. If given an expansive treatment, they could provide as broad a terrain for potential liability as exists in US tort law. For instance, 'against proper customs' seems very similar to the common law concept of negligence. Unfortunately, the summary nature of Mexican judicial opinions published in the *Semanario Judicial de la Federación* do little to help elucidate this norm by reference to detailed analysis of the law and facts.

[52] *See* e.g. FCC Articles 1929 and 1930 (liability of animal owners); FCC Articles 1931–1933 (liability of owners or inhabitants of buildings).

[53] Bejarano Sánchez, *supra* note 10, at 221 and 222.

As discussed in the section on damages, below, the severe limitations on tort damages mean that even if a theory of liability is well established, the amount of damages recoverable is very modest, and this has served to limit the development of tort liability generally.

6.1.2. *Strict Liability* (Responsabilidad Objetiva) *(FCC Article 1913)*

The other principal source of tort liability is similar to the common law concept of strict liability: that is, a person or entity may be held liable under certain conditions even if the person has not been guilty of negligence or misconduct. This form of liability, referred to as *responsabilidad objetiva* or *riesgo creado* ('created risk'), is contained in FCC Article 1913, and has been incorporated into most civil codes of the Mexican states.[54] FCC Article 1929 (liability of owners for damage caused by animals) and FCC Article 1932 (liability of landowners for damage caused by certain listed defects, such as explosions, gas leaks, falling trees, etc.) similarly provide for liability without requiring the plaintiff to show negligence or misconduct on the part of the plaintiff.

FCC Article 1913 states the general rule of strict liability:

> When a person makes use of machines, instruments, apparatuses, or substances that are inherently dangerous, because of the speed they may develop, because of their explosive or flammable nature, because of the power of the electric current that they conduct, or because of any other analogous reason, that person is liable for the damage caused, even though the person may not be acting unlawfully, unless [the person] proves that that damage came about as a result of the inexcusable fault or negligence of the victim.

FCC Article 1913 is sufficiently general that it gives rise to strict liability in many instances where US common law would not recognize strict liability. Thus, an automobile is a 'dangerous machine' due to the speed it can develop, and therefore the driver of an automobile will be held strictly liable for damages caused by any accident, without regard to negligence, as long as the victim was not guilty of contributory negligence.[55] In addition, if the owner of the vehicle is someone other than the driver, the owner is jointly and severally liable under strict liability (but with the possibility of an indemnity action against the driver). The same is true of aeroplane pilots, boat operators, and other operators of modes of transport. As discussed below, the effect of requiring strict liability for such common accidents, without regard to the fault of the victim, is mitigated by the severe limitations on damages recoverable by the victim. In addition, Mexican judges tend to take a conservative approach to such cases, setting a high standard for proof of the causation required between the dangerous act and the injury to the victim.

[54] *See* e.g. Civil Code of the State of Quintana Roo, Article 115; Civil Code of the State of Mexico, Article 1742; Civil Code of the State of Nuevo León, Article 1810.

[55] SJF, 8a, Tribunal Colegiado Circuito, T. XIII, p. 432 (1994).

6.1.3. Product Liability

The Mexican civil codes do not have specific provisions covering the liability of manufacturers for damage caused by defective products (product liability). Thus, if Fulano, the driver of an automobile, has an accident with another vehicle, causing serious damages to the driver and passengers of the other vehicle, he is liable under FCC Article 1913. If Fulano can prove that the accident was caused by a defect in the design or manufacture of the automobile, he may sue the manufacturer for liability based on FCC Article 1910, and may seek not only indemnity damages, but also damages for his own injuries.[56] In asserting liability under Article 1910, he must show negligence or misconduct on the part of the manufacturer. Such actions are extremely uncommon, due to the reluctance of courts to recognize the liability of manufacturers for defective products. In contrast with the United States, Mexican society tends to rely on governmental protection of citizens through enforcement agencies, such as the Federal Consumer Protection Agency (*Procuraduría Federal del Consumidor*, or PROFECO),[57] rather than through the use of civil litigation by private parties.

6.2. The Effect of Contributory Fault or Negligence of the Victim

FCC Articles 1910 and 1913 provide a defence for persons or entities whose intentional misconduct or negligence has caused injury to others, if 'the damage came about as a consequence of the fault or inexcusable negligence of the victim'. The person who causes the injury has the burden of proving the contributory negligence of the victim.

There is little published scholarship on the subject of contributory fault, although Bejarano has written that the concept 'does not have to do with every act of negligence (*falta de conducta*) committed [by the victim], since a minor act of negligence by the victim will not exonerate the party who causes the damage. The only fault that operates as a defence is *inexcusable* fault, that is, serious or wilful negligence, unusual conduct of a negligent type that is committed by persons who are careless or reckless.'[58] The case-law (*jurisprudencia*) on this subject unfortunately sheds little light on the doctrine.

6.3. Tort Liability Stemming from Criminal Conduct

Civil liability stemming from criminal acts, or *delitos*, is known as *responsabilidad civil delictuosa*.[59] Such liability may result from a criminal act that causes

[56] SJF, 8a, Tribunal Colegiado Circuito, T. XIV, p. 528 (1994).

[57] Article 26 of the Federal Law of Consumer Protection (*Ley Federal de Protección al Consumidor*, D.O. 24 Dec. 1992, allows PROFECO to bring suit against the manufacturer of a defective product or service on behalf of persons injured by the product or service, and if successful, the defendant must indemnify the parties who can establish proof of injury. The Federal Law of Consumer Protection contains numerous other provisions relating to guarantees and indemnification for damages. *See* e.g. Articles 61–82. (For more information on PROFECO, *see* www.profeco.gob (site visited Jan. 2004)). D.O. 24 Dec. 1992.

[58] Bejarano Sánchez, *supra* note 10 at 234.

[59] *See* Borja Soriano, *supra* note 10 at 348 *et seq*.

damages to the victim. In accordance with Article 7 of the Federal Criminal Law (*Ley Penal Federal*),[60] material damages caused by criminal acts or failures to act may produce criminal liability. Traditionally, however, if the victim of a criminal act wishes to seek compensation for such damages, this must be done in a civil action that is separate from the criminal action, and the elements of civil liability must be separately proven. Thus, if Fulano deceives Mingano by selling him a worthless debt instrument, and is found guilty by a criminal court of criminal fraud, Mingano may file a civil action against Fulano, and may offer into evidence proof of the criminal conviction; however, to hold Fulano liable for return of the funds, Mingano must prove *de novo* the elements of civil liability under FCC Article 1910.

The preceding paragraph discussed the traditional approach taken in Mexico to tort liability that arises from criminal conduct. Recently, a federal appeals court ruled that a criminal judge could, as part of a criminal sentence, require a criminal defendant to indemnify the victims of his crime for damages suffered because of the criminal act, rather than leaving the matter to the victim to bring a separate civil action.[61]

6.4. Tort Damages

The key to understanding the limited development of Mexican tort law is contained in the strict limitations placed on damages. Mexican law recognizes only compensatory damages for non-contractual liability (*responsabilidad extracontractual*): that is, the purpose of damages is to restore the victim, through payment of compensatory damages or otherwise, to the position the victim was in prior to the injury. The Courts are not allowed to award punitive damages in such cases, either in contractual or non-contractual cases.[62] Furthermore, in awarding compensatory damages, the generosity of the courts is limited by both law and legal tradition.

FCC Article 1915 begins with the following sentence: '*At the election of the victim*, compensation for injury should consist of restoring the situation to its previous state, when that is possible, or in the payment of damages or loss of income (*daños y perjuicios*)' (emphasis added). The underlined phrase makes it clear that the plaintiff may choose to ask the court either to award monetary damages (*daños y perjuicios*), or to order the defendant to restore a thing that has been damaged to its previous condition. Thus, the plaintiff in an automobile accident may seek from the defendant, as *daños*, the amount needed to pay all hospital and medical costs and to repair or replace the plaintiff's damaged automobile. There is no limit expressed in FCC Article 1915 to such damages for hospital care, and other expenses related to curing the injury. In addition,

[60] D.O. 17 Sep. 1931, as amended.

[61] Contradicción de tesis 2/2002-PS resolving conflict between the First Collegiate Court of the Fifteenth Circuit and the Second Collegiate Court of the Fourteenth Circuit, SJF, 9a, Primera Sala, T. XVI, Tesis 1a J 51/2002, at 160, Nov. 2002) (opinion of Olga Sánchez Cordero Dávila).

[62] SJF, 9a, T. V, Tribunales Colegiados de Circuito, Tesis VI, 20. 93c at 92, Feb. 1997.

the defendant may be required to compensate the plaintiff for *perjuicios*, or loss of income due to wages the plaintiff was unable to earn while incapacitated.

Beyond these damages for the cost of hospitalization and loss of income, the Federal Civil Code, and its progeny, place severe limitations on the amount of compensatory damages for physical injuries. These limitations are contained in the second paragraph of FCC Article 1915, which deals with damages for physical disabilities that result from personal injuries. That paragraph reads as follows:

> When personal injuries are caused and produce death, total or partial permanent disability, or total or partial temporal disability, the degree of compensation will be set in accordance with the Federal Labour Law [*Ley Federal de Trabajo*]. To calculate the corresponding indemnification, [the court] will take as its base [a figure] that is four times the amount of the highest minimum daily wage in effect in the region and will apply such figure to the number of days that are indicated in the Federal Labour Law for each of the mentioned disabilities. In case of death the compensation will be paid to the heirs of the victim.

In requiring the courts to set damages in relation to the provisions of the Federal Labour Law, FCC Article 1915, which has its counterpart in most, but not all, state civil codes,[63] has placed a strict limit on the amount of damages recoverable in personal injury cases. Articles 483–497 of the Federal Labour Law set forth the amount of damages that workers who are injured at work may receive as compensation from their employers.[64] These provisions were drafted to provide compensation to persons who could not work because they had become disabled in the workplace. By making reference to them, FCC Article 1915 makes these provisions applicable to all persons injured by anyone in any place. Because they are drafted with a daily labourer in mind (minimum daily wage), the amounts are extremely modest, especially by US standards.

6.4.1. *Federal Labour Law Provisions Relating to Personal Injury and Death*

Article 477 of the Federal Labour Law (LFT) sets forth a list of the types of bodily injury that a person may suffer: temporary disability, permanent partial disability, permanent total disability, and death; the first three are defined in LFT Articles 478–480. For example, according to LFT Article 492, when an injured worker has lost the use of a leg (permanent partial disability) he is entitled to receive indemnification based on the percentage of his disability, as set forth in a long table of disabilities contained in LFT Article 514. In Mexico City, the daily minimum wage in 2003 was equal to approximately $US4.00. As a result, an injured person who has lost the use of a leg will collect a grand total of 1,095 days (i.e. 3 years) of salary but this amount may not be more than $US8.00 × 1,095 = $US8,760.

[63] For instance, the Civil Code of the State of Quintana Roo, which includes the tourist centres of Cancún, Cozumel, and Playa del Carmen, contains no reference to the Federal Labour Law. *See* Civil Code of Quintana Roo, Article 124.

[64] *See* Chapter 13 above, at text accompanying note 28

The Federal Labour Law is even more penurious when it comes to indemnifying the survivors of a person who has been killed. According to LFT Articles 500–503, the decedent's survivors are entitled to recover an amount equal to two months of the deceased's salary to cover funeral expenses, and in addition an amount equal to 730 days (two years) of salary. As in the case of personal injury, if the salary of the deceased was greater than twice the daily minimum wage in the region, then the latter will provide a maximum limit on recovery for wrongful death (LFT Article 486). Thus, the total amount of damages that can be awarded for death of a worker cannot exceed 730 days times $US8.00, or $US5,840 (and an additional $US480 for funeral expenses).

6.4.2. Application of the Federal Labour Law Provisions to Civil Liability in Tort

In recognition of the modest nature of the amounts of indemnification under the Federal Labour Law, FCC Article 1915 quadruples the amount applicable to personal injuries in general. Nevertheless, because the minimum daily wage set by the federal government is so small (in December 2002, the equivalent of 43.65 pesos, approximately 4.35 US dollars)[65] the amounts recoverable are extremely small by US standards. As a result, the maximum amount that may be claimed under Article 1915 for wrongful death by the family member of a deceased will be four times the minimum daily wage (approximately $US4.00) multiplied by 730 (the number of days specified in LFT Article 502), which amounts to $US11,680.

Significant ironies can be produced by the limitations on damages awardable under FCC Article 1915. For instance, if the driver of a vehicle runs over a pedestrian, the driver will be strictly liable for damages in accordance with FCC Article 1913. If the pedestrian's legs were broken in the accident, the driver will have to pay damages under FCC Article 1915 for the following: out of pocket losses (*daños*) such as hospital and medical costs; the loss of income incurred by the pedestrian while unable to work (*perjuicios*); and temporary loss of the use of his his legs, in accordance with the figures set forth in the Federal Labour Law. Depending on the amount of medical costs, the damages could be significant, at least by Mexican standards. However, if the pedestrian is killed instantly the above losses are not incurred. Instead, the driver will be strictly liable for the wrongful death, in the amount of $US11,680, a modest amount in comparison with damages due to injuries that do not result in death. Of course, moral damages may be significant in wrongful death cases, but as discussed below, the courts have not been aggressive in awarding large sums for moral damages.

Despite such ironies, there seems to be little support for amending the civil codes in Mexico to create a more generous system of personal injury compensation. The reasons are rooted in Mexican culture, in which personal losses are

[65] D.O. 23 Dec. 2003.

traditionally remedied in communitarian rather than adversarial ways: through community support systems, both informal (family, village, etc.) and formal (insurance, governmental agencies), rather than by resort to litigation on behalf of an individual. This may well be an area in which the Mexican legal system will resist influence from US legal models.

6.4.3. *Moral damages* (Daños Morales)

In Mexico, as in most countries that follow the civil law tradition, the law of non-contractual obligations recognizes a special class of damages known as moral damages (*daños morales*). Moral damages may be characterized as damages that are awarded to compensate the victim for intangible losses suffered due to the defendant's wrongful misconduct. FCC Article 1916 defines *daño moral* as 'the adverse effect a person suffers in his or her feelings, affections, beliefs, respect, honour, reputation, private life, physiognomy and physical appearance, or in the way in which other people regard the person. Moral damages will be presumed to have been suffered when a person's freedom or physical or psychological well-being has been endangered or diminished through misconduct.'[66]

To a lawyer trained in the common law, 'moral damages' may appear similar to certain classes of damages that are frequently awarded in personal injury cases under the common law system: emotional distress, loss of consortium, or mental anguish. Unfortunately, however, they are not well defined in Mexican case-law or commentary. The *jurisprudencia* that exists on moral damages tends to repeat the language of the code provisions, with little insight into their application.[67] Borja Soriano, an authority on Mexican civil law since 1939, reflects the traditional, conservative view towards moral damages, and appears to question whether moral damages should be awarded in cases where the plaintiff has not suffered any physical injury or diminution in income or property.[68] Borja Soriano's view reflects the conservatism of the original Civil

[66] The final sentence of this paragraph from FCC Art. 1916 refers to actions that take place *ilegítimamente*. We have translated this term as 'misconduct'. The term *ilegítimamente*, like the term *ilícitamente* in FCC Article 1910, is not limited in application to acts that contravene a law. For instance, a breach of contract may be considered an action that takes place *ilegítimamente*, in the sense that it contravenes the private law of the parties. Such a breach may also give rise to extra-contractual liability, either to another party to the contract or to a third party who is injured by the breach.

[67] *See* e.g. Novena Epoca. Instancia: Tribunales Colegiados de Circuito. Fuente: Semanario Judicial de la Federación y su Gaceta. Tomo: XIV, septiembre de 2001. Tesis: 1.3°.C.243 C. Página: 1305. Octava Epoca. Instancia: Tribunales Colegiados de Circuito. Fuente: Gaceta del Semanario Judicial de la Federación. Tomo: 85, enero de 1995. Tesis: 1.5°.C.J/39. Página: 65.

[68] Borja Soriano, *supra* note 10 at 295: 'On one hand, there exist [moral damages] that have to do with what is referred to as the social aspect of one's moral "property": injury to a person's honour, reputation, esteem. On the other hand, there exists a category [of moral damages] that touches upon the "affective" part of a person's moral being; they injure a person's feelings towards others, and have to do, for example, with the sorrow that a person experiences due to the death of a loved one. The first category is always, or almost always, related to a pecuniary damage: the lack of consideration suffered by a person has financial repercussions, perhaps requiring him to abandon a job or other position, and compromising

Code on the subject of moral damages. On the other hand, newer works[69] take a more liberal view regarding the application of moral damages, which should be available as a compensation for the 'immaterial losses' of feelings and affection even though the plaintiff has not demonstrated a loss of income or damage to physical property.

Amendments to the Civil Code for the Federal District, that have been carried over to the Federal Civil Code, would appear to support a trend towards a more expansive view of moral damages. The second paragraph of FCC Article 1916 states that a person whose misconduct causes moral damage must indemnify the victim by the payment of monetary damages.[70] Until 1994 the Civil Code had been interpreted to disallow moral damages in cases in which no damage to tangible property had resulted from the misconduct. However, in that year the Civil Code was amended[71] to add to the second paragraph of FCC Article 1916 a statement that a person may be liable for moral damages 'independently of whether material damages may have been caused'.[72] Thus, for example, a person who has been defamed by another may claim moral damages even if he or she is unable to demonstrate tangible property damage or loss of income.[73] This change would seem to undermine the implication that moral damages may only be awarded when there has been a demonstrable pecuniary loss.

The amount of moral damages recoverable is not limited by the Civil Code, which simply states that '[t]he amount of indemnification [for moral damages] shall be determined by the Judge taking into account the rights that have been injured, the degree of liability, the economic situations of the party who is liable and the injured party, as well as the other circumstances of the case' (FCC Article 1916, fourth paragraph). Theoretically, therefore, a judge could award a sizable amount, equal to millions of dollars, as moral damages to tort victims.

his future or that of his children, or putting his business in danger. In such a case, there is little difficulty in admitting the need for compensation. [. . .] As to the second type of damage [feelings towards others], there are numerous cases in which [the courts] refuse compensation for feelings towards others. Thus, *daño moral* is often free of any connection [with actual physical damage]. The pain and suffering are the only detriments suffered; the victim has not actually suffered a pecuniary damage. In these cases, [. . .] a question arises whether they are compensable. An enumeration of such cases is impossible; we may only cite examples [of recovery] [. . .] that have to do with physical injuries that do not affect a person's ability to work: pain, scars, and injuries to the person's appearance' (authors' trans.).

[69] Ochoa Olvera, S., *La Demanda Por Daño Moral* (Mexico: Montealto, 2nd ed., 1999) at 138: 'In Mexican law, the time is ripe to remove this type of civil liability from atavistic, medieval concepts' (author's translation).

[70] The same paragraph states that moral damages may be awarded in cases involving strict liability under FCC Article 1913, as well as in matters involving governmental liability for acts of public servants under FCC Articles 1927 and 1928. The final paragraph of FCC Article 1916 permits the judge, in a case in which the moral damage has injured the plaintiff's reputation, to order the defendant to publish extracts of the opinion as an additional remedy.

[71] D.O. 10 Jan. 1994.

[72] *See* Ochoa, S., *La demanda por daño moral* (Mexico: Mundo Nuevo, 1991) at 31.

[73] Defamation is actionable under FCC Articles 1910, 1916, and 1916*bis*. In addition, defamation may be punishable as a crime in accordance with Federal Penal Code Articles 348–355.

However, research of Mexican case-law shows that judges have been reluctant to interpret the language of Article 1916 in a way that is generous to plaintiffs. The moderate nature of awards of moral damages is due to several factors. First, there is simply the weight of tradition: in the past, judges have not seen fit to award generous moral damages, and this conservative attitude is hard to overcome. Second, there is no jury in Mexico; decisions on the amount of damages are made by judges: government bureaucrats not easily swayed by sympathy or by the legal rhetoric of litigating attorneys. Third, the fourth paragraph of FCC Article 1916 states that the judge is to take into account the economic resources of both the victim and the tortfeasor. Thus, if either the victim or the tortfeasor is of humble means, a court is unlikely to award large sums in damages.

6.4.4. *Two-Year Statute of Limitations; Governmental Immunity*

The Federal Civil Code establishes a two-year statute of limitations (*prescripción negativa*) for civil injuries that are actionable under FCC Article 1910, starting from the time that the act of misconduct took place (FCC Article 1161, section V; FCC Article 1934).[74]

Government agencies are liable for damages caused by their employees in accordance with FCC Article 27. In addition, in 2000 Congress adopted the *Ley Federal de Responsabilidades de los Servidores Públicos.*[75]

[74] Compare the Civil Code for the Federal District, Article 1161.
[75] *See* Chapter 9, above, section 7.1.3.

18

Commercial Law

1. Introduction

As in other countries with modern economies, commercial law in Mexico has its roots in the *lex mercatoria*, the law merchant, that was developed by merchant traders after the Middle Ages and spread throughout the world. The law merchant departed from the formality of Roman civil law, being more pragmatic and attuned to the needs of commerce. The law merchant also influenced France's first Commercial Code, the *Code de Commerce* of 1808, which left its mark on Mexico with the publication of Mexican commercial codes in 1854, 1884, and finally in 1890. The French Commercial Code (the *Code Napoléon* of 1808) and the Italian Commercial Code of 1882 established legal frameworks for certain transactions, the definition of certain obligations, and the creation of certain forms of commercial enterprises or businesses as 'acts of commerce', in addition to defining the category of actors considered merchants. In so doing, commercial law became institutionalized and a special written law was developed,[1] covering a list of 'acts of commerce'.

1.1. Exclusive Federal Jurisdiction to Legislate on Matters of Commercial Law

Article 73, section X of the Mexican Constitution of 1917 grants to the federal Congress exclusive power to legislate in the field of commerce. The genesis of this provision dates back to 1883, when Article 72, section X of the Constitution of 1857 was amended to grant the Federal Congress the exclusive power to 'issue codes binding on the whole Republic in mining and commerce, [with] banking institutions [being] included in the latter [of these two fields]'. Prior to this reform, in the Constitutions of 1824 and 1857, and in light of Mexico's federal structure of government, commercial matters had been the responsibility of the states and the Federal District, and consequently each state would issue its own commercial codes (as did the States of Mexico (1854) and Tabasco (1878)) or, instead, would adopt the Federal Code of 1854 for their

[1] Barrera Graf, J., *Instituciones de derecho mercantil* (Mexico: Porrúa, 2nd ed., 1991), at 2–4.
On the history of Mexican commercial law generally, *see* Pallares, J., *Derecho mercantil mexicano* (Mexico: UNAM, 1987); Mantilla Molina, *Derecho Mercantil* (Mexico: Porrúa, 29th ed., 1998) and Pina Vara, R., *Elementos de Derecho Mercantil Mexicano* (Mexico: Porrúa, 26th ed., 1998).

own local jurisdiction.[2] The decision to make commercial law an exclusively federal concern was an important factor in standardizing commercial practices throughout the nation, warding off potential conflicts of law between different states. In civil law matters, by comparison, each state has the power to adopt its own civil code.

Federalizing commercial law has not resulted in absolute federal control over commercial practices, however. The constitutional grant of exclusivity applies only to substantive law (*la parte sustantiva*), including the identification of merchants, forms of business organizations, acts of commerce, public registry of commercial acts, bankruptcy, and certain procedural aspects. Commercial litigation, however, is a matter of concurrent jurisdiction, and either state or federal courts are competent to hear matters stemming from commercial disputes, at the discretion of the plaintiff.[3] Even where commercial cases are brought in state courts, however, the state courts must follow federal procedural law, as established in the Commercial Code and in the Federal Code of Civil Procedure.

Furthermore, while the Commercial Code includes many provisions that relate to basic contract law (*obligaciones contratuales*), they do not establish a complete set of contract rules. Rather than adopting a separate Commercial Contract Code, the Mexican Congress determined that the rules of contract law established in the Federal Civil Code supplement the Commercial Code.

Commercial practices in the age of global commerce and electronic means of communication seem to have little in common with nineteenth-century concepts of doing business. It is surprising to note, then, that the Commercial Code currently in force in Mexico is the same Code that was adopted on 15 September 1889, and became effective on 1 January 1890. The Commercial Code of 1889 (hereinafter Commercial Code)[4] was intended to codify in one place every facet of commerce. As commercial practices have become more complex and specialized, however, the Commercial Code has gradually been

[2] *See* Barrera Graf, *supra* note 1 at 22–25.

[3] Section I-A of Article 104 of the Mexican Constitution states: 'Federal courts have subject matter jurisdiction over all civil [including commercial] and criminal controversies resulting from compliance with and application of federal laws and international treaties to which Mexico is a party. If such controversies affect only private parties, the judges and courts of the states and of the Federal District, at the election of the plaintiff, may also assert jurisdiction.
Despite the backlog of cases in federal courts and the lack of confidence in the impartiality of state courts, both state and federal district courts are swamped with commercial matters, many of them involving the relatively simple processing of claims to enforce promissory notes; as a result, commercial matters account for a high percentage of the total caseload in state courts. According to recent statistics of the Superior Court of Justice of the Federal District, 46.45% of that court's docket involve commercial law. Coordinación de Estadística Judicial, Año Judicial Fiscal 2000, Tribunal Superior de Justicia del Distrito Federal.
The inadequacies of the judicial system appear to make the use of commercial arbitration attractive. However, as pointed out in section 4.2 *infra*, Mexico lacked a legal framework for commercial arbitration until the adoption of reforms to the Commercial Code in 1993, and the Mexican business community has been slow to embrace the use of commercial arbitration.

[4] D.O. 13–17 Oct. 1889.

supplanted and augmented, by the repeal of many original provisions and by the adoption of more specialized legislation that lies outside the Commercial Code.

This Chapter focuses primarily on the general principles of commercial transactions, as governed by the Commercial Code and supplemented by the Federal Civil Code. The reader should be aware that many types of commercial transactions are governed by specialized laws that have supplanted the Code, including the General Law of Business Corporations (*Ley General de Sociedades Mercantiles*);[5] the General Law of Co-Operative Corporations (*Ley General de Sociedades Cooperativas*);[6] the Law of Negotiable instruments and Credit Transactions (*Ley de Títulos y Operaciones de Crédito*);[7] the Financial Institutions Law (*Ley de Instituciones de Crédito*);[8] the General Law of Organizations and Auxiliary Activities of Credit (*Ley General de Organizaciones y Actividades Auxiliares del Crédito*);[9] the Securities Law (*Ley de Mercado de Valores*);[10] the General Law of Institutions and Mutualist Corporations of Insurance (*Ley General de Instituciones y Sociedades Mutualistas de Seguros*);[11] the Law of Commercial Bankruptcies (*Ley de Concursos Mercantiles*);[12] the Federal Law of Bonding Institutions (*Ley Federal de Insitutiones de Fianzas*);[13] the Federal Copyright Law (*Ley Federal de Derechos de Autor*);[14] the Law of Industrial Property (*Ley de la Propiedad Industrial*);[15] the Law of Navigation and Maritime Law (*Ley de Navegación y Comercio Marítimo*);[16] the Law of Foreign Trade (*Ley de Comercio Exterior*);[17] the Law of Foreign Investment (*Ley de Inversión Extranjera*);[18] the Law of Investment Corporations (*Ley de Sociedades de Inversión*);[19] and the Federal Law of Economic Competition (*Ley Federal de Competencia Económica*).[20]

Despite the application of specialized laws, the Commercial Code of 1889 has never been repealed, and basic notions of the Commercial Code still have relevance. The Commercial Code still serves as a supplementary source of substantive and procedural rules, and has particular relevance in the most general commercial matters, such as rules concerning obligations, the definition and responsibilities of merchants, the rules relating to judicial procedure in commercial cases, and arbitration.

Finally, Mexico adheres to several important international conventions the rules of which have direct application to commercial transactions in Mexico,

[5] D.O. 28 Aug. 1934, discussed below in Chapter 19.

[6] D.O. 30 Aug. 1994, as amended D.O. 4 Jun. 2001.

[7] D.O. 26 Aug. 1932.

[8] D.O. 18 Jul. 1990 as amended D.O. 23 May 2000, discussed below in Chapter 20.

[9] D.O. 14 Jan. 1985, as amended D.O. 4 Jun. 2001.

[10] D.O. 21 Jan. 1975, as amended D.O. 1 Jun. 2001, discussed below in Chapter 20.

[11] D.O. 21 Aug. 1935, as amended D.O. 16 Jan. 2002.

[12] The current *Ley de Concursos Mercantiles* was published in D.O. 12 May 2000 replacing the previous Law of Bankruptcies and Suspension of Payments (*Ley de Quiebras y Suspensión de Pagos*), D.O. 20 Apr. 1943.

[13] D.O. 29 Dec. 1950, as amended D.O. 16 Jan. 2002.

[14] D.O. 19 May 1997.

[15] D.O. 27 Jun. 1991, as amended D.O. 17 May 1999.

[16] D.O. 21 Nov. 1963.

[17] D.O. 27 Jul. 1993.

[18] D.O. 27 Dec. 1993, as amended D.O. 4 Jun. 2001.

[19] D.O. 4 Jun. 2001.

[20] D.O. 24 Dec. 1992, as amended D.O. 23 Jan. 1998.

including the United Nations Convention on Contracts for the International Sale of Goods (CISG).[21]

1.2. Legal Formalities and Commercial Transactions

Just as the common law of contracts favours a general rule of freedom to contract, commercial contracts in Mexico are governed by the principle of the autonomy of the will of the parties, which is recognized in broad terms in the Commercial Code. Thus, Commercial Code Article 78 states that 'In commercial agreements each of the parties is obliged in whatever manner and under whatever terms it appears each party intended to be obliged'.[22] While this provision seems to indicate a certain disregard of form and formality, in practice there is a strong predilection in favour of adherence to formalities in commercial contracting. An important aspect of this is the practice of registering commercial instruments and transactions in a public registry.

The Office of the Public Registry of Property, which is located in each state, is entrusted with maintaining the Public Registry of Commerce (*Registro Público de Comercio*).[23] The Registry is charged with maintaining a public record of the names of merchants who are registered to carry out commercial acts in Mexico, as well as a record of their specific transactions. Registration as a merchant is voluntary for individuals (*personas físicas*), but mandatory for corporations (*personas morales*);[24] merchants generally choose to be registered to secure the enforceability of their business dealings. Individual commercial transactions are not generally required by law to be registered. However, certain commercial transactions are not binding on third parties unless they are registered with the Public Registry. These include contracts for the purchase and sale of real property for speculative purposes; agreements for the incorporation, dissolution, liquidation, merger, or acquisition of business organizations; the purchase and sale of shares and obligations or the issuance or acquisition of the capital stock of companies; and agreements related to maritime commerce or

[21] The leading Mexican authority on the application of the CISG is Adame Godard, J., *Contratos Internacionales en America del Norte* (Mexico: UNAM/McGraw-Hill, 1999). Other relevant conventions applicable in Mexico include the Inter-American Convention on the Law Applicable to International Contracts, 33 ILM 732 (17 Mar. 1994); the United Nations Convention on Representation for the International Sale of Goods, D.O. 22 Feb. 1988; and the United Nations Convention on Prescription for the International Sale of Goods, D.O. 6 May 1988.

[22] For a more detailed discussion of this principle, *see*: López Velarde, R., 'Derecho aplicable en materia de contratos internacionales', in: Revista Mexicana de Derecho Internacional Privado, October 1998, at 37 *et seq.*; and Pereznieto, L. and Silva, J., *Derecho Internacional Privado*, Parte Especial (Mexico: Oxford University Press, 2000) at 249 *et seq.*

[23] The Public Registry of Property is under the local jurisdiction of each state, and maintains records of real property. The Public Registry of Commerce is under federal jurisdiction, and maintains a registry of merchants and commercial transactions. Commercial Code Article 18. The Regulations of the Public Registry of Commerce were published in D.O. 22 Jan. 1979.

[24] A non-registered corporation has an irregular status, and those who act as representatives or proxies (*mandatarios*) of such entities may be held jointly and severally liable for obligations of the corporation *vis-à-vis* third parties. *Ley General de Sociedades Mercantiles*, Art. 2.

ship mortgages, among others.[25] In general, many businesses and individuals choose to register commercial agreements in the Public Registry as a matter of course, simply to facilitate proof of the transaction in case of future disputes.

The following types of information are required by the Commercial Code to be recorded in the Public Registry of Commerce when a commercial transaction is registered:[26]

(i) the name, domicile, type of business, and starting date of operations in which the merchant engages;
(ii) the charter of the corporation, any amended articles of incorporation, rescissions, dissolution, or spin-offs;
(iii) the minutes of the first general assembly meeting, and attachments required for publicly traded companies;
(iv) the general powers of attorney and appointments that are granted to managers, dependent commercial agents, or any other proxies;
(v) increases or decreases in the capital stock of publicly traded companies;
(vi) issues of shares of stock, bonds, and other forms of corporate obligations, stating the series and the number of the instruments of each issue, their interest rate and amortization schedule, the total amount of the issue, and the property, works, rights or mortgages, when applicable, that are pledged to support their payment;
(vii) commercial notary guarantees (*fianzas de los corredores públicos*).

Registration is carried out by the notary public or the *corredor público*, as discussed in Section 3 below. The public document citing the commercial transaction must be filed before the Public Registry of Commerce located in the domicile of the merchant.

Originally centralized as a federal agency, reforms in 2000[27] resulted in the opening of branch offices of the Public Registry of Commerce under the local control of state governments,[28] in order to facilitate commercial registration throughout the country. Unfortunately, this measure has also given rise to uneven quality of registration services: in urban centres the Registries are staffed with highly trained personnel equipped with modern technology, while in other areas registration continues to be conducted through entries by hand in books and under unsound management practices. The increasing use of interconnected computer databases should help to alleviate this problem.

In addition to the Public Registry of Commerce, there exists a National Maritime Public Registry (*Registro Público Marítimo*), which was created by the Law of Navigation (*Ley de Navegación*)[29] and is under the Secretariat of

[25] Commercial Code Articles 25, 26. [26] Commercial Code Article 21.

[27] D.O. 29 May 2000.

[28] Through the *Dirección General de Correduría y Registros Comerciales* of the Secretariat of the Economy, the federal government co-ordinates with state governments the operation of the Public Registry of Commerce in each state. If a transactions involves property located in a state other than that of the domicile of the merchant, the transaction should also be recorded in the Registry of the state in which the property is located.

[29] D.O. 4 Jan. 1994. *See* the Regulations of the Public Maritime Registry, D.O. 29 Aug. 1980.

Communications and Transportation. The maritime registry maintains records of: Mexican vessels and naval craft; contracts of maritime acquisitions or assignments, as well as acts that grant maritime-related rights *in rem*; transactions related to property rights in maritime property, including mortgages and liens; contracts of charter; contracts for shipbuilding in Mexico, or ships that are built abroad and are intended to be registered as Mexican; and any other contract or document relating to sea vessels, maritime commerce, and port activity, which, according to the law, must be registered.

1.3. Mexican Business Culture

Foreign parties who transact business in Mexico should be aware that Mexico's business culture, that is, the set of unwritten practices that help determine the way business is conducted, may differ significantly from that of other countries, depending on the type of business or transaction. An analysis of Mexican business culture is beyond the scope of this book,[30] but one should be aware that customs and cultural practices will be important factors in determining the rights and obligations of parties, in addition to the rights and obligations established by law. Here we merely draw the reader's attention to some salient features of Mexican commercial practice.

1.3.1. Size of Markets and Concentration of Wealth

First, while Mexico's economy is large by comparison with other countries in the hemisphere, it is approximately one-twentieth the size of the US economy.[31] Mexico's economy is large enough to be a sophisticated industrial country, but its relative size and its economic integration with the United States (more pronounced since NAFTA's entry into force) makes it dependent on US economic forces. Because of this, and because of the historic legacy of interference from foreign powers (noted in Chapter 1 above) there is a tension in Mexico between embracing and profiting from US influence, and resisting or controlling the adverse effects of this influence. This tension is often felt at many levels, institutional as well as political, but it may also surface in personal relations and negotiations.

The relative size of Mexican markets is also reflected in a second characteristic of Mexican business: a concentration of wealth and economic power in

[30] *See generally* Kenna, P., *Business Mexico: A Practical Guide to Understand Mexican Business Culture* (Lincolnwood, Ill: Passport Books, 1994); Leppert, P., *Doing Business with Mexico* (Fremont, Calif: Jain Pub. Co., 1996); Malt, R., *Passport Mexico: Your Pocket Guide to Mexican Business, Customs and Etiquette* (San Rafael, Calif: World Trade Press, 1996).

[31] Mexico's Gross Domestic Product (GDP) in 2001 was equal to approximately 617 billion US dollars, as compared to Canadian GDP of 677 billion US dollars the same year. By comparison, the GDP of the United States in 2001 was over 10.1 trillion dollars. *Per capita* income in the United States in this period was seven times that of Mexico's *per capita* income, and 50% higher than Canada's. Source: www.worldbank.org/data-query (site visited Jan. 2004).

a small number of families that dominate certain sectors of the Mexican economy. One hundred years ago the Rockefellers, Vanderbilts, and others held considerable power over major sectors of the economy, but this is no longer the case. Bill Gates, the founder of Microsoft, is reputed to be almost as wealthy as John D. Rockefeller was at the height of his power, but Gates and others like him face a much larger and more competitive marketplace than did the Rockefellers. Mexico, with a smaller economy and a political economy that stifled competition for many decades, still shows a high concentration of economic power in several large extended family empires (the Garza Sada family in Monterrey, the Slim and Servitje families in Mexico City, and others) that have had inordinate influence over particular sectors because of their majority ownership of financial and industrial enterprises. In some instances, the privatization and sale of government-owned enterprises to wealthy families has added to the power of certain family groups; the acquisition of Telmex and Probursa by the Carlos Slim family is an example. In addition, protection of the newly privatized sector from competition has also aided the growth of these businesses.

This concentration of wealth, coupled with venture capital markets that are relatively underdeveloped, affect the financing of new business operations in Mexico. In the United States, the owner of a start-up company has access to diverse forms of venture capital, which may be available depending on the future company's potential. In Mexico, a similar entrepreneur has traditionally been obliged to use family connections and networks to achieve financing, a much more personal approach. This characteristic of Mexican business began to change in the 1990s, with the emphasis on neo-liberal economics and the breakdown of governmental controls that stifled competition. However, the use of family connections and networks to achieve financing continues to play an important part, since interest rates continue to be high for the small amount of venture capital available.

1.3.2. Mexican Business and Government Relations

Over the course of the seventy years that the PRI maintained an authoritarian grip on Mexico's government, merchants and their organizations became tied to the corporatist system of government, as described above in Chapters 1 and 5.[32] In 1941 Congress adopted the Law of the Chambers of Commerce and Industry (*Ley de Cámaras de Comercio e Industria*),[33] which required all merchants to form chambers categorized by industrial sector in order to represent the interests of the members. In reality, these mandatory chambers of commerce enabled the government to negotiate effectively with a highly regimented private sector, setting conditions for economic growth. While the *sector privado* was not one of the pillars of the PRI, the industrialists who controlled the country's private

[32] For a discussion of how businesses fit into the corporatist model, *see* Newell Garcia, R., and Rubio, L., MEXICO'S DILEMMA: THE POLITICAL ORIGINS OF ECONIMIC CRISIS (Boulder, Colo: Westview Press, 1984).

[33] D.O. 26 Aug. 1941.

economy adhered to a tacit agreement with the government: the government would provide stability, protection from external competition, and government contracts in exchange for private business leaders co-operating generally with the PRI machine.

In the wake of Mexico's economic and political opening up, the Mexican Supreme Court has ruled that forcing anyone to join or become a member of a chamber of commerce was inconsistent with the constitutional principle of freedom of association.[34] As a result of the Court's decision, the 1941 law was repealed and replaced by the Law of Business Chambers and Their Confederations (*Ley de Cámaras Empresariales y sus Confederaciones*),[35] which has done away with mandatory membership.

2. Structure and Scope of Application of the Commercial Code

2.1. Structure of the Commercial Code

The Mexican Commercial Code consists of over 1,500 Articles divided into five Books, or *Libros*. However, as explained above, many of the Code's provisions have been supplanted by subsequent federal laws, and for this reason almost half of the Code's original Articles have been abrogated (*derogado*). The five Books of the Commercial Code cover basic provisions, including: *Libro Primero*, Articles 1–74, general rules for merchants, commercial registration, accounting, and commercial notaries; *Libro Segundo*, Articles 75–640, commercial acts, commercial contracts, commissions, factoring, sales and exchanges, transport of goods and legal tender, warehousing,[36] provisions on letters of credit, payments, and check (abrogated and replaced by the General Law of Title and Credit Operations, *Ley General de Títulos y Operaciones de Crédito*);[37] *Libro Tercero*, Articles 641–944, maritime commerce (abrogated, and replaced by the Law of Navigation, *Ley de Navegación*;[38] *Libro Cuarto*, Articles 945–1048, bankruptcies (abrogated, and replaced by the Law of Navigation and Maritime Commerce, *Ley de Navegación y Coimercio Marítimo*);[39] *Libro Quinto*, Articles 1049–1500, commercial procedure, including litigation and arbitration.

[34] 'The freedom of association enshrined by Article 9 of the Constitution is the right enjoyed by private individuals, both natural as well as artificial entities, to create a new legal entity that shall have its own legal status [personality, which is] distinct from that of their associates. Such a right is violated by Article 5 of the Law of Chambers of Commerce and of Industry, in imposing upon merchants and industry workers, whose capital [stock] is listed with the Secretariat of the Treasury (*Secretaría de Hacienda y Crédito Público*) as being 2,500 pesos and above, the obligation to register in the corresponding Chamber [of their jurisdiction]'. Tesis P/J.28/95, SJF, 9a, T. 11, October 1995.

[35] D.O. 20 Dec. 1996.

[36] The rules on warehousing have been superseded by the General Law of Organizations and Auxiliary Activities of Credit (*Ley General de Organizaciones y Actividades Auxiliares del Crédito*), D.O. 14 Jan. 1985.

[37] D.O. 27 Jan. 1932.

[38] D.O. 4 Jan. 1994.

[39] D.O. 20 Dec. 1996.

2.2. Application to Merchants

The Mexican analyses of commercial law usually begin with a discussion of two definitional subjects: to whom does commercial law apply, and what are the 'acts of commerce' that are regulated by it?

In the United States, most provisions of the Uniform Commercial Code (UCC) apply to merchants and non-merchants alike. By contrast, in Mexico the Commercial Code applies only to merchants. Commercial Code Article 54 states that a merchant (*comerciante*) is anyone who, having the legal capacity to engage in commerce, makes this his or her everyday occupation.[40] As is apparent from the broad language of Article 54, the definition of merchant covers Mexican nationals as well as foreign nationals, and individuals (*personas físicas*) as well as organizations (*personas morales*). The Commercial Code classifies merchants on the basis of the nature of the person and the activities engaged in by the person. Therefore, a public stock corporation (*sociedad anónima*, or S.A.) or a limited liability company (*sociedad de responsabilidad limitada*, or S. de R.L.), for example, which have been chartered under the General Law of Business Organizations (*Ley General de Sociedades Mercantiles*), are considered to be merchants, so long as the nature of their activity is commerce. An individual is considered to be a merchant if commerce is his or her regular occupation. Furthermore, if an individual occasionally engages in a transaction that is considered by law to be an act of commerce, then that person is also subject to commercial law.

2.3. Notaries Public (*Notarios Públicos*) and Commercial Notaries (*Corredores Públicos*)

In a formalistic legal system such as Mexico's, notaries public and commercial notaries serve to confer official, legal recognition of the acts for which they are called upon to perform notarial functions, and also as public registries of commercial transactions.[41] The parties to such transactions may also seek legal advice from notaries, although most businesses in need of certification from a notary public or commercial notary seek expert advice from commercial lawyers who draft the documentation required for certification, and who present the documentation to the notary public.

As noted above,[42] many commercial acts are required by law to be authenticated and recorded in the Public Registry of Commerce in order to have legal

[40] CC Article 54, section I: 'Any person who according to local laws is eligible to enter into contracts and take on obligations, and who these laws do not prohibit expressly [from engaging in] the profession of commerce, has the legal capacity to exercise it'. *See* Mantilla Molina, *supra* note 1 at 77.

[41] *See generally* Raigosa Sotelo, L., NUEVA CORREDURÍA PÚBLICA (Mexico: ITAM, 1994), and 'Opiniones y estudios jurídicos sobre algunos aspectos de las funciones notarial y de correduría', in Colegio de Notarios del Distrito Federal, April 1996.

[42] *See supra*, text accompanying notes 23–25.

effect. Prior to 1992, notaries public in Mexico held a monopoly of this function, which guaranteed a significant income for notaries but also served as a bottleneck in the successful completion of business transactions, since the number of licences awarded to notaries public was limited. Generally respected within the legal system, notaries public are organized into associations (*colegios de notarios públicos*) which administer a closed system of rigorous examinations and admission requirements to enter the profession, severely limiting the growth in the number of notaries that might relieve the congestion caused by the expanding volume of commercial transactions.[43] In 1992 Congress responded to criticism of this system by adopting the Law of Commercial Notaries.[44] By this Law, Congress took an existing professional institution, the *corredor público*, or 'commercial notary', a form of commercial intermediary or broker, and expanded its role. Under the new Law, the commercial notary is authorized to perform some of the functions of a notary public,[45] most importantly the role of *fedatario público*, or public authenticator of documents.[46] *Corredores públicos* are restricted to commercial activities that take place within the particular state in which they are licensed. In 2001 there were 228 commercial notaries located throughout Mexico.

The early experience involving the use of *corredores públicos* has been mixed. Commercial notaries are generally considered honest and professionally qualified, although they are occasionally criticized for exercising functions that are

[43] In most Mexican states, the appointment of notaries is made by the state governor, and therefore such appointments have been susceptible to political favouritism. It is advisable to consult with experienced attorneys to identify notaries on whom one can rely for efficiently carrying out business.

[44] *Ley Federal de Correduría Pública*, D.O. 29 Dec. 1992, as amended, D.O. 28 Jan. 1998. *See also Reglamento de la Ley Federal de Corredurría Pública*, D.O. 4 June 1993.

[45] Under Article 6 of the Law of Commercial Notaries, a *corredor público* is an attorney who, after passing an exam, is licensed by the Ministry of the Economy to perform the following functions:

(i) to act as a mediator in transmitting and exchanging proposals between two or more parties in commercial transactions, and to act as an adviser to the parties on entering into or adjusting any commercial contracts;
(ii) to act as expert appraiser who estimates, quantifies and values property, services, rights, and obligations;
(iii) to provide legal advice to merchants;
(iv) to act as an arbitrator, at the request of the parties, in the resolution of disputes stemming from commercial acts;
(v) to act as notary public in the recording of contracts, agreements, acts, and events of a commercial nature, with the exception of real property transactions;
(vi) to record debt instruments (*obligaciones*) and other negotiable instruments (*títulos valores*);
(vii) to record mortgages on vessels, boats, ships, and aircraft that are entered into before the *corredor público*, and to grant loans for the purchase of equipment or working capital loans;
(viii) to act as public authenticator (*fedatario público*) in the creation, modification, merger, splitting, dissolution, liquidation, and expiration of business corporations.

[46] On *fedatario público*, *See* Chapter 2 above, at text accompanying notes 128–133.

still the exclusive province of notaries public.[47] The addition of commercial notaries has somewhat relieved the congestion caused by the limited number of public notaries, but it has not resulted in as dramatic a reduction in notarial fees as had been hoped. Administrative and professional control over commercial notaries is exercised by the *Colegio de Corredores Públicos*, which is charged with regulating the compliance of the professional code of ethics of the *corredores públicos*, and there have been few charges of dishonesty against this new profession. However, commercial notaries are sometimes criticized for exercising powers beyond their control, and which should instead be carried out by public notaries. As one might expect, it is the notaries public who make these complaints.[48]

3. Acts of Commerce

Unlike the Uniform Commercial Code adopted in the United States, which in general applies to merchants and non-merchants, the Commercial Code only applies to 'acts of commerce', which are defined as certain types of acts carried out between merchants, or between a merchant and a non-merchant. Thus, an agreement to transport goods made between a seller of goods and a trucking company would be considered an act of commerce, as would a contract between a homeowner and a trucking company to move furniture to a new home. However, contracts between non-merchants (e.g. if a person who is not in the used car business sells his car to a neighbour) are not covered by the Commercial Code. Similarly, the sale of real property to a commercial developer by one who speculates in commercial properties is an act of commerce, whereas the sale of a home by one homeowner to another is not so considered. An 'act of commerce' is normally defined by the nature of its author. However, in some cases it may also depend on the nature of the act: for instance, a contract for the sale of stocks or bonds is normally considered a commercial act. Any act undertaken by a company chartered under the General Law of Business Organizations is considered a commercial act, as are certain acts that employ commercial instruments (cheques, letters of exchange, promissory notes, maritime trade contracts, etc.).[49]

[47] Administrative and professional control of commercial notaries is exercised by the College of Commercial Notaries (*Colegio de Corredores Públicos*), which enforces compliance with a professional code of ethics.

[48] For more information in connection with commercial notaries in Mexico, *see* Bravo Vieytez, S., 'La Correduría Pública en México' at http://www.corredorpublicodf.com.mx (site visited Jan. 2004).

[49] *See* Barrera Graf, *supra* note 1 at 76 and 77. Thus, for instance, if a person sells his car to a neighbour, this is a non-commercial (civil) act, and the rules of the relevant civil code will apply to the contract of sale. But if the neighbour pays with a cheque, the payment becomes an act of commerce, and the rules of the Commercial Code will govern aspects of the contract having to do with the payment by cheque (e.g. if there are insufficient funds to pay the cheque).

Article 75 of the Commercial Code of 1889 lists twenty-three types of acts that are considered acts of commerce, but includes a catch-all provision stating that 'other acts of an analogous nature' shall also be considered acts of commerce, including a number of acts and instruments that are covered by legislation adopted after 1889. Some of these are discussed below.

3.1. Negotiable Instruments (*Títulos de Crédito*)[50]

In Mexico, negotiable instruments include *titulos de crédito* (credit instruments) and *títulos valores* (securities). According to the General Law of Negotiable instruments and Credit Transactions (*Ley General de Títulos y Operaciones de Crédito*, or LGTOC),[51] negotiable instruments are physical documents that provide evidence of rights that are recorded in them,[52] and include cheques, letters of credit, promissory notes, shares of stock, and certificates of deposit.

3.1.1. *Characteristics of Negotiable Instruments*

Negotiable instruments share the following characteristics:

Enforceability (*ejecutividad*) is the most important characteristic of a negotiable instrument, and refers to the fact that the negotiable instrument (a cheque, letter of credit, or promissory note) constitutes a guaranteed debt, enforceable in a court of law. In practice, attachment of property is available to creditors through an expedited judicial proceeding that takes places at the beginning of the suit after the debtor is served with process, and is known as an *embargo precautorio*, or attachment of property to ensure the satisfaction of a judgment. Negotiable instruments are considered *prima facie* proof (*prueba preconstituida*) of a debt,[53] and 'contain a preliminary admission by the debtor that he owes money or, at least, that an obligation was indeed undertaken; and at the same time, negotiable instruments establish in the eyes of the law, prior to the trial, that the plaintiff is using the action at his or her disposal to execute, demand and collect'.[54] This expedited proceeding of bills of exchange (*letras de cambio*), promissory notes (*pagarés*), and other negotiable instruments is highly valuable in a judicial system that is marked by procedural delays.

Formality (*formalidad*) means that negotiable instruments must contain certain information and fulfil certain requirements set forth by law in order to

[50] As in the United States and other countries, the term 'negotiable instrument' is commonly used for documents that represent value. This does not mean that all such documents are negotiated, i.e. sold to third parties, with equal ease. This depends on the type of negotiable instrument, and the representations contained in it. The leading authorities on Mexican negotiable instrument law are Cervantes Ahumada, R., TÍTULOS Y OPERACIONES DE CRÉDITO (Mexico: Herrero, 1979); Dávalos Mejía, C., TÍTULOS DE CRÉDITO (Mexico: Oxford University Press, 3rd ed., 2001); and Mantilla Molina. E., TÍTULOS DE CREDITO; LETRA DE CAMBIO, PAGARÉ, CHEQUE (Mexico: Porrúa, 2nd ed., 1983).

[51] D.O. 27 Aug. 1932, as amended, 23 May 2000.

[52] LGTOC Article 5.

[53] This presumption does not affect the rights of a party based on the transaction underlying a negotiable instrument, as discussed *infra*, in note 59.

[54] Dávalos Mejía, *supra* note 50 at 66.

achieve the legal effects accorded to negotiable instruments, such as *prima facie* evidence of the debt. Mexican courts have held that if specific requirements of content are not met, an instrument shall not have the legal effects attributed to a negotiable instrument.[55]

Incorporation (incorporación) means that a right is inherently attached to the physical document that expresses that right; consequently, if a physical document does not exist, there can be no negotiable instrument.[56] The bearer of an instrument is obliged to present the document in order to exercise the right that is recorded on it, and payment must be made against delivery of the actual document. Similarly, recovery or repossession of any merchandise represented by an instrument can only be accomplished by presenting the instrument itself; and transfer of the instrument entails transfer of title and rights associated with it.

As noted below,[57] changes in information technology have altered these rules, as electronic instruments have begun to replace paper documentation.

Literalness (literalidad) refers to the delimitation of the right that is attached to the instrument; i.e. the debtor may not demand anything that is not mentioned in the instrument.[58] This characteristic is evidence of the formality with which negotiable instruments are adjudged, and means that the literal text of the instrument shall govern any transaction related to that same instrument: the maturity or due date of the instrument (LGTOC Article 127), the monetary value of the instrument (LGTOC Article 167), and the place of redemption or of exchange (LGTOC Article 126).

Autonomy (autonomía) means that the right attached to the instrument is independent of the underlying transaction that gave rise to the existence of that instrument. Thus, any underlying contractual rights that could be enforced against the original maker of a negotiable instrument cannot be enforced against the holder (a concept familiar to US lawyers as rights of a holder in due course).[59]

Legitimation (legitimación), a concept similar to the common law principle of 'negotiability', means that the only person who has the legitimate right to redeem an instrument is the holder or owner of the instrument, who may not be the original beneficiary of the instrument but rather a person to whom the instrument has been legitimately transferred. Negotiable instruments are intended for free circulation and, therefore, if the original and successive

[55] SJF, 5a, T. LXXII, 1980, p. 1461. [56] Dávalos Mejía, *supra* note 50 at 68.

[57] *See infra*, Section 3.3. [58] Dávalos Mejía, *supra* note 50 at 68.

[59] 'The documentary right is autonomous not only because it is detached from the legal event or transaction that brought it into existence, but also because, assuming that the instrument is already in the hands of a subsequent holder, the holder cannot be affected in any way by any defects or lack of force or effect that by chance impair the right on the head of the person who transferred it.' Tena, F., DERECHO MERCANTIL MEXICANO (Mexico: Porrúa, 11th ed., 1984) at 328 (author's trans.). *See also* Gómez Gordoa, J., TÍTULOS DE CRÉDITO (Mexico: Porrúa, 5th ed., 1998); and Astudillo, P,. LOS TÍTULOS DE CRÉDITO (Mexico: Porrúa, 5th ed., 1998). On the concept of holder in due course under US law, *see* Uniform Commerical Code Section 3-302, and White, J. and Summers, R., UNIFORM COMMERCIAL CODE (St. Paul, Minn: West Pub. Co., 4th ed., 1995), section 13-3.

beneficiaries transfer instruments either by physical delivery (when they are to the bearer), by endorsement, or by any other means permitted by law (for example, judicial notice of transfer in cases of inheritances or bankruptcy), such transfers of instruments legally transfer the rights and, unless an agreement to the contrary has been entered into prior to the act, it is understood that the person who possesses the instrument is its owner.

3.1.2. Who is Obliged to Pay on a Negotiable Instrument?

It is important to distinguish between the person who is obliged by the negotiable instrument (the obligor, who in most cases will be the original maker who signs the negotiable instrument) and the person who is liable to pay on the instrument (who may be the maker, or may be an endorser (*aval*) who purchases or otherwise assumes the obligation if the maker does not pay). Thus, the following parties are liable for payment under a negotiable instrument:

(i) *The maker of the instrument* The person named in the negotiable instrument as the maker is obliged to pay. In the case of shares or stock, the company that issues the instrument is subject to the obligations that are created by it.
(ii) *The payer or obligor* This applies to bills of exchange or cheques, in which a bank or other financial institution is obliged as payer on the instrument, although in the case of bank cheques, payment is dependent on the availability of funds in the maker's account.
(iii) *A third party who acquires the obligation attached to the instrument* This is the case of guarantee by endorsement (*aval*).[60] The *aval* is commonly used in lending transactions, where a third party signs an instrument to guarantee performance of a person under the financing agreement.

3.1.3. Types of Negotiable Instruments

The principle negotiable instruments recognized in Mexico are the bill of exchange (*letra de cambio*); the promissory note (*pagaré*); the cheque (*cheque*); corporate stock shares (*acciones societarias*); corporate bonds (*bonos societarios*); certificates of patrimonial contribution (*certificados de aportación patrimonial*); investment certificates (*certificados de participación*); housing investment certificates (*certificados de vivienda*); dividend coupons (*cupones de dividendos*); mortgage-backed securities relating to boats and sea craft (*cédulas hipotecarias navales*); bills of lading (*conocimientos de embarque*); bank bonds and coupons (*bonos bancarios y cupones*); passbook savings accounts (*libretas de ahorro*); and certificates of deposit (*certificados de depósito a plazo*).

Advances in information technologies that are taking place worldwide are gradually being introduced in Mexico. The use of electronic payments and

[60] A guarantee by endorsement (*aval*) creates joint and several liability. This means that the party endorsing an instrument is jointly and severally liable with the original obligor for the entire debt.

electronic documentation is in the process of revolutionizing the way these traditional negotiable instruments are processed. These developments lie beyond the scope of this work, and the following descriptions are based on the traditional concepts that have been applied in Mexico for many decades.

Bills of exchange (letras de cambio) Since the early Renaissance, bills of exchange have played an important role in business transactions worldwide as well established means of assuring payment. Thus, for instance, bills of exchange are often used as negotiable instruments in conjunction with letters of credit (*cartas de crédito*) in international trade. The basic concepts of bills of exchange in Mexico conform to international customs, and are governed by the *Ley General de Títulos y Operaciones de Crédito* (LGTOC),[61] as well as by the international conventions on bills of exchange to which Mexico is a party.[62] These instruments entail a process of triangulation between: the drawer of the draft (*girador*), as the party who creates the bill of exchange; the drawee of the draft (*girado aceptante*), as the party (usually a financial institution) who acquires the obligation to pay the bill; and the beneficiary (*beneficiario*), the holder of the bill, to whom payment is to be made.

Bills of exchange are subject to requirements set forth in the LGTOC.[63] The words 'bill of exchange' (*letra de cambio*) must be expressly set forth in the text of these notes. The notes must also state: the place, day, month, and year of issue, in order to ascertain the law applicable to the instrument; what court has jurisdiction (when instruments are intended for circulation abroad); and the date of expiration of the instrument and applicable statutes of limitations.[64] Drafts must also contain: an unconditional order to the drawee to pay a particular sum; the name of the drawee; the place and date of payment (should this not be established, the place of payment shall be considered to be the domicile of the drawee); the name of the person to whom the payment must be made (drafts must be registered to someone's name; bills of exchange registered to the bearer are therefore not possible); and the signature of the drawer or the person who creates the draft at the request of the drawer (in this last instance, the bill of exchange must be signed before a notary public or a commercial notary).

[61] *See* LGTOC Articles 76–169.

[62] Mexico is a party to the United Nations Convention on International Bills of Exchange and International Promissory Notes, signed in New York on 1988, and to the Inter-American Convention on Conflicts of Law Regarding Bills of Exchange, Promissory Notes and Invoices, signed in Panama on 30 Jan. 1975. When instruments regulated by these conventions are involved, express mention thereof must be made on the note itself. Most public and private foreign debt has been evidenced by international promissory notes covered by these conventions.

[63] *See* LGTOC Article 76. On bills of exchange generally, *see* López Goicochea, F., *La Letra de Cambio, su mecánica y funcionamiento* (Mexico: Porrúa, 5th ed., 1980) and Gaxiola, O., 'El cheque y la letra de cambio en el derecho norteamericano y mexicano', in Boletín del Instituto de Derecho Comparado de México, 10, Mexico, 1951.

[64] This is the interpretation of Mexican courts in 'Letra de cambio. Requisito de la expresión de lugar de la expedición' A.D. 664/89, SJF, *Informe* 1989, part 3, p. 647.

Mexico is party to several international conventions that establish rules for bills of exchange.[65] When instruments regulated by these conventions are involved, express mention thereof must be made in the note itself. Most public and private foreign debt has been evidenced by international promissory notes covered by these conventions.

Promissory notes (pagarés) Promissory notes are widely used and versatile negotiable instruments that contain an obligation by the maker of a note to pay on a date certain. They are common in transactions between merchants, as well as in banking transactions. Promissory notes are governed by LGTOC Articles 170–174, as well as by the international conventions to which Mexico is a party.[66] An essential feature of a promissory note is the absence of any conditions to the promise to pay.[67] The notes must contain in writing an unconditional promise to pay a specified sum of money by the person who signs the instrument, and, when applicable, by the guarantee of endorsement, or *aval*.[68] The law also requires that the following be expressly stated: the name of the person to whom payment must be made (bearer promissory notes do not exist);[69] the time and place of payment (should this information be missing, the domicile of the person who subscribes the note shall be taken as the place of payment and, in the absence of a date, the debt shall become due on demand); the date and place of the making of the note; the signature of the subscriber or the person who at the request of the subscriber has subscribed the note.

Cheques (cheques) Cheques are common instruments of payment in Mexico, just as they are in most countries. The law governing the treatment of cheques is contained in LGTOC Articles 175–207. Cheques, like bills of exchange, involve a triangular relationship between the drawer of the cheque (*librador*) (the depositor), who wishes to make payment using funds deposited with the bank; the bank (*banco librador*), in which the chequing account is opened; and the payee (*beneficiario*) or bearer (*portador*) of the cheque.[70] Cheques differ

[65] *See* the U.N. Convention on International Bills of Exchange and International Promissory Notes, New York, 1988; and the Inter-American Convention on Conflicts of Law Regarding Bills of Exchange, Promissory Notes and Invoices, Panama, 1975.

[66] *See supra*, note 61.

[67] Mexican courts have held that incorporation of the term *pagaré* on a document renders the promise to pay unconditional. 'Serial promissory notes. Cases in which no conditions exist even though the text of the note itself does not employ that word.' A.D. 458/74, SJF, Segundo Colegiado Civil del Primer Circuito, 7a, T. 68, p. 57.

[68] In contrast with bills of exchange, promissory notes do not require acceptance or approval of a party other than the maker of the note, except when a third party becomes committed under *aval*. The *aval* is the third party who is jointly and severally liable with the obligor for the payment of the promissory note. The name of the *aval* must appear on the note or on an annex to the note. It should state '*por aval*' and should contain the signature of the party endorsing the note. If the amount payable by the *aval* is not limited in the *aval*, the endorsing party is liable for total payment of the note. *See* LGTOC Articles 109–116 and 174.

[69] 'Promissory notes [made out] to the bearer, are not [to be paid to a bearer]'. A.D. 21/1942, SJF, Tercera Sala, 5a, T. LXXXII, p. 5179.

[70] *Cf.* Tena, *supra* note 59 at 548. Cheques in Mexico involve three different relationships: an exchange relationship between the drawer and the beneficiary; a contractual relationship between the bank and the drawer; and a relationship between the beneficiary and the bank, which is incidental to the releasing of funds for payment. Dávalos, *supra* note 50 at 225.

from bills of exchange in several ways. In paying a cheque, the bank uses money belonging to the drawer rather than its own funds, in accordance with the terms of the deposit agreement. Consequently, the obligation to pay does not rest on the bank, but rather on the account holder or drawer; in the event that payment cannot be made due to lack of funds, a collection proceeding cannot be instituted against the bank, but only against the drawer of the cheque.

Cheques can only be drawn against banks, and only when the drawer has a chequing (sight deposit) account with the bank that is adequately funded to cover the amount of the cheque.[71] The word *cheque* must be expressed in writing in the text of the document, as well as the place and date of issuance, the unconditional order of payment of a specified sum of money, the name of the bank, the place of payment, and the signature of the drawer.

Corporate shares of stock (acciones societarias) Shares of stock, or *acciones*, represent the capital that investors contribute to a corporation or partnership.[72] *Acciones* permit the owner to exercise rights recorded in them (e.g. voting rights, patrimonial rights) in accordance with the LGTOC and with Mexican corporations law.[73] In addition, they represent negotiable instruments, since they are intended for free circulation among investors (LGTOC Article 6 and LGSM Articles 130–131); and they grant to shareholders the patrimonial and corporate rights inherently attached to the instrument.

The corporation, as the issuer of *acciones*, grants shareholders a variety of rights, in particular the ability to vote in the general meeting of shareholders, the right to receive dividends on profits, and the right to a share in case of an increase in capital, as discussed below in Chapter 19. Corporate shares of stock must be name-bearing instruments (*nominativos*), and in order to exercise their rights, shareholders must be registered in the book of shareholders that each corporation is required to keep.

As negotiable instruments, shares of stock are traded on the Mexican Stock Exchange (*Bolsa Mexicana de Valores*), which is discussed below in Chapter 20.

[71] LGTOC Article 175. *Ley de Instituciones de Crédito*, Articles 46 and 58. When a cheque is drawn without funds to back it with intent to profit improperly, the act is considered a criminal offence. Federal Criminal Code, Article 387.

The *Cámara de Compensación* is an autonomous, privately owned corporation whose shares are owned by Mexican banks, and under the authorization of the *Secretaría de Hacienda y Crédito Públic* (SHCP), it serves as the clearing-house for interbank payments including cheques. The *Cámara* is regulated by the central bank, the *Banco de México*. *See Ley Orgánica del Banco de México*, D.O. 23 Dec. 1993, as amended, D.O. 19 Jan. 1999, Article 2, section II.

[72] The Spanish term *acción*, usually translated as 'a share of corporate stock', connotes several things. In some contexts, it may mean 'a fraction of ownership in the capital stock of a corporation' or any other company that issues this type of instrument. Rodríguez, J., DERECHO MERCANTIL (Mexico: ed. Porrúa, 25th ed., 2001) at 463. It may also mean the 'status of partner and is used to express thereby the complex [set of] rights attributed to or belonging or corresponding to a partner'. *Id.* Finally, the term may 'designate the note or negotiable instrument in which these rights are incorporated, while stating the existence of a share of ownership of the capital stock'. *Id.* All three meanings are relevant here.

[73] LGTOC Article 5. *See also* Articles 130–131 of the *Ley General de Sociedades Mercantiles*, the Mexican corporations law, discussed in more detail below in Chapter 19.

Corporate bonds (bonos, or obligaciones societarias) Corporations often raise capital by issuing bonds, which constitute evidence of the interest of the bondholder (*obligacionista*) as the creditor of a loan to the corporation (LGTOC Article 208). Bonds are treated as securities (*títulos valores*) and are subject to the LGTOC, as well as to the Mexican securities law (*Ley del Mercado de Valores*, discussed below in Chapter 20). The corporation that issues the bond receives the amount stated in the bond from the person who acquires it; in turn, the corporation has the obligation to pay to the bondholder (either the original party or a subsequent holder) the principal and interest on the date of maturity set in the bond. In practice, the issuance of corporate bonds is carried out by a brokerage firm, which also acts as common representative of the bondholders.[74] Bonds may be converted into shares of stock if they are expressly issued as convertible instruments.[75]

Investment certificates (certificados de participación) These represent rights to a proportional ownership interest in trusts, property, and income from property. They are issued by lending institutions in their capacity as trustee or fiduciary (*fiduciario*), and are governed by the *Ley de Instituciones de Crédito* (LIC) Article 46 and by LGTOC Article 350.[76] The trustor (*fideicomitente*) endows the trust with property or resources, and directs a lending institution as the trustee (*fiduciario*) to issue investment certificates (*certificados de participación*), which represent for the acquiring party a proportional share or percentage (*alícuota*) of the property or resources contributed by the trustor in irrevocable trust.[77] Pursuant to the purposes set forth in the trust agreement, investment certificates provide a variety of benefits to the beneficiaries or certificate holders (*fideicomisarios*) such as a percentage share in the net proceeds of their sale.

Housing certificates (certificados de vivienda, or certificados inmobiliarios) Governed by LGTOC Article 228a*bis*, these are widely used in financing the sale of housing, as alternatives to mortgage financing, particularly in low- and middle-income housing financed under various government-sponsored programmes. As with investment certificates, housing certificates are created pursuant to a trust agreement established with a bank, which issues the certificates. Under the trust (*fideicomiso*), the bank (*fiduciario*) holds title to the property for the benefit of the buyer, who is the trust beneficiary (*fideicomisario*). Once the beneficiary makes a final payment to the bank, title to the property passes to the beneficiary.

Warehouse receipts (certificados de depósito) and *collateral certificates* (bonos en prenda) A warehouse receipt is an instrument that verifies ownership

[74] Bondholders may exercise their right to collect directly or, in certain instances, as a group. In the latter case, bondholders are organized by a representative to make decisions by majority vote.

[75] For a discussion of bond issuance and trading, *see generally* Frisch Phillips, W., SOCIEDAD ANÓNIMA MEXICANA (Mexico: Oxford University Press, 4th ed., 1999).

[76] For a discussion of trusts (*fideicomisos*), *see* Chapter 9 above, section 2.4.

[77] *See* Dávalos Mejía, *supra* note 50 at 307.

of property or merchandise deposited in a bonded warehouse, which is responsible for issuing the receipt. *Bonos de prenda* are certificates that are collateral to warehouse receipts, and which prove the existence of a secured loan (*crédito prendiario*) that is secured by the property or merchandise deposited with the warehouse.[78] Warehouse receipts and collateral certificates are governed by the General Law of Organizations and Auxiliary Activities of Credit (*Ley General de Organizaciones y Actividades Auxiliares de Crédito*, LGOAAC, Articles 5, 11, and 12), and by LGTOC (Articles 19, 229–251, and 287). The bearer of the *certificado de depósito* exercises dominion over the property covered by the instrument, and is entitled to retrieve it at any time against surrender of the receipt (and of the collateral receipt, if any exists) after settling storage costs and taxes. These instruments are of general use in commercial transactions, and their purpose is to facilitate the financing and sale of merchandise without the need to withdraw it from the warehouse. Like cheques, warehouse receipts may only be issued by authorized institutions, in this case, the bonded warehouse (*almacén general de depósito*). The certificates must be identified by name with the term *certificado de depósito*, or *bono de prenda*, as applicable.

Bills of lading (conocimientos de embarque)[79] Bills of lading are instruments that evidence merchandise delivered to an ocean carrier for transport on a vessel to a port of destination. Like bills of exchange and warehouse receipts, they have been common instruments of commerce throughout the world for centuries. Bills of lading stem from maritime transportation contracts in which the merchant enters into a contractual agreement with a shipping company for transportation of merchandise by sea. The bill of lading is thus both a contract of carriage and a document of title to the goods. Bills of lading are governed by Articles 98–105 of the Law of Navigation (*Ley de Navegación*),[80] and by the rules of applicable international treaties on bills of lading.[81] A valid bill of lading is required to list: the name and signature of the shipper; the name and the domicile of the carrier; the name and domicile of the party to whose order the bill is issued (and that party shall be the consignee, unless this party is the

[78] Bonded warehouses are auxiliary lending institutions, and warehouse receipts and collateral certificates are governed by the General law of Organizations and Auxiliary Activities of Credit (*Ley General de Organizaciones y Actividades de Crédito*, or LGOAC), D.O. 14 Jan. 1985, Articles 5, 11, and 12; and by LGTOC Articles 19, 229–251, and 287. On warehouse receipts and collateral certificates generally, *see* Fuente Rodríguez, J., *TRATADO DE DERECHO BANCARIO Y BURSÁTIL: SEGUROS, FIANZAS, ORGANIZACIONES Y ACTIVIDADES AUXILIARES DE CREDITO, GRUPOS FINANCIEROS* (Mexico: Porrúa, 2000).

[79] For a general discussion of bills of lading under Mexican law, *see* Salgado y Salgado J., *EL CONOCIMIENTO DE EMBARQUE Y SU RÉGIMEN INTERNACIONAL* (Mexico: UNAM, 1994).

[80] D.O. 4 Jan. 1994.

[81] Mexico is a party to the 1978 United Nations Convention on the Carriage of Goods by Sea (the 'Hamburg Rules'), the International Convention fo the Unification of Certain Rules in Connection with Ocean Bills of Lading ('Hague Rules'), the Protocol Notifying the Convention for the Unification of Certain Rules in Connection with Ocean Bills of Lading ('Visby Rules'), and the United Nations Convention on the Liability of Operators of Transport Terminals in International Trade.

bearer); the bill of lading number; a description of the merchandise, its quality, and the means to identify the merchandise; the cost of freight and transportation expenses, fees, as well as the [form of] payment, if payment has yet to be made or is about to be collected; the port of departure and the destination; the name and registry of the ship; and the rules for determining compensation in the event that the shipper is responsible for loss or damage.[82]

Market-traded negotiable instruments (títulos de crédito bursátiles) Certain of the negotiable instruments described above are regularly traded on the Mexican Stock Exchange, the *Bolsa Mexicana de Valores*.[83] According to Dávalos Mejía, five generic types of instruments are traded on the Mexican stock exchanges: publicly subscribed shares of corporate stock (*acciónes societarias de suscripción pública*); bonds or debt instruments (both corporate and government bonds); certificates of investment (*certificados de participación*); bills of exchange (*letras de cambio*); and promissory notes (*pagarés*).[84]

When these instruments are offered on the Mexican *Bolsa*, the normal, general characteristics of negotiable instruments may no longer apply to them. For example, incorporation of property rights into a physical document is no longer applicable.[85] In such cases, the stocks or other instruments become more than mere negotiable instruments, but rather securities exchange-related instruments (*valores bursátiles*). Since thousands of such instruments may be exchanged daily, the transfer of physical documents (stock certificates, etc.) would be too cumbersome, and therefore electronic systems have been developed to credit and track the transfer of securities.[86]

Government securities (títulos gubernamentales) Until the opening up of the Mexican economy in the early 1990s, the trading of government securities represented a large percentage of Mexican securities trading. Even today, the trading of securities issued by government agencies is a significant part of the Mexican financial market, and is essential in financing governmental activities. The issuance of government debt instruments is subject to a variety of constitutional, statutory, and budgetary safeguards. Thus, for instance, the states of the Mexican Republic are precluded from going into debt to foreign entities or in foreign currency (Mexican Constitution, Article 17). The General Law of Public Debt (*Ley General de Deuda Pública*)[87] is the statute that regulates

[82] *See generally* Enriquez Rosas, D., DERECHO MARÍTIMO (Mexico: Porrúa, 2000).

[83] On regulation of securities markets, *see* Chapter 20 below, section 4. For basic information on the *Bolsa Mexicana de Valores*, *see* www.bmv.com.mx (site visited Jan. 2004). Even though the Mexican Securities Exchange Law allows for the creation of stock exchanges in different markets of the Republic, since the market for stocks in Mexico remains small, the only existing stock exchange is located in Mexico City.

The Mexican Stock Exchange is small by comparison with exchanges in the United States. Based on 2001 figures, the total amount of trading on the New York Stock Exchange alone was over 200 times the amount of trading on the Mexican *Bolsa*. NASDAQ trading was 250 times the volume of the Mexican *Bolsa* for the same period. Source: 2001—International Federation of Stock Exchanges.

[84] Dávalos Mejía, *supra* note 50 at 375.

[85] *See supra*, text accompanying note 54.

[86] *See Ley del Mercado de Valores*, Articles 14*bis*7, 14*bis*8, and 15.

[87] D.O. 31 Dec. 1976.

the issuance of debt instruments by the federal government, pursuant to congressional authorizations of indebtedness and amortization.[88]

The most common securities issued by the Mexican government are Treasury Certificates or (*Certificados de Tesoro*, known by their Spanish acronym CETES). CETES are issued by the Federal Government through the Secretariat of Treasury and Public Credit (SHCP), and are underwritten by the central bank, the *Banco de México* (the underwriter of a security is the *agente de colocación*). CETES are short-term debt instruments (91, 182, and 364 days) and are auctioned off weekly on the basis of their yield at maturity. There is an active market of trading of CETES on the Mexican Stock Exchange, making CETES a liquid form of investment that is subject to the general forces that affect financial markets.[89] Other bonds of governmental or quasi-governmental agencies for which an important market exists are development bonds (*bonos de desarrollo*, or BONDES) of the federal government; promissory notes of the federal treasury (*pagarés de la Tesorería de la Federación*, or PAGAFES); Federal Treasury Bonds (*Bonos de la Tesorería de la Federación*, or TESOBONOS); federal government adjustable bonds (*bonos ajustables del gobierno federal*, or AJUSTABONOS); Federal District Urban Renewal Bonds (*bonos de Renovación Urbana del* Distrito Federal, BORES-DF); and monetary regulation bonds of the Bank of Mexico (*bonos de regulación del Banco de México*).

3.2. Commercial Contracts

As discussed earlier in this Chapter, the Mexican Constitution (Article 73, section X) provides that the federal Congress has the exclusive power to legislate on matters of commercial law. However, the applicable federal legislation in commercial fields, the Commercial Code and the more specialized commercial laws mentioned previously, do not cover the basic aspects of contractual obligation, such as when contracts are formed, who is obliged, defences for non-performance, etc. As a result, therefore, while contracts of a commercial nature (i.e. contracts between merchants, or between a merchant and a consumer) are governed by the applicable provisions of the Commercial Code, the basic principles of contractual obligation are determined according to the rules stated in the civil code applicable to the transaction.[90] The question arises as to which civil code supplements the Commercial Code in these instances. Fortunately, the Mexican Supreme Court has settled this question by ruling that all commercial contracts that are made in Mexico are to be governed by the terms of the Federal Civil Code.[91] As already noted, however,[92] both federal

[88] In turn, each State of the Republic has its own law regulating public debt.

[89] For a discussion of the trading of CETES, *see* Heyman, T., *La inversión en México: (acciones, cetes, obligaciones, oro, plata, petrobonos)* (Mexico: UVM, 2nd ed., 1981).

[90] On the Mexican law of contractual obligations, *see* Chapter 17 above.

[91] 'The Federal Civil Code is only supplementary to the Commercial Law when the institution or applicable rule of law is not specifically cited in the Commercial Code; or if such is the case, if its regulation is incomplete or inefficient'. SJF, 7a, Tercera Sala, 181–186, p. 121.

[92] *See supra*, text accompanying notes 3–4.

and state courts have jurisdiction to decide disputes arising out of commercial matters, and in cases before state courts the local civil procedural laws supplement the procedural rules contained in the Commercial Code (Commercial Code Article 1054).

While many of the rules of commercial contracts conform to the civil law of obligations, there are particular aspects of commercial contract law that deserve mention here.

3.2.1. Joint Obligation (Mancomunidad) *and Joint and Several Liability* (Solidaridad)

When several debtors are bound under a commercial contract, provisions of the *Ley General de Sociedades Mercantiles* (LGSM),[93] the Federal Civil Code, and the LGTOC establish rules of joint obligation (*mancomunidad*) and joint and several liability (*obligación solidaria, or solidaridad*). There is a subtle difference between these two concepts under Mexican law.

Mancomunidad applies when a plurality of creditors or debtors are bound by the same negotiable instrument. According to Article 1985 of the Federal Civil Code,[94] the credit or the debt is divided into as many parts as creditors or debtors exist, and each party, presumed to be equal to the others, has a separate and partial obligation.[95]

Solidaridad applies when a negotiable instrument is endorsed and each of the endorsing parties is responsible for the payment of the total amount of the debt owed to the creditor. The creditor may decide to enforce the debt against any of the endorsers, or the original obligor, and that party is entitled to seek payment from the others. In commercial law there is no presumption of *solidaridad*; rather, it must be established by proof of the express agreement of the parties.[96] For example, in accordance with LGTOC Article 159, when several debtors have jointly acquired debt in a negotiable instrument, a creditor may sue by means of a summary action for attachment and execution (*acción ejecutiva*)[97] based on the negotiable instrument, and thus 'create joint and several liability of the debtors [who are] contractually bound to each other as one (*mancomunados*)'.[98]

3.2.2. Time and Place for Performance

Breach of a commercial contract is a potential source of litigation in Mexico,[99] as it is in the United States, and therefore the date on which a party's performance is due is crucial in determining whether a breach has occurred. Under

[93] D.O. 4 Aug. 1934. *See*, e.g. LGSM Articles 7 and 21.

[94] Articles 1984–2010 of the Federal Civil Code are applicable to collective commercial debts.

[95] If the creditors document the debt with promissory notes, the debtor or debtors assume joint and several liability (*solidaridad*) in accordance with Articles 159 and 174 of the LGTOC.

[96] *See* Díaz Bravo, *infra* note 98 at 27 and Dávalos Mejía, *supra* note 50 at 88–91.

[97] On summary proceedings in commercial litigation, *see* Chapter 10 above, section 10.

[98] Díaz Bravo, A., Contratos mercantiles (Mexico: Harla, 2nd ed., 1987) at 25.

[99] *See generally* Vázquez del Mercado, O., CONTRATOS MERCANTILES (Mexico: Porrúa, 10th ed., 2001) at 155.

the rules applicable to non-commercial contracts, when one party is required to provide something to another (delivery of goods, etc.) and the time for payment is not fixed in the contract, payment is deemed to be due within thirty days of the date on which a payment demand is made, before either a court or a public notary in the presence of two witnesses.[100] In commercial contracts, when no time limit for performance of an obligation has been set by the parties, performance may be demanded within ten days of the date of contracting, although in cases involving summary attachment and execution procedures (*aparejada ejecución*) performance may be demanded the day after a contract has been signed.[101] Unlike the general rule for civil obligations, commercial law does not provide for the recognition of grace periods, as does civil law.[102]

Article 86 of the Commercial Code establishes that obligations shall be fulfilled in the place agreed upon by the parties, and if the contract does not specify the place, performance is to take place in any place that, according to the nature of the particular business, is considered adequate. To avoid confusion, it is obviously preferable to specify the place for performance in the contract.

3.2.3. *Formalities Required for Commercial Contracts*

Article 78 of the Commercial Code states that commercial contracts are enforceable without regard to the observance of any particular formalities. In practice, however, formality abounds in the Mexican legal system. To protect themselves, most merchants are careful to commit agreements to writing, and are often induced to record the agreement with a notary public or commercial notary to protect their rights *vis-à-vis* third parties.[103] Merchants are granted considerable freedom in the forms of contracts they may wish to use;[104] however, contracts between merchants and consumers are subject to special laws intended to protect consumers.[105]

3.2.4. *Commercial Contracts with Mexican Corporations: Elements of Particular Interest to Foreign Contracting Parties*

Business corporations are generally empowered by their corporate charters to undertake legal acts in furtherance of their corporate purposes (*objeto social*). In practice, it is not always easy to prove a corporation's capacity to undertake

[100] Federal Civil Code Article 2080. [101] *See* Commercial Code Article 83.

[102] Compare Federal Civil Code Article 2079, Article 404 of the Federal Code of Civil Procedure, and Article 84 of the Commercial Code.

[103] *See* e.g. Commercial Code Article 25 (acts not registered with a notary are null and void). *See also Ley de Propiedad Industrial* Article 8 (acts not registered before the IMPI do not affect third parties).

[104] *See* Federal Civil Code, Articles 1796, 1807, 1832 and 1834 *bis*, and Commercial Code Articles 78, 79, 80, and 82.

[105] *See* the Federal Law of Consumer Protection, *Ley Federal de Protección al Consumidor*, D.O 24 Dec. 1992, as amended D.O. 5 Jun. 2000. Enforcement of this law is carried out by the Office of the Federal Prosecutor for Consumer Affairs (*Procuraduría Federal del Consumidor*), a decentralized agency of the federal government. This Office also has the legal authority to serve as a mediator of disputes between merchants and consumers. *See* www.profeco.gob.mx.

legal acts. When a corporation is involved in proceedings before government authorities, the powers of representation of the corporation (that is, the proof that a corporation has authorized a particular act) are usually straightforward matters, as the corporation can employ a public notary to file a document certifying the corporate authorization.[106] In litigation, however, proof of the standing of a person to represent the corporation in a judicial proceeding is a highly formalistic matter and is often contested as a procedural tactic in litigation. Corporate records must be produced proving that the person who granted the power of attorney had the legal capacity to do so.[107]

Any act of commerce carried out by a corporation that falls outside its corporate purpose is subject to nullification. Accordingly, to be assured that a contract is enforceable in Mexico, it is important to verify (1) that the purpose of the contract is consistent with the corporate purpose, and (2) that the person who signs the instrument on behalf of a Mexican corporation has the legal capacity to do so. The former can be established by consulting the corporation's articles of incorporation, and the latter by reviewing the general or special powers of attorney granted to such person for acts of ownership or acts of administration.

Article 8 of the Mexican Monetary Law (*Ley Monetaria de los Estados Unidos Mexicanos*)[108] requires that debts denominated in foreign currency that are to be satisfied by payment within Mexico shall be settled by delivery of Mexican pesos at the market rate on the stipulated date. This provision is not affected by the rules of NAFTA applicable to contracts with US and Canadian investors, since the provisions of NAFTA that assure free transferability of funds in North American business do not require the enforceability of payments in foreign currency.[109]

3.2.5. Breach, Defences to Non-Performance, and Damages[110]

If a party to a commercial contract fails to perform an obligation, the other party may initiate a civil suit, or *juicio ordinario mercantil*, to declare the defendant in default and seek damages. However, one who declares a contracting party in default must be able to prove the charge, and failure to do so may subject the claiment to a counterclaim (*contrademanda*) by the defendant, who

[106] Proof of such authorization requires registration with a public notary of a document by which the board of directors of a corporation grants power of attorney to a specific person to undertake an act on behalf of the corporation.

[107] For general information about representatives and granting of powers of attorney, *see* Pérez Fernández del Castillo, B., *Representación, Poder y Mandato* (Mexico: Porrúa, 10th ed., 1998).

[108] D.O. 27 July, 1931.

[109] NAFTA Art. 1109(2) requires each party to permit transfers in a 'freely usable currency at the market rate of exchange'. The provision appears to be satisfied by payment in Mexican pesos, as long as these can later be exchanged for US or Canadian dollars.

[110] On the law of contract damages in commercial transactions, *see generally* Rojina Villegas, *Compendio de Derecho Civil, Teoría General de la Obligaciones*, vol. III, (Mexico: Porrúa, 18th ed., 1993); and Borja Soriano, M., *Teoría General de la Obligaciones* (Mexico: Porrúa, 13th ed., 1994).

may allege that the original moving party acted with *dolo*, i.e. took legal action without any basis or right to do so.[111]

As in other legal systems, non-performance of a commercial contractual obligation may be excused when the failure to perform was due to reasons beyond the control of the party obliged to perform (*caso fortuito*) or to *force majeure* or acts of God (*fuerza mayor*).[112] The grounds that excuse non-performance must be proven by the person relying on the defence.[113]

Damages for breach of commercial contracts are covered in Articles 2104–2110 and 2117 of the Federal Civil Code, and in Articles 88, 376, and 385 of the Commercial Code. As is the case with tort liability,[114] the damages that may be awarded for breach of contract are relatively restricted. The Commercial Code only permits a court to award interest on amounts in default at a rate of 6 per cent, which is well below historic inflation rates (Commercial Code Article 362). In addition, courts generally tend to be conservative in assessing monetary damages. For that reason, many contracts incorporate liquidated damages clauses (*cláusulas penales*). As in the United States, contractual clauses that set a liquidated amount as damages in case of breach are enforceable, although they may not be set at a level that would be considered punitive rather than compensatory.[115]

3.2.6. Particular Types of Commercial Contracts

Lending contracts (contratos de crédito)[116] Commercial banks monopolize the commercial lending market in Mexico, although non-banking institutions may also be authorized to make loans, in accordance with the *Ley de Instituciones de Crédito*, which applies both to banks and to other lending institutions. Mexican commercial and retail lending markets are small by comparison with the United States, which enjoys a broad array of financing markets and mechanisms for

[111] According to Roman law tradition, *dolo*, in the context of civil matters, encompasses elements of gross negligence, intentional misconduct, wanton and wilful misbehaviour, fraud, and abuse of process. Under Federal Civil Code Article 106, abuse of process is expressly considered a breach of contract, making the original moving party liable for damages to the original defendant.

[112] *See* Federal Civil Code Articles 2112–2116. Mexican law makes a distinction between these two concepts. *Caso fortuito* is identified with acts of man, such as a change in legislation that precludes fulfilment of the obligation, like the establishment of exchange controls making it impossible for the purchaser to pay for merchandise in the agreed upon currency. On the other hand, *fuerza mayor* is identified with the classical concept of *force majeure*, that is, acts of nature that prevent fulfilment of the obligation (earthquakes, hurricanes, etc.). *See generally* Pereznieto, L. *Introducción al estudio del derecho* (Mexico: Oxford University Press, 4th ed., 2001) at 167.

[113] *Cf.* Federal Civil Code, Article 1847. *See* Morineau, M., 'Comentarios al caso fortutio en la jurisprudencia mexicana y romana', in 7 Rev. Derecho Privado (Jan.–Apr. 1996). González Delgado, J.A., 'La exoneración de responsabilidad contractual por caso fortuito en derecho puertorriqueño y español', in 18 Revista Derecho Privado.

[114] *See* Chapter 17 above, section 6.4.

[115] 39–58 (April 1996).

[116] For related discussions of Mexican lending markets, *see* Chapter 20 below, sections 3 and 6.

businesses as well as consumers. Financial markets in Mexico are gradually improving and becoming more sophisticated, as Mexican financial institutions in recent years have received considerable injections of capital and technical services from foreign financial institutions, especially Spanish banks, which have invested heavily in commercial banking in Mexico.

The scope and depth of commercial lending in the United States benefits from a sophisticated system of secured transactions laws, in accordance with the Uniform Commercial Code and related statutes. In Mexico, while the commercial lending market has improved, it still suffers from the need to improve the protection of creditors' remedies for the financing of movable goods and real estate.[117]

The principal types of commercial lending contracts used in Mexico include: lines of credit; working capital loans (*créditos de habilitación y avío*); equipment loans (*créditos refaccionarios y de avío*); letters of credit (*créditos documentario*); foreign currency loans; simple loan contracts (*contrato de mutuo*); and gratuitous loan contracts (*contratos de comodato*).[118]

Although NAFTA has opened up Mexico's financial services sector to US and Canadian lenders, it has not remedied Mexico's antiquated system of commercial and consumer secured lending. Mexico has not adopted far-reaching legislative changes similar to those found in Article 9 of the Uniform Commercial Code and in the Personal Property Security Act (PPSA) effective in most of the Canadian provinces. The Mexican legal system has been highly suspicious of and even antagonistic toward personal property security, particularly when left in the debtor's possession, in part because of the difficulty of repossessing and foreclosing on property. Recognizing the need for change, several key representatives from Mexico's private sector have been preparing initiatives to amend legislation and registration requirements.[119]

(i) *Lines of credit* In a line of credit, one party agrees to put a sum of money at the disposal of the other, or to take on a debt in the name of that party, who agrees to pay back the amount of money or pay for the obligation (LGTOC Article 291). A simple line of credit (*crédito simple*) is created when a sum certain is made available to the borrower until it is exhausted; in a chequing account line of credit (*crédito en cuenta corriente*), the line of credit, subject to lending limits, remains in effect as long as the chequing account is open. Commercial lines of credit are used by sellers of goods and services to finance their operations and inventories.

In Mexico, revolving lines of credit (*lineas de crédito de fondo revolvente*) are commonly granted by banks but, in contrast with US law and practice, revolving lines of credit in Mexico are usually subject to unilateral termination by the lender, when exigencies (sudden changes in exchange

[117] *See* the discussion in Chapter 20 below, at section 3.2.

[118] For an authoritative work on commercial lending contracts, *see* Dávalos Mejía, C., *Títulos y Operaciones de Créditto* (Mexico: Oxford University Press, 3rd ed., 2002).

[119] For more information in connection with the foregoing *see* Nelson, Todd, 'Secured Financing Project' at http://www.natlaw.com/pubs/sfproj.htm (site visited Jan. 2004).

rates or other fundamental conditions) demand it. The right of unilateral termination is generally established in the credit agreement.

(ii) *Equipment loans and working capital loans* Equipment loans (*créditos refaccionarios*) are used in the acquisition of machinery, overhauling, upgrading, retooling, or replacement of equipment, as well as in expanding and improving facilities.[120] Working capital loans (*créditos de habilitación y avío*) are used for the purchase of raw materials, payment of workers' salaries, and any direct costs of doing business.[121] In both types of credit, the lender receives a security interest (*garantia*) in the goods produced by the borrower, and in some instances may attach proceeds of the sale of products.[122]

(iii) *Letters of credit* (cartas de crédito, *or* créditos documentarios) Letters of credit have been used worldwide for centuries, and it is not surprising, therefore, that Mexican law on letters of credit is similar to the rules that customarily apply to letters of credit in other countries.[123] In the letter of credit, the bank[124] ('issuer', or *banco emisor*) pledges to its client, the 'customer' (*cliente*) to pay a third party, the 'beneficiary' (*beneficiario*) either directly or through a corresponding bank (*banco corresponsal*). The beneficiary of the letter of credit is entitled to the proceeds of the letter of credit only upon the presentation to the bank of the precise documents that are specified in the letter of credit. The two basic types of letters of credit—commercial or trade letters of credit, and standby letters of credit—are both available in Mexico. The former are used to finance and provide payment for the sale of goods; the latter are issued to guarantee the customer's performance to the beneficiary.[125]

(iv) *Trusts* (fideicomisos)[126] A trust (*fideicomiso*) is a commercial contract that involves three key parties: the trustor (*fideicomitente*), or person who provides the resources that are placed in the trust; the beneficiary (*fideicomisario or beneficiario*), the party entitled to enjoy the benefits of

[120] LGTOC Article 323 alludes to 'acquisition of work tools or equipment, instruments, farming supplies, fertilizers, livestock or breeding cattle; cyclical or ongoing planting or cultivation, clearing of land for farming, the purchase or installation of machinery and, in construction work, materials for the development of the borrowing company'.

[121] LGTOC Article 321.

[122] *See* LGTOC Articles 322, 324, 327, 330, and 333. *See* Dávalos Mejía, C., *Derecho Bancario y Contratos de Crédito* (Mexico: Oxford University Press, 2nd ed., 1992) at 327–337.

[123] *See generally* LGTOC Articles 316–320, and *Ley de Instituciones de Crédito* Article 71. The Uniform Customs and Practice for Documentary Credits (UCP 500) of the International Chamber of Commerce is recognized in Mexico, and Mexican courts will apply the rules of the UCP if the letter of credit itself specifies that it is subject to the UCP. *See Uniform Customs and Practice for Documentary Credits* (UCP 500) (Paris: ICC, 1993); and *see* Schutze, Rolf A. and Fontane, G., *The law of documentary credits* (Paris: ICC, 2001).

[124] In Mexico, only banks are authorized to issue letters of credit. *See* Dávalos Mejía, *supra* note 50 at 338–352.

[125] The leading authority on Mexican letter of credit law *see generally* Dávalos Mejía, L., Titulos y Operecaiones de Crédito: Análisis Teórico Prácticode la Ley General de Titulos y Operecaiones de Crédito y temas afines (Mexico: Oxford University Press, 3rd ed, 2002) at 477–482.

[126] For more information on Mexican trust law, *see* Chapter 9 above, section 2.7.1.

the trust; and the trustee (*fiduciario*), the bank that holds title to the proceeds of the trust. Because they are highly flexible instruments, *fideicomisos* are used throughout Mexico as vehicles for commercial and investment purposes. For example, *fideicomisos* permit foreign nationals to purchase interests in land in Mexico's forbidden zones.[127] *Fideicomisos* are also used by private parties for investment plans and retirement funds;[128] as guarantee trusts (*fideicomiso de garantía*), used to place collateral in trust as security under a loan agreement; as means for administering estates after death; and for philanthropic and social purposes. *Fideicomisos* are also used extensively for public purposes, as quasi-governmental vehicles for carrying out a wide range of activities, from the purchase and sale of Mexican folk art to the construction of housing for government employees.

Commercial banks and development banks are the only institutions in Mexico permitted to serve as trustees of *fideicomisos*.[129] Mexican *fideicomisos* are similar to trusts in the United States. The bank, as trustee, receives funds (or title to property) from the trustor and holds the funds or property for the purposes specified in the trust agreement (*convenio de fideicomiso*).[130] The beneficiary of the trust (*fideicomisario*) may be either the trustor or a third party. The *fideicomiso* may be established in such a way that a technical committee (*comité técnico*), the members of which are usually appointed by the trustor, oversees the trust operations and may exercise decision-making functions.

3.3. Electronic Commerce[131]

Electronic commerce refers to any commercial transaction that employs data processing and electronic transmission of texts, sound, and images. Advances in electronic commerce are having profound substantive and procedural effects on commercial transactions.[132] While Mexico has not been a leader in electronic commerce, with the opening up of the economy Mexican companies and governmental entities have been working together to adapt commercials laws to technological changes in forms of contracting, documentation of commercial transactions, and taxation and regulation of commercial acts. Thus, in response to the demands imposed on the antiquated Commercial Code by new forms of electronic communications, the Mexican Congress amended the Commercial Code in 2000 by adding Articles 89–94, dealing with certain aspects of electronic commerce. The Mexican Congress also amended certain provisions of

[127] *See* Chapter 16 above, at text accompanying notes 50–56.
[128] *See generally* Dávalos Mejía, *supra* note 50 at 865–867.
[129] *See* LGTOC Articles 36 and 46, section XV.
[130] LGTOC Article 346. *See also* the discussion in Chapter 20 below, section 3.4.
[131] On electronic commerce in Mexico, *see* Barrios Garrido, G., *Internet y Derecho en México* (Mexico: McGraw-Hill, 1998).
[132] *See* Reed, C. and Angel, J., *Computer Law* (London: Blackstone Press, 4th ed., 2000) at 300.

the Federal Civil Code (*Código Civil Federal*), the Federal Civil Procedure Code (*Código Federal de Procedimientos Civiles*), and the Federal Law of Consumer Protection (*Ley Federal de Protección al Consumidor*).[133]

As in many other countries, electronic commerce creates new legal challenges in Mexico involving a wide range of issues, from security in transactions, to privacy, customs protection, intellectual property rights, electronic crimes, taxation of transactions, recognition of evidence, and many others. Mexico is party to the UNCITRAL Model Law on Electronic Commerce and the UNCITRAL Model Law of Electronic Signatures,[134] and is participating in other international forums that address these issues.

4. Commercial Litigation (*Procedimientos Mercantiles*)

As already mentioned, many of the substantive rules of the Commercial Code have been supplanted by more recent legislation. At the same time, however, numerous procedural provisions of the Commercial Code still apply in commercial litigation. Indeed, according to a prominent Mexican expert in commercial litigation, in practice the Commercial Code operates as a commercial procedural code.[135] The LGTOC, the Law on Insurance Contracts, and the Law on Commercial Bankruptcies also contain specific procedural rules.[136]

There are no specialized courts with jurisdiction over commercial litigation; instead, federal and state courts have concurrent jurisdiction over commercial matters.[137] Consequently, the applicable codes of civil procedure, whether state or federal, are supplemented by the procedural rules contained in the Commercial Code.

4.1. Commercial Litigation before Mexican Courts

As in the United States, commercial litigation is common in Mexico; however, the character of commercial litigation in Mexico differs markedly from that in

[133] When the Federal Civil Code of 2000 was adopted, Congress added a provision stating that electronic means of communication could be used to accept an obligation in any transaction (*see* FCC Article 1803, Section 1). Article 210–A of the Federal Code of Civil Procedure was also amended to recognize information produced or delivered by electronic means of communication as evidence of official acts such as court judgments. Finally, Articles 89–94 of the Commercial Code were amended to permit the use of electronic means or any other technology in all commercial transactions, and to establish rules for delivery and receipt of information using electronic means of communication. *See* D.O. 29 May 2000.

[134] *See* www.unictral.org (site visited Jan. 2004).

[135] Zamora Pierce, J., Derecho Procesal Mercantil (Mexico: Cárdenas Editores, 5th ed., 1991) at I–V. *See* Commercial Code Articles 1049–1414.

[136] *See* e.g. LGTOC Articles 4268 (procedures for cancellation or reposition of negotiable instruments).

[137] *See supra*, text accompanying note 3. The choice of state or federal court is at the election of the plaintiff. *See* Mexican Constitution Article 104, section I-A.

the United States. In the United States, commercial litigation may concern a wide range of business-oriented disputes, while in Mexico most commercial litigation is a matter of summary commercial proceedings involving the collection of a debt due under a negotiable instrument. While arbitration and mediation are gradually becoming more acceptable in settlement of business disputes, there is still a reluctance on the part of many Mexican lawyers and businesses to use them.

Mexican commercial litigation has also been characterized in the past by a disturbing tendency to employ criminal law as a litigation tactic. This may occur when a party to a commercial dispute alleges that the other party has committed a fraud, which amounts to an accusation of a crime or *delito penal*. The accusing party may then convince authorities to arrest the alleged perpetrator of the 'fraud', forcing the other party to capitulate.

Commercial litigation in the courts of Mexico is of two basic types: ordinary commercial proceedings (*juicio ordinario mercantil*) and summary commercial proceedings for execution (*juicio ejecutivo mercantil*). Detailed procedures applicable to commercial litigation are set forth in Articles 1049–1414*bis*20 of the Commercial Code. We highlight only some features here.[138]

4.1.1. *Ordinary Commercial Proceedings*

The stages of an ordinary commercial proceeding are: the filing of the complaint and answer (*fijación de la litis*); the evidentiary stage (*las pruebas*); arguments (*alegatos*); and judgment (*sentencia*). The first stage is the filing of the complaint (*demanda*) and answer (*contestación*) to the complaint. The defendant has up to nine days to submit the answer and, during this stage, the defendant must plead any defence (*excepciones*); the defendant may also present a counterclaim (*demanda reconvencional*, or *contrademanda*), to which the plaintiff also has nine days to respond.[139]

The procedural rules contained in the Commercial Code are intended to expedite the litigation process. Thus, the evidentiary period in commercial litigation (that is, the period for receipt and examination of evidence by the judge) is forty days, and includes introduction by the parties and admission by the judge of all pertinent evidence.[140] In many cases, however, arguments on the suitability and appropriateness of the evidence significantly extend this period, and interlocutory appeals about the evidence may suspend the proceedings while such appeals are being considered.[141] Furthermore, Mexican courts have held that waiting to introduce evidence until the very end of the forty-day evidentiary period is prejudicial to the process, and a judge may refuse to receive

[138] On commercial litigation generally, *see* Pallares, E., FORMULARIO Y JURISPRUDENCIA DE JUICIOS MERCANTILES (Mexico: Porrúa, 11th ed., 1990).

[139] Commercial Code Articles 1378–1381.

[140] Commercial Code Article 1383.

[141] Ovalle Favela, J., DERECHO PROCESAL CIVIL (Mexico: Oxford University Press, 3rd ed., 2000) at 188.

important evidence that is submitted at the last minute when it could have been submitted earlier.[142]

Evidentiary hearings are highly formal in commercial litigation. Attorneys for the litigants must submit questions in writing for the judge to use in examining witnesses, and the judge may either admit or reject the questions. There is no cross-examination of witnesses in Mexico, and the examination and transcription of evidence takes place in the offices of the court and is conducted by a secretary of the court, rather than the judge.

After the evidentiary term has expired, the evidence that has been admitted is made available to the parties to aid in the formulation of arguments. The court file (*expediente*) containing all the evidence is first made available to the plaintiff for a ten-day period, and then to the defendant for the same period of time. After the argument stage has concluded, the judge summons the parties for the rendering of the judgment, which according to law, must be issued by the judge within fifteen days of the parties' submission of their arguments. However, these time periods are usually drawn out because the Mexican procedural system allows for consideration and review of a variety of motions and appeals, some of which may bring proceedings to a standstill.[143]

Commercial litigation is conducted almost exclusively in written form; the examination of witnesses is rare. The judge is the sole trier of fact and determines the judgment without the involvement of a jury. The judgment must be limited to the dispute presented to the court; the judge may not, on his or her own initiative, depart from the scope of the litigation and rule on issues not raised by either of the parties. In addition, the judgment must be based on the applicable law, taking into account the logical interpretation of the law, including general principles of law where specific rules are lacking.[144] Finally, the judgment must be complete, in that it must address each issue raised in the case.

4.1.2. Summary Commercial Proceedings (Juicio Ejecutivo Mercantil)

While ordinary commercial proceedings are supposed to be conducted expeditiously, in accordance with the procedures outlined above, in fact ordinary commercial litigation in Mexico is as drawn out as it is in the United States. This is not the case with summary commercial proceedings, however. In most Mexican jurisdictions, summary proceedings are generally concluded within twenty-five months of the date an action is commenced.[145] As mentioned

[142] 'Taking into account that the period in this proceeding was to decide on the evidence and not only to offer it, the judge acted properly when he threw out the evidence offered by the appellant on the last possible hours of the last working day of the established period'. Anales de Jurisprudencia, Tribunal Superior de Justicia del Distrito Federal, T. XLIII, p. 185; T. LIII, p. 281; T. LXI, p. 215; and T. LXXII, p. 327.

[143] Proceedings may be suspended, for example, if an interlocutoary procedure is used to challenge an irregularity in the proceedings.

[144] Zamora Pierce, *supra* note 135 at 123.

[145] *See* Sarre, M. and López Ugalde, A., 'Administración de Justicia en México. Indicadores en materia mercantil e hipotecaria' in ESTE PAIS, 137, Aug. 2002, at 79 *et seq*.

previously, the value of certain negotiable instruments to creditors—promissory notes (pagarés) and bills of exchange (*letras de cambio*), for example—consists precisely in the ability to use summary judicial proceedings (*juicios ejecutivos mercantiles*) to expedite collection of an amount certain.[146] The summary proceeding is brought by filing a complaint (*demanda*), to which the negotiable instrument must be attached. Once the judge confirms that the instrument can indeed be the subject of a summary enforcement proceeding,[147] he or she issues a court order called a warrant of attachment (*auto de embargo*), compelling the debtor to pay the amount owed; if the debtor does not obey the court order, the creditor can attach assets of the debtor of sufficient value to satisfy the debt.[148] A creditor may request that the Court authorize the use of provisional remedies such as the use of the local police power to attach assets of the debtor. Attached assets may be held in possession by the creditor, deposited with a person appointed by the creditor, or (with the creditor's permission) left in the possession of the debtor. To be binding on third parties, the warrant of attachment must be recorded in the Public Registries of Property and Commerce where the property is located.[149]

The debtor's ability to contest attachment and execution is limited. When a warrant of attachment is issued, a copy of the complaint is served on the debtor, who has a period of five days to answer the complaint, either by paying off the debt or by challenging the judgment, using one of the few defences that are permitted by law.[150] Since the negotiable instrument itself is proof of the plaintiff's right to collect, the plaintiff offers proof positive (*prueba preconstituida*) of the claim simply by presenting a copy of the note to the court; the issue of a warrant of attachment takes place without further presentation of evidence or

[146] On summary commercial proceedings generally, *see* Dávalos Mejía, *supra* note 50 at 414–441.

[147] The following instruments can be the subject of summary proceedings: public instruments; judicial admission of indebtedness by the debtor; promissory notes; bills of exchange; cheques; bank bonds; warehouse receipts; subordinate obligations; the CAPS; insurance and bail policies; and others expressly mentioned in Commercial Code Article 1391.

[148] The debtor has the right to decide which assets shall be subject to attachment. If the debtor fails to do so, the creditor is entitled to choose the assets based on a scale of priority: first merchandise, then readily collectible loans, then personal property, real property and other securities (stocks and bonds), and finally contract rights that are the property of the debtor. Generally speaking, assets that are part of a business are attachable, while assets that are the property of a family are not. A number of assets are non-attachable, in particular personal effects and instruments and equipment used in the debtor's line of work. Wages and salaries of workers are also not attachable. *See* Federal Code of Civil Procedure, Articles 534–563.

[149] *See* Dávalos Mejía, *supra* note 50 at 448.

[150] These defences are found in Articles 1397 and 1403 of the Commercial Code, and in LGTOC Article 8. They include: incompetence and lack of legal status of the plaintiff; failure to sign the instrument; proof that the party bringing the action on which the judgment is based lacked proper authority to represent the plaintiff; incapacity of the defendant upon signing the instrument; failure to fulfil the requirements of a negotiable instrument; tampering with the note; evidence that the instrument is non-negotiable; defence based on a reduction of the debt or a partial payment that are on record in the text of the document; defence based on the paying off of the instrument or a court-ordered suspension of payment; lapsing of the statute of limitations; and expiration.

argument, unless the defendant presents a defence that requires the introduction of evidence.

After the answer of the complaint by the debtor, the judge opens a fifteen-day evidentiary period, during which creditor and debtor have an opportunity to offer evidence for or against the attachment and execution. The parties then have five days to view the exhibits and prepare a final argument. The final judgment must be handed down within eight days of the final arguments.[151]

Summary commercial proceedings are designed to be quick and automatic. In practice, they may be much more complex and drawn out, especially when large sums of money are at stake. Judgments issued by trial level judges may be appealed to the state supreme court or to the federal courts of appeals where the original proceeding took place, and the decision of that court may be appealed by *amparo* before a federal circuit court panel of judges (*Tribunal Colegiado de Circuito*).[152] A recent study by Moody's indicates that there are significant differences from state to state in the efficiency with which state courts deal with commercial cases.[153]

4.2. Commercial Arbitration[154]

Mexico's opening up to international commerce after its accession to the General Agreement on Tariffs and Trade (GATT) in 1986[155] included a realization by key government leaders that in order to attract investment Mexico should revise its procedural laws to promote the use of commercial arbitration, which has become a preferred form of dispute settlement in international business. Prior to reforms in 1993, Mexican judges were reluctant to enforce arbitration clauses in private contracts, and also reluctant to enforce arbitral awards, in part for cultural reasons (and lack of familiarity with arbitration procedures) and in part for legal reasons.[156] To overcome this reluctance, the Mexican Congress in 1993 amended Title IV, Book V of the Commercial Code (Articles 1415–1463) to facilitate the availability of commercial arbitration in both domestic and international disputes.[157] The Commercial Code provisions on commercial

[151] CC Article 1407. *See* Dávalos Mejía, *supra* note 50 at 452.

[152] *See* Chapter 6 above at text accompanying notes 34–35.

[153] '*Calificaciones de Ejecutabilidad de Contratos Mercantiles e Hipotecarios*', published in Moody's Investors' Service, Global Credit Research, April 2002. The study was carried out by ITAM University in Mexico City and based on questionnaires sent to practising lawyers in each state. Grades were assigned to each state based on four criteria: institutional quality, duration of summary commercial proceedings, effective use of resources, and efficient execution of judgments. The highest scores were received by the states of Aguascalientes, Nuevo Leon, Queretaro, and Quintana Roo, and the lowest were received by Chihuahua, Guerrero, Michoacan, Sonora, Tlaxcala, and Veracruz.

[154] On Mexican commercial arbitration, *see* Chapter 10 above, section 7.2.

[155] *See* Chapter 12 above, at text accompanying notes 20–25.

[156] For example, the Commercial Code previously required that any arbitration conducted in Mexico must be conducted in the Spanish language.

[157] The reform was published in D.O. 22 Jul. 1993. For a discussion of Mexican arbitration law after the 1993 reforms, *see* Graham, L.E., *El Arbitraje Comercial Internacional*

arbitration are based on the 1985 UNCITRAL Model Law on International Commercial Arbitration, although the Mexican Congress added certain provisions which deviate from the UNCITRAL Model Law, as noted below.[158]

Mexico has acceded to several international conventions on international commercial arbitration.[159] An advisory body to promote international commercial arbitration in the NAFTA region was created pursuant to Article 2022 of the North American Free Trade Agreement (NAFTA).

4.2.1. General Aspects of Arbitration

Commercial Code Articles 1415–1463, modelled on the UNCITRAL Model Law, covers both domestic and international arbitration; these Articles apply if the place of arbitration is in Mexico, unless other treaties or laws state otherwise. According to Commercial Code Article 1051, parties may choose to submit a commercial dispute either to the courts or to arbitration. The key to arbitration, of course, is that it represents an alternative to judicial dispute settlement, and is therefore only applicable if both parties voluntarily submit to arbitration, either by employing an arbitration clause in the underlying commercial agreement, or by agreeing to arbitrate after a dispute has arisen.

Commercial disputes in Mexico are normally submitted to one of several arbitration centres that have been established to administer arbitrations. Since arbitration was discouraged for so long, such centres are relatively new in Mexico.[160] Arbitration centres are likely to become more important as both businesses and lawyers become more confident in the effectiveness of commercial arbitration. Normally, the parties agree to the rules to apply to the arbitration, and the method for selection of arbitrators. However, if the parties are unable to agree, Commercial Code Article 1427 allows a party to seek a judicial order from a judge appointing an arbitrator or arbitral panel.[161] This provision, which the Mexican Congress added to the UNCITRAL Model Law, is a potential source of troublesome litigation (something arbitration is supposed

(Mexico: Themis, 2000). The Federal Code of Civil Procedure, Articles 609–636, which date from 1928, also include general provisions related to arbitration for non-commercial civil disputes.

[158] *See* Siqueiros, J.L., 'Mexican Arbitration: The New Statute', in 30 Texas Int'l L.J. 229 (1995).

[159] Mexico is a party to the Convention for the Recognition and Enforcement of Foreign Arbitral Awards (New York Convention); the Inter-American Convention on International Commercial Arbitration (Panama Convention); and the Inter-American Convention for Extraterritorial Validity of Foreign Judgements and Arbitral Awards (Montevideo Convention).

[160] The *Centro de Arbitraje de México*, located in Mexico City, carries out educational programmes as well as administering a set of arbitration rules (based on the UNCITRAL model rules) and maintaining a list of approved arbitrators. *See* www.camex.com.mx (site visited Jan. 2004). *See also* the National Chamber of Commerce (*Cámara Nacional de Comercio*, or CANACO), with headquarters in Mexico City, and the Mexican Association of Mediation and Commercial Arbitration (*Asociación Mexicana de Mediación y Arbitraje Comercial*).

[161] According to Commercial Code Article 1422, federal and state courts in the place designated by the parties as the proper venue for arbitration have concurrent jurisdiction to hear matters related to the arbitration.

to avoid) and it is advisable to ensure that the arbitration agreement leaves as little doubt as possible in order to avoid litigation.[162]

In contrast with their US counterparts, Mexican courts do not have the power to compel the parties to submit to arbitration. However, if a party attempts to litigate a matter which is the subject of an arbitration agreement then, at the request of the defendant, the court shall order that the lawsuit be dismissed and that the parties arbitrate their agreement.[163]

Where judicial intervention is required, unless otherwise provided in the arbitration agreement or applicable rules, a court located in the place designated by the parties as the venue for arbitration will have jurisdiction over matters related to it. The parties may request a court to provide provisional remedies, such as the attachment of property (*embargo de bienes*) which is the subject of the arbitration. Courts may also be involved in the recognition and enforcement or arbitral awards. With the authorization of an arbitral panel, the parties may also request judicial assistance for the production of evidence.

As a general rule, private rights may be subject to arbitration unless otherwise provided by law. The law usually prohibits matters from being arbitrated where the government or the public at large has a direct interest. The Commercial Code contains no specific provisions regarding the limitation on types of disputes that might be arbitrated. However, certain limitations arise from other laws. The Federal Civil Code provides that private parties can only determine their private rights so long as such determinations do not affect the public interest or the rights of third parties. According to Article 615 of the Code of Civil Procedure for the Federal District, the following matters are to be settled by a court of law, and are not subject to arbitration: the right to alimony; divorce, except for monetary settlements; nullification of marriage; and matters concerning civil status, except for pecuniary rights of legally acquired filiation.

4.2.2. Recognition and Enforcement of Arbitral Awards

In the past, it has been more common for commercial disputes between Mexican enterprises and foreign companies to be arbitrated in foreign countries, under international arbitration mechanisms, than in Mexico. This is changing, as commercial arbitration in Mexico becomes increasingly common. Nevertheless, because of the degree of international business conducted by Mexican enterprises, the arbitration of commercial disputes between foreign parties and Mexican parties may still take place outside of Mexico, under the auspices of the International Chamber of Commerce in Paris (the forum most commonly used by Mexican parties), the American Arbitration Association in the United States,

[162] The *Centro de Arbitraje de México* publishes model arbitration clauses, at www.camex.com.mx (site visited Jan. 2004). For instance, the parties should choose an institution to administer the arbitration that has well established rules for the selection of arbitrators in case the parties cannot agree on the arbitrators. Many institutions can serve as appointing authorities for this purpose, without having been designated as the administering body for the arbitration.

[163] Commercial Code Article 1424.

or by some other arbitration centre. For this reason, the recognition and enforcement of foreign arbitral awards in Mexico is an important subject.

The final three articles of the Commercial Code, Articles 1461–1463, are devoted to the recognition and enforcement of arbitral awards, both domestic and foreign. When presented with the original or certified copy of the arbitral award, and a certified copy of the agreement to arbitrate, a judge of competent jurisdiction in Mexico may undertake to enforce the award by ordering the losing party to comply with the award.[164] The judge is not to re-examine the merits of the case, and may only refuse recognition if one of six obstacles to enforcement listed in Commercial Code Article 1462 is proven to apply. These obstacles are the same as those listed in Article V of the United Nations Convention on the Recognition and Enforcement of Foreign Arbitral Awards of 1958 (the 'New York Convention').[165]

The proceeding to enforce an arbitral award is supposed to be summary, in accordance with Commercial Code Article 1463 and with Article 360 of the Federal Code of Civil Procedure. It should consist of a single hearing, after which the judge either issues an order recognizing the award, or rejects the award due to one of the exceptions to enforcement listed in Article 1462. In practice, delays often occur, and the possibility of attacking a judicial order through an *amparo* action may cause an enforcement proceeding to be drawn out.

[164] Commercial Codes Article 1461. If the arbitral award is not in Spanish, an official Spanish translation must be provided. For the recognition of foreign arbitral awards, concurrent jurisdiction is granted to federal or local judges of the domicile of the defendant, or of the place where the property is located. Commercial Code Article 1422.

[165] Adopted by Mexico, D.O. 22 Jun. 1971. Since Mexico is a signatory to the New York Convention, Mexican courts are required to enforce foreign arbitral awards issued in other countries. *See* the New York Convention, Article 3.

19

Business Organizations

1. Introduction

Mexican corporate law, which owes much to US and European influences, is an example of the centralizing power of the federal government in economic and commercial matters. Unlike the law of the United States, the Mexican law of corporations is entirely federal.[1] All corporate charters are granted pursuant to federal law, and there are practically no state laws that directly affect the matters discussed in this Chapter. Since the laws on securities and the stock market are also federal, many of the policies that affect corporations are set at a national level by Congress and by the federal agencies that administer these laws.

Throughout much of the twentieth century a closed economy profoundly influenced the development of Mexican corporations. Due to limitations on foreign investment, the Mexican private sector was protected from competition.[2] One result was the creation of large, family-owned corporations and holding companies that were closely held by individual family networks, such as the Garza Sada family in Monterrey, or the Truyet, Díaz, and Legorreta families in Mexico City. Even after the *apertura económica* of the 1990s, and the subsequent influx of foreign investment, these family groups still dominate some industries. The shares of most Mexican corporations are still held by a relatively small number of individual and institutional investors.

Some aspects of Mexican corporate law are vestiges of the distrust of foreign investment that comes naturally to a country in which the economy has been subject to domination by foreign interests at various times in its history.[3] This includes limits on foreign participation in companies within certain sectors of the Mexican economy which restrict the ability of foreign shareholders to control company decisions, as well as a requirement that foreign investors and Mexican corporations with foreign shareholders must register the foreign ownership of shares with the National Registry of Foreign Investment.[4] Registration

[1] *See* Mexican Constitution, Article 73, section X.

[2] The 1973 Foreign Investment Law placed severe restrictions in foreign investment in Mexican corporations. For a discussion of the 1973 law and the 1993 law that replaced it, *see* section 2 below.

[3] *See* Chapter 1 above, section 3.

[4] The requirement of registration of foreign investors is contained in the Foreign Investment Law of 1993 (*Ley de Inversión Extranjera*), D.O. 27 Dec. 1993, Article 32. *See also* Article 30 of the *Reglamento de la Ley de Inversión Extranjera y del Registro Nacional de Inversiones Extranjeras*, D.O. 8 Sep. 1998. The National Registry of Foreign Investment is maintained by the Secretariat of Foreign Relations. If foreign investors are not allowed an ownership interest in a Mexican corporation, this prohibition must be included in the legal documents establishing the corporation (*estatutos*).

includes a requirement that the foreign investor agrees to be subject to Mexican laws and not to invoke the protection of his government investments, requirements which are discussed below.[5]

Mexican corporate law has been relatively unchanged over the years, despite major economic changes such as the opening up of the economy. From 1 January 1994 to 31 December 2003, foreign direct investment in Mexico increased by a total of 142.5 billion US dollars.[6] Some of this represented continuing investment in industries already owned by foreign corporations, such as automobiles and computer hardware, but a considerable amount of investment during this period also found its way to new sectors and industries. While this influx has not changed corporate law *per se*, the opening and increased competition has resulted in other legal changes of importance to corporations, such as the development of antitrust laws.[7]

2. Principal Forms of Business Organizations[8]

Under Mexican law, all legally chartered corporations (*sociedades*) are classified under one of two broad categories: *sociedades civiles* or *sociedades comerciales* (also known as *sociedades mercantiles*).

2.1. Non-Profit and Civic Corporations (*Sociedades Civiles*)

Sociedades civiles are non-commercial organizations: generally they are established not for lucrative ends but rather to promote public welfare or the interests of their members or supporters. *Sociedades civiles* are regulated by the civil code of the state (or of the Federal District) in which they are established.

The Mexican civil codes distinguish between two major categories of *sociedad civil*. The first type is the *asociación civil*, a non-commercial and non-profit organization, which is identified by the letters A.C. after the name. *Asociaciones civiles* are commonly established as educational, philanthropic, or artistic organizations, or as social welfare organizations. *Asociaciones civiles* may acquire property, receive donations, and raise funds for the purposes of the association, but they may not be created for an economic purpose.[9] The A.C. has been the principal vehicle used by non-governmental organizations (ONGs in Spanish) involved in social welfare, such as *Amnistía Mexicana*, a human rights group, or environmental groups. As in other countries, NGOs have become increasingly important actors in Mexican society.

[5] *See infra*, text accompanying notes 22–24.

[6] Source: www.economica.gob.mx (May, 2004). This figure includes reinvested earnings and intra-company accounts.

[7] *See* Chapter 12 above, section 5.

[8] Leading treatises on Mexican corporations law include Rodríguez y Rogríguez, J., and Mantilla Molina, R., *Curso de Derecho Mercantil* (Mexico: Porrúa, 25th ed., 2001); Frisch Phillips, W., *La Sociedad Anónima Mexicana* (Mexico: Oxford University Press, 1997).

[9] Federal Civil Code (FCC) Article 2670.

The second type of *sociedad civil* is the *Sociedad Civil*, identified by the letters S.C. Like the *asociación civil*, the S.C. is considered a non-commercial organization: it may not carry out the activities listed in Article 75 of the Commercial Code, which are reserved for *sociedades mercantiles*.[10] However, unlike the A.C., an S.C. may have an economic purpose, and for this reason it is often used as a vehicle to offer professional services, such as legal, medical, or accounting services. An S.C. may acquire property and obtain profits from its activities, and distribute the profits to its members. An S.C. is not a shareholding corporation, but its members have ownership interests that may be limited to particular classes of persons, or may be subject to the approval of the members, as established in the association's rules. *Sociedades civiles* are relatively simple organizations to control, and are often used when the number of members is limited. Members involved in the administration of an S.C. have a subsidiary, unlimited liability for the operations of the S.C., while general members have a liability limited to the amount of their contributions.

2.2. Business Corporations (*Sociedades Mercantiles*)

Business corporations, or *sociedades mercantiles*, are subject to the general provisions of a federal law, the General Law of Business Organizations (*Ley General de Sociedades Mercantiles*, or LGSM).[11] As noted above, there are no state laws that regulate corporations, although corporations are subject to state laws on matters (contract law, real property law, etc.) that are governed by the civil codes, as well as public laws (land use, health and safety, etc.) that are not exclusively assigned to the federal government. In addition to the LGSM, other federal laws and statutes have been enacted to regulate particular aspects of corporate activities.[12]

[10] FCC Article 2688. The activities listed in Article 75 of the Commercial Code amount to virtually any type of commercial activity. An S.C. that carries out such activities is automatically subject to the provisions of the Commercial Code. FCC Article 2695.

[11] D.O. 4 Aug. 1934. The LGSM has been amended many times. The most recent version of the LGSM may be found at www.juridicas.unam.mx/infjur/leg (site visited Jan. 2004) and is also published in looseleaf editions by commercial publishers.

[12] The the issuance and sale of securities is regulated by the Stock Market Law (*Ley del Mercado de Valores*), D.O. 2 Jan. 1975, which regulates the sale of shares in companies listed on the stock exchange. This and other laws connected with securities and banking are discussed in Chapter 20 below. Other specialized laws relevant to this Chapter include the Regulatory Law of Article 131 of the Constitution, also known as the Law of Foreign Commerce (*Ley de Comercio Exterior*) D.O. 27 Jul. 1993, which regulates companies engaged in the importation and exportation of goods. Transportation companies are regulated by the Law of General Means of Transportation (*Ley de Vías Generales de Comunicación*) D.O. 19 Feb. 1940, as well as by specialized laws enacted for each mode of transport, such as the Law of Shipping (*Ley de Navegación*) D.O. 4 Jan. 1994. The Regulatory Law of Article 27 of the Constitution, D.O. 29 Nov. 1958, regulates corporations engaged in the exploration, extraction, and profiting from mineral substances. The Regulatory Law of the Secondary Petrochemical Industry, D.O. 29 Nov. 1958, governs companies that deal in this sector. The Forestry Law (*Ley Forestal*) D.O. 22 Dec. 1992. regulates companies engaged in logging, lumber, paper pulp, and related activities.

Following a brief background section on the general rules for incorporation and operation of business corporations in Mexico, this Chapter focuses on the most common form of business corporation in Mexico,[13] the *sociedad anónima*,[14] or registered stock corporation. The LGSM contains detailed rules applicable to the *sociedad anónima* (S.A.) and many of these rules also apply as supplementary rules to cover gaps in the regulation of other forms of *sociedades mercantiles*. We also survey briefly the main characteristics of the *sociedad de responsabilidad limitada* (S. de R.L.), or 'limited liability company', which a growing number of foreign investors use to conduct business in Mexico. Finally, we discuss the formation of partnerships, which may be used as alternatives to the *sociedad anónima* in carrying out commercial activities.

3. Incorporation of Business Organizations in Mexico

The Mexican legal system is marked by attention to formality in many areas of public and private law,[15] and this trait pervades the way in which business organizations are required to be chartered and operate in Mexico. Mexican legal scholars usually explain Mexican corporate law by following a list of requirements that all companies in Mexico must fulfil in order to be legally chartered as a business corporation. These requirements, which apply to partnerships as well as to corporations, are set forth in Article 6 of the LGSM, and include the following:

(1) *consent*, i.e. the voluntary consent of the parties who form the corporation;
(2) *corporate objective*, or *finalidad*, as established in the articles of incorporation (*contrato de sociedad*);
(3) *contributions* that the shareholders or partners are required to make;
(4) *corporate purpose* (*objeto social*), i.e. the lines of business that the corporation will pursue; and
(5) *formalities* that must be fulfilled in order for the organization to be granted legal personality.

3.1. Consent

This requirement is traditionally divided into two separate components: the legal capacity (*capacidad*) of the parties to enter into the incorporation agreement, and the legal defects that may vitiate consent.

[13] The other business corporations covered in the LGSM are: *sociedad en nombre colectivo* (general partnership), *sociedad en comandita simple* (limited partnership), *sociedad de responsabilidad limitada* (limited liability company), *sociedad en comandita por acciones* (partnership limited by shares), and *sociedad cooperativa* (co-operative).

[14] On the history of the *sociedad anónima*, *see* Barrera Graf, J., Las Instituciones de Derecho Mercantil (Mexico: Porrúa, 1999) at 387 *et seq*.

[15] *See* Chapter 18 above, section 1.2.

3.1.1. Legal Capacity

Chapter 15 above discusses the basic elements of legal capacity, and we therefore concentrate here on the particular factors that make a person unable to enter into a contract of incorporation or partnership.[16] Persons who are precluded by the Commercial Code (*Código de Comercio*) from conducting business also lack capacity to form a corporation. These persons include *corredores públicos*;[17] people who have been officially declared bankrupt and have not yet been discharged of their obligations; and persons convicted of crimes against property, including crimes such as fraud (*falsedad*), embezzlement or misuse of public funds (*peculado*), bribery (*cohecho*), and extortion [by a judge or public official] (*concusión*) (Commercial Code Article 12).

3.1.2. Defects in Granting Legal Consent (Vicios del Consentimiento)[18]

Under Mexican law, there are four valid defects that may lead to the nullification of consent: mistake (*error*); using fraud or misrepresentation to induce another party to enter into an agreement (*dolo*); bad faith (*mala fé*); and coercion or duress (*violencia*). *Error* is 'a belief contrary to reality; that is to say, a subjective state of mind that is in conflict with reality or with the accuracy that scientific knowledge provides us'.[19] *Dolo* or fraud occurs when 'any trick or deception is employed to induce an error or to keep any party to an agreement labouring thereunder' (FCC Article 1815; CCDF Article 1815). *Mala fé*, or bad faith, takes place when one party to the agreement is aware that the other is labouring under a false notion, and fails to advise that party. *Violencia* (duress or coercion) occurs when acts of physical or psychological force are carried out against a person in order to induce that person to participate in an otherwise legally enforceable act. Should any of these defects in consent be proven, it constitutes a sufficient ground for nullification of the agreement of incorporation or partnership.[20]

3.2. Goal (*Finalidad*) of the Incorporation or Partnership Agreement

In Mexican law, a clear distinction is made between the goal or investment objectives of the founding shareholders (*finalidad* or *fin de la sociedad*), which consists of profit-making, and the line of business the organization shall pursue

[16] For a more thorough discussion on incorporation or partnership agreements in Mexico, *see* Rodríguez y Rodríguez, J., *TRATADO DE SOCIEDADES MERCANTILES* (Mexico: Porrúa, 1965) at 15 *et seq.*

[17] *Corredores públicos* serve a quasi-public role in Mexico, and thus are limited in undertaking commercial ventures on their own behalf. For a discussion of *corredores públicos*, *see* Chapter 18 above, section 2.3.

[18] *See generally* Chapter 15 above, at text accompanying note 17.

[19] *See* Rojina Villegas, R., COMPENDIO DE DERECHO CIVIL 138 (Mexico: Porrúa, 19th ed., 1994) at 371.

[20] *See generally* Pereznieto, L., INTRODUCCIÓN AL ESTUDIO DEL DERECHO (Mexico: Oxford University Press, 3rd ed., 1997) at 171 *et seq.*

(*objeto social*), which is covered below. The *finalidad* is very general, and refers to the 'immediate and typical end that the founding shareholders are pursuing, which consists of sharing in the profits and the losses [of the corporation]'.[21] Thus, the articles of incorporation must expressly state that all shareholders shall share in the profits and losses, as it is illegal to exclude any party to the agreement from benefiting from profits or sharing the burden of losses.[22]

3.3. Contributions of Shareholders or Partners

A corporation's articles of incorporation (*acta constitutiva*, or *contrato de sociedad*) must include a 'statement of what each member is contributing in money or in other property, the value attributed thereto, and the criteria followed for assessment thereof' (LGSM Article 6, section VI). Aside from the contribution of money, the founding shareholders may also make contribution to the capital of a corporation in the form of property, goods, or intangible rights (such as intellectual property rights), provided that these things are definable and quantifiable. With regard to *sociedades anónimas*, or stock corporations, these contributions must be reflected in the number of respective equity shares, or *acciones*, of the corporation that are owned by each shareholder.

3.4. Business or Corporate Purpose (*Objeto Social*)

According to LGSM Article 6, section II, the articles of incorporation must also set forth the business purpose of the corporation, i.e. the lines of business that the shareholders aim to engage in by means of creating the corporation. According to one authority, this amounts to 'the entire set of operations and business dealings that constitute specialized activities of artificial entities'.[23] Due to the highly formalistic nature of Mexican corporation law, specificity in stating the corporate purpose in the articles of incorporation is essential, since in Mexico a corporation may only engage in a business which is described in its charter; business dealings conducted in a field that is not expressly defined in the charter may be viewed as unacceptable by the parties with which the organization has dealings, or may be challenged as null and void. Furthermore, as discussed below, a possible ground for early dissolution of the corporation is its inability to fulfil its corporate purpose. For this reason, the corporate purposes must be worded in the most detailed and exhaustive way possible in order to avoid complications during the life of the company.

3.5. Formalities of Chartering a Business Organization in Mexico

Chartering a business organization under Mexican law requires compliance with certain formal procedures in order to bring the organization into legal existence. The LGSM requires business organizations to be chartered before

[21] García Rendón, M., *Sociedades Mercantiles* (Mexico: Harla, 1993) at 47.

[22] *Id. See also* LGSM Article 16.

[23] García Rendón, *supra* note 21 at 57.

a notary public (*notario público*), who must either grant the organization a charter or deny it, based on whether its incorporation meets the requirements of the law (LGSM Article 5). Before a notary public may charter a corporation, authorization for the right to use the corporate name must be obtained from the Secretariat of Foreign Relations (*Secretaría de Relaciones Exteriores*, or SRE); this requirement must be met even if the corporation does not include foreign ownership. The Office of Legal Affairs (*Dirección General de Asuntos Jurídicos*) of the SRE keeps a registry of the corporate names (*denominación social*) of all corporations or business organizations chartered in Mexico, and authorizes applicants to proceed to a notary for incorporation so long as the proposed name has not already been taken. Registration of a corporate name should not be confused with registration of trade marks or copyrights.[24]

The notary public who carries out the act of chartering the corporation usually files for permission from the SRE on behalf of the applicant. When the corporation plans to admit foreign shareholders or partners, an additional special authorization is required. This requirement is found in Article 27 of the Constitution, section 1, which provides that only Mexicans and Mexican companies are entitled to acquire dominion of land or water and accession thereto, and that the state shall have the power to grant the same right to foreign nationals, provided that 'they [the foreign nationals] agree before the Secretariat of Foreign Relations to consider themselves [Mexican] nationals with respect to said property and not to invoke, because of this [status], the protection of their government with regard to that [property]'. This provision of the Constitution is Mexico's 'Calvo clause' (*Cláusula Calvo*),[25] named for the Argentinian jurist Carlos Calvo, and is a throwback to the days when Mexico was the target of attacks and invasions by different foreign powers. The Calvo clause stands as an important principle of resistance to the political and military power that has occasionally been brought to bear by foreign investors and their governments against acts taken by the Mexican government.[26] Fortunately, throughout much of the twentieth century the principle expressed in the Calvo clause has proved more symbolic than real: the provision in the Mexican Constitution has only been actively invoked once, during the controversy surrounding damage caused to the property of US citizens after the Revolution of 1910. At that time, after a period of negotiations between the members of the joint US–Mexican Claims Commission,[27] Mexico agreed to compensate foreign nationals for damages

[24] On registration of intellectual property rights generally, *see* Chapter 21 below.

[25] On the Calvo clause generally, *see* Shea, D.R., *The Calvo Clause* (Minneapolis, Minn: University of Minnesota Press, 1955); R. Nuñez Escalante, 'La Cláusula Calvo', 2 Revista de Investigaciones Jurídicas, Escuela Libre de Derecho 71 (1978).

[26] Foreign interference and invasion were a constant threat to Mexican sovereignty throughout the nineteenth and early twentieth centuries. One author cites 285 instances of 'plundering, injuries and invasions' that the US government and individuals carried out against Mexico from 1799 to 1918. García Cantú, G., *Las Invasiones Norteamericanas en México* (Mexico: Era, 2nd ed., 1974) 125–301.

[27] On this subject, *see* Pereznieto-Castro, l., 'Dos mitos en el derecho internacional privado mexicano: la cláusula Calvo y la zona prohibida', in 2 Revista mexicana de derecho internacional privado 125 (April 1997).

suffered as a result of the Revolution, at the same time reserving its rights under the Calvo clause.

While untested (fortunately, modern governments rarely attempt to use undue diplomatic or military pressure to protect a private investor) the Calvo clause nonetheless remains an important consideration for foreign investors. By merely invoking the diplomatic protection of the investor's government, a foreign investor becomes exposed to the threat of forfeiting all property in Mexico to the Mexican state. The Mexican government has not attempted to use the Calvo clause in this way, but investors should be aware of the sensitivity of Mexicans to overbearing actions by foreign governments or foreign investors.

All notaries public in Mexico have the power to charter any type of business organization,[28] whether corporations or partnerships. The notary records the act of incorporation (*acto de constitución*) in the notarial record book (*protocolo notarial*), along with the following documents, which are maintained as a public record, and which together comprise the corporate charter:

(i) the Calvo clause as included in the text of the articles of incorporation;
(ii) the articles of incorporation (*contrato de sociedad*) that the parties or founding shareholders or partners have agreed upon. The *contrato de sociedad* contains the organization's rules of operation, or corporate rules which in Mexico are called *estatutos de la sociedad*;
(iii) the names of the members of the Board of Directors, or the name of the sole director in cases where the founding shareholders opt for a sole director regime;
(iv) the amount of initial capital stock that makes up the corporation;
(v) the names of the shareholders;
(vi) the amount of capital contributed and the number of shares owned by each shareholder; and
(vii) the name of the person in whom the powers of the corporation are vested.

The LGSM requires that corporations must also be recorded in the Public Registry of Commerce (*Registro Público del Comercio*) of the place where the corporation has its domicile (Commercial Code Article 18). This requirement is crucial, since according to LGSM Article 2 only corporations or limited partnerships that have been recorded in the Public Registry of Commerce have legal personality (*personalidad jurídica*) separate from that of the shareholders or partners. Under the same Article, if a corporation is not so registered, the shareholders can be held jointly and severally liable to third parties for undertaking acts on behalf of the corporation, and may also be held criminally liable if third parties are injured.

LGSM Article 6 sets forth the documents that must be made part of the notarial record in order legally to charter a business corporation.

[28] For a discussion of notaries public, *see* Chapter 18 above, at text accompanying notes 40–46.

Article 6. The charter [*escritura constitutive*] of a corporation shall contain:

—the names, nationality and domicile of the founders of the corporation, whether individuals or entities;
—the corporate or business purpose [*objeto social*];
—the purpose [*razón social*] or name [*denominación*] of the corporation;
—the duration of the corporation;
—the total amount of capital stock;
—a statement of the monetary or property contributions of each shareholder or partner, the value attributed thereto, and the criterion used to determine the value;
—when the capital stock is variable, this shall be stated along with the required minimum value of the capital stock;
—the domicile of the corporation;
—how the corporation shall be administered and the powers of the administrative officers;
—the procedure for appointment of the administrative officers and the appointment of those that shall have the power to execute documents on behalf of the organization;
—how profits and losses shall be distributed among the partners or shareholders of the business organization;
—the total amount of the reserve fund;
—under what circumstances the corporation shall undergo early dissolution;
—rules for proceeding to liquidation of the corporation and the procedure for electing liquidators, when they have not been previously designated.

All of the requirements to which this Article refers and any other rules that may be established in the public document of incorporation concerning the organization and operation of the corporation or partnership shall constitute the rules thereof.

In addition to the requirements of Article 6, which apply to all business organizations, including partnerships, LGSM Article 91 sets forth additional requirements that apply only to *sociedades anónimas*, or stock corporations. Under Article 91, the documents to be recorded by the public notary must also include a list of the holders of paid-up capital shares; the number, par value, and types of shares into which the capital stock is divided, except for temporary stock certificates; the terms under which any unpaid shares are to be paid; the share of the profits granted to the founding investors; the appointment procedure for examiners or internal auditors (*comisarios*);[29] and the voting powers of shareholders. The number of shares held by each shareholder must be registered in the registry of shares (*libro de capital*) maintained by the corporation, which lists the names, addresses, and number of shares held by each shareholder. This registry is usually held in the custody of the sole director or the secretary of the board of directors, and may be kept at the corporate headquarters or any other place.

[29] The *comisario* is a person appointed by shareholders to oversee the acts of the board of directors and the financial viability of the corporation. Unlike the United States, corporations in Mexico are not required to undergo independent audits, and the *comisario* is the closest thing that exists to ensure the financial integrity and viability of a corporation.

4. Limitations on Direct Foreign Investment in Mexican Business Organizations

Foreign investment has played an important historical role in Mexico, but that role has not been unequivocally positive: foreign capital and the technologies that accompany it have helped build the modern economy, but they have also generated business conflicts, accentuated clashes between social groups, and brought occasional tensions between the Mexican and foreign governments. Foreign investment was limited during the early years of the Republic, due to political uncertainties and limited investment opportunities. By the mid-nineteenth century, however, companies from Europe and the United States had begun to invest heavily in mining, railways, and agricultural lands, helping Mexico to achieve a more modern, and less feudal, economy. Unfortunately, foreign investment did not alleviate the endemic poverty that plagued the country, especially in the rural regions, and the Mexican revolutionaries of 1910 associated foreign interests with the landed aristocracy (not an unfounded assumption). Thus, when the post-Revolutionary Constitution of 1917 was adopted, it imposed important restrictions on foreign ownership of land.[30]

Even after the Mexican Revolution, foreign investment continued to be accepted in Mexico, and was important in certain sectors, especially in petroleum and mining. The expropriation of the oil companies in 1938[31] brought an end to foreign investment in that important sector, a prohibition that remains in effect to this day. In most areas, while foreign investment was permitted, it operated according to a series of restrictions that emanated from presidential decrees issued during the Second World War for national security purposes. In 1973, under the direction of President Luis Echeverría, Congress consolidated these decrees into a single law, the 1973 Law for the Promotion of National Investment and Control of Foreign Investment (*Ley de Promoción de la Inversión Nacional y Control de la Inversión Extranjera*).[32] The 1973 Foreign Investment Law (1973 FIL) was highly restrictive, and reflected the state-centred political economy of President Luis Echeverría; it would remain in place, virtually intact, for twenty years, until the economic opening up of the 1990s brought its abrogation and replacement by the current law regulating foreign investment.

4.1. Background: The 1973 Foreign Investment Law

In addition to reiterating the Calvo clause requirement of the Mexican Constitution (Article 3), the 1973 FIL recognized four different types of

[30] *See* Chapter 16 above, section 2.6.

[31] *See* Chapter 1 above, at text accompanying note 138.

[32] D.O. 9 Mar. 1973. The leading commentator on the 1973 FIL was Jorge Barrera Graf, a renowned expert in commercial law, who wrote the leading book on the subject. On historical antecedents of the 1973 FIL, *see* Barrera Graf, J., *La Regulación Jurídica de las Inversiones Extranjeras* (Mexico: UNAM, 1981) at 11–26.

investment activities. The first represented those activities that were reserved to the government by virtue of the reservations in Article 27 of the Constitution or prohibitions in particular laws (1973 FIL Article 4). These included hydrocarbons, basic petrochemicals, radioactive materials, certain types of mining, electricity, railways, telegraphs, and any other activities reserved by law. Since these activities represented many of the most important industrial sectors in Mexico, this cemented the government's control over the economy.

The second type of activities were those reserved exclusively to Mexican investors, including Mexican corporations (*sociedades anónimas)* whose articles of incorporation indicated that they excluded the possibility of foreign ownership of shares. These activities, listed in 1973 FIL Article 4, included radio and television, certain forms of motor transport, domestic air and ocean transport, forest exploitation, natural gas distribution, and any other activity reserved by law to Mexican investment.

1973 FIL Article 5 set forth a third type of activities in which foreign investment was permitted, but limited to minority foreign ownership of an enterprise, i.e. less than 49 per cent of the shares of a company could be held by foreign investors. These activities, and the maximum percentages allowed for foreign investment, included mining in national reserves (34 per cent), secondary petrochemicals (40 per cent), manufacture of autoparts (40 per cent), and any other activities in which the amount of foreign investment would be limited.

The fourth category of activities included everything else, and represented the greatest restriction on foreign investment occurred. The restrictions on activities listed above had already existed prior to the 1973 Law. Article 5 of the 1973 FIL established a new, comprehensive restriction on *all* foreign investment in *any type* of activity.

The final paragraphs of 1973 FIL Article 5 read as follows:

> In all cases in which laws or regulations do not specify a particular maximum percentage [of foreign investment], foreign investment may participate in a proportion that does not exceed 49 per cent of the capital of the businesses, subject to the requirement that the foreign investor does not have, for any reason, the ability to control the business.
>
> The National Foreign Investment Commission may increase or decrease the percentage referred to in the previous paragraph when, in the judgement of the Commission, this may be convenient for the economy of the country, and may set conditions under which foreign investment may be authorized in specific cases.

This fourth category of restriction, the '49 per cent rule', was the most dramatic of the Law's provisions. Companies wishing to invest in a foreign subsidiary are loath to accept a minority position that would compromise their control of the business, including the use of their proprietary technology and know-how. However, the 49 per cent rule was consonant with the import substitution policies advocated by President Echeverría, which argued in favour of protecting local business from foreign competition, to allow local industry to grow.[33]

[33] *See* Chapter 1 above, at text accompanying note 144.

The 1973 FIL created a National Foreign Investment Commission (*Comisión Nacional de Inversión Extranjera*) to administer the law. The Foreign Investment Commission, which still exists, is composed of representatives of key federal ministries, supported by a highly qualified professional staff. As stated in 1973 FIL Article 5, the Foreign Investment Commission had broad authority to waive the 49 per cent rule, 'if convenient for the economy of the country'.[34] Nevertheless, during the *sexenios* of Presidents Echeverría (1970–1976) and López Portillo (1976–1982) the prevailing policy was to protect the economy from foreign influence, not to welcome it, and foreign-controlled investment was rarely permitted.

The control on foreign investment may have seemed odd to foreign visitors to Mexico in the 1970s and 1980s, since many foreign-owned companies—automobile manufacturers (Ford, General Motors, Volkswagen, Nissan),[35] consumer products manufacturers (Proctor & Gamble, Nabisco, Coca Cola), and others—were allowed to remain in the country, even with 100 per cent foreign ownership. However, even these companies had to apply to the Foreign Investment Commission to approve any significant change or expansion of their activities. Any new proposal of foreign investment faced the virtual brick wall of the Foreign Investment Commission, if the foreign investor had designs on exercising control over Mexican investment.

The international business community, as expected, reacted negatively to the 1973 FIL.[36] When coupled with the contemporaneous (and similarly restrictive) Transfer of Technology Law of 1973,[37] the 1973 FIL led Mexico to a predictable result: by the late 1980s the Mexican economy had the smallest amount of foreign investment, as a percentage of the total economy, of any major economy in the hemisphere. At the time Mexico appeared to be immune from any adverse effects of this; as an oil exporting country, Mexico was able to take advantage of the rise in oil prices of the 1970s to expand the economy, and the government (as owner of all oil reserves, production, and marketing) monopolized the economy, leaving a relatively limited role for major private investment, domestic or foreign.[38]

The economic crash of 1982 changed all this. The import substitution model, coupled with direct governmental control of the economy, proved to be

[34] Article 13 of the 1973 FIL stated the criteria to be used by the Foreign Investment Commission in considering whether to permit foreign-controlled investment. The 1973 FIL was supported by Regulations first adopted the same year. D.O. 28 Dec. 1973.

[35] In addition to the 1973 FIL, the automotive sector was subject to a confusing array of additional laws restricting the way these companies could do business.

[36] Pat Murphy, a prominent US lawyer specializing in international investment, presented cogent criticism of the 1973 FIL, in Murphy, E., 'The Echeverrian Wall: Two Perspectives on Foreign Investment and Licensing in Mexico', 17 Tex. Int'l L.J. 135 (1982); and Murphy, E., 'Expropriation and Aftermath: The Prospects for Foreign Enterprise in the Mexico of Miguel de la Madrid', 18 Tex. Int'l L.J. 431 (1983).

[37] *See* Chapter 21 below, at text accompanying note 42.

[38] Government control of the economy, and the crash of 1982, are discussed in Chapter 1 above, at text accompanying notes 1–2.

unsustainable. The transition to an open economy began during the *sexenio* of President Miguel de la Madrid (1982–1988), when the Foreign Investment Commission began to view foreign investment in a new light.[39] With the election of Carlos Salinas de Gortari, an economist, as President in 1988, the days of broad restrictions on foreign investment were numbered. Even before the drafting of a new law, President Salinas signed a new Foreign Investment 'Regulation' in 1989 that, in effect, amended the 1973 FIL by 'instructing' the Foreign Investment Commission automatically to accept 100 per cent foreign ownership of businesses under certain conditions.[40] At the same time, Mexico began negotiations with the United States and Canada that would eventually lead to the conclusion of the North American Free Trade Agreement (NAFTA), which the US and Canadian investors saw, correctly, as a major turning point in Mexican attitudes towards encouraging, rather than discouraging, foreign investment.

4.2. Current Restrictions on Foreign Investment[41]

Mexico's balance of payments crises of the 1980s[42] helped to end the restrictive foreign investment policies exemplified in the 1973 Foreign Investment Law. In 1993, before the NAFTA negotiations were even concluded, President Salinas submitted to Congress a new law, the *Ley de Inversión Extranjera* (1993 FIL), to replace the restrictive 1973 FIL.[43] While much more permissive than the 1973 FIL, which it abrogated, the 1993 FIL nevertheless contains certain restrictions and controls on foreign investment, reflecting the constitutional restrictions that still exist. Most importantly, Article 4 of the 1993 FIL declares a general rule that 'foreign investment may participate in any proportion in the shares of Mexican companies, acquire fixed assets, enter new areas of economic activity or manufacture new lines of products, open and operate business establishments, and expand or relocate existing businesses, except as established by this Law'. In sharp contrast with the 1973 FIL, which stated in Article 5 that foreign investors could not own more than 49 per cent of a Mexican company unless the Foreign Investment Commission approved a higher percentage, the

[39] This period is discussed in Maviglia, S., 'Mexico's Guidlenies for Foreign Investment: The Selective Promotion of Necessary Industries', 80 AM. J. INT'L L. 281 (1986).

[40] *Reglamento de la Ley para Promover la Inversión Mexicana y Regular la Inversión Extranjera*, D.O. 16 May 1989. The 1989 Regulations of the 1973 FIL are discussed in Vargas, J., 'Mexico's Foreign Investment Act of 1993', in *MEXICAN LAW: A TREATISE FOR LEGAL PRACTITIONERS AND INTERNATIONAL INVESTORS*, vol. 1 (St. Paul, Minn: West Group, 1998) at 105, 119–126. *See also* the articles published in 'Symposium: The New Environment for Trade and Investment in Mexico', 12 HOU. J. INT'L L. 181–361 (1990); and *see* Koslow, *supra* note 32.

[41] On the 1993 FIL generally, *see* Robles Farías, D., *EL RÉGIMEN JURÍDICO DE LOS EXTRANJEROS QUE PARTICIPAN EN SOCIEDADES MEXICANAS* (Mexico: Themis, 1999); and Vargas, J., 'Mexico's Foreign Investment Act of 1993', in *MEXICAN LAW: A TREATISE FOR LEGAL PRACTITIONERS AND INTERNATIONAL INVESTORS* (St Paul, Minn: West Group, J. Vargas, ed., 1998) vol. 1, at 105.

[42] *See* Zamora, S., 'Peso-Dollar Economics and the Imposition of Foreign Exchange Controls in Mexico', 32 AM. J COMP. L 99 (1985).

[43] D.O. 27 Dec. 1993.

default rule of the 1993 FIL clearly states that majority foreign ownership is permitted, unless expressly limited by provisions of the law.

The continuing limitations on foreign investment are contained in Article 5 of the 1993 FIL. These limitations include the constitutional reservations of certain activities to the state (private investment in hydrocarbons, etc.) that were carried over from Article 4 of the 1973 FIL. Article 6 of the 1993 FIL lists activities reserved exclusively to Mexican investors, similar to the list in Article 4 of the 1973 FIL (radio and television broadcasting, etc.); this reflects prohibitions contained in other Mexican laws. Articles 7–9 of the 1993 FIL include special provisions, similar to those in Article 5 of the 1973 FIL, that limit the percentage of foreign investment permitted in certain sectors which, by virtue of other laws, are still reserved to majority Mexican investment (such as certain forms of domestic transport, certain financial institutions, etc.). However, these percentages may be surpassed when investment is carried out through the acquisition by the foreign investor of a new type of ownership interest, called 'neutral capital' (*instrumentos de inversion neutra*, or *capital neutro*), created by Articles 18–23 of the 1993 FIL.[44] The 1993 also liberalized the rules regarding investment trusts (*fideicomisos*)[45] and carried forward most of the provisions concerning the Foreign Investment Commission (1993 FIL Articles 23–30).

The effects of the new, liberal approach to receiving foreign investment were felt almost immediately. This was aided, in part, by the enthusiasm with which the US and Canadian business communities approached Mexican investment in the wake of the NAFTA opening. The 1993 FIL achieved the effect that the Salinas government wanted: despite a brief recession in the mid-1990s, foreign investment grew appreciably. From 1994 to 2003 Mexico added 82 billion US dollars in new foreign investment.[46]

5. Shareholder Corporations (*Sociedades Anónimas*)

The *sociedad anónima*, usually abbreviated with its Spanish language initials, S.A., refers to a corporation made up exclusively of shareholders whose liability is limited to the amount of shares held by each shareholder; shareholders cannot be held personally liable for debts incurred by the *sociedad anónima*[47] (LGSM Article 87). To give notice to third parties of the limited liability of

[44] *See* Robles Farías, *supra* note 41 at 38 *et seq.*

[45] Regarding *fideicomisos*, *see* Chapter 9 above, section 2.4., and Chapter 16 above, section 2.7.1.

[46] Source: Secretariat of the Economy. If one adds to this figure reinvested earnings, intercompany accounts, and new investment in *maquiladora* plants, new direct foreign investment from 1994 to June 2003 amounted to 139.8 billion US dollars. US investors accounted for about two-thirds of this new investment. Source: www.economía.gob.mx, 'Inversión extrangera directa en México', figures compiled 30 Sep. 2003 (site visited Jan. 2004).

[47] On this topic, *see* Frisch Phillips, W., *La Sociedad Anónima Mexicana* (Mexico: Oxford University Press, 1999) at 175 *et seq.*

owners, LGSM Article 88 requires that the corporate name must be followed by the words *Sociedad Anónima*, or S.A.

For an S.A. to be chartered, a minimum of two shareholders must subscribe at least one share each. Their share equity may not be less than 50 thousand pesos (approximately US$5,000[48]) and at least 20 per cent of the value of each share must be paid in cash (LGSM Article 89). In practical terms, it is sufficient for the founding shareholders to declare to the notary public that the said amounts of money have been paid to the corporation. Each shareholder accepts the commitment to pay the proper amount, and the corporation is entitled to demand fulfilment of the obligation to contribute paid-up capital.

There are two different ways to charter shareholder corporations in Mexico: by simply chartering a corporation through a public notary, using the procedure described above in section 3.5; or by public subscription of shares (initial public offering). In the second method, in addition to meeting all the requirements for corporations chartered by a notary public, LGSM Article 90 also requires that a subscription schedule be recorded along with the company's rules in the Public Registry of Commerce (*Registro Público del Comercio*); in addition, all the shares of the initial public offering must be subscribed within one year of the date of issuance, or in a shorter time if one is fixed by the founding shareholders.[49] Finally, because the public sale of shares is a highly regulated activity, the initial public offering of shares in Mexico is regulated by the Mexican Stock Exchange Law.[50]

5.1. Share Subscription

The shares, or *acciones*, into which the capital stock of *sociedades anónimas* in Mexico are divided must be represented by registered certificates for the purposes of accreditation and transfer of the status and rights of a shareholder.[51] Bearer certificates (shares owned by parties whose identity is not identified) are not permitted in Mexico (LGSM Article 111). Since shares are considered to be securities (*títulos de valores*), these financial instruments are also regulated by the General Law of Securities and Credit Transactions (*Ley General de Títulos y Operaciones de Crédito*, or LGTYOC),[52] although the final sentence of LGSM Article 111 makes it clear that the LGSM is the principal law governing the issuance and ownership of corporate shares and is to be supplemented by the LGTYOC.

[48] At the exchange rate of January 2003.

[49] For generations, even sizable Mexican corporations were closely held companies, that is, their shares were not publicly traded on the Mexican stock exchange. This characteristic is changing with the increased modernization of financial markets in Mexico.

[50] *See* Chapter 20 below, at text accompanying note 53.

[51] Stock certificates are required to contain specific information, specified in LGSM Article 125, for the purposes of identification of the shareholder, and must also be equipped with detachable coupons which shall be returned to the corporation upon payment of dividends or interest (LGSM Article 127).

[52] D.O. 27 Aug. 1932, as amended.

The principal types of shares issued by Mexican corporations, and their characteristics, are the following.[53]

5.1.1. *Shares with Limited Voting Rights* (Acciones de Voto Limitado)

As a general rule, all shares must have equal value and confer equal rights on all shareholders, in keeping with the general requirement that shareholder agreements may not produce legal effects that exclude any shareholder from sharing in the profits (LGSM Article 17). There are important exceptions to this general rule, however, and LGSM Article 112 allows shareholders to agree that the capital stock may be divided into several different classes of shares, and that special rights may be granted to the respective holders of each type.[54] Thus, the articles of incorporation may limit the rights of the holders of certain classes of shares to only one right: the right to vote at extraordinary shareholders' meetings where fundamental matters are decided. Such 'shares with limited voting rights' (*acciones de voto limitado*) give shareholders priority in the payment of corporate dividends, and a higher dividend may be given for these shares than is given for shares of common stock.[55]

LGSM Article 113 guarantees minority holders of *acciones de voto limitado* two important rights, referred to as 'corporate privilege' (*privilegio corporativo*): the power to oversee or review the profit and loss accounts and books of the corporation, and the power to challenge decisions taken by majority shareholders in shareholder meetings, when shareholders representing at least 33 per cent of the shares file a challenge in a court of law to a decision taken by majority shareholders in a shareholder meeting (LGSM Article 113, last paragraph).

5.1.2. *Treasury Shares* (Acciones de Tesorería)

Mexican law also provides for the issuance of another type of share, *acciones de tesorería* or 'treasury shares', which are not distributed to shareholders, but are kept out of circulation by the corporation that issues them. Mexican treasury shares are *potential* shares that may only be issued as a result of a decision by the shareholders, by the Board of Directors, or by the sole director, if the shareholders so designate, and they may only be issued under certain predetermined circumstances and conditions. If the corporation should decide to increase its capital, treasury certificates may become part of a public offering on the stock exchange, and upon their purchase they become normal voting shares;[56] until such time they have no utility.

[53] *See generally* Barrera Graf, *supra* note 14 at 500–513.

[54] Thus, for example, it is common for the issuance of shares with limited voting rights in special shareholder meetings (*asambleas extraordinarias*); such shares commonly have preferential treatment in the issuance of dividends (LGSM Article 113). In this way, a corporation is able to attract investors who are interested in investment, but are not interested in influencing the management of the enterprise, and are therefore willing to give up certain voting rights for this purpose.

[55] Shares with limited voting rights and guaranteed dividends are considered 'preferred shares' (*acciones privilegiadas*). *See generally* Rodríguez and Rodríguez, *supra* note 16 at 118.

[56] Barrera Graf, *supra* note 14 at 512–513.

Under LGSM Article 134, it is illegal for Mexican corporations to acquire their own shares, unless this has been authorized in the company rules (*estatutos*). This Mexican rule stands in stark contrast with US law, which enables companies to purchase and sell their own shares, which can influence the price of those shares on the market.

5.1.3. *Partly Paid or Callable Shares* (Acciones Pagadoras)

Corporations occasionally issue shares the price of which are only partially paid into the corporation by the shareholder, if the corporate rules so provide. In such instances, LGSM Article 89, section III, requires that the shareholder pay in at least 20 per cent of the value of the share at the time of incorporation. The shareholder remains indebted to the corporation for the unpaid amount, which may be claimed (called) by the corporation at any time.[57]

5.1.4. *Employee Shares* (Acciones de Trabajo)

LGSM Article 114 provides that a corporation may provide in its rules for the issuance of a particular type of share to persons who work for a company. This type of share, called *acciones de trabajo* or *acciones especiales*, may be issued to employees in fulfilment of the requirement under Mexican law that corporations provide to employees a right to share in the corporate profits.[58] *Acciones de trabajo* do not represent ownership shares with voting rights in the corporation, nor are they considered securities (*títulos de valores*), but they do represent obligations of the corporation that issues them.

5.2. Payment of Dividends

Shareholders are entitled to receive dividends, but this right is only enforceable in the following circumstances, and provided that the financial statements of the corporation have been approved by the shareholders (LGSM Article 19).

(a) The corporation must not have suffered losses of paid-up capital (*capital social*), which must be reconstituted prior to payment of dividends (LGSM Article 18).

[57] According to LGSM Article 117, subscribers and purchasers of partly paid or callable shares 'shall be responsible for the unpaid amount of the shares of stock for 5 years, counting from the date of record of the transfer, but they may not claim payment from the transferor without first excluding [the possibility of assessing] the property of the purchaser'. In the event that the shares have a specific deadline for payment, the corporation is entitled to demand payment through the courts, or demand that the shares be sold (LGSM Article 118). If the shares have no time limit, a public notice must be given in the official gazette of the domicile of the corporation 30 days before the stipulated payment date (LGSM Article 119).

[58] Article 123, section IX of the Mexican Constitution establishes a requirement of profit-sharing for workers. The granting of *acciones de trabajo* does not of itself fulfil the obligation of the management in accordance with the profit-sharing mandate in the constitution. Most companies fulfil the profit-sharing requirement by making a single yearly lump-sum payment during the month of May, without issuing *acciones de trabajo*. *See* Barrera Graf, *supra* note 14 at 511–512. On profit-sharing, *see* Patiño Camarena, J. E., *Instituciones del Derecho del Trabajo y de la Seguridad Social* (Mexico: Oxford University Press, 1999).

(b) Before any dividends may be paid out, 5 per cent of the company's profits must be set aside to make up corporate reserves, until such time as the value of said reserve is equivalent to one-fifth of the capital stock of the corporation (LGSM Article 20).
(c) If limited voting right shares (*acciones de voto limitado*) exist, a dividend equal to at least 5 per cent of the total amount of dividends distributed must be given to the holders of these shares before proceeding to distribute dividends among other holders of common stock (LGSM Article 113, second paragraph).
(d) Where the corporation has issued partly paid or callable capital stock, (*acciones pagadoras*), distribution of profits shall be carried out in proportion to the total amount paid for these shares.[59]

Investors from the United States and Canada are protected by provisions of the North American Free Trade Agreement, by which the governments of the three NAFTA states are committed to allowing international payments relating to the transfer of dividends and other forms of profits to an investor located in the NAFTA party.[60]

5.3. Registration and Transfer of Shares

Corporations are required to maintain separate record books for different types of information. One of these books is the registry of shareholders.[61] According to LGSM Article 129, whoever appears as the registered shareholder in the company registry shall be considered the owner of the shares. Any subsequent transfers of shares that may take place throughout the life of the corporation must also be recorded in the same registry. Such registration of the owners of shares is considered crucial to the government's need to monitor the beneficial ownership of companies, both for purposes of tax enforcement and to ensure that limitations on foreign ownership and other requirements are met.

Restraints may be placed on transfers of shares of stock in keeping with the provisions of the rules of the corporation. For example, the rules may stipulate that shareholders may only transfer their shares of stock after giving the other shareholders a right of first refusal. Another possible arrangement is provided for by LGSM Article 130, which says that corporate rules may dictate that share transfers may only take place with the prior consent of the board of directors, who shall have the power to deny authorization of a transfer by

[59] This conclusion is an extension of the requirement in LGSM Article 17 that all shareholders must have a share of profits. García Rendón, *supra* note 21 at 267.

[60] NAFTA Article 1109. *See* NAFTA Article 1139 for definitions of investment, investor and transfer.

[61] LGSM Article 128 requires stock companies to keep a registry of the shares of stock issued by the corporation, containing the name, nationality, and domicile of the shareholder, and showing the number, series, and of shares belonging to each shareholder, and other special information.

designating that the shares in question must be sold to a particular purchaser at the current market price. The ability to control the sale of shares through restrictions in the rules has been used extensively in Mexican corporations, and is one reason why even the largest of Mexican corporations continue to remain in the hands of relatively small groups of investors, mostly connected with influential families.

In addition to registration, a share transfer must follow the rules governing the sale and transfer of securities (*títulos de valor*). For example, under the LGSM and the LGTYOC, share certificates must be endorsed by the party that transfers ownership to another in order to be effective. In addition, in cases in which the transfer of shares is restricted by the rules, the Board of Directors must authorize the transfer. In addition, the transfer must be recorded on the stock certificate (LGSM Article 131). For corporations whose shares are quoted on the Mexican stock exchange, or for banking institutions, additional requirements apply to share transfers such as the rules set forth in Article 53 of the Securities Law (*Ley del Mercado de Valores*), or Article 82, section II(b) of the General law of Credit Organizations and Auxiliary Credit Activities (*Ley General de Organizaciones de Crédito y Actividaes Auxiliares de Crédito*).[62]

5.4. Increases in Capital Stock: *Sociedad Anónima de Capital Variable* (S.A. de C.V.)

Before a *sociedad anónima* can increase its capital stock, several formal requirements must be fulfilled. First, the shareholders must vote their agreement to an increase at an extraordinary shareholders' meeting (LGSM Article 82, section III). The decision of the shareholders must then be formalized by a public notary and recorded in the Public Registry of Commerce, in order to meet the requirement that the fixed minimum amount of capital stock in existence is the exact amount of capital stock set by the founding shareholders. To avoid the need for repeated registrations, most major corporations in Mexico are incorporated as 'variable capital stock companies', or *sociedades anónimas de capital variable*, or S.A. de C.V. The advantage of a 'variable capital corporation' is that the variable portion of the capital stock may increase or decrease as determined by the procedure set out in the company rules (*estatutos*), without the obligation to fulfil any formal procedural requirements other than recording increases or decreases in the minutes of the general ordinary shareholders' meetings and in the corresponding registry in which the ownership of the shares is recorded. The same general rules apply to this variable capital corporation (*sociedad de capital variable*) as those that govern the amounts of capital stock of fixed-capital companies.

LGSM Article 132 states that shareholders shall have preferential rights to subscribe any new shares that are issued in the event of an increase in capital stock, in proportion to the number of shares owned by the shareholder.

[62] D.O. 14 Jan. 1985, as amended.

This right must be exercised within fifteen days following public notice in the official periodical of the domicile of the corporation, of the shareholders' decision to increase the capital stock. The company rules may also provide for a requirement of written notice to shareholders of the opportunity to exercise preferential rights.

5.5. Management of *Sociedades Anónimas*

Corporations in Mexico may be managed by either a sole director (*administrador único*) or a board of directors (*consejo de administración*) (LGSM Articles 142 and 143). A board of directors is created when two or more directors (*administradores*) are appointed. In practice, both modes of administration are usually provided for in the corporate rules, thus permitting the shareholders to decide on either of the management structures without requiring an amendment of the rules. In fact, as in the United States, most large Mexican corporations, other than closely held corporations, are managed by a board of directors, rather than by a sole director.

The procedure for election of board members by the shareholders is governed by law, and is not subject to amendment by the shareholders.[63] In practice, the names of the individuals who are to become the initial executive director or the members of the board are specified at the time the organization is incorporated, through registration of the appointment with the articles of incorporation. Appointments of directors take effect immediately upon formalization of the corporate charter by a notary public.[64] Subsequently, changes in the directors or officers of a corporation must be recorded in the corporate records (*libro de actas*), and this change must also be recorded by a notary public and filed with the Public Registry of Commerce in the place of the company's domicile.

The rules for appointment, representation, and operation of the board of directors—which in some instances are applicable to the sole director—can be summed up as follows.

(a) Unless otherwise agreed upon by the shareholders and reflected in the rules or at the time of appointment, the chairman of the board of directors (*presidente del consejo de administración*) shall be the member of the board who is appointed first; when the chairman is absent, the person who follows in order of appointment shall serve as chairman (LGSM Article 143, second paragraph).
(b) In order to satisfy the quorum requirement for an official meeting of the board, at least one half of the board members must be present, and the board's resolutions shall only be valid if they are made by a majority of

[63] *See* Frisch Phillips, *supra* note 8 at 365 *et seq*. The procedures for convocation and voting of the shareholders are contained in LGSM Articles 178–206.

[64] *See* Primer Tribunal Colegiado de Circuito en materia administrativa del Primer Circuito, SJF, 10a, vol. 47, p. 39, Sexta Parte, p. 58275, 1972.

the members present. In the event of a tie the chairman shall have the casting vote (LGSM Article 143, third paragraph). The rules can alter these minimum requirements by requiring a greater majority.

(c) The rules may stipulate that decisions made outside of board meetings may be ratified by subsequent vote of the board, provided that such decisions are unanimous and are confirmed in writing (LGSM Article 143, final paragraph).

(d) When a board consists of three or more members, the rights of the minority members must be set forth in the company's rules. According to LGSM Article 144, when a minority shareholder holds at least 25 per cent of the capital stock, the shareholder has the right to appoint at least one member to the board.[65] The percentage of shares required to appoint at least one member to the board is lower (10 per cent) for companies whose shares are quoted on the Mexican stock exchange.

5.5.1. Qualifications of Directors

The LGSM sets forth the following qualifications for sitting on the board of directors of a Mexican *sociedad anónima*.

(a) Board members must be natural persons and must directly exercise their own voting rights, and cannot be representatives of others (LGSM Article 147).

(b) Board members must have full legal capacity to enter into contracts and binding obligations for the corporation Article 5 of the Code of Commerce, and Articles 647 and 2709 of the FCC; board members may not be individuals who are disqualified by law (Article 12 of the Code of Commerce).

(c) Foreign nationals may be board members of a corporation, provided that their immigration status qualifies them legally to serve in such capacity and perform such acts of representation. In order to serve on a board of directors of a Mexican corporation, foreign nationals must have the immigration status of 'immigrant' (*inmigrante*), with the additional qualification of 'fiduciary or trustee' (*cargo de confianza*) or 'investor' (*inversionista*).[66] Furthermore, the number of foreign nationals that may sit on a corporate board may not be out of proportion with the percentage of foreign capital invested in the corporation, as measured by the number of shares owned by foreign nationals. This provision of the law serves to prevent foreign investors from controlling a Mexican corporation when such control is prohibited by Mexican law, or from having a greater percentage than may

[65] The right of minority shareholders to appoint members to the board has come under criticism because the rule does not take account of the total number of members that comprise the board. Therefore, appointment of only one board member by the minority may have little effect in cases where the board consists of many members. Consequently, it is advisable for all corporations to write into the original draft of the rules a maximum and proportional number of members of the board that the minority may appoint. Barrera Graf, *supra* note 14 at 573.

[66] *See generally* Pereznieto Castro, L. and Mansilla y Mejía, M.E., *Manual Práctico del Extranjero* (Mexico: Oxford University Press, 1999) at 90 *et seq*.

be legally permitted for corporations in those sectors specified in the Foreign Investment Law for which foreign investment is either prohibited or limited (Foreign Investment Law Articles 5–9).

(d) Both shareholders and non-shareholders may be members of the board of directors of corporations in Mexico. The appointment of board members is temporary, and the shareholders may revoke appointments at any time (LGSM Article 142).

5.5.2. Duties of Directors

As already mentioned,[67] the administration of a corporation may be carried out either by a sole director (*administrador único*), or by a board of directors (*consejo de administración*), as determined by the articles of incorporation and decisions of the shareholders. The basic duties of directors, whether the corporation operates under a sole director or a board of directors, are virtually the same, and are determined by the law and by the corporation's by-laws.[68]

Under LGSM Article 158, sections I–IV, the basic duties of directors are:

(a) to ensure that contributions to capital made by shareholders are actually paid in or otherwise delivered;

(b) to ensure that dividends paid to shareholders fulfil the requirements set forth by law and the rules of the corporation;

(c) to ensure that all decisions agreed upon by the shareholders are carried out; and

(d) to ensure that the permanent systems of accounting, control, record-keeping, filing, and reporting required by law or the company's rules have been put into place.

In general, while Mexican law is not known for emphasizing conflict of interest principles, Mexican corporations law takes conflicts seriously. Thus, board members who have a conflict of interests (*conflicto de intereses*) in any transaction of business of the corporation must apprise the other board members of the situation, and must refrain from participating in all deliberations concerning the matter in question (LGSM Article 156). Where such conflict exists, a director is usually required to leave the board of directors meeting while a decision is made by the remaining directors.

5.5.3. Decision-Making by the Board of Directors

The hierarchy of corporate governance in Mexico is similar to that in the United States and in many other countries: the ultimate decision-making power for major decisions lies with the shareholders, who exercise their voting powers

[67] *See supra* the paragraph preceding note 41.

[68] LGSM Article 157. On responsibilities of directors generally *see* Galindo Garfias, I., SOCIEDAD ANÓNIMA, RESPONSABILIDAD CIVIL DE LOS ADMINISTRADORES (Mexico: 1957); and Llebot Majo, J.O., LOS DEBERES DE LOS ADMINISTRADORES DE LA SOCIEDAD ANÓNIMA (Madrid: Civitas, 1996).

in annual or extraordinary meetings, as discussed below. Many important decisions are delegated by the shareholders to the directors; as noted above, this may consist of a board of directors (*consejo de administración*) or, less commonly, a sole director (*administrador único*). The powers of a sole director are virtually identical with those of a board of directors, and we therefore concentrate on the latter in this Chapter. Day-to-day and operational decisions are delegated by the shareholders and the board to the corporation's officers, as discussed in the following section. Finally, Mexican corporations also include a unique, semi-independent control mechanism, the *comisario*, discussed below in this section.

The board of directors is required to act in conformity with the provisions of the LGSM and of the corporation's by-laws. Board meetings must be convened by the chairman of the board (*presidente del consejo*). Board sessions must be attended by at least half of the board members in order to achieve a quorum, and board decisions must be adopted by a simple majority vote, unless otherwise stipulated in the company rules (LGSM Article 143, third paragraph). As previously mentioned, this same provision establishes that the chairman of the board has the casting vote.

As a practical matter, when foreign investors hold a minority interest in a corporation, it is common to establish 'negative controls' (*controles negativos)* to protect the interests of the foreign minority shareholders. Such measures may include agreeing with the Mexican investors a higher quorum requirement for board meetings, so that the board members designated by the foreign investor(s) must be present for the board to convene officially and make decisions. Another example of such measures is to require special (high) majorities for important decisions by the board. Nevertheless, in setting a higher voting majority for certain decisions, corporations should be careful not to hamstring the board from making the normal decisions that are vital to the daily operations of the company. Minority shareholders may also protect themselves by requiring that the company rules include a provision that disputes between shareholders must be settled by arbitration between them. One method of protection of minority shareholders is *not* permitted: according to LGSM Article 198, '[a]ny agreement that restricts the freedom of shareholder votes is null and void'.

It is common practice for the shareholders to appoint alternate board members (*consejeros suplentes*), whose duties are defined in the company rules. The election or appointment of alternates is particularly important when foreign investment represents a minority interest in the corporation and the board member or members appointed to represent the foreign interest are required to be present whenever the board of directors holds meetings. If the board member appointed by a minority foreign investor cannot be present, then it is common for the rules to recognize the right of an alternate board member to be present at board meetings to represent the foreign investor's interests.

One of the main functions of the board of directors is to review the financial statement of the corporation, which is prepared by the *comisario*, as discussed in the following section. The financial statement is part of the annual report which the board members are obliged to present at the annual shareholders' meeting (LGSM Article 172). Under Article 172, this document must contain information such as a report on the general condition of the corporation, an explanation of the policies and accounting standards used by the *comisario*, and a report on the state of financial affairs of the company.

As a general rule, neither board members nor the *comisario* (discussed below) may vote at board meetings on matters in which they have had prior involvement or for which they have been partly or wholly responsible. Thus, board members who are responsible for undertaking and filing corporate reports, such as compliance with the requirement that shareholders contribute paid-up capital, and the *comisario* (who is responsible for confirmation of the accuracy of the corporation's financial statement), may not participate in a decision to approve such reports (LGSM Article 197). The law does not specify a penalty for violation of this rule.[69]

5.5.4. *Liability of Directors*

In performing their duties, members of the board of directors may not act outside or beyond the scope of the business purpose of the company (*objeto social*). Any act carried out by board members that is inconsistent with the corporate purpose, as set forth in its rules 'would be overstepping their powers and would be acting *ultra vires*, without representation'.[70] In such instances, the sole director or the board member or members in question may be held personally liable for such acts, unless the shareholders recognize the need to have performed such acts and specifically ratifies them *a posteriori* by a unanimous vote of all shareholders with voting rights (LGSM Article 178). Directors can be held jointly and severally liable if they were aware of illegal or irregular acts regarding the corporation and failed to report the irregularities to the auditor (*comisario*) (LGSM Article 160). However, a director may not be held liable if he or she demonstrated disagreement with the decision to undertake an illegal act (LGSM Article 159).

LGSM Article 158 states that individual board members may face joint and several liability (*responsabilidad solidaria*) for illegal acts undertaken by other board members, or by the board as a group. According to Barrera Graf, 'the conduct of the body which gives rise to liability [the board of directors] may derive from the unlawful conduct of any one of its members, in which case all board members are jointly and severally liable'.[71] The corporation itself may also be held jointly and severally liable for the misconduct of its board members, pursuant to the principles of liability established in FCC Article 1918.[72]

[69] Macedo Hernández, J.H., LEY GENERAL DE SOCIEDADS MERCANTILES (Mexico: Cárdenas, 1984) at 189.

[70] LGSM Art. 160. *See also* Barrera Graf, *supra* note 14 at 581.

[71] *Id.* at 590.

[72] *Id.* at 590 *et seq.*

Mexican corporate law doctrine generally divides the liability of directors into four subtopics: (1) the scope of directors' liability (*contenido de responsabilidad*); (2) who has standing to sue a director (*legitimación para el ejercicio de la acción de responsabilidad*); (3) agreements or decisions on the limitation of and exemption from directors' liability (*pactos de limitación y exención de responsabilidad*); and (4) the statute of limitations on liability actions (*prescripción*).

Scope of liability Directors may be subject to civil liability, but if the misconduct committed by board members also entails a criminal offence (*delito*) under the provisions of the criminal code, they may also be subject to criminal prosecution.[73] Civil liability may encompass either the obligation to refrain from doing certain acts, as when a director fails to bring to the attention of the board a conflict of interest in a matter pending before the board,[74] or the failure to act when the director has a duty to act, such as the duty to report errors in the financial statements of the corporation of which the director is aware (LGSM Article 159).

Directors of corporations whose shares are publicly traded may be liable for disclosure of insider information if such information is provided to third parties or is used by board members for personal gain.[75] Under Mexican law, such liability is generally civil, although criminal liability may also be incurred if the acts committed by the director also constitute a crime.

Standing to sue If a director's acts cause damage to the corporation, LGSM Article 161 states that a claim for civil damages against the director may only be initiated, on behalf of the corporation or on behalf of the shareholders in general, if the shareholders agree to take such action by majority vote in a general shareholders' meeting.[76] A director may also be liable for damage caused to a third party if the director undertakes wrongful acts beyond those contemplated in his duties as director, and if a basis for liability based on such acts exists under the Civil Code.

Limitations of liability Limitations may be placed on board members' liability either in the company rules, or subsequently by agreement among the shareholders. The limitation of or exemption from liability must be stated in precise terms. For example, the rules may exempt directors from liability with regard to administration of the corporation or certain areas of the company's business. Such limitation of directors' liability is valid only as regards liability

[73] For example, a director may be found guilty of the crime of embezzlement (*abuso de confianza*). *See* Mexican Federal Criminal Code, Article 223.

[74] LGSM Article 156. Barrera Graf notes that under the Mexican Civil Code (*see* e.g. FCC Article 1916) a director could be liable for damage to someone's reputation. Barrera Graf, *supra* note 14 at 591.

[75] Article 16*bis*1 and 16*bis*2 of the Law of the Securities Market (*Ley del Mercado de Valores*).

[76] According to Barrera Graf, *supra* note 14 at 592, the principles of liability established in Articles 2104 *et seq.* of the FCC and CCDF may be used to assert civil liability against a director. Under LGSM Article 163, minority shareholders that represent at least 33% of the shares may also initiate a civil action on behalf of the corporation against a director, if the minority shareholders disagree with a decision by the majority not to take action against a director.

to the corporation or to its shareholders; it does not affect the potential liability of directors to third parties.

Agreements to limit directors' liability are invalid if they are contrary to public policy (*contrarios a disposiciones de orden público*). Examples of limitations against public policy would include any limitation that contradicted the obligations established by the LGSM, such as the duty to avoid conflicts of interest (LGSM Article 156), the duty to report wrongdoing of shareholders (LGSM Article 160), or the basic duties of a director (LGSM Article 158).

Statutes of limitations The statutes of limitations (*prescripción*) on the liability of directors is derived from the statute of limitations applicable to the underlying cause of action against the director. Thus, a cause of action against a director arising from a wrongful act (*hecho ilícito*), such as fraud or embezzlement, must be brought within two years of the date in which the damage was caused, according to Article 1934 of the FCC and CCDF.

5.6. Company Monitoring: The *Comisario*

In the United States, the financial affairs of a corporation are monitored on an annual basis by an independent auditor, usually an accounting firm that examines the financial records of the corporation and makes an annual report that is submitted to the board of directors. The independent audit is a key element in the transparency of a corporation's financial state of health, which is important to the operation of a public stock market.

In Mexico, a company's financial condition is monitored not by an independent auditing agency, but rather by a semi-independent corporate officer (or officers) within the corporation known as the *comisario*. The *comisario* has no equivalent in US corporate law, and was imported to Mexico from Italian law, which has influenced Mexican commercial law. As the following discussion shows, the *comisario* is not completely independent of the corporation, and yet is expected to act independently. This model of 'semi-independent' auditing is not surprising when viewed against Mexico's historical background, in which transparency has not been a highly valued goal.

LGSM Article 164 requires every legally chartered company, whether a corporation, partnership, or other form, to provide for oversight by one or more *comisarios*, or 'examiner/auditors', who may be either shareholders (of no more than 25 per cent of the shares) or non-shareholders. The *comisario* of a corporation is appointed by the shareholders by majority vote (LGSM Article 181); however, the law permits corporations to adopt rules that give a minority of shareholders the right to appoint at least one *comisario*, in addition to any *comisarios* appointed by the majority.[77] (A *comisario* is usually an

[77] *See* e.g. Barrera Graf, *supra* note 14 at 610 *et seq*; and Frisch Phillips, *supra* note 8 at 418, interpreting LGSM Article 144, which grants minority shareholders the right to appoint one board member when the board numbers 3 or more directors, as support for the right of minority shareholders to appoint a *comisario* to protect minority interests.

accountant, often a member of a firm of accountants which acts as auditors for the corporation. A *comisario* may act for more than one corporation at a time.)

The *comisario* is expected to act independently of the corporation in performing its duties, which include the following:[78]

(a) the power to demand information from board members on a monthly basis, including at least one financial report and a profit and loss account;
(b) the power to examine or audit transactions, documents, records, and other supporting evidence, to the extent that the body deems necessary;
(c) the power to file an annual report to the shareholders expressing the *comisario*'s view on the accuracy, adequacy, and reasonableness of the information presented by the board of directors to the shareholders;
(d) the power to issue opinions on the policies, accounting, and reporting standards that are used by the corporation, and whether those policies have been consistently applied by the board members;
(e) the power to issue opinions on whether the information provided by the board of directors is consistent with the actual state of affairs in the corporation;
(f) the power to request that particular points of discussion be included on the agenda at shareholders' meetings that the examiners/auditors consider pertinent, and even to convene shareholders' meetings when the board of directors fails to do so, and to attend such meetings with the right to speak but without the right to vote; and
(g) the power to examine the operations of the corporation without any constraints at any time.

The functioning of the *comisario* system has at times come under criticism as an ineffective control against corporate corruption: a charge that has also been levelled at systems of independent auditing used in the United States. *Comisarios* depend solely on information provided by the same board of directors that they are seeking to monitor, which limits their ability to exercise independent judgement. In practice, the success of the *comisario* in effective monitoring depends on how much the shareholders want the *comisarios* to act efficiently and independently.

Comisarios may be held individually liable to the corporation for any violation of the law or of its rules. They may also be held liable under the same principles as board members, as discussed in the previous section.

5.7. Corporate Officers

In Mexico, as in the United States, broad corporate policies result from the decisions of shareholders and boards of directors, but the continuing operations of

[78] LGSM Articles 165, 166.

the corporation are managed by corporate officers. In Mexico, corporate officers may consist of a general manager (*gerente general*) who may or may not be a member of the board of directors; managers (*gerentes*); deputy board members (*consejeros delegados*);[79] and legal representatives (*apoderados*).[80] The director general and other officers are appointed by vote of the shareholders, by the sole director, or by vote of the board of directors, depending on the company's rules.

The legal qualifications of corporate officers are the same as those required of board members, such as not having been disqualified from engaging in commerce, and having full legal capacity to carry out their duties.[81] According to LGSM Article 146, '[m]anagers shall have the powers expressly conferred on them, shall not require special authorization from the sole director or the board of directors to perform their duties, and shall enjoy, within the scope of the attributions that have been assigned to them, the broadest powers of representation and execution'.

Companies with significant foreign investment may wish to be assured of the ability to appoint senior officers to manage the company's operations in Mexico. In Mexico, no general laws limit the appointment of foreigners to management positions, although special rules apply in some sectors, such as the banking sector (discussed below in Chapter 20, section 2.3.1.).

For investors from Canada and the United States, the NAFTA provides that no NAFTA party can require a foreign investor to appoint persons to senior management who are of any particular nationality, although the government may require that a majority of the board of directors be of a particular nationality or domicile (NAFTA Article 1107). Chapter 16 of NAFTA also sets out commitments of the NAFTA parties to permit the temporary entry of business persons by foreign investors.

5.8. Shareholders

The shareholders are the highest governing body of a *sociedad anónima* (LGSM Article 178). Acting through the general shareholders' meetings (*asamblea general de accionistas*), they are empowered to decide upon and approve the activities and operations of the company. Decisions of the shareholders are carried out by the person or the persons designated by the shareholders: either the sole director, or the board of directors.

[79] Deputy board members are board members who are specifically appointed by the board to carry out particular acts delegated to them on behalf of the board (LGSM Article 148). For example, the board of directors may appoint *consejeros delegados* to negotiate an important acquisition on behalf of the corporation.

[80] *Apoderados* are persons who are granted power of attorney, in the name of the corporation, to carry out specific acts: for instance, when the corporation grants a power of attorney to execute a contract, initiate or defend litigation, or conduct business negotiations. The members of the board or the managers may, in keeping with the scope of their respective powers, grant powers of attorney in the name of the corporation, and such power of representation may be revoked at any time (LGSM Article 149).

[81] *See supra*, section 5.5.1.

In understanding how the rights of shareholders in Mexico are protected, it is necessary to keep in mind that many Mexican corporations are controlled by persons connected with each other by family or other ties. This is true even in corporations whose shares are publicly traded on the Mexican Stock Exchange, and are therefore subject to increased transparency and other controls. A family group may control a corporation even if the public controls a large percentage of the shares of the corporation, since the shares that are publicly held may consist of non-voting shares, as described above.

5.8.1. Shareholders' Meetings

The law differentiates between two types of shareholders' meetings: ordinary shareholders' meetings (*asambleas ordinarias*), and extraordinary shareholders' meetings (*asambleas extraordinarias*) (LGSM Article 179). The distinction between these two types of meetings is important, because the decision-making powers that may be exercised by shareholders at each type of meeting, and the validity of decisions taken by them, vary.

Under LGSM Article 182, certain types of decisions must be taken at extraordinary shareholders' meetings (discussed below). All other decisions may be made at ordinary shareholders' meetings (LGSM Article 180), which must be held at least once a year.[82]

According to LGSM Article 181, ordinary shareholders' meetings must be held at least annually within four months of the close of the fiscal year, and must deal with, in addition to the matters listed on the agenda, the approval of the annual report submitted by the board of directors, covering the matters listed in LGSM Article 172 (operations, financial accounts, etc.) including the report of the *comisarios*. The annual meeting should also deal with any necessary appointments, either of directors or of *comisarios*, and the amount of remuneration each is to receive (if not covered in the rules).

Extraordinary shareholders' meetings may be called periodically to resolve matters of high importance, such as the capitalization, structure, and basic functions of the corporation. LGSM Article 182 specifies the types of decisions that must be taken at an extraordinary shareholders' meeting.[83] Since important matters are dealt with at such meetings, extraordinary shareholders'

[82] Both ordinary and extraordinary meetings are generally held at the main office of the company, or at an alternative place designated by the shareholders. As a practical matter, for regularly convened meetings at which no controversial decisions are to be taken, the formality of a shareholder's meeting may often be dispensed with; instead, lawyers representing the corporation draft minutes covering the routine matters that require approval, and present these minutes to shareholders (or their legal representatives) for signature and approval. When competing interests are engaged in shareholder decisions, dispensing with a formal meeting is risky, since one group may demand nullification of the minutes.

[83] The 12 types of decisions to be taken at extraordinary meetings include: dissolution; increase or decrease in capital stock; change in the corporate purpose; change in the nationality of the corporation; mergers with other corporations; issuance of preferred shares of stock; redemption of its own shares of stock by the corporation; modification of the company charter; and any other matters for which the law or the rules require a special quorum.

meetings have special quorum requirements and voting procedures. Due to the highly formalistic nature of Mexican corporate law, the notice of shareholders' meetings and the quorum requirements may determine the outcome of conflicts between shareholder factions. Control of a corporation may be gained or lost as a result of the strategy followed in convening shareholders' meetings.

The sole director or board of directors is usually responsible for convening shareholders' meetings (LGSM Article 183). The law also permits *comisarios* to convene both ordinary or extraordinary meetings, in the event that the board of directors of the corporation does not do so at the required time or when, in the view of the *comisario*, it is appropriate to do so (LGSM Article 166, section VI). Shareholders may request the board of directors or the *comisario* to convene a shareholders' meeting; if the directors or *comisario* fails to convene the meeting, the shareholders themselves have the right to call a meeting if at least 33 per cent of the capital stock is represented by the group that requests such a meeting (LGSM Article 184). If necessary, such shareholders may present their stock certificates to a judge and request that a court of law within the jurisdiction of the corporation's domicile convene the meeting.[84]

Even if the shareholders' equity in the corporation consists of one share, a single shareholder is also entitled to call for a shareholders' meeting in the following instances: when no meeting has been held for the past two years, in violation of the law; when annual meetings have been held and no report has been filed by the board and approved for two consecutive years; and when shareholders have failed to elect board members or *comisarios*, as required by law (LGSM Article 185).

5.9. Mergers, Changes of Corporate Form, and Spin-Offs

The LGSM regulates the merger of one corporation into another (*fusión*); the transformation of one type of corporation into another type of corporation, for example a limited liability corporation into a stock company (*transformación*); and the creation of two new corporations from the same entity (*escisión*). This Chapter highlights only the general aspects of these three subjects, which are covered in detail elsewhere.[85]

[84] LGSM Article 184, second paragraph. While it may be expeditious for shareholders to convene a meeting directly, without judicial intervention, notice of a shareholders' meeting of this type could be challenged by dissident shareholders before a judge, who may enjoin the meeting from being held while the court ascertains whether those calling for the meeting hold 33% of the shares of the corporation; if held, the validity of such a meeting may later be challenged. Therefore, as a usual practice, when 33% of the shareholders wish to call a meeting, they do so with the aid of a judicial order, after the judge has verified the right of the shareholders to convene the meeting.

[85] *See* e.g. Vázquez del Mercado, O., *ASAMBLEAS, FUSIÓN Y LIQUIDACIÓN DE SOCIEDADES MERCANTILES* (Mexico: ed. Porrúa, 1992); and Gómez Cotero, J. De J., *FUSIÓN Y ESCISIÓN DE SOCIEDADES MERCANTILES* (Mexico: Themis, 5th ed., 1998).

5.9.1. Mergers and Acquisitions

Mergers (*fusiones*) must be approved by a majority of the shareholders of each of the merging companies (LGSM Article 222); in the case of *sociedades anónimas*, this approval must be by an extraordinary shareholders' meeting (LGSM Article 182, section VII). A merger may only take effect three months after its registration in the Public Registry of Commerce and after public announcement of the merger in the official publication (*gaceta*) of the domicile of the corporation (LGSM Articles 223 and 224).

LGSM Article 224, paragraph 2, provides that during the three-month period between the registration of the merger and the time the merger takes effect, 'any creditor of the merging corporations may oppose the merger in court, in a summary proceeding, [and] the merger shall be suspended until a final judicial ruling may be issued declaring the objection without merit'.

Mergers or acquisitions may be opposed by shareholders if either the decision to merge is improperly made, or the effect of the merger will violate the company rules or any other provision of law. In the latter sense, the recent development of Mexican competition law (discussed in more detail in Chapter 12 above) requires notification to the Federal Competition Commission (CFC) if a merger results in the formation of a corporation valued at a sum greater than the figure set in the Federal Law of Economic Competition (approximately 60 million US dollars in 2003).[86] It is the responsibility of the CFC to study the anti-competitive effects of the merger, and as discussed above in Chapter 12,[87] if the CFC finds that the merger would result in an improper concentration, it may prevent the merger from taking place.[88] Since mergers and acquisitions involving foreign companies often exceed these threshold levels, it is advisable to receive a favourable ruling from the CFC prior to attempting to finalize a merger.

To fulfil the requirements of registration and public announcement, corporations are required to convene an extraordinary shareholders' meeting, properly record the merger in the minutes of the meeting, and file the minutes in the registry of a notary public. Once these requirements are fulfilled, corporations may proceed to registration of the merger. With regard to public notice, the final corporate balance sheet must appear in the Registry, and the corporation or corporations that will cease to exist upon the merger must also provide an account of the system that will be used to settle their liabilities (LGSM Article 223).[89]

[86] Article 20 of the *Ley Federal de Competencia Económica*, D.O. 24 Dec. 1992, discussed in greater detail below in Chapter 20. On Mexican competition law, *see generally* Pereznieto, L. and Guerrero, R., *Derecho de la Competencia* (Mexico: Oxford University Press, 2002) at 21 *et seq*.

[87] *See* Chapter 12 above, section 5.2.

[88] Federal Competition Law (*Ley Federal de Competencia*) Article 17.

[89] A more expeditious procedure also exists to facilitate mergers. At a joint extraordinary shareholders' meeting of both the merging corporations, a decision may be adopted that all debts of the corporations that are to merge into one single corporation shall be paid off or that payments for those debts shall be deposited with a credit institution (LGSM Article 225). To

5.9.2. *Transformations*

In general, the same rules that apply to mergers also apply to changes of corporate form (*transformaciones*). LGSM Article 227 allows any legally chartered business organization of any type or class described in LGSM Article 1 (other than a co-operative) to adopt any legal form business enterprise.

5.9.3. *Spin-Offs*

Unlike conversions of corporate form, specific rules have been formulated to govern corporate spin-offs (*escisiones*), which may be of two types. The first type arises when the *escindente*, or parent company, decides to split up and divides all or part of its assets, liabilities, and capital stock into two or more parts. The separate parts are conveyed in a single operation to other newly created corporations, called *sociedades escindidas* (companies resulting from the split) and the original corporation ceases to exist. The second type of spin-off occurs when a corporation, also called *escindente*, transfers at one time part of its assets, liabilities, and capital stock in order to form a new, spin-off corporation (LGSM Article 228*bis*). In this instance, the corporation that initiated the spin-off continues to exist. The shares of a parent corporation in a spin-off must be totally paid-up and 'each of the shareholders of the resulting corporation (*escindida*) shall initially hold shares of the capital stock of the resulting company equal to the number of shares held in the parent company' (LGSM Article 228*bis*, section III).

Escisiones, like mergers and changes in corporate form, must be approved by an extraordinary meeting of the shareholders (LGSM Article 221*bis*). The shareholders must approve a charter or document (*acta*) that details the exact terms of the spin-off (LGSM Article 228*bis*, section IV, paragraph a). Each of the spin-off companies shall be responsible for fulfilling its individual obligations, but in case of non-performance, all of the resulting companies will be held jointly and severally liable for a period of three years *vis-à-vis* creditors who have not provided their express consent. The decision of an extraordinary shareholders' meeting to spin off one or more companies from the parent company must be registered in the record book of a notary public and in the Public Registry of Commerce and public notice must be given in the local government official publication (*gaceta oficial*) and in one of the newspapers of widest circulation of the domicile of the spin-off company (LGSM Article 228*bis*, section V).

Within forty-five days of such publication, shareholders who represent at least 20 per cent of the capital stock, or creditors who have a legal interest, may challenge the spin-off. Should no opposition exist, after this period elapses,

dispel any doubt about the payment of these debts, irrevocable trusts may be set up with the express mandate to pay off a previously stated amount for each creditor having a legitimate claim. When corporations opt for this fast-track method, it is important to report the amount of each debt of each corporation, and contact creditors to apprise them of the deposit in their favour for debt payment, to avoid lawsuits that could jeopardize the merger.

the spin-off takes full effect and the parties may proceed to filing the company rules with a notary public, and registration (LGSM Article 228*bis*, sections VI and VII).

5.10. Dissolution and Liquidation of Business Organizations

A *sociedad anónima* may be dissolved either by decision of the shareholders, or by a judicial action filed by a third party having an interest in the corporation, such as a creditor. According to LGSM Article 229, there are five possible causes for dissolution of a corporation:

(1) expiration of the term set in the corporate charter;
(2) the corporate purpose has been fulfilled or has become impossible to realize;
(3) by agreement of the shareholders (Article 182, section II);
(4) because the number of shareholders or interested parties is reduced to one; or
(5) due to the loss of two-thirds of the capital stock (i.e. when the assets of the corporation are worth less than one-third of the capital stock issued).

If a corporation is dissolved for any reason other than the first two causes listed, the corporation must record the cause in the Public Register of Commerce. This registration may be challenged in court within thirty days of the day of filing.

Once the formal procedures authorizing dissolution have taken place, the process of liquidation proceeds. Liquidation must be conducted by one or more liquidators who are appointed by the same shareholders who agreed upon the dissolution (LGSM Articles 234 and 235), and it must occur under the terms agreed upon in the company's charter, or in accordance with a decision of a general meeting of the current shareholders (LGSM Article 240). The liquidators are required: to complete any pending transactions, collect any outstanding payments owed, and sell the assets of the corporation in order to calculate the final liquidation balance that shall be deposited in the Public Registry of Commerce where the request shall be filed for cancellation of the Registration of the Corporation (LGSM Article 242). Should any assets remain, they must be distributed among the shareholders in accordance with the final balance that shall be made public on three occasions, every ten days in the official government publication of the domicile of the corporation. After thirty days, the liquidators shall convene a general shareholders' meeting during which the balance shall be given final approval (LGSM Articles 247, sections II and III, and 248).

5.10.1. Bankruptcy[90]

Bankruptcy results from the inability of a corporation to continue making the payments necessary to service its debts and carry out its operations.

[90] A detailed account of bankruptcy lies beyond the scope of this book. On Mexican bankruptcy law generally, *see* Dávalos Mejía, L.C.F., *Introduccion a la Ley de Concursos Mercantiles* (Mexico: Oxford University Press, 2002). *See also* the discussion at notes 101–102, *infra*.

As in the United States and other modern economies, Mexican law includes provisions for both voluntary and involuntary bankruptcy. Voluntary bankruptcy, known as *conciliación*, is commonly used in Mexico by creditors and debtors to refinance the obligations of viable corporations that lack the funds to meet their cash needs in the short term. *Conciliación* is not uncommon in economies that fluctuate as much as that of Mexico. Involuntary bankruptcy, however—the dissolution of a corporation and liquidation of its assets—has been relatively rare in Mexico. The reasons for this are cultural and historical, as well as economic. In a highly competitive and open economy such as exists in the United States, corporate bankruptcies are in part a function of the ease with which corporations may be established and capitalized, by access to credit from third parties. If an economic downturn occurs in a competitive economy, a corporation may be unable to meet its obligations, and will face bankruptcy. In short, in the United States it is relatively easy to start a corporation and to borrow funds, and relatively easy for the corporation to be sacrificed to satisfy its creditors when the competitive economy falls into recession.

In Mexico, by contrast, corporations are not easily capitalized, since independent sources of capital are much more limited than in the United States.[91] Historically, corporations in Mexico have been linked to large networks of family holdings, from which they could draw investment capital, and they were insulated from competition, at least until the recent economic opening up. Compared with corporations in the United States, Mexican corporations were less at the mercy of independent creditors, and could rely on the double protections of closed markets and access to capital from affiliated family enterprises. In such an environment bankruptcy laws were relatively unimportant, because bankruptcies themselves (especially large, corporate bankruptcies) were uncommon.

Since the economic opening up of Mexico in the 1990s,[92] bankruptcy and the protection of creditors' rights have become vital subjects of corporate law.[93] Since the adoption of the NAFTA, and with increased competition from imported products, many small and medium-sized Mexican companies that were formerly protected from competition were forced into bankruptcy. In response to the increase in bankruptcies, and to create a system of creditor protection consonant with a free-market economy, in 2000 Congress adopted a new Law of Commercial Bankruptcy (*Ley de Concursos Mercantiles*, or LCM).[94]

[91] *See generally* Chapter 20 below, at text accompanying note 64.

[92] *See* Chapter 12 above at text accompanying notes 1–16.

[93] The drafters of the LCM also benefited from efforts by the World Bank to promote legal reforms that would improve credit systems, and promote financial stability, in member states. Working with other international agencies, the World Bank has produced a set of 'Principles and Guidelines for Effective Insolvency and Creditor Rights Systems'. The Guidelines are available at www.worldbank.org/gild (site visited Jan. 2004).

[94] D.O. 12 Mar. 2000. According to *Artículo Quinto Transitorio*, the 1943 *Ley de Quiebras y Suspensión de Pagos* will continue to apply to proceedings filed prior to 12 May 2000, the effective date of the LCM.

The LGSM itself does not expressly refer to bankruptcy as a cause of liquidation of a corporation, but LGSM Article 229, section II, states that liquidation may occur

The LCM abrogated the former bankruptcy law, the *Ley de Quiebras y de Suspensión de Pagos*,[95] which was subject to inefficient and dilatory procedures and poor administration.[96] The LCM was based in part on the Model Law on Cross-Border Insolvency, which was adopted in 1997 by an UNCITRAL commission working in close co-operation with the International Association of Insolvency (INSOL).[97] While still in its infancy, the LCM is expected to improve the protection of creditors' rights while preserving the ability of debtors to respond to the economic pressures of increased competition.

A petition for commercial insolvency (*demanda de concurso mercantil*) may be filed with the federal district court of the debtor's place of domicile. A bankruptcy proceeding begins when a federal court[98] issues a *sentencia de concurso mercantil*,[99] in response to a petition for declaration of commercial insolvency that may be filed either by the debtor itself, by a creditor, or by the Office of the Attorney General (*Procurador General de la República*) (LCM Article 9). According to the LCM, a debtor is considered insolvent if it is determined to be generally in default of its obligations (*incumplimiento generalizado en el pago de las obligaciones*), by the triggering of either of the following two conditions: that 35 per cent of the debtor's liabilities are at least thirty days overdue, or that the debtor does not have liquid assets equal to 80 per cent of its obligations that are due and payable (LCM Articles 9 and 10).

LCM Article 2 states that *concurso mercantil* consists of two stages, or types: conciliation (*conciliación*), which is covered by LCM Articles 145–166, and bankruptcy (*quiebra*), which is dealt with in LCM Articles 167–196. According to LCM Article 3, the goal of conciliation is to secure the continued viability of the commercial enterprise by means of an agreement with the business's creditors. Conciliation is similar to the 'voluntary bankruptcy' measures, referred to under the former law as *suspension de pagos*. By contrast, the goal of bankruptcy is the sale of the assets of the corporation in order to satisfy creditors (LCM Article 3).

'due to impossibility of continuing to carry out the corporate purposes'. In other words, if a corporation is unable to continue operations due to a failure to meet its financial obligations, it may be liquidated. The essence of bankruptcy, of course, is the equal treatment and protection of creditors in cases of liquidation, and this is carried out pursuant to the LCM.

[95] D.O. 20 Apr. 1943.

[96] *See Ley de Concursos Mercantiles*, 'Exposición de Motivos', Cámara de Senadores, Periódico Oficial 8-I, 12 May 2000, at 5.

[97] The text of the model law is available at www.uncitral.org, 'Adopted texts' (site visited Jan. 2004).

[98] The federal courts have exclusive subject matter jurisdiction over bankruptcy proceedings (LCM Article 17). Unlike in the United States, there are no specialized courts for this purpose, and bankruptcy proceedings are brought before the same federal district courts that consider *amparo* and other federal matters.

[99] The term *sentencia* in civil or criminal law generally refers to a final judgment; in bankruptcy law, however, it refers to a preliminary adjudication by the court that a debtor is insolvent.

Once a debtor is adjudged insolvent, the federal judge appoints a *conciliador*,[100] or mediator, who is responsible for restructuring all outstanding obligations with creditors in order to allow the debtor to regain solvency. This period of *conciliación* is expected to be short: LCM Article 145 states that *conciliación* should last no longer than 185 days, with the possibility of two extensions of ninety days if requested by a sufficient number of creditors. If, at the end of the conciliation period, the debtor and creditors have not agreed a restructuring of debt (by the conclusion of agreements, or *convenios*, with the principal creditors) then the bankruptcy stage begins; the debtor or *conciliador* may also request the initiation of bankruptcy (*quiebra*) whether or not the period has run (LCM Article 167).

The *síndico* may consider the possibility of maintaining the corporation in existence, but if the sale of assets to satisfy the creditors leaves the corporation without the means to continue operations, all assets will be sold and the corporation will be liquidated (LCM Articles 198–199).

5.10.2. International Co-operation

LCM Articles 278 to 310 set forth special rules dealing with international insolvencies, and with the need to co-ordinate judicial procedures with courts in other countries. Increases in foreign direct investment in Mexico in the past decade, especially by US corporations, has made this subject particularly relevant, and of great interest to Mexican and foreign creditors and lawyers. In the mid-1990s, the American Law Institute began a project to develop principles and procedures by which courts and other relevant agencies might manage insolvencies resulting from a default of an economic enterprise having its centre of interest in a NAFTA country and having assets, creditors, and operations in other NAFTA countries.[101] While the project has yet to develop binding international rules or procedures, it has generated valuable summaries of the bankruptcy laws of Canada, Mexico and the United States, and has also concluded a set of principles of co-operation in transnational insolvency cases.[102]

[100] The LCM established an Institute of Specialists in Commercial Insolvency (Instituto Federal de Especialistas de Concursos Mercantiles, or IFECOM) to register and help train professionals in bankruptcy: *visitadores, conciliadores*, and *síndicos*. *See* LCM Articles 311–338.

[101] Information on the project, 'Transnational Insolvency Project: Cooperation Among the NAFTA Countries', is available at www.ali.org.

[102] The ALI Project resulted in several useful studies and reports, including *International Statement of Mexican Bankruptcy Law* (Philadelphia, Pa: ALI, 2003, Miguel Angel Hernández Romo and Carlos Sánchez Mejorada, Reporters); *International Statement of Canadian Bankruptcy Law* (Philadelphia, Pa: ALI, 2003, E. Bruce Leonard and Jacob S. Ziegel, Reporters); and *International Statement of US Bankruptcy Law* (Philadelphia, Pa: ALI, 2003, Jay Westbrook, Reporter); International Statement of Canadian Bankruptcy Law Statements of Bankruptcy Law Reports include *Principles of Cooperation Among NAFTA Countries* (Philadelphia, Pa: ALI, 2003, Jay Westbrook, Reporter). These publications may be ordered from the ALI at www.ali.org, 'Publications Catalog'.

A discussion of the ALI Principles of Co-operation, and of international co-operation in commercial insolvency generally, has been published by Professor Jay Westbrook, the US Reporter who oversaw this project. Westbrook, J., 'International Judicial Negotiation', 38 TEX. INT'L L. J. 567 (2003).

6. Other Types of Business Organizations

While the *sociedad anónima* is by far the most common form of business organization in Mexico, other forms do exist, and are sometimes chosen for particular types of activities.

6.1. Limited Liability Company (*Sociedad de Responsabilidad Limitada*)

The *sociedad de responsabilidad limitada*, or S. de R.L., which usually takes the form of a limited liability partnership, is often chosen by foreign investors (whether individuals or corporations) for three reasons. First, in the United States partnerships have historically been taxed at a lower rate than publicly traded stock corporations. Second, the legal regime governing S. de R.L.s is strict enough for the parent company to be able to maintain control of the company. Finally, a limited liability partnership can yield a high return to investors while exposing the investor to little liability. The S. de R.L. has most often been used in small and medium-sized businesses. Larger companies tend to use the corporate model, since they are dependent upon the issuance of shares that are publicly traded in order to raise capital.

LGSM Article 58 defines a *sociedad de responsabiidad limitada* as an organization that 'is created among partners who are only obliged to pay their contribution, without the shares of the partnership being able to be represented by negotiable certificates, either as order or bearer instruments, since they may only be transferred in accordance with the requirements established by law'. Limited liability companies may bear a company name or the name of one or more of the partners, which in either case must always be followed by the initials 'S. de R.L.' (LGSM Article 59).

The S. de R.L. can be formed by a minimum of two or a maximum of fifty partners (LGSM Article 61). The capital stock may not be less than 3 million pesos (approximately US$300,000) and partners' interests are represented by shares with limited transferability. Every partner has the right to membership of the partnership (*parte social*) (LGSM Article 68), and holders of partnership shares are presumed to have equal rights, including equal voting rights in partnership meetings (LGSM Article 78). Nevertheless, some partners are exceptionally allowed to have two or more memberships in the partnership, and may therefore have greater rights (LGSM Article 68). No single share may be worth less than one thousand pesos (US$100) (LGSM Article 62). Shares may not be offered for sale through public subscription (LGSM Article 63). When the partnership is created, at least 50 per cent of the value of the capital stock must be totally subscribed and paid into the partnership (LGSM Article 64). Unless otherwise stated in the partnership agreement, priority for increases in capital shall be proportionate to each partner's shares in the partnership.[103]

[103] The partners of a limited liability company may contribute additional amounts (*cantidades suplementarias*) beyond their initial partnership contributions, and they may provide

Decisions are made by partners whose votes are counted in accordance with their respective shares in the S. de R.L. Partners may agree that a unanimous or special majority vote is required to transfer ownership or membership (*parte social*) in the partnership to a third person (LGSM Article 65). Nevertheless, when a decision is adopted by a majority vote to permit transfer of an interest to a third person, the existing partners may exercise their right to acquire the ownership in the partnership that is being transferred (LGSM Article 66).

Under LGSM Article 73, the partnership must keep a special register of the partners containing the personal information on each partner and the amount of their respective contributions and, if applicable, any transfer of their contributions. Even though this same provision establishes that 'any person who proves that he or she has a legitimate interest' has the right to consult the registry, in practice this is not a simple task, as partnerships usually wish to maintain the anonymity of the partners and may very well object to such consultation. In such a case, the interested party may file suit to obtain permission to check the record book of the partnership, although a proceeding of this nature is lengthy.

The *sociedad de responsabilidad limitada* is administered by one or more managers (*gerentes*) who may be either partners or non-partners; performance of these managerial functions may either be temporary or for an indefinite period (LGSM Article 74). The general partners have the right to file suit against the managers for breach of obligations (LGSM Article 76).

The partnership meeting represents the supreme governing authority of the S. de R.L. At this meeting, decisions are made by majority vote, by holders of at least half of the capital stock of the partnership, unless a higher percentage had been previously approved in the partnership agreement (LGSM Article 78). Unlike *sociedades anónimas*, the law does not distinguish between different types of partners' meetings, but provides for only one type of meeting, at which the partners have authority to make a wide range of decisions.

Partners' meetings must be convened by the managers or by the oversight board (*consejo de vigilancia*); should both of these two bodies fail to convene meetings, a group of partners representing more than one-third of the capital stock may do so. Notice of a partners' meeting must be sent by certified letter, addressed to each individual partner, at least eight days before the meeting is to be held (LGSM Article 81). Given the personal nature of this type of partnership, the law permits partnership agreements to contain a clause stating

accessory services (*prestaciones accesorias*) to the partnership. *Cantidades suplementarias* are of a monetary nature and may be provided in the form of loans to the partnership, in which case the partner takes on an additional responsibility over and above the initial capital contribution. *Prestaciones accesorias* occur when the partners take on an obligation to perform services for the benefit of the partnership, such as carrying out the distribution of a product of the partnership, or produce an input required by the partnership. These accessory services, however, must be the result of a decision adopted by the partners and may not be set forth in the partnership agreement (*contrato social*), and may not be considered the performance of professional services (LGSM Article 70, second paragraph).

that holding a meeting of the partners is not necessary and that matters may be settled by simply sending the appropriate documents to all of the partners who may vote by letter.[104] (LGSM Article 82).

Amendments to the partnership agreement may be approved by a majority of partners holding at least three-fourths of the capital stock. However, when the partners wish to amend the official purpose of the partnership or the rules to determine an increase in the obligations of the partners, decisions must be approved unanimously (LGSM Article 83).

All business organizations chartered in Mexico must be registered with the tax authorities; when foreign nationals are shareholders, the corporation must also be registered in the National Registry of Foreign Investment.[105] Strict deadlines apply to the registration requirements: thirty days for tax registration, and forty for foreign investment. Should a partnership fail to register with either of these authorities, the partnership and foreign partner(s) shall be fined. The limited liability partnership must also have a specific domicile within the Mexican Republic in order to file for registration with the required authorities, and may also be required to join an industrial association or chamber of commerce.

6.2. General Partnership (*Sociedad en Nombre Colectivo*)

A general partnership form is used in certain types of enterprises in which all the partners have more or less equal responsibility, and, like the *sociedad civil*, is a vehicle commonly used by professional groups: lawyers, engineers, accountants, etc. In a general partnership, all partners are jointly and severally liable for all liabilities and obligations of the partnership (LGSM Article 25). The partnership name shall be made up of the name of one or more partners, and the words '*y compañia*' ('and company') or a similar term ('*Abogados*'), shall appeal at the end of the name (LGSM Article 27). Partners may not transfer their rights in the partnership without the consent of the other partners, nor can new partners be admitted without such consent (LGSM Article 31). Amendments to the partnership agreement (*contrato social*) must be approved by unanimous vote, unless the partnership agreement provides otherwise. If the charter can be amended by majority vote, the minority shall have the right to sever their relationship with the partnership (LGSM Article 34).

The partners may not engage individually in business that is of the same type as that of the partnership (LGSM Article 35). The administration of the partnership may be conducted by partners or non-partners (employees) (LGSM Article 36).

6.3. Limited Partnership (*Sociedad en Comandita Simple*)

A limited partnership is made up of one or several partners who are jointly and severally liable for all partnership obligations. However, unlike the general

[104] Given the slowness of the government postal service in Mexico, businesses commonly use courier services for these purposes.

[105] *See supra*, text accompanying note 4.

partnership, in which all obligations must be shared, in a limited partnership the partners (*comanditarios*) can agree that one or several of the limited partners shall only be responsible for payment of their respective financial contribution to the partnership (LGSM Article 51). Limited partnerships are rarely used today; they are generally governed by the rules applicable to general partnerships.

6.4. Joint Ventures (*Asociación en Participación*)

Unlike the types of organization mentioned previously, this type of association does not stem from a corporate charter or partnership agreement. Rather, a joint venture is created under a contract in which one person or legal entity grants to another the ability to contribute goods or services, and to share in the profits and the losses from one or several business transactions (LGSM Article 252). This type of association is of a temporary nature in that, as soon as the business deal is completed, the association is terminated; the joint venture (referred to in the LGSM as the *asociante*) therefore does not have a corporate name, nor does it possess legal capacity or standing to sue (LGSM Article 253). Such an association lacks legal personality and therefore cannot celebrate legal acts, which may only be celebrated by the *asociantes* acting in their own capacities.

In the past, joint ventures were used in Mexico to combine foreign capital and technology with Mexican property or other interests. This was particularly true before the adoption of the more liberal rules on foreign investment in 1993, which severely limited foreign corporations from controlling Mexican corporations. As a result, US and other corporations would enter into joint ventures rather than attempt to use a corporate form of enterprise.[106] With the liberalization of the laws on foreign direct investment, joint ventures agreements are still used, but generally in conjunction with other structures, such as corporations or partnerships.

[106] *See* Mears, R., 'Contracting in Mexico: A Legal and Practical Guide to Negotiating and Drafting', 24 St. Mary's L.J. 737 (1993).

20

Financial Institutions

1. Introduction

The regulation of financial institutions in all countries has become complex, reflecting the complexity of the financial markets themselves. In Mexico, in addition to complexity, financial regulation has also had to respond to dramatic shifts in financial markets. To say that the Mexican banking industry has experienced a bumpy ride over the course of the past few decades would be an understatement. The nationalization of all private banks in 1982, the subsequent privatization of the banks ten years later, and the government's 'FOBAPROA' bailout of banks ten years after that, have all tested the resilience of the Mexican financial system. They have also given rise to numerous changes in banking law, as well as in the structure of the public institutions that are charged with banking regulation.

While Mexico's financial markets are small in comparison with the United States, they are sufficiently large and modern to be diverse and complex. Financial intermediaries in Mexico include many types of institutions: banks, which can broadly be divided into full service banks and development banks; auxiliary credit institutions, such as bonded warehouses (*almacenes generales de depósito*); financial leasing companies (*arrendadoras financieras*); savings and loans associations (*sociedades de ahorro y préstamo*); credit unions (*uniones de crédito*) and financial factoring companies (*empresas de factoraje financiero*); securities firms, such as brokerage firms (*casas de bolsa*), securities deposit institutions (such as INDEVAL) and stock brokerage firms (*especialistas bursátiles*); mutual fund companies (*sociedades de inversión*) and other investment companies; insurance companies; retirement funds (*Sociedades de inversión Especializada en Fondos para el Retiro*, or SIEFORES); non-bank banks (*sociedades financieras de objeto limitado*, or SOFOLES); thrift savings banks (*sociedades financieras populares*); savings and loan co-operative societies (*sociedades cooperativas de ahorro y préstamo*); and foreign exchange dealers (*casas de cambio*).

Unlike the US banking system, regulation of financial intermediaries in Mexico falls exclusively under federal jurisdiction,[1] which explains the uniformity of financial laws nationally.

[1] Mexican Constitution, Art. 73, section X. Exclusive federal jurisdiction over financial institutions has been upheld by the Mexican Supreme Court. *Controversia Constitucional*

2. Types of Financial Intermediaries

2.1. Historical Background

Modern banking was introduced in Mexico in the mid-nineteenth century, when the Mexican government permitted the opening of a branch of the foreign-owned *Banco de Londres, México* y *Sudamérica*, which introduced the concepts of deposit banking and trust accounts. In 1884 a newly chartered Mexican bank was created, the *Banco Nacional Mexicano* (BANAMEX), with the goal of establishing a central bank that would manage the government's accounts and be the exclusive issuer of bank notes for use as currency. In practice, just as in the United States and other countries during this period, BANAMEX lacked a monopoly on the issuance of banknotes, and its notes competed with those of the *Banco de Londres, México* y *Sudamérica*. Throughout much of the nineteenth century banking remained a relatively undeveloped industry in Mexico.

The turmoil caused by the Mexican Revolution (1910–1917) impeded the development of the Mexican banking industry. Finally, by the 1920s the Mexican economy began to stabilize. Economic stability was aided by the establishment, in 1925, of a central bank, the *Banco de México*, which was granted the monopoly over the issuance of banknotes in Mexican currency, the peso. The *Banco de México* was created as a corporation (*sociedad anónima*) through the issuance of two types of shares: Series A shares, owned by the government, which held 51 per cent of the total shares; and Series B shares, which are held by Mexico's commercial banks.[2]

2.2. The National Banking System

The national banking system is made up of the *Banco de México*, full-service banks (*instituciones de banca múltiple*), development banks, the *Patronato de Ahorro Nacional*,[3] and public trusts (*fideicomisos públicos*). Full-service banks, also known as commercial banks, are privately owned lending institutions that offer major banking services directly to the public, similar to those offered in the United States and referred to as universal banking; they are distinguished from other financial institutions by the fact that they both accept deposits and make loans, as well as conducting other banking business.

Banking regulation in Mexico stems from the 1990 Lending Institutions' Act (*Ley de Instituciones de Crédito*, or LIC),[4] passed in 1990 in response to the

56/95. *The President of the United Mexican States v. the Honorable Mayor's Office of Guadalajara, Jalisco*, issued on 16 July 1977, unanimous decision of 9 votes.

[2] For more information on the *Banco de México*, *see* www.banxico.gob.mx (site visited Jan. 2004).

[3] *See Ley Orgánica of the Patronato de Ahorro Nacional*, D.O. 26 Dec. 1986.

[4] D.O. 18 July 1990.

decision to privatize the commercial banks that had been expropriated from their owners in 1982.[5] The sale of the expropriated commercial banks to private bidders took place in 1991 and 1992; by the end of the privatization process, the government only retained ownership of development banks.[6]

The banking privatizations were intended to restore order to the Mexican banking sector, which many observers felt had been disrupted by the government takeover. Yet while bank administration generally improved after the privatization (partly through the addition of foreign investment and technology) economic uncertainties during the 1990s and frequent changes in banking and related legislation[7] have continued to pose a challenge to bankers and bank regulators.

2.3. Full-service Commercial Banks (*Instituciones de Banca Multiple*)

Full-service commercial banks are the most important financial intermediaries in Mexico. Compared with the United States, which has a highly fragmented banking sector composed of approximately 8,000 national, regional, and local banks, Mexico has a small and relatively unified banking market. There are thirty-three full-service commercial banks in Mexico, all of which are authorized to carry out retail and commercial banking operations throughout the country (even though some of them have concentrated their activities in certain regions). Unlike the United States, Mexican banking law has never restricted nationwide bank branching or ownership.

As banks evolved in Mexico, the functions of specialized financial institutions (finance companies, mortgage finance companies, trust companies, etc.) became melded into larger banking corporations (*instituciones de banca múltiple*) that

[5] On 1 September 1982, faced with an international banking crisis, President José López Portillo, by simple decree, expropriated the assets of all commercial banks in Mexico, with the exception of the one foreign bank operating in the country, Citibank. D.O. 1 Sep. 1982. On the banking expropriation and its aftermath, *see* Quintana, A., *Aspectos Legales y Económicos del Rescate Bancario en México* (Mexico: UNAM, 2002); Davis, B., 'Mexico's Commercial Banking Industry' 10 Ariz. J Int'l & Comp. L 77 (1993); Murphy, E.E., 'Expropriation and Aftermath' 18 Tex. Int'l LJ 431 (1983).

[6] Administrative regulations adopted pursuant to the 1990 LIC to carry out the banking privatization were published in D.O. 25 Sep. 1990. The privatizations were carried out by the *Comité de Desincorporación Bancaria*, which operated within the SHCP. Between 1991 and 1992 a total of 18 banks were privatized: *Multibanco Mercantil de México, Banpaís, Banca Cremi, Banca Confía, Banco de Oriente, Bancrecer, Banamex, Bancomer, Banco BCH, Banca Serfin, Multibanco Comermex, Banco Mexicano Somex, Banco del Atlántico, Banca Promex, Banoro, Banco Mercantil del Norte, Banco Internacional*, and *Banco del Centro*. Eventually, with the opening of the Mexican banking sector to foreign investment, controlling interests in many of these banks were sold to foreign banks. *See infra*, text accompanying notes 23–26.

[7] The LIC was modified on numerous occasions, as published in D.O. 23 Jul. and 23 Dec. 1993; D.O. 23 May and 22 Jul. 1994; D.O. 2 Feb., 28 Apr., and 17 Nov. 1995; D.O. 30 Apr. 1996; D.O. 5 May 1997; and D.O. 4 Jun. 2001. The main changes included increasing the possibility of foreign investment in Mexican banks, the creation of the Savings Protection Institute (*Instituto de Protección al Ahorro Bancario*) and the Commission for the Protection of Users of Financial Services (*Comisión de Defensa de los Usuarios de Servicios Financieros*), as well as measures designed to protect the interests of the public and shareholders.

provide a full range of banking services under one corporate roof.[8] Under current Mexican law, a financial institution must fulfil several requirements to qualify as a full-service commercial bank or *banca múltiple*: it must obtain authorization from the Secretariat of the Treasury (*Secretaría de Hacienda y Crédito Público*, or SHCP); be duly chartered as a fixed capital-stock company whose purpose is to provide banking and lending services; have a corporate existence for an indefinite period of time; have the amount of capital stock and the minimum amount of capital required by law;[9] and be domiciled on Mexican soil (LIC Article 9).

Full-service banks are limited to carrying out the banking activities listed in LIC Article 46, although other bank-related activities can be performed with the authorization of the SHCP. Banking regulations are enforced primarily by the SHCP; by the *Comisión Nacional Bancaria y de Valores* (CNBV), discussed in section 11.2.2. below; and by the *Banco de México*. Banks must submit regular, detailed reports to CNBV on their operations and financial condition, including level of capitalization.[10]

2.3.1. Bank Management

As in other modern economies, the central role that banks play in national credit and monetary policies means that their governance and operations are subject to more regulation and oversight than other sectors of the economy. Mexican banking law requires a commercial bank to be controlled by a director general and a board of directors (*consejo de administración*) numbering five to fifteen persons, each of whom must be respectable and experienced in banking (LIC Article 21). To represent the public interest, at least 25 per cent of the members of the board must be independent (i.e. not involved in the direct management of the bank).[11] The majority of a bank's directors must reside in Mexico but foreign citizens are permitted to serve on the board of directors, so long as not more than 49 per cent of the directors are foreign citizens.[12]

[8] The formation of financial groups which bring together several types of financial institutions was first authorized in 1970. *See* De la Fuente Rodríguez, J., TRATADO DE DERECHO BANCARIO Y BURSATIL, Vol. 1 (Mexico: Porrúa, 3rd ed., 2000) at 33.

[9] The amount of capital that a full-service banking institution must have is no less than 0.12% of the net capital of all of banking institutions in Mexico combined, as measured on 31 December of the prior year. The capital must be fully paid-up, except when it exceeds the required minimum amount (LIC Article 19). CNBV is required to publish the minimum amounts, and lending institutions are required to disclose their paid-up share capital and create a capital reserve fund as provided for by law or the corresponding regulatory agency. Mexico's rules on bank capitalization meet the standards of the 1988 Basel Capital Accord. For information on the Accord, and on proposed revisions of it, *see* the web site of the Bank for International Settlements, www.bis.org (site visited Jan. 2004).

[10] Banks must comply with capitalization requirements by setting aside at least 10% of their net profits on an annual basis, until capital reserve funds are equal to the total amount of paid-up capital. LIC, Art. 99-A.

[11] LIC Article 22. Bank employees or executives, shareholders who have power of attorney over the executives, bank customers, suppliers or debtors, creditors, partners, board members, or employees of companies that are clients, suppliers, or bank creditors, among others, do not qualify as independent members of the board.

[12] LIC Art. 23, section VIII.

The Board of Directors is headed by a director general, who must be a person of recognized moral integrity, and may be a foreign citizen, but must be a Mexican resident. He or she must have at least five years' experience in senior decision-making positions in the field of finance and administration, and there must not be any legal impediment to his or her serving on the Board. The director general of a bank may not hold any position which requires the person to engage in regulatory supervision of any lending institution (LIC Article 24). The holders of series 'O' stock must appoint at least one statutory auditor or inspector, known as a *comisario*, who is responsible for oversight of the company; shareholders of series 'L' shares, if they exist, must also appoint one *comisario*.[13]

The appointment of executive officers of a bank is heavily regulated by law. The CNBV has legal authority to approve the appointment of officers, and is expected to keep a list of persons whose participation in banking is deemed inappropriate. The CNBV may also remove or suspend members of the board, general directors, statutory auditors or inspectors (*comisarios*), independent external auditors, executive officers and managers, fiduciaries, and any other official whose signature is binding on the company.[14]

2.3.2. *Foreign Banks*

Prior to the economic opening up of the early 1990s, the ability of foreign banks to operate in Mexico was severely restricted. The restrictions on foreign banks reflected Mexico's policies of protecting local industries from foreign competition. Just as restrictions on trade and investment had adversely affected the international competitiveness of Mexican manufacturers, the decades of protection had left Mexican banks uncompetitive, under-capitalized, and technologically inferior to US, European, and Asian banks.

The strict limitations on foreign bank presence in Mexico contrasted sharply with the importance of foreign banks as lenders to both the private and public sectors in Mexico, especially during the 1970s and early 1980s. This lending was carried out offshore, however, through dollar loans that were concluded and payable outside Mexico. Until 1999 foreign banks were only allowed to maintain representative offices in Mexico; as explained below, foreign bank representative offices are permitted to contact Mexican clients and act as information centres, but are not allowed to undertake the business of banking. The prohibition on foreign banks[15] was motivated by the same impulse to

[13] LIC Art. 26. For a discussion of the role of the *comisario* under Mexican corporations law, *see* Chapter 19 above, section 5.6.

[14] LIC Art. 25. Removal is authorized when the CNBV considers that the members in question lack technical, professional, or ethical standards with which to exercise the function of officer.

[15] Prior to the reform, the LIC allowed banks to issue two classes of shares: series 'A' shares, which could only be held by Mexican nationals or Mexican companies without foreign investment; and series 'B' shares, which could be held by foreign nationals. The LIC did not permit foreign holders of shares to have more than 5% of the total shares outstanding. Despite Mexico's entry into NAFTA, the limitation of foreign investment in existing Mexican banks was reserved under NAFTA Article 1405 and Annex VII.

control foreign influence that prevailed in other sectors in the mid-twentieth century.[16]

The limitations on foreign bank presence began to change with the general opening up of the economy and with the entry into force of NAFTA. Under the provisions of NAFTA, Mexico agreed to allow foreign banks from Canada and the United States to purchase 100 per cent of the shares of newly established Mexican banks, subject to severe limitations on the total share of Mexican banking assets that could be held by foreign-owned banks.[17] This was only the beginning of liberalization, however. The threat of bank failures in the mid-1990s (a legacy of ten years of mismanagement and weak loan portfolios) created a climate for major reforms that eventually opened the Mexican banking market to foreign investment. The LIC was again amended in 1999[18] to permit two types of shares of banking institutions: ordinary shares (*capital ordinario*, or series 'O' shares), which may be purchased by Mexican nationals and companies; and additional shares (*capital adicional*, or series 'L' shares), which may be purchased by Mexican or foreign nationals and companies, with no limit on the amount of foreign investment (LIC Articles 11–14).[19]

Currently, there are several different ways in which foreign banks may operate in Mexico. As a result, there is significant foreign investment in the Mexican banking industry.

Representative offices Foreign banks are allowed to establish representative offices with prior authorization of the SHCP. These offices are not permitted to conduct any business on the domestic market as financial intermediaries or brokers, nor may they engage directly, or through an intermediary, in attracting deposits from the public, either on their own behalf or on behalf of anyone else.

Branch offices Foreign banks may establish branch offices with prior authorization from the SHCP, which shall require a minimum amount of local capital in accordance with international banking practices. Foreign bank branches in Mexico are allowed to accept deposits only from non-residents and may make loans only to non-residents. The parent bank of a foreign bank branch shall be liable for the transactions of its branch office. Branches are subject to inspection and monitoring by the CNBV (LIC Article 7).

Banking agencies Banking agencies (entities that can carry out most banking services, but which cannot accept deposits) are not recognized under Mexican law.

Newly created subsidiaries of foreign banks The LIC was amended in 1993 to permit foreign banks to invest in newly created, wholly owned Mexican banking institutions, a departure from the prohibition of foreign bank ownership of

[16] During this period, the only foreign bank allowed to operate in Mexico was Citibank, with two small branches in Mexico City.

[17] *See* NAFTA, Art. 1405, and Annex VII.

[18] D.O. 19 Jan. 1999, amending Art. 11.

[19] There is a restriction still in effect which prevents foreign governments or their agencies from owning shares in any Mexican bank. LIC, Art. 13.

Mexican banks that had prevailed throughout the second half of the twentieth century.[20] As discussed above, in the early 1990s Mexico negotiated a commitment under NAFTA to permit Canadian and US banks to purchase controlling shares in Mexican banks, with important limitations. In anticipation of this commitment, the Mexican Congress adopted the 1993 reforms, applicable to banks from NAFTA and non-NAFTA countries, permitting foreign ownership of Mexican banks. Under this reform, foreign banks could create wholly owned subsidiaries in Mexico that could operate as full-service commercial banks. As a result, from 1993 to 1999 a number of foreign banks established Mexican banking subsidiaries.

A foreign financial institution may establish a bank subsidiary (*filial*)[21] in Mexico to operate either as a commercial bank or as a limited purpose financial company (*sociedad financiera de objeto limitado* or SOFOL, also known as a non-bank bank). Foreign financial institutions may own shares, including 100 per cent ownership, in a Mexican *filial* so long as the foreign institution is engaged in the same type of business as the subsidiary (LIC Articles 17 VII, 45-D, and 45-E). The shares of bank subsidiaries (*filiales*) are divided into two classes: 'Series F' shares, which must represent 51 per cent of the stock, and 'Series B' shares, which represent the remaining ownership. Only series 'F' shares may be acquired by a foreign financial institution or indirectly by a foreign-owned holding company; series 'B' shares are not subject to any restrictions with regard to ownership. All purchases and sales of Series F shares require prior authorization of the SHCP, except when the transfer is pursuant to a pledge of shares as a guarantee, or when the shares are the property of the *Instituto de Protección al Ahorro Bancario* (IPAB)[22] (LIC Article 45-G).

As distinctions between different types of lending institutions have become more blurred, and banks have been allowed to engage in a greater variety of transactions on the domestic market, the regulation of subsidiaries has become increasingly similar to the regulation of full-service banks, and the CNBV has the same powers to act with *filiales* of foreign banks as it does with domestic commercial banks.

Foreign acquisitions of existing Mexican banks The 1993 reforms of the LIC did not give foreign banks unlimited freedom to acquire Mexican banks; foreign banks *at the time* were only permitted to acquire 100 per cent ownership of *newly created* banking institutions, but they still could not purchase more than 5 per cent of the shares of any existing Mexican bank.[23] However, as already mentioned, the weakened financial positions of Mexican banks in the mid-1990s and the threatened bankruptcy of numerous Mexican banks had a

[20] *See* the amendment adding LIC, Art. 45-A to 45-N, D.O. 23 Dec. 1993, establishing a new Chapter III, entitled '*De las instituciones financieras del exterior*' ('Of Foreign Financial Institutions'). Those foreign-owned banks that were established in this period operated in wholesale, rather than retail, markets.

[21] The term *filial* is used to distinguish a foreign-owned bank subsidiary from a subsidiary (*subsidiaria*) owned by a Mexican bank.

[22] *See infra*, text accompanying notes 95–103.

[23] Original LIC Art. 7, since amended.

dramatic effect in liberalizing the banking laws. In 1999, to attract new capital and shore up the banking system, the Mexican Congress again amended the LIC by removing the impediment to foreign control contained in its Article 7, although the law does provide that a majority of the board of directors must be either Mexican citizens or residents of Mexico.[24] After the 1999 reforms, such acquisitions are still subject to SHCP and CNBV approval, but there no longer exists an outright prohibition of foreign control. As a result, a number of foreign banks (principally Spanish, US, and Canadian) have purchased controlling interests in Mexican banks, establishing a complete turnaround from the earlier practice of strict controls on foreign influence in Mexican banking.[25] By 2002, twenty-two of the thirty-three commercial banks operating in Mexico were controlled by foreign banks. After Citicorp's purchase in 2001 of *Grupo Financiero Banamex-Accival* (Mexico's second largest and its oldest banking conglomerate), foreign bank holding companies controlled 83 per cent of the total assets of the domestic banking industry in Mexico.[26]

2.3.3. Revocation of Authorization to Operate as a Bank: Dissolution and Liquidation of Banks

The central role played by banks in the allocation of credit and the purchasing power of money justifies special regulatory measures to ensure their proper operation, and banking regulators thus have special authority to try to prevent bank crises. Thus the SHCP, with the advice of *Banco de México* and the CNBV, has the power to revoke a bank's authorization to do business in a number of instances specified in the Law.[27] However, this Draconian power of revocation has never been used, despite apparent anomalies in Mexican lending practices that have affected banks' assets and helped bring about a controversial bailout of Mexican commercial banks in the 1990s.

[24] D.O. 19 Jan. 1999, amending the last paragraph of LIC Art. 23.

[25] *Cf.* De la Fuente, *supra* note 8 at 467.

[26] *La Jornada*, 18 May 2001, at 1. The three largest Mexican commercial banks are controlled by foreign banks: *Banamex* (Citibank), *Bancomer* (Banco de Bilbao y Vizcaya, BBV), and *Banco Santander Serfin* (Bank of Nova Scotia).

[27] LIC, Art. 28. The reasons listed in LIC Art. 28 include: when the articles of incorporation of a banking institution are not submitted to the SHCP by the institution within a period of 3 months following the granting of authorization to do business; if a bank does not begin to engage in business within 6 months of approval of the charter; if the minimum amount of capital has not been paid in by the time the corporate charter has been approved; if a bank posts losses that have an adverse effect on the minimum amount of capital; if a banking institution repeatedly conducts unauthorized transactions, despite warnings from the CNBV; when a bank does not maintain the legal ratio of assets to capitalization; if a bank does not meet its loan portfolio rating or the required reserve level; if a bank tampers with the books and accounting records; when, in the SHCP's opinion, the bank does not properly perform its banking and lending functions; if a bank does not diversify its asset and liability portfolios in accordance with sound banking practices, or puts the interests of depositors and investors at risk; if a bank seriously and repeatedly violates the laws and regulations; or if a bank does not cover payment of its fees to the IPAB (*Instituto de Protección al Ahorro Bancario*), the Mexican deposit insurance organization, as established by the organic law of that agency. *See Ley Orgánica del Instituto de Protección al Ahorro Bancario* (LOIPAB), Art. 27, D.O. 31 Dec. 2000.

Similarly, despite the detailed provisions of Mexican law covering dissolution and liquidation of banks,[28] no commercial bank in Mexico has ever been declared bankrupt. This record is due less to the stellar performance of Mexican banks than to the government's recognition of the economic disruptions that a major bank failure would cause. Thus, in 1990, when a number of Mexican banks were threatened with failure by a combination of weak loan portfolios and economic recession, the Mexican Congress, responding to a presidential initiative, created the Savings Protection Banking Fund (*Fondo Bancario de Protección al Ahorro*,[29] known as FOBAPROA) to help banks liquidate their large portfolios of non-performing loans. The cost of the FOBAPROA bailout has been estimated at 270 billion pesos (27 billion US dollars). This sum, equivalent to 2.4 times the annual federal budget for education, was funded entirely by government debt.

2.4. Development Banks

Development banks are entities of the federal government and are created by organic laws passed by the Mexican Congress.[30] They receive their funding from government allocations, deposits, or from borrowing, and they are important lenders in certain sectors of the economy. Each development bank has its own legal charter and its own assets.[31] (Similar institutions exist in the United States, such as the U.S Export-Import Bank or the Overseas Private Insurance Corporation.[32])

Mexican development banks have been used for decades to channel resources through medium- and long-term loans at preferential interest rates to end users in particular sectors, often through the use of other banking and non-banking intermediaries with expertise in the sector. This role was particularly important in the second half of the twentieth century, when government-controlled development banks served as conduits for funding provided by the World Bank and

[28] LIC, Arts. 28 VII, 29, 64. *See also* aplicable provisions of the *Ley General de Sociedades Mercantiles*, Arts. 3, 6, 8, 23, 113, 234–249; and the *Ley de Protección al Ahorro Bancario*, D.O. 19 Jan. 1999, Arts. 55–57; and the *Ley de Concursos Mercantiles*, D.O. 13 May 2000, Arts. 104, 111, 279-IV. According to LIC Art. 29, in a bankruptcy proceeding (*concurso mercantile*) the IPAB (an institution similar to the FDIC) shall assume the position of liquidator (*liquidador*) and trustee (*síndico*). The CNBV and the IPAB may request suspension of payments or bankruptcy proceedings to be held.

[29] D.O. 18 Jan. 1990. FOBAPROA operated pursuant to LIC Art. 122, since abrogated. For an informative discussion of FOBAPROA and its aftermath, *see* Quintana, *supra* note 5, at 76–113.

[30] Development banks include *Nacional Financiera, Sociedad Nacional de Crédito*, created by law published in D.O. 26 Dec. 1986, amended on 24 May 1986); *see* www.nafin.com. *See also Banco Nacional de Obras y Servicios Públicos* (BANOBRAS), D.O. 20 Jan. 1986 (*see* www.banobras.gob.mx); *Banco Nacional de Comercio Exterior* (Bancomext), D.O. 20 Jan. 1986 (*see* www.bancomext.gob.mx); and *Financiera Nacional Azucarera* (converted to *Sociedad Nacional de Créditto*), D.O. 12 Jul. 1985 (all sites visited Jan. 2004).

[31] LIC, Art. 30.

[32] *See* www.eximbank.gov, and www.opic.gov (both sites visited Jan. 2004).

other sources, reflecting the predominant role that the federal government played in the national economy.[33]

The role of development banks has diminished under post-Salinas neo-liberalism, in response to criticism that their operations in the past responded more to political pressure and cronyism than to economic arguments. Nevertheless, a number of development banks continue to be important, serving, among other things, as financial agents of state, municipal and federal governments for carrying out public works projects;[34] as agents for the issuing, trading, and marketing of government securities and bonds; and as financial agent of the federal government in international financing (the Constitution places restrictions on the ability of states and municipalities to take on foreign debt).[35]

The capital of development banks consists of shares called *certificados de aportación patrimonial* (certificates of capital contribution), which are divided into two series: 'A' and 'B'. Series 'A' certificates represent 66 per cent of the share capital and may only be subscribed by the federal government; series 'B' shares, which make up the remainder of the share capital, may be subscribed by individuals, or by public or private entities[36] (LIC Article 32).

The administration of development banks is the responsibility of its board of directors and director general. Appointments to the board of directors are governed by the development bank's organic law, and generally reflect the federal government's overwhelming interest and influence in them.[37] Nevertheless, in certain development banks, such as the *Sociedad Financiera Rural*, trade associations have significant decision-making authority.

Under LIC Article 44, two statutory inspectors (*comisarios*) are charged with independent oversight and inspection of the records and operations of development banks. One *comisario* is to be appointed by the Secretariat of Public Administration (SFP), which oversees quasi-governmental agencies, and the other *comisario* is appointed by the members of the board elected by series 'B' certificate holders.[38]

[33] *See* Chapter 12 above.

[34] *See Banco Nacional de Obras y Servicios Públicos* (BANOBRAS), www.banobras.gob.mx (site visited Jan. 2004).

[35] *See Nacional Financiera* (NAFIN), www.nafin.com (site visited Jan. 2004).

[36] The ownership of Series 'B' shares is limited to certain individuals or institutions, and since development banks are not operated with a profit motive, these shares tend to be held by other government entities. LIC, Art. 22.

[37] For example, *Nacional Financiera* (NAFIN), the federal government's principal vehicle for financing development projects, has a board of directors made up of 9 members, 6 of whom represent series 'A' certificate holders (the Secretaries of Treasury, of the Economy, and of Energy, and the Director of the *Banco de México* are among these 6 members); and 3 members representing series 'B' certificate holders, who are appointed by the Treasury Secretary acting for the President. *Ley Orgánica de Nacional Financiera* (LONF) Art. 17, D.O. 24 May 1996.

[38] Every development bank must have an advisory commission made up of shareholders of series 'B' certificates. The advisory commission issues opinions and gives advice on policies and performance of the development bank, and helps to elect board members and *comisarios*, but it lacks sufficient voting power to hold real decision-making authority. *See* LIC, Art. 45.

3. Permissible Banking Activities

Permissible banking activities in Mexico are divided into three broad categories: liability transactions (*operaciones pasivas*), asset transactions (*operaciones activas*), and services. The LIC provides for extensive regulation of banking transactions. Since such transactions are also regarded as commercial acts (*actos mercantiles*), the provisions of the Law of Negotiable Instruments and Lending Transactions (*Ley de Títulos y Operaciones de Crédito*) and of the Commercial Code (*Código de Comercio*) are also applicable. LIC Article 46 contains a list of permissible banking transactions; the list is not exclusive, since the SHCP, upon receiving advice from the CNBV and *Banco de México*, can permit additional types of transactions not specifically listed. The LIC also includes numerous provisions and limitations on specific banking transactions and the obligations of banks performing them, and on the obligations of bank regulatory agencies (the CNBV, IPAB and CONDUSEF, discussed below) with regard to banking operations.

3.1. Liability Transactions (*Operaciones Pasivas*)

As the name suggests, the common element of *operaciones pasivas* is the creation of a 'debit' or liability for the bank. This includes accepting deposits (demand deposits and time deposits), issuing bankers' acceptances, and issuing bank bonds and subordinated debentures (*obligaciones subordinadas*), since each of these presupposes an obligation of the bank to pay at some point in the future.

3.1.1. Deposits

Bank deposits are the principal source of funding of bank operations, and are key to the banks' role as financial intermediaries. A depositor transfers ownership of funds to the bank, which is obliged to hold it and give it back under agreed conditions, interest rates and time period being stated in the deposit agreement.[39] Demand deposits require the bank to have money available at any time in the event that the customer wishes to withdraw the deposited funds; demand deposits in Mexico generally provide for payment of interest. Time deposits may not be withdrawn on demand, but only on predetermined dates (in the case of a certificate of deposit), or when a specified period of time has elapsed after the notice of withdrawal. According to LIC Article 59, savings deposits must earn compound interest.

Savings or time deposits must be evidenced by a valid written document, either a savings account passbook or a certificate of deposit. This makes it possible for the depositor or holder of the certificate to have recourse to a summary judicial proceeding in the event of non-payment by the bank.[40] Funds deposited

[39] *Cf.* Dávalos Mejía, C., *Derecho bancario y contratos de credito* (Mexico: Harla, 2nd ed., 1992) at 288.

[40] On summary commercial proceedings, *see* Chapter 18 above.

with banks are subject to special rules in regards to settlement of the depositor's estate in the event of death.[41] A bank may modify the conditions of the deposit agreement (except with regard to time deposits) in response to changing financial conditions, but prior notice to depositors is required (LIC Article 58).

The ability of Mexican banks to accept deposits in currencies other than Mexican pesos is regulated by *Banco de México*. Currently, deposits in foreign currency are accepted from companies or from individuals who reside in states bordering the United States.[42]

3.1.2. Bank Bonds (Bonos Bancarios)

Bank bonds are negotiable instruments that give holders the right to summary collection proceedings (*acción ejecutiva*),[43] and are sold to investors by banks under the supervision of the CNBV. Bank bonds have been important sources of financing for commercial lending operations. Banks pay interest to the bearer of the bond periodically at the interest rate established in the bond, and are required to pay off the principal amount of the bond at maturity, under the conditions set forth in the bond (LIC Article 63). Bank bonds are negotiable instruments, and there is a secondary market for them, since the value of the bonds fluctuates with movements in interest rates.

3.1.3. Subordinated Debentures (Obligaciones Subordinadas)

Subordinated debentures are negotiable instruments that also entitle their holders to summary collection proceedings. As subordinated debt, in the case of liquidation of the issuing bank payment shall be made on a pro rata basis after covering higher-ranking obligations of the bank, but before distributing the corporate assets among the shareholders (commercial banks) and holders of certificates of capital contributions (development banks) (LIC Article 64).

In general, the regulations that apply to bank bonds also apply to these instruments. However, given the subordinated (and thus riskier) nature of these debentures, the LIC provides for certain special rules for them, allowing for more flexibility in their issuance and sale. For instance, unlike bank bonds, subordinated debentures may be issued either in Mexican pesos or in foreign currency, so long as the issuing bank receives prior authorization from the *Banco de México*.

[41] The depositor must specify a beneficiary in the deposit agreement, and upon the depositor's death the beneficiary may have access to funds on deposit, provided that the amount withdrawn falls within certain limits established in LIC, Art. 56.

[42] During the external debt crisis of 1982, dollar deposits that had been placed in Mexican banks, dubbed *mexdólares*, were converted by presidential decree to Mexican pesos at unfavourable exchange rates, an action that generated considerable litigation in US courts. *See* Zamora, S., 'Peso-Dollar Economics and the Imposition of Foreign Exchange Controls in Mexico', 32 *Am. J. Comp. L.* 99 (1985). On the aftermath of litigation in US courts, *see* Zamora, S., 'Recognition of Foreign Exchange Controls in International Creditors' Rights Cases: The State of the Art', 21 The International Lawyer 1055 (1987).

[43] On summary commercial proceedings, *see* Chapter 18 above section 4.1.2.

3.2. Asset Transactions (*Operaciones Activas*)

Bank assets represent obligations by third parties to pay money to the bank. The principal bank assets are generated by granting loans and revolving credits; by creating credit card accounts; and by acquiring assets from third parties (based on credits granted, by means of endorsement, guarantees, and letters of credit).

Because the value of a bank's assets is important to the bank's financial health, the LIC sets forth numerous rules to ensure that the bank's assets are secure investments (LIC Articles 65–76). Before granting loans, banks must assess the economic viability of their investment projects, and the creditworthiness and managerial effectiveness of borrowers; failure to do so may result in administrative sanctions.[44] The CNBV (discussed below) is responsible for periodically analysing banks' asset portfolios in order to assure the banks' financial stability.[45] Until recently, Mexico lacked a comprehensive national credit reporting system with detailed records of individuals' borrowing histories, making it difficult for banks to make accurate assessments of borrowers' creditworthiness. This contributed to weak loan portfolios that precipitated a banking crisis in 1994, resulting in a government bailout. In 1996 a national credit reporting system, called the *Buro de Crédito*, was created, significantly improving creditors' ability to assess the creditworthiness of debtors.

Banks must adhere to special rules regarding the formalization of contracts. For example, working capital equipment loans (*créditos refaccionarios de habilitación o avío*) may be formalized either before a notary public or before a commercial notary, or they may be entered into by private contract before witnesses and ratified before a notary public, a trial court judge, or the chief of the public registry (LIC Article 66). Mortgages on real property may be created under the same procedural formalities[46] (LIC Article 67). Banks must obtain special approval from the board of directors for related-party credit transactions, such as those between the bank and a potential borrower who owns more than 2 per cent of the bank's share capital; a member of the board of directors; or family members of shareholders or relatives of board members.[47]

3.3. Regulation of Interest Rates

Interest rates, like other aspects of liability and asset transactions (such as commissions, awards, discounts, etc.) are generally subject to regulations adopted

[44] The failure of banks to assess creditworthiness may result in administrative sanctions, but this may not affect the validity of the credits extended by the bank.

[45] Pursuant to the LIC, the CNBV has adopted detailed regulations on the types and amounts of assets that may be held by banks. Thus, a bank cannot make equipment loans (*créditos refaccionarios*) if the total amount of such loans exceed 50% of bank liabilities.

[46] Non-compliance with these procedures may lead to nullification of the contract, preclusion from registering the mortgage in the public registries of property and commerce, and greater insecurity of the creditor towards third parties.

[47] LIC, Art. 73, 73*bis*, added in June 2001, require that when persons related in any way to the institution apply for loans that exceed two million investment units (equal to 6.2 million pesos) the application must be approved by the board of directors.

by *Banco de México* for the purpose of implementing monetary and lending policy.[48] As discussed below,[49] before the opening of Mexico's economy in the 1980s the *Banco de México* exercised close control of bank interest rates. Since the relaxation of strict government controls, interest rates have been set by the market.[50]

3.4. Banking Services

As in the United States, under LIC Article 46, full-service banks in Mexico can only conduct certain authorized activities and provide certain services, such as: safety deposit services; trust transactions; acting as an escrow agent for the bearers of negotiable instruments; collection, deposit, and payment services (*servicios de caja y tesorería*) for issuers of negotiable instruments; accounting and bookkeeping services for corporations; acting as executor of wills; acting as trustee under a trust agreement (*contrato de fideicomiso*); court-ordered liquidations related to settlements, estates, or bankruptcies; and property appraisals.[51]

4. Regulation of Securities Markets[52]

The Securities Market Act of 1975 (*Ley del Mercado de Valores*, or LMV)[53] governs the initial public offering and the trading of securities on Mexican securities exchanges, and establishes rules for the operation of intermediaries in these markets. Securities are shares of stock, obligations, bonds, certificates, and other negotiable instruments that are issued and sold to the public, and which are intended to circulate on the securities markets. All securities sold to the public must be registered on the National Registry of Securities (*Registro Nacional de Valores*),[54] which is under the responsibility of the CNBV and has two sections: the Securities Section and the Special Section. Only securities registered with the Securities Section of the National Registry may be traded on Mexican securities markets. Securities issued in Mexico by Mexican or foreign companies (or that are issued by Mexican companies in any jurisdiction) and offered for sale in a foreign country must be registered in the Special Section of

[48] LIC, Art. 48; *Ley Orgánica del Banco de México* (LOBM) Art. 33.

[49] *See infra*, text accompanying note 121.

[50] The Supreme Court recently affirmed banks' freedom to set interest rates contractually in several controversial decisions. For example, the Court held that under freedom of contract principles, banks may contractually agree with their customers to charge compound interest on loan payments that are overdue, or may capitalize overdue interest (i.e. add overdue interest payments to the principal amount due on a loan), a practice common in Mexico during severe recessions. SJF, 9a, T. VIII, Pleno, p. 375, Tesis 49/98, Oct. 1998 (interpreting Articles 291–301 of the *Ley General de Títulos y Operaciones de Crédito*).

[51] LIC, Art. 46, sections XIII, XV, XVII–XXII.

[52] For a commentary on Mexican securities laws generally, *see* De la Fuente Rodríguez, J., *Tratado de Derecho Bancario y Bursátil* (Mexico: Porrúa, 4th ed., 2002).

[53] D.O. 12 Jan. 1975, as amended.

[54] LMV, Arts. 10–20 set forth rules for maintaining the National Registry.

the National Registry. Registration of securities is a prerequisite for the bearer's right to use summary commercial procedures for execution.[55]

Securities trading is carried out by securities specialists (*especialistas bursátiles*) and brokerage firms (*casas de bolsa*) which must be registered as securities intermediaries in the National Registry. A securities intermediary may: conduct any type of commissioned brokerage transaction or other transactions intended to match supply and demand for securities; conduct transactions on one's own behalf with public securities issued or guaranteed by third parties; and handle the administration and management of third-party securities portfolios.

Registration in the National Registry is intended to assure the quality of securities and of securities intermediaries. To qualify for registration, and thus be eligible for trading on a Mexican exchange or market, securities must meet the requirements specified in the LMV.[56] These requirements are aimed at providing the public with access to accurate information about securities offered for sale.

4.1. Regulation of Securities Firms

4.1.1. Brokerage Firms

To obtain an operating licence, brokerage firms must meet certain legal requirements[57] and obtain prior authorization from the SHCP, upon a favourable advisory opinion of the CNBV.

Historically, brokerage firms in Mexico were required to have majority Mexican ownership. In 1999, in line with the liberalization on foreign ownership of Mexican banks, discussed above, restrictions on foreign ownership of Mexican brokerage firms and specialist firms were removed.[58] Currently, ordinary share capital is represented by series 'O' shares and additional capital may be represented by series 'L' shares (up to 40 per cent of ordinary share capital); as in the banking industry, there are no restrictions on ownership of either series (LMV Article 19).

Mirroring banking regulations, the board of directors of a brokerage firm or specialist firm must have five to fifteen members, with at least one quarter of the membership being independent (an independent member is a person who is not an officer or employee of the firm). Any minority shareholder who represents at least 10 per cent of the paid-up capital of the corporation is entitled to appoint a member of the board. A majority of board members must be Mexican residents. Brokerage and specialist securities firms must also have a director general and a normative comptroller, as part of their management (LMV Article 17*bis*2).

Brokerage firms are permitted to carry out only those activities listed in LMV Article 22. Brokerage firms may: act as intermediaries on the securities markets; receive money funds to perform securities transactions; provide advice regarding

[55] *See* Chapter 18 above, section 4.1.2. [56] LMV, Art. 17*bis*, 17*bis*1, 17*bis*2.
[57] *See* LMV, Arts. 14 and 19-V. [58] D.O. 19 Jan. 1999.

securities trading; act as fiduciaries in securities transactions; trade in derivatives; receive and grant loans for securities transactions; provide securities-backed loans; act as agent for bearers of obligations (debentures) and of other securities, negotiable instruments, and notes; invest in shares of foreign financial institutions; and issue subordinated obligations that are convertible into shares, in addition to numerous other activities listed in Article 22.

4.1.2. Securities Specialists (Especialistas Bursátiles)

Securities specialists (*especialistas bursátiles*) may only engage in certain types of transactions, which are subsets of those conducted by brokerage firms. Securities specialists may carry out transactions as intermediaries on their own behalf or on behalf of third parties, may only deal in the specific types of securities for which they are registered, and may only trade on certain securities exchanges of which they are members. Securities specialists may conduct trading in stock directly with the public only when authorized to do so by the CNBV (LMC Article 22*bis*).

Individuals or groups (through an investment company incorporated as a professional association [*sociedad civil*] or as a corporation [*sociedad anónima*]) may also manage securities portfolios,[59] even though they do not qualify as *casas de bolsa* or *especialistas bursátiles*. The officers, members of the board of directors, and employees of an investment company may not own shares, be involved in the administration of, or have any dependent relationship with, brokerage firms, securities specialists, operators, or distributors of investment companies, securities rating institutions, or issuers of companies traded on the securities market. These individuals or companies must provide formal notice of commencement and termination of their trading activities to the CNBV (LMV Article 12*bis*).

5. The Mexican Stock Exchange

Currently, there is only one stock exchange in Mexico, the *Bolsa Mexicana de Valores* (BMV), located in Mexico City.[60] The BMV is incorporated as a *sociedad anónima de capital variable* and operates under a concession granted by the SHCP.[61] Pursuant to the *Ley de Mercado de Valores* (LMV),[62] several different stock exchanges could, in theory, operate in the country, given the SHCP's discretionary power to grant concessions.[63] However, efforts to increase the number of exchanges have failed to generate interest among investors.

[59] Management of securities portfolios includes advisory services, supervision, and/or making investment decisions on behalf of a third party.
[60] LMV, Art. 29 sets forth the general powers of securities exchanges.
[61] For information on the BMV, *see* www.bmv.com.mx (site visited Jan. 2004).
[62] *See* note 53 *supra*. [63] LMV, Art. 19-V.

Compared with stock exchanges in the United States and other developed financial markets, the BMV is very small, both in terms of the number of listed securities and the value of shares traded. In 2001 only 172 companies had securities listed on the BMV, and the total market capitalization of the BMV was 125 billion US dollars; in comparison, the market capitalization of the New York Stock Exchange equalled 11.4 trillion dollars, and the exchanges of several emerging country markets—Brazil (226 billion US dollars), Taiwan (247 billion) and Korea (148 billion)—were larger than Mexico's capitalization. The monthly value of trading on the BMV was 2.7 billion US dollars in 2001, as compared with 909 billion dollars of trading on the New York Stock Exchange.[64]

Articles 29–39 of the LMV set forth rules for the operation of stock exchanges. Stock exchanges must be established as corporations (*sociedades anónimas*) in which the share capital is fully paid-up; the authorized share capital may not be higher than twice the paid-up capital; its shares may only be held by brokerage firms or securities specialists (*especialistas bursátiles*). The BMV is managed by a board of directors (*consejo de administración*) composed of no less than five and no more than fifteen members, at least one-quarter of whom must be independent (i.e. not shareholders of the exchange). Shareholders who hold at least 10 per cent of the shares of the BMV are entitled to appoint a member of the *consejo de administración* (LMV Article 31). Other requirements of members of the *consejo* are set forth in LMV Articles 17*bis* 4 and 17*bis* 5; for instance, a majority of the members must be either Mexican citizens or foreign citizens resident in Mexico.

The LMV recognizes the power of stock exchanges to issue rules and by-laws. In addition to covering governance, and the admission, suspension, and exclusion of members, the *Reglamento Interior de la Bolsa Mexicana de Valores*[65] includes rules regarding: the registration of securities traded on the exchange (LMV Articles 11–20); the rights and obligations of issuers and the terms under which trading must be conducted; the way in which records must be kept; suspension of trading of specific securities;[66] self-regulation of members and enforcement procedures; and the obligations of brokerage firms to investors.

[64] Source: *Bolsa Mexicana de Valores, Informe Annual*, 2001, at 28, 31, 32. Annual Reports of the BMV can be found at www.bmv.com.mx (site visited Jan. 2004).

[65] The rules are available online at www.bmv.com.mx, '*Marco Legal: Reglamento Interior de la BMV*' (hereinafter *Reglamento Interior*) (site visited Jan. 2004).

[66] If normal operations on the exchange are disrupted, or transactions take place that do not constitute sound market practices, the BMV reserves the right to and may, at its own discretion, suspend quoting of securities trading merely by providing same-day notice to the CNBV. If the suspension lasts longer than 5 days, the CNBV must give its approval. After receiving authorization from the CNBV, the Exchange may also suspend or cancel registration of particular securities, when a stock or its issuer fails to meet the requirements for trading on the Exchange (which are basically, for the issuer and stock to be registered in the National Registry of Securities and Intermediaries, for the issuing party to have applied for and obtained registration on the exchange; and to abide by the internal rules or the Exchange). *Reglamento Interior*, *supra* note 65, *Título Décimo*.

5.1. Securities Deposit Institutions

The safe-keeping, administration, clearing, liquidation, and transfer of securities is a public service carried out by a corporation called the Institute of Securities Deposit (*Instituto para el Depósito de Valores* or INDEVAL), which holds an exclusive concession from the SHCP.[67] Once a public institution, INDEVAL was privatized in 1987; since privatization, its formal name is S.D. INDEVAL, S.A. de C.V. para. LMV Articles 54–85 govern the requirements for a securities deposit institution. For instance, securities deposit institutions must be established as corporations; only *Banco de México*, brokerage firms, specialist firms, lending institutions, and insurance and bonding companies may be shareholder-members; each member may only own one share; and the number of members of the institution may not be less than twenty. Administration is carried out by a board of directors composed of no fewer than eleven members. *Banco de México* and *Nacional Financiera* are both members of the deposit institution, and their representatives automatically sit on the board of directors. As with the BMV, INDEVAL's operations are governed by its internal regulations (*Reglamento Interior*), which are available, along with its operating manual, at the institution's web site.[68]

INDEVAL provides services such as: taking securities on deposit from brokerage firms, specialist firms, and other financial institutions; receiving certificates or notes from such financial institutions; managing securities held in deposit or trust, including the power to help assert property or ownership rights (*derechos patrimoniales*) on behalf of their clients; executing corporate rights of depositors domiciled in foreign countries who may request such services; and transfer, clearing, and liquidation services involving securities deposited with the security deposit institution. INDEVAL is required to maintain confidentiality of information on deposited securities and may only provide information to the depositor, his or her legal representatives, or whomsoever is deemed to have a legitimate interest therein, except when judicial authorities request such information as a result of a ruling issued in a legal proceeding to which the depositor or beneficiary is a party, or when federal treasury officials request such information through the CNBV for tax purposes (LMV Article 72). Violations of these provisions may result in administrative and criminal penalties, in addition to any civil damages that may be payable to affected parties.

5.2. Initial Public Offerings

To provide greater transparency in the issuance and trading of corporate securities, reforms in 2001[69] strengthened the regulations governing the initial offering of securities for sale to the public. For instance, the issuer must be registered

[67] Only one such institution may be authorized to operate in each market. LMV, Art. 55, para. 2.

[68] *See* www.indeval.com.mx (site visited Jan. 2004).

[69] D.O. 6 Jan. 2001.

in the *Registro Nacional de Valores*; must submit an application to the CNBV and BMV through a brokerage firm, with accompanying financial, economic, and legal information; and be in compliance with the rules of the CNBV and with BMV's listing requirements. In addition, the reforms required: mandatory submission of a draft prospectus to the CNBV by the issuer prior to issuing the securities; submission to the CNBV of financial statements approved by independent auditors at the time of issuance; a legal opinion on the status of the issuer; a favourable opinion from a brokerage firm on the issuer; and other similar requirements.[70]

5.3. Securities Trading

Transactions between brokerage firms and investors are governed by securities brokerage contracts (*contratos de intermediación bursátil*), under which the customer grants a general power of attorney so that the brokerage firm, on behalf of the customer, may trade in accordance with the requirements of the LMV and the applicable exchange rules. The transaction may be conducted in the name of the brokerage firm, unless it is agreed upon that the specific trade must be conducted in the name and representation of the customer. LMV Article 91 sets forth rules concerning the brokerage firm's handling of instructions from the customer, including the use of electronic forms of communication for orders and confirmations.

Contracts celebrated between brokerage firms and their customers are subject to verification by the CNBV, and to guidelines issued by this body.[71] Failure to enter into a written contract that sets forth the terms and conditions for the brokerage firm transactions on its customer's behalf will result in the CNBV declaring such transactions null and void (LMV Article 100).

Mexican brokerage firms may engage in securities transactions on foreign markets and, in so doing, are bound both by Mexican domestic laws and by the laws and regulations of the country where the transactions take place. Likewise, public offerings of foreign securities, certificates, or notes may also take place in Mexico provided that the issuer registers the securities with the Securities Section of the National Registry of Securities and Intermediaries and obtains the approval of the CNBV (LMV Articles 104 and 106).

5.4. Self-Regulation

Through self-regulation, participants in the stock market adopt rules of conduct and operation, oversee compliance with such rules, and impose penalties for

[70] For the rules governing issuance of securities, *see* www.bmv.com.mx. BMV's rules are based on *circulares* issued by the CNBV, and on the *Reglamento Interior de BMV* (Title IV), available at www.bmv.com.mx, 'Marco Legal'. Issuers must also adhere to the *Código de Mejores Prácticas Corporativas* and the *Código de Ética Profesional de la Comunidad Bursátil Mexicana*, also available on the BMV web site (site visited Jan. 2004).

[71] The guidelines can be found at www.bmv.com.mx (site visited Jan. 2004).

violations. This is not to say that entities subject to self-regulation are not also subject to governmental regulation; rather, governmental regulation serves as a parallel and more general regime, with the understanding that specific regulations are adopted by the entities to govern themselves. Under LMV Article 126, rules of self-regulation must be submitted to the CNBV for review, and the CNBV is empowered by the law to veto such rules.

Pursuant to LMV Article 125, stock exchanges, central counterparts (discussed below), and certain other associations (such as the *Asociación Mexicana de Intermediarios Bursátiles*) are all self-regulatory entities. Accordingly, and following the example of other major stock exchanges in the world, the BMV follows a self-regulation system that was put in place in response to the regulations adopted by CNBV in June 2001. Self-regulation is intended to strengthen adherence by BMV members to the complex rules that govern trading and protect the interests of customers, while contributing to the integrity and transparency of the market.

As mentioned above, licensed intermediaries, known as central counterparts (*contrapartes centrales*) operate as self-regulated entities. The purpose of central counterparts is to reduce or eliminate the risk of default of stock market intermediaries with respect to securities transactions. Central counterparts must be granted a concession by the SHCP in order to perform this function (LMV Articles 86–89).

6. Auxiliary Lending Institutions

Auxiliary lending institutions include bonded warehouses, financial leasing companies, credit unions, and financial factoring companies. Professional trading in foreign exchange is also considered an auxiliary lending activity. Such institutions are subject to the provisions of the General Law of Auxiliary Credit Organizations and Activities (*Ley General de Organizaciones y Actividades Auxiliares del Crédito*, or LGOAAC),[72] and are regulated by the SHCP. As of June 2003, credit unions, discussed below, are also regulated by the CNBV.

6.1. Bonded Warehouses

Bonded warehouses (*almacenes generales de depósito*) are employed to store, market, or distribute merchandise left in their custody or that is in transit. They issue to the owners or agents warehouse receipts (*certificados de déposito*) that provide evidence of the deposit. Bonded warehouses may also engage in manufacturing or processing, such as the transformation, repair, or assembly of deposited merchandise in order to enhance their value, without altering the essential nature of the product (LGOAAC Article 11).

[72] D.O. 14 Jan. 1985.

There are three different classes of bonded warehouses. The first includes warehouses that receive goods of any type in deposit and engage in value-enhancement processing, but do not provide customs warehouse services (*régimen de depósito fiscal*) or financial services. The second type is similar to the first but is also authorized to receive merchandise for processing through customs warehouses, and for this reason is similar to a bonded customs warehouse in the United States. The third type combines the functions of the first two, but is also authorized to provide financing.

6.2. Financial Leasing Companies (*Arrendadoras Financieras*)

Financial leasing companies (*arrendadoras financieras*) acquire property for subsequent leasing under financial lease agreements. Leasing companies make the property available for use by a lessee for a fixed time period, in exchange for payments that reimburse the leasing company for the cost of the property, debt service, and other fees. *Arrendadoras* are commonly used to finance large equipment used in construction, or other capital-intensive equipment, such as aircraft, vessels, or trains. Leasing companies are permitted to obtain loans and financing from domestic lending, insurance or bonding companies, or from foreign financing companies, and may use the loans to acquire property for leasing. Upon expiration of the leasing agreement, the lessee must choose one of three different options available, as established in the agreement: purchase of the property, at a price that may be established in the original agreement or thereafter; extension of the lease period, at a rate that may be negotiated; and agreement for the lessor and lessee to share in the profits from the sale of the property to a third party (LGOAAC Article 27). The risk of loss of property lies with the lessee, who usually insures against such risks (LGOAAC Article 31).

6.3. Credit Unions (*Uniones de Crédito*)

Credit unions (*uniones de crédito*) are variable capital corporations whose purpose is to provide readily available credit to the union's members. They may also act as guarantor for their members. Governed by LGOAAC Articles 39–45, credit unions may only receive loans from their members or from insurance and bonding institutions, domestic or foreign financing companies, and may issue negotiable instruments (but not subordinated debentures), in series or in mass, to be marketed to the general investing public. Credit unions may also associate with third parties in the creation and administration of industrial or commercial enterprises. They may also market or process products generated by their members.

In addition to the general restrictions applying to all auxiliary lending institutions, credit unions are also prohibited from discounting negotiable instruments, lending to persons other than their members, or trading on their own or on behalf of others in merchandise other than those permitted under their official corporate purpose (LGOAAC Article 45).

6.4. Factoring Companies (*Empresas de Factoraje Financiero*)

Factoring companies (*empresas de factoraje financiero*) are authorized to enter into financial factoring agreements with individuals or corporations. Factoring companies are governed by LGOAAC Articles 45-A–45-T, and are important in the financing of retail operations such as supermarkets and department stores. In a factoring agreement, the factoring company acquires secondary creditors' rights pertaining to the provision of goods, services, or both. Factoring companies finance transactions through loans or credits secured for this purpose from domestic funding sources, such as insurance and bonding companies; or from foreign financial institutions, or by issuing subordinated debentures and other negotiable instruments, in series or in mass, for sale to the investing public. Under a factoring contract, the factoring company acquires creditors' rights in debts (receivables) owed to the client by a third party on account of goods or services provided by the client. Factoring contracts may be denominated in pesos or in foreign currency, with the option to accept one of two different arrangements: (1) the client is not liable for payment of the underlying debt, which is collectible against the third party; (2) alternatively, the client becomes jointly and severally liable with the third party debtors for the payment of the debt (LGOAAC Article 45-B).

6.5. Foreign Exchange Firms (*Casas de Cambio*)

Foreign exchange firms (*casas de cambio*) are governed by LGOAAC Articles 81–87-B, which govern the sale and purchase of foreign exchange in general. Foreign exchange firms are not the only firms permitted to engage in foreign exchange trading; many full-service banks undertake foreign exchange activities, both on their own account and for customers (LIC Article 46). Nevertheless, LGOAAC Articles 81 and 82 permit, with SHCP approval, the establishment of a corporation to carry out the foreign exchange-related activities listed in Article 82. Banks and brokerage firms, which may also engage in foreign exchange activities, are not required to obtain separate SHCP authorization for these activities.

Casas de cambio are common in most Mexican cities. To be approved by SHCP, a *casa de cambio* must engage exclusively in the regular and professional purchase of foreign currencies in the normal forms used in modern-day business: currency notes, documents (such as travellers' cheques) payable on demand, etc. The operations of *casas de cambio* are regulated by the CNBV, and are also subject to relevant regulations of the *Banco de México* concerning foreign exchange operations.

6.6. Administrative and Criminal Enforcement of Laws Regulating Auxiliary Lending Institutions

The law provides for both criminal and administrative sanctions for violations of the provisions of the LGOAAC. The CNBV is responsible for monitoring the activities of the auxiliary lending institutions and for imposing administrative sanctions, and the SHCP has the responsibility of executing such sanctions. LGOAAC Articles 88–101*bis*2 cover administrative and criminal law sanctions that may be levied against companies and individuals who breach any provision of LGOAAC, with the amount of the penalty varying according to the seriousness of the breach. Corporate officers, members of the board of directors, external auditors, employees, and even customers of an auxiliary lending institution are all subject to such penalties if implicated in the violations.

7. Insurance and Bonding Companies (*Compañías de Seguros y Fianzas*)

The insurance business is the responsibility of three types of companies: insurance companies, mutual insurance companies, and bonding companies. Insurance companies (*compañías de seguros*) are fixed or variable capital stock corporations authorized by the SHCP to operate commercially as insurance companies. Mutual insurance companies are non-profit corporations organized for the benefit of their members.[73] Bonding companies (*compañías de fianzas*) are fixed or variable stock corporations authorized by the SHCP to issue bonds, sureties, and guarantees to guarantee performance of an obligation. Insurance companies are governed by the General Law of Insurance Institutions and Mutual Companies (*Ley General de Instituciones y Sociedades Mutualistas de Seguros*, hereinafter referred to as the Insurance Law),[74] and by the Law on Insurance Agreements (*Ley Sobre el Contrato de Seguro*).[75] Bonding companies require prior authorization from the SHCP, and are regulated by the Federal Law of Bonding Institutions (*Ley Federal de Instituciones de Fianzas*).[76]

Insurance and bonding companies are regulated by the National Commission of Insurance and Bonding (*Comisión Nacional de Seguros y Fianzas*, or CNSF), an independent agency (*órgano desconcentrado*) within the SHCP.[77] The CNSF is similar in composition and function to the CNBV, which regulates banks.

[73] Mutual insurance companies are non-profit businesses based on mutual interest (*solidaridad*) of the members of the company (*mutualizados*). The number of members may not be less than 300, and the members pay an annual premium to be insured for a particular amount. *See* Insurance Law Arts. 78–98.

[74] D.O. 31 Aug. 1935, as amended.

[75] D.O. 31 Aug. 1935, as amended.

[76] D.O. 29 Dec. 1950.

[77] For information on the CNSF, *see* www.cnsf.gob.mx (site visited Jan. 2004).

7.1. Foreign Investment in Insurance and Bonding Companies

Historically, Mexico has been an under-insured market, both in commercial insurance and in retail or personal insurance. In part, this may be attributed to the relative lack of tort liability in Mexico,[78] but the more prominent factor is the relative under-insurance of developing country markets, a by-product of budgetary limitations in emerging economies. In addition, long-standing limitations on foreign investment in Mexican insurance companies also prevented foreign firms from strengthening this sector.[79] However, in 2002 the Insurance Law was amended[80] to permit foreign companies to purchase up to 100 per cent of the shares in Mexican insurance companies or bonding companies (Insurance Law Article 33-A to 33-K). As a result, foreign investment in the Mexican insurance market has risen dramatically, with the promise of greater development of Mexican insurance markets and modernization of the industry.[81]

8. The Retirement Savings System

Until recently, the retirement system in Mexico was monopolized by the Mexican Social Security Institute (*Instituto Mexicano del Seguro Social*, or IMSS). In addition to operating public hospitals,[82] since 1943 IMSS has operated a retirement programme for private sector employees. All private sector workers and their employers were required to contribute to the IMSS,[83] as well as disability and death benefits. Workers did not have individual accounts, based on their contributions; instead, so long as they were registered beneficiaries, they were eligible for benefits based on their status and characteristics; this was referred to as the *sistema de beneficio*. All contributions were provided to a central IMSS fund; payments were small, and were not related to the amount contributed by the worker.

In 1992, with the social security system on the verge of collapse due to inadequate funding and mismanagement, Congress adopted a new programme, the *Sistema de Ahorro para el Retiro* (known as SAR-92).[84] The former *sistema de beneficio* was replaced with a *sistema de contribución individualizada*, whereby workers contributed payments based on a fixed percentage of salary to individual retirement accounts administered by the government. The SAR-92 system was

[78] *See* Chapter 17 above, section 6.

[79] Under NAFTA Annex VII, Art. 29, Mexico reserved its limitations on foreign investment contained in the Insurance Law.

[80] D.O. 16 Jan. 2002.

[81] According to the CNSF, in 1990, prior to the liberalization permitting increased foreign investment, only 9 Mexican insurance companies had minority foreign partners. By 2000, of the 62 insurance firms operating in Mexico, 31 had majority foreign ownership; 16 other firms were subsidiaries of financial groups, some of which are foreign-owned. Source: CNSF, www.cnsf.gob.mx, 'Módulo de información: Información Estadística' (site visited Jan. 2004).

[82] *See* Chapter 13 above, section 5.2.

[83] In reality, as in other areas of employment law (*see* Chapter 13 above), not all businesses complied with this requirement.

[84] D.O. 23 May 1996.

refined by further reforms in 1996, when Congress created the retirement system currently in force under the Retirement Savings Systems Act (*Ley de los Sistemas de Ahorro para el Retiro*, hereinafter referred to as the Retirement Savings Act),[85] under which the administration of individual retirement accounts was transferred to private companies.

Under the Retirement Savings System Act, contributions to pension funds made by the government, by employers, and on a voluntary basis by individual workers, are managed by private pension management companies, called *Administradoras de Fondos de Ahorro para el Retiro* (AFORES). AFORES are authorized to administer individual retirement accounts and to use the funds in them to manage mutual investment funds known as *Sociedades de Inversión de Fondos de Ahorro para el Retiro*, or (SIEFORES). AFORES and SIEFORES are regulated by the National Commission of the Retirement Savings System (*Comisión Nacional del Sistema de Ahorro para el Retiro*, or CONSAR),[86] an independent agency (*órgano desconcentrado*) within the SHCP.

The Retirement Savings Act and the Regulations adopted pursuant to it[87] provide for a variety of measures aimed at guaranteeing the stability of the AFORES and the proper oversight of government agencies. Thus, CONSAR has established guidelines (*circulares*) specifying the types of investments in which AFORES and SIEFORES[88] may engage, discouraging investment in speculative enterprises and promoting investment in productive activities (housing, infrastructure, regional development, etc.). Protection of the customers of AFORES is the responsibility of CONDUSEF, which is discussed later in this Chapter.

This new retirement system has helped increase the national savings rate by offering attractive rates of returns to investors and, as with its counterparts in other countries, the pension funds created by this law have provided an important new source of investment financing for domestic enterprises. The system is still in its infancy, however, and according to critics improvements are still needed in the performance of AFORES and SIEFORES.[89]

9. Financial Groups (*Grupos Financieros*)

The consolidation of financial service companies, long resisted in Mexico even before the nationalization of the banks in 1982, has now taken hold in Mexico.

[85] D.O. 23 May 1996.

[86] *See generally* www.consar.gob.mx (site visited Jan. 2004).

[87] *See* www.consar.gob.mx, '*Normatividad*', for the Regulations and related norms (site visited Jan. 2004).

[88] *See* www.consar.gob.mx, '*Normatividad: Circulares*' (Circular CONSAR 15-1, as amended). CONSAR is assisted by a Risk Analysis Committee (*Comité de Análisis de Riesgos*) made up of representatives of the main regulatory agencies (CONSAR, SHCP, CNBV, *Banco de México*, and CNSF). *See* Retirement Savings Act, Art. 45.

[89] Administration fees charged by AFORES are among the highest in the world; as a result, 26% of the total value of funds accumulated by AFORES through contributions and investment returns are charged to users by AFORES. Whitehouse, E., 'Administrative Charges for

Financial groups (*grupos financieros*) now control the financial markets in Mexico, and in many cases are themselves controlled by large foreign financial companies. *Grupos financieros* in Mexico are governed by the Law to Regulate Financial Groups (*Ley para Regular las Agrupaciones Financieras*, or LRAF),[90] adopted in 1990 at the beginning of the bank privatizations. The LRAF permits the formation of corporate holding companies (*sociedades controladoras*) consisting of a holding company (*sociedad controladora*) and any combination of the following types of subsidiaries: bonded warehouses, financial leasing companies, financial factoring companies, foreign exchange firms, bonding companies, insurance companies, limited-purpose financial corporations (SOFOLES, or non-bank banks), brokerage firms, full-service banking institutions, and pension management companies (AFORES). A *grupo financiero* must be made up of at least *two* different types of the following entities: full-service banking institutions, brokerage firms, or insurance companies. If the financial group does not include at least *one* of the three types of entities mentioned in the previous sentence, it must be made up of at least three different types of financial entities, none of which may be an AFORE (LRAF Article 7).

Financial groups may be formed upon authorization from the SHCP, based on an advisory opinion of the *Banco de México* and the CNBV, CNSF, or CONSAR, as applicable (LRAF Article 10). The creation of a financial group permits affiliated financial entities: to co-ordinate the offering of financial services to the public; to offer supplementary services and bill themselves as members of their particular group; to use the same or similar names to identify themselves to the public as a member of the same group; and to offer services through offices of other companies belonging to the group (LRAF Article 8). A financial holding company must own at least 51 per cent of the shares with voting rights of the paid-up capital of each of the members of the group, and the holding company must have the power to appoint the majority of the members of the board of directors of each one (LRAF Article 15).

Subsidiaries of the *grupo financiero* may not acquire ownership interests in the financial holding company itself, or in any other financial companies that are affiliated with the group. Subsidiaries of financial holding companies may make limited investments in securities issued by foreign financial institutions, with prior authorization of the SHCP, but only if the amount of the investment does not exceed 1 per cent of their paid-up capital (LRAF Article 31).

Financial groups are subject to inspection and supervision by the agency (CNBV, CNSF, or CONSAR) that has regulatory authority over the predominant subsidiary of the holding company, as determined by the SHCP. Under LRAF Article 30A, failure to address irregularities of the holding company or its subsidiaries exposes the company to administrative sanctions, and in serious

Funded Pensions: An International Comparison and Assessment', *World Bank Discussion Paper* No. 23140, (Washington, D.C.: World Bank, June 2000) at 28, available at www.worldbank.org (site visited Jan. 2004).

90 D.O. 18 Jul. 1990, as amended.

cases to administrative intervention (*intervención gerencial*), although the latter has never taken place to date. If the irregularities affect the financial stability of the group, the relevant commission may place the group in managerial receivership (*intervención gerencial*) and appoint a manager-inspector (*interventor gerente*) to take charge of the company; this may occur even if only one of the subsidiaries has been the subject of the takeover. The manager-inspector shall have all of the discretionary powers that may be required for administration of a holding company in receivership, and full powers of attorney for acts of ownership, administration, the filing of lawsuits, and collection. All legal representatives of the company and the board of directors shall be subordinate to the manager-inspector (LRAF Article 30B).

9.1. Foreign Investment in *Grupos Financieros*

As mentioned above,[91] liberalization of foreign investment laws in the banking sector has revolutionized banking in Mexico, a majority of Mexican banks now being controlled by foreign financial institutions. In each case, the foreign financial institution has established or acquired a *grupo financiero* to oversee its Mexican subsidiaries. Article 27-A to 27-N of the LRAF contains special rules governing foreign-owned *grupos financieros*.

9.2. Non-Banking Activities by Financial Holding Companies

A key component of US banking law is the separation of financial businesses from manufacturing and other businesses. Thus, United States banking law prohibits US banks and bank holding companies from holding controlling interests in non-banking enterprises (e.g. manufacturing or other enterprises),[92] and also prohibits industrial groups from controlling bank holding companies. In contrast, in Mexico there is no principle of separation of banking from manufacturing or other industries. Indeed, the last sentence of LRAF Article 7 expressly states that the SHCP may authorize financial groups to acquire any type of company. Thus, Ford Motor Company has incorporated a *grupo financiero* in Mexico to provide financial services related to its automotive manufacturing business, and the company obtained SHCP authorization to include other Ford subsidiaries in the financial group.

10. Protection of the Public Interest

10.1. Financial Privacy and Banking Secrecy Laws

Under Mexican law, financial institutions and the government agencies that regulate them owe a duty of confidentiality to clients of these institutions. Financial

[91] *See supra*, section 2.3.2. [92] 12 U.S.C. section 1843, as amended.

institutions (including financial holding companies[93]) may not disclose to third parties information regarding deposits, services (including trust services), or any other type of transaction on behalf of a customer except when required by the judiciary in the course of a trial to which the customer is a party, or to the SHCP for tax purposes (LIC Article 117). With regard to the securities markets, all intermediaries and anyone who has access to information must maintain confidentiality, not only to protect the customers but also to ensure market transparency and stability (LMV Article 25). Exceptions to the duty of confidentiality are limited. For instance, a financial institution may provide information about asset transactions to a credit reporting company (LIC Article 33-A, penultimate paragraph).

10.2. Money Laundering Legislation

In 1990, joining international efforts to control drug trafficking and organized crime, Congress adopted reforms to the Federal Penal Code to criminalize money laundering,[94] but it was not until 1997 that government prosecutors began to focus attention on this problem, in co-operation with the Mexican Bankers' Association. The federal Attorney General's Office (PGR) has special units that deal with money laundering, and Mexico is now a member of the Financial Action Task Force (FATF), an intergovernmental body that combats money laundering.[95]

10.3. Creditor and Depositor Protection, and the Bank Savings Protection Institute (*Instituto de Protección al Ahorro Bancario*)

One result of the highly criticized bailout of Mexican banks by the Mexican government[96] was the adoption in 1999 of the federal Law for the Protection of Bank Savings (*Ley de Protección al Ahorro Bancario*, or LPAB),[97] which created the Savings Protection Institute (*Instituto para la Protección al Ahorro Bancario*, or IPAB). The IPAB fulfils the same role in Mexico as the Federal Deposit Insurance Corporation (FDIC) in the United States: it is a decentralized federal agency charged with administering a deposit protection system, through the exercise of regulatory powers that serve to promote the stability of the banking system and the maintenance of a fund that can be used to compensate depositors in the case of a bank failure.[98] However, whereas the US deposit insurance programme applies only to banks that are members and contributors

[93] LIC, Art. 33-A. [94] *See* Federal Penal Code Art. 400*bis*.

[95] *See* www.oecd.org/fatf (site visited Jan. 2004).

[96] *See supra*, text accompanying note 31. [97] D.O. 19 Jan. 1999.

[98] LPAB, Art. 2. The IPAB is governed by a Governing Board (*Junta de Gobierno*) and by an Executive Secretary (*Secretario Ejecutivo*). The Governing Board is made up of 7 voting members, including the Secretary of the Treasury, the Governor of the Bank of Mexico, the President of the CNBV, and 4 voting members appointed by the President and approved by a two-thirds vote of the Senate (LPAB, Art. 75). Terms of office are for 4 years. For information on IPAB, *see* www.ipab.org.mx (site visited Jan. 2004).

to the FDIC, the IPAB guarantee programme covers all commercial banks (*instituciones de banca multiple*).[99] The IPAB is governed by a board of directors composed of representatives of the SHCP, the Governor of the *Banco de México*, the President of the CNBV, and appointees of the executive branch.

The IPAB is required by law to guarantee the liabilities of covered institutions in an amount up to 400,000 inflation-adjusted 'investment units' (*unidades de inversión*, or UDI)[100] per individual or corporate customer. Unlike the FDIC, which only guarantees demand and time deposits up to a set amount, IPAB protection covers any class of liability owed by a financial institution to a customer[101] (LPAB Article 11). Compensation is available directly to customers from IPAB resources only after the financial institution has been liquidated pursuant to bankruptcy or suspension of payment proceedings.[102] If a customer is not fully compensated from the resources of IPAB, a claim may be filed in bankruptcy against the financial institution (LPAB Article 7). After compensating a customer for losses, the IPAB assumes the creditors' rights against the financial institution (LPAB Article 17).

IPAB support is not limited to compensating depositors or other creditors directly against losses due to insolvency of financial institutions. The IPAB is authorized to provide financial assistance to troubled institutions themselves, by purchasing shares or subordinated debentures, assuming liabilities, granting loans, or acquiring properties from the financial institution. The IPAB will only take such measures, which are short of a complete takeover of the institution, if it determines that the institution is viable and support would be effective in keeping the institution in operation. In such cases, a bailout plan is submitted to the Governing Board of the IPAB, and the Board may either approve or reject the plan (LPAB Articles 28, 29, and 31).

When the IPAB becomes involved in rescuing a financial institution, then in addition to any power the IPAB may exercise as a shareholder, it is required to subject the institution to special controls and oversight, as determined by the IPAB and the CNBV. In serious cases, this control consists of intervention in the administration of the enterprise.[103]

[99] LPAB Art. 5.

[100] Investment units or UDIs are account units established in 1995 to counteract the effects of inflation by adjusting values for inflation. The UDI was originally valued at one peso; in June 2002, the value of UDIs was equal to 3.155 pesos (0.32 US dollars), making 400,000 UDIs equal to approximately 128,000 US dollars.

[101] LPAB, Art. 11. Obligations guaranteed by the IPAB include only deposits, and not other liabilities.

[102] On bankruptcy proceedings, *see* Chapter 19 above, section 5.10.

[103] Several types of control exist. The first, precautionary takeover (*administración cautelar*), may be declared when emergency financial support is first granted to a troubled institution. In such cases, the IPAB becomes the sole administrator of the institution, appointing a person who acts as executive manager. In addition to having the discretionary power needed to operate the institution, this person may override decisions of the shareholders or the board of directors. The second, and most dramatic, type of intervention is liquidation and trusteeship (*liquidación y sindicatura*). The IPAB performs this function when institutions are in the process of liquidation, suspension of payment, or bankruptcy, and designates a person to conduct this process.

The funding of IPAB operations comes from ordinary and special fees charged to financial institutions by the IPAB, in accordance with LPAB Article 20.[104] If the IPAB lacks the funding necessary to deal with the insolvency of a failing institution, it may seek funding from the *Banco de México* to meet its liabilities.

10.4. Consumer Protection: The National Commission for the Defence of Users of Financial Services (*Comisión Nacional para la Defensa de los Usuarios de los Servicios Financieros* or *CONDUSEF*)

CONDUSEF is a decentralized agency of the federal government, established in 1999 by the adoption of the Federal Law for the Protection and Defence of Users of Financial Services.[105] Like the IPAB, the creation of CONDUSEF stems from the public controversy surrounding the federal government's bailout of Mexico banks in the mid-1990s. Its purpose is to help protect the interests of consumers of financial services; in this regard, CONDUSEF took over duties formerly performed by the CNBV and the CNSF.

All financial institutions are under CONDUSEF's jurisdiction.[106] CONDUSEF provides guidance and legal advice to users of financial services who request assistance, as well as legal services to consumers who lack the economic means to retain private counsel (LPDUSF Articles 85–92). In addition, CONDUSEF serves to facilitate conciliation and arbitration services in disputes between consumers and financial institutions (LPDUSF Articles 60–84). A consumer may present a claim before CONDUSEF when he or she believes a financial institution is not providing services in accordance with its contractual obligations. The rules of procedure governing arbitration proceedings are found in the Commercial Code, supplemented by the Code of Civil Procedure for the Federal District of Mexico. When insurance companies and financial institutions are involved, the General Insurance Law and the Federal Law of Bonding Companies (both discussed above) also apply. Awards granted to a claimant by CONDUSEF may be challenged through an *amparo* action.

CONDUSEF also has limited regulatory authority. It may impose fines ranging from 20 to 1,000 days' salary (doubled in cases of repeated breaches) when institutions commit violations of the law, such as not providing information requested by the Commission, not appearing before the conciliation board at hearings, or not making good on payment of an award, among others (LPDUSF Article 94).

[104] These fees may not be less than four one-thousandths of the total amount of liability transactions of the insured institution. LIC, Art. 22. The IPAB may also charge special fees in order to meet its obligations, but the total annual fees charged to an institution may not exceed 8 one-thousandths of the total liabilities of the financial institution. For information on IPAB fees, *see* www.ipab.gob.mx (site visited Jan. 2004).

[105] *Ley de Protección y Defensa al Usuario de Servicios Financieros*, D.O. 18 Jan. 1999, hereinafter the LPDUSF. For information on CONDUSEF generally, *see* www.condusef.org.mx (site visited Jan. 2004).

[106] LPDUSF, Art. 2, section IV.

11. Bank Regulatory Agencies

Financial institutions in Mexico are subject to complex systems of federal regulation. As in the United States, compliance with banking laws and regulations is conducted by not one, but several federal agencies: the SHCP, the CNBV, the *Banco de México*, and the IPAB. Unlike the United States, because of the federal monopolization of commerce, state agencies are not involved in the regulation of financial institutions. Due to the importance of financial institutions to the national economy, federal agencies are expected to monitor tightly compliance with numerous regulations governing banking and non-banking activities. Non-compliance may give rise to administrative sanctions and criminal penalties.

11.1. Transparency in Regulation

As discussed elsewhere,[107] the demise of Mexico's authoritarian political and economic regimes has resulted in the adoption of laws that are intended to promote greater transparency in government regulation. Thus, in accordance with Federal Transparency Law (*Ley Federal de Transparencia y Acceso a la Información Pública*),[108] Mexican federal agencies are required to make available to interested parties, for comment, copies of draft regulations and other administrative dispositions. (Draft regulations applicable to the CNBV may be found at www.cnbv.gob.mx.)

11.2. Regulatory Agencies

11.2.1. Secretariat of the Treasury and Public Credit (Secretaría de Hacienda y Crédito Público, *or* SHCP)

The Secretariat of the Treasury, or SHCP, is the governmental agency charged with insuring the health of the nation's financial system, under broad regulatory powers delegated to this executive agency by Congress. Most enterprises engaged in financial services are subject to regulation, either directly or indirectly, by the SHCP.[109] The SHCP is responsible for granting authority to financial intermediaries, both Mexican and foreign, to operate in the country,[110] and also maintains the General Registry of Foreign Financial Institutions and Reinsurance Companies. With the exception of financial institutions engaged in the Retirement Savings System, which receive authorization directly from CONSAR, the SHCP is responsible for granting licences to all financial institutions.

The SHCP is the agency responsible for issuing interpretations of laws and regulations, which are published in the *Diario Oficial*. It may hear challenges to

[107] *See* Chapter 9 above, section 5.
[108] D.O. 11 June 2002, discussed in Chapter 9 above, section 5.2.
[109] *See generally* Hegewish Díaz Infante, F., Derecho Financiero Mexicano. Instituciones del Sistema Financiero Mexicano (Mexico: Porrúa, 2nd ed., 1999) at 56.
[110] *See id.* at 36–56.

administrative rulings of the regulatory commissions: the CNBV, CNSF, CONSAR, IPAB, and CONDUSEF.

The SHCP has some influence over the semi-independent regulatory commissions discussed below. In addition to approving the commissions' budgets, SHCP appoints a minority of the members of each commission; SHCP also appoints the chairmen of the CNBV and CNSF, and the Secretary of the Treasury sits as chairman of CONSAR.

11.2.2. *The National Banking and Securities Commission* (Comisión Nacional Bancaria y de Valores)

The CNBV is a semi-independent agency (*órgano desconcentrado*) established by law[111] and loosely attached to the SHCP. It has a Governing Board (*Junta de Gobierno*) made up of ten voting members, plus the chairman. Five of the voting members are appointed by the SHCP, three by the Bank of Mexico, one by the CNSF, and one by CONSAR. The Chairman is appointed by the SHCP and must be a Mexican citizen.

The CNBV issues regulations of general application that govern banks, auxiliary lending organizations and activities, and securities markets.[112] These regulations are issued in the form of circulars (*circulares*) and agreements (*acuerdos*), which deal with CNBV administration. The CNBV is the most important regulatory body[113] governing banks, financial intermediaries in securities, SOFOLES, *casas de cambio*, and financial holding companies, and as such has the legal authority to request information, conduct inspections, investigate alleged violations, issue warnings, and require officials of the institutions to appear before it for examination. The CNBV may remove or suspend executive officers of financial intermediaries, and disqualify these officers for periods of up to five years; it may also remove or suspend external independent auditors, and veto appointments of auditors. In rare instances, when the stability or solvency of the institution or the interests of the public or creditors is threatened by irregularities, the CNBV may take over the executive management functions of a bank or financial group.[114]

11.2.3. *The National Commission of Insurance and Bonding* (Comisión Nacional de Seguros y Fianzas, *or* CNSF)

The CNSF, like the CNBV, is a semi-independent agency attached to the SHCP, and was established pursuant to the *Ley General de Instituciones y Sociedades Mutualistas de Seguros*.[115] Its Governing Board (*Junta de Gobierno*) is made up

[111] *Ley de la Comisión Nacional Bancaria y de Valores*, D.O. 28 Apr. 1995, as amended (latest D.O. 1 Jun. 2001), available at www.cnbv.gob.mx (site visited Jan. 2004).

[112] Copies of *circulares* and *acuerdos* may be found at www.cnbv.gob.mx: '*Normatividad*'.

[113] The CNBV's role in this regard does not preclude the SHCP or the *Banco de México* from asserting regulatory powers over financial institutions in matters under their jurisdiction.

[114] *See* the discussion of intervention *supra*, at the end of section 9.

[115] D.O. 31 Aug. 1935, as amended. For information on CNSF, *see* www.cnsf.gob.mx (site visited Jan. 2004).

of the Chairman (appointed by SHCP), two Vice Chairmen, and nine voting members, six appointed by the SHCP (two of whom may not be federal employees), one by the CNBV, one by the *Banco de México*, and one by CONSAR. The CNSF regulates the creation, dissolution, liquidation, merger, and splitting up of bonding and insurance companies, and with regard to operations, inspection, and oversight. In order to fulfil these functions, the CNSF may require institutions under its jurisdiction, as well as financial groups, to provide information on such institutions' finances and operations.

The CNSF may remove and disqualify officers, and may intervene in the management of the insurance or bonding companies in cases of severe irregularities. It may also impose fines upon companies or executive officers for violations of financial reporting or other laws, and in appropriate cases it may order the removal or disqualification of executive officers.

11.2.4. The National Commission of the Retirement Savings System (Comisión Nacional del Sistema de Ahorro para el Retiro, *or* CONSAR)

CONSAR is a semi-independent agency of the SHCP created by the *Ley de los Sistemas de Ahorro para el Retiro*,[116] charged with the oversight of AFORES and SIEFORES (discussed above in section 8). CONSAR is headed by a Governing Board (*Junta de Gobierno*) comprised of the Secretary of the Treasury (who presides), the Chairman of CONSAR, and eleven voting members. The eleven voting members are the Secretary of Labour and Welfare (STPS), the Governor of the *Banco de México*, the Under-Secretary of the Treasury, the Director General of the Mexican Institute of Social Security (IMSS), the Director General of the Institute of the National Workers' Housing Fund (INFONAVIT), the Director General of the Institute of Security and Social Services of Workers of the State (ISSSTE), the Chairman of the CNBV, the Chairman of the CNSF, and three voting members appointed by SHCP, two from among representatives of national workers' organizations and one from employers' organizations.[117] The regulations governing the Commission are found in the LSAR and regulations passed pursuant to it.[118]

In contrast to other financial institutions, which are chartered by the SHCP, intermediaries that wish to operate AFORES and SIEFORES in the Retirement Savings System must apply for authorization directly from CONSAR.

CONSAR's regulatory powers over AFORES and SIEFORES are similar to those of the regulatory commissions just discussed. CONSAR issues regulations governing the operation of the retirement savings system, rules applying to the

[116] D.O. 23 May 1996, amended D.O. 23 Jan. 1998, 18 Jan. 1999, 17 May 1999, and 5 Jan. 2000. LSAR, Art. 2.

[117] LSAR, Art. 7. CONSAR also includes an Advisory Committee made up of representatives of workers and management and of the federal government. This Committee has 19 members in all, 6 representatives of workers, 6 of management, and 1 representative each of the SHCP, STPS, IMSS, INFONAVIT, and the Bank of Mexico.

[118] The LSAR and regulations adopted pursuant to it can be found at www.consar.gob.mx, '*Normatividad*' (site visited Jan. 2004).

participants in the system, rules concerning the chartering, organizational structure, working procedures, operations, and participation in the retirement savings system.

CONSAR oversees institutions that operate in the retirement system, and in co-ordination with the CNBV and the CNSF, also oversees other institutions that are related in some way to the system. For this purpose, CONSAR may: request information; hear cases of or investigate alleged irregularities that arise in the institutions under its supervision; suspend, remove, or disqualify officers of the institutions; and even take over executive management.

As in the case of the CNBV and CNSF, CONSAR is authorized to take extraordinary measures, including intervention in the management of an AFORE or SIEFORE, except in cases in which the AFORE is owned by a financial institution subject to the regulation of the CNBV or CNSF, in which case that agency will have principal responsibility for taking action.

11.2.5. The Banco de México: *Mexico's Central Bank*

The *Banco de México* (also referred to as BANXICO) is Mexico's central bank, that is, the governmental institution principally responsible for carrying out monetary policy. Because financial intermediaries are crucial elements in the monetary system, the *Banco de México* has certain regulatory authority over banks and other financial institutions, in co-operation with the SHCP, CNBV, CNSF, and other agencies.

The creation of a central bank was authorized by Article 28, paragraph 6 of the Mexican Constitution of 1917, but budgetary problems prevented creation of the *Banco de México* until 1925.[119] As originally drafted, Article 28 of the Constitution established the central bank 'under the control of the government', which placed the *Banco de México* firmly under the authority of the President. Consequently, in Mexico as in many other countries, the function of the central bank to operate as an independent entity, safeguarding the nation against inflation and preserving the value of the currency, was undermined by political expediencies related to successive presidents' desires to expand government programmes. Thus, for much of the twentieth century, in addition to carrying out monetary policies, the *Banco de México* also served as an important instrument of public finance through reserve requirements that channelled national savings to the government's use.[120]

In 1993, as part of the package of reforms to privatize the banks and re-establish and stabilize the financial system, Congress amended the Constitution to remove the *Banco de México* from direct presidential control, thus initiating a new era of independence.[121] As a result, inflation rates in Mexico have

[119] For an excellent history of the *Banco de México*, *see* www.banxico.gob.mx, '*Acerca del Banco de México: semblanza histórica*' (site visited Jan. 2004).

[120] *See* Zamora, S., 'Peso-Dollar Economics and the Imposition of Foreign Exchange Controls in Mexico', *supra* note 42.

[121] D.O. 20 Jul. 1993 and D.O. 23 Jul. 1993, amending paragraphs 6 and 7 of Article 28.

dropped dramatically, and monetary policies have been generally effective and free of overriding political influence.

Prior to the constitutional amendment, the officers of *Banco de México* had virtually no independence from the office of the President. Under the constitutional reform, the officers of its Board of Governors are appointed by the President after approval by a majority vote of the Senate. Under the amended organic law of the *Banco de México* (*Ley del Banco de México*, or LBM),[122] the Bank is administered by a *Junta de Gobierno* consisting of five officers, a Governor (*Gobernador*) who serves a six-year term, and Assistant Governors (*Subgobernadores*) who serve staggered terms of eight years (LBM Articles 38, 40). These officers can only be removed for cause (LBM Article 43). The reforms also granted the Bank administrative autonomy, particularly with regard to budget and disciplinary measures (LBM Article 46-I to 46-XXI).

The *Banco de México* is responsible for: pursuing stability in the value of the Mexican peso;[123] regulating the issuance and circulation of money by operating as a reserve bank for lending institutions; and acting as financial agent of the Federal Government. In addition, the *Banco de México* regulates certain activities of financial institutions, particularly in regard to matters that may influence exchange rates or the money supply. In regard to banks, it administers reserve requirements, monitors interest rates, and establishes other rules related to growth of the money supply. It also regulates transactions of any institution involving foreign exchange, and the sale of gold and silver. Because the operations of foreign exchange firms may influence the exchange rate of the Mexican peso, they are closely supervised by the *Banco de México*, which may order the temporary suspension of activities of such firms when market conditions make such a measure necessary, or when laws of a general nature are violated.

[122] D.O. 23 Dec. 1993, as amended. Information on the LBM, including amendments, and regulations adopted pursuant to it, can be found at www.banxico.gob.mx, '*Régimen Jurídico*' (site visited Jan. 2004).

[123] Together with the Secretaries of the Treasury and the governors of the central banks of the United States, Canada, and Mexico, the *Banco de México* participates in the North American Financial Group, created on 26 April 1994, to provide support for exchange stability of the 3 countries. *Cf.* Hegewish, *supra* note 109 at 59.

21

Intellectual Property Law

1. Introduction

This Chapter deals with the rights and obligations of the creators of artistic, literary, scientific, industrial, and commercial works, referred to as 'authors' or 'inventors', and of their beneficiaries, who are known in legal parlance as 'assigns and successors' or 'successors in title'.[1] In the United States, intellectual property law is a broad term, and includes patents, copyrights, trade marks, service marks, and other forms of intangible rights of invention or creation. In Mexico, the comparable term, *propiedad industrial* (industrial property) refers to patents; the term *derechos del autor* (rights of the author) refers to copyright; and the term *marcas* refers to trade marks. This Chapter focuses on patents and copyrights, and touches lightly on other forms of intellectual property rights, such as utility models, industrial designs, industrial secrets, commercial advertisements, trade names, and appellations of origin.

The Mexican Constitution does not expressly grant the federal Congress exclusive power to legislate in matters of intellectual property law. However, patents and copyrights in Mexico are in practice exclusively regulated by federal laws adopted pursuant to Articles 3 and 28 of the Constitution,[2] and the enforcement of each field is the responsibility of a distinct federal agency. Patents are governed by the Law of Industrial Property (*Ley de la Propiedad Industrial*),[3] referred to below by its Spanish acronym LPI, and are administered by the *Instituto Mexicano de la Propiedad Industrial* (IMPI). Copyright is governed by the Federal Law of Copyright (*Ley Federal del Derecho de Autor*),[4] referred to as the LFDA, which is administered by the *Instituto Nacional de Derechos de Autor* (INDA).

In the past, foreign holders of patents and copyrights, as well as the US government, have criticized Mexico for the inadequacy of its intellectual property laws, and the laxity with which those laws were enforced. Until the mid-1990s Mexico was considered one of the countries least protective of intellectual property among all the major trading partners of the United States.[5] With the adoption of a new industrial property law in 1994, Mexico has attempted to improve

[1] *See* Rangel Medina, D., Derecho intelectual (Mexico: McGraw Hill-UNAM, 1998) at 1.

[2] Article 28, paragraph 9 of the Mexican Constitution states that the rights granted to authors, artists, and inventors, for a limited period of time, are not to be considered prohibited monopolies.

[3] D.O. 27 June 1991, as amended D.O. 2 Aug. 1994.

[4] D.O. 24 Dec. 1996.

[5] Zamora, S. 'The Americanization of Mexican Law: Non-trade Issues in the North American Free Trade Agreement', 24 Law and Policy in Int'l Bus. 391–459 (1993).

the recognition and enforcement of intellectual property rights, in part to avoid the increasingly rigorous trade restrictions imposed by the United States for violation of such rights. The 1994 law is a major improvement, and respect for and enforcement of property rights have improved. As in other areas of public and private law, enforcement of intellectual property rights has been primarily a matter of governmental action; private litigation to enforce the law has not been significant, especially in comparison with the United States. Unfortunately, despite attempts to improve enforcement, government agencies still lack the resources to carry out rigorous enforcement efforts.

2. Industrial Property

The present-day Law of Industrial Property (*Ley de la Propiedad Industrial*, or LPI) replaced the former Law of Inventions and Trademarks (*Ley de Invenciones y Marcas*)[6] and the Law on Control and Registration of Transfer of Technology and the Use of Exploitation of Patents and Trademarks (*Ley sobre el Control y Registro de la Transferencia de Tecnología y el uso de Explotación de Patentes y Marcas*).[7] This legislative reform coincided with Mexico's economic opening up, and the demise of the economic policy of import substitution and 'inward growth', as discussed elsewhere.[8]

In addition to the LPI (the sole existing Mexican law governing patents) Mexican patent law is governed by international treaties to which Mexico is a party. Such treaties include the Paris Convention for the Protection of Industrial Property of 20 March 1883, as modified in Stockholm on 14 July 1967;[9] the Convention Establishing the World Intellectual Property Organization, signed in Stockholm on 14 July 1967;[10] the Lisbon Agreement for the Protection of Appellations of Origin and their International Registration, signed on 31 October 1958, and its respective Regulations;[11] the Nairobi Treaty on the Protection of the Olympic Symbol, signed on 26 September 1981;[12] the Patent Co-Operation Treaty and its Regulations, adopted at Washington on 19 June 1970, modified on 3 February 1984 and 29 September 1992;[13] the Trademark Law Treaty and its Regulations, adopted in Geneva on 27 October 1994; the Brussels Accord of 27 May 1997 between Mexico and the European Community on Mutual Recognition and Protection of Appellations of Spirits;[14] and the International Convention for the Protection of New Plant Varieties, revised in 1991.[15] Mexico is also a member of the World Trade Organization (WTO), which includes the WTO Agreement on Trade-Related Intellectual Property Rights (TRIPS).

[6] D.O. 10 Feb. 1976. [7] D.O. 11 Jan. 1982; revisions published on 9 January 1990.
[8] *See* Chapter 12 above, at text accompanying notes 1–27. [9] D.O. 27 Jul. 1976.
[10] D.O. 8 Jul. 1975. [11] D.O. 11 Jul. 1964. [12] D.O. 2 Aug. 1985.
[13] D.O. 31 Dec. 1994. [14] D.O. 21 Jul. 1997. [15] D.O. 29 Dec. 1995.

In addition to the preceding treaties and conventions, Mexico is a signatory to several free trade agreements that include sections on industrial property. The most important of these is the North American Free Trade Agreement (NAFTA) with Canada and the United States,[16] chapter 17 of which establishes trilateral guidelines for protecting and enforcing intellectual property rights.

As supplemented by detailed regulations (*Reglamento de la Ley de la Propiedad Industrial*, or RLPI),[17] the LPI represents a marked advance in Mexican intellectual property law. Mexican authorities have pointed out that the LPI is in many respects a state-of-the-art compilation of patent laws;[18] nevertheless, criticism of Mexican patent law protection continues, based on US perceptions of the shortcomings of relying heavily on governmental prosecution of patent offenders, instead of private rights of enforcement.

2.1. Protection of Industrial Property Rights

The LPI establishes three separate categories of industrial property rights that are entitled to patent protection: inventions (*invenciones*), utility models (*modelos de utilidad*), and industrial designs (*diseños industriales*). The term patent (*patente*) is used only for the protection of inventions.

2.1.1. Inventions

Breaking with prior legal tradition, which failed to define the term 'invention',[19] the LPI defines an invention as 'any human creation that enables matter or energy existing in nature to be transformed to be used by man, in order to satisfy his needs'.[20] To qualify for protection under the LPI, inventions must meet the requirements of novelty, inventive step,[21] and industrial applicability.

[16] D.O. 20 Dec. 1993.

[17] D.O. 23 Nov. 1994.

[18] Serrano Migallón, F., *MARCO JURÍDICO MEXICANO DE LA PROPIEDAD INDUSTRIAL* (Mexico: Porrúa, 2001); Pérez Miranda, R., *PROPIEDAD INDUSTRIAL Y COMPETENCIA EN MÉXICO* (Mexico: Porrúa, 1994).

[19] According to LPI Article 19, the following are not considered to be inventions: theoretical or scientific principles; discoveries that involve announcing or revealing some pre-existing aspect of nature, even though prior to their public release such information was unknown to man; outlines or sketches or models, plans, rules, or methods designed for the purpose of performing mental acts, playing games, or conducting business or mathematical methods; computer programs; forms of presentation of information; aesthetic creations and artistic or literary works; methods of surgical treatment, therapy, or of diagnosis applicable to the human body or to animals; and the juxtaposition of known inventions or mixtures of known products, variations in their use, form, dimensions, or materials, unless combined or merged in such a way that each component cannot operate on its own, or the characteristic qualities or functions thereof are modified in order to obtain an industrial result or an obvious use by a technician in the particular field.

Exclusion of the above-mentioned categories from being considered an invention does not mean that such items are not eligible for protection; such items may qualify for protection under copyright law.

[20] LPI Article 15.

[21] The concept of 'inventive step' stems from European patent law, and is similar to the US doctrine that requires that an invention not be obvious.

However, the following biological inventions are not considered patentable: biological processes designed for use in the production, reproduction, or propagation of plants and animals; biological and genetic material identical to those that exist in nature; breeds of animals; the human body or parts thereof; and varieties of plants.[22] Mexico has not yet adopted legislation in connection with the human genome project, but in 2001 a draft law was submitted for review by the Mexican Congress which, if adopted, would provide that the complete sequence of the human genome shall be considered to be part of the public domain, and therefore not eligible for patent protection in Mexico.[23] The proposed legislation is still under study by government agencies.

According to Mexican patent law,[24] a patent is a privilege granted to inventors and to those who make improvements on existing inventions, conferring upon them the exclusive right to use their own invention for a specified length of time. Since the right to hold a patent is a constitutionally guaranteed right, patents constitute an exception to the antitrust laws prohibiting monopolies, as well as an exception to the laws of economic competition, which are designed to promote free and fair competition.[25]

The President of the Republic enjoys the discretionary power to grant patents,[26] which is exercised through the Mexican Institute of Industrial Property (*Instituto Mexicano de la Propiedad Industrial*, known by its Spanish acronym IMPI). This institution is a decentralized public agency (*organismo público descentralizado*) with quasi-independence from central government. Created by Presidential Decree in 1993,[27] the IMPI has its own legal identity and assets, and is governed by Regulations[28] and by an Organic Law adopted in 1999.[29]

Although a young federal agency, the IMPI is generally recognized in Mexico as a professionally managed agency, but it has faced a stiff challenge in attempting to respond to a growing and increasingly competitive market in Mexico, which has generated increased demands on its capabilities. The IMPI's professional staff is considered honest, but the agency has lacked the resources to hire and train a sufficient number of employees to meet the growing number of applications received by the agency each year. Since Mexican industrial, scientific, and

[22] LPI Article 16. One may conclude from a reading of Article 16 that it is possible to receive patent protection for biological and genetic materials that do not exist in nature.

[23] The draft law is entitled 'Law for the research, promotion, development, control and regulation of the genome' (*Ley sobre la investigación, el fomento, el desarrollo, control y regulación del Genoma*) and is available at www.senado.gob.mx, 'Gaceta Parlamentaria' (site visited Jan. 2004).

[24] LPI Articles 9, 10, and 19.

[25] Mexican Constitution, Article 28, paragraph 9.

[26] Article 89, section XV of the Constitution states that it is the exclusive right of the executive branch of government 'to grant exclusive privileges for a limited period of time in accordance with the respective law, to discoverers, inventors, or people who improve any branch of industry'.

[27] D.O. 10 Dec. 1993.

[28] *Reglamento del Instituto Mexicano de la Propiedad Industrial*, D.O. 14 Dec. 1999.

[29] *Estatuto Orgánico del Instituto Mexicano de la Propiedad Industrial*, D.O. 27 Dec. 1999.

educational industries generate a very small number of patent applications each year (especially in comparison to the United States), much of the IMPI's workload is generated by patent applications generated by patent owners in other countries, as discussed in section 2.4, below. The IMPI's official publication, the *Gaceta de la Propiedad Industrial*, is published monthly and serves as the official source of information, including registrations and enforcement actions, concerning industrial property. The agency also carries out programmes of public education, and co-operative programmes with other public and private entities to promote innovation and technology development. Information on the IMPI can be found on the agency's web site.[30]

Rights of patentees of inventions As in other countries, exclusive rights to exploit an invention do not arise unless the inventor or someone representing the inventor applies for and receives a patent through the legal procedures administered by the IMPI. Even though an invention may be the product of human creativity, legal rights to protect that invention do not necessarily belong to the human being or beings that created it. Such is the case when inventions are the product of individuals who have entered into an employment agreement for the purpose of producing inventions, or when the invention is the product of performance of the everyday duties of an employee; in these cases, the patent may be held by the corporation that employs the inventor, rather than by the inventor, under rights set forth in the Federal Labour Law (*Ley Federal del Trabajo*, or LFT).[31] According to LFT Article 163, an employee is entitled to have his or her name appear on the invention as the author, in addition to being entitled to bonus pay, the amount of which shall be set forth in an agreement between the employee and employer or shall be determined by the Board of Conciliation and Arbitration (*Junta de Conciliación y Arbitraje*) when the importance of the invention and the benefits that the employer may reap from it are not commensurate with the salary earned by the inventor. However, the employer shall enjoy all proprietary rights to the invention when the job for which the employee was hired is focused on research and development or improvement of company procedures, and when the inventor's work is funded by the company. In other circumstances the invention shall be the property of whoever may be its creator and, all things being equal, the employer shall have prior claim (*derecho de preferencia*) to the exclusive use and acquisition of the invention and the respective patents.

Patents on inventions remain in effect for a period of twenty years, counted from the date of the filing of the application and payment of the filing fee.[32] This period, which may not be extended, is an extension of the ten-year period of patents that applied under the *Ley de Invenciones y Marcas* of 1976, which the LPI replaced.

[30] *See* www.impi.gob.mx (site visited Jan. 2004).

[31] D.O. 1 Apr. 1970, as amended, D.O. 23 Jan. 1998. LFT Article 163. On Mexican labour law generally, *see* Chapter 13 above.

[32] LPI Article 23.

After a patent on an invention has been obtained, the patentee enjoys the following rights:

(a) the right to file claims for damages against third parties who exploit the patented product or process without the patentee's consent. This right covers exploitation that occurs even before the patent is granted, since the patentee's rights are established at the date of publication of the patent application in the monthly Gazette of the IMPI (LPI Article 24);
(b) the right to prevent other individuals from manufacturing, using, selling, marketing, or importing the patented product without prior consent of the patentee (LPI Article 25). This right is enforced by the IMPI, as discussed below;
(c) the right to prevent other persons from using the patented process and from using, selling, marketing, or importing the product obtained directly from that process without prior consent of the patentee (LPI Article 25 (b)); and
(d) the right to grant a licence to exploit a patent, and to assess fees therefor (LPI Articles 62–63).[33]

Filing of patent applications covering inventions The LPI and the RLPI set forth the requirements and procedures that must be fulfilled and followed respectively in order to obtain a patent, including filing for a patent in Mexico when a patent has already been granted for the same product or process in another country.

Applications must be filed with the IMPI on a standard form which requests information such as the identity and location of the inventor, successor in title or legal beneficiary, applicant or representative, as the case may be; identification of the invention; the name or title of the invention; the patent application public disclosure date; any priority right claims that the applicant may be asserting; the signature of the applicant; and the place and date of application. Additionally, applicants must attach to the standard application form: a description and summary of the invention; any technical sketches or photographs that may be needed to comprehend the description; claims for rights to any products or processes; and any necessary drawings (LPI Articles 38–61). Inventions involving biological material whose description alone cannot provide sufficient detail require that written record be attached of deposit of the material in an institution recognized by the IMPI.[34]

When an applicant has already filed for a patent in another country, the filing date in that country may be recognized as the priority filing date, provided that the filing date of the patent application in Mexico falls within the grace period established by international treaty[35] or, in the absence of such an

[33] Such transfers must be registered with the IMPI in order for third parties to assert rights.
[34] Articles 38, 38*bis*, 39, 43, 45, and 47 of the LPI, and Articles 50, 60, and 70 of the RLPI.
[35] Both Mexico and the United States are parties to the Patent Co-Operation Treaty (PCT) adopted in Washington on 19 June 1970, and published in Mexico in D.O. 31 Dec. 1994. Pursuant to the treaty, an interested party can submit to the receiving office a patent application,

international provision, within twelve months of the filing date in the original country. In order to be granted priority, official written records must be attached to the application authenticating the filing date of the application in the original country; offering proof that the patent application being filed in Mexico does not seek any additional rights other than those being sought in the foreign country; and attesting to compliance with the requirements of any relevant treaties, the LPI, and the regulations of the LPI (LPI Articles 40–41).

The first obstacle an applicant must overcome in order to be granted a patent is to provide all of the information requested and fulfil any other preliminary requirements set by the IMPI. Should the applicant fail to meet any requirement, the IMPI may request that the applicant file all of the documents once again before the end of a grace period of two months, otherwise the application shall be considered withdrawn. Once the IMPI has verified that the applicant has complied with all preliminary requirements (provided all the necessary information and records), the application shall be published in the IMPI Gazette as soon as possible after eighteen months have elapsed from the time the application is first filed. After the application has been published, a thorough and substantive examination is conducted to determine if the invention in question qualifies as a novelty, is the result of a creative endeavour, and has some applied use in industry. Should the IMPI deem that a more thorough analysis is necessary, or that the invention does not meet any of the above-listed patentability requirements, it may require the applicant to present any additional or supplementary information or documentation that it may need, including any records pertaining to searches or examinations performed by foreign patent offices, or to change or correct any claims, descriptions, or sketches, or to clarify any information that the Institute may feel is pertinent.

Patent application procedures have one of three outcomes: the patent may be granted; the patent may be denied; or the patent application may be considered withdrawn.[36] In the first instance, the IMPI notifies the applicant in writing that the patent has been granted and that the prospective patentee has a period of two months to file a record of payment of the title issuance fee with the IMPI in order for the patent to be officially published. Should the applicant not fulfil this requirement, the application is considered withdrawn. An extension may be granted in this case, provided that the fee has been paid.

The IMPI issues one title for each patent, which must include the number and class of the patent, the name and domicile of the person or persons to whom it is issued, the name of the inventor or inventors, filing dates and priority filing dates, the name of the invention, and the expiration date of the patent. Should the patent be refused, the applicant receives a written notice stating the reasons

known as an International PCT Application, avoiding the submission of the same application in every country in which the interested party wishes to obtain protection. Such application shall be entitled to the right of prioirity based on a prior filed PCT Application, as specified in the Convention.

[36] *See* Rangel Medina, *supra* note 1 at 28 and 29.

for denial of the patent application. Such notice must be supported both in fact and law (*motivación y fundamentación*). As mentioned previously, the application is considered withdrawn when applicants do not meet deadlines established by the law (LPI Articles 56–59). Once a patent is granted, the IMPI must publish it in the IMPI Gazette.

Table 21.1 shows statistics on the number of patents on inventions granted and the main countries of origin of patent holders for the period 1989–2000.

As Table 21.1 shows, Mexican patent holders are responsible for only a small percentage (8 per cent in the early 1990s, declining to 3 per cent in 2000) of all patent applications for inventions filed with the IMPI. The United States, Germany, France, Japan, and the United Kingdom are responsible for over 75 per cent of all patent applications in Mexico, and the United States alone is responsible for over 57 per cent of the total. These figures are not surprising in a country that is more intent on industrialization through the importation of foreign investment and foreign technology (Mexico's emphasis since the economic opening up of the 1990s) than on investment in local research and development. Given its formidable budget constraints and the many needs of its economy, the Mexican government has not been able to provide as much support for scientific research and development as its NAFTA partners.[37]

2.1.2. *Protection for Utility Models* (Modelos de Utilidad)

Under Mexican industrial property law, in addition to patents on inventions, protection is available for rights in utility models.[38] Utility models are objects, utensils, devices, or tools that, as a result of a modification of their make-up, configuration, or structure, function differently from how the parts that make them up function, or offer certain utilitarian advantages, provided that they qualify as original or novel and have an applied use in industry (LPI Articles 27 and 28). Utility models may not meet the strict standards required to obtain patent protection, but instead represent incremental advances in the function, use, utility, or applications of technologies that have already been developed. Utility models are often developed by smaller companies and independent inventors, and their protection is therefore considered a stimulus to development. Staplers and paper items (folders, envelopes, etc.) are examples of utility models. Utility models are common in the chemical, metallurgical, textile, and paper industries, as well as in electrical products, construction, mechanical, and other industries. According to figures compiled by IMPI, the agency receives between 300 and 500 applications per year for registration of utility models; in contrast with patent applications, the majority of applications for utility models are filed by Mexican companies.[39]

[37] Mexico is not alone in this characteristic, of course. The differences between the technologically advanced countries and developing countries in the ability to invest sizeable amounts in research and generate new patents help explain why the latter nations have been less-than-zealous advocates of strict intellectual property regimes.

[38] Protection of utility models in Mexico was first established by the adoption of the LPI in 1991.

[39] *See* www.impi.gob.mx (site visited Jan. 2004).

Table 21.1: Patent applications by nationality of holder (1989–2000, Mexico)

Year	Total	Mexico	*Germany*	USA	*France*	*Italy*	*Japan*	*United Kingdom*	*Spain*	*Switzer-Land*	*Other Countries*
1989	4,574	757	368	2,415	154	50	131	212	32	n/a	455
1990	5,061	661	348	2,824	199	92	114	215	32	n/a	576
1991	5,271	564	370	3,087	199	78	152	211	44	163	403
1992	7,695	565	645	4,358	311	194	270	317	56	289	657
1993	8,212	553	633	4,948	280	125	225	348	51	289	760
1994	9,944	498	742	6,191	360	156	262	389	71	304	971
1995	5,393	432	513	3,139	267	89	210	69	55	216	403
1996	6,751	386	581	3,835	327	108	307	157	62	261	727
1997	10,531	420	856	6,023	497	179	334	396	85	383	1,358
1998	10,893	453	992	6,088	521	151	402	435	70	347	1,434
1999	12,110	455	1,155	6,869	624	159	397	412	93	327	1,619
2000	13,061	431	1,252	7,249	701	171	466	453	102	415	1,821

Note: Includes 159 PCT applications in 1995; 2,558 in 1996; 6,559 in 1997; 7,188 in 1998; n/a: no available information.

Source: www.impi.gob.mx.

Most of the regulations applicable to patents are equally applicable to utility models, with one important exception: it is not necessary to show that the creation of a utility model involved an inventive step. As with inventions, utility models must be registered with the IMPI. Registration of utility models is an administrative function designed to protect the rights of holders against third parties for a period of ten years from the date of filing, in contrast with the twenty-year protection afforded to inventions. This protection is similar to the rights of patent holders for inventions, and includes exclusive rights to exploitation, to prevent other persons from manufacturing, using, selling, or importing the model without prior consent of the patentee; and the ability to transfer the rights and to grant licences for exploitation of the utility model.

2.1.3. *Protection of Industrial Designs* (Diseños Industriales)

LPI Articles 31–37 include provisions that permit protection of industrial designs. According to Article 32, industrial designs include industrial drawings, including any combination of figures, lines, or colours incorporated in an industrial product with ornamental purpose; and industrial models consisting of any three-dimensional shape which may serve as a model or pattern for the manufacture of an industrial product. Industrial designs that are new and capable of industrial application are eligible for registration. For an industrial design to be considered new, it must be created independently of known designs or combinations of known features of designs, and must differ significantly therefrom. Examples of industrial designs include styling designs for automobiles, and the shapes of household goods, sporting goods, office products, wallpapers, fabric patterns, etc.

Industrial design registration lasts for fifteen years from the date of filing. Registration and protection of such designs is similar to that for patents.

2.1.4. *Protection of Trade Secrets* (Secretos Industriales)

The adoption of the LPI in 1991 enhanced the protection of trade secrets in Mexico; prior to the LPI, trade secrets had been protected only through the application of general principles of labour law and criminal law. The LPI defines a trade secret as 'any information relating to an industrial or commercial application that an individual or corporation keeps confidential, for the purpose of obtaining or maintaining a competitive or economic advantage for the individual or corporation *vis-à-vis* third parties in conducting business activities and for which sufficient measures or systems have been adopted in order to preserve their confidentiality and in order to restrict access thereto'. The information must relate to: the nature, characteristics, or purpose of products; to production methods or processes; or to the means or forms of distribution or marketing of products or the provision of services. Information that is public knowledge, obvious to technical experts, and information which must be disclosed pursuant to a legal or judicial order, is not a trade secret (LPI Article 82).

The information must be recorded either in documents, on electronic or magnetic media, on optical discs, microfilm, or film, or in any other similar instruments. Trade secrets may be transferred to or authorized for the use of third parties; in such cases, third parties shall be bound to maintain or protect the confidential nature of the information. Employees of companies that keep trade secrets have the same obligation, as are any administrative and judicial authorities who may become aware of any such information in the course their professional duties and may not provide this information to any persons with no legal interest (LPI Articles 83–85).

Violators of the duty to maintain the confidentiality of trade secrets may be held liable for criminal,[40] labour,[41] or civil and administrative infringement. Trade secrets are enforceable not only against any person who illegally obtains the secret from the premises of the owner, but also against third parties who acquire the trade secret from another third party and use it for economic gain or to damage the owner of the trade secret. If a trade secret must be disclosed in a judicial or administrative proceeding, the receiving authority must adopt measures necessary to prevent its disclosure to third parties not connected with the controversy.

3. Distinctive Marks

This broad category of protection encompasses trade marks, trade names, appellations of origin, and commercial advertisements (slogans).

3.1. Trade Marks (*Marcas*)

The legal definition of a trade mark is any 'visible sign that distinguishes products or services from others on the market of the same kind or class' (LPI Article 88). Trade marks protect exclusive rights of use, achieved by registering marks with the IMPI. Trade mark registration remains in effect for ten years, and may be renewed for subsequent periods of the same length of time (LPI Article 95).

Registered trade marks in Mexico originally emerged as a distinctive mark whose purpose was to identify only products, but in 1976 Congress passed the

[40] For the offence of 'disclosure of secrets', Article 211 of the Federal Criminal Code (*Código Penal Federal*) establishes a penalty of from 1–5 years in prison, a fine of 50–500 pesos (currently equal to approximately 5–50 US dollars), and suspension from exercising one's profession should the circumstances so merit. A sentence of between 2 months and 1 year in prison applies when disclosure is made by a person who provides professional or technical services, or by a public official or employee, or in cases involving disclosure of industrial secrets.

[41] According to Article 134, section XIII of the Federal Labour Law (*Ley Federal del Trabajo*), it is the obligation of workers to 'Scrupulously guard technical, commercial and factory secrets regarding products in whose manufacture or processing they are directly or indirectly involved, or any [secrets] that they may be aware of by virtue of the job they perform, as well as any confidential administrative matters whose disclosure may cause harm to the company', and violation of this obligation may be cause for termination of employment.

Law of Inventions and Trademarks (*Ley de Invenciones y Marcas*),[42] which also allowed for registration of service marks. The 1976 Trade mark Law was eventually abrogated and replaced by the LPI in 1991.

The LPI defines four different categories of physical trade mark types: (a) names or visible figures that are distinctive enough to help distinguish the products or services they apply to, or are intended to apply to, from others of the same kind or class; (b) three-dimensional shapes; (c) trade names, or corporate or firm names; and (d) the proper name of an individual, provided that it is not confused with a registered trade mark or a published trade name (LPI Article 89). Although trade marks may exhibit a broad range of physical traits, the law also places specific restrictions on what may *not* be registered as a trade mark.[43]

3.1.1. *Trade mark Registration*

Unlike the rights over inventions, which require examination by the IMPI to assure uniqueness before a patent may achieve protection, the rights to trade marks are generally obtained simply by following the proper procedures for registration with the IMPI, in accordance with the LPI and RLPI. The first stage of the procedure is filing the standard application form prepared by the IMPI and attaching thereto a record of payment of filing fees, as well as the required documentation describing the trade mark (labels, photographs, and sketches or drawings when three-dimensional trade marks are involved), the rules of use and transfer of rights, and, in cases involving joint ownership of trade marks, the legal documents attesting to the joint owner's grant of a proxy to the co-proprietor.

The procedure consists of three stages:[44] first, examination to determine whether the applicant has met the formal and procedural requirements (i.e. has filed all the necessary information and documents); second, examination to determine whether the trade mark sought by the applicant meets the statutory requirements and constitutes a unique or novel distinctive sign when compared with other registered trade marks or trade marks, and whether any other impediment exists to grant registration; and finally, granting or denying registration and issuance of the title of registration. The final decision of the IMPI must be published in the IMPI's official journal, the *Gaceta de la Propiedad Industrial*.

[42] D.O. 10 Feb. 1976. Adopted at the height of the import substitution era, the 1976 Law was much more limited and restrictive of trademark protection than the LPI, and for this reason was the object of criticism by US and other commentators. For instance, the 1976 Law imposed a requirement that foreign product and trade names must be coupled with local names ('Nabisco—Famosa' and 'Goodrich—Euzkadi' are examples) although the requirement was not rigidly enforced. The 1976 Law also imposed pricing and other restrictions on the transfer of technology, causing foreign owners of technology to avoid transferring technological advancements to Mexico.

[43] LPI Article 90 includes a long list of the types of marks that may *not* be registered, such as technical or common names of products or services (such as 'movie') that have come to be the usual or generic designation of these products or services, or three-dimensional shapes that are in the public domain (such as a crucifix).

[44] *See* Rangel Medina, *supra* note 1 at 68. Regulations for the trademark registration procedure are found in Chapter V of the LPI, and in Articles 53–62 and 113–135 of the RLPI.

After a mark has been registered, it is fully protected by law, and the proprietor enjoys all rights inherent thereto but must also fulfil the obligations that such rights may entail. Hence, in principle, a registered trade mark protects the particular class of products and services for which it has been granted (this concept has come to be known as the 'principle of trade mark speciality', or *principio de especialidad de la marca*),[45] except in instances involving well-known trade marks.[46] Trade mark protection is coextensive with Mexico's territorial jurisdiction; under the territorial principles underlying trade mark law (known as the *principio de territorialidad*)[47] a trade mark registered in Mexico is protected anywhere within the territorial jurisdiction of Mexico.

Rights of trade mark proprietors include the exclusive right to exploit the trade mark (i.e. to use the mark on products or services); to grant licences or franchises for use thereof;[48] to transfer the rights to the mark; to renew the mark; to assert administrative defences with the IMPI;[49] to file a civil suit (such as to bring an action for damages against someone who infringes the trade mark); or to bring a private criminal complaint (*querella*) in conjunction with the Ministry of the Public Prosecutor when criminal offences are committed against industrial property.

Proprietors of trade marks are required to use the mark within Mexican territory on at least one of their products or services on a continuing basis without interruption for at least three years. They are also required to use the mark without any modifications that may alter its distinctive character; to affix the caption '*Marca Registrada*' (registered trade mark) or the Spanish acronyms 'M.R.' or 'R.' to any product associated with the mark; to refrain from using the trade mark as a generic name; to cease to use the trade mark when the IMPI

[45] The categories of products and services can be found in RLPI Article 59, which contains 34 classes of products and 8 classes of services.

[46] When a trademark is well-known throughout the world (such as Gucci, Cartier, Bulova, etc.) protection may extend to products or services that are not encompassed within the classes specifically listed in the register entry of the trademark. This protection can be found in LPI Article 90, section XV, which prohibits registering as trademarks 3-dimensional names, figures, or shapes that are identical or similar to a trademark that the Institute deems widely known in Mexico. According to LPI Article 90, a mark is considered 'widely known' when 'a particular sector of the public or of business circles in the country is familiar with the mark as a result of commercial trade taking place in Mexico or in a foreign country that is conducted by persons who use that trademark with relation to their products or services, as well as the degree of familiarity that people may have of the trademark within the borders of the country, as a consequence of marketing and advertising thereof.'

[47] Mexico is not a party to the Madrid Agreement Concerning International Registration Marks of 1891, or its Protocol, which establishes a system of international recognition of trademarks registered by contracting parties to the convention.

[48] A set of special rules for licensing and transferring of rights to trademarks can be found in LPI Articles 136–150. Although trademark proprietors enjoy the freedom to enter into contracts with third parties, the law requires that licensing, transferring, or franchising agreements, as well as any fees that may have been charged, be registered with the IMPI, in order for these acts to be considered valid. LPI Articles 136, 142–143.

[49] Defences include the right to seek an administrative declaration of infringement, or to request that the authorities prevent or stop the circulation and marketing of goods or the provision of services in violation of the mark. LPI Articles 187, 188, and 199*bis*.

so orders; and to file a record with the IMPI of any transfers of rights, any fees charged for such transactions, and any licences or franchises granted to third parties (LPI Articles 128, 130, 131, and 136).

The number of trade marks registered in Mexico has risen each year, in direct proportion to the increase in international business transactions that have accompanied the economic opening up of Mexico since the early 1990s. In the early 1990s slightly more than 25,000 trade mark applications were filed in Mexico each year; by the year 2000 the number of applications received by the IMPI had risen to almost 60,000. Approximately 60 per cent of these applications are filed on behalf of Mexican companies and individuals; the United States is the second most prolific generator of trade mark applications, with approximately 20 per cent of the applications,[50] reflecting the United States' position as Mexico's largest trading partner and foreign investor.

3.1.2. Protection of Unregistered Trade marks

Registration is the most effective way to protect a trade mark. Article 151, section II of the LPI can be used by the owner of an unregistered trade mark that is already in use to nullify the registration of a new trade mark with which it would be confused. However, under LPI Article 87, only the owner of a registered trade mark has the exclusive right of use and can prosecute infringers. Parties using existing unregistered trade marks who are acting in good faith have the right to file for registration of the unregistered trade mark within three years of the date of publication of registration of the competing trade mark, and nullification of the earlier registration must be resolved in advance (LPI Articles 92, section I and 151, section II).

3.1.3. Forfeiture of Registration

Pursuant to the LPI, registration of a trade mark can only be forfeited as a result of one of three administrative procedures: nullification, lapsing, or cancellation. These may be determined in proceedings before the IMPI.

A trade mark registration lapses: when a trade mark ceases to be used for three consecutive years, when a trade mark is used in a way that alters its distinctive character, or when the proprietor fails to renew the trade mark (LPI Article 152). A registration can be cancelled either at the request of the proprietor, or whenever the trade mark owner has provoked or tolerated the transformation of the trade mark into a generic term within the class of products or services for which the mark is registered (LPI Articles 153, 154). Registration may be annulled in the instances set forth in LPI Article 151, which include: when the trade mark was unlawfully granted; when the trade mark was granted on the basis of bogus information; when the trade mark is identical or similar enough to lead to confusion with another trade mark that was used within Mexico or in a foreign country prior to the filing date of the application for

[50] Source: www.impi.gob.mx (site visited Jan. 2004).

trade mark registration; when a mistake or an oversight has been committed; or when registration was granted to the agent, representative, distributor, or user without the authorization of the proprietor of a registered trade mark in a foreign country.

3.2. Commercial Advertisements and Slogans (*Avisos Comerciales*)

Commercial advertisements are phrases or sentences whose purpose is to make the public aware of commercial, industrial, or service establishments or businesses, or products or services, so as to distinguish them from others of their kind. Examples of legally protected commercial advertisements are advertising slogans, such as '*Soy totalmente Palacio*' ('I'm totally Palacio'), used by the department store chain Palacio de Hierro. Such advertising may be protected by registering the material with the IMPI, and remains valid for a period of ten years from the date of filing the application (LPI Articles 99–104). The rules pertaining to trade marks (registration, proprietary rights, forfeiture, etc.) also apply to commercial advertisements.

3.3. Trade Names (*Nombres Comerciales*)

Trade or corporate names are the names of companies or industrial, commercial, or service establishments. It is not necessary to register these names in order to protect them, even though a request may be filed with the IMPI to publish such names in IMPI's *Gaceta de la Propiedad Industrial.* Registration and publication in the *Gaceta* carries a presumption of good faith in the adoption and use of the trade name. The trade name is valid for a period of ten years from the date of filing of the application, and the request may be renewed (LPI Articles 105–112). Any statutes or regulations pertaining to trade marks that may be relevant are also applicable to trade names.

3.4. Appellations of Origin (*Denominación de Origen*)

The LPI defines appellations of origin as 'the name of a geographic region of the country that serves to designate a native product from that location, and whose qualities or characteristics are solely the result of the geographic surroundings or environment, which encompasses both natural and man-made factors' (LPI Article 156).

Even though an appellation of origin grants the right to producers from the geographic region to use it, after obtaining authorization, these producers are not proprietors of the right;[51] ownership rights belong to the Mexican

[51] When the IMPI authorizes a private individual or business to use the appellation of origin, the Institute is essentially granting certain administrative rights which, in turn, may be transferred to other manufacturers, provided that they fulfil the requirements set forth in the Law. Authorization remains valid for 10 years, after which time it may be renewed. Authorization may be annulled if any infringement of the law is declared, or when it is determined that the

government.[52] Once the declaration of appellation of origin (*declaratoria de denominación de origen*) is published in the *Diario Oficial*, any use of the appellation on products not originally from the territory encompassed in the declaration shall be subject to penalty. A violation may occur even if the appellation is combined with terms such as 'generic', 'type', 'fashion', 'imitation', or any similar adjectives which create confusion in the minds of consumers or amount to unfair competition (LPI Article 137).

The procedure for a declaration of appellation of origin may be initiated either by the IMPI itself, or at the request of the individuals or companies who are in the business of the extraction, production, or manufacture of the products at issue. Local chambers of commerce or associations of producers, as well as offices or entities of the federal or state governments, may also apply to the IMPI for declaration of appellation of origin.

IMPI has registered, *inter alia*, the following declarations of appellation of origin to date: Tequila, Mezcal, Madera de Olinalá, Talavera de Puebla, and Mango Ataulfo. The appellation 'Tequila' applies to the distinctive Mexican liquor distilled from the fermented blue agave plant, and encompasses certain regions within the states of Jalisco, Guanajuato, Michoacán, Nayarit, and Tamaulipas.[53] The appellation 'Mezcal' (the liquor colourfully marketed in bottles containing the *gusano de maguey*, or maguey worm) refers to liquor produced within certain regions of the states of Oaxaca, Guerrero, Durango, San Luis Potosí, and Zacatecas.[54] The appellation 'Olinalá' applies to traditional lacquered wooden handicrafts made in the Municipality of Olinalá in the state of Guerrero.[55] The appellation 'Talavera' protects ceramics made in certain judicial districts in the State of Puebla.[56] Ataulfo is a distinctive variety of mango.

Under the terms of the North American Free Trade Agreement (NAFTA), Canada and the United States 'shall recognize Tequila and Mezcal as distinctive products of Mexico. Accordingly, Canada and the United States shall not permit the sale of any product as Tequila or Mezcal, unless it has been manufactured in Mexico in accordance with the laws and regulations of Mexico governing the manufacture of Tequila and Mezcal'.[57] The US appellations 'Bourbon Whiskey' and 'Tennessee Whiskey' and the appellation 'Canadian Whiskey' are similarly protected.

authorization was granted on the basis of false information and documents, or authorization may be cancelled when the appellation of origin is used differently from the authorized terms and provisions.

[52] LPI Article 167. According to Article 168, the IMPI shall file for registration of appellations of origin with the International Bureau of Intellectual Property, in collaboration with the Mexican Secretariat of Foreign Relations, in order to provide for their protection in foreign countries, pursuant to the Lisbon Agreement for the Protection of Appellations of Origin and their International Registration, adopted by Mexico and published in D.O. 11 Jul. 1964.

[53] *See* D.O. 9 Oct. 1974 and 13 Oct. 1977.

[54] D.O. 28 Nov. 1994.

[55] D.O. 28 Nov. 1994.

[56] D.O. 17 Mar. 1995, as amended by the resolution published in D.O. 11 Sep. 1997.

[57] NAFTA Annex 313.

4. Enforcement of Industrial Property Rights

4.1. Administrative Procedures for Declaration of Infringement

In addition to being the administrative authority responsible for granting patents and registering distinctive marks, the IMPI assumes responsibility for applying administrative penalties for conduct that infringes industrial property rights. The IMPI may act unilaterally in this capacity, i.e. it may proceed against offenders on its own initiative, or at the request of a presumptively aggrieved party.

The LPI sets forth a specific administrative procedure for the filing of petitions for declarations lapsing and nullification of a patent, industrial design, or utility model, or the lapsing, cancellation, or nullification of trade marks and other distinctive signs, or for an administrative declaration that a property right has been infringed. The proceeding takes place within the IMPI before the Office of the General Deputy Director for Intellectual Property (*Dirección General Adjunta de Propiedad Industrial*). The IMPI may act on its own initiative or at the request of a party. Before proceeding to administrative adjudication, the record must reflect that attempts have been made to reach a settlement with the alleged violator and that such attempts have not been successful, and that both parties are aware that the proceeding is not of a judicial nature and the IMPI does not act as a judge.

During the administrative proceeding, the disputing parties substantiate claims or offer defences, introduce evidence, and put forward legal arguments. At the conclusion of the proceeding, the IMPI official in charge of the matter[58] decides whether the law has been infringed. The IMPI may impose sanctions in accordance with LPI Articles 213, 214, 223, and 224. A property holder who wishes to recover lost profits or other damages must then bring a civil proceeding (*juicio ordinario civil*) before a federal court to seek damages against the infringer.[59] Federal courts have been granted jurisdiction over such disputes and other measures arising from the implementation of the LPI. However, when such disputes affect only private interests, they may be heard before state courts if the plaintiff so chooses, without prejudice to the right of the parties to submit the dispute to arbitration. LPI Article 229 require that products or services must be adequately identified as protected by intellectual property rights, in accordance with LPI Articles 26 and 131, or otherwise indicate that the property right is protected, in order to bring an effective action.

If as a result of this proceeding the IMPI issues an administrative declaration of infringement (*declaración administrative de infracción*) of any of the rights

[58] *See Reglamento de IMPI*, Article 8, section V. IMPI regulations may be found at www.impi.gob.mx (site visited Jan. 2004).

[59] Article 221 and 221*bis*. This provision states that damages may never be less than 40% of the sale price to the public for each product or service that entails an infringement of any of the industrial property rights covered by the law.

provided for by the LPI, the Institute may take any of the following different measures, in accordance with LPI Article 199*bis*:

(i) issue an order requiring merchandise to be removed from the shelves of stores, or preventing goods from being sold;
(ii) order the withdrawal of advertisements, signs, labels, and utensils or instruments meant for or utilized in the manufacture of the prohibited items;
(iii) prohibit the marketing of the prohibited products;
(iv) order the securing of the goods;
(v) order the offender to suspend unlawful acts or cease to provide service and close the establishment, should such a measure be necessary.

The LPI establishes a list of acts that are considered to be administrative offences that may serve as the basis of an administrative declaration of infringement.[60] It is the responsibility of the IMPI to investigate any alleged offences and, should the investigation reveal that irregular conduct was indeed involved, the Institute has the discretionary power to impose punitive measures. The possible penalties are a fine of up to twenty thousand days of the general minimum wage in effect for the Federal District (an amount equal to approximately $US 84,300 in August 2003); an additional fine of up to five hundred days of the general minimum wage in effect for the Federal District for each day that the infringement persists after the declaration of infringement; temporary closure of an enterprise for up to ninety days; permanent closure; and administrative arrest of up to thirty-six hours (LPI Article 214).

Articles 1714–1718 of the NAFTA Agreement commit the parties to minimum standards of intellectual property enforcement. NAFTA Article 1715 requires Mexico to 'make available to right holders civil judicial procedures for the enforcement of any intellectual property right' provided for in the NAFTA. NAFTA Article 1714 also states that the provisions of NAFTA 'shall be construed to require a Party to establish a judicial system for the enforcement of intellectual property rights distinct from that Party's system for the enforcement of laws in general'. There have been no assertions to date by US or Canadian authorities that Mexico's system of intellectual property enforcement fails to live up to its commitments under NAFTA.

[60] Article 213 provides a long list of acts considered to be administrative infringements or offences, such as carrying out acts that go against proper usage or business customs which involve unfair competition and relate to the subject matter of this statute; and making unpatented items appear as if they were legally patented. Should a patent have expired or be declared null and void by the authorities, after a term of one year has lapsed, as of the date of expiration or, as the case may be, the date of issuance of the judgment of nullification of a patent, use of this patent is considered an offence; using a trade mark that is similar enough to another so as to cause confusion with another product, in order to protect, goods or services of the same class, is also considered an infringement.

4.2. Criminal Enforcement of Industrial Property Laws

In addition to civil enforcement, the LPI establishes special criminal offences regarding industrial property, as set forth in LPI Article 223.[61] Possible penalties are from two to six years in prison and a fine of 100 to 10,000 days of the general minimum wage in effect for the Federal District (LPI Article 224).

Criminal offences for violation of the LPI are prosecuted by the federal Attorney General's Office (*Procuraduría General de la República*), to which the IMPI refers any criminal action. As already noted, the IMPI may act upon its own initiative, or in response to a complaint filed by an affected party (LPI Article 6). In 2001, 561 criminal cases were filed against alleged violators of intellectual property laws (including copyright), as compared with 150 cases the previous year. In 2002, 783 criminal cases were filed.[62]

4.3. Civil Actions for Damages due to Violations of Intellectual Property Laws

The LPI does not specifically provide a cause of action for private parties to bring civil actions for damage caused by infringers of intellectual property rights. However, the provisions of the civil codes relating to extra-contractual liability for wrongful acts[63] are sufficiently broad to permit a holder of an intellectual property right to sue a party for infringing a patent or trade mark.

5. Copyright

As with patent and trade mark law, in recent years Mexico has strengthened its copyright laws. In 1996 Congress adopted the new Federal Law of Copyright (*Ley Federal del Derecho de Autor*),[64] known by its Spanish acronym LFDA, which replaced the outdated Federal Law of Copyrights of 1963 (*Ley de los Derechos de Autor*).[65] The enactment of the new law represents an attempt to increase the level of copyright protection by incorporating international standards of international

[61] LPI Article 223. Examples of such offences include, among others, forging trade marks for deceitful purposes on a commercial scale; disclosure of industrial secrets to a third party, which are acquired as a result of a job, position, office, professional practice, business relationship, or by virtue of a licence for use of such secrets without the consent of the proprietor of the secrets, after being warned to keep such information confidential, in order to obtain some economic benefit for oneself or for a third party, or in order to bring harm to the proprietor of the secret; and appropriating an industrial secret without right and without the consent of the proprietor or of the authorized user.

Certain offences, such as committing trade mark forgery, or importing products with forged trade marks, when the person is aware of the forgery, are considered to be serious offences, and in such instances alleged offenders do not have the right to post bond for pre-trial release (Article 194, section VII of the Federal Code of Criminal Procedure (*Código Federal de Procedimientos Penales*)).

[62] Source: www.pgr.gob.mx (site visited Jan. 2004).

[63] *See* Chapter 17 above, Section 6.

[64] D.O. 24 Dec. 1996, as amended.

[65] D.O. 21 Dec. 1963.

regulation and by modernizing the institutional framework responsible for enforcing the copyright laws. The LFDA is supplemented by the regulatory law of the LFDA (*Reglamento de la Ley Federal del Derecho de Autor*, or RFLDA),[66] which are administered by the *Instituto Nacional de Derechos de Autor* (INDA).

In addition to the LFDA, Mexico is signatory to a number of international treaties that, pursuant to the Constitution, are applicable within Mexico. These international instruments include the International Convention on Copyrights;[67] the Universal Convention on Copyrights, revised at Paris in 1971;[68] the Inter-American Convention on Copyrights in Literary, Scientific, and Artistic Works;[69] the Convention on Literary and Artistic Property, signed at the Fourth International American Conference;[70] the Berne Convention for the Protection of Literary and Artistic Works;[71] the Paris Agreement pertaining to the Berne Convention;[72] the International Convention for the Protection of Artists, Performers, or Producers of Phonograms and Broadcasting Organizations;[73] and the Convention for the Protection of Producers of Phonograms Against Unauthorized Duplication of Their Phonograms (29 October 1971).[74] In addition, as stated above, the TRIPS Agreement of the World Trade Organization, as well as NAFTA chapter 17, commit Mexico to the observance of multilateral standards of protection of copyrights.[75]

In contrast to the Anglo-American common law tradition,[76] Mexican law makes a distinction between 'moral rights' (*derechos morales*), which are rights inherent to the author and are inalienable, and 'patrimonial (economic) rights' (*derechos patrimoniales*), which can be transferred to others (LFDA Article 11). As a practical matter, the retention of inalienable 'moral rights' permits the author to exercise some controls over the work, so as to protect those rights most connected with authorship, even after transferring the rights to another party.

5.1. 'Moral Rights' (*Derechos Morales*)

An author has sole ownership over the moral rights to his or her work. Moral rights are non-transferable and held in perpetuity; thus, they extend even beyond the period of any copyright, and cannot be attached or otherwise appropriated. Only the creator of a work or the heirs of the creator are entitled to exercise moral rights. However, in the absence of any heirs, or after works enter the public domain, insofar as they are considered to be an important part

[66] D.O. 20 May 1998. [67] D.O. 6 June 1957. [68] D.O. 9 Mar. 1976.
[69] D.O. 24 Oct. 1947. [70] D.O. 23 Apr. 1963. [71] D.O. 20 Dec. 1968.
[72] D.O. 24 Jan. 1975. [73] D.O. 27 May 1964. [74] D.O. 29 Oct. 1971.

[75] *See* e.g. NAFTA Articles 1701, 1705, and 1706. NAFTA Article 2021 provides that '[n]o Party may provide for a right of action under its domestic law against any other Party on the ground that a measure of another Party is inconsistent with this Agreement'.

[76] 'Unlike civil law countries, the US has no "moral rights" [. . .] [federal law] provides only limited rights respecting mutilation, which is deformation by leaving out parts of the work and attribution with regard to a very narrow category, called works of visual art'. Davis, M., 'Intellectual Property', in *United States Law of Trade and Investment*, vol. IV (B. Kozolchyk and J. Molloy, eds.) (Littleton, Colo: Rothman, 2001) at 35–35.

of the nation's cultural heritage, the State may exercise these rights (LFDA Articles 18–20).

Owners of moral rights are entitled to determine the form of dissemination of their work, or whether or not their work shall remain unpublished; to demand recognition of their capacity as authors, or to direct that their works be disseminated anonymously or under a pseudonym; to object to any deformation, mutilation, or modification of their works, or any conduct that may detract from their works or cause any harm to themselves; to modify their works; and to withdraw their works from commerce and object to a work that is not of their own creation being attributed to them.[77]

5.2. Economic Rights (*Derechos Patrimoniales*): Transferable Rights to Exclusive or Restrictive Use of Literary, Artistic, and Scientific Property

Patrimonial rights consist of the right to exclusive exploitation of the works of an author, or authorizing others to exploit an author's own works in any form that the author may deem appropriate. In addition to authors being the original holders of economic copyrights (*titulares originarios*), patrimonial rights are also passed on to the heirs of authors and may also be transferred to third-party assignees (*titulares derivados*), either voluntarily or by any other means, such as by sale or assignment, or by operation of law (e.g. final judgment of a court).[78] When a literary, artistic, or scientific creation is the product of a written contract of employment, unless the contract states otherwise it is presumed that patrimonial rights are divided equally between the employer and employee. The sole exception to this rule involves computer programs, in which case the employer is entitled to sole patrimonial rights.[79]

Patrimonial rights encompass the following acts: reproduction, publication, editing the works or physically copying the works in any medium; public dissemination of the works whether by representation, recitation, execution, or public exhibition in the case of artistic or literary works, and public access by means of telecommunications; public broadcast or radio broadcast of the works, by any means; distribution of the works, including sale or other forms of transfer of physical property, as well as any other form of transfer of use or exploitation; importation of unauthorized copies of the works; dissemination of derivative works in any form, such as translation, adaptation, paraphrasing, arrangements, and transformations; and any public use of their work.[80]

Patrimonial rights remain in effect throughout the lifetime of the author, and after his or her death for a period of one hundred additional years. When works

[77] These rights are part of a comprehensive list of rights attributed to authors under LFDA Article 21.

[78] The fruits of patrimonial rights may serve as collateral, and may be subject to attachment or enforcement of a security right. LFDA Article 41.

[79] LFDA Articles 84 and 103.

[80] LFDA Article 27. When a work is distributed by sale, the owner's right to object expires after the first sale is finalized; however, in cases involving computer programs, the author may reserve the right to authorize or prohibit leasing. LFDA Article 104.

are created under contract with, or commissioned by, federal, state, or municipal government agencies, and in the case of posthumous works, patrimonial rights are valid for a period of seventy-five years from the date of the initial release or debut (provided that the initial release or debut occurs within seventy-five years of the death of the author). Once these terms elapse, the work becomes part of the public domain.[81]

The law allows authors to enter into contracts that permit others to exercise patrimonial rights of copyright material, but the LFDA contains specific rules providing special protection to copyrights and placing restrictions on the freedom to enter into such agreements. Thus, the law establishes that all transfers of patrimonial rights create a legal obligation to compensate the author in some way,[82] and are of a temporary nature.[83] A work that is to be completed at a future date may not be transferred in its entirety,[84] and all acts of transfer must be put into writing and registered with the Public Registry of Copyrights (*Registro Público de Derechos de Autor*),[85] which is maintained by the *Instituto Nacional de Derechos de Autor* (INDA).

The LFDA establishes rules covering special types of contracts for the publication of literary works, and for the production of musical works, staged productions, radio broadcasts, audio-visual works, and advertising productions.

Literary works Contracts for the publication of literary works are defined by the law as agreements in which the author or owner of patrimonial rights makes a commitment to deliver the work to a publisher, and the publisher makes a commitment to reproduce, distribute, and sell the literary work, paying the owner of patrimonial rights any benefits that were previously agreed upon.[86]

Musical works Contracts for the printing and publication of sheet music permit the author or owner of patrimonial rights to assign the rights of reproduction to the publisher. The publisher is thereby granted the right to carry out the phono-mechanical setting and reproduction of the work, audio-visual synchronization, public dissemination, translation, arrangement or adaptation, and any other form of exploitation that may be agreed upon. The publisher has the obligation to disseminate the work in printed form (as opposed to performance, recording, etc.) receiving as consideration a share of any economic

[81] LFDA Article 29. When patrimonial rights belong to someone other than the author of the work, and that person dies without leaving any heirs, patrimonial rights belong to the author. If the author does not come forward to claim these rights, or should he or she be deceased, patrimonial rights revert to the State.

[82] LFDA Articles 30–31.

[83] When no time limit is specified, the contract remains in effect for 5 years; the parties may agree on a term greater than 15 years when such a term is justified by either the nature of the work or the required investment. LFDA Article 33.

[84] LFDA Article 34.

[85] Contracts that have not been registered have no effect against third parties. Once such contracts have been registered, however, they create enforceable rights (*títulos ejecutivos*), making it possible to resort to more expeditious remedies in judicial disputes.

[86] LFDA Article 42. LFDA Articles 43–57 set forth special rules governing such contracts, such as the obligation of the publisher to show the author's name or pseudonym, the name of the translator, the year of the edition, the International Standard Book Number (ISBN), or the respective number for periodical publications (ISSN) on the edition.

benefits that may be obtained from exploitation of the work, according to the terms of the contract.[87]

Stage productions With regard to contracts for stage productions of musical or other works, the owner of the rights may grant an individual or corporation the right to stage or publicly perform a literary, musical, dramatic, dramatic musical, dance, pantomime, or choreographic work, in exchange for monetary consideration; and the producer of such a work has the obligation to stage and present the work in accordance with the terms agreed upon by the parties.[88]

5.3. Protecting Copyrights

Original and derivative works A distinction is made in copyright law between 'original' and 'derivative' works. An original work, as the name implies, is a version created for the first time; a derivative work is created by the author on the basis of an original work that was not created by that author, who adds some novel characteristic to it, such as editing, record production, artists, performers, etc. Mexican copyright law does not treat these two types of works in the same way: rights to original works are considered *bona fide* copyrights or rights of authorship; rights to derivative works, however, are only considered 'related' rights (*derechos conexos*).

For example, a person whose name appears on a work is considered to be the author thereof, unless proven otherwise. The author owns both moral and patrimonial rights to that work, and is therefore entitled to avail himself or herself of administrative or judicial procedures to protect the work.

Derivative works, on the other hand (arrangements, compendiums, enlarged versions, translations, adaptations, paraphrased versions, compilations, collections, and transformations of literary or artistic property) are protected to the extent that they are original, but may only be exploited when authorization has been granted by the owner of the patrimonial rights to the original work (*obra primigenia*).[89]

Visual artistic works LFDA Articles 85–93 provide special protection for photographic, plastic, and graphic works (e.g. paintings, sculptures, lithographs,

[87] LFDA Article 58. Express authorization by the owner of patrimonial rights of musical works is required in order to carry out audio-visual synchronization, adaptation for promotional purposes, translation, arrangements, or transformations of the work. The contract may be rescinded: when release of the musical work does not take place within the period stated in the contract, without the owner being responsible for the delay; when the publisher fails to meet its obligation to disseminate the work without good reason; and when the work has not brought economic benefits to the parties within a period of 3 years, without the publisher being responsible for the lack of profitability. In all other instances, the provisions of the LFDA that pertain to contracts for publishing of literary works shall be applicable (Articles 59–60).

[88] LFDA Article 61. If the agreement contains no time limit, the contract is deemed to be valid for 1 year, the period in which the producer is required to stage the work.

[89] When a work is in the public domain, only the original part of a derivative work is protected; furthermore, the owner of the derivative rights does not have exclusive control over the original work, nor may that owner prevent other versions of the work from being made. LFDA Article 78, paragraph 2.

graphic designs) as well as restrictions on authors when the content of such works involves third parties. If an author transfers ownership of a pictorial, sculptural, or plastic work of art, such transfer entitles the acquiring party to exhibit the artwork and portray it in catalogues, but not to reproduce it; authorization to reproduce the artwork does not grant the right to reproduce it in any article nor to market commercially or promote the work. The author of artwork thus retains, in every case, control over any future reproduction of the work (e.g. publication of a book or poster that contains a copy of a painting or sculpture). Authors of photographs may only exhibit commissioned photographs after receiving authorization from the client who commissioned them. Portraits of persons may only be used by the author or published with the express consent of either the subject of the photograph, his or her legal representative, or the owner of the applicable rights thereto; such authorization may be revoked by any of these persons at any time.

Film and video Film and audio-visual materials[90] are protected as original works. The director, author of the screenplay, the creator of the adaptation, or the scriptwriter; the musical composer; the photographer and the animators or cartoon or comic strip creators are considered to be the authors of these types of works. The producer[91] is considered the owner of the patrimonial rights to the work, and may take whatever action is necessary to exploit the work; and once the authors have been engaged by contract to make their respective contributions, they are precluded from legally objecting to any efforts that may be made by the producer to reproduce, distribute, represent and publicly execute, subtitle, or dub the texts of the work.

Video producers enjoy the right to authorize or prohibit reproduction, distribution, and public dissemination of their videos (LFDA Articles 136–138). These rights remain in effect for fifty years from the first video recording of the images.

Computer programs and databases The LFDA was amended in 1991 to include protection of computer programs[92] and databases by assimilating operational software and application programs into the subject matter of literary works (LFDA Article 102). Computer programs that are intended to cause damage to other programs or equipment (e.g., viruses) are not protected, however. Patrimonial rights to computer programs include the right to authorize or prohibit the following acts: permanent or temporary reproduction of all or part of a computer program; translation, adaptation, arrangement, or any other

[90] LFDA Articles 94–100. Audiovisual works are understood to be works expressed by means of a series of associated images, with or without an accompanying sound track, that are made perceptible by technical devices producing the sensation of movement.

[91] The producer is the individual or corporation that takes the initiative, co-ordinates, and is responsible for the realization of the work or who sponsors it. LFDA Article 98.

[92] LFDA Articles 101–114. LFDA Article 101 defines a computer program as the original expression in any form, language, or code, of a set of instructions that, with a particular sequence, structure, and organization, is designed for a computer or other device to carry out a specific task or function.

modification of a program, and the reproduction of programs resulting therefrom; distribution of programs or of copies thereof, such as by leasing; and decompilation processes for re-engineering computer programs and disassembly (LFDA Article 106).

Even after the sale of computer programs or databases, copyrights to these products reserve the copyright owner's right to authorize or prohibit leasing or lending of such copies to third parties.[93] A legitimate user of a program is entitled to obtain authorized copies of the program when such copies are indispensable for utilization and are meant for safe-keeping, but copies must be destroyed when the term of authorization elapses.

Owners of the patrimonial rights to databases may authorize or prohibit the following acts: the permanent or temporary reproduction by any means of all or part of the database; the translation, adaptation, rearrangement, and any other modification of the database; distribution of the original or copies of the database; and public distribution of any derivative acts that may be authorized (LFDA Article 110). Databases fall under the category of compilations but the individual data and materials contained therein are not legally protected. Non-original databases are protected for a period of five years for the exclusive use of the person who creates the database (LFDA Article 108).

Right to privacy Mexican law is generally silent on the question of personal rights to privacy. Nevertheless, Congress did include in the LFDA provisions protecting the right to privacy and access to personal information contained in databases. Accordingly, when information concerns the personal lives of individuals, access to such information requires the authorization of the individual involved. Authorization is not required when information is used in investigations conducted by the authorities in charge of criminal prosecution or the administration of justice (prosecutors and judges); or when the information is contained in public archives or records (LFDA Article 148, sectons VI and VII).

The LFDA sets forth several different rules that apply specifically to performing or executing artists, book publishers, record or phonogram producers, videogram producers, and broadcasting organizations.

Performing artists Performing or executing artists[94] enjoy the right to recognition of their name in relation to their performance or the execution of their work, as well as the right to protest or object to any deformation, mutilation, or other attempt against their performance that may cause harm to their prestige or reputation (LFDA Articles 116–122). Additionally, these artists have the right to object to any publicly disseminated information regarding their performances or executions of artworks, the physical installations of their

[93] An exception exists when the sale of the software is an incidental part of another contractual relationship, such as a franchise agreement (LFDA Article 104).

[94] Performing or executing artists include actors, narrators, readers of prose or poetry, singers, musicians, dancers, or any other person who interprets or executes a literary or artistic work, or an expression of folklore, or who carries out an activity similar to these, even though no prepared text exists to guide its development. This does not include extras or understudies. LFDA Article 116.

performances or execution, and to reproduction of the physical installation of their executions and performances; however, these rights expire once the artist has authorized the incorporation of the act or performance into a visual, sound, or audio-visual installation or work. Protection of the artist is valid for fifty years as of the date a recording is first produced, the first performance or realization of works not recorded on a phonogram, or the first broadcast by radio, television, or any other means.

Book publishers The rights of the publisher of a book (*editorial*) differ from the rights held by authors, photographers, or others who create material published in book form. As already discussed, under Mexican law authors have both moral and patrimonial rights to their works. Book publishers, on the other hand, have rights over the editing, production, printing, distribution, commercialization, and reprinting of a work in accordance with the terms of contract between the publisher and the author. The author retains the right to make such corrections, amendments, additions, and improvements to his or her work as he or she considers appropriate before it goes to press.

In accordance with LFDA Article 125, book publishers are entitled to authorize or prohibit the first public distribution of the original version and distribution of each copy of their books, as well as the direct or indirect, total or partial reproduction of their books (subject to the rules on fair use, discussed below). They may also block the import of copies of their books made without their authorization. Book publishers also enjoy exclusive rights to the typographical characteristics and diagrams (tables, charts, and graphs) of each book insofar as they are original. Periodical publications enjoy the same protection. Protection remains in effect for a period of fifty years from the date of the first edition.

Sound recordings[95] Under LFDA Articles 129–194, producers of sound recordings have the right to: authorize or prohibit the direct or indirect, partial or total reproduction of their recordings, as well as direct or indirect exploitation thereof; to prohibit importation of copies of recordings made without the authorization of the producer; to authorize public distribution of the original and of every copy of the recording either by sale or by any other means of distribution including broadcast and signal transmission; to authorize or prohibit adaptation or transformation of the recording, before and after sale, provided that the owner of the patrimonial rights has not exclusively reserved such rights. This protection is valid for a term of fifty years as of the first recording of the sound.

Broadcasting Under LFDA Articles 139 to 146, broadcasting organizations[96] are entitled to authorize and prohibit the following acts: rebroadcast,

[95] Such recordings include any physical recording of sound, such as records, cassette tapes, compact discs, etc. *See* LFDA Article 129.

[96] A broadcasting organization is defined as the entity with the concession or permit to emit or broadcast sound, or visual signals, or a combination of both, that are perceptible to a plurality of receiving subjects. LFDA Article 139. Activities of broadcasters are regulated by the General Direction of Information of the Ministry of Government (*Dirección General de Información de la Secretaría de Gobernación*) pursuant to the Federal Law of Radio and Television (*Ley Federal de Radio y Televisión*) D.O. 19 Jan. 1960, as amended.

delayed broadcast, simultaneous and delayed broadcast, by cable or any other system; the physical recording, reproduction of the recording and public dissemination by any means that entail a for-profit venture. When someone unscrambles (decodes or deciphers) a coded (scrambled) programme-carrying satellite signal, receives and distributes a scrambled programme-carrying satellite signal that has been unlawfully unscrambled, or participates or aids in the manufacture, import, sale, leasing, or realization of any act that enables someone to have a device or system that is of primary utility in unscrambling a scrambled programme-carrying satellite signal, without authorization from the legitimate distributor, shall be liable to pay damages to the broadcasting organization. Radio broadcasting rights are valid for a period of twenty years from the date of the first broadcast or original transmission of the programme.

5.4. Limitations on Copyrights

The LFDA creates exceptions to copyrights in certain instances. The first category of exception involves works considered to be of public benefit, for which the State pre-empts the author's right to claim a copyright. The second category consists of works that do not require any authorization of the owner of patrimonial rights, nor payment of royalties and, therefore, use thereof is not considered a copyright infringement.

Works of 'public benefit' Certain literary or artistic works that are deemed necessary for the advancement of science, culture, or education in Mexico are considered to be of public benefit, and such works may therefore be reproduced without the express permission of the copyright holder (LFDA Article 147). If the Secretariat of Public Education (*Secretaría de Educación Pública*) considers a work to be of public benefit, it may authorize publication or translation of that work, even without the consent of the author of the work. This may occur if the author is unknown, or if the author denies authorization to publish the work without justification for the denial (LFDA Article 39). This does not preclude the author from filing a claim for and receiving compensation for the publication. The copyright regulations, or RLFDA, set forth the procedures for declaring material to be of public benefit, in proceedings before the *Instituto Nacional de Derechos de Autor*, in which the affected owner of the copyrights to a work has the opportunity to be heard in his or her own defence. The President of Mexico is responsible for issuing the Decree declaring the limitation on the patrimonial rights by virtue of a determination that such an act is of public benefit (LFDA Articles 38–43). Examples of the use of 'public benefit' include primary and secondary school textbooks that are distributed by a federal agency, the National Commission of Free Text Books (*Comisión Nacional de Libros de Textos Gratuitos*, or CONALITEG).

'Fair Use' As in the United States, Mexican copyright law includes certain 'fair use' exceptions that allow copyrighted works to be reproduced or displayed without the author's permission, and without the need to compensate

the copyright holder (LFDA Articles 148–151). LFDA Article 148 lists the following instances in which the exception applies: quoting of texts, provided that such quoting is not a simulated and substantial reproduction of the entire work; reproduction of articles, photographs, illustrations, and commentaries regarding current events, published by any means, provided that such reproduction has not been expressly prohibited by the owner; reproduction of parts of a work for review or critique and research; one-time or single-copy reproduction for personal and private use, in non-profit endeavours by educational institutions; single-copy reproduction by a library in order to preserve the work, when the work is out of print, not registered in the catalogue, or at risk of disappearing; reproduction in order to make a record for a judicial or administrative proceeding; and reproduction, dissemination, and distribution of works by means of drawings, paintings, photographs, and audio-visual means that are visible from public places.

Authorization by the owner of the copyright is also not required in any of the following instances: when using literary and artistic works in stores or establishments that are open to the public and that trade in copies of said works, provided that no admission is charged and that usage does not transcend the premises of the place of sale and the purpose of such use is to market or promote sales of the works; and temporary recording[97] of artistic or literary works, provided that broadcast takes place within the time agreed upon by the copyright owner and user, no transmission or broadcast takes place concomitantly or simultaneously, and only a single broadcast is made. Royalties are not required to be paid when a transmission is received by home radio or television receiving devices, the public is not charged for watching or listening to the transmission, and the receiver is a small-scale or minor user or a small business. Finally, the following acts are not considered infringements of the rights of artists, performers, or executing agents, producers of sound or video recordings, or broadcasting organizations: use of performances, sound or video recordings, or broadcasts when no direct economic benefit is pursued, when acts involve brief fragments for use in news reports on current events, for educational or scientific research purposes, or when such acts involve the limitations listed in the LFDA (LFDA Articles 149–151).

5.5. Registration of Copyrights

Registration is not required in order for literary and artistic works to be protected, although today most literary works are registered with the *Instituto Nacional de Derechos de Autor* (INDA). In the case of non-literary or artistic works, registration is mandatory in order for the author to be entitled to claim rights of protection. The Public Registry of Copyrights (*Registro Público del*

[97] Just one broadcast of the recording is authorized, and the recording must be destroyed after transmission. *See* Serrano Migallón, F., NUEVA LEY FEDERAL DE DERECHOS DE AUTOR (Mexico: Porrúa, 1998) at 169.

Derecho de Autor), an office of INDA, is responsible for registration, safeguarding, and enforcing the legal interests of authors, owners of related copyrights, and owners of the respective patrimonial rights and their assigns and successors in title.[98]

Registration of works may not be denied on the grounds of immorality, invasion of privacy, or disturbance of the peace, unless a court ruling so determines, nor can registration be denied for political, ideological, or religious reasons (LFDA Articles 165–166). Registration may only be denied for: works in the public domain; trade marks (unless they are artistic works), publicity or advertising campaigns and promotions; when a judicial or ministerial order includes a suspension of registration; and when acts that infringe the provisions of the LFDA or that fall outside the purview of the law are involved (LFDA Article 164).

5.6. Reservation of Rights to Exclusive Use

In addition to the rights of copyright holders already listed, Mexican law provides for the protection of certain rights to protect the exclusive use of titles, names, appellations, physical and psychological characteristics (including caricatures of human figures, fictitious or symbolic characters, persons, or groups) that are used in artistic activities, advertising, and marketing (LFDA Article 173). The right to exclusive use protects the marketing interests and goodwill associated with performing groups (e.g. Los Tigres del Norte), newspapers (e.g. Reforma), magazines (e.g. Proceso) or comic strips (e.g. 'La Chilindrina').[99]

[98] LFDA Articles 163–164. Not only are works registered in this office, but also articles of incorporation of collective bargaining associations (*sociedades de gestión colectiva*, discussed *infra*, at section 5.7) agreements reached between these associations and other foreign companies, acts pertaining to patrimonial rights, powers of attorney granted to the legal representatives of authors and owners of copyrights in order to be qualified to submit filings with the INDA, judgments in favour of collective bargaining associations, and agreements entered into by performers or artists for performances or works.

[99] One must distinguish between the content of the comic strip, and the character portrayed in it. According to LFDA Article 188, exclusive use of titles, names, etc, may *not* be reserved under the following circumstances: when they may be easily identified with or are similar to subjects of other reserved rights to exclusive use that have already been granted, or are in the process of registration, and may therefore lead to confusion (for example, the name *Procesos* may not be used because the magazine *Proceso* already exists); when they are of a generic nature and are meant to be used in isolated fashion (for example, the name *Diario*, which means daily newspaper); when they indicate sponsorship of an organization or institution without the authorization thereof; when they reproduce or imitate official signs, marks, or symbols; when they include the name, pseudonym, or image of any specific person without his or her consent, regardless of whether the name, pseudonym, or image is identical or similar to the point of being readily confused with other well known names, pseudonyms, or images; subtitles; graphic characteristics; legends, traditions, or events that are identified with the names that are characteristic of them (e.g. *Navidad* (Christmas)); isolated letters or numbers; translations into other languages, fanciful spelling variations or contrived constructions of non-reservable words; names of persons utilized in isolated fashion, except when such names are requested to be used as artistic names, caricatures of human figures, or fictitious or symbolic characters; and the names of countries, territorial divisions, the names of the native people from a particular place or derivations thereof used in isolated fashion.

Rights to exclusive use of such names, figures, etc., may be perfected by applying to the INDA for a certificate of registration. Once issued, the certificate guarantees the holder a reservation of rights to exclusive use for a period of one year from the date of issuance of the certificate, in the case of titles to publications, broadcasts, and periodicals, and for five years for all other categories (LFDA Articles 189–190). The validity of the protection may be renewed for periods of equal length, except in cases of advertising promotions, which expire at the end of their initial period of validity (LFDA Article 191). Termination of the reservation of rights to exclusive use may come about by annulment, cancellation, or expiration under the terms set forth in LFDA Articles 183–185.

5.7. Collective Bargaining Associations (*Sociedades de Gestión Colectiva*)

In Mexico, non-profit associations have been created to protect both national and foreign authors and owners of related rights, as well as to collect and distribute to the rightful individual any payment for royalties that may be generated from copyrights and related rights (LFDA Article 192). As a practical matter, these organizations, which are similar to the US-based organization ASCAP (American Society of Composers, Authors, and Publishers), protect the rights of their members by licensing and distributing royalties for public performances of their copyrighted works. Thirteen such organizations have been formed in Mexico.[100]

These associations are considered public interest entities and they require prior authorization from the INDA to operate.[101] The law grants these associations the right to perform several functions: to exercise patrimonial rights on behalf of their members, negotiate licences for use of the repertoires that are administered by them with users, and enter into contracts or agreements; to supervise the use of repertoires; to collect royalties and deliver them to the rightful owners, after deducting administrative expenses; to provide assistance to members; and to collect donations and accept inheritances and bequests. The

[100] They include the *Sociedad de Autores y Compositores de Música* (SACM) [Society of Authors and Composers of Music], the *Asociación Nacional de Intérpretes* (ANDI) [National Association of Performers], the *Sociedad General de Escritores de México* (SOGEM) [General Society of Writers of Mexico], the *Sociedad Mexicana de Ejecutantes de Música* (SOMEN) [Mexican Society of Music Performers], the *Sociedad de Autores de Obras Fotográficas* (SAOF) [Society of Authors of Photographic Works], the *Sociedad Mexicana de Artes Plásticas* (SOMART) [Mexican Society of Plastic Arts], the *Sociedad Mexicana de Caricaturistas* (SMC) [Mexican Society of Animators and Cartoonists], the *Sociedad Mexicana de Directores-Realizadores de Cine, Radio y Directores de Televisión*) [Mexican Society of Movie, Radio, and Television Directors], the *Sociedad Mexicana de Escenógrafos* [Mexican Society of Set Designers], the *Sociedad de Compositores de Música de Concierto de México* [Mexican Society of Composers of Concert Music] and the *Sociedad Mexicana de Historietistas* [Mexican Society of Writers of Comics]. *See* Rangel Medina, *supra* note 1 at 157. Other organizations include the *Sociedad Mexicana de Autores de las Artes Plásticas*, (SOMMAP) [Mexican Society of Authors of Plastic Arts], the *Centro Mexicano de Protección y Fomento a los Derechos de Autor* [Mexican Centre for the Protection and Promotion of Copyrights] and the *Sociedad de Autores de Programas de Computación* [Society of Authors of Computer Programs].

[101] Authorization must be published in the *Diario Oficial*.

obligations of these associations set forth by law include: intervening in the protection of the moral rights of their members; accepting the administration of any patrimonial rights that may be entrusted to them; negotiating the amount of royalty payments with users of their members' repertoires; filing annual reports to their membership on any business affairs that may be conducted by the association and on the amount and description of any financial operations that the association may carry out; delivering to copyright owners records of liquidations; and liquidating royalties and any interest that may have been generated for the person entitled to them.

5.8. Copyright Enforcement

There are two classes of copyright enforcement in Mexico: administrative enforcement, and private copyright enforcement. Administrative enforcement is carried out by the *Instituto Nacional del Derecho de Autor*, or INDA, an autonomous, quasi-independent agency (*órgano desconcentrado*) established under the Secretariat of Public Education (*Secretaría de Educación Pública*) and led by a Director General who is appointed by the President.[102] Private enforcement involves civil litigation brought by copyright owners or other interested parties.

As noted elsewhere, Mexico has been criticized in the past for lack of enforcement of intellectual property rights. As regards administrative enforcement of copyrights, Mexico has been wanting: it still ranks among the top countries of the world for copyright infringement, although the INDA is credited with improving enforcement.

5.8.1. Administrative Enforcement

The LFDA establishes a list of administrative copyright infringements that may be investigated and penalized by the INDA. Administrative infringements tend to involve matters in which the government protects the public interest. Administrative infringements include: when a publisher, impresario, producer, broadcasting organization, or licensee enters into a contract or agreement for the purpose of unlawfully transferring copyrights; when a licensee infringes the terms of a licence granted for reasons of public benefit; to falsely claim to be an association of collective bargaining (*sociedad de gestión colectiva*); when an association of collective bargaining does not provide information or reports

[102] The duties of INDA are to protect and promote copyrights and literary and artistic creations; to maintain the Public Registry of Copyrights (*Registro Público del Derecho de Autor*); to conduct investigations of alleged copyright infringements; to request that authorities perform inspections; to implement measures to prevent practices that infringe copyrights and related rights; and to enforce the rules set forth in the LFDA. The INDA is also responsible for the registration of copyrights; for the granting of reservations of rights to exclusive use; and for issuing administrative authorizations set forth in the law (e.g. use of public benefit, certification of associations of collective bargaining). Additionally, the Director General is in charge of investigations of infringements and application of administrative penalties.

that are requested by the INDA; failing to insert in a literary or artistic work any information that is required by law, or including information therein; publishing a work without including the name of the author, translator, compiler, arranger, or the person who adapted the work; publishing an official government literary or artistic work before the Federation, a state, or municipality has done so; fraudulently or deceitfully using a title in a work that may lead to confusion with a prior work; establishing, representing, publishing, disseminating, or utilizing a literary or artistic work in any way, without mentioning the community or ethnic group or region of the Republic that it is characteristic of; and any other infringements that may stem from interpretation of the LFDA and its regulations[103] (LFDA Article 229).

The above-mentioned offences may be penalized by fines that range from 1,000 to 15,000 times the minimum daily wage for the Federal District, which is currently equivalent to about $US4.35 (LFDA Article 230). Moreover, should the infringement persist, an additional fine of up to 500 days' minimum daily wage may be assessed. Offenders may challenge imposition of penalties by means of the remedy set forth in the Federal Law of Administrative Procedures (*Ley Federal de Procedimiento Administrativo*), discussed above in Chapter 9.

In addition to administrative infringements, the LFDA lays out several other administrative infractions of a commercial nature, which the Mexican Institute of Industrial Property (*Instituto Mexicano de la Propiedad Industrial*), or IMPI, is responsible for investigating. These offences consist of conduct intended to profit either directly or indirectly from protected material, such as public dissemination or use of a protected work without authorization of the owners of copyrights; using the image of a person without his or her authorization; producing, reproducing, storing, distributing, transporting, or marketing copies of protected works without authorization; marketing protected works that are mutilated, deformed, or modified without authorization; importing, selling, leasing or carrying out any act that enables someone to have a device or system whose purpose is to deactivate the electronic protection of computer programs; or using material to which the rights of exclusive use are reserved by someone else (LFDA Article 231). These offences may be penalized by fines that range from 500 to 10,000 times the minimum daily wage, according to the classification of each individual offence set forth in the Law (LFDA Article 232). Any challenge of penalties imposed is governed by the Law of Industrial Property (*Ley de Propiedad Industrial*), under LPI Articles 213–219.

5.8.2. Private Copyright Enforcement and Dispute Resolution

The LFDA also permits private parties to protect their copyright interests, either with or without the help of an administrative agency. The LFDA provides for

[103] The infringement established in the last clause appears to grant broad discretionary power to officials who interpret the LFDA, and the lack of clear limits on this discretion arguably makes the provision unconstitutional as a violation of Articles 14 and 16 of the Mexican Constitution, although this has not been tested in the courts.

three different ways of dealing with disputes that arise out of private copyright enforcement: settlement, arbitration, and judicial proceeding.

Settlement (*avenencia*) is an administrative proceeding conducted by the INDA to allow parties involved in a dispute over copyrights to reach a friendly out-of-court resolution of any dispute that may arise over the interpretation or application of the LFDA. In such a proceeding, both sides have the opportunity to be heard, but a settlement may only be reached if both parties are in agreement; the INDA's role is one of mediation, not judgment, and the INDA is precluded from issuing any opinion on the merits, substance, or facts of the case (LFDA Articles 217–218).

Arbitration[104] (*arbitraje*) of disputes may be held before a panel of three arbitrators, with each one of the two parties involved in the dispute appointing one arbitrator and the third arbitrator being appointed by the other two. The arbitrators must be selected from a pool of prospective arbitrators who appear on a list published by the INDA.[105] The arbitral award must be issued within seventy days of the date the arbitrators agree to hear the case.

Finally, if a dispute between a copyright holder and another party is not settled or decided by arbitration, the copyright holder may bring a civil action in the Mexican courts. LFDA Article 227 establishes that judicial proceedings regarding copyright law shall be the exclusive jurisdiction of the federal courts. The INDA shall be called as a party during the case, shall be made aware of any judgment regarding copyrights that is handed down by the court, and the court shall send copies to the INDA of any notice of judgment that may modify, assess a fine, terminate, or uphold copyrights, so that the respective entry may be entered into the Public Registry of Copyrights (*Registro Público de Derecho de Autor*).

5.8.3. *Criminal Enforcement of Copyright Law*

In addition to the offences listed in section 5.8.1 above, the following acts are considered criminal felonies, and are punishable by confinement of three to ten years in prison, and fines from 2,000 to 20,000 times the minimum daily wage: wilful production, reproduction, importation, storage, transportation, distribution, sale, or leasing of works or copies of works, sound or video recordings, or books protected by the LFDA, on a commercial scale and without authorization of the owner of the copyrights or related rights.[106]

[104] LFDA Articles 219–228 cover arbitration of copyright disputes, but these provisions must be applied in conjunction with the rules of arbitration established in Articles 1415–1463 of the Code of Commerce (*Código de Comercio*) and the applicable provisions of the Federal Code of Civil Procedure, as discussed in Chapter 18 above, Section 4.2.

[105] Under LFDA Article 221, this list is to be published in January of each year, in the *Diario Oficial de la Federación*, although to date the last list of arbitrators was published on 28 January 1999.

[106] Article 424*bis* of the Federal Criminal Code (*Código Penal Federal*), as amended D.O. 17 May 1999 and D.O. 6 Feb. 2002. The same sentencing range applies to anyone who knowingly contributes, or provides in any way, raw materials or components meant for production or reproduction of literary or artistic works, sound or video recordings, or books to which the paragraph in the text refers, and to anyone who engages in the manufacture for profit of deactivation devices for systems of computer program protection.

Lesser crimes include wilfully using protected copyright works for profit without authorization from the owner; speculating in free text books distributed by the Secretariat of Public Education (SEP); or arranging for the intentional overproduction of copies of a protected work beyond the amount authorized by the owner of the copyrights on the part of publishers, producers, or record companies.[107] Sentences for the commission of these offences range from six months to six years in prison and from 300 to 3,000 days' wages in fines.

Investigation of such offences is carried out by the INDA, and if sufficient grounds exist for prosecution the matter is referred to the local office of the federal prosecutor, or *Procuraduría General de la República* (PGR).

5.8.4. Conclusion: Efforts to Strengthen Copyright Protection

As the previous sections illustrate, Mexican copyright law contains a full array of enforcement procedures for ensuring the rights of copyright holders. This is not to say, however, that all these procedures have been vigorously employed. Sales of counterfeit materials, such as 'pirated' music cassettes or CDs, have been commonplace in Mexico's streets and markets for many years, and until recently the authorities ignored these violations. To deal with this problem, and to help strengthen copyright enforcement, in 1999 the Mexican Congress introduced reforms of the Federal Criminal Code (*Código Penal Federal*) that make it a crime for anyone to wilfully sell to a final consumer on roads or highways or in public places, for purposes of commercial speculation, copies of literary and artistic works, sound or video recordings, or books, without the authorization of the owner of the copyright or of the related rights. The penalty in this instance ranges from six months to six years in prison, and a fine of 1,000 to 30,000 days' minimum daily wage.[108] The effectiveness of this provision is uncertain, especially in the many instances in which the sales are carried out by unemployed persons who, for lack of more meaningful employment, work in the 'informal' sector. The law may become effective in prosecuting organized criminal enterprises involved in such commerce, although it is still too early to make an assessment of its effectiveness.

[107] *Código Penal Federal*, Article 424.
[108] Article 424*ter* of the Federal Criminal Code, added D.O. 2 Feb. 2002.

22

Conflict of Laws

1. Introduction

In the United States, the term 'conflicts of law' refers to subjects that deal with the jurisdiction of courts to adjudicate disputes; to the choice of the particular law applicable to a dispute; and to the judicial enforcement of foreign judgments, among other matters. In Mexico, as in most other countries, these subjects are identified by the phrase 'private international law' (*derecho internacional privado*). This Chapter deals with three important subjects included under this rubric: choice of law, jurisdiction to adjudicate, and enforcement of foreign judgments.

Conflict of laws in Mexico were traditionally decided according to strictly territorial principles: if a person or matter was deemed to be 'present' in Mexican territory, then Mexican courts would have jurisdiction and Mexican laws would apply, and this could not be changed by the parties or supplanted by other countries' laws or interests. After the Mexican Revolution, Mexican conflicts rules based on territorialism were supported by nationalistic sentiments, as post-revolutionary *caudillos* (local political bosses) were eager to consolidate their power and protect the country from outside influence. This adherence to territorialism was reinforced by the Mexican Constitution of 1917, which included in Article 121 an extensive 'full faith and credit' principle that was intended to settle jurisdictional conflicts within Mexico arising from the application of the laws of the different states. This principle drew on elements of Article VI of the US Constitution, but was more grounded in specific territorial principles than its US counterpart.[1] Territorialism was also reflected in

[1] Article 121 of the Mexican Constitution reads as follows:
In every State of the Federation, full faith and credit shall be given to public acts, records and judicial proceedings of all other states. The Congress of the Union, by means of laws applying to the general population, shall prescribe how such acts, records and proceedings shall be proven, their effects being subject to the following rules:

I. The laws of a State shall only have an effect in their own territory and, consequently, may not be binding outside it;
II. Personal and real property shall be governed by the law of their location;
III. Judgments issued by the courts of one State over rights *in rem* or to real property located in other States, shall only have force of a final judgment in the latter state when its own laws so provide.

Judgments regarding personal rights may only be enforced in another State when the losing party has expressly submitted to the State, or by reason of his or her domicile, to the justice system that issued them the judgments, provided that the person has been personally summoned to appear in court;

the choice of law and jurisdictional rules written into the Mexican substantive and procedural codes which controlled civil and criminal procedure.

As the twentieth century drew to a close Mexico began a new period of economic and political opening up (*apertura*).[2] In 1987 and 1988 Mexican substantive and procedural codes were amended to discard the most exaggerated elements of Mexican territorialism; these changes are discussed in more detail below. To date, relatively few Mexican courts have been called upon to apply these rules, and given the strong adherence to territorial theories of jurisdiction, it may take some time before Mexican judges begin to interpret and apply the new rules in an expansive fashion by accepting the application of foreign law or the jurisdiction of foreign courts.

2. Choice of Law Principles

2.1. Background

While Article 121 of the Constitution sets forth the general rules for resolution of conflicts of law within Mexico, these rules lack implementing legislation; for this reason, Article 121 has seldom been cited by Mexican courts. A general lack of concern over conflicts of law may have been due in part to the undeveloped nature of tort litigation in Mexico:[3] in the United States, many conflicts of law rules have been worked out in the context of extensive tort and products liability litigation; in Mexico, the relative unimportance of both has narrowed the terrain for jurisdictional conflicts.

In the absence of a comprehensive 'Law of Conflicts of Law', the CCDF, and now the Federal Civil Code, served as the closest thing to a comprehensive set of conflicts rules. The conflicts rules exemplified in Mexico's civil codes can be divided into two phases of development: the traditional territorial phase, which held sway until the late 1980s, and the modern approach to conflicts, exemplified by reforms to the civil and procedural codes (CCDF, CPCDF, and CFPC) in 1987 and 1988.

At the outset, it is important to note that under the Mexican civil codes, separate choice of law rules apply to persons (*personas físicas*) and to legal entities (*personas morales*). Consequently, we treat these two subjects separately.

IV. Legal acts affecting marital status that conform to the laws of one state shall be valid in the others; and
V. Professional degrees issued by the authorities of one State, shall be respected in other states and subject to their laws.

Article IV Section 1 of the US Constitution states: 'Full faith and credit shall be given in each state to the public acts, records and judicial proceedings of every other state. And the Congress may by general laws prescribe the manner in which such acts, records, and proceedings shall be proved, and the effect thereof.'

[2] Discussion of economic *apertura* can be found in Chapter 12 above. Mexico's political opening up is discussed in Chapters 1 and 5 above.

[3] *See* Chapter 17 above, Section 6.

2.2. Choice of Law Rules Applicable under the Mexican Civil Codes Prior to Reforms in 1987 and 2000

A relative lack of interest in developing conflicts of law rules in Mexico can be understood in the context of a country in which centralism dictated a pull towards uniformity of the law. Ever since the development in Mexico City of the first Civil Code of Mexico in 1870, the states have tended to adopt virtually verbatim the civil code rules developed in the capital.[4] Although the 1932 Civil Code of the Federal District (CCDF) was applicable only to local matters in the Federal District and to federal matters nationally, it served as a model for state civil codes throughout the country. As a consequence, the territorial approach of the 1932 CCDF is reflected in the state civil codes. Such uniformity also applied in commercial law, thanks to a constitutional amendment in 1883, by which Congress made commercial law a matter of exclusive federal jurisdiction.[5] One result of the relative uniformity of Mexican private law and the centralization of business law was to reduce the incentive towards forum shopping, which could give rise to conflicts of law.

The choice of law rules of the original CCDF of 1932 were contained in Article 12.[6] Article 12 followed a strict territorialist approach, requiring that Mexican laws be applied to all persons found within Mexican territory, whether the persons are Mexican or foreign citizens, and whether their presence is permanent or transient. Such a nationalistic, territorial approach was not surprising in the period after the Mexican Revolution, when the leadership was intent upon resisting undue foreign influence. As the end of the twentieth century drew near, however, it became apparent that the simplistic, territorial approach was increasingly out of step with the needs of a modern economy. As a result, the rules surrounding conflicts of law in Mexico were amended, to internationalize the legal system and incorporate more modern conflict of laws principles.

[4] *See* Chapter 14 above, Section 4.2. As explained there, the 1932 Civil Code of the Federal District (CCDF) originally applied to federal matters throughout the Republic. In May 2000 the CCDF was amended by the Legislative Assembly of the Federal District and lost its character as supplementary law in federal matters throughout the country. Shortly thereafter, Congress adopted a separate Federal Civil Code (FCC), based verbatim on the original CCDF, to apply to federal matters generally.

[5] *See* Chapter 18 above, text accompanying note 2. In 1889 Congress adopted the Commercial Code that is still in force today. Article 2 of the Commercial Code originally stated that in the absence of any provisions in this Code, 'those [codes] of local jurisdictions [i.e. the state civil codes] shall be applicable to acts of commerce . . . ', as supplementary rules. The Mexican Congress, to ensure complete uniformity, decided in 2000 (D.O. 28 May 2000) to require that the 1932 CCDF, rather than the state civil codes, be of supplemental application for the entire Republic in all federal matters, including commercial law. As a result, Article 2 of the Commercial Code now states that 'in the absence of provisions in this code of law and other commercial laws, local law contained in the Civil Code applicable to federal matters [i.e. the CCDF] shall be applicable to acts of commerce'.

[6] CCDF Article 13, even prior to the reforms of 1987 and 2000, stated that the form of acts that have legal effect shall be governed by the place where the act is concluded.

2.3. Choice of Law Rules under Current Mexican Civil Codes

Starting in 1975, a group of Mexican experts selected by the Secretariat of Foreign Relations (SRE) began attending the OAS-sponsored Inter-American Specialized Conferences on Private International Law (CIDIP, from the Spanish initials), with the goal of modernizing Mexico's rules concerning choice of law and jurisdiction. Armed with principles gleaned from these conferences, the experts organized national seminars on private international law, which led to proposals to amend Mexican laws. As a result, beginning in 1987, a series of reforms were proposed to the Civil Code for the Federal District (and federal territories) (CCDF) to modernize the choice of law rules applicable in Mexico.[7] Simultaneously, reforms were made to the Code of Civil Procedure for the Federal District,[8] to the Federal Code of Civil Procedure,[9] and to the Commercial Code,[10] to modernize the jurisdictional rules and promote acceptance of commercial arbitration and international judicial cooperation.

The 1988 reforms to the Civil Code for the Federal District had the effect of softening the rigid territorialism of the 1932 CCDF. Article 12, referred to above, was amended to read as follows:

> Article 12. Mexican laws apply to all persons within the Republic, as well as to acts and events that take place within Mexican territory or under its jurisdiction, and to those persons who submit themselves [or their acts] thereto, *unless [Mexican] law provides for the application of a foreign law, or the application of foreign law is otherwise provided by treaties or conventions to which Mexico is a party* (emphasis added).

The addition to Article 12, the words emphasized above in the 1988 reforms specifically authorized Mexican courts to apply foreign law where appropriate: a major departure from rigid territorialism. It is important to note, however, that the statement in Article 12 'unless [Mexican] law provides for the application of a foreign law' is still highly restrictive. Under the civil law tradition, judges are not expected to invent rules, whether of a substantive or a procedural nature. Therefore, in the absence of an applicable treaty, a Mexican judge will still refuse to apply foreign law unless a specific Mexican law provides therefor; the judge is not allowed to invent choice of law rules that point to application of the foreign law. Examples of such rules are not copious, but they do exist.[11]

[7] D.O. 7 Jan. 1988, amending Articles 12–15 of the CCDF.

[8] D.O. 7 Jan. 1988, adding Title Seven, Chapter Five, Section Four, to the Code of Civil Procedure for the Federal District (CPCDF), Articles 599–603, establishing new rules on enforcement of judgments. The reform also added a new Chapter Six to the CPCDF on international judicial co-operation (Articles 604–608).

[9] D.O. 7 Jan. 1988, amending the Federal Code of Civil Procedure (CFPC), adding Book Four, on international judicial co-operation (Articles 543–577).

[10] D.O. 4 Jan. 1989, adding Articles 1415–1463 to the Commercial Code ('On commercial arbitration').

[11] *See* e.g. FCC Article 13, para. IV (application of the law of the place of execution of legal acts); FCC Article 1593 (application of foreign law to wills made in foreign territory); FCC Article 2736 (law of the place of incorporation applicable in determining existence, capacity, dissolution, etc., of a corporation).

In addition, a new Article 13 was added to the CCDF in 1988. This Article, adopted almost verbatim in the Federal Civil Code of 2000, for the first time created specific choice of law rules which, while still general, provide at least some guidance to Mexican courts in choosing the law applicable to disputes between parties in different jurisdictions. As amended in 1988, CCDF Article 13 read as follows.

Article 13. The choice of applicable law shall be made in accordance with the following rules:

I. Legal acts generated within the Mexican states [*entidades*, including the Federal District], or within any foreign state in accordance with its laws, shall be recognized as valid.

II. The status and legal capacity of persons shall be governed by the laws of their place of domicile.

III. The creation, type of tenure, and termination of estates in realty, as well as leasing agreements and rental contracts of realty or personal property, shall be governed by the laws of the place where they are located, regardless of the foreign nationality of their holders or owners.

IV. The formalities required of legal acts shall be governed by the laws of the place where they are executed. However, when such acts produce effects within the Federal District, they may be subjected to the formalities prescribed in this Code.

V. Except as provided in the preceding paragraphs, the legal consequences of acts and contracts shall be governed by the laws of the place of their performance, unless the parties have validly designated a different law.

The rules to be followed by a court in actually applying foreign law were contained in a new Article 14 of the 1988 reforms to the CCDF.

Article 14. In the application of foreign law, the following rules shall be observed:

I. Foreign law shall be applied in the same manner as a foreign judge would apply the law, for which purpose the [local] judge shall take notice of all necessary information regarding the text, effectiveness, meaning, and scope of the foreign law.

II. Foreign substantive law shall be applied unless, by reason of the special circumstances of the case, the conflict of laws rules of the foreign state should be taken into account, in exceptional cases, thus making the substantive laws of Mexico or a third party state applicable.

III. The application of foreign law shall not be prevented because Mexican law does not provide for the same institutions or procedures as required for application of the foreign institution, if there are analogous institutions or procedures available [under Mexican law].

IV. Antecedent, preliminary, or incidental issues that may arise in connection with the main issue shall not necessarily be resolved in accordance with the law applicable to the latter.

V. When different aspects of the same legal relationship are governed by different laws, such laws shall be applied harmoniously with the aim of achieving the intended purposes of each of these laws. Problems arising from the simultaneous application of

> different laws shall be resolved by taking into account equitable principles regarding the specific case.
>
> The provisions of this Article shall [also] apply if the laws of a different Mexican state are applicable.

Finally, FCC Article 15 provided grounds, common in most jurisdictions, on which foreign law should not be applied for the purpose of evading fundamental principles of Mexican law, or if such application would be contrary to public policy.

The rules summarized above were those applicable in the Federal District until May 2000. In that year, as explained elsewhere,[12] the Legislative Assembly for the Federal District adopted the Civil Code for the Federal District, applicable to local matters within the Federal District. In the same month the federal Congress adopted the current Federal Civil Code, applicable to federal matters throughout Mexico, which virtually copied the former CCDF, as amended in 1987. The *new* CCDF, however, as adopted by the Legislative Assembly, included certain departures from the liberalized rules that now apply under the FCC.

Choice of law rules in regards to the status of legal entities such as corporations differ from those just described for persons. The choice of law rules applicable to corporations are, in fact, much simpler. For one thing, the rules of the current FCC and CCDF are the same. Article 28 of both the FCC and CCDF states that *personas morales* (i.e. legal entities, such as corporations) shall be governed by the corresponding laws (of their place of incorporation), and by their articles and rules. (See also FCC and CCDF Article 2736, applicable to foreign corporations.)

2.3.1. Choice of Law Rules for the Federal District under the CCDF of 2000

The CCDF of 2000 added a number of provisions in substantive areas of family law that deviated from the 1932 CCDF, as amended. Insofar as choice of law rules are concerned, the major departure from the previous CCDF, and from the current FCC, was a reversion to the strictly territorial rule of Article 32 of the original CCDF: 'Article 12. The laws of the Federal District shall apply to all persons present within its territory, whether citizens or foreigners.' In other words, the CCDF excises the language of FCC Article 12 that opens the way for the application of foreign law, and in theory at least, leaves no possibility for the application of foreign law to a person present in the Federal District. In addition, CCDF Article 13, section II, states that the marital status and capacity of persons [present within the Federal District] shall be governed by the laws applicable in the Federal District.

These reforms represent an attempt by the government of the Federal District, dominated by populist politicians, to assert control over the status of persons within the largest population centre of Mexico.

[12] *See* Chapter 14 above, at text accompanying notes 30–34.

2.4. Choice of Law Rules in Mexican Commercial Law

Book Five (*Libro Quinto*) of the Mexican Commercial Code (Articles 1049–1463) sets forth numerous procedural rules to be followed by state and federal courts in commercial disputes. However, the Commercial Code does not have specific choice of law rules. (Commercial law is uniform by virtue of being exclusively federal in nature, and therefore the need for choice of law rules is diminished within Mexico.) Since the Federal Civil Code (FCC) serves as the source of supplementary rules for the Commercial Code,[13] Articles 12–15 of the FCC, discussed above, serve as the applicable choice of law rules for commercial matters.

2.5. International Treaties and Applicable Law

Since 1978, Mexico has become a party to more than sixty international conventions which directly or indirectly affect choice of law.[14] Like the United States, Mexico is also a party to the United Nations Convention on Contracts for the International Sale of Goods (CISG),[15] which establishes that rules of contract law apply automatically to contracts for the sale of goods between a Mexican party and a party from another contracting state.

2.5.1. The Status of International Law before Domestic Courts

Unlike the United States, which follows a dualistic approach to the recognition of international law by domestic courts, Mexican conflicts of law theory follows the monistic approach to international law:[16] treaties to which Mexico is a party automatically become part of the supreme law of the land.[17] Consequently, treaties are directly applicable within the domestic legal system, even when their content deals with subjects that are assigned to the Mexican states under the savings clause, Article 124 of the Mexican Constitution.[18] The monistic theory of international law presents problems when an international treaty requires

[13] *See* Chapter 18 above, at text following note 3.

[14] For a review of the conventions ratified by Mexico, *see*: Pereznieto Castro, Leonel, Derecho Internacional Privado, Parte General (Mexico: Oxford University Press, 7th ed., 1998) at 274 *et seq.*

[15] D.O. 22 Feb. 1988.

[16] *Dualism* refers to the recognition that the international and domestic legal systems exist in two separate spheres, and that international law must somehow become incorporated into domestic law to have effect within a country (as opposed to having effects between nations). *Monism* refers to the recognition that international and domestic laws are part of a single legal system, and as a result, there is no requirement that international law be incorporated into domestic law. *See generally* Brownlie, I., Principles of Public International Law (New York: Oxford University Press, 4th ed., 1990) at xxx; Verdross, Derecho Internacional Público (Madrid: Aguilar, 1967) at 36 *et seq.*

For US rules on the recognition of treaties in domestic law, and on the rules of incorporation of self-executing and non-self-executing treaties into domestic law, *see* Restatement (Third) of Foreign Relations Law of The United States (Philadelphia, Pa: American Law Institute, 1987) Section 111.

[17] Mexican Constitution, Article 133.

[18] Ortiz Ahlf, L., and Vázquez Pando, F., Aspectos Jurídicos del Tratado de Libre Comercio de América del Norte y sus Acuerdos Paralelos (Mexico: Themis, 2nd ed., 1998) at 23 *et seq.*

contracting states to adopt implementing legislation and Mexico has failed to do so. For instance, in 1994 Mexico adopted the Hague Convention on Child Abduction. However, since Mexico has never adopted implementing legislation, Mexican courts have failed to apply the Convention, despite hundreds of cases in which a child has been brought to Mexico (in many instances from the United States) without the consent of the parent who is a resident of another country.

Evidence of the respect shown for international law in Mexico can be found in two recent Supreme Court opinions. In isolated cases (*tesis*) decided in 1999[19] and 2001,[20] the Supreme Court held that the correct hierarchy of Mexican law places treaties above domestic laws, including laws adopted after a treaty enters into force; only the Mexican Constitution takes precedence over treaties. The full effect of this opinion is as yet uncertain,[21] but it appears to be consonant with the *apertura*, or increased openness to external influence, that has been taking place in Mexican public law.[22] Coupled with the Supreme Court's recognition that the federal executive, with advice of the Senate, may enter into treaties that deal with subjects assigned to the states under the Constitution,[23] the potential impact of international treaties on Mexican domestic law is significant.

Despite the Supreme Court's acceptance of the primacy of international law, many Mexican judges, like their counterparts in the United States, are not well versed either in conflicts of law principles or in the rules of international treaties, and they may ignore the applicability of an international convention if it is not brought to their attention by counsel for the parties.

2.5.2. *NAFTA and Choice of Law*

NAFTA, an agreement between governments, has little direct application to conflicts of law issues. It does, however, include several provisions that underscore the precedence of national laws in subject matters covered by NAFTA.[24] By its own

[19] SJF, 9a, Tercera Parte, T. X, Tesis aislada LXXVII-99, p. 46, Nov. 1999. Previously, the Supreme Court gave equal weight to treaties or domestic laws, applying the 'last in time' test used in the United States to settle conflicts. *See* vol. XCVIII, third part, at 61. On the US rule of 'last in time', *see* Rotunda, R. and Novak, J., TREATISE ON CONSTITUTIONAL LAW: SUBSTANCE AND PROCEDURE (St. Paul, Minn: West Group, 3rd ed., 1999) at 581–585.

[20] SJF, 9a, T. LXXVIII (Amparo en revisión 2119/99). This decision is discussed in: Pereznieto, L., 'SUPREMACÍA DE LA CONSTITUCIÓN Y DE LOS TRATADOS INTERNACIONALES EN MÉXICO', in EL FORO no. 1, 2001, at 245.

[21] *See* e.g. Siqueiros, J.L., 'Tratados internacionales se ubican jerárquicamente por encima de las leyes federales y en un segundo plano respecto de la Constitución Federal', in REVISTA MEXICANA DE DERECHO INTERNACIONAL PRIVADO, no 8, Apr. 2000, at 111 *et seq.*

[22] *See also* Amparo en revisión 140/2002, Quejoso, Ricardo Miguel Cavallo, in which a criminal judge in the Federal District granted extradition of a former Argentine military officer accused of a crime in Spain (defendant accused of responsibility in the disappearance and torture of political prisoners in Argentina) in response to a request by letters rogatory from the Spanish Court, even though the statute of limitations of the crime attributed to the alleged convict had lapsed, and even though the Mexican Constitution establishes that criminal laws must be strictly enforced, including statutes of limitations.

[23] *See supra*, note 11.

[24] *See*, for instance, the following provisions of NAFTA chapter 7B (Sanitary and Phytosanitary Provisions), Articles 712.2 and 713.3; chapter 17 (Intellectual Property), Article 1702. *See also* the

provisions, NAFTA declares that private parties do not have standing to assert the rights contained in the NAFTA Agreement, although private parties do have rights under the dispute settlement procedures contained in chapters 11 (Investment), 14 (Financial Services) and 19 (Antidumping and Countervailing Duties). These procedures give private parties access to international dispute settlement facilities (ad hoc arbitral panels).[25] The panels themselves are expected to apply national laws, in the same way that a domestic court would apply the law, and NAFTA itself gives no guidance as to the choice of law rules to be applied by panels.

3. Jurisdiction to Adjudicate

The thirty-one Mexican states and the Federal District have the power to adopt their own civil and criminal codes, as well as to establish their own rules of judicial procedure, including judicial jurisdiction. The civil and criminal codes for the Federal District have served as a model for state codes, as have the Federal Code of Civil Procedure[26] and the Federal Code of Criminal Procedure.[27] Uniformity in the rules of judicial jurisdiction relating to commercial matters may also be attributed to the fact that commercial law is exclusively a federal matter; thus, while both state and federal courts have concurrent jurisdiction over cases that involve the application of commercial law,[28] in commercial litigation state courts are required to apply jurisdictional rules contained in the Commercial Code, or CC (see e.g. CC Articles 1090–1121).[29] CC Articles 1092 and 1094 provide the basis for the courts to accept jurisdiction based on the parties' selection of the forum (choice of law clause).

Since the state procedural codes[30] were modelled on the Federal Code of Civil Procedure (*Código Federal de Procedimientos Civiles*, or CFPC) this Chapter focuses on the federal model.[31] Both state and federal theories of jurisdiction

North American Agreement on Environmental Co-Operation, Article 3; and the North American Agreement on Labour Co-Operation, Article 2. Agreements available at www. sice.oas.org (site visited Jan. 2004).

[25] On dispute settlement under NAFTA, *see* Coe, J., 'Taking Stock of NAFTA Chapter 11 in its tenth year: An interim sketch of selected themes, issues and methods', 36 *Vand. J. Transnat'l Law* 1381 (2003).

[26] *See* Chapter 10 above, text accompanying note 6.

[27] *See* Chapter 11 above, text accompanying notes 62–63.

[28] On the application of commercial law, *see* Chapter 18 above, at text accompanying notes 3 and 92, and section 4.

[29] On commercial procedure generally, *see* Chapter 18 above, Section 4. *See also* Arellano García, Carlos, Practica Forense Mercantil (Mexico: Porrúa, 13th ed., 1998); Castillo Lara, Eduardo, Juicios Mercantiles (Mexico: Oxford University Press, 2004). In commercial cases brought before a state court, the court will first apply any procedural rules specifically contained in the Commercial Code, and will in addition apply the state code of civil procedure, if they are not in conflict with the former. In case of conflict, the rules of the Commercial Code prevail.

[30] State procedural codes may be found at www.juridicas.unam.mx, at 'Legislación de Entidades Federativas' (site visited Jan. 2004).

[31] *See generally* Pereznieto Castro, *supra* note 14 at 189 *et seq*; Pereznieto Castro L., and Silva Silva, J., Derecho Internacional Privado, Parte Especial (Mexico: Oxford University Press, 2000).

are founded on concepts common to the civil law tradition,[32] as discussed in the following section.

3.1. Historical Background

Jurisdictional concepts in the United States have been determined primarily by judicial opinions, especially those of the United States Supreme Court, which has developed jurisdictional tests in interpretation of the due process clause of the US Constitution. By contrast, as discussed in Chapter 3 above, the ability of judges in the civil law tradition to create rules, even rules of interpretation, is severely limited. Even in cases in which a particular code or law does not resolve an issue in question, judges are reluctant to invent rules, preferring instead to apply a law or code by analogy in order to resolve a problem.[33]

Jurisdiction under the civil law tradition may be assumed only to the extent that a law specifically authorizes the exercise of jurisdiction by the particular court in the case before it. Jurisdictional rules, like rules of procedure, must be strictly followed, and judges are considered to possess very little flexibility or discretion in the application of the rules. Thus, the CFPC, as well as the state procedural codes, contain a list of requirements that must be followed by the judge in assuming jurisdiction.[34]

Common law jurisdictional concepts were inherited from a traditional British society composed of small communities, one that prized practical and swift conflict resolution by judges who possessed considerable authority to interpret the law and exercise their jurisdiction. The roots of the civil law, on the other hand, lie in Roman public law, in which the State (Roman Empire) played an omnipresent role. As a consequence, the court system in the Roman Empire developed a high degree of formalism, the product of an ever-growing state bureaucracy and the desire to prevent judges, who served at the pleasure of political elites, from exercising authority unconstrained by political power.[35]

The other major influence on Mexican concepts of conflicts of law was Spanish procedural law, which largely replicated the formalistic nature of Roman Law.[36] In addition to being charged with the evangelization of the indigenous populations, the Spanish *conquistadores* were expected to administer the Crown's justice in New Spain. The Spanish system of colonial justice was founded on territorial power as the dominant theoretical construct, and this carried over into Mexico after independence.

[32] On concepts of jurisdiction under the civil law tradition, *see generally* Virgós Soriauo, M., DERECHO PROCESAL CIVIL INTERNACIONAL: LITIGACIÓN INTERNACIONAL (Madrid: Civitas, 2000).

[33] Beginning with the Second Restatement of Conflicts of Laws (1971) Article 6 established an ample list (actually called a 'laundry list') of standards under which judges may take on jurisdiction and can use to decide with broad discretion. Cramton, Curie, Kay, and Kramer CONFLICTS OF LAWS (St Paul, Minn: West Group, 1993), at 117 *et seq.*

[34] CFPC Articles 18–38.

[35] *See generally* Lewald, H., 'Conflicts de lois dans le monde grec et romain', in REVUE CRITIQUE DE DROIT INTERNATIONAL PRIVÉ, 1969, at 419.

[36] Gómez Lara, C., TEORÍA GENERAL DEL PROCESO (Mexico: Oxford University Press, 1995) at 243 *et seq.*

3.2. Rules Governing Jurisdiction to Adjudicate

Under common law theories used in the United States, the power of a court to judge a dispute is divided into two elements: *subject matter jurisdiction* (the power to decide the particular type of dispute that is before the court), and *jurisdiction over the parties* (the power to judge a dispute involving the particular litigants who are before the court). (For the purposes of this Chapter, we often use the common law dichotomy to describe Mexican rules.) Mexican legal theory does not employ such a distinction. In Mexican law: *competencia* refers to the power of the court to assert jurisdiction over both the parties *and* the subject matter of the dispute before it.[37] *Competencia* is determined in accordance with the Organic Law of the Judicial Power applicable to the particular court in question, as well as with specialized laws, such as the Commercial Code (Articles 1090–1121). Rules relating to federal court jurisdiction are covered by the Federal Code of Civil Procedure (*Código Federal de Procedimientos Civiles*).[38]

In Mexico, as in the United States, a judge's assertion of jurisdiction over the parties and over the subject matter of a dispute is subject to constitutional limitations. The US Supreme Court has developed a number of specific rules, or analytical tests, that govern the exercise of jurisdiction by state and federal courts, pursuant to the Supreme Court's broad power to ensure compliance with the due process clause of the US Constitution. In Mexico, this broad power of oversight of due process is carried out by means of the *amparo* doctrine: if a Mexican court asserts jurisdiction that is not in accordance with the rules laid down in a procedural law and applied by a judge, the decision may be challenged in several ways. First, a party may contest jurisdiction initiating a *recurso por inhibitoria* with a court that has jurisdiction over the matter under dispute, requesting that court to notify another court that the latter lacks jurisdiction in the matter. Second, a party who contests jurisdiction of a court may file a *recurso por declinatoria* directly with the court in question, asking the court to recognize lack of jurisdiction and to refer the matter to a court of competent jurisdiction (see CFPC Article 34). Finally, if all else fails, a party may contest jurisdiction by filing an *amparo* action (*amparo directo*) with the appropriate collegiate appellate court, asserting that the due process clause of Article 14 of the Mexican Constitution has been violated.[39]

One major difference between US and Mexican Supreme Court analysis consists of the tendency of US courts to adopt flexible rules that involve the

[37] In Mexico, two terms are used to refer to judicial power. *Competencia*, the most commonly used term, refers to the authority of a specific judge to administer justice in a particular case, and is tantamount to the way jurisdiction is generally used by US conflicts authorities. *Jurisdicción* is used more narrowly in Mexico to refer to the geographical demarcation of a court's power. Both concepts, *competencia* and *jurisdicción*, are included in the US term 'judicial jurisdiction', which is defined as 'the power and authority of a court that binds the parties to any matter property brought before it' (Black's Law Dictionary (St. Paul, Minn: West Group, 7th ed., 1999).

[38] D.O. 24 Feb. 1943, as amended.

[39] On *amparo directo*, *see* Chapter 8 above, text accompanying notes 34–35.

balancing of numerous factors, including policy implications of the court's decision. Mexican judges, in line with the civil law tradition, abjure flexibility and detailed policy analysis in favour of a more rigorous adherence to the apparent meaning of the applicable specific code provision.

3.2.1. *Jurisdiction over the Parties*[40]

The federal rules governing jurisdiction over the parties, and over the subject matter, are set forth in Articles 23–38 of the CFPC. Even though the CFPC is a federal code, it has served as a model for state procedural codes,[41] and therefore the rules summarized below are generally followed by state courts. In addition, CFPC Articles 30–33 set forth very basic rules concerning the allocation of concurrent jurisdiction between federal and state courts, and between courts of two or more states.

The rules of jurisdiction set forth in CFPC Articles 23–29 are highly territorial in nature. The most important instances in which a federal court located in a particular territory has jurisdiction over the parties and the subject matter are the following:

(i) where real or personal property that is the subject of the dispute is located within the territorial jurisdiction assigned to that federal court (CFPC Article 24, section III);[42]

(ii) where a debtor is domiciled within the territory assigned to the federal court, whether the debt is based on real property or is a personal debt, including marital property (CFPC Article 24, section IV);

(iii) cases in which the parties consent to the jurisdiction of the court, either through a choice of forum clause (discussed below, in section 3.2.3) or because the parties have agreed to enforce an obligation within the court's jurisdiction (CFPC Article 24, section II);[43]

(iv) in bankruptcy cases, the court of the domicile of the debtor has jurisdiction to hear the matter. All creditors, therefore, must appear before this court in order to make their claims known in one centralized jurisdiction (CFPC Article 24, section V);

[40] *See generally* Pereznieto Castro, *supra* note 14 at 191 *et seq.*

[41] State procedural codes can be found at www.juridicas.unam.mx, 'Legislación y Jurisprudencia' (site visited Jan. 2004).

[42] Certain actions involving real property may be filed by a single party and do not require the presence of a defendant or opposing party. One of the most common actions of this type is a 'survey and demarcation of land', (*apeo y deslinde*), by which a court confirms or modifies the measurements and limits of a parcel of land. In the beach resort areas of Mexico land boundaries contained in contracts of sale or other documents are often faulty and do not match the measurements on record at the public registry. In some instances, actions of *apeo y deslinde* may be brought by adjoining landowners to delay construction and force a settlement of a property dispute. To avoid delays, the developer of the disputed property may be forced to enter into a settlement agreement in order to continue construction.

[43] CFPC Article 24, section II recognizes the jurisdiction of a court in '[t]he place agreed by the parties for the enforcement of an obligation'. This language may be interpreted as authorizing the recognition of choice of forum clauses.

(v) in cases involving inheritance, the court of the domicile of the deceased has jurisdiction to hear the matter (CFPC Article 24, section VI);
(vi) in cases having to do with the guardianship of children or of handicapped persons, a judge located in the place of residence of the child or handicapped person has jurisdiction (CFPC Article 25); and
(vii) in cases involving judicial intervention in marital contracts, to anul a marriage, or in matters involving divorce or abandment of a spouse, a judge in the place of domicile of the spouses (or, in the latter case, of the abandoned spouse) has jurisdiction (CFPC Article 27).

A considerable volume of case-law (*jurisprudencia*) exists concerning the application of these rules. Published federal courts are usually cited as authority by litigating attorneys. However, as discussed elsewhere,[44] since the opinions of the federal courts published in the *Semanario Judicial de la Federación* are generally worded, they rarely contain specific recitals of facts or precise explanation of the rulings. As a result, federal court opinions seldom represent instructive disquisitions on the application of rules of jurisdiction. Nevertheless, some commentators have compiled surveys of *jurisprudencia*, and have attempted to present them in a systematic way in interpreting conflicts of law principles.[45]

3.2.2. *Jurisdiction over the Subject Matter*

Exclusive jurisdiction of Mexican courts in certain cases According to CFPC Article 568, Mexican courts (either federal or state courts, depending on the matter) have *exclusive jurisdiction* to decide disputes relating to the following matters, among others:

(i) cases involving lands and waters situated within the territorial limits of Mexico, including matters relating to the subsoil, air space, territorial waters, and continental shelf, whether or not the matters involve real property rights, rights derived from concessions, exploration, exploitation, or use of such properties, including properties contained within the exclusive economic zone[46] of Mexico (CFPC Article 568, sections I and II);
(ii) cases involving official acts of either state or federal government agencies (CFPC Article 568, section III);
(iii) cases involving the internal operations of Mexican embassies and consulates located in foreign territories (CFPC Article 568, section IV); and
(iv) cases in which other laws have granted exclusive jurisdiction to the Mexican courts (CFPC Article 568, section V).

[44] *See* Chapter 3 below, at text accompanying note 88.
[45] Silva, J.A., Derecho Internacional Privado, Su Recepción Judicial En México (Mexico: Porrúa, 1999); Ovalle Favela, J., Garantías Constitucionales Del Proceso (Mexico: Oxford University Press, 2nd ed., 2002).
[46] On the exclusive economic zone, *see Ley Federal del Mar*, D.O. 8 Jan. 1986, Articles 46–56.

Subject matter jurisdiction of federal courts generally The subject matter jurisdiction of federal courts springs from Articles 103 and 104 of the Constitution, as supplemented by the *Ley Orgánica del Poder Judicial de la Federación* (LOPJF).[47]

According to Article 103, federal courts have subject matter jurisdiction over the disputes that arise from any of the following matters. In each of these cases, federal courts have exclusive jurisdiction; such cases may not be brought in state courts:

(i) laws or other governmental actions that violate constitutional rights of citizens;
(ii) laws or other official acts by the federal government that restrict the sovereignty of the Mexican states or of the Federal District; and
(iii) laws or other acts by state governments, or by the government of the Federal District, that impinge upon the jurisdiction of the federal government.

Article 104 of the Constitution grants to federal courts jurisdiction over civil and criminal cases involving the application of federal laws or international treaties (similar to 'federal subject matter jurisdiction' in the United States). Federal subject matter jurisdiction in Mexico also includes maritime law and cases in which a federal agency is a party. Article 104 also grants to the federal courts jurisdiction over cases involving diplomatic officials and those involving disputes between state governments; Article 104, section I-B grants jurisdiction to federal appeals courts to decide appeals from federal administrative tribunals. Article 104, section IV, grants to the Supreme Court exclusive jurisdiction over cases involving constitutional challenges (*controversias constitucionales* and *acciones de inconstitucionalidad*), which are discussed in Chapter 8 above.

Finally, Articles 103–107 provide a sweeping grant of jurisdiction to federal courts in *amparo* cases. As discussed in more detail above,[48] the broad use of *amparo* as a remedy for any wrongful act of government, including state judicial decisions, has given the federal judiciary a preponderant role in the interpretation of both state and federal laws.

In cases involving the application of federal law that affect only the interests of private parties, federal and state courts have *concurrent subject matter jurisdiction*; in such cases the complaining party may elect the forum (Mexican Constitution, Article 104, section I). For example, when a consumer sues a merchant for breach of contract, and asserts rights under the federal Commercial Code, the case may be brought in either a state or a federal court. Alternatively, of course, the consumer may file a complaint with the Federal Consumer Protection Agency (*Procuraduría Federal del Consumidor*) seeking a negotiated settlement with the merchant.[49]

[47] The current *Ley Orgánica* was adopted in 1996 (D.O. 22 Nov. 1996). The *Ley Organica*, referred to as the LOPJF, is discussed in Chapter 7 above.
[48] *See* Chapter 8 above, section 2.1.
[49] *See* www.profeco.gob.mx (site visited Jan. 2004).

Federal courts in Mexico, unlike their US counterparts,[50] do not possess jurisdiction in cases in which the plaintiff and defendant are residents of different states of the union (known in the United States as 'diversity jurisdiction'). Furthermore, while state courts in the United States are required to apply federal constitutional principles in cases involving private or public litigants as plaintiffs or defendants, in Mexico a state court never bases its decision on federal constitutional law. Such cases are always brought in the federal courts, under federal subject matter jurisdiction.

Subject matter jurisdiction of state courts Article 116 of the Constitution grants to state courts the jurisdiction to hear all disputes that are not expressly reserved to the federal courts. The particular rules concerning subject matter jurisdiction of the state courts can be found in the applicable state constitution and state procedural codes.[51]

Private law matters are generally governed by state law, i.e. by the civil codes and other state laws (discussed above in Chapters 15, 16, and 17). Thus, state courts have jurisdiction to decide disputes involving rights in tangible property (both real property (*bienes inmuebles*) and personal property (*bienes muebles*)) located within the state. (Federal courts have jurisdiction when the property in question belongs to the federal government.) State courts also have jurisdiction to decide family law matters that affect parties domiciled within the state.[52] Thus, the state court where a minor or other person without legal capacity resides has jurisdiction to decide custody and guardianship. State courts have jurisdiction over adoptions of persons who reside within the state, although they may share jurisdiction with federal courts in the case of international adoptions.[53] In matters involving marriage, such as parental consent to the marriage of a minor, the court where the marriage application is filed shall have jurisdiction and shall also have the legal authority to decide whether any other impediment exists.[54] In divorce cases, the court where the marital domicile is located and the court where the domicile of an abandoned spouse is located have jurisdiction.[55] Finally, state courts have jurisdiction in disputes involving the law of obligations, both contractual and extra-contractual (tort). However, in tort cases (*responsabilidad extra-contractual*) a federal court will have jurisdiction if

[50] 28 U.S.C. Section 1332.

[51] State constitutions and procedural codes may be found at www.juridicas.unam.mx (site visited Jan. 2004).

[52] *See* Pereznieto and Silva, *supra* note 31 at 129–130.

[53] Mexico is a party to the Inter-American Convention on Conflict of Laws concerning the Adoption of Minors (available at www.oas.org/juridico/english/Sigs/b-48.html), and to the 1996 Hague Convention on Protection of Minors. These Conventions establish rules for 'international [i.e. cross-border] adoptions', and may be applied by either federal or state court judges in assuming jurisdiction over adoption cases in Mexico. State court judges have jurisdiction over adoption matters by virtue of their subject matter jurisdiction over the application of state family law, while federal jurisdiction is possible due to the application of an international treaty. Since the case-loads of most federal judges tend to be heavier than those of most state courts, it is usually advantageous to file such a case in state court to expedite the decision. Of course, even where adoption is involved, state court judgments may be subject to delays resulting from the filing of *amparo* actions.

[54] Pereznieto and Silva, *supra* note 31 at 171.

[55] *Id.* at 130.

the tort occurred on federal territory or federal property, such as a federal highway or in territorial inland waters.[56]

3.2.3. *Consent as a Basis of Jurisdiction: Choice of Forum Clauses and Arbitration Clauses*

Mexican courts recognize the ability of private parties to determine a court's jurisdiction by mutual consent: for instance, by including a choice of judicial forum clause in an agreement, or by otherwise consensually submitting a dispute to the jurisdiction of the court or arbitral tribunal. The power to give effect to choice forum clauses in civil and commercial matters is conferred by Article 24 of the CFPC and Article 1051 of the Commercial Code, and by similar rules of state procedural codes. Arbitration clauses, on the other hand, are enforceable pursuant to Article 1051 of the Commercial Code, and by the arbitration rules set forth in Title Four of the Commercial Code (Articles 1415–1463). CFPC Article 24 permits the parties to a contract to accept the jurisdiction of a court to decide disputes arising out of the contract, although there are important exceptions to this rule. For instance, a choice of judicial forum clause is *not* enforceable in an agreement involving real property rights, or to a dispute arising from the lease of real property, if application of the clause results in a foreign court having jurisdiction over a case involving real property located in Mexico; in both instances, Mexican courts shall have sole jurisdiction.[57]

If there is no formal impediment to enforcement of a choice of forum clause, then a choice of forum clause will be given effect so long as the application involves no 'actual impediment or denial of access to justice'.[58] The courts have considerable discretion to determine whether enforcement of a choice of forum clause will cause a denial of justice. Thus, a court will determine whether litigation in a distant forum, as agreed to in a choice of forum clause, will put one of the parties at a serious disadvantage due to expense. Mexican courts will not give effect to a choice of forum clause that allows only one party to choose an appropriate forum, if the same right is not granted to the other parties (CFPC Article 567).

It is important to note that, while Mexican courts will give effect to arbitration clauses in commercial contracts, arbitration in non-commercial civil contracts, such as contracts of marriage, are not enforceable absent a law specifically authorizing arbitration.

Arbitration clauses For many years, Mexican courts, like other Latin American countries, failed to recognize the validity of arbitration clauses, which were seen as ousting the judiciary of its inherent power to decide disputes over which it had jurisdiction.[59] For this reason, international commercial arbitration, regularly employed in much of the world, was not favoured in Mexico. Mexico's reluctance to promote commercial arbitration was finally altered in

[56] SJF, 9a, Primera Sala, Part I, 1a XVII/95, p. 63, June 1995.

[57] CFPC Article 568.

[58] CFPC Article 566.

[59] Vargas, J., 'Enforcement of Judgments and Awards in Mexico' 5 U.S.-Mex. LJ 137 (1997).

1993, when Congress, as part of the economic opening of Mexico and the attempt to attract increased foreign investment, amended the Commercial Code to insert, in Articles 1415–1463, specific rules that now make commercial arbitration an effective method of alternative dispute resolution in Mexico. These reforms permit parties to commercial contracts concluded in Mexico to incorporate an arbitration clause to settle disputes arising from the contract. The provisions also established procedures in Mexican courts for the acknowledgement and enforcement of foreign arbitration awards, in accordance with Mexico's commitment to the United Nations Convention on Recognition and Enforcement of Foreign Arbitral Awards, discussed below.

Articles 1415–1463 of the Commercial Code establish arbitration rules for both domestic and international arbitrations (i.e. those involving foreign parties). These rules are based on the UNCITRAL Model Law on Commercial Arbitration and on the United Nations Convention on the Recognition and Enforcement of Foreign Arbitral Awards (New York Convention), which is discussed below.

An arbitration proceeding may take place under the auspices of a foreign arbitration centre, such as the International Chamber of Comerce (ICC),[60] the American Arbitration Association (AAA),[61] or other international arbitration centres, such as the Inter-American Commercial Arbitration Comission.[62] Thanks to legislative changes favouring arbitration, Mexican arbitration centres have become active; these include the *Centro de Arbitraje de México* (CAM),[63] and the *Centro de Mediación y Arbitraje* of the *Cámara Nacional de Comercio de la Ciudad de México* (CANACO).[64] An arbitration may also be conducted as an *ad hoc* arbitration by the parties in accordance with an agreed set of arbitration rules, in conformity with the provisions of the Commercial Code. Upon the request of one of the litigants, Article 1424 of the Commercial Code requires a judge to refer parties to arbitration, rather than continue a judicial proceeding, if the parties have agreed to arbitration, so long as the agreement to arbitrate is not defective. The arbitration will be conducted in accordance with the rules of the arbitration institution designated by the parties, and if the parties have not so specified, in accordance with the rules set forth in CC Article 1427. Additional rules regarding the scope of arbitration, the procedures to be followed by the arbitral tribunal, and the execution of arbitral awards (as well as rules for contesting awards) are contained in CC Articles 1432–1463.[65]

[60] *See* www.iccwbo.org (site visited Jan. 2004).

[61] *See* www.adr.org (site visited Jan. 2004).

[62] *See* the list of arbitration rules and centres at www.sice.oas.org/DISPUTE/comarb_e.asp (site visited Jan. 2004).

[63] *See* www.camex.com.mx (site visited Jan. 2004).

[64] *See* www.arbitrajecanaco.com.mx (site visited Jan. 2004).

[65] On commercial arbitration in Mexico, *see*: Uribarri, G., El Arbitraje en México (Mexico: Oxford University Press, 1999); Pereznieto, L. ed., Arbitraje Comercial Internacional (Mexico: Fontamara, 2000); Santos Belandro, Ruben, Arbitraje Comercial Internacional (Mexico: Oxford University Press, 2000); Silva Silva, Jorge Alberto, Arbitraje Comercial Internacional en México (Mexico: Oxford University Press, 2002); Derains,

Mexican lawyers and businesses are gradually acquiring greater experience with and confidence in commercial arbitration. Nevertheless, to the extent that arbitration proceedings may require judicial intervention (to enforce the agreement to arbitrate, or to enforce the award itself), the threat that a disgruntled party may file an *amparo* action to deter the arbitration may render arbitration more problematic and time-consuming than it would otherwise be.

3.3. Service of Process

Proper service of process is a necessary element of a court's jurisdiction over the parties to a lawsuit. As pointed out elsewhere,[66] Mexican judicial procedure is highly formalistic, and by comparison with that of the United States may be characterized as relatively rigid. While many US procedural laws are strict (e.g. statutes of limitations, or proof of service of process), flexibility it built into many rules. Thus, service of process in the United States is effected pursuant to relatively flexible, and open-ended, state 'long arm' statutes; proof of service of process may be made by a private agent, or process server, hired by a litigant. By contrast, in the Mexican system, service of process and other official acts of notification must follow strict procedural formalities.

Federal rules regarding proper notification of judicial proceedings, including the initial service of process (*emplazamiento*) on a named defendant, are contained in Title 7 of the First Book of the CFPC, Articles 303–321. Service of process may only be carried out by an administrative assistant of the court, called the *actuario*,[67] who must describe in a certificate filed with the court the precise circumstances under which the person was served (CFPC Articles 67–69). That record becomes part of the formal court record (*expediente*) in the case. The CFPC makes no provision for service of process or notification by mail.

Specific rules governing service of process are contained in CFPC Articles 327–328. Once the judge accepts the complaint and asserts jurisdiction, an officer of the court (*actuario*) is responsible for providing specific notification (*notificación*) of the fact that a judicial process against the defendant has begun (*emplazamiento*). The defendant then has nine days in which to file an answer, although if the defendant is a foreign resident this period can be extended by the judge. The defendant has the right to contest the jurisdiction of the court without submitting to general jurisdiction. Failure of the defendant or his representative to answer a complaint within the allotted time will be taken by the judge as an admission by the defendant of the facts alleged in the complaint (CFPC Article 332).

Yves and Schwartz, Eric A., EL NUEVO REGLAMENTO DE ARBITRAJE DE LA CÁMARA DE COMERCIO INTERNACIONAL. GUÍA DE ARBITRAJE COMERCIAL INTERNACIONAL (Mexico: Oxford University Press, 2001).

[66] The formalities of Mexican procedural law are discussed in Chapter 10 above.

[67] In exceptional cases, such as when no *actuario* is available, service may be effectuated by a notary public or by a *corredor público*. CPFC Article 128. For a discussion of notaries public and *corredores públicos*, *see* Chapter 18 above, section 2.3.

When the defendant is a foreign person or entity, service of process may be made either upon a legal representative of the foreign party,[68] or in accordance with the procedures applicable under one of the international conventions on service of process to which Mexico is a party. The United States and Mexico are both parties to the Inter-American Convention on Letters Rogatory,[69] an international convention that facilitates service of process, notifications, and subpoenas for evidence requested by US courts to Mexican courts.

3.4. Judicial Co-operation in General

As mentioned previously, reforms to the CFPC in 1987 liberalized Mexico's procedural rules in regard to international litigation. These reforms were motivated by Mexico's adherence to international treaties dealing with conflict of laws, in particular the Inter-American procedural conventions.[70] The reforms added a new section to the CFPC, *Libro Cuarto* (Articles 543–577), entitled 'Concerning International Judicial Co-operation'. The rules on judicial co-operation are detailed, and cover matters from service of process, to taking of evidence, to certification of documents, and enforcement of judgments.

4. Enforcement of Judgments in Mexico

Judgments rendered by Mexican state or federal courts are entitled to full recognition and enforcement within Mexico pursuant to Article 121 of the Mexican Constitution, Mexico's 'full faith and credit' clause. There are very few exceptions to recognition of a judgment in Mexico by another Mexican court. The full faith and credit clause does not apply to judgments of courts from other countries, however, and Mexico is party to only two international treaties for recognition and enforcement of judicial judgments (as opposed to arbitral awards, discussed below).[71]

In attempting to enforce a domestic or foreign judgment, the plaintiff may file for attachment of assets (*embargo de bienes*) or collateral belonging to the

[68] To appear before Mexican courts, either as plaintiff or defendant, a foreign national (person or entity) must appoint a duly authorized attorney domiciled in Mexico as their legal representative; this representative is granted proper power of attorney under Mexican law to represent the foreign party. Service of notices and summons to appear at hearings in a proceeding may be made on the legal representative, instead of on the party. CPCDF Art. 260, Section II.

[69] The 1975 Convention, as well the Additional Protocol of 1979, can be found at www.oas.org/juridico/english/tresigsu.html, 'Judicial Cooperation' (site visited Jan. 2004).

[70] These conventions are available on the OAS web site; *see ibid.*

[71] One is the Inter-American Convention on Jurisdiction in the Internacional Sphere for the Extraterritorial Validity of Foreign Judgments (available at www.oas.org/juridico/english/Sigs/B-50.html (site visited Jan. 2004)). Neither the United States nor Canada are parties to this Convention. The other is the 1989 Convention between Mexico and Spain on the Recognition and Enforcement of Judgments and Arbitral Awards in Civil and Commercial Matters.

defendant if the parties had agreed to such attachment in a contract. Attachment is carried out in a special precautionary proceeding called a *procedimiento precautorio*. The plaintiff may initiate such a proceeding before the court of any jurisdiction in which assets of the defendant are located. The codes of civil procedures of the states and Federal District contain provisions (*providencias precautorias*) that govern the attachment of property involved in litigation. A litigant may file a request for attachment (*petición de embargo precautorio*) when the danger exists that the opposing party may attempt to flee the jurisdiction or hide assets.[72]

4.1. Enforcement of Foreign Judicial Judgments in Mexico[73]

Given the attention to formal requirements in Mexican civil procedure, and the territorialism that we have alluded to previously, it is not surprising to find that an attempt to enforce a foreign judgment in Mexico may be time-consuming, expensive, and fraught with uncertainty. Nevertheless, enforcement of a foreign judgment is possible, in accordance with CFPC Articles 564–577. Under CFPC Articles 564–566, a foreign judgment is enforceable in Mexico if the foreign court issuing the judgment had jurisdiction in the matter, in accordance with rules of jurisdiction compatible with Mexican law. The Mexican court will recognize the legitimacy of the foreign court's jurisdiction where the parties, by means of a choice of forum clause, have submitted to the jurisdiction of the foreign court, so long as this does not result in a miscarriage of justice. As noted elsewhere, certain subjects (e.g. title to real property located in Mexico) are considered to be the exclusive jurisdiction of Mexican courts,[74] and foreign judgments are not enforceable in such matters (CFPC Article 564).

According to Articles 569–571 of the CFPC, judgments (*sentencias*) rendered by a foreign court against any individual or entity are enforceable within Mexico upon proof of the following conditions: first, that the person who suffered the judgment was properly served with notice of the judicial proceeding; second, that the person received a fair opportunity to assert his or her rights in the case; and third, that at the time of the filing of the suit upon which the judgment was rendered, the party had its legal domicile or habitual residence within the territory of the country where the judgment was issued. There must be some nexus that ties the foreign judgment to the jurisdiction in which it is rendered. Thus, when the judgment debtor is a corporation or other legal entity, the judgment debtor's main office, or other offices, must be located in the territory of the country where the judgment was issued, or the judgment debtor must have conducted business activities in the territory that gave rise to the judgment

[72] *See* e.g. CPCDF Article 235. Such *providencias precautorias* may even be initiated prior to the filing of a lawsuit (CPCDF Article 237).

[73] On enforcement of foreign judgments in Mexico, *see generally* Pereznieto L., Pereznieto Castro, *supra* note 14 at 191 *et seq*. *See also* the authorities cited in note 77 *infra*.

[74] *See* Chapter 16 above, at text accompanying note 7, and section 4.4.2. below.

within the territory. The provisions of the CFPC give considerable discretion to the Mexican judge in determining whether these territorial links of the judgment to the judgment debtor have been met (CFPC Article 564).

4.2. Recognition of Foreign Judgments Stemming from Application of Choice of Forum Clauses

In addition to the requirements mentioned in the previous section, there are two additional requirements where the foreign court that renders the judgment has jurisdiction pursuant to a choice of forum clause.

First, where a foreign court has rendered a judgment pursuant to the exercise of jurisdiction under a choice of forum clause, the party claiming the benefit of the judgment most show evidence to the Mexican court of the other party's acceptance, in writing (either by contract or subsequent agreement), of the jurisdiction of the court that issued the judgment (CFPC Article 566). In accordance with CFPC Article 572, the plaintiff must file a certified copy of the foreign judgment with the court.

Second, the court carries out a brief proceeding called *homologación*, by which the judge may confirm the foreign judgment and proceed to execution in satisfaction of it; the defendant has a period of nine days from the initiation of the *homologación* in which to raise a defence to the enforcement of the foreign judgment (CFPC Article 574). This sounds simple, but in practice many delaying motions are often filed, and even if a judge does confirm the judgment, the defendant is entitled to file an *amparo* action, which will further delay enforcement.

4.3. Enforcement of Foreign Arbitral Awards

Awards stemming from an arbitration proceeding may be recognized if they meet the requirements set forth in Articles 1461–1463 of the Commercial Code, which establishes the same rules of recognition as the New York Convention on Recognition and Enforcement of Foreign Arbitration,[75] to which Mexico has

[75] *See* Commercial Code Article 1462. Under this Article, as under Article V of the New York Convention, recognition or enforcement of foreign arbitral award may only be denied when:

I. The party against whom the award was issued, proves before the proper judicial authority [a judge having jurisdiction to hear the case] of the country in which recognition or enforcement is being sought that:
   a) One of the parties to the arbitration agreement was affected by some legal impediment or that said agreement is not valid by virtue of the law to which the parties submitted, or if nothing was stated in this regard, by virtue of the law of the country in which the award was granted;
   b) It [the party] was not duly notified of the designation of a member of the arbitration tribunal or of the actions of the arbitration, or that it was unable, for any other reason, to assert its rights;
   c) The award involves a dispute that is not foreseen in the arbitration agreement or contains decisions that exceed the terms of the arbitration agreement. Nonetheless, if the provisions of the award involving matters that were subject

been a party since 1971. Unfortunately, judicial enforcement of an arbitral award may give rise to the same delaying tactic, through an action of *amparo*, that faces any final judgment by a state or federal court in Mexico.[76]

4.4. Procedures for the Enforcement of Foreign Judgments[77]

Numerous opportunities exist to contest enforcement of a foreign judgment, however. For instance, under CFPC Article 571, section III, a Mexican court may enforce a foreign judgment only if the court rendering the judgment had proper jurisdiction in accordance with international rules that are compatible with Mexican law. (As noted previously, CFPC Article 568 sets forth a list of matters over which the Mexican courts are considered to have exclusive jurisdiction, and any judgment issued by a foreign court in such a matter shall not be recognized by Mexican courts.) If the party against whom a foreign judgment was rendered is a Mexican citizen (person or entity), the judgment will not be recognized by a Mexican court unless there has been appropriate service of process in accordance with Mexican law.[78]

The procedures for enforcing foreign judgments in federal courts are set forth in Articles 564–577 of the CFPC. In enforcing foreign judgments, Mexican courts make a distinction between procedural and substantive requirements.

4.4.1. Procedural Requirements

Several formal procedural requirements, contained in Articles 564–577 of the CFPC, must be fulfilled in order for a judgment issued by a foreign judge to be enforced in Mexico. First, an authenticated copy of the foreign judgment to be enforced must be provided to the court. The copy must be translated into the Spanish language by a certified translator (*perito*) who has been duly accredited by the Mexican courts. The translation, in turn, must be authorized and certified by a consular officer of the Mexican government in the country in which the judgment was rendered. Finally, the party who has filed to enforce a judgment

to arbitration can be separated from those that were not, acknowledgement and enforcement may be given to the former [those that are subject];

d) The composition of the arbitration tribunal or the arbitration proceeding did not adhere to the law of the country where the arbitration took place; or

e) The award was still not binding on the parties or would have been thrown out or stayed by the judge of the country under whose law that award would have been issued; or

II. The judge confirms that, according to Mexican law, the subject of the dispute cannot be subject to arbitration; or that acknowledgement or enforcement of the award are contrary to public order.

[76] *See* Chapter 8 above, at text accompanying notes 34–35.

[77] On enforcement of judgments in Mexico, *see* Bennack, L. and López Velarde, A., 'La ejecución de sentencias extranjeras: Contraste entre México y los Estados Unidos de América', 24 Jurídica (Universidad Iberoamericana) 261–280 (1995); Pereznieto Castro and Silva Silva, *supra* note 31 at 392 *et seq.*; Pereznieto Castro, *supra* note 14 at 163 *et seq.*; and Silva Silva, Jorge Alberto, Codificacion procesal civil y Mercantil Internacional (Mexico: Harla, 1995) at 195.

[78] CFPC Article 571, section IV. *See* Section 4.4.2. below.

must specify an address within the jurisdiction of the court where notifications may be received. (CFPC Article 572) Other important procedural formalities are contained in CFPC Articles 573–577.

4.4.2. *Impediments to the Enforcement of Foreign Judgments*

In addition to procedural formalities, the CFPC lists several impediments to enforcement of foreign judgments, as follows. The foreign judgment must not attempt to affect rights to real property, whether located within Mexico or elsewhere (CFPC Article 571, paragraph II);[79] the court that rendered the judgment must have had jurisdiction to hear and adjudicate the matter in accordance with internationally recognized rules compatible with those of the CFPC (CFPC Article 564); and the judgment debtor must have been given proper service of process and an opportunity to appear in court and exercise a defence (CFPC Article 571, paragraph IV). In addition, the judgment must have the status of *res judicata* in the country where it was issued, and no appeal or motion may be pending against it (CFPC Article 571 V); and the action that gave rise to the judgment must not be the subject of litigation pending between the same parties before a Mexican court, in a matter in which the Mexican court was the first court to take jurisdiction of the dispute, unless the letters rogatory to serve process under the foreign litigation had been filed prior to the filing of the lawsuit in Mexico, and had been submitted to the Secretariat of Foreign Relations or the state authority in the place where judicial process is being served (CFPC Article 571, paragraph III). Finally, enforcing the judgment must not violate Mexican public policy (CFPC Article 569).

Even if all procedural and substantive requirements are met, Mexican law permits a judge to refuse to enforce a foreign judgment if the judgment debtor can show that the courts of the country in which the judgment originates would not enforce a Mexican judgment under similar circumstances (CFPC Article 571, section VIII, paragraph 2). The burden of proof of lack of reciprocity is generally understood as resting with the party contesting enforcement of the judgment, and it may be difficult in many instances to provide sufficient proof that a foreign court will not enforce a Mexican judgment. The opinion of the Secretariat of Foreign Relations is usually relied upon by the courts as certification of lack of reciprocity. Insofar as judgments of US courts are concerned, it is generally understood that the reciprocity requirement is met, since the laws of most states of the United States provide for enforcement of foreign judgments, particularly money judgments.[80]

In addition to the formal means of resisting enforcement of judgments, some 'informal' or tactical means of avoiding judgments also exist. For example, if

[79] CFPC Article 571, paragraph II, states that foreign judgments or arbitral awards are not enforceable if they are based on an *acción real*. As used here, the term *acción real* means actions that pertain to rights in either real or personal property.

[80] *See generally* Restatement (Third) of Foreign Relations Law of the United States (Philadelphia, Pa: American Law Institute, 1987) Section 481 (including comments and Reporters' notes).

the judgment debtor is a company, the officers of the company may collude with labour leaders to call a strike at the time a judgment is issued. (Such a tactic is unlikely with large, established companies.) Under Mexican labour law, a strike renders unenforceable any judgment that would diminish the assets of the company.[81] Alternatively, a judgment debtor may withhold property from enforcement of judgments by means of a bogus pledge of assets to another person or company; while such an act may be criminal, if it is not detected it may relieve the debtor's property from attachment and execution. Finally, in cases in which it appears that a judge will enforce a judgment, the judgment debtor may file suit against the plaintiff. As noted above, a foreign judgment cannot be enforced in Mexico while a lawsuit between the same parties is pending in Mexico, and thus enforcement of the judgment must await the pending action.

These and other tactics have made enforcement of domestic and foreign judgments a problematic enterprise, and have caused many companies to make cash settlements for less than the full amount of the judgment, rather than risk delay and lack of enforcement. Furthermore, since any interest, fees, or expenses due to the plaintiff resulting from a delay in fulfilment of a judgment are calculated from the date of issuance of the Mexican court judgment,[82] rather than the original foreign judgment, it is in the interests of the debtor to prolong the proceedings to delay a Mexican enforcement action. Mexican judges are unlikely to require the defendant to pay the plaintiffs' costs or attorneys' fees.

Finally, judgments of Mexican courts, or enforcement of foreign judgments by Mexican courts, may involve the need to calculate the amount in pesos that becomes payable to satisfy the judgment, if the original debt was payable in a foreign currency (US dollars, euros, etc.). According to the Monetary Law of Mexico,[83] all judgments rendered by Mexican courts must be denominated in Mexican currency, the peso.

[81] *See* the discussion in Garcia Sámano, F., DERECHO PROCESAL LABORAL (Mexico: Themis, 2000) at 27.

[82] Bergman, M. and Kossik, R., 'La ejecución de las Sentencias en México, vol. II. no. 3, REVISTA DEL INSTITUTO DE LA JUDICATURA FEDERAL (2003) at 11–28.

[83] *Ley Monetaria de los Estados Unidos Mexicanos*, Article 8, D.O. 27 Jul. 1931, as amended.

Index

www.ingramcontent.com/pod-product-compliance
Ingram Content Group UK Ltd.
Pitfield, Milton Keynes, MK11 3LW, UK
UKHW020851150926
475595UK00003B/118
* 9 7 8 0 1 9 8 2 6 7 7 7 5 *